Also by Roland McHugh

The Sigla of "Finnegans Wake"

The "Finnegans Wake" Experience

Annotations to FINNEGANS WAKE

REVISED EDITION

ROLAND McHUGH

Baltimore and London
The Johns Hopkins University Press

With love to my wife, Elizabeth

The Johns Hopkins University Press, 701 West 40th Street, Baltimore, Maryland 21211
The Johns Hopkins Press Ltd., London

The paper used in this book meets the minimum requirements of American National Standard for Information Sciences—Permanence of Paper for Printed Library Materials, ANSI Z39.48–1984.

Library of Congress Cataloging-in-Publication Data

McHugh, Roland.
Annotations to Finnegans wake / Roland McHugh.—Rev. ed.
p. cm.
Includes bibliographical references.
ISBN 0-8018-4226-3 (alk. paper). — ISBN 0-8018-4190-9 (pbk. alk. paper)
1. Joyce, James, 1882–1941. Finnegans wake. I. Joyce, James, 1882–1941. Finnegans wake. II. Title.
PR6019.09F59357 1991
823'.912—dc20 90-23512

Preface

The first book-length commentary on *Finnegans Wake* was Campbell and Robinson's *A Skeleton Key to "Finnegans Wake"* (New York: Harcourt, Brace, and World, 1944). Campbell and Robinson's approach was to identify as many of the *Wake* components as possible and then to string them together into running prose, using the extant sentence structure as a model. Since that date, the number of identifiable components has been multiplied considerably, and several attempts to improve on Campbell and Robinson have been made. It is quite possible to isolate most of the ingredients in some short passage and produce from them a coherent and readable narrative. Unfortunately, when treated in this manner the text ceases to possess any real attraction or interest. When Adaline Glasheen states that Joyce's early drafts of *Finnegans Wake* (FW) 'are amazingly dull, discontinuous, and read as distressingly as any dozen pages of *A Skeleton Key*', this is not so much a rebuke to Campbell and Robinson as to their method in general. The substitution of a continuous narrative 'translation' for the FW text has the effect of distracting the reader from direct confrontation. Were the *Wake* written in standard English, the reader could perhaps expect to retain enough of it in memory to evaluate the interpretation, but no beginner could conceivably do this with a speechform as complex as Joyce's. Instead, all attention will be absorbed by the 'translation', and its connections with FW will be taken on trust.

The 'ability to read FW' can hardly be acquired thus. The pleasure of articulating its sentences, perceiving the beauty and justice of their condensation, the humor of their imagery and their reconciled irreconcilables, is the only legitimate objective. *Annotations to Finnegans Wake*, on account of its format, brings this ideal within the range of the feasible. It provides a single page for every page of the *Wake*, of size larger than those in the current Viking Press edition. For every line of FW text, *Annotations* can accommodate glosses, not normally exceeding two lines of small print. (The third and subsequent Faber editions are one line out in pages 548–54). Hold a page of FW alongside its counterpart, allowing the eyes to slip momentarily across to *Annotations* at the end of every line. By all means stop and ponder at intervals. If possible, try to find an area of the *Wake* which strikes you personally as intriguing or beautiful, and contemplate those things in it which the *Annotations* illuminate. Try to develop a feeling for the different qualities or atmospheres of the various FW chapters. Try to stay away from digressive accounts until you have developed some confidence in your own interpretations.

The reader of a mathematical or philosophical study can seldom afford to take any step on trust for fear of being caught out a few pages later. He has developed a disposition to worry over the justification of any obtruding strut: if he fails to resolve it he will question the utility of proceeding. This is precisely the wrong technique for Joyce. Reading *Finnegans Wake* is far more like learning a language: one unconsciously inculcates background material while focusing upon odd nuclei of sense, which are due to aggregate at some future date.

In 1962 Clive Hart stated in *Structure and Motif in "Finnegans Wake"* that 'in spite of all the excellent exegetical work that has appeared in recent years, the bulk of the long text of *Finnegans Wake* remains almost entirely unexplicated. Until such time as a complete exegesis is available, every commentator on *Finnegans Wake* who attempts to pursue a reasoned critical argument will constantly be troubled by the necessity to pause and offer explications of those passages which he quotes in substantiation of his points.'

How much closer are we now to a 'complete exegesis'?

1. *Finnegans Wake* contains thousands of words taken from foreign languages, either reproduced verbatim or comprising elements in new coinages. Some of these have been treated systematically in language lists: D. B. Christiani, *Scandinavian Elements of "Finnegans Wake"* (Evanston: Northwestern University Press, 1965); H. Bonheim, *A Lexicon of the German in "Finnegans Wake"* (Berkeley and Los Angeles: University of California Press, 1967); B. O Hehir, *A Gaelic Lexicon for "Finnegans Wake"* (Berkeley: University of California Press, 1967); B. O Hehir and J. Dillon, *A Classical Lexicon for "Finnegans Wake"* (Berkeley: University of California Press, 1977). *A Wake Newslitter* (University of Essex) published important lists of Dutch, Slavonic, and many other languages from 1962 to 1984.

2. Many *Finnegans Wake* words function echoically, their principal signification that of some English word that is 'not orthographically present', as Hart notes in *A Concordance to "Finnegans Wake"* (new ed., New York: Paul P. Appel, 1974). In the Overtones section of the *Concordance* is a lengthy compilation of such words. However, as the list is alphabetical rather than arranged in the order of *Wake* pages, the student can detect overtones on a given page only by scanning the entire list, a tiresome process to repeat.

3. There are thousands of references to historical, mythical, and fictitious persons, which Adaline Glasheen has attempted to catalogue in her three censuses, the most recent being *A Third Census of "Finnegans Wake"* (Berkeley: University of California Press, 1977). These books use an alphabetical listing like the *Concordance*, with the same consequent drawback.

4. Titles of, and quotations from, songs are listed in *Song in the Works of James Joyce*, by Matthew J. C. Hodgart and Mabel P. Worthington (New York: Columbia University Press, 1959).

5. Literary allusions are listed by author in J. S. Atherton, *The Books at the Wake* (new ed., New York: Paul P. Appel, 1974).

6. Geographical allusions are indexed in L. O. Mink, *A "Finnegans Wake" Gazetteer* (Bloomington: Indiana University Press, 1978).

7. Many books and articles dealing with *Finnegans Wake* include original explanations of specific words and phrases, often concealed among endless pages of colorless critical drawl.

8. A galaxy of little specks of insight has appeared in *A Wake Newslitter*. Some information circulates privately among a few favored enthusiasts, for example, the late Mrs. Hope Wright's unpublished typescript "Chinese Words and Allusions in *Finnegans Wake*," but most exegetes possess answers they will never reveal. Either the illumination seems too local to warrant writing up into a note, or the visionary fails to suspect that he has surmounted someone else's problem. It is not always entirely obvious what items are, and what items are not, in need of glossing.

It does not take long for the initial dilemma (what do the words mean?) to become the dilemma of surfeit of information. How is it to be stored? Clive Hart, Matthew Hodgart, Leo Knuth, Charles Peake, and Fritz Senn, for example, found it necessary to annotate their personal copies of the book (and also kindly permitted me to examine their annotations). Without this kind of safeguard it is risky to publish any interpretation of *Finnegans Wake*. The statements already made by others about the passage may totally invalidate the things one wishes to say.

Considering the drawbacks it is truly astonishing that so many people get anywhere at all with the book. The repetitive reading that is so important in assimilating it is surely obstacle enough for most of us. The present work attempts to cope with the formidable secondary task of identifying the components of the text, by supplying the cream of all available exegesis in as condensed and accessible a form as possible.

Acknowledgments

I began production of this book in 1972 by typing all the useful annotations then at my disposal onto sheets of paper numbered for the pages of *Finnegans Wake*. Carbons of these sheets circulated among several experts for the next five years, and they inserted a great deal of their own material and also corrected many of my errors. The greatest number of meaningful additions were received from Matthew Hodgart and Leo Knuth, but useful contributions were also made by Adaline Glasheen, Clive Hart, Louis Mink, Fritz Senn, and Petr Skrabanek.

The first edition of *Annotations* having appeared in 1980, I began the following year to prepare the second. Ian MacArthur sent me a very extensive list of addenda and corrigenda, much of which I employed. The critical stance of MacArthur is shaped considerably by his studies of Joyce's manuscripts, and his notes indicate a type of approach which may attract some readers and repel others. All readings that can be confirmed by reference to the manuscripts are acceptable. Thus in an area of the book where use is made of some minor language featuring as a wordlist in one of Joyce's notebooks, each word must be presented with allowance for errors or inaccuracies on Joyce's part. Any words not in the original list are disallowed. A similar approach colors the recent *Understanding Finnegans Wake* by Danis Rose and John O'Hanlon (New York: Garland, 1982).

In making use of this approach I have tried to restrict its use to identifications that are 'reasonable', as most in fact are. Fritz Senn has remarked to me that once one claims that the reason x equals y is 'because Joyce thought it did', one admits instant defeat. A host of fanatics will rise up, insisting that their own strained and subjective interpretations have every bit as much validity.

I have responded to MacArthur's suggestions, and also to a similar but shorter list received from Laurent Milesi, by trimming away certain glosses that are not substantiated by manuscript material. I have also increased the direct quotation from Joyce's often enigmatic MSS. Most of the material in question comes from the sixty-six notebooks preserved at the State University of New York at Buffalo (numbered VI.A, VI.B.1–47, and VI.C.1–18). There is also helpful material among the FW manuscripts in the British Library.

Another manuscript-based aspect of the interpretation of FW is the use of *sigla*. These are signs invented by Joyce to encapsulate the ultimate characters of the *Wake*, themselves conglomerates of real and fictitious persons from all epochs. The twelve questions into which chapter I.6 (p. 126–68) is divided are labeled in the British Library MSS with twelve sigla (reproduced here). Other sigla lists may be found on pages 219–21, 555–58, and elsewhere.

Sigla are printed in *Annotations* at points where this seems valuable for the reader, but a complete treatment would flood the pages and also require some rather arbitrary decisions where affinities are uncertain. My use of sigla does not specifically confirm manuscript usage at the point in question but is intended rather to illustrate their presence in a number of structurally significant contexts. The reader should eventually recognize such sigla as ᗰ, often seen facing ⊣ ⊢ and having his back to Λ∆⊏⊏, as standard Wakean configurations. I have slightly increased the number of printed sigla in this edition. A revision of my study *The Sigla of "Finnegans Wake"* (Austin: University of Texas Press, 1977) is unlikely to occur before all the Buffalo notebooks have been transcribed and published.

A large quantity of additional glossary was received in letters from Adaline Glasheen, and in a copy of the first edition annotated by Charles Peake. This material was far more 'maximalist' than MacArthur's, but very illuminating and has been used extensively. Other sizeable lists were received from Harald Beck, Vincent Deane, and Don Gifford. For further insights I am grateful to Jeremy Addis, Andrée Alverhne, Jacques Aubert, Ruth Bauerle, Peter Bekker, Patricia Berger, Richard Brown, Peter Chrisp, Maurice Craig, Brigid Cunningham, John Dillon, John Duffy, Edmund Epstein, David Evans, A. C. Ganter, Matthew Hodgart, Raymond P. Hylton, Vivien Igoe, Claude Jacquet, John Kidd, Terence Killeen, Leo Knuth, Oliver Mahon, Reinhard Markner, Tom Mathews, Leni McCullagh, Tony Mulqueen, Gerry Murphy, Robert Nicholson, Riana O'Dwyer, Gerry O'Flaherty, Danis Rose, Noreen O'Rourke, Luigi Schenoni, Petr Skrabanek, Daragh Smyth, Bruce Stewart, Yukio Suzuki, Ian Wibberly, and members of the James Joyce Institute of Ireland. Reviews by Wilhelm Füger, John Garvin, and Ulick O'Connor have also provided data.

The list of books from which I have drawn information includes all those mentioned above. Additionally, the following studies have provided valuable material:

Bauerle, Ruth. *The James Joyce Songbook*. New York: Garland, 1982.

Begnal, Michael H., and Senn, Fritz, eds. *A Conceptual Guide to "Finnegans Wake."* University Park: Pennsylvania State University Press, 1974.

Benstock, Bernard. "Persian Elements in *Finnegans Wake*." *Phil. Quarterly* 44 (1965): 100—109.

Dalton, Jack P., and Hart, Clive. *Twelve and a Tilly*. Evanston: Northwestern University Press, 1966.

Ferrer, D., Kim, S., Rabaté, J-M., Jacquet, C., Milesi, L., Brun, B. and Derrida, J. *Genèse de Babel: Joyce et la Création*. Paris: C.N.R.S., 1985.

Garvin, John. *James Joyce's Disunited Kingdom*. New York: Barnes and Noble, 1976.

Gifford, Don, and Seidman, Robert J. *Notes for Joyce*. New York: Dutton, 1974.

Hart, Clive, and Senn, Fritz, eds. *A Wake Digest*. Sydney: Sydney University Press, 1968.

Higginson, F. H. *"James Joyce's Revisions of Finnegans Wake."* Ph.D dissertation, University of Michigan, 1954.

Jacquet, Claude: *Joyce et Rabelais*. Paris: Didier, 1972.

Jarrell, Mackie L. "Swiftiana in *Finnegans Wake*." *ELH* (Baltimore) 26 (1959): 271–94.

joycenotes (London). Three issues edited by Lena Inger, 1969.

Kelleher, John. "Notes on *Finnegans Wake*."*Analyst* (Evanston) 12 (1957): 9–15; ibid. 15, 9–16.

——. "Identifying the Irish Printed Sources for *Finnegans Wake*." *Irish University Review* 1, no. 2 (1971): 161–77.

Knuth, Leo, and Brown, Carole. *The Tenor and the Vehicle: A Study of the John McCormack/James Joyce Connection*. Colchester: A Wake Newslitter Press, 1982.

Lernout, Geert: "Dutch in *Finnegans Wake*." James Joyce Quarterly 23 (1986): 45–66.

Rose, Danis, *James Joyce's "The Index Manuscript": Finnegans Wake Holograph Workbook VI.B.46*. Colchester: A Wake Newslitter Press, 1978.

——. *Chapters of Coming Forth by Day*. Colchester: A Wake Newslitter Press, 1982.

Schmidt, Arno. *Arno Schmidts Arbeitsexemplar von Finnegans Wake by James Joyce*. Zurich: Arno Schmidt Stiftung im Haffmans Verlag, 1984.

Senn, Fritz. "Some Zürich Allusions in *Finnegans Wake*." *Analyst* (Evanston) 19 (1960): 1–22.

Thornton, Weldon. *Allusions in Ulysses*. Chapel Hill: University of North Carolina Press, 1968.

Troy, Mark L. "Mummeries of Resurrection: The Cycle of Osiris in *Finnegans Wake*." Ph.D. dissertation, University of Uppsala, 1976.

Tysdahl, B. J. *Joyce and Ibsen*. Oslo: Norwegian Universities Press, 1968.

Whitelock, G. K. *Cricket in the Writings of James Joyce*. London: By the author, 1975.

The following articles appearing in *A Wake Newslitter* deserve particular mention as having been very valuable to me:

Old Series

Hart, Clive, and Senn, Fritz. "Gloss on 143.03–28" (I.3–9; II.1–15; 1962).

——. "Gloss on 338.04–33" (IV.4–8; V.4–9; 1962).

Hart, Clive. "Australiana in *Finnegans Wake*" (IX.1–5, 1963).

New Series

1964 Hodgart, M. J. C. "Word-Hoard" (Albanian, Kiswahili and Basque) (I.1.1–5; I.2.9–10)
1964–5 Misra, B. P. "Sanskrit Translations" (I.6.8–10; II.1.9–11)
Staples, Hugh C. "The Epithets of H.C.E." (I.6.3–5; II.2.9–13, II.3.25–8)
1965–66 Broes, Arthur T. "The Bible in *Finnegans Wake*" (II.6.3–11; III.5.102–3)
1966 Bates, Ronald. "Finnish in *Finnegans Wake*" (III.1.3–4)
Senn, Fritz. "Ossianic Echoes" (III.2.25–36)
——. "The Aliments of Jumeantry" (III.3.51–4)
Bird, S. D. "Some American Notes to *Finnegans Wake*" (III.6.119–124)
1967 Hart, Clive. "His Good Smetterling of Entymology" (IV.1.14–24)
Senn, Fritz. "Litterish Fragments" (IV.3.52–5)
1968 Knuth, Leo. "Dutch Elements in 75–78" (V.2.19–28)
——. "Malay Elements in *Finnegans Wake*" (V.4.51–63)
1971 Senn, Fritz. "The Localization of Legend" (VIII.1.10–13)
Knuth, Leo. "Dutch in *Finnegans Wake*" (VIII.2.24–32; VIII.3.35–43; VIII.4.4–62)
Glasheen, Adaline. "Rough Notes on Joyce and Wyndham Lewis" (VIII.5.67–75)
1971–73 Ioannidou, Ioanna, and Knuth, Leo. "Greek in *The Mookse and the Gripes*" (VIII.6.83–8; X.1.12–16)
1972 Skrabanek, Petr. "Slavonic List" (IX.4.51–68)
Goodwin, David. "Hebrew in the *Wake*" (IX.4.68–75)
Swinson, Ward. "Macpherson in *Finnegans Wake*" (IX.5.89–95)
Atherton, James. "Sus in Cribro" (IX.6.111–13)
1973 Skrabanek, Petr. "More Hebrew" (X.6.88–91)
1974 Schenoni, Luigi. "Amaro in *Finnegans Wake*" (XI.4.68–70)
1975 Ioannidou, Ioanna, and Knuth, Leo. "Greek in *Finnegans Wake*" (XII.3.39–54)
MacArthur, Ian. "More Bog Latin and Shelta" (XII.3.54)
——. "Hungarian in *Finnegans Wake*" (XII.5.85–6)
1976 Bosinelli, Rosa Maria. "Italian in I.1–8" (XIII.2.19–32)
Barsch, Karl. "Finnish Words in *Finnegans Wake*" (XIII.4.73–4)
Skrabanek, Petr. "Anglo-Irish in *Finnegans Wake*" (XIII.5.79–84)
Rose, Danis. "Corrections to Jacquet's *Joyce et Rabelais*" (XIII.6.106–8)
1977 Staples, Hugh C. "Legal Language in 573.33–576.09" (XIV.4.55–60)
1978 Aubert, Jacques. "Breton Proverbs in Notebook VI B. 14" (XV.6.86–89)
Rose, Danis. "Breton in ʌ a/b" (XV.6.90–92)
1979 O'Hanlon, John. "In the Language of Flowers" (XVI.1.9–12)
Senn, Fritz. "Seeking a Sign" (XVI.2.25–8)
Manganiello, Dominic. "Irish Family Names in *Finnegans Wake*" (XVI.2.30–1)
O'Hanlon, John, and Rose, Danis. "Specific use of Yeats' 'A Vision' in *Finnegans Wake*" R (XVI.3.35–44)
Rose, Danis, and O'Hanlon, John. "Swedish in Four" (XVI.5.73–5)
1980 Rose, Danis, and O'Hanlon, John. "Constructing *Finnegans Wake*: Three Indexes" I (XVII.1.3–15)
Rose, Danis. "More on Huck Finn" (XVII.2.19–20)
MacArthur, Ian, Nersessian, Verej, and Rose, Danis. "Armenian in II.4" (XVII.2.26–7)
Rose, Danis, and O'Hanlon, John. "Finn MacCool and the Final Weeks of Work in Progress" (XVII.5.69–87)

I also made use of further Italian word-lists prepared by Luigi Schenoni, and a German list from Wilhelm Füger to supplement Bonheim's *German Lexicon*. These lists were intended for publication in the *Newslitter*, but regrettably had still not appeared when production ceased in 1984. *A Wake Newslitter* has now been replaced by *A Finnegans Wake Circular*, edited by Vincent Deane. Copies may be obtained from him at 38 Anna Villa, Ranelagh, Dublin 6, Ireland. The issues that have so far appeared have been most useful. I have made particular use of Petr Skrabanek's studies of FW 483–5 (in Issue 1) and Armenian (in Issue 3).

For permission to quote from Joyce's works and MSS I am grateful to the Society of Authors, literary representatives for the Estate of James Joyce. The Buffalo Notebooks are used by permission of the State University of New York at Buffalo. I wish to thank the Viking Press, New York, and Faber and Faber, London, for permission to quote from *Finnegans Wake* and from *Letters of James Joyce*, vol. 1, edited by

Stuart Gilbert, and vol. 3, edited by Richard Ellmann; the Viking Press and Jonathan Cape, London, for extracts from *A Portrait of the Artist as a Young Man*; and Random House, New York, and the Bodley Head, London, for extracts from *Ulysses*.

A rather longer interval is anticipated before the appearance of a third edition of *Annotations* than that which separated the first and second. I should be glad to receive comments from readers for use in preparing the third edition. They should be sent directly to me at Jonquil Cottage, Blacklion, Greystones, Co. Wicklow, Republic of Ireland.

Abbreviations

It is difficult to decide what educational standard the user of this kind of book should be assumed to have acquired. Certain foreign words, particularly the French, are so commonplace that a definition almost constitutes an insult. I feel that anyone capable of digesting *Ulysses*, an essential preliminary to *Finnegans Wake*, should be able to handle *Annotations* without difficulty. There are of course an enormous number of echoes and overtones in the text that seem far too obvious to gloss; the effect of glossing them would be to obscure the really useful matter by pointless distraction of the reader. I have tended to include any such additions when specified by my corresponants, for I assumed that for those exegetes the words in question were not obvious. Future editions of *Annotations* may require the excision of some of these notes to make space for more arcane glossary.

Certain items appearing frequently in *Finnegans Wake* are glossed merely by a tag. The full explanation would necessitate inordinate repetition of data such as the following:

Giambattista Vico (1668–1744) is the author of *Principi di Scienza Nuova* (*The New Science*), in which is expounded his theory that a common cyclical pattern identifies the histories of diverse nations. The cycle consists of (i) the age of gods, represented in primitive society by the family life of the cave, to which God's thunder had driven man; (ii) the age of heroes, characterised by the continual revolutionary movements of the plebians against the patricians; (iii) the age of people, the final consequence of the levelling influence of revolutions. The three ages are typified by the institutions of birth, marriage and burial, respectively, and followed by a short lacuna, the *ricorso* (resurrection) linking the third age to the first of a subsequent cycle. These four periods are illustrated by the four books into which *Finnegans Wake* is divided, and also by concise references to attributes to the ages (e.g. their institutions).

Annotations simply states 'Viconian cycle' in such instances.

The ultimate male protagonist of the *Wake*, designated Ш in Joyce's MSS, is often discovered in the text as a formula 'HCE'; for example, in the first sentence as 'Howth Castle and Environs'. In such cases *Annotations* gives 'HCE' (or in scrambled cases, 'ECH,' etc.) Similarly, the ultimate female protagonist Δ is indicated by 'ALP', 'LAP', etc.

Rival male particles ⊏ and Λ are sometimes demonstrated by the presence of specific emblems. The tree (⊏) and stone (Λ) are indicated by the words 'tree/stone' (or 'stone/tree'). Further designations for ⊏/Λ are 'Nick/Mick' (Old Nick and St Michael), 'Jerry/Kevin' and 'Nolan/Browne'. The latter unit is usually given with Λ first, to recall the Dublin bookshop 'Browne and Nolan' and the sixteenth-century philosopher Giordano Bruno of Nola, who discussed the coincidence of opposed contraries and whose name is made to illustrate the principle. ⊏ and Λ sometimes fuse to create a further unity, Λ⊏ who stands opposed to Ш. The attack of Λ⊏ on Ш is often identified with Buckley's shooting of the Russian General (see the gloss at 335.14–17) and may be alluded to simply by the gloss 'Buckley'. Further, in so far as Ш can be identified with Charles Stewart Parnell, the Λ⊏ attack is partly the attempt of the forger Richard Pigott to incriminate Parnell in the Phoenix Park Murders of 1882 by means of false letters. Pigott was trapped at the enquiry into these letters by his spelling of the word 'hesitancy' as 'hesit*e*ncy', and the latter form is used here as a gloss in reference to the incident.

Rival female particles ⊣ and ⊢ are occasionally indicated by 'dove/raven' when these emblems appear in the text. Components in the love-triangle Λ⊏ ⊣ Ш include the legendary Tristan (Λ⊏), Isolde (⊣) and King Mark (Ш). The parallel Irish legend features Diarmaid (corresponding to Tristan), Grania (corresponding to Isolde) and

Finn MacCool (King Mark). These persons may be casually referred to at points in *Annotations*. As Finn is an example of ᗰ, his demise in the *Annals of the Four Masters* is of consequence. The Masters themselves illustrate an aged male tetrad, ✕, and the date they give for the event, A.D. 283, multiplied by their number, 4, gives 1132, an important recurrent number in the *Wake*. Its appearance is simply marked '1132' here.

Certain frequent quotations appear in simplified form: Parnell's words when about to be deposed as leader of the Irish party were not exactly 'When you sell, get my price', but Joyce takes them to be so. Wellington denied having said 'Up, guards, and at 'em' at Waterloo, but the phrase is here attributed to him as Joyce uses it in Wellington contexts. The name 'Eblana' used by Ptolemy has been taken erroneously to refer to Dublin, and is treated here as such, in keeping with Joyce's usage. The prayer beginning 'Exsultet jam Angelica turba caelorum', which accompanies the lighting of the Paschal candle during the Roman Catholic service of Holy Saturday, includes the phrase 'O felix culpa, quae talem ac tantum meruit habere Redemptorem!' ('O happy fault, that merited such a redeemer!'). This is rendered ''Exsultet'': 'O felix culpa!' The abbreviation 'Ppt' (i.e., 'poppet') used by Swift in the *Journal to Stella* for his and Stella's name is given ''Swift: 'Ppt' ''. The relationship of Swift with Stella and Vanessa is an illustration of that between ᗰ and ⊣ and ⊢. Lady Morgan's phrase 'Dear Dirty Dublin' occurs too often to be repeatedly glossed with her name. There are also certain parts of the city that must be memorized.

In addition to the principal rivers passing through it, the Liffey, Tolka, and Dodder, we have the following specific areas:

Baile Átha Cliath: Irish name of Dublin, 'Town of the Ford of the Hurdles'.

Blackrock: Urban district on the coast five miles south of the city center.

Chapelizod: Village on the Liffey three and a half miles west of the center. The name derives from Isolde, who is said to have had a bower there. Chapelizod is the setting for Joseph Sheridan Le Fanu's novel *The House by the Churchyard* (page references here are to the 1904 edition).

Clontarf: Coastal parish three miles east-northeast of the center, the scene of a battle in A.D. 1014, when high king Brian Boru defeated the Danish invaders, although himself assassinated in the process.

Dalkey: Coastal urban district nine miles south of Dublin.

Dún Laoghaire: Maritime borough between Blackrock and Dalkey. 'Dun Leary' in old accounts was renamed Kingstown in honor of George IV's visit to Ireland in 1821. Original name restored after Irish independence.

Howth: Promontory and peninsula on north side of Dublin Bay. Name derived from Danish *hoved*, a head. Highest point is the Ben of Howth, rocky summit with heather and gorse. Supposedly a hiding place of Diarmaid and Grania when pursued by Finn. Howth Head in *Finnegans Wake* equated with ᗰ. Grania O'Malley, the sixteenth-century Irish pirate, was refused admission to Howth Castle and in revenge kidnapped the Earl of Howth's son (used in FW 021–3).

Leixlip: Village six miles west of Chapelizod. Its name means 'salmon leap' and refers to the adjacent salmon leap on the river Liffey.

Lucan: Village between Chapelizod and Leixlip, noted for its spa. Birthplace of Patrick Sarsfield, Earl of Lucan, hero of the Irish Jacobite wars.

Phoenix Park is described as follows in *Thom's Dublin Directory* ' . . . contiguous to the N.W. boundary of Dublin city, and N. of the river Liffey, comprises an area of 1,760 statute acres, and is about seven miles in circumference. Irish antiquarians derive its name from a spring of limpid water, in Irish *fionn-uisge*, pronounced *fin-uiske*, and gradually corrupted into *phoenix* . . . enclosed for a deer park by the Duke of Ormonde, in the reign of Charles II. Several additions were subsequently made to it, and the whole was laid out in an ornamental manner by the Earl of Chesterfield, when Lord-Lieutenant of Ireland, who also erected in it a pillar thirty feet high, surmounted by a phoenix rising out of the flames, in allusion to its popular name, and caused it to be thrown open as a place of recreation for the inhabitants of the city. There is also a splendid equestrian statue of General Gough [now removed]. In the Park are also the Wellington Testimonial, a lofty obelisk of granite, 150 feet high; and the Zoological Gardens.'

Tallaght. Parish seven miles southwest of Dublin; supposed burial place of Parthalonian invaders of Ireland.

The exact epoch from which my data is presented is variable, but normally the statement that a certain institution exists may be taken to mean it existed during the period of the composition of FW (1922–39). Institutions only existing in previous centuries will usually be given some indication of date, but in view of the very extensive demolition of old Dublin buildings over the last thirty years, it has been impossible to find space to indicate whether or not they are still standing. Frederick O'Dwyer's *Lost Dublin* (Dublin: Gill and Macmillan, 1981) is a useful guide to the phenomenon. New constructions have also affected Joyce's calculations. For instance, statements at 254.12–13 and 547.30 about the Liffey bridges are invalidated by the appearance of two recent road bridges seaward of the Loop Line.

The same considerations which apply to visible artefacts apply also to dialect. What was Dublin slang at the turn of the century overlaps to some extent with present usage, but changes are rapid in the vulgar tongue and it can be dangerous to extrapolate. The process of geographical demarkation of slang or colloquial expressions is an awkward one: many so-called Dublin expressions are also current elsewhere in Ireland, and often in parts of Northern Britain and Scotland also. To what extent Joyce would have been aware of this spread it is impossible to say, and whether it matters is a question for the reader. The pointers I use—dialect, slang, colloquial, and so on—are, I hope, not too inaccurate. FW is very partial to such items and the research necessary to exactly delimit them would be enormous, and perhaps ultimately of no great help to the reader.

General Abbreviations

An asterisk at the bottom of a page, followed by a reference, indicates that all asterisked items on that page are taken from the source specified. The system of conventions adopted in Hart's *Concordance to "Finnegans Wake"* is complied with; for instance, locations in the text are given as five-digit references with a period between page number and line number. A bracketed page/line reference means that the reader's appreciation of the point at which it occurs should be enhanced by his examining the area indicated, either in the *Wake* or in *Annotations* itself.

Am.	America(n)
Arch	archaic
Aust	Australia(n)
BVM	Blessed Virgin Mary
Coll	Colloquial
C	century
ca.	circa
cg	children's game
D	Dublin
Dial	dialect
11th E.B.	*Encyclopaedia Britannica* (the 11th edition, possessed by Joyce)
Eng.	England, English
FB	Frank Budgen, friend of Joyce
Fr.	France, French
FW	*Finnegans Wake*
Her	heraldry
HF	*Huckleberry Finn* (with chapter from which quote taken)
HSW	Harriet Shaw Weaver (Joyce's patron)
Ir.	Ireland, Irish
J	Joyce
L/R	a type of consonant split in Celtic languages
Ms	song in John McCormack's repertoire (used in III.1–2 only)
Mil	military
Naut	nautical

nr	nursery rhyme	*Sl*	slang
P/Q	a type of consonant split in Celtic languages	*U*	*Ulysses* (page numbers from 1961 Random House edition; 'emended' means form cited is that in Critical edition, Garland, 1984)
ph	popular phrase or saying		
pr	proverb		
Portrait	*A Portrait of the Artist as a Young Man*	*Univ.*	university
r	river	U.S.	United States
R.C.	Roman Catholic	VI.B.	reference followed by number and page of one of Joyce's notebooks at the University of Buffalo
Rh. Sl	rhyming slang		
s	song (including hymns, etc.; airs to which songs sung are in square brackets)	WW	World War
		⚔	battle

Details of the L/R and P/Q splits are given in O Hehir's *Gaelic Lexicon for "Finnegans Wake."*

Language Abbreviations

Where a given word is identical in several languages, the best known of them will normally be specified (e.g., German in the event of an overlap between German, Dutch, and Danish). However, evidence of Joyce's intentions from the manuscripts can influence attribution. For example, many words that could be given as Spanish are found in Joyce's listings of Portuguese, and labeled here accordingly.

Exceptions to the overlap principle occur where a high concentration of one of the secondary forms is found in a restricted area of the text. Thus, in pages 075–78 there are so many Dutch words that identical spellings in German will be overlooked, and in pages 311–32 Norwegian, using pre-1930s spelling, will be used in preference to Danish. The languages known as Bog Latin, Shelta and Bearlagair Na Saer are examples of the 'Secret Languages of Ireland' described in R.A.S. Macalister's book of that name (Cambridge, 1937). The reader is referred to Adaline Glasheen's paper "*Finnegans Wake* and the Secret Languages of Ireland," *A Wake Digest*, 48–51. Where alternative characters are possible (e.g., Danish å = aa) the tendency is always to employ the form closest to that on the FW page, or if there is no difference, the more usual of the two.

Alb	Albanian	*G*	German
Am	Amaro (Italian underworld slang)	*Gi*	Gipsy
AngI	Anglo-Irish	*Gr*	Greek
AngInd	Anglo-Indian	*Heb*	Hebrew
Ar	Armenian (Eastern dialect)	*Hin*	Hindustani
Arab	Arabic	*Hu*	Hungarian
Bas	Basque	*I*	Irish (modern spelling)
BL	Bog Latin	*Ice*	Icelandic
BLM	Beche-la-Mar (Melanesian pidgin)	*It*	Italian
BNS	Bearlagair Na Saer	*J*	Japanese
Bre	Breton	*Ki*	Kiswahili
Bul	Bulgarian	*L*	Latin
Bur	Burmese	*Li*	Lithuanian
C	Chinese	*Ma*	Malay
C.f. rom	Chinese with French romanisation of characters	*ME*	Middle English
		MGr	Modern Greek
C. Pi	Chinese pidgin	*N*	Norwegian
Cz	Czech	*OCS*	Old Church Slavonic
Da	Danish	*OE*	Old English
Du	Dutch	*OF*	Old French
Es	Esperanto	*O Ice*	Old Icelandic
F	French	*ON*	Old Norse
Fi	Finnish	*Per*	Persian

Port	Portuguese	*Sh*	Shelta
Pro	Provençal	*Skt*	Sanskrit
PS	Pan-Slavonic	*Sp*	Spanish
R	Russian	*Sw*	Swedish
RR	Rhaeto-Romanic (Roumansch)	*SwG*	Swiss German
Rum	Rumanian	*T*	Turkish
Rut	Ruthenian (Ukrainian)	*Vo*	Volapük (artificial language)
Sa	Samoan	*We*	Welsh
SC	Serbo-Croat		

The only serious problems arising from differences between spelling and apparent pronunciation should be with the Irish words, where the reader must remember that the aspirated forms 'bh' and 'mh' have a sound value corresponding to 'v' or 'w'.

Adam & Eve's Church, D, beside *r* Liffey, on site of tavern of same name
riverain: pertaining to a river *It Dial* riveran: they will arrive
Commodus: Roman Emperor Vico Vico Road, Dalkey
L vicus: street, village vicious circle
*'Sir Amory Tristram 1st earl of Howth changed his name to Saint Lawrence, b. in Brittany (North Armorica)'
HCE
F violer: violate viola d'amore (musical instrument) *F* pas encore: not yet
*'viola in all moods and senses' *Naut* short sea: one with close waves * 'ricorsi storici of Vico'
The legendary Tristan (Malory's Sir Tristram) spent youth in Brittany, returned to Cornwall & thence to Ir. to fetch
Isolde for his uncle, King Mark North America happy Xmas
(Isthmus of Sutton [*Gr* isthmos: neck] *G* wiederfechten: refight Peninsular War (Napoleonic) (Howth
joins Howth to mainland) is a peninsula)
Topsawyer's Rock: formation on *r* Oconee *L* exaggerare: to mound up
*'themselse: another dublin 5000 inhabitants'
*'Dublin, Laurens Co, Georgia, founded by a Dubliner, Peter Sawyer, on r. Oconee. *Sl* mumper: halfbred gypsy, beggar
Its motto: Doubling all the time' *It* gorgo: whirlpool *Gi* gorgio: a non-gypsy
*'flame of Christianity kindled by St Patrick' *'bellowed: the response of the peatfire of faith to the windy words
afar of the apostle' *I* mise: me
G taufen: baptise Matt 16:18: 'thou art Peter' Moses, Moses (burning bush)
*'The venison purveyor Jacob got the blessing meant for Esau' very soon
scad: trick As a boy Parnell was called 'Butthead' Thackery: *Vanity Fair*
*'Parnell ousted Isaac Butt from leadership'
*Swift's Stella & Vanessa both had name Esther saucy two-one
F sosie: double, counterpart Vanessa wrote a rebus deriving Jonathan Swift's name from those of the biblical Joseph
s O, Willie brew'd a peck o'maut Jameson whiskey Guinness brewery *L roridus: dewy & Nathan
*'Noah planted vine & was drunk' *C* shen: god, spirit *'At the rainbow's end are dew and
G Regenbogen: rainbow *G* ringsum: around the colour red'
(7 clauses; 7 rainbow colours) *AngI* bloody end to the lie: no lie
(stuttering) *J* kaminari: thunder
Babel *Hin* karak: thunder *Gr* brontaô: I thunder *F* tonnerre: thunder
It tuono: thunder *Sw* åska: thunder *I* tórnach: thunder
Port trovão: thunder *Old Rum* tun: thunder *Da* tordenen: the thunder
Wall Street parr: young salmon *F* père retailed
Old Parr: Eng. centenarian accused of incontinence
early to rise Christy's Minstrels ministry

F chute: fall
entail: an inheritance not to be disposed of
'The Solid Man': W. J. Ashcroft, D music hall performer (If Howth is head of a sleeping giant, his feet stick up in
Humpty Dumpty Phoenix Park)
enquiring inquest

(5 toes) Castleknock, W. of Phoenix Park (' knock' means 'hill')
Turnpike in Chapelizod
Orange & Green factions *Du* rust: rest
Basque word for orange etymologised 'the fruit which was first eaten'

*letter, 15/11/26, to HSW

⚔ Catalaunian Fields, A.D. 451. Attila & G gegen: against U.13: 'fishgods of Dundrum'
Ostrogoths beaten by Aetius & Visigoths: most significant conflict of these rival Gothic tribes
Aristophanes: *The Frogs*: 'Brekekekex koax koax' (chorus of frogs' ghosts in Hades)

* badelaire: type of sword artists Vernon family
* partisan: type of pike supposedly possesses
s Master Magrath * migraine: fire grenade Brian Boru's sword
* malchus: type of sword Malachi Mulligan * verdun: type of sword ⚔ Verdun
* baliste, catapulte: Whiteboys: C18 Ir. insurrectionists, hoodie: hooded crow
siege engines cannibalism dressed in white shirts
Howth Head assegai boomerang God's blood!
* aze gaye: type of lance maelstroms (Ireland's people)
F sang: blood *G* Lärm: noise
St Lawrence (003.03) *F* larme: tear
AngI ph at all, at all chance-medley: chance encounter *ph* castles in the air
St Lawrence O'Toole: patron saint of D *AngI* cashel: stone fort
s 'Bid me to live, . . . thy *L* ego te absolvo: I absolve you (R.C.)
Protestant to be' seduced
s There's Hair Like Wire Coming out of the Empire
(Jacob's deception of Isaac) hay straw
Jacob how hath sprawled *Du* met: with
Howth prowled *ph* my stars!
dust (devil/angel)
dusk
finespun Isa 48:13: 'my right hand hath spanned the heavens'
fane: flag, pennant, weathercock
First words sung by Wagner's Tristan: are you sure? bog-oak: coniferous wood preserved in peat-bogs
'Was ist? Isolde?'
alder peace sleep fall
In Norse myth the ash (Askr) was the first man, the elm (Embla) the first woman
Macpherson: *Fingal* II.52: 'If fall I must, my tomb shall rise'
'will . . . must'–indeterminism (free will) v. determinism (necessity)
farce for the nonce Phoenix (from ashes)
nuns finish
Ibsen: *The Master Builder* (*Bygmester Solness*) *G* Freimaurer: freemason
(Parnell & Lewis Carroll stuttered)
Broadway imaginable *Sl* rushlight: liquor *D Sl* farback: house with
rushlight: candle made from rush dipped in grease 2 back rooms
messuage: dwelling house plus JOSHUA JUDGES
adjacent land & buildings NUMBERS
Helvétius, freethinker yesterday Sterne/Swift (also Swift's
LEVITICUS (commit to writing) DEUTERONOMY predecessor was John Sterne)
r Styx *F* tête: head Swift: *Tale of a Tub*
wash the features of his face
Swift/Sterne Moses wrote Pentateuch (1st 5 books of Bible)
s Finnegan's Wake 1):
'Tim Finnegan lived in Walkin Street, GENESIS EXODUS
A gentleman Irish mighty odd, evaporated Guinness (ousted meanwhile, 272.22–7)
He had a tongue both rich & sweet, Pentateuch Punch & Judy *Jean-Jeudi: penis
An' to rise in the world he carried a hod. *G* panschen: mix (water & wine)
Now Tim had a sort of a tipplin' way 80 'man of God' (Deut 33:1) = Moses HCE
With the love of the liquor he was born,
An' to help him on with his work each day, *G* Bildung: education *L* supra: above
He'd a drop of the craythur every morn' tope: drink heavily thorp: village
r Hwang-ho ALP had a little wife
so-&-so Alice P. Liddell: Lewis Carroll's model for *Alice in*
to ugg: to fear hare & hounds *Wonderland*
hugged with her hair hands take up your partner (*s* Finnegan's Wake, chorus:
Balbus: Roman who bibulous mitre on head 'Dance to your partner')
built a wall (*Portrait* I) balbulus: stuttering
L habitaculum: dwelling place fancied
St Patrick's father supposedly maintained lighthouse at
Haroun-al-Raschid, caliph of Bagdad in *Arabian Nights* Egbert Boulogne built by Caligula
HCE 2 Frankish kings were called Childeric calculate by multiplication
Sl in one's altitudes: drunk malt night light
Round Table
steeple
wondrous (dressed stone) Woolworth Building, N.Y.C. (skyscraper)
Da opstandelse: resurrection originating
fire escape (Parnell alleged to awful Howth Ir. philosopher John Scotus Erigena
have escaped from Cap. O'Shea down one) Eiffel Tower height *L* erigo: I erect

*Lazare Sainéan: *La Langue de Rabelais*, Paris, 1922

L caeli: heavens   Caelestius, disciple of heretic Pelagius, was probably Irish
G Himmel: sky, heaven   Himalaya
toploftical: haughty   Moses' burning bush   Tower of Babel
bush on top of newbuilt tower   Bush is sign of an inn or place where liquor sold
St Laurence O'Toole, patron of D, contemporary of St Thomas à Becket
F larron: thief   *Da* klatre: climb   *AngI* clittering: noise of hurrying feet

Hamlet V.1.29: [Adam] 'was the first that ever bore arms'   Vasily Buslaev, hero of ballad cycle of Novgorod   wassail, booze
I laoch: warrior   Riesengebirge (Sudetic Mts)   *G* Hure: whore   *Her* vert: green
R buslai: drunkard   *G* Riesen: giant   (D coat of arms)
L ancilla: handmaiden   *Her* argent: silver   he-goat   *AngI* horrid horn: fool
F troublant: perturbing   Poursuivant: an officer of the College of Arms
escutcheon   *Her* fesse: a third of the field, enclosed by 2 horizontal lines   *Gr* hêlios: the sun   *Her*, 'of the second': 2nd colour in description of heraldic object
nr A Was an Archer (e.g. 'T was a tinker & mended a pot')
US Sl hooch: liquor
Monday morn
comedy
wine sours to vinegar
fine   Sunday eve

G eigentlich: really   *Gr* tragodia: tragedy   *G* Donnerstag: Thursday

original   Cubehouse: lit. trans. of Ka'aba, centre of Islam   Earwicker
eyewitness
(Vico's thunder)   farts   'Our Father' (Lord's Prayer)
Pilgrim must visit Arafata, hill near Mecca
T shebi: likeness   Koreish: ruling tribe in Mecca at time of Mohammed, persecuted him
shabby chorus of unqualified Moslems   Kali: Hindu death-goddess   caliph
Black Stone of Ka'aba at Mecca (came down white but was blackend by sin)

righteousness

5 set times of day for Mohammedan prayer: just after sunset, at nightfall, at daybreak, just after noon & in mid-afternoon
Mohammed used toothpicks
Koran, Sura 8: 'ownership of leather beds'

pr A nod is as good as a wink to a blind horse
neighbour   *Arab* nabi: prophet
It santi: saints   prophet's coffin (that of Mohammed is eversuspended)
absent
Arab jebel: mount   Egyptian   *F* herbe: grass
ph between the devil & the deep blue sea
Friday

second sight   occasionally answers   Ansars ('helpers') took down the Koran

dromedary

L collapsus: fallen in

premises

Arabian Nights ('The Thousand Nights & a Night')   Sarah/Abraham

s The Holly & the Ivy   Valhalla   Rollright Stones: stone circle nr Chipping Norton
bite Eve's apple   Abel   Rolls Royce
Carnac, Brittany, site of megaliths   Stonehenge   kistvaen: box-shaped tomb   *I* fág a bealach: clear the way
I carraig: rock, stone   *Da* engen: the meadow   Tristram used name Tramtris in Ireland
M Gr autokinêton: automobile
Gr hippos: horse   Fleet St, D   Thurn und Taxis: rich Austrian family, ran postal service
turning taxis
megaphones   basilicas   Areopagus: Supreme Court at Athens
Du kerk: church
Sl hoys: shoplifter   brool: to murmur   *s* The Peeler & the Goat
Mecklenburg St, D (in Nighttown)   *Sl* bite one's ear: borrow money   Marlborough Barracks, D
Merlin entombed alive
burrock: wicker basket for catching fish   *I* bóthar mór: main road
The Four Courts, D

The Twelve Pins, mts in Galway omnibuses
walkingsticks twelvepence *It* nubi basse: low clouds
sliding
Seventyfirst dirigibles: airships, balloons
Horace: *Odes* III.29.12: 'Fumum et opes strepitumque Romae' ('The smoke & the grandeur & the noise of Rome')
Sick & Indigent Roomkeepers' Society, D
L 'durum et durum non faciunt murum': 'stern measures do not build a protecting wall'
G Turm: tower
G Aufruhr: commotion, revolt
G Aufruf: call, summons
cg Ring-a-ring o'roses: 'One for me, & one for you, & one for little Moses'
Butt Bridge, D
s Finnegan's Wake 2): 'One morning Tim was rather full, Howth hod it
His head felt heavy which made him shake. *Da* hodet: head
He fell from the ladder & broke his skull, in course of *G* stottern: stutter
So they carried him home his corpse to wake'
s 'Needles & pins, blankets & shins, when a man is married his sorrow begins' Egyptian Mastaba tombs

Lute is a Chinese emblem of matrimony

AngI shee: fairy
Gr schizô: split *I* síodh: tomb *s* Pretty Molly Brannigan: 'When I hear yiz crying round me "Arrah,
G Scheisse!: shit! Finn MacCool why did ye die?"' Finn MacCool
fine Thursday morning sighed

s Hooligan's Christmas Cake Sullivans (573.06–7)
duodecimally
dismally
ululation: wailing *s* Johnny I Hardly Knew Ye: 'With drums & guns, & guns & drums'
s Hooligan's Christmas Cake: 'There were plums & prunes & cherries, Raisins & currants & cinnamon too'
s Phil the Fluter's Ball: 'Then all joined in wid the utmost joviality'

Gog & Magog, legendary giants

C . . . HE *Da* han: he *Da* hun: she
Chinese Han Dynasty & their chief enemies the Huns
Dial: kinkin: small barrel Kincora, Brian Boru's home can-can
chorus
(4 comments by ✕)
(rhythm of *s* Brian O'Linn)
s Brian O'Linn King Priam of Troy daylabouring
L prius: before *L* olim: once
pillowstone: grave marker Jacob used stone for pillow (Gen 28:11) *Du* bier: beer
Stone of Destiny (Coronation Stone) brought from Scone in Scotland
G sich: himself Vulg Ps 129:1: 'De profundis' *s* Adeste Fideles: 'O come all ye faithful'
Finnegan Oscar Wilde: *De Profundis*
I bradán: salmon Apocalypse
L finis: end *It* bocca: mouth
I fionn-uisce: clear water barrow: burial mound Genesis
s Finnegan's Wake 2): 'They rolled him up in a nice clean sheet, & laid him out upon the bed,
With a gallon of whisky at his feet, & a barrel of porter at his head'
s Phil the Fluter's Ball: 'With the toot of the flute & the twiddle of the fiddle, O'
'There is but one God' (Islam) whole
old
tautologically
(letter, 13/5/27, to HSW: 'Ш The sign in this form means HCE interred in the landscape')
flat of his back Tower of Babel
Hom: Iranian divine drink, anthropomorphised as a demigod who is broken in a mortar but revives
Humphrey Chapelizod, D (Isolde's chapel) Ashtown, nr Phoenix Park
Bailey Light on Howth Bailywick: area under a bailiff Howth
I barr an: the top of
Howth Head *ph* to foot the bill
hill Ireland's Eye: small island nr Howth HCE
Bill: name applied to some promontories
I ochone!: alas! *N* fjell: mountain bay windows *Gr* boes: cries oboes
N fjord: bay

livelong

Howth

telltale ALP Anna Livia Plurabelle

(this para. has many names of fish & musical instruments) *It* flutti aflitti: wailing waves trochee (metrical foot: long-short) Ocarina: a musical instrument *It* o carina!: that's nice!

Swift's Vanessa Peter, Jack & Martin: Catholic, Anglican & Lutheran Churches in Swift's *Tale of a Tub*

ins & outs *Tale of a Tub*

houses tomb

ph Dear Dirty Dublin Grace: 'For what we are about to receive may the Lord make us truly thankful'

G taub: deaf

Poolbeg lighthouse & Kish lightship, D

AngI kish: basket craw: stomach *s* London Bridge Is Falling Down

It gran pupo: big baby grampus: name for various whale species

spreads *Arch* whase: who is, what is

on the point of death

the First what is by *Du* baken: beacon St Patrick

King Lear III.4.187: 'Fie, foh, & fum' *Sl* bake: head

Kennedy's Bread (D) (bread & wine: Communion, Last Supper &c.)

O'Connell Ale from Phoenix Brewery owned by Daniel O'Connell's son *s* Dobbin's Flow'ry Vale

Danu: mother-goddess of Tuatha Dé Danann

foodstuff

(Real Presence of God in Eucharist)

bogey Behemoth (Job 40.15): prob. the hippopotamus,

Arch pyth: pith flourwhite (Eucharist) emblematic of mystery of God's creation

Noah finish! photograph *G* Gestern: yesterday

nowhere more

Salmo salar, salmon Agapemones: C19 religious community practising

Gr (hypothetical) agapemonides: sons of a loved one 'love-feasts'

smolt: salmon after parr stage *G* wohlbekannt: well known

midst woebegone

Mil Sl dead off: of meat, &c., spoiled *ph* hook, line & sinker

dead on salmon *G* schlucken: to swallow *Yiddish* shlook: shoddy person

ph neither fish, flesh nor good red herring

good riddance

Gr brontê: thunder *Gr* icthys: fish

Brontosaurus & Icthyosaurus (both extinct)

edge

HCE

L hic cubat aedilis apud libertinam parvulam: here sleeps the magistrate with the little freed-girl

ALP *Sl* flag: apron

Sunday *F* choses

F ric-à-rac: with rigorous exactitude

pennyweight *s* Little Annie Rooney

L unda: wave umbrella

Da med: with *U*.176: 'on Ben Howth rhododendrons a nannygoat'

Du slaap: sleep *I* Binn Éadair: Howth

It brontolone: grumbler *I* Seipéal Iosaid: Chapelizod

cranium

yondmost Howth *I* clé: left (side) verdigris

U.520 (of Jesus): 'He had two left feet' *ph* feet of clay

G Mund: mouth

mound

Prussians called ⚔ Waterloo 'La Belle Alliance'; centre of Fr. lines was La Belle Alliance Inn Hill 60, near Ypres, changed hands frequently during WWI

Da bagside: back, rear (Magazine Fort, Phoenix Park)

all hallowed hill Tara: ancient capital of Ireland

ambushes attributed to Wellington at Waterloo: 'Up, guards, & at them'

lying *r* Liffey

s 'Wait till the clouds roll by, Jenny' bird's-eye view

mountain's Wellington Monument, Phoenix Park (not a museum)

Waterloo

here show off

⊣ ⊢
L minxit: she urinated
foliage

Tommy Atkins Napoleon's tomb at Les Invalides
Cambronne commanded a division of Old Guard at Waterloo

F pousser: push push-pram (wheelchair for crippled war veterans)
L janitrix: female doorkeeper
genitrix Katherine Strong (079.27)

precious
Prussian

cup & saucer Admiral Byng executed (shot); Wellington had a Gen. Byng at Waterloo

(rhythm of *nr* The House That Jack Built) (English)

⚔ Salo, 1796 Crossguns Bridge, D
⚔ Loos, 1915
De Valera, on 1916: 'If only you'd come out with knives & forks' hat trick (3)
Sl to put down one's knife & fork: to die
Gr lipos: fat

Wellington's horse Copenhagen Sir Arthur
L/R
⚔ Magenta, 1859 (McMahon's victory) Iron Duke (Wellington)
⚔ Golden Spurs (Guldensporenslag), 1302
duck trousers ⚔ Quatre Bras, 1814 Magna Carta
L dux: leader Orange Toast to William III: 'who saved us from . . . brass money & wooden shoes'
F goliard: minstrel, jester Peloponnesian War, 431–404 B.C.
Goliath

Waterloo
trews Λ ⩘ ⊏
Napoleon's Marshal Grouchy at Waterloo death
⚔ Boyne, 1690 ditch
Royal Inniskilling Fusiliers at Waterloo *Sl* scotcher grey: louse
L inimicus: enemy Angel Scotch Greys (regiment) at Waterloo Devil
(many jokes begin: 'There were an Englishman, a Scotsman & a Welshman') *I* beag: small
Λ Mordred: King Arthur's nephew ⊏
Wellington: ⚔ Gawilgarh, ⚔ Argaum, 1803 ⩘ *F* petit

Wellington: ⚔ Assaye, 1803 *ME* assaye: try Tom, Dick & Harry
I say, I say *F* assez, assez! touch-hole of cannon *Sl* touch-hole; dyke; hairy ring: cunt

Thomas
Armenian verminous Delia: Artemis Julian Alps, N. Italy
varmint Delian League: Greek confederacy, organised 478 B.C.
⚔ Mons, 1914 Mont St Jean: name Eng. army gave to Waterloo, from village which Napoleon thought the key to Wellington's position
engine
Crimea hoping shellshock
crinoline used for hoop-petticoats
1796, Napoleon seizes Leghorn feigning
leghorn: straw hat
handmaid's astrology *It* strale: arrow water undies
strategy
DOVE

RAVEN *F* bander: to have erection
ravin: robbery
Wellington Monument: upright column in Phoenix Park *U*.721: 'Wonderworker, the world's greatest remedy for rectal complaints'
tallow scoop (waxworks) telescope
Excalibur (sword) Rosse, Ir. telescope maker
6 cylinder (car) *O Ice* hross: horse

Belgium (Waterloo in)　filly
⚔ Philippi, 42 B.C.
Arthur Guinness, Son & Co., Ltd.　⚔ Hastings, 1066

irritate
The Dispatches of the Duke of Wellington during his Various Campaigns, 1834–9
Thin Red Line: Argyll & Sutherland Highlanders; later used for all British Infantry
shirtfront　**S**
G Lieber Arthur, wir siegen. Wie geht's deiner kleinen Frau?:　*Du* hoogachtend: yours faithfully
Dear Arthur, we conquer. How's your little wife?　⚔ Orthez, 1814
Napoleon　tactics　⚔ Fontenoy: George II found Ir. soldiers facing him (1745)

jealous　⚔ Agincourt, 1415
again courting
Captain Boycott, Ir. land agent, ostracised　⚔Crécy, 1346
Sergeant-Major Cotton: *A Voice from Waterloo*

OE bode: messenger　Blücher's famous reply to troops that they must go on, as he had pledged his word to Wellington, led to victory at Waterloo

hurled dispatch　displayed　rear
deployed
Wellington: ⚔ Salamanca, 1812　*F* chère　*F* fichtre!　Christ cursed fig tree　yews
Wellington wrote to 'Dear Jenny' to　fuck you　(Matt 21:19)　*F* victorieux: victorious
'publish & be damned'　*F* foutre: fuck
F ça ne fait rien, votre: that doesn't matter, your (in *WWI Sl*, anglicized 'Sam fairy Ann')　First Duke of Wellington
F du tic au tac: tit for tat

'ten-league' boots　caoutchouc　retreat　⚔ Stamford, 1470

F Sl foutre le camp: go, leave

steal (Ir. pron. 'stale')
store stale stout
U.596: 'Irish missile troops' (infantry with rifles)
mistletoe (*The Golden Bough*)
cannonfodder　*G* Futter: food　100 days between Napoleon's escape from Elba, & Waterloo
Portrait I: 'the pope's nose'　papal indulgence
F blessés　*L* terra　widows　⚔ Torres Vedras, 1810
Tara: ancient capital of Ireland
AngI bawn: white
bluchers: kind of halfboot named after Blücher　red hose
F tonnerre: thunder

AngI bullsear: a clown　⚔ Camel, A.D. 656　⚔ Flodden Field, 1513

⚔ Solferino, 1859 (Napoleon III defeats Franz Josef)
submarines　⚔ Actium, 31 B.C.　⚔ Thermopylae, 480 B.C.　⚔ Bannockburn, 1314
Wellington: ⚔ Almeida, 1811, Orthez, 1814,　Sainéan, *La Langue de Rabelais* II, 205: 'Brum, a brum!
Almighty God!　Toulouse, 1814　pour se reprendre d'un lapsus'
G brummen: to rumble　*G* Donnerwetter!
General Cambronne said to have shouted　*G* Unwetter: storm　*G* Gott strafe England: God
'merde' at ⚔ Waterloo　*G* rinnen: to flow　punish England
⚔ Austerlitz, 1805 (Napoleon won)
⚔ Bunker Hill, 1775

s Tipperary: 'But my heart's right there'

thank you　*F* s'il vous plaît　*ph* scotching the snake　grape & canister: grape-
cool crape: shroud　shot & canister-shot
Dial canister: head　*F* pour le pays/paix　Prince Bismarck v. Napoleon III
'The Canister' at intersection of Main St & Napoleon St, Jamestown, St Helena　kiss
⚔ Marathon, 490 B.C.
⊣⊢ Martha & Mary
F se branler: to masturbate　*L* marmor: marble　telescope
brandish　*F* sauve-qui-peut: save himself who can!
W.G. Wills: *A Royal Divorce* (play about Napoleon's divorce)
Sl key: penis
Giambattista della Porta: *I'due Fratelli rivali*　*It* porca: sow　Wellington: ⚔ Talavera, 1809, Vimeiro, 1808
It gamba: leg　*It* bariste: barmaids　Deliver us from errors

nr 'Taffy was a Welshman, Taffy was a thief'
⚔ Spion Kop, 1900
Copenhagen 'Stonewall' Jackson: Am. Confederate general
Cape of Good Hope
Sl maxie: big mistake matrimony young bachelors
one too many
1806, Napoleon's victory over Prussians at Jena (Iena) *I* fhionn: fair ∧ P.F. Dunne: *The Dooley Philosophy* &c.–featuring Mr Dooley & Mr Hennessy, whom he calls 'Hinnissy'
hyena
1815, Napoleon's defeat by Prussians at Leipzig *I* dubh: dark ⊏
G Krieg *ME* funk: spark
hinnessy & dooley *I* siomar sin: trefoil ∧
Shem and Shaun
Sl waxy: angry G.E. Pickett: Am. Confederate general
trefoil (shamrock) from out battlefield
hinnessy & dooley *Sl* pumpship: urinate
(i.e. to light bomb)

Duke of Wellington

(suggests story of Buckley shooting Russian General because insulted when he wipes arse with sod of turf: cf 338–55) telescope crupper
Copenhagen *L* culpa: fault
Fr. Marshal Soult at Waterloo *L* insulto: I jump
Napoleon called Wellington 'general of sepoys'
Fr. Marshal Ney at Waterloo

Mahratta attack on Madras, 1741 Wellington in Mahratta War (Assaye &c.)
ph mad as a hatter Wellington: 'Up, guards, & at them'
Anglnd pukkaroo: seize! *Sl* Pukka: sure, certain bugger yourself! *Sp* usted: you Wellington, asked if he were Irish: 'If a gentleman happens to be born in a stable, it does not follow that he should be called a horse'
⚔ The Nile, 1798, fought in Aboukir Bay tinderbox
Ghent tenders his matchbox Corsican (Napoleon)
Sp usted: you 1st Marquis of Dufferin: Indian governor-general
Wellington: ⚔ Busaco, 1810

HCE

long cooling
killing
whereabouts

Jack O'Lantern: a will-o'-the-wisp; something misleading Howth
Castletown House said to have a window for each day of the year
(29) windows *s* The Three Ravens: 'Down in yonder green field Down a down hey down hey down There lies a knight slain 'neath his shield'
twentynine ○

Napoleon: ⚔ Wagram, 1809 Piltdown Man (hoax: pieces of skull supposed prehistoric)
a-waltz around
Fomorians: mythical Ir. colonists

early bird one . . . two . . . three . . . &c.

veritable tableland blackbird
Henry V II.3: Falstaff's death: 'a table of green fields' amended to 'a babbled of green fields'
Rothschild *F* L'empereur *Arch* glav: sword
Da skud: shot (Raven & Dove) ⊣⊢
unhorsed endorsed Alfred Northcliffe, Ir. newspaper magnate, born in Chapelizod

s The Three Ravens   suddenly   *Du* kraai: crow   débâcle
Λ⊼ ⊏   *Du* kraak: crash
Da kvarter: district   three boos
quarters
Thon, once worshipped in England, may be Thor
G Anschauer: observer
(lightning)   *G* Nixe: water nymph   (thunder)

Macbeth IV.1.117: 'cracke of Doome'   *RR* nebla: fog   *Da* liv: life
L nubes: cloud   *L* nubo: I cover   no, never on your life
AngI freet: superstition
much afraid
dead in the world   *King Lear* III.4.187: 'Fie, foh & fum'
RR fè: faith   *RR* fö: fire   *RR* fom: hunger
pr Boys will be boys
ph let bygones be bygones   Moore: *The Peri at the Gate of Paradise*
Da fugl: bird   bird of paradise   Fairy Godmother
(dove represents peace)   *Gr* peri potmon: concerning fate   *Heb* peri: fruit
Du kip: hen   *Da* i land: on land   *Da* i skip: on board ship   *Cz* peří: feather
Es pinglopiki: pinprick   landscape
piggyback   beak

pixillating   *L* pax   rainbows (pact of peace, Gen 9:16)
Gr euhemerema: success, good luck
blunderbus   armistice tonight

Es milito: war   tomorrow   Merry Christmas
Es paco: peace
munition   HCE

Heb nebo: height   *L* susurro: I whisper
nearby   *G* neben: beside
celebrate   coach's

s (*I*) 'Siúl, siúl, siúl arún, Siúl go socair, Agus siúl go ciúin' ('Go, go, go my dear, go securely & go calmly')
shoots around
knapsack

spatee: gaiter in imitation of Highland stocking   scapular: 2 squares of cloth, worn on priest's chest & back
flags   clavicles & scapulas (bones)
1724–copper coinage for Ireland produced by Wm Wood: a swindle. Swift wrote tirades against 'Wood's halfpence'
moonlight
bloodstone: heliotrope   Boston, Massachusetts (see 111.09–20)

Nick/Mick   Father Michael   lovely parcel of cakes

cates: choice food   how is yer, my dears?   Howitzer gun   *F* il
how are you Maggy
F elle   loff: a measure of corn   Plurabelle   *F* pleur: tear
lots of love   *s* Ah! The Syghes That Come fro' the Heart
Buckley   first
hart, buck
I cearc: hen
I ceart: correct
unto life's end   *I* slán: farewell
stain (tea stain)
booty   true to life   *G* streng: stern

historic present (tense)

Lord Mayors & Lady Mayoresses
Book of Common Prayer: Burial of the Dead: 'In the midst of life we are in death'
fish

applause   mirth
F pleures   birth control
F napperon: tray cloth   *F* sabots   Sarah: mother of Isaac   *Da* sa sær: so odd
an apron
Isaac   Hou: a god of Gurnsey   bricks   Greeks
(tell)   pricks
trousers   sides   to every
Troy

worth living *It* città: city
G zitter-: tremble

G Bettler: beggar

s While London Sleeps anything
(money)

lie of the land (liquidation of debt)

G Flut At subsidence of Universal Flood in Norse myth, Ymir's bodv became the world, his hair the trees
F flute! & his eyebrows the grass & flowers glaubrous: hairless
face *G* Herrschaft: mastery Avesta: sacred writings of Zoroaster
G Der Herr schuf die *G* Schuft: scoundrel vesta: match
Welt: The Lord *It* sarchiare: to weed with a hoe
created the world
cg '& I'll do all that ever I can, to push the business on' *G* paffen: to smoke
nr Humpty Dumpty
laziness

s Kafoozalum

The Grand Remonstrance, 1641: document produced come the morning
by Parliament giving account of royal mismanagement & recommending radical reforms
s 'Be like two fried eggs, Keep your sunny side up'

hen

favourite Queen Anne's Bounty: provision for maintenance of the poor clergy
behaviourism
Jewish Day of First Fruits time

Revue des Deux Mondes: say *G* Himmel
major Fr. literary review pimples
ph at sixes & sevens: disordered *G* Hügel: hill *AngI* colleen: girl
F colline: hill
AngI aroon: my dear St Bridget & St Patrick (003.09–10)
sitting around
G taufen: baptise Wharton's Folly: 'the Star Fort', unfinished fortress in
taffeta Phoenix Park
tripartite *Es* planco: ground

'Move over, Mick [Michael Collins], make room for Dick [Richard Mulcahy, his successor]': D graffito after Collins'
death, 1922 Nicholas Proud: secretary of D Port & Docks Board in J's time
G Berge: mountains burghers
Alf Bergin: law clerk in City Hall, D (Cork Hill)
Cork Hill, Arbour Hill, Summerhill, Misery Hill & Constitution Hill (all in D)
chest of viols: viol*in*, viola d'*amore*, viola d*a gamba*, viol*oncello*, viol*one*

contrabass ECH
s 'As I was going to St Ives, I met a man with seven wives, & every wife had seven' &c.

legend that 3 brothers, Aulaf, Sitric & Ivar, founded D, Waterford & Limerick, apparently originated with Giraldus
Cambrensis on the right
on the left Olaf Rd, Ivar St & Sitric Place nr Arbour Hill, D

squeeze out a livelihood

rebus: word-puzzle *s* Phil the Fluter's Ball: 'Hopping in the middle like a herrin' on a griddle, O!'
Romulus & Remus
F mont

Howth Head (Magazine in Phoenix Park) *F* pied: foot
Pie Poudre: a court formerly held at a fair for quick treatment of hawkers &c. (*F* pied poudreux: vagabond)

Swift: *Epigram on the Magazine* (in Phoenix Park): 'Behold a proof of Irish sense! Here Irish wit is seen! Where nothing's left that's worth defence, They build a magazine '

pound Peter's Pence: donation to R.C. church

I feach!: Look!

M.J. MacManus: *So This Is Dublin* (1927) derides J

HCE

HCE

F gravure

illkept unkempt
innkeeper
chapel shuffler

musical
magical

L murus: wall

buried dolmens incubus

Ptolemy's account of Ireland, A.D. 150

F prétendant: claiming Jubal: 'father of all such as handle the harp & organ' (Gen 4:21) exhausted

Feardorcha O'Farrelly (fl. 1736), Ir. poet

Butt Bridge, D well-known optophone which ontophanes

using A = 1, B = 2 &c., D + B + L + N = 32; W + K + O + O = 64

magazine
mausoleum
funerall: slow sad pavan danced at wakes
fun for all

optophone: instrument to enable blind to read by sound

Wheatstone invented box shaped like a lyre, into which piano's vibrations passed, & which then appeared to play itself

struggling for Ivor
lichens on weathered stones

listening for Olaf *Da* forover: forwards

G vorüber: past, gone harpsichord

AngI ollav: sage

Herodotus ✕ (Mamalujo = *Ma*tthew, *Ma*rk, *Lu*ke & *Jo*hn)

hereditary

Annals of the Four Masters (written in Donegal, which was called Boreum by Ptolemy)

Blue Books: official reports of Eng. Parliament

N f.t.: for tiden, 'at present'

I baile: town four things Dyfflinarskidi: territory around Norse D

HCE

G vier: 4

L unum: 1 Ben Bulben, mountain, Co. Sligo

Teetotum (orig. T. totum): 4- sided disk with letter on each side. In game of chance spun to see which side finished uppermost *L* duum: of 2

Months of Jewish Year: 1. Nisan. Rain stops; 4. Tammuz. Hot: fruits ripe; 8. Marchesvan. Sowing time; 12. Adar. Rain begins

 m

△ Poor Old Woman (name used for Ireland) ⊣

L trium: of 3

Goldsmith: *The Deserted Village* (Sweet Auburn . . .')

(sighs of ✕ in II.4: 'Oh dear,' 'Ay ay,' 'Ah ho,' 'Ah dearo dear')

Dysart O Dea, Co. Clare *L* quodlibet: what you please

⊏ (penman) mightier ∧ (postman) Succoth: Jewish Feast of Tabernacles

Bulwer-Lytton: 'pen is mightier than the sword'

L innocens: harmless

Anacletus II, antipope, opposed Innocent II, pope

The Book of the Dead

Grand National (horse race) *F* facile *G* Passah: Passover

A.D. 283, death of Finn MacCool (*Annals of the Four Masters*)

283 ✕ 4 = 1132 emmet: ant *G* wandern *Du* groot: great

O'Hanlon: *Life of St Laurence O'Toole* [patron of D], II: Laurence . . . O'Toole was born in the year 1132'

A.D. 1351, a shoal of whales cast ashore (*D Annals*)

Da hvid: white m

G Walfisch: whale

Eblana: Ptolemy's name for D

283 ✕ 2 = 566. Baal: Semitic fertility god (postdiluvian)

Da baal: bonfire Old Ir. Baal Fire rituals (on eve of 1 May) △

wicked wish I kish: basket turf
Kish lightship off D turds
Sothis: Egyptian name of Sirius, star of Isis: rose at beginning of Egyptian sacred year satisfy cow sacred to Isis
Saul, son of Kish Sackville St (now O'Connell St)

Da svært gode: mighty good elegant
Goody Two-Shoes (children's story) *AngI* brogues: shoes (013.25; *ph* ignorant as a kish of brogues)
D is Town of the Ford of the Hurdles (trans. of Ir. name Baile Átha Cliath)

⊣

Sp sobre las olas: over (on) the waves *G* Puppe: doll (her sister)
sob sob Swift: 'Ppt'
'pia e pura bella': religious wars of Vico's heroic age Baile Átha Cliath
Europe *AngI ph* bloody wars!

∧
⊏ *We* primas: primate, chief

nr 'St Patrick was a gentleman & came of decent people' Santry, district of D
nr 'Taffy came to my house & stole a piece of beef' 'o peace', a farce
a piece of verse

In Norse Eddas the Ginnunga-gap is the interval between aeons
apparently

ECH

Empyrean: the Highest Heaven (thunder)bolt
L excelsissimus: very highest
earthquake Danny Mann, hunchback in Boucicault's *The Colleen Bawn* Biddy Doran (112.27)
callous *L* gallus: cock *Da* døren: the door
let off

ninepence (faces on coins)

(for killing the copyist)

sinecure (der. from *L* sine cura, 'without care')
Gr gynê: woman

9th Commandment: 'Thou shalt not covet thy neighbour's wife'

Annals of the Four Masters by Farfassa O'Mulconry, Peregrine O'Clery, Peregrine O'Duignan & others

L liber lividus: blue book
Livy: Roman historian
It toh!: look! paisible: peaceable eirenic: of peace

Da fædreland: native land
N fred: peace
pricket: buck in 2nd year

pricket's sister: female fallow deer in 2nd year amid
shamrock St Patrick supposed to have used shamrock to explain Trinity
looking glasses
(donkey is the 5th province) Heber & Heremon: legendary progenitors of Ir. race
Gen 27:11: 'Esau my brother is a hairy man'
Ballymun: district of D

(compare 281.04–13) Goatstown, district of D tulips
muskrose (white) goats chew hedges
together Rush, village, Co. D, site of tulip townlands: Ir. areas of twilight
sweet rush, *Juncus* cultivation 'Holland in Ireland,' 526.06 land, size very variable
variegated Moyvally, Co. Meath

Knockmaroon Hill in *G* rings 'rum: all around
Phoenix Park
chiliad: millennium Fomorians & Tuatha Dé Danaan: legendary antagonistic Ir. colonisers
perihelion: point when nearest to the sun Tim Healy, opponent of Parnell
'Ostman': Viking (Viking occupation of D)
Firbolgs: legendary Ir. colonisers
giants *Sl* firebug: arsonist
Jerry/Kevin (⊏/Λ)
Little Green Market, D hear hear!

laughters *L* pax 404.23 'sealingwax buttons'
peace pact sealed (flowers)

Killaloe, site of Brian Boru's palace

Tower of Babel tongues (God created diversity of tongues after Tower of Babel attempt,
I teanga: language to restrict power of mankind)
Da tigge: beg
I tuigeann tú?: do you understand?
Swift's Houyhnhnms in *Gulliver's Travels* *F* parlez-vous français?

F fiancée *I* tá: is, are *It* sussurrare: to whisper, hum hummed 'sir, sir'
(often begins sentence)
Da elsker du mig, min kære pige?: do you love me, my dear girl?
(repeats sequence *I*, *It*, *N*, *F* of .13–14)
G dunkel: dark *G* hell: light
Ireland in C8–11 overrun by hordes of 'dark foreigners' (Danes) & 'light foreigners' (Norse)
F où est ton cadeau, espèce d'imbecile?: where is your present, fool?

nowadays

flora & fauna call

fuck

Howitt Mts, Australia *F* lave: wash *s* Finnegan's Wake (chorus):
Howth *ph* old as the hills 'Whack fol the dah, dance to your partner,
Welt the flure, yer trotters shake,
Wasn't it the truth I told you
Lots of fun at Finnegan's Wake'

Adam *Arch* carl: churl *Du* kopje: small hill (in S. Africa)
I ainm: name
Parthalón: legendary Ir. coloniser *ME* for-shapyn: transformed pigmy
path alone Joseph Biggar: hunchbacked supporter of Parnell
shrunk lockjaw

oh, by all that's spectral mammary
pectoral: of the chest
Mousterian man = Neanderthal man
mysterious taking nuncheon: light refreshment of liquor
the Dragon Man in Blake's *Marriage of Heaven & Hell* *ph* on the *qui vive*: on the look-out
dragoman: interpreter, in Arabic-, Persian- and Turkish-speaking countries
fief: an estate in land (Vico discusses fiefs in Roman history) January February
S Constable Sackerson Gin contains juniper brewery
March April sack *F* pluviose: midwinter month of Fr. Revolutionary calendar
arrack: Eastern liquor *It* brillo: drunk (pouring rain)

G fror: froze *Du* soort: sort *AngI* mahan: bear *Sl* miching: skulking

(fire at mouth of cave) kraal: stockade, pen

L cave! perhaps propose to us

Neanderthal Man cracked & sucked marrow bones

billowy way (sea) *F* Comment vous portez-vous aujourd'hui, mon blond monsieur?: How are you today, my fair sir?

Pillars of Hercules, Gibraltar *MGr* koulos: one-handed porter (drink)

L hirculus: little goat Sorley Boy MacDonnell, rebellious Ulster chief

Jespersen, *Language* XX.4: 'Panamanians, when addressed, used to reply "No spiggoty (speak) Inglis"'

Da Taler de Dansk?: Do you speak Danish?

r Tolka, D *NautSl* scowegian: Scandanavian

saxophone Pigott (hesit*e*ncy)

Do you speak Saxon? *G* also

shake hands strong & weak verbs in German

haphazard *Du* bloot: naked

about the bloody Greeks

Mutt & Jeff: Am. comic-strip characters

you too!

much pleasure had (at meeting you)

deaf

deafmute

Noah utterer: one who passes counterfeit coins

G Stummer: mute person

stammer

audible to be coarse

horrible to be sure

L apud: with bottle *L* surdus: deaf

surd: stupid

r Poddle, D Erin

1014: ⚔ Clontarf, D. Brian Boru defeats Danish army of occupation

('Clontarf' means 'bull meadow', hence Dungtarf = bullshit) where you ought to be

inaudible

G a bisschen: a little visible

Arch bit-kin: little bit

Brian Boru

'hesit*e*ncy'

wrath in my mind Rathmines, D district

remember him (Moore: *s* Remember the Glories of Brian the Brave)

It mi rimiro: I look at myself

G Augenblick: moment *Sl* bison: nickel (U.S. coin)

ph bygones are bygones (two sons)

ph cross your palm with silver P/Q *G* Trinkgeld: tip gilt trinket

guineas

Wood's halfpence (see 011.21) *ph* Guinness is good for you

coyne & livery: billeting practised under Brehon Laws by Ir. chiefs

F l'ouie: hearing *It* lui, lui!: it's him! ᗰ indelible

louis (coins) Wotan untellable

Harald Graycloak ruled W. Norway in C10 *I* céad míle fáilte romhat: 100,000 welcomes to you

Sitric Silkenbeard led Danes at ⚔ Clontarf

(some of his coins are preserved) grilse: salmon after smolt stage

Dublin Bar *Sl* bar: 1 pound sterling

poached salmon identical

poached egg

coyne & livery (016.31) *Gr* monomachos: gladiator
Liberties: district of D
Manneken-Pis: statue in Brussels of a child urinating

Tacitus mentions Ireland (has concise style)
ph to make a long story short
dumped the wheelbarrow of rubbish *Dial* rubbage: rubbish
Humpty Dumpty cabbages

puddingstone: conglomerate rock *F* Bruxelles

Liverpool

Lord Almighty
with what noise
similar to Clontarf (the name means 'bull meadow')

SwG schnore: chatter

s Brian O'Linn; he made breeches with 'the skinny side out & the woolly side in' Black Linn: highest point on Howth Isthmus of Sutton, joining Howth & mainland sitting
Arthur Wellesley, 1st Duke of Wellington

Baldoyle & Raheny, districts of D *I* beurla: Eng. language
Turkish to Finnish barely
Da forstand: understanding Sturk, in Le Fanu's *House by the Churchyard*, lives in Chapelizod & is stunned in Phoenix Park but briefly recovers *F* patois
G Götterdämmerung *Du* on (prefix): un- *G* umsehen: look around
obscene
good afternoon! *ph* I'll see you damned first
get after (behind) me
a dream Dunsink Observatory, D

'peninsula' means 'almost-island'
Prince Albert Island, Canada
Moyelta: the old plain of Elta, where the Parthalonians died of plague & were buried. Prob. area adjacent to Howth, perhaps also S. of D *G* Eltern: parents
whimbrel & peewee (lapwing): birds occasional on Bull Island, Clontarf salting: meadow flooded by tide

Isthmus of Sutton droit de seigneur: supposed right of a feudal overlord to deflower bride of any of his tenants on 1st night of her marriage
Da bygning: building
Gen 1:1; John 1:1: 'In the beginning'
Cape Finisterre: N.W. tip of Spain; Celts supposedly came thence to Ireland Phoenix Park Moore: *s* Let Erin Remember the Days of Old [The Red Fox]
G Punkt *G* Ruhm: fame
R svet: light white & black *s* Moddereen Rue (= little red dog, i.e. fox)
sweet & brack (salt) *R* brak: marriage
HCE crashing estuary insurgent
HCE

G niederfallen: fall down plague *F* plage: beach
place, thick as snowflakes
blizzard
Du waas: haze, mist
ON Heimskringla: world's whirl *F* tomber *F* monde
Order for the Burial of the Dead: 'ashes to ashes, dust to dust'
Gr gês: earth *G* Erde (500.30 'Brinabride, my price!')
F merde

lye: strong alkali (burial of plague victims in quicklime) *Da* smal: narrow
L fiat: let it be *L* fuit: it was *N* ly: shelter
Oslo also the stranger Babylone: district of Paris
F l'étrange: the strange Rev 17:5: 'BABYLON THE GREAT'
A. Bennett: *Grand Babylon Hotel* ALP Earwicker
nr 'Tit-tit-tittlemouse Lived in a little house' *G* Alpdruck: nightmare
Da drukne: to drown *N* ild: fire

cemetery Wagner: *Tristan & Isolde* III.3: *s* Liebestod ('love-death')

F merde! *G* Mord: murder
It morte
Wagner: *Tristan & Isolde*: Liebestod: 'Mild und leise wie er lächelt . . .' *G* behauptet: asserted
Moore: *s* By the Feal's Wave Benighted [Desmond's Song].
Slough of Despond in *Pilgrim's Progress*
Gr thanasimos: deadly swallowed
ancestral
this earth of ours
human *pr* He who runs may read rune-stones
L humus: earth Hab 2:2: 'he may run that readeth it'
G Rede: speech *nr* See Saw Sacradown, Which is the way to London Town?
3 Castles on the Arms of D
Newcastle & Crumlin (555.13)

also softly, mister

I Bí i bhur thost (*AngI* whist)!: be quiet

Forficula: genus of earwigs Morgana le Fay, King Arthur's sister, sorceress
(because they are here) *L* amnis: river
Howe: site of the Norse parliament (Thingmote) in D during Viking occupation
howe: burial mound
Viceroy *G* Grab: grave
Viking's □
Da hvad: what

N øre: ear astonished
Stone Age
N øye: eye thunderstruck Thingmote
Thor
OE abecede: alphabet *F* clef □

alphabet *G* Rede: speech

In the Koran, 'We' refers to God, 'Thou' to Mohammed & 'Ye' to the audience

MENE TEKEL

L forsan: perhaps UPHARSIN Thingmote
Dan 6:25–8: 'MENE, MENE TEKEL UPHARSIN . . . Thy kingdom is divided, & given to the Medes & Persians'
(writing on the wall at Belshazzar's feast)
Neanderthal Man
Heidelberg Man (Old Stone Age) HCE
After enlightenment Buddha walked the world *G* Heiden: heathen Edinburgh
The Buddhistic 12-fold chain of dependent origination: ignorance→impression→knowledge→name & form→
the six senses→sensation→desire→attachment→existence→birth→old age & death→ignorance

During enlightenment of Buddha a reed grew *U*.38: 'Gaze in your omphalos. Hello. Kinch here. Put me on to
from his navel Edenville'
reredos: altar screen Rama: avatar of Vishnu *L* terricola: earth-dweller

MGr vivlion viou: book of life earthquake hatch: hatchet HCE
celt: prehistoric chisel
F pourquoi *F* casser CEH
purpose P/Q assay
Gr boustrophêdon: turning like oxen in ploughing: writing with lines read
left-right, then right-left &c. (2nd sentence is 1st read backwards)

bellicose: warlike futhorc: the runic alphabet
ph billing & cooing effigy
Da forfalde: fall into decay *cg* 'Face to the east, Face to the west
fire-lighting flint Face to the one you love the best'
west Wellington: 'Up, guards, & at them'

F petit — *Gr* holos: whole

alphabet — several Q/P — *F* petits pois cuits
silver

L pecunia: money

F parole — *ON* Ragnarøkr: destruction of the Norse gods
soldiers' parole
rocks orang-utan — *AngI* wisha: indeed, well

thorn: *OE* letter(th)

midnight — Hebrew alphabet begins: aleph, beth, ghimel, daleth

(see 120.20; owls to Athens = coals to Newcastle)
alpha, beta, gamma, delta
Greekish — *F* fromage

epsilon — Ws — *L* haud: not
epicene
(hiss) — dustbin
D

F Angleterre — Gen 3:3: 'the tree which is in the midst of the garden'
F touche-à-tout

F pomme — *L* fructus — (St Patrick banishing serpents from Ireland)
(Eve's apple)

scotched

Gen 2:23: 'she shall be called Woman, because she was taken out of Man' — pick
Ottoman

bootleggers

if x = 1 & y = 36, (x+x+x)(x+y) = 111 — plus

(is three 1s) ΛΛ⊏ — ⊣⊢ 2+1

3 — Crow: *Master Kung: The Story of Confucius* 49: (examples of omens) 'Three-legged calves, big snakes' — *L* idem: the same — *Boa boa,* boa constrictor
Du kalvers: cows — calver: epithet of salmon & other fish — evergreen — Wm Archer: *The Green Goddess*
Before Confucius's birth his mother saw fabulous animal with jade tablet in mouth bearing message of prophesy — Igraine, mother of King Arthur
An ancient Chinese scholar read 'a hundredweight daily'
111 — *L* liberorumque: & of children
Conan: one of the Fianna — All Hallows — Neanderthal

F petit-fils: grandson

Paps of Ana: mts in Co. Kerry, shaped like breasts
G Ahn: ancestor
L In illis diebus (formula to introduce lesson & gospel in Mass): in those days
G Lumpenpapier: rag paper
man-mountain: Gulliver as giant in Lilliput — fountain pen
Horace: *Ars Poetica* 139: 'parturient montes, nascetur ridiculus mus' ('the mountains are in labour, a laughable little mouse is born') — (boots given to Stephen by Mulligan)
(mute religious acts the language of Vico's 1st age) — *AngI* signs on it: consequently
L quis: who — *L* quid: what
(asked you for £1)
quad — world-mind
L quod: because
righting — wrongs
rules

Lane-Poole: *Speeches & Table-Talk of the Prophet Mohammad:* 'The last milch-camel
Arch ban: curse must be killed rather than the duties of the host neglected'
Mohammed's eyebrows were divided by a vein which throbbed visibly in moments of passion

Moore............Thomas cousin-german
Mohammed married his cousin & lived chiefly Charmian: Cleopatra's attendant in *Antony & Cleopatra*
on dates & water Mohammed called Judgement Day 'the hour, the smiting, the day of decision' &c.
ancient Arabs tied camels to graves (Lane-Poole)
sheepskin parchment

It terracotta: baked earth

Gutenberg, printer, associated with beginning of era of printed books
G Mutter: type-mould *G* Guten Morgen Cromagnon Man Magna Carta
G Tintingfass: inkwell Great Primer Type
L omnibus: for everybody
rubric: heading of section of book, printed in red winepress

al Koran Mohammed's 2nd revelation (Sura *nr* What Are Little Girls Made Of, Made Of
alcohol LXXIV): 'O thou who art wrapped, rise up & warn!'
misprints

G endlich: finally

L typus: figure, form, image *Gr* topos: place full stop
tope: drink heavily

topsy-turvy typical (1 for each year of man's life)

Mohammed's imprecation: 'May his forehead be darkened with mud!'
(end of FW join) Solemnisation of Matrimony: 'What God hath joined, let no man put asunder . . . till death
Dublin's giant us do part'
daleth, Heb. letter Mahamavantara: Sanskrit world cycle
delta, means 'door'
Heb dor: i) generation; ii) dwelling

Moore: *s* Fly Not Yet, 'Tis Just the Hour mile to Babylon *N* sytti: 70
L nondum: not yet (003.10 &c.) *It* sette: 7
nr 'How many miles to Babylon? Three score & ten, sir. Will we be there by candlelight? (cf. *U.* 195)

handsel: first specimen of something; auspicious
Sl movables: small objects of value
movable type
sing-song
zig-zag
earwig storytale
Whigs & Tories
Leixlip

The Strawberry Beds, Chapelizod * C16 storytellers would begin with formula 'Au temps que les bêtes parlaient'
Du strubbeling: difficulty & end with 'Il y a de cela bien longtemps quand les poules avaient des dents'
F bégayeur: stutterer
bray * 'Car si ne le croiez, non foys je, fist elle'
Sl cuddy: donkey *pr* Walls have ears

'Forty Bonnets': nickname of Mrs Tommy Healy of Galway hopes hoopskirts
L/R *Da* barnets: the child's * *pr* Du temps des hauts bonnets (C15)
Noah, Ark *F* homme *F* femme
F pomme
ph gilded youth

medieval chansons de mal mariée *Mal maridade: Provençal dance
relate wife's escape from jealous husband * revergasse: old dance
* la Frisque: a dance * la pyrrichie: a dance
F frasques Deucalion's wife Pyrrha (parallel with Noah)
F ma foi! * la Gaye: a dance * Trippière: a dance
Morgana le Fay, King Arthur's sister, sorceress *(Mélusine transformed into snake-woman)
*Expect un pauc: a dance *la Valentinoise: a dance

*besch: S. W. wind *flouin: boat
pr it's an ill wind that blows no one good *F* flou: loose, blurred

*Lazare Sainéan: *La Langue de Rabelais*, Paris, 1922

gentlemen hearing Norway earwig

F comme ceci *G* wissen It was of a night listen!
Du het was of ie wist: it was as if he knew
HCE *F* corne: horn ALP
(Grace [Grania] O'Malley, Ir. pirate, was refused admission to Howth Castle & in revenge captured the Earl's heir)

stone/elm Old Stone Age
Gerald Nugent: *Ode Written on Leaving Ireland:* 'From thee, sweet Delvin, must I part' *Arch* eld: old
John Ball: 'When Adam delved & Eve span, *s* 'Madamina' from *Don Giovanni* watered silk
Who was then a gentleman?' delve: dig Adam
Montenotte, site of Fr. defeat *Arch* leal: lawful, loyal
of Austrians in 1794 & 1796; name means 'night-mountain'; also district of Cork
rib (Eve) Fleming: *St Patrick* 48: 'in those days, when rivers had at all times their own way'

alone

Arch Jarl: earl Howth
Van Houten's Cocoa
Laying on of Hands (in blessing, confirmation &c.) *L* gemini: twins

Giordano Bruno (see 092.06–11) had motto: In tristitia hilaris hilaritate tristis (In Sadness Cheerful, in Gaiety Sad) dummy: teat
Homer HCE
Bartholomew Vanhomrigh: father of Swift's Vanessa (innkeeper)
Diarmaid (Dermot) & Grania: equivalent of Tristan & Isolde in Fenian myth

Heroine of *s* Tam Lin pulls roses at castle *Sl* to pluck a rose: urinate
door to announce her presence *Sl* quean: whore (red rose: Lancaster)
water door
wait *Angl* forenenst: opposite
St Patrick's foreknowledge of the 3 orders of Irish *Le Petit Parisien,* journal of '20s
saints resulted from 3 visions: i) Ir. all ablaze (others at 022.03–4 & .27–8) Peru
King Mark, Tristan's uncle look as like as two peas in a pod
once (i.e. finished)
Piesporter (wine) skirmishes

Du antwoordde: answered Dutch Nassau shit! Grace O'Malley
not so (door remained shut)
Alice *I* seanda: old
Sterne: *Tristram Shandy*
wilderness

wirelessed *I* Dubh-ghall: Dane *Du* dief: thief deaf
lovecall *s* Come Back to Erin
Da svarede: answered not likely!

Grannuaile: another name of Grace O'Malley *Heb* sabaoth: armies
Da branne: fire angels
Legend that Grace O'Malley sailed for 40 years

'Tours du Monde en Quarante Jours', widely advertised in Paris before WW I Dermot had a 'lovespot'
Gulliver

owlers: those who carried wool to the coast by night, for illegal export
Annals of the Four Masters *G* tauchen: dip *L* convorto: I turn around
St Patrick said to have served 4 masters Lutheran *G* Luder: scoundrel
I ludramán: lazy idler
Dermot

summers

Henry II granted D to the citizens of Bristol
hostelry
Bartholomew Vanhomrigh down

G ringen: to wrestle
Brodar assassinated Brian Boru at ⚔ Clontarf, 1014
brother & sister
(white rose: York)
G flackern: flare
Patrick's visions (021.16–17), ii) only the mountains on fire
water
wicket window
Mark Twain
Arch twy: 2, double
shit!
G antworten: to answer
Lilliput
no man's land
I Fine Gaedhil: tribe of the Irish
Da svarede: answered
Grannuaile
St Lawrence family, Earls of Howth
'Tours du Monde en Quarante Jours' widely advertised in Paris before WW I
AngI ph the curse of Cromwell on (someone)
Crom Cruach: Celtic idol destroyed by St Patrick
F même
Caisleen-na-Cearca, castle where Grace O'Malley kept the heir of Howth, was ruthlessly demolished by Cromwell
Swift: *Tale of a Tub*
L monitrix: instructress
L provorto: I turn forwards
St Patrick said to have served 4 masters
perverted
Christian
Tristan ('sad')
Dermot
be damned to her
Hilary
apron
Mansion House, D (Lord-Mayor's residence)
Mansion House Ward, D
night
late
time
cow has 4 stomachs
Tristopher
AngI pogue: kiss
I Naomh Pádraig: St Patrick
I Naomh Brighid: St Bridget
Moore: *s* The Valley Lay Smiling before Me
Patrick's visions, iii) lamps lit in the valleys
F arc de triomphe
Tristan
s The Campbells Are Coming
Mark 3:17: 'Boanerges, which is, The sons of thunder'
Brian Boru was called 'The Terror of the Danes'
3 castles on D coat of arms
Brobdingnag (*Gulliver's Travels*)
civic collar
Isthmus of Sutton
G Hemd: shirt
Balbriggan, Co. D, site of unsuccessful cotton industry in C18
socks & gloves
Ragnar Lodbrok, Viking chief, is said to have had snakeproof pants
catgut
bandoleer
Saxon
Kattegat: sea between N. Denmark & Sweden

farfamed gumboots *PS* rud-: red (colours of rainbow)
The Peninsular War combats *F* bottes rude yelling
L panuncula: thread wound on a bobbin
indignation
Strongbow, leader of the Anglo-Normans who invaded Ireland right

ECH ordured speech spoke
N ord: word
s Polly Put the Kettle On
Per barg: thunder duppy: ghost *Arch* dup: to open
Lettish perkons: thunder *T* gök gürliyor: thundering sky *Ma* guntur: thunder
Bre kurun: thunder *Li* griauja: it thunders *R* grom gremit: thunder thunders
Rum thuna: thunder *Ki* radi: thunder *Arab* dill: thunder *Fi* ukkonen: thunder
Ice þruma: thunder *Sa* faititily: thunder *Alb* bumulloj: thunder
tea (stock ending of Ir. fairy tales: 'They put on the kettle & they all had tea')
(contraceptives)
U.588 (from Swift: *Drapier's Letters*: 'Eleven men well armed will certainly subdue one single man in his shirt')
G Schürze: apron alliterative poetry
We porthor: doorkeeper, porter
(fire, water, air [flatulence], earth)
how Kersse the tailor made a suit of clothes for the Norwegian Captain (see 311.05–09)
tiler: masonic doorkeeper unclose door = open it so far
Job 38:8,11: 'Hitherto shalt thou come, but no further' Gen 9:12: 'the covenant which I make between me
Parnell, speech in Cork, 1885: 'No man *AngI* betune: between & you'
has a right to say "Thus far shalt thou go & no farther"'
(pirate ship)
ph get the wind up *G* gehorsam: obedient

Motto of D: Obedientia civium urbis felicitas (Citizens' Obedience Is City's Happiness) *Gr* polis: city, state
Persius: *Satires* 1.84: 'De nihilo nihilum' ('Nothing can come out of nothing')
'Exsultet': 'O felix culpa!' *'Ex nihilo nihil fit (out of nothing comes nothing)' *L* malum: apple
Cz nicky: nulls, zeros *'Ex malo bonum fit (–evil–good)' *'Mickelmassed (Michael, his conquerer =
*'Hill = ᗰ Rill = Δ' *'Less be proud of, be proud of them but naturally, as hill much heaped up)'
*Arthur Guinness, Sons & Company, Ltd (go up it) as river (jump it)'

(they won't tell the secret of their source)
*'Norronesen = Old Norse, warrior' *'Irenean = Irish born, peace *L* quare siles: why are you silent?
*'The quarry & the silexflint suggest Ш silent' (eirene)' *Victoria Nyanza (089.27)
L silex: flint *Albert Nyanza **L* unde gentium festines?: 'Where the dickens are you hurrying from?'
I ní h-annsa: not hard (formula for answering riddles) Hill of Howth often cloud-capped
Du wolkenkap: cloud cap *'woollen cap of clouds' *'Audi *urio* (I long to hear)
*'he is crowned with the frown of the deaf' Es *urio* (I long to eat)'
eavesdrop *'close at hand' *'mous = Chaucerian battles *djinn *din 'the noise of an angry armed
*'his house's e(a)ve Δ water' form to suggest distance in time' battles spirit, to suggest
*'far ear = far east' King Mark distance in space'
*'His hill begins to be clouded over in the effort to hear'
such & such so & so
*'twig = AngloIrish = understand'
had to laugh *G* verflucht! (curse) but *'twig = beat with a twig'
*'Herrfluch = the curse of the Lord on you for not talking louder, he tries to grab her hair which he hopes to
abhors appears *'Manus habent et non palpabunt' (Vulg Ps 113:7) catch by a fluke'
adheres abear: tolerate *G* abhören: listen to *F* tromper: deceive
*'His ear having failed, he clutches with his The 4 Waves of Ireland: 4 points on Ir. coast (the Waves of
hand & misses & turns away hopeless & unhearing (he abhears)' Rory, Tuath, Cleena & Scéina)

landlocked *AngI* Lochlann: Scandinavian neighbours
round towers supposed to lie beneath Loch Neagh, appearing on certain days
perpetuated Ps 8:2: 'babes & sucklings'
petrifying properties attributed to waters of Lough Neagh *ph* Ireland, isle of saints & sages
morning papers Co. Louth

loaf *G* hold: handsome
G Leib
L pudor: shame *L* liber: wine
G Puder: powder
bread & water
windfall: apple; unexpected fortune
holy spire vessel floating
Sl vestal: prostitute
F plein: drunk vowels: u, i debt (I.O.U.)
F à plein voiles: in full sail

*Letter, 13/5/27, to HSW

F cache-cache: hide & seek   *L* novo: new   Dublin by Lamplight Laundry, D (cf. letter, 13/11/06, to Stanislaus explaining)
AngI ph at all at all   conveyance
& not a
skin of his teeth

brow
Gen 3:19: 'In the sweat of thy face shalt thou eat bread'   dead
Hospice for the Dying, D   earned his bread   *F* dragon volant: a sort of cannon

laws   from all evils
boll weevil: pest of cotton
Humphrey Chimpden Earwicker

Shaw: *Widowers' Houses* (Mark 12:40)   *ph* blushing from ear to ear   year's end (December)

s Finnegan's Wake 5): 'Then Micky Maloney raised his head
When a noggin of whiskey flew at him,
It missed & falling on the bed,   May . . . December
The liquor scattered over Tim;   disembarks (phoenix rises from ashes)
Bedad he revives, see how he rises
& Timothy rising from the bed,
Says "Whirl your liquor round like blazes,
Thanam o'n dhoul, do ye think I'm dead?"'

AngI usquebaugh: whiskey   Ad . . . am
L usque ad necem: even unto death
AngI thanam o'n dhoul: your souls from the devil!   *ph* dead as a doornail

Herold: *La vie de Bouddha,* describes Buddha's horse as being like a god

the phoenix burned at Heliopolis
When Tim Healy became Gov.-General of Ir. Free State, Dubliners called the Viceregal Lodge in Phoenix Park 'Healiopolis'   *I* capall a mhaistir: his master's horse
Buddha born in Kapilavastu   *It* il paese di Vattelappesca: Nowhere Land
Northumbrian   Phibsborough Road, N.D   Watling St, Roman Road   Watling St, S.D
Northumberland Road, E.D   *I* sráid: street
I bóthar mór: main road (373.05, W.)   *s* The Foggy Dew
Moore St, D
Buddha met an old man, a sick man & a corpse outside his palace & thus learned of age, sickness & death   *I* Cothraighe: old name for St Patrick by P/K; etymologised 'belonging to 4' ✕
Kantaka, Buddha's horse
Katachanka, Mohammed's horse

Gerald Nugent: *Ode Written on Leaving Ireland* ('From thee, sweet Delvin, must I part')

F infranchissable: impassable
F en franchise: duty free

L primo signatio: 1st signing

After enlightenment Buddha learned of his past lives

corpse of Osiris was embedded in a sycamore   Tory Island off Ir. coast; said that rats cannot live there & that mainlanders use earth from the island against rat infestations
F briquet: lighter; short sword

umbrella

s Groves of Blarney: 'But were I Homer, or Nebuchadnezzar'   Lonan: chieftain converted by St Patrick
Brian Boru   Browne . . . Nolan   Onan
Genghis Khan
Guinness   *Arab* khan: inn
ombre: C18 card game for 3
It ombre: shadows, ghosts

Fenians: revolutionary brotherhood of 1860s, but name erroneously applied to the Fianna, Finn's army
Medicine men annoint with spittle
Shabti images buried with Egyptian dead penny dreadfuls

city sweet stores
suttee: Hindu widow who immolates self on pyre with husband's body
I míle deóra: a thousand tears
F miel: honey *Gr* dôron: gift medicine man
(opium) *F* passe-partout: functioning in all circumstances; a master key

Swift in *Battle of the Books* calls wisdom of the ancients HCE
'honey & wax . . . furnishing Mankind with the two Noblest of things'

Gr basilikos: kingly *It* basilico: herb basil, once used for skin disorders Fintan Lalor
in *Barber of Seville* Don Basilio sings aria about spread of calumny Fife Players
overboard

Bothnia (named after) menhir: tall, upright monumental stone

Du meinherr: gentleman

pig under roof (*C* character): home
sacred roof tree, symbol of Osiris
pr Every bullet has its billet *Da* til drengen: to the boy dregs The Salmon House, Chapelizod (mentioned in *The House by the Churchyard*, place of entertainment)
shillelagh: blackthorn cudgel

L manus: hand *Sl* toothpick: shillelagh

Gr eirênê: peace Wellington Monument, erected on site of old Salute Battery
ph chip off the old block
bought & sold

honour of the Lord *L* onero: I burden Eng. 'planters' in Ireland
owner of the land VI.B.45.148: 'paddy planters walk bowed'
points attach hose to doublet *ph* lap of the gods

classes

Michael Gunn, manager of Gaiety Theatre, D *Da* skaal!

game old Gunne
'The Grand Old Man': Gladstone
after *Heb* sores: a root *Heb* ṣedeq: justice

Buddha
Cz hoch: boy buttock
Tuskar lighthouse off S.E. Ireland had 1,000,000 candlepower light
moil: to labour; to wet
Moyle: sea between Ireland & Scotland
Da Bretland: orig. Wales, now poetic for all Gt Britain 'Pike-County' dialect used in *Huckleberry Finn* according to introductory note
I árd rí: High King (of Ireland) Hong Kong
Sl bung: drunk

tree/stone
I Liam: William *I* Lía Fáil: monolith at Tara that shrieked at coronations of rightful High Kings; supposedly now British coronation stone
James Maculla, projector of a copper coinage for Ireland funnyman
MacCool *I* mór: great *G* Reise: journey
Huckleberry Finn

Huckleberry Finn's 'Pap' was 'most fifty' (*HF* 5)

shuffle & cut cards
s Phil the Fluter's Ball: 'the shuffle, & the cut'

Hopkins & Hopkins, D jewellers

eggnog: drink containing eggs General

Buckley (see 335.13) Sigurd the Jerusalem-farer: C12 king of Norway Asia Minor
NautSl buggerlugs: offensive term of address *Sl* be going to Jerusalem: be drunk
gamecock Peter, Jack & Martin: Catholic, Anglican & Lutheran churches in Swift's *Tale of a Tub*

Budge: *Gods of the Egyptians* I.331, mentions the 9 Worms of Restau (*Book of the Dead* I.B.4)
Egyptian Book of the Dead LXIII.B: 'The Chapter of not being Scalded with Water'
Papa Westray: one of the Orkney Islands (named from Papae, Celtic clergy there in Viking period)
Osiris introduced cultivation of wheat *L* vester pater: the pope
s As Your Hair Grows Whiter I Will Love You More *r* Lethe
Buddha renouncing luxury cut off his hair & threw it to heaven;
he had previously been addressed 'Hero' by a monk After his enlightenment Buddha was saluted 7 times
Hep: the Nile god
included

tropic of Capricorn *Gr* koproi kaprôn: pig shit
Egyptian hymn to Ptah Tanen states that his head is in the heavens while his feet are on the earth

Sahu: incorruptible habitation of souls, in Egyptian myth *Arab* sahel: shore
HF 29: 'sure as you are born' *HF* 20: shuck tick: a kind of mattress
HF 12: texas: officers' cabin on steamboat
HF 20: tow linen: material for shirts
HF 31: 'the road to Lafayette' *HF* 31: 'dropped in my tracks'

Du onrustig: disturbed bodysnatcher Chapelizod Isis
bottlewasher *AngI* mether: wooden drinking vessel
Tut-ankh-amen (totally calm) messenger Methyr: a name of Isis
Egyptian Book of the Dead XL: 'Osiris Rā, triumphant, saith . . . I have performed upon thee all the things which the company of the gods ordered concerning thee in the matter of the work of thy slaughter. Get thee back, thou abomination of Osiris . . . I know thee . . . O thou that comest without being invoked, & whose [time of coming] is unknown'

precentor: leader of singing in a church

Christ Church & St Patrick's: D cathedrals

howe: hill, tumulus Howe: site of Norse parliament during Viking occupation of D
Howe!: cry of sailors
sleep well

appears

Da holmsted: homestead coffins

AngI bad scran to you: an evil wish influenza *HF* 35: 'breakfast-horn'

Aesop's fable of the Belly & the Members

Isle of Man

Jacob's Biscuit Factory, D *U*.635: 'Dr Tibble's Vi-Cocoa'

Edwards' Desiccated Soup Mother Seigel's Syrup (tonic)

Persse O'Reilly (see 044.24) fell

lessons
Church of the 3 Sons of Nessan, Ireland's Eye
business hesit*e*ncy tableturning
Sl bee's knees: acme of perfection
multiplication

F tombeau *Sl* toss: masturbate Disraeli

P/K L/R

progenitor grandfather

Matt 6:3: 'let not thy left hand know what thy right hand doeth'

Jerry/Kevin Λ (Angel) ancient Ir. Ogham alphabet ochres

(404.13) tricks
Nick's
(110.26–35) *Du* zeep: soap milksop

Moore: *s* Lay His Sword by His Side [If All the Seas Were Ink]
HF 32: 'law sakes' Synge: *The Playboy of the Western World*
G Knirps: mannikin ⊏ *We* taran: thunder
Black & Tans: Eng. recruits in 1920–1 serving in Royal Ir. Constabulary
costive: constipated
L encaustum: purple-red ink
birthday suit Children of Mary: Catholic girls' association
F Bourse: Stock Exchange

'House of Gold, Tower of Ivory' (Litany of BVM, associated with Eileen in *Portrait* I)
(green, white & orange of Ir. flag) *L* felix
ivy . . . holly (*s* The Holly & the Ivy)

Moore: *s* You Remember Ellen, Our Hamlet's Pride [Were I a Clerk] Holy Mary
Our Lady's *L* Luna
'Pia e Pura Bella': religious wars of Vico's heroic age

Williams & Wood's jam
William Wood's halfpence (011.21)
jam door-jamb

Katty Lanner: D soubrette

tam-tam: gong; tom-tom *s* Mr Whirligig Magee
F faire du tam-tam: kick up a row cachucha: a Spanish dance
taborin: delight
small drum

'Timothy' means 'honour's lord' Zekiel Irons: parish clerk and fisherman in Le Fanu's *The House by the Churchyard*

'Ezekiel' means 'God strengthens' spawning
G spüren: sense, feel the effect of

s Enniscorthy: 'Dimetrius O'Flanigan McCarthy'

Portobello: district of D Pomeroy, Town, Co. Tyrone

R vechnyi pokoi, na vechnuya pamyat: eternal peace, for eternal memory: R.I.P.
I Binn Éadair: Howth

G Angst: fear limbo *L* lumbus: loin
he slumbers
G Mischer: meddlers

so be it
S **K**
Katherine Strong (079.27)

memorial
L murus: wall

HF 32: 'up a stump'

HF 19: 'stern-wheel'

Guinevere (parallel of Arthur, Mark & Finn triangles)
queen of Eire

It grassa: fat

AngI devil a hap'orth: not a halfpennyworth

Lex Salica: a Frankish lawbook (excluding females from succession)
leg's *I* salach: dirty *Da* salig: blessed *G* selig: happy
Castor & Pollux Round Table tabouret: low seat for 1 person

ph stick to one's last

(birds) hell of a lunch avalanche
F à l'aval: downstream
pr It's an ill wind that blows nobody good

'best of men' = the Buddha *Du* gulden: golden
gold & silver
AngI findrinny: silver-bronze

Earwicker

last post: bugle call at burial
or end of day

I cál ceannfhionn: potatoes & cabbage mixed with butter apple dumpling
Cain & Abel
merlin chair: aseated *Evening World:* N.Y.C. newspaper, 1887–1931
invalid wheelchair invented by J.J. Merlin
full-length or swagger coats

Fez: city, Morocco Stormont: N. Ireland parliament
fellah: peasant, in Arabic countries
It stilla: drop
It stella: star

Dick, Tom, Harry ∧ ∧⊏ ⊏

knows

Da elsker: loves
Selskar Gunn, son of Michael Gunn (025.22)
F pervenche: periwinkle Norwegian's *Da* viv: wife

Du zee: sea Congreve: *The Way of the World* track law (horse racing)
teastain (111.20) see
last time switch: bunch of false hair

Gr anastasê: resurrection *AngI ph* , how are you! worth her weight

J. Adams & Sons, D auctioneers *F* actionnaire: shareholder
would-be
It vivi: alive

John 8:11: 'sin no more'

namesake sibling (Finn & Salmon of Wisdom)

Smollett: *Roderick Random*
Heb ram: high

Conn of the Hundred Battles, legendary Ir. king Chapelizod
F bordel bottles illicit drink shop
Lord-Mayor *Ma* buah: fruit
baboon *G* Baum: tree
dollop lee side & weather side of ship Lord Ardilaun: Sir Arthur Guinness

Lord Iveagh: Edward Cecil Guinness, Ardilaun's brother, philanthropist
L evoe: shout of joy for shame!
Phineas Barnum, Am. showman

G senken: submerge, lower
Heb shekhem: a shoulder
It farfalla: butterfly pocketknife Smollett: *Peregrine Pickle* *Sl* in pickle: venereally infected
ph pig in a poke firefly
Smollett: *Humphrey Clinker* *Da* twilling: twin *F* pucelle: virgin *F* puce: flea
Sl clinkers: faecal deposits in anal hair Barnum showed midgets
It ricorso: recurring (Vico)

stool pigeons

with alone
Heb 12:1: 'compassed about with so great a cloud of witnesses'

AngI shee: fairy

Heb eset: form of 'isha (= woman) zephyr (West)
East Aesop's *Fables* fiddle Sephiroth: 10 emanations of Ain Soph, (9th is Yesod), in kabbalistic lore a star *L* astra: star

white dwarf, red giant (types of star) theocracy: priest-rule
White & Red politically
coalescing
Heb qoheleth: Ecclesiastes ('preacher')
Heb Torah: law
Heb śaraph: (poisonous) snake
Heb mappiq: a dot on the letter HE HCE

Sl overseen: somewhat drunk *Heb* mayim: waters

time-honoured *Heb* raqia': firmament

time or *Sl* get the bum's rush: *ph* hell of a hurry
(*pr* Time & tide wait for no man) be forcibly turned out
wherry: shallow boat dhow: native vessel in Arabian Sea
D Bay bey: Turkish governor
Willow Pattern
Co. Wicklow
dugong: marine mammal perhaps responsible for mermaid stories
reproaching

fishmonger *F* soixante-dix: 70 Sheba *T* shebi: likeness
Heb šebi: captivity
T adi: ordinary *Heb* adi: wreath Horus & Set
Heb ʿade ʿad: for evermore Tut(-ankh-amen)'s curse
Cain & Seth cellulose (sugar turned into starch for storage, e.g. over winter) *It* tutto cessa: everything ends
T batin: belly *It* annebbiato: clouded, foggy
bating: leaving out of account inebriated
HCE incestuous
L humilis: lowly

G Beinamen: surnames
Heb lašon: tongue, speech *Heb* ḥanneni: pity me
lashings Motto of the Garter: Honi soit qui mal y pense (Shame Be [to Him] Who Evil Thinks of This) *Heb* ḥamišim: 50
Heb ḥamiša ḥumše: 5 fifths, i.e. Pentateuch
Pigott's forged Parnell letter begins 'Dear E! . . . let there be an end of this hesitency'

L timendum: to be feared responsible *Heb* hibbub: love Edinburgh

Eden & Burgh Quays, D, face one another

Iris Tree, Eng. actress
(trees are green)   *s* Orange Lily, O

agnomen: name added to family name, generally on account of some exploit

Gr prodromos: forerunner   Enos: son of Seth, magician   ECH
Gr arithmos: number   *Heb* enos: man   *Sl* chalk: to slash, scratch

pivotal: central, cardinal, vital

tombstones commemorating the names Glue, Gravy, Northeast, Anker & Earwicker in churchyard at Sidlesham in the Hundred of Manhood, W. Sussex

'Wapentake' of some Eng. counties corresponds to 'Hundred' of others   Herrick: maiden name of Swift's mother
Arch hem: them
Talmud (Hebrew commentary on the Pentateuch)

Du hoofd: head   *I* Binn Éadair: Howth Head
Heb ben: son of

Sl cabbage: to purloin (mostly of tailors)

Cincinnatus assumed Roman dictatorship while danger lasted, then immediately returned to plough
Tennyson: *Lady Clara:* 'The grand old gardener and his wife Smile at the claims of long descent'
s Chevy Chase: 'Under the greenwood tree'   HCE
Heb hag: feast   *s* Chevy Chase
Gr hagios: saint

madhouse   Royal Marine Hotel, Dún Laoghaire

ethnarch: governor of a people or province

Four Courts, D   (pub)   topee: pith helmet; can be made of plant *Sola*
surcingle: band holding on the cassock
Heb adam: i) red; ii) earth
plus fours: long wide knickerbockers   puttee: strip of cloth wound round leg

L flagrantia: heat, vehemence   there was a turnpike at Chapelizod
fragrant
fixed bayonets

Inverted flowerpots on sticks used to trap earwigs   notice on box: 'this side up with care'   EHC

cause & effect

paternoster line: fishing line with hooks & weights at intervals
silver doctor: type of fishing fly
Hu három: 3

Arch cotch = catch
Ulster thon: those
William IV 'The Sailor King'

Sl Adam's ale: water   *Heb* qarban: offering   *AngI* gorb: ravenous eater
corban: anything devoted to God in fulfilment of a vow

William I ('the Conqueror')

spindle side: female line of descent

Gladstone had lost part of his left forefinger in an accident   Parnell's great-aunt Mrs Sophia Evens, practical joker
gallowglasses: heavily armed Ir. soldiers
Arch etheling: member of a noble family
Leix & Offaly: 1st Ir. plantation; was devastated by Mountjoy   Drogheda devastated by Cromwell
mayors of Drogheda named Elcock in 1554, 1568, 1592, 1607 & 1916
U.S. scattergun: shotgun
Gr prôtosyndikos: first advocate
It giubilei: jubilees

Clonmacnoise: famous Ir. monastic settlement   typical

L puritas: purity, purulency   *L* doctrina: teaching   (may suggest white, orange & green of Ir. flag)

hemlock   *s* The Garden Where the Praties Grow
It preti: priests
St Hubert, patron of the chase   William II (William Rufus)
Pomerania   pouring rain

bailywick: area under a bailiff   (fisherman)

s 'Do ye ken John Peel with his coat so gray, Do ye ken John Peel at the break of day, Do ye ken John Peel when he's far far away, With his hounds & his horn in the morning'

Gladstone's friend Lord Clarendon called him 'Merry pebble'

tree/stone   *ME* holm: holly   Holmpatrick: old name of Skerries, Co. D
In Cornwall glas-tann (green sacred tree) meant evergreen holm oak
massive   Ghibelline   outside
pr A rolling stone gathers no moss
bourn: domain

L nomen gentile: clan name   collated
accolade   *F* accolé: coupled, bracketed

anthropomorphic   *Rum* fata: face
L Fata: Fates
L fas: possible, right
L nefas: impossible, wrong

s Home, Sweet Home: 'There's no place like home' *Heb* melekhi: my king
Bohemia Nehemiah rebuilt Jerusalem after Captivity 2 Ir. high kings named Malachy
Abel, Cain

ponkes: elemental spirits Sechseläuten: Zurich spring festival
ping-pongs that bell *L* cum sceptris: with sceptres Angelus: 'et concepit de Spiritu Sancto'
Heb Hokmah: 2nd Sephira, divine wisdom ('& she conceived of the Holy Ghost')
Heb methegh: bridle (gram. term)
ph method in madness (*Hamlet* II.2.207)

Gen 3:19: 'unto dust shalt thou return' punic: treacherous, perfidious
Punic: Carthaginian Finnegan

⊣ ⊢
nightwalkers Shahrazad relates the stories constituting the *Arabian Nights* to her sister Dunyazad to entertain
skirts are raised *It* scherzi: jokes King Shahryar
rapparees: Ir. plunderers

muses Bessy Sudlow, wife of Michael Gunn, who managed Gaiety Theatre, D
Sl amuser: robber who throws snuff in victim's eyes
Mistinguette, Fr. dancer (Jeanne Bourgeois, 1875–1956) pantomime
patronised Galatea
ph pay through the nose *Gr* miliodôros: of a thousand gifts

Hu három: 3

dine out with Duke Humphrey: go dinnerless Hungarian

Angl spalpeen: landless labourer
Chapelizod; Lucan
Thomas Nashe: *Works* III.147: 'To his worthy good patron, Lustie Humfrey, according as the townsmen doo christen him, little Numps, as the Nobilitie & Courtiers do name, & Honest Humfrey as all . . .'

Here Comes Everybody: nickname of H.C.E. Childers, C19 politician

Moore & Burgess, minstrels, had catchline 'take off that white hat!' (*U*.167)
Ido (artificial language) basvoco: bass

When Finn was 15 he defeated the High King's hurleyplayers. The King asked 'Who is that white hat?' (MacCool). Finn's nurse said 'MacCool he shall be called'

King Street (address of Gaiety Theatre)
Satan: Puritan term for theatre
asphalt veldt oxgang: the 1/8 part of the carucate, varying from 10 to 18 acres

W.W. Kelly's Evergreen Touring Company performed W.G. Wills' *A Royal Divorce*, about Napoleon's divorce *G* immer
L semper: always

hundred & eleventh (Δ's 111 children)
humdrum
millennium
century

At success of Limerick soprano Catherine Hayes, her mother said 'I'm at the summit of my climax'

Balfe: *The Bohemian Girl* Benedict: *The Lily of Killarney*
hosiery D Horse Show
Booth: Lincoln's assassin (shot him in theatre) J wore a Borsalino hat

cuckoo-spit: protective froth surrounding some homopterous insects (his hat hangs slightly below their hoods) Little Red Riding Hood (pantomime)
McCabe succeeded Cullen as Archbishop of D. Both were antinationalists, & cardinals (have red hats & are addressed 'your Eminence')

Da folkeforfatter: popular author

tuxedo: a dinner jacket

clawhammer: tailcoat of full evening dress

Annals of the Theatre Royal, D 104: 'The cast was thus'

parterre: the pit under the gallery HCE

F habitué: regular attender

bruit: to noise, report, rumour *Heb* maḥarath: tomorrow

F vase de nuit: chamberpot
Heb athma: breath

Shane Leslie's review of *U.* in *Quarterly Review* CCXXXVIII: 'There are some things which cannot and, we should like to be able to say, shall not be done'

(reptiles are cold-blooded)

Lady Campbell said Oscar Wilde was like a great white caterpillar

Am. Juke & Kallikak families: hereditary degenerates

People's Park, Dún Laoghaire *s*: 'Ho, ho, ho. He̱, he, he, Little brown jug don't I love thee'
People's Gardens, Phoenix Park *Heb* ḥay: alive *G* Hoch! *Heb* ḥoq: a statute, law

viceregal
excellently

L quondam: formerly, for some time
G pfui! *L* fuit: he was
L interdum: sometimes *L* quidam: a certain one Voltaire: *Epitres* XCVI: 'If God did not exist it would be necessary to invent Him'
Sl qui tam: informer
L quoniam: because, seeing that Stamboul = Istanbul stumbling

Haroun-al-Raschid (*Arabian Nights*): Caliph of Bagdad dark *I* tearc: scant
VI.B.32.199: 'sneakers (white shoes)' *Fi* tarkka: accurate
romantically Abdullah: father of Mohammed
Gr to pan: the whole, completely
Da gammel lax: old salmon John Mallon: superintendent of D police at time of Phoenix Park murders

Caliph: 'Commander of the Faithful'

Heb sulḥan: table spread with food dropped dead
seated
L fiat: let there be food (turn to be fed)
Jewish Day of First Fruits
chop & cabbage *L* alicubi: somewhere Cubehouse, Ka'aba (see 005.14)
Fi kapakka: tavern J.S. Le Fanu: *The House by the Churchyard*
Heb Rosh Hashana: Jewish New Year Oliver Lowe, magistrate in *The House by the Churchyard*
'Old House': Theatre Royal, Hawkins St, D
obscene market *Sl* nark: police spy at
I ar: on
bowels calabash: name of various gourds
Ps 68:12: 'She that tarried at home divided the spoil'
Homer known as Son of Meles (river)
homer: Hebrew measure of capacity
Southron: native of South

Souvenir of the 25th Anniversary of the Gaiety Theatre, 1896, 34: [Edward Terry] . . . 'that–as "Jeames" would say–most "homogeneous" actor'
woodwards & regarders: forest officers protecting venison
Heb šomer: watchman

Du on (prefix): un- *F* gentil: nice
ungentlemanly immodesty

⊣ ⊢
The Hollow, Phoenix Park

F laine: wool

warp weft

ph 'The oversight of verte & venyson', 1445
Arch vert: right to cut green trees in a forest

garth: piece of enclosed land
gad: of plant, to straggle *PS* gad: snake goeth
ME hwer(e): where it is said that if St Swithin's Day is wet, 40
sokeman: a tenant holding land in socage days of wet weather will follow
Song of Sol 2:1: 'I am the rose of Sharon, & the lily of the valleys'
Isa 11:1: 'stem of Jesse'
rescue

s The Memory of the Dead: 'True men like you men' *Vo* zesüd: necessity
Vo led: red *Vo* lol: rose *Vo* kadem: academy with a
Volapük (artificial language) Fresh Nelly, D whore (*U*.214 &c.)
with a *Vo* Fikop: Africa *Vo* Nelij: England *Vo* flen: friend
s 'Lillibullero, bullen a law' *G* Maler: painter abused
Lilith: Adam's wife before Eve, in kabbalistic lore

HCE

calcium chloride absorbs moisture
Chloe *Gr* chlôroeidês: greenish
happy-go-lucky Ides of April: 13 April
Ides of March (Caesar assassinated)
in one's birthday suit: naked

(confusion of tongues after fall of Tower of Babel)

tired

tigerwood: variety of citron wood

(Phoenix Park) kepi: Fr. military cap; top slopes forwards
F caoutchouc: rubber; (obs.) raincoat
The Great Belt, Denmark *G* blau *G* Funke: spark Ironsides: nickname of Cromwell
hide & seek a blue funk
Bhagavad Gita: Hindu spiritual treatise Inverness cloak, overcoat: one with a removable cape

L luciferens: light-carrying (i.e. for pipe) *It* oriuolo: a watch

Dagobert: King of Franks 629–639; in comic song wears trousers back to front
thereabouts
AngI bamer: straw hat *G* Schuld: guilt *s* Brian O'Linn (see 017.11)

country

I Conas tá tú indiu mo dhuine uasal fionn?: How are you today my fair gentleman?

ouzel: blackbird; fig., a person of dark complexion
The *Ouzel Galley*, believed lost, reappeared unexpectedly off Poolbeg in 1700

'Dublin' means 'black pool' old days (Florestein in *The Bohemian Girl* is stopped by
Poolbeg lighthouse, D Devilshoof, who asks the time & then steals his watch)

Gr bradus: slow Hesitency HCE ECH
Joe Brady, one of perpetrators of Phoenix Park murders evitated: avoided
We honni: assert, allege, pretend homicide
Honi soit qui mal y pense (Order of the Garter) (Shame Be [to Him] Who Evil Thinks of This)
L nex: murder

Civil Law noxal: relating to damage or injury done by person or animal belonging to another
L noxa: harm
Kimmage Outer (072.20); St Patrick's Day: *17* March; Fenian Rising, 1867; result, 1767
Knights of St Patrick: D association (Le Fanu's *The House by the Churchyard*, ch. 1, begins
'A.D. 1767')

softnosed bullets used by republicans in Easter Rising, 1916

Taff (338.05; Butt in .34)
tipstaff: a sheriff's officer carrying a tipped staff
Jurgensen: a type of watch
Waterbury: watch made in Waterbury, Conn.
usucapion: acquisition of ownership by long use or enjoyment skirling: shrill crying

(wind)

It tonante: thundering

s Cuchulain's Call
Heb kohen: sacrificing soothsayer
sidereal: of time, measured by stars

pondus: moral force
L pondus: weight *Sl* copperstick: policeman's truncheon; penis
confusion chopstick
Confucius

chopsticks used in Confucius's home Confucius liked chewing ginger root
In ancient Chinese medicine, sours used to nourish bones, acid for muscles, salt for blood, sweet for flesh and bitter to improve general vitality

J haku: say

G Morgen: morning
Morning Post: D newspaper
parr: young salmon

triple-headed
Hydra: manyheaded mythological snake

Marcel Jousse: *Études de psychologie linguistique: le style oral rythmique & mnémotechnique chez les verbo-moteurs,* 1925
quiritary: in accordance with Roman civil law
G zusammen: together
Noah Webster's dictionary

redaction: edition

price one shilling, postage free *L* gigas: giant
Gygas: King of Lydia
Dundrum, district of D
Gr chronometron: time-measure

chopstick (035.36) CHE hough: hollow behind knee ELEVEN
Berlin glove: one knitted of Berlin wool (Placing right fist in bent left elbow imitates letter E backwards) *G* Ellbogen: elbow
THIRTY TWO (013.33)

F duc de fer (The Iron Duke: Wellington) Wellington Monument, Phoenix Park, once popularly called the 'overgrown milestone'

F gage: pledge, token *F* rendez present: make present

HEC

HCE

Sinn Féin: nationalist movement in Ireland
Howth fingers
Milton: *On his having arrived at the age of twenty three*: 'my great Taskmaster's eye'

St Michan's Church, D (Church of Ireland) HCE
G Mitwohner: person sharing living-quarters soul

Gaping Ghyl, vertical shaft in Yorkshire make errors
SWIFT others STERNE
Eustachian tube joins ear & nose *G* es war zu machen: it had to/could be done

gigantism caused by excess of 1 pituitary hormone Heidelberg Man (Old Stone Age) HCE
G männlich *G* Leiche: corpse
G Luft: air (hat) Svyatogor: giant in a Russian epic (lit. 'holy mount')

Serbian dobro noc: good night greatly

Noah's sons Shem, Ham & Japhet seeing
⊏ ⋀ ∧

taken aback
F bock: glass of beer
all

taskmaster (036.27)
Da tysk: German
Ps 68:33: 'lo, he doth send out his voice, & that a mighty voice'

molecules
monticule: small conical mound left after volcano
snarler (dog)

L verbi gratia: for instance
verbigeration: repetition of same word or phrase in meaningless way
Wilde to Douglas in *De Profundis:* 'but I met you either too late or too soon'
pr The early bird catches the worm
Da tak for ilden: thanks for the light
warm
G verboten: forbidden
L balbus: stammering
verbatim
badly palpably
Da kveld: evening
twittering of birds

ph between the devil & the deep sea
Charlemont Mall, beside Grand Canal, D come
Charleville Mall, beside Royal Canal, D
Grand & Royal Canals, D *SwG* Fluh: precipice, rock-face

G müde: tired a softer

AngI pogue: kiss *r* Arvanda acquiescent
cowshit *L* aqua
Castle Browne renamed cowshot: flat scooping legstroke made by the batsman (cricket)
Clongowes Wood blue Giordano Bruno the Nolan Browne & Nolan, D booksellers
Mosaic Dispensation: Moses' religious system

I má's é do thoil é: if you please
I seile: saliva
Anglo-Irish Ascendency
F ascendances: ancestries
(gentleman would have concealed recollections instead of letting wife know)

expectorate: to spit

belcher: any particoloured handkerchief
G Spucker: person who spits *G* Tuch: cloth
pocket thoughts

dubbed

Peach Bombé *nr* 'Georgie Porgie pudding & pie' *I* pocán: little he-goat
really Lucan *G* Pilz: mushroom
RR senaf: mustard *RR* pibe: pepper

boiled *I* minnseóg: young she-goat after first kidding white malt vinegar proviant: food supply
bilk: deceive snivel
horse radish

HEC pot-valiant: valiant through effect of drink

F plat regional: local dish favourite (Benjamin was favourite son) *F* bouilli: boiled beef
benjamin tree: American spice bush Polish
Heb zayit: olive *It* porco grasso: fat swine
Es porcograso: lard
Erebus: place between Earth & Hades Phoenix Brewery
arabesqued Irish insurrection of 1798
F Grand Cru

tablets bouquet: odour of wine

Moore: *s* Though Humble the Banquet, 'Tis a Lover's Farewell [Farewell, Eamon]
leman's

Rh.Sl bit of strife: wife *s* Annie Laurie: 'Maxwelton braes are bonny'
F née
cleaned up (after meal)
F glaner: glean
dumb beast *RR* persic: peach *Prunus armeniaca:* apricot
domestic Persians Armenians
RR pomaranza: Pomerania *RR* clav: key
orange (fruit) *It* clava: club, mace
▲'s 111 children

whispers *It* pispigliando: whispering
RR secret: lavatory *RR* ama-da &c.: loved amid
RR lavurdi: weekday but one

Hegesippus: i) Athenian orator; ii) early Chr. writer; iii) supposed author of *L* adaptation
of Jewish War (means cup of tea
'horse-commander')

HF 1: 'I couldn't stood it much longer'

hosch = *H*; intra (enter) = *C*ome in; just a tablespoon! = *E*nough
RR hoscha!: come in! *RR* intrar: to enter
coupled *s* Annie Laurie

E . . . CH *L* cum: with *RR* pitschen: slight, small
RR peclas: a cake made on Shrove Tuesday
gospel & epistle sides of altar

RR vinars: brandy *L* volatilis: flying
L in vino veritas (Pliny): in wine, truth *L* vale: farewell
Vincentian: member of Congregation of Priests of the Mission founded
Bruno of Nola; Browne & Nolan by St Vincent de Paul
(037.23)

Paul Saul
poor soul
Heb ruaḥ: spirit (lit. 'puff')
Ecclesiastes, book of Bible
St Augustine of Hippo *ph* 'have a banana'
Heb Hawah: Eve
Mohammed: 'Women were created out of a crooked rib
of Adam'
Marie Louise/Josephine
F mère l'Oye: Mother Goose
Baudelaire: 'mon semblable! mon frère!'
brother
Balfe: *s* The Secret of My Birth (from *The Bohemian Girl*) PERSSE

O'REILLY (044.24)
F oreille: ear
ortho-: straight, correct

hit & run   Baldoyle: district of D, has racecourse   Winny Widger (.11)
F hippique: relating to horses
Sl go through the card: win every race on the programme

Dublin Details: a newspaper column about D race horses   Perkin Warbeck: pretender to Eng. throne; obtained Ir. support
Peter & Paul   CEH

Vo ek: some   *I* each horse
Vo nek: none   neck & neck
Vo evelo nevelo: ever never

Blount family = Mountjoy

Raheny: district of D   *Sl* drummer: horse with irregular foreleg action   nondescript
hinny: offspring of stallion & she-ass   St Doolagh: village near Baldoyle & Raheny

J.W.Widger: most famous of Waterford racing-associated family, amateur rider
U.423: 'Thou art all their daddies, Theodore'

bantamweight   topped
Sl timber topper: horse good at jumping
tinkers   Song of Sol 2:11–12: 'For, lo, the winter is past, the rain is over & gone . . . & the voice of the turtle is heard in our land'
Sl cove: fellow   *G* Renn: race
L vox: voice   'the turf' (horseracing)   *F* lande: heath

Sl Treacle Town: Bristol   *Sl* out of pawn: out of prison

Kehoe, Donnelly & Pakenham: D ham curers
Phoenix Park
Eoin MacNeill: *Celtic Ireland* 55: 'Lugaid Cichech . . . reared the two sons of Crimthann, Aed & Laegaire, on his breasts. It was new milk he gave from his breast to Laegaire, & blood he gave to Aed. Each of them took after his nurture, the race of Aed being marked by fierceness in arms, the race of Laegaire by thrift'

Sl hulks: prison ships
Sl oofbird: rich person   *Sl* Jimmy O'Goblin: a sovereign

Sl thick 'un: sovereign or crown piece   Seaforth Highlanders (regiment)

Dion Boucicault: *The Colleen Bawn*
hear the parson
low   *Esp* edzo: husband
& so on
(Sunday papers)

Sl gargle: a drink   Butt (compare 341.24–9)
D Sl butty: drinking companion

Yeats: *Countess Cathleen*
I capaillín: little horse

Gr methê: drunkenness
ph hail fellow well met
Sl red biddy: cheap red wine fortified with methylated spirit
Sl blue ruin: bad gin   eglantine: dog rose (used for rosehip wine)
RR spoken in Engadine, Swiss valley
ECH   *I* deoch an dorais: parting drink
Duck & Dog Tavern, D (C18)
The Cock, D pub (C18)

Little Old Man: the last sheaf, in some harvest customs
pr All's well that ends well
Arditi: *s* The Stirrup Cup
I leaba: bed
(039.11)
s Abide with Me

The Liberties, D
Vo motapük: mother-tongue
Pump Court, London (in Dickens' *Martin Chuzzlewit*)
It molta piu: much more
Volapük: artificial language
It una volta di piu: once more
s (from *The Lily of Killarney*) The Moon Hath Raised Her Lamp Above: ('. . . I come, I come, my heart's delight')

Martial: *Epigrammata* XII.57: 'Rus in Urbe' ('the Country in Town')
Buckley & the Russian General
busybody
Bul rusin: Russian

HF 10: 'sun-bonnet'

eyot: small island
I Márta: March
Welsh fusiliers
Ides of March
Behan **S**
Kate **K**
RR lavina: avalanche
monthlies
Skt kātyā: widow
R Katya: Catherine
L mens: mind
Punch & Judy show
Sl pumpship: urinate
wild horses
Moore: *s* Oft in the Stilly Night

epithalamium
Gr met 'agona: with struggle
cash drapery
'The Drapier': Swift
Kloran: sacred book of Ku Klux Klan
'ex-private secretary': expression of Henry Adams, Am. historian
Joseph O'Mara, Ir. tenor, sang in *Tristan*
s 'Liebestod' from *Tristan* begins 'Mild und leise'

Bank of Ireland, College Green, D

stone of destiny = Lia Fáil (025.31)

HF 17: 'no slouch of a name'
L hostis: stranger, enemy
F sans
Sl scrape: butter
HF 16: 'to suspicion'
HF 11: 'take a cheer [chair] . . . she set still'
Sl rootie: bread
toadstool
selfabuse
HF 8: 'you must be most starved'

barman
F birman: Burmese

Da nattergal: nightingale
Bur nat: spirit
Bur -gale: suffix denoting offspring
Bur nwa-no: milk
It nano: dwarf
Onan
HF 12: 'towhead' (small island)

if he'd a licence
HF 2: 'how in the nation'

parabellum: type of pistol
Sl wing: penny

HF 19: 'sidewheel'

Dalkey, Kingstown [Dún Laoghaire] & Blackrock Tram Line
s Daffydowndilly
HF 11: 'throw true'
suicidal
HF 9: 'worth two bits'

beatitude
quietus

Grisel Steevens founded Steevens' hospital, D
calendar months

Sir Patrick Dun's Hospital, D
Jervis St Hospital, D (name of street der. from Sir Humphrey Jervis, sheriff 1674)
Kevin (Jerry in 041.03)
St Kevin's Hospital, D
Adelaide Hospital, D
St Kevin's Bed: hollow above Upper Lake, Glendalough

Garrett Wellesley founded Hospital for Incurables on Lazar's Hill, D, whence pilgrims with cockleshells in their hats embarked for the Shrine of St James the Less, at Santiago de Compostella (Sterne calls him 'Saint Iago'), patron saint of lepers

s Ophelia's Song: 'by his cockle hat & staff'

(040.17)

Shelley: *Epipsychydion* *L* hostis: stranger, enemy

L odor insuper: smell above

L petro: old sheep; a rustic; by Peter *L* perfractus: frustrated

Swinburne: 'great sweet mother' (*U*.5)

Shaw

shaw: thicket

Yeats Wilde *Sl* tweeny: a maid

meed: merit, reward ant

Byron: 'Maid of Athens, ere we part'

linkboy: boy with torch to light streets grasshopper (ant in .10)

HF 52: 'ash-hopper'

bed & breakfast

bacon & eggs

F rêve: dream *G* Schinken: ham

Henry James Byron: *Our Boys* (play)

'The Barrel': area on W. side of Meath St where Friends' Meetinghouse stood (soup-run there)

ECH *s* Sweet Molly Malone 'In Dublin's fair city'

Eblana: Ptolemy's name for D their *L* linea: lines

L superficies: surface *F* correspondant: corresponding *L* puncta: points

London Tube, Paris metro

twopenny halfpenny

G Oberfläche: surface writing

(routes, linea) (restings, puncta)

We crwth: bowed lyre *I* crónán: hum, drone

Cremona violin possessed by Emiliani, D Theatre Royal violinist

ALP

Finnachta Fledach, king of Tara, 'the festive'

The Strawberry Beds, between Chapelizod & Lucan

F fraise: strawberry

A. Peter's account of old D street cries includes those of the honey man, the 'sweet lavender' man & a man selling 'Boyne salmon alive' (sounded like 'foin salmon'). Elsewhere she mentions 'The Old Sot's Hole', Essex Gate (Swift used to frequent it).

Rev. S. Hughes: *The Pre-Victorian Drama in Dublin* 6: 'John Barrington . . . sang & danced here his Roratorios in derision of the Oratorios in Fishamble Street'

Handel's *Messiah* first performed in Fishamble St Music-Hall, D

U.763: 'sweeeee theres that train far away'

prosthetic: pertaining to replacement of lost teeth, &c. prothetic: of prothesis, placing of elements &c. ready for use in Eucharistic office

Sl house of call: lodging-place for tailors

Sp cuja: bedstead viz. Old Sot's Hole: D pub frequented by Swift

rue Cujas, Paris

St Cecilia, patron of music Liberties, D *I* ceól mór: great music

Handel: *Ode for St Cecilia's Day* Medical School of National University was in Cecilia St

Griffith's Valuation: a rent reduced to the government rating valuation of the farm

premier Gladstone Parnell: speech in Cork, 1885: 'No man has a right to fix the boundary of the march of a nation'

Charles Stewart Parnell

James II last reigning Stuart *F* peut-être

Cork ph touch weekly insult: get wages paid

L fuit: it was

J.J.&S.: John Jameson & Sons D whiskey

private secretary (040.16)

Leixlip

How Buckley shot the Russian General
I rosca: attack
I seinn: play music
I buachaillín: little boy
I rosc-catha: battle hymn
I fíon: wine
I Sinn Féin Amhaín: Ourselves Alone (slogan)
I ámhran: song
Da ballader: ballad-singer

I cumann: club, society
community
Gr melos: song
F bégayeur: stutterer
bugger
G Eier: eggs

G Lieder: songs
cg follow-my-leader
Pro riau: river basin
Pro colo: mountain
col: mountain pass
river Liffey
hill of Howth

Gr eleutherios: free
Gr dendron: tree
s Woodman, Spare That Tree
fulfilling

Souvenir of the 25th Anniversary of the Gaiety Theatre 32: '& oh! the choristers of old! Probably no set of men & women were ever so single-minded . . . these operatic supers . . . the "crowds" were always agreed'
Souvenir of the 25th Anniversary of the Gaiety Theatre 31: 'Mrs Bernard Beere made a great success in "Masks and Faces" in February 1887'

Watling St, Erning St, Icknild St & Foss Way: Roman roads in Britain
hackney
Viscount Harmsworth: Alfred Northcliffe, Ir. newspaper magnate
s The Irish Jaunting Car
newspapers: *Northern Whig* (Belfast)
Manchester Guardian

Cutpurse Row, now W. end of the Cornmarket, D

Earwicker
L videlicet
poplin manufacture a major industry in C17–19 D

F croûte de pain: crust of bread
The Pale: in C15, that part of Ireland where Eng. jurisdiction was established
Daly's: D club, closed 1823
Dundreary whiskers: long side whiskers
Rutland Square, D
HEC

Hume St, D (sedan chairs)

Wandering Jew

(pigs, i.e. legs of ham) *I* amalóg: simpleton During James II's reign, Protestant aldermen in D took refuge in Skinner's Alley

Mosse built Rotunda Hospital, D, & used part of site as garden for fêtes &c.

The Oblate Fathers, D religious congregation

tabinet: Ir. watered fabric

F fumant: smoking

Hammersmith, district of London *D Sl* chiselurs: children

Rev. S. Hughes: *The Pre-Victorian Drama in Dublin* 2: 'The impression left by Shirley's prologues is that bear-baiting & cudgel-playing were more to the taste of our ancestors than plays'

braxy: splenic apoplexy in sheep

'blue-coat scholars' from King's Hospital, D

Simpson's hospital, D

Simpson's-on-the-Strand, London restaurant

F tasse: cup

tasting

A. Peter (*Dublin Fragments*) mentions Turkey coffee & right good orange shrub (orange juice & spirits)

There were 4 old established D poplin manufacturers: Messrs Pim Bros, Elliott & Son, Messrs Fry & Co. & Richard Atkinson & Co.

blains: blisters annuitant: one receiving an annuity

corns Diana: goddess of the hunt

Particularism: doctrine of particular election of redemption

Celtic Particularism: support of Old Ir. against R.C. church doctrines, esp. about date of Easter

Prebendary: canon of a cathedral holding a prebend

Celtic monks developed own kind of tonsure 'The Lace Lappet': head-dress shop in C18 D

uniate: member of the Greek church retaining its liturgy but acknowledging pope's supremacy

Hebrew letter HE means 5 & a window

just

Sl juiced: drunk

Sl uncle's : pawnshop

s The Wake of Teddy the Tiler

F plume *F* drôle (Shem the Penman)

Pro plumo: pen *Pro* drole: young boy

Weaver's Almshouse: Townsend St Asylum, D *Pro* chat: young boy

J's parody of 'Pretty Molly Brannigan': 'But if I cling like a child to the clouds that are your petticoats' (Gorman 283)

L curio: priest Caoch O'Leary: aged blind piper in poem by John Keegan

s A Nation Once Again

F Félibre: member of Provençal literary brotherhood founded 1854

Pro taiocebo: earwig *Pro* casudo: fall *Pro* Poulichinello: Punchinello

Pro atahut: bier, coffin

black & white

Blanco White: Ir.-Spanish priest; changed his religion

rough & ready

redwood

Delville: Glasnevin estate owned by Dr Patrick Delany, where Swift's 'The Legion Club' (1735) was privately printed

F rose des vents: compass-card

black hand: a lawless secret society

(Ireland was divided into 5 provinces at one stage; now there are 4)

Picts & Scots Mohammed: 'May your hands be rubbed in dirt'

Scotia Minor: old name for Scotland

Wagner: *Parsifal*

percival: horn used in fox hunting

Parnell 'the uncrowned king of Ireland' Pigott's forgery of letters incriminating Parnell *It* cielo: sky

Guillaume de Machaut called organ the 'king of instruments' Pigott's music warehouse, D

Mr Patrick Delaney released from life imprisonment for Phoenix Park murders after he gave evidence against Parnell at Parnell Commission

Pigott: cello player at Theatre Royal, D

It liuto: lute applause

Du soort: sort *Parsifal*

(042.05)

G sputen: make haste

It sputa: spit

s The Snowy-breasted Pearl mountain hare

s A Wild Mountain Air

L ductor: leader (elevation of host & ritual of chalice in *Parsifal*)

'The Doctor': Tommy Robinson, C19 D organist

(knights of the Grail) chase (singer)

L silentium in curia: silence in court

F chanté: sung

Annona: Roman corn-goddess

St Andrew's Street & Church: site of Thingmote, Norse parliament in D

I rann: verse *G* rann: flowed

boys & girls *I* caile: girl skirts & breeches

D.W. Cahill: Ir. author 6' 5" high; died in Boston

tree/stone story

Here lie the remains of Viking

We llyn: lake, pond Finn Lug Lamhfada: leader of Tuatha Dé Danann

(earwig) Dunlop (tyres) *L* lex Michael Gunn: Manager, Gaiety Theatre, D

Daniel O'Connell lax: salmon Guinness *We* arth: bear

Bartholomew Vanhomrigh, father of Swift's Vanessa 'Old Nol': nickname of Cromwell

F perce-oreille: earwig Pearse & O'Rahilly (Easter Rising)

John Boyle O'Reilly of Ir. Rep. Brotherhood: his unit produced treasonable ballads

Ir. children used to take a wren from door to door collecting money on St Stephen's Day. They chanted: 'The wren, the wren, The king of all birds &c' (*U.*481)–'wren' pronounced like 'rann'

have you heard of . . .

G brummen: buzz

General Cambronne (009.27) said to have shouted 'Merde' at ⚔ Waterloo

F claque: clap *G* Klatsch: clap *It* battere: to clap

glass crash: theatrical sound effect *R* khlopat: clap

I greadadh: clapping

Signor Arditi: conductor in C19 D, nicknamed 'Nelson's Pillar'

It arditi: dare!

It audite: listen

Music Cue (theatre): note on prompt copy of play indicating music

Oliver Cromwell
Olaf: 1st Norse king of D

Magazine Fort, Phoenix Park

D Castle
cg I'm the king of the castle

Green St Courthouse, D

Mountjoy Prison, D

D Sl Joy: Mountjoy

Immaculate Conception

We pr The butter is in the cow's horns (i.e. she gives no milk)

'The Wren, the Wren, The king of all birds' (044.15)

It balbo: stuttering
It -accio: pejorative suffix *It* -uccio: diminutive suffix
Sl chow chow chop: last lighter containing the sundry small packages to fill up a ship

HCE

U.S. Sl bucketshop: unauthorised stockbroker's office

Sl trash & trumpery: rubbish

Long John Clancy, subsheriff of D at time of *U.*

Hammerfest, port in Norway

hooker: type of Ir. fishing boat

God's curse!

Eblana: name of D used by Ptolemy

I gall: foreigner

Black & Tans: Eng. recruits in 1920–1 serving in Royal Ir. Constabulary

Poolbeg Lighthouse, D

F donnez-moi

Copenhagen

wife & family

Oscar Fingal O'Flahertie Wills Wilde

Boniface: generic as proper name of innkeepers

Sl bargearse: person with round behind

Da gammel: old, ancient

Sl moniker: name

Da og: &

as they are

garden party

Nursing Mirror, periodical

*U.*471 (emended): 'Innocence. Girl in the monkey house. Zoo. Lewd chimpanzee. (*Breathlessly*) Pelvic basin. Her artless blush unmanned me'

general: slavey, maid-of-all-work

ph to bill & coo

Noah's Ark

G Popo: buttocks

Buckley (335.13)

in arrears

G Frau

'There will be wigs on the green': colloq. expression, orig. *I* for coming to blows or sharp altercation

Sophocles Shakespeare Dante Moses (author of anonymous Pentateuch)

Oxmantown: part of N. D (named from 'Ostman'–Eastman, Viking)

nr Humpty Dumpty: 'All the king's horses & all the king's men'

L corpus

Cromwell: 'Go to Hell or Connacht' (from a Parliamentary act of 1654)

ph raise Cain: create a disturbance

Souvenir of the 25th Anniversary of the Gaiety Theatre 31, describes old-fashioned tenors delivering their 'famous chest C' Jesus! *It* corpo di Bacco!; by Jove! *It* barraggio: dam spook
freak fog stench

Blackfriars Lane, site of Dominican Monastery where Henry VIII was granted divorce from Catherine of Aragon
s The Shan Van Vocht (*AngI*, means 'poor old woman', i.e. Ireland)
Alice Liddell: friend of Lewis Carroll, model for *Alice in Wonderland*

kingsrick: kingdom Numidia Arthur Barraclough: D tenor
Hibernia *Sl* barrage: an excessive quantity
(heard or redelivered Hosty's Ballad)

Vergobret: chief magistrate among ancient Ædui of Gaul caracul: Asiatic sheep
Caractacus: British chieftain, resisted Roman invasion
Eccles 44:9: 'they were as they had never been'

hear
Annals of the Theatre Royal, D 46: 'The Zouave Artistes . . . original Founders of the Theatre at Inkermann . . . the female parts being performed by men' 'The mime of Mick (Λ), Nick (⊏) & the Maggies (○)'
suave Zouave: Fr. corps for defence of the pope, 1860–71 –FW II.1 (219.18–19)
U.664: 'usual hackneyed run of catchy tenor solos foisted on a confiding public by Ivan St Austell and Hilton St Just and their *genus omne*' St Just & St Austell: Cornish towns
Annals of the Theatre Royal, D 67, mention Vyvyan & S. Vincent in 'Maritana' played by Mr Frank Smith & Mr J.F. Jones; 68: 'Valjean . . . in which Mr Coleman assumed four characters'; 49: 'Collins . . . of . . . Lucan'
(twelve)
The Dáil (pron. 'doyle'): seat of government, D
'Fin M'Coul & the Fairies of Lough Neagh': pantomime at Theatre Royal, D, 1844 Finn MacCool in anger tore up a sod of turf thereby creating Lough Neagh & the Isle of Man
F féerie: fairy-play
Gulliver's Travels Harlequin (frequently in Theatre Royal pantomimes)

merry men: followers of a duet *It* persi: lost *Eyrbyggja saga:* one of the great Icelandic sagas
Earwicker
from end to end

ph a tissue of falsehood
factitious
(Hosty) *It* oste: innkeeper, host
It ostia: Eucharist; sacrificial victim

G Tenorist: tenor

purely military

Tennysonian *Fi* tuoni: figure of Death
It tuono: thunder
It animando vite: giving life

Arch doom: judgement   down   *It* ei fù: he was

I a chara: friend (voc.)
(O'Mara)
I sasanach: Englishman   *I* árd-rí: high king
G Dass noch!: That too!   *Sl* take the king's shilling: enlist
ph sown his wild oats

Moore: *s* Alone in Crowds to Wander On [Shule Aroon]
Wild Geese: Ir. Jacobites who went to continent after defeat in 1691; subject of 'Shule Aroon'
After 1607, Earls of Tyrone led Ir. volunteers in Spanish military service
Irish whites: type of potato
Viscount Wolseley, Ir. field marshal in Crimea   Buckley
Blanco White, Ir.-Spanish priest, changed his religion
I cathair: city, citadel   *s* I Dreamt That I Dwelt in Marble Halls
caw (raven)
Pump Court, London   dove/raven
The Pigeonhouse, D   *L* columbarium: dovecot; sepulchral chamber
Poe: 'Quoth the raven "nevermore"'

L cornix: crow

Papal Legate   (book bequeathed to his father)   raw chocolate
Co. Louth   *R* byl: he was   (Peter Cloran)

Arch doomster: judge   Master in Lunacy
Thom's Directory: 'Four Courts'—lunacy department: 'Registrar in Lunacy', 'Chief Clerk in Lunacy'
Dublin Intelligencer: C18 D newspaper   *D Sl* Ridley's: mental hospital ward

utility man: actor of the smallest speaking parts in a play
Annals of the Theatre Royal, D 211: 'utility men'; 219: 'the young soprana, at a short notice, sustained the part'
(Treacle Tom)   *ph* Dear Dirty Dublin

Ham, son of Noah
(Frisky Shorty)
Isrāfīl: angel who will blow trumpet on Mohammedan Judgement Day
('The Summoner')
Epsom Downs (horse racing)   *It* ebbro: drunk
ups & downs
state of nature (theology): natural moral state as opposed to state of grace
Spenser: *Colin Clouts Come Home Againe*   atlas: 1st cervical vertebra
s The Coolin
flesh & blood

Parnell & O'Shea
Parnell: 'Do not throw me to the wolves'
Moore: *s* Though the Last Glimpse of Erin [The Coolin]   drunkard
Da glimt: gleam; glimpse
dubbed
Robert Barton, violinist & pugilist, often hailed as 'Boxing Bob' when performing at Theatre Royal, D
thought   (occurred to him)

Bass's Ale   thrust into   bankrupt   my dreams have come true
Sl cogged: fraudulent   *F* drame: drama, play
AngI Lochlann: Scandinavian   centuple: hundredfold
Domhnall & Muirchearlach O'Lochlainn: high kings of Ireland
ego urge   Michael Cusack: original of 'The Citizen' in *Cyclops*
Nicholas de Cusa: philosophy of coincidence of contraries
demission: action of giving up or letting go from oneself
Leibnitz: 'identity of indiscernibles' (principle that no two things ever absolutely identical)

Arch baxter: baker (butchers)
nr 'the butcher, the baker, the candlestickmaker'
F poing: fist Baron Ping, in Confucius's home state, concealed mustard in feathers of a fighting cock, to blind his opponent's bird, but opponent supplied his cock with metal spurs
Hotspur (*Henry IV* [1 & 2])
St Patrick pother: choking smoke
mustardpot
outstanding candlestick Bruno . . . of Nola *Da* han var: he was

Drury Lane Theatre, London

(042.05) (Frisky Shorty)

ph take a leaf out of someone's book French loaves available (writer of calumny)
French leave: departure without permission or notice
numerous spurious 'prophecies' attributed to St Colmcille (Columba) astral
The Book of Kells 'sometimes called the book of Colum Cille' *G* spurlos: without a trace
L mare transeo: I cross the sea St Colmcille's unauthorised copy of Finnian's copy of the Psalms was returned to Finnian, under principle 'to every cow belongs her calf'
In Islam theology, the Koran is supposed to be copied from 'The Mother of the Book', preserved under the throne of God *L* tabula rasa: clean writing tablet
L involucrum: wrapper, covering erasing

'Paganini Redivivus' ('Paganini come alive again') Valentine Vousden: D music hall entertainer played at Dan Lowry's Musichall; may have been R.M. Levey, co-author of *Annals of the Theatre Royal*

L transtulit: he has transferred Cape Finisterre: N.W. tip of Spain habitat *G* finster: dark *I* bhí sé: he was
latitat: a writ supposing the defendant to lie concealed, summoning him to answer to the King's Bench
Father Henry Browne rejected J's *Day of the Rabblement* for U.C.D. magazine

G treu *Da* trøster: comforter

I Iar-Spáinn: W. Spain
I Iar-Connacht (Spanish influence in W. of Ireland)
eupeptic: promoting digestion
Church of Discalced (= barefoot) Carmelites, D
reverend

Bruno of Nola Father Bernard Vaughan: *The Sins of Society*
Browne & Nolan: D bookshop
(Cad's wife) see press, passim

(Cad)

(Carroll's Mad Hatter had ticket on hat)

handle pen HEC his Eminence: title of a cardinal
angle
Dial canary-fit: a fit of anger

cark: burden of anxiety cork
Dunhill, make of pipe, London
(the cad) Dun Hill on Howth
G Meerschaum (pipe)

Maynooth *L* fuit: he was
F jeudi: Thursday (Jove's day)
Percy French: *s* Phistlin Phil McHugh Gray: *Ode on a Distant Prospect of Eton College:* 'Where ignorance is bliss 'Tis folly to be wise'
once
Percy French: *s* 'Has anybody ever been to Mick's Hotel, Mick's Hotel by the salt say water? . . . Never again for me!' hunting
L nix: snow see
Sl nix: nothing
L nebula: fog autodidact: self-taught
nevertheless

face Moore: *s* Has Sorrow Thy Young Days Shaded? [Sly Patrick]
Sl phiz: countenance
alter ego passing
AngI possing wet: saturated

It scherzo: joke Shahrazad (*Arabian Nights*)—1001
charade
(sword of Damocles) bonafide

scratch-wig (theatre): untidy
wig used in comedy

square-cut: a coat with square skirts regatta (.22)
stock collar: a *F* lavallière: loose necktie oxter: armpit
kind of stiff, closefitting, St Patrick Lad Lane, D *We* llan: church, village
neckcloth *Sp* llana: page (of book &c.)
area baldness: hair
disease causing bald patches

three *Sl* shirkers: truants

trenchcoats overalls will, can & ought to

over a gate *F* vouloir, pouvoir & devoir: will, can & ought to (infinitives)
pissabed ghost story
Da haard: hard HCE *Da* eventyr: fairy tale HCE curch: kerchief
Sl haberdasher: publican
Da enkel: bachelor
G Enkel: grandchild
Du jongens: boys a lot since Thorgil (Turgesius): Viking invader; tried to
repaganise Ireland
Lancashire sheep-tally: 'yan, tyan, tethera, methera, pimp, sethera, lethera, hovera, dovera, dick'

halfsister (Confucius had 9)

our brother
wholebrother
Parents of Confucius prayed for a male child *It* fungo: fungus, mushroom (beard)
at a shrine on Mount Mu Mungo Park: explorer of W. Africa

game of battledore & shuttlecock

—Juxta-Mare: beside the sea (in Eng. placenames)
in lieu of
Lu: Confucius's home state
Co. Meath Mecca X-ray

local colour
Loki, in Norse myth, caused Balder's death with mistletoe
Clonturk Park, D Chapelizod
Capel St, D
We craog: rock

We bryn: mountain Lesser Pilgrimage: Mohammedan journey to Mecca (but not Arafat) Silures: ancient British
Ordovices: ancient British tribe in N. Wales tribe in S.E. Wales (D has some Silurian & Ordovician rocks)
G Insel Shaw: *John Bull's Other Island*
I Muicinis (lit. 'pig-island'): ancient name for Ireland
Regifugium: Roman ceremony, Litany of BVM: 'refugium peccatorum' (refuge of sinners)
'flight of the king', festival celebrating expulsion of kings *L* persecutorum: of the persecuted
his headquarters

s Londonderry Air: 'Oh Danny Boy, the pipes, the pipes are calling' ['Would that I were a tender apple blossom']
Betting Sl ten to one, bar one: odds against any
own doldrums ABC horse in race except one

charlotte: apple marmalade covered with bread crumbs
panomancy: divination by bread
fragrant calabash: name of various gourds (can be adapted to
contain smoking pipe)

Annie Oakley: sharpshooter
U.658: 'alternately racking their feelings (the mermaids') with sixchamber revolver anecdotes'

I ruadh: red read

Macbeth V.1.57: 'all the perfumes of Arabia will not sweeten this little hand'

repeater (watch, revolver)

F revenant: ghost

r Tolka, D

I dearbhbhráthair: true brother
'my dear little brothers in Christ' (*Portrait* III)
G Sippe: kindred, relations

Buddha (Siddhartha the Compassionate)
Bismillah: 'In the name of God, the Compassionate, the Merciful'
dementia praecox *Es* Spegulo ne helpas al malbelulo. Mi kredas ke vi estas prava, Via doto, la vizaĝo, respondas fraŭlino: A mirror doesn't help an ugly person. I believe you're right, Your fortune (is) your face, replies a young lady

(*nr* Where are you going, my pretty maid: 'My face is my fortune, sir, she said')
F habillement: clothing *Da* farfar: grandfather
author of our doom *s* (Ir. air) Arthur of This Town
Arthur Major Doyne erected near D a statue to the horse he rode at Waterloo

Chinese king Yu Weng, to amuse a whimsical court beauty, ordered lit the fires of wolf bones on hilltops signalling a barbarian attack (with disastrous result) Old Ir. Baal Fire rituals on eve of 1 May
ph airy nothings (from *Midsummer Night's Dream* V.I.16)

son of a bitch
Sl soor: pig
(7 articles of clothing, cf. 022.34–023.01)
beaver: a hat of beaver's fur
F baver: to drivel puggaree: thin scarf wound round a sun helmet & falling behind as a veil *US Sl* calaboose: a common prison
buggery
C k'ang: overbearing *G* toll: mad Elba elbowroom surtout: overcoat
Kung the Tall: father of Confucius four-in-hand: long narrow tie, with flat slipknot & dangling ends
unmentionables (underwear)

Viscount Wolseley: Ir. field marshal in Crimea *G* Knopf: button
Arthur Wellesley, Duke of Wellington *Angl* findrinny: silver-bronze

D'Esterre, killed in duel by O'Connell
mighty

Gr legomena: (words) said (Irish)

G suchen Sie das Weib: find the lady

senses: touch, sight silence insolence *Da* stilling: situation, pose night hear a pin drop (fall) *Sh* fin: man *Du* boom: tree 'Like a scene on some vague arras, old as man's weariness, the image of the seventh city of christendom was visible to him across the timeless air, no older nor more weary nor less patient of subjection than in the days of the thingmote' (*Portrait* IV) *It* rombare: to rumble, roar

Wilde: *The Picture of Dorian Gray*

to keep mum: to be silent mirage 42nd cousin: Scottish expression for 2nd generation down *Sw* kusin: cousin

audible *Da* os: us wireless air senses: hearing, taste, smell

L os: mouth; bone 'winedark sea'(Homer) *G* oede: desolate

F mère liss: release, migration, peace, rest

Da ting: court *Sl* prigged: stolen

Thingmote: Viking parliament in D

Val Vousden: *s* The Irish Jaunting Car

Sl vis-à-vis: jaunting car (because passengers sit face to face)

s Boys of the Old Brigade ('steadily, shoulder to shoulder') Jew & Christian

jehu: furious driver Christiania (Oslo)

ph Ireland, isle of saints & sages

buttocks *I* capall: horse

couple

Howth belfry *Da* tyr: bull

dry tears clothes

nose noesis: sum total of mental processes of a rational animal paradise arise *Du* eren: honour Erin

Eden

vindicative lo & behold! *L* arbor: tree

indicating

L petrus: stone Saintsbury: *The Peace of the Augustans*

peace be to them

U.S. pine barren: level sandy tract of land with pines Motto of House of Savoy: Fortitudo eius Rhodum tenuit (His Strength Has Held Rhodes) Ajax

Gr rodinos: pink, rosy Angelus is rung morning, noon & sunset (6 pm)

F ustensile: utensil do re mi . . .

G Reh: deer doe

Good Friday Mass of the Presanctified: 'Adoremus . . . Flectamus genua . . . levate': 'Let us adore . . . Let us kneel . . . rise'

s When Midnight Is Striking the Hour *L* laetate: gladden!

late

smallish sort quite

Gr oideô: to swell

manfully *I* pluc: cheek *I* leicean: cheek Lucan

Lecan, castle, Co. Sligo

bloody

Da krigsmænd: warriors Thor

L sorer: sister

Old High German

Sw sprog: speech Alphonse de Lamartine to Louis Philippe, 1830: 'Sire, you are the best republic'

Da bedste: grandfather *Sl* bester: swindler ECH

Eagle Tavern, Eustace St, meeting place of Corp. of Cooks & Vintners, D

St Laurence O'Toole: patron of D bannocks: hard biscuits (i.e. starchy)

3 tailors of Tooley St sent a petition to Commons beginning 'We, the people of England'

I beannacht Dé agus Muire agus Brighid agus Phádraic: the blessing of God & Mary & Bridget & Patrick

AngI gort: enclosed field *Du* gort: barley *I* Brí: Bray (means 'hill')

Morya: supposed coauthor of Blavatsky's 'Mahatma Letters' St Thomas's Church, D

Gort, Connacht Morya, Ulster Bray Head, Leinster or Munster stomach

Charles X, 1829: 'I have, like all Frenchmen, only a place in the pit' perplex

L floruerunt: they flourished *G* Hochzeit ('high-time'): wedding

is

L turris: tower *G* Hitze: heat

chee-chee: minced Eng. used by half-breeds Crom abú!: war cry of Fitzgeralds

King Billy: William III (of Orange) Cromwell

Wellington: 'Up, guards, & at them' albeit (oil paintings of
AngI Down aboo!: Up with Down! ancestors lost brightness)
Rembrandt
remembrancer: city representative
Villon: 'Where are the snows of yesteryear?' Vercingetorix: Gallic chieftain who revolted against Caesar
L/R Poor Old Woman (poetic term for Ireland) = *AngI* Shan Van Vocht
Caractacus: British chieftain, resisted Roman invasion
G Vogt: overseer, warden

Horace: *Odes* III.1.2: 'favete linguis' ('listen all in silence')
L intendite: attention!
to list: to like *ph* at sixes & sevens: disordered
listen
Halley's comet has 76-year period Ulema: Moslem group in pre-war Turkish government
VI.B.10.35: 'Ulema (Pers. Parl.)'
Parliaments: Sobranje (Bulgaria), Storthing (Norway), Duma (Tsarist Russia, 1906–17)
Black & Tans: Eng. recruits in 1920–1 serving
It casa concordia: house of peace *OE* huru: at all events in Royal Ir. Constabulary
Sw Hur maar ni, mina fröken: How are you, my young ladies?
Da Hvorledes har De det: How are you? last door on the left m'ladies, thank you
PS mlad-: youth, young
It millecentotrentadue: 1132 *It* scudi: crowns *Gr* Tipote, kyrie, tipote: Why, Lord, why?
L triginta: 30 *Sp* cien(to): 100 *Hin* chā kī pattī: tea
Hin makkhan rotī: *Sp* usted: you *Port* senhor: sir
bread & butter *Sp* dispénseme: excuse me *Sp* en son de: in the guise of
I Ó tá brón orm, a Chothraighe, (an) tuigeann tú Gaedhealg: I am sorry, St Patrick, do you understand Irish?
Sp sabes: you know P/K
C hai-p'a: suffer fear *C* lang: wolf *F* et puis allo, écoute *Rum* batiste: handkerchiefs
so long *Gr* epi allo: upon another thing *F* Baptiste (Christian name)
F tu vas venir dans le petit: you're *Rum* izmene de bumbac: cotton drawers Portugal
going to go in the little *Port* e meias: & stockings
O.O.: sign on toilets in S.E. Europe *Sp* mios: my *Rum* portocallie: orange colour
Port os: the *Port* pipos: barrels *Sp* demasiada: too much *Sp* grueso: large *Port* por: for *Port* o: the
It piccolo: small *It* pochino: a little bit *Sp* es: is *F* merci, et vous?
G wie viel: how much? one dollar *Hu* kocsis: cabman *Hu* szabad: may I?
I go maith: well (adv.)
Da tak
cad, *Sl* mugger: broadnosed Indian crocodile
(crocodile tears: false ones)
F liard: small coin ○ Maggies Nick/Mick

Louis XII said of heir to throne (Comte d'Angouleme): 'This fat fellow will spoil all'

U.550 (emended) 'THE NANNYGOAT: (*bleats*) Megeggaggegg!' universe
get
G sicher: surely *ph* Sure as eggs are eggs
Moyliffy, Magh Life: ancient territory in Co. Kildare
G Haushälter: householders *G* Jahrhundert: century
Hundred of Manhood, W. Sussex (030.08)

G Kuhhandel: shady business

(Wellington Monument)

globe

Firbolgs: mythical Ir. colonisers

boater: straw hat
(Ir. & Fr. tricolour flags)
Stetson hat oleaginous: oily
It sgocciolava: dripped

Mutsohito: Japanese emperor 1867–1912 *L* conciliabulum: place of assembly
Es senkapetulo: without money
U.16, &c. 'Agenbite of Inwit'
inviting

(036.27)

L atrox: cruel   Atreus: father of Agamemnon   Il'ya Muromets: popular hero-warrior of Russian folklore
Hermes cursed House of Atreus   in the dust   *L* Ilium: Troy
L maeror: mourning   Moore: *s* Avenging & Bright (Moore's   mountebanks   *G* Mund: mouth
Miramar: castle nr Trieste   note says name of its air means 'The Fenian Mount')
fenny: boggy   dead bones   *I* mór: great   *MGr* mourounomatês: having cod's eyes
s These Bones Gwine to Rise Again
venison (Esau & Jacob)

take it or leave it
live it   (die it)
corpse
crops
legend that when Confucius born the phrase 'established the world by law' was found written on his chest
pertinently   pretty neatly
Macbeth IV.1.80: 'of woman born'   *I* bán: woman
ph to the manner born
HCE

E . . . CH   Custom House, D

(retire at age 65)

G Hemd: shirt   dicky: detached shirtfront
Tom, Dick & Harry
L quid pro quo: something in return   Browning: *Pippa Passes*   (pointing with his pipe)
G Jagd: hunt   pea-jacket: a sailor's heavy overcoat

Francis Xavier   *ph* in his day

Mother of God have mercy   mastic: a gum exuded by evergreens   pullman
Gr mastix: a scourge, whip
Trans-Siberian Railway

G durch & durch: through & through
(with one eye)
cyclically
G Rundreise: tour

s The Irish Jaunting Car
Intourist: Russian travel agency
Keating: *Forus Feasa ar Eirinn* (begins: 'Ireland has been thrice clad & thrice bare')
interestedness
frore: frozen

four-leaved
(clover)
Da blomster: flowers   *Phoenix dactylifera*: date palm
G Baum: tree
HCE   cacuminal: pointed   erubescent: blushing   *Sl* root: penis
iridescent
G Asche: ash   clusters   *G* Pein: pain   pines   Swift:: *Cadenus & Vanessa* (Cadanus is anagram
A . . . L . . . P   lustre: 5-year period   penis   of Decanus = Dean)
Irish Field & Gentleman's Gazette, D

'Castlebar Races': British retreat from Fr. army in Co. Mayo, 1798

Annals of the Theatre Royal, D 194: 'new reading' (of Balfe's 'The Secret of My Birth')

Gr dyas: 2   Dyas: equivalent of Zeus in the Vedas
L Deus ex machina: providential interposition
David Garrick, actor   Joseph Grimaldi, clown   hypostasis: metaphysical substance, that which underlies
Rev. S. Hughes: *The Pre-Victorian Drama in Dublin* 4: 'Garrick's school of grimace'
L ore rotundo: with rounded mouth   Thomas Elrington: Ir. actor

Francis Elrington Ball, Ir. historian, edited Swift's letters (the factferreter)
Copernicus copycat (the namecousin)
all (the tourists, 055.13)

L pro tempore locum tenens: holding the place for a time
transported across *Du* kors: across
cockshy: a shy at an object set up for the purpose
Dial cockshot: twilight
(the porty, 051.24–052.03)
(O'Connell, 052.29) plangent: making sound of waves beating on a shore

I tonn a' mhaith sháile: wave of the good salt-sea silkhatted silhouetted *G* Walross: walrus mighty odd
Valhalla
Da skumring: dusk
muezzin: Mohammedan public crier who proclaims hours of prayer
holy blazes!

ghazi: Mohammedan fanatic devoted to infidels' destruction
Frank 'Ghazi' Power: Ir. journalist (521.22)
word
'overgrown milestone': old name for Wellington Monument
(imitates gesture, 036.18) *MGr* molybdokondylon: lead pencil
O'Connell Monument (round tower), Glasnevin Cemetery Steyne: pillar in D erected by Vikings
(Daniel O'Connell) *Da* stod: stood *G* Meise: titmouse *Da* skulde: should
Odin *Du* meisjes: girls
ph a Roland for an Oliver all over Roland: bell in Longfellow's *Belfry of Bruges*, at Ghent (035.32)
F sillon: furrow *F* joue: cheek
F joujou: toy

Moore: *s* The Young Man's Dream [As a Beam O'er the Face of the Waters May Glow]

Da akkurat: exactly O'Connell said Peel's smile was like 'a silver plate on a coffin'

Da bygning: building

Goldsmith: *The Traveller:* 'Remote, unfriended, melancholy, slow, Or by the lazy Scheld, or wandering Po' (cf. .30)
van Dieman's Land: Tasmania VI.B.6.154: 'innsigns
skald: ancient Scandinavian poet Weary Willy in an Eng. comic strip bottleneck = poteen
wandering maunder: move dreamily; ramble in speech broken cup = tea
zoo (animal constellations) zodiac old shoe on pole = ?
I teach: house wisp of straw = bed
(sign for Aires looks like flask neck, Taurus cup, Cancer rolled lawn turf) broom = whiskey
(constellation Gemini is vaguely shoelike, Leo looks like broom, Aquarius like cabbage stalk) sod of turf = tobacco'
Da blad: leaf *Da* stockfisch: dried cod
Pisces
The Angel, Islington (many Irish in this part of London) *AngI* praties: potatoes
G Herberge: inn *AngI* poteen: illicit whiskey ('flask neck')
J.H. Voss: 'Wine, Women & Song'

F presqu'île: peninsula

Wyndham Lewis
nous: intelligence
Wyndham Lewis: *Time & Western Man:* 'there is not very much reflection going on at any time inside the head of Mr James Joyce' (.21)
Gr pragma: deed, act formal cause (Aristotle)

Moore: *s* O Breathe Not His Name (let it sleep in the shade) [The Brown Maid]

Hin kis wāsṭe: why *Hin* kiskā: whose
Hin kidhar: whither *Hin* bajā: suitable time *Gi* tem: country *Gi* gav: town, village
Hin kitnā: how much tell Tem: creator in *Egyptian Book of the Dead* Swift: *Tale of a Tub*
G Grube: hole, mine *Gi* Match-eneskey gav: fishy town, i.e. Yarmouth
Gi Cudgel players' country: Cornwall *Gi* Pov-engreskey tem: potato country, i.e. Norfolk
Du Luilekkerland: land of Cockaigne *R* po-vengerski: in Hungarian *Gi* Paub-pawnugo tem: apple-water country, i.e. Hertfordshire *G* regnen: to rain
Gi Leek-eaters' country: Wales

Mound over Confucius's parents' grave washed away by heavy rainstorm points of compass

Gr melos: song stages of Confucius learning to play zither: 'I have practised the melody, but have not yet acquired the rhythm', 'I have not yet caught the mood', 'I have not yet ascertained the kind of man who composed the music', 'Now I know who he was . . . his eyes when they looked into the distance had the calm gaze of a sheep' (occurred in state of Tsi) *nr* Rich man, poor man, beggar man, thief

✕ four *G* Völker: peoples Marquis of Tsi proposed a prize of 2 peaches to the 2 best of his 3 ministers; all committed suicide

Meng, Chi & Shuh-sun: principal families of Confucius's native state

A disciple of Confucius met woman whose relatives were eaten by tiger. Asked why she did not move somewhere safer, she replied: 'But the officials here are not oppressive' as young man Confucius became tithe collector

F hanter: haunt habitat zones

Blake's Four Zoas, see *Jerusalem* 43 [38]: 'Urizen, cold & scientific; Luvah, pitying & weeping; Tharmas, indolent & sullen; Urthona, doubting & dispairing'

the roar Armagh (Ulster)

s One More Drink for the Four of Us

Clonakilty, town, Co. Cork (Munster); nicknamed 'Clonakilty–God Help Us!', because of appalling conditions there during famine Deansgrange, Co. D (Leinster)

Barna, town, Co. Galway (Connacht) (ass)

fell ill ALP

Hell

G um: around termites (build mounds)

Hill of Allen, Co. Kildare, Finn's HQ

I an: the *Da* Jotnursfjaell: 'giant's mountain': mt range in Norway *G* Grummel: distant thunder

thunderstruck

(show of legs)

It irreperible: undiscoverable *L* adjugo: I fasten together

seemingly

Sl judy: whore *L* judicandum: to be tried & judged (adj.)

Madam Tussaud's Waxworks

Gr kudos: glory *Sp* dos: 2 three National Gallery

escudo: Portuguese coin

Horace: *Odes* III.30.1: 'Exegi monumentum aere perennius' ('My work is done, the memorial more enduring than brass')

umbrella (Sarah Gamp) *F* de grâce!: for pity's sake!

Lewis Carroll an amateur photographer Tom Quad: quadrangle in Christ Church College, Oxford, where Lewis Carroll lived

roundabout Alice

L sol blandus: the pleasant sun word 'slithy' in Carroll's *Jabberwocky* nevermore

Carroll's real name C. L. Dodgson

Magdalen College, Oxford corrugate cogitate *Sl* mildewed: pitted with smallpox

maudlin agitate

ta-ta (goodbye) Alice

FSl tata: pederast

G ehe(r): ere, before overread

I céad: first, chief *L* urbs: city

I Áth Cliath: Hurdle Ford (D)

Eblana: Ptolemy's name for D outlander: foreigner *Du* dik: fat *L* maladictus: accused

L tertia: the third *F* maladif: sickly *Cz* mladík: youngster

L multi vult: many faces Rota: supreme court of R.C. church

L magnopere: very much

Sl thieves' kitchen: law courts 'Pillow-talk' opens The *Tain Bó Cúailgne* (dialogue between Maebh & Aillil) shithouse

Marlborough Green, N. D, C18 Molesworth Fields, S. D, up to C18

pro & con Jedburgh justice: hanging first & trying after (from the Scottish border town)

pro: before

benefit of clergy: orig., clergymen's privilege of exemption from secular court trial; later extended to all who could read
Thingmote: Viking parliament in D
ph done him in

Mark 5:9: 'My name is Legion: for we are many'
J.B. Dunlop invented pneumatic tyres

behold
Isaac
bicycles

Ivy Day
Blake: letter to Cumberland, 12/4/1827: 'the Mind, in which every one is King & Priest in his own House'
L ulva: sedge
Da ulv: wolf
Caesar: 'I came, I saw, I conquered'
holly, ivy, mistletoe
F loué: praised

s Wrap the Green Flag Round Me, Boys
The Golden Bough: ritual murder of divine king (compare 006.07–27)
L uxor: wife
Sp muerte: death, murder
mortification
expiration
G Schrei: shriek
It grida: cries
De Quincey: *Suspiria de Profundis* ('Sighs from the Depths')
Vulg Ps 129:1: 'De profundis' ('Out of the depths')
F soupirs: sighs
Manneken-Pis: statue in Brussels of child urinating
nr London Bridge Is Falling Down
Grania
s Adeste Fideles
s Phil the Fluter's Ball
s Phil the Fluter's Ball: 'With the toot of the flute & the twiddle of the fiddle, O!'
G Flucher: one who curses

G wohl
chin chin (toast)

s Phil the Fluter's Ball: 'Then all joined in wid the utmost joviality'
F boire: to drink
s Johnny I Hardly Knew Ye: 'guns & drums'
Beaune: a red wine
negus: mixture of wine, hot water, lemon & spice
s Hooligan's Christmas Cake: 'There were plums & prunes & cherries, Raisins & currants & cinnamon too'
Ibsen: *Bygmester Solness*
strangers
Bögg ceremonially burned at Sechseläuten (Zurich spring festival)
G seufzen: to sigh

Horace: *Odes* II.14.1: 'Eheu fugaces, Postume, Postume, Labuntur anni' ('Ah me, Postumus, Postumus, the fleeting years are slipping by')
threne: song of lamentation
Da treenige Gud: threefold God
Pope: *Essay on Criticism*: 'to err is human, to forgive divine'
status quo
C kuo: country, nation
HEC
SwG Kuo: cow
C kuang: light
C shu: tree
C wang: king
Joshua, Judges (Books of Bible)

⚔ Fontenoy: Lord Hay (Eng. captain) falsely supposed to have cried: 'Gentlemen of the French Guard, fire!'
Λ ⊏ ⊏
F messieurs
firstshot: weak poteen of 1st distillation
C ping: soldier
Sechseläuten: Zurich spring festival
s 'We be soldiers three, Pardonnez-moi, je vous en prie'
Sl tommies: Eng. soldiers
cock-a-leekie soup
cap-à-pie: head to foot
Coldstream Guards (regiment)
Montgomery St, D, in Nighttown

Finner Camp: military establishment between Bundoran & Ballyshannon, Co. Donegal

Arthur Wellesley, 1st Duke of Wellington

OE mod: mind
Da ældre: elder
Da far: father
Da mod: against
Redruth, town, Cornwall
Du stilstand: standstill
G (Waffen)stillstand: truce
L retro: backwards
(032.02)
Santoy: musical comedy at turn of century & name of its heroine
It santo: saint
Vauxhall, London

Sarah Siddons, actress
interviewed
Westend
beauty
vestpocket
beautiful

Anne Bracegirdle, actress A. Peter: *Dublin Fragments* mentions that: 'The Half Moon & Seven Stars, Francis St, sold Irish poplin. The Blackamoor's head sold paduasoys, russets &c. A chimney sweep lived at the Eagle & Child. The Black & All Black sold corn & hay'

HEC *L* emptor: buyer CHE

F.A. = Fanny Adams an aside (acting)

stage whisper *Souvenir of the 25th Anniversary of the Gaiety Theatre* 32: (old fashioned soprano) 'was always provided with a patient *confidante*' ⊢ recovering

F chapeau Thomas à Becket

F capote (anglais): condom

Laurence O'Toole (patron of D) Sir Arthur Guinness

F Sl baquet: cunt *Sl* lance: penis Siddhartha: Gautama Buddha

Christmas present *nr* Oranges & Lemons

(*Bhagavad*) *Gita*: Hindu spiritual treatise

holly & ivy Feast of the Innocents

F fée: fairy

world had been unkind 'Comparisons are odorous' (*Much Ado* III.5.18)

Cain

spring flowers of his birthday virid: green

fruits ripened at birth of Buddha veritable

Abel gardenparty *G* Regenworm: earthworm charlatans

G rein: pure ringworm scarlatina

climates *Climatis vitalba:* Traveller's Joy (abundant in Ir. hedgerows)

dermatitis night

Bur maha: royal

Maya-prajapati: Buddha's stepmother

L obiter dicta: incidental remarks *Gr* entychia: conversation

(proper name) *Gr* properispômenon: word with circumflex accent on penult. syllable

Sl dustman: gesticulating preacher

charcoal + saltpetre + sulphur = gunpowder

Sevenchurches: place near Glendalough Peter (stone)

ash (tree) Glendalough, site of St Kevin's monastic settlement

collation: lunch liver & bacon

buckrams: wild garlic steak & kidney pie wash-house

hash: chopped meat dish

Kevin

thank heaven

propaganda nullity (law): judicial declaration of invalidity of a marriage

says

days ages

I aratar: plough *L* calamus: pen, reed demented prick fuck

avatar Arata–Kalama: hermit who sheltered Buddha

s The Irish Jaunting Car ('It belongs to Larry Doolin')

Sl runabout: car

Ginger Jane (in British Museum): oldest complete human body in world

rewritten Earwicker *Sl* pink: secret

re right men

Brehon Laws: old Ir. legal system

G Eiskaffee: iced coffee

Escoffier: famous chef

Brillat-Savarin, gastronomist *F* ma foi!

F foie: liver

G mein Leber: my liver *G* mein Lieber: my dear

pr You can't make an omelette without breaking eggs

F poêle: frying pan *G* unbedingt: certainly

un-bedimmed & be damned!

knew how hard 'twas to collect *L* infamatio: calumny different pair of flannels

correct

I bradán: salmon

Mary Elizabeth Braddon: *Lady Audley's Secret* (about bigamy)

It troterella: little trout

11th Avenue, N.Y.C., once called Death Avenue (railway tracks down centre of street)

to wit   *L* ehim: ha!, what!

pr it's too late to shut the stable door after the horse has bolted   harlot
'shall I whistle for it?' (jocular offer of help when someone slow to start urinating)

Mrs Siddons, actress (058.35)   *L* meretrix: whore

revolver
vulva
health   Drom-Choll-Coil: old Ir. name of D

Board of Trade

Moore: *s* O, Blame Not the Bard [Kitty Tyrrel]   *Da* benklæder: drawers

unison   jury leg: wooden leg   *s* Brian O'Linn
God forgive
Ballynabragget, townland, Co. Down

bawl   bark   mark you
burk: to kill by suffocation
L cave canem: beware of the dog   Wellington: 'Up, guards, & at them'
lashed   lynched
Asita: hermit who recognized new-born Buddha   asita: loathing (more correctly, want) of food
L sanitas: health, sanity
Buddha's sister tried to teach him to wear bracelets   martyrs tortured on grill
Sl bracelets: handcuffs   *F* à point: medium (steak)

Sakya Muni: name of Gautama Buddha   monkey tricks
Moody & Sankey, Am. revivalists
mistletoe   Apsaras: maidens set to entertain Buddha when young; dropped on him from mango tree
Buddha, meditating under tree, was suspected to be Indra, thunder-god
F torréfier: to roast, scorch   interdiction
Cuxhaven: German port

incident   interfering   grenadiers

Layamon: *Brut*   Daniel McGrath, grocer & publican, 4–5 Charlotte St, D (in J's time)
A letter published in 1894 *Sydney Bulletin* proposed name 'Eastralia' for E. Australia   perusers
Sydney Parade, D

172.24–5: 'we're spluched'   cabler   met too early (037.13–14)
Aust Sl cobber: mate   (bootmaker, 618.30)
Captain Boycott

toreador   *s* Call Me Early, Mother Dear
(makes sweeping gesture with his cape)   matador
precentor: leader of congregational singing   Smock Alley Theatre, D   *L* proba verba: honest words

L ipse dixit: dogmatic assertion   snuffbox
L mutatis mutandis: the necessary changes being made
Lady Morgan ('Dear Dirty Dublin') & her friend Lady Moira

'dirty Dubs' (D Militia) performed echoes in *Der Freischütz* at Theatre Royal, D. When Caspar calls 'one!' they were to follow 'one! one! one!' but second man roared 'two!'   open
one two three   dainty   *Sl* drab: whore
flies: space above stage where scenery hung until needed   daily

It una mona: a silly cunt Sylvia Silence: character in Eng. schoolgirls' magazine of 1920s

L scaenitae: actresses *L* memini: remember Minerva: Roman goddess of wisdom

turtledove (039.15)

ph 'Dear Dirty Dublin'

facts

John-a-dreams (*Hamlet* II.2.295): generic for 'a dreamy fellow'

muse

(lisp) reporter

1132

Wilde was charged under section 11 of the Criminal Law Amendment Act 1885

s Master Dilke Upset the Milk When Taking It Home to Chelsea: 'He let the cat, the naughty cat, Slip out of the Gladstone bag' (refers to divorce case over Sir Charles Dilke—parallel with Parnell)

glad-rags rating: enlisted naval man (as opposed to officer)

cromlech: prehistoric structure—large flat unhewn stone supported by 3 or more upright ones setts: granite blocks used in paving

Fishamble St, D aeration

s 'Questa o quella' from Verdi's *Rigoletto* Ir. P/Q split

Cromlechs called 'quoits' in W. Cornwall

(sinking feeling in stomach) what's what

Nirvana

Buddha's mother chided him for neglecting his body *Sw* fastrer: aunts *Sw* systrer: sisters

foster sister

pants (211.11)

Port cor: colour

L mea: mine

Horniman Museum, London

Annie Horniman: patroness of Abbey Theatre, D

how can I *L* piscis: fish

L puella: girl *F* siège: seat, chair Troy

ph bet your bottom dollar

Sl drummer: trousers-maker Keyser's Lane, medieval D (vulgarly named 'Kiss-arse lane' because steep & slippy in frosty weather)

G Meer: sea Merchant Tailors' Guild of St John the Baptist, D, 1704

right reverend

Oedipus Rex Marie Antoinette: 'I have seen everything, & have forgotten everything'

Pope: *Dunciad:* 'To hatch a new Saturnian age of lead'

Covenanter: Scottish presbyterian

G bejaht: assented to

Uruvela, where Buddha obtained enlightenment

'seventh city of christendom' (D, *Portrait* IV) *Da* viv: wife

citadel

Adriatic (Trieste on it)
Buddha, renouncing luxury, changed clothes with a god dressed as a hunter
clothes hejira: any exodus (from Mohammed's flight from Mecca in 622)
Ibsen: *Bygmester Solness* *G* Burgermeister *F* silencieusement: silently
Herold: *La vie du Bouddha,* relates that Buddha left his palace 'dans la nuit sonore'

Wasawarthi Mara: demon who tempted Buddha Rahoulas: son of Buddha 'Ostman': Viking

Da by: city The Old Vic, London theatre laughter . . . merriment

Viconian cycle: birth, marriage, death, divine providence
Dead Sea
Buddha, who had for years looked for the *G* Bilder: pictures dip
builder of the house, was enlightened: the spirit, tired of rebirth, learned how to attain Nirvana
Movietone: newsreel of 1930s *F Sl* patte: hand (female papish)
AngI shee: fairy
Da min kvinde: my woman (marriage ceremony) *G* Hosenband: belt
Da gifte: marry husband
lotus *It* ottuso: dark
T.S. Eliot: *The Waste Land* *L* luctuosus: sorrowful Ireland, 'Emerald Isle'

L Ilium: Troy R.C. Catechism: 4th Commandment: 'Honour thy father & thy mother'

King Edgar's forged charter, A.D. 964: 'By the abundant mercy of God who thundereth from on high . . . divine Providence hath granted me . . . the greatest part of Ireland, with its most noble city of Dublin'
F franchissable: that can be passed

Gr astea: cities, towns *Gr* agora: place of assembly, market helot: serf, bondsman
Gr philos: loving

I Cor 15:53: 'For this corruptible must put on incorruption'

'Garden of Erin': Co. Wicklow

convict

HCE Cheops built Great Pyramid exarch: under Byzantine Empire, governor of a distant province. Otherwise, in Eastern Church 'Archbishop', Patriarch's deputy &c.
proper: own

Amenti: Egyptian underworld

Egyptian Book of the Dead: Chapters of Going Forth by Day
six seals on tomb of Tut-ankh-amen
Wednesbury, town, Staffs

A London particular: London fog

Moore & Burgess, rivals of Christy's Minstrels. Used catchline 'Take off that white hat!'
'Barkis is willing': indication of person's willingness to do something (Dickens: *David Copperfield*) *Sl* barker: pistol

Lotta Crabtree: C19 Am. soubrette *L* Pomona: Roman fruit-goddess
crabapple *F* pomme
Chapelizod See of D & Glendalough
Lucan

Little Britain: Brittany (Tristan)
Little Britain St, D (*Cyclops*)

grasshopper
AngI crawthumper: ostentatiously devotional Roman Catholic
Reade & Co: D cutlers Hobson's choice
Sl shoot: fuck

ant *Sl* pistol: penis
Sl aunt: prostitute

G geil: lascivious *I* gall: foreigner Ned Thornton: original of 'Tom Kernan' in *U.*
Po wodka (from 'water of life')
Cain Matthew Kane: original of 'Martin Cunningham' in *U.*

G Mittwoch: Wednesday
Wednesbury 062.28
Abel

gentle reader six feet one

person . . . gender . . . number . . . case (grammar)
L mira me: admire me

(rainbow) the Flaggy Bridge: roadbridge 5 km east of Derrybrien on Gort-Portumna road
Da liv: life 'There is but one God & Mohammed is his prophet' (Islam)
New Bridge, in Leixlip, is probably oldest bridge in Ireland
shrievalty: sheriff's jurisdiction

Abel *ph* one man one vote
able-bodied seaman *ph* one flesh, one blood
Sir Edward Creasy: *Fifteen Decisive Battles of the World*
single: mild ale or beer

HCE emerods: hemorrhoids

paralysingly
soliloquy
*U.*200: 'Murthering Irish'

Hengest & Horsa: brothers who led Saxon invasion of Kent
I (a) thoise efíon: (his) capacity of wine
Peter's *Dublin Fragments* lists D pubs: House of Blazes, The Parrot (in district then called 'Hell'), The Orange Tree, Glibb, The Sun, The Holy Lamb
ph last but not least

The Mohammedan Ramadan fast begins at dawn, defined as time when a black & a white thread are distinguishable
Ship Hotel & Tavern, 5 Lr Abbey St, D
Angelus: 'The Angel of the Lord declared unto Mary . . .'

Mary *s* Phil the Fluter's Ball
Murray: J's mother's maiden name

caterpillar

hobbledehoy

'Joacax': nickname of J when at university
L jokax: joker
process server: sheriff's officer who serves processes or summonses *Ali Baba* (pantomime): 'Open Sesame!' bottle of stout
Zozimus: D bard & beggar
G Staub: dust *L* magnum bonum: great good
Charles Martel ('the Hammer'): Charlemagne's grandfather magnum: large wine bottle

Charles Selby: *The Boots at the Swan*; the boots' name is Jacob Earwig; he is deaf & impersonates a policeman

I bara: palm of hand tintack *I* teinteach: fiery (*Coll*, lightning)
I barra: bar, hindrance *I* tinnteach: scabbard lamp

Ham, Shem & Japhet   *s* The West's Awake
hop, step & jump
obi: bright Japanese sash worn round the waist   *Sl* choker: cravat   noise
G ohne: without   *s* The Rocky Road to Dublin
General Deland at Waterloo   Ragnar Lodbrok: Viking chief   *ON* Ragnarøkr: destruction of the Norse gods
Cato: 'Delenda est Carthago' ('Carthage must be destroyed')   *We* Dulyn: Dublin
s I Dreamt That I Dwelt in Marble Halls
Land of Beulah (Isa 62:4): Blake's country of dreams

Moore: *s* While History's Muse [Paddy Whack]
R byelo: white   Moore: *s* While Gazing on the Moonlight [Oonagh]

U.S Sl blind pig: place selling illicit liquor
Mullingar Inn, Chapelizod

all over
Tower of Babel (Babel related to *Akkadian* bāb-ilu: gate of the god; hence 'door')
Beelzebub
s The West's awake: 'Connaught lies in slumber deep'

s Marseillaise   marches   *G* Musikant: musician
Mars, war-god
overture   Bulwer-Lytton: *The Last Days of Pompeii*

F Sl pomper: to booze   meaningless
popery
nocturne   rain
F reine
r Liffey   *F* pleurer   *F* plainte: wail   as mad as
Gr potamos: river   *L* ploro: I wail
butchers'   *G* Schurz: apron   bakers'
G wischen: to wipe   boucher: treasurer, cashier
G Waschhandtuch: washing glove   chandelier   *L* Regina Coeli: Queen of Heaven
(*D by Lamplight* laundry   (candlestick maker)   (BVM); name of jail in Rome
employed reformed prostitutes)   *F* Chandeleur: Candlemass   *G* Welt: world
G waschen
(216.04–5)

pr A stitch in time saves nine

Athos, Porthos & Aramis, Dumas's *Three Musketeers*   Australia   Jerry
Astraea became the constellation Virgo   astrologers
Scots saunts: saints   Kevin   *Sl* pike:
Heaven   depart
Rum pamint-ul: the land   *s* 'O weel may the keel row, the keel row, the keel row'

Heroine of Patrick Kennedy's story *The Twelve Wild Geese* is called Snow-White-and-Rose-Red

(213.14)   *F* cherchez la femme
F Coll filons!: let's scram!   *Sp* flamme: pudding

knobbly   *L* non oblitus: not forgotten
Ido (artificial language) nonnobli: base
barebacked   facial   *It* sprezzabile: contemptible
G Fisch: fish   visual expression   *It* scapolo: bachelor
doesn't ask you   bachelor's button
It macellaio: butcher
Noah Beery: Am. film star   1 stone = 14 lbs
(Guinness, 549.34)

autumn *L* auctus: increase

pins

F collé hairs on your head

Sl Sweet Fanny Adams: nothing at all

F tableau vivant:
representation of statuary group by living persons

s The Young May Moon

(Bloom's astronomy)

every night
very nice
razzle-dazzle

F compris

Peter Robinson: London Department Store
Robinson Crusoe
ABC Charles Chance: original of J's 'M'Coy'
Charley Chan: film hero
Mr Hunter corresponded to Bloom gaga
in J's early plan for short story 'Ulysses' Dada movement

drawers Emerson: *Civilization:* 'Hitch your wagon to a star'

trousers *U.S. Sl* clean dippy: totally crazy

Furphy: Australian latrine bucket manufacturer;
hence 'furphy' = latrine-rumour
bravo!

Coll canoodle: fondle

Sl mashed on: fascinated by

Peaches & Daddy Browning: a young girl & old man involved in scandal in 1920s

cherubim
Sl Cherrybums: 11th Huzzars
(wore red pants)

s Tea for Two zoo (Noah's ark)
how d'ye do?
G taufen: baptise HCE
(003.09–10)

r Tippecanoe
Sl tippy: unstable

F finis
WWI Sl (*signalese*)
ack ack ack: fullstop (Viconian cycle: thunder, marriage & burial) 1132
F soudainement: suddenly
Dickens: *Our Mutual Friend*

ph in the same boat *G* sozusagen: so to speak

Angl ph never put a tooth in it: to speak out clearly

G Nacht *G* Tag

L in rebus publicis: in public affairs

L per omnia saecula saeculorum: for ever & ever

L futuete!: fuck!
(acrostic)

Vercingetorix: Gallic chieftain who revolted against Caesar *Da* det er: that is losel: profligate
Arch hight: called
hawks (stamps) *G* Gummi: rubber

HCE □ chain letter shades
John O'Donovan on J.C. Mangan: 'One short poem of his exhibits *seven different* inks'
F blanchissage: laundry pothook: hooked stroke made in writing
F lavandière: washerwoman
subpoenaed ALP

afterwards Pious Catholics put 'S.A.G.' HCE Edinburgh
afterwit (St Anthony Guide) on letters hide & seek
G läppisch: childish (LAP)
L lapsus linguae: slip of the tongue
(111.16 'how are you Maggy') *F* Sem: Shem composed
Finno-Ugrian languages: Lappish,Magyar (Hungarian) superimposed
Siamese twins

Tristan Jolly Roger: pirate flag
'twixt Sterne/Swift Roger Cox: Swift's clerk
Percy French: *s* 'Are ye right there, Michael, are ye right? . . . & it might now, Michael, so it might!'

Mme Blavatsky, neé Hahn-Hahn *G* Hahn: rooster

what was mother after
what's the matter
herm: Greek 4-cornered pillar surmounted by head or bust, usually of Hermes

□ pillarbox: mailbox

□

hard work to distinguish

Cain's descendants: Jabal (father of cattle owners); Jubal (ancestor of those who use harps & organs); Tubal (instructor of brass & iron artificers)
invented

Oetzmann & Co.: D & London furnishers *Sl* gone west: died

Lalouette's carriage & funeral establishment, Marlborough St, D: 'funeral requisites of every description'

G rattenkahl: quite bare

Sl oscar: money

s Lillibullero *L* nubilis: marriageable
bolero: girl's small jacket *L* nivis: snow *L* nubis: cloud
s We Don't Want to Fight, But, by Jingo, If We Do

G mit: with *G* Mitternacht: midnight
G nackt: naked

horses & their asses

air = appx. 80% nitrogen, 20% oxygen

analects: gleanings, esp. literary chimaera
analyse electrolyse
waterworks

some more hydrogen up the atmosphere helium
G heiter: merry *Gr* eliôse: melted

Black & Tans: Eng.
recruits in 1920–1 serving in Royal Ir. Constabulary
The Little Church Around the Corner, N.Y.C. Norwegian tailor (311.05–09)

I táilliúr: tailor

G schnorren: to cadge queer sort of a man (016.01) blouse
Der Querschnitt published poems by J, 1923 *Da* mand: man (blue butcher's apron)
continued evening opening

Mutt & Jute meatjuice
mutton chops
Eastmans Ltd, victuallers, D
North, South, East & (Limerick is in West)
I dún an doras: shut the door

rules

apple-pie order why, upon my oath 'Exsultet': 'O felix culpa!'
Apophis: Egyptian god
deeply
kneedeep
Tom King & Phelps, D actors

salaam: oriental salutation

nickname Gen 4:5: '& Cain was very wroth & his countenance fell'
playful with his brother
Sl peeler: *Sl* phiz: countenance
policeman
velveteen: cotton or silk cloth like velvet
dimity: stout cotton cloth with raised stripes
HCE

(034.20) The Hollow, Phoenix Park

It magretta: rather thin *s* I've a Terrible Lot to Do Today

Lupita, sister of St Patrick
F Sl lorette: whore (they went to church at Notre Dame
de Lorette) carbolic acid: phenol
pale (red at 068.10)
peeled

Sl soiled dove: prostitute Luperca: she-wolf that suckled Romulus
Luperca: priestess of Pan

strip-tease

F jambes James Joyce

nautch: E. Indian exhibition of dancing girls (got big-headed)

mow: stack of hay; place in a barn where hay heaped up

I grianán: sunny house (the finest building in ancient Tara, reserved for the ladies of the place) *L* ad hoc fuck *G* hucken: to squat

love-stories
lavatories
leave

Lupita proved her chastity by carrying hot coals without getting burned

It alla zingara: gipsylike

coney: rabbit

Grania

Oscar was Finn's grandson houri: nymph of Mohammedan paradise

Wilde's father found guilty of assaulting Mary Travers HCE

ALP *L* lacesso: I provoke Boucicault: *Arrah-na-Pogue*

'Muslim' means 'one who is resigned' & 'Islam' means 'self-surrender'

Eva, daughter of Diarmaid MacMurchadha, king of Leinster, married Strongbow (.19)

Ice dottir: daughter Diarmaid Cromwell's Quarters, flight of steps, D, known as 'The Forty Steps'

Valkyries

Gr kyriê eleêsôn: Lord have mercy

bugger

It sfidare: to challenge

It ti sfido: I challenge you

L angelus Dei: angel of God *L* mei: of me

giaour: Turks' term of reproach for non-Mussulmans, esp. Christians

It arco: bow *It* bisavolo: great grandfather

It forte: strong ('Strongbow') *Da* farfar: grandfather

do, re, mi, fa, so, la, ti, do

G Teufelsdreck: devil's dung *F* reine *AngI* shee: fairy Sheba

Teufelsdröckh: hero of Carlyle's *Sartor Resartus* *AngI* shebeen: illicit tavern

Prankquean (021.15)

Koran: Suras X & XVII: 'Extolled Be His Glory'

(398.29)

rippling rills (L/R) lips voice

beard of the prophet

up to beddy

stele: upright sculptured slab Asia Minor obelise: mark a word or passage with obelisk

on the spot *I* pobal: folk *I* cloch: stone Folkestone & Dungeness on S. Kent coast

'Lapis tituli' at Folkstone marked landing place, like the 'Long Stone' at D

Ir. forces at ⚔ Clontarf were in Tomar's Wood (prob. originally devoted to service of Thor) *Arch* bewray: expose, make known

G erpressen: to blackmail off the red (billiards)

damnation *Gi* tatcho: true

Gi tawnie yecks: little ones, grandchildren Patrick Colum: 'As in wild earth a Grecian vase' (069.03)

Gi pattin: a leaf *Gi* patrin: trail

women he'd
womanhood
(lit. trans. of *I* for 'the times   *s* Lilly Dale ('O the wild rose blossoms')   Oscar Wilde
when the fairies existed')   Padraic Colum: *A Portrait* (poem): 'As in wild earth a Grecian vase'

s By Memory Inspired   The Hole in the Wall, pub nr Phoenix Park
we
Sir Blyaunte rescued Launcelot after his madness, & when the Grail had cured him both lived some time in the castell of Blyaunte (Malory)   *Da* blyant: pencil   *I* peann-luaidhe mór: big pencil
Portrait I: 'Once upon a time and a very good time it was'   (gate: 063.19, 34; door: 067.19)
Du hoog: high   Valhalla
Ar ôrė ôr: day by day   *Da* aar: year   *Ar* dėr: form of address to secular clergy   Da(d)   *Ar* hayr: father
(before metal or anger in Ireland)   *ph* there's hair!
Ar digin: Mrs   *Ar* orti: son   *Ar* ôriort: young lass
*U.*214 'Ay, I will serve you your orts and offals'
Garden of Eden (traditionally sited in Armenia)   *Paradise Lost*   Adam & Eve's Church, D
L ave: hail!   *G* Armen: poor people   *Ar* doun: house   *Ar* minag: solitary, alone
Armenia   Amen
lucifer   match   *Ar* barekeac: living a good life
Ar Lousavoric̆: Illuminator (title given to St Gregory, 1st patriarch of Armenia)
Ar s̆ous̆an: lily;   *Ar* šoudov: hastily   shut up
Sousan: fem. name   *ph* sure as eggs are eggs
Swift's Stella & Vanessa both had name Esther   Easter eggs   *R* drema: somnolence
Ishtar: Babylonian mother-goddess   *Gr* astêr: star   drama
SAD,   deceased   Stonehenge
I Saorstát Eireann: Ir. Free State (1920s)
Soroptimist movement: women's society in 1920s

Caddy & Primas (014.12)
cadet: younger son

hog   kid
hug   kiss
remnants
ruminants

F prétendre: to maintain

jakes

gate

goat   *G* lockt: beckons
padlocked
Du poort: gate
Du poorter: citizen
Arch enaunter: lest, in case

(Easter Sunday)

lest   George Petrie's collection of Irish airs (ed. Stanford): *s* The Wee Bag of Praties

G Betreffender: the person concerned   summer holidays
G herbetreffend: before mentioned   *G* Zimmer: room
Heinrich Zimmer: C 19 Celtic scholar

Dirty Dick's Free House, Bishopsgate, London   Leixlip ('Salmon Leap')   sockeye salmon: a small Pacific species

G Kommerzialrat: councillor of commerce   *G* zentral   *G* Europa: Europe
It corpo di Bacco: by Jove!   *G* rauchen: to smoke

G Österreich: Austria God save the mark!: expression of impatient scorn 1132
mark (*G* coin) 11 shillings (abbr.)
Holy Romans (rent)

the first day of July *G* weil: because *G* zwischen: between business with pleasure
(tourist season) *F* blessure: wound
'the broken lights of Irish myth' (*Portrait* V) *G* gebrochenes Deutsch: broken German
swopping The Brocken, Harz Mts, Germany *G* mit *G* Brocken: morsel
G der Fall Adams: the case of Adam *Frankfurter Zeitung*, periodical, misattributed
It franco furto: unpunished theft a short story to J, 1931
Da Fastland: mainland, continent *G* er constate: to assert
periodical
s Brian O'Linn (017.11–12) made woolly trousers *G* Lammswolle: lamb's wool *G* und weiter: & further
melton: heavy material used for coats *G* wieder: again
Zurich
G zurückschicken: send back
G tausend und abertausend: thousands & thousands *G* Donnerwetter! *Sl* monkey: £500
Du fransman: Frenchman take heart to grass (C17 corruption of 'heart of grace')
*I'll make my love a breast of glass

*Paddy O'Snap *F* obus: artillery shell abuses Roebuck: district of D
Rubek, in Ibsen's *When We Dead Awaken*, dies on the mountain
s 'Lots of Fun at Finnegan's Wake'
*I will go to the Roebuck pinnacles
Buckley *The Butchers' March
*Ancient Clan March
HEC *The highly excellent good man of Tipperoughny town *The Belfast Mountain
*Alas, that I'm not a little starling bird *Long Dance entitled

*Adieu, ye young men of Claudy green *F* bock: glass of beer what-you-may-call-it

Quaker Oats oaths Titus Oates, invented the Popish Plot (by Catholics, to assassinate Charles II, 1678)

gate *The taylor of the cloth

hog-calling (head) Bolshevik

(feet)

Languedoc

stirabout: a kind of porridge the other one the emperor

pr Blood is thicker than water Attila killed his brother Bleda & his bloody step brother's

Brodar: assassin of Brian Boru wood alcohol: methyl alcohol (poisonous; in methylated spirit)
bargain
s My Grandfather's Clock *Gr* tachys: fast

Dan O'Connell *R* izba: cottage
O'Connell Ale (formerly from Phoenix Brewery)
open *Da* irsk: Irish *I* uisce: water whiskey

Attila
artillery
mixed metaphors
Mookse (152.15)
1132

HCE God

Joseph Biggar: hunchbacked supporter of Parnell
Jupiter
Dionysius' Ear: name of an amplifying prison chamber in Dionysius' palace in Sicily

*George Petrie's collection of Irish airs (ed. Stanford)

Attempts to provide construction work in Ireland during the famine included 'famine walls'

Gr rhipis: fan flabel: fan whiskey bottle toothpick

Wild Geese: Ir. Jacobites who went to continent after defeat in 1691

Paradise Lost

compiled *The rejoicement of Fian Ladies

I foinne: to knead, bake Milton *The Humours of Milltown
I fionn: fair fine ladies (D pron.) Milltown: district of D
collection Eckermann: *Conversations with Goethe*
⚔ Inkerman, Crimea, 1854
low Waterloo

Clontarf (theatregoer)

wheat-ear: Gnostic appellation for Christ; small bird backside *s* Yes, We Have No Bananas
guilty god *Du* geit: goat Bogside: Catholic district of Derry
'York' means 'boar-wick'; boar was Richard III (York)'s emblem *s* At Trinity Church I Met My Doom
Sl porker: Jew Baggot St, D
Vico discusses auspices in Roman history Cain Abel
openair hospices
Swift called Bank of Ireland 'The Wonderful Wonder of Wonders' Parnell: 'When you sell, get my price'
Jack London: *Moonface* (murder story) *U*.482: 'Bloom's weather. A sunburst appears in the northwest' (*Circe*, midnight)
'Take away these baubles' (Cromwell ordering removal of mace on dissolution of Rump Parliament) *Revue Hebdomadaire* (weekly) Tamerlane
dromedary
B.C. *I* Baile Átha Cliath: D (pron. roughly 'blau clay')
G blau *G* Klee: clover
Pentateuch A.D. 'God Bless the good Duke of Argyle' (said when rubbing one's back against a post)
disgrace Behemoth D Bay
W.G. Grace, cricketer *Heb* gibbor: giant
Mundzuk, father of Attila *Sl* growler: 4-wheeled cab
G Mund *G* Zucker *G* Mondsucher: moon-seeker, lunatic
Burnham light at Bristol Barnum & Bailey Circus in U.S. from 1880
Bailey light on Howth
Patrick Cotter, Ir. giant, resembled Brian Boru Waterford was a Ribbonmen stronghold (C19 secret society)
terra cotta *Your welcome to Waterford
*The Ribbonman's March *The Lobster Pot Sir Arthur Guinness
Sl lobsterpot: cunt *Sl* lard: copulate *Arthur of this Town
*Hush the cat from the bacon *Leather bags Donnel

Popery *O'Reilly's delight *Kiss the Maid behind the Barrel
*The Ace & Deuce of Pipering
Du borrel: a drink Gog & Magog: biblical giants Yeats: *Countess Cathleen*
'Oedipus' means 'swollen foot' *Sl* swad: i) bumpkin; ii) soldier Ghibelline family in C13 Italy
(Luther suffered from constipation) give a cock's egg: send on a fool's errand
HCE leg before wicket (cricket)
tanner: sixpence make: halfpenny

Cromwell: 'Go to Hell or Connacht' (from a Parliamentary act of 1654)
St Helena (Napoleon sent there)
Burke's *Peerage* barbarian Peculiar People: i) the Jews; ii) a denomination founded 1838, practising baptism & divine healing
Burke's pub ('Oxen of the Sun')
Grey Owl (Indian chief)-totem 'Grand Old Man' (Gladstone)
factotum
lycanthrope: werewolf *s* 'Yankee Doodle went to London just to ride a pony'

looney Clontarf
G Dorf
Lord's Cricket Ground, London stage Irishman
G Arsch: arse *G* Mann
Iron Duke Thomas Furlong: *The Plagues of Ireland* archdeacon *Sl* cabbager: a tailor
Dial yuke: itch archduke
if gone

*George Petrie's collection of Irish airs (ed. Stanford)

cover (cricket) *MilSl* up in Annie's room: reply to enquiry about person's whereabouts
G Tritschtratsch: prattle, gossip (implies he is a 'bit of a lad')
Dial twitchbell: earwig Lombard Street West (where the Blooms used to live)
all out (cricket) *G* Bratsche: viola Lombard St, London (finance)
Sublime Porte: the Ottoman court at Constantinople; hence, the Turkish Government Tzar
Angl Ban: Lord-Lieutenant of Ireland Belgians
of all the Russias 'Exsultet': 'O felix culpa!' caprice *C* wan: 10,000 or a large number
Gr ôphelimos: useful
111 (201.27–31) *Castle Costello *A bed of feathers & ropes

Horace Walpole called gossip 'rattle'
*Horace the Rake
*The sons of Fingal Moore: *s* Sweet Inisfallen
Fingal: district N. of D
*A woman & 20 of them *Mammie will you let me to the fair P/Q

nr Pop Goes the Weasel *Plough song or whistle H(CE)

William Beaverbrook: newspaper magnate *nr* A Was an Archer sour grapes

Edomites: tribe of Esau (Gen 36:9) Eamonn De Valera
Armenia occupied by Turks from 1405; nationalism John Devoy: a founder of Ir. Free State
in C19–20 met with systematic massacres Bad Homburg: German spa
raven/dove *G* Händler: dealer
Da raab: shout *G* Kuhhandel: shady business *Sl* mitch: play truant both
Da rabrab: 'quackquack'–'duck' in baby talk Karl Zeller: *Der Vogelhändler* (opera)
Woolworth's stores Asiatic philosopher guinea pig
ECH *Gr* apistos: unfaithful
Du boos: wicked

Bell's *Standard Elocutionist* (note: this list contains 111 items)
BAD

Wedgewood china
ph easy as kissing hands cuneiform letters (wedgeshaped)

Gripes (152.15) Kimmage, district of D

(035.24) Le Fanu's *The House by the Churchyard,* ch. 1, begins 'A.D. 1767'

G Fuchs: fox socialist party
future
Romish devotion

holy rosary *G* ihm

Bullocky, cricketer

G glatt: smooth *pr* People who live in glass houses shouldn't throw stones Mookse
Gladstone (152.15)
Gripes wicket (cricket)
wicket: casement
I so slán abhaile: here's a 'safe home' (farewell)

change the bowling (cricket)

L grumus: hillock, little heap

grand old *I* lionndubh: melancholy (black bile)
I lionn dubh: porter, stout
P/K

briskly

*Petrie, Irish airs

paleology: science or study of antiquities
self-denying ordinance: act of 1645 preventing members of Parliament from holding civil or military office
G Heiland: the Saviour   dissecting
C. Hyland, manager of Gaiety Theatre, D, in 1920s

(stuttering)   Waterloo

Crumlin, district of D   bloody   *Da* gud: god   Visigoths
*U.*13: 'fishgods of Dundrum'
day

ph you go bail: you can be sure   Pott's: a type of bone fracture in heel   Ketil Flatneb, Viking, father of the queen of D
ph the pot calling the kettle black
Ulysses (calling himself Noman) with Polyphemus   (bury)

1132

Charles Martel ('the Hammer'): Charlemagne's grandfather, defeated Saracens at ✕ Poitiers, A.D. 732   *I* ag briseadh: breaking   *I* ag stracadh: tearing
I ag milleadh: destroying
I ag buaileadh: beating   Marlborough
s Malbruk s'en va
His Master's Voice: gramophone record company
His Majesty   jester/king antithesis   heroic couplet consists of two 10-syllable iambics
trope   1132   abeyance
G Elf
Finn burnt his thumb while cooking salmon of wisdom & bit it to ease pain, thereby obtaining wisdom   biting thumb an expression of contempt in Italy
s 'With my bundle on my shoulder
There's no one could be bolder
& I'm off to Philadelphia in the morning'   polder: land reclaimed from sea
Hurdle Ford (D)

slips (cricket position)   ECH   *Et Tu, Healy:* poem written by J in 1891 or 1892, on Parnell's death
L cur: why
2 deaf-&-dumb institutions in D

pat self on the back
G Bach: brook
Vo adyö: adieu

Bully's Acre: oldest D cemetery, Kilmainham
Balfe: *The Siege of Rochelle* (opera)   *L* exitus: a going-out
G siegen: to triumph

I deoch an dorais: parting drink
Bar-le-Duc: town, France, staging area for siege of Verdun, 1916
Bergen-op-Zoom, town, S.W. Holland, frequently besieged

Vo yed: yet   made   Ostman: Viking, hence Oxmantown (N. D in Middle Ages)

chambered cairns (archaeology)

H . . . C . . . E   eolith: primitive stone instrument
ph up hill & down dale   The Coombe, street, D   *Gr* neo lithostrôton: new stone pavement
H . . . C . . . E   Coolock: district of D   Enniskerry: village, Co. Wicklow

rectilinear: forming a straight line

Hugh Miller: *The Testimony of the Rocks,* 1857   Oliver's lambs: Ir. name for Cromwell's soldiers
Oliver & (074.05) Roland were 2 of Charlemagne's 12 paladins
Da skatter: treasure

paladin: knightly hero, knight errant   cumulus cloud
L nubila: clouds
Da hvem: who   save   (legend that King Arthur will awaken & return to earth when his horn blown)

Sinn Féin, Sinn Féin Amháin: Ourselves, Ourselves Alone (slogan) *F* avant: before
haven't *Da* skal: shall
HCE *ph* vale of tears
Sl greenmans: the country
U. 43: 'Of lost leaders' Browning: 'The Lost Leader' (poem)
Green Man Rise–O: game in which Hero & Leander *I* dún: fort
child concealed under coats suddenly jumps up & chases others
Da ulv: wolf Roland's horn (cf. 073.33)
s Roll, Jordan, Roll Byron: 'Roll on, thou deep & dark blue ocean, roll'
Tilton's poem 'Toll! Roland, toll!'
'In those days' (formula before lesson) *L* Deus Gen 22:1: '. . . God did tempt Abraham & said unto him,
Abraham: & he said, behold here am I'
L adsum: here am I

s Finnegan's Wake: 'Thanam o'n dhoul, do you think I'm dead' (024.15)
L anima ad diabolum mene credidisti mortuum: soul to the devil did you believe me dead
Moore: *s* Silence Is in Our Festive Halls [The Green Woods of Truiga]

Moore: *s* There Are Sounds of Mirth in the Night Air Ringing [The Priest in His Boots]

Gr pantria: wedding Constantinople
patriarch
(getting up, not properly awake)

L/R (liver damaged by boozing) *ph* 'keep your breath to cool your porridge'

G nass: wet *s* Piff Paff (Meyerbeer: *Les Huguenots*) (breath)

C feng: wind Pembroke, S.E. D district
Finglas, N.W. D district
Kilmainham: S.W. D district doze
Baldoyle: N.E. D district ('is in his' is lit. trans. of *I* for 'is a')
Rathfarnham: district of D

It sdoppiare: to uncouple, open out

G Tiergarten: zoo Lyons' tea rooms nenuphar: water lily, lotus (der. from *Skt* nīl: blue

Ar ar̃iudz: lion *Ar* ariun: blood *Ar* Bôghos: Paul *Ar* paregam: friend

Sl gam: leg

Ar marmnasėr: carnal *Ar* marmin: flesh *Du* tot weerziens: 'au revoir'

s Mademoiselle from Armentières *Gr* marmara: marbles that

Du negen en twintig: 29 sigil: seal (i.e. on letter) *Du* brievenbus: letterbox

Du postzegel: postage stamp with mysterious powers Sihlpost: Zurich G.P.O.

G besiegt: defeated *Du* stil: silent Lilith: Adam's wife before Eve in Kabbalistic lore

Matt 6:28: 'the lilies of the field'

undefiled

Du fooi: tip, gratuity

Du foei!: fie!

Du kamermeisje: chambermaid *Du* in't zeepsop: in soap suds *Du* zijn: to be; his

Gr zôê: life *Du* laars: boot

Du we moesten ons haasten: we had to hurry

Du te: to

Byron: *Don Juan:* 'The Isles of Greece, The Isles of Greece, Where burning Sappho loved & sung'

Chapelizod Shem & Shaun *Du* we hebben: we have *Du* opzoeken: look up

Du door: through *Du* courant: newspaper *Du* want: for *Du* 't: it

deep sea

shaman: witch doctor Steyne: pillar in D erected by Vikings

shamiana: in India, a cloth canopy Broadstone Railway Terminus, D

Da by: town HCE King Billy: William III (equestrian statue, D); also name of last male Tasmanian aborigine, whose grave was robbed

be white-horsed: obtain job through influence *Du* kunt u niet: can't you

William III stayed at Finglas after ⚔ Boyne, 1690 anxious seat: (fig.) state of anxiety

can ye not give me to boot a pair of soft boiled eggs

G Saft: juice

3½ hours *L* ex profundis malorum: out of the depths of evil

Devotions of the Three Hours' Agony (in honour of Christ on the Cross)

prayed *G* Engel: angel

(abuser, cf. 071.05–6)

L nomen: name *Heb* nahash: snake

Heb nasha: cunning *Heb* gur: exile *Heb* hasha: silence

Hu rab: slave

I rab: hog

*U.*516: 'Serpents too are gluttons for woman's milk'

posteriors: descendants

'Blackfaced Connemara': a breed of sheep ECH

L pace: by leave of

Clonmel, town, Co. Tipperary means 'meadow of honey'; site of prison for Tipperary *G* gastfreundlich: hospitable Mountjoy Prison, D
HCE *Sl* crib: house, shop &c.
Castle of Ham on the Somme, upper-class prison
Sl crack: burgle

yegg: travelling burglar or safebreaker

St Augustine: 'Securus iudicat orbis terrarum' ('the verdict of the world is secure')–phrase influenced Newman (cf. *Apologia*) *L* sic *L* vindicare: lay claim to
L sicarius: assassin, ruffian
G sicher: secure *Du* taal: language

D motto: Obedientia civium urbis felicitas (Citizens' Obedience Is City's Happiness)

Du nu goed: all right

God again Pugh & Co.: D glassworkers

P/K *L* corpus: body cause & effect *Du* liever: rather

Howe: hill in D upon which Norse Thingmote was held howe: hill, tumulus

Tom, Dick & Harry

court order *Du* koorts: fever
G kurz: short

Du grondwet: constitution

Du voorschot: overdraft
Du maatschappij: company; society
Du een nieuw pak: new suit of clothes cards

L pro tem: for the time Magh Elta (Moyelta): plain in D region where Parthalonians died of plague & were buried (city supposed to lie beneath Lough Neagh)
Gr misos: hatred; nêsos: island (almost no islands in Lough Neagh)

Du wacht even: wait a minute!
Gr limnê: lake; phobos: fear (almost no lakes on Isle of Man)
ph kettle of fish Fianna: Finn's army
Finn in anger tore up handful of turf, thereby creating Lough Neagh & Isle of Man
ph Dear Dirty Dublin

Old Nol: nickname of Cromwell *r* Troutbeck
I linn: pool Ben Jonson's Old Knowell acted by Shakespeare
osiery: basketwork (osier: a willow species used in same)
Dial sally: willow
uncle angle Izaak Walton: *The Compleat Angler* *s* Phil the Fluter's Ball: 'Twiddle of the fiddle'

their Peter Browne was in theological dispute with Berkeley
s The Quilt (Oh Molly, I can't say you're honest): 'May the quilt lie light on your beautiful form' *L* lutensis: living in mud
R Bog: God
The O'Donoghue: chieftain supposedly living under Lake of Killarney
G erst ECH *G* treu *F* bleu *G* Donau: Danube don't know who
Du hunebed: megalithic grave Strauss: *The Blue Danube*
Du best: very well! Huns frequently threatened Roman Empire from far side of Danube

Gr pharos: lighthouse; plough

John Foster's Corn Law, 1784, imposed heavy duties on its importation into Ireland
Paris cemetery Père-la-Chaise, where Wilde is buried obsecrated
F peur: fear *F* chasse: hunting *L* occaecatus: made blind

petrify another such (masterpiece)
(supposed property of Lough Neagh water)
St Thomas à Becket & St Laurence O'Toole were contemporaries (005.03)

Osiris, known as First of the Westerners Ibsen: *The Master Builder* Cassivellaunus: British ruler defeated
G Bilder: pictures by Caesar
I Samhain: Allhallowtide: beginning of winter half year
I Bealtaine: May Day: beginning of summer half year

ahead 1132 *L* circiter: about, near to starboard

torpedo *Gr* auto dynamikon: self powerful

Viking boats carried row of shields along each side trip up
tholus: cupola the holes
Tholsel: D Corporation Guildhall
ph as different as chalk and cheese

Du oorlog: war Sygtrygg = Sitric
F horloge: clock six strokes
I an ríoghan bhocht: the poor queen (Ireland) ten to five
Da Rhine Vogt: the Watch on the Rhine *G* Pfeife: pipe
G Blätter: leaves
blather
step *s* Woodman, Spare That Tree

face to face heptarchy: strictly, state with 7 rulers, but
L fossa: ditch also used for a group of 7 separate states
turrets Towers of Tower of London: Beauchamp, Byward, Bell, Lion, White, Wardrobe & Bloody

Du instappen, alstublieft: get in, please

Du hoofd: head

Du afdeeling: department *Du* ledikant: bed *Du* te huur: for hire
Du ik houd wel van: I am pleased with
staple: class of medieval Eng. towns whose merchants had special rights *L* et a.u.c. (anno urbis conditae): in the year of building Rome
F pompes funèbres: funeral arrangements

Abraham purchased the cave of Machpelah for family tomb (Gen 23:9, 19)

false etymology

G gehellt: illuminated *Du* Heer: Lord *Du* overgeven: give up
Du geheel: entirely *G* übergeben: hand over *Sl* skidoo!: depart!
Du t'huis: at home all aboard ship

Du bier: beer brasses

Du hoedendoos: hatbox *Du* reukwater: scented water
G Hoden: testicle *G* Dose: box *Du* bekers: cups
Du braakmiddel: emetic *Du* eetlust: appetite
Du zoutzak: salt bag *MGr* soutzoukia: smoked sausages
Du rookworst: smoked sausage *Du* varkenspootjes: pigs' trotters
Du vleeschhouwer: meat-hewer = butcher
Du jawel: yes, indeed Javel water: a dilute bleach & disinfectant
javel: corn cut ready to become sheaf
Gladstone *Du* met deze trein: with this train

Du konditie: condition H . . . CE
Sl follow: attend funeral
Du wandeling (noun): walk, stroll

Du lente: spring

Du stofferig: dusty   wailing   *Gr* hypnos chilia aiônôn: sleep for thousands of ages
whiling
HCE   *Gr* lêthê: oblivion (river of)

G Donnerwetter!   *G* Hundert   *G* Kopf: head   *Gr* megapodos: large foot
G Donau: Danube   *G* Donar: Thor   VI.A.1: 'Greeks believe thunderbolts form mines'
F d'un grand âge: of a great age

G Zeit: time   summons serving   *G* Blitz: lightning
G blitzblau: black & blue
(worms entering coffin at hinges)

G geh: go   *G* hinnen: from hence
Gehenna: the Underworld
G Unterwelt: underworld   Sheol in the Bible usually means the grave, sometimes Hell
Heb šeol im šeol: sheol by sheol
Sl upper crust: the human head; the aristocracy   *Gr* sidêreia: iron mines
Uppercross Barony includes part of Chapelizod   *L* siderea: starry   Siberia
L progeniem: offspring

Du in binnenland en buitenland: at home & abroad

Du spoorweg: railway, track

⚔ Heights of Abraham, 1759
Ides of April 035.03
G Vater Unser: Our Father
'Attila' means 'little father'
Attila became king of Huns after murdering his brother Breda
In Ir. myth the 3 murderers of Cian had to bury him 7 times because the earth kept casting him back
monad: ultimately simple unit of being (studied by Bruno & others)   *Du* vigilantes: cars
G Monat: month   minutes
Du spuitwijn: sparkling wine   *Du* aardappel: potato
apple fritters
putrefaction   Dreyfus affair (Fr. anti-Semitism)   *s* Tramp, Tramp, Tramp, the Boys Are Marching
Du hoedenwinkel: hatshop   blotting

G Patrizier: patrician   scarce
Du patrijzen: partridges
Du groenten: vegetables   *Du* druiven: grapes   muscat: type of grape

Celtiberians: ancient people of N.-central Spain

I Uladh: Ulster   Blue Men: name given to Moors captured & taken to Ireland by Vikings in C9   palefaces
L vetera: old
more or less

L dives: rich   *I* mór: great

defensive   always

Bellona: Roman war-goddess
black bottom: U.S. dance popular 1926–8
It ohibò: fie!

be damned to it

enough
Lough Neagh

cirque: arena
Sir
Low Church Whiggery bugger

Macbeth II.2.62: 'incarnadine' incarnate
Swift called Thomas Tickell 'Whiggissimus'
Billy-in-the-Bowl: legless strangler in old D

G Erwacker: awakener

semidetached (house) J.C. Mangan: *The Time of the Barmecides*
(Barmecides were C8 Persian noble family)
Barmecide's Feast: not eating (story of illusory food in *Arabian Nights*)
(between soup & savory course)
(done to a turn)
VI.B.18.121: 'taerts (young salmon)'
Macbeth IV.1.80: 'For none of woman born Shall harm Macbeth' Great Crested Grebe (eats roach)

Ps 90:10: 'The days of our years are threescore years & ten'

Leixlip ('Salmon Leap') socage: freehold tenure of land
fish-ladders enable salmon &c. to ascend dams & falls

Irish Times, newspaper

earliest Danu: mother-goddess of Tuatha Dé Danann
(Danish Kings of D) *pr* a friend in need is a friend indeed
(Legend that Cain got idea of burial from seeing an earwig by Abel's body)

Moore: *s* When in Death I Shall Calmly Recline [The Bard's Legacy] [air unknown]

Venus, wife of Vulcan *L* tentatrix: temptress

wide world chockfull *Forficula:* a genus of earwigs

I inghean: young woman *Hamlet* III.1.76: 'bare bodkin'
Arch hem: them look at!

F Sl tapette: tongue

s I Know Where I'm Going ('. . . the dear knows who I'll marry')

nr Rich Man, Poor Man, Beggarman, Thief
ABCD

F tirer: draw, delineate; pull
Lane Pictures: a collection claimed by both
Katherine Strong: C17 D scavenger & tax collector, a widow, D & London galleries; subject of great controversy
much disliked **K** tip: rubbish heap vidual: widowed, of a widow
(050.06)

Dublin knew HC . . . E Elvan: Cornish name for quartz-porphyry dykes

G stinkend: stinking *Sl* moggies: cats
Sl biddy: chicken Moggy's Alley, D
vegetables *Sl* beggars' bullets: stones

(stones thrown, 072.27) *Salmonella:* bacteria causing food-poisoning
Salmo fario: species of trout

Earwicker
pr The weakest goes to the wall

Hamlet (name derived from Danish prince Olaf) *G* Gulden (coin) Dane
s The Vicar of Bray: 'In good King Charles's golden days'
Sir James Carroll, Lord-Mayor of D, on Katherine Strong: 'she cleans but sparingly & very seldom'
bosom

Neapolitan
Gr nekropolis: cemetery
I bóthar: road Giant's Causeway
(anglic. 'batter') Jacob Bryant, C18 mythologist, identified Noah's Ark with the Moon
Angl sorra a foot knows: no one knows
wood-sorrel (sometimes mistaken for shamrock)

Serpentine: lake in Hyde Park, London Phoenix Park
L fornix: arch, vault; brothel
find, keep *G* Tau: dew *G* taub: deaf St Patrick's Purgatory: cave on an island in
baptised *G* taufen Lough Derg Pride's Purge (355.13)
J.S. Le Fanu: *The House by the Churchyard.* In it Mr Dangerfield (Charles Archer) stuns Dr Sturk in Butcher's Wood
& Mr Nutter, Lord Castlemallard's agent, fights a duel with Lt Fireworker O'Flaherty, also in Phoenix Park
nr A Was an Archer

Nutter left boot marks at scene of murder in *The House by the Churchyard*; p. 224 has drawing of one
representing tracing made of it by characters
and so on

world *L* castra: military camp

I leabhar: book Thor
(Ir. monks hid books from Vikings) *Da* brand: fire
lost

s Home Sweet Home *G* übergeben: deliver

(384.15)
(digging for letter)
Du sprak: spoke Krishna: Hindu De Propaganda Fide: papal HQ for all
Du Heer: Lord god of fire & storm missionary work

mortal man *F* pomme de terre:
Gr morphê: shape potato (*Sl* Murphy)
terrine: Fr. dish of meat, poultry &c. *L* terra
cooked together under earthenware *Skt* māyā: illusion
Agni: Hindu fire-god Mithra: Persian god of light Siva: Hindu god of destruction
oriflamme Araf: Limbo, region between Paradise & Gehenna
alluvial (*r* Lethe) Noah (flood)
Gr nauarchos: admiral
G gehorsam: obedient *Du* timmerman: carpenter
in ancient Ireland, ritual lighting of fire on 31 October on Hill of Ward, Co. Meath (Prometheus)
flamen: Roman priest
(King of the Wood in *The Golden Bough*)
nr 'This is the rat, That ate the malt, Posidonius: a Stoic
That lay in the house that Jack built' Poseidon
L lave: wash stone/tree

rear of the minster

Heytesbury St, D
ph bury the hatchet
pinafores Sheridan: *School for Scandal*

Chapelizod–Lucan (tram fares)
Aix-la-Chapelle

vicinal way: local common way
Julius Caesar: 'Veni, vedi, vici' ('I came, I saw, I conquered')
HCE LA . . . P
G platschen: to splash
Flaminian Way, Rome, lined with tombs
L flumineus: of a river
paved the way

Gr gigas: giant
L (artificial): multipopulipater: many peoples' father
I céad míle fáilte: 100,000 welcomes

F trame: thread (of life)
G Strecke: track, lines Hermes leads souls to Greek realm of death
L per omnia
saecula saeculorum: for ever & ever
L rhaeda: travelling carriage
Angl Ben Edar: Howth *I* seo mórbhothar Uí Chonaill: this is O'Connell Street

swallow way up yonder fiacre: hackney coach *G* halte: stop
(cockleshells in hats of pilgrims to St James's shrine; cf. 041.02) St Fiacre, C7 Ir. saint
hard by: close by house Halt! Who goes there? (sentrybox) howe: hill, tumulus
Howe: site of Thingmote (D Viking assembly)
Buchan cold spots: certain dates with colder weather
rupestric: pertaining to rocks
Henry Luttrell: D colonel whose grave was violated (skull broken with pickax) during 1798 rebellion Brenner Pass, Alps
Killiney Hill once called Malpas High Hill, bears Malpas obelisk verst: Russian land measure, appx 2/3 mile
Mal Pas: stretch of mud in Béroul's *Tristan*
Malpas Place, D *G* Traum: dream *I* Beinn Éadair: Howth
(there was a tramline over the top of Howth)
Livland: Baltic province Oscar Wilde

Peter Kropotkin: Russian revolutionary (height)

off colour I Peter 5:8: 'your adversary the devil'

Oglethorpe, C18 philanthropist, founded state of Georgia
Genghis Old Parr: Eng. centenarian accused of incontinence
Sl gink: fellow
s Johnny I Hardly Knew Ye: 'Ye eyeless, noseless, chickenless egg'

C . . . H . . . E hemispheres

bloody bugger's

Paternosters Λ ⩘ ⊏ chaplet (prayers) Hail Mary ⊣ ⊢
Knockpatrick (= Patrick's hill) *I* Muire: Mary (BVM only)
s Rien n'est sacré pour un sapeur (popular, 1930s) *s* La femme à barbe (popular, 1930s)
F homme-nourice: male nurse
ghost

G Holst: holly
catching hold of

C wei: awe *C* tau: way, path *F* razzia (fr. *Arab*): a military raid
Napoleon & Wellington *C* ling: honourable Jean de Reszke: a tenor

Buckley & the Russian General

(080.17)

action & reaction

'all in' wrestling

Purple Top, Tipperary Swede: types of turnip
Ruhr district, Germany
John Toller (d. 1819) was 8 feet tall   *G* toller: madder
Da taler: speaker   taller (062.28)
Billy-in-the-Bowl: legless strangler in old D   minor

worm: condenser of whiskey still

Sl stiff: money; corpse

AngI poteen: illicit whiskey
s Johnny I Hardly Knew Ye
(festivals at solstices)   refreshment

vernacular   ugly   6 Victoria 15: Act of 1843 against African
vermicular: wormlike   slave trade
Offa in *Widsith* defeated Saxons singlehanded
VI.B.14.157: 'strongfella–master'   De Valera 'the Long Fellow'
four

L collidabantur: they were brought into collision   tries to convert (rugby)

Woden = Wotan   Webley: make of pistol

L in illo tempore: at that time (beginning of gospel readings)

In crypt of Christ Church Cathedral, D, are skeletons of cat, & rat it chased behind organ pipes; both were trapped & died
Moore: *s* Believe Me, If All Those Endearing Young Charms
float

(German word order)

chance
strange

territorial   loose
It tenitore: holder, keeper

addling: pay accumulated on a voyage
weeks

G Juni   *G* Juli (070.03)

Billy-in-the-Bowl: legless beggar in old D; strangled bypassers
F boule: ball
hesitency

HC . . . E

change

G Judenfest: Jewish holiday

Mad Hatter & March Hare in *Alice in Wonderland*

G Bach: brook John Jameson & Son: Ir. whiskey
We bach: little

2 minutes silence observed on Armistice Day

J.J. whiskey

Macaulay: *Lays of Ancient Rome:* 'Lars Porsena of Clusium By the nine gods he swore'
Sheol: Hell (078.10) Sheofon: Jewish ramshorn
Zakkūm: in Islam theology, a thorny tree growing up from the bottomless pit *OE* heofon: heaven
'Grace' in *Dubliners:* 'lux upon lux' do sometime
a point of law *L* lex: law appointed Nietzschean
mark for it *ph* chip off the old block *G* nichtig: invalid, empty
Seaghán Ua Neachtain: author of an C 18 Ir. dictionary
Jespersen: *An International Language,* quoting Dr Sweet: 'the ideal way of constructing an *a posteriori* language would be to make the root words monosyllabic . . . & to make the grammar *a priori* in spirit'
Da nat (pron. 'not'): night sense of the word

AngI ph ignorant as a kish of brogues
Da sprog: language

to wit coct: boil, digest, bake Langue d'oil: Romance dialect of N. France

Red Bank oysters *G* Perlmutter: mother-of-pearl

Sl the boy: champagne
I ruadh: red Red Cow Inn, Tallaght, scene of fighting between rapparees & Crown forces, 1717

The Good Woman Inn, Ringsend, D Conway's Tavern, Blackrock

of all *ME* atte: at the

I fé'n riaghail: under the government Adam & Eve's Church, D, on site of tavern
Sir James Barrie: *Quality Street*
Grace: Prankquean (021.05–023.15) Tailte: queen of Firbolg, in whose honour Tailtean games were established (043.33)
South Downs, Sussex, not far from Sidlesham

lexicon
⚔ Lexington 1775
F blanche (488.30) Bonaparte

delight

'southdowner' (.24) *U.S.* & *Aust* sundowner: tramp who arrives at station about sundown, to obtain food & night's lodging; an evening drink
spat *G* Faust: fist tope: drink copiously
Ir. practice of spitting in hands before shaking them to conclude deal
take French leave: to go away, or do anything, without giving notice
letters
portfolio *pr* Marry in haste & repent at leisure
L pax (liturgical)

AngI pogue: kiss *Gr* pux: with closed fist (as in boxing)

s Lillibullero, Bullen a Law

2 gun truce
I tuargain: battering, bombardment 1531–47: Treaty of Schmalkalden
called Treaty of Cognac, 1526 face Menai Strait
fez: Turkish hat

Moscow
Arab Bismillah: in the name of Allah
Mecca
'Tubular' railway bridge over Menai Strait
R khorosho: very well
Cain's descendants Jubal & Tubal Cain
levant: to abscond
Jubal Early: Confederate commander at ⚔ 2nd Bull Run, 1862
L pons asinorum: the asses' bridge: a first difficulty
(broken in fight)
F en route
(suspension road bridge over Menai Strait)
danegeld: annual tax, orig. to fund protection of Eng. against Danes

lignum vitae: hard Am. or W. Indian wood used in medicine
reminiscent

tobacco pipe
Sl pluck a crow: settle an unpleasant affair

Rialto Bridge, D & Venice
⚔ Pea Ridge, 1862 (Am. Civil War)
It rialto: height, rise
⚔ Little Big Horn, 1876
(043.33)

⚔ Bull's Bluff, 1861 (Am. Civil War)

G Wunder

contusions
coccyx: tip of the spinal column

excellence
General O'Duffy led Blueshirts, Ir. Fascist movement
'This was the Noblest Roman of them all' (*Julius Caesar* V.5.68)
Macaulay: 'Lars Porsena of Clusium' (083.07–8)
L (artif.) sitisfactura: a making thirsty
gentlemen's agreement
Cornelius Agrippa: platonist & 'natural magician'
L deinde: thereafter
(opium)
fomentation: application of hot wet flannel to body

Jenner invented vaccination

Vicar St, D
Vico Road, Dalkey
Red Cross
nonfoetal

defence
pavilion: the pinna or flap of the outer ear

hatter's hares (083.01)

human body contains appx. 206 bones & 650 voluntary muscles

torso
worse
It in corso: in progress
It corpo: body

isinglass: very pure form of gelatine

G Wurm: worm, snake

Olympiad: 4-year period between Olympic Games
Steyne: pillar erected by Vikings in D
1132
Olaf, Danish prince, source of name *Hamlet*

(Napoleon)

It fiamme: flames
It parafoco: fireguard
G politisch: political

Dunawly (Olaf's fort) in Clondalkin, Co. D
Dunn, bass at Theatre Royal, D, called himself 'Dunelli'
Venetian Dial el don de dunele: the gift of women, a Don Juan

bottom cruisers *ph* lock, stock & barrel

I burral: bit, jot *Angl ph* by the black of your nail: only just
burial

other fellows
Vedda: an aboriginal people of Sri Lanka
K.O. (knock out)

Huguenot Peter the Painter, anarchist, involved in Siege of Sidney St, hence, type of gun

Pacific Ocean
chant in Norman Douglas, *London Street Games*: 'I - N spells in . . . Hit him on the belly bone'
Humphrey cemetery *G* Durchfahrt: passage
L semita: path
to wit *Sl* curb: thief's hook

nostrum: quack remedy oxter: armpit alpenstock

(Ulster) HCE

ALP Ibsen: *John Gabriel Borkman*
L acta legitima plebeia: daily record of lawful acts of common people
(lit. trans. of *G* Platz nehmen, take a seat) to wit *Da* bare: just

Butt Bridge, most easterly road-bridge over *r* Liffey in J's time Black Pool: lit. trans. of 'Dublin'
Blackpool Bridge: part of Roman road from Bristol to Lydney
Da naturligvis: of course
G natürlicherweise: naturally
wellbehaved

fasting

Atlantic Ocean Phoenix Park
Phoenicia

conundrum

Maamtrasna: scene of murders in 1882 for which Myles Joyce executed after unsound trial
Festus King: shop in Clifden, Co. Galway

G Mansch: mixture Mayo of the Saxons: C7 monastery in Mayo, resorted to by Eng. monks farfamed
Romansch language
Angl poteen: illicit whiskey

calends of March: 1 March, 1st day of Roman year incompetently

fetch: apparition; double of a person *pr* One man's meat is another man's poison
fish *F* poisson
cushats: ringdoves *F* fesses: buttocks fesse, field: heraldic terms
Sl to fly pigeons: steal coal faces amongst
'oyez!' opens court session (070.27)

Ambrosius Aurelianus, semimythical champion, led Romanised Britons against Hengest in C5

Kersse (311.05–09)

nightshirt (Parnell; 388.03)

trousers

We cymry: Welsh bespoke: tailor-made Mamertine: medieval Roman prison
meantime deposing: testifying

L exutio: an exclusion　　flowers of speech　　*L* fluor: flow　　Constabulary
fluorspar: native calcium fluoride
Peter, Jack & Martin: Catholic, Anglican & Lutheran Churches in Swift's *Tale of a Tub*
tripartite　Piezo-electricity generated in quartz crystals by pressure
copperas: cupric, ferrous or zinc sulphate　　quartz　　3-piece suit　　soot & sulphur, i.e. traces of gunpowder
quite
Adam & Eve　　*G* Feuer anstecken:
fluorspar, copperas, quartz & alum all crystalline　　light a fire
I feacht: turn, time
in fact
Coleraine, town, Co. Derry; distilling once principal industry
Police Constable　　alias
Sl crowbar brigade: Ir. constabulary　　*Sl* Robert: a policeman　　climbing boy: boy chimneysweep
Cathal Crovdearg deposed Roderick O'Connor, last High King of Ireland　　Malachy II succeeded Brian Boru as High King of Ireland
Arab melecky: king
pieces　　ALP　　smear　　*I* pluc: cheek
L pix: tar
I pusa: mouth　　Clontarf　　Clane, village, Co. Kildare
clean turf
Middlewhite: a class of pig　　Mudford: village, Somerset　　Thor
AngI Thoor: tower
I feiste: entertainment　　Peter & Paul
G feist: fat　　*Sl* peeler: policeman
Festy King & Crowbar　　St Anthony, patron of swineherds
Anthony: smallest pig of a litter
telephone

Eire
3 brothers, Heber, Heremon & Ir, led Milesian invasion of Ireland
AngI cry crack: give in

s Paddy Whack

amidst

maelstrom

The Ir. Agricultural Organisation Society founded by Sir Horace Plunkett　　*I* muc: pig
pastoral　　*F* ouragan: hurricane
(competition from Denmark as obstacle to Ir. bacon industry)

pig totem animal of Jews
Christians　　*Gr* to spiti: the house
Scattery Island, Co. Clare
scattery: dispersed, scarce
Ballybrickan: suburb of Waterford once inhabited by pig-brokers

Sl the fancy: prizefighting　　*Du* doorweg: way through　　*Sl* pikey: tramp
Sl mains: cockfights　　(damage to door, 067.09)
AngI gentleman who pays the rent: pig　　St Francis called all animals his brothers & sisters

It tròia: sow　　*It* qui sta Troia: here is Troy　　Hissarlik: Turkish city, supposed site of Troy
It questa tròia!: what a whore!

(082.12–13)

^
Oliver St John Gogarty, ear, eye, nose & throat specialist

W.C.: water closet; Wesleyan Chapel
W.P.: 'warming pan' (meant a *locum tenens*, esp. among the clergy)
MacDonald's *Diary of the Parnell Commission* abbreviates 'Parnell witness' P.W.　　OO (toilet sign)
Merrion Square, D
Sl square: latrine

solemnly

Moore: *s* One Bumper at Parting [Moll Roe in the Morning]

solicitor

Norse Ir. pubs once open on Sundays only to bona-fide travellers
morse: walrus *It* mustacci: moustache *Sl* bona: girl
'Please to remember The 5th of November Gunpowder, treason & plot' (Guy Fawkes Day chant)
hat in a ring (challenge) jubilees *F* giboulées d'avril: April showers
June
s 'days of Auld Lang Syne' (Jupiter, husband of Juno)

descend ephemerides: diaries (now means astronomical almanacs)

today, yesterday & tomorrow *Temora:* Gaelic 'epic' by James Macpherson. 'Temora' is his spelling of 'Tara', seat of Ir. High Kings
Tournay, city, Belgium
particularly

Shem, Ham & Japhet Tennyson: *Charge of the Light Brigade:* 'Theirs not to reason why'

life Hyacinthus: youth loved by Zeus & Apollo; killed by Zeus
John Macdonald, B.A.: *Diary of the Parnell Commission* W.P. (086.34)

L si vis pacem para bellum: if you want peace prepare for war (040.28) Fair Green: area S.W. of wall of medieval D
L civis: citizen Celtic *I* Gaedhealtacht: Irish-speaking areas
Bully's Acre: oldest D cemetery bellicosity
Ballycassidy, town, Co. Fermanagh
G Friedhof: cemetery
G Friede: peace *G* hoffen: to hope

crying changeling: fairy child substituted for human one Lucan
⚔ Wallop Fields (Vortigern v. Saxons)

Mise of Lewes: the agreement between Henry III & his barons (1264)

bears & bulls: speculators for falls & rises, respectively, on Stock Exchange
Bull Island, D
(tonsure question, 043.12–13) Gripes Mookse (152.15)

Ondt Gracehoper (414.20) Nuvoletta (157.08)
Sl nippy: a Lyons' tea-shop girl
mishe mishe (003.09) Mutt & Jeff
deaf
Roderick O'Connor died at Cong Abbey Aran Islands Annual coronation of King of Dalkey Island: burlesque ceremony
s Land of Hope & Glory Tory Island, Co. Donegal, originally elected king Puck, male goat, annually crowned at Killorglin Fair
Kings of Mud Island, gang of desperadoes in Ballybough ca. 1650–1850

Strongbow: leader of Anglo-Normans who invaded Ireland Carthaginian women in 146 B.C. siege cut off their hair to make bowstrings
Carthaginian carrotty
Isod's Tower, Essex St, D, demolished 1675

thickets

Bohernabreena, townland in Glenasmole, once wrongly thought site of Da Dearga's hostel *AngI* 'that bangs Banagher' (reaction to something unusual)
mixer (.13)
s O'Donnell abú (O'Donnell to victory!) *I* tungc mór: big push

'. . . Dead Man's Dark Scenery or Coat) is one of these jacket-games, where one party has to hide, covered up in their coats'—Norman Douglas: *London Street Games*
exanimation: loss of life, swooning case-hardened: hardened on the surface
L testis: witness
night of nights tripartite

speaking

Waterhouse's Clock, D
Central European
HCE *L* virens: being green appletree all
G Abfall: garbage; apostacy

(087.13)

G Baselbut: region around Basel

Gautier: 'Je suis un homme pour qui le monde visible existe' (086.32-3)
H. Travers Smith: *Psychic Messages from Oscar Wilde:* 'I was always one of those for whom the visible world existed'
conative: desiringly, willingly
cogitabund: meditative

Gr morphoô: form *Gr* sophos: wise
Morpheus *Gr* melos: music *Gr* pan krates: all-powerful

G Lüge: lie *F* truie: sow
Sl lug: ear
morbus pediculosus: ancient disease in which body swarmed with lice belie
Hu szerda: Wednesday

Othello III.3.191-2: 'O, beware, my lord, of jealousy; It is the green ey'd monster'
Sunday Saturday Wednesday
poll: pass, in ordinary B.A.
crossgrained: perverse
mighty *Du* oog: eye ears Inquiline: commensal
(086.32-3) *It* 'naso inquilino' for 'naso aquilino', common blunder of uneducated people
G Nase: nose treacherous beat you out

tankardful *G* Aas: carrion *Hu* balra: on the left
Hu jobbra: on the right
Hu tányér: plate *Hu* asztal: table *Hu* igen: yes a Guinness redenominated
Sp majar: to be tiresome *Hu* magyar bor: Hungarian wine
Acrostic: HERE COMES EVERYBODY Egbert: king of W. Saxons
Burke's *Peerage* lists 'Lyulph Ydwallo Odin Nestor Egbert Lyonel Toedmag Hugh Erchenwyne Saxon Esa Cromwell Orma Nevill Dysart Plantagenet (*Bentley*', b. 1876, under 'Tollemache-Tollemache'
Vercingetorix: Gallic chieftain, revolted against Caesar
Ethelwulf: king of W. Saxons
Yggdrasil: the World-Tree in Norse myth
holly & ivy

devil & the deep sea
daffodils
were praising *I* de bholóig: from an ox *ON* Ragnarøkr: destruction of the Norse gods
eau de Cologne Matt 27:51: '& the rocks rent'
uncles Moore: *s* Fairest! Put on awhile [Cummilium]
The Three Wicked Uncoverings : a Welsh Arthurian triad
art thou *J* yube: night *s* Cummilium Ostman: Viking, hence Oxmanstown

Thing: Viking council *Da* hvad: eh? what? refreshed *F* fresque: fresco

s 'There is a green island In lone Gougane Barra'
s 'There is a happy land'
Lord Edward Fitzgerald, Ir. rebel
Lord Edward St, D
Sir Philip Crampton: D surgeon (his monument had drinking fountains attached)

The Five Lamps: 5-way junction, D; Portland Row adjoins *Fi* portteri: porter *Da* virkelig: real
Virgin
Black Pool: trans. of 'Dublin'
living his lifetime
Tem: creator in *Egyptian Book of the Dead*

bet anytime

In Islam, evil jinn or devils supposed to be eavesdroppers in heaven; 2 angels, a driver & a witness, talk with God

ph like as two peas in a pod *Gr* dromios: twins
N drøm: dream
Esau sold his birthright for pottage of lentils

L coram populo: in public

Machiavelli: *Il Principe*
It ma che vuole! : what do you expect!
Roscommon *G* Kamerad: comrade Galwegians: old inhabitants
Russian Rooskay, village, Co. Roscommon of Galloway, Scotland
bishop

smoked burst into flames
J's uncle supposedly resembled Marquess of Lorne
Ajaccio, capital of Corsica *s* Cruiskeen Lawn ('full jug')
Ajax *It Dial* cossa: what?
s Father O'Flynn: 'sláinte & sláinte & sláinte again' *L* in cursu: in progress
It corso: course *It* ricorso: recurring (Vico) Grace O'Malley
⚔ Yellow Ford, 1598

Esau Moore: *s* O Doubt Me Not [Yellow Wat & the Fox]
easily

pedigree pig (086.14) Jacob
be Jaysus! *AngI* gentleman who pays the rent: pig
(door-eating, 086.26) *ph* useful as damn it!

Sterne: *Sentimental Journey* II.175: 'God recognised
tempers the wind, said Maria, to the shorn lamb' Ir. letters t, c & d are eclipsed by d, g & n
Ir. riddle: 'Londonderry, Cork & Kerry, Spell me that without an R'. Answer: 'THAT'
I gort: letter G; tilled field heliotrope (223.28) hardly a drop
Londonderry (Ulster), Cork (Munster), Skerries (Leinster), Gort (Connacht)
L magistra: mistress
martinet: rigid disciplinarian
HEC

velocipede: early form of bicycle or tricycle kitcat: a ¾ length portrait

Mandarin Ezra Pound translated Chinese poetry further orders *F* ourdir: to hatch (a plot)
'Tuscan tongue in a Roman mouth': definition of good Italian Our Father

L quare hircum: why the goat? *L* unde gentium festines: where are you hurrying from? (023.19–20)
Albert & Victoria Nyanza: lakes nr source of Nile Noah
edge *I* siar: westwards, backwards
'We are dancing on a volcano' (Comte de Salvandy, speaking to King of Naples at a party, 1830, before July revolution) indeed
Pali
pulu: yellowish vegetable wool
R.A.S. Macalister: *The Secret Languages of Ireland* lists types of Ogham ciphers:
Shirt-of-two-strokes Ogham Mac Ogham Finn's-ladder Ogham (3 forms)
Finn's-three-shanked Ogham Head-in-a-bush Ogham Head-under-a-bush Ogham

Ogma Sun-face supposedly invented Ogham Serpent-through-the-heather Ogham
Millrace Ogham
Arm, Bird & Colour Oghams ABCDEF *Sh* glonsk: man

Macalister notes that Bog-Latin may replace a letter by its name 'as if a Greek meaning Jason called him "Jotalphason"' epexegesis
G Ture: door *ph* sure as there's a tail on a cat
(*Laudabiliter*, 090.03) italic
glory be to God really truly Hankow: centre of revolution prior to Chinese Republic
C. Pi joss: god handkerchief

Sun-Yat-Sen, father of a Chinese revolt, 1st president of the Republic (tones significant in Chinese)
kow-tow: Chinese custom of touching ground with forehead as mark of respect
Da bukser: trousers
L sol: sun
Boxer Rising, China, 1900
Defiance: black colt raced in '20s
Pope Adrian IV's Bull *Laudabiliter* granted Ireland to Henry II being
labouring writer
Heb tob: good
laud: praise
which displeased
Tom, Dick & Harry
Sir Charles Dilke: subject of a Victorian divorce scandal (parallel with Parnell)
venue
King's Head: name of several old D pubs

L pugnax: fond of fighting
L evinxi: I wound round
Antepost bets are placed before day when horse runs
Flag falls at start of horse race
F effroi: terror
beck: stream
Du regens: rains
Father Time's backside
Regent's Park, London
Du plantsoen: park
Da skide: rotten
G Morgen: morning
N morken: rotten, decayed

Walpurgis Night

Katty Gollagher: hill near Bray
Mick/Nick
St Michael's sword
I gealach: moon
G Schreck: fright
welkin
(devil's fork)

tunny fish's swimbladder
Gen 1:3: 'Let there be light'
Du vocht: moisture
In Norse Eddas the Ginnunga-gap is the interval between aeons
Disraeli, repudiating Darwinism: 'I am on the side of the angels'

Midgaard: the Earth in Old Norse literature
garth: piece of enclosed land

(prostitution)
s Slattery's Mounted Foot

Da ja: yes
L gemellus: twin
Gamal & Camel: doorkeepers at Tara during reign of King Nuad
F parfait

D.A. Chart mentions the Hole in the Wall in Phoenix Park; voter to be bribed put hand in & was given guineas
The Hole in the Wall: pub at Cabra Gate of Phoenix Park, also called 'Nancy Hand's'

s The Man That Broke the Bank at Monte Carlo
Multyfarnham, town, Co. Westmeath, where 1641 rebellion concerted
Sl pox (clap in .28): venereal disease

Thomar: Danish invader defeated by Malachy
ruddiest
Roebuck: district of D

Japanese

ABC
omega alpha (094.21–2)
G Auge: eye (086.32–3)
G Ohr: ear
Gr rhino: nose
G Kehle: throat
(3 items)

Persse O'Reilly
F oreilles: ears
really & truly
R blyad': whore
Mecklenburg St, D (Nighttown)
bloody awful
L scortum: whore
Gr pornê: whore
Li kekše: whore

Sh stripu: whore
It puttana: whore
I striopach: whore
BL Oinciu: Ireland
F merde!
'shite & onions!' (expression of J's father)
I méirdreach: whore
I an: the
I óinseach: harlot, giddy woman

Punic: treacherous, deceitful
Penal Laws enacted against Catholic Church in Ir., C17–18

⊏ *Sl* pegger: a hard drinker stucco

I muc: pig (stuck pig)

cloudburst Brythonic: of Celtic languages, employing initial Ps, e.g. Welsh

Eng. spelt as *I*: 'with best wishes for a very merry Christmas'

I peist: beast *I* mhuise: indeed, well

Dean Kinane: *St Patrick* 197–8n: 'the pigs have eaten our son . . . Patrick commanded the boy's bones to be collected' (& resuscitated him) *I* as fearra: best

I buachaill: boy 'Ireland is the old sow that eats her farrow' (*Portrait* V)

storybook Cleopatra Clio: muse of history

Benches in Four Courts, D: KING'S

Dundalk: town, Co. Louth (*I* Dún Dealgan)

I tighearna: lord

turkies

(086.32–3) ('Pegger', .01)

Mark & Arthur

s Killaloe: 'You may talk of Boneyparty
You may talk about Ecarte
Or any other party
& *"comment vous portez vous!"*'

Mark Antony

Baal & Astarte: paired sun & moon deities worshipped in ancient Near East

Labour

sockdologer: decisive blow or argument

nor'easter: waterproof coat

'Sunlight' soap Sir Jonathan Trelawney: in opposing king's papistry became popular figure in Cornwall

COMMON PLEAS Lord Jesus

please God! *We* llwydd: president

Jury's Hotel, D *Annals of the Four Masters*

of the jury

years

ABCD

amrita: immortal, ambrosial *I* inis: island

continental Natal, town, S. Afr. Giordano Bruno burned at stake, 1600

F canton natal: native canton, district

Moore: *s* The Dawning of the Morn [The Market Stake]

s The Rising of the Moon *Da* skulde: should

Tír na nÓg: land of the Young; legendary island W. of Ireland Tyre, town, Lebanon

AngI usquebaugh: whiskey unknown

G Abgott: idol

Valhalla EXCHEQUER HECH

CHANCERY

baptised *s* The Holly & the Ivy

Castleknock Hill, Phoenix Park *AngI* kithogue: lefthanded person

his holiness the pope

lift (his hand) Goidelic: of Celtic languages, employing initial Cs, e.g. Irish

Arch faix: faith *WW I Sl* xaroshie: very good *WW I Sl* zdrast: be healthy (greeting)

Catholic Faith Jesus Christ!

Gr ecsthra: hatred
L ex cathedra: from the chair
It seguire: to follow *Sp* olla podrida: rotten pot (savoury stew) *G* Gelächter: laughter

metheglin: Welsh spiced mead testifier (∧)

Bruno's motto: In Tristitia Hilaris Hilaritate Tristis P.W. (MacDonald's abbr. for 'Parnell Witness') *L* cum: with
'Every power in nature & in spirit must W.P. *L* isce et ille: this & that
evolve an opposite as the sole means & condition
of its manifestation, & all opposition is a tendency to reunion. This is the *G* einsam: single
universal law of polarity or essential dualism, first promulgated . . . by Giordano Bruno' (Coleridge, *The Friend*)
L iste: that of yours *G* hin und her: hither & thither

Gr symphysis: growing together

synthesis/antithesis *Gr* duas: 2

∧ barmaids 30 - 2 = 28 ○ 28 day lunar month
peerless *F* trente: 30
Gr êranthos: spring flower Shaun the Post

Moore: *s* Sweet Inisfallen, Fare Thee Well [The Captivating Youth]

I fíon: wine *I* deur: tear blushes
Arch buss: kiss
I oiris: knowledge, science *Du* kleur: colour
s My Wild Irish Rose nice
'legato' opposite of 'pizzicato' (music) *It* pizzicare: to pinch
It legando: tying *It* pizzicagnolo: porkbutcher
s Handy Spandy *AngI* machree: my darling
chant in N. Douglas, *London Street Games*: 'Charlie likes whiskey . . . O sugar-de-candy'
s Pastheen Fionn (fair-haired child) Moore: *s* Believe Me, If All Those Endearing Young Charms
(postman)
Anglican morning prayer: 'Give peace in our time, O Lord' Hymen

defend
defame
It gemma: gem
chant in N. Douglas, *London Street Games*: 'Three little children sitting on the sand All, all a-lonely'
Macgillycuddy's Reeks, Co. Kerry WP

tactile (smell only, 095.19, 23)

chant in N. Douglas: *London Street Games*: 'I'll tell Ma when I get home'

I sí: she *I* sé: him

season

⊏

Pontius Pilate

L nolens volens: willing or unwilling
Bruno of Nola

Da tomme lommer: empty pockets

blind Patrick
black patch
Bridget
breeches
The Curia: Papal Court; cf. Papal Swiss bodyguard
L Quomodo vales hodie, Arator generose?: How fares your health today, noble gentleman?
Waterloo

Motto of House of Savoy: Fortitudo eius Rhodum tenuit (His Strength Has Held Rhodes)
vilesmelling acronym: FART *Li* raudonas: red
Latin latten: brasslike alloy, used for crosses Thomas Aquinas (said to have been very fat)

J.J.: *Gas from a Burner*
Sl gush: smell
30 - 2 = 28 ○

G Krieg: war Shem the Penman
'Jim the Penman': James Townsend Savard, forger
(092.18) parish priest impromptu
Paris
AngI make a hames of: make a mess of home Gratiasagam: nickname for St Patrick from his *Gratias agamus* reiteration in the Mass ('let us give thanks')
L donatrices: female donors inkbottle
G bis: right to, all the way
Venus' son Aeneas venison purveyor Jacob doves associated with Venus
Robinson Crusoe *ph* timid as a deer
Bottom in *A Midsummer Night's Dream* I.2.85: 'I will roar you as gently as any sucking dove'
(soccer, 174.25, 176.30–1)
I dún: fort chastity belt *L* conclamo: cry out together
F Sl chasser: to flirt
ph gift of the gab *Da* farver: colours *It* gridando: shouting

F honte: shame *I* naire: shame *L* pudor: shame *Da* skam: shame
It vergogna: shame *L* putor: foul smell *G* Scham: shame
The Four Ends of Life: artha (success), kāma (pleasure), dharma (duty) & moksha (enlightenment) *Skt* kavya: poet
plaintiffs
AngI plausy: flattery Written on letters by Ir. children: 'Deliver the letter, The sooner the better'
U.5: '*Thalatta! Thalatta!*' (in Xenophon's *Anabasis*, the cry of the Ten Thousand on sighting the sea) sweeten bitter
eyebrow pencil & lipstick

thunder

Mangan: 'O my dark Rosaleen, do not sigh, do not weep!'

Moore: *s* Lesbia Hath a Beaming Eye *s* Kevin Barry *s* The Arrow & the Song
F louche: squint (Matt 7:3–5) *s* 'There is a green island in lone Gougane Barra Where Allua of songs rushes forth like an arrow'
anagram (John is the anglicized form of Sean)
John Kells Ingram: *s* The Memory of the Dead: '. . . Who blushes at the name'
T.D. Sullivan: *s* God Save Ireland [Tramp, Tramp, Tramp]

Dufferin: *s* Lament of the Irish Emigrant ('I'm Sitting on the Stile, Mary') *s* Kathleen Mavourneen 'It may for years & it may be forever'
John Philpot Curran: *s* Acushla Machree

s Off to Philadelphia in the Morning (about Paddy Leary)
Ptolemy II Philadelphus founded library at Alexandria *Gr* philadelphos: brother lover
Charles Lever: Ir. novelist; wrote *Charles O'Malley*
Samuel Lover: Ir. novelist & songwriter
s The Bowld Sojer Boy *s* Finnegan's Wake

ph More power to your elbow! *I* samhail: ghost
lots

s The Wearing of the Green　　Gretna Green　　*Sl* joyboy: homosexual
greatness
s Widdicombe Fair (rhythm)　　*ph* Looks like Muldoon's picnic (means everything is untidy)
Moate, village, Co. Westmeath　　Muldoon: Irish-American wrestler, 'The Solid Man of sport'
W. J. Ashcroft, D music hall performer 'The Solid Man'
ph like a house on fire　　In 1717 or 1718 Swift, walking with others in the evening, stopped &
cracking jokes　　looked up at an elm: 'I shall be like that tree: I shall die at the top'
Lia Fáil: monolith at Tara that shrieked at coronations of rightful high kings

Urdu syce: groom　　(postman)

F trouver: to find (201.01)
retrieved

L perlectio: a reading through

I úna: famine　　*I* íde: thirst
St Itą's early Ir. religious poetry
Cornelius Agrippa, Platonist, 'natural magician'　　triple
tribulations
threne: dirge, lamentation　　49 of the Danaides, daughters of Aegyptus, killed
G fürchte Früchte: fear fruits　　their husbands; punished with thirst in Hades
Aeneid II.49: 'Timeo Danaos et dona ferentes' ('I fear the Greeks,
through they bring gifts')　*Gr nr* 'ena melo, melo mou' ('one apple, my apple')　*s* Tea for Two　　two is three
G Frau: wife　　*L* malum: bad; apple　　*Arch* amygdal: almond
'sycophant' derived from *Gr* syko, fig
G Obst: fruit　　Humpty Dumpty　　medlar fruit

Da fra sin fromme søn: from his pious son
G fromm: pious
a city arose

alpha

omega

s One More Drink for the Four of Us

Muniment Room in City Hall, D　　Marshalsea Prison, D
auspices
Yeats: *The Tables of the Law*

Solon: Athenian legislator
solan: gannet
tried　　for a drink　　evidence
sovereign lord, the king　　king's evil: scrofula
so help me God & kiss the book　　*F* bouc: goat　　Festy, Hyacinth & Gentia
gentian　　beetroot　　petticoat
Betsy Ross: Am. woman reputed to have made first Am. flag
s 'Glory be to God that there are no more of us For the four of us will drink it all alone'

pass the port　　be it so

Sinbad

monopoly

War of the Roses　　seamen's　　*G* Priester: priest

papal dispensation   pope   Minos
menace
York Minster (Cathedral)   *Sl* gush: smell   Ballybough, district of D (had vitriol works)
(Lancashire in .18)
G Bock: he-goat
Grace O'Malley
s Silent, O Moyle
AngI rossy: impudent girl   blush
s Sweet Rosie O'Grady
Prankquean (021.15)   *Sp* todo: everyone

Da ber om forladelse!: beg your pardon!

s Comin' through the Rye: 'Gin a body meet a body'

Gasometer, Sir John Rogerson's Quay, D   whooping cough (*U*.90)   Dion Boucicault (wrote *Arrah-na-Pogue, The Colleen Bawn* &c.)
Copenhagen
nr Cock Robin: 'All the birds of the air'   Minnie Cunningham: male impersonator in Dan Lowrey's Music Hall   *L* minxi: I have urinated
ph Dear Dirty Dublin   Burns: 'John Anderson, my jo, John'   *Sl* jo: sweetheart

HCE
H_2S (stink)

North Wall Quay, D   1132   lamelooking

sesame seed   White-Eyed Kaffir: G.H. Chirgwin, C19 music hall entertainer (*U*.335)   James Whiteside defended O'Connell
seaweed   semen's
St Patrick

Sl cabbage: cheap cigar

s Pastheen Fionn ('fair-haired child')   *G* Danke schön
I go barradh: excellently   Lancashire
Begorrah!   *AngI* when I was in my: when I was a

Da farfar: grandfather

Dan Lowrey's Musichall, Sycamore St, D

P/K   *G* Bett   P/K   P/K   P/K
pissabeds

Sl sip: kiss

AngI mountain dew: illicit whiskey

give a brewer's fart: befoul oneself

four-bottle man: one who can drink 4 bottles of port at a sitting   *Annals of the Four Masters*
I ungaim: I anoint
s Father O'Flynn: 'Sláinte & sláinte & sláinte again'   *G* Anschluss: connection
L umquam: ever   *L* nunquam: never   *I* longaim: I lap up

G fern: distant   found dead

pantings   cuckooings

G munkeln: to whisper   Poor Clares: an order of nuns

(386.12–14 &c.)   dying   reading & writing
pr A bird in the hand is worth two in the bush

some fellow's *Gr* rhino: nose rose
hunting
pr All roads lead to Rome contradicting

N Lille Trille laa paa en hylle (nursery rhyme eq. to Humpty Dumpty)
Niall of the Nine Hostages: Ir. High King, father of Leary (610.09)
corsages: bodices King Mark *N* bestefar: grandfather
marquis *AngI ph* at all, at all

Sir Amory Tristram: 1st Earl of Howth Le Fanu: *The House by the Churchyard*

Chapelizod

Da gammeldags: old-fashioned

Milltown Park, D: Jesuit house of studies
(Milton's park is paradise)
laugh *U.*78 'Language of flowers'
(003.09–10)

bad *I* a dearbhráthairín óg mo chroidhe: o young little brother of my heart
bold *F Sl* saucisse: whore saucy sisters
Moore: *s* The Meeting of the Waters Swift: 'Ppt'
F maman: mummy

Ulster, Munster, Leinster & Connacht (the 4 provinces of Ireland)
(4 statements: .×.)

s '. . . We'll tak a cup of kindness yet for the sake of Auld Lang Syne'

Ma orang: man

G schenk uns mehr: pour us more, give us more Christ sake Succat: St Patrick's baptismal name
I An Seanchas Mór: corpus of early Ir. law 'The Great Register' be it so
Sir James Craig: 1st prime minister of Ulster

(constellation)
Da forhøre: examine subspecies Vico says mankind's first words were onomatopoeic
sib: amity, clan, family
G stottern: stutter
Ibsen: *Samfundets Støtter* (*Pillars of Society*)
amongst mental specialists

St Augustine, 'Securus iudicat orbis terrarum' ('The verdict of the world is secure')–the phrase influenced Newman (cf. *Apologia*)
Gr hagios: saintly HCE *Gr* kurios: lord brush: fox's tail
to play possum: lie still feigning death
coparcenors: co-heirs of an undivided estate hairs tailzie: in Scottish Law, the limitation of a freehold estate to a person & his heirs
the pope's address: 'Urbi et Orbi' ('To the City & the World')

given law (hunting): of a hunted animal, given a start
quarry view (hunting): footprints of a buck or fallow deer
worry: seizing of fox by hounds in hunt holt: a wood
crossland: land belonging to Church in Irish palatinate Mullinahob: house near Ratoath, Co. Meath
Townlands in vicinity of Ratoath, Co. Meath: Peacockstown, Tankardstown, Raystown, Harlockstown, Cheeverstown, Loughlinstown, Nuttstown, Boolies (area hunted by Ward Union Staghounds)
Outlier: animal outside fold Nolan 'Fitz Urse' means 'son of bear' Reginald Fitz Urse: chief murderer of Thomas à Becket
Noel, Yule *G* Löwe: lion tail *G* Teil: share
beaters: persons rousing & driving game *Du* bruin: brown swart: black
Bruno

ph looping the loop ECH
F loup
Dublin

Rutland Square, D (sloping) thicker

hessians: boots with tassels at the top in front
G Coll Pfennigfuchser: miser *G* fuchs: fox
Ben Jonson: *Volpone (The Fox)*: Volpone takes to bed & pretends to be dying Elijah was fed by ravens
covert: woods & undergrowth that shelter game
ruminant's 4 stomachs: rumen, reticulum, omasum & abomasum

Abraham

Da Mikkelræv: Reynard the Fox Mick/Nick
syllabub: drink made of wine & cream whipped together

(fasting) *ph* get the bulge on: have the advantage of
030.06–7: tombstones of Glue & Gravy families at Sidlesham

G Vorort: suburb

attack

L pons: bridge enrage

L humus: earth mogul: autocrat

hesitency

nr Humpty Dumpty

Reynard: the fox in the *Roman de Renart*

liver *Sl* gush: smell pong
eruct: to belch out
O Lord

Fugger's Newsletter: collection of letters sent by agency to Count Edward Fugger in C16

triduum (R.C. church): 3 days of prayer before a feast
Roman Saturnalia (in December) lasted several days
G Zwilling: twin
wellingtons (boots)
Scotland Yard

F houx: holly *G* Efeu: ivy mistletoe (used to kill Balder)

The Hundred of Manhood (030.08) *G* wimmern: whimper *G* Weib: woman

Fama: personification of rumour

noise L/R L/R *Da* dreven: driven

lull *Sl* blem-blem: crazy

stone blind *Ali Baba & the 40 Thieves* (pantomime): 'Open Sesame'

H . . . CE Sidlesham (030.07)

G Anker: anchor

bottom/arse Arsa: an Arabian goddess

converts to Islam take new forename

Cornelius Magrath: Ir. giant befriended by Berkeley who claimed he owed his stature to tar water *Da* karakter: character

Turko the Terrible: Xmas pantomime at Gaiety Theatre, D

first house: in U.S. primary schools, key signature

piastre: Turkish coin *Du* buikdanseuse: belly dancer omnibus

street arab *Old T* bumbashaw: head of 1,000 men

T para: money

Peter's pence: contribution to R.C. church

Da til: to

I sagart: priest

Charing Cross, London

venereal HCE

L vulgo: publicly

James Joyce

C wang: king Moore: *s* As Vanquished Erin [Boyne Water]

*U.*208: 'birthaiding hands'

(fishermen's)

feet *G* frisch: fresh *Sl* mush: umbrella

L fas: possible, right fast

Arch eke-name: additional name, nickname *L* acnomina: surnames

G auch: eke, also *L* ecnumina: outside the power of the gods

Hansard: official report of proceedings of House of Commons *Arch* gar: make *G* ganz: all earwig

It città: city

Du Heer: master, lord pencil sharpener Cope St, D

Bull Alley, D

Romulus & Remus earwig e'er a one, ne'er a one

G Wiege: cradle *G* Waage: scale *G* still: quiet *G* immer: always

I immór: very big

L toties testes quoties questus: how often complaints, so often witnesses

(letters of *I* alphabet are names of trees)

HCE

s The Young May Moon ('. . . glow-worm's lamp is gleaming')
Hermetic Order of the Golden Dawn: ceremonial magicians of late C19
loquacious   taciturn

L ruina: a falling down

L esto perpetua: be perpetual (said of Venice & also by Grattan at establishment of Ir. parliament, 1782)
stout   *F* est tout pour: is all for (porter)
F piste cyclable: bicycle track   sludgy

Da puste: be out of breath   Morse code

G Standbild: statue

L corpulenta: corpulent   Jocasta: mother & wife of Oedipus
Gr gigas: giant   hat trick
L omnibus: for everyone   ABC
F homme
Da øre: ear   *Da* bror: brother   budget: in C15, leather pouch or wallet   fillibeg: kilt   tuft: cap tassel
tabard: loose sleeveless upper garment   Bruce Bairnsfather's famous WW I cartoon 'If you know a better 'ole, go to it'
Victoria Palace Hotel, Paris, where J lived 1923–4   Scaldbrother's Hole: subterranean cavern in Arbour Hill, D, where Scaldbrother, robber, kept his plunder
Dean Kinane: *St Patrick* 184–5: 'The same price was laid upon the head of a wolf or friar' (in penal times)   croppies
Da hvid: white
I fionn: fair   *Da* lykke: joy
N sverte: black   *G* lockt: beckons   *Du* Pinkster: Whitsuntide
G drohnen: to drone   Valkyrie

filiform: threadlike   purgatory bigotry   Pigott's forged Parnell letters
'Move over, Mick [Michael Collins], make room for Dick [Richard Mulcahy, his successor]: D graffito after Collins' death, 1922   Nicholas Proud: secretary of D Port & Docks Board in J's time
Gr grêgoros: quick

*name O'Reilly said to derive from Ir. words for 'a race' & 'learned or skilful'
O'Reilly motto: Fortitudine et prudentia (By Fortitude & Prudence)
*'Count Alexander O'Reilly, who was a Spanish general, Count Andrew O'Reilly, who was an Austrian fieldmarshal & thereby exemplified the name "gregarious" '   Myles the Slasher: Maelmora O'Reilly, chieftain
AngI meela-murder: 'a thousand murders', great commotion & destruction
Breffni: anc. area in (now) Cos Cavan & Leitrim. Tullymongan Hill: place of inauguration of O'Reilly chiefs
E. Breffni: territory of O'Reillys   W. Breffni: territory of O'Rourkes; Tiernan O'Rourke's wife's adultery led to Anglo-Norman invasion of Ireland
I O Ragheallaigh: O'Reilly
Rosicrucian   Reginald Fitz Urse, Becket's principal murderer, is said subsequently to have come to Ireland & founded MacMahon family
Verdun   *Her* rampant: rearing up
field of valour   *Sp* verdor: green
lying   *Her* dexter: right   *F* purée de pommes: applesauce   resurrected
shield of E. Breffni O'Reillys: dexter hand apaumée couped at the wrist proper, dropping blood, & 2 lions
Her proper: in natural colouring
Her apaumée: showing open palm
Milesius O'Reilly died at ⚔ Clontarf   John Boyle O'Reilly of Irish Republican Brotherhood; his unit produced treasonable ballads
Tiernan O'Rourke (.27)   *L* ferox: wild, warlike
for example   *L* amplus: large, glorious
stories by C.B. Kelland about 'Scattergood Baines' in 1930s in *Saturday Evening Post*   *Da* aften: evening

L quasi cum tribus sodaliciarius: as it were comrade with 3

**Weekly Irish Times* 21/1/1933: article on name O'Reilly

*U.*8: 'beastly dead' *transition:* magazine which published parts of FW during composition

Gr atalos: shaky *U.*5: '*Thalatta! Thalatta!*' (Xenophon's Ten Thousand on sighting sea)
Moore: *s* Shall the Harp Then Be Silent? [Macfarlane's Lamentation]
Lac Leman (Lake Geneva)

Bartholomew Deep, S. Pacific
Macfarlane means 'Son of Bartholomew'
G Achtung! *Cz* pozor: attention! *Da* vicekonge besøger smukke unge skolepiger: Viceroy visits beautiful young schoolgirls
I Trí Páistíní Éireannaigh: Three Little Irish Children *Da* med: with
Da eventyr: adventure *I* Lochlannach: Scandinavian
I Fathach i bPáirc an Fionn-uisce: Giant in Phoenix Park Ballyhooly, town, Co. Cork
Da haven: the garden *AngI* bannalanna: alewoman *AngI* ballyhooly: a tongue-lashing
AngI buddaree: rich vulgar farmer Father Murphy, Ir. rebel, was P.P. of Boulavogue
AngI bullavogue: rough fellow

Shield of Heath House O'Reillys includes oak tree with snake descending trunk

Liquidamber: genus of gum trees

Balsam Poplar *Populus trichocarpa* Parteen, Co. Clare, famous for salmon
PAL lax: salmon
Canadian Red Fir *Abies magnifica*; Noble Fir *Abies nobilis* *I* fir: men
noble sir
resipiscency: repentance for misconduct (papal infallibility) (Smoke signal announces election of new pope)
Hawthorne: *House of the Seven Gables* *L* Quintus Centimachus: Conn of the 100 Battles
Gr porphyroeidês: purplish porphyroid: a rock resembling porphyry (High King of Ireland)
Butter Towers of Rouen &c. paid for by sale of dispensations to eat on fast days 10.30
L en caecos harauspices: behold the blind soothsayers ECH ALP *L* annos longos patimur: we endure long years
lamps of maintenance lighted at TocH meetings to commemorate dead Disraeli was 1st Earl of Beaconsfield ziggurat: artificial hill
G innerhalb: inside (Babylonian archaeology)
Arch brevet: authoritative message, esp. a papal indulgence (075.01: lion's mane & paw)
wyvern: winged dragon with eagle's feet, used in heraldry
s Swing Low, Sweet Chariot

G litten: suffered Macaulay: *Marriage of Tirzah & Ahirad*: 'How long, O Lord, how long?'
(church windows with stained glass light up)
Finglas: district of D

'prisoner of the Vatican': the pope

Ivar Beinlaus & Olaf the White invaded D in 852 Einstein (born in Ulm; see .36)
(the pope, Matt 16:18)
L venter: belly

G Bauch: stomach Tristan
G Bauchredner: ventriloquist
G Weltraum: space

Du dode: dead *Da* sammen: together
Gr dodeka: 12 O

Du dijk: dyke

L aliquis: of some consequence
canonicity: canonicalness
C . . . HE tesseract: regular 4-dimensional polyhedron bounded by 8 cubes
(193.29)
L ulmus: elm

(097.28) (fast river)

(196.02) Gaea Tellus: Greek earth-goddess

ladylike

window

Notes & Queries (periodical) *Answers* (magazine) *ph* long & the short

Titbits (magazine) *AngI* liss: fort

I árd: high Ards of Down: baronies in Co. Down

ups & downs

(4 women) Swift met Stella at Moor Park, Surrey Jane Waring, whom Swift wooed as

Unity Moore: early C20 actress 'Varina'

L quarta quaedam: some fourth woman *s* Tommy, Make Room for Your Uncle

Sl quaedam: whore King Mark *Du* oom: uncle

Da piger, hold op med jeres leg: girls, cut out the nonsense

G volkreich: *Da* folkreig: populous

Lucan HCE

Chapelizod

L homo capite erectus: man erect as to the head George Peabody: Am. philanthropist

H . . . C . . . E

Cainozoic: pertaining to 'Who struck Buckley?': phrase used in C19 to

3rd great geological period annoy Irishmen

(puberty)

Boucicault: *The Colleen Bawn* (means the fair-haired girl)

Gr 'etoimologies: repartees *AngI* aroon: my dear *Sl* redflannel: tongue

Tolstoy: *War & Peace*

F flamme: flame, passion

ph sure as eggs is eggs

Po jaja: eggs Buckley & the Russian General (338–355)

blotting paper

Napoleon, 1793, dictating letter when a bullet covered it with earth: 'Good, we shall need no sand' (to blot)

R da: yes (the Cad)

full-paid a Paul Pry: a nosy person

3 castles on D coat of arms

AngI ph in the pay of the Castle (Eng. spy)

Peter (*Dublin Fragments*) says old stamps ('Queen's Heads') did not stick well

F affranchissant: liberating; paying postage on,

(a postage stamp could cover) stamping (letter) lounge-lizard: gigolo

ph a nine days' wonder *Po* praczka: laundress

G Pratschen: anecdote

(all Poland)

R plach: crying

G platsch! (exclamation)

Po pisma: writings *Po* żony: wives

Owen's: U.S. glass manufacturers Owlglass (Eulenspiegel): a jester, buffoon (upper reaches of river)

Bas izara: star twins

woman

The Mother of the Maccabees martyred with her 7 children ca. 168 B.C.

Da mormor: grandmother *I* maca mhic: sons of a son Matt 5:38: 'an eye for an eye, & a tooth for a tooth'

s Father O'Flynn ('Sláinte & sláinte & sláinte again')

breeding mothers said to lose a tooth for every child 111 (201.27–31)

G O je!: Oh dear! Caddy & Primas (014.12)

pr a hungry man, an angry man

thine sheltered

without Cain

Abel wives of Lamech (Gen 4:19): Adah (dawn) & Zillah (shadow); also wives of Cain & Abel in
(held azeleas to each nostril) arc *L* Noe: Noah Byron's *Cain*
G rasten: rest *Gr* archê: beginning

Gr ôkeaneios: of the ocean

HCE ALP

Da perlemor: mother-of-pearl *Bas* burni: iron
Bas ur: water *Bas* uri: rain *Bas* gori: red
L gorgonia: coral *Bas* gogor: deaf

funicular railway: cable railway

F Sl Louis: a whore *F* cul: arse bustle (578.22)
Sl quean: whore colander
s 'Lillibullero bullen a law' curlicue: fantastic curl or twist
(40 bonnets 020.28)
spectacles *nr* 'Rings on her fingers & bells on her toes' *F* yeux: eyes
G Speck: bacon *G* Eier: eggs *F* oreilles: ears
crucifix *F* nez: nose

Bas Egueri: Xmas
Bas egun: day
Septuagesima *It* sola: alone *AngI* pooka: hobgoblin
steeplechase pawns, bishops, rooks (chess)
pelota, Basque game piecebag: bag of HCE *Bas* Eskuara: Basque
pieces of cloth for quilts &c. *Bas* handi: big
Basque *G* Slange: serpent
Gen 3:14–15: '& the Lord God said unto the serpent . . . I will put enmity between thee & the woman . . . it shall bruise thy head' *I* mórán mó: much more *F* Notre Dame de la Ville:
very Our Lady of the Town
G Barmherzigkeit: charity *Po* ogrodnik: gardener
O'Growney helped form Gaelic League: brought
Po herbata: tea *G* Drogist: druggist back to Ireland for burial
G Wort: word *Po* drogi: dear *Po* bulki: loaves of bread

curse supposed to be put on those who opened Tut-ankh-amen's tomb

s There's a Mother Always Waiting

s Her Golden Hair Was Hanging Down Her Back
G holden: lovely
(rainbow colours) red poppies *Hu* narancs: orange
It gialla: yellow
Gr chlôris: greenness *Cz* Marinka: name for a skivvy; Parma violet (flower) *s* As I Was Going to St Ives
marine blue nickname for Mary Aniline, source of many dyes, orig. obtained from indigo
humours *Scots* ilk: each
amours *Da* hvilken: whatever *Sl* whilk: a silly girl
cg Ring-a-ring o'roses: 'One for me, & one for you, & one for little Moses'
(003.09–10)

Gen 3:19: 'In the sweat of thy face shalt thou eat bread'

AngI goo: a useless person, a fool *Du* groot: great gudgeon: person easily duped
C.O.D.: cash on delivery

Island bridge: district of D, where *r* Liffey becomes tidal

Ebba Atterbom translated *Portrait* into Swedish (1921)

s At Trinity Church I met My Doom:
'She told me her age was five-&-twenty,
Cash in the bank of course she'd plenty,
I like a lamb believed it all,
I was an M—U—G— (Drum)
At Trinity Church I met my doom, (Orchestra)
Now we live in a top back room, (Orchestra)
Up to my eyes in debt for "renty",
That's what she done for me' (Drum)

ears hues & cries

Nabucodonosor = Nebuchadnezzar

II Kings 5:14: Naaman cured of leprosy in Jordan

r Na'aman

stone/tree bids

Ps 137:1–2: 'By the rivers of Babylon, there we sat down, yea, we wept, when we remembered Zion. We hanged our harps upon the willows in the midst thereof'

Suras of the Koran begin: 'In the name of Allah, the Merciful, the Compassionate'
T anā: mother *T* mazi: olden times Livia
Plurabelle *Lord's Prayer:* 'Hallowed be Thy name, Thy kingdom come, Thy will
be done, on Earth as it is in Heaven' Hallow Eve (Halloween)
unhymned *Da* hemme: to check, hamper
manifesto

Hamlet I.5.189: 'The time is out of joint'

Aengus: Ir. love-god Sebastos: Greek name for Augustus, whose wife was Livia
L angustissimus: closest *L* Augusta: highness Rockabill Lighthouse off Co. D
nr Rockabye Baby, in the Tree Top *D Sl* relic of old decency: souvenir of better times

Gr anastasis: resurrection Anastasia: supposed Russian duchess Michael Gunn, manager of Gaiety Theatre, D
It stessa: herself kneel down (knighthood ceremony) dead & gone
I arís: again gun/cannon *Da* selver: silver
nr 'Will you walk into my parlour? said the spider to the fly'
F amour *Du* stam: bole of tree Peter Sawyer founded Dublin, Georgia *It* strame: litter
Sir Amory Tristram, 1st Earl of Howth Isolde *F* seul *Da* til: to *Du* Ik: I
Du dik: fat, bulky *Et Tu Healy:* J's poem on Parnell's death *L* mihi: to me birthright (Esau)
Du ik doop: I baptise *Richard III* V.4.7: 'my kingdom for a horse'
(.10–13, compare 003.04–15) *L* hesternus: yesterday tomorrow woebegone Browning: *Pippa Passes:* 'God's
Swift: 2 Esthers (Stella & Vanessa) marry in His heaven, All's right with the world'
water on the brain *nr* 'Rings on her fingers & bells on her toes'
letter, 26/7/27, to HSW: 'Chinese (Chinks) . . . no record of a Deluge' free drinks
G Flur: floor, meadow Swift: *The Drapier Letters* *F* arc-en-ciel: rainbow
Vallancey: *Collectanea de Rebus Hibernicis* 'Groans of the Britons': plea to Rome, A.D. 426
nr 'Peter Piper picked a peck of pickled pepper' *It* popolino: the lower classes
Huguenots' poplin industry in old D
Da hus: house

G Hosenband: trouserbelt

Moore: *s* Ne'er Ask the Hour, What Is It to Us? [My Husband's a Journey to Portugal Gone]
G Huhn: chicken *Da* hans baad: his boat
W.S. Gilbert: Ought We to Visit Her? A . . . Z

Cleopatra's Needle, London featuring Abraham & Sarah
Aldborough House, D
G Kamm: comb pyramids
s The Campbells are Coming
Papa Westray, one of Orkney Islands
L placeat vestrae: may it please your
letter from Ezra Pound, 15/11/26, about FW III: 'nothing short of divine vision or a new cure for the clapp can
possibly be worth . . .' potatoes gander
Massinger: *A New Way to Pay Old Debts* *s* The Gipsy's Warning: 'Gentle maiden, trust him not'
s Over There: 'Oh, potatoes they grow small . . . Oh, I wish I was a geese'

Merchant of Venice *s* Anacreon in Heaven: 'When the myrtle of Venus joins with Bacchus' vine'
s Wife, Children & Friends: 'Pledge me high'
Stewardship of the Chiltern Hundreds is conferred on member of Parliament wishing to resign his seat Ormond Quay, D *L* oremus: let us pray
G Mund: mouth *F* queue: tail
Grania Finn MacCool
Hundred of Manhood (030.08)
Eighty ten (*F* quatrevingt dix) = 90; 20 + 90 + 1 = 111 one seat
L ceterum: the rest
John Maddison Morton: *Box & Cox* (play about John Box & James Cox)
Boxer Rising of 1900: last Chinese peasant rising
House of the Golden Stairs: brothel in Shanghai *s* Little Annie Rooney: 'She's my Annie, I'm her Joe'

Zemzem: well at Mecca

After his father's death, Confucius and his mother moved to Zigzag Hill (Chufu) Confucius born in dry cave called 'The Hollow Mulberry Tree'
Du taal: language *G* taub: deaf logarithm to base L
Swift: *Tale of a Tub* *G* Taube: pigeon analogy *Sl* dant: prostitute
Napper Tandy, United Irishman, 1740–1803 *Po* napiwek: tip tipped the wink *Po* motyl: butterfly *Po* przy: near
naughty little dancing girls Danzig *Po* przeszyć: to pierce
PS orel: eagle Persse O'Reilly interior monologue
s 'The Wren, the Wren, The king of all birds' *Po* olbrzym: giant *G* Minne: (courtly) love
Moore: *s* Drink to Her Who Long [Heigh Ho! My Jackey]
L extorreor: be parched monolith
Moore: *s* If Thou'lt Be Mine, the Treasures of Air [The Winnowing Sheet]

HCE Victoria Nyanza & Albert Nyanza: the 2 western reservoirs of the Nile *I* ní h-annsa: not hard (formula for answering riddles) Noah
G Ahn: ancestor
s 'Daisy, Daisy, give me your answer do' handsel: first specimen of something
R da: yes St Barbara: patron of armourers & gunners
rag, tag & bobtail *L* usque ad mortem: even unto death (Matt 26:38)
s 'Jumbo said to Alice: "I love you"' (refers to a famous elephant shipped from London Zoo to America in C19) anisette: liqueur
'Exsultet': 'O felix culpa!' *ph* Dear Dirty Dublin *s* My Old Dutch
F cul: arse
Walter Pater: *The Renaissance:* 'She is older than the rocks on which she sits' (Da Vinci's Mona Lisa) *AngI* whist!: silence!
s '& they call me the jewel of Asia'
Ayessha: heroine of Rider Haggard's *She*
s 'Lots of fun at Finnegan's Wake' How Buckley shot the Russian General
LAP
Rush, town, Co. Dublin J.L. Motley: *Rise of the Dutch Republic*
Macbeth II.3.125: 'Look to the lady'
Shirley's play 'Look to the Lady' played in theatre in Werburgh St, D Bastille *Book of the Two Ways*: Egyptian papyrus
G Postille: book of family sermons
Egyptian Book of the Dead XXIII: Chapter of Opening the Mouth
Egyptian Book of the Dead CXXV: '. . . I know the names of the two-&-forty gods . . . I have not turned back the water at the time when it should flow' *It* attraente: attractive Tartar

Tory Island: Fomorian stronghold off Donegal coast Galatia Abbey & Gate Theatres, D
Gr gala: milk
Crow St Theatre, D (C18) rift in the lute: small defect marring general result Mookse & Gripes (152.15)
in the nude lude: ashamed Smock Alley Theatre, D (C18)
Ondt & Gracehoper (414.20) *L* ludus: game *F* tirer un coup: fire a shot ('tirer' means 'to pull')
Sl aunt: prostitute horoscope
Osiris dead to the world (drunk) *s* In the Glen of Aherlow
Horus was conceived magically by Isis after death of Osiris
Waterlow, painter faith *Da* suk: sigh aspirations 3
Waterloo expirations

St Colmcille Gage St, Hong Kong, brothel area *Sl* crany: clerk
L columba: pigeon
trio of bottlewashers

D Sl totties: girls who
duet
copyright
cowboy
U.S.A. *F* sou: small coin

Du thee: tea   wild horses   *nr* 'All the King's horses & all the King's men'
Moore: *s* Of All the Fair Months That Round the Sun [Song of O'Donohue's Mistress]

O'Donohue's white horses: waves on a windy day
s 'You're the cream in my coffee . . . I'd be lost without you'
backside
Da Norsker: a Norwegian

Da torsk: cod   *r* Poddle, D   Persse O'Reilly

Burke's *Peerage*   Samuel Lover: *s* The Angel's Whisper ('A baby was sleeping, its mother was weeping')
a ton of bricks   ⚔ Tannenburg, 1410
Sl pit: cunt

Tommy Moore's Melodies   too many more
AngI ph top of the morning! (greeting)
Polynesian   valentine   *G* Brautschauer: man looking for bride
breeches
219.18–19: 'The Mime of Mick, Nick & the Maggies' (FW II.1)
League of Nations
pictorial   periodical

Stationers' Hall, D   Ziegfeld Follies (1920s & 30s)   *F* homme   *F* faux pas
G Sieg: victory   *F* faut pas: must not
Genesis, passim   (prison sentence)
(end & beginning of FW)
thick   Moore: *s* As Slow Our Ship

thunderbolt

Captain John Smith's life saved by Red Indian princess Pocahontas. Subject of Brougham's *La Belle Sauvage*
F honteuse: shameful   wait
s McGilligan's Daughter Mary Ann   J. Fenimore Cooper: *The Last of the Mohicans*
R velikan: giant   William III & Mary   *R* dochka: little daughter   *Thom's Directory:* 'County of D' section
says people living N. of Howth 'popularly known as Fingallians'
Stock Exchange   beautiful
Custom House, D (head of Liffey carved on keystone)   China Mission
three cheers   *L* mictio: urination
Dickens: *Pickwick Papers*   *nr* Humpty Dumpty ('had a great fall')

F Sl lice: prostitutes

Souvenir of the 25th Anniversary of the Gaiety Theatre 28: 'Amongst the most successful engagements . . . the Vokes family'   The Spread Eagle (in The Coombe, D): corsetry shop
corsets   *Sl* Maggie: whore   magistrates   *Sl* strap: fuck   ALP
Sl cursitor: pettifogging attorney   bench   Alyosha Popovich: hero of Kiev epic cycle
G Popo: buttocks   *G* fett: fat   HCE   *ph* See Naples & then die
catch   Hawkeye: hero of J. Fenimore Cooper stories
Du als het U belieft: if it pleases you, I beg you   Earl of Essex on death of Earl of Stafford: 'Stone dead hath no fellow'

exit   *r* Delvin   re-enter   *r* Liffey

nr This is the house that Jack built: 'that ate the malt'

Abraham, Sarah, Isaac

Sir Isaac Newton (apple)   taught him common sense   Esperanto established common-sex substantives
Brahma: Vedic creator, persuaded Buddha to teach the law
Arthur Guinness, Sons & Co., Ltd

s As I Was Going to St Ives: '7 wives'   Dukas: *Ariane & Barbe-bleu* (opera; story by Perrault)
barber   *G* Blut
ALP   HCE   heads   *L* umbella: umbrella
eats
canes   good better best   *Da* hoved: head
brace, triple: bellringing terms   Lord of Howth (021.05–023.15)
Grace O'Malley   Dame St, D

manifestations   College Green, D   University College, Stephen's Green (originally)

ECH   back, centre-half (football)   tree/stone

Messrs Earwicker Ltd
L.S.D.: pounds, shillings & pence

Chapelizod
fool Lucan

unmentionables: underwear Redcoats

proteiform: varying in form *L* graphicus: writing
L scriptus: writing
naif: naïve (described it as)

(copy) delinquent recidivist: one who habitually relapses into crime
deliquescent: liquifying by absorption of atmospheric moisture

HCE

entomologist entomophilous: of plants, insect-pollinated *Gr* nympheus: wedding
sexual mosaic or chimaera: organism with some male parts, some female
ECH Orion, hunter
nymph: immature nonmetamorphosing insect
leaf
lief: beloved
God's truth

s Johnny, I Hardly Knew Ye (' . . . & guns & drums') (earwig's forceps)
Some moths emit sexual attractant odours at night *Sl* forceps: hands
quest Stella (Swift) *Vanessa*, a genus of butterflies
L persequor: to pursue flower to flower
Ar kidout'iun: science *Ar* madènakrout'iun: literature
Mother Nation
Ar lour: news *Ar* heṙou: far *Ar* kišer: night
lour: gloominess of the sky
Ar hazar: 1,000 (& 1: *Arabian Nights*)

Ar zereg: day *Ar* pou: owl giaour: term of reproach applied by Turks to non-Mussulmans, esp. Christians
Ar gouyr: blind
Ar aysôr: today *Ar* amousin: husband

F bordereau: inventory

chiaroscuro: disposition of darker & brighter masses in a picture

L semper: always simple as ABC Hebrew letters: Aleph means 'ox', Beth means 'house', Gimel means 'camel'

Ar Lousadour: Light-giver Hell *Ar* khaghal: to play *R* durnoi: bad
Ar baron: Mr

party-wall: wall between 2 buildings or pieces of land, in the use of which each occupier has a partial right

rainbow

Gilbert & Sullivan: *s* A Right Down Regular Royal Queen (*The Gondoliers*)

(two-paned: spectacled)

ph racy of the soil: characteristic of Ir.

Gilbert & Sullivan: *Patience*

Master Kung: name of Confucius

rules of propriety (in ancient China)

Carp Primus: son of Confucius

Confucius's grandson wrote *The Doctrine of the Mean*

God's truth

sinking fund: one formed by periodically setting aside revenue, usually to pay a debt

Edward & Robert Bruce went to Ireland in 1315

Robert Bruce learned to be patient after watching spider climb wall

ECH

Elberfeld Calculating Horses tapped answers to sums

Ar kinedoun: tavern

Sl tubthumper: parson

Ar kini: wine

Ar k'ahana: priest

Ar djardar: clever

gardener

Chinese Han dynasty & their chief enemies, the Huns

Ar misen: the meat

Ar manoug: child

darn all

I méar: finger

meatmonger

Ar taṙnal: to return

F maison manager

Ar barbaṙ: language

Ar karedchour: beer

carriage horse

'Barbarians' supposedly der. from *Gr*, expressing 'stammering' sound of foreign languages: 'ba-ba'

Barbour's account of Bruces' expedition

ascendant: ancestor

I fionn: fair

HCE

Gr epi: upon

Ancient Chinese wrote on silk with mixture of brick dust and water

samite: rich silk fabric worn in Middle Ages

Kohl: black colouring agent

(ink from nutgall)

Shem, Ham & Japhet

Tophet: place of burning dead bodies, S.E. of Jerusalem

'where in Sam Hill': C19 U.S. expression meaning 'where in the world'

Ar glor: round

Wyndham Lewis called *U.* 'an Aladdin's Cave of incredible bric-a-brac'

L sol: sun

Ar k'aghak': city

Aust slip us the dinkum oil: tell us what it all means

cage

sagacity

It cagare: to shit

L odia: hatreds

CEH

pr Look before you leap

J rarely uses quotation marks

Du kant: side *Du* kwestie: question, affair

Sl josser: chap

ratiocination: process of reasoning

Feng-Yang: birthplace of Hung Wu, the founder of the Ming dynasty

Finnegan Lao-tze told Confucius 'He who is only the son of another has nothing for himself'

Kung family, descendants of Confucius

nr Where Are You Going, My Pretty Maid ('My face is my fortune, sir, she said')

A Chinese historian pointed out that Confucius was superior to other men, who are imperfect in 1 or 2 features, because he was imperfect in all

'my ancestral stair' (Yeats: *Blood & the Moon*)

Yen Ying, Tsi minister, deriding Confucius: 'It would take generations to exhaust all that he knows about the ceremonies of such a simple thing as going up and down stairs' (naked)

Yeats: *A Vision*

etiquette vital in ancient Chinese society

blinkered

certainly

left

Mr Best in *U.* keeps saying: 'don't you know'

'For our purposes the simple fact that such a Naked World is possible, nay actually exists (under the Clothed One) will be sufficient' (Carlyle: *Sartor Resartus* X)

pr truth is stranger than fiction

Crow: *Master Kung: The Story of Confucius* 37, says for Chinese the sea was 'a symbol of oblivion. The fact that the brine-laden water . . . gave them this wonderful salt, which river water could not provide, probably added to the mystery' *s* Brian O'Linn

Bruin

dried bear's paw a delicacy in ancient China

familiar din-din: dinner

Meanings of Chinese names of China: 'Under Heaven', 'The Flowery Kingdom', 'The Middle Kingdom'

certainly *ph* Isle of Saints (Ir.)

Sir John Pentland Mahaffy: 'In Ireland the inevitable never happens, the unexpected always'

Arch mayhap: perhaps

is it a chapel?, has it a book in?

Chapelizod Lucan

Alb ultë: low *Alb* naltë: high *Alb* madh: big *Du* vaal: faded

L ultimum aut nullum: last or nothing vale of tears

Alb verdhe: yellow Phaethon drove the chariot of the Sun too near the Earth, scorching the surface

Alb paiton: car

Alb tambel: milk rain *Alb* trendafille: rose Ophelia

Crow: *Master Kung: The Story of Confucius* 39, says there were no teapots in ancient China

Aristotle: *De Poetica* 24: 'Accordingly, the poet should prefer probable impossibilities to improbable possibilities'

ph the Holy & Undivided Trinity (Mahaffy was Provost of Trinity Coll.,D)

Hamlet III.1.63: 'To be or not to be, that is the question' *Alb* me kene: if, seeing that

Quiztunes: U.S. radio programme *ph* hit the nail on the head

Alb Zoti: God *G* Zot: obscenity *Heb* zot: this, that *Du* zot: fool toenails

(remains shuffled in grave)

wool worn about his person Aristotle or the Bible

Aristophanes

unbiassed *It* boia: executioner

Alb boje: colour

G Hahn: cock, rooster

Gr to hen: the One (philosophy) *G* früher: earlier *Fi* kuura: hoarfrost

original sin

Alb prandverë: spring *Alb* Prill: April *Alb* kishë: church

It primavera: spring (bells chimed the hour)

s Love's Old Sweet Song bantlings: brats, bastards

Alb sahat: hour bantams

behaviourist psychology

Impey: *Origins of the Bushmen* 49 mentions a prehistoric 'chip instrument factory'. 45 mentions pottery with a 'conical bottom' *Du* kopje: small hill (in S. Africa)

busman's holiday: one spent following one's usual occupation *L* limen: threshold *F* limon: mud

L illico: there, on the spot *Du* strandlooper: beachwalker; bird

G Mist: garbage

Tara Brooch (in National Museum, D) found in 1850 by a child on the strand near Drogheda

freezing Acts 9:11: 'the Street that is called Straight'

F trouver

AngI street: backyard euchre: outwit opponent in game of Euchre

Ardagh Chalice, C8, in National Museum, D. It was found accidentally by a child *G* heilig: holy

Tipperary   *Da* puteter: potatoes   New Zealand   sight
Dial ree-raw: confused, topsy-turvy   Reerasta, Tipperary, where Ardagh chalice found
Boucicault: *s* I've a Terrible Lot to Do Today

F Goddam: Englishman (derisive, from 'Goddamn')   sticks & stones
'bigot' supposedly derived from 'by God'

Jacobites
Jacob's Biscuits (D)

Belinda: heroine of Pope's *Rape of the Lock*

L quinquaginta: 50   *T* terzi: tailor   *Alb* sërmë: silver   CHE   Chapelizod
It terzo: third
Da hane: cock   hen exhibition
Alb hane: inn
Da klokken tolv: 12 o'clock   *Alb* zog: bird   Zog I: King of Albania from 1928

Boston Transcript
Le Fanu: *The House by the Churchyard* 224: 'The sod just for so much as a good sized sheet of letter-paper might cover, was trod & broken'
31 January

heat turned the milk

Van Houten's Dutch Cocoa   General Elections
erections

Christine Beauchamp (280.22)

funeral   life's end (011.28)
fun for all

twins

F tache   tea   carelessness   *ME* cautel: crafty device; precaution
Gr kautos: boiling

Ibsen: *The Master Builder*
bilk: deceive
ph on the spur of the moment   Charlotte Brooke: *Reliques of Irish Poetry*

peasant poetry   ladylike   Lydia Languish, in Sheridan's *The Rivals*, wrote letters to herself

U. 186: 'Horseness is the whatness of allhorse' (parody of Aristotle)

milkwhite

son   turd
sod of turf
wipe   boucher: treasurer; (obs.) butcher

s Love Me Little, Love Me Long

Sl pecker: nose

pure & simple jumble of words

Swift called Wood (of Wood's halfpence) a son of a beech paltriest
Samuel Beckett *G* Buch(e): beech *G* Buchstabe: letter poultry
forest it 4 gospels
Matthew Arnold: *The Scholar Gipsy* *It* zingari: gypsies
Targum: each of several Aramaic translations *G* Schülerin
nr Peter Piper picked a & interpretations of parts of Old Testament shooler: vagrant
peck of pickled pepper kindlings: broods, litters *Da* hensyn: regard, consideration
s 'We'll tak a cup of kindness yet for the sake of Auld Lang Syne'
Newman: *s* Lead, Kindly Light

pr birds in their little nests agree

volucrine: of, or pertaining to, birds

genetic *Gr* gamos: marriage
Sl gammon: humbug, chatter

'auspice' der. from *L* 'avis specere' (cf. augury of birds, *Portrait* V)

ph with a vengeance (.10 fly)

egg (.10 moult) 'White man's burden' (Kipling)
age
(.11 hatch)

Sl lioness: prostitute

Isa 11:6: 'The wolf also shall dwell with the lamb, & the leopard shall lie down with the kid'
(.11 agreement in the nest)

Poe: *The Raven:* 'bleak December' *F* Janvier palmy days
Guinevere *Du* veer: feather

U.636: 'Marcella, the midget queen' majesty

Master of Arts *Gr* anomos: lawless
Arthur anomalous amorous anonymous
Stephen Hero mentions McCann's review, including a lady's verses, copy
'The Female Fellow': '(a swallowflight of song) . . . signed "Toga Girilis" ' *Alb* cope: piece
(*L* toga virilis: garment worn on reaching maturity) T.C.D. (Trinity College, D) tea (111.20)

s The Jolly Young Waterman Au Bon Marché: Paris department store
(temperance song) Notre Dame Cathedral, Paris
iron *Alb* ar: gold *Alb* lumë: river *Alb* me fol: to speak *Alb* falemi nderës: thank you
Heb ari: lion *Ma* ari: snake *Alb* ari: bear Aran Islands falls
Alb nadje: (in the) morning straw will show
Shaw
windbag *F* blague: humbug *F* rudess: rough *L* robur: oakwood, anything strong
robber calling
fantasies *F* frisette: bunch of curls
Shaw spells 'show' 'shew' *F* grisette: young workingclass woman

I graithe: business, duty
Lewis Carroll's portmanteau words great accoutrement
Baptiste Mantuanus: writer glossaries *F* lapin: rabbit from the Latin & the Greek
of school Latin eclogues Virgil came from Mantua grigs: short-legged hens
Nut: Egyptian sky-goddess, laid cosmic egg Grabar: Old Armenian
ph not on your life! good & grand
Armenian etymologists *Per* daryā: sea *Ar* zov: sea
Per muye: hair *Ar* mazerov: with hair
Ar meṙav: he is dead damn!
Merovingian
L sine: without anyone, anyone other
Ainu šine ainou: 1 man *Ainu* ainu utara: men
Ainu e-kik-an: you are beaten *Gr* anakar: upward *I* anacair: affliction, distress
no right to *Da* kik: peep anyone other *Ainu* šine, tu, re, ine, ašikne: 1, 2, 3, 4, 5
Da faar: sheep other hand asking
Du rand: edge
L tutus: secure forwarder six days' licence
'titties' (*U.*753)
can-can (dance)
F daim: fallow-deer, buck
F Mesdames, Madamoiselles, Messieurs, s'il vous plaît *F* cerf: deer
'marmouselle': term for young girl in Rabelais' *Pantagruel* (Sainéan) *L* silva: woodland
G Schwanz: tail *G* Schweiz 'ischt' is Swiss pron. of *G* 'ist' *Alb* kapak kapak: little by little
she wants, she writes, is to tell the God's truth about him *G* Trut: turkey
Alb minzë: pupil of eye fully
no mincing matters
black & the white
Alb plak: old *Alb* smût: sick
foibles

charlotte: apple marmalade *Alb* molle: apple *Alb* vogel: small specially
covered with breadcrumbs *G* Vogel: bird
F péché: sin Motto of the Garter: Honi soit qui mal y pense pants
(Shame Be [to Him] Who Evil Thinks of This) *F* camélia: prostitute
Ann
Dublin
Tristan Isolde Ancient Arabs believed mts kept the earth steady, as pegs do a tent
tree/stone ⋀ *We* ysol: consuming, devouring *L* mons: mountain
PAL Waterloo Bunyan: *Life & Death of Mr Badman*

C14 rivalry between Genoa & Venice led to defeat of former

please

G mein *G* ich bin *G* frisch *G* frech: insolent
F pardonnez-moi *G* bin so frei: permit me
It parlo turco: he talks double-Dutch
U.S. Sl talk turkey: talk business man to man
Mick/Nick nihilists

Bruno of Nola; Browne & Nolan
L nolens: unwilling

Vulg Ps 113:5–7: 'Oculos habent, et non videbunt. Aures habent et non audient. . . . Manes habent, et non palpabunt' ('Eyes have they, but they see not. They have ears, but they hear not. . . . They have hands, but they handle not')

Lord Avebury introduced Bank Holidays
mason (STONE) stone circles near Avebury
jolly *Da* Glælig Jul: Merry Christmas
s 'Christmas comes but once a year, & when it comes it brings good cheer'
Joyce anxious to please *Sl* bobbies: police terribly sorry
bourgeois joist (TREE) monopolize *U.*47: 'Aquinas tunbelly'

time to go home again *ph* see eye to eye

smell nose noesis: sum total of mental
tell processes of rational animal

Alb Nemc: Austrian, Hungarian Bucharest, cap. of Romania
Alb búkur: beautiful *Alb* rahat: quiet
Alb mal: mountain Belgrade, Bulgaria
Malaysia
nestling incunabula: books printed before 1500
L incunabula: cradle

Sir Edward Sullivan: Introduction to *The Book of Kells:* 'The black is lamp black, or possibly fish-bone black'

shillelagh: black-thorn stick

'the evolution of humanity from savagery to barbarism . . . Michael & his angels against the Dragon & his angels' (George Birdwood: *Sva*)

geodetic: pertaining to surveying *L* domesticus = *Gr* oikonomikos: pertaining to the house

(boustrophêdon; compare 018.33–4)

Anne Hathaway

Osiris, 'lord of the ladder' *I* Sem: Shem sematology: study of
cemetery meaning

Japhet Hamlet Hamlet
Ham Hum.Lit.: literae
west Humaniores (Oxford 'Greats')

pounce: powder used to prevent ink spreading, or to prepare parchment
(blotting paper) *Alb* vet: person *Alb* hângër: to eat
G Anhänger: adherent
Alb sot: today *Alb* ftofte: cold
Alb odë: room
Alb qiri: candle *Alb* karrigë: chair *I* duisín: dozen
sherry *Alb* darkë: supper, dinner
Alb ve, vœ: egg *Alb* gote: glass, tumbler *Alb* raki: brandy
Albania *Sl* any God's quantity: abundance *Alb* portogal: orange
Alb bukë: bread sofa *Alb* sofer: table

Alb motër: sister

Alb bir: son *Alb* nip: nephew *Sl* nippy: a Lyons' teashop girl
Alb bije: daughter *Alb* mbesë: niece
terrestrial (in mudmound) (111.20) timestained

It is considered unlucky for an actor to say the tag (last speech) at rehearsal
(teastain at end of letter)
ph be in a brown study: be withdrawn

trademark Portrait of the Artist

✠ Boyne, 1690: victory of William III (of Orange) (teastain may be author's mark)

lesser evil

arabesque: mural decoration with flowing intertwined lines

Lapsang Souchong: a type of China tea

'Clove' is derived from *F* 'clou' (nail)   Drinkers used to chew a clove to mask breath

Sl coffin-nail: cigarette

s The Lark in the Clear Air

Tiberias, Palestine, was chief centre of rabbinic scholarship

salacity: quality of being lecherous   *Gr* gerontophilos: lover of old men

U.S. Sl hardnosed: tough, practical

underlined passage

Arch mayhap: perhaps   erroneously   *ph* it's a case of spoons with them: they are sentimentally in love

It prostituta in erba: budding prostitute   VI.A.271: 'dinky pinks (drink)'

L herba: grass

1, 2, 3, & away!   perpetual curate: in Ir., an assistant R.C. clergyman

Grace O'Malley   chased

G und so weiter: & so forth   psycho-

Gr sykon: fig

-analysis   Jung

Alice in Wonderland

Freud

auricular confession   *Stephen Hero* XXI: [Cranly] 'to describe the hymeneal tract . . .

compression   called it *oracle* & all within the frontiers he called *oracular*'

L in camera: privately; in the room

variegated

virgated: made straight, rodlike

undemonstrable

ph settle one's hash   Mark Twain: *Innocents Abroad*   *ph* all aboard

neurasthenia: nervous debility

pineal body: endocrine gland in the brain; disease leads to hypersexuality

nympholept: one inspired by violent enthusiasm, esp. for an unattainable ideal

G Traum: dream   priapic: relating to cult of Priapus, Roman god of procreation; priapism: persistant erection of penis

trauma   drama

agnate: descendant from a common male ancestor   cognate: descended from a common maternal ancestor

lubricity: slipperiness, lasciviousness

meiosis: deliberate understatement; reduction division of nuclei, as in sex organs

feller

Song of Solomon
salmon
Esra, book of Bible Ezra Pound liked cats *Gr* mêtêr: mother
arse *Eng. upperclass nursery Sl* 'Who's *she*? The cat's mother'
Sl better half: spouse

F ph revenons à nos moutons: let's
return to our sheep (i.e. to the subject)

Shaw: *Shewing-Up of Blanco Posnet* Buckley *G* Schotten: Scots
shooting of Russian General Bolshevism
G Baum: tree 'Red Terror': Communist government repression in Hungary, 1919, followed by similar
(parody of 'Aesopian language' of early Bolshevism) anti-Communist 'White Terror'
(111.13–15)

Communist 'cells' *s* Thou Art Not Conquered Yet, Dear Land
Spartacus: leader of Roman slave revolt, a hero in Communist hagiography; name used by German revolutionaries, 1918 Ir. Volunteers *s* The Foggy Dew (one song of this name about Easter Rising)
s The Dying Soldier: 'Sweeter far for thee to die'
s We Shall Rise Again: 'In Dublin's fair city'
s 'Twas on a Glorious Easter Day: ''Ere one more year is o'er'
turned our coats

s We Shall Rise Again: 'From Swords to the sea' *s* My Old Howth Gun

s Bishop O'Dwyer & Maxwell: 'Then answer made the brave O'Dwyer' Horace: 'Est modus in rebus' ('A middle course in all things') (*Sat.* I.1.106)
Gr prostas: porch, vestibule

L fornix: arch, vault; brothel curate: in Ireland, a barman
Phoenix Park Magazine Wall
TLS review of *Dubliners,* 18/6/14: 'The reader's difficulty will be enhanced if he is ignorant of Dublin customs; if he does not know, for instance, that "a curate" is a man who brings strong waters'
pr There is many a slip between the cup & the lip

G Ausland: foreign country present of wedding cake

Sl Kate: prostitute (094.21)

milkman Mick/Nick sweethearts heat

(094.22) grasped

Basic English: simplified English with 850 words, intended as international secondary language

*U.*432: 'Metaphysics in Mecklenburg Street!'

road *Du* advokaat: barrister vowels *F* semi-voyelles: semivowels linguals
vocatives *F* voyou: guttersnipe *F* langue
labials dentals gutturals *G* Furz: fart
F dentelle: lace

(Pythagoreans tried to keep mathematical truths secret)
sesquipedalian word: a very long word epistemology *Gr* panepistêmion: university (universal knowledge)
epically Volapük: artificial language
R grom: thunder I Sam 4:21: '& she named the child I-chabod' (lit. 'where is the glory?')
Cromwell Habakkuk, book of Bible
hapax legomenon: a word of which only 1 use is recorded (lit. 'once said')

pr When all fruit fails welcome haws

horsecart

testis *AngI ph* tare & ages! (expletive)

Carl Bohm: *s* 'Still wie die Nacht, tief wie das Meer, soll deine Liebe sein' ('Still as the night, deep as the sea, should thy love be')
(compare 398.29)

Viconian cycle: birth (with thunder), marriage, burial, ricorso

fire & air & earth & water
G Feuer: fire *I* agus: & *It* aria: air *Da* jorden: the earth
Gen 6:2: 'the sons of God saw the daughters of men' before
(thunderclap: Viconian cycle) fair
s 'There was an old man called Michael Finnegan, Lot & his wife
He grew whiskers on his chin again
The wind came up & blew them in again
G grün: green Poor old Michael Finnegan. Begin again . . .'

Henri Estienne: 'Si jeunesse savoit! Si vieillesse pouvoit!' (*Les Primices,* esp. 191) ('If youth but knew! If age but could!') June . . . Yule (i.e. summer & winter) *s* Tell Me the Old, Old Story
Gr stolion: small garment Edgar Quinet & Jules Michelet helped to popularize Vico
F Dial quiqui: chicken (003.09)
Giambattista Vico Giordano Bruno (he was burned at the stake) in order that
F jambe *F* brule (stuttering) *L* ut: in order that
so as to Universal: an artificial language polyglot

Sp sordo: deaf *L* mutus: dumb (deaf-&-dumb language) *Sh* Sheltafocal: word of Shelta
Idiom Neutral: an artificial language (language of flowers)
F con *Sp Sl* cuba: the pros & cons *G* Strasse: street
concubine cunt prostitute street arab tutu: a ballet skirt
naughty *No, No, Nanette* (musical comedy of 1920s) Anne Boleyn & Henry VIII
It nozze: wedding palmy days
spitfire

F souffle: draught petti(coat)s table set for tea *Du* thee: tea
(003.10)
r Tolka, D till Tibbs his eve, i.e. forever (there is no St Tibbs; Tibb's Eve means 'never')

*Roland dies of thirst

kicked the bucket *ph* business is business

millennia

s Three Cheers for the Red, White & Blue

Peter Stuyvesant: governor of New Amsterdam (became N.Y.C.) Sankt Pauli: brothel quarter of
r Amstel (in Amsterdam) Peter & Paul Hamburg *F Sl* poule: prostitute
Rome spelt his end died off South America

*donner le moine (lit. 'give the friar'): trap by deceit Catholic
Sl kettle: cunt

L epistola: letter

(Viconian cycle)

F combler: heap up, fill up *G* fesch: stylish maid-of-all-work
Du versch: fresh
(compare 281.04–13) saucer
I cupán té: cup of tea
It caldo: hot Dutch oven: a cooking utensil told the tale of the town

Swift: *Tale of a Tub*
Du toon: toe
*capnomantia: divination by smoke (capnomancy) *ph* as right as two trivets
tea-leaves used for divination; tea is an infusion Fusionism: C19 Fr. mystical sect
Wee Free Kirk: minority group in Scottish Church
Ir. Free State (1920s)
prostitute

*Lazare Sainéan: *La Langue de Rabelais,* Paris, 1922

Irish Independent (newspaper)

holus-bolus: all at once

bickerings Butler family, Earls of Ormonde
F voltiger: perform on horseback
vault desultory: devious
*Rabelais' Gargantua learned to jump from horse to horse while riding; the horses were called 'chevaux désultoires'
Buffalo Bill

(Cock & Bull story–*L* taurus, bull; *L* gallus: cock)
L lanius: butcher

possibly *G* wer tiefer trinkt: he who drinks more

*bacbuc: Pantagruel's divine wine bottle *ph* in the back of his mind
back pocket
ph all my eye!: nonsense!

Heb soferim: writers *Heb* lebab: heart
suffering Tower of Babel Bible
hue & cry

(Belshazzar's feast, Dan 5) (show) *OE* Mod: mind, spirit *N* møte: meet

'noun' denotes a person, place or thing cosmos *G* Alle

F turquerie: harshness, cruelty
goddamned turkey

Aesop's fable of the hare & tortoise

*L'Hostel du Roy Pétaud (of the fraternity of beggars)

hyacinth

delightful *à l'aube des mouches: towards evening, or 3-4 hours after sunrise (lit. 'at flies' dawn')

ph take it or leave it *G* Luft: air

*Dieppe fishermen never mention priests or cats while in their boats
ph let the cat out of the bag
HCE corners
coigns

*Sainéan: *Langue de Rabelais* (continued)

*Swiss military rite of kissing ground & throwing earth over left shoulder before charging enemy
G Kuss: kiss *L* terra firma worse luck
omoplate: shoulder blade *pr* A drowning man will clutch at a straw

*filofol: term for 'philosophy' suggesting 'fine folie' (lit. 'fine madness')

Gr phôs: light *saige-fol (lit. 'wise-crazy'): epithet of character Triboullet
forsake
quarter

ph please the pigs: if
circumstances permit

Francis Jeffrey's review of Wordsworth's *Excursion* in the *Edinburgh Review*: 'this will never do'
G Frau fowl *écorcher le renard: vomit (lit. 'flay the fox')
*calamite: lodestone *L* calamus: reed-pen *L* incolumitas: safety *F* flair: sense of smell playful
beginning of Sir Edward Sullivan's introduction to *The Book of Kells:* 'Its weird & commanding beauty; its subdued & goldless colouring; the baffling intricacy of its fearless designs; the clean, unwavering sweep of rounded spiral; the creeping undulations of serpentine forms that writhe in artistic profusion through the mazes of its decorations; the strong & legible minuscule of its text; the quaintness of its striking portraiture; the unwearied reverence & patient labour that brought it into being; all of which combined go to make up the Book of Kells, have raised this ancient Irish volume to a position of abiding preeminence among the illuminated manuscripts of the world '

gloriole: scrap of glory, aureole, halo *F* plume

L ambi: on both sides
Tiberian vocalisation of Hebrew consonants (placing vowel points under them) introduced in Old Testament MSS from C10 *Gr* chrêsmon: oracle trilithon: megalithic structure: 2 uprights & a lintel
Sullivan: 'The XPI . . . was known as the Chrismon' (medieval note-mark)
hesitency
N hes: hoarse
fondly
counterclockwise
Theology state of nature: natural moral state as opposed to state of grace

Tennyson: *Locksley Hall*: 'Better fifty years of Europe than a cycle of Cathay'
Cathay: a name for China
C Hsiang-kang: Hong Kong
r Siang-Chang
C san-shih-erh: 32 (with Fr. transliteration 'erh' is 'eul')

9th from the 20th = 11th A.D. 432: St Patrick lands in Ireland (013.33)
Blavatsky, *Isis Unveiled*, discusses Hindu cycles of history, all based on 432 years

SIGLA: ᗰ ▲

×
pothook: a stroke in writing ⊏
□ T

⊣ has one side missing

(cemetery) Champ de Mars, Paris *G*: ,nicht?: ,isn't that so? interior monologue
L mors: death

114.10–11: 'lampblack and blackthorn'
kettle pot
Ir. P/Q split Sullivan: 'a string of Q's with which are intertwined a number of droll & impish figures in
(capitals) various grotesque positions, with legs tucked under their arms, and tongues protruding'
G Ohr: ear

***Sainéan:** *Langue de Rabelais* **(continued)**

P/K serpent with tail in mouth on *Tunc* page of *Book of Kells*

P/K P/K P/K P/K

(W)

(T)

ph 'knows not a B from a bull's foot'

dumb-show: in medieval theatre, mimed preamble summarising play's action

pronomial: acting as pronoun

Modern Greek 'mp' has sound value of 'b'

Hamlet III.3.399: 'very like a whale' (*U.*40) farced: stuffed pemmican: condensed food; fig. condensed thought & matter

Huysmans: *A Rebours* 265: 'Le roman . . . deviendrait une communion entre un écrivain magique et un idéal lecteur'

ph sink or swim ('The novel should be a communion between a magic writer & an ideal reader')

Sullivan mentions 'raddle' (red ochre) among pigments used in *Book of Kells*

Sullivan's introduction: 'Attention is drawn to these errors by four obeli in red' (obelus †)

peppercastor

(031.10)

*U.*279: 'Remember write Greek ees'

L supercilium: circumflex accent

ph owls to Athens = coals to Newcastle

(G)

occident: West kakography: bad spelling; bad handwriting

Ostrogoths: Gothic tribe often in conflict with Roman Empire

Etruscan language never deciphered tabletalk

Dean Kinane: *St Patrick*, 'Approbations' 12: 'the learning, the deeply religious spirit, betrayed in almost every page' life's end

1132 (horsepower)

ghimel: 3rd letter of Hebrew alphabet (means 'camel')

Matt 19:24: 'It is easier for a camel to go through the eye of a needle'

iota: Greek letter 'i' *L* sinistrogyro: I turn around to the left

(W)

Mediterranean

agglutinative, as distinct from inflexional & isolating languages

doubleyou *G* ganz kurz: quite short *G* Doppelvau: W

*U.*40: 'W is wonderful' (in *Proteus,* which begins: 'Ineluctable . . .')

(F) *ph* horns of a dilemma

Digamma: original 6th Greek letter; looks like *F*, sound value of 'w'

born a barbarian

L lapsus linguae: slip of the tongue hetaira: Greek courtesan; demimondaine

Emperor Claudius, linguist, name means 'lame'

insertion mark *F* frequent in FW MSS

stage foliage

Sullivan: 'The fret pattern, which is employed in a considerable number of forms as a filling for panels in both borders & initials. . . . Diaper work is occasionally introduced to brighten small spaces'

basket wreaths of bayleaves worn by Roman emperors

basque: the extension of a lady's bodice

fret ('fidget', 'dejectedly')

Sullivan's introduction to *Book of Kells:* 'Symbol known in Irish MSS as 'head under the wing' or 'turn under the path' . . . indicates that the words immediately following are to be read after the end of the next full line'

L ipsissima verba: very same words

Arbutus: genus of evergreens including Strawberry Tree. In Ireland its berries called 'cain-apples'. Abundant in Killarney

Cain Abel

J: *The Mirage of the Fisherman of Aran:* 'He . . . wears a big black hat with a wide brim'

When Irish is written in Roman characters, the dot placed above a letter to indicate aspiration is removed & an extra 'h' is added (H)

'j' & 'i' interchangeable in Latin

initial, medial, final or isolated positions of characters in Arabic words

principial: initial (Bacon) jimjams James Joyce

Eng. riddles about j being in jam jim: name of Arabic 'j'

'Jam Sahib': K.S. Ranjisinhji, cricketer

threadworm: rectal parasite

underwear Sullivan: 'The frequently recurring presence of serpentine forms all through the decorations of the manuscript has given rise to the suggestion that these forms are in some way connected with the worship of ophidian reptiles'

(St Patrick banished serpents)

frequent *G* Wetter: weather *nr* 'Ride a Cock Horse, to Banbury Cross, See a fair lady, upon a white horse'

Theology invincible ignorance: that shared by a whole race or class

lacertine: lizardlike

arts: writing, music, painting, sculpture, black arts

Podatus: in Gregorian chant, a figure indicating that a single syllable is to be sung as 2 notes, the lower first

uproarious

cannons *Sh* Sheltafocal: word of Shelta

canon, fugue

(last sentence of FW joins first) Matt 19:30: 'The last shall be first'

gravediggers (*Hamlet*) Shakespeare left Anne his second-best bed by inserting sentence in draft of will

Hamlet I.2.180–1: 'the funeral-baked meats Did coldly furnish forth the marriage tables'

G Butterbrot: piece of buttered bread

van Hoother, Howth (021.10)

Cod. = codex *Du* pap: porridge breakfast lunch dinner

Pap. = papyrus

supper ⚔ Boyne, 1690 scholiast: commentator on a writer

Sl deadman: baker foreshortened

ampersand: & (4 in letter 111.10–20) *Gr* glyphô: carve
Sl ampersands: the posteriors glimpse
Russias

L lapsus: fall; *F* lapsus: slip vocative & accusative cases
(e.g. of the tongue); *G* der Fall: the case
aphasia: loss of faculty of speech

Ares: Greek god of war
(R)
L ars bellica: art of war Tom Kettle: D friend of J; killed in WW I
kettledrum

God's bones! (oath) Red Hand of Ulster
(red, rubric, ruby, blood, rouge, ruddy, Rufus)
truth with beauty *L* oremus pro Romulo: let us pray for Romulus

Angl within an aim's ace: very near

Rubaiyat (= 'quatrains') *of Omar Khayyam* (metre, imagery duplicated)
are

Roe's Distillery, James's St, D
Fire at Marrowbone Lane Distillery, D, ca. 1860: whiskey ran down gutters in Cork Street
Mallarmé: *Un Coup de dés* Whang the Miller in Goldsmith's *Citizen of the World*

6 loyal Northern counties (Ulster) *Sl* ooman: woman

Angl rossy: impudent girl Omar (Khayyam)
It rossi: the reds
King William Rufus
(Matthew leads a red six, Mark plays a red queen, Luke plays a red king but Johnny trumps it with the five of spades, the highest trump in spoil five)

Sl kisser: mouth Omar Khayyam
K.M.: King's Messenger; Knight of Malta
then (*L* tunc)

L basia: kisses (passionate) *L* oscula: kisses VI.A.981: 'osculum (cheek)'

In some letters & MSS ††† written next to signature
Guests at the *Chemical Marriage of Christian Rosencreutz* travel in 3 adjacent ships to Tower
Rosicrucian *Tunc* page of the *Book of Kells* has 3 marginal panels; text Matt 27:38: 'Tunc crucifixerant XPI cum eo duos latrones' ('Then were there two thieves crucified with him')

Sullivan: *Book of Kells* 'is often called the book of Colum Cille'

pr two's company, three's a crowd

L labiolingualis: pertaining to the lips & tongue *L* suavium: kiss
L basium: kiss (passionate) VI.A.981: 'basium (lips) suavium (tongue)

Four Masters (M) em: unit for measuring amount of printed matter in line, page &c. dog

P.W. Joyce: *English as We Speak It in Ireland: 'the dear knows* (correctly the deer knows) . . . a translation from the Irish . . . *thanssag Dhee* = God knows changed to *thans ag fee* (the deer knows)' X & Y 'Ithaca' (chapter uses 'impersonal catechism')

Ulysses has 18 chapters, *The Odyssey* has 24 books

Maurice Darantière printed 1st ed. of *U.*: his name occurs at end Z

'Penelope' (end of *U.*) paraphe: flourish added to signature

colophon: inscription formerly placed at end of book

732 pp. in 1st ed. *U.*

(Molly) ancient Ir. Ogham alphabet

deaf-mute

AngI duff: black

Scophony system of supersonic light control: mechanical forerunner of TV tube

Gr dektos: a receiver

looked for

Gr (artificial) chrômophilos: colour-lover

F centime (coin) microamp: small unit of current

William Carleton: *Paddy-Go-Easy* happy-go-lucky *Da* ulykke: misfortune, accident Ulyssean *Gr* tetracheir: having 4 hands *L* quadra: 4 *L* manus: hand

dots & dashes

G Vorstellungen über das Studium: conceptions of the study schizophrenia

saxophone phonology: phonetics

Jung Freud

tonguetied

Muggleton: Eng. tailor; founded sect of Muggletonians

periplus: circumnavigation

bestseller Coleridge: *The Ancient Mariner*

Sainéan: *La langue de Rabelais* I.167: 'Chapeau à prunes sucées, en forme de noyau ou d'amande' ('sugar-plum hat in form of nut or almond')

shopkeeper V. Bérard's theory that *The Odyssey* is a hellenisation of the log (*periplous*) of a seafaring Semite Macpherson's *Ossian*

Jesus Christ

Jason & Argonauts

Dodecanese Islands, Aegean Sea

Baedecker's guidebooks to European cities & countries

Sl goose: prostitute

Tiberian vocalisation of Hebrew consonants (placing vowel points under them) introduced in Old Testament MSS from C10

L duplex: twofold

It hanno o non hanno: they have or have not (295.L2) Hanno left account of African voyage, written in Phoenician

unbreakable (code) ('Penelope')

verso, recto (sides of sheet) *Sl* rushlight: liquor

rushlight: primitive candle, rush dipped in grease

Morse Code

Moses wrote Pentateuch

The Book of Kells has 4 types of full stop. Sullivan dates it on basis of punctuation

L circumflexus: bent; a vault

bits of broken glass & split china

Scotland Yard

by a fork

O.W. Holmes: *The Professor at the Breakfast-Table*

plane surface

G Punkt
punching holes

old Italian writing placed 'i' before an 's' followed by consonant, e.g. *ispazio* (space)

Du thee: tea

Da smørrebrød: buttered bread
butter

Ham
ham

newlaid eggs

G Brotfresser: professor (jocular)

G Brotfresser: breadeater

Rev. Patrick Prendergast's tailor cut up a valuable collection of MSS accidentally (name means 'taker of guest' or 'host')

Gr pneuma: spirit

unwittingly

Gr rheuma: current

pr a boy's best friend is his mother

Sullivan: 'The dots are, in the Kells volume, almost always square in shape or quadrilateral—not round'

natural selection

(peck-marks)

Dame Partlet in Chaucer's *Nun's Priest's Tale*. The expression means 'hen', & figuratively, 'woman'

It prati: meadows

grown in praty-land (Ireland) only = *S*hamrock; fowl = *H*en; mi in Sol-fa = *E*; *M* not you (U); *-US* a case ending. *SHEMUS*

F bis
bees

shame

Sainéan: *La langue de Rabelais* II.353: 'le Petit Bonnet rouge' (name used for devil)

Finn MacCool (MacCumhall)

N kvinne: woman

Queen's County: Leix

first instant: first of this month

yours most faithfully

Stevenson: 'Home is the sailor, home from the sea, & the hunter home from the hill'

Fox and Geese: district of D

F L'Auberge du Père Adam: Father Adam's Pub (003.01)

St Cummian, regarded as heretic at time of Paschal dispute justified himself by claiming compliance with Rome, Jerusalem, Antioch & Alexandria

huffsnuff: person liable to take offence (term used in Sainéan II. 402)

St Jerome, translator of Vulgate

Cassandra, prophet

(S . . . HE . . . M) mishmash
Noah (drunk, Gen 9:21)

Song of Songs 1 version of * published by Ossianic Society, D
*'howbeit, we heard not a son to leave by him'
*'without a thing in his ignorance' *Tulcha MacCumhall, Finn's brother
*'in his old man' (old age)

Angl the day was in it: that day, on that day *'on (lit. after) the morrow' Diarmaid
*There were tears of blood 'every time' & a vomiting of blood 'the other time'
*'What name is on thee?' *prob. taken from the Psalter of Cashel
L 'juxtajunctor': harnesser-together
Diarmaid *'out of each desert into its fellow'

*'daughter': woman looking *Torba, one wife of Finn's father

*Morna the Fair-Neck, warrior military service

D Sl totties: girls
Sl Tommy Atkins: British soldier *G* formell: formal
another

lowclass

Du Hans de Koerier: Shaun the Post

According to Ben Jonson, Shakespeare had 'smalle Latine & lesse Greeke'

worried 'bulb of percussion' on flints (archaeology)

D ph It is as true as Essex Bridge

Joseph

Lewis Carroll: *Jabberwocky* flowering chestnuts

Brasenose College, Oxford
Bruno of Nola

R kak vy pozhivaete, moy chërny Gospodin?: how are you, my black sir?
Du kak: shit *Du* foei: fie! for shame! *Angl* poteen: illicit whiskey
'Jim the Penman': James Townsend Savard, forger

**Macgniomharta Fhinn* (*The Youthful Exploits of Finn*)

tonight

(no one answers except echo) backwoods: uncleared forest land

G Briefträger: postman

John Jameson & Son D whiskey 110%

quiz
L qui, quae, quod: who, which
apostles misunderstood an M for an L

riposte: counter-stroke (fencing)

Fine Arts

ᗰ myth erector *PS* most: bridge Maximos tries to bridge gap between Christianity & paganism in Ibsen's *Caesar & Galilean*
L Pontifex Maximus: high priest, pope (lit. 'great bridges-maker') Jack & the Beanstalk (pantomime)
Bluegum: tree *Eucalyptus globulus* *G* Baum *Sequoia (Wellingtonia) gigantea:* redwood
(tall) Baobab: African tree with very thick stem
It nudi: bare trousers Lafayette

twenties Conciliation Hall, D, where O'Connell wore a green cap, speaking after release from prison, 1844
CEH *AngI* esker: sandy ridge *Sl* chaingang: jewellers, watch-chain makers Albert: kind of watch chain
Howth (often cloud-capped)
CHE *Du* Hollander: Dutchman opulence
epulation: action of feasting
Newton & the apple

HCE yesterday & tomorrow

seven (colours of rainbow) servantmaids
several sere: withered; wanton
hearthrug Wilberforce
Lord's Prayer: 'Thy will be done'
Lord's Prayer: 'on Earth as it is in Heaven' *r* Vartry: water supplies D
party
s The Protestant Boys ⚔ Boyne, 1690
It prode: brave
five: Noah, wife, 3 sons *Da* marken: the field *F* Allemagne
G Marken: borders, districts
'ge-' before German past participles HCE King Mark of Cornwall
'The Irish Tutor' given at Theatre Royal, D

ph the toll of the road: its cost in damage, injury & lives
It rotabile: of vehicles, wheeled
leap year daughter finny

HCE prisms

F fausse (hunchback in suit; see 311.05–09) indument: endowment; clothing
phosphorus
(earth) (fire) (water)

(air) *s* Bill Bailey, Won't You Please Come Home? *Sl* tile: hat

Judge Toler tried Robert Emmet long on (cricket position)
N legge: lay *I* cad a chlog: what o'clock offer chances (cricket): said of a batsman who hits ball to a player
Leg before wicket (cricket) CEH stands up (cricket): said of a wicketkeeper fielding
It legge: law St Augustine: *Confessions* VIII.12: 'tolle lege' ('take it & read') immediately behind stumps
scenes postern: back door

F.E.R.T.: motto of House of Savoy ECH
Buckley
Houdini, master of escaping Harrods, Barkers, Shoolbred's, Whiteley's: London department stores
Hamlet III.2.13 : 'outherods Herod'
rightly Mecca evacuated by Koreysh for 3 days while Mohammed undertook
Lesser Pilgrimage
Germans, Huns old Ir. zoomorphic brooches with animal heads

(Ir. coins have omniana: bits of everything *L* omne animal: every living creature
pictures of animals) animalism: i) animal activity, sensuality; ii) doctrine viewing man as mere animal
Eddystone lighthouse sunbeams
Edison invented electric bulb Swann invented a lamp

Meilhac & Halevy: *Frou Frou* (opera) *Gi* dook: ghost Richard III (Crookback) killed in ⚔ Bosworth
G Frau *ph* by hook or by crook
Du boos: angry *Du* baas: boss
I bás: death
G Aas: carrion Luke Plunkett, D actor, played Richard III, riding a donkey, & so amused audience with
Richard's death that they insisted on its repetition
S O S so-&-so Susanna (book in Apochrypha)
Annals of the Theatre Royal, D 16: 'Opera, written by a lady of this city'
W.G. Fay: *A Short Glossary of Theatrical Terms* (1930): 'Business—All movements & actions used by actors in playing
a scene, such as opening & reading letters, eating or preparing meals, fights, smoking, etc.'

mineral waters 'Wash & brush up': service juju: magical object in W. Africa
advertised in Eng. men's public toilets jujube

Heb adam: red; earth, clay Sarah, wife of Abraham oxide of iron
red sandstone *s* The Exile of Erin
AALLPP *ME* attaint: convict *It* lite: lawsuit
arraign: indict, impeach
cashes back *Da* indgang: entrance endorses
Bank of England *Arch* doom: judgement
Chapelizod Damiri: 'Wisdom hath alighted on 3 things, the brain of the Franks, the hands of the Chinese,
& the tongue of the Arabs'
Commendatore (*Don Giovanni:* the statue invited to supper) *Sl* block a hat: knock a
block: customer's mould at hatter's man's hat down over his eyes
Da morgen: morning afternoon *G* Geheimrat: privy
J. Morgan, hat manufacturer, D nuncheon: lunch councillor rat . . . mouse
G ernst Howth mauser rifles *G* lustig: merry
G mausig: cheeky *Angl* mausey: having heavy buttocks
Rump Parliament, 1648–53
Early English: architectural style typical of C13
transoms marigold window: rose window many gilt lights
trademarks
hagioscope: opening to make altar visible from aisle Woolworth
myrioscope: kind of kaleidoscope piscinae: stone basins for discharge of ablutions
aumbries: recesses in church wall *ph* from the year dot: from long ago

horloge: clock *s* The Wren: 'The king of all birds' *L* fuit: he was
Big Ben *G* ist (*L* est): is
L heri: yesterday *D Sl* mouldy: drunk *Quercus:* genus of oak trees
L herit: he will be
plane tree Megalopolis: ancient capital of Arcadia

ph blot on the scutcheon

hidalgo: one of lower Spanish nobility HCE HEC *G* hold: gracious old
carucate: in feudal system, as much land as could be tilled with 1 plough in 1 year
hide: unit of land, 60–120 acres biglooking

(defaecation) graminivorous: grass-eating *Cz* dům: house
Arch doom: judgement
F manoir: countryseat villa
vill: feudal territorial unit corresponding to modern
London Underground civil parish
(air, earth, water, fire) aqueduct
cockahoop forth
D superstition that gasworks' air cures whooping cough (*U.*90) fart
carbon monoxide, a constituent of coalgas hold

G Puder: powder *Sporting Times (The Pink 'Un)*: newspaper; hostile review of *U.*

'Pink pills for *s* Slattery's Mounted Foot
pale people' (advert.) The Pale: Eng.-governed part Lundy Foot, D tobacconist, sold 'superfine pig-tails
of medieval Ireland for ladies'. John Philpot Curran told him to inscribe
L ceresia: cherry 'quid rides' (*L*, what are you laughing at) on his carriage
Titus Andronicus: Caius & Sempronius are also characters in it

Napoleon called the Eng. 'a nation of shopkeepers' (Wellington)

queens, castles (chess) 3 castles on D coat of arms
Sl shot: fucked *Sl* quean: whore caskets
draughts Stromboli, volcano

man must be *F* fier à: to trust be fair to him
Arch mote: may *F* fier: proud
Pietà: representation of white & gold: liturgical colours coarse
Mary mourning over dead Jesus
(heather on Howth; violet is liturgical colour of repentance)
F chaperon: medieval headdress
Ir. P/Q split Dublin Metropolitan Police
P's & Q's *L* quies: rest *Souvenir of the 25th Anniversary of the Gaiety Theatre* 37: 'Miss Cissy Graham's
Da by: town entertaining "Triple Bill" followed'
Da hoved: head Matt 7:7: 'seek, & ye shall find'
L plenus: full Browning: *Saul:* 'If Death laid her hand on him & Famine devoured his store'
filth earth HCE
(horserace) Bruno of Nola *Sl* pole: penis polar bear
Browne & Nolan *F Sl* passer: fuck
G Ahn: ancestor *Gr* orchis: testicle
Sl orchestra: testicle

Da fandt sted: took place

delicious
L delictum: crime, transgression
cg Ring-a-ring-o'roses: 'One for me, & one for you, & one for little Moses'

360 idols in Ka'aba, destroyed by Mohammed

Before Mohammed's birth a prophet was expected: women hoped for male children & 'Hanīfs' denied popular
El-Khalasa: stone block in Ka'aba colossal superstitions
AngI flahoolagh: princely St Patrick's Paschal fire (609.24ff.)
(Father . . . Son . . . Spirit)
'Forgive us our trespasses as we forgive those who trespass against us' (Lord's Prayer)

cinders *L* Pelion on Ossa (*Odyssey* XI):
mountain on mountain (piled up by Titans)
Pillars of Hercules, Gibraltar Oedipus complex
F pilule: pill *L* pilula: little ball *L* hircus: goat

Co. Westmeath Co. Carlow
G Wurst: sausage
very truly yours

Sl futter: fuck *G* Vater *G* Magd: maid Cahermohill, Co. Limerick CHE
In 1885 the Gaiety Theatre, D, put on *Private Secretary* with 'Hill, that "mountain of flesh" as "Cattermole"'
ph making a mountain out of a molehill

Sl tout: spy: solicitor of custom for tradesman *F* en-tout-cas: umbrella/sunshade

nr Sing a Song of Sixpence surcease: cessation
Circe
'While stands the Colosseum Rome shall stand' (Byron) HCE
Sl frails: women Celbridge, village, Co. Kildare
educated abroad prayer: 'As it was in the beginning . . .'
ejaculated *Arch* gan: began Guinness
bottle of Bass Roderick O'Connor, last high king of Ireland
⚔ New Ross

busman's holiday: one spent following one's usual occupation Quakers' meeting: when silence falls on a group Witch's Sabbath
Gr 'omos: same *Gr* 'eteros: other HCE *s* Johnny I Hardly Knew Ye: 'Ye eyeless, noseless, chickenless egg'
insane

HEC Via Aemilia: road from Placentia to Rimini rebuilding of Paris by Baron Haussmann & Jean Alphand
half a million *G* Hausmann: tenant, lodger
orphaned Samuel Lover: *Handy Andy* Allegheny Mts, in Appalachians
Andes elegant
nr Humpty Dumpty *L* Patricius: Patrick
patricians
phlegmatically
plebians
Grace O'Malley was refused entrance to Howth Castle as gates were closed for dinner (021.04) Rothschild
Du rots: rock
Dublin Rockefeller *Sl* fly: cunning, artful hemispheres
traces

homing pigeon *G* Heim Merrion, district of D Roebuck, district of D
Pigeonhouse, D 7 cities have been considered Homer's birthplace: Smyrna, Rhodos, Kolophon, Salamis, Chios, Argos, Athenae Howth
Clonskeagh, D district Seapoint: district of Dún Laoghaire Ashtown, nr Phoenix Park Raheny, D district
Lord Chamberlain censors plays; D alone was exempt from his power

Moore: *s* I Saw Thy Form in Youthful Prime [Domhnall]

Bel Paese cheese Ireland's Eye: small island nr Howth
It il bel paese: the home land *L* quot: how many
tetrains *G* tot: dead *Hu* szombat: Saturday
L tot: so many sunbath
Hu vasárnap: Sunday
G Wassernapf: water basin
Lecocq & others: *Giroflé, Girofla* (an opera; also a singing game. In the opera they are twin sisters)
F giroflée: stock (flower) Poe: 'Quoth the RAVEN "nevermore"'
L columba: DOVE (Noah's ark) goalkeeper
Protestantism: every man his own priest
fullback (football) *It* arco: bow *It* forte: strong
Allblacks: New Zealand rugby team (Strongbow)
stumps pulled at end of play (cricket) *ph* thick & thin
I 'tuigeann tú: do you understand?
Arch thew: thigh crater

J.S. Wyss: *Swiss Family Robinson* *F* les nouvaux riches
It colle: hill Swiss Alps relatively new rocks (*F* roches)
far off I Cor 13:13: 'faith, hope, charity'
pharoahs

Futurism: C20 art movement   send   sense   *F* souriantes: smiling   VI.B.32.118: 'chorus girls they hang their legs like censers'
L futuete!: fuck!   *Sl* leglifter: fornicator
F grommellants: grumbling

Ulysses & *Iliad*   lasses and lads
Moore: *s* Though the Last Glimpse of Erin
I lug: mountain-hollow; name of several mts   Mangan & Berkeley valued tar water as medicine
Lug: Celtic sungod   Thor   Wotan   wodka
Asama: Japanese volcano   (Heroes in Valhalla live perpetually on 1 boar)   stave off   *ON* Ragnarøkr: destruction of the Norse gods
Asa = Odin   asthma   pigsty
pedestal
Du paddenstoel: mushroom, toadstool
G winken: beckon   (obituary)

Christmas, Advent, New Year, Lent, Easter, Pentecost   lengthy   reverend

peritonitis   costitis: inflammation of ribs   no flowers by request   fun for all
Easterling: Viking (used for invaders of Ireland)   follower: one who attends funeral   funeral   funfair
Moore: *s* Go Where Glory Waits Thee

James Clerk Maxwell, physicist   committed   commenced   *L* comminxit: he defiled
U.109: 'Spurgeon went to heaven 4 a.m. this morning. 11 p.m. (closing time). Not arrived yet. Peter'
Borgia popes   *F* bière   *F* beurre
finished a burgess   *Du* vat bier: draught beer
battle of the Boyne   *G* roh: crude
AngI bawn: white
felt fond   *Huckleberry Finn*   stuck
huckleberries: blueberries
toss up: prepare food quickly   youngster   foul   hock   *G* Becher: beaker
F fou   *Scots* fou: drunk
gained the age of reason   *F* raisin: grape   VI.B.32.140–1: 'ad = eat/da = give/ rup = break/sa = sow/su = squeeze/ hang = state/hoek = dynamic'
tames

pursues   Vico: *New Science* 401: 'the first language in the first mute times of the nations must have begun with signs, whether gestures or physical objects'
Irish

L hic, haec, hoc: this   himself   rafters   Rialto Bridge, D

Annesley Bridge, D   Ball's Bridge, D   at all
Binn's Bridge, D   Tolka Bridge, D   Newcomen Bridge, D
U. 25: 'How, sir? Comyn asked. A bridge is across a river'
s 'The flea on the hair of the tail of the dog of the nurse of the child of the wife of the wild man from Borneo has just come to town'

tried

(rainbow)   natural dyes used in Scottish tartan manufacture: rue root (red), dulse–a seaweed–(brown), bracken root (yellow), teasel or Fuller thistle (green), ash tree root (dark green), sundew (purple), wild cress (violet)
long gone but not forgotten

cousin germane   Dillon Cosgrave (*North Dublin, City & Environs*) claims there are 24 places called 'Dublin' in the U.S.

(Lublin, Poland)

(BUD)

(*F* NIL: Nile)   (NULL BID)
Christie's, London auction house
Eve made of Adam's rib

Bishop of Glendalough (post declined by St Laurence O'Toole)   *Du* hoed: hat
Earl of Howth
surrounded   *We* brwnt: foul, dirty   L/R (also Chinese pron. of Eng.)
Sorrento: part of Dalkey   brown buildings   dUblIns
free port (Chinese treaty ports controlled by West before WW I)
polt: blow, knock   *C* hwang: yellow   *C* huang-shang (*f. rom.* 'chang'): a term for Emperor
HCE   Hwang Ch'êng = Imperial City (part of Pekin)
Sl highty-tighty: uppish, quarrelsome

Slemish, mt, Co. Antrim, where Patrick tended herds for 6 years   Magh Meall: Ir. Elysium (Honey Plain)
virtues
capital sins

P/K   blessed virgin Humphrey   B.L.G.: Burke's Landed Gentry   V.B.D.: Volta Bureau for the Deaf
P.P.M.: postage paid in money   T.D.S.: Ter die sumendum (to be taken 3 times a day)
T.C.: Trinity College (D)   (4 meals)
L.O.N.: League of Nations   *G* Diener: servant
gold   Tipperary

ph 'Dear Dirty Dublin'

HCE   *G* Wehr: defence   *G* Mörder: murderer
Ottoman   Ostman: Viking
Effendi: Turkish title of respect for officials   *Du* baas: boss, master   Priam of Troy, father of Paris
Padishah: Persian title applied to ruler
Les Rois Fainéants: last Merovingian kings
(papal infallibility)   *I* Liam: William   Tara of the kings: ancient cap. of Ir.
According to Keating, C17 Ir. historian, the Coronation Stone in Westminster Abbey is the Ir. Lia Fáil from Tara, brought to London from Scone, Scotland, by Edward I
William Gladstone 'failed' Parnell in Westminster when Home Rule Bill defeated   Saul (converted on road to Damascus, then took name Paul)
Damascus   Paul   us

pest: plague   alpenstock

Liffey on fire   *pr* Spare the rod & spoil the child
lightning, marriage, burial (Vico)
pr Marry in haste & repent at leisure   *s* Sweet Rosie O'Grady: '& when we are married, O how happy we'll be'
Sl punk: prostitute
Wilkins Micawber in *David Copperfield*, always waiting for something to turn up
Arch welkin: sky
Osiris is called the god at the top of the staircase & sometimes depicted at the top of 10 steps

A spiderweb across the mouth of the cave in which he hid & a bird which laid eggs before it, saved Mohammed from his enemies
Sw spindel: spider
G Unsichtbarkeit: invisibility   live in

Arbutus: genus of evergreens, including strawberry tree (abundant in Killarney)   *s* My Love's an Arbutus

Viceregal   *F* foi   Macpherson: *Fingal* I.39: 'Four stones . . . rise on the grave of Cathba'
sworn foe   Swaran: Norse leader defeated by Macpherson's Fingal
Macpherson: *The Death of Cuthullin* 109: 'He offered him the shell of joy'   Mora & Lora: 2 hills in Macpherson's works
(Kings on hilltops view the conflict of their armies beneath)
hell
'firm look in readiness', 'forward spear', 'feet of wind', 'the last of his fields': phrases from Macpherson's *Temora*
Macpherson explains 'Curach' as 'Cu-raoch . . . the madness of battle'
Macpherson: *Ossian:* 'I went in suit of the maid to Lego's sable surge: Twelve of my people were there, the sons of the streamy morven'   *Temora* VII describes mists over Lego

In *Temora* VIII, Fingal's companions 'darkened', i.e. grieved
'fidhil' is Eng. 'feel' spelt as Irish   *Fingal* II.51–2: 'stars dim-twinkled'
Fithil: an 'inferior bard' in *Temora*   fiddle
Fingal IV: 'To begin a battle is expressed, in old composition, by *lifting of the sunbeam*'

HCE   HCE   *Gr* hagios chitôn eripheios: holy garment of a kid
L hereditatis columna erecta: the lofty column of inheritance
ecumenical

simultaneous equation   eliminated integrals

³⁄₁ is an improper fraction   comical headpiece (Confucius had strange bump on forehead)
codpiece
hair on him   name 'Chinese' taken from short-lived rule of Chins
Confucius and his mother moved to Chufu after father's death
Confucius (Kung Fu-tze) born after prayer at shrine from which Tai Shan (a sacred mt) visible
Festy King (085.23)   L/R   *AngI* shanty: old house
Sl gasometer: voluble talker   annular
lithium: lightest metal

Regent Circus, London cobblestone
It raggiante: radiant Cabal: King Arthur's dog
Da København: Copenhagen cabin (faithful dog) *It* ammirare: to wonder at
cavern
approximate *F* à peu prés: almost Atlas alignment
'paroxysm' from *Gr* par oxys, preciosity *F* allongement: elongation in space or time
'beyond acute' ⚔ Badour, won by Arthur
Booterstown: district of D Batterstown, Co. Meath
Finn's hunt for the magic boar *I* madradh: dog Mordred: Arthur's nephew, killed by him
bare Twrch Trwyth: boar hunted by Arthur in *Mabinogi*, killed by Mordred moderates
Arthur died at ⚔ Cammlan *The Book of Aneirin:* 'an Arthur in the exhaustive conflict'
Camden St, D HEC Otho: Roman emperor; suicide
Hamlet I.4.2: 'a nipping & an eager air' *F* aigre: chill, bitter (earth)
(fire) aiger: a tidal bore
(water)

struggle for life Browning

Nathaniel Lee: *The Rival Queens* (a play) *Grimshaw, Bagshaw & Bradshaw*
(performed at Theatre Royal, D)
licence granted

White Horse Hill, Berks, England

It costellare: to constellate, spangle
Luke 14:21: 'bring in the poor & the maimed, the halt & the blind'
Tom, Dick & Harry
It miraculone: big miracle applause
It culone: big arse *It* uccellino: little bird
the stage
'terrier' der. from *L* terra, hence burial
nr Rich Man, Poor Man, Beggar Man, Thief *I* támh: sleep, death Olaf: 1st Norse king of D
Mr Fox: alias of Parnell (Viconian cycle, 414.31) Tav is last letter of Hebrew alphabet; aleph (= ox) is
Ostman = Viking, hence Oxmantown, part of N. D first letter of it *Da* tavs: silent
U.10: 'Turko the terrible': first Xmas pantomime *F* vespasienne: street urinal
at Gaiety Theatre, D Thorgil: Turgesius (051.16) Vespasian: Roman Emperor
Marcus Aurelius: Roman Emperor Whigamore (original of 'Whig') *It* traditore: traitor socialist, communist
somersault *AngI* tory: robber Socians: sect denying Christ's divinity

hands *ON* Ragnarok: fate of the gods
Raglan Road, D
Marlborough Place, D Cromleach & Crommal Hill, Co. Antrim, in Macpherson

Sl lurcher: rogue (pissed)
r Lubar, Co. Antrim *G* Marschall Grand Court of Wardmote in Guildhall, London, receives election returns
wardmote: assembly of citizens
net weight (before he eats)
gross weight
grace before meat
ton *I* Banba: Ireland (poetic)
U.80: 'Prayers for the conversion of Gladstone they had too'
I Beurla: Eng. language 'Grand Old Man' (Gladstone)

It melarancia: orange (fruit)
It mela: apple
Sp El Gran Turco: Sultan of Turkey Luxemburger Leix . . . lip
It granturco: maize *F* orge: barley *It Arch* formento: wheat *G* Lachs: salmon
'The sparkle . . . benevolence' is part of the inscription on bust of Sir Philip Crampton (surgeon) in D, verbatim

forbear *L* quare: why, how
James Carey informed on Invincibles
L cur: why *Sl* burked: smothered *Da* Irsk: Irish *Da* holm: islet
The Invincibles murdered Cavendish & Burke in Phoenix Park Partition of Ireland
swig *Da* svig: deceit Gorky: *The Mother* *Gr* methy: wine
United Irishmen: nationalist group founded by Tone, 1791 Methyr: a name of Isis
tasted a bit corky (wine) *R* gor'kii: bitter *Da* svigermoder: mother-in-law
R gorkii: hot
G komm *G* eile dich: hurry up! CEH *Huckleberry Finn* *Tom Sawyer*
Tom, Dick & Harry

G stark Howth
Macpherson: *Temora* I.221n: 'Mor-annal, *strong breath*'
roam America
Europe
O'Connell scruff

isobars: lines joining areas of equal atmospheric pressure

(Adam) *G* Riesengebirge: Bohemian/Polish mts

s Sweet Rosie O'Grady

planters: Eng. settlers on forfeited Ir. lands in C17 *G* Liebster: dearest
F plantureux: copious
makes aquascutum: mackintosh quay
lobsterpot *Sl* gay women: whores
G. men: detectives

Persse . . . O'Reilly (insurance: Vico's Providence)

fire earth (water) (air)

Pigott: hesitency

bigotted *L* silvicola: inhabiting woods
Union of Great Britain & Ireland, 1800
G Matrosen: sailors
G Hosen: trousers
chest of drawers fief: an estate in land 939 year lease
(Vico discusses) *King Lear* III.4.187: 'Fie, foh, & fum'
Gr polemos: war The doors of Janus' Temple in the Roman Forum were always open in time
Gr politeia: citizenship of war & closed in time of peace
elixir Eleazar in Halevy's opera *La Juive*
Raoul: hero of Meyerbeer's *Les Huguenots* (Catholic)
silks poplin
*U.*168: 'poplin . . . The huguenots brought that here' *G* über marshal *G* Schall: reverberation
Bonaparte Wellesley *G* Meer: sea
Blücher: Prussian marshal at Waterloo *Sl* Mudson: Adam
Ibsen: *The Master Builder* Andrew Ducrow: horseman, performed in Theatre Royal, D ('The Napoleon of Equestrians')
Punch & Judy
Gardiner St, D *L* judex: judge
AngI brehon: judge HCE *F* cauchemar: nightmare ectoplasm: in spiritual seances, materialised astral substance
ph full of beans: lively
nr Baa Baa Black Sheep, have you any wool? quite

dramatised Alice Milligan: *Last Feast of the Fianna*

Schubert: *Die Forelle* ('The Trout': setting of poem by G.F.D. Schubart) W.J. Fitzpatrick: authority on social life of past Ireland
s The Boys of Wexford indemnified Brian Boru etymologised 'Brian of the tributes'; defeated Danes
Babu: Mr (Hindu term of respect) identified Boru tribute was extracted from Leinstermen by Ir. high king
Du schenken: to give (Henry II gave D to Bristol) *G* drei
G Schenke: inn *ph* sent to Coventry: ostracised (*U.*332: 'three birthplaces of the first duke of Wellington)
G Ortschaft: village, place *L* triplex: threefold terra-cotta
tumulus (buried) *F* cuite: burned, fired
ph Liberty, Fraternity, Equality

ph make a virtue of necessity

pr Necessity is the mother of invention

Hall: *Dublin & Wicklow:* 'In population & size, Dublin is the second city of the British Empire' tenterhooks (cloth stretched on tenter)
points attach hose to doublet *Rh Sl* lath & plaster: master
Da Althing: national assembly each of us
L rex regulorum: king of princes
I árd-rí: high king Ibsen: *Kongs-emnerne* (*The Crown-Pretenders*) *r* Dee (2, in Scotland & Eng.)
Gr basileus: king St Patrick landed at Inverdea, mouth of *r* Vartry (anciently *r* Dea)

Balaclava G Klee: clover Ultima Thule: extreme limit of travel or
I Baile Átha Cliath: D discovery
thole: endure *F* fou *Scots* fou: drunk pubcrawl
kraal: in S. Africa, a village or cattle enclosure
Sir John Lavery, portrait painter paid
Sl lavery: Ir. £1 note with portrait of Lady Lavery played
double or quits buggers
treble quadruple quintuple
Cadmus sowed dragons' teeth & armed warriors sprang up
Deucalion & Pyrrha created people by throwing stones behind their backs (sodden-after Flood)
Gaudio Gambrinus: Flemish king,
brewed the first beer Potter's Field: pauper section of
Peter the Great (four suits) demi-monde cemetery in many cities

Cambronne (009.27) *Sl* nurse: prostitute *Sl* drum: brothel

It tre: 3 *It* uno: 1 Anne Bracegirdle: actress

Sl silver screen: cinema

Richard III, 'Crookback' Richard Burbage: David Garrick & Spranger Barry: rival London
Shakespearian actor & D actors
(controversy between old Ir. & Roman churches over the date of Easter)
22 March (first possible date of Easter)
L vigintiquinque: 25 *F* Germinal: 1st spring month in Fr. Revolutionary calendar
25 April last possible date for Easter
(7 syllables) Have papooses everywhere (535.34–5) *Gr* (artificial) arithmosophia:
Ojibway Indians of N. Ontario skill in counting
Plough & the Stars: flag used by Ir. rebels
7 stars in Ursa Major (The Plough) Wapentake: division of some Eng. counties
Earwicker Vico's cycles
'Pike-County' dialect used in *Huckleberry Finn* according to introductory note
mew: moult
renews

L equa docta: skilled mare terracotta (pipe)
Portobello bridge, D aqueduct
(Aphrodite) HCE
Persse O'Reilly Shelbourne Hotel, D
Watling St borders Guinness's Brewery
Wall St
Giant Ivy flourishes in Glenasmole (Finn's hunting ground)

I Tír-na-nÓg: Land of Young
younkers: young men bewitched *The War of the Gaedhil with the Gaill* 79–81: 'They carried away their soft,
G Gewitter: thunderstorm youthful, bright, matchless girls; their blooming, silkclad young women; &
bewildered their active, large, & wellformed boys' (Ir. plunder of Viking-held Limerick,
blossom 968)

Harald Fairhair: 1st king of Norway (Isolde theoretically Tristan's aunt)
Olaf the White: 1st Norse king of D
L nepos: grandson

words of Brazen Head in Robert Greene's *Honourable Historie of Friar Bacon & Friar Bungay:* 'Time is! . . . Time
was! . . . Time is past!' beck, burn, brook = stream
G Brücke: bridge wath: a ford scale: landing-place rainfall in D ca. 30″ per annum
scow: coracle, punt

(32° F) boilingpoint

trulls: whores Ibsen: *Et Vers:* 'To live is—war with trolls in the heart's & mind's vault.
To write,—that is to hold doomsday over one-self'
HEC eschatology: science of the 4 last things, death, judgement, hell & heaven

Henry Humphreys: *The Justice of the Peace in Ireland*
J.P.: Justice of the Peace
Theban recension of *Egyptian Book of the Dead*

Mark of Cornwall G melken: to milk G mürrisch: morose
nr 'The king was in his countinghouse, counting out his money, The queen was in the parlour, eating bread & honey, The maid was in the garden, hanging out the clothes, Down came a blackbird & pecked off her nose'
armour arbour Furry Glen, Phoenix Park, also called Hawthorn Glen
showing off

Sl pump ship: urinate fathers (past) stone/tree
Da fortælle: tell, recount
mothers (future)
Sl put the comether on: coax, wheedle
Eliot: *The Waste Land:* 'Mrs Porter . . . *s* The Sun Shines Bright on Mrs Porter
They wash their feet in soda water' *I* eanach: marsh, fen
s 'O Mr Porter, Whatever shall I do, I want to go to Birmingham & they're taking me on to Crewe'

Pimlico, street, D

s 'Deutschland, Deutschland über alles' London churches: St Edmund, King & Martyr; St Dunstan-in-the East; St Peter-le-Poer; St Bartholomew the Great; St Bartholomew-by-the-Exchange
F pitre: clown Petrin: highest hill in Prague
Peter & Paul
Da hesten: horse Westmoreland St, D
King Billy's statue, D, had back to Trinity College & faced Dame St (he was Prince of Orange)
Oranje Nassau: Dutch Royal family
Nassau St, D, runs S. of Trinity College
Drom-Choll-Coil, old Ir. name of D, means 'the brow of hazel wood'
Billy-in-the-Bowl: legless strangler in old D
name 'Dublin' means 'black pool' Blowyk: old name of Bullock (place nr Dalkey)
artesian well Phoenix lived in Arabian desert
Phoenix Park was named thus through misunderstanding of Ir. name Fionn-uisce, which means clear water (from a well there) writing on wall at Belshazzar's feast
Charles Collette: *Cryptoconchoidsyphonostomata* (patter farce, lit. 'hidden shell-like tube-mouths') played at Theatre Royal, D expressions
Hellespont
Hero & Leander (Hero drowned in Hellespont)
Glasnevin (D cemetery) sounds like *I* Glaisín Aoibhinn, which means 'pleasant little field' oldest *L* plena: full
Yildiz Kiosk: seat of Turkish Government under Abdul Hamid
youngest *ph* 'island of saints & scholars' (Ireland)

Thousand & One Nights

1 hectare = 2.471 acres 'hugecloaked' (*U*.93) Daniel O'Connell killed D'Esterre in duel on the Fifteen Acres, Phoenix Park
White horse is symbol of William III, painted on walls by loyalists

'Amerikay' (*Portrait* II)

sons daughters *s* The Memory of the Dead: 'But true men, like you, men, Are plenty here today'

birth thunderbolts falchion: broad curved sword
s Adams & Liberty: '& repulse with his breast the assaults of the thunder . . . & conduct, with its point, every flash to the deep' fashioned

L vehiculum: vehicle

circulation Eblana: name of D used by Ptolemy
flood . . . ebb
support Howth Castle HCE equerry: gentleman of the Royal Stables; officer attending Eng. sovereign
Hewitt: name used by Robert Emmet
we're delighted

rhododendrons (on Howth Head) sea level
Dundrum, district of D
(mountain) leguminiferous zone: that in which podbearing plants grow Balfe: *s* 'When other lips & other hearts . . . & you'll remember me'

Portrait II: 'night mail to Cork . . . telegraph poles held the galloping notes of the music between punctual bars' (Birds on telephone wires look like notes)
AngI sagart: priest

mosque synagogue Dilmun: Sumerian garden of Paradise in which
mouse Tree of Life is date palm
Arthur's companions: Sugyn, who could suck up seas; Gillia, chief Ir. leaper; & Gwevyl, who could let 1 lip drop below his belt & turn the other on to his head Dublin
applaud
Moore: *s* Come O'er the Sea, Maiden, with me [Cushla ma Chree]
Glewlwyd of the Mighty Grasp: Arthur's gateman in *The Mabinogion*
Mabinogion: Culhwch & Olwen: 'Thou shalt receive *Arch* baxter: baker
the boon . . . as far as wind dries, as far as rain wets, as far as sun runs, as far as sea stretches'
Broadway
(air, earth, fire, water)

delighted disgusted
come back = revenant = ghost
(earth, fire, water, air) *R* ostrov: island inferno *Heb* mabbul: flood
Mare Inferus: Tuscan Sea, W. of Italy
flew Moyle: sea between Ireland & Scotland
gracefulness
A long Sumerian poem on Paradise includes words 'None said, "O disease of the eyes, thou art disease of the eyes". None said "O headache, thou art headache". . . . Thou hast founded a city, thou hast founded a city, to which thou hast assigned its fate. Dilmun the city thou has founded. . . . Like fat, like fat, like tallow'
scorbutic: afflicted with scurvy
URU: Sumerian ideogram for 'city'

pirate boats of D Danes had raven flags *I* dubh: black *Du* raaf (pl. raven): raven *Du* duif (pl. duiven): dove
F gueulant: bawling *N* fjell: mountain *pr* No man is a hero to his valet
peacock boar *It* boaro: cowherd
Sl ph son of a seacook (abusive) emmet: ant
L taurus: bull
G Österreich: Austria
old age
ostrich mongoose
nettlerash tiler, lodge (Masonic)

attributed to Henri IV of France: 'I want there to be no peasant in my realm so poor that he will not have a chicken in his pot every Sunday' *L* dapifer: waiter *L* panis et circenses: bread, & circus contests
L Pontifex Maximus: high priest; pope tope: drink heavily
L (artificial) hortifex: garden maker
ph gets our goat: annoys us

AngI man in the gap: a sturdy defender
Moore: *s* Oft in the Stilly Night: 'the light of other days'
ph Dear Dirty Dublin Chas Matthews: *My Awful Dad* (played at Theatre Royal, D) *L* timor: fear
M.G. Lewis: *Timour the Tartar* (played at Crow St Theatre, D)
Annals of the Theatre Royal 63: Irving's interpretations 'startled some, puzzled many, but set all a-thinking'
Kingsbridge Station, D
Thomas Burgh built old Custom House, D gibbous: hunchbacked gibus: opera hat (collapsible)
old Guinness steam barge on Liffey, lowering funnel at bridges
Bridge of Sighs, Venice (joke about genuine old cutlass with new blade from 1 owner & new handle [helve] from another) *G* Heft: hilt
ph old head on young shoulders

CHE
s Caller Herring
tarpon: giant relation of herring
chameleon

CEH endocrine glands: ductless glands living his life bannock: barley- or pease-meal cake
'Forty Bonnets': nickname of Mrs Tommy Healy of Galway
deaf
DOVE
(statue) Ballsbridge, district of D RAVEN *I* dubh: black
Basle, Switzerland
G König: king

G Stein *It* tronfio: puffed up *L* triumphus reipublicae: triumph of the state
Kingstown Harbour (Dún Laoghaire harbour) repertory comfort *L* prosperitas publica: public prosperity
idol had feet of clay *I* Baile Átha Cliath: D

The Hollow, Phoenix Park Tristan vacuum
tree/stone
mountain boulder
molten butter
mountain dew: in Ireland, whiskey *L* lumen: lamp
lemon peel

lump of sugar in boiling water   penny
s Boyne Water   'Paddy' Ir. whiskey
Grania was daughter of Cormac MacAirt   *I* Ní: Daughter of

Diarmaid (Grania placed magical injunction on him to elope with her)   Diarmaid
pr Diamonds cut diamonds
Grania   Diarmaid   Grania

watch out   Wynn's Hotel, D

liquor   big white horse (008.21)

tip   Goldsmith: *The Deserted Village:* 'Sweet Auburn, loveliest village of the plain'   *L* cantare: to crow
Blake's Albion (in *Jerusalem*)   piece   HCE
hen & cock (egg producers)   egotists
Cantrell & Cochrane: D mineral water manufacturers
s Slattery's Mounted Foot   Finn MacCool built Lund Cathedral; a St Lawrence had to guess the builder's name or forfeit his eyes
Tom Tit Tot: class of folk tale in which demon loses his power when his name is discovered
flesh & praties (potatoes)   fish & chips   Arthur Wellesley, Duke of Wellington
wily   sly
Huckleberry Finn   *Da* kukkuk: cuckoo   HCE
Am. Juke & Kallikak families: hereditary degenerates
born   wenches   Buckley (338–55)
boon (blessing . . . ban (curse)
HCE   (engendered . . . foetus . . . born)
Da født: born
presumably   plough . . . share

evince: make manifest   travelled
at all events   travail (childbirth)
footprints   Magazine   *Sl* meg: wench   hetman: Polish commander   *Sl* sear: cunt
Miocene (26m. years ago)   *N* het: hat   unhorsed   Ringsend, district of D
HCE

stock collar: a kind of stiff, close-fitting neckcloth

ECH
Kersse (311.05–09)
Coleridge: *The Ancient Mariner* 141–2: 'Instead of the cross, the Albatross About my neck was hung'

Thersites (Trojan War)   *ph* set the Liffey on fire

Parnell's hobby was assaying gold

(flying machine)

polish

Justius 187.24; Mercius 193.31   cornucopia

awry   rucksack   *Du* rook: smoke
G sacht: soft   *G* Rücksicht: regard, lit. 'back-sight'
alpenstock   New York

SC jugo: South   *L* jugo: I marry

Gordon Selfridge: 1920s director of Selfridges, London chain store
selfrighteousness
A.C.W. Harmsworth, Viscount Northcliffe: newspaper magnate, born in Chapelizod
La Belle Alliance & Mt St Jean (Waterloo)   William Gerard Hamilton: Ir. M.P.; made brilliant maiden speech; said never to have spoken again
F larme: tear   (earth, fire, air, water)
Anthony Hamilton: *Memoires de la vie du Comte de Grammont.* Grammont married Elizabeth, La Belle, Hamilton

Elizabeth Hamilton: *s* My Ain Fireside George Hamilton: *Introduction to the Study* *G* Himmel
James Hamilton: *Book of Psalms & Hymns* *of the Hebrew Scriptures* Hamilton
Sir William Rowan Hamilton: Dubliner; James Archibald Hamilton, astronomer at Armagh Observatory,
discovered quaternions studied transit of Mercury (mercury = quicksilver)
grabbed

(the P/K split)
garden pest sweet peas

ECH

fresh newmade *F* nué: cloud *F* mots plural
John 1:14: 'the Word was made flesh' *D Sl* mott: girl *L* prurire: feel sexually aroused
Plurabelle excessively

I Áth Cliath: Hurdle Ford clear whisper chemise Themis: titaness; represents divine justice
John 3:8: 'The wind bloweth where it listeth'
The Irish Hudibras or Fingallian Prince, 1689 *AngI* hoolies: wild parties Hodge's Ireland-Holyhead ferry
The Hiberniad, 1760 Hodge: name for Eng. rustic worry
carry *F* Brabançon: Belgian

Wilde was convicted of indecent practices with Charles Parker *Du* beschoten: shot at
Sl Fritz: a German (245.08) *Sl* barker: pistol (031.15)
Buckley hicuppy *ph* in his cups: boozing Jacob's biscuit factory, D, makes arrowroot biscuits
Berkeley Jacob bought Esau's birthright with pottage of lentils (Gen 25)
time after time waifs & strays on the parish

HCE Hans Christian Andersen evenings of the week

Ivan the Terrible Sunday *Sl* softsoap: to flatter
Shaun *L* taurus: bull with soft words
G badend: bathing

Mullingar Inn, Chapelizod

I nua: new *ph* born with a silver spoon in his mouth
Nuad of the Silver Arm: king of the Tuatha Dé Danann
Erin left hand to the sea (i.e. clockwise)

(C) Eblana: name of D used by Ptolemy *Du* dubbeltje: a Dutch coin
T.T.: teetotaller
Amsterdam *Du* damp: haze, vapour nightmare

Sir Richard Steele on Lady Elizabeth Hastings (*Tatler* 49): olive oil chrism: consecrated oil christened
'to love her was a liberal education' St Olave's Church, Fishamble St, D
St Laurence O'Toole's Church, HCE ALP
Seville Place, D Dickens: *The Cricket on the Hearth*
Du predikant: preacher deaf Darius: Persian king defeated at Marathon

maneh: Hebrew coin o'clock
among many
s Home, Sweet Home HC . . . E

Da liv: life moonshine whiskey Champagne

stout bottled William I, Henry VIII, Charles II, Richard III
G Hahnrei: cuckold
G Alte: old person

Mandrake supposedly shrieks when uprooted *G* Weib: female
convulsions birds: drake, shrike, vulture, Ibsen: *The Wild Duck*
bitterly wild duck, bittern

moonlight (gains girth) sundown

Troilus & Cressida III.3.175: 'One touch of Nature makes the whole world kin'

J: *The City of the Tribes:* 'In [the parish house of St Nicholas] there is a curious document in which the writer says that . . . he had never seen at a single glance what he saw in Galway —a priest elevating the Host, a pack chasing a deer, a ship entering the harbour under full sail & a salmon being killed with a spear'

G Blick: glance

F saumon: salmon

flattery

Canute reproached those who flattered him (commanding the sea to turn back)

Cincinnatus assumed Roman dictatorship while danger lasted, then immediately returned to plough

Da farfar: paternal grandfather

Father Knickerbocker = N.Y.C.

Da morfar: maternal grandfather

Lord's Prayer: 'Our Father . . . on earth as it is in heaven'

athwart   *Sl* crack a quart: drink a quart bottle   *Sl* crack: deflower   *Sl* quaint: cunt

G stehen: stand

foot-hills

Sl footle: nonsense, twaddle

Tim Finnegan   early

morning light   *Arch* an: if   sunbaked

place

△   *G* Mutter

s Cecilia (1925): 'Does your mother know you're out, Cecilia?'

myopic eyes   suburban

s The Bells of Shandon: 'With deep affection & recollection
I often think of those Shandon bells,
Whose sounds so wild would, in days of childhood,
Fling round my cradle their magic spells'

pontifex: lit. 'bridge builder'

circumvallate: to surround with a rampart or ditch

asleep

Man alive!   grig: tease, entice

G Berg

icebergs

It spondo: riverbank   tickle me   on the knees   underneath   righteous

spondee: metrical foot (2 long syllables)   *F* onde: wave

Ossian, son of Finn

ocean

Sl rudder: penis   wet dream   Hammurabi: king of Babylon

HCE   Prankquean (021.05–023.15)

Ecclesiastes

Du min: love

□   prototype   mother-in-law   *I* tig: house (S.)

I teach: house (W.)   *Du* wit: white   with

tit-for-tat   hatchment: escutcheon

of prey   *Sl* rookery: brothel

Sudermann: *Magda*   monkeyhouse   *Du* paard: horse   leopard (spotted)

G Magd: maid (046.28–9)   *Du* nÿlpaard: hippopotamus

witchcraft   *G* Vorort: suburb   *G* drei   *G* Schloss   *G* Schluss

3 castles on D coat of arms

Vatican   husband & wife

L nox atrabilis: gloomy night   'Exsultet': 'O felix culpa!'

G wohnen: live   *G* Ecke: corner   Epsom Downs   Le Decer: C14 mayor of D

Eblana: Ptolomy's name for D

F le mieux Benjamin Lee Guinness of Guinness brewery Bartholomew Vanhomrigh & Dick Whittington
letter, 24/9/26, to HSW: 'Antwerp I renamed Gnantwerp for I was devoured there by mosquitoes' (Lord-Mayors)
Moscow *I* cora: weir 2 Corry's pubs, D (ca. 1900) The Arch, pub, Henry St, D
L musca: fly Weir's pub, Burgh Quay, D
The Scotch House, pub, Burgh Quay, D *I* úbhall: apple *L* uva: grape
The Oval, pub, Middle Abbey St, D
L erat: it was *L* est: it is

Michael & Lucifer
L erit: it will be *L* non mihi sed lucifero: not to me but to the light-bringer
D motto: Obedientia civium urbis felicitas (Citizens' Obedience Is City's Happiness)

× 389.20: 'Ah, dearo, dear!' *L* dea: goddess
I a dhia: o god! *Book of Common Prayer:* Burial of the Dead: 'dust to dust'
Delphic oracle *I* nuin: letter N
(beginning with D & ending with N) ruinous
boast a) Phoenix Park

b) Guinness's Brewery

c) O'Connell Street

Gr (artificial) philohippikos: horse-loving paupers
hiccup *Gr* theos: god *L* bibosus: given to drinking

a) Belfast (shipbuilding industry) Jay Gould: Am. financier
GOLD
flaxy lass
flax (Belfast linen industry)
thunderbolts

sinful
Ulster Dial cope-curly: Orange (Ulster loyalists)
head over heels
cornucopia (launching)
Dial conny: canny
wedded b) Cork

'The Marsh': district of Cork
Sl on the mash: in constant pursuit of women

Da beundre: admire

'vineleaves in his hair' (*Hedda Gabler*) loof: palm of hand

(Blarney stone) SILVER c) Dublin *I* 'uise: well, indeed
soapstone: a variety of talc *pr* Speech is silver, silence is golden *Heb* isha: woman
AngI mavourneen: darling

Brooklyn
Brookline, Rathgar, D
Mansion House, D (Lord-Mayor's residence)
D noted for Leinster Lawn, Leinster House, D
Georgian architecture COPPER Irishtown, E. D district
Dublin, Georgia Irish whiskey (Power's Distillery, E. of
Guinness's Brewery, James's Gate (W. of Watling St) arrears Watling Street)

boose combative CEH
L erroribus: comparative battled
follies (abl. pl.) *ph* turning over a new leaf *AngI* more power to you (encouragement)
Power's Ir. whiskey
Atlanta, Georgia
Dublin, Georgia, on *r* Oconee
Da gaarden: the yard d) Galway

Spanish Place, Galway

Mayo, Sligo, Galway: Connacht counties
Tuam, Co. Galway
chub, dace: fish IRON

L aequalis: equal *s* The Bells of Shandon

& we'll on Christmas

Guinness a) North b) Shandon (Cathedral, Cork city)

AngI moy: plain (8 bells in Shandon Cathedral)
c) mills' money d) aequal
S *Da* hvad slags: what sort *AngI* Lochlann: Scandinavian *Da* rettan: serve up flasks
Da smussig: dirty
Da melk: milk vicious *Da* geit: goat *Da* fra tid til anden: from time to time
old man: overflow waste in pouring draught stout *RhSl* Jack & Jill: till
toothpick wastepaper basket

newspapers, tobacco & sweets

general: slavey, maid-of-all-work *Da* kirke: church *G* Fusstritt: kick
Ir. pubs used to be open on Sundays to bona-fide travellers only *Da* hjælp!: help!

burglars *Da* underholde: support *G* putzen: to clean
Luggelaw: lake, Wicklow Mts *Da* barnet: the child *s* The Croppy Boy *F* crotte: dung
F botte: boot *Da* glimtfyr: flashing beacon *Du* baas: master
Sl glim: a fire, a candle *Da* til: to *I* bás: death
Da kniv: knife

now & then *Du* thans: now *Da* sporvogn: tram
Du nieuws: news *Du* spoorwagon: railway carriage
Y.W.C.A.
X or Z: no Y (not young)
water closet

HEC *Da* skrive: write

Sl bacon: rustic *Da* begripe: understand *Da* Irer: Irishman
Da fullstendig: complete
Da jublende: exulting North Wall Quay, D bugger *G* kein: no
Jutlander Norwegian Joseph Biggar: hunchbacked supporter of Parnell
G ernst combative
earnings commission
professional drinkers abstain *Du* zondig: sinful

Ibsen: *Peer Gynt:* 'Han er faderligt sindet imod min Person;–men ökenom,–nej, det er han ikke!' ('He [God] is fatherly towards my little self, but economical–no, that He is not!') aleconner: inspector of ale

s Poor Ole Joe

K *s* (*U*.443): 'There's someone in the house with Dina'

Da tak: thank you Glory be to the Saints of God now &
I go leor: enough, plenty
parks
AngI clauber: mud from animals' feet
floor arse cunt
ashcan
maiden name *s* 'You are the honey–honeysuckle, I am the bee'
middle P/K (008.11ff.)
broke candles

L/R blackcurrant tomorrow Temora: Macpherson's name for Tara
After Black Monday massacre of D settlers by Ir. tribes at Cullenswood, Dubliners feasted there every anniversary to defy the Irish Gomorrah picnic
Primate of all Ireland

grackles: name for various birds of genus *Graculus* crackles sandwiches

ate

gooseberries

who let the cat steal the chop?

Kilkenny cats: 2 cats who fought until only their tails remained (used allusively)

Saint Luke

Da tak: thank you

parts society state

Janus: god of doors (January) *L* Februarius: 'the cleansing month'

car-man mushrooms (peak season September) black & blue

(dog-days of July) (touring: August, holiday month)

Gunpowder Plot (5 November) Christmas box (December)

F prés salés: salt marshes Donnybrook: district of D, had fair Roebuck: district of D

L pratum: meadow *L* campos: fields

L ager: field Crumlin: district of D Kimmage: district of D

Roundtown = Terenure, district of D

F champs: field Ashtown: district of D Cabra: district of D

Finglas: district of D

Santry: district of D Raheny: district of D

Baldoyle: district of D

L retro-: backwards

L conflingens: striking 1 thing against another

L vox: voice vaticination: inspired prophecy

L numen: authority *L* in nomine domine: in God's name

Gr daimôn: god

four

L misericordia: compassion

(574.31–2) The Dáil, seat of government, D (573.06–7)

12 apostles: Matthias, Thaddaeus, Simon the Canaanite, John, Simon Peter, Andrew, Bartholomew, Philip, James the son of Zebedee, Thomas, Matthew, James the son of Alphaeus

I Mór: great, the Great Jacques McCarthy (pron. Jakes): journalist of D *Evening Herald,* famous for wit

Murphy: any Irishman

Morpheus: god of sleep

how are you Maggy (111.16)

(14 linked phrases)

forlorn

(14 words forming a 'word-ladder': string of words each differing by 1 letter from the next)

G holen: get, fetch H . . . CE leap year

s Peg O' My Heart

⊕ panorama

flaws Alexander: *Space, Time & Deity* duty
flowers (discussed in Wyndham Lewis, *Time & Western Man*) gaiety
city planxty: Ir. harp tune GOAT weekends
time off
SHEEP Edward Moore: *The Gamester* II.2: 'rich beyond the dreams of avarice'

Hamlet, Prince of Denmark
Camelot: King Arthur's castle
future preterite (Latin grammar) *L* exanimatio: terror
suspended animation
exanimation: loss of consciousness (camel in .07) nearsighted
Matt 19:24: 'It is easier for a camel to go through the eye of a needle'
Copenhagen *L* ingrediens: entering
(rainbow) entrance/exit
Whigs existence
egregious
history *It* ricorso: recurring (Vico)

(Viconian cycle) (thunder)
As You Like It II.7.26–8: '& so from hour to hour we ripe & ripe/& then, from hour to hour,
eyes we rot & rot,/& thereby hangs a tale' ears
(marriage) (burial)
Hoel: father of Isolde of the White Hands
anon.
Roman watches of the night: Vespera, Conticinium, Concubium, Intempesta Nox, Gallicinium (evening, growing
even(ing) *s* Come Live with Me & Be My Love quiet, lying down, deepest
Nox: Roman goddess of night Lucan night, cock-crowing)
L lucens: shining
behold

pr One man's meat is another man's poison *F* poignées: handfuls *L* folium: leaf
Poyning's Law restricted Ir. Government
Nimb took Ossian to the Land of the Ever Young curly
L nimbus: cloud *L* nihil: nothing Galahad
wrestlers gain, lose
Jacob & Esau struggled in the womb (Gen 25:22)
Gr aster: star *G* starr: stiff Hengest & Horsa, brothers, led Saxon
invasion of England
Shem, Ham & Japhet: sons of Noah (gentiles eat pork)

rainbow fails falls

Yeats: *To the Rose upon the Rood of Time* rosered *G* gelb: yellow (rainbow colours) indigo
F orage: storm
stargazer

dreaming

kaleidoscope
collide or (e)scape
⊣ what's our lovematch
Rosseter: *s* 'What then is love but mourning, What Desire but a self-burning, Till she that hates doth love return'
AngI shee: fairy

Swift: 'Ppt'

Pro pitouet: young boy

It angiola: angel

vanity: dressingtable

jot

by my soul

F espèce Clancarthy footballer association
Pro espés: thick football
Du gast: guest
F pendre: to take
innkeeper mauler: one who wrestles for ball
when it is held over goal line
Hurling has 15 players a side Dagos: generic name for Spaniards
baiting: eating
Roger Boyle, Earl of Orrery eggcup egg & spoon race
awfully Baldoyle, district L/R accent
of D, has racecourse Eily O'Connor: heroine of Boucicault's *The Colleen Bawn*
Sp admiración: admiration

Prussians called ⚔ Waterloo 'La Belle Alliance'; centre of Fr. lines was La Belle Alliance Inn *Sp* soso: dull, insipid
& you must not *Sp* celoso: zealous, hot
Sp do: in *Sp* todo: all *nr* 'Come a little closer, said the spider to the fly'
pr moderation in everything please
Pro romeu: pilgrim *Romeo & Juliet* felt so tuckish
Pro jolio: jolly
reminds me exquisite
delicious

three halfpence Swift: 'Ppt'

let me *s* Come Back to Erin
ph pull one's leg

size in stockings

trousseau
trousers
VI.A.901: 'clothes extend personality'

garters

a million times (older than her)

Rev. Matthew Pilkington's wife was friend of Swift *L* quondam: at one time *Sl* fleshmonger:
Sl quoniam: cunt procurer, wencher

s Brown October Ale
a pox on it!
Shanks' pony: one's own legs as a means of conveyance air, water, earth, fire
frosty corncrake *F* terre
thanks ever (so much) your poor *Sl* tickler: penis
put him in my mouth

in birthday suit: naked *It* tutti i sensi: in full sense Isolde Blanchemains, blancmange

F tutu: short ballet skirt wife of Tristan mange

(When Isolde's adultry was discovered, she was maggies

given by Mark to lepers instead of being burnt, and was rescued by Tristan)

F fleur: flower

stomach

s Tea for Two

G Angst: fear

thanks so much

(003.09–10)

acquiescence make my acquaintance *Sl* codling:

Pro acqueste: this a raw youth

bicyclist

silence, exile & cunning

tears *Sp* pelele: man of straw, insignificant fellow

medlar: fruit eaten only when decayed

cheat

dancing once through & through

daughters

G übernehmen: take over hear

(060.26)

poetry Shakespeare

pastries

jaculation: action of hurling *Garden of the Soul:* a prayer book

Gregorian choral

Du of: whether *G* Leib: flesh

believe in immortality

struggle for life & the survival of the fittest often have

F causeries: discussions

The *New Freewoman* serialised *Portrait*; later called *The Egoist* & edited by Harriet Shaw Weaver, who donated large sums of money to J

surplice

AngI gentleman who pays the rent: pig pious

Bram Stoker: *Dracula* thrill

brimstone (hell)

keepsake fuss

for Christ's sake

curse you Solomon *PS* Bog: God

curfew

Sl have a banana: have sexual intercourse

godmother reason *It* riso: laugh
Pro risou: hedgehog

around Tristan (095.23) *Sl* puff: sodomist

assailing

vestry
Pro vèspre: evening

Sl phiz: countenance
Dean Swift

G Schwips: drunkenness bless us
Schweppes mineral waters
Belshazzar: last king of Babylon Sardanapalus: last king of Assyria
F sourd: deaf
associations

(age 21: possession of key of door)

Roman collars *Pro* gleisoun: church
what women call ours gleesome (glee: song)
nr 'Hushabye baby, in the tree top' La belle Isabeau: child prophet of Camisards Lancelot
Isa Bowman, friend of Lewis Carroll, played title in *Alice in Wonderland* adaptation luckless
Bow Bells

engineer

French College, Blackrock, Co. D my husband *F* nom d'un chien! (expletive)

Pro encò: home *L* ego te absolvo: I absolve you
Pro encho: tap, cock *Pro* tencho: tint, ink

ph please God!

Eros
heroes
King Mark desired Isolde after seeing one of her hairs

Diarmaid *F* mot
D Sl mott: girl

Grania

Sl pullet: young girl

Robert Prezioso: journalist who was attracted to Nora Joyce in Trieste
I mórán mó: much more

bye bye!

tree/stone *Da* grav: grave
Gladstone ('Grand Old Man')
hesitency *Da* ond mand: bad man *Pro* cigalo: cicada gigolo
It cigolìo: squeaking
love of Michael *G* Ich gehe dir vor: I will precede you
Pro fournigo: ant passdoor: door between stage & house in theatre

apron stage in Elizabethan theatre

angel/devil

F tête-à-tête hear hear! The Four Courts, D

F de tout au tout: entirely

The Old Sot's Hole, Essex Gate, D; a discussion there in 1757 led to the 'Commissioners for Wide Streets'

ph commit no nuisance Mick v. Nick *L* aves silvae: birds of the wood

L ave, salve, atque vale: hail, good health & farewell eight & twenty

L aquae vallis: waters of the valley *nr* Sing a Song of Sixpence: 'four & twenty blackbirds, baked into a pie'

arithmetic

eurhythmic: harmony

selftaught

ph in the name of God & all that's holy mistletoe

s The Holly & the Ivy

ivy *Du* hoest: cough ○ (28 names)

St Ives, town, Cornwall

I íde: thirst

St Ita: Irish, wrote religious poetry

I úna: famine *Gr* xenia: hospitality ('ph' & 'th' from Greek alphabet)

going in

confessed grasshoppers

comfort

absolution ant *R* pravda: truth penance mortal

L pravitas: deformity myrtle tree sacred to Venus (Blake)

nr Sing a Song of Sixpence: 'When the pie was opened, the birds began to sing'

nr Ring-a-ring o'roses

pr the wish is father to the thought

nomenclature

(nurse is chaperone) world

Charlemont Mall, D

Bellini: *Norma: s* Casta Diva ('pure goddess')

chaste *PS* chista diva: immaculate virgin

Sunday *F* amour

s 'In the gloaming, oh, my darling'

All Saints Church, Phibsborough Rd, D, has a dome St Andrew Undershaft: London church

sacred

underwear

underworld

Swift: 'Ppt'

Arch buss: kiss

Smock Alley Theatre, D *L* pudor: shame

It pupetta mia: my little darling

L lingua: tongue

lingo

Prezioso (146.31)

blackguard *It* silenzioso: silent

delicious isn't it bad for you? before you
baffling you
(003.09) *L* misi: I sent

darkness

(bat) *F* ennui: boredom, annoyance

duveteen: velveteen

princess dress: one in which lengths of bodice & skirt are cut in 1 piece
J.F. Molloy: *The Romance of the Irish Stage* (1897) II.230: in late C19 'a new dye was spoken of as the Rutland blue'
gone out of fashion

F chère: dear (both senses)
Ship St, D, orig. Sheep St

Isolde

conversation lozenges: sweets with inscribed words

Wordsworth: *Daffodils:* 'twinkle on the milky way'
jewels

'my intended': my fiancé

actor *F* expliquer
L auctor: creator
existence *Du* nieuw: new *Pro* nivoulan: cloudy sky
Pro nieu: cloud
Pro brinbrou: a commotion *Pro* troucho: trout
Brian Boru treacherous
Goths & Visigoths *Pro* gibo: a hump
give us *Pro* gibous: hunchbacked
Pro bosso: a hump Serafim
Saracen words in Provençal
Sw tron: throne *Pro* tron: thunderclap *Pro* alpin: Alpine
Iron *Pro* uiau: lightning
I canntal: sorrow close
Cantal: mt in Auvergne
chambermaid marvellous
mermaid
liar *G* liebst: dearest

G muss wissen: must know

tearstreaming

forbidden *G* Frucht: fruit
far better
Anglican marriage ceremony: 'With this ring I thee wed'

Sir Amory Tristram, 1st Earl of Howth *L* amor: love
I mórán mó: much more
George Colman the Younger: *Love Laughs at Locksmiths* so long as luck will last

^ Thomas Campbell: *s* 'Then came down to the beach a poor exile of Erin Ealing L/R
The dew on his robes was heavy & chill; For his country he sighed when at twilight repairing, To wander alone by the wind-beaten hill. But the day-star attracted his eye's sad devotion, For it rose on his own native isle of the ocean,
wake Where once, in the flow of his youthful emotion, He sang the bold anthem of Erin go bragh'
F rugir: to roar
s Brian O'Linn *Sl* maunder: ramble in speech *Sh* mislier: walker, tramp

AngI box & dice: used to denote the whole lot

F Dieu   *L* Dominum Nostrum: Our Lord   for something to eat
deaf & dumb

whimper
Quimper, town, Brittany
a blue Monday: one spent   flesh
away from work in dissipation
ph hook, line & sinker   devil

I Sinn Féin: We Ourselves (slogan)   *Sl* shinner: member of Sinn Féin, Ir. nationalist movement
begged you to save his immortal . . . soul
schoolmastered   how d'you do?

J.H. Voss: 'wine, women & song'
homemade

No, thank you!   bolshevism

wax   (earwig)

ph begging the question

hesitency

time

G Blickpunkt: point of view

specialist   *G* Schotte: Scot

Gr sophologia: wise speech   Wyndham Lewis: *Time & Western Man:* 'Bergson had said that the intellect "spatialized" things. It was that "spatialization" that the doctrinaire of motion & of mental "time" attacked'
Demiurge   *F* cache-cache: hide & seek

ph for the nonce
nonsense   Fairy Godmother
misfortune   Proust: *À la Recherche du temps perdu* (*temps perdu* = lost time)
last time
F recherché

D.B.C.: Dublin Bread Company
*U.*248: 'We call it D.B.C. because they have damn bad cakes'
behaviourist psychology   *F* pailleté: spangled   homemade

D.B.C.

s There's Hair Like Wire Coming out of the Empire
G der Erzherr: the arch-lord   Einstein
clumsily
surrogate
sorrow gate
Gerald Griffin: *Talis qualis*
L qualis . . . talis: as . . . so

Harrogate: town, Yorkshire   arrogate: to ascribe to another without just reason
case

L talis: such, such like, this   persons   *L* passim: in every part
passions
Quantum theory: theory that energy in radiation is discharged in discrete units, quanta   tantalizing
L tantum . . . quantum: so much . . . as

L talis: such, such like, this optimism/pessimism

Sl a three cold Irish: three pennyworth of Ir. whiskey & cold water

tiptoe *F* à la sourdine: on the sly if you please?
to a sardine
Bulwer-Lytton: 'pen is mightier than the sword' Criterion Theatre, London
It tal dei tali: Mr So-&-so
(Shem the Penman) no, thank you!

Daily Mail, newspaper

Lewis & his followers called themselves Vorticists
postmortem police investigation
Postvorta: goddess of childbirth
L fustigo: to cudgel to death
determinism: doctrine of necessary causation chain determining everything
Spinoza, who lived in The Hague, used term 'extension'

scissors Drs (doctorandus): Dutch academic title
Caesars *Du* als het U belieft: if you please *Du* beleefd: polite

G Vater *G* Macht: might, power *G* Gedanke: thought Stuttgart (Hegel born there)
as a matter of fact *Du* dank je: thank you wetting his whistle
tersely coarsely *G* weil du bist ein Sohn der Welt: because you are a son of the world *Du* zoon: son
hoarsely son of a whore

L qualis: of such a sort

Professor Lucien Lévy-Bruehl, anthropologist
G Loewe: lion *G* bruellen: to roar
Shalmaneser V, king of Assyria, carried the Israelites into captivity. He was followed by Sennacherib, who invaded Judah

R.L. Stevenson: *Dr Jekyll & Mr Hyde*
shekel: chief silver coin of Hebrews
L toto coelo: by the whole heaven

Jerry
gone to Jericho: gone no one knows where; also, to have been drunk
Kevin Cavan
sent to Coventry: ostracized

pr diamonds cut diamonds

Leonine convention: one made on terms 'that one should take all the profits & another bear all the loss'; held by Cassius not to be binding
Lewis in *Time & Western Man* says that *U.* tells us nothing about Jews & criticises Stephen for 'trying to be a gentleman'
Gentile/Jew
Wilde on fox hunters: 'The unspeakable in full pursuit of the uneatable'
G Feigenbaum: fig tree *G* Blatt: leaf
Budapest 5688 Anno Mundi = A.D. 1927: date of *Time & Western Man* *G* Jude: jew
Merchant of Venice I.3.109: 'spit upon my Jewish gaberdine'
doughty

pr All's well that ends well (time)
Darwin: *The Descent of Man*
obscurity fire escape (388.03)
It faro: lighthouse

Gr têle-: afar

refrangible: capable of being refracted
Pythagoras' Theorem: the square on the hypotenuse equals the sum of the squares on the other 2 sides

CE . . . H

onus microcosm: man as an epitome of the universe

radio

R manda: cunt *s* Sweet Molly Malone: 'In Dublin's fair city'
L feracitas: fruitfulness veracity
Farinelli: castrato singer with great power of breath retention anthropology
L ob: before

school of thinkers *G* Spengler: tinsmith
L schola: place of learning Oswald Spengler: *The Decline of the West* (used much in *Time & Western Man*)
F queue C4 revolt of Volscians was subdued by Rome
F parce que revulsion
toes Levy-Bruehl F.D.: Fidei Defensor (defender of the faith)
It brullo: bare

G eitel: vain
Saxe-Weimar-Eisenach: grand duchy, Thuringia
Nuremberg egg: early watch, globular shape (joke of absent-minded professor who holds egg in hand & boils watch) Lewis: *The Childermass* (1928) 150: 'your witch's cauldron, Time'
upon the other ostensibly *ph* the pot calling the kettle black
1549: Robert Ket's rebellion boiling
square feet

couple of

Thomas Tompion, watchmaker, invented the deadbeat escapement
HC . . . E
Du het: it *G* Mitleid: pity accordance

Malory: *Morte d'Arthur* Tara: ancient capital of Ireland purest common or garden
mortadella: type of sausage tradition

Book of Taliessin: C6 Welsh poetry overcast
retaliation *Sl* loos-wallah: rascal, thief *Sl* bolo the bat: speak the language
take heed Lewis Waller played Satan in adaptation of Marie Corelli's *The Sorrows of Satan* bowl *The Tyro:* review edited by Wyndham Lewis, 1921–2
Moore: *s* Let Erin Remember the Days of Old: 'When Malachy wore the collar of gold' *Gr* tyros: cheese
It tiratore: shot, marksman Mulligan (*U.*)

specific gravities deglutible: capable of being swallowed *L* lapsus linguae: slip of the tongue

liquor associated *The Royal George* sank in 1782; Cowper wrote poem about it
The Royal Gorge: canyon, Colorado
Gr pneuma: breath *Gr* dipsios: thirsty

G Meinung: opinion Myrrdin = Merlin, in early Welsh accounts
F Merde alors!
General Cambronne: famous for using word *merde* in public Levy-Bruehl
Giraldus Cambrensis: wrote on Ireland in C12 Wyndham Lewis
G Brille: spectacles
F.D.: Fidei Defensor (defender of the faith)
ph stuff & rubbish melodic melodeon
melodramatic
candour *L* quando: when *G* Dank
pr One man's meat is another man's poison *Du* denk je?: do you think?
pr all's fair in love & war

arse are
s Pretty Molly Brannigan: 'The place where my heart was you'd aisy roll a turnip in'
ring true two-three several popes named Innocent

s The Holly & the Ivy
honey in his hives

'my dear little brothers Little Britain: Brittany
in Christ' (*Portrait* III) brats
Cadwan, Cadwallon & Cadwalloner: kings of ancient Wales

expletive: serving to fill out *L* sermo: speech
explicit
middleclass

lessons etcetera
Cicero (oration)
Bruno of Nola

Japanese *F* javanais: cant in which extra syllables inserted into words
Javanese: of Java
in Eng. public schools, older & younger
pupils with same surname called 'N Major' & 'N Minor'
Litany of Saints: 'Christe, audi nos. Christe, exaudi nos' ('Christ, hear us. Christ, graciously hear us')
Jupiter
Aesop's fable of the Fox & the Grapes

ladies & gentlemen semicolons hyphens

highbreds & lowbreds

G eins Butler: *Erewhon* (nowhere)
'Once upon a time and a very good time it was there was a moocow' (*Portrait* I) *G* wohnen: live
Du er woonde eens: there once lived
G einsam: lonely all too lonely *Gr* archôn: ruler
bloody awful *s* A Frog He Would A-wooing Go: 'gammon & spinach Heigh ho! says Anthony
Rowley' *pr* Hood maketh not frere (487.21)

flabellum: fan of ostrich feathers carried on either side of pope's chair in procession
L pilleolus: skull cap (formerly worn by prelates) vaticinated: prophesied
depilated vacated
pallium: vestment worn by R.C. patriarchs *F* impermeable: raincoat

The Harp & Crown: C18 D pub

Prophecies of St Malachy, no. 5: 'De rure albo' ('of the white Ibsen: *The Master Builder*
country')–refers to Pope Adrian IV so-called because chockfull
Borgia popes Villa Borghese, Rome Pentecost
gorgeously laid out *It* cascata: waterfall
Pinacoteca: art gallery in Vatican Catacombs *We* Caerludd: London
L hortus: garden aqueducts orthodox (Ludd's town)
It a spasso: (to go for) a walk Voltaire: *Candide*: 'best of all possible worlds'
pr business is business worst
F pensable: conceivable

s The Minstrel Boy: 'His father's sword he has girded on' *It* lancia spezzata: lit. 'broken lance'; a prince's
bodyguard
heels

Nicholas Breakspear: Englishman, became Pope Adrian IV & granted Ireland to Henry II in his
bull *Laudabiliter* thinking
treetop *King Lear* IV.6.109: 'every inch a king'
(triple crown of the pope)
Gr pentas: 5 parsec: unit of interstellar distance

asylum St John Lateran, cathedral, Rome There were 5 Oecumenical Councils of Lateran
Azylian culture in the Mesolithic Shem Shaun lantern

St Nicholas Without-the-Walls, D *L* secundum: according to 111

Prophecies of St Malachy, collection of 111 Latin phrases applying to the popes from Celestine II to the last pope ALP *L* amnis limina permanent: the bounds of the river remain

F colline: hill dubbing *Gr* nun ôn: ever present
AngI colleen: girl
Ninon de Lenclos: C17 Fr courtesan

G rinnen: to run ALP

s 'Ha, ha, ha, He, he, he, Little brown jug don't I love thee'
I donn: brown brown stream

perched *Du* olm: elm tree

Sl fit to be tied: furious

deuce

nearly *It* polpa: flesh, pulp

changing colour other forgetting

disdain *L* frons: forehead; leaf
design
forgiving backside
Wyndham Lewis: *The Caliph's Design, Architects! Where's Your Vortex?*
F cul de pompe: pompous arse specious: beautiful, but of little value
heavens believed
L Optimus Maximus: Best & Greatest (epithet of Jupiter) *G* Bruder: brother

-in-law

Pope Adrian IV new assumed name stuck still

vis-à-vis *L* accessit: he approached Aurignacian culture in upper Paleolithic
Sl phiz: countenance indignation
All roads East or West
auster: South
waterways *pr* All roads lead to Rome *Heb* sor: stone
G Raum: space *L* hic: this he saw
L illud: that one *L* hoc: this Peter *G* satt: full in state

G Popo: buttocks acclimatation = acclimatization
pope preposterously
thereupon infallible encyclical
G Unfall: accident
Wilde on fox hunting: 'The unspeakable in full pursuit of the uneatable' *F* ouest: West amethyst *Gr* athemistos: illicit, illegitimate
patriarch *G* Wüste: desert
Pope St Deusdedit, 615–18
Prophecies of St Malachy, no. 86: 'Bellua insatiabilis' ('insatiable beast')–Innocent XI
ph cheek by jowl Fisherman's Ring: pope's ring of investiture *F* blaque: pouch
jewel Giordano Bruno: *Il Spaccio di Bestia Trionfante*
day wallet Wallace collection of paintings, London (in Hertford House)
It addetto: assigned (to a service)
the longer he thought *G* Vetter: cousin Father, Son & Holy Ghost
G fett: fat, rich *G* Summe: sum
Heb micah: prophet (also an Old Testament book) laic: secular, lay
5 popes named 'Sixtus'

13 popes named 'Leo' 45

F bon appetit
good hap betide us!
maudlin Magdelenian culture in upper Paleolithic
whig (tory at .26) Magdalen College, Oxford

AngI within the bawl of an ass: too near 'pray for . . . intentions' (R.C.)

Scottish Dial. tod lowrie: familiar name for the fox *L* rarum: few *L* rerum omnium: of all things
L ominosum: ominous pleased
Mousterian culture in middle Paleolithic
master mouse
It Santità: (your) Holiness Anna Livia (196.02–4)
F aulne: alder *Gr* lithos: stone

also

It miserandissimo: most pitiful *L* retempto: I try again

bellowed Pope Telesphorus 125–136 *L* concionator: preacher
papal bull *Gr* telesphoros: efficacious
Gr sussômos: united in 1 body
Pope Sisinnius 708 *Gr* zôsimos: capable of living
Robenhausian culture Pope Zosimus, 417–18 *L* Mus: mouse
houses Tardenoisian culture in Mesolithic noise
pr You cannot make a silken purse out of a sow's ear Wyndham Lewis edited magazine 'BLAST'
noose mouse
anathema *L* inferioribus: from the dead *Prophecies of St Malachy,* no. 93: 'Animal rurale' ('rustic beast')–Benedict XIV
L Pontifex Maximus: high priest; pope baldaquin: canopy over altar
F poncif: unoriginal artistic subject *U.*40: 'Get down, bald poll!' (Joachim Abbas)
Matt 16:23: 'Get thee behind me, Satan' *G* Rotz: snot
satrap: subordinate ruler *Du* rots: rock

wine

by the way timepiece please
time/space *L* pace: by leave

F figurez-vous ça!: imagine that!
Index Librorum Prohibitorum Achille Ratti became Pius XI
index finger *G* Mund Achilles tendon *Gr* obolos: a coin, money given to church
mind *Gr* achilleios periodos: 2nd Paleolithic period worship
G Nase: nose
Nazarenes: an early Jewish-Christian sect
Various popes were called Clement, Urban, Eugenius & Celestian formous: beautiful, comely
urbane Pope Formosus
Pope Gregory (several) *L* quota hora est?: what's the time?

Adrian IV's bull *Laudabiliter,* granting Ireland to Henry II
audibility
Barbarossa: German emperor who opposed Adrian IV; also a kind of grape *Du* oorlog: war *Gr* eirênê: peace
Thor was also called Orlögg
beaten *F* rousse: russet *F* horloge: clock
Beeton: town eaten up by Los Angeles
well, sir?
sour grapes
2-dimensional

L fuerit: shall it be?
Sp Como?: How?, What do you say?
L sancta patientia: holy patience

It dial culla vosellina: little voice

rhyme reasons Canossa, where Henry IV humbled himself before Gregory VII

cannot

wanhope: dispair I shall also bound be, well so thou too sez it temple *Laudabiliter*

velocity is two feet in one second stocking
G stockend: hesitatingly
special *L* in excelsis: in the highest bellow *L* ab ovo: from the egg
spatial below above
Pope Honorius (several) (nearly fell off tree)
holiness

J's father from Cork but sodawater

what o'clock it is

I teampal: church *Prophecies of St Malachy*, no.11: 'sus in cribro' ('sow in a sieve')–Urban III (who was exiled) *L* semper: always *D Annals*, 1286: all D citizens excommunicated
It tugurio: hut Turkey divided into Turkey-in-Europe for encroaching on the ecclesiastical rights & Turkey-in-Asia New Rome = Constantinople
believing *Da* blivende: lasting Leo IV fortified Vatican Lyon
Leonine City: area around Vatican Lion is Zurich's heraldic animal

elocution pontifically
L consistorium: assembly place pompously
Constantine: Roman Emperor Archbishop Thomas Cranmer burned at stake *Sl* crammer: lie
converted to Christianity concluded *MGr* krima: judgement, punishment, offence
shipwrecked

Wilde to Douglas (in *De Profundis*): 'but I met you either too late or too soon'
nowhere so early
(.04)

decretals: the collection of papal decrees forming canon law 'Our Father' (Lord's Prayer)
Shaw: *Widowers' Houses* (Mark 12:40) *Arch* halidom: holy place, sanctuary
ph safe as houses
(Act of Union of Great Britain & Ireland, 1800) paresis: incomplete paralysis
F tu sais Union Jack (*Laudabiliter*) yoke *MGr* parisos: equal Paris
Prophecies of St Malachy, no. 101: 'Crux de Cruce' praises
('Cross from a Cross')–Pius IX perishes in Paris
(pressing grapes into wine) present

wait a moment *G* mein Gott! *G* mein gut gospel
Wyndham Lewis: *The Enemy* (journal)
Lewis: *Constantinople Our Star* voluminous
Lewis: *Enemy of the Stars* fulminous: pertaining to thunder & lightning
'Quas primas': beginning of an argument in the *Summa*
Caddy/Primas (014.12) compote: fruit preserved in syrup
L fructus: profit, fruit

G Pein: pain *G* Blick: glance (153.28)
point
almighty ceiling Lucky Strikes blood *Da* ild: fire would-be
It cielo: sky (cigarettes) blue milk (215.06–7)
satellites star cluster stirabout: a kind of porridge *Da* Lucia lys: St Lucia's light
It santo: saint *It* scintilla: spark Maple's Hotel, D *It* lucciole: firefly
St Madeleine Sophie Barat founded Congregation of Sacred Heart gathered
together odd dozens odds & ends *Da* Graesk: Greek Greek, Latin, Russian
docent: teaching volumes *Sh* gresko: voice Churches
Rosicrucian Last pair of prolegs (caterpillars' abdominal legs) form claspers
prologues
waterproof

hundred *G* drei-und-dreissig: 33 *R* vremya: time *F* tu cesses: you stop
F vraiment, tu sais
Nick/Mick *Gr* alôpêx: fox
5 popes named 'Nicholas' Aloysius: J's saint's name
proper number Euclid
L nomen: name *L* nimbus: cloud
Anaxagoras, philosopher Erasmus
inexact Mommsen: wrote Roman history
Arminius: Dutch theologian *Prophecies of St Malachy*
Anacletus the Jew: 3rd pope, 76–78
Capponi: enormous collection of documents on Church history

Ippolito Aldobrandini became Pope Clemens VIII & ordered Bruno's execution
formalin: preservative

G sondern: but *L* alter: the other over

Binomial Theorem
diorama: partly translucent picture changing with direction of light
Punic Wars R.H. Barham: *Ingoldsby Legends*

Du hoop: crowd lessons of experience
F blesser: to wound
L judicans: judging Pontius Pilate manuscripts
Egyptian mummy
junkroom *Egyptian Book of the Dead* xxxvi: 'The Chapter of Knowing the Chapters of Coming Forth [by Day] in a single Chapter'
fox, cunning
dictated letter to FB: 'All the grotesque words procession of holy ghost (see .18)
in this are in russian or greek for the three principal dogmas which separate Shem from Shaun. When he gets A & B on to his lap C slips off & when he has C & A he loses hold of B' procession of Holy Ghost
Gr diplous: doubly *L* ipso facto

L sed contra: but, in contradiction all but succeeded
R raskol: schism
Monophysite heresy that there is only 1 nature in Jesus; subsect of Byzantine Church
R sobor: cathedral subordinates as often as
Gr sêmeion: identifying mark *It* buccinare: blow (the trumpet)
G nakt: naked combine
Gr syllepsis: conception *Gr* aspilos: immaculate *Gr* porizô: to originate
Gr archê: beginning *Gr* poreia: march, procession
Gr hagion pneuma: Holy Ghost *Gr* synerethizô: excite mutually synthesise *R* proshestvie svyatogo dukha: procession of Holy Ghost
loggerheads *Gr* sakellarioi: ecclesiastical dignitaries
logothetes: functionaries under Byzantine emperors
found *Gr* sympôleô: to sell together

R papskii: papal *R* nepogreshimost: infallibility

L Filioque: & the Son (The Great Schism between Eastern & Western Churches arose through 'Filioque' controversy over procession of Holy Ghost from Father & Son or from Father alone)
Da efter: after years *L* con: with (read, know) (sheepskin parchment books)
blind (drawn) said Pope Pius (several)
We encyd: space
We amser: time Pope Gregory (several)
answered gregarious
god of Mohammed
sheep/goat
AngI bothered: deaf

Matt 19:30: 'the last shall be first' (date)
Henry King: *The Exequy*: 'Stay for me there; I will not faile / To meet thee in that hollow Vale'
Valhalla (heroes chosen from slain & taken there by Valkyrie) observed Act of Union unicorn
L unicum: unparalleled
Elijah the pope's address or blessing: 'Urbi et Orbi' ('To the City & the World')
Elizabeth I (1st statute: Act of Supremacy) constabulary stable *L* stabulum: dwelling, tavern (papal ring & robe)
bless them
passim
Yardley's perfumes Army Cut cigarettes
Bond St, London
Macaulay: *Review of Ranke's History of the Popes:* 'She [the R.C. church] may still exist in undiminished vigour when some traveller from New Zealand shall, in the midst of a vast solitude, take his stand on a broken arch of London Bridge to sketch the ruins of St Paul's'

confessed

(date) Valhalla

43rd statute of Elizabeth: Poor Relief Act, 1601 perfect
Egyptian Book of the Dead XLIII: 'The Chapter of Not Letting the Head of a Man be Cut off . . .
G unsichtbar: invisible embouchure: arrangement of lips &c. for producing a musical tone
unsightly ambusher (bad breath)
F haleine: breath current adverts: 'it could have been a lovely evening if . . . '
houri: nymph of Mohammedan paradise

vituperated Viterbo, papal residence in Italy *Prophecies of St Malachy*, no. 98: 'Canis et coluber'
G weiter: further berated ('dog & serpent')–Leo XII
'Asphalt' (11th E.B.): 'The solid or semi-solid kinds of bitumen were termed *asphaltos* by the Greeks: & by some ancient writers the name of *pissasphaltum* was also sometimes employed'
eunuch unicorn *It* un corno!: fuck you!
I chorn: horn
L ungula: hoof, claw

I ubh: egg
L uvula: grape
AngI usquebaugh: whiskey

wilfully

It nuvoletta: little cloud Sistine Chapel (Vatican)
nightdress sixteen summers
banisters

frightened shoulders

G Glaube: belief *G* Hochzeit: wedding *Arch* welkin: sky
(raised sky-high his walkingstick, 155.23–4)
overcast *G* Zweifel: doubt *Sl* acting the mick: playing the fool

Paul Moore: *s* 'Tis the Last Rose of Summer: 'All her lovely companions'
balls *It* nubi: cloud

(squirrels hibernate) *Sl* mivvy: woman

G erst: first first quarter (lunation)
moon *G* Fürst: prince
(28-day cycle) father Scandinavian Norwood: district of London

soda parlour Viking's blancmanage Relish

H . . . C . . . E

Latria: the supreme worship due to God alone
constellations emanations of Ain-Soph, 10 Sephiroth (Kabbala cf. 261.23)
far

Gr adiaptôtos: infallible

systematically Old Catholics changed doctrine on auricular
schismatically confession
L ens: a being *Love's Labour's Lost*

It nuvoluccia: little cloud *Gr* Theotokos: Mother of God (Virgin Mary)

Gr gnôsis: knowledge *Prophecies of St Malachy:* 'Fides intrepida' ('intrepid faith')– boundless curiosity
curia: Papal court a future pontiff
(conclave of cardinals to elect a new pope, at the end of which they burn the ballot papers) Heliogabalus & Commodus: Roman emperors
H . . . C . . . E
Enobarbus: character in *Antony & Cleopatra*

G Rauch: smoke *G* Buchstaben: letters of alphabet
papyri
L spiratio: breath duplicate
separate
such

It sfumato: hazy *It* stella: star *F* la princesse de la Petite Bretagne

Isolde of the White Hands was princess of Brittany (Little Britain) *F* mignon: dainty

Mrs. Cornwallis-West (Mrs Patrick Campbell), actress
West Cornwall (Tristan story)
(Isolde of Ireland)

Tristan L tristis, tristior, tristissimus: sad, sadder, saddest
It madonnina: demure young lady

dogmatic *It* accanito: dogged, ruthless *L* canis: dog
mad dog Queen Victoria: 'We are not amused'
Dublin boozed Catholic dog/cat painfully oblivious
Gr bous: ox
G Männer

G seufzen: to sigh

s The Green Grass Grew All Around *L* arundo: reed *L* in medias res: into the midst of a subject (epic convention)
G vergrossern: to enlarge The reeds repeated that King Midas had ass's ears
glitter Gripes Mookse
Book of Common Prayer: Burial of the Dead: creeping
'ashes to ashes, dust to dust'

Voltaire: *Candide:* 'best of all possible worlds' *Gr/L* (artificial) metamnisia: land beyond the river
worst all soon one uniform brown
F brune either Spain or *I* an: the *F* eau Holland *L* nemorosus: wooded
Citherior ('hither') Spain: Roman province, N. Spain *It* spiano: open space, plain
Browne . . . Nolan (German word order)

years

Da tung og træt: heavy & tired

death

Ondt (414.20) Wilde: *De Profundis* morrow

escape Christ grace
Arch grice: steps
Gracehoper (414.21)

Luke 1:28: 'Ave Maria, gratia plena, Dominus tecum' ('Hail Mary, full of grace, the Lord is with thee') grassy plain
It dormi!: sleep! *F* adieu
F Dieu

G wecken: wake up *F* parapluie
F par la pluie

Wilde: *A Woman of No Importance*

Song of Sol 1:5: 'black but comely' (.33) children

his holiness *F* mot *F* amour
metamorphosis

Prophecies of St Malachy, no. 97: 'Aquila Rapax' ('rapacious eagle')–Pius VII
that is hight (called)
butcher's apron (213.26)

F il avait raison

hank of rope &c.
(since he resembled handkerchief, 213.28)
Gr ton panike autochthon: the panicstricken aboriginal
We angeu: death
We cariad: love beatitudes

shieling: hut on a piece of cattle-grazing pasture   *Prophecies of St Malachy*, no. 74: 'De Rore Coeli' ('Of heavenly manna') --Urban VII   'got wrong' is lit. trans. of *Da* fik uret (was wrong)

poll: cut off top or branches of a tree   Paul & Peter tree/stone   *F* piètre: mediocre, feeble

F pierre stone/tree   sierra   *F* saule: polled willow   Saul became Paul after conversion   alas

*U.*205: '–A myriadminded man, Mr Best reminded. Coleridge called him myriadminded'

engagements   banisters

F nuée: rain cloud   nightdress

years

Du stout: naughty   married name

r Liffey   single

r Mississippi   *L* singultus: sobbing

Ivan Krylov: Russian fabulist

commonplace   Hope Bros; Harrods: London department stores

leap year   laughing

broke   *G* Weh, O weh: woe is me

s 'Ha, ha, ha, He, he, he, Little brown jug don't I love thee'

sorry to be going

It basta!: stop it!   *OE* Romescot: papal tax of 1 penny per household

rattlesnake

L diu cursus: long race

in due course

in Eng. public schools, older & younger pupils with same surname called 'N Major' & 'N Minor'

Bruno of Nola   Jupiter

reasons   excess   assure

much more

sympathy   Tennyson: *Charge of the Light Brigade:* 'Half a league onward'

Gr syn bathos: with depth   *It* gnocco: dullard   Jim   smallpox   *pr* half a loaf is better than none

letter, 14/8/27, to HSW: 'an "ever devoted friend" (so his letters are signed) . . . the appelation "darling X" has also been addressed to me who am hopelessly given to the use of signorial titles' (is discussing Lewis in I.6)

R khorosho: well, good   *L* ambo: both

D Horse Show

I Baile Átha Cliath: Hurdle Ford Town (D)   St Cyril & St Methodius: apostles to the Eastern Church

bally clever   Balaclava (Light Brigade)   awful careless

St Theobald: anchorite

G Bild: picture

Charge of the Light Brigade   According to Colum, Lewis was always telling J he should go to S. America

Bartholomew's Handy Reference Atlas of the World, 10th ed., says Tristan da Cunha has 105 inhabitants   Isle of Man

Inaccessible: small island near Tristan da Cunha

Moore: *s* The Meeting of the Waters   by the way, reminds me

umbrella pine (conifer)

shelter belt (forestry)   true service tree *Sorbus domestica*

bowels weeping beech: *Fagus sylvatica* *L* picea: spruce fir *L* tilia: lime tree
Weeping Bitch (Canicula): medieval folk tale concerning transformation of girl into bitch
cricketbat willow: *Salix caerulea*

Norsemen

reflect *Du* nat: wet sweet gum tree,
butternuts (from N. Am. white walnut tree) *Liquidamber styraciflua*
manna ash: *Fraxinus ornus* etcetera *It* edera: ivy prevalent
red cedar
hawthorns Curragh Chase Wood, Co. Limerick plane tree
Howth Curragh of Kildare, racecourse *ph* as plain as a pikestaff
larch pine
'lodgepole pine', *Pinus contorta* terra-cotta
pinacotheca: art gallery Paul Rubens composed *Under the Deodar* (tree, *Cedrus deodara*) *L* pingere: to paint
Verney: Fr. painter raspberry, *Rubus* *ph* dear dirty Dublin tinctured
G Stand: condition *L* verni rubeus: russet-leaved habit
pure stand of timber (forestry): trees growing in seclusion from other species

elevation
L olivetum: olive grove
ECH Old Conna Hill, nr Bray *I* conadh: firewood False-Acacia: *Robinia pseudacacia*
Acacians: followers of Acacius, bishop of Cesarea, or Acasius, patriarch of Constantinople
sallow: willow history
L vox populi: voice of the people *L* nux: nut *L* populus: poplar hickory tree
nr Hickery Dickery Dock Arbor vitae: an evergreen, genus *Thuja*
aqua vitae: brandy
mourn elm alder tree
F aune: alder
Gr dikaios: just O.K.
whitebeam tree *J* daikyō: scoundrel

Jonah
Daniel Jones: *An English Pronouncing Dictionary*
whale's belly barefaced robber

L laetificatio: gladdening *Gr* sidêro: iron dromite: kind of meteorite
edification *L* sidereus: starry (meteorites often contain iron)
Lewis said that *Circe* was indebted to his *Enemy of the Stars* *U.*734: 'the apathy of the stars' (after urination in Bloom's back garden)
iron

falter throat

Moore & Burgess minstrels
murmur
voices overheard

Belfast Cork coalscuttle is full of Dublin
G Faust: fist (red hand of Ulster) *U.*510: 'behind the coalscuttle . . . the bearded figure of Mananaan MacLir'
West (Galway) whatnot: stand with shelves
Dial beyind: beyond
sick of each other Faust of *It* sconosciuto: unknown
ph thick as thieves
Es S estas preter la tapiŝo malgranda. Li legas al si en sia ĉambro. Kelkefoje funkcias, kelkefoje ŝrumpas ŝultrojn. Hodiaŭ kiel vi fartas, mia nigra sinjoro?: S is beyond the small carpet. He reads to himself in his room. Sometimes functions, sometimes shrinks shoulders. Today how are you doing, my black sir?

point of view

trying all fours feebleminded

ablebodied

recall with a great pleasure

newspaper correspondance columns: 'may I trespass on your space'

'fools rush in where angels fear to tread' (Pope) myself
Michaelangelo St Michael (Mick)
satisfaction *F* sottise: nonsense object *L* quicquid: whoever
so! 'tis fiction
It ciondolone: idler, lounger hypothecated: mortgaged *G* Bettler: beggar
hypothesised *G* Übermensch
pastime

(you)

grade of *pr* Time is money
degraded

dogmas of Origen
Darwin: *Origin of Species*
L spurios: bastards

cheese

Brutus & Cassius
F beurre caseous: cheesy simultaneously
Gr sys: together shoulder to shoulder
sailor soldier
s Love's Old Sweet Song: 'Once in the dear dead days beyond recall'
by & by
Primas (014.12)

grease *G* Stoff: stuff
grace milksops
regicide
L risus: laugh absolutely unadulterated
obviously reverse
caseous: cheesy
choice means butter
cheese
rival *G* Käse: cheese
F arriviste: ambitious person
jealous can possibly be

selfsame Roman history *U.*102: 'Same old six and eightpence' hide & seek
(i.e. unchanged)
preparatory

s Polly Put the Kettle On
Du op: up *G* Mutti: mummy
(ingredients in salad) *L* acetum: vinegar *L* oleosus: oily *F* sel: salt
L eheu: alas
sal volatile: smelling salts paprika Old Parr: Eng. centenarian accused of incontinence
L petrus: stone whole
saladbowl *G* Pfarrer: parson salmon

sprig *G* Petersilie: parsley

Morphios (142.29) Capel St, D
Sl Murphy: potato caper: type of bud used in pickling
Leticia Greene *s* Greensleeves
lettuce
(theory of Bacon writing Shakespeare's plays)
pr Handsome is as handsome does
pr Many a slip betwixt cup & lip chewing

course schools

Borgia motto: 'Aut Caesar aut nihil', from Suetonius, *Caligula* 37: 'Aut Caesar aut nullus' ('either Caesar or no-one') outknowledged

Caesars sizar: at Trinity College, D, a student receiving college allowance up to a certain age

unbearable *F* fromage composer Verdi: *La Forza del Destino*
F beurre Caesar assassinated before he
(thunder beginning Vico's first age) made himself king, as tyranni-
trumpet triple cide was a lesser crime than
It pieno: full *G* Fürst: prince duke regicide
pianoforte joke
Caesar killed by knives duly
cat of nine lives
commentary

F souffler: to blow South Sea Bubble: scheme inaugurated 1720 to take up the National Debt by trade with
the South Seas, but which collapsed the same year *Sl* bubble: a dupe, gullible person
Sandhurst: Eng. military academy champagne
campaign
G Krieg *F* frère
ph flat as a pancake built
reappearance new neck-&-neck

F champ de bataille: battlefield cursory
F bouteilles: bottles
Persse O'Reilly Hosty (040.21) Finn MacCool
Ural Mts history
(i.e. name *champ de* *L* nomen: name *U.*13: 'collector of prepuces'
bouteilles) *N* propp: *L* numen: divine will *L* colluctatio: contest prefaces
Elamite cork permitting connoisseur *F* coucou: Corsican upstart (Napoleon)
sunkuk: king *F* permiennes: Permians, Finnish tribe cuckoo Caucasian offspring
son of a gun P/K certain Tobol'sk: old Siberian town *It* ostia: the Host
Satan *L* ostia: entrances *Fi* for 'I don't come' is lit. Ostiak Vogul: district in Siberia; Ostiak & Vogul
('cunt of Virgin Mary') 'I deny the fact of coming' deny wanting languages

wanting to waste paint
West Point: U.S. military academy
painter's wash *ph* man alive! no nonsense *Hu* onson: in my dream
Fi & *Hu* inessive case, *F* mort Mordvin: a Finno-Ugric language *F* live: Livonian
also called 'locative' *L* in esse: actual *L* in posse: possible *Hu* kéz: hand
G essen: to eat *ph* easy as kissing hands *Hu* három: 3
interlocutor *F* con: cunt hussy
Hu ház: house
husband in her house *F* avoir quelqu'un dans le nez: dislike someone strongly
has-been *Hu* házban: in the house
sort of a cavalier richly roundhead
caviller: one who raises frivolous objections
soft *L* Fidei Defensor: defender of the faith *L* lac: milk lack
Thoth *Arch* thoft: thought *F* lac: lake
wisdom tooth *F* dent laughter *Da* lofter: lofts, ceilings
(bumps on head indicating wisdom to phrenologist)
Fi onni: luck, happiness, fortune *Fi* linnut: birds *F* tête de linotte: scatterbrain
Fi vesi: water (milk tooth) *Fi* unin: stove linnets
onion Union of Eng. & Ir., 1800 *Da* og: & low *Selkup Samoyed* (Finno-Ugric) hajôg: 2 eyes
Fi uni: sleep, dream he hasn't the eye & he hasn't the ear (for singing)
Fi puhua: to speak since Michaelmas he wishes
boohoo
same again *F* Sem: Shem correctly lion is royal beast
Ostiak semgen: 2 eyes *L* corrigo: I make straight really
L ex ungue leonem: (we know) a lion by its claws (reconstruction of whole from part)

G Kraft: strength wheelbarrow St Petersburg
F poutre: beam
avalanche pitchblack

ostrich *G* Auge *G* Strich: line Ireland's Eye: small island nr Howth
(head in sand) Matt 7:5: 'see clearly to cast out the mote out of thy brother's eye'
'tell the truth, the whole truth & nothing but the truth, yonker: young man
so help me God' (legal oath) *G Dial* Janker: folk costume, jacket
charming *ph* at sixes & sevens: disordered (family line; painted line)
kingly
Keats' *Endymion:* 'A thing of beauty is a joy forever' *Sl* jaw: talk *s* Cherry Ripe

Pre-classical L medius fidius: by the god of truth!
God

Marina
anyone
Ormuzd & Ahriman: principles of good & evil in Zoroastrianism   element   *ph* list of fame   famine
F faim: hunger
someone   *G Dial* Salm: psalm   *L* comedet: he may eat
Isa 7:15 (Vulg): 'Butyrum et mel comedat ut sciat reprobare malum et eligere bonum' ('Butter & honey shall he eat, that he may know to refuse the evil, & choose the good') (This sentence is regarded as prophecy of Jesus)

G Haensli isst ein Butterbrot, mein Butterbrot! Und Koebi isst dein Schinkenbrot! Ja! Ja! Ja!: Little Hans is eating a piece of bread & butter, my piece of bread & butter! & Jacob's eating your ham sandwich! Yes! Yes! Yes!
G stinken: to stink (pron. 'schtinken')   *G* Kot: shit

butterscotch

Gr tyros: cheese   jinks

G Wurm   Jesus!

ph beggar my neighbour   dumbshow: in medieval theatre, mimed preamble summarising action of a play

L ex quovis butyrum num fit merus caseus: from any butter there is not made pure cheese   ascribed to Pythagoras: 'Non ex quovis ligno fit Mercurius' ('You cannot make a Mercury out of just any piece of wood')   *L* nex: murder   *Sp* burro: ass
Nicholas de Cusa: *De Docta Ignorantia* (Of Learned Ignorance)

bottom   aubergiste: innkeeper
F Sl aubergine: red nose (from drink)

L primum mobile: prime mover (outermost sphere of Ptolemaic universe)

obilisk

L sine quam: without as much as   Giordano Bruno: *Gli Eroici Furori* (*The Heroic Enthusiasts*)

Theophilus: Bruno's mouthpiece in several works
L in principio: in the beginning
starting point   otiose   *Much Ado about Nothing* III.5.18: 'Comparisons are odorous'

(Humpty Dumpty)   world   *F* beurre

Brie, kind of cheese

Gr tyros: cheese   *Gr* dynamon: powerful machine
Silkeborg: Danish town manufacturing dairy machinery
electrolysis   *L* ambo: both   *L* adipes: fats

Sp burro: ass
It burro: butter
Lewis said in *Time & Western Man* that he hoped J would be 'influenced by my criticism'

editio princeps: 1st printed ed. of a book

much to the good

Poole's Myriorama: a show of projected maypoles picture *L* pictor: painter
pictures in D before cinema Picts & Scots
F ombre: shadow *Gr* skotia: darkness, gloom

undistributed middle: term in logic meals

wistfully want
wastefully

milkmaid
cowry shell (Maggy)

boiling point Platonism
margarine produced with platinum catalyst
Saul, son of Kish, went out to look for his father's asses

arses

Chamber Music

F entrée

'entry of subject' (music) chest of viols plum pudding
viands
ph cart before the horse 'Work in Progress' (J's name for FW before publication)
F hors d'oeuvre
s I Dream of Thee, Sweet Madeline

Gounod: *Faust* IV.12: Si le bonheur: 'O Margarita! (golden margarine)
O Margarita! Still on the bough is left a leaf of gold'

AngI drisheen: stuffed sheep's intestine cooked as pudding
Pudding flavoured with tansy is eaten at Easter to remind of 'bitter herbs' of Passover
heartbreaking

L crinis: hair

bowl

F betterave: beetroot

full-bottom: a full-bottomed wig

'Cuticura' soap sold in D; advertised as promoting hair-growth

notice Hair 'Harlene' hair restorer sold in D

area called *It* il tempo: the time
ph kill time ill temper
L in illo tempore: at that time (beginning gospel readings)

diagram

roulade: quick succession of notes, prop. as sung to 1 syllable
It colpo di glòttide: burst from the glottis, glottal stop *Sl* lug: ear Joseph Maas: tenor
inclined to overdo

deadbeat

space
nr 'Close your eyes & open your mouth & see what I will give you'
cantatrice: female professional singer

G B-Dur: B flat major
troubadour
(spatialist measuring lines of print)
years
orchestral Tonhalle: Zurich concert hall
architectural townhall
vivarium *pr* One man's meat is another man's poison Lewis: *Plans & Planners*
beef *G* beissend: pungent, acrid
argot
argon: an inert gas
for the moment

isosceles triangle

goulash: a highly seasoned stew gouache: painting with opaque colours ground in water
don't you know?

Lewis's painting *Girl Sewing* at the present
Sl needlewoman: harlot
National Gallery, London, when first built called the 'National Cruet-Stand'

terse bush soul: among Negroes of Calabar, the external soul embodied
torse: heraldic wreath in an animal

wallaby

zoological kangaroo tail (Lewis didn't like cubists)
conger eel teal: small bird *L* in excelsis
rhomb trapezoid: quadrilateral with no sides parallel
princesses of Trebizond, Turkey, once much in demand by Christian & Mohammedan princes

Gr klimax: ladder
Lewis: *Cantelman's Spring-mate* (has characters called A, B, C & D)

Eocene & Pleistocene: geological periods

F ébahi: astonished *Gr* philadespoinis: mistress-loving good, better, best
F ahuri: flabbergasted Philadelphia Illinois
F coup de grâce: finishing stroke *F* boîte à surprises

F pour poorbox 'Worth a guinea a box' (advert for Beecham's pills)
per box
Sherlock Holmes

roots
Sl roof: hat
classes *L* reductio ad absurdum *L* de facto: in fact
L deductio ad dominum: a leading away to the Lord *L* de tactu: from a touch
L mirabile dictu: wonderful to relate
L mobile tectu: moveable by means of a roof

Lewis studied at Slade School of Art
slate Henry Slade: C19 medium

'Fragments of the True Cross' hawked abundantly in Middle Ages place
true cost

(spatialist) semi-literary

ethel: type of dress

(three shillings & ninepence)

shortness

Sl (1927) 'it': sex appeal (Clara Bow) evidently
Ovid: *Ars Amatoria*

Lewis, in *Time & Western Man*, attacks 'the child cult' & associates J with it
mixed biscuits Charlie Chaplin

Sl shover: chauffeur butler
bootlegger
secretary HIM
U.357: 'Of course his infant majesty was most obstreperous at such toilet formalities'
make matters worse
Lewis, in *Childermas*, mocks J in the person of 'James Pulman' ('Pulley') reasons
(spatialist)

L infantulus: little baby boy *It* seducente infanta: seducing infanta

muscular

L tota mulier: complete woman *L* verus vir: real man

parturiency: parturient quality *L* matres: mothers

L mictorius: urinative

particular attention

VI.A.51: 'Mary Ann she is very fond of flirting, Mary Ann she is very fond of tea'

cheese

tay (*I* pron. of 'tea') Cleopatra
F morceau: morsel

mastery

Antony & Cleopatra　*U.S. Sl* wop: mid- or S. European immigrant in U.S. (esp. Italian)

she's of all shades
cheese　trades
pantomime　Lewis: *Art of Being Ruled*　*F* beurre
antinomian

L qualis: of such a sort　*L* talis: such, such like, this

Quantum theory (149.35)　HCE

Aquinas: *s* Tantum Ergo ('so great, therefore')　irradiate (quanta of energy radiated)
Gr ergon: work　illuminate　x is to y　whey: milk after separation of cheese
y is to z
hayseed　ABC　caddy (golf; 014.12)
Gr philadelphos: brother-loving (man)

amethyst hued　Newtonian　cross-legged patricide　*L* ex lege: according to law
Gr athemistos: illegitimate　low-tone　*L* exlex: lawless, outlawed
Sl green: inexperienced　frightfully　*Sl* blue: obscene
contending green & blue factions in C6 Constantinople
Lewis, in *Time & Western Man,* questioned originality of J's
phrase 'great searching eyes' (*U.*5)
stronghold of Acropolis　Lewis: *Blasting & Bombardiering*

blasphemous
Gr blasphoros: harm-carrying
cannot　tell　*Sl* pineapple: bomb

will not　Psalms of Solomon　congregational

A New Dictionary of the terms ancient & modern of the canting crew, ca. 1698 (canting crew: criminals & vagabonds)

Sl topsman: hangman　Tarpeian rock in Rome from which traitors thrown

nefand: unspeakable, execrable　*G* Sauerstoff: oxygen　alkalis + acids = salts + water
Du zout: salty
find time　firstclass

nitric acid　(tastes: sweet, salt, acid, bitter)
saltpetre
Thundering Legion = 12th legion　Mt Olympus

Law of the 12 Tables: ancient Roman law whose decay　*L* merus genius: pure genius
is described by Vico
careous: rotten　*L* morituri te salutant: they who are about to die salute you (gladiators to spectators)
L salutat: he salutes
Themis: titaness, representing divine justice　*Gr* phemis: speech
L themis: law, custom　Lewis was antidemocratic　*ph* let the devil take the hindmost
Abraham Tripier: first silk weaver mentioned in D municipal records

Solon: Athenian legislator
badtempered

espouse

Marriage service: 'till death us do part'
venerate　*L* nuptias: marriage

Solon made law that words of Homer could not be changed

Law of the 12 Tables VI.1a: 'Si quis nexum faciet manucipiumque, uti lingua nuncupassit ita ius esto' (' If anyone shall make bond or conveyance, as he has declared with his tongue, so shall it be binding'—called by Vico the great fount of all ancient Roman Law)
Ibid. III.7: 'Adversus hostem aeterna auctoritas esto' ('let there be eternal authority over the enemy')　*L* semper sic: always thus　*L* fulmen: thunderbolt
appear　hoyden: ill-bred girl　heathen　infidel

Merchant of Venice V.1.83–8: 'The man that hath no music in himself Nor is not moved with concord of sweet sounds . . . let no such man be trusted'

Scott: *The Patriot's Song:* 'Breathes there the man with soul so dead, Who never to himself has said, This is my own, my native land! –Whose heart hath ne'er within him burned, As home his footsteps he hath turned, From wandering on a foreign strand?' *s* My Heart's in the Highlands

highlows: laced boots reaching over ankles

beach *s* The Exile of Erin: 'Sad is my fate, said the heartbroken stranger'

Haydn: *The Creation*, chorus 'The heavens are telling the glory of God'

ph his bark is worse than his bite

Noah's Ark

Japhet four-in-hand: vehicle with 4 horses, driven by 1 person

bred sired

Donne: *The Flea*: 'in this flea, our two bloods mingled be' *It* galantuomo: gentleman

Gr hêmikapnousi: of the same family (smoking together) cheek by jowl

Sl dingo: tramp who does no work

⊏ *Law of the 12 Tables* VIII.21: 'Patronus si clienti fraudem fecerit, sacer esto' ('If the patron abuses the client, let him be accursed')

(Originally a penalty where a man was sacrificed, but 'sacer' came to mean a man disgraced, outlawed & deprived of his goods) *F* Sem: Shem same *L* sumus: we are

Shem, son of Noah   Shemus: man in Yeats' *Countess Cathleen* who sells his soul to devil
letter 18/8/26 to HSW: 'the Irish change J into Sh e.g. James Sheumas'   *Low L* Jacobus: James
U.S. Sl roughneck: a 'tough'   getatable: accessible   *F* prétendre: affirm   aboriginally: from earliest known times

(illegitimate child)   *L* lex: law

Ragnar Lodbrok: Viking chief   *F* barbe   Harald Fair Hair: 1st king of Norway
G Blaubart: Bluebeard (wife-killer in Perrault's story)
Beardwood: friend of J's father   Bloggs: mock Eng. working-class name
F de trop: superfluous

ph put two & two together

St Patrick was called 'Adzehead' because of his tonsure
lark's eye: mischievous eye   hole   *ph* something up his sleeve

(not real)
'uncrowned king of Ireland' (Parnell)
barbel: filament hanging from mouths of some fishes   *F* saumon: salmon   *U*.550 (emended): 'THE NANNYGOAT (*bleats*) Megeggaggegg!'
Gr mega-: great
I meigead: goat's chin
ph all ears
ph not a foot to stand on   *ph* handful of thumbs (awkward)

blind gut: caecum

gleet: slimy matter; morbid discharge from urethra   avoirdupois   *Sl* manroot: penis
Gladstone   stone: 14 lbs   *Sl* stone: testicle
I Tim 6:10: 'the love of money is the root of all evil'
kelt: salmon after spawning
distended
F triste
debouch: (fig.) to emerge   *L* prôtohistoria: first knowledge

It brefotrofio: orphanage   Threadneedle St, London (Bank of Eng.), once called Pig Street   (Δ's 111 children)   shovel . . . hoe
It grifo: snout
pounds, shillings & pence

Λ Ʌ ⊏ Δ anna: 1/16 Indian rupee

⊂⊃ lira: Italian coin O *Sl* bob: shilling *Sl* tester: sixpence
F Sl lorette: whore X
groat: orig. 1/8 oz. silver; in 1351 was fourpence S *Angl ph* not for Joe: definitely not *Sl* Joe: dinner
dinar: Yugoslav coin K *Sl* joe: fourpenny piece *L* dictito: I say often
G Schwester: *I* siuirín: sister Haeckel: *Riddle of the Universe*
soup tureens

G Jungfrau: virgin *pr* Time & tide wait for no man *Arabian Nights*: Tale of Nur al-Din & his son:
Arch youngfry: child 'His day was as a month' (i.e. grew up quickly)
crabapple

(no copper coinage)

Balfe: *s* (from *The Bohemian Girl*) Then You'll Remember Me: 'When other lips . . . '
Quakers, Bohemian Protestants & Gnostics: all heresies
agnostic
Sl gnostic: a knowing fellow
Sl kick the bucket: die

pr When the wine is in the wit is out Whitsun
ph be at one's wits' end
The Vicar of Wakefield: 'When lovely woman stoops to folly' *Sl* conk: to hit on the head
Goldsmith: *She Stoops to Conquer*
F Sem: Shem *s* When Papa Papered the Parlour

Yeats *R* yabloko: apple cooking apple *R* zmeya: snake
G Apfelkuchen: apple tart
Du zelf: self *Du* zo: so
shocking *R* zhuk: beetle Yeats: 'when you are old & grey & full of sleep'
Ibsen: *When We Dead Awaken* (*Naar Vi Døde Vaagner*)
Sl deader: corpse
circumcised

s Yes, We Have No Bananas
Sp mañana: tomorrow
ph when pigs begin to fly: never *G* Luft: air
Du loof: foliage
ph take the cake

Matt 28:20: 'I am with you alway, even unto the end of the world. Amen'

shamrocks riddle of Sphinx: answer: a man
Matt 27:51: 'the earth did quake, & the rocks rent' *ON* Ragnarøkr: destruction of the Norse gods

Ibsen's

lax: salmon; later, a particular kind of salmon parr & smolt: stages in development of salmon
gaff: stick with iron hook used for landing salmon Island Bridge: bridge over Liffey at point where becomes tidal
Leixlip (name means 'salmon leap')
botulism: poisoning from eating food (often canned) infected with *Clostridium botulinum*, leads to coma

G schmeckte: tasted ananas: the pineapple
Ananias: liar (Acts 5:1–6), tried to deceive apostles
Gluckstein & Salmon: owners of Lyons' Corner Houses
Adam Findlater's Mountjoy Brewery, founded by Findlaters & Robert Gladstone CHE
martyrs burned at the stake
beef

L grex: flock, crowd
Greeks (Russian & Greek heretics)
go-upons (i.e. pigs' trotters)

bog oak: coniferous wood preserved in peatbogs chickenhearted youth *F* rosbif:
G Jude: jew Fielding: 'Oh! the roast beef of old England' roast beef
F attouchement: touch, contact

somatophage: body-eating vegetarian

Da hun: she *Da* far: father *Da* sønner: sons
Da forsone: to atone
Esau sold his birthright for a mess of pottage of lentils (Gen 25:34)

G irr: mad, mistaken Ir. P/Q split

piscivorous: fish-eating citron

Hu hiba: defect, deformity
habit
glottal stop (phonetics) *Fi* kukka: flower (J ate very little)
Ps 92:13: 'The innocent man will flourish as the palm tree flourishes: he will grow to greatness as the cedars grow on Lebanon' citron
'Cedar' said to derive from Kedron, stream in Jordan
F limon: mud

firstshot: weak poteen of 1st distillation W.G. Barrett & Co, distillers, D
ph first come, first served Gilbey's gin (D)
whey: milk after separation of cheese
(rainbow colours)
rhubarb (red) mandarins (orange)
Da funkle: sparkle indigo
blue funk *G* dunkelblau: dark blue iodine vapour is violet
sentimental *Sl* cupshot: drunk
pr There's many a slip 'twixt the cup & the lip
gulped

Hu jó: good

J liked a Swiss white wine, Fendant de Sion, which he said looked like the urine of an archduchess
Magyar, Hungarian majesty *Hu* az: the
F douche: shower
I deoch an dorais: parting drink Tennyson: *Charge of the Light Brigade:* 'Cannon to right of them Cannon to left of them'
Feherbor: a white wine *Hu* bor: skin
Hu fehér: white *Hu* bőr: wine it's not archduchess

Gi pea-mengro: drunkard

any God's quantity: abundance

'black beetle': oriental cockroach time

unremunerated National Apostle (St Patrick)

We caer: town; castle
Caer, worshipped by Aengus, was obliged to change into a swan
steamship slipstream Prydwen: King Arthur's ship in *The Spoils of Annwfn* every winter
according to Colum, Wyndham Lewis was always telling J he should go to S. America
ph bury the hatchet *L* exeunt exit *G* Nummer

Sp tren: train *It* patata: potato
Gi desh ta trin: 13 *It* papaveri: poppies
It ciao!: hello *Gi* chavi: girl, child, daughter *Gi* shillipen: cold
Gi sar shin: how are you?
Bridewell: prison, D
Belfast man

next time time

Wyndham Lewis: *Cantelman's Spring-mate*

John 21:15–16: 'Feed my lambs. . . . Feed my sheep'

cheap speciality

moreover *ph* for love or money
Gi morava: to kill, slay *Gi* luvvo: money

Sl do for himself:
commit suicide

Eden Quay, D

antinomian: one who holds that the moral law is not binding to Christian in a state of grace
(fire, water, air, earth)

explode explain
L explaudo: I drive out, clap off stage
pneumatics suffocate
semantics Saffron cakes in *Egyptian Book of the Dead* stand for 'Osiris' or 'heaven & earth'
devil's leaf: virulent, tropical stinging nettle
foreign devil: a foreigner in China (disparagingly)
It anzi: on the contrary taking the words out of his mouth *G* Maul: mouth *It* guardacoste: coastguard
malt
Leporello: servant to Don Giovanni Jesus Christ! *It* quanto costa?: how much?
Hu százas: 100 *Hu* krajcár: obsolete copper coin Neapolitan (Vico)
David & Jonathan (In Italy J frequently made urgent requests for money to his brother Stanislaus)
ph to consult brother Jonathan today Tokay: a sweet Hungarian wine tomorrow
spliced wireless

Treacle Frisky

long & the short Mulligan calls Stephen 'the bard'
Treacle Tom & Frisky Shorty (039.16–18)
(J's habit of jotting down overheard conversation) condign: worthily deserved
Du trek: appetite wife (9th commandment)

Monday Munda: an E. Indian language commote: put into commotion
It conversazione: conversation committed
titbits
tippit: game in which object held in player's hand is to be detected
HEC

Gr kydos: glory, renown
Hu kid'ō: snake
dash it all

F sosie: double, counterpart

across transpiciously: manifestly *F* canaille: rabble, scoundrel
L crux: cross

Swift: *Gulliver's Travels*
Ringgold Wilmer Lardner the Elder: *Gullible's Travels* (1917)

answering to

33 years

pig

pencil *G* Lauscher: listener (hence outer ear of game)
pensile: hanging
Parnell Prattling Parnel: a plant, 'London Pride' sweating
prunella: material used for academic robes
Jesus Christ Cornelius Jansen maintained perverseness & inability are for good of the natural human will
Albion (English) gentleman
Albigensian heresy
let alone

Tamil & Samtal: Indian languages *It* conclamazione: acclamation
Da Tommelise: Thumbelina *Da* samtale: conversation conversazione (172.31)

agricultural manufacturers sacristans
L agricola: farmer
panesthesia: sum total of individual's perception at a given moment

HE . . . C In 1902, when J visited Paris, he stayed at the Hotel Corneille *F* canaille: rabble
carnal Pierre Corneille: C17 Fr. playwright, often impoverished
s Ta ra ra boom de ay
Tara: ancient capital of Ir.
I mór: big

HCE

sept: Ir. clan date heavens hears how

L vice versa *I* cruach: conical heap
Fi isän vieressä: next to the father cracking *F* cracher: to spit
3 cheers *AngI* beg: little paper bag
'Pepper's ghost': theatrical illusion

G Himmel-Schimmel! (expletive)
Ham, Shem
Aeschylus: *The Seven against Thebes* *Oliver Twist*, ch. 43: 'Wasn't he always top-sawyer?' (Fagin lamenting the Artful Dodger)
Tom Sawyer no one *s* Home Sweet Home
bottom sawyer: man who stands below in sawing pit
eavesdropper

snickers
F Sem: Shem smirks

features
F se ficher: regard with indifference

for instance

cultivating
cuttlefish 'ink'

warp & woof place person
word (a 'substantive' denotes a thing, place or person)

cull: one who is cheated or imposed upon
F cul

slangwhanger: slanging match

J had a limp handshake

F monsieur *Sp* gracias: thanks

I'm sure, see what I'm *G* also, gut: quite so

quite so *G* wieso?: why *Sp* muchas gracias: many thanks

Irish *AngI* is there Gaelic on you?: do you understand Gaelic?

G selber: self your servant (.11)

antagonist

Gr Haimoptysia diadoumenos: in blood spits crowned with a diadem

tantalus: stand for decanters
fill his tumbler
halcyon days
colcannon: cabbage & potatoes & butter, traditional Ir. dish for All Hallow's Eve

parson

soccered socked Goldsmith: *The Deserted Village*
AngI sagart: priest
Dublin on the Liffey Bartholomew Vanhomrigh: father of Swift's Vanessa *F* bis
U.475: 'ZOE: No, eightyone. Mrs. Cohen's'
Mabbot St, D *U*.729: 'Mrs Bella Cohen, 82 Tyrone Street, lower'
Haliday: *The Scandinavian Kingdom of Dublin:* 'tried the river from Mr Vanhomrigh's house . . . to Green Patch . . . as far as opposite Mabbot's Mill . . . Salmon Pool bank, running southwards to the Brick Fields' (advice of a committee on embankment of the Liffey)
J: *The Shade of Parnell:* 'The citizens of Castlecomer threw quicklime in his eyes'
F pierre *L* contra lime (tree)
really Piers . . . Rahilly (Persse O'Reilly) detained rather lateish (upper class British accent)
ph business is business

Goldsmith: *The Deserted Village:* 'Sweet Auburn'

rugger: rugby football

Arch cullions: rascals; testicles 'Troubles' (Ir. Civil War, 1922–3)

Old Contemptibles: British Expeditionary Force, 1914

Wicklow

All Souls College, Oxford Belial: a devil *Dial* mickle: a great many nil *L* nihil: nothing
Balliol College, Oxford Mick v. Nick (St Michael v. Lucifer)

(003.04–14) (Eve from Adam's rib)

(Adam & Eve after Fall)

emperor from Corsica (Napoleon) *We* arth: bear *F* Angleterre
imp Arthur (Wellington) *G* Engel: angel
G Sachsen: Saxony Jute sound (misunderstanding)
G Jude: Jew Jute on mound (015.29–018.16)

witch on the heath heather on Howth often on fire (*U*.378)

Howth
on High
It arcobaleno: rainbow peace upon earth (Noah & God)
G vorsprechen: pronounce, announce *G* versprechen: promise
(Lucifer falls) *G* Himmel *G* Tümpel: pool (Adam)
tumble blameful

F poursuivre: follow *ph* from the egg to the apples
pr Where there's a will there's a way
nr 'Humpty Dumpty sat on a wall'

(Howth) (Liffey)

rill's trill His Majesty laugh

foreshores Tory Island: Fomorian stronghold off Donegal *F* douze *G* dumm earwigs
Da til: to ✕ deaf & dumb Tory . . . Whig ○
F railler: jeer at; jest
rail: utter abusive language
chirp

F perce-oreille: earwig
Ballad of Persse O'Reilly (044.24)
'Exsultet': 'O felix culpa!'
L O fortunata causalitas: O lucky causality (170.22)
(devil) took

Gr misoxenos: hostile to strangers misogynic Ghazi Power: Ir. journalist (521.22)
G.A.A.: Gaelic Athletic Association

L niscemus: we do not know *L* nomen: name
L nemo: nobody
cg hornies & robbers (i.e. cops & robbers)
Sl honey: semen *Sl* rubber: condom
George du Maurier: *Trilby:* 'Vincent sang. "Old Joe kicking up behind & afore & the yaller gal a-kicking up behind old Joe"'

Thom's Dublin Directory *s* Tom, Tom, the Piper's Son
Thon, once worshipped in England, may be Thor
*retort: 'Piss up yer leg, an play wiv the steam'
Sl peeler: policeman breeches
Mick v. Nick

*Mademoiselle went to the well (girls' rope chant) 'they have forgotten what "mademoiselle" means & now call it "Adam & Ell"' *Humble-Bumble *Moggies on the wall
*Twos & threes *American jump Magazine Wall
*Fox come out of your den
*Broken bottle *Writing letter to Punch *Tiptop is a sweets store

HCE Henry Crump: C14 Ir. theologian convicted of heresy *Postman's knock
Val Vousden: *s* Are We Fairly Represented?
*Solomon silent reading *'Appletree, Peartree, Plumtree pie How many children before I die?' tree/stone
*I know a washerwoman *Hospitals anyone's
*As I was walking
Percy French: *s* 'There's only one house in Drumcollogher' *Battle of Waterloo *Colours CEH
*Eggs in the bush
*Telling your dream *What's the Time
*Haberdasher isher asher om pom tosh
*Nap *Ducking mummy *Last man standing *Ali Baba & the Forty Thieves* (pantomime)
Tim Healy: opponent of Parnell
Teague: familiar name for Irishman fusiliers
(masturbated)
Finnegan *s* Old Zip Coon

s Turkey in the Straw *s* 'Here we go gathering nuts in May, On a cold & frosty morning . . . This is the way we wash our hands'
s: 'Lots of fun at Finnegan's Wake'
Millikin wrote *s* The Groves of Blarney
U,128 (emended): 'It was Pat Farrell shoved me sir' *s* The Priest in His Boots

s Enniscorthy: '& the steam was like a rainbow round McCarthy'
Rembrandt
Bloody Sunday, 21/11/1920, when Black & Tans murdered civilians at Croke Park
Germans v. Gaul (Fr.) *I* gall: foreigner *s* Finnegan's Wake: 'Shillelagh law was all the rage'
Ulster HARRY
TOM Tommy (Atkins) pathetics
Wellington
DICK Marshalsea Prison, D *s* When Irish Eyes Are Smiling
s La Marseillaise
Roth pirated *U.* *G* rot: red *G* weiss: white *G* blau: blue

F noir *F* blanc *F* rouge green, white & gold (Ir. tricolour green, white & orange)

The Black & Tans: Eng. recruits in 1920–1 serving in Royal Ir. Constabulary maxim: type of gun
Kant: *Groundwork of the Metaphysic of Morals*: 'categorical imperative'

leveret: young hare *Fi* talvi: Winter *I* ochón!: alas! *Hu* honn: - at home
Hu haza: homeward

Koskenkorva: a district of Finland

The Inkbottle House: Church of the Seven Dolours, Botanic Avenue, D (shape said to have been suggested by Swift)

fear of his life

pianoforte

black vamp

Switzer's: D department store Albert Schweitzer on Bach
tick: sort of mattress Switzerland (neutral in WW I)
Telemachus *s* Lillibullero sunbonnet (nightcap) hotwaterbottle
telemac: overcoat somnolence

*given in Norman Douglas's *London Street Games*

The Awful Disclosures of s Yankee Doodle: 'So 'tarnal long & 'tarnel deep', 'a nation louder'
Maria Monk (*U.*235) Maid Marian: Robin Hood's woman monotone
Mount Merrion, district of D *L* ampulla: flask

St Patrick's Purgatory: cave on an island in Lough Derg
knicker bocker
tong: a Chinese secret society *Sl* shemozzle: uproar *Daily Mail*
Angelic Salutation:
'Hail Mary, full of grace. Holy Mary, mother of God' *C. Pi* joss: god

U.S. Sl (gangsters', 1920s) gat: gun; croak: die

ladies & gentlemen *ph* 'dog of a Christian!'

Crossguns Bridge, D Cairo Koran *Fi* koira: dog
Karakorum: ancient capital of Mongolia, established by Genghis Khan
Sheol: in Bible usually means the grave; shoals of herrings *It* stella: star
sometimes hell houri: nymph of the Mohammedan paradise chemises
Swift's Stella & Vanessa
vespertine: of evening
Cz ryba: fish *F* poisson: fish
F poisse: i) bad luck; ii) ponce

Nebuchadnezzar
no book is honester

Vanessa lovenest *F* grogner: to grunt grognard: a grouser, grumbler
quintessence lowness
F guignard: unlucky person

L a latere: from the side private secretary
Sucat: name given to St Patrick by his parents
Hu kávéház: café one day Bruno of Nola
coffeehouse
heavenly *Sl* hambone: amateur *Gr* pseudô: beguile
(Castor & Pollux born from eggs laid by Leda) *pr* give a dog a bad name & hang him
agnomen: name added Bethgelert: grave of Gelert, dog wrongfully killed in Welsh story
to family name, generally on account of some exploit *G* gelehrt: learned
Gipsy Bar, Paris, frequented by J

Old Bailey Court, London manjack: a single person

F sou last of next month
L nex: murder
ph as sure as there's a tail on a cat *It* stòrico: historic Stoics' fortitude
R starik: old man
say only twenty minutes more Molière: *Le Malade Imaginaire*

J.H. Voss: 'Wine, Women & Song' waterclosets

Guy Fawkes fucks letter 11/11/25 to HSW reports a magazine wanted J
thinks & talks to write 'What you feel & do when you are going blind'
Thackeray: *Diary of C. Jeames de la Pluche, Esq.*
F plume: pen
(writing can be read by holding up to mirror) (hiccup)

Shakespeare

antithesis precisely the same (hiccup)

Scott, Dickens & Thackeray

foxed: cheated *Sl* bunny: cunt *Sl* to roger: to fuck bishop Wyndham Lewis: *The Lion &*
face to face Dickens: *Barnaby Rudge* *the Fox* (1927, about Shakespeare)

Sl lioness: prostitute *Sl* drum: brothel Scott: *Ivanhoe* *L* lapsus linguae: slip of tongue
Lyons Tea Shops, London Dundrum, district of D gaga: crazy *Fi* lapsi: child
L linquo: I leave Swinburne: *A Ballad of Francis Villon:* 'Villon our sad bad glad mad brother's name'
Hu rövidäbb: shorter short temper *Fi* -empa: comparative suffix *G* fad: stale
Thackeray: *Vanity Fair* consequences causality case (some Finnish postpositions require noun
Hu nad: big *Fi* vanha: old in genitive case)
crosswords murrain

ph without rhyme or reason *Fi* lanka: thread

life line (palmistry) *G* alle any English speaker metaphorically
spooks
speaking puking earth (Ireland)
Fi -ksi: translative suffix
St Swithin's Day: 15 July

Exod 12:7: '& they shall take of the blood, Lucan, Chapelizod
& strike it on the two side posts & on the upper door post of the houses' (Passover)
Du eerstgeboren: firstborn
G erst: first
Arch welkin: sky

F cul *F* vert
culverts
Balaam: biblical prophet stirabout: a kind of porridge

Hu maassa: (in) land
F en masse *It* massa: crowd, mob *Da* baad: boat
Du waden (stem waad): wade *G* baden: bathe
Mon Khmer yām: die; p-yām: kill; pan-p-yām: put to death Munster

Peter & Paul patriotic poetry *L* nunc et semper: now & always
Attic Verdi: *Aida:* 'Morir! si pura e bella!' junk, sampan: Chinese boats
L in saecula saeculorum: 'pia e pura bella': religious wars of Vico's heroic age
for ever & ever avocation: diversion, distraction
r Avoca, Co. Wicklow
National Schools (Ireland)
Intermediate Examination (Ir.)
intermittently

⚔ Ladysmith (Boer War)
'Avenge Majuba!': rallying cry in Boer War
Isaac Bickerstaff: name used by Swift in parody of Partridge's
astrological predictions
Rainbow Bridge (Wagner, *Das Rheingold*) *It* ponte dei colori: bridge of colours
WWI Sl plinkity plonk: white wine Ponte dei Sospiri: Bridge of Sighs (Venice)
ph war to end war: WWI

Port dia dos finados: All Souls' Day, 2 November

Peeping Tom *It* finestrella: small window (*U.* has 3 books & 18 chapters) horsepower
Pip & Estella in Dickens' *Great Expectations* *It* pipistrello: bat *Port* estrella: star
Gi dur-dicki mengri: telescope, i.e. far-seeing thing larboard
Valery Larbaud assisted in Fr. translation of *U.*
Nassau St, D, used to have streetlamps on S. side only
G Strasse: street
G Wetter: weather *It* porco: pig *Port* outono: autumn

Selkup Samoyed (Finno-Ugric) kule: crow *Kalevala:* Finish national epic
I cúl: goal *Fi* parka: poor *L* ovum: egg owing cod's eggs *Fi* kala: fish
massacre by Black & Tans of Ir. leaving football cock's eggs (071.27) *Fi* tavala: in a way
game in Croke Park, D, 1920 *It* tavola calda: buffet (table of hot dishes)

Du duvel: devil *G* Sache: thing; cause
('see me', 'my see' & 'my seeing' *Gi* Duvvel: God DOVE *Gi* Duvel: God sake
are lit. translations of Selkup Samoyed *It* corvo maggiore: RAVEN
constructions for 'I see' & 'what I see') *Fi* korva: ear

s My Lagen Love

L hic sunt leones: here are lions *L* hic sunt lenones: here are pimps
(on medieval maps) Judge Lennon attacked J in *Catholic World*, 1931
Anti-Treaty forces of Ir. Civil War, 1922–3, were called Irregulars

Sl bulldog: pistol

Unknown Warrior (grave, Paris)

snout

AngI creased: beaten

Jack the Ripper dayboys
Wellington: 'Up, guards, & at them' *AngI* go-boy: sly harmful fellow
L exemplum: example *Port* para: for *Port* são: saint Deucalion & Pyrrha: equivalent of Noah & his
Para: Finnish spirit, bearer of milk, cream, butter wife, in Ovid
by St Paul! Roman pantries had guardian spirits

Stator & Victor: epithets of Jupiter *Port* mesa redonda: round table
ph cut & run
St Laurence O'Toole, patron of D
Port Lourenço: Laurence *Port* convocação: convocation
CCC . . . BBB . . . AAA

L cloaca: sewer Biloxi: seaport, Mississippi *L* aper: boar
L bilis: anger, gall
L atrox: cruel, savage *Port* preciso + verb 'to be' indicates necessity qualify
clarify

ABC

daddies Stephen Dedalus *Port* dedal: thimble
dedal: labyrinth *Port* dedo: finger
favoured HCE

Port popa: poop (of ship) *Port* navio: ship
Port preto: black
Sl flicker: drink

habit
megalomania ALP

uncial: of letters, capital HEC

Boswell: *Life of Johnson,* 16/10/1769: 'inspissated gloom'

glaucous: dull green *Ulysses*

Eccles St, D *F* édition des ténèbres
early printings of *U*. bound in blue paper Blue Books: official reports of Eng. Parliament
Most Reverend Bowdler expurgated Shakespeare
AB . . . C
3 sheets in the wind: very drunk

Port espelho: mirror
Port no: in the *I* mór: great
I aisling: vision, dream

that is to say *G* Esche: ash tree *s* My Love & Cottage near Rochelle
G Schelle: bell
try-on Liberty's: London department store ewer
The Liberties: district of D (Fendant: 171.25)
Port branco: white *Port* padeiro: baker six
blancmange, pudding or pie *Port* monje: monk

standing

queue
F Sl queue: penis

proscenium: enclosure of the stage   obscene   inamorated   *Port* justilho: bodice, stays
prosboscis   *Port* âmago: pith, essence, heart   *Sp* amago: threatening gesture
pantomimes at the Gaiety Theatre, D
Pantheon
Port acordár: waken   acoustic   *G* im: in the
according to all accounts   *Port* im: in
s The Dear Little Shamrock (of Erin)   d'you hear that *fa*?   so pure
hemlock
Rom 9:29: 'Lord of Sabaoth'   *Heb* sabaoth: hosts, armies
Port sabão: soap   just like a bird   boy
baritone   Barton McGuckin: D tenor
Port barato: cheap   *G* Glück: joy   Gluck, composer
(Ir. tricolour, green, white & orange)   Trinity College, D

Port amarello: yellow
Amaryllis: genus of flowering plants named for a country girl in Theocritus & Virgil
Kersse (311.05–09)   poniard: dagger
closest   Spaniard's
Port alfaiate: tailor   *Port* azul: blue   *Port* lenço de assoar: sheet of nose-blowing (handkerchief)
Port alfinete: pin   *L* punxit: he has punctured
L pinxit: painted (used on paintings with signature)

riddle: 'Londonderry, Cork & Kerry, spell me that without a K.' Answer: 'THAT'   Londonderry (Ulster)   St Laurence O'Toole
Cork & Kerry (Munster)   of D (Leinster)
It occidente: west (Connacht)   (013.26)   *ph* Dear Dirty Dublin
It accidentaccio!: damn!   Derby (horserace)
D: Town of the Ford of the Hurdles   on the other hand   (178.05) and all that sort of thing

C18 inhabitants of Liberties, D, called *r* Poddle 'Pottle'   an itchy palm (Shakespeare): lascivious
bottle

Sauvé: *Proverbes & dictons de la Basse-Bretagne*, no. 190: 'La conscience avec son tic-toc
Est la clochette de Saint-Kollédoc'
heat of

F gorge: throat   bone   *Sl* lugs: ears   ballocks
pain   *I* bolg: belly
squint   *I* súil: eye   echo   *R* ukho: ear   hearer

tetter: pustular herpiform eruption of the skin

ph rats in the attic = bats in the belfry (madness)   *Sl* bamboozle: deceive

memorize
mumble
hake: fish related to cod   Jim Fisk: U.S. financier. Vanderbilt said 'Who's Fisk?'
Da fisk: fish

worries

James Clarence Mangan: 'If anyone can imagine such an idea as a human boa-constrictor, without his alimentative propensities, he will be able to form some notion of the character of my father'   *Da* min fader: my father
L lex: law   lexicon   *F* parole

stage Irishmen

Sir Charles Russell at Parnell inquiry trapped Pigott by asking him to spell 'hesitancy'

F cul: arse

Lewis Waller played   *G* Sprache: language   speech!

Satan in adaptation of Marie Corelli's *The Sorrows of Satan*

G schick: elegant, stylish   Klondike (gold mines)   *G* Reich: country (Switzerland)

F pioupiou: soldier

F Pays Bas: Netherlands   land of Nod: sleep; place where Cain went after killing Abel   *F* pension: boarding school

Swabia, Germany   *Sl* swab: uncouth fellow

r Danube   *L* barbarus: foreign, savage

hebdomadary: weekly

Sunday, Monday (moon day), *F* mardi (Mars, god of battle), Wednesday, *F* jeudi (Jove's day), *F* vendredi (Venus, lecherous), Saturday (sated = full)

abominable   *It* puzzo: stench

It pozzo: well, privy   tutoring (J's occupation in Trieste)

pothook: a stroke in writing   *L* niger: black, wicked, false

It vulgaria: ordinary things

(James Townsend Savard, 'Jim the Penman', was a forger)

Dublin   *Portrait* V: 'a church which was the scullerymaid of christendom'

s Slattery's Mounted Foot

Sl owl: prostitute   *G Sl* Futt: cunt

I Dial taytotally: utterly, entirely

Sl conk: nose   Carlyle: 'the unspeakable Turk'

Wilde on fox hunters: 'The unspeakable in full pursuit of the uneatable'

Greece & Armenia occupied by Turks from C15, Armenian nationalism in C19–20 met by systematic massacres

point-to-point racing

prefects (i.e. police)   *r* Liffey

low hyacinth (087.12)

law

Budgen (*Further Recollections of JJ*) says J claimed to be interested only in women's underwear, not their bodies

wadmel: type of woollen cloth

F culottes   undergarments

Hamlet I.5.190: 'The time is out of joint! O cursed spite That ever I was born to set it right'

Ten Commandments

advertisement

abortion

L status quo ante: conditions before

ante: price (from poker)

low   hypochondriac

Drumcondra, district of D

F née   *Hu* hamis: false, base

L natus: born   Ham

shamiana: in India, a cloth canopy
palimpsest: parchment &c., written over twice
Pelagius, heretic, was possibly Irish plagiarist

light fantastic (dance) Gnostic heresies
gnosis: intuitive knowledge of various spiritual truths
'Lucifer' means 'lightbearer'
lucifer: match
Macpherson: *Temora* I.220: 'the red eye of his fear is sad'

F enseigner: to teach J worked for Berlitz School in Trieste & Pola madness (method in his)
It educande: girl boarders in convent schools *ph* hue & cry

Du gember: ginger *G* Ingwer: ginger *L* zinziber: ginger
F gingembre: ginger *It* zinzero: ginger
Sl tincture: whiskey his Nibs serif: fine cross stroke at top or bottom of a letter
seraph
sheepskin parchment lantern (his nose)

L simul: at the same time *ph* flash in the pan *Ar* kirk': book
Gr chronikos: of time lavatory *Ar* kin: price
I scríobh: write
I scríob: scratch

scrivener
Sw skrev: wrote
Irish terriers'

Old Father
Ulfada: warrior in *Fingal*, glossed as 'long beard'
Portrait of the Artist
Sardanapalus: last king of Assyria; burned himself, wives & treasure when his subjects rebelled

It hanno o nonhanno: they have or have not
Machiavelli *F* monologue intérieur Hanno: Carthaginian navigator
Nick into yer ear *Hamlet* III.1.56: 'To be or not to be, that is the question'
It autore: author (*It* essere o non essere, questo è il problema)
Sir Arthur Q.E.D. = which was to be demonstrated
Paolo loved his brother's wife, Francesca (*Inferno* V; also operatic role) girls in his eyes isles
Ibsen: *Little Eyolf*
plaintive tenor voice ducal income

drachmas year Broken Hill Estates: Australian mine-owning corporation Cambridge
landed cambric
manners

Oxford Thursday
burled: of cloth, tufted
party ALP & a lovely moustaches

frangipane: perfume resembling jasmine

Mrs O'Shea: Parnell's wife *It* qui va piano, va sano: he who goes quietly goes safely
It pieno: full
The School House, Glasnevin, built in shape of ink bottle, at Swift's suggestion

rats

J sometimes wore black eyepatch

I fuinneóg: window Macpherson: *Battle of Lora* 143: 'Son of the distant land, who dwellest in the secret cell'

Jesuits' bark: *Cinchona* bark, which contains quinine
ph his bark is worse than his bite *ph* the biter bit

It zolfo: sulphur J was treated with scopolamine, which he disliked, for his eyes *It* scoppia la mina: the mine blows up

U.712: 'Qui si Sana'('here one is healthy')

Coue, psychologist, had his devotees repeat: 'Every day in every way I am getting better & better'

Synge: *The Playboy of the Western World*

In Le Fanu's *The House by the Churchyard* the mysterious characters Dangerfield & Mervyn live, respectively, in the Brass Castle & the Tyled House. Brass Castle was in Chapelizod, Tyled House in Ballyfermot, districts of D *G* nichts

Da ting som ingen ting: thing like no thing

It puzzone: stinker *s* Killarney: 'Angels often pausing there Doubt if Eden were more fair'

personal to the writer as a matter of fact

Edam: a Dutch cheese my word!

It imposte: shutters Montesquieu: *Persian Letters* (1721)

It persiana: shutter French letters

ph every picture tells a story stickyback: small photo with gummed back

Exiles boucher: prehistoric hand axe amygdaloid: almond-shaped

G Bücher: books

rhyme reason alphabet biblical biasses

L obiter dictum: incidental pronouncement made by judge, not binding *L* visus undique: seen from all sides ineffable

L visus ubique: seen everywhere him & her

I.O.U.s 'The sootcoated packet of pictures which he had hidden in the flue of the fireplace' (*Portrait* III)

Ibsen: *Little Eyolf*

lucifers: matches (used Vesta matches)

(turncoats)

horsehair scapular: 2 small squares of cloth, worn on priest's chest & back

francs *pr* The road to hell is paved with good intentions

Latin syntax Matt 18:6: 'it were better for him that a millstone were hanged about his neck'

brass latten: brass beaten very thin

currant buns mashed potatoes P/Q quotations Esau sold his birthright for a mess of pottage

F mots

tissue paper

pr It is no use crying over spilt milk stale chestnut: old joke

Leon & Stein: *The Merry Widow*, musical comedy, 1907 *Sl* abbess: bawd

'Silent sister': C19 name for Trinity College, D, because few books produced & little public school support

Brandon Thomas: *Charley's Aunt* (play)

press clippings right, left & centre

milk

Sl bilk: statement devoid of truth or sense

eyebrow lotion (*Nausicaa*) kiss my arse

notions

F plume: pen

wine carbon dioxide devil you care

(carbon paper)

John 1:27: 'whose shoes' lachet I am not worthy to unloose' (also Mark 1:7 & Luke 3:16) Isa 40:3: 'the crooked shall be made straight'

Mercury is old remedy for syphilis

undiluted delight gleet: slimy matter glee Exod 21:24: 'Eye for eye, tooth for tooth'

war loans

F oui = *It* si = *G* ja = *Sw* jo = *It* già = *Gr* ney = *I* tá: yes   *U*.783: 'yes I said yes I will Yes'

Chamber Music

Christ called James & John Boanerges ('sons of thunder', Mark 3:17)
Isis Unveiled I.xxviii: 'Dervishes, or the "whirling charmers" . . . will never reach beyond his second class of occult manifestations'
'Red Terror': Communist government repression in Hungary, 1919, followed by similar anti-Communist 'White Terror'   *N* redd: afraid
Ps 91:5–6: 'Thou shalt not be afraid . . . for the destruction that wasteth at noonday'   *U*.37: 'Ineluctable modality of the visible'
mercy
misery   history

pr No man is a hero to his valet

Stourbridge: Eng. town noted for firebrick works

litharge: lead monoxide   lithagogue: medicine expelling calculi from kidneys   galena: lead sulphide   eggs aches
Sp gallina: hen   *Sp* galeno: doctor
pr The apple does not fall far from the tree   *nr* Humpty Dumpty

'The Harmonious Blacksmith', harpsichord music by Handel
Moore's Melodies   *It* moro: black
(i.e. against destroying eggs)   Moore: *Lalla Rookh* (poem, made into cantata)

Ben Travers: *Rookery Nook* (play)   Diogenes, Cynic philosopher, looked with a lantern for an honest man   *F* brûler   broiled & cooked
G gekochtes Ei: boiled egg
poached   athanor: digesting furnace used by alchemists

It frullino: egg whisk   *F* fredonner: to hum (tune)   *Sp* mas blanca que la blanca hermana: whiter than the white sister
Meyerbeer: *Les Huguenots:* 'Plus blanche que la blanche ermine'
Sp amarilla: a gold coin
Sp muy bien: very good   Matt 3:4: 'his meat was locusts & wild honey'
carrageen moss: an edible seaweed   C . . . B . . . A
plaster of Paris
Swift's Stella & Vanessa both had name Esther   micturition   Elliman's yellow embrocation
G Huster: cougher (i.e. cough mixture)
paté   according
Rev. Pilkington: friend of Swift (.25) & Sheridan   *F* cure-dent: toothpick
Thomas Sheridan: 'The Art of Punning'   regale: a feast
(frying pan)
F legs: *s* The Girl I Left behind Me   *Du* leven: life
legacy   Laetitia Van Lewen became Mrs Pilkington, friend of Swift. Delany called her 'Letty'
cantrip: a spell of necromancy   *L* culorum: of the posteriors
L colubra: snake
F oeufs à la   Gaby Delys: Fr. revue artist   *M Gr* avga: eggs
Église de Saint-Gabriel, Paris
G mein   *G* Feld: field   *Du* eiers: eggs   *L* usque ad mala: until the apples   *F* ciel
ph from the eggs to the apples: from start to finish   *F* pomme de terre
It uovo: egg   *L* ova: eggs   *I* ubh: egg   *F* sulfate de soude: sodium sulphate   *Rum* ochiuri: poached eggs
It uova sode: softboiled eggs   *It* occhio: eye
F sauté   *F* saumon: salmon   *F* monseigneur   suffusion   *Du* oog: eye
soufflé
some cat on toast   Mère Poulard: Paris restaurant; famous for 'omelettes de Mère Poulard'
letter 28/5/29 to HSW: 'Mme Puard, my old clinic nurse'
fried eggs   Carême: Fr. gastronome
fennel   *F* Carême: Lent
(013.26)   *Annals of the Four Masters*

Father T. Mathew: Ir. temperance advocate   lion, noble beast (emblem of apostle Mark)
F le père
St Luke   *Sp* águila: eagle (emblem of apostle John)   Baldwin: ass in the Reynard cycle
F baudet: ass
costive: niggardly   antinomian   James Clarence Mangan
antimony   lime   litmus paper

George Roberts: manager of Maunsel & Co, D, was to publish *Dubliners*, but after 3 years' delaying, the printer, John Falconer, decided against it & destroyed the 1st edition

public (books destroyed
pulpit by pulping)

L codex: book *L* podex: posterior

(pulped)
benefaction benediction

L flammeus: flaming

home rule

ph wild goose chase katharsis (J: *The Holy Office*)
Wild Geese: Ir. Jacobites who went to continent after defeat in 1691

'where in Sam Hill': pop. C19 U.S. expression meaning 'where in the world'

The Sporting Times had hostile review of *U.* in April 1922

P/K *It* porpora: purple cardinal & ordinal numbers *The Anglican Ordinal* (rulebook)
Vatican Sl purpurandus: one fit to be purpled, i.e. made a cardinal
Ice Dönsk tunga: Danish tongue
Rev 17:4–5: 'the woman was arrayed in purple & scarlet colour . . . & upon her forehead was a name written, MYSTERY, BABYLON THE GREAT, THE MOTHER OF HARLOTS' (Puritans applied to R.C. Church)
The Pink 'Un: subtitle of *The Sporting Times*

Luke 6:41: '& why beholdest thou the mote that is in thy brother's eye, but perceivest not the beam that is in thine own eye?'

L (translation): 'First the artist, the eminent writer, without any shame or apology, pulled up his raincoat & undid his trousers & then drew himself close to the life-giving & allpowerful earth, with his buttocks bare as they were born. Weeping & groaning he relieved himself into his own hands. Then, unburdened of the black beast, & sounding a trumpet, he put his own dung which he called his "down-castings" into an urn once used as an honoured mark of mourning. With an invocation to the twin brethren Medard & Godard he then passed water into it happily & mellifluously, while chanting in a loud voice the psalm which begins "My tongue is the pen of a scribe writing swiftly". Finally, from the foul dung mixed, as I have said, with the "sweetness of Orion" & baked & then exposed to the cold, he made himself an indelible ink'

St Colmcille: *s* Altus Prosator
Vulg Gen 3:7: 'et fecerunt sibi perizomata' ('& made themselves aprons')

Litany of BVM: 'vas honorabile' ('honourable vessel')

St Medard & St Gildard are invoked to bring rain

Vulg Ps 44:2: 'Lingua mea calamus scribae velociter scribentis' ('My tongue is the pen of a scribe writing swiftly')

Orion's *L* orina: urine

The Aeneid refers frequently to 'Pious Aeneas' fulminant: developing suddenly; thundering firman: order issued by Oriental sovereign

tremulous *F* terre

nychthemeron: period of 24 hours
G nicht: not

U. was not protected by copyright in U.S. & pirated editions appeared

Gr Ourania: 'Heavenly', muse of astronomy *Du* dood: dead *Gr* kopros: dung
Supposedly Orion originally named Ouriôn because generated from *Gr* ouron, urine
ph double-dyed villain

solution of gallic acid + solution of a ferrous salt = blue-black ink firstly
Dean Kinane: *St Patrick* 134: 'O God, through the bowels of Thy mercy'
lastly Esau *R* menshevik: Russian Socialist of moderate party

alchemist

corrosive sublimate: mercuric chloride

integument: hard outer covering   marivaudage: preciosity in writing

Viconian cycle: unfold (birth), marry, mould (death), wheeling (ricorso)

transaccidentation: transmutation of accidents of bread & wine in Eucharist   dividual: shared amongst a number

Squid squirts inklike screen

Wilde: *The Picture of Dorian Gray* (idea came from Balzac's *Le Peau de chagrin*)   *Da* dødhud: dead skin   *We* hud: magic, illusion, charm

went

Meillet & Cohen: *Les langues du monde* 358 (Dravidian languages): 'maram und endu kangiren (un arbre existe ayant dit je vois)'   devil

Santali (*Samtal*) dal: strike; dapal: strike each other; cover; danapal: covering   agglutinative genre: a feature of Munda languages, e.g. Santali

speaking   at last   *Li* arklas: plough   *Li* arklys: horse

ph putting the cart before the horse

squaring the circle (Bruno attempted)

St Ignatius Loyola   A LITTLE CLOUD   open

6 October: Ivy Day, anniversary of death of Parnell

(IVY DAY IN THE COMMITTEE ROOM)

(pen)

Li žasis: goose   *Li* žasinas: gander

pr What is sauce for the goose is sauce for the gander

right

THE SISTERS   *Du* kruis: cross   *Du* kroon: crown

Da -en (postposition): the   Ku Klux Klan   kraal (S. Africa): village, enclosure

by the . . .   (religion, sovereign & home)

police station

polite society

Li stotis, stoties: station   *L* quemquem: whoever   *L* qum: when, as, while

duties

(from being pelted)   CLAY   A LITTLE CLOUD

libellous   foul play

AN ENCOUNTER   EVELINE

IVY DAY IN THE COMMITTEE ROOM   *Da* rum: room   The Virgin appeared at Knock, Co. Mayo, 1879

Journalese omnium gatherum: gathering of all sorts

business

Sl pigeon: business

whore   Iris: Greek rainbow-goddess   nickname   *Li* mergyte: little girl

F arc-en-ciel: rainbow

Da rand: edge   round the corner

Hyde   Jekyll

Sl have a hideful: be drunk   *Heb* beth El: house of God

THE BOARDING HOUSE   *G* Fenster: window   *Li* gražus: beautiful

F bordel: brothel   *Li* oras: weather

Da Hvorledes har De det i dag, min sorte herre?: How are you today, my dark sir?

Li sergantis: sick

F Sl sergot: policeman

hat   AFTER THE RACE

GRACE

prince

fandango (dance) *Li* šiltas: warm *Li* silpnas: weak
Li šaltas: cold *Li* stiprus: strong
Li sveikas: hello Poor Law Guardian palpably Baltic
astonished *Li* baltas: white
G Stimmung: mood 'Is that called a tundish in Ireland? asked the dean. I never A PAINFUL CASE
G stumm: dumb heard the word in my life' (*Portrait* V) *G* Sache: case
stemming *G* Stamme: family, race

G während: during where in

what the son of a bitch

COUNTERPARTS *Li* Kaledos: Christmas
Caledonian: Scottish

lieutenant whiskey caftan: an Oriental undertunic
Li Lietuviskas: Lithuanian captain
'it was said him' is lit. trans. of *Da* det blev sagt
ham (' he was told')

on the *N* utgift: expense THE DEAD *Da* med: with
Li aciu: thanks *G* von *G* Ausgabe: edition
ARABY conspue: express detestation Dominican Order (Bruno asking
congruent belonged to, 1563–76)
nobody's permission *Da* kun at bringe hjem: only to bring home

TWO GALLANTS of porter *Da* til: to A MOTHER Wellington: 'Up, guards, & at them'

poltergeist *G* kotzen: vomit *Du* donder op: get the hell out of here! applause
hoplite: Greek soldier *Li* kiek: how much? A MOTHER
L pater: father intelligence
indulgence: herring
Guinness porter (dark brown)

printing

Da silde: herrings *F* hareng
Zuider Zee, Holland King Harry
s Herring the King: Jan. Feb.
'Herring our king'
Mercy & justice contrasted *Li* lova: bed *Li* labas rytas: good morning
in Portia's speech in *Merchant of Venice* IV.1.194–215 *Gr* labyrinthos: labyrinth
rest existence *Li* Tamsta: sir, your grace Penman
master Ham, son of Noah

to his brother BRUNO Shaun Λ

G Breite: breadth

brain burn Brown Bess: old regulation musket
F brune BROWNE
I bás: death
G bauz!: interjection if something falls
Nayman: Nestorian shepherd who became Odysseus, lit. 'no-man Zeus'
the fabulous king, Prester John NOLAN
oblique case

hesitency tenses Deponent verbs are passive or middle in form,
but active in meaning
imperative indicative
vindictive
vocative case direct discourse jolly: to entertain, beguile

G Zwilling: twin

son of Adam (Cain)

It scemerie: stupidities interim
uterus

deathbed

L conifiteor: I confess

I a mhic: my boy

45 papal bull Bill of Attainder: bill passed (first in 1459) for attainting any one without a judicial trial to boot

pray *Confiteor:* 'in thought, word & deed' *L* cur: why *L* quicquid: whoever

(questions asked by confessor to determine gravity of sin) *L* ubi: where

L quando: when *L* quomodo: how *L* quibus auxiliis: with whose help

L quoties: how often

controversy between Roman & old Ir. churches over date of Easter

Sl piejaw: admonition, moral advice

Easter Island, Pacific

(hell) Tennyson: *Charge of the Light Brigade:* 'Cannon to right of them, Cannon to left of them'

catch-as-catch-can nigger *Du* blanke: white man

F blanc *Sl* blankards: bastards

AngI forenenst: opposite

heresiarch United Kingdom

Tiresias (bisexual seer)

U.207: 'founded, like the world . . . upon the void'

dog in the manger (Aesop's fable)

'I will not serve, answered Stephen' (*Portrait* V)

ph live & let live

ph pay the piper

ph by the by

Swinburne 'Sea of Sodom': the Dead Sea (II Esd 5:7)

King Solomon

solemnities

Bathsheba: mother of Solomon

G Bad: bath

L caldor: heat apropos *Sl* pipe: penis

candour *L* opprobro: I reproach

Jacob's pipe: pipe with porcelain head representing one of the patriarchs

(genitals)

G Abgott: idol heart of hearts

penis

Penal Laws: restrictions on Catholics in C 17–18 Ir.

Mrs Centlivre: *Bold Stroke for a Wife* (play, 1717)

Sauvé: *Proverbes & dictons de la Basse-Bretagne,* no. 478: 'Dieu te fasse, cher enfant, devenir aussi grand Que le prêtre qui t'a baptisé' ('May God make thee, dear child, to grow as big as the priest who baptised thee')

In blessing of the baptismal water on Holy Saturday, the celebrant dips the paschal candle into it

wise *I* piseóg: superstition sophist
pious wish
elenchus: logical refutation

*U.*47: 'Morose delectation Aquinas tunbelly calls this'
the love philtre drunk by Tristan & Isolde
small p's passibility: susceptibility to suffering
Tristan died at Cliff of the Penmarks (Penmarc'h)
Sir John Lubbock: *The Pleasures of Life*
four
Butler's *Lives of the Saints* strabismal: squinting; fig., displaying perversity of intellectual perception

cockeyed Popeye ablative

cantred: district containing 100 townships Yeats: *Countess Cathleen*
G Minne: love 'Congested Districts' in rural C 19 Ir.

acres, roods, poles, perches: square measure used for land

It educande: girl boarders in convent schools

Edward Moore (1712–57): *The Gamester* II.2: 'rich beyond the dreams of avarice'
arrivisme: unscrupulous ambition

books in some versions Sorge is the son of Tristan & Isolde
F bouche *G* Sorge: sorrow
King Anguish: father of Isolde *L* solus cum sola sive cuncti cum omnibus: [a man] alone with [a woman] alone or else the whole lot with everybody
best man (wedding)

(marriage) obituary verses

bolivar: basic monetary unit in Venezuela
Sl collarwork: laborious work
wide wide world

owl: 'tu-whit, tu-whoo!'

Macpherson: *Fingal* II.54: 'Thy spouse high-bosom'd, heaving fair'
In Macpherson's *Fingal*, Morna is glossed as 'woman beloved of all' (Fingal's mother)

We pr Seek the nest of evil in the bosom of a good word

accurately Japhet Matt 13:57: 'A prophet is not without honour, save in his own country'

impetiginous: scabby

Elijah fed by ravens (I Kings 17:6) & predicts rain from a little cloud (I Kings 18:44)

Du rook: smoke *F* parler: to talk
superstition that rooks hold 'parliaments' to try & execute offenders
D Annals note public records were burned in 1304
D Annals, 1833: fire in Custom House Record Office in Four Courts, & Custom House burned 1922

Book of Common Prayer: Burial of the Dead: 'dust to dust'

Sl mudhead: stupid person   obtundity: dulness   I Cor 15:55: 'O death, where is thy sting? O grave, where is thy victory?'
F peste!: good gracious!

Sl murphies: potatoes

bully beef

crackerhash: biscuits & salt meat

pr He who sups with the devil hath need of a long spoon

AngI ph more power to your elbow! (encouragement)
Sl elbow grease: hard work

birthright

J: *The Holy Office*

L pro anno: per year   J's father urged him to seek a clerkship in Guinness's: Stanislaus thought he should take it
'Guinness is good for you' (slogan)
agape
bishop of York   *Du* doodskop: death skull
Yorick's skull (*Hamlet* V.1)

Hamlet III.1.79: 'from whose bourn No traveller returns'   *ph* vale of tears
ph separate the wheat from the tares
divine providence (Vico)

crib-biter: nervous person; cantankerous horse: persistent grumbler

pr Once bitten, twice shy

Armenia occupied by (Islamic) Turks from 1405; nationalism in C19–20 met with systematic massacres

pr Every bullet has its billet

Boulanger: Fr. general with whom the Ir. conspired
F boulanger: baker
s I'll Sing Thee Songs of Araby   *L* alibi: elsewhere
Macpherson's *Fingal* glosses placename Cuthon as 'mournful sound of waves'
Fingal V.101: 'grey-bounding' (dogs)
Macpherson: *Carric-Thura* 160: 'slow-rolling eye'
Macpherson: *Temora* I.221: 'an oozy rock'   *L* praeposteritas: inversion

L anti nos: against us   shamming   scheming
Antinous: suitor of Penelope, represented in *U.* by Mulligan & Boylan
scatophily

thoroughpaced proselyte
prosody
sum   Lady Dufferin: *s* Lament of the Irish Emigrant: 'I'm sitting on the stile, Mary'
L mus: mouse

nr There was a Crooked Man (mentions 'crooked sixpence' & 'crooked stile') Black Friars: Dominicans

love of Shakespeare J provided last line for Gogarty's prizewinning poem 'The Death of Shelley'

serendipity: faculty of making sudden & happy accidental discoveries

(4 continents) *L* afer: African

Macpherson: *Fingal* IV.75: 'Nine times he drowned it [his dagger] in Dala's side'

G bis jetzt: until now (194.06–7)

Fingal II.55: 'a stranger in the hall of her grief'

'Heil Hitler! Ein Volk, ein Reich, ein Führer' (slogan)

Novara Avenue, Bray *L* patrimonium: paternal estate *G* am: at the *G* Bummel: stroll

novena: a 9-day devotion

AngI on his keeping: in flight from authorities *s* Zip Coon: 'I pose you heard ob . . . Sings po'sum up a gum tree'

Gen 4:9: 'Am I my brother's keeper?' possum feigns death to avoid capture

'aint (got) the gumption *L* immaculatus: unstained

altruist

Fingal I.46n: states that 'of other times' means 'of old'

Celestine heresy der. from Pelagians (359.01–3); also name of a Benedictine order of monks

celibacy

celebrity

counterfoil Lincolnshire lottery

F feuille: leaf, page Koran: Sura LVI: 'Amid thornless lote-trees'

Reporters: in Islam, 2 angels who record good & bad deeds of every man

F petit particularly

little brother

come home kindergarten please bring

Da død: death terrify

Mohammed on death: 'the soul cometh out like the smell of the best musk, so that verily it is handed from one angel to another'

F toilettes

5 set times of day for Mohammedan prayer: just after sunset, at nightfall, at daybreak, just after noon & in mid afternoon Donnybrook, district of D

dawning

teatime

nuncheon: light refreshment of liquor

s 'One Fine Day in the Middle of the Night Two dead men got up to fight'

ON Muspell: name of the realm of life

frontispiece

spectacles

Ibsen: *The Master Builder*

It babbo: daddy *G* Bürgermeister

G Himmel: sky, heaven *Du* punt: point, full stop (003.09–10)

Marcion: heretic, believed he was Christ

schism (heresy)   How Buckley shot the Russian General

gonorrhea   Aesop's fable of the Fox, the Wolf and the Ape

It lupo: wolf

Eva, daughter of Diarmaid MacMurrough, married Strongbow after his invasion of Ir.

J's father worked for the Collector-General of Rates

meantime   Hamilcar: father of Hannibal

Parnell accused of misappropriating the Paris funds   *G* schämen: be ashamed   Kitty O'Shea: Parnell's wife

Christ's crown of thorns

Christ's robe preserved in Trèves Cathedral   so help you

F pitre: clown   *F* poule   cock crow (Peter betrays Christ, also in *Hamlet*)

St Peter & St Paul   gape: disease of poultry

F pas mal de: a fair amount of   Reynaldo: Polonius' servant in *Hamlet,* also one of the 12 peers of France

F siècle: century, age

demotic

Hasdrubal: son-in-law of Hamilcar   cost

roubles

pound of flesh (*Merchant of Venice*)

E . . . H . . . C

Sydney Grundy: *In Honour Bound* (play, 1880)

crucifiction   *F* Saint-Esprit: Holy Ghost   Saturday   holiday

Sauvé: *Proverbes & dictons de la Basse-Bretagne* no. 37: 'Mon souper dans mon ventre je voudrais qu'il fût nuit,

pr There is many a slip 'twixt the cup & the lip   Que dimanche vint demain et fête après demain'

King Lear I.2.15: 'Got 'tween asleep & awake'   (between sleep at end of *U.*, & FW)

Parasceve: day of preparation for Jewish sabbath, esp. Good Friday   cock crow (*Hamlet*)

F estomac: stomach   simian: apelike   (monkeys don't cry)

'Jim the Penman': James Townsend Savard, forger

shaman

Moore: *s* Oft in the Stilly Night   Tennyson: *Break, Break, Break:* 'O! for the touch of a vanished hand'

I arís: again

AngI naboclesh: pay no attention to him/it   handmade   *F* rêve

two gates of sleep: true dreams pass through gates of horn, false through gates of ivory (*Aeneid* VI.893, *Odyssey* XIX.562)

obedience of Ruth (Bible)

Chamber Music XXI: 'His love is his companion'

the fleshpots of Egypt & the hanging gardens of Babylon

Euston & Marylebone, London railway stations

dormer: bedroom   *AngI* shee: fairy   *Gr* Selene: moon-goddess

moonshee: interpreter, secretary   serene

G Scheinwerfer: headlamps, searchlights (lit. 'light-thrower')

snickered

nest egg: money laid by

(170.22)

ph have one's cake & eat it   Gray's *Elegy*

Temple Mount: Mt Zion in Jerusalem, site of David's tomb

references in Macpherson's *Temora* to i) the traveller in the future who will pass Cathmor's tomb, whistling; ii) the unhappiness of souls of those buried without funeral song; iii) the pre-Christian custom of naming persons only after they had performed some distinguishing work

It balbettare: to stutter   baptised

F bêtise

(Prodigal Son)

E . . . H . . . C review of *U.* in *The Sporting Times:* 'The main contents of the book are enough to make a Hottentot sick' Dubliners *AngI* crawsick:
*U.*783: 'yes I said yes I will Yes' sick & thirsty after night's drinking

holy fire *Gr* leon: lion (sheepfold)
Luke 12:27: 'lilies of the field'
VI.B.31.102: 'old sooty (devil)' Mookse
loan shark: one who lends money at extortionate interest rate
Mulligan

Gripes (Serpent) *F* ver solitaire: tapeworm
gripe: pain in bowels
gem James Joyce

Othello III.3.191–2: 'jealousy; It is the green ey'd monster'

Hamlet *pr* Silence is golden
damn it! *pr* Silence means consent
Isa 1:16–17: 'cease to do evil; Learn to do well' *AngI* whist!: silence!

Herr Studiosus: nickname of Ibsen; Earwicker
ironical phrase to describe zealous student wig in your ear: gossip
whist drive parishoners *WWI Sl* barishnya: unmarried girl

Cadbury's make crackers *WWI Sl* crackers: mad
*U.*6: 'cracked lookingglass of a servant'

astigmatism *WWI Sl* boozeliers: fusiliers
M Gr stigmê: moment *WWI Sl* iggri: quickly
Alfred Shaw, Johnny Mullagh: cricketers mullah: a Mohammedan religious man *Sl* mull: simpleton
Sl lamppost: tall thin person Mulligan
Blue Coat School, D (King's Hospital) Guy Fawkes
Boylan in *U.* wears socks with sky-blue clocks
Potiphar's wife tempted Joseph rantipole: a wild or reckless person
F pot-au-feu: beef stew (typically French)
confessed

F follette: merry, gay, wild

I Cor 13:13: 'faith, hope, charity' (FAITH)
F encore: still
s Rock of Ages HOPE

Host supposedly able to choke guilty CHARITY

Witch doctors use bone to curse II Tim 4:1: 'the quick & the dead'

L insomnia, somnia somniorum: sleeplessness, dreams of dreams
L per omnia saecula saeculorum, amen: for ever & ever, amen
mercy ⊏ *L* vopiscus: 1 of a pair of twins, born alive after premature death of other
L Dominus vobiscum: the Lord be with you *Confiteor:* 'through my fault,
Richard III V.4.7: 'A horse, a horse, my kingdom for a horse' through my own fault, through my own most grevious fault' utterly
Luke 11:27: 'Blessed is the womb that bore thee, & the paps that gave thee suck'

Sl jigs: delerium tremens

James Joyce compulsory
U.S. Sl jimjams: delerium tremens convulsive

when Boabdil, last Moorish king of Granada, went into exile, his mother said 'You do well to weep like a woman over what you could not defend as a man'
Cathmor & Cairbar: contrasting brothers in Macpherson's *Temora*

L de profundis: from the depths　　attrite: repentant through fear of punishment, not through love of God
Temora III.262–3: 'days of youth were mixed with mine'

compline: hour of the last service of the day　　attends　　Atha: seat of Cairbar, in *Temora*
Temora II.241: 'Fingal begins to be alone'　　is at hand
Temora III.259: 'Never shall they [souls] rise, without song, to the dwelling of winds'
L spiritus: breath, spirit
F gouttelette: droplet　　(031.11)

(031.03, 030.19)　　(031.17)

nr 'Wednesday's child is full of woe'　　*F* jeudi　　(005.10–11)

I lá: day

wastepaper basket

Temora II.239: 'O Trenmor! High dweller of eddying winds . . . thunder'　　Ulerin: star in Macpherson's *Temora*, glossed as 'the guide to Ireland'
Campbell: 'Lord Ullin's Daughter'　　Dog Star: Sirius
Temora V.289: 'all its trees are blasted with winds'
Gen 2:9: 'the tree of knowledge of good & evil'
Temora III.244: 'Trenmor, clothed with meteors'　　horizon
L metuor: I am feared　　*L* horrescens: shuddering
troglodyte　　*Gr* dynamo-: power-　　Beelzebub (spelled like JHWH, Jehovah)
logos: universal reason governing world (Heraclitus); lit. 'word', as in John 1:1
Gray's *Elegy:* 'Full many a flower is born to blush unseen'　　Moore: *s* 'Fairest! put on awhile these pinions of light I bring thee' [Cummilium]　　*L* cubilibus: to, for, by beds
Macpherson: *Fingal* III.63: 'the hall of her secret sigh'

Temora VI.305n: 'the warning voice of the dead'

only

ALP　　alpha, beta, gamma, delta

all

Punchestown Races, Co. Kildare

resourceful　　ricorso (Vico)　　bells (peal)

G drei: 3　　'Old Sod': Ir.　　'Forty Bonnets': nickname of Mrs Tommy Healy of Galway

F mesdames　　*G* Knie: knee

knows how　　tipsy cake: cake saturated with wine or spirits

beck: brook

G Tasche: pocket, handbag
tramtickets (floating in river)
innuendo

Green Hills: area near Tallaght

Poulaphuca: chasm of Liffey S.W. of D　　Blessington: town, Co. Wicklow

Sallynoggin: district of Dún Laoghaire
Sally Gap: crossroads in Wicklow Mts nr source of *r* Liffey
deluging delighting
AngI deludhering: deluding
AngI sloothering: blarney

Wyndham Lewis: *Time & Western Man* 170: 'The materialist of today is still obsessed with the wish to make this dead matter *real*. . . . So he brings it to life, by pumping it full of "time"'

F quoi

Isa 35:6: 'Then shall . . . the tongue of the dumb sing'
Luke 11:14: 'when the devil was gone out, the dumb spake'
quack (ducks)

F eau
omega (end of alphabet)
(delta shape)

r Cheb *Sl* to go phut: fizzle out
r Futa

(their heads bang together over river)
AngI hike!: stop! (call to a horse)
∧ ⋌ ⊏ ⊣ ⊢

r Repe

r Blackwater
('Dublin' means 'black pool')
r Steeping *r* Upa
r Stupia
r Heart

r Saale *ph* Dear Dirty Dublin
soil *F* salir: *r* Duddon
to dirty

r Battle battledore: wooden bat *r* Moldau
bottle used in washing clothes mildew
r Dnieper *r* Ganges

AngI ph at all at all *L* Anima Sancta: Holy Spirit
r Sendai
A city is supposed to lie beneath Lough Neagh
lock & key *r* King
r Nisi *L* nisi prius: unless before (a writ of summons to jurors) Charles Humphreys: Wilde's solicitor
L fieri facias: cause to be made (type of writ) *r* Fier versus *r* Illisos
Sl fieri facias: red-faced *r* Tom *r* Till illicit
pr time will tell Wm Whewell made 1st British cotidal
pr Time & tide wait for no man *pr* As you sow so shall you reap chart
Odysseus (Outis: no man) *r* Spring spring & neap tides
r Roughty *L* minxit: he urinated *Du* loof: foliage *r* Loo
love *Sl* oof: money

letter, 7/3/24, to HSW: 'It is a chattering dialogue across the river by two washerwomen who as night falls become a tree and a stone. The river is named Anna Liffey' [as on old maps]

F rive gauche: left bank *F* rive droite: right bank *It* sinistra: left
reeve: official, bailiff, steward, overseer *I* droichead: bridge

Howth *r* Elde Deucalion: equivalent of Noah in Ovid

r Wiesel *r* Rat *r* Derry
weasel (arched back walking)
(Derry . . . Cork . . . Dublin . . . Galway represent 4 provinces of Ireland)
AngI blather: garrulous nonsense
L lictor: magistrate's assistant (carried fasces, bundle of
L lector: reader rods surrounding an axe)
I gárda: policeman else *r* Elster HEC
r Gard Henry the Fowler: C10 German king
AngI ph at all at all *r* Qu'appelle HCE Hugo Capet: king of Franks; stands for HCE
F que s'appelle: what's he called? returned divine times in Vico *L* caput: head
r Ur Goths Tristan
Gotland: Swedish island in Baltic *Da* tvist: discord
Kattegat: sea between Denmark & Sweden in North Huns
Mark Sullivan: *Our Times, 1900 to 1925*, 70 gives chant used in teaching geography: 'Maine, Augusta, on the Kennebec.
blacksmith (marriage over anvil at Gretna Green) New Hampshire, Concord, on the Merrimac.'
Sl block: fuck *Da* saft: juice
r Bann licensed Adam & Eve's Church, D
(marriage banns never announced)
(married by the captain) *Da* Ederfugl: eider duck Ibsen: *The Wild Duck*
Sl splice: marriage (Anglican marriage service) *r* Duck take *r* Drake Creek
Da vildgæs: wild goose (river & mountain)

fishes & weirs Happy Christmas
isthmus of Sutton
r Line Stock ending of Ir. fairy story: '& if they don't live happy that you &
marriage lines: marriage certificate I may'
r May *r* Pasmore *r* Oxus *r* Don
ask us *ph* Dear Dirty Dublin
Du dom: foolish les Dombes: lake area near Lyon health insured
Hu domb: hill *Hu* folyó: river
Stork & Pelican: 2 D insurance companies third party risks
r Pelican
Sl tin: money *r* Delvin *r* Devlin
r Tin *L* delvo: I wash
rape of Sabine women *r* Sabrina (the Severn) *AngI* asthore: darling
r Astor
treacherous *r* Deva deltas cat & mouse

r Adda *F Sl* flic: policeman

alderman *r* Min *F* maison-dieu: hospital
'Old Man's House': Royal Hospital, Kilmainham, D Min: ithyphallic god
F fou Alpha Hospital for Incurables, Donnybrook Rd, D

s The Rocky Road to Dublin
quagmire *r* Waag *G* Weg: way
r Quagua pemmican: condensed food; hence, *r* Grass grasshopper
condensed thought & matter (wedding ring)
r Ant *F* or: gold *r* Ore scabbard gabbart: barge; lighter *F* barque
Koran: Sura XCIX: 'an ant's weight of good' *r* Arques
Gr okeanus: ocean *r* Till *Naut* loom: appearance
'Ivernia': Ptolemy's name for Ir. of land on horizon
Naut landfall: first sight of land (Noah sent out birds from Ark to see if *r* Tilt kilt
dry land had appeared) tilt: awning over a boat
r Gran *r* Pheni *ph* sweat of his brow (after Gen 3:19)
V. Bérard thought Ulysses a Phoenician
Pigeonhouse, at S. side of mouth of Liffey
r Pigeon
timoneer: helmsman, steersman *F* suivre: follow scutties: small boats
r Marchan *r* Suie *Sl* scut: cunt scut: rabbit's tail
The Wash: part of E. Anglia coast burnous: hooded cloak worn by Arabs & Moors

r Runa *Sl* bow: penis *r* Bow *r* Riss *Du* borst: breast *r* Pilcomayo
renegade runagate: fugitive bowsprit burst
r Saskatchewan Burns: *s* The Deil's Awa' wi' the Excise Man grayling: fish of family *Salmonidae*
r Whale Grail

s Doran's Ass: 'So he tuned his pipes & fell a-humming' idiot (D pron. 'eejit')
Egypt
Late Egyptian kings called Ptolemy tell me soon Eskimo
Alexandrian Ptolemy (90–168 A.D.): gave early description of Ireland *Port* escuma: froth
r Swift Solomon & Sheba (I Kings 10)
r Seba *L* vagina: sheath
salmon *r* Solomon N. & S. Bulls (sandbanks), D roaring surfeited
may have been named for roaring of surf *r* Ruhr *G* rühren: stir
spray *I* buadh: victory *r* Buëch *r* Erne earned *Da* lille: little *r* Lille
r Spree *r* Boyarka *r* Bua *r* Bojana *R* boyarka: wife of a boyar (348.10) *I* Banba: Ireland (poetic)
stale (hard) daily bread *r* Trader Beck *ph* earning his bread in the sweat of his brow
steely-bred traitor (after Gen 3:19)
Da kaldt: called

r Winterbourne Charles Kingsley: *The Water Babies* *L* Ave Maria: Hail Mary
G Wasser
HCE eye *r* Syr Darya *r* Bhader
Da fisk: fish

N bak: back *N* vande: water, tide *Ki* nyumba: house *Ki* chamba: hiding place *r* Chu
(200.22–32) *r* Salso girls *Ki* noo: whetstone *r* Chambal *Ki* choo: privy
Morley called Parnell Ireland's erring chief *r* Chef pontiff ('bridgemaker') *r* Oise
Da til: to HEC *r* Error
r Gota *r* Yssel *r* Limmat *r* Negro
God above! isn't that the limit as the nigger said when he looked in the glass
(took one look) *r* Plate

how oft she was left at the side *r* Ladder *r* Conewango Creek coney: rabbit bunny
Antiphon for Paschal time: 'a latere dextro' ('from the right side') bunting used to make flags
(high) *Ki* sina feza: I have no money *L* me absente: in my absence
(flag falls at start of race) *r* Sina *r* Santee *Ki* ahsanthe: thanks
r Asse proxenete: one who negotiates something, esp. a marriage; in *F Sl* a bawd what is that?
man in possession: bailiff's man
F merde pour votre . . . *G* russischer: Russian Hindu lingua franca: mixed jargon used in
r Emme *r* Reuss *r* Honddu *r* Cher *r* Jarkon Levant
spate: sudden rising in river show you Hebrew
ph call a spade a spade *r* Shari *r* Ebro
Da skole: school Dublin Abecedarian Society (extreme Anabaptists)
r Skollis
F par exemple Blavatsky's 'Mahatma Letters' came from Tibet by
telekinesis (movement produced by medium, at a distance)
prosecute *r* Cocytus *r* Cox but little
r Sake *r* Botletle
r Loa *ON* vindauga: window
low *r* Windau *G* Aug: eye
osier: species of willow used in basketwork
easychair *r* Meuse music
cuneiform letters *r* Ribble *r* Reedy *r* Derg
L cunnus: cunt fiddle dirge
G Bogen: bow *r* Bandon *r* Sure fiddle-de-dee *r* Dee
r Bogan abandon *r* Fiddown
r Bow *r* Tista just a *r* Suck
G Dial ist a' Sach': It's as follows! What an affair!
Cliffs of Moher, Co. Clare most
more
r Humber Glomman grampus: whale *r* Tar door
gloomy *ME* gloumben: look sullen tare: vetch
r Bubu *D Annals* records for 1575 a storm so violent that 'neither bowman nor shot could go
buboes: inflamed swellings abroad'
r Bale *G* brannte *r* Brantas (bonfires on hills) ne'er a *Heb* ner: lamp
G Alprand: edge of mts Rocky Mts *r* Nera
old Ir. Baal fire rituals on eve of 1 May Giant's Causeway, N. Ir. Death Cap: a poisonous
Grafton St, D toadstool
fungus Fingal's Cave, Hebrides *r* Barrow
Finglas: district of D; means 'clear streamlet'
Daniel O'Connell *r* Sittang *r* Sambre *r* Sette *r* Drammen
darnels: tares accumulated sitting sombre on his seat dreaming
Da drømmende: dreaming *r* Usk Don Quixote was Knight of the Rueful Countenance
r Drome asking questions *r* Rufu
D Annals, 1729: 'Linen scarfs worn at funerals to encourage the linen manufacture'

deaths in the morning *Times*, by question & answer hop, step & jump
r Mormon *r* Thames *G* Handzettel: handbill *r* Hop
deep end (burial at sea) births in the *Daily Mail* to moil: labour hard
r Moi Moyle: sea between Ireland & Scotland
(mouth) twelve to four guttersnipes sandpipers & plovers remove leeches from mouths
G zwölf: 12 snipe (birds) *r* Peck of crocodiles
F Sl crocs: teeth Ibsen: *Et vers:* 'At digte,–det er at holde Dommedag over sig selv' ('to write–that
r Crocodile is to bring oneself to Judgement')
Da hunselv: she herself *r* Weir dander: anger
r Hunse to dree one's weird: to suffer one's destiny *r* Dande
Du droomen: to dream
r Drome on high
G Stern: star *Du* zwart: black *Du* kous: stocking *Du* wijde: baggy *Du* broek: trousers
(night) *r* Zwarte *r* Kowsha Willibroek Canal *Du* wit: white
r Buda *r* Pest Ibsen: *Peer Gynt* Henri IV: 'Paris vaut bien une messe' ('Paris is worth a mass')
r Worth *r* Thet
Jacob's mess of pottage (Gen 25:29–34) *r* Dodo *r* Durme
r Mess *F* dodo: sleep *s* I Dreamt I Dwelt in Marble Halls
r Adra *r* Drance *r* Durance *r* Vaal *r* Severn
trance Burns: *Esopus to Maria* 57: 'in durance vile'
r Darent *r* Wink

Ki wanda: a finger's breadth
r Wende *r* Wandle
Lapland has short summer *r* Amazon wish him
r Ishim
F bonjour *SC* dobar dan: good day! new potatoes salt sault: waterfall
ph Dear Dirty Dublin *r* Dan Dapper Dan: *r* Euphrates
his maggers (031.10) nickname for a smart man
r Maggia *r* Bloem
Da fisk: fish *r* Lay *Ki* yayi: egg

Danish bacon on toast & a cup & a half *Da* København: Copenhagen (weak)
coast
green tea *r* Tay *F* soupçon *r* Oup Mocha coffee *F* sable: sand
r Dzubgan *r* Dzo dozen (cups) *r* Kafue *r* Mokau *r* Au Sable
r Sikiang *F* sucré *r* Ale Matt 16:18: 'thou art Peter & upon this rock' *r* Shinko
r Sukri
G Schinkenbrot: ham sandwich *Ki* hujambo, bana?: a *Ki* greeting *F* jambon *Da* og: & or stay his
r Ham *r* Jambi *r* Bana *r* Jam *F* plaise: please
r Tomi Pyrenees pair of knees
stomacher: kind of waistcoat Pyrrha: wife of Deucalion (197.03)
double joints shook with gout rush
toggle joint: 2 pieces hinged edgeways *r* Goyt *r* Russ
(mt peak) *r* Vivero rivers up her sleeve towering rage swells & rises
packload *Sl* vivers: food *r* Sieve *r* Metauro *r* Swale
G Riese: giant *r* Hardey Hekla: volcano, Iceland *r* Frome stare
Da kaste: throw *r* Stour
r Sow so-&-so *r* Sozh

r Platte *r* Tawe
the plate on her toe
ask to whistle to him Balfe: *s* The Heart Bowed Down
r Esk *r* Vistula *r* Heart
s The Rakes of Mallow Michael Kelly: D composer & tenor
The Barber of Seville: (*s*) 'La Calunnia è un venticello' ('Calumny is like a
Balfe: Ir. breeze') fuff: puff of wind
composer, wrote *The Bohemian Girl* *r* Suchio
beat *r* Hen

terrace Tower of Babel
L turris: tower
Sl mag: talk

mangel-wurzel *F* fait: fact
mangle weight: washerwoman's tool writing
Moore: *s* *r* Roya *r* Romanche *L* Annona: Roman corn-goddess *r* Aroostook *r* Nive
Rich & Rare *F* La Manche: English Channel *G* geboren *r* Ebro aristocrat
Du dochter: daughter *r* Sense *r* Arta *r* Pyriphlegethon *G* funkeln: sparkle
science
r Fan & her frostifying fireflies *Du* vlies: fleece
r Anner *r* Dasht *r* Vire Vlie Strait

promenade shrieked sleeked 'neath their bearskins
r Nith
(green water) r Jade r Robe r Wood
jade: deceitful girl rob the world
archbishops of D: Paul Cullen & Edward MacCabe s Mother Machree

AngI blatherskate: nonsense *It* porpora: purple r Brahmani
purple patches of prose
Da femtyfyx: 56
r Fem
powder tumbling *Da* vuggeborn: child in the cradle
L pudor: shame
Du mand: basket

waterclocks

Alma Gluck: soprano Nellie Melba, soprano, was Juliet to Jean de Reszke's Romeo
Gluck (composer) delta
s Phoebe Dearest

Da hun var: she was
Da holmen: the islet r Var
Da sang: song r Holme *Da* Jeg elsker saaledes hine smukke lille unge piger: I so love those beautiful little
r Sanga (back home) young girls
Soay Island, Hebrides r Soar so on Firth of Forth r Tone
r Pigg
r Sonora Louis 'Oom' Botha: Boer general *AngI* bothered: deaf r Bheri Sunday
F ton sonore: *Du* oom: uncle r Botha beri-beri from malnourishment r Sandy
resonant tone r Umvolosi r Yaw *L* stultus: foolish
(unwilling)
r Dee r Yare *Da* liv: life r Chalk
ph as God is my judge
r Sorgue socks r Doon

r Douro door *AngI* dudeen: short tobacco pipe r Shirvan
r Dudhi servant
r Siligir r Wensum r Farmer Creek Pile Ends: end of S. Wall in C18 D
winsome Mile End Road, London
r Daer Milucra & Aine loved Finn r Grawe
(seven girls) Grania
sallyport: opening in a fortified place for passage of
troops making a sally
Sihlpost: Zurich G.P.O.

blackbottom (dance) r Shubenacadie
Sl block: fuck *J* shoben: urine
r Sihl
sill
(legs)

Prov 30:19: 'the way of a man with a maid'

r Silver *Sl* shiner: a silver coin
r Siller
r Neisse r Little

r Inny (capture of river by another)

r Pleisse r Adda two and a tanner r Tamar r Liz r Lossie
pleaseful Tamar falsely accused of prostitution (Gen 38:24)
r Hab

weary *It* rima: rhyme *Da* O det: O that!
r Wye r Rye r Rima r Odet
r Trent hell Denis Florence MacCarthy wrote *Underglimpses*
trend
combs (combinations, *G* Flut: flood r Pian Creek
undergarment) *Fi* pian: soon playing piano *It* piena: flood
learn s Cusheen Loo
r Lerryn r Cushing Creek

r Rede *G* Rede: speech, language *F* trouver *F* poule
read pool
It parco: park *G* tummeln: i) make haste, ii) romp about
(111.05–9) *r* Tummel
r Tarn
turn

Da øre: ear listen in
r Ore *r* Ouse *r* Essonne *r* Inn
backside

bedamned

F petit
petty gaping
r Dane *r* Hodder *r* Dodder Order for the Burial of the Dead: 'In the
Sl hoddie-doddie: a squat midst of life we are in death'
person, a cuckold

r May *r* Honey Creek May & December *r* Embira
s The Young May Moon honeymoon
tidal bore

r Irwell *r* Shire
anywhere
Sl dace: twopence

brose: made by pouring boiling *r* Milk
water on oatmeal
r Brittas (joins Liffey nr Blessington)

T lep: shore sloblands of Fairview nr mouth of *r* Tolka, D *F* plage au: beach at

Clontarf Dublin Bay
r Feale *r* Gaya *r* Aire *r* Salt
seawind *F* embouchure: river mouth; mouthpiece

r Onon *Arch* anon: at once *Da* tegn: sign
anonymous *r* Teign thing
r Ingul *r* Potters *r* Fly
inkling otters
r Jagst vessels *r* Vesle *Du* vet: fat *Ki* homa: fever
Jack's *r* Vet homesickness *r* Fever
home *r* Mahu *r* Mahon *r* Horse Creek
womb man of the house but heard
Ki bunduki: gun *Ki* boi: houseboy *Ki* askari: soldier *r* Hazel Creek
boy *G* mit girl Hazelhatch: townland, Co. D (on Grand Canal)
Clondalkin: village, Co. D (on Grand Canal) *r* King's King's Inns Quay, D
r Inn
fishnet freshet: stream of fresh alevin: young fish at all in tow
water running into sea elevens *r* Leven *F* élève: schoolchild
r Rede Maxwell Henry Close described Ir.
glacial geography, esp. of D
C wan: 10,000; a large number

Ki mia na kumi na moja: 111 Hebrew letters: aleph means 1; lamedh, 30; pe, 80
r Mean *r* Acu *r* Cumina *r* Moy *r* Ola 1 + 30 + 80 = 111
Kierkegaard
(churchyard)

r Bishop's Brook Cain K . . . E . . . Y Abel apple of eye
r Box *Sl* box the bishop: masturbate *r* Cane
Ibsen: *Little Eyolf* Kierkegaard: *Either/Or* *r* Yea

Lorelei: siren of the Rhine

r Loddon *C* ho: river
lot of lodes: open ditches

Da tvillinger: *Da* trillinger: spoil five: a card game *F* Nord: North
pr The more the merrier twins triplets 2 . . . 3 . . . 4 . . . 5 . . . 6 . . . 7 . . . 8 . . . 9 *r* Nord
r Sud *PS* sever: North yes & no *G* nein farthing nap: a card game
F Sud: South eights & nines
Napoleon *It* messa: Mass
r Missouri
(ass is 5th province) gadabout: wanderer

r Shoal egad! few men
sure *L* flumen: river
I abhainn: river *Gr* thanatos: death *Gr* zôe mou, sas agapô: my life, I love you (last line of
r Owen *r* Töss *r* Nare ne'er Byron's *Maid of Athens*)
r Cam *r* Camlin

r Neckar *r* Dive Bellini: 'Casta Diva' : (from *Norma*)
G necken: tease (little devil) *ph* pearls before swine
r Font Thames is tidal to Teddington
It fonte in monte: the spring on the mountain
Da til havet: to the sea
r Link
r Tapti *r* Jutaí jetty Paul & Peter *r* Pietar
petering out
r Clyde estuary *r* Waihou *r* Thur
Coleridge: *The Ancient Mariner* 105–6: 'We were the first that ever burst Into that silent sea'
whoever *r* Huebra *L* tactus: touch
Sp huebra: day's work
r Tilar *r* Sauldre *r* Salor *r* Pieman *r* Peace
nr 'Tinker, tailor, soldier, sailor, rich man, poor man, beggar man, thief'
r Polista *r* Elwy *r* Esk
policeman always ask
r Vardar headwaters
harder farther
Waterlow: Eng. painter Henry Grattan & Henry Flood: Ir. statesman of late C18
low water ⚔ Waterloo *r* Aherlow
Joan of Arc *r* Arc Hosty *r* Fidaris
(rainbow girls) hosting: raising of army *L* fides: faith
r Doubs *G* niemand: *G* nirgends: nowhere *r* Nile
nobody *r* Niemen *L* nihil: nothing
(023.19–20) *G* albern: silly *I* ní h-annsa: not hard *Sl* gemman: gentleman
L anser: goose mystic knots (Burns): entanglements in bride's nightdress made by bridesmaids
r Nuanetzi Albert Nyanza & Victoria Nyanza: the 2 western reservoirs of the Nile

r Tez *r* Thelon *r* Langlo *s* Tipperary: 'It's a long way to go'
r Wear *r* Loon *r* Wabash
r Sid *r* Huon
Sl gravel: confound said who in
r Gravelly Diarmaid MacMurchadha: king of Leinster (patronymic means 'sea warrior')
D Annals, 1431: 'McMorogh, dynast of Leinster' *r* Wolf
r Blyth

how often *r* Jumna who (marriage or betrayal)
r Ofin *r* Jump *Sl* jump: fuck

r Silva *L* silva: forest
silver moonlight
the Curragh of Kildare, racecourse *r* Hay
r Sun Kildare means 'church of the oak' peace
pr Make hay while the sun shines
'Killing Kildares': Kildare Foxhounds

G Forst: forest *r* Foss *r* Sankh
Da fossefald: waterfall sank
r Neath

r Tigris 'Exsultet': 'O felix culpa!'
L tigris: tiger tiger's eye: a gem
horribly *r* Acheron anachronistic
r Corrib, Ireland
L nulla: none nullah: a watercourse
r Nula

Eden Quay, D leave
Co. Wicklow known as 'the garden of Ireland' *F* lave: wash
Kilbride, Co. Wicklow, on *r* Brittas Horsepass Bridge, over Liffey, nr Poulaphouca
(joins Liffey) *r* Bride
The Great Southern & Western Railway Co. & the Midland Great Western Railway of Ireland Company
have lines running near Liffey in places tresses *r* Grain
r Asat
asearch *r* Robec (in Rabelais)
Marriage Ceremony: 'to have & to hold . . . for better, for worse, for richer, for poorer'

r Liffey pennylands: lands valued at 1 penny/year Humphreystown Bridge, nr Poulaphouca
Barley-fields, D, site of Rotunda Lotts, street, D
Town of the Ford of the Hurdles = D Land-Leaguer (C19 Ireland) landlubber willing to nurse her
F Sl St Lago: the St Lazare prison for prostitutes, Paris Wellington Quay, D
Alice *r* Lesse *r* Lagos *It* lago: lake (Holy Ghost) *r* Dove *r* Duna
alas First words sung by Wagner's Tristan: 'Was ist? Isolde?'
r Sarthe *r* Suir *r* Finn
AngI sarthin shure: certain sure
r Mourne *r* Nore leave Slieve Bloom, Ir. mt (*r* Nore flows away from)
Lieve Canal *Du* bloem: flower *r* Bloem
Dryden: *Alexander's Feast:* 'None but the brave deserves the fair' *r* Moy drains Lough Cullin, rather
r Braye *r* Divatte diverts wayfarer than the adjacent Lough Conn, closer to sea
Lough Cullin & Lough Conn run together *r* Colne Neptune rowing club, D

Tritonville road, D Hero & Leander
Triton, son of Neptune Leander Boat Club, London
r Neya *r* Narev *r* Nen *r* Nonni *r* Nos *r* Ow
I ná raibh: that was not ballad jingle: 'hey nonny no'
r Avoca (Ovoca) East with West *r* Yokanka
r Ystwith *r* Yukon
r Dell Creek very first *r* Fairy Water *r* Ferse
St Kevin retreated to Luggalaw before Glendalough
Moore: *s* No, Not More Welcome, the Fairy Numbers [Luggelaw] (tempted by Cathleen in both places)
r Dinkel *r* Dale *r* Lugg
G Eremit: hermite Dingley Dell: country village reverend
in *Pickwick Papers*
aspersed: lava beds *L* lavabrum: bathtub
Low L dies Veneris: Friday sprinkled *r* Lava
the Venusberg (*Tannhäuser*) *r* Oso
r Derg Wednesday *r* Juna *r* Juny
r Nance Creek Abbé Prévost: *Manon Lescaut* Ninon l'Enclos: C17 Fr. courtesan
nixie: female water sprite *r* Escaut
r Sycamore Creek

AngI cushla: pulse *r* Singimari struma: swelling Macpherson glosses Strumon
r Struma streams 'stream of the hill'

s By That Lake, Whose Gloomy Shore (about Glendalough)
red bog: peatbog in central fountain of Vaucluse, where Petrarch lived
r Red lowlands of Ir. *r* Vaucluse *r* Lucy Creek
(colours of rainbow) red *r* Orange arranged around
r Arrone L'Arronge: C19 German dramatist
aphrodisiac *L* galbus: yellow (blue eyes) *r* Eye indigo
enamoured
F vierge (wish on seeing rainbow) *r* Mavri
to the verge of violating Mavrodaphne, a Greek wine
laughing through Laura, to whom Petrarch wrote sonnets Daphne: river nymph, turned into
r Tees laurel tree daft
St Petrock: patron of Cornwall *Ki* maji: water *Ki* wavu: net *Ki* elfu: 1,000 *r* Mesha
Petrarch *r* Maas *Thousand & One Nights*
Ki Simba: lion *r* Simba Uranga Sinbad the Sailor *r* Ogi lewd could
Siva the Slayer: Hindu god of destruction *Ki* oga: to bathe
r Thurso
thirst
F baiser: kiss
r Baïse
r Lippe *r* Acis *r* Kiso *r* Kushk
F lippe: thick (lower) lip
r Nive *r* Neva Dion Boucicault: *Arrah-na-Pogue*

pass parch *F* secheresse *G* hielt: held herself
Val de Ruz, Switz.
F souffler rose higher *r* Aisne own estimation *L* aestus: undulating
D Annals, 1452: 'The Liffey was entirely dry at Dublin for the space of two minutes' *L* aestuarium: estuary
Kiswahili *r* Tura Bantu
banter

nautic = nautical *r* Na'aman Lake Naama *Du* naam: name *Da* navn: name
Naamah: sister of Tubal-Cain
r Went

Lugnaquillia: highest summit in Wicklow Mts noblest peaks
Scots & Picts *F* noblesse
Sl fanny: cunt

r Birch *r* Canoe (old Guinness steam barge)
Coll canoodle: fondle (065.24ff.)
Leda & the swan *G* leider: unfortunately unready *r* Raidak
r Lea *r* Leda *nr* Mary, Mary, Quite Contrary
r Cygnet

r Chirripo *r* Po
doing
headwaters of the Liffey nr Mt Kippure
s Bird Song at Eventide

Devil's Glen, on *r* Vartry, Co. Wicklow, Sally Gap is near the source of the Liffey
where Act II of *Arrah-na-Pogue* takes place
sloot: ditch; narrow water channel spillway: channel for overflow water

r Lay
'Dublin' means 'black pool' *r* Rainy cow
Raheny, district of D
Inishfree: island, Co. Sligo

r Findhorn *Ki* mtu: man *Ki* mti: tree *Ki* mto: river
findhorn: smoked haddock
somebody witness *r* Flinders
bugger

marcel wave: deep, soft wave made in hair with
curling iron
weir (on river) which side did they drop their gloves
merely
r Fleury *Arch* flory: flower *r* Back West waist
clothes in their flurry hurry flory-boat: boat for landing passengers from steamers
r Loth

ph in the swim: in luck, in fashion

r Rother rather!

F guimpe: i) nun's wimple; ii) tucker (easy to wash)
Sl snouty: haughty
job St Veronica wiped face *r* Wieprz *r* Rance
r Jub of Jesus (6th station of Cross) *Sl* wiper: handkerchief rinsing
Aaron Arrah!
Arran Quay, D
vestry
r Vesdre *F* vrai: true
F eau de Cologne *r* Colo
F cul
r Oder *r* Magra
odour
r Aird just
aired
r Baptiste
on entering confessional: 'Bless me, Father, for I have sinned'

HCE river catchment basin *ph* free & easy hip hip hurray

F dentelle: lace *r* Paar pair Old Parr: Eng.
don't tell parr: young salmon centenarian accused
r Old all *r* Welland of incontinence
Moyelta, the Old Plain of Elta, where Parthalonians died of plague & were buried
who will?

*U.*561: 'Ask my ballocks Belvedere College, D exhibitioners: boys who won exhibition in
that I haven't got' exhibitionists secondary school exam
s What Ho, She Bumps!

r Nuble jubilee *r* Ellis Ellis Quay, D
nubile L & K (initials)

L calor: heat *r* Annan *r* Exe Laura Keene: star of play Lincoln watched when
& an X after assassinated
r Keowee *M Gr* diabolos: devil *r* Wiske *G* Seife: soap
r May *Sp* diablo: devil diabolo: a game safety pin
(618.04) Lilith: Adam's wife before Eve in 'Then he tears the leg of my drawers'–
Children of Mary: Catholic girls' association kabbalistic lore line in girls' rope-chant quoted in
ph pull my other leg, the one with the bells on it Norman Douglas's *London Street Games*

hasten
Aston Quay, D

r Amstel *r* Garonne
am still go on
Mater Misericordiae Hospital, D Mendicity Institution, D (Usher's Island)
(after it was put in the papers) *r* Meriç *r* Corda Saturday
Monday *G* Wochenschrift: weekly magazine
r Zindeh Sunday *r* Mun makeshift
r White kidgloves chicken & bacon

r Egg

Da sne: snow Mt Snowdon *Scottish Dial* take a skunner against: be disgusted with
snowed on *r* Kunna
I tá: it is so *r* Sava *r* Savuto HCE
snow thaws
r Erriff *r* Arve
ever ever
4 taverns in which the Ouzel Galley Society met: (i) The Rose & Bottle, Dame St
city
(ii) Phoenix Tavern, Werburgh St (iii) Jude's Hotel, S. Frederick St
(iv) Power's, Booterstown
r Nanny Water (N. boundary of *r* Vartry (runs out at Wicklow)
D admiralty jurisdiction)
Porta Latina, Rome Latin Quarter of Paris icon *r* Ikom *r* Etsch etched
ECH = HCE backwards
upside down *r* Cammock mocking Guy Fawkes
Sl cornerboy: loafer cammock: crooked staff, hockey stick
Morris & Rolls Royce cars *U.*10: E.W. Royce as *Turko the Terrible:* 1st Christmas pantomime at
r Ross Gaiety, D *F* roi *r* Turco *r* Evros
G Hahn ECH suet *F* yaourt: yoghurt *Per* hamman: bath
European peacock Swift's yahoos
Per adam: person Fatima: Mohammed's daughter

Sl local: nearby pub *r* Peiho banjos
r Ubangi
Oddfellows: a fraternal society *r* Tiaret papal tiara (turning)
Rotunda, D, used as skating rink in late C19
The Scalp: pass near D *r* Neva *Du* meer: lake
G Meer: sea
G Hausmann H . . . C . . . E *r* Cabin Creek
Baron Haussmann rebuilt Paris
nr The House That Jack Built: 'This is the priest all shaven & shorn, That married the man all tattered & torn . . .
That tossed the dog, That worried the cat' C . . . H . . . E *r* Enna *r* Egg

maudlin *r* Mauldre Areopagus: supreme court at Athens
G Maul
r Caguán tin pan *Dial* crowders: fiddlers
tympani
r Ma *G* hing: hung *r* Hong agnomen: name added to family name,
Ma: Cappadocian war-goddess generally on account of some exploit
s 'Lillibullero, bullen a law' *r* Alaw acrostics crucifix
The gods swore by *r* Styx Crosstick Alley in old D
wynd: narrow cross street *AngI* snags: gangs
r Wynd Brook snakes
AngI vulnerable: pregnant Church of St Mary del Dam, D (occupied site nr present St Werburgh's)
venerable *r* Virgin
I Sinn Féin: We Ourselves (slogan)
ph make a shine: make a fine show
never *r* Dungu don't go so cruel
r Nievre
r Meurthe make *Du* bergen: to store, put *Du* zak: sack
what the murder *r* Maguera *G* borgen: to borrow *r* Zak

lampion: lamp, usually of coloured glass Sean the Post: postman in Dion
Boucicault's *Arrah-na-Pogue*
chapbooks Old Tom Moore's Almanac
r Boucq *r* Moore John Casey: *Sequel to Euclid*
tidy

masquerade *r* Giguela
F mascaret: tidal wave in estuary
Sp rizo: curl *r* Rabbit
It riso: laugh *Sl* rabbit it!: 'Minnehaha', Hiawatha's girl in Longfellow's poem,
r Minho confound it! means 'Laughing Water'

(rhythm of *Hiawatha*)

r Dargle Mulhuddart: village nr *r* Tolka; a well there much frequented on Nativity of BVM

r Chanza *r* Tirry *F* mont-de-pieté: pawnshop
chance of Terry Kelly: D pawnbroker
r Avre
every
r Woman

ph I have the bent of his bow: I understand him
r Bow
avoirdupois *r* Slaney *r* Deel *G* langsam: slow
r Oise tell me
take *r* Thet *r* Thouet
r Tongue that's the way
F pr hâtez-vous lentement: *r* Scheldt *r* Lynd
hasten slowly (i.e. more *G* schnell: fast lend us
r Ash haste, less speed) *r* Cannon *r* Owenmore

Ki polipoli: slowly

r Fal *G* Fluss
flowed
r Teviot curls *r* Sampu
devious shampooed
r Gala *r* Fragua *r* Wupper upper & lower *r* Laua
Gr gala: milk Pistany: Czech spa
noted for mud packs *r* Reese *Du* keel: throat
r Greese *Sl* keel: backside
r Warthe *r* Wear *r* Mole *r* Itchen butterscotch
warts wharves weirs mole: large breakwater *Sl* itcher: cunt
pr Time & tide wait for no man *r* Serpentine *r* Leaf
turpentine leaf-mould: rotted leaves (compost)
Usher's Island, D *F* prunelle: pupil of eye *r* Esla *r* Dun quincunx
r Prunelli *r* Isle islets
Sl little Mary: 'tummy' *r* Gold *r* Belly
Little Mary St, D *r* Mary *r* Peel

r Anguille ankle
F anguille: eel

flag: iris (flower) leaves
Iliad XIV: Hera preparing to beguile Zeus: 'With ambrosia first did she cleanse every stain from her winsome body, & annointed her with olive oil . . . & with her hands plaited her shining tresses'

Moore: *s* Rich & Rare Were the Gems She Wore
r Richmond
r Rehr *r* Rhine Rhinestones

dawk: impression *r* Ey *I* ean-uisce: marsh water
eyes *L* luteus: muddy *L* Lutetia: Paris
Anna Pavlova: dancer, 1882–1931 Lilliput *r* Lippe
lips
F pommettes: cheekbones The Strawberry Beds, Chapelizod
r Birrie
(rainbow colours) *r* Endre *F* boue de *r* Loire
F boudoir
It ciliegia grande: big cherry *G* Kirsche: cherry (*Sl* cherries: young girls) cousins
r Grandê Grand Canal & Royal Canal, D *r* Real
r Mississippi *r* Missouri

Da passe: wait on, serve minute *AngI* minnekin: little pin
F passe: pass Manneken-Pis: statue in Brussels of a child urinating
F arroser: to water *It* sprizzare: sprinkle clock striking
r Arros
r Mine stars brightly shine *r* Zambezi
nine *r* Bride *s* Somebody's Waiting for Me
(Source of Liffey is less than half its length from D)

mealie: mailbag *r* Slang
Du slang: snake
r Oyster *r* Forth *r* Bassein
Sl oysterfaced: needing a shave river basin

pr Strike the iron while it is hot
r Spiti *L* Ierna: Ireland
r Irthing *r* Neath
anything on earth
r Lomba *L* gaudium: joy *r* Moselle
Lombard Street (Stock Exchange) must
r Ogowe *It* lesto: quick Julius Caesar *r* Ishikari *r* Washimeska
o go *It* presto: quick *r* Julia is she was she masked
It carissima: very dear *r* Caratirimani
r Arish duodecimoroon: person with one twelfth negro blood
r Bonaventura *r* Malagasy *r* Liddel *r* Oudon
It buona ventura: good luck Lewis Carroll's Alice Liddell, *Du* oud: old
(weigh) model for *Alice in Wonderland*

L amnis: river HCE

Gr alektoris: hen *ME* angin: beginning ancient
pr Necessity is the mother of invention
Indians *r* Test

r Peace

All Souls

(the door) ugly *r* Iglau
r Hooghly
r Bush *r* Moma

r Ems *r* Embarrass

r Aue *r* Awe *r* Judy Creek *r* Queen

elbow *r* Saisi riddle: 'Little Nancy Etticoat': 'The longer she stands the shorter she grows'
r Elbe *F* saisir: to seize quick bigger (a candle)
r Save *r* Tagus *r* Werra
take us
r Ourthe lamb
where on earth Lambay Island, N.E. of D
r Epte
apt to forget
s Love Me Little, Love Me Long length
r Liddel *r* Longa *r* Linth

Sugarloaf Mts, Co. Wicklow *r* Guadalquivir
r Hat Creek
r Arno *Iliad* XIV: Hera preparing to beguile Zeus: 'she girdled it with a girdle arrayed
ornament with a hundred tassels, & she set earrings in her pierced ears'
r Guil *r* Owl bifocals
Owlglass: Eulenspiegel (jester)
r Eye *G* netzen: moisten *Iliad* XIV: '& with a veil over all the
r Fish *r* Netze peerless goddess veiled herself'
r Hydaspes *r* Boucq buckled *r* Aube *G* Laub: leaves
lobes of her ears
G Laut: sound salmon genus *Salmo*

r Gallego *Sl* shimmy: vapour *Cz* výpar: haze *It* tinto: coloured
calico chemise *r* Vaipar *r* Tinto
Sheridan: *The Rivals* *r* Line

r Blood *r* Orange Knickerbockers have 2 legs in 1 garment

fancy-free: not in love (*Midsummer Night's Dream* II.1.164) *r* Black
Black & Tans: Eng. recruits
r Tan joseph: riding cape worn by C18 women (furlined) in 1920–1 serving in Royal Ir. Constabulary
r Joseph sequin *r* Sequana (Seine)
r Lea Leda & the Swan
let down
r Swan *r* Gaspereau *r* Hay *r* Roper
Swan is royal bird *Sl* gasper: cheap cigarette Europe
corduroy *r* Alpheus
r Codroy alphabet
Sl bar: pound (sterling)

r Windrush

Fi joki: river

r Somme *It* fiume: river *PS* reka: river

F fleuve *J* gawan: river *I* siubhlóir: vagrant
gown *r* Sioule
Ir. mile = 2240 yards along the road
r Lunga *r* Rhodanus
r Gumti
gumption
Du welk: which naze: promontory, headland
r Nazas
F douce *r* Deli

Lao-tse *r* Poddle puddle
r Lotsani *r* Trothy
fall in the sea *r* Fenny *G* Hexe: witch *r* Char C.J. Kickham: C19 Ir. novelist
funny *r* Hex char (fish)
marshmallow
r Musha *r* Mullet mullet (fish)
r Chariton charity *r* Queen
Gr Charitôn: of the Graces
r May Princess May of Teck was betrothed to Prince Albert Victor, Duke of Clarence &
Queen of the May Avondale ("Collars & Cuffs"). When he died she married the Duke of York
r Regnitz therefore *r* Darling *r* Murray *r* Mirror
reckon *r* Wharfe *Da* hvorfor: why muddied
r Mersey *r* Körös *Gr* koros: surfeit; youth
mercy me! chorus

Du boom: tree *Du* slang: snake plug tobacco (Lotus-eaters)
surfaceman: road labourer *Du* boomen: to chat idly
undulation
unification

('waving of her hair') lazing North Wall, D *r* Waal
Lazar's Hill, D

hellfire Duke of York
r Eel *r* Jucar *r* Oich
r Meander grass widow

AngI twig: get the point, realize *r* Bonnet *r* Avon
VI.B.9.93: 'Avondale Clarence Grillroom' Parnell's home at Avondale
pr One man's meat is another man's poison *r* An *G* neben: next to neighbour
r Fish *r* Clarence *F* poisson *r* Anabar one to another
r Crouch Master Bates: Gulliver's teacher *r* South
masturbates *r* Bates Creek
r Granite Creek facelift: form of cosmetic surgery

game (as meat) mixed bag baccarat: a card game
r Bhagirathi *r* Hatti
Ki tembo: palm wine *Ki* tumbo: belly *Ki* pilipili: pepper *Ki* saa: watch, clock, hour
r Tembe *r* Pili Saas Thal valley, Switzerland
Ki taa: lamp *Ki* bizaa: merchandise *r* Thunder
r Taas spices *Ki* bizari: a spice
r Battle *Da* efter: after *Da* frisk: fresh
s Just before the Battle, Mother *s* After the Ball
r Aube *r* Bearba
Soo Canal I bet my beard
r Son bitch

r Worth

Sl goodfor: promissory note *r* Spey *r* Prut
spare
r Arun *r* Gironde *r* Waveney *r* Lyne *r* Garumna
L arundo: reed, cane round & round in a wavy line *It* aringa: herring *Fi* roume: stream
G rund: *F* rond: round *r* Boulder Creek *r* Narova
r Arrow
I duileasc: edible seaweed *r* Vet
Moore: *s* Oh! Where's the Slave: 'The friends we've tried Are by our side, & the foe we hate before us' wild west wind
r Curaray *r* Medway

r Weser *r* Eder *r* Eider *r* Chattahoochee
whether either (chattering)
r Ain *r* Cree
r Chichui own children *I* croí (pron. 'cree'): heart
r Nisling *r* Isole
listening
Isolabella: island in Lake Maggiore Romulus & Remus
r Rom *G* Reim: rhyme
r Lech *r* Dart hands
leech *r* Hans
r Box Creek *r* Aisch *r* Ivari
each & every one
gave spoils
G Gabe: gift, present

r Fleet (subterranean London river,
with history of flooding city)
inundation *OE* flod: river to sea *r* Glashaboy

r Polly *pr* Out of the frying pan into the fire
r Polimounty pawnshop
(theatre) *L* ingenuina: belonging to a freeborn woman
ingénue: naive young woman, especially on stage
Artizan Dwelling Co. buildings, D Smyly Boys' Home, Dún Laoghaire
artesian wells levee: embankment against river floods
Viceroy's levée *r* Vivi *r* Vienne *G* -chen: dim. suffix *F* vieillot: oldish
F reine *It* vivi: live
solo *r* Susurluk *L* Ausonia si dulcis: Italy so
suras of Koran *r* Sula *L* susurrus: whisper pleasant
timbre cheer
r Tambre *r* Chir

r Jary r Dive r Neb nab Culdee: Ir.-Scottish religious order from C8
jeer *It* cul di sacco: cul de sac r Sacco rubbish r Wabash
r Raab maundy: (fig.) almsgiving, largesse *F* pour souvenir
robbed r Maun *G* Meerschaum (lit. 'sea foam') merchandise
It per ricordo: as a keepsake *G* Erinnerung: remembrance tinkers & tailors
r Arigna
firstborn tributary
r Ribble r Derry
Arabian Nights (1001 Nights) r Wicker r Pot
pot luck in wicker pot
ever & ever kiss the book *G* Buch
kick the bucket
r Bann George Borrow wrote about gipsies (hence tinkers) r Lee
tinker's damn r Barrow *Aust* billy: teapot Lee: famous gipsy name
Cock-a-leekie soup is made of a cock Tommy (Atkins)
boiled with leeks *Sl* chummy: soldier
Altoids, 'the original celebrated curiously strong peppermints'

(T.B. symptoms) *F* petite r Macfarlane
It piccolina: little
s 'Needles & pins, blankets & shins, when a man is married his sorrow begins'
r Shin
Brasenose College, Oxford

r Walker *AngI* beg: little L/R papal
Johnnie Walker whisky r Papar
stars & stripes (locomotive)

nightmare Tiger Tim: nickname of Healy
March Hare r Tech r Tombigbee
Bully Hayes: Am. pirate
r Hayes
fatted calf in parable of Prodigal Buck Jones: manager of Crow St Theatre, D; owned
Son (Luke 15:11–32) r Heart Clonliffe House
r Val

Skibbereen, town, Co. Cork *I* Baile Átha Cliath: D
Val Vousden: *s* The Irish Jaunting Car ('It belongs to Larry Doolin') *AngI* jackeen: Dublin man (derisory)
Teague: nickname for Irishman

mousetrap
Peter's pence: contribution to R.C. church
r Mackenzie harelip clackdish: wooden beggars' dish with clacking lid Pierce Penniless: *Supplication to the Devil*
J.M. Barrie: *The Twelve Pound Look*
twelve-tone music G.V. Brooke: D actor; drowned Pliny the Elder thought that drowned women floated face down
F morte *F* mer Anne Mortimer: Richard III's grandmother r Blanche
Parnell's sister Anne drowned herself waterfalls *F* blanchisseuse: laundress
Peg Woffington: Ir. actress who played Sir Harry Wildair in Farquhar's *The Constant Couple*

Sam Dash: C18 master of revels at D Castle pigs in clover: a game
to dot one's i full stop r Snake (139.31)
Picts & Scots scotched snake (Patrick banished snakes) *Gr* presbys: old man
MGr presbys: ambassador
G Reiz: tickle; stimulation r Reisa Standfast Dick: rock reef across Liffey *Sl* morning drop: gallows
Medical Dick: subject of Gogarty's verse
Medical Davy (Gogarty's verse) St Brigid established religious institution at Kildare (means 'Church of the oak')
Dial jordan: chamber pot
r Tweed r Mobile Saar: wife of Finn r Jordan
Rigoletto: s La donna è mobile r Saar Sarah Philpot Curran: Emmet's fiancée
('Woman is fickle') *L* aeva mobilia: moveable ages r Powder *s* Eileen Aroon r Arun
r Orne tea urn r Box Creek Aruna is the Phaeton of Indian myth
r Rhone

s Kitty of Coleraine (she breaks a pitcher of buttermilk on seeing the song's narrator, but is consoled by him)
pr Penny-wise, pound foolish Ellen Terry played Puck

I púcán: little goblin r Dniester r Egg
Easter egg
Irish/Roman Church controversy over date of Easter *R* Pavl: Paul

James Clarence Mangan wrote under pseudonym G starr: stiff Star & Garter (pub name)
'Man in the Cloak'; died of cholera morbus It collera: anger Girton: 1st women's college at
Dean Swift: *Drapier Letters* L cloaca: sewer F Sl cloaque: brothel Cambridge
r Dean Bernard Shaw & William Butler Yeats received Nobel Prize (Sweden)
mangold: mangel-wurzel Oliver Bond: United Irishman, condemned,
swede r Bitter r Olivera but died first of apoplexy
Inishfree: island, Co. Sligo James the Little: brother or cousin of Jesus
James Stephens: *The Adventures of Seumas Beg*
r Tiber Clongowes Wood College Cross of Cong: processional cross now in National
libertine's r Congo r Wood r Cross Museum, D
When J was a child, his family called him 'Sunny Jim'
Moore: s Remember the Glories of Brian the Brave
r Bravo
r Lubilash lashings of: lots of r Olona
Olona, Lena & Magdalena are resp. Italian, Russian & S. Am. names of Magdalene
r Lena r Magdalena r Cam r Drome Camilla & Mamilla: Robert Greene heroines
r Shannon

Tuam, town, Co. Galway r Dora Riparia r Hope F douche
L riparia: frequenting riverbanks soap
Blarney Castle, Co. Cork
breeks
Sl pencil: penis Eílís Óram: folklore character; notorious liar
Sl toby: cunt
r Volga

r Belle It bellezza: beauty L Missa pro Messa: Mass for the Harvest (003.09–10)
blue-bag used in washing clothes r Misa
r Taff nr Jack & Jill AngI the broth of a boy: a real (essential) boy
Sl spoon: flirt, sweetheart
Robinson Crusoe's Man Friday L Caducus Angelus: Fallen Angel r Rubicon
Sir John Rogerson's Quay, D
Atkinson's warehouse on Wellington Quay stored poplin ties
366 = a year & a day r Tyne
Victor Hugonot: D tie salesman
Huguenots introduced poplin manufacture in D
I.S. Varian's brush factory, D: trademark is a pig (I muc) When singer forgets next verse of song he says
(079.27) Katherine Strong: C17 D scavenger 'There's a hole in the ballad'
(044.08–047) (055.17)

Dolphin's Barn: district of D
U.161: 'give every child born five quid' F dauphin: prince
Sp infanta: princess r Maggia
Lusk: village, Co. D

L spes: hope 'Speranza': Wilde's mother, poetess in 1780 was incorporated Simpson's
It speranza: hope Hospital, D, for 'decayed & blind & gouty men'
statue of Sir Hugh Gough, who was blind name choice r Ill
& partially deaf, in Phoenix Park L naves: ship hills
Sir Amory Tristram, 1st Earl of Howth, changed name to St Lawrence
r Amur r St Lawrence
Robin Redbreast hanging (hemp rope)

s Brennan on the Moor r Oconee conditor: founder Jonathan Sawyer: settler of Dublin, Georgia (003.07)
(in song he is caught & executed)
mosquito bites r Scott WW I classification of men: C3 = unfit VI.A.984: 'C3 arm weak'
r Mosquodoboit peduncle: stalk Skt karma: action, occupation
letter to HSW, 24/3/24: 'Shaun's map: for this see any postage stamp of the Irish Free State. It is a
philatelic curiosity. A territorial stamp it includes the territory of another state, Northern Ireland'. Some
Free State stamps show map of Ir., others the 'Sword of Light' Jekyll Hyde
Shemus sells his soul (*Countess Cathleen*) Sean the Post (206.11)
Bruno of Nola Don Giovanni & the statue
William De Morgan: *Joseph Vance*
Lock Hospital, D (for V.D.) Honor Bright: prostitute found L meretrix: whore
ph lock stable door murdered at Ticknock, Co. D Lambeg drums on anniversary of ⚔ Boyne, 1690
King Billy: ⚔ Boyne, 1690 Dunboyne, town, Co. Meath r Goldene Aue
gilt
r Ida The Hushabys & Billy & Ellie Dunn nr Rock-a-bye Baby *Il Trovatore*
are characters in Shaw's *Heartbreak House* F elle trouve tout: she finds all
2 Gentlemen of Verona IV.2.39: 'Who is Silvia? What is she' r Swilly

Guinness r Yenisei r Laagen r Niger Festus King: shop in Clifden, Co.
r Yun Hennessy brandy lager r King Galway
(039.16–18) r Ob

(495.01–3) s Master Magrath (commemorates Ir. greyhound winning Waterloo
r Magra (040.16) Cup in 1869)
O'Donovan Rossa Bridge, D
r Delaware r Rossa

r Selinus r Susquehanna r Pru
Gr Selênê: moon r Salina Creek
r Ward canal (the P/Q split) r Brosna
I brosna: bundle of firewood
r Ena r Maas r Zusam r Cammock (Camac), D
Croatian camac: boat
r Bradogue, D r Fox (035.30)

r Greaney r Leza
Gretna Green
r Licking r Leytha r Liane r Rosanna r Rohan It simpatica: nice
liane: climbing forest plant
r Sohan r Una r Bina r Laterza It la terza: the third Gr philomênê: moon-lover
I sohan: pleasant L una: 1 L bina: a pair L trina: triple OF mesme: same
T irmak: river r Joseph r Foyle r Snake

r Fountain Creek r Laura r Marie L Agnus Dei: Lamb of God
⚔ Fontenoy, 1745 r Noya
St François de Sales: patron of writers Scottish Dial ilka: every It madre: mother
r Frances r Macleay ph every mother's daughter r Ilek r Madre de Dios
(menstruation) r Bloodvein (testicles)

raisin Isa 63:3: 'them that tread out the winepress' chambermaid
r Devi
beyond her years 'Jim the Penman': James Townsend Savard, forger

passed before his time

my colonial! (oath) r Wardha r Baker baker's dozen = 13 r Sind
what a Da dusin: dozen
AngI tilly: small quantity of anything given Swift: *Tale of a Tub*
over the amount purchased r May
Markets were forbidden on the Nones of the month
Hibernian (c.f. Caledonian Market, London)
r Seal (sealed book of Rev 5–6)
(Pandora's box) US pork barrel: Federal Treasury viewed as source of grants for local purposes
r Pison r Hudson
poison Hudson's soap
AngI 'could you give me the least taste in life of a bit of soap?' r Raft
Clane, village, Co. Kildare
r Marne most mild G Mulde: trough
morn r Merced r Mulde mercy me!
Reckitt's Blue r Lohan G lohnen: to pay (making rinsing easier)
Fi lohi: salmon

Sl wide: (paper cones for snuff) crack of dawn
shrewd
r Dvina cracked divine (Swift, mad clergyman) yesteryear
Swift's Esthers (Stella & Vanessa)
Narcissus Marsh founded library nr St Patrick's Cathedral, D
Thackeray: *Vanity Fair*
Chinook: jargon originating from trade with Henry Dodwell: Ir. theologian
r Chinook Oregon & Columbia Red Indians r Dodwell
titlepage
J's friend Ottocaro Weiss heard a boy imitating a Slovene priest preaching in Italian: 'Senior ga dito: Faciasi Omo! E omo fu fò. Senior ga dito: Faciasi Hidamo! Hidamo se ga facessà' ('God said: Let there be man, & man was. God said: Let there be Adam, & Adam was')
r Omo Wilde: *Lady Windermere's Fan*

G Dichter: poet Joseph Sheridan Le Fanu: *The House by the Churchyard*
(lake poets)
John Stuart Mill: *The Subjection of Women* H.R. Wheatley: *What Is an Index* 66: 'Mill on Liberty
George Eliot: *The Mill on the Floss* *G* Ja *r* Altmuehl —on the Floss'
G alt Muehle: old mill Aston Quay, D *r* Floss millrace

Du blauw: blue whiskey & soda *r* Iskar *r* Suda
cauld: cold *L* sudor: sweat washing soda
(patterned) *r* Chay Tonkin
Mrs Tulliver in *The Mill on the Floss* talks about her 'chany' (chinaware)
r Hoangho (also called 'China's Sorrow') *r* Lost

L ai mihi: woe is me! turbary: ground where turf is dug
r Aimihi turbid
r Gihon *r* Lovat gabber: deceiver, talker *r* Maur
go on Lovat's Court, D jabber
r Morava *Da* regn: rain *Du* onder: under
more over *r* Regen *It* onde: wave
this is the life for me

ken it
r Kennet
tailing out (ending) *ph* that's the long & the short of it
r Taling
*'At this point the woman who is to be turned into a tree sees herself pictured upside down in the water, in the form that she later takes' left right *r* Root
*'This statement comes *r* Cher *'chair (seat)' *r* Ashley *r* Fie 'Filou' ('scoundrel'), shouted across Rhine by
from the woman who is later to become a stone' *F* chair: flesh Frenchman, was heard by German as 'wie viel
r Saône *r* Senne Uhr?' ('What's the time?')
G schon: already since I or anyone *Butler: *Erewhon* (Nowhere) *r* Erewon
Waterhouse's Clock, D *I* clog: clock *r* Hurd
r Clogh
Mrs Conway, original of Mrs Riordan in *G* Bach: brook
Portrait, used to say 'Oh, my back, my back, my back!'
r Ache ALP Aix-les-Bains *r* Ping *r* Pongo *r* Belle (032.02)
(6 o'clock ringing of Angelus)
Sechseläuten: Zurich Angelus: 'et concepit de Spiritu Sancto' ('& *r* Pang
spring festival *G* Leute: people she conceived of the Holy Ghost)
Tennyson: *Ring Out, Wild Bells*: *r* Godavari *r* Vert
'Ring out the Old, ring in the New!' avert
r Thaya *r* Amana *T* aman: pardon
Amen

r Churn *G* der Wind
turning *r* Derwent
r Lay *r* Bride

Sl embrace: copulate

6 + 10 + 9 + 1 + 12 + 1 = 39 articles of clothing (39 Articles of Church of Eng., 534.12)
*'strollers are (thieves). The meatman's garment is put among 6 + 10 = 16 = P 12 =L 1 = A
the linen & is so badly washed that no one will take it' cold (if means 9 of the 10 kerchiefs total no. = 29)
*'In the war, notes in secret writing were sent on face cloths'
gossip *'As the story goes on the river gets wider & the 2
r Joseph *r* Joss women become parted' who said?
*'Their words are no longer *'Deo Gratias: Said to a person who gives a sneeze'
clear to one another' *G* Mutter *L* taceas: be quiet *r* Wharnow *G* alle *r* Alle
r Mutt Dea Tacita: nurse of Romulus & Remus
Lord's Prayer: 'Thy kingdom come . . . power & the glory . . . Glory be to the Father'
alluvial
Sp lluvia: rain
r Lost *F* à l'étranger: abroad 211.09: 'for Nancy Shannon a Tuami brooch'

r Shannon

*'dunce . . . Duns Scotus School of Thought' *'Markland's wineland is a Northman's name for
ON Markland, Vinland: parts of N. America America, & Brendan's Sea for the Atlantic'
r Yang-tze Agnès: Paris milliner *r* Hat Creek bid a bead: say a prayer
*'the American Irishman has a very high opinion of himself'

*C.K. Odgen: *Notes in Basic English on the Anna Livia Plurabelle Record* (J appears to have collaborated in production of these notes)

210.29: 'scruboak beads for beatified Biddy' r Lost last yestereve
L hesternus: yesterday's history L Ister: r Danube
marigold window in church r Main
*'person being given a high place in the church after death'
*'man's-in-a-hurry . . . here used for a place for making water'
r Manzanares Bachelor's Walk, D (beside Liffey)
Du in de loop der jaren: in the course of years
r Loup
211.11: 'a pair of Blarney braggs for Wally Meagher' (nothing left after laundering but buckle & hooks)

Sp orar por Orbe y por las Animas: to pray for the Earth & the Souls
r Orara r Orbe r Las Animas
I 'uise: well I olla: splendid L umbra: shadow
r Ussa r Ulla r Umba r Mezha AngI musha: well, indeed
G Ufer: bank, shore
r Ufa over & over G Spund: bung, plug It sponda: bank, shore r Dee
earwadding r Irrawaddy r Stoke stuck in my ears r Aar
Du aars: arse
r Lethe r Orinoco
least sound
Adam Findlater: grocery magnate & politician in Edwardian D Joachim of Flora: theologian
r Finn kimono r Joachim Creek
Hengest & Horsa: brothers who led Saxon invasion of England r Otter
ph on his high horse AngI forenenst: opposite 'Father of Waters': r Mississippi
r Yonne r Horse Creek I falairín: little pacing horse
r Isset Fallarees Commons: place on Liffey nr Ballymore Eustace
Astley's Amphitheatre, Peter St, D, equestrian circus. Later used to house blind women

Samuel Lover: *The White Horse of the Peppers*
r Horse Creek 'Pepper's ghost': stage illusion produced by projector & glass screen

C19 temperance slogan: 'Ireland sober is Ireland free' Angelical Salutation: 'Hail Mary, full of grace, the Lord is with thee'
r Maria Creek r Greese
Lord I thought so r Madame Lecocq: *La Fille de Madame Angot*, an opera.
load of laundry r Isonzo r Amman
lifting elbow: drinking *'Carrigacurra. Town on Liffey where Conway had a beer house' [actually a stretch of land nr Poulaphuca] r Conway
Sl canteen: inn

gate's Graeco-Roman but your buttocks buttresses
rheumatic Gr rheuma: stream
St Margaret Mary Alacoque: visionary who preferred drinking water in which laundry had been washed
r Mary
Corrigan's pulse: disease discovered by D doctor of that name varicose Alice Jane Donkin: friend of Lewis Carroll
r Alice

r Son (Christ, who washes away sins of world)

F lavandière: washerwoman r Limpopo

'Collars & Cuffs': nickname of Duke of Clarence (visited D) throne

s Follow Me Up to Carlow r Scamander r Isar
I saw
Golden Falls is on r Liffey The Isis: The Thames r Seint *'See there'
*'My blood is ice' r Zêzere
r Hamble
Sp burro: ass

Dwyer Gray: owner of *Freeman's Journal*: *'He gave the town its water. The *ass* here is representative of the Apocrypha'
r Me Nam r Lyons r Gregory r Meyne

s One More Drink for the Four of Us r Drave
drives
*'That go-in-the-mist: another name for a "long-ears" or ass'
waives & strays: unclaimed cattle

***Ogden: *Notes* (continued)**

Poolbeg lighthouse, D   *Gr* pharos: lighthouse
Dial beyant: beyond   *r* Pharphar   far, far
near   Kish lightship off D
r Nyar   *r* Kistna
r Garry   *r* Indus   honeymoon
Indies
r Lune   *'She's dead, little Eve, little Eve she's dead. The boys & girls at play send one another back &
s (children's) Die, dog. Little dog, die   forward in the air a hundred times, & then let them
*Strange things are seen in the eyes   *cg* Die die little dog   come slowly to rest, saying those words with the
of persons on the point of death   *r* Eye   die   name of the person in question'
*The stone is a sign of space, & the tree, which has growth, of time
r Milk
*Milky Way   *r* Bubye
r Evenlode   *r* Save
lodestar   safe
r Jurua
r Sow   *r* Moy   my
Moyvally, Co. Kildare, on Liffey
r Valley   *r* Towy   so will I too by mine
Rathmines, district of D
AngI old skeowsha: old friend
ph Dear Dirty Dublin
fosterfather   *r* Fingel   gill: brook   gammer: female
AngI fooster: bungler   daughter-girls   equivalent of gaffer
letter, 7/3/24, to HSW: 'The splitting up towards the end (seven dams) is the city abuilding'
s 'As I was going to St Ives, I met a man with 7 wives, & every wife . . . ' &c.
hue-&-cry   The Sudd: mass of floating vegetation
in *r* Nile   *Sl* suds: ale
cg Ring-a-ring-o' roses: 'One for me, & one for you, & one for little Moses'
r Biferno   Margarets   cheek by jowl
bifurcate (213.14)   *r* Pink
ECH   *'The colours of the colour-band seen   *r* Lim   McBirney's: draper's stores on Aston Quay
by moonlight, so that all their dresses are in light shades'   *G* Birnen: pears
Da turkis: turquoise   indigo   *r* Milk   burnous: women's hooded cloak
r Indian   Michaelmas, 29 September
Da tys: hush!   *Da* elve: small river
Bartholomew's *Handy Gazetteer:* *r* 'Tys Elv'   *r* Elfenland   *Du* elvenland: fairyland   *r* Tees   *r* Teme
Many happy returns. The same to you   *It* vi ricordo: I remember you
r Seim   *'Vico's order but natural, free'
ALP   *ph* Limerick was, Dublin is & Cork shall be, the finest city of the 3   Ordovician rocks nr D

*'The high place on which the Norwegian Thing had its meeting has now become Suffolk Place' [actually site of St Andrew's, Suffolk St]   *'What number of places will make things into persons? Play on the statement that a "substantive" is the name of a person, a place or a thing'
r Trinity   Trinity College, D   pure   *r* Eure   Sanskrit (an Aryan language)   *F* sans
r Our   HCE   *L* Hircus civis Eblanensis: goat citizen of D   your
(goat = thing; citizen = person; D = place)
primitive adoption ceremony of sucking male paps: St Patrick refused to submit to it   *C* ho: river
r Ho
r Save
AngI chittering: constantly complaining
G Fledermaus: bat   *r* Liffey
r Save   *G* Fuss   *r* Moose
r Oos   *G* Moos: moss
r Elm   *Macbeth* V.5.30: 'a tale told by an idiot'
my old head falls   *r* Halls Creek
whole   *G* hallen: to echo

***Ogden: *Notes* (continued)**

r Elm

r Stone

5

II

D newspapers used to give lighting-up time for cyclists

Phoenix
G nichts (no fee)
Sl diddlem club: lottery gods: gallery in theatre *BNS* scrab: shilling
downstairs gad: to wander (hence, wanderers, vagrants)
AngI the quality: the gentry built weekday
large shilling: brass coin minted in James II's Gunmoney Coinage of 1689–91
performance Sundays matinees Massine: ballet dancer arrangement CHE
perfume *L* somnus: sleep some days 'Children's Hour': B.B.C radio programme
expurgated in some early Ir. cinemas returnable jampots were
explicated accepted from children for admission (porter bottles)

St Genesius: patron of actors
Gr archimimos: chief actor

From the respective cities of Findias, Murias, Gorias & Falias, 4 magic objects were brought by the Tuatha Dé Danaan: Nuad's Sword of Light, the Dagda's Cauldron of Plenty, the Spear of Lug & the Stone of Fal (destiny)
Coarbs: an order of old Ir. monks
I Claidheamh Solais: Sword of Light *R* pobeda: victory *F* pierre du sort: stone of destiny
glorious galore (cauldron of plenty)
senate
sennet: trumpet call announcing entrance on stage
Adelphi Theatre, D (became Queen's) *PS* brat: brother
Gr adelphoi: brothers Bratislava: capital of Slovakia
nr Humpty Dumpty: 'All the king's horses & all the king's men'
umpteen: very many
Queen's Men: a company of Elizabethan actors wirelessed
Judas Aristobulus II unseated his brother John Hyrcanus II, high priest of the Jews, 78–40 B.C.
Gaiety Theatre, King St, D

cloudburst Celtic Hellenic Teutonic Slavic Zend Latin Sanskrit (Rev. John Roche Ardill, *St Patrick*
broadcast *A.D. 180*, 122 calls these 'The seven sister tongues')
tabloids *BNS* fern: man *It* caldo: hot firn: snow of former winters
tableaux Finn MacCool
St Michael & Lucifer (Old Nick) adapted *s* Ballyhooly Blue Ribbon Army
Le Fanu: *The House by the Churchyard*: 'There was a man near Ballymooney, Was guilty of a deed o'blood'
Blue Chin: character in *The House by the Churchyard* *Sl* bluechin: an actor
Black Dillon: doctor in *The House by the Churchyard* who revives Sturk otherwise

⊏ (penman)
AngI glugger: empty noise; a foolish boaster
dress circle & gallery in theatre gangster
(barrel)
Du bleek: palefaced
Blake black
rogues' gallery: collection of portraits of criminals
tabs (theatre): curtains

letter, 22/11/30, to HSW: 'The scheme of the piece I sent you is the game we used to call Angels and Devils or colours. The Angels, girls, are grouped behind the Angel, Shawn, and the Devil has to come over three times and ask for a colour. If the colour he asks for has been chosen by any girl she has to run and he tries to catch her. As far as I have written he has come twice and been twice baffled. The piece is full of rhythms taken from English singing games. When first baffled vindictively he thinks of publishing blackmail stuff about his father, mother etc etc etc. The second time he maunders off into sentimental poetry of what I actually wrote at the age of nine: "My cot alas that dear old shady home where oft in youthful sport I played, upon thy verdant grassy fields all day or lingered for a moment in thy bosom shade etc etc etc etc." This is interrupted by a violent pang of toothache after which he throws a fit. When he is baffled a second time the girl angels sing a hymn of liberation around Shawn. . . . Note specially the treatment of the double rainbow in which the iritic colours are first normal and then reversed'

too much forced

disgraced in divorce court
caught
○ St Bride: St Brigid

(February of a leap year has 29 days)

Valkyries
Gr kyriê eleêsôn: Lord have mercy

⊣ *Sl* beauty spot: cunt

graceful ⊢

∧ (postman)
AngI chuff: full *Sl* chuffed: pleased sanguine: red pencil or
pictograph: a pictorial symbol or design chalk, used in drawing
tophole: (fig.), the
highest point attainable

L gemini: twins generally Castor & Pollux gat (gun)
VI.C.18.12: 'pud: shoe'
shooting Russian General (338–55) adumbrate: to typify, foreshadow (fig.)
F chute redskins (game)

△ *Sp* corriente: (adj.), *RR* Grischun: Grisons, area where *RR* spoken
running; (sb.), stream *RR* scoula: school
pod (suffix): foot distributes Maundy Money
F pied: foot mandamus: writ, letter &c. issued by sovereign or court
RR perdunaunza: saint's day *L* ovum: egg *F* entrée
hundred and eleven entries *It* pulcino: chicken
It Pulcinella: Punch, Neapolitan mask
Easter egg
law
F lieu
ᗰ Michael Gunn managed Gaiety Theatre, D *Laxdæla saga* (Icelandic)

King Eric of Sweden could alter wind's direction by turning his cap
G Schweden: Sweden
cap-à-pie: from head to foot
cad with a pipe (035.11)
coat of arms is surmounted by crest & flanked by supporters

Book of Common Prayer: Litany: 'the World, the Flesh & the Devil'

AngI glugger: egg that fails to hatch
psychological
setting sail
studding-sail: one beyond the leeches of jib: triangular staysail on large ships
any principal sail during a fair wind royals: largest sails on a ship of any sort
umbra: ghost

remnants emblem revealing *L* quondam: at one time

supercargo: officer superintending Copenhagen
ship's cargo Vatican (Peter = rock) pope in heaven
The Custom House, D CHE esker (geology): an Ir. name for ridge of
Caerleon-upon-Usk: site of Arthur's court postglacial gravel

O (drinking after hours)

L Patricius: Patrick annuary: priest who says annual masses
St Patrick's College, Maynooth (trains priests) diary
colporteur: hawker of books, bibles &c.
subsection (sucking porter)
inquest

S *Da* øl: beer Tuesdays tiff: to drink Wednesdays
Da svinge: to brandish Taff (Butt in .11)
bed *Du* aap: ape
Da bad: bath VI.B.27.105: 'apes bear torches at Cena'
Da rullepølse: rolled meat sausage Glen of the Downs, valley, Wicklow
roly-poly: steamed jam pudding
Gungnir: Odin's spear gasworks earthquake Loki, in Norse myth, caused Balder's death
Lucky Strike with mistletoe *Da* o.s.v.: og saa videre: & so on
G Scheren: scissors (cigarettes)

mildew
F Dieu
K Rachel & Leah: wives & nieces of Jacob bachelors
Isaac S. Varian: D brush manufacturer fortunes bashful
purdah: curtain, esp. to screen women from sight of men delta
divination from cards, palms, tea-leaves *Sl* tosspot: heavy drinker
palm card: conceal it in hand, to cheat witch
pauses
Le Fanu: *The House by the Churchyard* Asgaard: home of the Norse gods
one thing, that

F pressant: urgent
present
Futurist school of painting (C20)
Sl one-horse: on a small scale

Everglades: mangrove swamp, Florida *G* Beobachter: observer blood & thunder
G Beauftragter: representative
AngI good people: fairies

It elanio vitale: *F* élan vitale (vital impulse) close-ups blackouts

toilets *G* Hexenschuss: 'witches' shot': stabbing pain at onset of acute lumbago
stage to let toilette *F* cauchemar: nightmare *It* incubone: big nightmare
ON Ragnarøkr: destruction of the Norse gods *F* de la mode
Bertha Delimita: J's niece
George Harley: C18 actor, Harlequin & Columbine *N* beina: legs
performed in D James Quinn: C18 Ir. actor cool limb
jorum: large drinking vessel or contents

lamented P/K rest in peace
Royal Ir. Constabulary
earwigs *F* oui *R* da: yes no *Da* ikke: not limelight & floodlight

Kreuger & Toll: firm of match manufacturers *Du* hoed: hat *Da* hovedpine: headache
copyright *Du* kopen: to buy *Da* pibe: pipe P/K Kapp & Peterson: D pipe & tobacco makers
Mrs J. Morgan, hat manufacturer, Grafton St Harriet Bosse, Strindberg's 3rd wife

hither & thither tree/stone granted
ALP
rack-rent: extortionate rent Venetian blinds *F* sourd *Du* doof: deaf *ph* deaf as a post
170.24: 'rending of the rocks' Phoenician Sardinian *Du* doofpot: extinguisher
F chauve-souris *G* Wohnbedarf: home furnishings *Du* eik: oak
Chauve-souris mime troupe Wild silkworms feed on oak but are cultured on mulberry
Silken Thomas, C16 Ir. rebel *F* chauve-souris *G* Grabstein: gravestone
Gladstone bag
G.O.M. ('Grand Old Man') = Gladstone J had a picture of Cork in a cork frame

fire in pit (hell) incidental providence (Vico)
ferment
J.F. Larchet, orchestra leader at Abbey Theatre from 1908 profusion
F archet: bow (musical) *F* la corde: the string otiose effusion
H . . . C . . . E *Da* bemærke: observe
Gen 1:1: 'In the beginning' hardly remark
H . . . C . . . E

exode: concluding part of a Greek drama

(imitation of voices in canon) *AngI* betune: between

Amphion & twin brother built Thebes: John McCormack, Ir. tenor
walls formed at sound of Amphion's lyre
John Sullivan, Ir. tenor
F sous le vin
s 'Oh, Mr Porter, Whatever shall I do, I want to go to Birmingham & they're taking me on to Crewe'
Sl soger: soldier *F* deux so pleased
F sauve-qui-peut: save himself who can *G* Oh Hoffnung der Rache, verlasse mich nicht: O hope of
revenge, abandon me not *G* Der Rasche: the quick one
climax (032.34)
Mick Nick
catastrophe Moussorgsky: *Night on the Bare Mountain* pull him up by the roots

Mädchen in Uniform (a film by Leontine Sagan, 1931)

thingamejig Gog & Magog, legendary giants

omitted titular: one who has title
admitted

transformation scene in pantomimes, e.g. *Cinderella*

Petit Journal called 70th wedding *G* Neid: envy
anniversary a radium wedding night

an angel sword flashed lightning

full stop prayer at end of Mass: 'Sancte, sancte, Michaelus, defende nos in praelio' ('Holy St
Michael, defend us in battle')
sign of the Cross
Sl make a shine: make a fuss, commotion
Devil himself *AngI* glugger: empty noise; a foolish boaster *N* lur: cunning
Dublin sulphur
G Punkt: full stop *It* sbuffare: to pant, puff, snort *L* tussio: I cough
It sputare: to spit anything
Gertrud Eyesoldt, actress gnashing his teeth *It* brividi: shivers privities: secrets, private
weeping his eyes out *G Dial* gnatchen: to wail *L* brevis dies: [our] brief day brevity of existence thoughts
utter John Lubbock, Lord Avebury: *Pleasures of Life* *G* Kelche: chalice
other *I* lúbach: deceitful *F* quelque chose accablé: something overcome
G Kleeblatt: clover leaf Rev 20:12: 'the book of life' *I* leabar: book
swords corr. to spades in Tarot pack; with clubs are 2 black suits
Matt 25:41: 'Depart from me, ye cursed, into everlasting I Cor 13:13: 'faith, hope, charity'
fire, prepared for the devil & his angels'
F jarret: bend of the knee djowr: giaour (term of reproach applied by Turks to non-Mussulmans)
athlete's foot (disease) *I* diabhal: devil appear!
amongst *Sp* nombre: name, reputation peaceful suggestiveness
F ombre *Dubliners:* 'Eveline'
jest early stars *G* Zittern: trembling
It zitte (f. pl.): silent glitterings of light
twinklings *Dial* twitchbell: earwig laughter
Arch rondel: circle; kind of dance
naughtily descended
musk-scented
stairs skylight beckonings behind his back semicolon
twilit

Mary, sister of Charles Lamb, suffered from mental illness

Marie Louise/Josephine archangel

L agnus: lamb *cg* Wolf ('shepherd' has to save 'sheep' from 'wolf') Irish
It (Obs) agnoli: angels *BNS* airig: a mason
deaf & dumb alphabet *I* an: the Ogham: ancient Ir. system of writing

s Old Mother Mason (chant in Norman Douglas's *London Street Games*)
G Mutter 'Mother Mason's': shebeen, S. King St, D
L calor: warmth, passion Seville oranges citron–lemon (yellow)
colour of her brightness (rainbow colours)
emerald *It* pervinca: periwinkle (blue) indigo

4 X 7 = 28 (days of February) month marmalade jar
It melme: muds
(mimed clues)
twenty-nine
pantomime
I druim/drom: back

nr Pop goes the weasel heliotrope *It* Isotta: Isolde

G stolpern: stumble GLUGG such a thing did I ne'er see

be my own you (if you call correct colour)
call my hue

face to face

Copenhagen: Wellington's horse
Marengo: Napoleon's horse
Glenasmole ('Valley of the Thrushes') in the D mountains was Finn's hunting ground, where Ossian, son of Finn, after 300 years in the Land of the Young, fell from horse, touched ground & became old
Patrick (subsequently met Ossian, cf. *U*.200)
scald (poet)–Ossian–meets evangelist
F arrête-toi!: stop! Scaldbrother's Hole, D: a subterranean cavern in Arbour Hill where Scaldbrother, robber, kept his plunder *Gr* evangelion: good news
F accusant St John's Wood, London St John's Road, Kilmainham, D
Mrs John Wood's Company played at opening of Gaiety Theatre
damned *F* il s'arretait
G dumm: stupid
trefoil (Patrick demonstrates Trinity with shamrock)

Λ (space): 'Who are you?' 'the cat's mother': reply to stop children asking questions

⊏ (time): 'What do you lack?' *pr* a cat may look at a queen

Arch prehend: seize, catch, apprehend puzzling his

G Feind: enemy
finder fender
G (ge)worden: become
Du woorden: words *G* Schall: echo; sound
G Dichtung kenning (anagram): heliotrope heliotrope heliotrope
Howth Macalister, *Secret Languages of Ireland,* mentions 'a dark tongue' (Ogham)

St Augustine: *Confessions* X.vi: 'I asked the earth, & it answered: "I am not"; & the things in it said the same. I asked the sea & the deeps & creeping things, & they answered: "We are not your God; seek above us." I asked the winds & the whole air with its inhabitants answered me: "Anaximenes was deceived; I am not God." I asked the sky, the sun, the moon, the stars. "Not" (say they) "are we the God whom thou seekest"'

G untergehen: submerge, set (of sun)
(fire . . . air . . . earth . . . water)
sought *G* Luft
(Matthew . . . Mark . . . Luke . . . John)
G Grund: ground *F* ongle: claw
G Blumen: flowers
groaning beck: brook (water)
growing (corn) *G* Bächlein: rivulet
jauntily Sheridan: *School for Scandal*
skand: disgrace, shame
word from the wireless ether

wet waiting
weeping weeting: witting, cognisant

otem: totem

for him gutta-percha

hint he was an engine driver L etiam: & also
india-rubber L ruber: red
ph at his wits' ends

Town of the Ford of the Hurdles (D)
fouled the ford water (ford), earth (stones), air (duck), fire (roast)
graving dock sat down Atem: creator in *Egyptian Book of the Dead*

G Urteil: judgement
ph thereby hangs a tale
Ah ho! (013.26) so sad

foot & mouth disease deplorable Ah, dearo dear! (013.27)

inherited Boucicault: *The Colleen Bawn*
G heben: to rise *It* colline: hills genitor: parent
something terrible *G* hehr: majestic *G* Antlitz: face
Tower of Babel hairy ('velvet' on deer's antlers prior to rutting)
bulging
belching
nocency: guilt interrogation (021.18)
F noces: marriage notes noses interregnum (question marks)
tender late & early

Moore: *s* Sing, Sweet Harp, O Sing to Me [air unknown] anon.
alone
L nescientia: state of not knowing
subconscious
scarce *G* Mörder: murderer
mother
bladder *G* Vogel: bird tympanum
vocal tones
schoolmaster trumpet missed his footing
skull *F* trompe: deceive flute
St Cecilia: patron of song
Ah ho! (013.26) precisely
Proust: *A l'ombre des jeunes filles en fleurs* *Sl* frill: a girl *G* schauen: to see, view
George Trobridge: *A Life of Emanuel Swedenborg* 213–4: 'delightsomeness . . . two married partners . . . consociate'
but *L* florilegium: bouquet associately
drawers (guessing colour of)
hindsight common or garden boyfriend

F pluriel troubadour thinking
prurient through a trapdoor (pantomime devil)
fand: examine, put to proof guesswork
find *Da* fand: devil
are tiretain: cloth of wool & cotton or linen
F tire-toi!, cache-toi!: go!, hide!
you
It nr 'O quante belle figlie, Madama Dorè! . . . Che cosa ne vuol fare, Madama Dorè?'
r Liffey ('Oh, how many beautiful daughters, Madama Dorè! . . . What are you going to do with them, Madama Dorè?')
(fished with)
Cinderella
too tiny brought *G* Angst
China (women wear tiny shoes) *G* Braut: bride ask
common or garden

either *I* toth: cunt
Thoth: Egyptian god; invented writing
brandished *F* maman
F bander: to have erection whole *F* ma main
release *Song o' My Heart*: film, 1930, with John McCormack *G* hast du vielleicht . . . ?: have you perchance . . . ?
carbuncle: red precious stone *L* apud: near upon *L* praecox: precocious

F tête-à-tête   la-do-mi-so-si

witchery   advised   *G* angestimmt: tuned   resoundingly
(lit.) *G* wortkarg: taciturn   Ringsend, district of D
F toutes ensembles

have a look   *Sl* frig: masturbate

ph tell it to the marines   noses
Ulster   ultramarine (blue)
Norman Douglas, *London Street Games*: retort: breeches
C ni: to urinate   'Piss up yer leg, an play wiv the steam'

beware   werewolf   taboo
I abú: to victory!
all for   toffee   tuck
Tophet: place of burning dead bodies, S.E. of Jerusalem
Du anker: anchor   *s* Soldier, Soldier, won't you marry me: 'very very best'
hunkers: hams
Mephistopheles

to wit   bread & butter & watercress (.16)

Wurra-Wurra ('Great Worm'): an idol destroyed by St Patrick
G Wurm   Shem shall have some
cg There stands a lady on a mountain, Who she is I do not know, All she wants is gold & silver, All she wants is a
It rigagnolina: (fem.) rivulet   nice young man . . . What's for tea love? What's for tea love?—Farewell.
It montagnone: (masc.) big mountain   Bread & butter, water-cress'
ken
golden syrup & plum jam   deaf & dumb

had   woo

G wollen: want   (003.09–10)
worry

moonbeam   (heliotrope also name of a gem)
moonstone   brimstone   (Glugg's first guess at colour: red)

G hell: bright   *G* Feuerstein: flint
hellfire   firestone: heat-resistant red sandstone

coral (pink)   Cora Pearl: Parisian courtesan whose father wrote music for *Kathleen Mavourneen*
Van Dieman's Land: Tasmania (rich in pearls)

church   Forward!   shake   ears

Browning: *Pippa Passes:* 'God's in His heaven, All's right with the world'

s O Dear, What Can the Matter Be?: 'He promised to buy me a bunch of blue ribbons To tie up my pretty brown hair . . . Johnny's so long at the fair'
L mater: mother

It pretti (m. pl.): pure   *Du* allebei: both
L alabi: elsewhere
L flos: flower   *s* Die Vogelhochzeit: 'Fiederallala, fiederallala, fiederalla-la-la-la. Der Sperling, der Sperling . . . '
VI.B.33.150: 'flossies in her hat'
(hat brim)

s Dinah: 'in Carolina'

s Roaming in the Gloaming

cg 'Poor Mary sits a-weeping' *F* étincelles

Isa Bowman, friend of Lewis Carroll, played title role in *Alice in Wonderland* adaptation

loveliness (neck)

F hélas *G* wofür: what for peripatetic Isolde

Alice

Isa Bowman Finn MacCool letter from Lewis Carroll to simper

Cant bowman: fancy man Isa Bowman: 'So *tremble*! Do you hear? sympathize

Be good enough to tremble!'

s Still I love him, Can't deny it: '& if he goes St Francis

nowhere, I'll go there as well'

St Clara founded Franciscan nuns (*U.*339: 'daughters of Clara')

F journeé close *cg* Jenny Jones: 'You can't see her now'

fiancée Tristan true

(215.24) *It* minuscoline (f. pl.): very tiny *r* Dee

unmarried dress up husband

cherub

high sheriff

seraph

angels *cg* Here We Go Gathering Nuts in May

Swedenborg discusses angels' garments in *Heaven & Hell*

cashmir Liberty's: department store, London; term quicksilver tricked out: decked

'Liberty' used attrib. to designate their textiles

It selve: woods

something *cg* Lubin: 'Here we come looby, looby, Here we come looby light, Here we come looby, looby,

All on a Saturday night'

Sl noose: to marry

with a sly glance in & a coy glance out

cg Lubin: 'Put your left foot in, Put your right foot out, Shake it a little, a little, a little, & turn yourself about'

right round

Alice Liddell: friend of Lewis Carroll, model for *Alice in Wonderland*

coloratura: florid ornaments in vocal music, runs,

trills, &c.

RAYNBOW *It* arancia: orange (rainbow colours)

It rubretta: red

odalisque: concubine in Eastern harem *F* fleurettes

Hamlet IV.5.174: 'rosemary, that's for remembrance' (purple flower, in bloom in November)

s 'Sur le pont d'Avignon, L'on y danse, L'on y danse'

cg When I was a young girl: 'This way went I'

I ainm: name Anna . . . Livia antediluvian

oodles of names (anagram) Luvius: Ptolemy's name for *r* Lee

s Dies Irae

The Merry Wives of Windsor

(the 7 in later life) *F* haricot: bean

helter skelter holds her skirts causeway first instant
quack doctor
she hears of a tinkle of thunder

cg Cat's cradle (greyhound on Irish sixpence)

confession

potty

It ricchissime (f. pl.): very rich many

Sl dust: money

nr 'Little Bo Peep She lost her sheep . . . dragging their tails behind them'
teen: injury
cg When I was a young girl: 'This way went I'

WOBNIAR (letter, 22/11/30: 'the double rainbow in which the iritic colours are first normal and then reversed')

Pansey: *Viola* *It* papaveri: poppies forget-me-not
F foncé: darkened (red) (blue)
(green) primrose (yellow) marigold (orange)
pr While there's life there's hope
Arch ancille: handmaid
angels' *F Sl* ancelle: whore

vice versa

Three Rock Mountain, D scarcely sight
G Monaten: months Macpherson: *Fingal* I.34: 'the scout of ocean'
livid with woe woad: a blue dye
L viridis: green *Du* woede: fury
The Devil's Punchbowl, chasm nr Killarney Burns: *Tam O'Shanter* (also hat)
Sl poll: head tummy's centre (navel) shent: disgrace
Catechism: 'an outward & visible sign of an inward & spiritual grace' (definition of sacrament)

(actor's cue)

who's who

fondly appreciate

Sl bit of fluff: girl *F* geste revèle l'inconnu: gesture reveals the unknown
uncouth
ph start from scratch

7 SACRAMENTS: BAPTISM CONFIRMATION
water Stuart: royal family
(solar plexus) EUCHARIST Holy Communion *Angl* gillie beg: little lad

PENANCE sins, mortal & venial Shrove Tuesday

Macpherson EXTREME UNCTION
(Ossianic poet) excrement emuncted: blew nose
MATRIMONY chest to chest *Much Ado about*
just in jest *Nothing*
tell a lie

Pro tartarin: monkey Alphonse Daudet: *Tartarin de Tarascon* (hero has split personality)
It tastare: to touch *Pro* tastarin: somewhat *Pro* tourtons: small cakes for children
Gr chlamydophagos: cloak eater *L* (artif.) vestimentivorus: clothes eater
It bretelle: suspenders, braces imbrate: defile HOLY ORDERS

It sicari: cutthroats *Arch* mak siccar: make sure
McGillycuddy's Reeks, Co. Kerry

Everallin: wife of Ossian & mother of Oscar in Macpherson

J. M. Flood: *Ireland: Its Saints & Scholars* 106: 'the holy Bishop Assicus was [St. Patrick's] coppersmith'

Tripartite Life of St Patrick *G* Sieg heil elsewhere
F tricher: cheat
Young Irelanders: C19 patriots' party *G* genug!: enough!
patriot's absolution *G* mach' nichts: doesn't matter *R* zhenikh: bridegroom
Macpherson: *Fingal* II.55n: 'Deo-gréna signifies a sun-beam'
ship Macpherson: *Temora* VIII.318: 'Erin rolls to war, wide-tumbling, rough & dark'
Fingal V.91: 'the bow of the shower' (i.e. rainbow)

three sheets in the wind: very drunk
R pogoda: weather permitting
(Robert Bruce: silence; Coriolanus: exile; St Ignatius Loyola: cunning)
plural singular
common *s* Come to the Bower neuter Macpherson's Brassolis kills herself after her brother kills her
I cumman: society, club lover
F au revoir *s* Good-bye, Dolly Gray Macpherson: *Carric-Thura* 158n: 'The circle of Loda is . . . a place of worship
Conan: a member of the Fianna among the Scandinavians'
G Schluss *s* Lochaber No More girl chaser missionary for the ministry
Fingal V.90: 'I see not Gelchossa, my love' *Heb* mišna: 1st part of Talmud
F Sem: Shem Aram, son of Shem *Heb* śimḥa: joy Eire
sons of Erin *I* siomach: kind of trout
Portrait V: 'silence, exile & cunning' DORA: Defence of the Realm Act, 1914
m, b, d, h & vowels = *Heb* mebhadeah: joyous hedge schools: private &
Heb sheol: abode of *G* dunkel Le Fanu: *Uncle Silas* diligence: stagecoach orig. openair Ir. schools
the dead (group of minor Ir. writers on this page)
Crone's *Dictionary of Irish Biography* uses entry 'brother of succeeding'
Macpherson: *Fingal* I.34n: 'Cairbre signifies a strong man'
corporal punishment Pennsylvania Armorica (Tristan) to meet
(mania for writing) *Da* Bretland: orig. Wales, now poetic for all Gt Britain
bankers' trust pronto!
F emprunté: borrowed
(evidently means 'divination *G* heiss *G* roh: raw Charles Lever: *Harry Lorrequer*
from meteors') liquified hydrogen Laracor: village, Co. Meath; Swift was incumbent, 1700–
F Sl Paname: Paris 1714
L Turicum: Zurich Trieste
Trieste once called *La città immediata* *F* aller et retour (return ticket) *G* Fahrkarte: travel ticket

G getrennt: separated William Carlton: *Rody the Rover*
twenty
L Libera nos: deliver us *L* beate Laurentie O'Tulie ora pro nobis: Blessed
Laurence O'Toole, pray for us (patron saint of D)
every man his own castle
Europe Cashel, ancient capital of Munster *AngI* cashel: stone fort
Da ligge: lie (down) *Pro* liogo: place *F* jambe
It luogotenente: *Pro* liòtenènt: lieutenant inclined jambs in Irish Romanesque doorways
pronaos: space in front of *It* deretano: behind, bottom Finisterre
temple, vestibule reredos: altar screen *L* fenestra: window
fire escape (Parnell: 388.03) *s* The Man on the Flying Trapeze: 'with the greatest of ease . . . her dear home'

weighing anchor *s* On the Raging Canal

s On the Other Side of Jordan (Am. revival hymn) *s* Waterboy
N jorden: the earth *Heb* Hawah: Eve heave ho!
Charles Joseph Kickham: *Knocknagow* Gerald Griffin: *The Collegians*
himself *It* collegio: college
John Mitchell: *Jail Journal* Sebastian Melmoth (name assumed by Wilde) fasse: interpolated
It giornale: newspaper 1st epistle vernacular comment
Hebrews highbrows *R* slon: bishop (in chess) sometime Samaria Macpherson: *Temora*
R chernila: ink Cornelius: centurion converted by Peter *L* praepositus: commander tomorrow
church in Antioch *G* ledig: unmarried ladies & gentlemen *R* touman: fog
I an teach: the house *L* salve: hail! *It* salvo: safe
Da tordenshjold: thunder shield *L* ebrio: I make drunk *Da* tilsammen: together
free love tea-leaves for everybody tinned salmon

yard ham & eggs till further orders
Da jord: earth
Da fremad: forward Samuel Lover: *Handy Andy*
F nom de plume
G Gott strafe England!: May God Punish England (slogan) St George merry England
don't you laugh *G* Weinschänke: wine shop *G* Schwemme: tavern
W.J. O'Neill Daunt: C19 Ir. novelist

Society of Authors (gave J a subsidy)
L Senatus Populusque Romanus–S.P.Q.R. (Imperial Roman motto)
(letter, 22/11/30: 'he thinks of publishing blackmail stuff about his father, mother')

Napoleon called English 'nation of shopkeepers' bloody truth
coper: one who barters, deals plighted troth
F maladie *We* melodi: melody *Pro* malodi: thanks to Horace & his friend Lalage
Gr lalage: prattle Tristan of Lyonesse in Cornwall
arrant: notorious knight errant Bulwer-Lytton: *The Lady of Lyons* Gilligan's maypole: wireless aerial
Rose Gilligan, fruiterer & florist, Capel St P.G. Smyth: *The Wild Rose of Lough Gill*
Michael Banim: *Croppy; Crowhore of the Billhook* crystal set (radio)

Calypso *Lotus-eaters* *Hades* *Aeolus*
L nemo in patria: no one in the fatherland
Lestrygonians *Scylla & Charybdis* *The Wandering Rocks*
(Bloom's lunch) *s* The Son of a Gombolier: 'I'm a rambling wretch'
The Sirens *Cyclops* (Polyphemus) *Nausicaa* *Oxen of the Sun* (maternity)
Mater Misericordiae Hospital, D
Circe (similarity to Walpurgis Nacht section of *Faust*)
G nackt: naked
I mailís: malice bear entire Leinster, Munster, Connacht, Ulster
my liege! *Sl* maleesh!: never mind!
strip poker (game) globetrotter
G Trottel: idiot
old fellow gaffer Trobridge: *A Life of Emanuel Swedenborg* 312:
'Some Sabbatarian observed' (that Swedenborg did not observe the Sabbath)
Sl beardsplitter: woman Omega, lit. 'big O'

Burns: *Tam O'Shanter* (also hat) ladyship (arsehole)
Gr mega: big *L* fundus: bottom 'Letty': Delany's name for Laetitia Van Lewen (friend of Swift)
gammer concealed sponsor *L* sponsa: bride ceased
Trobridge 201: 'congenial consorts will be found' (in the next world by the unmarried, or unhappily married)
making water Jameson's whiskey *G* Kluft: chasm delta
malt
microcosm Gap of Dunloe, Co. Kerry
(cunt)
ph kettle of fish
formula to end fairy tale: 'So they put on the kettle & made tea, & if they don't live happy that you & I may'
muffins *Gr* thea: goddess just set it all right down
all had tiffin for tea
rightfully right black & white

his

Act of Contrition: 'I am heartily sorry' *G* Beichtstuhl: confessional

G Fläschchen: little flask *F Sl* quille: penis *Sl* bone: penis
foreskin
Caxton, early printer
Castor & Pollux
miraculous Jeremiad *G* Sündenbock: scapegoat

duchess of so & so *G* Heldin: heroine
F sceau: seal
F en bloc Bayreuth (Wagner)

utterly Otto Wesendonk, whose wife Wagner admired during period of composition of *Tristan*

who stole his innocence *Da* grusomhed: cruelty
sold

eureka spectroscope

imposed *L* ambo: both
ambushed
ph cheek by jowl St Michael (angel) *Pro* besoun: need, requirement
besides

Old Joe Beelzebub

Provençals *Pro* drollo: girl expelled *nr* Humpty Dumpty
L domus: home
R národní dům: *L* domum: home *Pro* osco!: bravo! *Pro* pesco: fish *Pro* bisco: i) soup; ii) ill
parliament (national house) *Pro* Basco: Basque humour
amulet *Pro* erbo: herb
F omelette aux fines herbes: omelette with fine herbs
L finis orbe: the end of the earth *G* Muster: pattern

neither sink nor swim socialism

blocking catalogue

Marie Corelli: *The Sorrows of Satan* (*U.*184) *F* comme il faut
L soror: sister *Pro* coume un fou: like a fool
Pro teto-dous: soft head Wagner's mistress, Mathilde Wesendonk, inspired *Tristan*
F tête-à-tête
tryst paradise *G* tausend
Tristan Paris *G* tosend: roaring
Eccles 11:1: 'Cast thy bread upon the waters'
making good
It casa nuova: new house *s* Mademoiselle from Armentières *F* oiseau
Giovanni Giacomo Casanova *Pro* nèblo: fog *Pro* nòvi: newlywed
Pro nivo: cloud *Pro* ennovia: to dress *F* Occitanien: Provençal
Pro nòvio: newlywed like newlywed *It* accidempoli: dash, damn
sigh centuries

F demi-pension
lifetime passion
P.W. Joyce: *Ancient Irish Civilisation:* 'The Irish musicians had various *styles*. . . . The 'Sleep-music' (*Suantree*) was intended to produce sleep'
go to sleep
personal company Gipsy
L ipse secum: himself with himself
G fing an: began *s* Phil the Fluter's Ball go to sleep music
MS of prelude to Wagner's *Valkyrie* is enscribed 'G. s. M.', i.e. Gesegnet sei Mathilde, 'blessed be Mathilde'
G vor- und rückwärts: forwards & backwards signs

HF 28: 'being brung up' *HF*, 25: 'soul-butter'

ricorso (Vico) *I* corónach: funeral dirge

Paradise Lost I.620: 'Tears such as angels weep, burst forth' (*U.*184)
W.H. Mallock: *Is Life Worth Living?* *Da* nej: no
Heb toledôth: histories *Heb* zachar: remember
tree/stone
grandstand *A Brilliant Career* (play written by J at age 18)
Pro grand carriero: main road *It* gran carriera: full speed largesse: liberality
lifesize satyrs *L* susceptor: support, defender
L sator: author; sower susceptible
L genetrix: mother *L* avus: grandfather
(originating)
L avia: grandmother
velocipedes *L* veluti: just as
F velouté: velvety
L abavunculus: *L* nurus: daughter-in-law *L* nepos: grandson
maternal great-uncle *L* noverca: stepmother
L circumpictus: painted around *L* sobrinus: cousin-german patriots
sober senses
L glos: sister-in-law *L* socer: father-in-law parents
L germanus (-a): full brother (sister) *It* socerine: little mothers-in-law
L vitricus: stepfather *L* patruus: paternal uncle levir: brother-in-law eke-name: nickname
patriots Archimedes: theory of levers *Gr* oikos: house
Moore: *s* Remember Thee? Yes, While There's Life in This Heart [Castle Tirowen]
Once prosperous trade street
tree/stone stoney broke I'll paint yous a *F* pomme you'll
poem

tell me the (answer) to havel: term of reproach riddle
'Tingsomingenting' (414.34); 'Nixnixundnix' (415.29)
Sl gussies: effeminate men
penny *Scottish* gussies: swine 'give it up?' (170.23) *Heb* ish: man
s 'Gin a body meet a body, Comin' through the rye' when it is home
Gi shom: I am

letter, 22/11/30: 'My cot alas that dear old shady home where oft in youthful sport I played, upon thy verdant grassy fields all day or lingered for a moment in thy bosom shade'

verdigris

F amour shed
amusement
J Shina: China *C* yung: eternal, lasting
shy young thing
J yoru: night here upon St Bonaventura
J yume: dream Timor Sea, between Indonesia & Australia
root of wisdom tooth

funeral 'Festy King' (085.23) Macpherson: *Fingal* I.43: 'king of shells' Liffey
Fonar: bard in Macpherson's *Temora* Shelley *Sl* goog: egg *Temora* III.260: 'by gurgling Moruth'
Temora III.262n: 'kings of Caledonia & Ireland had a plume of eagles' feathers' (minor Ir. poets:)
John Boyle O'Reilly plus
Thomas D'arcy McGee plus Kevin Isod O'Doherty plus

Denis Florence MacCarthy *G* Zahn: tooth sawn in two
letter, 22/11/30: 'This is interrupted by a violent pang of toothache after which he throws a fit'
L sanguis: blood features of his face
all his anguish flooded
Sl phiz: countenance temperature

have at you! (toast) Jesus Christ Croesus: last Lydian king, world's richest man
Isis Unveiled II.256: 'Joshua, son of Nun (called *Jesus* in the Greek & Slavonian versions)' none
Silius Italicus: C1 poet In Egyptian myth, Nunn slept till creation
Egyptian Book of the Dead CLXXV: 'It is decreed that thou shalt live for millions of millions of years, a life of millions of years'
rainbow: red to violet vilest lustre: 5-year period

Pegasus holy hell's bells! Bloody Acre, part of Glasnevin Cemetery, D

nothing on earth

Jesus Christ some *L* summus: highest beat his breast
Gr Chronides: son of Chronos (time)
St Patrick's hymn 'Breastplate' birthplace

(repossessed)
attrition: imperfect contrition *OE* mid: with

exorcism *G* so ist es recht: that is good
asceticism *It* esercizio: exercise
Malthos: enemy of Fingal in *Temora* ('slow to speak') *I* mór: great *Temora* I.220: 'Cairbar, after being frightened . . . "at length resumed his soul"'
fuck off to hell *U.S. Sl* stein song: drinking song Old Steine: place in Brighton
Fingal IV.90: 'Go, Ferchios, go to Allad, the greyhaired son of the rock'
feet *Arch* aer: ear *Gr* polygonia: fecundity

Sl blowing the gaff: giving away the secret *U.S. Sl* hopjoint: opium den
Sl pipe: penis
s Little Brown Jug Am. Democrats in 1844 called 'locofocos'
It Arch loco: place *It Arch* foco: fire
turnspit (in hell) *s* Old Rosin the Beau *G* Ratskeller: restaurant in basement of town hall
U.S. Sl rathskeller: tavern
s Frankie & Johnny: 'He was my man, but he was doin' me wrong'
Ben Travers: *Rookery Nook*, play
Mookse/Gripes (152.15)

F grippe

turkish delight
Berkeley advocated use of tar water as cure-all
colitis *s* The Man That Broke the Bank at Monte Carlo
Gr chrôma: skin; colour
L carbo: coal *L* inflammabilis: inflammable *L* comburenda: things requiring
F poursuivre to be burned
ph 'a long pull & a strong pull & a pull all together'
(in *The Dead*, Michael Furey 'was in the gasworks')
Crone: *Dictionary of Irish Biography:* twopenny
'Dub.Uni.Mag.' = *Dublin University Magazine*
go to pieces Dinneen's Ir. dictionary
pressgang go to press Denis Florence MacCarthy (minor Ir. poet) *I* caínteach: satirist
Michael Moran ('Zozimus'), D street singer, known as 'the last of the gleemen'
Gr zozimôs: capable of living
L inculminatio: a placing on the highest point

Pip . . . pet (.25 Swift)

escapes Hertzian waves: a class of ether waves
N skip: ship *G* Herz: heart
Vanessa/Stella Venus *Vanessa*, genus of moths
s Call Me Pet Names
Astarte: Babylonian equivalent of Venus

Four Courts, D 'I'll wait for you, O darling' (words of fiancée of Ir. poet poetaster
Kevin Isod O'Doherty when he was transported)
s Still Growing: '& all around his college cap I'll bind a band of blue, For to let the ladies know that
he's married'
marid: in Mohammedan demonology, *Sl* blackballed: refused
a jinn of the highest class Pim Bros: S. D drapers
It leste: nimble Claribel: pseudonym of Charlotte Barnard, composer of 'Come Back to Erin'
Todd, Burns & Co.: N. D drapers
thank you, madam
(leaving telegraph office)
good afternoon, madam

surrender *s* Dermot Asthore

Isa Bowman: *The Story of Lewis Carroll* 39:
'One of my stays at Oxford' language of Tintagel (King Mark's castle was there)
Bédier: *Tristan & Iseult:* 'Mais, à Tintagel, Tristan languissait'
jealous mighty loud
Connolly: *Green Pastures:* 'Did you bow, Mighty Lord?'
unconditionally *s* Certainly, Lord
Satan *U.S. Sl* can that: cease that
AngI mavrone: my grief

Swift: 'Ppt' M.D. ('my dears'): Swift's abbreviation in letters to Stella

Invincibles: perpetrators of
Phoenix Park murders, 1882
(Glugg comes back on receiving Isod's message) dashes & dots (telegraphy) *F* dot: dowry
(J returns from the continent) *pr* As the old cock crows, the young cock learns
Du zoo vader zoo zoon: like father like son Bran: Finn's dog
Sifadda: horse in *Fingal*
obstreperous *Temora* VII.310n: '*To travel on the winds,* a poetical expression *I* sos: peace
for sailing' S.O.S.
hop, step & jump epilepsy,
upsadaisy!
didn't do a tishy (1922 phrase): fall with legs in a tangle
L didando: I broadcast
glacier Atlantis
gladiator
Heb daghesh: point, *Heb* diacritic *G* Esche: ash tree
double disguised (Tristan returned to Isolde disguised)
orlop deck of a ship: the lowest
all up tailormade
ph storm in a teacup Trobridge: *A Life of Emanuel Swedenborg* 234, mentions delight taken
by masters of vessels in having Swedenborg as a passenger

toothache tall tale picture

well future *F* mouton (sheep); *L* caper: goat
cut capers: act or dance fantastically

P.W. Joyce: *English as We Speak It in Ireland*: 'Did you ever see the devil With the wooden spade & shovel Digging praties for his supper & his tail cocked up'

Sinbad rainbow
doorstep

see knowledge
cg Three Sailors: 'Shall we have lodgings here?'
s 'A-hunting we will go, A-hunting we will go, We'll catch a fox & put him in a box, & then we'll let him go'

French (*Portrait* IV: '*Les jupes* . . . articles of dress worn by women' &c.) socks
fringe
so-&-so

(Glugg has to guess colour of Isod's drawers) worth

wild guesses *ph* wild goose chase *cg* London Bridge: 'my fair lady'
Wild Geese: Ir. Jacobites who fled to continent after defeat in 1691
Exiles *I* con- (pfx): dog, canine
for example *F* chien
England
VI.B.32.202: 'those who will be exiled speak 'can' for dog/those who will rise in life speak 'now' for no'
about

VI.B.33.77: 'mitre = fish's head'
Godhead *Sl* codhead: a fool *L* sinistra: left hand
3 ostrich feathers on badge of Prince of Wales as Heir Apparent
L rex regum: king of kings balderdash
L servus servorum Christi: 'slave of the slaves of Christ' (title of the pope)
C.K. Ogden: *The Meaning of Meaning* 3, gives example of match being struck as engram complex leading to expectation of flame

F jaune: *I* fearg: anger (Glugg's second guess at
yellow Joan of Arc of eggs colour: yellow)
C nao: vex, disturb, brawl
U.347–8: '-Nao . . . Nao . . . Nao'
F méchantes
jaundice
C hao: good

L per causas nuntiatas belli: through the declared causes of the war
It per caso: by chance (letter 5/1/21 to Italo Svevo: 'a rubber band having the colour of a nun's belly')

Bas aski: enough go on! *Bas* gau on: good night! *Am* micco: victim, simpleton
We gau: a lie, lying *It* mi caco: I shit (in my pants; really or fig. for fear)
C P'ing-an: peaceful

annoyance *J* anaya: in an instant
chant in N. Douglas, *London Street Games*: 'The black man said . . . You can sling your hook away'
Bas alegera: happy *Bas* tšimista: lightning
F à la guerre comme à la guerre *It* in camicia: in one's shirt
hurricane hotfoot: quickly *Bas* zango: leg *Bas* segur: true, sure
Bas harrika: a blow from a stone *Bas* zingor: mean, miserly
N utskud: scum; rabble *Arab* jamal: camel *Arab* yallah!: go!
awkward
It ciappa: take *Da* skarp snakk: sharp talk undefiled *G* Engel: angel
It Arch cioppa: teat *Da* underfallen engelsk: undershot English
Gr melanos: black *J* tsuki: moon *J* suppon: turtle *Da* rask: quick
J soppu: soup Rask spoke 25 languages
Basque *F ph* il parle français comme une vache espagnole
J makoto: indeed!

what a *Gr* gala: milk nauseous

s Hokey Pokey, Five a Plate *It* uova in camicia: poached eggs
It affogate (fig.): of eggs, poached
fallen to wit Gripes
N sperre: rafter
bedazzled Tristan *Sp* caballero: gentleman
F triste F. Hals painted *The Laughing Cavalier*
G Bruder shilling *Don Quixote*
bloody hell
bezant: coin formerly current in Eng.
peso: coin formerly current in Spain
Sp sin: without Sancho Panza *Sp* panza: belly
After enlightenment Buddha walked the world, then remained immobile with his eyes open
winsomer *G* Kerl: man
s The Girl I Left behind Me
L candidatus: clothed in white (Ir. tricolour: green, white, orange) *L* sine labes: without fault,
L viridosus: greened *L* aurolucens: gold-shining blemish
Greek HEC *BL* cotan: hero *BL* breiche: green

stood there Mookse Kevin ʌ
Most heavenly
antirevolutionary tonsor: barber

almoner: hagiography: the writing of saints' lives *J* sumi: ink
distributor of alms *L* duodetriginta: 28
The Buddha was once reborn as a 6-tusked elephant *L* Cynosura: the Little Dipper (Ursa Minor)
L septimus: 7th *L* optimus: best Maya: mother of the Buddha cynosure everybody
narcissus *D Sl* micky dazzler:
a would-be dandy
Sp curro: handsome *R* solntse: the sun vestals
loose curls Lewis Carroll Solness, the Master Builder *R* zvezda: star
Buddha married daughter of Dandapani & was surrounded by eyelash-fluttering women
s John O'Reilly the Active
Cockspur liquid

G suess: sweet *F* sourire Isa Bowman: *The Story of Lewis Carroll* 36: 'the sweetest smile that ever a man wore' *Da* sprit: spirit
G Lustspiel: comedy *It* piena: flood *It* ripida: steep *Arab* arbada: to be
F les pelerins: the pilgrims *It* rapida: swift noisy
Pilgrim's Progress P/K Eucharistic Congress, D, 1932
L princeps: first, chief, leader
congratulations alluding
lauding

nicknames
G Leichnam: corpse
Dulcinea (beloved of Don Quixote) employing

(intended husband)
ear
satisfy tease him
set on fire
It rigoletto: circle of dancers holding hands recollect *F* rigoler *Arab* jismī: bodily, physical
Arab jamaša: to caress
fairhaired vouchsafe
F bouche
as far as (I) dare assume *It* Assunta: the Virgin
Arab aŝfār: lips *Arab* šafr: lip *Arab* asunn: tooth
Gr kyriê eleêsôn: Lord have mercy endure the injuries *G* im Bett: in the bed
BL anduiriu: today *BL* anduire: yesterday *BL* imbethrar: tomorrow
S's *BL* liber: sea
L liber: book; free
say certainly
BL certne: nevertheless
ABC

s Tantum Ergo organ

Isa Bowman: *The Story of Lewis Carroll* 5: 'Happy little girls who had such a master'

Gr adelphos: brother

enchant *F* encore choir
in chorus

Arab salāt: prayer *Arab* mahdi: holy man *s* The Maiden's Prayer *Heb* nabi: prophet his nibs
'Tantum Ergo' includes 'salus', 'honor', 'blessing' & 'alleluia' Messiah
prostituting Fatihah: 1st sura of the Koran, means 'opening'

Islam prayer involves sequence of postures heavings
Isa Bowman: *The Story of Lewis Carroll* 4: 'For ever that voice is still; be it mine to revive some memories of it'
G bloss: naked *I* blas: taste absolution
blissful
'In the name of the Father & of the Son & of the Holy Ghost, amen' (blessing) *L* amamus: we love
G Färbung: dye, colouring heliotrope
mist white slogan: 'White as Osman Towels'
Arab masquid: a mosque Ottoman

westward
T.S. Eliot: *The Waste Land* 41: 'Looking into the heart of light, the silence'; 278: 'Weialala leia / Wallala leialala';
Arab La ilaha ill-Allah: there is no god but Allah (call to prayer) 433: 'Shantih shantih shantih'
Turk turquoise
L Sanctus, Sanctus, Sanctus: 'Holy, Holy, Holy' (prayer)
Gr xanthos: tawny
L fuit: he was *F* fuite after
F tout de suite

manager 'your obedient servant' (bank jargon)
Midland Bank Ltd
Burke's Landed Gentry nobility rosary Ailesbury Road, Ballsbridge, D (wealthy families there)
mobility: the mob, the lower classes *F* la roseraie: the rose garden

neighbourhood uncle's Lucombe oak,
BL onncaill: bury *Quercus hispanica* var. *Lucombeana*
Turkish hazel, *Corylus colurna* Incense cedar, *Calocedrus decurrens* etcetera hypsometer: instrument which measures altitude
Grecian fir, *Abies cephalonica* cedars
Mt Anville, Dundrum, D: convent of sisters of Sacred Heart orthodoxy heart attacks
Athrataxis: genus of Tasmanian cedars
ultima thule: extreme end of the world *L* larix = larch Ranelagh, district of D
St Laurence O'Toole, patron of D Wych elm, *Ulmus glabra*

Polly Peachum: heroine of John Gay's *Beggar's Opera*
pillarboxes love letters affixed
affianced
battlelines (clotheslines)

F boites envious

embrasure: bevelling on sides of window
rere *L* fiat: he was; may it be
Fiat cars
Gr autokinêton: self-moving thing (i.e. automobile) our only

Chuff Tristan *G* uns Isolde entries
tea
cousin-german announce
F gourmand: greedy
misnomers colours Siamese (cat)

pr a cat has 9 lives hearty

(fire) marmalade shortbread

marchpane: marzipan switch: a false tress

F poire Sunday
pierrette: a female pierrot sundae (ice cream)

Booterstown, district of D

F charmeuse clothes
U.416: 'Glycera or Chloe' (girls in Horace's *Odes*)
glittering jewels Lydia & Cynara: girls in Horace's *Odes*
glycerin ladylike fanlights perfumed cigarettes
lemonade
F la monade: the monad, ultimate unit of being

G Stichwort: cue, keyword pincushion
swordstick *G* sticken: to embroider
Highness *pr* Handsome is as handsome does
BL luis: arm, hand
cg How many miles to Babylon: 'Will I be there by Candlemass?' (2 Feb.; J's birthday)
Cantalamessa: Italian family name ('he who sings Mass')
St Tibb's Eve: never (there is no St Tibb)
BL nionon: heaven
cg 'The farmer's in his den, The farmer's in his den, He I Hedy Ho, The farmer's in his den'
Fomorians: race of early Ir. colonisers *G* hin & her: hither & thither Parthalón: early Ir. coloniser
G Paar: pair adin: to deafen Song of Solomon
It parolone: big words, bombastic speech *nr* 'Sing a song of sixpence'
Yule
VI.B.18.73: 'the single month (Yule)'
chorus *s* 'God rest ye merry, gentlemen, Let nothing you dismay'
G Weib: woman
Prufrock (T.S. Eliot) jolly *s* 'The Holly & the Ivy, Now they are both in bloom, Of all the trees that are in the wood The holly bears the crown'
Da fru: Mrs *Da* frøken: unmarried woman
lively *F* billet doux
ph bill & coo Christmas Night
mistletoe
s Wassail Song: 'sing a wassail too'
s 'Whip jamboree, whip jamboree, O you longtailed blackman, poke it up behind me, Whip jamboree, whip jamboree, O, Jenny, get your oatcake done'
s Polly Put the Kettle On: 'Jessie, pass the plumcake round'

(compare 281.04–13) Romulus & Remus pavan: a grave, stately dance
G Reh: deer
striding through the streets of Chapelizod *F* valses: waltzes

me & you purlieus Ballybough, district of D on muddy estuary of *r* Tolka
met & yodelled
s Miss McCloud's Reel daintily

Harcourt St Railway, D (terminus) rigadoon: lively, complex dance for 2
Grangegorman: district of D, site of Richmond Lunatic Asylum, & also Broadstone Railway terminus, on plateau-like prominence
J's father was secretary of United Liberal Club in D during 1880 general election. The Liberal candidates, Maurice Brookes & Dr Robert Dyer Lyons, ousted Sir Arthur Guinness & James Stirling lion: C15–16 Scottish gold coin
rains
Thyme is a seasoning *Sl* seasoner: person in the fashion

astute indigestibles
(stew made with left-overs)
daffodils can-can *G* Stimme: voice simmering

F bégayeur: stutterer deaf & dumb past aeons *L* obcaecitas: blindness about something opacity
beguilement post horns
past epochs limb from limb
P/K
Song of Momus to Mars (Dryden; Boyce)

style: prolongation of ovary, in a flower gnats pollinate flowers
s Still wie die Nacht *Da* natte: night

stamens of flower see *F* tournesol: heliotrope
understatements
sideways *F* s'accordant: corresponding corsets
courses

feminine towards heliolatry: sun worship

chalices calyx: cup of leaves at base of flower heliotrope (turns towards sun) parachutes
G als
masculine pistil: ovary & style & stigma, in a flower
L musca: fly (pollination) HCE
papers

cg Mulberry Bush

bridal & so on

G leicht *G* sie

precious dutifully *nr* Ding Dong Bell

Alice love elixir

enchanted Stanislaus Joyce

gladiators to emperor: *L* morituri te salutant: they who are about to die salute you *G* bloss: bare blossom *L* O coelicola te salutamus: O heaven-dweller, we salute thee
patron *G* Unschuld: innocence postmaster *F* billet doux (lit. 'soft missive')

Verne: *Around the World in Eighty Days* (Shaun the Post)

Ki barua: letter *Ki* chepa: stamp panpipe cutaway (coat)

BNS gab borab: clerical student

(5 senses)

s Father O'Flynn: 'in all Donegal'

blessed blasé arise & let us pray conceive
I ceilteach: denying Celtic Holy Ghost *BL* cetech: hermit, ecclesiastic

Leopardstown racecourse, Co. D Loki, in Norse myth, caused Balder's death by mistletoe
Skt karma: action, occupation

untouchables in Indian caste system

Egyptian Book of the Dead CXXV: 'I am pure. I am pure. My purity is the purity of that great *Bennu*' *L* pueritia: innocence, boyhood
Egyptian god Neha-hau: name means 'stinking members' *It* amanti: lovers *It* belle mani: beautiful hands
Amenti: Egyptian underworld
F petit *F* peton: little foot

'Harlene' (164.31)

'Cuticura' (164.30) (face cream) scented *G* Jüngling: youth

F demain *Ki* demani: spring in E. Africa magical
Ki masika: autumn in E. Africa
yore *Ki* baraza: veranda *Ki* siku: day seeker balmy
ph as sure as sure can be bread & butter *Du* brood: bread

Baile Átha Cliath
BL cliath: cleric
clock The Great Cackler: goose in *Egyptian Book of the Dead* sweepstake Abelard & Heloise

familiar perhaps

strictly necessary *F* toutes Philomela metamorphosed into nightingale

wear drawers BVD & BVD dot: men's underpants
magdalene: reformed prostitute
lots post haste
postmortem
Isabel

F deshabillé (meanings of Latin cases: genitive, accusative, dative, ablative)
in

all the more intimate

Campbell: *Lochiel's Warning:* 'Coming events cast their shadows before' seem

elsewhere passed suspense

It sensitiva: the sensitive plant, *Mimosa pudica*, whose leaves fold up if touched

(rainbow colours) red brick jonquil: type of narcissus (yellow) (marine blue)
F fauve: fawn (sort of dull orange) sprig of (green) vegetation
s Smiling through Swedenborg discusses angels' garments in *Heaven & Hell*
violet bruise

s Auld Lang Syne H . . . C . . . E

selfishness

promise us *Pro* requist: precious

busy things *pr* Satan finds work for idle hands to do
BL bisi: finger tutu: ballet skirt
Sl peach: blab, inform *s* We Don't Want to Fight, but, by Jingo, If We Do
Buddha did not wish to preach the law but was persuaded by Brahma
G wie ernst: how seriously

tup: copulate

Confiteor: 'mea culpa, mea culpa, mea maxima culpa' colp: a blow

Aesop's fable of the hare & the tortoise
'I talked with a hare': part of the *Law* taught by the Buddha *BNS* mus: personality
perverted *It* bianca: white *It* mutandini: panties

It conversa: lay sister full-length *G* Herzog von: duke of
obverse
G Fürst: prince
Wellington ravin: beast of prey cousin
RAVEN coo (DOVE)
our we others Bonaparte

wholesale Assumption of the BVM

we am

Smith Robinson Jones *G* nutzlos: useless, unprofitable

what-you-may-call-'em
white limbs
trial *Du* eer: honour earwax dum-dum
trio here's *F* sourd: deaf
Iris: rainbow-goddess queen bees
Irish Rifles: regiment; (*Sl*) small combs
Pro caro: face Motto of the Garter: Honi soit qui mal y pense (Shame Be [to Him] Who Evil
L caro: flesh *Pro* carissime: sweetest Thinks of This)
L mel: honey *L* spondere: to pledge busy in minutes
Hellespont (Strait of the Dardanelles) *G* Minne: love
fact *Da* fuld: full, drunk *BL* Teo: God *BL* Daur: God
It Dio mio!: my God! *L* timeo: I fear
Buddha preached the law at Gazelle Park

The Buddha, when established as 'The Master', lived in the Bamboo Wood communicate
It bimbo: boy *Hu* bimbó: bud
Original Sin learning
sense
F mille *F* cent *F* centimes (coins)
F sentiments
snake sloughs skin snake/apple
King of Snakes encircled & warmed the Buddha (Genesis)
so long as dead certain II Tim 4:1: 'the quick & the dead'

Buddha's story of Visvamitra's lost children, who were recognized by their eyes
It questua: begging, collection
Buddha plays lute Lutine Bell in Lloyds was rung Buddha's begging bowl
while teaching to announce losses of ships
tickling: method of catching trout enticements

F ma chère

L sursum corda: lift up your hearts (Mass) nuns
L cauda: tail Luke 1:38: 'Behold the handmaid of the Lord' (Angelus)
immature amma (surg.): a band or truss welcome hope
amateur
G Hochzeit: marriage

giving in marriage
Vulg Eccles 1:2: 'Vanitas *F* ménage
vanitatum, et omnia vanitas' ('vanity of vanities, all is vanity')

L Domine: O Lord

G Hochzeit: marriage, Luke 1:38: 'Be it done unto me according to thy word' (Incarnation)
lit. 'high time' *ph* down & out
votes for women as well *G* fett

Lord's Prayer: 'On Earth as it is in Heaven' clitoris *Du* meid: maid
Clytie pined for Apollo & turned into a heliotrope scullerymaid
Sl yard: penis *Sl* cullions: testicles *G* Stimmrecht: suffrage

Roman Catholics emancipated
L amans: lover
majesty

Arch gytt: get
begettings *F Sl* cocotte: whore

F la chérie John 1:14: '& the Word was made flesh & dwelt among us'
dickens 'the word is made flesh' (Angelus)
Virgin Mary *G* wofür

It giro giro tondo: 1st words of Italian equivalent of 'Ring-a-ring o'roses'
rondo (music)
bride elect

hillside angel in chief
It ciuffo: forelock
Erebus: place of darkness between Earth & Hades meaning
whereabouts *Angl* mearing: boundary
R.A.S. Macalister: *The Secret Languages of Ireland.* He translates a sentence from Bearlagair Na Saer: 'I saw pigeons bringing fire to boil meat in Dublin' *F* carrefour: crossroads *F* viande
merry hell & so forth *cg* Oats, peas, beans & barley grow
bulging forsooth
Beelzebub hullabaloo *Sp* diablo: devil

Ahriman: Zoroastrian god of evil where else? *cg* 'London Bridge Is Falling Down'
remaining Lucifer
and could not bridged by pins & needles *F* brocher: to stitch

riddles *cg* Ring-a-ring o'roses *Da* rund: round *R* brat: brother

J Yasha: a female Demon
J sasage: something to eat
picnic

no honorary guest on our social list *AngI* glugger: a foolish boaster
special
cg 'Old Roger is dead & is laid in his grave'

s What Shall We Do with the Drunken Sailor?: pitiful
'Low, boys, & up she rises'
woebegone *Heb* (Bible) ephphatha!: be opened! *G* Examen
booze *Ali Baba & the 40 Thieves* (pantomime): 'Open Sesame! *T* susamis: thirsty
It scemato: lessened

no *Da* nu mere: now more *Da* siden: afterwards *Da* stolen: the seat Thomas Aquinas
s Lament of the Irish Emigrant: 'sitting on the stile' *L* tumescens: swelling up *L* inquinans:
sight *Da* domstol: judgement seat defiling, polluting
Da dag: day
synagogue expressly E . . . HC *L* Trinitatis: of the Trinity
Da senga: the bed *BL* sgeng: bed
s At Trinity Church I Met My Doom: 'I was an M-U-G' paid for free L/R
It peccato: sin, fault
BL munchaol: bad *G* Maden: maggots *Du* brood: bread duly *Gr* doulos: slave
Dooley (010.04)
recant Albigensian Heresy *BL* betchennacht: blessing *BL* goll: blind
Genesis Guinness Hennessy *G* Macht: power gods
pray for him international
proffer his penance
ex-commander-in-chief (sport of) *It* colori: colours (game, version of 'Angels & Devils')

dust throws lava bed plenty *Am* rosso: gold
death throes *It* polenta: a cornmeal dish *Am* polenta: gold
God save our queen *s* Die stem van Suid-Afrika (S. African National anthem, lit. 'The voice of S. Africa')
OE swith: strong *Da* aftræk: outlet
Charles Bianconi, greatest Ir. mailcoach owner of early C19 *Du* aftrek: sale; demand
Am bianco: silver *It* bianconi: the white ones
Nijni Novgorod, Russia *Am* Terracuta: Italy assets

liabilities Repeal of the Union (of Great Britain & Ireland) Trinity (College, D)
eternity
calembour: pun
St Columbanus
Du soep: soup whiteheaded (Finn) *L* pater & mater
AngI whitehaired boy: a favorite
ph chip off the old block *G* Heide: heath, heather
s Phil the Fluter's Ball
(he'll tell the whole story even if he has to go to jail [*BLM* calaboosh] for it)
G Teufel: Devil (003.09–10)
BLM belong: of

BLM he make what name: what does he make volcanic
G Wolken
BLM belong: of Anakim: giants killed by Joshua (Josh 11:21) Anak: father of St Gregory
*331: 'this remarkable man' *L* molimen: effort *Gr* anax andrôn: lord of men (069.12)
polyglot Jebusites: Canaanite tribe dispossessed 100% Erse speaking Erzerum: town, Armenia
by David of Jerusalem; credited with goat-worship *Du* procent: percent
*307: 'when in a trance condition would sometimes lie in bed for several days without eating'
BL drogmall: back *303: 'Swedenborg was fond of the society of ladies'
Augustine Aloysius (J's middle names) shantung: a soft Chinese silk
(Anaks Andrum) Pekin
Farmer Giles gaining flesh face
HF 8: 'set back considerable'
saying avalanche *299: 'he looked so innocent & so joyful out of his eyes'
lunch
*298: 'his smiling skyblue *Aeneid* frequently refers to 'Pious Aeneas'
blue eyes' Kibla: point towards which Islamic prayer alias
asked must be said

G Herrgott: Lord God (233.03)
sheep/goat
Chronicles (book of Bible) brimful King Priam of Troy (means 'buyer')
Lewis Carroll's 'portmanteau words' (*Through the Looking-Glass*)

*George Trobridge: *A Life of Emanuel Swedenborg* (2nd ed., 1912)

In Ireland, potato wards were   ditchdiggers   N akter: after
those won by bribery   G dumm   G krumm: crooked   actor
R lososina: salmon meat   Summanus: Latin god of nocturnal thunderbolts   SILVER
assassinated by someone   Silver penny introduced into England by King Offa, 735
It offa: biscuit   blood oranges   G Kandiszucker: lumps of crystallised sugar
BL bloa: apple   in Amsterdam Swedenborg used to bring home sweets
Lilith: Adam's wife before Eve   for his landlady's children   blow his nose
F midinette
purest polygamous intentions   *24: 'value of the wife to her husband, both   peculiarity
prurient   Sl polly: whore   in a pecuniary sense & also as a companion'
BL ailmin: beautiful   HCE   gale days: days when payment made
Heathcliff (Emily Brontë, *Wuthering Heights*)
F souffrant   plenitude   G Haustorte: cake
Sh wart: one   platitude   *22 mentions husband's liability for wife's
Colossus of Rhodes   G wert: worth   BRONZE   torts (civil wrongs)   so is he
rhodomontade: brag romantic   Rhadamanthus: one of the judges in Hades   It scolarina: little schoolgirl
Lady Campbell said Oscar Wilde was like a great white caterpillar
big   (finger)
G Weg   N femtifem: 55   Sl funt: pound (sterling)   Sl nest: cunt
worth
Pro uei: eye

Pro auriho: ear   Caledrwlch: Arthur's sword, in the Welsh *Triads*
L aurum: GOLD   BNS kalidh: goat
G Leidenschaft: passion

smoke pipe   meerschaum pipe   cupric: of bivalent COPPER
(lit. 'sea foam')   (blue or green)
feminine   ampersand   G Aas: carrion   G Doktor   Sh talop: belly
Aphrodite born from the foam   Rembrandt's painting *The Anatomy Lesson of Dr. Tulp*
anatomy lecture   St Mary
Pro gients: men, a tribe

G Meister   Viking   Du noord: north   G kämpften: fought
Mistral: Provençal poet   Norwegian Captain (II.3)
& wind   G Wogen: waves   ozone
dolomite: a rock, various colours   N osean: ocean
ocean breezes   Da bedstefar: grandfather
F brise: to break   It nave: ship   G Pfarrer: priest
Da svigermore: mother-in-law   agnomen   prime assignation
Whiggamores: group of C17 Scottish insurgents   L primo signatio: 1st signing
Milchu: owner of Patrick during his slavery   United Kingdom
G Milchkuh
aircraft
F aidant: helping
Lough Neagh (076.21)   (dope hidden in knob of stick)
knock-kneed   G Versunkener: one who has sunk, esp. morally
rheumatism   Tommy Atkins: nickname for   curse of God
tommy rot   British soldier
Barbarossa: German emperor who   Berbers & Bedouins
opposed Adrian IV
Heb beghedh: clothes   Heb kol beth yiśrael: all
neighbours   Heb na'ar: young man   the house of Israel
BNS gudth: whore   F sou: small coin
good   Heb zuz: ancient coin
Sl dromedary:
burglar, thief
Caledonia   calumny   not   shake
askers   reports
his hand   BL ur: bad
Sh grifi: female
Oscar   Lionel in *Martha* (in *U.* context)
Ar osgi: gold   Sw fröken: young ladies   brokenhearted
It sempre: always

2 satellites of Jupiter observed from Lick Observatory, California, 1904

John Peter   It sodali: companions
Jupiter   satellites
bears witness to   'Justification' sent to courts of Europe by William
Bubwith, Bishop of London, 1406–7   whiteness   of Orange

*Maud I. Crofts: *Women Under English Law* (1925)

volumes Swedenborg was Assessor Extraordinary of the *I* Saorstát Éireann: Ir. Free State
Du heer: master, lord Royal College of Mines Nelson
deceased adenoids *G* den Leixlip
Ar adenok': formerly
Trobridge: *Life of Emanuel* butler *L* recte: rightly
Swedenborg 299: 'the last great change which he knew must come to him before long'; 301 mentions buckles on his shoes

coupon *F* coupole: cupola
Leopold Bloom, 7 Eccles St, D *G* Wochenbett: childbed
household Howth *G* Nummer Numbers, book of Bible roundabout
Swedenborg usually wore black velvet Georgian mansion since many years *Da* mange:
Da senest: at the latest many
Yeats was greatly concerned by the controversy over Hugh Lane's bequest of paintings to D Corporation, which was not honoured for many years
Da daarlig: bad baby tooth

Sl gobstick: spoon Nerses the Gracious: C12 Armenian patriarch
goodness gracious! *Sp* gracias!: thanks!
Swedenborg claimed a new set of perks up Michael Gunn, manager of Gaiety Theatre, D grandfather
teeth was growing in his mouth at age 81 *54: 'the "Parks" . . . of guns . . . great rows of cannons'
Ecclesiastes, book of Bible prime ministers
ecclesiastics Confucius became Minister of Crime
HF 12: 'Mornings, before daylight' *HF* 21: 'spoon vittles' prave: wicked
HF 11: 'a power of money' *L* prava verba: crooked words Proverbs, book of Bible
Greek or Roman feminiser letter 23/10/28 to HSW:
L persona erecta: an upright person *Gr* glykys: sweet 'They have been giving me . . .
Gilbert & Sullivan: Confucius was first to make use of jury system injections of arsenic'
Trial by Jury *37: 'the two purses that he carried'
*336–7: 'in order that it should draw properly he would walk incoherent
about the room swinging the teapot from side to side for exactly ten minutes'
L bis: twice C.G. Jung things simply for inducing

teapots rainy days nine & twenty
Sl daisy: cunt
It tutto: all
*16 (Carroll) 'said that modern professional photographers spoilt all their pictures by touching them up'
Gr poiêtographia: poetry *G* Alt *12: 'oldmaidishly prim'
photographies (Lewis Carroll's hobby) *19: 'suddenly he turned round & saw what I was doing . . . &
BNS samhar: podex *BL* tionnor: podex turned very red, frightning me very much'
tinned salmon
s It's Your Last Trip, Titanic, Fare You Well Revelations, last book of Bible *ph* true bill: that's right
Maud I. Crofts: *Women Under English Law* 12: 'the grand jury either brings in a 'true bill' in which case the trial
Humpty Dumpty is held before the court of quarter sessions'
Crofts 14: 'Jury of Matrons' (female jury for pregnant women condemned to death)
Stoneybatter: street in D *U*.444: 'a holy show'
ph to cut a long story short
St Andrew's, Suffolk St, D, on site of Norse Thingmote (parliament)
whole right up suffragette
L toga contrastata: a put-on-instead-of toga fairy godmother Lao-tze (208.30)
Gen 2:18: 'I will make him an help meet for him' (Eve) *Mother Goose,* pantomime
Grant Allen: *The Woman Who Did* (novel, 1895)

HF 19: 'soured on him' Judges & Kings, books of Bible *HF* 26: 'brisken up a room'
Liffey given as Avenelith in Charter of Prince John, 1192
Heb mem: water viviparous: giving birth to Chapelizod
Heb ebhen: stone live young (not laying eggs)
fen: marsh fulgor: splendour *Arch* (& *Du*) laat: late *HF* 17: 'a saw-log'
funny vulgar *L* fulgor: lightning *Du* hoe laat: what time? (floated down river)
nr Sing a Song of Sixpence, a pocket full of rye
Psalms, Apocrypha (Bible)
VI.B.33.18: 'cheekmole of Allah a city' Aulaf Cuaran, King of D, called Aulaf
Olaf . . . Ivor (012.31) Quaran in Haliday's *Scandinavian Kingdom of D*, 96
Koran (discusses divorce) VI.B.33.18: 'be the owner of thyself (divorce)'

Da eget hjem: own home Howarden: Gladstone's country place
G Ecke: corner HCE
L Ierne: Ireland *L* flamen: priest flaming waistcoat Vesta: goddess of hearth
In *A Tale of a Tub* the doctrine of purgatory is represented by flame-coloured clothing fibula: clasp, brooch
Du wintermantel: winter coat *L* pontifex: chief priest

F couler: flow spawife: female fortuneteller lord of manor
(river)

*Isa Bowman: *The Story of Lewis Carroll told for Young People by the Real Alice in Wonderland* (1899)

than 111 *Da* elskere: lovers *G* Jahr
yards
I anam: soul *I* ainm: name *It* fiumi: rivers river mouth
names *L* annus: year fuming
Da hvem ved noget: *I* mo ghrádh mo chroidhe: takes the rap takable aback
who knows something my love of my heart Magrath (060.26)
Ani: Egyptian scribe *G* vierte
Ali Baba & the Forty Thieves (pantomime) anima (Jung)
mere names of mountains furibund: raging

mountain (river) bed *G* Schi: ski *G* feig: cowardly
F chichi: affected manners frightened
ping-pong pain *RR* stummi: stomach 'pura e pia bella': religious wars of Vico's heroic
RR pign: pine tree *RR* pugn: fist, ball age polar bears
G pur: pure jactitation: false claim to be married gesticulating
RR pur: clean to another (*27 mentions)
Gr Panellênismos: idea of 'Parnellism & Crime': title of articles in *The Times* in which were published (river)
Greek national unity Pigott's forged Parnell letters *39: 'harbours' (wife who has left husband)
*35: feme sole (Law): sovereign lord & governor-general
unmarried woman *Ar* zôravar: general *Rut* givno: shit
The Antient Concert Rooms, D *F* durant coverture (Law): condition of a feme covert,
*39: 'Right of Consortium' *G* Ruhm: fame overture married woman (*33 mentions)
*40: 'At Common Law a husband & *G* Herr *G* Damen
wife were incapable of stealing from one another'
bereaved chicken broth *33: 'a deed to which the husband & wife were both parties'

Finn MacCumhail (= MacCool) *39: 'a wife is under no . . . liability with regard
hetman: Cossack commander *Sl* foots: pays for to her husband's funeral expenses'
jacent: recumbent *T* elma: apple *RR* giantar: (to have) lunch *RR* tschaina:
It nutre (v.): nourishes 11th E.B.: 'Eskimo' describes prostrate male eskimoes being fed by their wives dinner
the same Signor Foli: name used by tenor Roumansch language
It assieme: together A. J. Foley, Ir. bass, 1833–99 *RR & It Dial* Signur: Sir
(singing loud) Ludwig II of Bavaria, patron of Wagner (rattling) kettle
fish the earwigs out of his lugs
Arch hayel: hail

unmentionables gesticulating Blowick: old name of Bullock, nr Dalkey
(underwear) blowy
G winden: reel, twist *G* wenden: turn

(give up smoking) bagpipes
Book of Common Prayer: Catechism: 'renounce the devil & all his works, the pomps & vanity'
Sl kip: brothel *AngI* streel: untidy wench
keep the streetwalkers steelworkers
place Nestle's milk The Coombe, D

cop *Ali Baba & the Forty Thieves* (pantomime) *G* Eule: owl *It* massa: much
Du kopen: to buy bubo: inflamed swelling (plague) *L* bubo: owl
dinar (coin) *RR* savunêr: to soap; persuade *s* The Nut Brown Maid
dinners saving *s* Savourneen Deelish dealing
Mayde Berenice dedicated her hair for her husband's safety in war

Oxmantown: part of N. D; its parochial church is St Michan's *L* mulier: woman

Mussulmen *It* ondulare: to wave Sugarloaf Mt,
undulate Wicklow aloft
BNS Ealp O'Laoghre: D *RR* viv: living
RR baselgia: church
the purple: the rank of cardinal

Vatican Monsignor Robinson: papal nuncio to
Macalister: *Secret Languages of Ireland* 240: Ireland in 1930s *L* crucis: of the cross
'ass is an old Irish word for milk' *G* Sohn *Robinson Crusoe*
glass of milk to his comrade chitterlings
quack . . . duck aqueduct *Cz* hrom: thunder *Ar* Hrom: Rome
L quaque: wheresoever *L* dux: leader honour of Rome
adored *It* mezzo scudo: half 'scudo' (coin) Persse O'Reilly
about *It* Sant: Saint
Josephine & Marie Louise (subject of W.G. Wills' *A Royal Divorce*) *L* Missa: the Mass
3 Gondoliers: Luiz, Marco, Giuseppe Mary & Joseph
3 tenors: Ludwig, Mario, Joseph Maas
votes *G* Widder: ram widows

*Maud I. Crofts: *Women Under English Law* (1925)

end of the *Gloria Patri:* 'World without end, amen' backwards beware

ph go Dutch: each to pay for himself
Sl do a Dutch: run away
(lamplighter resembles Earwicker
cf 031.01–3) pyre *Heb* lubab: festive palm branch
olive carried during Feast of Tabernacles
s The Rising of the Moon: 'Out from many a mud-wall cabin'
Ps 120:5: 'Woe is me that I sojourn in Mesech, Neomenia: in Jewish antiquity, the time & festival of
that I dwell in the tents of Kedar!' *Da* ceder: cedar new moon
Feast of Tabernacles: Jewish commemoration shop shuts up shipshape *I* Inis Fáil: Ireland
of Exodus at full moon *I* tobar: well John 7:2: 'Now the Jews' feast of tabernacles was at hand'
synagogue sing-song *BL* Ondslosbu: Britain
Da senga: the bed *G* Sänger: singer *Da* by: town
F couvre-feu: curfew
Heb hag: festival, feast

roost

werewolf *Scots* gae: go

F chez log fire
F foyer: hearth
darkle: grow dark *'*tinct, tint:* disparition graduelle de la lumière,–*tinct* perdant le c,–et le son des cloches qui
faiblit' Ting! ting! phenomenal
BL ruodmarg: bog *L* alveus: riverbed
s Ave Maria
It marea: tide enveloped *L* circumvallatus: walled-around *It* belve: wild beasts
L alveum maris: basin of the 'sea' (in Temple, Jerusalem) *Sp* obscuridad: darkness
G frieren: to freeze *AngI* there is a wish on them: they wish

Du zoo: so *Du* koud: cold Deucalion (parallel to Noah in Ovid)
D Zoo, Phoenix Park *'Le sens de la phrase est: deaf old man put coal on the fire & busy
pyre peeress woman of the house sees that it catches fire'
Pyrrha (wife of Deucalion) (Japanese polite formula)
J haha: mother
huzoor: Indian potentate
*'*to's pitty:* en grec: chez soi' Nancy Hand's: 'The Hole in the Wall', pub at Ashtown,
'tis pity D (Nancy Hand was hostess there) *J* tsheetshee: father
Isengrim: wolf in the Reynard
cycle
G Fahr wohl weddingbells
Da faar: sheep *Du* wol: wool
*'*Gill* . . . nom de la personne qui attaque le héros H.C.E.; il laisse tomber des cailloux de sa poche pour marquer
le chemin: allusion à la légende de Deucalion & Pyrrha' (037.12; 072.33)
s The Rocky Road to Dublin
*'en paraît dans le ciel sous l'aspect de la voie lactée: the milky road to Juno'
o'er Erin *G* lang *It* cielo: sky
*'Quelle heure astronomique est-il? L'heure qui sonne . . . It is long past eight' *D Sl* sail on!: scram!
Moore: *s* Sail On, Sail On, Thou Fearless Bark *'*Say . . . Amune!* trois phrases annonçant . . . neuf heures moins un
*'la lune & les étoiles . . . *Gr* selênê: moon a moon quart' [*U.* 85: 'Heigho!']
leurs barques lumineuses' Jacob Bryant identified Noah's Ark with the new moon

It tranquille (f. pl.): quiet
(deer in Phoenix Park) Randle Holme: *The Academy of*
Da dyrhaven: deer park *Armory & Blazonry* III.3.78: 'Terms for Carving . . . *Unbrace* that
Pro adew: goodbye Duck . . . *Unjoynt* that Bittern. *Untach* that Curlew . . . *Allay* that Pheasant'
*'ii: deux petits oiseaux, mâle & femelle . . . lançant leurs petites prières . . . les deux points sur les i'
Da Tommelise: Thumbelina *BL* luathan: bird
Du avond: evening conticent: keeping silent
* (*r* Avon) *L* Conticinium: 1st Roman watch of the night
lion *G* scheut: avoids shut eyes (sleep)
C lao-hu (coll): tiger *C* shih-tzu (coll): lion *L* Concubium: 2nd Roman watch of the night
L Intempesta Nox: the 3rd watch *L* Gallicinum: the 4th watch (cockcrow)
G nicht *F* aube: dawn *L* Aurora: dawn
L Pater Noster *'adressé au monstre ancestral' *L* sed libera nos a malo: *Da* løvedom: lion kingdom
Panther: legendary father of Jesus *I* leaba: bed but deliver us from evil *Da* løv: foliage
sheep *F* L'enfant **Bur* siang: elephant *Gr* elephas: elephant
s While London Sleeps sang Acts 18.34: 'Great is Diana of the Ephesians'
Gr megadontos: of great teeth Behemoth (Job 40:15) prob. the hippopotamus mammoth

***Jacques Mercanton: 'L'Esthétique de Joyce', *Études de Lettres,* Lausanne, XIII.39–40 (J collaborated in production of these notes)**

Tuskar Lighthouse off S.E. Ireland   *Arab* salam salaleikum: peace be with you   snout is not so big

*'le rhinocéros: pig. Es geht ihm wurst: au propre & au figuré'   *G* Popo: buttocks   *F* dormir: sleep

G ihm ist ganz wurst: he doesn't give a damn   gone west   *J* kiku: listen   hippopotamus   Hippodrome

so be it   Urquhart's *Rabelais* III. 13: 'nuzzling of camels . . .   *It* Ho popo: I've got to shit

frantling of peacocks . . . charming of beagles . . . gurieting of apes, snuttering of monkeys'

pr Boys will be boys

*(*s* Matthew Hanigan's Aunt)   hurricane lamp   *s* Then You'll Remember Me: 'When other lips & other hearts'

Hanukkah: Jewish Feast of Lights

I Iúl: July   Yule   *Du* Mei: May   Moore: *s* 'The young may moon she's beaming, love' (*U.*740)

G Mohn: poppy   *G* Blume: flower   'low' in 'Wicklow' perhaps from Old *Da* loe (blaze)

hooker: type of Ir. fishing boat

sapphire   E.&W. Siemens fitted out lighthouse at Arklow   Arklow, Wexford & Waterford all S.E.

Henry II first landed in Ireland at the Crook, over against

westward   Hook tower, Waterford Bay, hence *ph* by hook or by crook

Brer Fox (Uncle Remus stories)   listened   *R* lisa: she-fox

somewhat torn   toran: sacred Buddhist gateway   integument

Heb śimḥath tora: rejoicing in Law; last day of Feast of Tabernacles   undergarments   arguments

It pesciolini: little fishes

r Liffey

Jonah & the whale   *L* feria quinta: fifth holiday (name for Thursday used by early Christians)   papal infallibility

procession of the Holy Ghost (subject of original split between E. & W. Churches)

F poisson   holy cross   *I* liobar na bóthair: a tramp

(ear)   river   *Heb* dâbâr: word; thing

G horchen: listen   *R* ryba: fish

din going on   *Heb* munt: dead

(because fish asleep)   Isa 21:11: 'Watchman, what of the night?'   *G* es

Bas ez: no   *It* notte: night   *G* geht's   *Pro* ges noun: not at all

echo   doves   Rosamund's Pond in St James Park, London: meeting place for lovers in numerous plays

Dumas: *The Three Musketeers*   girls   boys   *F* beau

Anne Bracegirdle, actress   brasse: kind of perch

HCE

cyclist

(216.04–5)

G vorsehen   *L* Hesperus: the evening star   mouth of Liffey

F espérons: let us hope

G wenden: turn   *HF* 21: 'jimpson weeds'   *HF* 7–11: 'Jackson's Island'

nr Who Killed Cock Robin?: 'Who'll pull the bell?'   none are unwelcome

Le Fanu: *The House by the Churchyard* 119 (quoting Swift's *Polite Conversation*): 'What, you are sick of the mulligrubs, with eating chopt hay?'   *The House by the Churchyard:* 'mulsum'   *Sl* mulligrubs: cholic

mulse: liquor made from honey   *HF* 31: 'No-siree-*bob*'

Mary Queen of Scots   *HF* 18: 'our duty to you, sir'

merely

G matt: exhausted

HF 20: 'Royalty'   Matthew . . . Mark . . . Luke . . . John

G johlen: hoot   treblebedded

expectation (for spitting on)

letter, 20/1/26, to HSW: 'Euston Hotel. 732 rooms, 2 wings, liveried porters . . . Mr E. H. Knight, manager. I met him every morning and wished him good kday'   tapster: tavern keeper

Da fru: Mrs   what's he like

s Home Sweet Home

Findlater's A.1 whiskey (sold in D)   *s* Chevy Chase

Heb hag shavout: Feast of Weeks (Pentecost)

s The Stirrup Cup   Purim: a Jewish feast   *Du* het oude huis bij het kerkhof: the old house by the churchyard

Le Fanu: *The House by the Churchyard*

***Mercanton: 'L'Esthétique de Joyce' (continued)**

Kierkegaard

Da gaard: yard

Jewish Feast of Weeks (Pentecost)

judge in chambers

Thirty Years' War

Remarque: *All's Quiet on the Western Front*

(lull in the game)

G Feld: field

The House by the Churchyard 447 (Phoenix Park): 'by the Star Fort, & through the thorn woods'

⚔ Gorey, Co. Wexford, 1798

God Almighty!

The Brass Castle, Chapelizod, Dangerfield's house in *The House by the Churchyard* (mutton candles flare there, cf. 364, 408)

Heb ghadhol: great

Heb ḥošekh: darkness

HCE

Heb qodes: holiness

Heb El: God

G Brandenburgertor: Brandenburg Gate, Berlin

The House by the Churchyard says Lord-Lieutenants wear 'a thunder-cloud periwig'

Thor   Asa: Odin   Arthur   order

HF 16: 'lightning-bugs'

HF 20: 'My souls, how the wind did scream along'

HF 32: 'By jings'

HF 31: 'work your jaw' (chatter)

HF 27: 'down the banks'

HF 26: 'hark from the tomb' (reproof)

It ansiosa: anxious

see if the soup be hot enough

Joyous Garde, Lancelot's castle, where Tristram & Isod stayed after break with Mark (Malory)

stirabout: a kind of porridge

ladylike

palace

winner   *G* ein: 1

Du twee: 2

F la pauvre

Napoleon

Josephine/Marie Louise

The Lily of Killarney: opera based on Boucicault's *The Colleen Bawn,* in which the heroine is admired by Hardress Cregan & Myles-na-Coppaleen

Florestan: husband of Leonore in Beethoven's *Fidelio*

Balfe: *The Bohemian Girl,* in which Florestein & Thaddeus are rivals

Ps 68:18: 'thou hast led captivity captive'

It far la bella: play the decisive game (in cards)

Iseult la Belle

I naoidheanán: infant

R.J. Gatling invented a machine gun

BL ninan: drum

s Tramp, Tramp, Tramp, the Boys Are Marching

horseshoe magnet

D Horse Show

(iron) filings

It educande: girl boarders in convent schools

fillies

Sorrento Point, Dalkey (Vico Road runs towards)

Vico Road, Dalkey

arraigned

Giambattista Vico

arranged

s Dolly's Brae (referring to site of a conflict with Orangemen)

s Good-bye, Dolly Gray: ' 'Tis the tramp of soldiers true In their uniforms of blue, I must say good-bye to you, Dolly Gray!'

BL bertrosar: brother

Battle of Waterloo

Adam Loftus suggested the establishment of Trinity College, D

ph devil take the hindmost

G vergiften: to poison

pineapple   Adam's apple

cain-apple: fruit of strawberry-tree

Cain (according to Kabbalists, offspring of Satan & Eve)

Jacob & Esau

Yin & Yang

'Exsultet': 'O felix culpa!'

Sl jerk off: masturbate

Harmsworth: Ir. newspaper magnate

F jour de l'an: New Year's Day

L de anno: from the year

W.H. Mallock: *Is Life Worth Living?*

F brune (Bruno)   Giordano (Bruno)

It tenzone: a duel, contest

G brav im Bettli: well-behaved in bed

BL betlim: contest

does for him

reintroducing Jerry (⊏)

chestnut

coulter: knife ('Kinch')

unchaste

colt

Du taal: language
I tál: flow
It mutualita: reciprocity time/space *G* Spassmacher: clown, joker peacemaker
L veloces ambos: both swift *F* vélos: bicycles
Arabian Nights tails wheels within wheels: a complexity of influences
Rubaiyat (of Omar Khayyam) (Ezek 1:16)
G Stück: piece elmtree/stone Stane St: Roman road in England
(Elm in Chapelizod; Steyne: pillar in D erected by Vikings)
away *L* sic: thus six
age of the use of reason: for RCs, age at which a child capable of committing sin
running amok break *G* lasterhaft: vicious *Du* helft: half (sb.)
left half
G Jugend: youth *G* Tugend: virtue

Am smorfire: to eat *Am* tondo: the world
It smorfia: grimace *Am* poltriero: bed
Am Bola dal ruffo: hell *Am* baito: house *I* mór: great *Low L* altruis: by others
Am larto: bread

Gr men, ti kanete sêmeron, ho emou mauro kyrio?: well, how do you do today, my dark gentleman? *AngI* mavrone: my grief
MGr ti pote: not too bad

God knows meaningless

L inde iterum: after that again truth

s My Sweetheart When a Boy *s* Eily Mavourneen, I See Thee before Me (from *The Lily of Killarney*)
Gr melainô: to blacken teacup white garters
maligned
Am Sant' Alto: God delicious *It* rosso: red
raise up
eyeballs oxide of mercury (red)
margarine (164.14)
iron Exod 20:16: 'Thou shalt not bear false witness against thy neighbour'
rust (reddish) *Arch* an: if
saltwater
cold water
BLM blong: of (Glugg washes his bruise. He doesn't want the girls—who belong to Chuff—to see it)

chestnut James Russell Lowell: 'once for every man & nation'
VI.A.17: '⊏ pain in lost limb (innocence)'
I mórán mó: much more *G* männisch: masculine
mannerish
Tara: ancient capital of Ireland (deserted after St Ruadhan cursed it)
s Ta Ra Ra Boom De Ay
short skirts *ph* change one's tune *G* ward: became
L scorta: whore
G verbannt: exiled struggle for life
N forbanne: curse
black revered Hell *Da* hvide: whites I see seven (colours)
Du blank: white veil (white light split into rainbow colours)

(telescope) *F* trompe-l'oeil

tantamount to a chiaroscuro (disposition of darker & lighter masses in a picture)
Sandymount, district of D
(28 colours) Bacchantes wore fawn skins Dove & green both represent peace
apple (red) custard (yellow) indigo, violet *G* feldgrau: fieldgrey
hematite: iron ore (eskimo blue with cold) mimosa: greenish-yellow
isinglass: a form of gelatin *Lucilia*: genus of greenbottle flies

L quasi modo: as if in the manner X-ray (colourless)
royal blue tangerine wisteria: blue-violet flower
Philomela, in Ovid, ravished by Tereus & became nightingale *AngI* shee: fairy (29th name)
Du theeroos: tearose
knew primary colours

complementary colours Aengus (Angus): Ir. love-god, son of Dagda

It piccioni: pigeons suspicions
(bright birds hover over Aengus's head)
G unsatt: unsatisfied *G* Spiegelei: fried egg (miming 'helio'—*Sl* helio: heliograph)
G Spiegel: mirror eagle eye
Gr astêr: star 'Turn again, Whittington, Lord-Mayor of London' (pantomime)
asters, type of flower *Gr* tropos: turning lodestone
Diarmaid was once loved by the daughter *It* lingua: tongue palate
of the king of Land-Under-Wave
(description of articulation of 'trope')
(T) (drum-roll sound RO) (PE)
Ally Sloper: character in Victorian comics

Achilles' weak point (HEEL) I O
Achill Island, Co. Mayo open
TROPE (in Gregorian music means a short closing cadence) *F* valse: waltz
L vulsus: smooth, hairless *F Sl* valseur: female rump
'heliotrope' orig. applied to sunflower &c. jolly well
Gr astêr: star starts *L* sol: sun
G Pilgerfahrt: pilgrimage H (1st letter of 'heliotrope') *G* Henker: hangman
'head of things' = ELITE 'halter' = ROPE
G Halunken: scoundrels

L cucullus non facit monachum: hood maketh not frere (garbled version of 'heliotrope')
Ir. pilgrims at Abbey of St Gall had tattoed eyelids
Da oldenborre: cockchafer
old bore *G* Floh: flea
beetle . . . fly . . . bee *nr* Little Bo Peep
Sl fly: artful, shrewd
Swift: 'Ppt'

luncheon Turkish delight
Gr hys: pig
Gr mys: mouse twelve horsepower Norman companions of Prince John in
Du twaalf: 12 walrus Ir. were described as 'proud belly swaines'
A form of colour blindness was named after John Dalton
uncle *G* dunkel: dark
In 1492 earls of Ormond & Kildare ceased *G* Loch: hole Swan Water: subterranean river,
their quarrel when they shook hands through hole in Chapter House Rathmines, D
door of St Patrick's Cathedral, D world's

voyeur *F* voyant Copenhagen Garrett, Earl of Kildare, replying to Wolsey's
charges in 1524: 'I serve under the cope of heaven . . . when you are . . . kneeled unto'
fact Moore: *s* I've a Secret to Tell Thee [Dennis, Don't Be Threatening]

trepanning Archbishop King, 1725: 'when any couple had a mind to retire to be wicked
a traveller's account of Drumcondra Rd, 1634: there [Glasnevin] was their harbour'
'As dainty a fine way as ever I rode' S.A.O. Fitzpatrick: *Dublin* 74: 'full of bushments &
underwoods'
basement *G* sprich: speak *AngI Sl* twig: understand

St Kevin's monastic settlement *L* benedixit: has blessed
at Glendalough *Sl* gape: cunt
Fitzpatrick 50: Long Entry, place nr the Coombe, D *L* intimus: innermost
'my Lord of Dublin'
s 'I gave the captain six thirteens, To carry me over to Park Gate!' (thirteens: C18 Ir. shillings)

Behind St, D Turn-again-lane, D

I Abha Beig: Little River I (one)
awabeg: Arabic H EL (*Heb* El: God)
O (cipher) TROOP *R* raduga: rainbow
Seven Sisters Road, London

Moore: *s* When He Who Adores Thee [The Fox's Sleep]

fucks backside
infuses
Layfield, an actor playing Iago in D, was striken with madness on stage & speaking the lines 'jealousy; it is the green ey'd monster' said 'green-eyed lobster'
Vieux Marc (liqueur)
King Mark of Cornwall

look!
(description of mouth: cheeks, teeth, tongue, uvula &c.) Book of Breathings: a funeral ritual in *Egyptian Book of the Dead*
(mouth)

G Rubinen: rubies *G* Elfenbein: ivory
(cheeks) (teeth)
It massiccio: massive Tyrian purple
(tongue)
G darunter: underneath
(uvula)

fondant
Arch union: a large & valuable pearl
L unio: onion *L* margarita: pearl
consonants & vowels
L consonantia: harmony
Hillel, Pharisee: 'My abasement is my exaltation'

ABC reverberates tegmen: hardened wing cover of some insects. Those of some Orthoptera resonate to the song
pomoeria: consecrated spaces running inside & outside city walls
Eng. equivalents of meanings of Hebrew letters: window: H; hedge: E; prong: L; hand: I; eye: O; sign: T
head: R eye: O mouth: P *s* The Absent-Minded Beggar: 'Pass the hat for your credit's sake & pay, pay, pay!'
G Auge: eye
F Sem: Shem ABC

s O! Fred, Tell Them to Stop: 'This girl which I do now adore'

G Obacht vor dem Zug!: Watch out for the train!
G Zug: procession *G* Weg

G Saum: hem, margin

cg Queen Mary: 'One morning I rose & looked in the glass'

Uggugg: villain of Lewis Carroll's *Sylvie & Bruno*

same
(003.09–10)

muttonchops Mutt & Jeff by the by left

lurch *I* ógh: virgin

G helfen shouted so as to
G schautet: looked
Arch prich: itch *ph* it is not cricket Sally Lunn: type of sweet, light teacake
G sprich: speak *F Sl* cricquet: penis
G Blumen *G* gegen: against *Du* een: one

L avis: bird; omen *ph* a little bird told me
thrilled

AngI rossy: impudent girl *s* (children's) Morgen ist die Hochzeit da!: 'Willst du dieses Mädchen haben, musst du rosa Bändchen tragen'
L simulo: I pretend tied in ribbons *G* Rumpf: rump *G* Kopf: head

Dial swart: dark *G* Schornstein: chimney
Schwarzer Hans: devil figure; fountain spirit in Grimm *s* (children's) Hänschen seet in'n Schosteen ('little Hans sits in the chimney corner')
F il fait semblant de: he pretends to sweeping their chimneys
G scheiden: to separate, divorce
VI.B.33.33: (?*cg*) 'adieu, adieu, frau scheiden'
L fingere: pretend scissors sisters
biting maidenheads *Sl* spit: deflower palefaces

G spucken: to spit

I Bi i dho husht: Be quiet *G* Seid Ihr ruhig, kleine Vögel: Hush, little birds
Sl puker: good-for-nothing
It grandicelli (m. pl.): rather grown *It* state zitti: shut up! *Du* zitten: to sit adults before
s 'Singing Polly Wolly Doodle all the day' coif: feminine headdress *F* tante *F* oncle (when you're older)
s Daddy Wouldn't Buy Me a Bow-wow: 'I've got a little cat, & I'm very fond of that, But I'd rather have a bow-wow-wow' *F* temps *G* jetzt: now
Macbeth V.5.51–2: 'till Birnam Wood Do come to Dunsinane' *Macbeth* II.2.54–5: 'Glamis hath murther'd Sleepe, & therefore Cawdor Shall sleepe no more: Macbeth shall sleepe no more'
burning world–doomsday *Arch* glamour: witchery

moider: confuse, bewilder *G* hierfür: for this
G lieb: dear

nr A was an Archer (e.g. 'T was a tinker & mended a pot') (005.09–10) *G* lieber Mann
Holinshed: *Chronicles* VI.21: 'the Liffie, named of Ptolome Lybnium' (Ptolemy's 'Libnius' is in N.W. Ireland) Father Liber: worshipped in Italian fertility rites, later identified with Bacchus *G* lieber Gott
G links: left (direction)

The *Grand Grimoire* begins with the invocation of Lucifuge Rofocale by means of the Blasting Rod, made of hazel with forked ends. A virgin kid, adorned with a garland of vervain, is decapitated & the skin used to form a circle, in which the operator intones 'I conjure thee . . . to appear without noise & without any evil smell' *L* vox: voice invokes sowed
road rood: cross The Rand, S. Africa, site of goldfields
rand: border or margin of land
Wyndham Lewis's publication *Blast* frequently said BLESS & BLAST to different people Luke 4:8: 'Get thee behind me, Satan'
s Oh! where's the slave so lowly: 'The friends we've tried, Are by our side, & the foe we hate before us'
Gr agathos: good *F* fleur
Evil spirits in the *Grand Grimoire* include Agaliarept, Fleurety, Nebiros & Lucifuge Rofocale

G Prunk: pomp (022.02–03) *Arch* kirtle: skirt

heliotrope

s Monkey Married the Baboon's Sister: 'What do you think the bride was dressed in?' *s* Vilikins & His Dinah woolly vest
nr Mary Had a Little Lamb: 'everywhere that Mary went the lamb was sure to go . . . It made the children laugh & play, To see a lamb at school' fauna/flora
Swedenborg records in his *Spiritual Diary* seeing angel children entering a garden: 'the beds of flowers, at the entrance, seemed to express joy by their increasing splendour'
L lignifer: one who carries wood Macbeth Macduff
Lucifer ABCD *I* cac: ordure
Thomas Francis Meagher, Young Irelander, popularly called 'Meagher of the Sword' *L* incoronatus: uncrowned incarnate *AngI* duff: black
s Camptown Races: 'I put my money on de bob-tail nag, Somebody bet on de bay'
piebald

AngI ph not for Joe: definitely not *PS* nic: nothing Attila the Hun ('the scourge of God')
Low L Jacobus: James attaboy!
God's curse *L* impluvium: skylight; square basin beneath to catch rainwater
westward migration of Huns caused invasion of Roman Empire by Visigoths
Da hun: she
*85: 'the spiritual principle of man had sunk so far into his natural'
stands there *I* maon: dumb *It* obliare: to forget
I mún: urine obvious amnesia
*114: 'the proprium of the angels, which is evil' *Du* potlood: pencil (lit. 'pot-lead') saucepan
Sainéan: *La Langue de Rabelais* II.386: 'latin de marmite' (lit. 'pot-Latin')
creak want made *117: 'Adam, when he was desirous to be wise . . . fell'
Greek *G* mit
Gr apo phôtos: away from light spoor: track, prints hate
*92: 'every man . . . in that world . . . thinks from its light & loves from its heat'
I Cor 13:13: 'but the greatest of these is charity'
*83: 'while a man reads of heat & light in the Word, the spirits & angels . . . instead of heat perceive charity'
*114: 'all angels have been men' *104: 'instead of times there are in heaven states'

G steht: stands anything

son of a bitch *Sl* black arse: kettle, pot
daughter of Bacchus
Malleus Maleficarum (Kramer & Sprenger's textbook for witch trials): 'The First Part. Treating of the Three Necessary Concomitants of Witchcraft which are the Devil, a Witch, & the Permission of Almighty God'. Question 2 deals with the Devil's cooperation *L* cupere: to desire
Tristan
spies sees South peers
*120: 'determination of the quarters in . . . [heaven] is not . . . from the south, but from the east'
West mercury
*121: 'the north [means] wisdom in shade' *G* Weisheit: wisdom
Swedenborg: *Spiritual Diary*: 'When [angels] see spots on their garments, it is a sign that they have had evil thoughts . . . when they see any of their garments missing from their chamber, they at once know that they have done wrong'
lapsang tea (leaves)
Imogen: heroine of *Cymbeline*, spied on when undressing
imagination
It bim bum bam: count out in children's games
It bimba: little girl

s Cherry Ripe

enough

G Lehnstuhl: easy chair
Du leerstoel: professorial chair
ph wax in his hands Dante
waxing tantalising
F dentelle: lace *Book of the Dead*

Galileo
Galehoult (*It* Galeotto) brought together Lancelot & Guinevere. Paolo & his brother's wife, Francesca, fell in love while reading about this (*Inferno* V: 'Galeotto fu il libro'—'The book was a pander')
F gauche/droit
Du doodgaan: die
Machiavelli *F* zut alors!
It smacchia: cleans *It* velluti: velvet
monitor: assistant in school

teacher *L* in omnibus moribus et temporibus: in all customs & times

letters

aspirated (Ir. letters) let us I.O.U.
aspirate: draw breath, blow

threes

Benjamine Rohan: Huguenot leader
Bruno meets Nolan
s Listen to the Mocking Bird (Spaeth, *Read 'Em & Weep*, says it concerns one of 'songdom's . . . swains')

Sodom & Gomorrah
G Gemurmel: murmuring

*Swedenborg: *Angelic Wisdom concerning the Divine Love* (paragraph numbers): early Swedenborg Society Translation

squaring his shoulders clenching my fists
G Schulter: shoulder
Faust we were
G Faust: fist
so were you

R dvoinya: twins *R* brat'ya: brothers
I bráthair: kinsman Eng. Parliaments: Mad (1258); Long
ramp: climb mankind's child (1640–53)–became Rump; Lack-learning
(1404); Merciless, or Wonderful (1388)

St Berchán, nicknamed Mo-Bhí, founded Glasnevin monastery; *I* Glaisín Aoibhinn: Pleasant Little Green (pron. glashínívíñ)
Prospect Cemetery, Glasnevin (Catholics)

G vielen Dank: thank you

Mount Jerome Cemetery, Harold's Cross, D (Protestants) Blake: *London* (*Songs of Experience*): 'harlot's curse'
better

L Gratias ago: I give thanks

brother
Gen 4:5: '& Cain was very wroth & his countenance fell'
'bivitelline' lit. means '2-yolked' (i.e. twins) *Gr* ametallikos: unmetallic Ibsen: *The Crown*
bimetallism: unrestricted currency of 2 metals at a fixed ratio *Pretenders*
L obscindo: I tear to *R* obshchina: community *G* Gemeinde: community Urus: extinct species of wild ox
Kipling: *The Absent-Minded Beggar* obsceneminded bickerers *G* Bekehrer: proselytizer(s)
superfetation: secondary implantation during pregnancy (also fig.)
(both use oil)

'twixt Timothy
Thomas (= twin) *HF* 13: 'for gracious sakes' orthodox *L* dux: leader
Arthur Duke of Wellington
heterotropic: not exhibiting equal physical properties in all directions heretic sheep . . . goat *AngI* bawn: white; pretty
heterodox born
slowly nursed
nurtured
G richten: set right boy if

Dial gar: make

G Wasserstoff: hydrogen
G Stickstoff: nitrogen
HF 12: 'not for pie'

natural selection (Charles Darwin)
s Charley Is My Darling
Darwin: *The Descent of Man*
breakfast

F fleur angel's garden
F ange: angel
r Gardon, Languedoc

crownless ain't no more
(head)
Sainéan: *La Langue de Rabelais* II.353 names Devil 'Celui qui n'a point de blanc en l'oeil' to a
Sainéan: *La Langue de Rabelais* II.399: 'Braguettodyte, qui habite la braguette (Rabelais III.27), composé burlesque
Sainéan II.299: Jonathan Swift Sainéan II.156: saquebutte: sackbut formé d'après l'analogie de *troglo-*
Sl quoniam: cunt *L* quondam: at one time *ph* son of a sea-cook *dyte*'; II.59: catadupe: waterfall
Sl John Thomas: penis *G* stammen: be descended from

Du de eerste de beste: any, the first you meet
G erstbeste: first *I* tá sé déanta agam: I have it done = I promise to do it

Peruvian/Russian: new v. old world languages
R russkii: Russian
R suchki: whores *G* Mundart: idiom Slav *PS* slovo: word
s Look At Me Now
It mappamondo: geographical globe
L mappa mundi: map of the world *G* Mund: mouth

F sauterelle: grasshopper
(Ant & Grasshopper)
nothing whatsoever
Eccles 1:9: 'there is no new thing under the sun' *L* sol: sun
L sol: sun *pr* 'Early to bed & early to rise Makes a man healthy & wealthy & wise'
tattling turtle soup bagful (earful)

aboriginals Sydney Grundy: *In Honour Bound* (play, 1880)
London Regional (BBC radio)
Sts Matthew, Mark, Luke & John

Sainéan II.354: 'Par sainct Bon' (bishop of Clermont ca. 710)

Campbell: *Lochiel's Warning:* 'Coming events cast their shadows before'

boxing gloves *AngI* noody-nady: hesitant in speech (fr. *I* niudaimi-neadaimi, a hesitant person)
total *s* 'Come into the Garden, Maud, For the black bat, night, has flown'
(Glugg's third guess at colour: violet) garner: granary
stars violets
thine eyes meaning iodine vapour is mauve
F évidemment tierce: a 3rd part
letter, 22/11/30, to HSW: 'the Devil has to come over three times'
P.W. Joyce: 'When a person singing a song has to stop because he forgets the next verse, he says (mostly in joke) "there's a hole in the ballad"' patently
paten: dish for bread at celebration of Eucharist
bucket through

AngI gossoons: young lads
duad: pair *ph* sure as there's a tail on a cat Ham, son of Noah
pomelo: citrus species called, in England, Forbidden Fruit

AngI fecking: stealing urine re-echo-able
Pro aurino: golden
Bur Myamma: Burma
Miami
young country

Dr Barnado: D-born founder of orphans' homes kindergarten
Barnado's furriers, Grafton St, D
G.H. Bingham, Lord Lucan, suddenly returned to his village & found the villagers burning his effigy *G* Hof: court
F vrai de vrai: as true as true *L* deus ex machina: providential interposition
Sainéan II.347: 'Vraybis! vrai Dieu, formule fréquent chez Rabelais' *F* blanc
vivisection
Barnstaple, town, Devonshire *L* mortisectio: I cut up (something) dead
Gr (artif.) mauromormô: dark bugbear mauro (poet): distant
Isaac Jackman: *The Milesian* (a play)
L -ibus: dative & ablative pl. suffix Sainéan II.346: 'Corbieu!'
F Morbleu! (oath)

pitched example diagnosed
Jones: *King Arthur in History & Legend* 81n quotes 'whose life was an ensample' (smelled out)
I Tonn Rudhraighe, Tonn Tuaithe, Tonn Chlíodhna: 3 of the 4 Waves of Erin (points on Ir. coast)
orgiast: one who celebrates orgies
Welsh Triad: *Three Stout Swineherds of the Isle of Britain* Marechal MacMahon: Fr. officer in Crimean War
Swein Forkbeard: Viking, son of Harald Bluetooth *G* Meer: sea
L ipse: himself Yspaddaden Penkawr: hawthorn as malevolent chief of gods in Welsh myth
quotidian: daily, trivial quotients
Layamon: *Brut* (Brut is legendary founder of Britain)
ME layaman: lawman

Arch yclept: called Clio: muse of history chronicler
(suspicius of unless he can see it)
Sulpicius Severus: *Chronica* Geoffrey: *Historia Regum Britanniae:* 'save he followed' (= unless he followed)
Arthur's nephew, Gawain, was sent to Pope Sulpicius to act as squire AL . . . P
HCE

St Polycarp knew St John & subsequently met the major theologian Irenaeus, thereby forming a link in a chain of tradition eyewitnessed Rev. John Roche Ardill, *St Patrick A.D. 180*, suggests Patrick may have met Irenaeus
r Liffey
Butler: *The Way of All Flesh* Sarah Bridge over Liffey (= Island Bridge) *I* droichead: bridge quarrelsome
Gen 21:5–7: Sarah laughed when God said she was to bear a child *L* extorreo: I am scorched
at age 90; hence name Isaac (means 'he laughed') last Liffey road bridges in J's time: O'Connell & Butt Brs
Isaac Butt: ousted from leadership by Parnell *I* minne: stuttering *G* Minne: love
F monologue intérieure *Perrichon: a dance *Bastienne: a dance
monolith
Ariane: wife of Bluebeard in Perrault's story *Ricqueraque: love & its ill consequences *jocquer: to perch
*brimballer: make love *Joly cas: (fig.) pregnant
how sayest thou **Dulcis amica:* a dance World Atlas of *Everyman's Encyclopedia:* 'A, aa (*Sw, Da-N*): river; ab (*Per*): water, river; abu (*Arab*): father; abiad (*Arab*): white; . . .
Bab-el-Mandeb (*Arab*): "the gate of tears"' (strait between Gulf of Aden & S. end of Red Sea)
Dublin Gulch, Montana
Sea of Marmora between Black Sea & Mediterranean Mermer: Sumerian storm-god
The hero is traditionally born with a caul *1001 Nights*

HCE *F* les Rois Fainéants: last of the Merovingian kings
hocus-pocus: mock Latin for 'hoc est enim corpus meum' (Mass) *L* Esquiline: largest hill of Rome *G* wie viel: how much

Ptolemy Soter founded Ptolemaic dynasty

Sardanapalus: last king of Assyria; buried himself, wives & treasure when his subjects rebelled
F sourd: deaf sour apples *U.S. Sl* lollapaloosa: wonderful
but

Ginger Jane: oldest complete human body in world Adam *L* costa: rib
Java Man
*'*Par Mahon!* . . . serment de géant qu'on entend encore à Montpellier' *OF* mesme: same psychoanalysis
space/time

sepulture: burial *G* grüss Gott! (S. German salutation) Merodach: Babylonian sun-god
Great Scott!
H . . . C . . . E

acute angle *G* Hut: hat *T* Hissarlik ('place of forts'): Troy's mt site
hennin: high conical womens' headdress of C15, like spire incidentally queen selm: bar of a gate
*quine: ape (female)
as a matter of course *magot: Barbary ape Selma: residence of Macpherson's Fingal
Sl maggot: whim
baritone singer *F* singe: ape *G* Sänger: singer isles of Scandinavia skald: ancient Scandinavian poet
Macpherson says 'Berrathon' means 'a promontory in the midst of waves'

Buncombe, N. Carolina (from which 'bunkum' derived)
Commission for Wide Streets, D
Macpherson: *Temora* VIII mentions Fingal's knowledge of herbs Artho: father of Macpherson's Cormac
gillyflower: clove-scented flower, wallflower

***Lazare Sainéan: *La Langue de Rabelais*, Paris, 1922**

AngI is the name is on: is the name of Chapelizod *G* Handschuh: glove

shadow of our lives

attack

BL tamor: earth
yesterday, today, tomorrow
awaken someone or other
summoner

weatherbeaten

tocsin: bell, esp. alarm klaxton his whereabouts

G Webwaren: textiles
Gibbon: *Decline & Fall of the Roman Empire* XXXV reports that Attila, about to relinquish his siege of Aquileia, observed a stork & family about to leave her nest in a tower in the walls. He deduced the tower must be unmanned, breached the wall there & destroyed the city
L aquila: eagle eyrie: eagle's nest

spillway: passage for overflow water
OE ruth: mercy
valley of Jehoshaphat: scene of Last Judgement (Joel 3:12)

I Magh Cille: plain of a church *Belgian Lion quarantine
*Wing of St Michael John Bull guarantee
Sp calavera: hot-headed fellow *the Slaves to Virtue *L* veritatem: truth
*Calatrava
*Polar Star *L* procul abeat: may he be far away Ivor, Viking king of D *Da* Danmark
aurora borealis ivory *Elephant (began in Denmark)
nr Hector Protector Valdemar: several Danish kings Gustavus Vasa, king of
*Wolodmir *Vasa Sweden (1496–1560)
ph peel your eyes *Saviour of the World *Labour (early trade union)
*Blood of our Saviour
Pliny the Younger (nephew of Pliny the Elder): *Letters*

L calamus: reed pen (281.04–5: 'de Pline et de Columelle') *L* lumen: light calumny *L* contumelia: insult
Columella wrote on agriculture Pliny the Elder, natural historian Aulus Gellius: grammarian: wrote *Noctes*
Mick Macrobius commented on Aulus Gellius *Atticae*
Vitruvius: *De Architectum Libri Decem*
Cassiodorus: historian, statesman, monk Book of Lecan: ancient Ir. MS Lucan
Lucan (epic poet): *Pharsalia*
The Coombe, street, D *Du* kooper: buyer
Lord's Prayer: 'Thy kingdom come' keeper of the
Du winkel: shop *I* deoch an dorais: drink at parting
G Winkel: angle
bed & breakfast

Punch & Judy

Giambattista Vico
John the Baptist
Gen 2:21: '& the Lord God caused a deep sleep to fall upon Adam . . . & he took one of his ribs' (creation of Eve)
aboulia: loss of willpower
(Adam's rib)

(tailor & captain: II.3)
The Forty Shilling Tailors: D tailor's shop
ship ahoy! ten stone ten pounds (150 lbs)
hoyden: ill-bred girl
(breasts)

ditto (waist)

(hips)

Quis separabit?: motto of order of St Patrick (Who Shall Separate?)
F cuisse: thigh
(calves) Sheridan: *School for Scandal*
(feet)

***orders of knights**

G eher: before
'ere
F sauve qui peut: *L* gallus: cock
save himself who can!
It Arch oreglia: ear (Isod)

ph thorn in their flesh *It* presto prestissimo: very quickly twinkling
It prestissima: very ready

s Who Killed Cock Robin: 'All the birds of the air fell *s* 'The Wren, the Wren, the King of All Birds'
Biddy (112.27) a-sighing & a-sobbing'
harns: brains *G* Bier: beer *G* Spirituosen: liquor
G Harn: urine *Du* wijn: wine 'licenced for consumption on the premises' (pubs)
Du advokaat: barrister, lawyer *Pro* marrit: bad Pa's
advokaat (liqueur) Ma's *Pro* poulit: merry
Pro flam: flame *Pro* galant: gallant
Pro festoun: a festoon *Pro* galantet: pretty *Pro* flour: flower
hue & cry H . . . C . . . E gillyflower: clove-scented flower, wallflower

Heb ḥalom: dream (v.) (Anglo-Irish writers:) Edmund Burke
Josh 6:6–20: 7 priests with trumpets of rams' horns demolish walls of Jericho
Crone's *Concise Dictionary of Irish Biography* gives title R.B. Sheridan
of Kendal Bushe's *Cease Your Funning* as *Cease Your Fuming* Moses' burning bush
Goldsmith Yeats Synge Wilde Shaw show Swift
yeas & nays
Sterne

come to pass

't in Dutch is short for *het* (it)
Du goed: good *Du* het beste: the best thing
thereto returning

task books homily
Du boekentas: satchel goody: a children's supper dish hominy: maize coarsely milled & boiled for bread &c.
jaggery: Burmese palm sugar juju: magical object in W. Africa
F grand-mère *Bur* ju: jam
Charles-Pierre Girault: *Grammaire des* *pr* Fine words butter no parsnips
grammaires (digest of grammatical opinion) *Angl* bothered: deaf parse (grammar)
Massora: Hebrew text of Bible Matthew, Mark, Luke, John
Annals of the Four Masters Lucan
1132
vulgar air

2 Gent. of Verona IV.2.39: 'Who is Silvia? What is she'
s 'What are the wild waves saying Sister the whole day long?'
went Mnemonic of *L* mas. nouns of 3rd declension: 'amnis, anguis, axis, collis'
(respectively meaning river, snake, axis, hill)
Bur nga-man: sea monster mango-fish: edible Indian fish
Bur nga: fish fishermen
F rancune: rancour Rangoon, capital of Burma *Sinbad the Sailor*
paddy bird: species of egret feeding on paddy fields *Bur* sin: elephant
sitting
Languedoc (Southern France)

I Dáil (pron. 'doil'): Ir. Legislative Assembly
Langue d'oil (Northern France)
F dernier cri: latest fashion Provençe *G* Zentrum
denier: a Fr. coin trams in D converged on G.P.O.
Dublin United Tramways Co. radii

Anglo-Indian crore: 10,000,000 (rupees) variations in the price
reflections
pices: Burmese copper coins
N. Circular Road, D S. Circular Road, D
diggings: lodgings
Dubliners: 'A Little Cloud' *It* nebulosa: nebula *I* uisce: water *Da* senga: the bed
We pr He who sings in bed will cry before he sleeps in sky Sinbad
We pr A mother-in-law's slice of bread & butter- *G* Alpdruck: nightmare
thick bread & thin butter *G* Druckhaus: printer's shop
Pro caspi! egad!
Tennyson: *Charge of the Light Brigade:* 'Cannon to right of them,
Gaelic League stinks Cannon to left of them'
garlic *F* guerre *ph* Gael & Gall (*I* gall: foreigner)

Du fijn hapje: appetizing little morsel Swift's Stella
Swift's Vanessa unhappy *L* stella vesperina: evening star whispering

rhomb, trapezium: types of quadrilateral *It* gran: great
Grandma
geometry grasshopper & ant coney: rabbit
Gr Gaia mêtêr: Mother Earth hop, skip & jump (lep)
cuneiform letters *L* lepus: hare merrily durian: prickly Malayan fruit Maid Marian: Robin Hood's sweetheart
Wilde: *The Picture of Dorian Gray* madcap
Pro lou: the Dariou: character in Mistral's *La Matieto*, Provençal poem

BLM longa house blong: to the house of

poor man's clock went (8 o'clock)
nr This is the way the ladies ride: 'Nimble, nimble, nimble, nimble' VI.B.46.27 (Burmese): 'nin (8)'
Lear: *O My Aged Uncle Arley* early
Ruth 3:2: 'Boaz . . . winnoweth barley'
platinum hips & haws: fruit of dog rose

Trinity College, D *Da* som hedder: who is called

toffeenose *nr* Old Daddy Dacon ('Bought a bit of bacon')

piece of bacon *ph* not hold a candle to

AngI fecking: stealing

woke hardly waddle swallow
follow

G Weg *Da* tilbage: back

pantomime
panties
Ruth 2:23: 'unto the end of barley harvest & of wheat harvest' old
Du boos: evil, angry Ruth gave herself to Boaz, who was much older than she
boss
pants

Punch & Judy
Jury's Hotel, D
(248.30)

(rhythm of *The Bells of Shandon*; see 139.16) *Gr* diaspora: dispersal (Jews dispersed after Captivity)
desperation of desperation
fond

Da luk døren: shut the door *It* chiudi l'uscio: shut the door! *F* fermez la porte *G* Türe zu: shut the door!
I dún an doras: shut the door Lucifer Fermoy, Co. Cork
M Gr sphalna portan: shut the door *R* zakroi dver': shut the door *Fi* kapakka: tavern *G* kaputt
sport one's oak: keep one's door shut *T* kapiyi kapat: shut the door
G Beifall: applause

applaud

Ellerton: *s* The Day Thou Gavest, Lord, Is Ended: 'The darkness falls at Thy behest'
Du schouwburg: theatre

I ludramán: lazy idler

Michael Gunn: manager of Gaiety Theatre, D *G* Gastspiel: starring tour/performance hell
gods: gallery in theatre gospel
what colour? (heliotrope) *L* orbita: track, course
arbiter: referee
Snorri Sturluson: Norse historian

ON Ragnarøkr: destruction of the Norse gods (no vowels in *Heb*)
170.26: 'the rending of the rocks' Matt 27:51: 'earth did quake, & the rocks rent'
G Götterdämmerung (Wagner) hills valleys *L* exeunt omnes: they all go out (stage direction)
hell's bells
manna man of God *HF* 14: 'how do dat come' *HF* 14: 'dad fetch him'
Heb lama: why?
hear that far Motto of House of Savoy (FERT): Fortitudo eius Rhodum tenuit *L* tonuit: thundered *L* quoque: also
L fulgor: lightning
Buckley *s* Yankee Doodle *s* Bunkey doodle-i-do skidoo! Ḳiddush: Jewish ceremony & prayer by which holiness of a festival proclaimed
Judg 5:7: 'At her feet he bowed, he fell, he lay down; at her feet he bowed, he fell; where he bowed, there he fell dead'
Gen 11:4: 'Go to, let us build us a city & a tower'
Azrael: angel of death
harps arks Hebrews brows James' Gate, D (Guinness's Brewery)
Deut 6:8–9: 'a sign upon thine hand, . . . between thine eyes . . . upon the posts . . . on thy gates' *s* Kafoozalem:
Jews put phylacteries (Tephilim) on their doorjambs (Mezouzah) hip, hip, hurrah! 'from old Methusalem'
s Finnegan's Wake: 'Souls to the devil, did you think I'm dead?' yes *Heb* yipol: to fall
Heb yareah: the moon Nephilim (giants, Gen 6:4)
Nick/Mick
I am Shem *F* Sem: Shem
Heb emi, 'ami, šemi: my mother, my nation, my name
Heb lebhabh: hearts *Da* og han var: & he was Opening of the Mouth (*Egyptian Book of the Dead*)
Babel (Tower of)
Gen 17:20: '& as for Ishmael . . . I will make him a great nation' (he was a son of Abraham)
Sh'ma (Jewish liturgy): 'Hear O Israel: The Lord our God is One Lord' (Deut 6:4)
Heb haavo: the sin heavenfallen Ps 115:16: 'the heaven & heaven of heavens'
Gen 4:24: 'If Cain shall be avenged sevenfold, truly Lamech seventy & sevenfold' Gen 11:4: 'Go to, let us . . .'
Ps 68:3: 'Yea, let them exceedingly rejoice' Ps 68:5: 'extol him who rides upon the clouds'

Ps 68:13: 'Though you have lien among the pots'
Exod 16:3: 'When we sat by the flesh pots' pisspots Ps 68:34: 'His excellency is over Israel'
Gen 17:20: '& as for Ishmael . . . I will make him a great nation'

Gen 9:29: 'Noah . . . & he died'

tumbledown

Tem: creator in *Egyptian Book of the Dead* world

megaphone *Gr* phônêma: utterance, speech phenomenon inhabitants
F terre *It* fime: manure
firmament
Tweedledum & Tweedledee (*Through the Looking-Glass*)

Litany of the Saints: 'Christ hear us, Christ graciously hear us'

H . . . CE Jer 21:13: 'Who shall enter into our habitations'

HF 19: 'I'm nation sorry' *HF* 28: 'shin for the raft'
HF 20: 'camp-meeting' (U.S. religious revival) governor

I gárda: policeman
ML didymus: twin
In *Acts of Thomas,* Judas Thomas is said to be Jesus' twin. 'Thomas' means 'twin' Opening of the Mouth (*Egyptian Book of the Dead*)

Du bode: messenger cherubim
crubeen: pig's or sheep's trotter
'Timothy' means 'honouring God'

R.A.S. Macalister, in *The Secret Languages of Ireland*, translates a sentence of Bearlagair Na Saer referring to the bonds of Masonry: 'Stone to stone, stone between two stones, & stone over stone'

tree/stone

we beseech Thee, O Lord

G litten: suffered

Anglican Morning Prayer: 'Give peace in our time, O Lord'

Commandments: 'Thou shalt not kill . . . Thou shalt not commit adultery'

C ming: name

L mingere: to urinate

F merde

murder

idolatry

have mercy

Book of Common Prayer, Holy Communion: 'Incline our hearts to keep Thy Law'

(5 vowels)

G Mumm: courage

Mum!: silence!

L unde et ubi: whence & where

The Pope's address: 'Urbi et Orbi' ('To the City & the World')

teetotum (orig. T. totum): 4-sided disk spun in game of chance

Tom Tit Tot: folk tale in which demon's safety depends on secrecy of his name

(progress of civilisation)

L sic

(children return to father's pub—to D—after II.1)

Howth (021.18)

shut

blackguard

'quick march . . . by the left' (army)

Mainly about people: C 19 weekly

Livius: historian

Mezzofanti: linguist

Lavater: physiognomist

(diagonally crossing)

Tycho Brahe: astronomer

Berkeley: philosopher

Berkeley Road, D

particular, as opposed to universal, propositions in logic

Solfa: do, re, mi, fa, so, la, ti, do

ut = do

Gainsborough: painter

G quer: across

carfax: i) crossroads; ii) (obs.) the '4 Arts'–music, arithmetic, geometry, astronomy

Guido of Arezzo: composer, inventor of tonic solfa

Da gade: street

Piazza Giambattista Vico, Trieste

Vico Road, Dalkey

G fahr: ride

far

I fear: man

Aquinas (*Summa Theologiae* II.II.19) distinguishes filial, initial, servile & wordly fear (*filialem, initialem, servilem & mundanum*)

Montanus, heretic, loved by Priscilla & Maximilla (see Flaubert's *St Antoine*) (215.19)

wedding

Sl wetting: fucking

ECH

rouge (red)

enthusiast

cuddling

hoyden: ill-bred girl

F1. *AngI* raumaush: romance, nonsense

does snuffle

(hard labour)

quoth she

s 'Twas off the Blue Canaries

Gaelic

I teanga: language

HCE

(Mark of Cornwall)

F2. Mary Mercer founded Mercer's Hospital

Mater Misericordiae Hospital, D

F3. W.G. Wills: *A Royal Divorce*

letter, end July 1939, to FB: 'the technique here is a reproduction of a schoolboy's (and schoolgirl's) old classbook complete with marginalia by the twins, who change sides at half time, footnotes by the girl (who doesn't), a Euclid diagram, funny drawings etc.'

Chinks (yellow) *F* jupe jade (green)
Gypsies said to colour Punch & Judy (rainbow colours)
their faces tawney blue indigo violet
F petit bleu: *G* Bluse: blouse *G* entdeckt: discovered
express letter (458.24) *Da* en elv, et fjeld: a stream, a mountain
Sw fjäll: mountain
Dial whins: gorse howe: hill, tumulus Howe: site of Viking
(on Howth) Thingmote in D home
many happy returns
taking time

seakale: shore plant with edible shoots
G befinden: consider, to all is said & done
find oneself
maid
7 Wonders of the World: Pyramids, Walls & Hanging (i.e. pensile)
Gardens of Babylon, Statue of Zeus at Olympia, Lighthouse
at Alexandria, Temple of Diana, Colossus of Rhodes,
Mausoleum at Halicarnassus
Diaphane ('Proteus')

cachinnate: laugh loudly *F* culottes: breeches

Edgar Pitt: *Sweeney Todd, the Demon Barber* (melodrama) *G* Tod: death
Euclid: 'A line is length without breadth'
'World without end, Amen' (*Gloria Patri*)
HCE *L* aevum: eternity
heavens
L sopor: deep sleep Zeus suckled by goat in cave
Hy Maine: tribal territory, Co. Galway
Gladstone bag *nr* Denary, danary
Glastonbury *G* glatt: smooth
ECH
ribs untiring
rubbish tumulus chthonic: dwelling underground
I árd-rí: high king
Cornwall mufti: plain clothes worn by someone with right to
Cromwell wear uniform
L dominium directum: direct ownership (for Vico an attribute
confession box of new barbarism corresponding to Roman quiritary ownership)
manifest
Yeats: *Dramatis Personae* XIV: 'I told him [George Moore]
that he was more mob than man'
Ain-Soph: Kabbalistic name of the unmanifest Diety, from which
were produced 10 emanations, the Sephiroth (principles, forces,
attributes)
Kabbalistic doctrine regards woman as intrinsically passive
naughty beside (10, ten)
horoscope *G* mehr mercury, salt, sulphur (alchemy)
Gr kurios: lord *G* kurios: strange *G* Salz: salt
Ps 91:5–6: 'Thou shalt not be afraid for the terror by night . . .
nor for the destruction that wasteth at noonday'
cryptogram
cryptogam: non-flowering plant

Gr deka: 10
dickens (10 questions; 10 Sephiroth of the Kabbalah)
decans: 36 divisions of zodiac in Chaldean astrology

F1. (strip poker) ALP *L* ludo: I play hypnotised
F2. Kellywick: a castle of Arthur in Cornwall VI.C.3.173: 'clingaround corset'
(address) 'The Long Fellow': De Valera Commons cake walk:
Salthill: district of Galway city Co. Monaghan dance from negro minstrel shows
F3. (Wine in Mass)
F4. *It* sotto voce *It Dial* poce: breast

decent ECH
L decem: 10
ALP
ATLOP: anagram: PLATO
Thom's *D Directory: 'Chapelizod*, a village partly in Palmerstown parish, Uppercross barony, but chiefly in the parish of the same name, Castleknock barony'

prolegomena: preliminary discourses

sidereal
ideal real

Persse O'Reilly
Padraic Pearse
I'll be damned!

O'Reilly

HCE

G Furcht: fear
G kracht: crashes *Du* kracht: force, strength
first crash of thunder (according to Vico drove men into caves)
blown to fuck
Jespersen: *Language* VIII.5: '*flutterby* for butterfly'

(St Lucia, patron saint of eyesight, .16)
G Erd
Ardnacrusha, Co. Limerick; hydroelectric scheme there subject of much boasting in 1930s
Mass for the Dead: 'Requiem aeternam dona eis Domine, et lux perpetua luceat eis' (Lord, grant them eternal rest & let perpetual light shine upon them')
ALP

the ounce of tea in the pot
Nicholas of Cusa: *Of Learned Ignorance*

so be it
Da bygge: build
ring to tether horse, stone to stand on while mounting it
gnosis: knowledge of spiritual mysteries
Boot Inn, Pickardstown, Co. D
Boötes: constellation (the ploughman)
Da skimmel: whitegrey horse (milkwhite horse, 111.30)
Du melk: milk stood still
Du overal: everywhere
Ice láfi: floor
outwards both
determinism: doctrine of necessary causal chain determining everything
I bás: death

Magazine Wall (013.14–15)
Ballyhoura Mts, Co. Cork
cg 'The farmer's in his den,
The farmer's in his den,
He I Hedy Ho, the farmer's in his den'
(publican makes money on raffles)
G drang: have entered
publican

F1. jussive: expressing command Joseph Smith founded Mormons beeline buryingplace
Arab Yusuf: Joseph merman
tidemark go to hell! *Sw* Göta Elv: *r* Gota
F2. (backwards): O love, look in the glass & see how Izod tips [you] what words are trouser drawers
Da salg: sale
F3. good riddance Godred Croven: Norse king of Isle of Man, reduced D Tynwald: Manx council
F4. ALP Apis: sacred bull of Memphis; begotten by ray of light from moon Swift's *A Tale of a Tub*
L means 'Bee loves altar, Moon reads book, Hen seeks pastures'
F5. after dinner
F6. blessed Mary Akenhead founded Ir. Sisters of Charity beatified
Matt Talbot: C20 D ascetic; always entered churches on his 'tummy'
F7. *Da* begge: both

VI.Ċ.2.231: 'seldomers—frequently/drunk than sober'

G eine erste Kraft: a good, well-qualified employee
ECH hake (fish)
St Ignatius Loyola (founder of Jesuit order)
L ignotus loquor: unknown I speak

Father Theobald Mathew:
Ir. temperance advocate
49 of the Danaides, daughters of Aegyptus, killed their husbands
Balder: Norse god killed by mistletoe Egypt (South)
Cyrus: king of Persia Asia Major & Minor (East)
has
smallpox

(West) Ostrogoths: barbarian tribe often in conflict with Roman Empire
pandemic disease postmortem
Gr pandêmia: the whole people

Castille: Spanish province
Hispanic: pertaining to Spain castilian: one living in castle
Cathay: a name for China HCE Euxine: the Black Sea
CEH (Irish) Hebrides (Scotland) *F* Espagnol Cymric: Welsh
pr The Englishman's house is his castle ECH
Hellenic Rolf Ganger: 1st Duke of Normandy (theoretically ancestor of Anglo-Norman invaders of Ir.)
ganger: one who travels on foot

ph let bygones be bygones

G bei: by, on, at *Da* Saaledes er det i denne vakre verden, mine bøørn: It is like that in this beautiful world, my children
It bei: governor
Michael Gunn: manager of Gaiety Theatre, D *Da* vild: wild
L primus: first *G* Alter: age
L alter: second
L idem: the same *The Emerald Table of Hermes Trismegistos:* 10 precepts, of which no. 2 reads: 'What is below is like that which is above, & what is above is like that which is below, to accomplish the miracles of one thing'
ECH
lath & plaster
love & pleasure
L non quod sed quia: not because but wherefore
Dunne: *The Serial Universe*
seriocomically

Eddington: *The Expanding Universe* *Arch* rimeless: countless
timeless
ph without rhyme or reason Original Sin

St Augustine: 'Securus iudicat orbis terrarum' ('untroubled, the world judges')
hearsay
HCE *L* haud certo ergo: not at all certainly, therefore
heresy in *Paradise Lost* (contains several heresies)
'Exsultet': 'O felix culpa!' *AngI* bad cess to him! (imprecation)
capability
archetype typtology: theory of spirit-tapping
architect

F1. Huntley & Palmers' alphabet biscuits
A to Z
F2. VI.B.45.148: 'cassowary = thunder' fletcher: arrow-maker flashes of lightning
back Spice Islands
in spite space *Du* punt: point, full stop Egyptians imported perfumes from Land of Punt
F3. *It* cima: top, peak *It* d'oro: golden
F4. Luther the gay Lothario: seducer in Rowe's *Fair Penitent*; the expression is used in *Two Gallants* VI.B.3.32: 'Luther = Arius' cenobite: member of religious community
VI.B.2.34: 'extraordinary clothes = heretics'

HCE ALP
It commercio: commerce
Cz proud: stream zelotypia: jealousy
luckless bride
HCE ALP *G* ernst Allsop's Ale
L odium theologicum: theological hatred
OE Hlyd-monath: Loud month (March) ⊣ ⊢ teleology: doctrine of ends or final causes
∧ ⩜ ⊏

Hill of Howth *r* Liffey *G* Backfisch: teenager
Rev 20:12: 'the book of life' amnion: embryonic membrane
L amnis amnium: river of rivers *L* flumen: river
L flamen: (m) priest; (n) wind
(lit. 'little stream of little priests')

HCE ECH Gen 9:25: 'Cursed be Canaan' (Noah's
L cum: with entrance words after Ham had seen him naked)

s Between a Kiss & a Sigh
star sough: swampy place
L petra: stone *L* ulma: elm

very

L (artif.) subdiurnemus: let us *s* Afton Water
sojourn Eblana: Ptolemy's name for D
carr: pond, bog living among *F* en amont: upstream

Salmenbräu: Swiss beer

freshet: stream of fresh water running into the sea

Gerald Griffin: *The Phantom City* faked film folk
latifundia: large estates
Earwickers of Sidlesham in the Hundred of Manhood (030.07–8)
bought & sold *'Chapelizod . . . comprising an area of 63 acres. Population 1,280'
(400 × [26 + 6] = 12,800)
ON fylki: district Ireland has 26 southern & 6 northern counties (Partition)
'Move up, Mick [Michael Collins, who accepted Treaty ratifying Partition], make way for Dick' [Richard Mulcahy] (D graffito after Collins' death, 1922) *I* mac: son
I muc: pig
*Riverside House *Sunnybank
It buona: good
*Buena Vista *Santa Rosa *Mayfield House
St Rosa of Lima: patron saint of the impossible
*Springvale *Orchard Lodge

*St Laurence Lodge buried
scented ever remembered
*Hillview *Ashview *G* Wald *Glenmaroon
eastward *F* marron: chestnut
*Glenthorn *Glenaulin (means 'pretty glen') *Ardeevin (means 'pleasant height')
*Norman Court

*Boundary-ville *'Its buildings are—a Church of Ireland Church, with an ivied tower, a Convent . . .'

*King's House

F1. Jespersen: *Language* X.1: '*stark-naked*, formerly *start-naked*'; X.6: 'saying *dood* . . . for "good" '
bored stiff *L* vivi-: alive very sorry sad *Du* dood: dead
F2. *s* I Dreamt That I Dwelt in Marble Halls Marble Arch, London
Poolbeg lighthouse, D
F3. *ph* 'Perfidious Albion' *Prophyrio albus:* White Swamp Hen of New South Wales, extinct
Porphyry: Neoplatonist holy rosary Rosemary
ph tell that to the horse marines (indicates disbelief)

*Chapelizod section of Thom's *D Directory*

*Stone House *Belgrove *Mulberry House *Phoenix Park Distillery,
beloved (with groves) *Mulberry Hill bld. orig. mill
*Mardyke Mills *G* Kloster: cloister no man's land
*Mount Sackville Convent
township *G* Vorangegangene: the dead

Le Fanu: *The House by the Churchyard.* Ch. 1 describes
Chapelizod: 'the village tree—that stalworth elm'
abovementioned
Da skaal! (toast)
Da skole: school *I* agus: and *Da* igen: again
*'a National School' Job 14:2: 'He cometh forth like a flower'
*Auburn self-raising flour
Goldsmith: *The Deserted Village:* 'Sweet Auburn' *G* reizen: attract
It fragola: strawberry *F* fraise: strawberry
*Strawberry Beds
Phoenix Park Phoenix Tavern, Chapelizod tripartite
(phoenix reborn from flames)
*Wren's nest *G* niedlich: pretty
(pub)
L turris: tower *Sabine-ter.
rape of the Sabine women
*The Cottage *The Bungalow

Brandenburger *Isolde-gardens
Rosary divided
into 3 sections, *I* an: the ALP of deepest peace
chaplets *Da* en lille plads: a little place ALP
(her colours) arride: to gratify (216.04)

F trou de dentelle: hole of lace *G* Wonne: delight

s The Holly & the Ivy Hollywood, village, Co. Wicklow

seem so yes

please *'It is said to derive its name from La belle Izod, daughter of king Aengus'
F angoisse: distress, anxiety *'Palmerstown parish, Uppercross barony . . . Castleknock barony'
Po tytón: tobacco *Po* włosy: hair

matrimonials *L* praesaepe prosapiae: the family's
Gr metromyrias: 10,000 tavern
Tabard Inn, Southwark, where Chaucer's *Canterbury Tales* one
begins one one *'The Tap' *'The Carlisle Tavern'
ribbon development (city planning) contract bridge (game)

Leixlip (on Liffey)
190,080 (inches in 3 miles) × 12 = 2,280,960
*'Chapelizod . . . three miles W. from the General Post Office, Dublin'
G Thausig (*Basle Dial*): 1,000
L radius luminis: ray of light westwards
G Wust: chaos *G* Wort
General Post Office *G* Wüst: waste, desert
Dillon Cosgrave (*North Dublin, City & Environs*) claims there are 24 places called 'Dublin' in the U.S. *Deserted Village:* 'loveliest village of the plain'
Stars & Stripes

F1. Jespersen: *Language* VIII.1: 'habit that mothers & nurses have of repeating . . . [e.g.] 'Now we must wash the little face'

F2. Summerhill: street, D
geriatric The homosexual in 'An Encounter' wore a 'jerry hat' (hard round hat)
catsup: ketchup

F3. handkerchiefs halfpenny

F4. VI.B.2.64:: 'googla = water (to drink) pluplu = water wash' (Jespersen, *Language* VIII.7: a child invents different words for different waters)

F5. *Po* szewc: shoemaker bloughs: bluffs sewed him the blouse & breeches
braces *Po* chory: sick *It* brache: breeches
peashooter Paul Suter: Zurich friend of J

Chapelizod section of Thom's *D Directory

D motto: Obedientia civium urbis felicitas (Citizens'
buxomness of the dahlias Obedience Is City's Happiness)
box hedge home Star & Garter: common pub name
Hodge: any rustic *I* linn: pool
Newcastle-under-Lyme, England (074.13–19)
3 castles on D coat of arms *It* riva: bank, shore
not a bit of it! *s Dies Irae* awry
Persse O'Reilly

Da by: town
May Oblong: D prostitute
zoo snore
Cz snu: dream
G Schein

assails *Gr* methysos: drunk
answers (methylated spirit in lamps)
bar below there Bedevere: King Arthur's butler;
barrel knight of the Round Table
Wace (Arthurian): 'the Table Round' *AngI ph* top of the morning
(past breakfast room & toilet)
Sir John Harington: *The Metamorphosis of Ajax* (describes
water closet)
(children's study upstairs) *G* Sturz: fall

Moore: *s* Here We Dwell, in Homeliest Bowers (Love & the
Novice) [Cean Dubh Delish]
SwG nigelnagelneu: brand new

It rifocillare: cheer up, revive

Doldor: a high part of Zurich (physics)

(family portraits) prehistoric
antithesis
St Athanasius:
opponent of Arius
Cambridge Univ. Sl wrangler: Maths Tripos student

face to face respecting: facing *Gr* panhysterikos: all-womb-suffering
Mutt *It* altrettanto: *It* bancarotta: bankruptcy
G mit just as much ABC
Jeff

☍ Catalaunian Fields, A.D. 451: Attila & Ostrogoths
temporarily defeated by Aetius & Visigoths
check & gambit in chess
booze-up
s Sweet Genevieve
St Genevieve's military advice saved Paris from Attila
fickle
Sw flicka: girl
F frondeur: scoffer
oft teased
eftest (Shakes.): *G* Aufzieher: *G* aufziehen: to tease
ready, convenient educator, tutor; scoffer
Sw flicka: girl *G* unterdrückt:
flapper: modish girl of 1920s repressed (Freud)

F1. (ref. from D motto)
F2. Chapelizod section of Thom's lists Thomas Halpin & then 'Hands, G., Martin's-row'
Glens of Antrim, N. Ir.
Swords, town, Co. D
F3. RAVEN/DOVE *s* Cean Dubh Delish (air to Moore melody in .13; means 'dearest dark-head')

lote: lotus
Gr mimos: mimic
Maida Vale, London mimetic
Mimosa: genus including Sensitive Plant
C.K. Ogden & I.A. Richards: *The Meaning of Meaning* *G* Meinung: opinion
G Minne: love *I* meann, minne: stuttering *s* The Young May
Gr elpis: hope graces speer: make peer Moon
ALP enquiries *L* sperare: to hope
Du thee: tea *Da* kongen: the king *Da* hus: house
nr 'The king was in his counting-house' *Sl* canteen: inn
knaves Decimus Magnus Ausonius, poet *L* audacior:
L Ausonius: Italian bolder
AngI gillie: lad, servant Λ ⊏ ⊏ *It* storiella: story, fib
I gall: foreigner *G* Ringel(ringel)reihen: Ring-a-ring o'roses (*cg*)
sung young *G* entsprechend: corresponding
James Millington: *English as She Is Spoke* (edited unspoken
version of a *Port*/Eng. phrasebook gestures platonically
by a man who knew almost no Eng.) nods no note yes
Sl gladrags: fancy clothes

called
G Cis: C sharp Pluto & Proserpine spells peace

Belisha beacon: traffic crossing sign

(rainbow colours) *Arch* grene: green *G* wider: against
orange (anagram)
wander flags sect
s 'The green isle of Erin, It beckons me yonder' sept: Ir. clan
domicile *L* septem: 7
do-mi-so: CEG, common chord
John 1:14: 'the Word was made flesh'
indigo
G Selbstlaut: vowel congenor: member of same
class as another
St Adamnán: Ir. biographer
of St Colmcille Adamman: an
I Émhe: Eve Ossian (pron. 'Usheen') artificial language
vowels: A, E, I, O, U; semivowels Y & W *N* Ygg: Odin
I agus: and *G* mag: may
& wife *G* Weib *G* O Wehoweh: oh dear! (Uwayoei = 5 vowels
shibboleth (Judg 12:6) & 2 semi-vowels)

Venus Moon
L vetus: old, aged *F Sl* mou: human body
Great Bear Virgo *L* nova: new nova (astronomy): new star
(constellation) *L* veto: I forbid
nereids: sea nymphs
Nereus: old name of constellation Eridanus

L una unica: one only
elm/stone *Arch* unshent: uninjured,
unharmed

Kristelig Forening
for Unge Kvinder:
the Danish Y.W.C.A. rambler rose

May bee *G* Maiblume: mayflower
Du Mei: May

F1. Ross Point close to Inishmacsaint (island in Lough Erne)
F2. Manneken-Pis: statue in Brussels of a child urinating
F3. sinfully simply desperate *F* d'esprit
F4. *I* anama: souls Jespersen: *Language* VIII.8: 'baby . . . babbles . . . ' "amama" . . . or "apapa" . . .
F5. father-in-law Adamnán's law provided heavy penalties for killing women or "ababab" '
s The Mermaid: 'I care more for my pottles & my kets' kettles & pots P/K
F6. all aboard Tara: ancient capital of Ireland copycat dog
Mt Ararat, where Noah's Ark landed look slippy!

F fleur floor

G anlocken: to allure (032.03) Sechseläuten: Zurich spring festival

s The Chimes of Love Are Pealing

Angelus: 'et concepit de Spiritu Sancto' ('& she conceived of the Holy Ghost')

(196.02) Conchita: temptress in Louy's *La femme & le pantin*

Amaryllis: a country-girl in Theocritus & Virgil

Senta: virgin; heroine of *The Flying Dutchman*

Sl (1927) 'it': sex appeal (Clara Bow)

Sl it: cunt

pleasure/business

Shem & Shaun

demijohns *L* geminus: twin

arithmetic Browne & Nolan: D booksellers & publishers

Irish *cg* 'Will you be my man?' 'Yes.' Will you carry my can?' 'Yes.' Will you fight the fairies?' 'Yes.' (Children then blow in one another's faces.)

stupid

Mookse Gripes groose: shiver Ondt (414.20)

mugwump: person holding himself superior to party views

F faire une grande gaffe: put one's foot in it

Gracehoper (414.21)

F tout petit peu *F* je m'en fiche fichu: sort of light shawl

It solfa: music *Alice in Wonderland* X: 'Soup of the evening, beautiful soup'

bodikin: diminutive body Thimble Theatre: U.S. comic strip (Popeye)

(to her, inborn) *It* intendere: to understand

herringbone

Alma Mater: school, regarded as 'fostermother'

Mather, D auctioneer

Charles-Pierre Girault: *Grammaire des Grammaires* (digest of grammatical opinion)

masculine, feminine or neuter

about Abaddon: angel of the bottomless pit must proceed prosody 3rd person of Holy Trinity procedes

second person (you)

ablative Oblate Fathers, D

L ob: for (dative case)

ablative absolute: Latin grammatical construction

L gramma: a writing, drawing, letter of the alphabet

imperative mood

reflexive verbs

Ir. Gavelkind: custom by which land, on owner's death, went into common use

deaf as your arse

G Potz tausend! (expletive)

It grappa: Italian 'uisce beatha' made of grape

G Dial hor emal uff: stop it! *Gr* hêdonê: pleasure dregs

G was die Leute sagen: what the people say analectual: fragmented

pickmeup

intellectual giant

F1. tell it

F3. jungle C.G. Jung young girl

F4. halfway house (half-knitted) lovers

F6. 'French Devil': Jean Bart, C17 privateer *G* frech: insolent red herring (river)

on entering confessional: 'Bless me, father, for I have sinned' *AngI* Lochlann: Scandinavian

Sl leap: fuck

syntax *G* dunkel: dark subjunctive (mood of verb)
subway junctions *L* subjunctiones: subjoinings
F pluriel
prurient perfect (tense)
hairiest chaperone *G* plaudern: gossip *L* plaudo: I clap
aorist: grammatical term denoting certain forms of verbs
petticoats *L* haec genua omnia: all those knees
ME anent: concerning *L* haec genera omnia: all such things
(future perfect) case (grammar)

Paul/Peter preterite patriot
Peter Wright published in '20s a scandalous book on Parnell, Gladstone &c.
tense (grammar)
accusative case
wallflowered geraniums *Sl* better half: spouse
gerundium (Latin grammar)
year or so It's a wise child

wilkin: ram

predicate
predictable
accent
accidence (grammar)

Cant fambles: hands

Ares: Greek war-god
Sts Boris & Gleb of 10 depicted on Russian icons alpha, beta, gamma, zeta, omega
Boreas: Greek god of N. wind Ganymede: cupbearer to Zeus
Hamlet III.1.63: 'To be or not to be, that is the question'
almightiest *Gr* ho megistos: very great
L satis: enough *G* Werbung: wooing *Da* jeg: I *F* je suis
L (abbr) verbum sap.: a word is enough to the wise
(I thought you were a gentleman. If you are, I'm a queen)
Sl quean: whore
Andante amoroso (music)
Dante *Da* kukkuk: cuckoo
It umoroso: full of humours
(metronome) (186.33) beggar maid

patriarch
Petrarch
F où (qu') est la bonne Pauline?
Gr ouk elabon polin: they did not capture a city
Inferno V.121–3: 'The bitterest woe of woes Is to remember in our wretchedness Old happy times; and this thy Doctor knows'
s The Barley Corn: 'O rum it is the comicalest thing How it tickles . . .' common noun (grammar)
pash: strike *Gr* ploutos: wealth pauper
have a pash for: love
egg & spoon race

final causes Lindley Murray: *Grammar of the English Language*
clothes
present participle (grammar)

deponent verbs orthodoxy indicative (mood of verb)
L hortatrix: she that incites hortative (mood of verb)

F1. W.H. Mallock: *Is Life Worth Living?*
F2. A. Mackirdy & W. N. Willis, *The White Slave Market*, quotes a 'missus': 'What are you going to do—follow suit, reneague, or go to the pack?' René Descartes
F3. *nr* 'Arithmetic it makes me sick' &c. fractions menstruation mensuration: act of measuring
F4. C6 Ir. lay schools were described in the *Small Primer* Lewis & Short: *Latin Dictionary* black & white witchcraft

conditional tenses (grammar)
future tense
pr Handsome is who handsome does
classical poetry scanned by quantity (long & short syllables)
rather than accents (stressed & unstressed) joking *L* oratio obliqua:
yoking (of subjects„ in grammar) indirect speech
passed *R* brat: brother *I* a leanbh: child (voc.)

(men choosing mates)
stick
G Leben: life *L* sollicitor: I am being seduced
lemon squash *Arab* lebban: milk apprentice
G Quatsch: nonsense

G aufgewachsen: grown up

Irish Distressed Ladies' Fund (for cases of nonpayment of rent)

Humphreystown House nr Poulaphouca

attack first, questions after
queck: to quack *L* quicquid: whatever
Gen 3:1: 'the serpent was more *G* Schlange: slander
hiss history subtil' snake
Persse O'Reilly *Her* vert: green *Her* embowed:
F oreilles bent
Her proper: in natural colour

Alice in Wonderland *s* Amo, Amas, I Love a Lass
(Paradise) little looker
Through the Looking-Glass *Du* lokker: tempter
Alice was based on Lewis Carroll's friend Alice Liddell
misery *F* pain (i.e. Eucharist)

Euclid's multiply Mick/Nick

Nike: Greek goddess kickshaws handlebars
of victory *L* volvo: I turn *Sl* kickseys: shoes
Publius Vergilius Maro (Virgil) Moore: *s* Take Back the Virgin Page (the 'o' a long syllable)
Sortes Vergilianae: divination by opening Virgil at random
I Béarla: Eng. language

G verschwindibus: hocus-pocus (verschwinden: disappear)
L sequentur: they follow mnemonic from a Latin school
frequent book: 'For *nemo* let me never say *neminis* or
G nimm: take *G* nehmen: to take *nemine'*
nights *ph* name the day (for wedding)
C . . . O . . . D: cash on delivery
G ja *Gr* moira: fate Ireland's Punic Wars

Ulster (North) *Du* ga: go (imp.)

F2. meat teeth
VI.B.36.308: 'grits = teeth'
G lang Long Worm: a Viking ship *Sl* old gooseberry: the devil *G* Wurm

F4. description

Munster, Leinster & Connacht
Bul monastir: cloister
Monastir: city, Yugoslavia (South)
Lenin, Star of Russia
(East) (West)
Clio: muse of history
Pascal: *Pensées* II.162: 'Cleopatra's nose: had it been shorter the whole face of the earth would have changed'

The 5 Bloods of Ireland: O'Neil, O'Connor, O'Brien, O'Lochlan, McMurrough
G mitsamt: together with (Ass) *L* appono: I lay by appendage
Sir Julius Caesar: Eng. judge
R da: yes *Da* gamle: old
Da torsk: cod
taskmaster *Da* mester: master
triumvirate
VI.C.2.249: 'rompers (skirt)'
Octavius, Lepidus & Mark Antony: triumvirate, 42–31 B.C.
L lapideus: made of stone *Gr* anthemion: little flower
Suetonius: historian & biographer of 12 Caesars

omen (Octavius would become emperor)
onus (Lepidus: weight)
obit: death (Antony's suicide)

L mutua: in return
caudle: a warm drink summer slumbering
Autumn (inverted spelling)
L trigeminus: triplet brothers
AngI coddle: type of stew *F* figure: face

harm Michael Gunn: manager of Gaiety Theatre, D
I gam: fool *It* gonna: skirt *AngI* gossoon: young lad
s O, Willie brew'd a peck o'maut: 'The cock may craw the day may daw' (014.35) Heber & Heremon: legendary progenitors of Ir. race

It eroico: heroic
It furioso: furious
Ariosto: *Orlando Furioso*
Giordano Bruno of Nola: *Gli Eroici Furori*
pr No man is a hero to his valet
Moore: *s* The Valley Lay Smiling Before Me [The Pretty Maid Milking her Cow]

L nolens volens: willing or unwilling, willy-nilly brewed *F* pensées
Bruno brume: fog split infinitive (grammar)
It brune: black-haired women

'As it was in the beginning, is now, & ever shall be' (*Gloria Patri*)
G Erdapfel: potato (snake)
E . . . C . . . H
Hail Mary *Heb* Hawah: Eve

the higher up the monkey goes the more

nr 'This is the man all tattered & torn, That kissed the maiden all forlorn, That milked the cow with the crumpled horn, That tossed the dog, That worried the cat, That killed the rat, That ate the malt, That lay in the house that Jack built'
G wir wissen: we know

Christ Charley

Sir Hugh Gough (statue in Phoenix Park) won battle whereby England gained the Punjab why it is

---

F1. VI.B.45.129: '32 = teeth/1 = moon/sixerords point hole' *Ar* vecerord: the sixth (vec = 6), hence 23 + 1 + 16 = 40
F2. *nr* 1, 2, 3, 4, Mary's at the Kitchen Door
F3. compulsory upholstery
F4. *Sl* understandings: legs *It* sostituto: substitute compliment
Gr gymnos: naked genuflect compline: last service of day
F5. appreciate *F* plisser: pleat
F charmeuse

G fromm: pious
who it's from *G* wir glauben: we believe
G hinter Leda was seduced by Zeus as a swan
nr 'Mary, Mary, Quite Contrary, how does your garden grow?'

'World without end' (*Gloria Patri*)
Browning: *Pippa Passes* *L* mamma manet: mother remains where what's
G Wut: rage (penises) what

(breasts, *U*.753) *Sl* totties: girls

F Sl pige pas: I don't understand daylight
combat *s* Come, Lasses & Lads

panoptical: pertaining to everything at once
purview: scope of a scheme, &c.
s Sally in Our Alley man-o'-war Minotaurs
mini-wars (270.30–1) manoeuvres
actions
⚔ Actium (Octavius v. Mark Antony), 31 B.C.
flowers A.B.C.

notes: B, C, A, D absent-minded

step at ease mess

misadventure jolly well right

Janus: Italian deity with 2 faces *G* blitzen
Holy Jaysus!
G Kopf Hengest & Horsa: brothers, led Saxon invasion of England
OE hengest: horse
Swift: *A Tale of a Tub*

Swift's Houyhnhnms H . . . C . . . E
hinny: offspring of stallion & she-ass
one, two, three

Seidlitz powder: a laxative understood
stuttered
since horse measured in hands

templates (004.22) (horses put heads in tub)
timepiece
pace: by leave of

G Herrn J's father was secretary of United Liberal Club in D during 1880 general election. The Liberal candidates, Maurice Brookes & Dr Robert Dyer Lyons, ousted Sir Arthur Guinness & James Stirling (004.21–4)
counted-outs (losers)
famous home brew

F gageure: wager against
F guerre bears & bulls: speculators for falls & rises, respectively, on Stock Exchange
Wellington: 'Up, guards, & at them'
hoplite: heavily armed foot soldier of ancient Greece
Staffordshire Hertfordshire Buckinghamshire Berkshire
varsal: universal

F1. *s* The Goat: '"What's that, ma'm?", says I'

F3. *r* Lethe litmus
F4. shellshock *G* Stimme: voice
Swift: 'Ppt'

s An Páistín Fionn: 'Cara mo chroídhe mo pháistín fionn' (friend of my heart, my fairhaired maid)
bosom friend

'Family hold back': jocular command to leave enough food for guests

Caudine Forks (prov.): a trap (from mt gorges where legions captured)
⚔ Cannae: legions destroyed by Hannibal: baskets filled with rings belonging to slain

(presents from Δ)
Napper Tandy: United Irishman (1740–1803)
Napoleon

(045.05–06)

L opprimor: I am oppressed *L* opima: rich

G heil rainbow, 7 colours, symbol of peace
Gr heptarchê: magistracy of one-seventh
L lex: law *L* nex: violent death
Mick, Nick & the Maggies (219.18–19)
G was ist das *G* wo: where
Lincoln: Gettysburg Address: 'government of the people by the people for the people'
L fas est: it is lawful
'Take away these baubles' (Cromwell ordering dissolution of Rump Parliament)
s Pack Up Your Troubles in Your Old Kit Bag
wampum used as currency
s Old Uncle Ned: 'Then lay down the shovel & the hoe, Hang up the fiddle & the bow, No more hard work for poor old Ned, He's gone where the good niggers go'
Merope: mother of Daedalus
Da ned: down Anna Liffey shoplifter

G nie never another *Sl* skidoo: make off
r Nièvre *r* Nore
you & I & I & you

Sl goy: gentile

pr Never buy a pig in a poke

a whole

Gr hekatoendeka: 111 *Da* mange: many mumbo jumbo jujubes
Hecate: Greek moon-goddess
Da mange tak: many thanks
Mutt & Jeff: U.S. comic strip
Sp muchas gracias *G* Freispruch: acquittal, absolution
AngI barcelona: silk neckcloth
Dial gar: make Anna Livia
□ basket/letter/museum *I* gair: laugh
G Hintergrund: background
G Laub: foliage
laughing

VI.B.2.40: 'trees laugh at old wind's joke'
Sl blowharding: boasting heliotrope

G Winker: signal
Marquis of Wellesley: lord-lieutenant of Ireland, Wellington's brother
emperor
Apollyon: fiend in *Pilgrim's Progress*, associated with Napoleon during Nap. wars
(008.21)
pr A nod is as good as a wink to a blind horse
Sp huir: escape *L* tricuspis: having 3 points
G Haube: bonnet

F1. A. Mackirdy & W.N. Willis: *The White Slave Market*, quotes a 'missus': 'They sky-pilots . . . don't own creation . . . I'll shake eternity to get even with you'
F3. *G* Huhn: hen
F4. Thom's 1922, p. 798 (advert): 'Pure Altar Wine Sweet, Medium & Dry'
F5. penny babies: type of sweet
F6. very grateful. Many thanks Morton Prince: *The Dissociation of a Personality* (see 280.22), quotes (p. 481) a letter from Christine Beauchamp in which her secondary personality added comment: 'Nobody asked you, Sir, she said' (parody of *nr* 'Where are you going, my pretty maid . . . My face is my fortune, sir, she said')
F7.
F8. (interpretations of baby sound 'da':) *R* da: yes; *We* tad: father; *I* an t-athair: the father

HCE coverchief: kerchief

s The Man That Broke the Bank at Monte Carlo
Mont St Jean: name Eng. army gave to Waterloo, from village which Napoleon thought the key to Wellington's position

Racine: *Les Plaideurs* I.1.15: 'point d'argent, point de Suisse' (referring to Swiss soldiers)

Dial syne: since then
Dathi: last pagan king of Ireland, killed by lightning while crossing Alps

Jespersen: *Language* IX.1: 'Sweet. In 1882 he reproaches Paul'
Matterhorn (Alps)

ECH *F* entre
Du donder: thunder
entre-chat: dance step
hobnob: chat, gossip
Hannibal, son of Hamilcar (crossed Alps)
ph shiver my timbers!
AngI 'more power to your elbow' (encouragement)

Ibsen: *The Master Builder* (defies God from tower)
Timothy: companion of Paul
barmbrack: Ir. speckled cake
1132

street

becoming *Du* toekomende: future (adj.)
sempiternal *L* semper: always
speel: ascend *Du* speel: play
datepalm *Phoenix dactylifera*

tints
calends: 1st of the month
eleven hundred & thirty-two

moreover
more than ever
elfshot: disease produced by evil spirits
(top of tree)
(tree vandalised by children from house)

purdah: veil, curtain, esp. to screen women from sight of men, in harem
(wondering . . . at . . . what the demons . . . they were sliding along)

as Shakespeare might put it *Sl* pitch a fork: tell a story

nr The House That Jack Built
jerry-built house
Sp hijo de puta: son of a whore

R starik: old man
G vielgesungen: much-sung

anemone, windflower
G Windstille: calm

Dagobert: C7 king of Franks, educated at Slane; in comic song wears his trousers back to front
Clongowes Wood College, Clane, Co. Kildare
preparatory
ph put a bold face on
L puer

bridge material
s 'Brian O'Linn had no breeches to wear' &c.

F2. *Gr* gnôsis: knowledge *L* genu: knee Genoa
F3. Archibald Clavering Gunter: *Mr Potter of Texas*

pussy *It* puzzo: stink
ph I smell a rat
(hairy trousers)
A Vision 16 (psychical phenomena): 'a smell of cat's excrement'

s Brian O'Linn EHC *L* hircus: goat
Aw!, lining (of trousers)
F culotte (Brian O'Linn made sheepskin trousers, inside out; Dagobert wore trousers back to front)
(common *Gr* & *L* formulae beginning paragraphs in historical works)
ceno (pref.): recent
L pacata: peaceful
Goldsmith: *The Deserted Village:* 'Sweet Auburn' untellably Thomas Stafford: *Pacata Hibernia*
Da gammel: old
Gr diagônistikos: disposed to fight
AngI one word borrowing from another: a quarrel

Sl make: halfpenny
microscope
telescope
L tellus: earth

G standfest: steadfast Mr Stand-Fast is tempted by Mme Bubble in *Pilgrim's Progress* tapioca topical typical
sago saga *AngI* sign's on it: consequently, therefore
King Arthur sometimes called Arthur Mab Uter
Sl belly-god: a glutton (hunchback)

lady in waiting

AngI fat as a hen in the forehead = very thin

Buffalo Times, newspaper
bison bygone
Arch hight: called

opera *Ariane & Barbe-bleu* (from story by Perrault) topsy-turvy
Sl blowhard: braggart
Fairy Palace of the Quicken Trees, where Finn & his companions were rescued by Diarmaid
tavern sign 'Goat & Compasses' is derived from 'God encompasseth us'
Wellington born 1769

ME eyen: eyes
velivolant: running with full sails

Cain & Abel Shem, Ham & Japhet

It lui: he *It* lei: her *Da* hun: she

Da ham: him
Ham, son of Noah

tell me the time told

We pr Today is thine, whose to-morrow?

L qui, quae, quod: who, what
quack quack, quotes
(children learn dates parrot-fashion)
curley Λ
⊏

F1. Jespersen: *Language* VIII.5 quotes a children's secret language in which *pegennepy* = penny & *wareechepes* = breeches

F2. (head)

F4. Henry Humphreys: *The Justice of the Peace for Ireland*

F5. boy Jones: youth who habitually penetrated Buckingham Palace in 1840s Herodotus no one Noah massa's
U. 370: 'arks' (arse) (so flat)

F6. traduce: defame, (*Arch*) translate English language Dolphin's barn: district of D
L ad usum Delphini: for the use of the Dauphin (the Delphin classics for schools)

(hear)

bead-roll: long list (orig. of persons to be prayed for)

gladhander: one who acts cordially towards everyone

L proprius: his own

dulcarnon: dilemma; the word is derived from Arabic for '2-horned'

Λ

⊏ doves said to have no gall as Noah's burst its gall from grief

prefers

Gael *I* blas: flavour; good accent in speaking Irish

blast *I* Dubhghall: Dane

s The Jackdaw's Nest *Gloria Patri:* 'world without end'

L omnis: all

platitudes

Du schedel: skull

nutshell

Moore: *s* She Sung of Love [The Munster Mare]

Hamlet II.2.562: 'What's Hecuba to him, or he to Hecuba'

Arch hem: them Hagar: concubine of Abraham

Macbeth V.5.27: 'Out, out, brief Candle'

(evening chorus of barking dogs)

G Auch, auch, brav' Kindli: that too, good little child

ph cock on a dunghill

anend: at last *L* vespertilio: bat

unending

L-bitur: he will be . . . ed

good shepherd

gabardine

goat *I* gabhar: goat

sit with Bacchus *G* Zum Bock 'at the sign of the goat'

It becco: cuckold *F* chèvre

Da Fadervor: Pater Noster

burgoo: oatmeal porridge eaten by sailors

kids (goats, children)

L aegis: goatskin

frumenty: hulled wheat boiled in milk & seasoned

Nippon: Japan ('yellow peril')

nr Sing a Song of Sixpence: 'dainty dish' *G* lecken: to lick

Eldorado in S. Am (West)

Sl gippo: greasy gravy

s Give us good ale

hochmagandy (R. Burns): copulation

offrandes: offerings

Sp diana: reveille

F flou: hazy *It* pipistrello: bat

through what's

(bats eat objectionable flies)

s Brennan on the Moor

s Tim Finnegan's Wake Johnnie Walker whiskey slogan: 'still going strong'

noctule: largest British bat

coming on *Sl* fluffy: tipsy

to box (the) lumber up

hoodie: hooded crow

caravan

Porterstown: townland, Castleknock, D

his war

follow: accompany corpse to grave

F1. palpitations Castle Howard: famous edifice in N. of England *Sl* coward's castle: pulpit

trousers baptising maiden name hoyden: ill-bred girl

F2. oldfashioned brother raving RAVEN

Maid Marian: Robin Hood's sweetheart *s* When Johnny Comes Marching Home

F4. *F* parlez-vous Eskimo Ashkenazi: a European Jew *ph* pot calling the kettle black

Zeus reared on goat's milk on Mt Ida Ido: an artificial language cattle (moo)

F5. upholsterer Apostles' Creed cradle last

capricious apple-pie bed

F6. Swift: 'Ppt' feel (feed birds)

F7. *Alice in Wonderland* *R* lis: fox

(085.23) suit *I* ochón: alas

O'Connell imponent: that imposes impotence
lampblack
Dial muckle: much MacCool (Ir. legends of bursting-forth of rivers at burial of heroes)
funeral
Flaminian Way leads N. from Rome women
weem: underground dwelling place in Scotland
L flumen: river *I* Fianna: Finn's army
(origin of rivers)
Wellington
(helmet resembles mtn)
HF 12: 'cottonwood' Mourne Mts, Co. Down (river flows from mtn)

D motto: Obedientia civium urbis felicitas (Citizens' Obedience Is City's Happiness)
meet document number one: the Treaty
make (name used by De Valera's followers)
(pretentions to importance) Paul/Peter (election poll)
poll: head, nape of neck
(003.09–10) tipped up *F* noblesse oblige
tiptop
'As it was in the beginning, is now, & ever shall be' (*Gloria Patri*)

Hin jaj: judge
daughter *F* nuit blanche: sleepless night (204.18)
Hin dāktar: doctor *I* druimin: a white-backed cow
Gautama Buddha *Da* drømme: dream sure
goddam butter *Da* hjem: home
theosophising included James Clarence Mangan: (trans.) *Dark Rosaleen* (lit.
cheese (161.12) (Liffey flows from W. Wicklow) 'The Little Black Rose')
Gr thea: goddess *F* drames: plays

(215.23) *G* sein: being
Hin bap: father
Malory: 'Some men say yet that King Arthur is not dead . . . I will not say it shall not be so'
Arthur's coming *G* Herbst: autumn, harvest
L alter . . . alter: the one . . . the other
I Baile Atha Cliath: D *I* blath: flower
Arthur's last battle against Saxons took place 'in the country around Castra Legionum (City of the Legions): Roman fortress at Bath'
Caerleon-upon-Usk (site of Arthur's court)
Layamon: *Brut:* 'ever yet the Britons look for Arthur's coming'
down eric: blood fine for murder of an Irishman Erin *I* abú: to victory!

s Phil the Fluter's Ball: 'Then all joined in wid the greatest joviality, Covering the buckle & the shuffle, & the cut, Jigs were danced, of the very finest quality, But the widda bet the company at "handeling the fut"' (111.27–35)
L pondus: weight
avoirdupois

F1. milk & honey (Exod 3:8 &c.) (085.23)
embalm

F2. *The Rape of Lucrece* toga *Sl* toggery: clothes
F3. Moore: *s* The Minstrel Boy: 'Warrior-Bard' bold
F4 (rainbow colours) *AngI* roe: red (William of Orange) *I* buidhe: yellow *I* gorm: blue indigo & violet
Macaulay: *Lays of Ancient Rome*
F5. stained glass Stanislaus Joyce surely milt: semen *ph* butter wouldn't melt in his mouth
dugs duck trousers
F6. *I* tuigeann tú?: do you understand? *It* sant: saint
F7. Moore: *s* O, Could We Do with This World of Ours [Basket of Oysters] fenian
Red Bank oyster restaurant, D

gobbet: lump of food gibbet
ph dodge the column: evade one's responsibilities
s Phil the Fluter's Ball: 'Ye've got to pay the piper when he toothers on the flute'
scribes
(illuminated MSS)
L circum: around CEH encomium: panegyric
torture of pitch cap minium: vermilion *L* inluminatus: illuminated
Improperia ('reproaches') in Easter liturgy 'pansy' der. from *F* pensée
L tunc: then
cg Pussy in the corner
(for ⊣, who has to write letter)
beware *It* fanciulla: young girl *L* incipit intermissio: intermission begins
G Beweise: proofs
willow, symbol of grief

St Colman, disciple of St Patrick, supposedly died at ringing of vesper bell
Fabius Maximus: Roman dictator
Luke 1:38: 'Behold the handmaid of the Lord'

L minimus: smallest

(Noun is name of a person, place or thing)

J.M. Barrie: *Dear Brutus*
Julius Caesar III.2.75: 'lend me your ears'
s '3 men, 2 men, 1 man & his dog Went to mow a meadow'

nr Rockabye, Baby *I* dún: fort
nr 'Humpty Dumpty sat on a wall'

Browning: *How They Brought the Good News from Ghent to Aix*
letters today from any people
son of a bitch uttermost

pussycat
postcard
wended
Tristan
footprints gill: ravine (036.35)

F1. *Sl* gezumpher: swindler *s* For He's a Jolly Good Fellow Alfred Jarry: eccentric Fr. playwright
F2. *s* 'I'm sitting on the stile, Mary' I was God bless him
bet her bottom dollar *F* cul curious (they . . . your . . . my . . . she . . . her . . . he . . . our)
Hamlet V.2.10: 'There's a divinity that shapes our ends'
F3. *It* stella: star *It* essa stessa: she herself Vanessa
Pohlmann & Co. (D), pianos
F4. Heavenly Twins (Gemini) (letters) nearly soon
F5.
pull the chain (toilet)
F6. On Her Majesty's Service (letters)
F7. turkey Tarquin the Proud, last king of Rome (in *The Rape of Lucrece*) cuckold
ECH *s* Adams & Clay *G* wegen: because of

anear
rhinestones cold
season of the year evergreen over
(summer)
what price pomp oscillation selection
osselet: little bone
Da omkring: roundabout *L* nomen est omen: name is omen
none
ph war to end war
pr All's well that ends well
'bring & buy' sales *nr* Baa, Baa, Black Sheep
athlete *I* Baile Átha Cliath (D: 'Town of Hurdle Ford')
fortress
early her sake
hearsay

F1.
brush gilded youths
lilac *Sl* Miss Laycock: cunt there's
St Cecilia: patron of song
F maladie melody
undeveloped *Da* proppe: gorge, cram sir senior
dues In Boucicault's *Arrah-na-Pogue,* Arrah's foster brother escaped from prison with help of a message
'k' in 'kiss' *L* quod erat faciendum: which was to be done she passed to him in a kiss
to get her, to lose her (conjugate verbs) *L* amare: to love *F* verbe de vie
s A Married Woman's Lament: *C* ai: to love (spine of book)
'you use me severe' *s* The Sorrow of Marriage: 'then rue' junior thrown
Pettigo: town, Co. Donegal *Univ. Coll.* Little Go: 1st B.A. exam
degree take sides *G* Seiden: silks Take silk: become a K.C. or Q.C. petticoat *Sl* plough:
Orlando du Lasso: Netherlands composer *It* lasso: weary *Univ. Coll.* ploughed: failed college fuck
L octo et viginti: eight & twenty
HF 29: 'nary a pale did they turn' *Skt* nārī: wife
(29 Feb.) *F* figurant: representing *nr* 'Sing a song of sixpence, A pocket full of rye' pigs begin to fly
29 husbands
rules of the game
Old Norse Åse: Peer Gynt's mother *Sl* trot: whore D'Oyly Carte Opera Co.
fucking arsewise (i.e. backwards) ways forwards olive oil Olive Oyl (Popeye)
vinegar *F* jupe raised *G* reizen: attract Solomon salmon salad dressing
pepper castor salt cellar *G* mit met *Sl* mustard pot: cunt between them
'the Mad Mullah': Mohammed bin Abdullah: Somali rebel, early C20 Mad Mullinx: C18 D beggar Tristan (Land's End)
Her bisse: snake erect & knotted *F* bisser: to encore
Thor's thunderbolt bolt the door Asa & Auden: names of Odin dogday *Da* dag: day
Skokholm: island off S. Wales *AngI* asteroid: meteorite druids' *I* cúil-deas: pretty-head (girl)
cool as a cucumber *Sp* cumbre: summit astride upon
clouds of incense
stage-struck afraid blancmange *G* Mensch
isabelle horse *F* ruelles rules of the road Samuel Lover: *Handy Andy* any man
s Swing Low, Sweet Chariot *s* Anacreon in Heaven: 'I'll swinge the ringleaders' (.29) father fother: cartload
betroth
Almighty God
pr Truth is stranger than fiction surplus

at night oneiric: pertaining to dreams
on air Eire

happily analyses scarce
Annaly: ancient territory in Co. Longford
sums new
L somnia: sleep

Bible bibulous
libellous history
Barbarossa: German emperor who opposed Adrian IV

Esther (Swift) Saturday afternoon Leixlip: place on
yesterday *L* lex: law *r* Liffey: name means 'salmon leap'
Anon. C19 poem: 'Or Leixlip smiling on the stream below'
(460.29) (salmon returns to native river to spawn)
month's mind: mass for person celebrated 1 month after death
Ann *L* Amati Nomen: name of beloved
she licks her (pencil)
Yiddish shikseh: young non-Jewish woman

(one 'f' in 'funeral')

shilling in coppers
shieling: rough hut on grazing land
parish soup always

Father Michael (111.15)
Finn MacCool
mark
AL . . . P
Persian cat

cakes she rubs her P (the P/Q split)
cates: bought provisions pothook: a stroke in handwriting
Vere Foster's handwriting books

how much is my trousers

Q (the P/Q split) (mother's)
curlicues
she rubs her other air

P.T.O.

hopes to soon hear

Cinderella: Prince Charming
Morton Prince: *The Dissociation of a Personality*, study of a case history, 'Christine Beauchamp', in Boston. He calls her most prominent secondary personality 'Sally' Isold(e) *It* soldi: money
heliotrope Parnell: 'When you sell, get my price'

charming

F les héros tombant seul sur la Champs de Mars (Paris): the heroes falling alone on the Champs de Mars
F jambe de marche: walking-leg

words ideal

kiss my arse she licks her other
Xs on letter (kisses)
Charlemagne pura e pia bella: religious wars of Vico's
F chêne: oak heroic age

Tree of Life (Kabbalah)

Du barnsteen: amber

Horace: *Odes* III.13.1: 'O fons Bandusiae' ('O spring of Bandusia') liquid
(111.20)

wonder (water, fire, earth, air)
Du droog: dry

It mai: never
F mais maintenant elle est venue: but now she has come

both *SwG* Wöschwib: chatterbox
ph at latter Lammas: never

Dial garth: enclosure, garden

Don Juans

Tommy Atkins
Sl totty: whore

Edgar Quinet: *Introduction à la philosophie de l'histoire de l'humanité:* 'Aujourd'hui, comme aux jours de Pline et de Columelle, la jacinthe se plaît dans les Gaules, la pervenche en Illyrie, la marguerite sur les ruines de Numance; et pendant qu'autour d'elles les villes ont changé de maitres et de nom, que plusieurs sont rentrées dans le néant, que les civilisations se sont choquées et brisées, leurs paisibles générations ont traversé les âges et se sont succédés l'une à l'autre jusqu'à nous, fraîches et riantes comme aux jours des batailles' ('Today, as in the time of Pliny & Columella, the hyacinth disports in Gaul, the periwinkle in Illyria, the daisy on the ruins of Numantia; & while around them the cities have changed masters & names, while some have ceased to exist, while the civilisations have collided with one another & smashed, their peaceful generations have passed through the ages & have come up to us, fresh & laughing as on the days of battles')

belletristic: pertaining to belles-lettres

L bellum: war
L pax: peace

L mutuo: reciprocally
Gr morphês: shape
(mutual exchange of shape)

Nietzsche: *Also Sprach Zarathustra*

margaritomancy: divination by movement of a pearl beneath an inverted pot
'jacinthe . . . pervenche . . . marguerite'
Brutus

Sortes Vergilianae: divination by opening Virgil at random
L sortes virginianae: fates of virgins

It Cassio: Cassius   trifid: 3-cleft
Cassio: Othello's lieutenant

Saxon Shilling: piece of antienlistment propaganda in D, 1905
Desdemona

It nel: in the
sexton
('Il fazzoletto' repeated by Otello in Act III of Verdi's opera)
nothing
It falso: false   *It* col: with the   *It* dal: from, by, at the
parish priest
It letto: bed   *It* fazzoletto: handkerchief   *It* lezzo: stink
L toties quoties: as often as the occasion demands   sycamore
quarry
awful silly   *Da* ærger: spite
Othello: Moor (Othello), 'sally' = willow (willow song, Desdemona), Ancient (Iago)

Julius Caesar III.2.22.: 'Not that I loved Caesar less but that I loved Rome more'   *G* Sieger: victor   *G* Ruhm: fame, glory
oxygen (comprises 50% of earth's crust; occurs in air uncompounded & in rock compounded)
occident

G Rauch: smoke   Kierkegaard: *Enten-Eller* (*Either/Or*)

F1. fossa (anatomy): cavity   native forefathers   Vercingetorix: Celtic chieftain who revolted against Caesar
L rex: king   Arc de triomphe

F2. translate   *G* geschwind: quickly   Turkish   Teague: nickname for Irishman   *PS* bog: god   boy
polish   *L* nates: backside   *G* nett's Weib: nice girl, woman   blotting paper

F3. Ignatius Donnelly: *The Great Cryptogram*
hidalgo: one of lower Spanish nobility   XYZ   (kisses)

F4. (Othello)   niggard
saying   Mick   Nicholas

Julius Caesar III.2.28: 'there is tears for his love; joy for his fortune; honour for his valour; & death for his ambition'

Arch boon: prayer *Da* begyndelse: beginning

L auspicium: watching birds for augury
L augurium: augury

L Ad Majorem Dei Gloriam: For the Greater Glory of God (Jesuit motto). At Belvedere, pupils put letters A.M.D.G. at beginnings of essays
G flink: quick freck: quick Sterne
Swift Franky

HF 22: 'sure-enough queens' because
arithmetic *HF* 8: 'bekase'

fingers *ph* giving him what for fight
figures five (fingers)

truckers'
trochee, dactyl, spondee (metrical feet)
Gr daktylos: finger

Sl boko: nose

(hand) thumb

(index finger)

(ring finger)

felt

left right lovetried cardinals HEC
L numen: divine will eminence (cardinal numbers)
Cardinal Newman enema: substance HEC Cardinal Manning
(Viconian (birth) injected into rectum marriage (Archbishop
cycle) HEC epulentic: Cardinal Wiseman of Westminster)
epileptic (?death) *G* weiss
HEC O.K. (cardinal points: 4 points of compass)
Cardinal MacCabe (archbishop of D)
Ki huja: argument *Ki* kuja: come

Gr panoplos: fully armed
peregrine: exotic, foreign
Sl piffle: nonsense

Rota: supreme court of R.C. Church
rote *Da* Fanden: Devil cataclysm first to last
John Fander: *A Full Catechism of the Catholic Religion,* 1863
Before C18 calendar reform, new year began in March
Decemvirs: council or ruling body of 10
thumbs down (gesture) = no alday: everyday

's true as you're there while
strue: destroy
Om = Aum (Brahmanic sacred syllable)
numerous

pippive	15+
poopive	25
Niall Dhu	-2
Foughty Unn	41
Enoch Thortig	31
endso one	1
	111

F1. bluebells widow's weeds
F2. *L* Laus Deo Semper: Praise to God forever. At Belvedere, pupils put L.D.S. at ends of essays
F3. *s* Where, O Where Has My Little Dog Gone?
F4. Pigott & Co, music warehouse, Grafton St, D la-di-da
Lancers (dance)

Parnell: speech in Cork, 1885: 'we have never attempted to fix the *ne plus ultra* to the progress of Ireland's nationhood'
4 Ir. sees: Armagh (in Ulster), D (Eblana), Cashel, Tuam
L nec castellum tuum: not your castle
AngI cashel: stone fort

Sw en och trettio: 31 & so on
Enoch: eldest son of Cain
P/K spillikin: game in which pile of rods are picked up
pitchcap (278.L1)
L Boreas: N. wind *L* Eurus: E. or S.E. wind
plus *L* Notus: S. wind
L Zephyrus: W. wind 1,2,3,4,5 *Sl* quim: cunt
multiply 'carry one' (digit, in multiplying)
traduce: defame, (*Arch*) translate
reduced
common denominator lowest

aliquant (math): contained in another but not dividing it equally
L sex, septem, octo, novem, decem: 6, 7, 8, 9, 10

Arch rakehelly: scoundrel values
(Le Fanu: *The House by the Churchyard* 297)
29 remainder
the 39 Articles of the Church of England

(mathematical tables) introduce thunder
(convert) *It* fulmine: lightning
100 links = 1 chain 1 Norfolk wey = 40 bushels *Da* til: to
1 York tod = 28 pounds *G* Tod: death
ounces lbs *L* ad: to thousands Townsend St, D
L ad lib: at will Townsend, D mathematician
imperial gallons
several tens, several
gills (liquor) Livingston
girls
1 nail = 1/16 yard (measure for cloth)

G Donnerwetter!
G Keibe! (expletives)
G Schicksal: fate
Gr kybos: dice
put the kybosh on someone: put bad luck on them
Sl kybosh: nonsense

acres, roods & perches
ph rule of thumb all
powers
nonpareil: having no equal 3 r's: reading, writing, arithmetic
Du allemaal: all-round (scored low marks)
Euclid algebra *HF* 17: 'they wouldn't took any money'
HF 19: 'nohow' *HF* 18: 'anywheres'

Hall & Knight: mathematics textbooks *Du* aap: ape
Todhunter: mathematics textbooks *Du* baas: boss, master
agnomen: a 'to-' name (030.03) *It* incognita: unknown quantity
(symbols a, b, y, z in algebra) beat
terribly Goethe: *Hermann & Dorothea*
diarrhoea
HF 17: 'they always give me the fan-tods' (fidgets)
HF 17: 'seemed to me'
HF 18: 'I ought to told her father' *HF* 24: 'every last word'
HF 21: 'every which way' *G* Kinder
kind of
HF 27: 'pison long'

F1. Classical meaning of 'adolescence' was age between 17 & 31 12 + 28 + 40 + 31 = 111 boys & girls 'Forty Bonnets': nickname of Mrs Tommy Healy of Galway
dad

F2. *Sl* gamester: wencher *ph* road to ruin Rouen (France)
L dies: day

HCE intersecting right angles
stage Englishman royde: var. roid, rigid
parallax (angle) bisects

(diagram 293)

electricity
brickbats imbroglio
umbrella
telegraph pole highest common factor (maths)

Co. Fermanagh certain inclination
sept: Ir. clan *F* inclination
mathematical functions

Co. Monaghan something is divisible
lowest common multiple (maths) reversible
by nothing involution: raising of number to assigned power
night time involved inverted
heroic couplet *We* pell: distant, long *G* gleich: equals
John Pell: mathematician Browning: *Pippa*
octagon oxygen (infinity sign) *Passes:* 'God's in his heaven, All's
inclined right . . .'
rust (oxidation) *G* Minne: love how many combinations & permutations
coefficient: numerical, as opposed to literal, part of mathematical
It mutande: drawers term
L permutandis: things needing to be changed
surd: irrational number its cube root being extracted
thunderclap
L exstructus: built up taking 'n' as five at a time

teachers

cxiii *R* tochka: dot

different dumbbells

F beugler continuation itineration
G ur-: primitive *U*.422: 'utterance of the Word' *L* tono: I thunder
Our Exagmination round His Factification for Incamination of Work in Progress: essays on FW by 12 contemporaries of J forth
antecedents

Issy (circles on 293) Clytie: sea nymph metamorphosed into
F bicyclettes: bicycles heliotrope
consequences Aysha: wife of Lilliput
U.S. Sl trike: tricycle Mohammed Anna Livia
(vowels missing in .14) *Sl* bigwig: person of high rank or wealth

F restant N. Circular Road, D
NCR (math): number of R-item
tandem bicycle combinations possible automatic
L tandem: at length with N original items Ottoman: Turk
Turko-Indian (rainbow colours)
turquoise indigo
giddy

L viridis: green *L* fulvus: reddish-yellow
L or: gold

F1. Henry Dudeny: puzzle expert *Sl* poll: head
F2. Charles Tottenham rode 60 miles & entered Parliament in his boots to vote against government. 'Tottenham in his boots' was long after a toast in D
F3. halfpenny hackney Richview Press, D *AngI* massach: person with large
F4. Brian Boru *The Apocalypse of Baruch* s Master McGrath buttocks
Victoria Palace Hotel, Hjalmar Ekdal: character in *The Wild Duck* *Da* kjaer: dear
Paris, where J lived, 1923–4 wedlock Lona Hessel: character in *The Pillars of Society*
F5. (099.13) Giant's Causeway, N. Ireland

G Lenz: spring HCE happy civic order
Lancelot epicyclic
G Erde: earth outrageously violated Merlin
order violet
table-turning *s* Here We Go Gathering Nuts in May St Zita: patron
Round Table (Arthur) *Sw* knut: knot of servants
G hier & dort: here & there *Sl* yegg: travelling burglar

middle

hodgepodge Tom, Dick & Harry

BLM, means 'they & their wives run to their house'

higgledy piggledy

Cincinnatus (030.13)
Cincinnati, Ohio

cat & dog exarch: bishop next in rank to
patriarch x = unknown quantity
simultaneously be hend: comely
G Himmel Hamilton (300.27–8) hand head
G erst first last man *Da* mand: man

G Uhu: owl last first

Le Fanu: *The House by the Churchyard* 155 (men carrying sedan
chair) 'the two-legged ponies, as Toole called them'
donkeys (399.29)

Sl gink: fellow
Adam & Eve
King Arthur
Arthur Guinness
nr Humpty Dumpty:
'All the king's horses &
all the king's men'
Guinevere
Evergreen Touring
Company (032.29)

MPM (math): number of M-item permutations rainbow pantomime
possible with M original items pandemonium-
equivalent *HF* 15: 'Dog my cats ef I didn' hear sumf'n'
L aqua *F* lavant
Fi kaksitoista: 12
HF 14: 'Well, now, I be ding-busted' *HF* 15: 'does tire a body like
Fi yksitoista: 11 *Fi* kymmenen: 10 *Fi* yhdeksän: 9 everything'

Fi kahdeksan: 8 *Fi* seitsemän: 7 *Fi* kuusi: 6

Fi viisi: 5 *Fi* neljä: 4 *Fi* kolme: 3 *Fi* kaksi: 2

Sp nombre: name
F nom de nom!
F nombres
barbarians
ballbearings

Fi yksi: 1 amalgamated caravanserai: Eastern inn
camels where caravans put up
Finnish twelve factorial (12 × 11 × . . . 1) = 479,001,600
Fi helvetti: hell in other words
(5 - 1 = 4) (2 + 5 × 1 = 7)

([5 × 2] - 1 = 9) (0) (0) (1) *F* mille: thousand
(millions)
(500 + [2 × 2 × 5 × 5] = 600) *I* Baile Átha Cliath

survey purview fractions
preview serve you fashionable
Iris: Greek rainbow-goddess evening binomials
I iris: record, report *Dubliners:* 'Eveline' by no means
comprehended
Yeats: *A Vision* 143: 'as inaccessible as God or thou'
bygone days The 5 axioms & the 5 postulates in Euclid's *Elements of Geometry*

F1. trilby: kind of soft felt hat titbits
F2. Society for the Prevention of Cruelty to Children protection
F3. purty (pretty) forty score *Angl* rossy: impudent girl diversion L/R
VI.B.45.133: 'Rurik 800 wh' (whores) Rurik: Viking settler in Novgorod (309.10)
F4. boneshaker: old bicycle freewheeling Merrion Square, D
(squaring the circle)
F5. *A Vision* 177: 'I think that in Asia it might not be difficult to discover examples at least of Phases 26, 27, & 28'; 151: Phase 20 'The Concrete Man'
abstract 4 quarters of lunation
face
F6. tomato—red marmalade—orange quince—yellow salad—green (rainbow colours)
indigo blue violet violin

algebra
neuralgic brawn
chaos (anagram)
Gr hepta: 7 (letters)
please to lick one and turn over (.18)
Tetragrammaton: word of 4 letters, spec. Hebrew name of God
begad
H . . . C . . . E
primary tincture: term used in Yeats' *A Vision* for objective quality at climax in Phase 1
Bagdad (Arabic numerals)

A . . . L . . . P
Medes & Persians (Dan 6:28)
L lustrale principium: beginning connected with purification
Comic Cuts: Victorian children's comic; included 'Casey's Court'
serious exercises
Xerxes: king of Persia
John Casey: *Sequel to Euclid*
Frost: *Treatise on Solid Geometry*
two & thirty
Hickey's: 2nd-hand booksellers, D (Bachelor's Walk)
VPH (284.F4) Victoria Palace Hotel, Paris, where J lived, 1923–4
Wellington Bridge (Metal Bridge) over Liffey, leads to Bachelor's Walk
(shuffle cards)

bid adieu
F atout: trump card
cardinals (282.20)

deal (cards)
I rad mo chroidhe: kick of my HEART
It rosse: red
pigs in clover: game
red & black suits of cards
Cullinan DIAMONDS
bagpipes
SPADES (*F* pique, i.e. pike)
CLUBS (*F* trèfle, i.e. clover)
s 'Dear harp of my country . . . farewell to thy numbers'

back numbers (algebra to replace arithmetic)
Euclid: *Elements,* proposition 1: 'Problem: To describe an equilateral triangle on a given finite straight line'
for it
please
Plato
G erst
the first
L aqua
equilateral triangle
littoral: on the shore
A . . . PL
problem
G Probe: proof
answer
Bass's ale (red triangle on bottle)
G drei
(thumb in his mouth)
pride bride
Mullingar Inn, Chapelizod
I an t-athair: the father
It tizzo: brand
ingenuous: free born
'In the name of the Father, & of the Son, & of the Holy Ghost' (blessing)
libertine: freed man
mathematical
tripos
be it so

N nei: no
L num: interrogative particle expecting negative response
Gr adelphos: brother
L prope: near
L procul: far off
no
I can't, can you?
L nonne: not?

yes
no

ph easy as kissing hands
vice versa
Ham, son of Noah
F Langue d'Oc (South)
F Sem: Shem
all
Euclid: *The Elements of Geometry*
F oui
me
F Langue d'oil (North)
F jument: mare
Sl Mudson: Adam
O glory

F1. Romulus & Remus rhomb rebus *pr* Rome was not built in a day
F2. Goldsmith: *The Traveller* *F* trouver
F3. Goldsmith: *The Deserted Village*

F5. putting a spoonful of sugar into a saucepan of chocolate hotpot

virtuoso   *L* olorum: of swans   O Lord!   devil
(more virtuous brother)   D.V.: Deo volente (God willing)
Du gans: goose
nr 'Goosey goosey gander'
forgiving

devil
r Deva
Euclid: 'There is no royal road to Geometry'   mother   *G* Mut: courage
s The Rocky Road to Dublin   Mut: Egyptian goddess
PS bog: god   *G* Bach: brook

washerwoman (I.8)   Matt 15:11: 'but that which cometh out of the mouth, this defileth
work   a man'   Anna Liffey
worst   *L* amnium instar: image of rivers
OE wyrd: fate

ALP   Howth
hold
bearings   prime
(points A & L on 293)
Naut box the compass: go completely round (compasses needed for construction on 293)   I can
Abel   not   Seth: 3rd son of Adam & Eve
mix   Pistany: Czech spa noted for mud packs

alpha   *I* mún: urine   A
Isle of Man   Mud Island, D
L bene: well   all in apple-pie order (complete order)
pineapple
R odr: bed (applepie bed)

Da husk: remember!   In Yeats' *A Vision,* 'husk' & 'spirit' are 2 of the 4 Principles of man's body
'Swift, prince of triflers'
Berkeley   Balbus: Roman who tried to build wall in Gaul (*Portrait* I)

Exod 16:3: 'Would to God we had died by the hand of the Lord, in the land of Egypt, when we sat by the flesh pots' (*sedentes super ollas carnium*)

L (translation): 'Come without delay, ye men of old, while a small piece of second-grade imperial papyrus, concerning those to be born later, is exhibited with more propriety in the Roman tongue of the dead. Let us, seated joyfully on fleshpots & beholding in fact the site of Paris whence such great human progeny is to arise, turn over in our minds that most ancient wisdom of both the priests Giordano & Giambattista: the fact that the whole of the river flows safely, with a clear stream, & that those things which were to have been on the bank would later be in the bed; finally, that everything recognises itself through something opposite & that the stream is embraced by rival banks'

take   Mick
currant cake
courage   *D Annals,* 1622: 'A university opened in Back-lane for the education of Roman Catholics'
Papal Zouaves   *It Dial* pisdrol: boy   bread & butter
suave pupils

F1. *nr* 'Will you walk into my parlour?, said the spider to the fly'

F3. *L* canorus: melodious   speech from the dock
s Ireland, Boys, Hurrah!: 'Deep in Canadian woods we've met'

F4. Basque, Finnish, Hungarian: European languages not Indo-European   Tintagel (Cornish)   *I* Teanga: language
pemmican: condensed food   goulash
F quiche: egg & cheese flan

nr 'A dillar, a dollar, a 10 o'clock scholar' changing *L* vice versa

F bons mots themes troubadours trope: figurative expression
Sl mott: girl schemes trapdoors
doublecrossing (305.L1)

content
L cunctans: delaying
HF 10: 'he druther see the new moon' XYZ *Da* ned: down
HF 11: 'Please to don't poke fun'
s Ole Man River: 'he don't say nothing' ordinal numbers *L* ungula: nail
(counting on fingers) uncles
L.F. Sauvé: *Proverbes & dictons de la Basse-Bretagne*, no. 156: 'Noed fait avec la langue ne se défait point avec les dents' ('Knot made with the tongue can't be undone with the teeth')
ph as long as it's broad

Finnish facts about *AngI* shee: fairy first *Sp* segundo: second
Kitty O'Shea *G* Faust: fist
(married Parnell) *s* It Is a Charming Girl I Love furthermore
occident barring accidents *It* barocco: awkward
fifthly Oxmantown: part of N. D paroxytone: having acute accent on penultimate syllable
oxytone: having acute accent on last syllable
proparoxytone: having acute accent on antepenultimate syllable *G* Hexenschuss: 'witches' shot': stabbing pain at onset of acute lumbago
hope to hell
fact Ireland's
Tristan, Patrick & Strongbow all landed in Leinster
David & Jonathan Tristan & Patrick both came twice to Ir.
Sir Thomas Lipton repeatedly failed to win America Cup with various yachts, all named 'Shamrock'
Strongbow: leader of Anglo-Normans who invaded Ireland. He married Eva, daughter of Diarmaid MacMurchadha *F* soute: ship's storeroom soutane
suit of sails: full set of sails required for ship

Sp madera: wood P.T.: German abbr. for *praemissis titulis* (= omitting the usual titles)
Anguish, father of Isolde Old English *G* Publikum: the public
G Schnickschnack: humbug zigzags soteric: pertaining to salvation Borsalino hats (J wore one)
PS znak: sign nick-nacks satirical *AngI* barcelona: a silk neckcloth
peccaminous: full of sins Dubliners addressed Swift 'Mr Dane' (i.e. Dean)
LowL corpulenta: sins *L* corpus: body
F bottes earshot

(St Patrick's Cathedral, D) celestine: heavenly

Tristan Patrick (put off hat .18) penny halfpenny
tri- (3) hat trick (3)
L dominum nostrum: our lord (genuflect before church .20) Timbuktu
nostrum: quack remedy hymnbook 2
L cultus Galloromanus: culture of Romanized Gauls

Lord have mercy in the Land of Nod: asleep
about
G Blut *I* braim: fart bile
brain
shed

massacred In 1172, Henry II held court in a wickerwork pavillion outside D, & there Strongbow surrendered D to him
F sang
pr a hungry man, an angry man

F1. Robert Greene: *A Groatsworth of Wit Bought with a Million of Repentance*
(onions for fake tears)
F3. *pr* A mountain & a river are good neighbours
F4. Ally Sloper: character in Victorian comics sloop (ship)
G Popo: buttocks
F5. *s* Hooligan's Christmas Cake: 'There were plums & prunes & cherries, Raisins & currants & cinnamon too'
F6. creepy-crawleys *F* parlé: spoken
Peter Parley's children's books Paul (Patrick banished snakes from Ireland)
s Ehren on the Rhine
F7. respectable *I* fear-feasa: wise man, seer moustaches *Sp* muchacha: girl
forefather *AngI* gatch: affected movement

forth ph hold the fort believe s Old Folks at Home: 'Way down upon the Swanee river'
Ford of the Hurdles (D) wights ways
It prence: (poet) prince It Propaganda: R.C. society for propagation of gospel by missionaries
(papacy)
chrism: holy oil (cross)

real reality believed all sorts

C19 attempts to obtain Aesop penny post all kinds
Protestant converts in Ireland by bribery with soup Esau sold birthright for pottage (Gen 25:34)
Indies ever induce
r Indus
our people steeplechase Gr ophis: snake Ophites: C2 sect worshipping serpent as god
office worship workshop

Sundays
The Pale: English-occupied part of medieval Ireland
Palestine Cain slew Abel s There's Hair Like Wire Coming out of the Empire
Pales: Italian god of flocks & shepherds G der Erzherr: the arch-lord
Benjamin Franklin (lightning) empyrean Da sin: his
G Funken: spark Benjamin (Gen 35:18) means 'son of the right hand'
Cumhal: father of Finn carefully interlocking (underwear) G Unterlack: primer coat
comma Yeats: *A Vision* 237: 'interlocking of the gyres'
29 (O) Benjamin Franklin elected to 2nd Continental Congress, 1776
comma

burn flaming furnace
Father Furniss: *Sight of Hell*
blaze hellishly hot the at Wickerworks (288.28)
Bully Hayes: Am. pirate L hoc: this thing here
(214.18) *Inferno* V.138: 'E caddi, come corpo morto cade'
('& fell like a dead body falls')

R ostrov: island
Ostrogoths: barbarian tribe often in conflict with Roman Empire
descendants It presto: quickly, soon colon
Duchess of Shrewsbury called Swift 'Presto' s Paddy Whack
R molniya: lightning
megalomaniacs
maids G Schlange: snake Murtagh of the Leather Cloaks: Ir. high king (941)
Macbeth III.2.18: 'We have scotch'd the Snake'
Martha & Mary G Magd: maid Mediterranean Uranian
*U.*167: 'Three Purty Maids' Turanian: name applied to non-Semitic & non-Aryan Asiatic languages
Peter the Great

It disparito: disappeared Sp desterrar: to exile
Sp despertar: to awaken
ph saving your presence beverage

Boucicault: *The Shaughraun*—in this play Conn revives during his wake

(time of snake worship; age of dinosaurs) (Patrick banished snakes; Tristan killed dragon) Anne Rivière: singer
F ainée: elder

Ides of March (*Julius Caesar*)
F trouvère: troubadour L vere: truly
Rudolf Valentino Moore: s Song of Fionnuala: 'Lir's lonely daughter' (*U.*192)
It come te chiami: what's your name? It prima vista: first sight
Medieval L comes: Count (title)
Parnell, 'Uncrowned King of Ireland'

F1. say vulgar & decimal fractions

F3. It patata: potato R padat: fall

F5. Sl fox: follow stealthily
F6. pr Walls have ears Henry II: Eng. monarch during Anglo-Norman invasion of Ir.
G modeln: to modulate s Herring the King
Ahriman: supreme evil principle in Zoroastrianism

sceptre nick *AngI* shee: fairy Kitty O'Shea (married Parnell)
deception *s* What are the wild waves saying?
(is) Tristan Isolde supposedly came from Chapelizod
F La Chapelle
s Peg o' My Heart temple tomfool

F lave semicupium: hip bath
lay *L* cupiens: desiring, longing
O'Shea A.D. 432 St Patrick p.m.
arrives in Ireland
Waterbury: watch made in aleph (1st letter *Macbeth*
Waterbury, Conn. of Hebrew alphabet)
beth (2nd letter) ghimel (3rd letter) (ticking watch)

G lauschen: listen centuries
(the 3 synoptic gospels) sinecures
St John's gospel *Much Ado about Nothing* daleth (4th letter)
quartan
(the donkey) foresight

G Vorsicht: caution Doge

mid delight *G* blinken: sparkle
Da med: with
soap bubblebath *F* propre: own; clean *Sl* mitts: hands *L* tunc: then (.23)
On his 1st visit to Ireland, Tristan was cured of wounds by herbal baths prepared by Isolde
F seigneur

lovenest

F douche (2nd visit)

in no time *BLM* bymby: (used to indicate *G* wusch
future tense) *BLM* salt water: ocean
We isel: low, humble Patrick as boy tended herds for Milchu on Slemish (Mt Mish); returned to Ireland as
F alors! result of hearing 'voice of those who were near the Wood of Foclut' & landed at mouth
F chemin de fer of *r* Vartry
F chemise de fer: suit of armour waterproof *L* multa lusi: I have played much
Sarah Siddons, actress: quite Winchelsea
'Will it wash?'
U. 339: 'daughters of Clara' Diogenes lived in tub & searched with a lantern to find an honest man
(Franciscan nuns) *nr* Rub-a-dub-dub *It* diacono: deacon
G Blick: look *s* She Was Poor but She Was Honest
lampblack (114.10–11)
F s'il vous plaît *L* nunc: now *L* tunc: then *L* semper: always
F par jour *s* Kathleen Mavourneen: 'It may be for years & it may be forever'
AngI mavourneen: my darling Arklow, Co. Wicklow Co. Louth (N. of D)
plural (S. of D)
s Come, Lasses & Lads *G* Spottpreis: ridiculously low price
Dubliners: 'Grace': 'Lux upon Lux'
suborn: to bribe

G Firma: firm *Sp* lagrima: tear *L* gemitus: groan HCE
old established
G Kraft: strength *Heb* nahash: snake
von Krafft-Ebing: specialist on sexual perversion grinding & gnashing of teeth

F1. Muckross Abbey, Killarney (snakes)
F2. *nr* 'Jack & Jill went up the hill'
F3. Matthew, Mark, Luke, John (donkey)

F5. Pomeroy, town, Co. Tyrone Portobello, district of D
F6. Dutch *R* dozhd: rain took veil: became nun
R oblako: cloud *L* obloquor: speak against a person obloquy: disgrace
F7. bookie Buckley (335.13) shat Prince Potemkin: lover of Catherine the Great
Bul rusin: Russian

L unicus: one only St Ives & Land's End, Cornwall (King Mark of Cornwall)

AngI mavrone: my grief dynamite

finale Tut-ankh-amen

foot insulated insulted

The Lovely Peggy: prisonship anchored off *F* seule: alone Crampton, surgeon, planted famous

Ringsend 1798–1804 given the bird: rejected pear tree in Merrion Sq., D

Gen 3:19: 'in the sweat of thy face shalt thou eat bread'

earn

Tom, Dick & Harry

subsequent timocracy: (Aristotelian) polity with property qualification for ruling class; (Platonic)

obsequious polity with love of honour rulers' dominant motive

grass widowhood Isle of Man

the 5 bloods of Ir.: O'Neil, O'Brien, Loughlinstown: area nr Killiney, Co. D

O'Connor, O'Lochlan, McMurrough

Stoneybatter: street in D *s* 'Cherry ripe, who'll buy'

G Juwel: jewel kickshaws *It* madornale: huge

Juliet *F* choses

L finis: end

fondling Elizabeth bust

finding (second Isolde, i.e. Blanchemains) *Arch* clip: embrace *Arch* buss: kiss

discovered

F nom de Dieu! left straight on down

F lieu

Vico Road, Dalkey

Papish Am. Confederate generals: Pickett; 'Stonewall' Jackson

thorpe: village

many a falsehood whispered

ear *L* ambo: both

yearling

athwart *G* umarmen: to embrace *Sl* miching: skulking

awkward *L* amare: to love (003.09–10)

Diarmaid (Dermot) & Gráinne (Grania): equivalent of Tristan & Isolde in Fenian myth

F que tu es

delightful

F pitre: clown lap

Matt 16:18: 'Tu est Petrus'

Southend-on-Sea, Essex Ally Sloper: character in Victorian comics

first edition

foist: cheat

dear me

(newborn) Diarmaid

F1. echo HCE

F3. *s* All around My Hat I Wear a Tricoloured Ribbon VI.C.17.157: 'dido (white print scarf)'

F4. *G* Stern: star Sterne ordained Dean Swift

butterfly fly button Emerson: *Civilisation*: 'hitch your wagon to a star'

F5. *s* The Vicar of Bray: '& so I got preferment'

F6. *Freeman's Journal* freehand caricature Cuticura soap

F7. *Sl* beauty spot: cunt

F8. Charles III ('the Simple') of France inferiority complex (Adler's term)

Livy: *History* V.48.9: 'vae victis' ('woe to the vanquished') *Inferno* V.100: 'Amor, che al cor gentil ratto s'apprende' ('Love, that soon teaches itself to the noble heart')
Grania
ME rathe: quick
wroth
Moore: *s* This Life Is All Chequered [The Bunch of Green Rushes]
choked
ph Devil take the hindmost more me displaced
diagrams St Lubbock's Day: August Bank Holiday
theorems dioramas
G Rundschau (-Zeitung): review fashionable W. end of London
Wyndham Lewis: *Time & Western Man*
India paper (used for books)

indexes begins to appear *F* par ma foi!
again appears
reproaching chase
pastorally preaching
throats Hoggen Green: site of the parliament in D during Viking
truths occupation (= the Howe)
trespass because ∵ (math): symbol for 'because'
∴ (therefore) they won't do it in short *U.*588: 'Shirt is synechdoche'
Rigoletto: 'La donna è mobile' ('woman is fickle') *Arch* an: if
It più la gonna è mobile: the more the skirt is moveable *L* ut: so that do = ut (sol-fa)
this 'ere
pr it's an ill wind that blows nobody good
good-for-nothing flotsam

Yeats: *A Vision* 75: '*Will* frees itself from contamination' Yeats: *A Vision* 194: 'discarnate *Daimons*'
littoral: on the shore *Convolvulus:* bindweed (means 'brain')
*U.*717: 'flotsam, jetsam, lagan and derelict'
lagan: goods or wreckage lying on seabed
derelict: that which is abandoned
searchlight Beach-La-Mar: Melanesian Pidgin *F* à la mer

far ahead into futurity *Convolvulus:* bindweed piccaninnies (head)
Gr pharos: lighthouse fatuity nitpicking
reel to just fancy *It* novo: new

Arch whilom: at times *Tempest* I.2.379: 'Foot it featly' fitly

cream crame: stall in a fair Spengler's *Decline of the West* refers to Western Man as 'Faustian' (mentioned in *A Vision* 260)
cream of fashion
G Laune: mood *G* Leichtsinn: frivolity *F Sl* soûlard: drunkard *G* Schwermut: melancholy
Faust's 'two souls', leicht (light) & schwer (heavy) *A Vision* 251: 'lunar south is solar east'
Swift

s Hark, Hark, the Lark symbolically *Cymbeline*
'Riding the Franchises' of medieval D mentions 'mears & bounds' separating city & Liberties
Parnell: speech in Cork, 1885: 'No man has a right to fix the boundary of the march of a nation'
Tennyson: *Charge of the Light Brigade:* 'Half a league, half a league, half a league onward' *I* méar: finger
Landsmaal: 'New Norse', based on rural dialects (lit. 'land's language')
G helfen, half, geholfen
beast of burden
gyres: conical helices of determined events, as described in *A Vision*
Eton collar Collar of SS (esses) presented by William III to Bartholomew Vanhomrigh (father of Swift's Vanessa & Lord-Mayor of D) in 1697
whisper Sterne Platonic love twixt Platonic (great) year (mentioned in *A Vision* 204n)
AngI whist!: silence!
A Vision 247: 'Nicholas of Cusa's undivided reality which human experience divides into opposites'

somewhere

F1. Buick car How Buckley shot the Russian General Rudge motorcycles in '30s
F2. *Matière de Bretagne* (Arthurian cycle) Layamon: *Brut* brute force
F3. *Arab* Bismillah: in the name of Allah Viscount Wolseley fought in Crimea (335.14–17)
Bushmills whiskey

VI.B.36.264: 'marginal notes change sides'

rule of Coss: algebra (from *Arab* cosa: unknown quantity x)
It cosa?: what? *G* was ist? I beg your pardon?
BLM you make what name?: what do you make?
Yeats: *A Vision* 231: 'the third state [after death] which corresponds to Gemini, called the *Shiftings,* where the *Spirit* is purified of good & evil' Yeats: *A Vision* 197: 'every month or phase when we take it as a whole is a double vortex moving from phase 1 to phase 28, or two periods, one solar & one lunar, which in the words of Heraclitus "live each other's death, die each other's life"'
verdict on suicide: 'when the balance of his mind was disturbed'

Somnium Scipionis (from Cicero's *De Re Publica* IV)
It sciupone: spendthrift
*U.*660: 'wrapped in the arms of Murphy' (Morpheus)
Sl Murphy: potato
myriad *I* míle marbhadh: thousand murders; great commotion
lapis lazuli (J had blue eyes) *L* lapis: lead pencil; stone

(diagram for Euclid's first proposition; Area enclosed by the arcs is a mystical figure, *Vesica Piscis,* symbol of the womb; ALP–delta of river)

uterus
L uter: which of 2
Babes in the Wood (pantomime)
Jacob & Esau struggled in the womb (Gen 25:22)

Views of Dublin V + V + D + V + L + I = 566 (014.07)
L lapis via: Philosophers' stone *L* vieo: I twist together
Moore: *s* 'Twas One of Those Dreams That by Music Are Bought [The Song of the Woods] Mearing Stone: stone in a wall near D Castle
G Ulme: elm *I* Aill-na-Mirem: Stone of Divisions
Einstein born at Ulm *I* méar: finger
HF 16: 'Give a nigger an inch an' he'll take an ell' in
AL (line on figure) Anne Lynch's D tea (1 inch to the mile)
algebraical

Sir Isaac Newton's name for algebra was 'Universal arithmetic'
Sarah (.F2)

Wyndham Lewis's 'Vorticism'; also vortices in *A Vision*
sprung rhythm: prosodic term used by G.M. Hopkins

aside

lend us

F1. Drumcondra, district of D *G* Traum: dream butterflies
F2. Sarah laughed when God said she was to bear a child at age 90, hence name Isaac (means 'he laughed')
Todhunter's edition of Euclid *L* pontifex: chief priest
Sir Edwin Arthur Burtt: *The Metaphysical Foundations of Modern Physical Science* Bart: abbr. for 'baronet' Thomas Kettle: 'secret scripture of the poor'

double eye presbyopia: form of long-sightedness Presbyterian
shill: to separate ink straight
shall & will strayed
first
Sl fig: cunt
ait: islet at Lambda *Du* modder: mud (Mud Island, D)
Fi aiti: mother Lambay Island N.E. of D
F encore
anchor
nothing & carry one
F eau
Lewis Carroll
Alice memorable corollaries
Lewis Carroll: *Through the Looking-Glass*
Skt sarga: process of world creation, letting go, voiding A.J. Ellis: *Algebra Identified with Geometry* *Heb* aleph: A
(with point of compasses on alpha & radius alpha lambda circumscribe a circle) lamb's tail spoke of wheel (radius)
Gr kyklon: circle *L* ter: thrice H . . . C . . . E

a leg

Plato: *Meno* (geometry dialogue)

discovery Macpherson's *Ossian*
discobolus: discus thrower
actually *G* entdeckt: discovered
actuary: statistician *G* Ente: duck
Du passer: pair of compasses
(passed an exam)
damned *Da* galehus: lunatic asylum gallows
L docere: to teach St Patrick's Hospital, D, founded by Swift as lunatic asylum
L discere: to learn much of a muchness Bagdad daddy
docetism: doctrine of incorporeal nature of Christ's body vaudeville *R* gorodskoi golova: mayor under Catherine's rule
F boue Boudeville organised D street-cleaning department
Skt Māyā: illusion de ville *Gulliver's Travels*
Skt tamas, rajas, sattvas: darkness, goodness, passion (3 qualities of all created things) *G* rauchen: to smoke Turkish
presence of ladies Merrion: district of D
smoking *Da* smuk: beautiful
Dollymount: district of D seaside (all these
Monkstown: district of D districts on coast)
corpulence Dalkey, Kingstown & Blackrock Tram Line
L aura: breeze *L* auris: ear
doggerel orison afar
Dockrell's: D decorators' store *G* Furz: fart
Popocatepetl, volcano Abraham Bradley King: Lord-Mayor of D, welcomed George IV & was knighted by him
Magazine Wall
magma: fluid matter under earth's crust
It bene: well! *The House by the Churchyard* 323: 'breathing turf & thunder, fire & sword'
Byzantine State important in *A Vision* & other works of Yeats

pr History repeats itself coalblack

r Guadiana
L gaudeo: I rejoice
tenor

continuously posset: hot milk curdled with wine &c. *G* quer: across
queer

F1. it's just up off Dogs' & Cats' Home, Grand Canal Quay, D *U*.550 (emended): 'Megeggaggegg!'
X.J.P.F. (055.18) Ibsen: *Et dukkehjem* (closest trans. is 'A doll's home')
F2. *pr* A friend in need is a friend indeed (walk up volcano)
F4. 'At the Creeke of Bagganbun, Irelande was lost & wonne'—refers to Robert Fitz Stephens' landing at the Bann, Wexford, 1170 *It* bagnare: to bathe wake
I Banba: Ireland (poetic)
F5. Alma Mater: school regarded as 'foster-mother'
animal matter

homologous hestern: of yesterday
Swift's Stella & Vanessa both named Esther *L* isto die: on that day
forever Eccles 1:2: 'vanity of vanities' (*L* vanitas vanitatum)
Swift's Vanessa
The Thousand Nights & a Night (*Arabian Nights*) night of 1,000 years in
II Peter 3:8: 'one day is with the Lord as a 'The Historical Cones',
thousand years' Shakespeare diagram in Yeats' *A*
A Vision 187: 'ultimate reality, symbolised as *Vision* 266
remember years the Sphere' mirror
(Xmases) *s* Little Mother of Mine
behind
mind
Santa Claus
A Vision 221: 'Certain London Spiritualists . . . decked out a Christmas
Tut-ankh-amen tree with presents that have each the names of
some dead child upon them'
cg Hunt the slipper

Commemoration of All the Faithful Yeats: *A Vision* 229: 'It is from
Departed: All Souls' Day the *dreaming back* of the dead . . .
that we get the imagery of ordinary sleep . . . so long as I dream in words
I know that my father, let us say, was tall & bearded. If, on the other
hand, I dream in images . . . I may discover him there represented by a
stool or the eyepiece of a telescope' Communion of Saints come-all-ye
chameleon *s* Cummilium sands sounds
s I Dreamed I Was in Derry
Du dro(o)men: to dream
awakened the eiderdown

wonderful memory

tomorrow *It* straordinario: extraordinary *F* binaire: binary down
It bene: well! (294.05–06) bring down O & carry O
F eau Nothung: Siegfried's sword (*U*.583) (maths)

midland *I* luis: letter L (means
quicken tree)
Lucan (on Liffey) (letter A on diagram)
elm, elder (trees)
(turn compasses other way) *pr* All's fair in love & war

In *A Vision,* Yeats says he is transmitting information given to him
by the 'instructors' *G* umstricken: to ensnare
HF 7: 'he 'lowed to tell it' gyres: conical helices of determined
F allo, allo! events, as described in *A Vision*
(now rotate compasses to produce right-hand circle)
It 'giro giro tondo': 1st words of Italian equivalent of 'Ring-a-ring o'roses'
Rotunda, public building & hospital, D
G um . . . herum: round about
G Nässe: wetness nice *G* nass: wet
Sl nace: intoxicating
identical compasses lasses *G* alles
dainty accomplices *Sl* pair of compasses: human legs
G Kunst: art *G* Kunsthandel: trade in works
of art Handel
It beve!: drink! *A Vision* 73: 'As will be presently seen the sphere
is reality'
Tew: Lord-Mayor of D trickling dewponds
two tricky (2 points where circles intersect)
Dublin meeting approximately
(N. & S. Circular Roads, D, parallel to Royal & Grand Canals)
F suite: *s* In the sweet by & by Daniel Dunlop, D theosophist
succession *It* poi: then, afterwards (points P & pi) Dunlop, (tyres)
each other look 'ee here! I see where you mean
I ochar: border, edge

F1. (Norwegian Captain, 311–32)
Am. Juke & Kallikak families: hereditary degenerates Killiney, Co. D
F2. say when! A tumblerful thimbleful *nr* Twinkle, twinkle, little star

the W.C. G nun: now lemma: subject for exploration; subsidiary proposition
G Quatsch: nonsense previous axiom
lemon squash (270.L1) *L* vide: see *R* pervyi: the first
I'm squeezing the lemon *Gr* stigmê: *L* punctum: point
F limon: mud
several *r* Araxes, Armenia
seminal reasons (.26)
make (point P at bottom of diagram, i.e. hell)

bottom Adam & Eve
Batum, Armenia hod (Finnegan)
Ibsen: *The Master Builder* bird of paradise
bilk: decieve
G Zweispaltung: bifurcation
Jacobus Arminius: Dutch theologian
Gr Armenios: Armenian
fundamental
(point pi at top, i.e. heaven) (*ph* pie in the sky)
G Wiederherstellung: reconstitution
ph eat humble pie (apologise)
epexegesis: addition of words to make sense clearer
apex
pint of porter 'going, going, gone' (auction)
point of order (parliamentary term)
visage P/K

P/K P/K keek: peep

(St Michael, angel, in heaven)
Percy French: *s* ' "Are ye right there, Michael? are ye right? Do you think that ye'll be home before it's light?" " 'Tis all dependin' whether The ould engin' howlds together & it might now, Michael, so it might!" '

dangerous Nick (devil)

mighty *Ar* yaghaks: for, about
Ar hokuots: for the souls
our acquaintance maddest thing
Ar ařak'inout'iun: virtue
here done matter
mother
flap lap *G* Pfanne: pan
(fried; egg hits fan)
Izaak Walton: *The Compleat Angler* brethren *Ar* bnout'ion: nature
complete the angles as in 'divine nature of Christ')
Ar hreštak-atz: of the angel (join alpha P & PL by dotted lines)

Gr spermatikoi logoi: the 'seeds' of individual things, in Stoic philosophy (Latinised *rationes seminales*, seminal reasons—.04)
spermatically (join L pi & pi A by continuous lines)

allow me a line while I enclose a space

Nike: Greek goddess of victory *Heb* peh: mouth, origin
like Pa I pee
a neat little boundary *ph* plain as a pikestaff
Sl pikestaff: penis
bucket
L aqua in bucca: water in the mouth
figuratively womb
fig leaf

F1. Percy French: songwriter J.F.M. ffrench: *Prehistoric Faith & Worship: Glimpses of Ancient Irish Life*
F2. splits
F3. *Ar* t'arkman: interpreter think Sukhum-kaleh: bathing resort on Black Sea
Magrath *I* Tuigeann tú Gaedhealg?: Do you understand Irish? *L* sursum corda: lift up your hearts
Heb goel: Saviour *ph* sink or swim Swinford, town, Co. Mayo
F4. hesitency has it a tense?

geometer *L* mater: mother (veil of Isis)
Gr Gaia matêr: mother Earth
Sl highlows: laced boots

Finn acquired wisdom by eating salmon hexagon
wise Solomon's seal (star *G* Seele: soul *G* Hexen:
formed by 2 superimposed triangles) witches
(serpent) Finn *ph* fe fo fum!
Hibernia
Siberia
attend Plato: *Meno* *Da* pisk: whip
(subtend an arc or angle) Hist! *L* piscis: fish
other circumstances being equal eke willed
serpent
pleases Shem, Ham & Japhet

jabot: neck frill jab *Da* trekant: triangle
on women's bodices *Da* spids: point
'Exsultet': 'O felix culpa!' capered
It calpestare: to trample
I ochón: alas *Gr* Calpe: Gibraltar
A Vision 69: 'All physical reality . . . is a double cone'
vertically
vortex (293.L2)
acute *G* Winkel: angle
twinkles
apex by & by

approach near me
I méar: finger it
match (Prometheus brought fire) see
R mech: sword *AngInd* jeldy!: quickly
watch *G* Schluss: close, end redneck: U.S. poor white
Sl sluice: cunt in South; also a R.C.
Brahman gayatri: holy formula to go & see
s 'Oh! hadn't we the gaiety at Phil the Fluter's Ball!'
AngInd punkah: large fan living spit: the very image
Town of the Ford of the Hurdles (D)
HF 9: 'the dead water under the bank' *Huckleberry Finn* (used in this
section for river associations)
discinct: ungirt isopleural: equilateral
Catechism: 'really distinct & equal in all things' 'soul to the devil' (trans.
(6 points of Solomon's seal) from *s* Finnegan's Wake)
sexual *Pro* flume: river *L* flumen, fluvius: river
L luteus: muddy middle way (*G* Weg)

bloody triagonal: triangular *Pro* fiho: young girl
F triage
Aqua Appia: fountain *L* lippia: having watery eyes
near Temple of Venus Appian Way, D ALP

valve equilateral triangles *L* luteus: muddy
vulva *I* uisce: water *L* usque: as far as
tailors used to sit crosslegged while sewing
R křeslo: armchair
s The Lass That Loves a Sailor affliction
Newtonian calculus was known as the 'Doctrine of Fluxions'
Skt mahā: great
Bur wetma: sow
tiddle: smallest tidal bore *G* rutschen: to slide
pig in litter titled rushes
Atlantic Al Koran *G* Bett und Bier: bed & beer
Olaf Cuaran: a Norse quar: of channels, to silt up
king of D, called Aulaf Quaran in Haliday's *Scandinavian Kingdom of*
D, 96 *Cant* quarrons: cunt

F1. shape *F* chape: cope, hood *Sp* doná: lady Speranza: Wilde's mother, wrote for *The Nation* *Sp* nacion: nation
F2. *R* ugol: angle *G* egal: equal *R* my vidim: we see *It* Il Capo di Buona Speranza: Cape of Good Hope
F3. G. Griffin: *s* 'Tis, it is the Shannon's Stream *r* Sangamon, Illinois
F4. mankind *G* mein Kind: my child
F5. *r* Whangpoo Whang the Miller: character in Goldsmith's *Citizen of the World*
nr Pop goes the weasel *G* wissen: to know (we know who)

ambage: dark language for deceit & concealment

N paa: on *N* laa: lay, was lying ALP Anna
N lik: body, corpse; like (lay like on like)
Sl it: cunt

ph go one better
get an VI.B.42.138:'⚭ egg-beater' (seen from end)
It di riffa o di raffa: by hook or by crook *L* quod erat faciendum: which was to be done
Q.E.F. appears after problems in Euclid (Q.E.F.)
L fossa: ditch *ph* Put that in your pipe & smoke it
F Sl fosse: cunt languid

L tunc: then (Tunc page of *Book of Kells*)
Luke 2:29: 'nunc dimittis' (now you release)
Euclid: 'A point is that . . . which has no magnitude' littlest
delta

last

first
delta
empt: discharge power of n
L emptum: purchase

Pseudo-Dionysius: *Celestial Hierarchies*
unity
ECH
L vectorius: for transport
(605–606)
victorious radius vector: variable line drawn to a curve from a fixed point as origin

Gen 28:12: '& he dreamed, & behold a ladder set up . . . & behold the angels of God ascending & descending on it'

circumflexion: bending circles
around *Sw* flickor: girls searchers
fill ellipses gyres (*A Vision*, cf. 295.23)
ellipsis
figures eternally reproductive
G ficken: fuck
impossible corollary

locus someone to the base (logarithms)
logos: universal reason governing world; lit. 'word' as in John 1:1
The decimal part of a logarithm is the mantissa; the other part is the characteristic nothing in the end
log 1 to any base = 0 n'th also
It orso: bear
no wit Sinbad sin (abbr. for sine) A . . . L . . . P
better Adam
cosin (abbr. for cosine) versed sine = 1 − cosine
cousin Lilith coversed sine: versed sine of complement of angle
cosecants & cotangents
consequences & contingencies
perpendicular right angles
tangles of red hair
abscissa limits: values of a variable between which a definite integral is taken
frivolous Sexagesima: 2nd Sunday after Lent expend
sexagesimal arithmetic based on number 60
Moore: *The Peri at the Gate of Paradise* perimeter

antithesis
allotheism: worship of strange gods

clear
G Perlmutter: mother-of-pearl

infinitesimal calculus

many calico

unmentionables

Eternal City: Rome shortness
G Schürze: apron

F2. *pr* Corporations have neither souls to be saved nor bodies to be kicked
F3. toast

Du scherts: joke there are 2 sides to everything
L scholium: interpretation 3 Tristan *F* triste: sad
G ich three *G* Euch
x x
Du vierde: 4th Q.E.D.: *L* quod erat demonstrandum—which was
to the fore to be shown (appears after theorems in Euclid)

Yeats: *A Vision* 72: 'my mind had been full of Blake from boyhood up & I saw the world as a conflict—Spectre & Emanation' my imagination
dimensioned Lourdes (miracles)
mentioned Lord!
HF 13: 'My George! It's the beatenest thing I ever struck'
A . . . B . . . C
superposition quite a coincidence
superb

✠ Cannae 216 B.C.: Romans defeated by Hannibal
aulic: courtly
Aulidis: city whence Greeks sailed to Troy

L omnes collidimus: we all collide Oliver Cromwell
G krumm: crooked
N slep: drag *G* über Grania
grandmother

believe *Arch* levin: lightning bold
thunderbolt
Mookse & Gripes
wholly mixed
place seeing *Faust* I.1338: 'Ich bin der Geist der stets verneint' (I am the spirit that evermore denies')
AngI forenenst: opposite
Du dom: stupid lieutenant's
damn letter-man's
Wyndham Lewis's magazine BLAST *Da* vandret: horizontally blushing
frequently said BLESS & BLAST to different people
(Kev is at top of diagram; see 296.09–18)
reflection fluxion
Da bølgelinie: waveline isn't he the picture!

picture *HF* 16: 'we didn't see her good'
(cunt)

exclusivism: practice of being within ourselves
L orsa: beginnings
L sors: fate, chance
L fors: chance
(monosyllables here, .21 & F3)

John Dee: mathematician & magician
Rowan Hamilton: mathematician (300.27)
William Gerard 'Single Speech' Hamilton: Ir. M.P.; made brilliant maiden speech; said never to have spoken again *G* Hammel: sheep
follow *U*.138: 'silvertongued O'Hagan' (Thomas O'Hagan, Lord Chancellor of Ir.)
arse *L* ars: art
rolls his r's
(says 'l' for 'r', i.e. Chinese pronunciation) *C* yang: sheep
Du slang: snake *C* feng: seam ALP
C lang: wolf *C* tsi: son *C* tzu: word
Cuchullain swears by 'the solemn contents of Moll Kelly's primer'
The House by the Churchyard (prologue): 'Oh! be the powers o' Moll Kelly!'
Tom Sawyer top-sawyer at top when wood sawed
a lesson to me all my life
G laufe: run laugh (it would have been better if we'd talked about money)
r Liffey
copperas: cupric, ferrous or zinc sulphate *BLM* copra: coconut
J's father urged him to seek a clerkship in Guinness's; Father Butt in *Stephen Hero* thought similarly

F1. 208.27: 'Hellsbells, I'm sorry I missed her!' misled

F3. *English as She Is Spoke* (267.08) includes 'Idiotisms' All Chinese words have 1 syllable *C* yü: fish
G.B. Shaw pointed out that GHOTI spells 'fish' (pronounce as in enouGH, wOmen & naTIon)

F4. sigla used by J in his MSS for, respectively, Earwicker, Anna, Issy, the 4 old men, the title of the book, Shaun & Shem

postcard, 18/4/29, to HSW: 'the book advertised in *Pearson's W[eekly]*. "Want to join the police?" That, at least is about something'

I Cor 13:13: 'faith, hope, charity' FAITH

divil's *L* aequalis: equal
AngI gossoon: young lad
unequal to any other angle

HOPE damned
dampened
infernal *It* invernale: pertaining to winter
vernal: pertaining to spring
CHARITY

whereupon sing us a song
ultimogeniture: right of succession pertaining to youngest of family. Opposite is primogeniture
sentiment
last

I mí-ádh: bad luck 'Sweet Marie' biscuits from Jacobs', D
MARIE to eat
toothache armchair darling

Vere Foster's handwriting books

candy kisses (sweets) *Du* opfrissen: refresh (one's memory)
G fress auf: gobble, eat up
G Erinnerung: memory
learn by heart *Sp* leo: I read
Sp escribir: to write microscopes myco-: fungus
(144.13) *L* scribebis: you will write and
ravenously I.H.S. his mum (▲)
R ravnostoronno: equilaterally
G Bewunderung: admiration to the wonder of his tutor
Sl chipper: lively, fit
A Vision 68: 'The first gyres clearly described by philosophy are those described in the *Timaeus* which are made by the circuits of "the Other" (creators of all particular things), of the planets as they ascend or descend above or below the equator. They are opposite in nature to that circle of the fixed stars which constitues "the Same"' *A Vision* 91: 'In an antithetical phase the being seeks by the help of the Creative Mind to deliver the Mask from Body of Fate. In a primary phase the being seeks by the help of the Body of Fate to deliver the Creative Mind from the Mask' corrective corrupt
mufti: civilian clothes unconsciously trafficking
It graffi: scratches
L sinister: left trigonometry

Sir William Rowan Hamilton discovered quaternions
Dolph
Earl of Godolphin (1645–1712) served under 4 monarchs
West Bruno of Nola; Browne & Nolan (D bookshop)

I tabhair: give quarter pouring

G Sturm & Drang: Storm & Stress (C18 literary movement carrying to furthest consequences doctrine of rights of individual)
jugular
Sl juggler: fornicator *F Sl* quille: penis
Napier invented logarithms *L* tamquam: as it were
Sl scrag: neck birthright (Esau sold)

F1. *Sl* pikey: a tramp picnics Nick/Mick
F2. Davy Stephens sold newspapers on Kingstown pier & met Edward VII when he visited D. Kingstown was named after George IV, the 'First Gentleman of Europe', who knighted the Lord-Mayor when visiting D
F3. *nr* 'Baa Baa Black Sheep, Have you any wool?' man in the street
F4. lovely white elephant

tightropes Bul spri: stop bloodletter

Bul lekár: doctor licker *Du* aars: arse *G* Es war etwas: it
Brasenose College, Oxford *Bul* brusnár: barber was something
preterite O.H.M.S. (On His Majesty's Service)
*U.*181: 'I.H.S. . . I have suffered'
peacemaker

Boston, Mass. (280.23)
I bastún: blockhead
nr Baa Baa Black Sheep

Browning: *Pippa Passes* I bet, as fine

L multa lusi: I have played much Mick/Nick
earwig
Christ Church versus Balliol (Oxford colleges)

scribble

our daily bread
born gentleman (111.13) born & bred

funeral *G* fröhliche Frau: gay wife

(Bruno's motto: 'In Sadness Cheerful, in Gaiety Sad')

(111.16) *L* anima: soul (499.30) is sorrowful
It mi sono mangiato il fegato: I ate my heart (lit. 'liver') out *It pr* Se non è vero, è ben trovato: if it is not true, it is a happy invention
Verlaine: *Romances sans paroles* VII: 'O triste, triste était mon âme' Thomas Harriot: mathematician
It son trovatore: I am a troubadour *Sl* so-so: tipsy
Michael Stifel: mathematician
G steif: stiff, pedantic *G* Teufel: devil
Gr mysterion: mystery
P/K on pension
F gouvernement Monday, Tuesday, Wednesday, Thursday
Friday, Saturday

Fear of the Lord: one of the gifts of the Holy Spirit his
(Sunday)
L quisquis: everyone, whoever

shittim wood: acacia wood, used in making the Ark of the Covenant (Exod 25:10)
Pope: *Essay on Criticism* 216: 'Drink deep, or taste not the Pierian Spring'
Artesian well Cartesian (Descartes)
dismal *G* diesmal: this time *L* dies mali: evil days

Ezek 4:1–6: 'take thee a tile . . . & portray upon it the city, even Jerusalem: & lay siege against it. . . . Lie thou also upon thy left side, & lay the iniquity of the house of Israel upon it . . . lie again on thy right side, & thou shalt bear the iniquity of the house of Judah' D Castle
Etienne Bezouts: mathematician *G* jenesmal: that time
besides that
Croagh Patrick, mt, Co. Mayo beware Olaf, name of several N. kings of D
Croke Park, football ground, N. D, scene of massacre by Black & Tans, 1920

F1. (311.22) sooterkin: sweetheart; also applied to imperfect literary productions
F2. Christian Brothers' Schools, D
F3. according to the *Agni Purāna*, the Indian *aśoka* tree flowers if touched by a beautiful girl's leg
F4. nasty low disagreeable
Bul mastilo: ink *Bul* igra: game
F5. Eros Erasmus In Bédier's account, Tristan dies at Cliff of the Penmarks right
Cornwall coroner

Skt bhagavat: fortunate, prosperous
Da biskop: bishop
& hopes to soon hear   lend me   lentil (171.05)
Tippoo Sahib defeated by Wellington   lent
Pascal   Paschal candle   *Gr* kondylos: knuckle, fist, box

G Punkt   apologies
pottage (of lentils; Esau sold birthright for)
many many

guerdon: reward   *R* bystryi: fast, quick
pardon
trespassing on your munificence
benefice
wagtail: bird, familiarly 'Willy Wagtail'

'Capital' tea   Flaubert: *Bouvard & Pécuchet*
(cf. Yeats: *A Vision* 160, 162)

HF 31: 'kept my eyes peeled'   'The answer is a lemon' (derisive reply)
satin   Satan   Euclid: *Elements of Geometry*   *Arch* leman: lover
sat on
F je le jure   *Skibbereen Eagle:* Ir. newspaper
sweetheart   whiteness

L calamus: reed, cane, pen
bifurcating   *Sp* bolsillo: pocket; purse, pocketbook
Du onderwerp: subject   found

Ali Baba & The Forty Thieves (pantomime): 'Open Sesame'
key signature (music)   Bolshevik
HCE   happiness

handwriting

stroke   *G* Ohr: ear
Matt 5:38: 'An eye for an eye'
OK   *G* Dolche: daggers
okeydoke
L ad lib.: at will   J wrote last line of Gogarty's poem 'The Death of Shelley' which won Vice-Chancellor's prize at Trinity College, D
Robinson

I remain, hope you been a good girl

G und   always my thoughts

L dies: day   J's essay, *The Day of the Rabblement* (1901), published with a paper by F. Skeffington
dice
eche: everlasting   *It* stampare: to print
bellyache   one penny each   (J's essay was privately printed in a leaflet, & privately distributed)

anonymous
Arch anon: straight on, straightway
Du ook: also, eke   thank you   characters
look, look, look   Franky (282.08)   caricatures
drama   *It* San: Saint

F1. knocking spots off   Macduff kills Macbeth
plum-duff: flour pudding with raisins
F2. leap year sends   souvenirs soft as summer snow
sweet-williams & forget-me-nots
F3. keep it to yourself

Heliopolis pardon me Edward Cocker: *Arithmetick* (whence phrase 'according to Cocker')

post penman

U.43: 'Old hag with the yellow teeth' (Queen Victoria)

AngI more power to her elbow! (encouragement)
(mathematical power) *AngI* pogue: kiss
Mrs Centlivre: *Bold Stroke for a Wife* (a play, 1717)
(strokes of writing)

yogic doctrine of Kundalini, 'serpent fire', able to pass up the 6 *chakras* or subtle centres: i) below genitals; ii) above genitals; iii) at navel; iv) at heart; v) at throat; vi) between eyebrows (position of 3rd eye)
It fontanella: fontanelle

AngI writers: Steele, Burke, Sterne, Swift, Wilde, Shaw, W.B. Yeats
Dublin Bay

(010.04–7) Daniel O'Connell (Catholic Emancipation)
reading his speech dispatch (009.03)
papers James Connolly: one of leaders of Easter Rising in D, 1916
arse

Charles Stewart Parnell (he stuttered) he goes
paraphernalia
s Londonderry Air: 'Danny boy'
Skt Upanishad: confidential information (Vedic & postvedic writings)
Wellington: 'Up, guards, & at them' Mohammed ben Musa al-Khwarizmi, C9 Arabian mathematician, began the Arithmetic section of his thesis 'Spoken has Algoritmi'
I Éire go bráth: Ireland until Judgement Day
Lady Gregory erege: heretic proof!
Gen 4:5: '& Cain was very wroth, & his countenance fell' (270.13)
brother
Jacob's biscuit factory, D forbidden Pig & Whistle (common pub name)
Matt 7:16: 'gather . . . figs of thistles'
HF 13: 'My George'

HF 28: 'I judge'
pappadams: Indian savory biscuits
Automatic writing of Yeats' wife led to *A Vision* 'families of curves' (math)
parables parabolae famelicose: very hungry
O.W. Holmes: *The Autocrat of the Breakfast-Table* *G* Hof: court
muddled the fruits HCE
culture etcetera wouldn't one Abel

rap Wyndham Lewis's publication *Blast* frequently said BLESS & BLAST to different people alright
L pergamen: parchment *HF* 33: 'it was a grand adventure, & mysterious, & so it hit him where he lived'
blessed saint Charles *HF* 35: 'whilst I think of it'
envious
letter 25/7/26 to HSW: 'how tactful it was of Abel to slit the throats of the firstlings'
nr Mary, Mary, Quite Contrary
L quare: why
bloody bugger (081.26)
F coup de grace
geometry, lit. 'measuring earth'
ph measured his length
ABC
adder (snake)
Franky (282.08)

BLM means 'he fought them to destroy your bloody face'

Cain
miso-: (prefix) hater of-

F1. *Du* speel: play able to spell heliotrope
terribly difficult devil cult
F2. thunder
F3. Bruno of Nola; Browne & Nolan
Castle Browne renamed Clongowes Wood College

once one's one Rest in Peace Gen 4:5: '& his countenance fell'
(295.15)
Wagner: *Tristan & Isolde:* Liebestod (love-death): 'Mild und leise'

Sp formaliza: put in its final form *L* Laus Deo Semper: Praise to God Forever. At Belvedere, pupils put L.D.S. at ends of essays
Da slutningsbane: end of the line
point carried, i.e. won *L* pix: tar

Primary motto of Rotary International: 'Service Above Self'
Jules Henri Poincaré: *La science & l'hypothèse* (gives account of non-Euclidian geometry)
way
euchre: outwit opponent in game of euchre
Eucharist
F merci beaucoup

weight, mass, momentum, potential energy (mechanics)

G Regenbogen: rainbow *G* rings rum: all around H . . . C . . . E
bogies *ph* run rings round
recommended

301.13: 'fun for all'
s Aboard the Bugaboo
blasted
VI.B.36.180: ' 'sit in a barrel'—funfair'
US pork barrel: Federal Treasury viewed as source of grants for local purposes (roll in barrel)

I mála: sack big toxin
mailbag bad taxi
Saxo Grammaticus: Danish historian

It nubilina: unmarried girl dynamite

G sie studiert, was: she studies, eh? glistening

England's (Land's End's) last day

presented

example

Gr katastrophê: down-turning
Gr anabasis: ascent
Xenophon: *Anabasis*
Rotary International (.L1)
L processus: advance

Delft earthenware
going daft
René Descartes
office *L* ambo: both
awful
picked crumbs

come
Descartes: 'cogito ergo sum'
alleluia *AngI* 'you cogged (i.e. cribbed) that sum'

F2. *s* 'Chin chin Chinaman, Chop, chop, chop!'
F3. glasses
F4. Moore: *s* I'd Mourn the Hopes That Leave Me [The Rose Tree] blacksmith
beef tea
F5. All Saints' & All Souls'
All Hallows

Second motto of Rotary International: 'He Profits Most Who Serves Best'
builds bilk: deceive

celebrated signature giaour: term of reproach applied by Turks to non-Mussulmans
It come si compita: how do you spell
salubrious
dispelled tea (111.20) hesit*e*ncy
R Sim ('Giant'): god of ancient Slavic people
L cunctatio: hesitancy
When J was a child, his family called him 'Sunny Jim' bleeding God!
Sheep/Goat shipshape
Einstein (General Theory of Relativity showed space non-Euclidian)
dartra: vague name for skin diseases
Dartry: district of D
ph dear dirty Dublin
celebrating
Celbridge, village, Co. Kildare
ph gift of the gab hesit*e*ncy
HCE
I céad míle fáilte: a hundred thousand welcomes *G* Wort: word
Old World
albeit capable
culpable
wilful murder
woeful mother
argument
Luggelaw, Co. Wicklow (Lough Tay)
energumen: enthusiast, devotee
Royal Blue Tubal-Cain: descendant of Cain, instructor of brass & iron artificers
prussic acid
Prussian blue Giordano Bruno: *Lo Spaccio della Bestia Trionfante*
L orexis: appetite
Blueshirts: Ir. fascists, 1930s
Gen 4:9: 'Am I my brother's keeper?'

John Jameson Ir. Whiskey

OK *ph* hook, line & sinker
Old Keane: actor who collapsed (to die) whilst playing Othello to his son's Iago
Jubal-Cain: brother of Tubal; father of cattle-owners
G Bitte sehr, mein Lieber: you're welcome, dear
brother man knows it not
Gen 4:9: '& the Lord said unto Cain, where is Abel thy brother? & he said, I know not: Am I my brother's keeper?' polar antithesis
emphasis
phthisis *ph* born with a silver spoon in his mouth
Nuad of the Silver Arm: king of the Tuatha Dé Danaan
sleeve *Skt* saṁdhi: peace *AngI* shanty: old house
Gr to Trishagion: the Thrice-holy (Trinity)
L 'sanctus, sanctus, sanctus' (*Trisagion*)

I bi i dho husht, tú: be quiet, you
bird in the bush
allow pen . . . post
penstock: sluice for regulating flow of water
chamberpot *L* ave: hail!
George Moore: 'Ave', 'Salve' & 'Vale' (parts of *Hail & Farewell*)
Vale of Remembrance *L* vale: farewell! evocation
Moore: *s* The Meeting of the Waters (refers to Vale of Ovoca or Avoca)
s Auld Lang Syne *L* salve: good health!
Steyne: pillar in D erected by Vikings *G* Stein: stone
defy *Arch* cullions: rascals; testicles
F je vous défends de chanter: I forbid you to sing
G Lob: praise *Annals of the Four Masters*
form-master

meed: reward

pilgrimage Erin
scrum

F1. shillings bloody
F2. guilty manager
F3. *Sl* giglamps: spectacles (sight) (wash behind ears) (smell) gustation
soap intensifies explosive boiling of geysers

(halos)

G Kropf: crop, maw
ph neck & crop: entirely, bodily
U.S. Sl heavy sugar papa: sweet old man with fat purse

G Gift: poison *G* uns Nobel Prize *F* noblesse oblige
Noblett's: D sweet shop
Adrian IV's bull *Laudabiliter,* granting Ireland to Henry II

signified Hong Kong
single (become one)
Heb mispeh: watchtower end of Mass: 'Ite, missa est'
Gen 31:48–9: 'between me & thee . . . Mizpah' (city in Gilead)
why the devil
E . . . C . . . H
Mookse & the Gripes *Fi* oikea: right (hand)
O.K.
St Augustine: 'Securus iudicat orbis terrarum' ('secure, the world judges')
L secures gubernant urbis terrorem: axes govern the city's terror (lictors' axes represented state's power)

s (Roman soldiers') Mille Mille Mille Mille
Mille Decollavimus *L* studivimus: we shall have studied
L manducabimus: we shall chew
In the Middle Ages the 7 Liberal Arts were divided into the Trivium (grammar, rhetoric & logic) & the Quadrivium (arithmetic, geometry, astronomy & music) intermediates
ALP ECH

Cato's policy was establishment of solidarity through traditional government
D Annals, 27/8/1892: 'The South City Market almost entirely destroyed by fire' Nero was rumoured to have instigated fire that destroyed half of Rome
Saul (book of Bible) contains stories of Goliath & the Witch of Endor
Orderliness & desire to classify major characteristics of Aristotle
pr a place for everything & everything in its place
Bulwer-Lytton: 'The pen is mightier than the sword. . . . To paralyze the Caesars' Pericles: reserved, incorruptible Athenian statesman for over 40 years Ovid's *Metamorphoses* includes much change of human into natural things

Domitian: emperor responsible for extensive military campaigns & public works
The Sphinx often depicted sitting on a column whilst confronting Oedipus
Socrates drank hemlock, refusing assistance to escape execution *L* portioncula: portion
Ajax fought Ulysses at funeral games for Patroclus

HAM
Homer
Longfellow: *The Wreck of the Hesperus*

Diarmaid & Gráinne (Grania): equivalent of Tristan & Isolde in Fenian myth Marcus Aurelius: *Meditations* (much concerned with morality)
Alcibiades accused in Athens & obliged to escape, then invited back & made general when needed
Lucretius went mad from a love potion made of Spanish Fly

F1. *WWI Sl* divvy: division *WWI Sl* babbling brook: cook *ph* going, going, gone (auction)
F2. Moore: *s* 'Strike the gay harp See the moon is on high' [The Night Cap]

F4. *s* Edy was a Lady
F5. Jespersen: *Language* VIII.8 quotes 'nyamnyam' as child's word for something tasting good
F6. ABC
F7. Catechism: 'Really distinct & equal in all things'

Gen 9:20–1: 'Noah . . . was drunken' Plato: *The Symposium* (170.05)
Horace: *Epistles* (personal letters to friends) son (Isaac confused sons)
Sarah laughed when God said she was to bear a child at age 90, hence
Tiresias lived both as man and woman name Isaac (means 'he laughed')
Marius drove barbarians from Rome
⚔ Clontarf, 1014: Vikings driven from D
ph to consult Brother Jonathan 'Diogenes' means 'Zeus-born'
'Jonathan' means 'given by Jehovah'
Brother Jonathan: C18 personification of U.S. (prohibition)
Procne & Philomela, embroiderers in Ovid (248.02)
Abraham Bradley King: Lord-Mayor of D when George IV visited city Alfie Byrne: Lord-Mayor of D in 1930s, known as 'our little Lord-Mayor'
HCE Hengler's Circus came annually to D in late C19
Nestor: horse trainer Cincinnatus (030.13)
Leonidas (Thermopylae) Thomas Kettle advocated parliamentary solution to Ir. question
Arthur Griffith founded Sinn Féin movement Moynihan, in *Portrait*
Jacob's travels (Gen 28–32) Projected hydroelectric scheme for D in V, signs the testimonial
1920s involved chief engineer Kettle, consulting engineer Griffith &
borough engineer Moynihan ALP Theocritus supposed inventor of pastoral poetry
Joseph interpreted dreams
Fabius Maximus was called 'Cunctator' (delayer) De Valera: 'our allies the hills'
Samson, strong man
(divorce) Sir Henry Tudor: leader of the Black-&-Tans
Henry Tudor Parnell, brother of statesman
Aesop said to have invented talking-beast fables
Prometheus gave gift of fire to mankind
fable of the Grasshopper & the Ant (414.20–1)
Sodom Pompeius Magnus: Roman commander
Greek Orthodox Church
Miltiades Strategos: Greek commander
Solon: legislator who tried to pacify unprivileged classes
Jimmy Wilde & Jack Sharkey: boxers
Ear of Dionysius: amplifying prison chamber in Dionysius' palace in Sicily
Sappho's book III.63 condemns an uneducated woman
St Patrick spent 40 days in retreat on Croagh Patrick, in imitation of
Moses Job, when smitten with boils 'sat among the ashes' (Job 2:8)
Cicero was able to destroy Catilina with the help of written evidence from Allobrogan envoys
Catilina: Roman conspirator 5 Cadmean letters introduced into Greek alphabet
Ezekiel prophesied during exile in Babylon (on *r* Indus, hence India)
Themistocles: Athenian, ostracised, died in Asia St Laurence O'Toole buried at Eu in Normandy King Solomon's tin mines
Vitellius took emetics so as to eat more
Darius: Persian king defeated at Marathon because Greeks attacked immediately

---

F1. pantomimes: *Jack & the Beanstalk; Little Red Riding Hood*
F2. *Hamlet* III.2.339: 'Very like a whale' (*U*.40) Thomas Moore: *The Veiled Prophet of Khorassan* (Jonah in whale) speakeasy
F3. sense pin money
F6. Mick/Nick pen . . . post
F7. *It* taglierini in brodo: noodle soup parts of speech
It toglieresti: you would remove
Sl phiz: countenance
F8. *F* où, Monsieur you *F* nenni!: nay!
F9. hit the hay: go to bed St Laurence O'Toole, patron of D, is buried at Eu in Normandy

pr Delays are dangerous
F vite
Xenophon managed to lead the 10,000 home despite attempts to hinder them
F Gobelins dix-sept . . . six . . . & neuf (275.17)
Ann Lynch's tea (D)
L mox: soon
Chancellor & Son, clockmakers, D

chancellor of the exchequer
ticker (watch)

Gr pantokratia: almightiness
Aum (sacred syllable)
(10 Sephiroth of Kabbalah & chimes of 10 p.m.)
Matthew, Mark, Luke
*U.*568: 'Mamma, the beeftea is fizzing over!'
I aon: 1
I dó: 2

I trí: 3

I ceathar: 4

superfetation: 2ary implantation during gestation; (fig.) superabundance
I cúig: 5
Cush: son of Ham
I sé: 6

I seacht: 7

I ocht: 8

I naoi: 9

I deich: 10

Gr kakopoiêtikos: prone to do evil
Gr kakao: cocoa

John Maddison Morton: *Box & Cox* (play about John Box & James Cox)
libido
unconscious

amalgamated

NIGHTLETTER: U.S. telegram sent overnight

Yuletide greetings

Dial beyant: beyond

r Liffey

prosperousness

New Year
New York

J.J.& S.: John Jameson & Son (whiskey)
F souci: preoccupation
F sosie: double, counterpart

F1. Kish lightship off D
Gr anticheir: thumb
ph back of my hand
freehand (writing)
Isis Unveiled II.259: 'In the Jewish *Kabala*, where the ten Sephiroth emanate from Adam Kadmon . . . [Messiah] comes fifth'
Roman numeral V said to represent 4 fingers & thumb extended

F2. X (Roman numeral)
skull & crossbones
hopes
enjoy himself
(292.31–2)

acrostic: 'I'm noman'

life tribal *L* balbutiens: stammering
(In Vico's 1st age, men driven into caves from fear of thunderstorms) *It* tribolo: affliction, distress
doombook: book of *Book of the Dead* light
old Teutonic lore *G* Standpunkt: point of view (marriage the institution of Vico's 2nd age, *G* Hochzeit)
bird's *G* Stamm: origin, stem letter, 2/3/27, to HSW: 'Chinese . . . 山. It means "mountain" and is called "Chin", the common people's way of pronouncing Hin or Fin'
(that man hides from thunder, but that marriage is the height of his life, yet that pride kills him, while the scheme is cyclical, was never much in dispute) weds a nymph lady when
L lympha: clear water
bogs: sinks *s* Enniscorthy: 'For the pride of balls & parties, & the glory of a wake'

(burial the institution of Vico's 3rd age) Rhythm of rumba is counterpoint of 3 beats against 4 (ricorso)
s Enniscorthy: '& the steam was like a rainbow round McCarthy'
allotheism: worship of strange gods
perhaps
C.M. Doughty: *Travels in Arabia Deserta* Edri Deserta: old name of Howth
King Lear III.4.187: 'Fie, foh, & fum'

Sinn Féiners *L* ruricola: rustic cosmopolite: citizen of the world
(fawning customers) Rurik: Viking settler in Novgorod
Milesians: last mythical colonisers of Ireland, came from Spain (Hiberia) Anglo-Norman (invaders) *r* Nore
PS svet: world Arklow, town, Co. Wicklow
The Birth of a Nation (film) Sviatoslav I: last Norse king of Kiev distinguishable from his Slavic subjects
Gr ôtion: little ear *G* Bruder: brother
Ibsen: *The Master Builder* first in the West Ibdullin & Aminah: parents of Mohammed

Hy Maine: tribal territory, Co. Galway *Da* tolv: 12 *I* dáil: assembly (the Dáil, seat of government, D)
tube: radio valve
fearing

I ruadh: red Duke of Wellington
rude Wollin: island off Polish coast
seemed to have the right time of day

Bellini & Tosi: pioneers of radiotelegraphy
Bellini & Tosti: composers (coupling of units in radio amplification)
sky bodies HCE (telegraph key)
(radio messages from aircraft & ships)
Vatican radio vacuum *Rigoletto: s* La donna è mobile ('woman is fickle')
L viaticum: Eucharist (vacuum cleaner interference with radio)
Pythagorean table of opposites makes motion a male attribute & rest a female one boiling whole ham shack: amateur wireless transmitting station
ph lock, stock & barrel
aluminium saucepan
It mele: apples
merrygoround electrically *s* Old Ireland's Hearts & Hands
mulligatawny soup *G* Raum: space eclectic (i.e. church censorship) hearths

ohm: unit of electrical resistance   homes   HCE   *L* ingenium: innate quality

1132   Peterson coil for lightning protection   & Sons
torpedo   *Da* synder: sins
Jomsborg: Viking settlement perhaps on Silberberg (Silver Hill) on Wollin Island (309.14)   triode valve (radio) (2 . . . 3 . . . 1)
Leixlip   *r* Liffey   living depended   *L* unda: wave
Sl pipeline: aerial   deep end
HCE   hydrocephalus: water on the brain   gain control (radio)
(radio waves around 100 megacycles per second)   antediluvian   *r* Libnius (Liffey)
(dial ranges through history)
I Saorstát Éireann: Ir. Free State   *HF* 25: 'Everybody, most, leastways women'
G Staat: State   *HF* 19: 'has brung'
pips (time signal on radio)   pipeline   penetrate
pinna: external part of the ear
earwig *Forficula auricularia*   Viking   *N* far: father   manufactured

I Piaras Ua Raghallaigh: Piers O'Reilly   ear tympanum
O'Reilly & Co., mantle manufacturers, 16 Eustace St, D   *I* ruamghail: rumbling   *Sl* lug: ear
I Baile Atha Cliath   external auditory meatus: passage from pinna to eardrum
Eustachian tube: passage from larynx to ear
condensing (radio)   conducting all & sundry   Santry: district of D   conch: pinna   capable
Naul: village N. of D   Enniscorthy, town, Co. Wexford   rods of Corti in ear
spaces of Nuel in ear   concerts   Brython: a Briton of Wales, Cornwall or ancient Cumbria
consortiums   *L* concerto: I dispute   Symmonds = var. Simon ('he who hears')
union   *Aramaic* bar: son   *Heb* goy: nation
Heb b'ni-b'rith: a son of covenant (= Jew), name of a Jewish association
brotherhood   ask old Alexander   Rus: old name for Kiev & environs
Askold: Viking who seized Kiev, succeeded by Oleg. They belonged to a tribe known as Varangians (*Gr* barangoi)   Ibsen: *The League of Youth*   *Da* o.s.v.: og saa videre: & so on
Woking, town, Surrey   Yahoos in *Gulliver's Travels*
lull   day   arborize: make treelike

front   back   *G* Buckel: hump   *G* Hummer: lobster
ructions
ossicles of middle ear: hammer, anvil & stirrup   HEC   (Iron Duke) Erin   Charlemagne
kill the   labyrinth of inner ear   latter end   otology: science of the ear   ontological
H . . . C . . . E   *G* Himmelsbrot: manna (lit. 'heavenbread')   cartomancy: divination by playing cards
Sl house of call: lodging-place for tailors   manse (i.e. house of cards)
C . . . H . . . E   *s* The Memory of the Dead

lure   *Arab* Nur: light   mirage in a mirror   error   thereby
Lur: tribe in W. Iran   Nur: region in N. Iran
Martinmas   muezzin   mizen-mast   byelaws   'Time, gents, please' (pub closing)
Koran: Sura 24 (*Nur*) states that God's light is like a lamp encased in glass
hunters' pink: scarlet   battlefield   watthour: work done by 1 watt in 1 hour
oriole: Am. bird   aureoled
PS orel: eagle   *It* oriolo: clock   about to be unbottling (drinking bout)
F oreille   Oriel: ancient principality N. & W. of D
O'Connell's Ale from Phoenix Brewery, D   *F* bock: glass of beer

Canterbury bells (blue flower)   *Da* indtil: until
stoup: holy water basin   *Arch* whilom: once upon a time   wick: corner of eye
tailor   *Da* øyne: eyes   Ostman: Viking   Scandinavian   (yet the drink is . . .)
Sheridan: *School for Scandal*
doublejointed   Finn MacCumhail in anger tore up a great sod of turf, creating Lough Neagh & the Isle of Man
Isle of Man   Hubul: idol in ancient Mecca
MacCumhail: son of Cumhal   Gorey, town, Co. Wexford   chicken chokers
Pythagorean   Patagonians (believed to be giants)
mighty giant   former
moiety
turkeycock (pull plug out)   grace of God   Lough Neagh
praises be to our holy Father, the pope gave his solemn benediction
R pop: orthodox priest   (cork pops out like bullet)
papal bull   Cathars: Albigense, C11–13 Fr. sect, persecuted   Catholic Emancipation
cathartic   emulsion

slippery side *I* sláinte: health George Alexander Stevens: 'Cease, rude Boreas,
slanted blust'ring railer! List, ye landsmen, all to me'
Isle of Man amen the Pope's address or blessing: 'Urbi et Orbi' *nr* 'Tinker, tailor, soldier, sailor'
ambit: circuit, compass, verge
Bass's ale

togethers
G Herr Gott Charles Godfrey Leland discovered the Shelta language offing
Charles Leland: poem about Flying Dutchman lee & luff sides of ship *Arch* leal: loyal
Ellmann: *JJ* 23: 'McCann's story, told to John Joyce, of a hunchbacked Norwegian captain who ordered a
suit from a Dublin tailor, J.H. Kerse of 34 Upper Sackville Street. The finished *N* öre: ear
suit did not fit him, & the captain berated the tailor for being unable to sew, whereupon the irate tailor
denounced him for being impossible to fit' tailor *G* Ohr: ear
s There Is a Tavern in the Town
matter of course (draws model of suit for Kersse)
amidships buttonholed
hailed

G Norweger: Norwegian
captain
lobster propensity

wax *Egyptian Book of the Dead* CXXV: 'Hail, thou whose strides are long, who comest forth from
earwig whisper Annu, I have not done iniquity' 'the god who is the lord of the ladder' = Osiris
meat-safe Ana: ancient Ir. fertility goddess
Gr ana: lady

Strongbow led Anglo-Norman
invasion of Ireland
ph Think of a number, double it, take your first thought away from it
letter *N* ledd: link *N* dubbe: bob up & down Dublin thirst
I Sinn Féin, Sinn Féin Amháin: *N* sval: cool (radio valves) Bass's ale *I* bás: death
Ourselves, Ourselves Alone (slogan) *AngI* aroon: my darling *Du* baas: boss, master
E . . . H . . . C cannibal
O'Connell's Ale
meat & drink Wellington: 'Up, guards, & at them'
N trygge: make safe *Sl* trig: fill up

Da sagde: said
ship's husband: agent appointed by owners to transatlantic
attend to business of a ship while in port Latin
Fi Norjankieli: *N* hvor: where (021.18)
Norwegian Celtic where can I get . . . a suit? (suit of clothes, marriage suit, *ph* suit of sails)
sooterkin: sweetheart, mistress
sowter: tailor suit! *F* zut!: go to the devil!
tailor *N* taleren: the speaker clothes shop
I a chara: friend (voc.) *Sp* ahora: new best
Naut cant: to swing around
tailor finished 'Exsultet': 'O felix culpa!' (*C Pi* seems to mean 'get plenty of money,
F coupure: cut, excision supreme salesman')
I an: the make a suit meaning to say, of clothes
N make: wife
of course *Port* precisão: need

pair of trousers Cossack cassock Judg 6:39: 'let me prove, I pray
thee, but this once with the fleece'
mens' garments (tailor) taking (cigarette out of mouth)

fist (083.28–30) begin
Ir. practice of spitting in hands before shaking them to conclude deal
baste: to tack (sewing) cub scouts in Britain: 'DYB' (do your best); 'DOB' (we'll do our best)
raw paste (pudding) *Sl* plank: to put down
N (C19) tog: took to take French leave: but a glad farewell Matt 5:38: 'An eye for an eye, & a tooth
to go away, or do anything, without giving notice for a tooth'
forsooth suit loy: Ir. turf-spade

HF 26: 'plenty good enough' Nor'east Norse *HF* 26: 'every bit & grain'
Sir John Norreys fought Tyrone
broadcast

stop thief! *G* tief: deep *I* Magh Éireann: Plain of Ireland
G stolpern: stumble *N* stolpe: post, mast *s* Come Back to Erin
Da svarede: answered *N* blaafisk: bluefish
N som: like *ph* school of whales
N lykke: happiness, fortune *J* taiyō: i) sun; ii) ocean *Naut ph* heave in sight
likelihood (021.24) *J* ika: below
as suffered back

loss of his voice weigh anchor *N* anker: anchor *N* Norge: Norway

N seilende: sailing (days) Brinabride (013.26–7)
Flying Dutchman only *G* Sonnen: of the sun
comes ashore once every 7 years Fram: Nansen's ship in polar expeditions
Butt & Taff (338–354) Franz Josef Land: archipelago near Spitsbergen
N til: to Cabo Tormentoso: Cape of Good Hope moon
evening star & rising sun
January . . . December *F* des ombres *N* fare: danger
40 days & 40 nights (the Flood)
Port enjoo: nausea *Port* o mar: the sea the tide makes (rises)
mermen
rear & fall of waves

didn't it rain
he run
(make the hump in jacket) brothers-in-law

Moore: *s* Quick! We Have But a Second [Paddy Snap] (song about drinking)

meaning (making the suit)

G nicht so? (hunch to imitate hump)
G nett: nice
n'th *N* regner: rains
the Ryehouse Plot, 1683: conspiracy to assassinate Charles II & the Duke of York
Naut Sl crimp: agent who presses flotsam & jetsam
dupes into becoming seamen *Sl* sharks: pressgang *J* to: &
G wohl nit: surely not *N* godt: good *N* haap: hope Earl Lawrence (St Lawrence family of Howth)
Du niet: not Godthaab: town, Greenland
tripartite (prankquean's 3 visits) *It* Maometto: Mohammed
F Sl lorette: whore mammet: doll, puppet
mountain
pr If the mountain will not come to Mohammed, Mohammed will go to the mountain
Prankquean

(It was surely not a good hope of Earl Lawrence their telling told, but it was surely a bargain what he always allowed of the customers)
house Howth (021.14–15)

Meal-tub Plot in C17 against Duke of York
meantime *G* wohl ja: surely yes Spitsbergen
occasional conformity: condition whereby dissenters Muckers: German gnostic sect
could qualify for Church of Eng. office Muggletonian sect founded by an Eng. tailor
concessions from monarch: Pilgrimage of Grace: anti-Reformation movement in N. of Eng. in 1536
Petition of Right: parliamentary declaration assented to by Charles I in 1628
blind customers

Gill, Berkeley, Wesley: theologians (Presbyterian, Anglican, Methodist) Arthur Wellesley (Wellington)
Waterloo *I* céilidhe: musical Gaelic *AngI* shanty: old house
G wünderlich: strange entertainment J. Tully: *Shanty Irish*, 1928, about Ir. emigrants in U.S.
Du maken (stem *maak*): make rosary
Rota: supreme court of R.C. church
Giaour of a Christian! (i.e. dog; term applied orthodox churches
by Turks to non-Mussulmans)
pr Boys will be boys (radio)
pubs

suras of the Koran quorum (12 of jury) O (12 occupations) Livery Companies of London included
Arab al: the lorimers, leathersellers, skinners, salters,
pewterers, painter-stainers (cited as 'Paperstainers' in Smith's *Dictionary of Dates*), parish clerks, fletchers, bowyers, girdlers, mercers, weavers, innholders & upholders

Matt 19:30: 'the last shall be first'

Arch Sl library: tavern open to the public

innholder: innkeeper *N* oppeholde: detain, stop
N inneholde: to contain, hold *Arch* opholder: undertaker; dealer in small wares
G setz an sofort: start immediately Bass's ale
G Seefahrt: navigation (at sea) bassooned
floor of the house *U*.10: 'Dedalus, come down, *N* skip: ship keep thy bible
flow of the hose like a good mosey' *s* Go Down, Moses, & set thy people free
Gideon

I a cháirde: friends (voc.) please God
Judg 6:36,37: 'by mine hand' codpiece
Pease Cods: girls' game *L* ructus: a belch rectified *Sl* nap: blankets
in *London Street Games* *ph* flip of a jiffy
occasion *ph* sober as a judge *Sl* godfather: juryman
(McCann-311.05–6—was J's godfather)
so whereupon truly
jury
satisfied *F* bon amours writer
Reuters: news agency
pneumonia atoms
no money
The Boyg: ogre in *Peer Gynt*
legal oath: 'so help me God & kiss the book'
Sovereign Lord the king & the prisoner at the bar
ON thing: assembly Pilsener beer
Du baar: bier Ragnar Lodbrok: Viking chief *N* rogn: fish spawn
ON Jarl: Earl (they called him reckoner, I'll call him roguenor)
N penge: money pig on Ir. halfpenny

coyne & livery: billeting practised under Brehon Law by Ir. chiefs hearing

statement *I* dearg-daol: earwig
ship-shape *It* sotto voce: in a whisper
Harvey Duff: police informer in Boucicault's dockland compass
The Shaughraun *AngI* duff: black dark
Da ind: in *N* vel: well *N* ut: out valid
end as well as *L* velut: just as *F* velu: hairy
emptied (bottles) often balance of his natural life

Ir. halfpenny had a pig on it, threepenny bit a hare & penny a chick cheating checking
Youthful Exploits of Finn: 'threw a cast' (& killed a duck)
my meaning Ragnar Lodbrok: Viking chief
'tribune's tribute': popular name for contributions given by Irish to O'Connell
L/R Sitric the Viking minted first (Danish)
I capall: horse (on half-crown) penny in Ireland
G Juwel: jewel *N* nummer: number
Youthful Exploits of Finn: 'the round-bag of jewels' *L* nummus: a coin *L* summus: the top
Bottomley: financier Tom, Dick & Harry David Digges La Touche: 1st governor of
L heres: heir Thomas Digges: mathematician, d. 1595 Bank of Ireland
friendship metals
Youthful Exploits of Finn: 'Finn of hard weapons'
Finn MacCool meant (tailor is paid for making suit)
Youthful Exploits of Finn: 'Finn MacGleoir' (name given Finn after his mother married Gleoir)
Ir. shilling had a bull
bullion *AngI* gauger: a ne'er-do-well
stiver: small Dutch coin, any small coin *N* indhold: contents finance
N pengepung: purse
Bray, town, Little Britain St, D. scene of 'Cyclops' queerest
Co. Wicklow 'little Britain': one who was for containing British in home islands around turn of century
feeling mishaps

himself descendant periplus: circumnavigation

tower readymade *I* Linn Dubh: black pool (Duibhlinn: D)
(of Babel, 314.02) *I* lionn dubh: porter, stout, black bile
hodden: coarse woollen cloth *I* púca: hobgoblin 'Let there be light' let there be day
N pukkel: hump (Gen 1:3)
Judg 6:40: 'dew on all the ground' (330.10–11) *N* gammel: old
earth how the hell camel (Matt 19:24)

devil Finnegan
Eiffel Tower eye (of needle, Matt 19:24)
Tower of Babel
babbling
readymade *ph* on the QT (quiet)
Magna Carta signed at Runnymede
(067.20–2)
Dyflinarskidi: territory round Norse D

both all characters coming around *G* ganz um: all round
someone or other
nr Humpty Dumpty: 'wall' *I* ludramán: lazy idler
Waterloo
A *U*.632: '–Neat bit of work, longshoreman one said.
–And what's the number for? loafer number two queried.
It palombaro: diver B –Eaten alive? a third asked the sailor'

G Rutsch: slide *Sl* rutter: swindler C *Sl* roe: semen
nr A was an Archer (e.g. 'T was a tinker & mended a pot') *Sl* ramp: to rob with violence
045.05: 'Of the Magazine Wall'
scrum (rugby)

furthermore *AngI* galore: plenty mortal sin

Humpty Dumpty aboriginally
We cwymp: a fall Burial of the Dead: 'dust *Sl* raised a dust: created a disturbance *L* arbor: tree
Leixlip to dust' Carlyle: *Sartor Resartus* (lit. 'tailor repaired
Osiris 'god at the top of the ladder' (Finnegan on ladder) again')
'Deliver the letter, the sooner the better' written on *G* hoch: high *G* lachen: laugh
letters by Ir. children Sinbad the Sailor
gibbous: humpbacked P/Q split
give us *ph* grist to the mill pushpull: type of electronic circuit
intervalve coupling (amplification) *G* Lauf: movement, course
vulva laugh
I Baile Átha Cliath

Parthalón: legendary Ir. colonist, *ph* talk like a Dutch uncle
anglicised 'Bartholomew' Bartolomeu Dias: spit of land in Mozambique
damn well Boers' Bartholomew Vanhomrigh: father of Esther (Swift's Vanessa),
& lord-mayor of D
ME save: unless *N* selv: self antenna (of radio) *AngI ph* run rings round (someone)
silver screen
(pips on radio: B.B.C. time signal first used 1924) (pips of Eve's apple)
ever since
cast aspersions subtitles

Norse made easy
Erse never mind
ph give the devil his due *G* Sohn: son *G* Blitz: lightning *ph* call the tune
Mark 3:17: 'Boanerges, which is, sons of a bitch *It* tuono: thunder
The sons of thunder' Judg 6:39: 'let there be dew' (330.10–11)
Thon, once worshipped in England, may be Thor turd
that's all mighty pretty but what about his daughter?
Murtagh of the Leather Cloaks: Ir. high king, 941 *N* döpe: baptise
hissed *Da* ungkerl: bachelor

yawn *I* buachaill: boy twill: a fabric
s John Peel: 'the sound of his horn called me from my bed' *Da* tvilling: twin
eyes associated with their wedding *ph* the apple of his eyes
lapel
Vulg Judg 6:37: 'Si ros in solo vellere fuerit' ('If the dew be *L* omnis: all
on the fleece only') sickened *L* hominis: man's
RR scoula: school slippers
L terra: land
peanuts *RR* famiglia: a family no wonder *RR* fama: fame
RR famaglia: servants

W.G. Wills: *A Royal Divorce* bachelor of arts *F* cul: arse
RR davos: behind, buttocks
Trinity College, D *s* Finnegan's Wake: 'a drop of the craythur' (whiskey)
didn't he have
s The Night before Larry Was Stretched *Du* niet waar?: is it not so?
stitched
s John Peel: '& the cry of his hounds has me oftimes led'

duck, drill (fabrics) Alice Liddell: friend of Lewis
plus-fours Carroll, model for *Alice in*
(more drink) *Scots* maut: malt (whiskey) *Wonderland*
(money)
I don't give a brass rap: I don't care full-length short shrift
rap: false or inferior coin
far

Boniface: generic as *N* efter: after angle of lag: angle whereby alternating current
proper name of innkeepers shortly lags behind electromotive force *Sl* lag: urinate
N hoste: cough *L* hostis: enemy, stranger
Heaviside Layer of atmosphere: reflecting zone for electromagnetic waves
cheek by jowl Three tailors of Tooley St (053.29)
joule: electrical unit tailor: measure of whiskey
s Come Back to Erin Moyle: sea between Ir. & Scotland bread & butter
my
G Reiter: rider *L* diluvium: deluge
divil's
Skibbereen, town, Co. Cork three sheets in the wind: very drunk
N skibb: ship
superstition that rubbing hunchback's hump brings good luck

rehearsing overall
horse: to raise

appearances
F appentis: outhouse
parasols taken aback exclaiming
F seul
HCE MacCool *Coll* brolly: umbrella
howe: hill, tumulus everybody
good morrow watt: electrical unit bastards *Port* boa tarde: good evening
marram grass (by sea) freshwater (sailors) boasters jill: of a boat, to move about
Castletown Bearhaven, Co. Cork *N* noksagt: enough said *Sp* segundo: second
beehive Nagasaki *Sl* whole caboodle: whole lot (i.e. hump)
made tracks *N* strak: straight Öresund: the Sound, *N* snarest: quickest
Du straks: presently strait between Denmark & Sweden *G* Weg
s The Rocky Road to Dublin *G* hören: hear *Sl* lug: ear in the lee of
hornpipe
(tilt hat) Burns: Tam O'Shanter *I* sláinte: health (toast)
(type of hat)
P.W. Joyce: *English as We Speak It in Ireland:* 'Did you ever see the devil With the wooden spade & shovel Digging praties for his supper & his tail cocked up'
how the h(ell)

N fanden: the devil morn *Du* met: with Kilbarrack Church once called Chapel of
N sjöulker: old salts moan Mone (S.W. of Sutton)
Isthmus of Sutton suddenly & knew *Da* endnu: still
joins Howth to mainland *I* indiu: today & you
straightways *Da* strandvegs: along the beach particular friend of mine *G* Fremd: stranger, foreigner
North Strand Road, D Sackerson peninsula pen & ink
N fordi: because *N* længsel: yearning take a hold of them ⚔ Clontarf, 1014
r Tolka, D *Arch* hem: them
Da ti og fjorten: 10 & 14 (⚔ Clontarf, 1014) (172.24) *N* oppe: up
N kable: to cable shutting today, opening tomorrow
we're beware Clifden (407.20) sailing arriving
POSH = port out starboard home (from most expensive booking of cabins on Orient ships)
N skipperen: the skipper Skibbereen, town, Co. Cork *F* nautique: nautical
s Sumer is icumen in *F* pneumatique: pneumatic communication system
Poe: 'Quoth the Raven, "Nevermore" ' *N* tælle: to count *I* labhair: speak
'Pourquoi Pas': Charcot's Antarctic exploration vessel (479.28–9) lowering *Du* lauw: law
sidekick *N* kikke: to peep Gaelic
Du kijker: spectator

N Pukkelsen: 'Humpson' *N* tiltalt: charged, accosted

s Let Erin Remember the Days invision: want of vision ultraviolet violence
of Old: 'the proud invader' Ulster volitant
infrared
let them in for raids
Aryan 2 hearts that beat as 1
Erin boats
witness Tom & Dick & Harry henry: electrical unit Patrick particularly *N* summe: collect oneself
N tysk: German *N* hanrei: cuckold
kismet (= bound to happen)
Kish lightship off D
customer was customer proof: measure of alcohol in spirits overproof: containing more alcohol than proof
Moore (.2) *ph* mears & bounds (292.25) spirit does
heft: weight eric: blood fine for Eric in *The Flying Dutchman:* rival of the Dutchman
murder of Irishman
ph heave to here's to you, Brian Boru Bruin Bear
ph spliced the mainbrace *Sl* sluice: to drink brewing baron (Ardilaun)
ph wet one's whistle

Elizabeth I to 18 tailors: 'Good morning, gentlemen both'
good morrow marram grass (by sea) godmother's
Mother Goose (pantomime) bent: unenclosed grassland
AngI gossip: friend skerries: rocks covered at high tide
world Kincora (where Brian Boru lived)
N borg: castle
N overleve: survive mountebank cold
'bunkum' der. from a N. Carolina representative 'talking for Buncombe'
metropolis deeds houri: nymph of the Hibernia
their meed (reward) Mohammedan paradise hibernating
(312.06)
✂ Sevenoaks, 1450: pretender John Cade claims name Mortimor (.21)
down *G* Dämmerung: twilight *N* tid: time *Port* peixe: fish
(*Götterdämmerung)* pixies
bottom of the sea *N* sess: seat his S.O.S. too (his ship)

bargain *Naut* bulgine: engine Davy Jones' locker liquor
N bölge: billow jorum: large drinking vessel *L* loquor: I speak
Ran: Norse sea-god, equivalent of Davy Jones kettle of fish
Morya: supposed author of Blavatsky's 'Mahatma Letters' really
F Mer Morte: Dead Sea Moore: *s* How Oft Has the Banshee Cried [The Dear Black Maid]
AngI ph Moryah! (expresses doubt) *I* mór: great *It* alla palla: to the ball
N holmgang: single combat
G gang: going Eire
FIRE EARTH
AIR (bird)
on his beam end: down on his luck 4 things (013.20) *HF* 21: 'You borry'd store tobacker & paid
HF 8: 'fo' in de mawnin'' back nigger-head'
HF 20: 'fitten for' WATER Vikings used to make the sign of the hammer of Thor
HF 18: 'the big water' (means the Mississippi) over their drinkinghorns
God's truth! days VI.C.7.18: 'sign of the hammer (auctioneer)'

Leif Erikson discovered America how life passes Hy-Brasil: fabulous island in Atlantic
I Baile Átha Cliath: D *Port* Brasíl: Brazil (Brazil was Portuguese colony) hawk
Sir John Hawkins supposedly brought potato to Ireland Basil the Blessed: Russian saint *G* Furt: ford
L/R L/R *N* brast: burst *Port* povo: people Jesus Portugal port of call
Town of the Ford of the Hurdles (D) vessel

*U.*195: 'a drug in the market' *G* Lurch: amphibious animal
on
(drowned) Hell's bells!
old fellow falls
Ice kampavín: champagne eye slant Iceland *Ice* handleggr: arm *s* Old Folks at Home
Da København: Copenhagen *Ice* fylkir: king (poetic)
Ice fólk: folk salmagundi: mixed dish; *Sl*, a cook
Ice heim (pron. 'hame'): home
Norwegian captain capon (was thought dead) very posthumous expression
It (vulg.) cappone: sexually impotent *U.*494: 'he was a very posthumous child' *L* expletio: satisfying (sb.)
Moore: *s* Oh! Where's the Slave So Lowly [Sios agus Sios Liom (lit. 'down & down with me')]
shall I shoot him
Du kiezen: teeth *N* til: to *Port* jantar: dinner
bit of cheese (*G* Käse) *Ice* til dæmis: for instance

stingray *Ice* t.d.: til dæmis (for instance) Kennedy: D baker of Patrick St
Port perú: turkey cock 'stinger': whiskey & soda thoroughbred dough
St Patrick (Japanese, *Ice* og svo fra: & so from *Port* relogio: watch
612.16–30) *F* sans saki: Japanese liquor religion's *Gr* logion: oracle
temper *s* Finnegan's Wake: 'Souls to the devil, did ye think I'm dead?'
Sp tiempo: time
(sound depth) *Ice* getá: to be able pussful
Ice get ég: can I pushpull: type of electronic circuit
L Tartarum: Hades okey dokey
Dalkey
Ship's husband *ph* deep as the north star
Ice sæla: bliss, happiness *Da* sold: pay
talk *N* tolk: interpreter *N* tanker: thoughts
nr 'Tinker, tailor, soldier, sailor' *Da* tolder: publican
pr Every man to his taste *I* ceathair: 4
HF 13: 'trading-scow' cater: 4 at dice or cards
I céad míle fáilte: 100,000 welcomes *Ice* áfram: onwards amen
God keep us all Fram: Nansen's ship in polar expeditions
Da ekspedient: salesman *Sp* hombre: man *Sp* hambre: hungry welcome
Humphrey *Port* comér: to eat
sign of the cross *ph* what's the good word?
God be praised!
Ice diskur: dish *Ice* ostur: cheese *Ice* svangur: hungry *HF* 10: 'carelessest'
dish of *It* alla balla: to the bale, pack
HF 27: 'stealthiest man *HF* 29: 'She *was* the best girl I ever see, & had the most sand'
I ever see'
N ven: friend *s* The Lone Fish Ball: 'one fish-ball
. . . fixin's' (extras)
Da ekspedient: salesman *s* 'I'm the son of a son of a son of a son of a son of a gambolier'
N sulten: hungry *Ice* sonur minn: my son Shackleton: Antarctic explorer
N opvarte: wait upon *N* ham: him angry Ostman: Viking (hence Oxmantown in N. D)
Wellington: 'Up, guards, & at them'
Valdemar: several Scandinavian kings

F mal de mer *Da* søsyg: seasick

ball of his foot *Du* meer: more *G* krank: sick
G Meer: sea
tide to turn in haste with the fare
Da Naut tov: cable
when (pouring drink)
G wehren: to defend
(021.18–19)

(drunk)
Humpty Dumpty merchantman

Matt 5:38: 'An eye for an eye' word for *N* mistænke: to suspect mistake
tailor 'the ninth part of a man' (316.11)
tailor *N* taler: speaker *Sl* the why for: the reason
N. Hawthorne: *Twice-Told Tales*
Sl uglyman: garotter *N* mand: man hump hemp (rope)
everyman for himself but God for us all
3 cheers for repeal of the Union please

Du groot: great apologised Thomas Power O'Connor: *The Parnell Movement*, 1889
put it on the bill *s* Bill Bailey, Won't You Please Come Home Bailey Lighthouse, Howth
descended The O'Connor Don: C19 Ir. M.P. (family of lineal descendants of Connacht premonitory
Daniel O'Connor Howth is a promontory monarchs)
oblivious of the Head of Howth
r Liffey
chiaroscuro: disposition semblance *Per* mard: man Martinmas
of darker & lighter masses in picture *R* zyemlya: land (Nova Zembla) mortal man
N mennesker: people Diarmaid Dolomites (mts) haar: a cold sea fog
Murmansk: Russian port *ph* Dear Dirty Dublin moulting *N* haar: hair mountain hares
clusters *s* Do Ye Ken John Peel: 'with his coat so gray'
pastures
Tristan *Gr* agape: love *I* grádh: love Grania
trustfully (Grannuaile, 021.25)

lovely mover walker

*U.*508: 'My mother's sister married a Montmorency'

(climbing mountain)

N aner: forefathers onerous
Scots 'dinna': do not *Gr* anêr: man *Gr* anêros: grievous amorous
ECH *Gr* anthrôpos: man Guinevere *I* duine: person *I* fear: man game's
enterprise *L* homo: man *L* virtus orig. meant 'manliness' *Indo-Eur. root* khom, khem: man
s 'Be it never so humble' *Du* zo: so small *L* absit omen: may there be no ill omen! *U.*190: '*absit nomen*'
There's no place like home' *L* obsitus: fastened up Nemon: Celtic war-goddess
Dan 7:9: 'The Ancient of Days' (God) yesteryear *L* nemo: no man

titmouse panorama (in C19 a huge painted landscape) macron: line placed Humphrey *G* Jungfrau:
Gr (artificial) panoramamakron: all that which is seen over long vowels maiden
in a long time *N* kursus: course 211.15: 'Jill, the spoon of a girl, for Jack, the broth of a boy'
watercourses *L* cursus: march, journey
hero of *Flying Dutchman* compelled to Alexandrian *Gr* andreia: manliness
wander by curse
Mt Etna: volcano Holy Spirit spate in river LAP
r Hooghly *Du* hoog: high
marriage ceremony: 'for richer, for poorer . . . until death us do part'
PAL von Suppé: overture *Dichter & Bauer*
s The Young May Moon: 'glow-worm's 'hand in hand we'll go'(cf. .27–8)
lamp is gleaming, love' *N* han i hende: he in her
Joel 2:25: 'I will restore to you the years that the locust hath eaten' American
Millikin: Ir.-Am. songwriter
milk & honey *I* bannóg: loaf
bannock: hard biscuit *s* Phil the Fluter's Ball
Rubaiyat of Omar Khayyam: '& wilderness is paradise enow'
Thom the toucher (506.28)
Valley of Mina at Mecca nevertheless

to my mind always wash & brush up
Archbishop Walsh of D (antiparnellite)
fash: weary oneself
Sl soup & fish: *Richard III* I.1.1: 'Now is the winter of our discontent'
full evening dress Baconian theory of Shakespeare's writings
Du brood: bread so much for Buckingham (beheaded in *Richard III*)
aurochs: extinct earwig *N* gammel: old
species of wild ox Legion of Honour (created by Napoleon)
Egyptian Book of the Dead CXXV: 'I live upon right & truth . . . I have performed the *L* fiat: let there be
commandments of men . . . be ye then my protectors' tav & aleph: last & first letters of Hebrew alphabet
Arab alif: letter A (ox) Mohammed sought refuge from persecution at Taif but eventually moved to Yethrib (Medina)

Annapolis: U.S. town with Naval Academy Mesopotamia

gods *pr* fair's fair

gentlemen's *G* Mensch: man pledge
386.09–10: 'woman squash'
Burns: 'John Anderson, my jo': 'Now we maun totter down, John, & hand in hand we'll
go; & sleep the gither at the foot, John Anderson my jo'
veiled the higher I hilltopped the more I missed
heeltapped
blessed way nickname
blizzard
monument *N* koldbrann: gangrene Northeaster *N* eldste: oldest
N natt: night
wafting warp . . . woof *L* nihil: nothing
source of Nile in Abyssinia
N ulv: wolf overtones Wolfe Tone: hero of 1798 rising
Ulverton Road, Dalkey
Iris: Greek rainbow-goddess Irish Sea
7 deady sins: pride, covetousness, calvity: baldness
(rainbow) giddiness lust, anger, gluttony, envy & sloth

tallyho Valhalla

s Do Ye Ken John Peel?: 'With his hounds & his horn in the morning'

should be shot Finn MacCool

AngI usquebaugh: whiskey erstwhile O'Connell's Ale barmbrack: Ir. speckled loaf
F ébaucher: to sketch out aleconner: inspector of ale
Balbriggan, town, Co. D rainbows Demetrias: ruined city, Greece think *Sl* wrinkle: to tell a lie
in *s* Enniscorthy, 'the steam was like a rainbow round' Dimetrius McCarthy
sure *L* stercus: dung histories
r Suir
begin to (281.04–05: 'de Pline et de Columelle')
Pliny the Younger describes eruption of Vesuvius in which Pliny the Elder (author of *Historia Naturalis*) died
Hamlet III.1.83: 'Thus conscience does make cowards of us all' *N* taler: speaker
plenary indulgence (005.09) tailor
malt (whiskey)
testing his tape *nr* A was an Archer (e.g. 'T was a tinker & mended a pot')
pr One swallow does not make a summer chalk, marble & limestone are all calcium carbonate

3 swallows: trademark of Power's whiskey Moselle wine
(united 3 drinks in 1) Mussulman = Moslem (doesn't drink wine)
fair pageant oesophagus slaked lime: calcium hydroxide
fiery his open guts
quicklime: calcium oxide *s* Phil the Fluter's Ball: 'With the toot of the flute & the twiddle of the fiddle, O!'
Portrait I: 'Once upon a time and a very good time it was'
day

ECH Amsterdam
crystal set: early radio receiver
nr Humpty Dumpty reminiscences Netherlands lumbago
rheumatism limbs
Ally Sloper: character in Victorian comics captain
It (vulg.) cappone: sexually impotent
liner (ship) here before
(plumbing depth of sea)
ph cut of his jib *It* gobbo: hunchback Richard the Third (hunchback)

godfather *G* Popo: buttocks *N* seiler: sailor Horus
N fatter: 'governor' apropos *N* buxe: trousers *Sl* buckshee: free
coat & trousers

Arch hem: them oasthouse: building for drying hops turning round
N Pukkelsen: 'Humpson'
tailor P . . . Q (split) double diode valve (radio)
doubledyed
Congreve: *The Double Dealer* Berkeley valued tar water as medicine
still Tara: ancient capital of Ireland
marine ran *Port* garganta: throat transatlantic *It* maroso: wave
Rabelais: *Gargantua* *It* tromba: tube
Du Golfstroom: Gulf Stream curse of Olaf *J* shitateya: tailor
Du gulp: trouser fly attire
vernacular *Da* at väre: to be (*Hamlet*) *N* sige: drop *HF* 26: 'stretchers' (lies)
L fornix: brothel war I'm telling no
cast *s* McPherson's Goat cotton trousers Nebuchadnezzar
coat & trousers (Book of Daniel)
G hops: hola!

G läuft: runs
laughed
ship's husband wished

told

fiery furnace (Dan 3:6–21) thrust metaphysically Omar Khayyam
L fieri: to be made *L* fornax: furnace
Hamlet III.1.64: 'a consummation devoutly to be wished'
situation
Humpty Dumpty *N* dæmpe: damp down

okey doke added *G* Änderer: one who changes something
N døpe: to baptise *N* ander: other *N* dyp: deep
Sl half seas over: drunk curse

N inunder: beneath tarpaulin *HF* 23: 'the shines that old idiot cut'
inundation
N skrædder: tailor *Sl* snider: tailor addicted nasturtiums
Sl stitch: tailor stich in my side
buttonhole Communist *J* fuyu: winter *J* fuku: suit
It budin: pudding *I* cumman: society, club fuck you *F* fou *J* fukkyū: revival
smoking boasting
bombast (orig. cotton padding for clothes)
the latest Savile Row fashion doublebreasted navigator
Civil War faction
Moore & Burgess, minstrels, had catchline 'take off that white hat!' (*U.* 167) back of my hand
N hvit: white *N* aske: ashes Aske: in Norse myth, the first man *Da* bag: behind
G Hemd: shirt *N* ham: him *G* toll: mad tailor penny bun *N* frokost: breakfast
Hansbrow's *Hibernian Gazetteer* claims Normans landed in 2 ships called Bag & Bun
s 'When I waltz with the band' Judg 6:37: 'Behold, I will put a fleece of wool in the floor' (Gideon asking
G mit God for sign—see 330.10–11) *Da* flis: splinter
behind *N* uthus: shed
oasthouse
curse of my ancestors upon

U. 200: 'Murthering Irish' call
G Mund: mouth
G Schimpfname: abusive name gutter goddamned condemned
ships' *N* gitter: railing, trellis
cousin invalid United States
valet
fit to light a kettle of fish worst
N fisk: fish worsted (cloth)
Westend suitmaker needle cloth

I a chara: friend (voc.)

s 'Wid my bundle on my shoulder, Faith! there's no man could be boulder, . . . & I shtart for Philadelphia in the
N skjorte: shirt morning'

dream come true
I druim a' dhreama dhruadha: ridge of the druidical adherents
Ireland's round towers *Da* bag: back *N* tretti: 30 *N* uke: week thirty hours a week
N lund: grove *N* rund: round *N* tur: tower *N* til: to *Du* hoer: whore
stop thief! several Taafes were exiled from Ireland *Da* rundtur: excursion ship's husband
Taff (Butt .29) interjected
s Come back to Erin L/R
I Magh Eireann: plain of Ireland
ill luck blasphemed the Norwegian captain *L* flatus: blowing inflating
Da ild: fire *Da* ilde: bad
through *N* gammel: old eye Earwicker
G wacker: brave
Arch fare: travel

L Afer: African *L* arena: sand *N* Blaaland: old name for Africa
G Affe: ape *Da* rik: realm nighed Bering Straits
battered by

didn't it rain!

infernal machine (time bomb) Bully's Acre: oldest D cemetery
nr Hickory Dickory Dock

pr finders are keepers great circle sailing time

remaining snippers (tailors)
Sl snip: tailor

N ölkjenner: aleconner literally Power's Ir. whiskey
(inspector of ale) *AngI ph* more power to your elbow!
Thomas Grey: *Ode on a Distant Prospect of Eton College:* 'Where ignorance is bliss 'Tis folly to be wise'
Tennyson: *Charge of the Light Brigade:* 'Their's not to reason why'
Viconian cycle: he is born, is married, he dies

lantern *N* stift: pin *G* Stift: crayon

Ir. pubs were open on Sundays to bona-fide travellers corolla: the petals of a flower, collectively

Some plant viruses transmitted by injection by feeding insects
disgusted itself

Dublin Bar at mouth of Liffey
Sl kipsie: cheap boarding house
outback (Australia) Gladstone *I* Bóthar na páirc: park road Bonaparte Nola
Glasthule: district of Dún Laoghaire Bruno Browne & Nolan
what's his name Charles Bianconi: greatest Ir. mailcoach owner in early C19
James Watt invented steam engine (by rail or road) Australians in Ireland
ilk

kiber galler: a peasant's toe anchor
Hamlet V.1.153: 'he galls his kibe'
gale Walensee: Lake, E. of Zurich *G* Was wollen Sie haben: what do you want?
Du zee: sea *N* haven: garden
bearings Bering Sea *Du* haven: harbour ECH
beer N. & S. Circular Roads, D
(pub is open) as hello! Longfellow: *The Wreck of the Hesperus:* 'the reef of Norman's woe'

Here Comes Everybody *nr* Mary, Mary, Quite Contrary: 'With silver bells & cockle shells'
hiccups
Phoenix Tavern: pub in Chapelizod mentioned in *The House by the Churchyard*

Lotts, street, D *N* funn: discovery *s* Lannigan's Ball till Erin wakes
s 'Lots of fun at Finnegan's Wake'
s The West's Awake: 'slumber deep'
saving
cutting

pr Business is business Copenhagen *Du* helpen: to help
Du koopman: merchant
(scene at pub counter)

HCE ears what's yours? (invitation to drink)
(landlord serving drinks)
VI.B.46.89: 'giel (hâte)' [haste] *Ar* kayl: wolf *F Sl* gail: racehorse *Ar* ôdaradzin: stranger
Gael & Gall (foreigner) *G* geil: lascivious *G* Gaul: horse odour ozone Armenian
N blande: mix Tom, Dick & Harry

N pattedyr: mammal

s The Wearing of the Green: 'Paddy dear & did you hear' animals on Ir. coins: hen (penny), hound (sixpence), horse (halfcrown), rabbit (threepenny bit), sow (halfpenny)
(Noah put animals in ark)
Ark of the Covenant
N dronning: queen encounter cubit: forearm high & dry
drownings *G* Drohung: threat
s Finnegan's Wake: 'Your souls to the devil, did ye think I'm dead'
Sl dodger: dram of liquor *G* trink: drink

F zut!
suit
Alice Springs, Australia *Aust Sl* fossicker: gold prospector
N fos: waterfall *Aust Sl* swagman: itinerant
'down under': Australia piped

mulga: an Australian tree
Mullingar Inn, pub, Chapelizod
(the tailor—see 311.24) *C* pei-wei: kerchief nankeen: Chinese cotton pantaloons
The Pei-wei dynasty was a Hun one: Nanking was the capital of several Han ones
Gideon was son of Joash cheerio!
SC zhivio: prosit!

(hat off)

Take off that white hat! (catchline of Moore & Burgess minstrels)
coming back speaking
lunching Baldoyle: district of D; has racecourse *Bur* rishi: sage, poet
U.306: 'drunk as a boiled owl' steeplechase
Daniel O'Connell dangling his overcoat over his shoulder *G* so was!: imagine!
Conan: one of the Fianna top-gallant flag on mizen mast
C lao: old, senior *C* shao: junior looks more like an officer in the Navy
so as *C* yü: compared with, together with novice
Take off that white hat! *Sl* botch: tailor course
white-hot son of a bitch
C ching: spirit *C* huan chang: return at a later stage making
F. rom. of *C* shang is 'chang'; huan shang: change lower garments
hullaballoo (Brewer *The Custom of the Country* (play by Fletcher & Massinger; custom is *jus primus noctis*)
says Ir. name for crying together at funerals)
Take off that white hat! so awful welsher: bookmaker at race meeting who escapes when he loses
tailor's tape son of a bitch
this, that & the other Confiteor: form of confession used at beginning of Mass
because
Du misvatten: misunderstand
misfitted
bitch's bastard such a suit of clothes the way his own father wouldn't know him

Arch wise: way, manner *C* hung: red *C.f. rom.* hoang tseu: inn sign, shop sign; son of the Emperor
N klok: wise how he poorly fitter

s 'Do ye ken John Peel with his coat so gray . . . With his hounds & his horn in the morning'

haik: Arab outer garment Baldoyle racecourse The Dáil, pron. 'doyle': seat of government, D
Bur kai-kon: a hurdle hurling How are you today, my dark sir?
ph a dark horse 186.33: 'search me' *T* terzi: tailor
F Zut!: go to the devil! kersey: coarse cloth for trousers

occurred
sliving: cutting sleeve-board (for ironing sleeves) Curragh racecourse
sliver: ribbon of wool ready for drawing start to finish
from sheep (lambskin) to tailor's board Phoenix Park
HF 21: 'laughed at him, & sassed him' tit for tat

as long as there's a tail on a cat
Bur kya: tiger

Judg 6:38: '& it was so' Judg 6:37: 'Behold, I will put a fleece of wool in the floor'
captain knew nothing horses
BLM two feller he feller go where: where are they going
a fact *ph* tit for tat

Sl knockingshop: brothel toper: drunkard
once upon a time
(electrical impedance) true

maltreating hearts' content
malt (whiskey)
C Pi methink: I think mho: unit of electrical conductivity
ph tit for tat
dielectric: nonconductor
dialectic
absolution obseletion: becoming obsolete Nelson's Pillar, D
L obsoleto: I degrade nil
King Billy (William III) had statue in D Wellington Monument, 'overgrown milestone'
N konge: king
Oliver Cromwell *L* Libera nos domine: free us, O Lord
(statue of Daniel O'Connell, Liberator)
so help me God *ph* cook my goose Emancipator (O'Connell)
L culpa: sin, fault goose: tailor's smoothing iron
It ricorso (Vico) 'Collars & Cuffs': nickname of Duke of Clarence (214.29)
recurring

Beau Brummel   *Coll* bummel: river   buccaneering   Van der Decken, the *Flying Dutchman*
G Bummel: stroll   bugger   *G* ducken: to stoop
Sl pump ship: urinate   ahoy!   Sandymount, D   'ship of the desert': camel
a whole   Sterne: *Tristram Shandy*   (may desert sand block his pumps!)

Corsair   highwayman
high seas
Chapelizod   *Du* bloed: blood   Harald Bluetooth, Viking   Baltic
how are you?   Erik Blodöks: Norwegian king, 'Bloodaxe'   oath   Beelzebub
xebec: small 3-masted Mediterranean ship   *Sl* creep in through the hawsehole: to be promoted (derogatory)
creeping   royal English Navy
Landsmaal: 'New Norse', based on rural dialects
small of his back (*L* lumbus)   arsehole   hawser: ship's cable
maiden voyage   Jonah & the whale

curse   *R* portnoy: tailor   befall   spit in his face
befuddle
(combat)   landslide   *s* Donnybrook Fair
G Donner: thunder   *G* Wolkenbruch: cloudburst
nr Taffy Was a Welshman   vestments
Sl reefer: midshipman
breach of promise   *Sl* muttoner: wencher
bitch   mutiny
According to Stanislaus Joyce's diary, J's father used to say 'break his bloody arse with 3 kicks!'

feud   *G* Meister   *N* gaas: goose
if I were a few years younger   *ph* cook his goose
sails (to trim)   sampling   leather

furbelows: like hell!   feel the weight of my fist
flounces on petticoats
G Faust: fist   *R* gora: mountain   gorbellied Pukkelsen   *R* gorbatyi: hunchback
horrid   *R* pushka: cannon (i.e. son of a gun)
bellows pockets: patch pockets with   potatoes (deform pockets; Bloom carries one)
expandable sidepockets in Norfolk jacket   *R* pochta: letters
disgrace to the   kith & kin
*U.*404: 'a wolf in the stomach'   *R* rimskii katolicheskii zerkov: Roman Catholic Church
We teilwra: tailor

G Zirkus: circus
Ir once had 5 provinces;   *Da* Island: Iceland   hullaballoo   Scandinavia
now there are 4   *We* isel: low, humble
Londonderry (N.)   Drom an Dún Daire: remnants   Mecca   Muckross, Co. Kerry (S.)
N dunder: thunder   ridge of the fort of the oak wood   Magrath   *G* Rasse: race
make a coat & trousers for a foreign fellow with such a
N foran: before   (seaman)
N tale: to speak   *N* hulle: hole   *N* bak: behind   Fascist!
tail   camel's hump   *Da* bakke: hill   fadge: to suit, fit
fudge: to patch up

dry cell (electric battery)   long ago
selenium cell: light-sensitive apparatus   halloo
Sh Rilantus: Ireland   *ph* crack of doom   Daniel O'Connell   O'Connell's Ale
Roland's horn (*Chanson de Roland*)   *Fi* ukkonen: thunder
inside of it   *Fi* salama: lightning   salmon
Power's Whiskey   saloon
salmagundi: a mixed dish   *N* tummelumsk: dizzy
lifted   back   hearing that
L ambilateralis: alien
belonging to both sides   ionized
Appleton layer: highest regular layer of ionosphere   *s* The Peeler & the Goat: 'O the Bansha peelers went out one night on duty & patrolling'
The Pale: Eng.-occupied part of medieval Ir.
It tuono: thunder
about   Tony Lumpkin: character (rascal)   *It* lampi: lightnings
in Goldsmith's *She Stoops to Conquer*
bound   least

s 'Oh! the French are on the sea, Says the Shan Van Vocht'   *N* bukk: he-goat
cramped back
s The Rocky Road to Dublin   gustatorily
ghost story
N spøke: joke   *N* gjenganger: revenant   then & there   dead spit   *G* Spuk:
N spøkelse: ghost   *G* den und der: this one & that one   *N* død: dead   ghost

prototype   how very unlikely
phototype: photographically produced printing block
U.216 (emended): '*And that filibustering filibeg*'   suit

atlas: satin   *Du* onder: under   (Gen 3:19) earning his bread in the sweat of his brow
N ond: evil   oxter   *N* ernære: support   *Ice* svelt: hungry
embrace   lighthouse on Lizard Point, Cornwall
Ambrose Lightship off N.Y.C.   Chapelizod
Tale told of Shem & Shaun

I ruadh: red   *N* rede: nest
to rede a riddle
Phoenix Park   *I* páirc: field   garden of Eden   (Eve created from Adam's rib)
Sphinx's riddle   *N* gardin: curtain
H . . . C . . . E   *F* enceinte
Coleridge: *The Ancient Mariner*   murrain: infectious disease
s The Lass That Loves a Sailor   Ulysses   *Gr* thalassa: sea

L terra firma   *I* magh: plain
I tulla: hill
HCE   empty bladder
here comes everybody
(311.22–3)   *F* saucissons: sausages

G Lumpenpack: riff-raff   *N* bund: bottom   *N* overrasket: surprised

N sot: soot   *N* opsitter: freeholder   Take off that white hat! (catchline used by Moore &
said   op. cit.   goblets   Burgess minstrels)
old Set (Egyptian mythology)   shut up & sit down   *I* Sinn Féin, Sinn Féin Amhain: Ourselves,
(radio set)   suit   Ourselves Alone! (slogan)
G ohne: without
all on
N skaal! (toast)

radio   Waterloo   'there is a personal message for'
R woda: water   S.O.S.   *L* Missa: Mass
coat & trousers   will any person believed to be present   passing
s The Croppy Boy: 'Good men & true'   '12 good men & true': jury
report   *N* hoved: head   *N* politi: police   'love' = nil in tennis
Hoved: Danish name of Howth in C9   H . . . C . . . E   *N* mester: master   ⚔ Clontarf, 1014
G vier   *N* ellers: otherwise   For the Greater Glory of God   postmaster
(telephone no.)   (Jesuit motto)
s Funiculi, funicula
U.472: 'Doctor Finucane pronounced life extinct when I succumbed'
L Ad Majorem Dei Gloriam: For the Greater Glory of God (Jesuit motto). At Belvedere, pupils put letters A.M.D.G. at beginnings of essays
weather forecast
G Welt: world
N nord: north
Joseph O'Neill: *Wind from the North* (novel about D Danes, 1934)
reverend   St Colmcille (Columba; spurious   *Du* predikte: preached   *Sermon on the Mount*   charity
column-filler   prophecies attributed to)   month's   *s* Slattery's Mounted Foot
Scandinavia   *N* bygmester: master builder
It schiuma di nebbia: foam of mist   *Da* byge: shower
G Muster: pattern, paragon   heralded by fog signals
Da vejr: weather   Harald Fairhair: 1st king of Norway
HCE   *Da* køkken have: kitchen garden   *N* hoven: swollen   enveloped in an unusual suit of clothes
Da København: Copenhagen   *Da* ekstra: extra
Da Middelhav: Mediterranean
middle half
St George's Channel between   way westwards   occasioned
Ir. & Wales
sudden ridge of low pressure, mist   local
sodden rush   Lucan
tomorrow   steamship   *N* mandag: Monday (washday)   being
N mandig: manly   seemed
brighter, visibility   *Sl* ability: sexual potency

omens   today   (news after weather)

Viconian cycle: 1) thunder, fall; 2) auspices   Eden
(divination by flight of birds), nuptials;   approaching   *Sl* nub: copulation

Viconian cycle: 3) burial; 4) divine providence R.I.P. *L* Requiescat in Deo: May he rest in God
lieutenant governor *Du* groeve: grave *ph* bury the hatchet
It previdenza: foresight

L Laus Deo Semper: Praise to God Always (Jesuit motto). At Belvedere, pupils put letters L.D.S. at ends of essays
L.S.D.: pounds, shillings & pence
Arthur Guinness, Sons & Company, Ltd Anne Lynch D tea
(advertisements) Anna Livia Plurabelle
111 'United we stand, divided we fall' (Morris: *Flag of the Union*)
even money offered
Irish Hospitals' Sweepstake Tuesday *N* dyr: expensive
stock derby
1001 pities Pepys: '& so to bed' dreams
thousand to one
the 4 imperatives of the Oxford Group (Buchmanites): absolute truth, absolute purity, absolute honesty, absolute love
midnight sun
(radio programmes due later in evening & week)
(bed) *Fi* keskiviikko: Wednesday *Fi* torstai: Thursday
Fi kalastus: fishing *Fi* tanssia: to dance
Fi perjantai: Friday *Fi* lauantai ja sunnuntai: Saturday & Sunday *Fi* kirjallisuus: literature
Fi pelejä: some games
(Christian literature programmes on Sunday) whilst his pullover is finished
palaver *G* finnisch: Finnish
Horus: enemy of Set (324.15) Judg 6:12: 'The Lord is with thee, thou mighty man of
I a chara: friend (voc.) *Sp* ahora: now valour' (Gideon) *I* Sinn Féin, Sinn Féin Amhain (324.15)
Chapelizod *C* ts'ai-feng (*F. rom.* has *fong*): tailor *C* tsei-fan: robbers
Typhon = Set *G* Laune: mood alone
r Laune & *r* Brick, Co. Kerry found you a father-in-law
gentlemen's tailor *G* Seelord: Sea Lord (rank) John Maddison Morton: *Box & Cox*
F gosse *F* bosse
Hengest & Horsa: brothers, Horus Elizabeth I to 18 tailors: John Jameson & Sons, Ir. whiskey
led Saxon invasion of England 'Good morning, gentlemen both' salesmanship
ph tell that to *N* tale: to speak scatological
the marines tailor godfather (McCann, of Norwegian Captain
captain story—311.05–6—was J's godfather)
L pax: peace between
N betvinge: conquer
r Maine & *r* Flesk, Co. Kerry *N* fisk: fish *N* flesk: pork
Gen 2:24: 'they shall be one flesh'
Amundsen: first man at the S. Pole Ironsides: nickname of Cromwell
Ostman: Viking
Humpty Dumpty Hardicanute: son of Canute; fought for throne with half-brother Harold
Paps of Ana: 2 hills nr Killarney
I Banba: Ireland (poetic) sailors & tailors
I Iodáil: Italy idol sailed boats . . . coats John Maddison Morton: *Box & Cox*
Judg 6:36: 'If thou wilt save Israel by my hand, as thou has said'
Coats brothers: threadmakers Gen 6:14: 'Make thee an ark of gopher wood'
sworn *N* svale: swallow Judg 7:2: '& the Lord said unto Gideon'
blood-brotherhood oath (*Götterdämmerung*) Norwegian right honourable
St Clotilda: wife of Clovis, who swore to be converted to the God of Clotilda if her God would grant him victory
Macpherson: *Temora* VII.309: 'Seven bosses rose on the shield' Pukkelsen
targe: shield
would believe in maritime *It* lupo di mare: seapike; (fig.) 'old sea dog' (lit. sea wolf) (4 footed: 4 provinces)
Wotan = Odin wooden wall: wooden fighting ship, rendered obsolete in C19 sheepfolds ship holds
G wüten: to rage
Hugh O'Neill (Red Hand of Ulster); Matthew, Mark, Luke & John *G* blass: pale
Mardyke, Cork (Munster); Lusk, Co. D (Leinster); Cong, Co. Mayo (Connacht)
first let us pray
ass (Neddy, bray)
kow-tow: Chinese custom of touching ground with forehead as mark of respect
Sp toros: bull *Port* criado: servant Tom, Dick & Harry
L credo: I believe altitude multitudes infallible (pope)
(only one God in Christianity) *L* ultio: revenge

N tabel: table Horus tailor Horrocks Ltd, textile firm, Lancs
Horace Taylor: Zurich friend of J & Budgen
commandments 1st martyr (St Stephen)
reverse (commandment not to kill) murder
quick *L* deus: god
St Patrick picked shamrock (pun on Trinity)
Matt 6:28: 'lilies of the field' *s* At Trinity church I Met My Doom: 'I was an M-U-G' that
L crux: cross *Du* boom: tree
poured *N* heil! *I* uisce: water
oasthouse
making a sign of the cross I baptise thee, Ossian (Patrick baptised but failed to convert Ossian)
L mingo: I urinate *I* crúisce: jug pope tithe
I uisce beatha: whiskey Viking
Our Father Oscar, Ossian's son Earwicker
triforium: gallery in church wall unconditional baptism *Da* forføre: seduce
L inter tribum trifariam trifoliorum: within the threefold tribe of *G* Fürst: prince
Gael & the Gall (foreigner) HCE explorer shamrocks Celtic clans
transatlantic
seahorse cuddy: ass *Naut* coalman: coal ship
N aas: hill
F douche holy apostle's *N* pukkelen: the hump
do *I* buachaillín: little boy
west Helsinki

Howth Roman Catholic religion
heathen damned Daniel (O'Connell) Romeo (Daniel) O'Connell
Moore: *s* From This Hour the Pledge Is Given [Renardine] Tara: ancient
It tera: earth capital of Ir.
ternate: arranged in threes chrysanthemums

anthem *Ice* osk: wish sailor
anathema Oscar, son of Ossian
N god kveld: good evening good day insure
G Gott got (caught) cold
Ossian Faroes (Danish) *Sw* hälsosam: healthy Ben Edar: Howth
against fairies Pharaohs wholesome home *Da* til: to
death sentence: 'Lord have mercy on your soul' for ever & ever
Lloyds of London heresy sail *I* I n-ainm an Athair: in the name of the Father
spit in his hand
It Spirito Santo: Holy Ghost
Nansen: Arctic explorer Norse *N* altid: always
HF 8: 'dey wuz a nigger trader roun' de place considerable, lately'
N overtro: supersitition wherefore *Da* pokker (a mild oath): the devil, the deuce
N hvorfor: why the hocus pocus
O Ice mikla: to make big *N* stor: big explorer Isolde
N mand: man wholesale
Du, N daad: deed *Du* doopen: baptise *N* gudfader: God the Father secondhand
duped *N* gudfar: godfather Sacred Heart
Dublin = Baile Átha Cliath *Ice* dómkirkja: cathedral St Patrick's Cathedral, D
St Isaac's Cathedral, St Petersburg
N aa, herre: O sir rear-admiral Peter/Paul (rivalry); Peter & Paul Fortress, St Petersburg
I a chara: friend (voc.)
suitor *L* sutor: cobbler
Sutor St, D
Moore: *s* Come, Send Round the Wine [We Brought the Summer with Us]
sponsor: godfather
N skole: school whether
Da skaale: drink health
talking about Leif Erikson & his discovery of America
eureka!
the roaring forties: ocean areas between 40 & 50 degrees S.

Pliny: *Nat. Hist.* XXV.10.36: 'Sutor ne supra crepidam judicaret' ('the cobbler should stick to his last')
RR crap: stone Horus Horace
Gr krismion: a watch Christian doctrine tailor popularly called the ninth part of a man
Gr chrismon: annointing, grace *Ice* dóttirin: the daughter *It* dottrina: catechism (316.11)
Da dyb: deep *N* skodden: the fog
Balscadden Bay, Howth (E. of D) isthmus
Leixlip (means 'salmon leap', W. of D) 173.05: 'Low Swine' *Da* lykke:
N lukke: shut happiness
Sweyne: son of Harald Bluetooth; fought Christianity *Du* soort: sort
laughed

smugglers Mutt . . . Jute duty free *N* forløper: precursor
N smuk: pretty (tailor will have smuggled goods when captain marries his daughter)
praises be to our good Saint Brendan *L* filius: son *I* a chara: friend (voc.)
AngI praties: potatoes Ibsen's *Brand* thinks he is sent by God *L* cara: precious
Fynlogue: father of St Brendan tailor = ninth part of a man (316.11) needlewoman
nicest little
Pro chato: girl *Pro* charmadouiro: charmer *Heb* bat: daughter of c.i.f.: cost, insurance
ph chit of a girl (small) *U*.737: 'Tinbad the Tailor' plus freight
It tesora: treasure *Port* tesoura: scissors *I* a stór: my treasure *Pro* lamp: lightning
Pro tesura: to measure *Pro* esluci: lightning
free on board dotes ALP *L* plus quam belle: more than beautifully
U.281: 'What are the wild waves saying?'
N foster: foetus leap year *D Sl* totty: girl
Ice tuttugu: 20
111 *It* tramite: through, via
Trinity (College, D) 3
Vanity Fair trend of the times
4 (grit of riverbed) *r* Trent *r* Thames
N saft: juice the (*r*) Dee in flooding hydrogen: lightest element
soft *d* in 'floo*d*ing'
Rhaeto-Romanic language
pr Look before you leap reading romances
RR inviern: winter *s* Little Annie Rooney *RR* lavina: avalanche
RR evna: saucepan, kettle evening in vain Rona: village in *RR*-speaking Switzerland Lavinia: wife of Aeneas
yesteryear *RR* pled: word, speak pierglass *We* peryglus: perilous *RR* glatsch: ice
RR ester: foreign *RR* prigulus: bad, unwell, dangerous
Esther (Swift's Stella & Vanessa) *RR* piz: peak piece
truckle bed: low bed on castors piss
G Stufe: step, ladder rung *RR* malaura: storm, bad weather
RR suffel: wind
primroses (springtime) *RR* tuot: all, entire
D Sl rossy: impudent girl
RR god: a forest Dingle: town & peninsula, Co. Kerry
glory *I* duine: person tingle
r Dargle, Co. Wicklow blunderbus Margadant: *Raetius* (Rhaeto-Romanic)
marching Mercadante *RR* marchadaunt: merchant
N fort: quickly follow my leader Ladin dialect of Rhaeto-Romanic
It forte: loud *RR* Furlan: Friulan (in *RR* family) ladies
lie of the land somewhere calling *It* caldo: hot
language summer
pianotuner *Dial* beyant: beyond beyond the beyond Cambria (latinized Welsh): Wales
RR tunar: to sound, thunder D Bay *F* ondes: waves *RR* combra: chamber, room
Welsh mts mutton *N* titte: peep dormer window
RR munt: mountain *N* drømmer: dreams
Wagner: *The Flying Dutchman* vistas
N flyende: flying
Kilbarrack Church (ruins) N. *Fi* saksalaisen: German Concessa: Patrick's mother
of Clontarf Sechseläuten: Zurich spring festival *It* concessa: granted
Angelus: 'et concepit de Spirito Sanctu' Dollymount: district of D nr Kilbarrack
('& she conceived of the Holy Ghost') Capt. Marryat: *The Phantom Ship* (about Flying Dutchman)
Sinbad Fortunatus Wright in C18 captured a winsome
the Sailor Fr. ship; considered piracy by French
s The Peeler & the Goat: '& took him for being a-strolling'
love Loe, Cornwall, famous for shipwrecks *Fi* rouva: married woman
Litany of BVM: 'Tower of Ivory, House of Gold' Parnell: 'When you sell, get my price'
Hu ivar: sex if *Da* gifte: marry
Swift: 'Ppt' poor lookout *Du* oog: eye *s* Black-eyed Susan
The Blue Lagoon: projected pleasure pool between Dollymount & Bull Island
season *F* mireilles *nr* Georgie-Porgie *N* Norge: Norway
Mistral: *Mireille* *N* borg: castle
N timer: hours
Irish Times, newspaper
VI.B.37.89: 'lovver (chimney' Aurora borealis

Earwicker alone *G* Popo: buttocks Bonaparte
r Irrawaddy hippopotamus
Du poorter: citizen ABCD scye (tailors' term): opening in coat for sleeve
water on the brain *R* azbuka: Cyrillic alphabet (named from 1st 3 letters, az, buky & vede)
L dulce: sweetly DOVE lovely
ph Dear Dirty Dublin
Huginn & Muninn: mind & memory, Odin's messengers, RAVENS privateer
carcase

pr There's no fool like an old fool polar bear
Du pool: pole *Sl* poor Rube: helpless rustic in N.Y.C.
Du beer: bear *Rh Sl* Brian O'Linn: gin
Isa 2:4: 'They shall beat their swords into plowshares'
battering ram *s* The Rocky Road to Dublin *s* Polly-wolly-doodle: 'my fairy fay'
Da pram: barge Watling St, D
Gideon was son of Joash cofounder
godfather
s Polly-wolly-doodle: 'curly eyes & laughing hair' talking about
AngI Andrew Martins: pranks, tricks
melton: type of cloth *N* lovsang: song of praise
Hood: *Song of the Shirt* (poem)
thoughts above 111
Judg 6:39: 'Let me prove, I pray thee, but this once with the fleece'
godfather apart

pr Marry in haste & repent at leisure bet true blue

Protestant parson tailor *We* bach: little *AngI* donochs: mugs
predestined arse *We* tyle: hill
s My Last Cigar: 'the volumed smoke' *s* Come Home, Father: 'The clock in the steeple strikes two'

s Rosin the Beau: 'When I'm dead & laid out on the counter'
s Lincoln & Liberty: 'the Slavocrat's giant he slew'
N skib: ship right honourable (the captain)
L onus: load
John & Henry Sheares: United Irishmen, defended by Curran but executed
r Nannywater *We* ni: daughter of sheers (tailor) *Port* marqueza: marchioness
house on the mountain *Port* Dinamarquês: Danish

Ice rúm: bed *Ice* elding: lightning
Ice herbergi: room *N* olding: old man
Erin depravity privacy *L* jus primus noctis: droit de seigneur, 'first night rights'
Ice líf: life *L* pravitas: deformity
Moore: At the Mid Hour of Night [Molly, My Dear]

thirty *Ice* annar: second Hellespont
Da fyrste: prince Hoppy Holohan ('A Mother' in *Dubliners*)
swamped sea chest remember *s* Molly, My Dear

rollcall 'sweetheart Emma': Lady Hamilton, Nelson's mistress
sailor proverbially has wife in every port ever he
Copenhagen (Nelson's victory) brothels
N hagen: the garden Battle of the Nile (Nelson's victory)
Moore: *s* When Daylight Was Yet Sleeping under the Billow [Ill Omens] [Kitty of Coleraine *or* Paddy's Resource]

In the *s* Kitty of Coleraine, St Martin's-in-the-fields, London
she breaks a pitcher of buttermilk
Ringsend, district of D HCE *L* heri: yesterday *s* See the Conqu'ring Hero Comes
(bells) *Da* seng: bed *Bas* (h)iri: village *Bas* concor: hunchback *Bas* ertzo: mad
reverend Fox Goodman (035.30) *s* I'll Tell the World *G* Welt: world *C* ehr: ear
Ice refr: fox *G* Fuchs: fox *G* gut Mann Bell of the well: bell of St Patrick (In Nat. Museum, D)
Du vanger: catcher *I* an Bhealaigh: of the way
steeple-boy's revenge Thingvellir: seat of Icelandic parliament; a great bell was
done dead sent there when Christianity adopted by Icelanders
raptest
aptest *U*.5: *'Thalatta! Thalatta!'* (in Xenophon's *Anabasis* *Du* hoop: hope
the cry of the Ten Thousand on sighting the sea; in ordinary *Gr*, 'Thalassa')
Moore: *s* Before the Battle ('By the Hope within Us Springing') [The Fairy Queen] embrace
(wooden, i.e. inert)
Sl quean: whore

Egyptian Book of the Dead XX: 'The night of the making to stand up of the double Tet . . . on the night of the things of the night . . . & on the night of making Horus to triumph over his enemies' (erection)

According to *Egyptian Book of the Dead*, Horus & Set fight; cry 'Humph!' H . . . C . . . E
Thoth separates them & gives Horus power over day & Set power over night
please Rothschilds
Du roede: rod, penis
Bas eliza belza: black church Lord's Prayer: 'Thy will be done'
It bellezza: beauty bedpan

Bas Jinko: God *Bas* Pazko: Easter *It* basco: Basque HCE
s Yankee Doodle Dandy *Bas* besta: fiesta Tabasco: hot pepper sauce
Siamese (twins) singlet: woollen garment
Fi suomea: Finnish
Coppinger (055.18) Tom, Dick & Harry
ME copener: paramour
Manneken-Pis: statue in Brussels of a child urinating Valdemar: several Danish kings
Horatia: Nelson's daughter
Brigadier AIM
brigantine
Da olivengrene: olive branches Oslo

husband heart *N* fosterfar: foster father North-Northeast
G Muss: necessity *Sl* gluepot: parson graving dock
tombstones commemorating Northeasts, Glues, Gravys, Ankers & Earwickers at Sidlesham in the Hundred of Manhood, W. Sussex

N anker: anchor 100%
chin-chin (toast)
C ch'en: sensual pleasure daylight *J* banzai: a cheer Nippon: Japan
G -chen (diminutive) bull's eye
nose landlubber Norwegian
U.625: 'the best bloody man widgeon: (fig.) fool
that ever scuttled a ship' *N* skib: ship

caw (raven); coo (dove)
Cat & Cage: D pub
Judg 6:40: '& God did so that night' (gave sign to Gideon) 'Fingal of Victories': title used by Macpherson
Fingal: region of N. Co. D
Canmathon & Cathlin: stars in Macpherson's *Temora* In legend the 3 sons of Tuireann had to give 3 shouts on a hill as part of penance
Matha: warrior in Macpherson's *Fingal*
s Erin Half-heard Their Harps Tuhal: character in *Fingal*
Macpherson: *Berrathon* 397: 'the half-viewless harp'
Macpherson: *Dar-Thula* In *Temora,* Cormac's daughter Roscrana marries Fingal
Bolga: according to *Temora,* a name for S. part of Ireland *N* bølge: wave, billow *AngI* boyo: chap, lad
MacArt Cormac: Grania's father *Temora* II: 'His [Fingal's] soul was rolled into itself'

government peace on earth

honeysuckle *Sw* Ryss: Russia

⚔ Prague, 1757 *F* bragues: breeches
'Battle of Prague' (piano piece) *s* The Keel Row: 'As I came thro' Sandgate'
s 'Gin a body meet a body comin' through the rye'

dunnage: clothes, baggage deaf-&-dumb
Sl doss: bed *G* stumm: dumb
doornailed mortmain: property left to corporation

Pompei destroyed by volcanic eruption Whiteboys: C18 Ir. insurrectionists, dressed in white
Goatstown, district of D
white heather (lucky) Luke J. Elcock: mayor of Drogheda, 1916

deaf-&-dumb *s* John Peel: 'his coat so gray'
G dumm: stupid
'trooping the colour': military ceremony awfully
Pro reire: rere
Du jool: fun Grand Duke Michael
Crown Jewels (Michael (031.19)
Peter the Great rue de la Paix, Paris *F* jeu
rue de l'Abbé de l'Épée, Paris
All Saints' *F* jour publicans hand in glove *Arch* glave: sword
All Souls' Free-Staters v. Republicans (Ir. Civil War)
treaties Himalaya
We cymylog: cloudy
I fathach: giant Co. Louth
Our Father
loudmouthing Holy Mary emphasis
Tim Healy (betrayal of Parnell) *We* enfys: rainbow
Reign of Terror Tara *pr* It's never too late to mend
We taran: thunder Nuvoletta (157.08)
HEC (rainbow) scapegoat

Skin-the-goat (in *U.*) *We* gafr: goat gaffer *G* Sünder: sinner (215.15–18)
'The Sinners' Bible' left out a 'not' from the 10th Commandment
guide
spurtle: steam with some force

now Peter/Paul Father Theobald Mathew: Ir. temperance advocate
Swift: 'Ppt'
teetotally troubled grinned down
I Dial taytotally: utterly, entirely
'Ja, vi elsker dette landet. . . . Med de tusen hjem' ('Yes, we love this country with its thousand homes')—1st & 4th lines of Norway's national anthem, by Bjørnstjerne Bjørnson
Ir. National Anthem: 'Mid cannons' roar & rifles' peal We'll chant a soldiers' song' *N* vill: wild Solveig's Song (*Peer Gynt*) *N* sang: song
R solovei: nightingale
Louis XIV, 1700: 'there are no more Pyrenees' *N* tyrann: tyrant
Tyrrhenia: Etruria lax: salmon Maréchal de Luxemburg, 'tapestrymaker for Notre Dame'
Our Lady's leader's Judg 6:40: 'for it was dry upon the fleece only, & there was dew on all the ground' (sign given to Gideon)

old wives' tales

feud nickname

arse
wicker . . . Ear 'Red Rowley' (pseud.) author of *s* Mademoiselle from Armentières

Berkeley (Buckley) Finn MacCool

G Feines: something excellent *G* Sinn: meaning, sense
fines *I* Sinn Féin: We ourselves (slogan) Percy French: *s* The Night Miss Cooney Eloped

Rollo (Rolf) Ganger: 1st Duke of Normandy (theoretically ancestor of Anglo-Norman invaders of Ir.)

bandbox *I* Banba: Ireland (poetic) tit for tat zigzag
polder: reclaimed land (birdsong) Laughing Jack Hooper: C18 hangman laughing jackass
s 'Wid my bundle on my shoulder, Faith! there's no man could be boulder, I'm laving dear ould Ireland widout warning, For I lately took the notion, For to cross the briny ocean, & I shtart for Philadelphia in the morning'
scorning *F* Boche: German motion pictures
G süss *G* mein *Da* holm: islet Finn's Hotel, D, where Nora Barnacle worked when J met her
G k(l)itzeklein: very small
N forening: union 'So they put on the kettle & they made tea & if they don't live happy, that you & I may' (formula to end fairytale)
L nova: new curtain
made free *N* du: you
if they don't live happy, that you & I may hook & eye

s 'I got a shoe, you got a shoe, All God's chillun got shoes' *F* ménage: household *G* wohl: well
birth . . . marriage . . . gone west, died (Vico) got to manage *F* (familiar) manège: stratagem
L mundum: world

cg Knock, knock, who's there J told James Johnson Sweeney that Cain & Abel were the origin of war & that the 2nd 'w' in 'Twwinns' was for Eve & meant 'without an apple', as she was born without an Adam's apple

Childermas: festival of Herod's slaughter of innocents one, ten & a hundred *N* uhindret: unhindered
Sl bee's knees: acme of perfection *Da* barn: child *N* danske: Dane
barn dance
Catherine wheel

N moder: mother
I modar: dark
Humpty

popgun *N* sky: cloud

(tea so strong that spoon stands upright in it) first 'Exsultet': 'O felix culpa!'
Sl sergeant major: strong tea famous couplets
hard of hearing (deaf) *ph* the case is altered

I lia: stone monument
coming & going limestone
Marriage ceremony: 'till death us do part'
stone-deaf wintry *AngI ph* top of the morning

L tellus: earth longer
tell us it all as if
sooner tumble to (it)

scream Mananaan MacLir supposedly had 3 legs, which revolved like a wheel
(symbol of Isle of Man)

two-lipped druidess Lord almighty!
Ludd founded London
G Durst: thirst

catch-as-catch-can Highland Fling
can-can
tell your parents
215.33: 'What Thom Malone?' tickle bare end

'In the name of the Father, & of the Son, & of the Holy Ghost' (blessing) holly
Balder: Norse god killed by mistletoe *N* sol: sun holocaust
N og saa videre: & so on *L* tri-: 3 *L* sex: 6 *L* nonus: ninth *N* aand: spirit
N ondt: hard, ill, wickedly

Ondt/Gracehoper (414.20–21) *Sl* moke: ass Mookse/Gripes
ON grosskorper: big bodies
what about plebiscite *Sp* aléman: German

Heb rib: dispute
boys & girls Mount of God: Mt Horeb (part of Mt Sinai) I Kings 3:4; I Chron 21:29: 'high place'
G Kerl: guy Deluge (Mt Ararat) the Lord (Gibeon)
the Lord Haram: enclosed area of Jerusalem including site of Temple
Heb har(-im): mountain(-s)
N munden: the mouth *N* Viken: old name thwaite: piece of land
mountain for the Oslo Fjord tarn: mountain lake
thorpe: agricultural village *N* fos: waterfall *L* fosse: ditch fell: hill *N* haug: hill shaw: thicket
withe: willow toft: homestead haugh: piece of flat land by river *N* lund: grove
garth: piece of enclosed ground measuring the magnanimous well as

Herzian waves: a *U.* 205: 'myriadminded' (Shakespeare) Eire every
class of ether waves toroidal coil: electrical transformer
(shark after diving) *s* Daffydowndilly

Fomorians: mythical Ir. invaders Nana: the Sumerian Aphrodite. She wore a
R velikan: giant Tolstoy: *Anna Karenina* *R* karlik: dwarf 'beauty belt'
N sommer: summer *Cinderella* (pantomime) *N* viv: wife *R* evna: daughter of
Somerled: Norse king of Argyll & Hebrides *ON* Val-tívar: gods of the slain *N* bil: car
Brian Boru gauge lavender water *N* vaade: danger
barometer (the wading girl in *Portrait* IV) *N* lavvande: low water
Le Fanu: *The House by the Churchyard* 366: 'the capriole-legged old mahogany table' twilight
cabriolet
month of the year
mouth of the (*r*) Yare
semen assault Magazine Wall
seamen imagination
L laetificus: gladdening *G* neu: new euhemerism: method of interpretation which derives myths
from real events
Kristiania: Oslo (name layer beguiled *N* begjærlig: desirous
used in Ibsen's time) first liar, the devil gaily waylaid
'Tout est perdu fors l'honneur' (erron. cited as François I after being
captured in 1525) *F* sauf
Judg 6:37: dew . . . floor . . . fleece

s 'The flea on the hair of the tail of the dog of the nurse of the child of the wife of the wild man from Borneo
has just come to town'
Bornholm: Danish island in the Baltic Sea

Da 'Snip snap snude, nu er historien ude' (formula to end fairy tale)

Da 'trip trap træsko' (expression used as call of victory in game) Ketil Flatneb, Viking, father of the queen of D

'so they put on the kettle & they made tea & if they don't live happy that you & I may' (formula to end fairy tale) HEC ALP

N han igjen: he again *N* hun igjen: she again Finn

Chinese Han dynasty & their chief enemies, the Huns Finnegan

Da derhen igen: there again *I* Piaras an Ua Raghailleach na Tulaige Mongáin: Piers the descendant of Reilly (*Raghallach*) of Tullymongan (in Breffni) (099.26)

'whack-fol-the-diddle' (refrain in songs)

Dublin

s Yankee Doodle unruly cracked Gestapo

CheKa: Russian Extraordinary Commission, 1917, i.e. secret police 'Turn again, Whittington' (in pantomime)

Frankfurt-on-the-Oder Finnegan *I* MacCumhail (MacCool)

Persse O'Reilly

God *r* Tolka *N* tolk: interpreter Doolin, village, Co. Clare

We goth: pride stopping the talk of Dublin

wattle & daub: twigs & clay or mud: used to build huts &c. pull

boat to ground together *L* testes: witnesses (touch wood for luck)

tree/stone

William Shenstone: poet *Du* pop: doll, human effigy mamma

emblems of 4 evangelists: man, lion (puma in *U.*332), bull, eagle

auspices *Gi* chal: person Romany Erin

G.A.A.: Gaelic Athletic Association *Gi* chi: child, girl, daughter roaming

Parnell: speech in Cork, 1885: 'No man has a right to say to his country "Thus far & no further shalt thou go" '

VI.C.6.263: '△ cavern woman hair dragged by it'

ECH ALP *Da* lik en and: like a duck

Anit: Egyptian goddess

r Liffey little bit

G Marsch: march O.K. *Da* kæmpedamper: giant steamship *N* dæmper: damper, moderator

It alto là!: who goes there? (mil.) *F* gué: ford *N* kjæmper: giants

wharf *F* mons *R* rebenok: child

(Eve created from Adam's rib)

N mand: man *N* haard: hard hearing

'Grand Old Man' (Gladstone)

Le Petit Tondu (Napoleon's nickname)

Bluebeard (wife-killer in story by Perrault)

S.I. Hsiung: *Lady Precious Stream* (a play)

Du landschap: scenery thingummyjig incident happy-go-lucky

Gr theogamia: marriage of gods

(035.03) June collided *ph* let the cat out of the bag

January

amidst funeral games utmost

Fianna G.A.A.: Gaelic Athletic Association (games in Phoenix Park)

forecast a breach of the peace

I Inbhear Life: 'Liffey Estuary' (D bay) *G* Sinnbild: symbol

meeting point Pontine Marshes

Da ikke sandt: isn't that true? *F* Nil: Nile

First Cataract of the Nile Aswan Dam (on Nile)

G Damm: dam

hairpins 'Exsultet': 'O felix culpa!'

pseudonym

F sourd: deaf *R* zdravstvuyte gospodin: how do you do, sir?

I conas tá tú, a dhuine uasal: how are you, gentle sir?

aurora borealis sticking

Martial: *Epigrammata* XII.57: Rus-in-Urbe ('the Country in Town')

s 'Boots, boots, boots, boots'

Czechozlovak diversion *Cz* dveře (pron. dverzhe): door

Ali Baba & the 40 Thieves (pantomime): 'Open Sesame' the door is it
Wenceslaus *Hu* szesz: alcohol *Cz* v: in *Cz* s: with
the door is means
(what does this mean?)
in the door fits
Cz z: out of *Cz* k: to, towards *Cz* ano: yes *Cz* ne: no
G Handschuh: glove Prince Potemkin: lover of Catherine the Great
Cz podomek: manservant
Cz ani slovo: softly – not a word *Po* Slowianie: Slavs
Hu szusz: breath, wind
mummified Confucius
L nummi: coins, money
everlasting *Cz* Kateřina: Catherine
LAP **K**
Cz daří dobře: keeping well Dantzig Corridor gave Poland access to Dantzig & Baltic Sea after WW I
s My Boy Willie
Cz vybojovaly: they won the battle
Cz kavárna: coffeehouse
mil. commands: 'ready!, present!, fire!' Corsican Upstart (Napoleon)
salute (008.09,010.22–3)
remarked to herself
von Moltke: Prussian field marshal
Ourselves Alone (Sinn Féin Amháin) *Cz* dříví: wood, timber paterfamilias
Cz vrbový: willowy
whippoorwill Bohemians home *Du* boef: criminal *Cz* baf: puff
bobby now you're in the museyroom (008–010) Jameson's whiskey
Shem
(008.33–4) hare Guinness' hound
Shaun *F* jeunesse: youth
Wellington
below
Milton: *Samson Agonistes* sari: dress worn by Hindu women
outside
fashion
It fascio: bundle
Da dronning: queen beeswaxed Nelson: 'Kiss me, Hardy'
meanders *Sl* phiz: Swift: *A Tale of a Tub* mundane
countenance Monday (washday)
fed up to the chops miracles
40 Bonnets (020.28)
F mots
Da fader: father *D Sl* mott: girl
G Vater Unser: Our Father
APL amnesty (1542): forgetfulness *I* Sinn Féin Amháin: Ourselves Hottentot
Alone (slogan)
L amnis: river praised
leap year *Cz* poduška: pillow, oreiller
Cz Praha: Prague
daughter
sons
s Cock Robin: 'The birds of the air were a-sighing & a-sobbing' dorter: dormitory
L formica: ant Lord's Prayer: '& lead us not into temptation . . . For thine is the Kingdom, The Power & the Glory . . . Amen'
Thingmote: Viking parliament in D (on mound) Gorey, town, Co. Wexford meals
R gora: mountain *R* gore: sorrow
Sl murphy: potato
nutmegs *Cz* brambory: potatoes *ph* 'Dear Dirty Dublin'
Cz dorty: cakes dumpling
I obaire: work, labour upset the pot *G* Pfote: paw *AngI* whist!: silence!
D Bay Mrs Beeton's cookery book *U*.190: 'caudlelectures'
Mrs Caudle's curtain lectures in *Punch*, 1845 *Cz* chesty: frequent chat *Cz* dobrý den: good day
lictor: Roman officer executing judgements on offenders; carried fasces *L* cauda: tail
Cz noviny: newspaper William Morris: *News from Nowhere* (describes a socialist utopia)
Naul, village, Co. D Teplitz & Marienbad: Bohemian spas Merrion Baths, D

parish priest's   curé   uncivilized   liturgies
F ensevelir: to bury   lethargies
very best   Moore: *s* Fly Not Yet, 'Tis Just the Hour [Planxty Kelly]

Chambers' Encyclopaedia   *Cz* milost: grace   *Cz* Panny: of the Virgin   *Cz* kostel: church
chamber pot   lycopodium: inflammable powder used as stage lightning   *Cz* milostpaní: *G* gnädige Frau
Cz žid: Jew   follow   *Cz* bílé boby: white beans
give us
wanting   Demerara (Gladstone's father was slaveowner there)
De Valera
tub
tumble
BROWNE   tall hat (Gladstone wore)   characteristic
G toll: mad (Gladstone popularly regarded as model for Tenniel's Mad Hatter)
'Man of Destiny' (Napoleon)
Delgany, village, Co. Wicklow   professed
volcano
Captain Nolan carried order causing the Light Brigade to charge
NOLAN   nightcap   recognize
L nates: buttocks
'Grand Old Man' (Gladstone)   mahogany
MacMahon: Fr. marshal in Crimea
s 'dog of the nurse of the child of the wife of the Wild Man from Borneo'

Wellington
Ranelagh, district of D   Danelagh: area in N. & N.E. Eng. settled by Danes in C9–10
Gladstone   Browne   Bonaparte   Nolan   Parnellite
G Brauen: brows
common denominator   Ʌ   Olaf the White: 1st Norse king of D
Cumhal, father of Finn
this is his big white horse (008.21)

reference   majesty   Dumas fils: *La dame aux camélias*
midget   come-all-you: type of ballad
matches to   statue of Sir Hugh Gough in Phoenix Park   *Cz* Prosit: to beg
It goffo: clumsy   *Cz* prosím: please   *G* Prosit!: cheers!, your health!
crick in your neck
Cz krk: neck
s The Barley Corn: 'O rum it is the comicalest thing, How it tickles . . . '
Sl pickled: drunk   Punch & Judy

together

s 'I got a shoe, you got a shoe, All God's chillun got shoes'

G Pöbel: rabble   magazine   (045.05–06)   chromo: chromolithograph
It mezzatinta: half-tint
G Krim: Crimea   Humpty Dumpty: 'All the King's horses & all the King's men'

Almanack's: London club in Regency   Tennyson: *Charge of the Light Brigade:* Cannon to right of them, Cannon to left of them . . . Volleyed & thundered'   *L* canis: dog
G Flunder: flounder

come & gone   *Cz* slečny: unmarried middle-class girls
Dial gang: go   slowcoach   *Cz* slíčnost: grace
G Duft: aroma

I dúnann an doras: shuts the door

(014.06, 501.06)
Ulster Dial thon: that
s 'Do ye ken John Peel with his coat so gray, Do ye ken John Peel at the break of day, Do ye ken John Peel when he's far far away, With his hounds & his horn in the morning'
Adam Findlater: grocery magnate & politician in Edwardian D   tallyho   Tallaght: district of D; supposed plague grave of Parthalonian invaders
Findlater's Church, D

s Donnybrook Fair   Millikin wrote *s* The Groves of Blarney
s Widdicombe Fair   Manneken-Pis: statute in Brussels of a child urinating
Chapelizod   like   Co. Carlow   Charlemagne's
Aix-la-Chapelle

tallyho

his majesty died down
drew rein

R izba: cottage
Izba: Polish Chamber of Deputies
(.23)

Grimm brothers' fairy tales

defiled baker's dozen = 13
eel
legs armour the phoenix burned at Heliopolis Phoenix Park (024.18)
F amour When Healy became Gov.-General of Ir. Free State, Dubliners called the Viceregal Lodge in Phoenix Park 'Healiopolis'

F valet de chambre

skirl: play bagpipes Ant hunt *s* Chevy Chase
G Hund: dog
Grasshopper lightning thunderpeal
tender appeal
wondering whether Waste Land hostile *G* Ost: East
Du vasteland: mainland (as opposed to island) West End, East End
G neu: new *G* Ziel: target
New Zealand Old Balaclava (Crimea) Buckley shot the Russian General
Ellmann: *JJ* 398: 'Buckley, he explained, was an Irish soldier in the Crimean War who drew a bead on a Russian general, but when he observed his splendid epaulettes & decorations, he could not bring himself to shoot. After a moment, alive to his duty, he raised his rifle again, but just then the general let down his pants to defecate. The sight of his enemy in so helpless & human a plight was too much for Buckley, who again lowered his gun. But when the general prepared to finish the operation with a piece of grassy turf, Buckley lost all respect for him & fired'

Du ons bereiden: prepare ourselves
'Ko Niu Tiireni, e ngunguru nei aa-ha-haa!'–part of a Polynesian *haka* ('It is New Zealand, rumbling here')

Maori (New Zealand race) *G* Sturm
Wellington, city, New Zealand
fiercer 'Ka tuu te ihiihi! Ka tuu te wanawana!'–from the same
fusilier *haka* ('Now is seen the fearfulness, the awfulness'–i.e. of the warriors in their dance)
Russian general

I bhuachaillín: little boy
Buckley weakling

Paderewsky: Polish statesman
R po russki: in Russian

Ferguson: *Hibernian Nights' Entertainment*
G Untertan: vassal love
Blessed St Barbara (patroness of artillery men; *U*.599) dozen & one (*1001 Nights*)
Du sint: saint Swift: *A Tale of a Tub*
O'Connell *It* colomba: DOVE hell's
St Columba
RAVEN *It* tutti: all Noah's ark
Tut-ankh-amen yacht
F aimée: Arthur, Duke of Wellington
beloved orthodox
Grace O'Malley: Ir. pirate *s* Phil the Fluter's Ball
(021.20 &c.)
long & the short of it
Lang & Greenwood had controversy about Shakespeare
(Wellington Monument in Phoenix Park) odalisque: concubine in Eastern harem

spendthrift spindrift: spray blown along surface of sea
F mathurin: sailor J.C. Mangan: 'Maturin, Maturin, what a strange hat you're in'
St Mathurin: patron of fools (C.R. Maturin, dressed eccentrically & wrote *Melmoth the Wanderer*, name used by Wilde)

suspicious

F piou-piou: soldier *L* in sæcula sæculorum: for ever & ever sign of the cross

army mess went to Mass *L* Introibo ad altare Dei: I will go unto the altar of God (the
Kierkegaard: *Enten-Eller* Mass; *U.*3)
Da at alle taler Dansk: that everybody speaks Danish *U.*425: 'Rugger . . . You hurt? Most amazingly sorry!'

s The Bowld Sojer Boy

Measure for Measure *G* Messer: knife cycling
F messieurs

loudmouth
Co. Louth Co. Meath

G (be)heizen: to heat, to fire

s 'Needles & pins, blankets & shins, When a man is married his sorrow begins'
ultimatum Shem/Shaun
(006.11–12) for all the world to see

Attila *G* waschen: wash W as in wash
Alaric: 1st Teutonic leader to conquer Rome
G frönen: drudge feoffee: one *Arch* insue: ensue Cain & Abel
G Fronherr: feudal lord who holds land had issue
Senta sings spinning song in *The Flying Dutchman*
spindle side: female line of descent
Abraham . . . Sarah behold
auburn brume: fog
It amore: love

s The Babes in the Wood (also pantomime) story book
John 1:14: 'the Word was made flesh'
ph start from scratch

'the truth, the whole truth & nothing but the truth' (legal oath)
Butt & Taff (338–54)
pr Truth is stranger than fiction *I* sláinte: health *J* shin: truth
AngI ph shin shin: there there chin-chin (toast)
Ulysses S. Grant led Federal 030.13: 'grand old gardener' gold medallist
army in Am. Civil War *G* Garten *L* qua: in so far as
public man funeral *nr* Where Are You Going, My Pretty Maid?: 'My face is my
T. Manlius Torquatus: federal fortune, sir, she said'; 'I'm going to market, sir, she said'
Roman consul who condemned his own son to death

The Liberator: Daniel O'Connell Le Petit Corporal (Napoleon's nickname):
Liberal leader (Gladstone) a cigarette brand *It* corpore: body
catnapping *ph* with baited breath
It lezzo: stink
G Jungfrau: virgin

tenderised Atalanta (running) reading
Sp tendero: Atlantic swell breathing
shopkeeper shimmy shake (dance) *ph* (from Gen 3:19) sweat of his brow
taut bight: a curve or bend in human body *G* Welt: world
11th E.B.: 'London': *pickadil*, stiff collar, source of name Piccadilly West End
VI.C.6.41: 'pickadillies = ruffs' peccadillo wit's end
Sl soiled dove: prostitute my wife & I thinks
L candidatus: clothed in white
softboiled egg apparent electorate
boiled shirt: a dress shirt aperient: laxative illiterates
nonentities (with no Latin)
It nullatenenti: have-nots
NOLAN calabash: type of gourd
snap (photograph)
William Ewart (Gladstone) antagonist by the same token
Arch whilom: once physiognomist *Gr* phôtognômos: one who knows light
upon a time St Bruno founded Carthusian monks
BRUNO St Bruno pipe tobacco
consumed panegyric what a lot
paregoric

G Piffpaffpuff: childrens' imitation of sound of gun W. G. Grace, batsman run getter: a great old free scorer in cricket

centuries (cricket): hundreds of runs

cg Blind Man's Buff leg before wicket: fault in cricket (stopping ball by interposing leg)
Papal Legate Po dupa: arse
eminence Papal dispensation
almoner: distributor of alms
Church of the Three Patrons, Rathgar, D Divine Providence (Vico)

milkman bonafides L bona facies: good face L sola fides: only faith
Po mlecko: milk Boniface: generic name for innkeepers
friends say 'Hutch' & 'Annabel': popular singers, 1920s–30s
G Freude: joy
vanished continent (Atlantis 336.27) ALP
VI.C.6.21: 'H = vanished consinant'
PAL prelude subliminal
L ludus: game seminal
the Salmon of wisdom caught & eaten by Finn (entrance & exit)
Solomon (wisdom)
mailbags Dickens: *Bleak House*
Da blækhuse: inkwells

Λ Bruno Nolan

William (Gladstone) Bonaparte Du twee: 2 G Rosen: roses suppose
Fr. Marshal Ney at Waterloo creamy
call Sylvia Silence: character in Eng. schoolgirls' magazine of 1920s (061.01–10)
imagine G Stotterer: stutterer suppose N bygmester: master builder
F poutre: beam, girder
Du bil: arse turn to the front & tread G tritt: step backwoods
omnibus Du bok: billy goat
imagine

Sl lobster: British soldier William Viscount Wolseley (Crimea)
ph Dear Dirty Dublin for instance Arthur Wellesley, Duke of Wellington
not improbably

appreciate practical jokers

participate worries dribbling

yourselves pr Walls have ears

M.J. MacManus: *So This Is Dublin* (1927) derides J darlings
slowly Bedlam
pleased pick flower (flora) pure
true
howdydo Finnegan
fauna
highty-ti likes monkey nuts how d'you do? Du dood: dead
Tahiti (Society Islands) Sl mankey: decrepit
Tom, Dick & Harry ballocks
Teague: nickname for Irishman Bullock: place nr Dalkey
how the hell
Butt

J wore a Borsalino hat shot the Russian General
Morris saloon (car)
⚔ Boyne, 1690. Defeat of Ir. Jacobites
belle of the ball Tancred: Norman leader of 1st crusade
Flavin: Lombard king Taff
TAF George Moore's *Evelyn Innes* includes 'Ulick Dean' (W.B. Yeats) BUD
Artaxerxes: name of 3 Persian kings F compère appear compare compete

malster: malt-maker
s Ireland Boys, Hurrah: 'We've heard How Buckley shot the Russian General
her faults a hundred times' Lord Burghley: Elizabethan statesman, suppressed recusants
G Ehren: honours *I* go bráth: until Judgement Day (i.e. forever)
L germanus: full brother Erin
house Ir. Citizen Army (1916)
place
White Friars: Carmelites 1132
Pied Friars: mendicant order prior to 1245
revelation *Skt* karma: action, occupation previous
elevation Carmelite Order privy
umbrella *Sp* paraguas: umbrella
(looks up expecting thunderstorm) paraphrastical
solution riddle rhyme writing *R* krasnyi: red
solatium: compensation *We* rhyfel: war *We* hedd: peace *D Sl* butty: drinking companion
General Blücher (⚔ Waterloo) what's he? Billy Walsh: antiparnellite
R moriak: sailor bloody red what say? D archbishop

middleaged clerical appearance (.05)

digester

F garce: slut & to die Buddha *G* da: there
disgraced *R* da: yes
Sh mwil, mwilsa: I, me Burns: 'Flow gently, sweet Afton' Sevastopol
(father) *Sh* suni: see *Da* aften: evening cesspool
promptly cesspool

put up a hare: put forward a point *s* Home to Our Mountains (from *Il Trovatore*)
very first
describe him to us, ant . . . the grasshopper Cain's descendants Jubal & Tubal
conscript
s Brian O'Linn—he had breeches with 'The skinny side out & the woolly side in'
R guberniya: province Sunday suit . . . Monday
governor-general & lord-lieutenant of Baltimore (Co. Cork) *R* Baltiiskoe more: Baltic Sea
L gubernator: steersman *Sp* gerente: manager *G* laut *R* liev: lion *L* tonans: thundering
L Cornu Amalthae: horn of plenty & use parliamentary language
Eng. gunboat shelled Liberty Hall, D, during 1916 Easter Rising military
lilies of the valleys don't (speak Shelta) *Sh* Sheldru: Shelta Shelta
I sail: willow *Cz* noc a den: night & day *F* parler: to speak
s Father O'Flynn: 'Sláinte & sláinte & sláinte again' tell us *It* strana: strange *Du* slang: snake
Tass: Soviet news agency Ir. Ogham writing *R* strana: country *It* malora: ruin *Sl* sling slang: to abuse
R Malorossiya: Little Russia (Ukraine) Sathenik: mythical Armenian queen *R* sotnik: captain of a group of
It razzia: raid speaks it, calling a spade a spade satanic (orig. 100) soldiers
Ar Siranouche (woman's name) ginshop man-o'-war
monosyllabic words (swearing; Chinese)
many symbols Ir. tinkers used Shelta tinker's damn okey doke for
monosyllables simple men damn it! *Fi* tammi: oak auto-da-fé O.K. though for
Charlemagne *C* meng: dream mandarin *F* airain: brass *Tom Sawyer* *C Pi* topside:
C ch'ang-li: usual procedure Iron Duke (Wellington) 'Man of Aran' (film) superior
pagan *F* géant: giant Ajax a jakes *F* rassembler
killer ejaculate all the night
Moore: *s* Remember the Glories of Brian the Brave [Molly MacAlpin] Wood's halfpence: monetary
F bruyant: noisy *F* bref swindle imposed on Irish,
against which Swift
wrote invective
Freud: *The Interpretation of Dreams* waking
'Terror of the Danes' (Brian Boru)
s The Moon Hath Raised Her Lamp Above breakfast killed our reverie
(erection)
Charlemagne OGPU: Russian secret police, 1922
Bobrikoff, Russian Gov.-General of Finland, shot on
s Let Erin Remember the Days of Old 16/6/1904 (*U.*134)
F braise: embers
drawing *F* blouson *It* meditabondo: thoughtful, pensive
bosom
Sh minker's tari: Shelta grasshopper's *G* weiter: onward whitehot lantern
G heiter: cheerful
fed on green isles hills of Erin
Moore: *s* Let Erin Remember: 'On Lough Neagh's bank, as the fisherman strays'

Nipponese language wamble: wriggle about
(Japanese) *Sl* wedge: penis rambles
I Uladh abú: Ulster to victory! Pukkelsen (316.01) *J* san: polite form of address
J sayonara: farewell see you nearer *Sl* poke-hole: cunt
It annoiato: bored *nr* 'Old Daddy Dacon, bought a bit of bacon' (257.14–15)

F Sl bicon: large cunt *R* gotovit: he cooks *s* 'I got a shoe, you got a shoe, All God's chillun got shoes'
Sh gåt, got: young *R* obed: dinner *R* chelovek: man
Sl fudden: semen *R* pishcha: meal (theme of eating the god) *BL* metchennacht: a curse
R povar: a cook poor old pissabed! *R* molodezh: the youth *G* Mitternacht
Sh laburt: a curse *R* myaso: meat because, & damn it, sir, he can't Gam cant: Shelta
belaboured *R* bog: God Czar
limber: detachable forepart of gun carriage *G* Hund: dog Λ K ⊏
Tennyson: *Charge of the Light Brigade:* 'Cannon to right of them, Cannon to left'
doe *L* ros: dew *s* Do Ye Ken John Peel?: 'With his hounds & his horn in
F dos ⊣ ⊢ the morning' *G* bellen: to bark
(so far so good; his bark is worse than his bite) enveloped by enemies *Gr* chrôma: colour
R sobaka: dog *ON* Ragnarøkr: destruction of the Norse gods
Crimean fashion cannibal *G* Wappen: Raglan-sleeved coat *G* Rock: coat
bastion coat of arms Lord Raglan (Crimea)
The Malakoff: fort nr Sevastopol Varna, where troops in Crimea lodged
F mal coiffé busby *Da* bygge: build varnished Russians (boots) Roscius, actor
Lord Cardigan (Crimea) jacket General Scarlett (Crimea) Prince Menshikov (Crimea)
G Jagd: hunt Perekop: isthmus, Crimea *F* manchette: cuff *J* manchaku:
3-coloured camouflage *Gr* perikopê: a section 'Gaelstorm': Ir. raincoat, 1920s deception, camouflage
camiknickers pendulous (medals) (7 items: colours of rainbow)
earwigs hire purchase *Cz* obr: giant *Da* berømtst: most famous Siege of Kars, Crimea
L pulcher: beautiful *Po* ubranie: suit of clothes Kersse (311.05–9) Castor & Pollux
F confectionneur: outfitter, clothing shop several shiners (coins)
Polikoff: D tailor *I* siomar: shamrock
(mademoiselles would look back at such clothes) thunder & lightning *J* tento: lightning
J musume: daughter, girl

Gr aster: star *Bul* terziya: a tailor *Bul* shumat na ratta: the noise of the battle

G horchen: listen Bulgarian Cuchulainn had 7-pupilled eyes
(wagging ears)
US Sl full of beans, full of hops, full of prunes: lively, actively foolish
(his eyes full of images from Butt's description of the general's uniform)
R groza: thunderstorm *Gr* arktos: bear Count Todleben (Crimea)
G grossartig: magnificent *G* Tod: death *G* Leben: life
Guy Fawkes sex appeal *s* Auld Lang Syne

Bosquet's comment on charge of Light Brigade: 'C'est magnifique, mais ce n'est pas la guerre'
Daguerre invented photography
has forgotten his night of glory passed among
gloze: flattery, deceit
s Flowers of the Forest all & sundry
Alexander
benefit of the doubt come all you Dukes of Wellington
F jupes women
grace Calf of Man, on the Isle of Man reigning heavenspun (rainbow)
raining
confirmation red, orange, yellow, green, blue, indigo & violet
coronation
In Tasso's *Gerusalemme Liberata,* Erminia disguises herself to enter enemy camp &
rescue her beloved ECH
Du dood: dead Steppe (Russia)
Sl hodmandod: deformed person
struggling *ph* 'Dear Dirty Dublin' Lublin, town, Poland remember
leal: loyal lusk: sluggard Lusk, village, Co. D
sign of the cross Macaulay: 'Every schoolboy knows who imprisoned Montezuma & who strangled
sickle Atahualpa' Attila ('little father'; .36)
Zuma: name of a pyramid field feeling willynilly
Wilno, city, Polish 1920–39
perhaps born midst Kremlin before he was baptised
Minsk, city, Polish 1919–20 Crumlin, district of D *Da* født: born
(feels his origins might have been unholy) Vatican water-can
G Vater
ant & the grasshopper (414.20–1) father son
It lettera: letter *F* lettres à cette terre

okey dokey Ukraine stutterer of guilt, he is notorious on every rota scutter: to squitter, have
Rut dobre: good scatterer of gold *Da* guld: gold *F* retour diarrhoea
F route: road *Rut* lyudskyi vischod: origin of man son of a bitch fitchet: polecat

wash & brush up: notice in Eng. men's public toilets
Archbishop Walsh of D Boney: Napoleon *s* 'On the bonny bonny banks of Loch Lomond'
ph tongue in cheek

R Rutene: Ruthenian impossible objects *Rut* misto: town *Rut* mist: bridge
routine Julian Alps, Yugoslavia *It* misto: mixed *Rut* mistomist: town of towns
Rut lyis: forest Ljubljana: cap. of Slovenia *Du* hoofd: head Howth Riviera
Rut luhy: meadows Dublin *Pro* ribiero: river
s Loch Lomond: 'But me & my true love will never meet again'
Trulock: D gun manufacturers
I carraig: rock *Sh* karnag: drawers Moore: *s* Forget Not the Field [Lamentations of Aughrim]
Carnac, Brittany, site of megaliths stone/tree *G* Feld
Loch Lomond Ogham writing The Furry Glen, Phoenix Park
Woeful Dane Bottom: valley in Gloucestershire, possibly site of a Danish defeat
Rut ne: no *Rut* tak: yes
Rut nji: no
prick ranks princesses bodies (hiding)
prink: to smarten prank: to dress showily
byre: cow house

Black Sea (Crimea) strives to recollect all the struggles for life
G Schwarzseher: pessimist regulate
road widow of Ephesus
Rut vidnova: renewing
ph black sheep of the family *D Sl* relic of old decency: souvenir of better times
overdraft
Requiem Mass: Dies Irae ('Day of Wrath') *s* Mother of Mine *s* O Sole Mio
Rathmines: district of D *Rut* selo moe: my village
It zulu: (fig.) boor Bjørnson: Ibsen's rival, MacMahon: Fr. marshal in Crimea northeaster
It lui: him 'son of bear' (also meaning of 'MacMahon') Oslo L/R bear
west *Bul* proletta: spring south
It proletta: small progeny sweat of his brow
Peter & Paul (rivalry) MacMahon: 'J'y suis, j'y reste' (when asked to leave
Malakoff fortification)
Brian Boru (bear likes honey)
Deadwood Dick
(bear) Maida Vale, London *R* medved: bear
Du meid: maid *R* med: honey
s Jerusalem: 'Hosanna in the highest' defiled the lilies of the field *G* Feind: enemy
De . . . lilah Lilias Walsingham: heroine of *The House by the Churchyard*
confronted Samson
Shem, Ham & Japhet jawbone of an ass (Samson's weapon)
G Gott strafe England: God punish England (slogan)
s 'God save Ireland say we all'
sycophants what with

psychopomp: a conductor of souls pulchritudes
to the place of the dead
Buckley & the Russian General whether VI.B.8,147: '⊥ girl lying on causeway with one
Rosh Hashana: Jewish New Year leg heavenward, lacing her shoe'
parish priest visitation: ecclesiastical visit
pollex: thumb mirage marriage
fancies painted
fantasies (lower): 'P a bishop going forth on rogations'
shoelaced
s The Wren: 'Up with the kettle & down with the pan' constellations
s 'Hi-de-di, how-de-do' *PS* pan: sir *Puss in Boots* (pantomime)
ph The pot calling the kettle black
Po pol: half *L* sol: sun dargsman: day labourer *L* luna: moon
Po but(y): boot(s) *G* soll: should *Cant* darkmans: night *Ar* targman: interpreter
follow my leader
'Piping Pebworth, Dancing Marston, Haunted Hillborough, . . . Drunken Bidford'—poem attributed to Shakespeare
refusing to resume drinking competition at Bidford *Rut* muzhytskyi charivnitsa: peasant witch Czar
G Wirt: innkeeper On His Majesty's Service *Ar* dzaṙa: servant
Ross rifle (WW I) Czar of all the Russias *Da* Russer: Russia my first
criss cross *G* Ross: steed *s* 'The Wren, the Wren, The king of all birds'
EAR *F* cul-de-sac second is made to sit on (WICKER chair) *F* perce-oreille

s You Should See Me Dance the Polka

F bouche *F* gorge: throat (roof of mouth) unbuttoned

sharpen signal
shrapnel

interior monologue *G* Spiel *s* Little Brown Jug

s Pop! Goes the Weasel *s* Merrily, Merrily (from *The Tempest*)
Whang the Miller: character in Goldsmith's *Citizen of the World* *s* The Protestant Boys
Mills bomb (shrapnel) (his snapshot was in Russian journal)
⚔ Boyne, 1690 *Sl* snapper: penis *WW I Sl* rumjar: German mortar bomb
general by *s* The Girl I Left behind Me
R lyub-: love
twostep symphony bones (mus. instr.) every
I cogadh: war *Gr* sumphôtia: giving of light
(black & white piano keys) *Il Trovatore* I.3: 'IL CONTE DI LUNA: 'Il Trovator! Io fremo!' ('the troubadour' –(his rival)–'I rage!') Balaclava, Crimea balaleika I tumble to it
s Phil the Fluter's Ball: 'With the toot of the flute & the twiddle of the fiddle, O!'
hammer & sickle scythe *G* Hummer: lobster
Rut hovoryty: to speak *s* Let Erin Remember the Days of Old: 'collar of gold' *Her* gules: red fullstrength
choler something
to the following effect Berkeley valued tar water as medicine
swallowing olfactory (smell)
bowels squitters: diarrhoea monarch
F boules: game (cf. skittles) monad: ultimate unit of being
pr Necessity is the mother of invention
ph making a virtue out of necessity
acting sergeant betwixt (Turkish flag has star & crescent moon)

Matt 7:20: 'By their fruits ye shall know them' *s* Piff Paff (militant Protestant song from *Les Huguenots*) *G* piff paff (onomatopoeic for gun)

Michael Glinka: *A Life for the Czar* *Po* mleko: milk Milky Way *s* The Rocky Road to Dublin
G Pfeife: pipe *s* 'When Malachy wore the collar of gold'
corkscrew bend verbal vocal visual

renounced CHE *We* caer: town, castle
renown Carholme: race track at Lincoln
hundred & eleven

ph fleet of foot

s The Wearing of the Green: 'O Paddy dear & did you hear the news that's going round?'
Gr hippos: horse
hip, hip, hurray! heliotrope wins or places (2nd) as the case might be
helioscope: apparatus for observing sun Winter Palace (Russian Revolution)
L meus deus: my god Windsor Palace, England (horseracing at Windsor)

NOLAN Penitent in confession must perform *satisfaction* as penance, & exhibit *firm purpose of amendment*
contrite
very reverend Epiphanes: race horse, sired 1932
Gr epiphanês: manifest, notable
Saint Doolagh: village & church BROWNE Brown Bomber: horse in a comic strip; also Joe Louis, boxer
L/R nr Baldoyle bowler
ossuary: urn for bones of dead *L* bonum: good horse theology
as sure bone in your osteology
Buckley shot the Russian General 'Isle of saints & scholars' (Ireland)
The Racing Calendar: horse-racing annual roistering roast chestnut
penitent (*metanoiac*) in confession must exhibit *supernatural sorrow & contrition* (.25)
guffaw (horse laugh) *L* nuper: recently *L* satur: sated exomologosis: public confession
Dick Whittington (pantomime): 'Turn again, Whittington, Lord-Mayor of London!'
chestnut: stale anecdote absolution after confession
nr Humpty Dumpty *s* 'Come lasses & lads, Take leave of your dads'

mamas flesh & blood

trefoil (shamrock) to be sure Coppinger (055.18)
trifles coppers
Slippery Sam: thief & tailor in Gay's *Beggar's Opera*; also a card game

In Ireland, worshippers outside a full church during Mass are considered morally present though physically absent knave of diamonds slouching
'Mick, Nick & the Maggies' (219.19) *ph* a penny for your thoughts
pittance penance (confession)
deck: cover

Gen 27:22: 'The voice is Jacob's voice but the hands are the hands of Esau'
In Jewish folklore Sammael is God's enemy (Sam & Tim) Boozer's Gloom: race horse, 1930s
sulking silken Baldoyle: district of D, has racecourse

clocks of six steeples
chic people
F ensemble *Youthful Exploits of Finn:* 'a chief-smith' *L* semper: always
several candlestickmakers
F midinette: workgirl *It* casa bianca: white house *WWI Sl* Casabianca: the last one
Mrs. Hemans: *Casabianca*
Spanish Inquisition *Sp* causas es quo stas: you are the cause; where do you stand?
L ad valorem: according to value 'Take off that white hat!' (catchline of Moore & Burgess minstrels)
De Valera Dominican Brothers
circumstances

distinguished patronage of the last governor-general (of Ir., Donald Buckley, 1932)
unwashed poltroon personage *Skt* jagannātha: 'lord of the world', Vishnu or Krishna
Punjab Great Jupiter, what was that
F gross
(7: lucky number) The 1,000 Guineas (horse race) *Sl* guinea to a gooseberry: long odds

Liverpool Summer Cup (horse race) *s* Right Little, Tight Little Island
pr There is many a slip 'twixt the cup & the lip (039.10–11) Persse O'Reilly

Town of the Ford of the Hurdles (D) cross of Christ phoenix burned at Heliopolis *Gr* holophulos: entire
G Ross: steed *Gr* 'X' = *L* 'Ch' all the populace
HCE shout of exclamation Punjab E . . . CH
shite excrement Emancipator: race horse, sired 1927
Crimean HCE

Prov 30:19: 'The way of an eagle in the air . . . & the way of a man with a maid'
Eagle's Way: race horse, sired 1919
bay (ink made by Shem, 185.25) Bailey Lighthouse, Howth
white hat (Finn MacCool)
F ratatouille *G* Fürstin: princess
P. Tuohy (painted J) first & second
Liffeybrink Spring Double: the Lincolnshire Handicap & the Grand National

heels *L* pater: father such a thing to happen here!

Garden of Eden thought of

such a thing Lord-Mayor profoundly annoyed amused *F* ennui
lock maker *L* pro forma: as a matter of form
chains that will be all for today

dream offered Butt & Taff

slapstick quick-change (artistes) *Sl* top-hole: superb
sweepstake

aware B.B.C. London Regional (racing)

corroborated liberated second sports flash
collaborated
different Big Dipper: Ursa Major *Sh* tasi: to read *I* tiomar: bequest *Ma* timor:
taking the time of day Timor: island in Malay Archipelago *L* timor: fear East

pungency poignancy *Ma* orang-utan (lit. 'man of the woods') Orient: East
Du Maleis: Malay *L* Ultonia: Ulster (orange) Orion, constellation
(constellation Draco lies between the Dipper and Sagittarius) cursed
Draco: Athenian lawgiver *Du* op de loer: on the lookout
corsair: pirate with bell, book & candle gamble
B.B.C.
Strongbow's tomb, Christchurch Cathedral, D celebrating *s* Tramp, Tramp, Tramp
(once place of business) Cerberus (hell gates)
Palace of St Sepulchre, D, nr Marsh's Library *G* Armee: army ⚔ Mons, 1914
Holy Sepulchre (crusades) armaments *F* Allemands: Germans
(cannonballs)

Giant's Causeway, Co. Antrim route stations of the cross
followed
gospel truth *s* Tommy Lad
(communist)
ph Perfidious Albion 'Tingsomingenting' (414.34) *s* Tinker, Tailor
think some other thing
said Galwegians: Norwegian Captain Europe and Asia
inhabitants of Galloway caftan: Oriental tunic Åse: Peer Gynt's aged mother
children *s* Mother Machree Myles-na-Coppaleen shoots hunchback Danny
Da skoledreng: schoolboy Mann in *The Colleen Bawn* (Boucicault)
L miles: soldier

goat/sheep surtout: overcoat shoulder of mutton

look more like the gentleman

Ginnunga-Gap: in Norse Eddas; the interval between aeons noy: annoyance
aggregate Jap . . . China (war, 1930s) behind *SC* Skupshtina: Yugoslav parliament
anger get up *L* a posteriori ⚔ Waterloo *F* val des ombres: valley of
⚔ Austerlitz shadows
below zero *pr* No man is a hero to his valet great state for fear
F valet de chambre greatest heat
erection susceptible might *L* a priori *G* Popo: posterior
Alb popo: alas proper
proportions *Alb* zotni: sir

bother doubt 'Nixnixundnix' (415.29)

Great Jupiter! (342.14) *Alb* me fol: to speak *Alb* shpirt: spirit
(I followed him by the light of a match) *Alb* shpirtua: match
Alb schkrepes: match *F* cuirasse: armour *G* Wehrmann: soldier
nr Humpty Dumpty: 'All the king's horses and all the king's men' *C* min: the people
Tragedies of the Ancients ant & the grasshopper (414–419) *Ma* gunong: mountain
Grand Opera son of a gun scandalous
Heb sabaoth: hosts, armies Mookse *ph* burning the candle at both ends
epaulettes *Arch* smook: smoke John of the Cross: *Obras Espirituales*
butt end fine doings! *F* foin! (expletive: disgust) *Rut* obraz: image
F Sl foin: tobacco *Alb* duhan: tobacco (from *Arab* duhan, smoke)
Da ejendom: possession *Du* leggen: to lay
(walking)
bandylegged *G* Pulver: powder *R* poroch: gunpowder *Rut* stolitsya: capital (city)
looking stool of ease: privy, commode
G nehmen Sie Platz: have a seat *Alb* frang: European celebrate lubricate
nemesis: retribution *G* platsch!: splash! *F* à la français *L* salubris: health-giving
orthodox sublime *Sl* pumpship: urinate
(military base) supine supreme
chorus parish priest Oliver Cromwell
L coram: in the presence of
Ragnar Lodbrok: Viking chief
reciting
I ceathar: 4 gospels all & sundry Santry, district of D
R chetyre gospoda: 4 gentlemen
chattery (breaking wind) farts
Heb haftara: excerpt from Prophets read in synagogue after having his breakfast (when Bloom defecates)
Rut kuropatva: partridge the gist ghost
AngI by the holy . . . ! aghast
G bibbern: tremble fear verst: Russian land measure: ca. 2/3 mile
ON vear: gods (poetic)
fjord opening line of *Paradise Lost:* 'Of Man's first disobedience & the fruit'

Siegfried Sassoon: WW I poet Anglosaxon is coming *Ar* sarsoun: shiver *Ice* jötnar: giants
G Unglück: bad luck, accident joining
highly *It* ligio: loyal, faithful sapper P/Q split
religious happy-go-lucky
tear in his eye *ON* bönd: constraining powers (class of gods)
ON -tyr: god
s Johnny I Hardly Knew Ye

Moore: *s* Weep On, Weep On, Your Hour Is Past [The Song of Sorrow] Goethe
Solomon
Shakespeare Dante *G* Papst: pope *AngI* gombeen man: usurer
Papist *Ma* jamban: latrine
coward's blow *Ma* ya (iya): yes *It* gamba: leg
We cawraidd: gigantic *Paradise Lost* cartridges'
Siamese twin acknowledgement
It scimmia: ape
WW I Sl strafe: to bombard *Bul* studen-: cold suddenly drops dead
communique, straight *WW I Sl* firetrench: front trench *Bul* drob: liver *PS* led: ice lead
sat on his heels changes uniforms *R* drob: buckshot
R ushi otchii: father's ears lifting
ph letting the cat out of the bag grows

blue eyes become brown Celtic twilight
F cul *F* toilette
(style of Synge's *Playboy of the Western World:* son tries to murder father)
Youthful Exploits of Finn: 'in his oneship' (= alone)
Nietzsche *Rut* nichnyk: night watchman *G* Kopf bandylegged
Nijni Novgorod, town, Russia *Sl* knob: penis waterlogged
Roman Catholic *ph* laying down his life
cathartic
Christianly Nebuchadnezzar *F* Messe: Mass exposing
'Kruschens': laxative salts *L* messa: harvest espousing
sinful teetotum: game in which 4-sided disk is spun open order (infantry formation)
Heb Sl totto: arse manure manoeuvring
remunerature cowards Irish peasantry thinked
It muratura: masonry cow herds *We* cawraidd: gigantic *I* ruad: brown
breath headquarters

Caucasus *ph* have the nerve *F* liard: small coin if
lewd
for love or money *It* inoccupato: at leisure
antimony (present in various base metal alloys)
view base metal *Alb* akshan: morning action pagne: loincloth
bimetallism: circulation of 2 monetary metals in fixed ratio
ping-pong (.27) Very lights (used to Nazi storm troopers
G vier: 4 illuminate battlefield)
heroes

I Sinn Féin Amháin: Ourselves Alone (slogan) Seraphim

fierce smell Urals *Ma* orang-utan *Du* stank: stench *WW I Sl* saphead: fool satrap
L aura: odour rank smell
Peter the Great *Alb* altipalter: revolver billet cf. 213.18–19: bell for Sechseläuten (.22–3)
T peder: father antipater
bullet babbling *Alb* yatagan: curved dagger
G gut *Youthful Exploits of Finn:* 'no lie is this'
blubbering ('me' precedes Albanian infinitives) knees *F Sl* gnaas: 'number one', 'moi'
Naas, town, Co. Kildare
feet to beat it (run away) so long! clemency clumsy
R patóm: after(wards) Seringapatam besieged 1792, 1799
L mea culpa Aram, Son of Shem (also early Armenian king)
Erzerum, Turkish base in Crimean War, once Armenian
R ushi: ears without prejudice
Ar dėr: expression used to *Ar* dirouhi: female equivalent of dėr
address secular clergy Czar of all the Russias
Ar sour: sword *Ar* hour: fire *Ar* Haroutioun: male Christian name
arse *G* Ärger: anger falling *F* travaille
weight of his age *Ar* ardch: bear *Gr* argia: idleness
stomach (*pr* An army travels on its stomach) *F* bosse brother
recognised the face *Youthful Exploits of Finn:* 'there was fear with her the sons of
Nuad: king of the Tuatha Dé Danann Morna for him'; 'heavy': pregnant
sons of Noah covered his nakedness (Gen 9:23)

Armenian Hail Maries *Ar* hayrmer: the Lord's Prayer
Ar hayr: father *Ar* mayr: mother among
OCS Gospodi pomilui ny: Lord have *I* a chara mo chroidhe: friend of my heart (voc.)
mercy upon us, Kyrie eleison *Ar* dkhour: sad I hadn't the heart to (shoot him)

matter of fact *F* penser *s* 'The wild man from Borneo has just come to town'
G Waldmann: forester, satyr
Ma Brunai: Borneo proposing *Ma* parang: jungle knife
BL bara: skirmish *Ma* perang: war

matter of fact bloody life
bowie knife
does so, surprised great Scot! *Alb* Zoti: God You hadn't the heart?
Bul suprúg: husband *G* Zote: obscenity *Du* zot: fool
I fonn: desire; tune
R vot: here What fun!
s Planxty Sudley sadly
someone or other rather suddenly
AngI whist: silence
WW I Sl valise: khaki knapsack falls asleep
Sh kuldrum: asleep anything at all
P.P.s (parish priests)
Ar mard: man Wilde to Douglas in *De Profundis:* 'but I met you either too late or too soon'
at all *F* merde! (too late to shoot general because defecating)
farewell *s* The Wearing of the Green

S. Lover: *Handy Andy,* ch. 6: 'Think o' this when you're smoking tobacco'
Baggot St, D
yard's notch
at arm's length
post sticking *It* tocca: touch *Ma* rumah: house
It stocco: dagger making room *Ma* rumah makan: restaurant
by omnium gatherum *Da* skat: treasure, tax

lagan: goods or wreckage *Ma* susu: milk
lying on seabed *Ma* biribiri: sheep
Ma jongos: waiter *pr* Speech is silver, silence is golden (right hand)
(ordering a drink)
Ma terima-kasih: thanks *L* nihil obstat: nothing prevents (form of approval by Church censor)
Ma kasih: give me *Bul* napred: before *F* naperie: household linen
Bul Coll momche: waiter
advert: 'Guinness is monstrance mumchance: silent
good for you' *L* prima facie: at first sight champagne something
s Nearer, My God, to Thee *Triestine* bon pro me fazzi: much good may it do me
ouzo: a *s* The Wearing of the Green: 'I met with Napper Tandy' *G* trink: drink scup: a fish
liqueur *R* uksus: vinegar Moore: *s* Drink of This Cup [Paddy O'Rafferty] (consecration)
Offertory (Mass) tobacco

whipped off *Sl* chimney pot: tall hat
doffed
tinopener takes up Saints

trespasses *It* centellare: to sip
G Trost: consolation, comfort
L Pontifex Maximus: high priest, pope *Port* hospedaria: inn hospitality
haruspical: functioning as haruspex, Roman soothsayer
salvation Moore: *s* The Meeting of the Waters: 'There is not in this wide world a valley so sweet'

send us delights

forces

like as *G* bösen: evil *G* Feind: enemy
Du boezemvriend: bosom friend
forgotten abused Mullingar Inn, Chapelizod

G Zwischenzeit: interval *G* teilweise: partly fashionable
television

frozen Crim Tartary (North) forces *F* affaibler
Frisian (cattle) fuses *F* affubler: to dress up
mackintoshes Nijni Novgorod, town, Russia (North)
I muc: pig *G* Schnee: snow galoshes
Spanish (South) ruddock: a gold coin; hence, money; also a kind of cider apple titivated tattooed
Antichrist *Sp* Habaneros: Havana cigars *L* Pax Romana Rome (South)
Anti-Greenback (dollar) Party (U.S. politics)
Abraham . . . Sarah *It* bella suòra: beautiful nun, sister (Abraham married half-sister Sarah)
Ibrahim: Sura 14 of the Koran happy Christmas
Arabian Nights (East) execute devil dances
rumba
jehu: furious driver *G* Johannisfeuer: St John's fire (lit on midsummer eve) Yale University U.S. (West)
atmosphere hemisphere nuns' talk nonce Turkish (East)
resolutions for the coming new year girls elding: firing, heating
rebel Dryden: *Alexander's Feast:* 'never ending, still beginning'
begetting *pr* It's never too late to mend etcetera
eat celery
Aunt Sally (throwing game)

Buckley shot the Russian General
Sochi (Fr. spelling 'Sotchi'): a port on the Black Sea
Trollope: *Phineas Finn* tomorrow afternoon
Finn
your funeral's a resurrection
Ixion chained to wheel in hell
passed the buck Peter the Piper: C15 anarchist
pr he who pays the piper calls the tune blackthorn stick *s* Peter Piper
It colligiano: living in the hills melting *SC* dober dan: good day!
I Colg a' tiuine: Fury of the tune beating
Du dom: stupid tombstone come & warm his limbs again
Adam *Hu* domb: hill *Du* stom: stupid, mute
I agam: at me
It gamba: leg
F parlez-vous le français Pidgin English *F* parler
s Polly Wolly Doodle parlour
Vercingetorix: Gallic chieftain who revolted against Caesar 6th Duke of Buccleuch defeated by Gladstone in Midlothian in 1879 rhetoric
Buckley shot the Russian General Ghazi Power: Ir. journalist (521.22) *Ar* hov: breeze
Po gatsi: drawers
Sea of Azov (Crimea) *Ar* gov: cow don't leave out the sod of turf
Ar dzov: sea *s* Father O' Flynn: 'Sláinte & sláinte & sláinte again'
I Páid a mhic: Pat, my son (you haven't gone off your song?) *I* áth: ford
s Paddy Whack *G* Abgott: idol Butt *We* bach: little hath yesterday
not ended? *Da* vær saa god: (lit.) be so good *Bul* ezik bulgarski: Bulgarian language
s The Day Thou Gavest, Lord, Is Ended *Ar* hay: Armenian Buckley
Ballygarry: town, Co. Mayo *L* saeculum: century what you may call 'em
Bulgaria Napoleon on pyramids: '40 centuries have their eyes fixed on you'
call the scapegoat's bluff *Huckleberry Finn*
Po skop: wether (sheep)
someone somewhere *I* siomar: shamrock Dingley Dell: country village in *Pickwick Papers*
howe: hill, tumulus *Charge of the Light Brigade:* 'someone had blundered'
s 'One fine day in the middle of the night, Two dead men got up to fight, Two blind men were looking on'
I Sinn Féin: Ourselves Alone (slogan) bog myrtle (shrub) *Da* stod op: stood up
Ma tuan: lord 'Turn again, Whittington, Lord-Mayor of London' (pantomime)
James Larkin: C20 Ir. labour leader
G Schneesturm: snowstorm nice change

We budd: gain, profit
HF 18: 'couldn't come it'
I cúisle: heartbeat godforsaken heart
Cush: point of land W. of Howth Howth
Sh spurk: flirt Nihilist
People's Park, Dún Laoghaire Niall of the Nine Hostages: Ir. high king
Upper Baggot Street, D all at once
gut (tract) *G* Wanst: belly
begod *R* khorosho: very well
Aengus: Ir. love-god
Taff I said I would 'Exsultet': 'O felix culpa!' it was
Bul az: I phoenix

wet Thursday *s* One Fine Day in the Middle of the Night midriff Bulgarian
12 July in Ulster: King Billy on white horse *Sh* Midril: Devil *I* bolg: belly
Bul sbogom: farewell, lit. 'with God' *HF* 27: 'along about noon-time' *R* cholodny: cold
roughly *L* arx: castle 1st equinox (21 March) calendar
Khorasan: N.E. province of Persia

bethel *G* elf 1132 years *Da* to: 2
Macbeth II.2.55: 'sleep no more' *N* elv: river *Sh* skimisk: drunk
as the crow flies *Po* krowa: cow Ghazi Power led a 'power' of skirmishes, odd adventurers
Rut krov; *Po* krew: blood Gen 9:29: '& he died' (Noah) & indeed
Flood lasted 40 days & *Bul* godina: year *Ar* heghegh: flood
40 nights *PS* den: day *Da* nat: night
Bul vreme: weather; time *R* veter: wind ever
rainy *G* Wetter: weather most mournful
doomsday *Po* dym: smoke I was in the Royal Irish
Po krzesa: to strike (fire) Persse O'Reilly
Chersonese: peninsula of Sevastopol as under Sir Arthur Wellesley (Wellington)
Milesians militia Sandhurst: military Siddhartha Gautama: the Buddha Woolwich:
donkeys' years Silesia college Crimean War military college
letters 1914–18 headed 'somewhere in Flanders' Cromwellian
Ma ayer: water *G* stumm: dumb *G* Prost!: to your health! prostitutes
Ireland *G* Waffenstillstand: truce
the fleshpots of Egypt & the hanging gardens of Babylon Marrowbone Lane, D
Eastcheap & Marylebone, places in London *Sl* marrowbones: knees
G Waffenstillstand: truce Boston, Mass. Julian (New Style) calendar did not replace Old Style in
Wapping: area of London Russia until after Revolution
Charge of the Light Brigade: 'Half a league onwards' *Bul* blagodarya: thank you
ph rue the day leg over a stile Finnegan blackguards
lose please God *s* The Peeler & the Goat: 'Bansha peelers' muskets
lues: plague, pestilence
who's who Mal 4:5: 'the coming of the great & dreadful day of the Lord' *It* San: Saint
VI.C.9.9: 'great day—1000 yrs'
St Patrick arrived A.D. 432+
heptahundred 700
1132

Gr hepta: 7 *L* anni Domini: years of the Lord Hodges Figgis: bookshop, D
Haji: pilgrim to Mecca tells
AngI is in it: exists Bog of Allen

Numerous spurious 'prophecies' attributed to St Colmcille (Columba) *I* Éire go bráth: Ireland until Judgement
The Book of Kells 'is often called the book of Colum Cille' prophecies Day (i.e. forever) broke
I can tell you incommixed: not mixed
I continue
HF 13: 'dead beats' *HF* 31: 'begun to study'
HF 18: 'took out after them'
HF 31: 'we would give them the cold shake, & clear out'
HF 8: 'Well, dey's reasons'
bloody *Army Sl* perisher: periscope *HF* 33: 'he lays over the yaller fever'
BLM means 'they looked & called at those who came to [villa prob. means village]'
Longaville: character in *Pro* toumba: to fall
Love's Labour's Lost *Pro* toumbado: fall (sb.)
Pro aclapa: cover with stones *s* The Peeler & the Goat: 'Bansha peelers'
Pro aclapadis: heap of ruins clapped
Vanessa . . . Stella (Swift) *It* stissa: anger

John Maddison Morton: *Box & Cox* (play about John Box & James Cox) Jonathan Swift
Boxer Rising, China, 1900
L exercitus: army *Bul* topka: ball, dance
exercise
Roman Catholics *R* oruzhie: weapon *R* patronna: cartridge
Rome & Carthage *R* horosho: very well *s* The Peeler & the Goat: 'on duty & patrolling, O'
G krumm: Crimean War by the way (breaks off laughing)
crooked Cromwellian

thunder & lightning *G* heiss: hot
skivvies
G Feuer: fire D motto: Obedientia civium urbis felicitas (Citizens' Obedience Is City's
Dublin obeisant *L* basia: kisses Happiness)
I smalcadh: devouring fulvous favourite Turkish (tobacco) *Du* rooken: to smoke
AngI kish: wicker basket (for turf)

Swift's Yahoos (in *Gulliver's Travels*) marriage ceremony: 'Whom God hath joined let no man put
ladies *C* hao pu-hao (colloq): how do you do? colonel asunder'
weren't you aide-de-camp?

Port difficultoso: difficult *Port* tresdobre: threefold
Cz dobře: good *R* bitva: battle
bottleful of stout *Du* borrel: drink, glass of genever
Bre staot: urine barrelful of beer
alpha omega megrim: migraine *G* Rasse: race *PS* posleden: last
awful associations
F plombe: lead futures
aplomb impervious
boodle: lot, memories bosom my tears run slow
money illegally acquired maimed Zozimus, D street singer, had 'buzzum' friends
R sleza: tear blimey! platonic love recall
F blême: pale gun recoil
chickens home to roost missionary post
dickens
boyars: rank of Russian aristocracy; erron. applied Valhalla
to Russian landed proprietors
Alma Mater: school *G* dringen: urge, press bygone fusiliers
⚔ Alma, Crimea, 1854 drink *G* Fusel: bad liquor
cully: fellow condensed *Rut* vody: waters
colour sergeant: one attending regimental colours
absinthe & vermouth *G* Wehmut: melancholy; absinthe gentlemen in agreement
contain wormwood *G* Mut: courage
Swaran: Norse leader defeated by Macpherson's Fingal throne-filler

W.G. Wills: *A Royal Divorce* rest

inhabitants New Ireland: island near New Guinea *F* mot *R* velikolepnyi: magnificent

me old attachés *R* kurgan: burial mound *Dial* keek: peep

ph more kicks than ha'pence happened Cedric or Sitric Silkenbeard, son of Gormfhlaith, led
Danes at ⚔ Clontarf
O'Donoghue Conchubar: uncle of Cuchulain

Youthful Exploits of Finn: 'It is these are their names'
Youthful Exploits of Finn: 'under that manner'
Clongowes Wood College
(*Portrait* I)
maladies Tuileries, Paris *R* plemyannitsy: nieces
F reinette: type of apple 1914–18 army jokes about plum jam (only jam they got)
F reine *R* vera: belief, religion, faith *R* dyadya: uncle
nr Old Daddy Dacon
King Mark of Cornwall for the purpose of warmth
AngI ph a great man for . . . jinking: winning game by taking all tricks in 1 hand
womb Tennyson: *Charge of the Light Brigade* lace
Da lys: light
Moore: *s* Lesbia Hath a Beaming Eye [Nora Creina]: 'But no one knows for whom it beameth'

hip, hip, hurray *Rut* raz: once *Rut* tre razy: thrice 'three times three' (cheer)
screameth
ancestors Wellington: 'Up, guards, & at them'
Lancaster v. York (Wars of Roses) anathema
heavensent heroines
houri: concubine in harem
when new arrivals *F* espionne: female spy
train (.31) *Sp* señoritas sinuous Spain
(robbed him) *ph* in the thick of battle battle of Waterloo
the attack Bakerloo line on London underground
toothbrush *s* Dashing Away with a Smoothing Iron
(his tongue)
multinational anfractuosities (set of teeth)
L infructuositas: unfruitfulness *Bul* sinya: blue *PS* sin: son
s 'The Wren, The Wren, The king of all birds' son of a bitch *R* sonya: sleepyhead
(Eve from Adam's rib) Eve, queen of Alburz, Zoroastrian mount of paradise *R* son: dream
nr Ride a Cock Horse ready tricolour given to Louis XVI infantry
Gr rhoda: cunt *R* rady: are glad in 1789 with words 'here is a cockade which will go round the world'
Ar khôsel: to speak *Ar* lezou: language *It* barbe: beards
lesbian Silesian St Barbara: patroness of gunsmiths

triggers *nr* 'Rings on her fingers & bells on her toes' where does the pain
Port dôr: pain *It* pene: penis
Mr Punch drumhead court martial: one summoned round *G* Generalstab: general staff
upturned drum, concerning offences during action
Ps & Qs (nursery): 'please' & 'thank you' Pigott forged letters implicating Parnell in Phoenix
the P/Q split if you please marshal Park Murders *Cockney* do your nut: act madly
Sl dingbats: mad Lortzing: *Zar & Zimmermann* (opera)
Bas zahar: old *G* Minne: love
Bas tšori: bird *Bas* elhur: snow
chorus aether (T.V. transmission)
heliotrope night time

Taff vice versa

Butt Baird invented T.V.

uranium teleframe: 1 complete sweeping of T.V. screen
step up: amplify (T.V.)
Tennyson: *The Charge of the Light Brigade* sync pulses added to output (T.V.)
Gr synkopê: cutting up
bits between their teeth *U.*596: 'Irish missile troops'
Butt . . . Taff misled
nr Hickory, Dickory, Dock carrier wave (T.V. transmission)
spray gun in T.V. tube bombards screen with electrons
split focus (in early form of T.V.) dynamite
Tsars Alexander & Nicholas scanning spot in T.V. traverses picture in parallel lines slightly sloped (.10)
Medieval L nichil: nothing to horizontal

rutilant six hundred (of the Light Brigade)

G Schluss: end caesium (sensitizes T.V. screens)
gospel truth casein (used in plastic mnfr)
fluorescent T.V. screen spectra mephitis: noxious emanation from earth, hence mephiticism
spectacular *I* caoch: blind coagulates
iconoscope: early T.V. camera fellowship of the Holy Ghost
(Phil 2:1: 'fellowship of the Spirit')
G wohl: well the Pope O'Donoghue General of the Jesuits

Russians eidolon: spectre
Sp idolo: idol
The Star & Garter: *G* starren: to stare *G* Gürtel: girdle Isabella la Catolica: patron of Columbus
pub name 'The Son of Heaven': Chinese emperor
Michael Palaeologus: Byzantine emperor Jan of Nepomuk: patron saint of Bohemia,
Mark 1:7: 'the latchet of whose shoes' whose tongue had not decayed when tomb
Peter & Paul (rivalry) opened 330 years after his execution
powder & ball
Great Belt: strait dividing Zealand from rest of Denmark O'Gorman: *Martyrology*
Buckley Herbert Gorman: J's authorised biographer
customary midweek service victor
vicar
R notnyi: musical breaths
not voice
hell, something's gone wrong with the switch! (In Extreme Unction, eyes, nose, mouth, hands & feet are
speech anointed)
television vices

G Fänger: catcher wipes his mouth with a sort of
(putting his fingers up his nose) mother
often *G* oben: above wanton
G unten: below
Da beundre: admire bundles altogether *L* manus: hand

L pes: foot
pederasts
accomplices confederates
L comfoedo: I pollute, defile
s 'the cat came back . . . for it couldn't stay away' *It* coda: end Jesus

Christ *s* 'the cat came back . . . for it couldn't stay away'
G Katz': cat because *L* cauda: tail
Gen 2:9: 'the tree of life also in the midst of the garden' *G* Erden: earth Eden
BL Add MS 47480.107: 'garerden (cemetary)' *Ar* gerer: tree
Hillel: Pharisee, interpreter of scripture
Hillel Men's Shelter, D up hill & down dale *Ma* dalem: under
Job 8:17: (the hypocrite) 'seeth the place of stones'

in point of fact just forgetting amoret: love sonnet
L in ponto fert: he carries in the sea
Russian General Buckley shot bugger
all over the whole bloody shop
G Schiff: ship (hen collects–011.10–19 &c.)

evensong honour ladies & gentlemen

gesture expressive Lady Campbell said Oscar Wilde was like a great white
caterpillar pollard: animal
sunflower (heliotrope) *F* beau point blank blackmail that has lost horns
(Wilde wore flower in buttonhole at his 1st trial)
mundane Old Bailey Court (Wilde) hesitency backfire

malevolence *Sl* lance: penis (aiming at general)
It melo: apple tree
lord of creation wife of his bosom last
wipe of his bottom *Sl* lad: penis
G Eltern: parents *R* prostite pozhaluista: excuse me, please *R* dovol'no, proshus: that's enough,
enter alter his mind behind prostitutes pure jealousy thanks
R prashchur: ancestor *Gr* prostates: leader *Port* circunstância: circumstance
Li prašau: please precious *F* defence: forbidden debaucheries
on pickpockets Ps & Qs prosecuted
picket (army) Paul/Peter
be at pains, please more by token

betake yourself other place *Port* praça: marketplace
hotter place (i.e. hell)
Cossacks am sure Bashi-bazouks: Turkish irregular soldiers
God's sake *F* basque: skirt Bezique: a card game
poor leprechaun Oscar Wilde *Bas* asko: much bellyful
Africa (*Ma* 'p' commonly replaces 'f') *Bas* esker mila: many thanks
Turkish delight fucking (*Ma* P/F) *Ma* puki: cunt *Romeo & Juliet* julienne: meat &
Cz pěkný: nice raw meat *I* ráiméis: romance, nonsense vegetable soup
N stoel: stiff Mary Lamb's tales (*Adventures of Ulysses*) (head)
toes in my kidneys sheep/goat (kid)
I Sasanach: Englishman *Alb* nji herë, dy herë, tre herë: once, twice, thrice

Osiris Byron: *The Destruction of Sennacherib*: 'The Assyrian came down like a wolf on the fold'

Players' cigarettes *R* trubka: tobacco pipe Tommy Atkins
prayers (pipe of peace)
s Sir Patrick Spens *Bul* pari: money *s* Slattery's Mounted Foot
Peter's pence: contribution to R.C. church *Bul* zlatar: goldsmith
Sl crimson dawn: shed a light *Cant* darkmans: night
cheap red wine shellite: explosive
R slava bogu: Glory to God Huguenots (massacred)
R slovo: word VI.B.14.31: 'huguenote (flatche bed)'
Daniel (in lion's den) reading
R spalnji: sleep
Revelations (Bible) Albigensians (massacred) *s* Father O'Flynn: 'sláinte & sláinte & sláinte again'
Genesis (Bible) *L* sanctus
ph still & all tit for tat *F* chanter

Sunday school whoreson warrior carries a comrade *R* komnata: room
Sunda: dialect in E. Indies *Du* schoon: clean Napoleon: 'Every French soldier carries a marshal's baton in
G Schnaps unless forgetful
G Schnappsack: knapsack enlist regiments his knapsack'
rudiments of civilised warfare hailfellow wellmet
Sl wildfire: strong liquor

s God Save the Queen: 'Send her victorious'
Nolan/Browne
Nowells, Brownings: firearms
Tom, Dick & Harry
G dumm
s 'Lots of fun at Finnegan's Wake'

apparel
Cant meggs: guineas
C19–20 *Sl* meggs: halfpennies
Chipping Norton, town, Oxfordshire
Isa 2:4: 'They shall beat their swords into plowshares'
Du eieren: eggs
Pro arc-de-sedo: rainbow
halcyon days
rainbow rumba
hell's own
Royal Leinsters
Sl lobster: British soldier
R radouga: rainbow
G Liebster: dearest
redoubt
raw recruits
Rosicrucians
Paddies
British
AngI praties: potatoes

Windward Islands, West Indies
wayward
Ma Inggris: English
s My Dark Rosaleen
Omar Khayyam
Rut yisty: to eat
Rut pyty: to drink
F homard: lobster
cayenne
windowed

carriage
J.H. Voss: 'wine, women & song'

Pushkin: *Tsyngany*
cigarettes
Rev. Stoddart Kennedy, 'Woodbine Willy', gave out cigarettes to troops in WW I
Po popiół: ashes
D Sl rossies: impudent girls
R papirosy: cigarettes with black tobacco
Charlie Chaplin
R chórnay: black
Po szklanka: drinking glass
Bass's Ale
R pivo: beer
I sláinte (toast)
J banzai! (shout of victory)
Peter & Paul (rivalry)
s Phil the Fluter's Ball: 'Then all joined in with the utmost joviality'
Novial: an artificial language
down
rebels
king
armistice
F petit bonhomme il vit encore: man in the street still lives ('Jacques Bonhomme' personifies France)
drinks
AngI bonham: sucking pig
tit for tat
Moore: *s* The Dream of Those Days [I Love You above All the Rest]
Gr dromos: race
Du droom: dream
R strast: passion

buckoo: Australian term of approval
Aust Sl bonzer: first-rate
private
(officers' stripes)
believe me
Du toegeven: give in
halfpenny damn
Ma wang: money
Humpty Dumpty
Sl wing: penny
(so-called)
genitals
Dan O'Connell
Korniloff: Russian officer in Crimean War
Ma tanah: land
I miliseach dílis: dearest sweetheart
Cornwall (King Mark)
R milusha: nice girl
WW I Sl militia's delicious: camp followers
flank movement (army)
St Petersburg (Petrograd)
Ma bagus: fine
some picturebook
care
idols
Earwicker
comminations: church recital of Divine threatenings against sinners
In legend of the 3 sons of Tuireann the sons had to give 3 shouts on a hill as part of their penance
Shem, Ham & Japhet
tinker's
private life
Petrograd
retrograde

Leningrad (Petrograd)
both
leanings
F Sl soeurs: whores
Sl sisterhood: brothel staff
Ma puteh: white
Lyndhurst Terrace: Hong Kong brothel area
It putti: cherublike figures
Ma chelana dalam: drawers
venting her anger can tell the truth
Sl belle: whore
vinting: making wine
Ma anggur: wine
Prussians called ⚔ Waterloo 'La Belle Alliance'; centre of Fr. lines was La Belle Alliance Inn
highness
hairyness
'Respectable' girls preferred in Oriental brothels
colonel
lightning
Ma guntur: thunder
Ma sawab: truth
It culone: having a big arse
Malay Street: Singapore brothel area
lieutenant-governor
F aimées
Salvation Army
down

bloody
pompadour
Sl tout: one who solicits clients for brothel; bludger & pimp live off earnings
Java (in Malay archipelago)
down
by Jove!
work
Du wolk: cloud
Youthful Exploits of Finn: 'at the head [end] of a week'
stumblebum: a clumsy person
R russkii volk: Russian wolf

Old Contemptibles: British Expeditionary Force, 1914–18 Scott's Road, Shanghai brothel area
Russian General *L* ursus: bear Ossian *L* gemini: twins Scots red
uniform *R* nemtsy: Germans nem. con.: no one opposing nonchalance
Youthful Exploits of Finn: 'He went before him' echelon: formation of troops in staggered parallel divisions
(went his way) *Da* domstole: courts of justice uplift
Tom Fool story apple fallen woman: prostitute
pitied James Whiteside defended O'Connell & O'Brien (.31 black)
Sl petted: of whore, reserved by pimp for private satisfaction
Britishers ricochet Bartholomew Vanhomrigh: father of Esther (Swift's Vanessa), lord-mayor of D
breeches shirt *Fi* vanhemmat: parents ham & eggs *F* vis-à-vis
harlot scarlet runner (beans) *Youthful Exploits of Finn:* 'gave love to'
General Scarlett (Crimea) *Sl* runner: brothel tout in Egypt
word

Maid Marian: Robin Hood's sweetheart (*Sl*: whore)
mermaid maddening
ph A Roland for an Oliver revolver splinters of Cork (009.23)
Richard III V.4.7: 'my kingdom for a horse' splendour of God Colt revolver
how goes the enemy?: what time is it? Persse O'Reilly *F* monsieur
enema
F Allemagne Almighty God above us ant & the grasshopper
BL almaig: night Armenian Goth *Almanac de Gotha* (record of European noble families)
Du meest: most Mme de Pompadour: 'After me, the deluge'
Louis XIV: 'L'État c'est moi' Co. Meath Dulwich, place in London
('The State it's me') Procurator of the Holy Synod hoary sinners
Sl procuress: woman who procures girls for brothel
R pulya: bullet paralysis I shot him
Gr polyergon: elaborate thing Lewis machine gun
white slaver Humpty Dumpty I'm believer
Raglan coat has wide sleeves (Lord Raglan, Crimea) unbeliever
since *Po* bron: weapon Browne & Nolan *Po* ulan: lancer
common sense *Du* bron: well (sb)
s The Volga Boat Song *Port* vermelho: red
R volk: wolf boasting Vermilion Sea: old name for Gulf of California
unseemliness rival's
R zemlya: land rifle
authorization
Gr autosôtêr: self-saver
behind homosexuality
sodality
s Lullay Mine Liking General Cambronne: 'Merde!' *Sp* cabron: he-goat, cuckold
F comprends? perhaps
Holy Russia
rasher of bacon
clever brigadier-general
Balaclava *R* braga: kind of beer
Parnell called Gladstone *G* hold: lovely Amsterdam
the Grand Old Spider *Youthful Exploits of Finn:* 'It is a name for Deimne, Fionn'
Carlyle: *Sartor Resartus* *G* Sieger besiegt: victor conquered

fishmongers counter a 'nation of shopkeepers' (Napoleon on English)
fieldmarshals *F* marchand: shopkeeper sharpshooters
Kipling: *Danny Deever* *Port* bigodes: mustaches
I déan deifir: make haste
Bul pet: 5 shoves his thumb & 4 fingers

three four five hee-haw . . . ass arse
ph fe fi fo fum ('oh's' & 'ah's' in .22–6)
buckshot unbottle
embezzle
Graves wine *Hound & Horn*, magazine *F* loup garou: *Ar* kayl: wolf *G* Geselle: companion
s John Peel: 'his hounds & his horn' werewolf
T kaptan: captain black backside beard
Le Mort Homme, Dead Man's *U*.226: 'Bad cess to her big face!' HCE
Hill, N. of Verdun, WW I Free State (Irish, 1920s) first rate Russian General
frustrated 4-star general (U.S. army) Rosicrucian
Daniel O'Connell, commander-in-chief
Heb aleph (letter) Koran
as best as he can with the help of God & His blessed mother *Bul* blazhen: blessed
asbestos
Bul maika: mother suffering save *It* pugna: fight
maker sulphur (in hell) purgatories

St Patrick's Purgatory: cave on an island follow theogony: generation of the gods
in Lough Derg (practicing sin) the agonies damned
Bul tresene: trembling Bismillah: 'In the name of Allah . . . the Merciful'
Mars
august gracious *R* sobor: assembly *G* sauber: clean
Holy Ghost egregious in sober truth
(civilian clothing) detriment Isle of Man

not so?

momentarily *Gr* apoxy-: pointed approximately ominously determined
scoffing *Gr* apaxioumenos: participle of 'disclaim as unworthy' disturbed
busman's holiday

bones
Gr hagios: holy diadem (heaven)
damned

Yes, sir! Tsar sabre-toothed tiger truth Savile Row (the suit) *It pr* se non è vero, è ben trovato (if it
R ya: I *R* yastua: food sombre is not true, it is a happy invention)
that he lives yet is my grief *Arch* grafe: work
R net: not
bedad *ph* cock a snook Kilturk, Co. Fermanagh
Lewis Carroll: *Hunting of the Snark*
L ursus: bear Viking victorious
Bjørnson, Ibsen's rival: name means 'bear-son' *L* taurus: bull
ph rats in his attic mad as 'Clontarf' means 'Bull Meadow'

Sitric Silkenbeard led Danes at ⚔ Clontarf, 1014 Moore: *s* O, For the Sword of Former Times [air
Oliver *F* sourd unknown]
(I) seen him *Da* klokken tolv: 12 o'clock rolling
s Klokke Roeland (about cathedral bell)
all over Ireland ('Old Sod') sod of turf
pr A Roland for an Oliver
clean his wipe himself *R* pudavik: weight of 1 pud undoing *It* tuoni: thunders
I claimhe: itch *G* Wolle: wool *s* Paddy Whack *Fi* tuoni: figure of Death intoning
F culottes Ps 113 (Vulg): 'In exitu Israel de Aegypto' (*U*.698) Jupiter instant
I tón: arse *L* deo: by the god at that insult to Ireland!
R igo: yoke, suppression *It* pronto: ready *Serbian* dobro noc: good night
(Igor-land, i.e. Russia)
crossbow *F* merde! = *Sp* mierda! *It* miro: I take aim like an arrow
bishop's crozier *nr* Who Killed Cock Robin?: 'I, said the sparrow With my bow & arrow'
Cock Robin *N* rogn: rowan tree sparrow
ON Ragnarøkr: destruction of the Norse gods *It* sparo: I shoot, fire
annihilation of the atom etymology *R* groza: thunderstorm
L ab nihil: from nothing *R* groznyi: terrible (epithet of Ivan)
G Gründer: founder *s* The Wild Man from Borneo Hurdle Ford (D)
Lord Rutherford splits the atom, 1919
explodes detonates Lucan: *Pharsalia* Ivan the Terrible
Persse O'Reilly Urals
fragor: loud harsh noise amid which confusion
It rombazzo: uproar confession
R molat: hammer escaping molecules country bumpkins
atoms *N* skape: to make, create Coventry, city, England
pumpkins Fairy Godmother London elegance of Piccadilly
Mother Goose (pantomime) Landau carriage (Cinderella's pumpkin)
pinkindindies: C18 D nocturnal strollers; slashed passers-by with their sword points
It scenata: scene senators Honolulu
Bulawayo Imperial Rome *G* Raum: space 'Modern Athens': Edinburgh *G* Atem: breath atoms
R balavayu: I play pranks Empyrean *G* Mord: murder Atem: creator in *Egyptian Book of the Dead*

(radio time signal; in Freemasonry the time is always noon)
sunset all day long *F* guerre *Da* Kongerige: kingdom Donnybrook: district of D
Danelagh: area in N. & N.E. England settled by Danes in C9–10
Eire

woolgathering Kremlin Crumlin: district of D
Oliver Cromwell
Bristol Artane: district of D with Christian Brothers' turn
borstal boys school Isolde's Tower, D
Ir. once had 5 provinces; now there are 4
Youthful Exploits of Finn: 'a big four' (= 5)

R dom: house, family   what are all the bulbs up in the air?   shot him?
dumdum bullet   chambers   hubbub upstairs   shadow
I mo mhic: my son
moving
G stark: strong   R dooch: spirit   I deoch an dorais: parting drink
(O'Connell's Ale, D)   R durak: idiot
Gen 4:13: Cain: 'My transgression is greater than pardon'   diminuendo (music)

Eccles 1:2: 'vanity of vanities'   sure enough
L vilitas: cheapness
Finn MacCool
Goll, defeated by Finn
desperate   despite   wage-slave (Communist   feudal unshackled
s The Soldier's Song: 'the despot or the slave'   propaganda): capitalist worker
s Bishop O'Dwyer & Maxwell: 'O'Dwyer upheld the right'

Butt & Taff   umbraged: i) shaded; ii) offended
s The Brave Volunteers: 'for a wee while'
L magister: master   living-by-owning (Communist propaganda): capitalist society
L magis quam: more than   ethic
surface of the globe   glebe: soil of the earth
s The Brave Volunteers: 'by craven & traitor'
s The Brave Volunteers: 'they had cause to revile'   Mauser Rifles used in Easter Rising, D
s Dublin: 'too foul for hell'   s Ireland to the British Empire: 'burning, With boiling lead
Youthful Exploits of Finn: Luichet 'fell by Goll'   & brands'
Moses' burning bush (Exod 3:2)   gillie: young attendant on a Celtic chieftain
Persse O'Reilly   St Cecilia: patron of music
Sicilian hurdy-gurdies
s The Soldier's Song: 'fonn na bhFiann' ('soldier's song'); 'bearna baoghail' ('gap of danger')
It concertone: augm. of concerto   concertina
Morehampton Road, S.E. D   makes love
Sheilmartin Avenue, Howth (N.E. D)
Meeting-house Lane, old D   embraced   Vergemount Hall,
embarrassed   Clonskeagh, D
father or mother   murmur   brotherhood of sisterliness
s We Shall Rise Again: 'without falter'   Da mormor: grandmother   blather   or   sophister
Fianna: Finn's army   U.S. Sl dook: hand
It pugna: fight   Comintern: 3rd Communist International
Sw fästman: fiancé   s Who Fears to Speak of Easter Week: palm (shaking hands)
Ar oukhd: vow   G fest: firm   'great men & straight men'   Ar Asdouadz: God
can-can   concatenation
Ar khaghaghout'iun: peace
when all the world was a garden   Anthea: epithet of Aphrodite as flower-goddess
Arch worm: snake   PS gad: snake   unveiled
wonderful   Wonderland   world was
Waterloo   how does the world wag?
Siamese twins   G Mutter
Samurai: class of military retainers in feudal Japan   U.200: 'Murthering Irish'
s Dies Irae   Ides of March
ideas
muscat   (281.04–05: 'de Pline et de Columelle')

magpie   Tower of Babel

(.22–8 form   raven/dove   you love the size   G loben: to praise
rhyming verses)   sexual mosaics can have the head & body different sexes
I hate the seat of his trousers   G Traube: grape
mice ate the   trouble
spindle side: female line of descent   F sourd

by-&-by   boys   girls   flotsam & jetsam
Gael & Gall (foreigner)   G Flossen: fins
Tom, Dick & Harry   Lucifuge Rofocale: Lucifer in the *Grand Grimoire*
carmine, silk & honey all insect products   Exod 3:8, 17 &c.: 'milk & honey'
deaf as a beetle for us   cousin   Coriolanus

more sweeter to me   Buckley shoots the Russian General
mouths water   *Ulster* thon: that
Germinal: 1st spring month   I bod: penis   Taff   bite
in Fr. Revolutionary calendar   ph chew the fat of his anger
Swift: *Tale of a Tub*   Butt

thumb & five fingers   pump & pipes of organ
nr Old King Cole: 'his pipe . . . & his bowl'
Peter & Paul (rivalry)

whereabouts

(5 senses)

G überlisten: to dupe

x = unknown (algebra)   as it were   *Da* stilhed: silence
L ad: to   stillhead: top of still

shut up!   Judg 6:40: '& God did so that night: for it was dry upon the fleece only, & there was dew on all the ground'   damn well   *U*.276: 'But Bloom sang dumb'
I Cor 13:12: 'For now we see through a glass, darkly; but then face to face'
(Butt stopped talking but those around him spoke)
L vociferor: I cry out   vice versa   *s* Abdul the Bulbul Ameer (his enemy is Ivan Slavinsky Skavar)
R Slavyanskii Slovar: Slavonic dictionary   old Jerusalem (Crimean War result of dispute over key to church of Bethlehem)
s Kafoozalem: 'from old Methusalem'
godfather   Hegesippus (038.16)   HCE   educe: bring out
L hircus: he-goat
pr Beauty is in the eye of the beholder   Pride's purge in Cromwell's House of Commons
Beauty of Bath: kind of apple
apart

I bi i dho husht: be quiet!   heresy

Jesus' Harrowing of Hell: descent between Good Friday & Easter Sunday   Harrow-on-the-Hill, London   *s* The Rollicking Rams
s The Rocky Road to Dublin

Moore: *s* After the Battle: 'Night closed around the conqueror's way' [Thy Fair Bosom]
AngI aroon: my precious

Solomon Islands
Saladin's Islam
modern Germany   Americas up to date   Amalekites defeated by Gideon
giaour: term of reproach applied by Turks to non-Mussulmans
ancient
Isis Unveiled I.528: 'Stevens . . . found railroads in Upper Egypt whose grooves were coated with iron'
Oxmantown: part of N. D (from 'Ostman', Viking)
VI.C.6.202: 'throat—where a camel is stabled'
Saturdays & Sundays
satellites

fallen from scaffold   skeleton
Solar System: satellites of the Sun
Hengest & Horsa: brothers, led Saxon invasion of England   condemns gangsters   *G* Herrscher: ruler, master   chainganger
Major Sirr noted for brutality to Irish
vintage master   *C Pi* topside: superior

G stumm: dumb   *It* misto: mixed
hunchback, stomach between his shoulders
comfort   *G* Kummerfett: 'sorrow fat' (corpulence)
Da kumme: water closet   *F* pet: fart
Anna Livia   *Da* dagblade: newspapers   coach-&-four

all   none but wanderers

wilderness
Wyndham Lewis: *The Childermass*
Da Alfader: Odin   much

L in vino veritas   God's truth
(attempts to use drugs as lie detectors)

iota of truth first last
Faust
ever true ⚔ Inkerman (Crimean War)
Scots ilka: every
G Kopf
God coffin coffeepot
astride broad shoulders
bought & sold
It sollecitare: hasten forward, speed up
G grob: coarse grovelling humbly
7 orifices in head Crimeans

God knows free & gratis stamps enclosed

studied *Da* jura: law
Jura Mts
read metaphysics *r* Mississippi wifebeater bachelor
It Messa: Mass *Sl* botch: tailor
HCE Thomas Taylor the Platonist
tailor
solve our thesis Praemium Nobelium: Nobel Prize *L* primum mobile: 'first mover'
G es gibt: there is (outermost sphere of Ptolemaic universe)
Haeckel: *The Riddle of the Universe* 170.04–24: 'the first riddle of the universe: asking, when is a man not a man? . . . when he is a . . . Sham'
anatomies
Du waarom: why *G* weil: because

for example point *G* zum Beispiel: for example

six secs *G* hurtig: nimble *F* soupçon
prove him heretic (6 points: 358.36–359.20)
fine when I was a kid
sowens: a kind of porridge made from bran
darkies supper be a fishfry
Per tariki: dark *I* Samhain: Allhallowtide
good red bread with sweet meat in the kettledrum

let us pray *14: 'I have been reading it'

notwithstanding Messrs John Long Ltd refused *Dubliners*

*Preface: 'The letterpress is good, the paper excellent'
negligible
bettered
*4: 'Your preceding works were eagerly seized on'
albeit *G* Notfall: emergency case turn aside
*2: 'worthy of the previous publications' *G* keiner: none
pasteurisation *G* Packpapier: wrapping paper
L uro: I burn *G* packen: grab, pack
asked
(burned)
heaped (up) *13: 'Enough, however, have I seen of it' *Da* bedst: best
helped
*5: 'I wish, & augur, a large circulation' *14: 'it will command a wide circulation'
*13: 'In the hurry of the times'
*9: 'heartily praying for it a circulation coextensive with its merits'
*12: 'the safe & pious hands into which have been entrusted such a mission . . . as you . . . so edifyingly . . . record'

*2: 'It is, I can see, well worthy' is embellished
ambush
*15: 'replete with information' accompanying active

passive first to last
passim
veneration

Du timmeren: to build God please
bless
overwhelmed Black Sea
back seat
Venetians
vignettes

*Dean Kinane: *St Patrick*, 'Approbations' (from a selection of church dignitaries)

G Grobschmied: blacksmith *It* oréfice: goldsmith
Du smid: smith
Per shukr-i-khuda: thank God! splendidly Aubrey Beardsley's illustrations for Wilde's *Salome* Oberon
chowder: fish soup
Per khub: good (adj.) *Per* arzan: cheap Woolworth's tryout
well worth a trial
Bushmills whiskey Bismillah (Mallarmé: *Un coup de dés: F* hasard: chance)
I míle fáilte: thousand welcomes *Per* hazaruyak: 1001 (*Arabian Nights*)
F cent pour cent *Per* farangistan: Europe
Per sad: 100 foreigners *Per* dast-i-chap: on the left
Per dast-i-rast: on the right *Per* khair: good Arabian aurora
Burial of the Dead: 'ashes to ashes, dust to dust' European
Per hamd: glory *Per* damida: blown damn it Hudibras's beard (described in detail in Butler's poem)
Aubrey Beardsley
G Wehrmann: soldier Greece conquers
vermin women
Persse . . . O . . . Reilly *G* Realismus: realism *Per* dard: pain *Sl* dard: penis
realise in us with perhaps a dart of pain
persons
It pene: penis
favourites of mine finger
moment
characteristic
catatonic catheter
fondly fingered frequently signet ring
cunt
significant *It* Corpo di Dio! (oath) *L* culpa: sin, fault
F sang *It* colpo: blow, hit Dido, queen of Carthage
G kunstvoll: ingenious *G* wie: as raven/dove
cunt ravishing
lovely
F oreille *F* longeur
oriental languidness
The Thousand Nights & a Night (*Arabian Nights*)—they were told to King Shahryar sherry-cobbler: a drink *G* wenn: if
s I Lift up My Finger & I Say Tweet Tweet raven's 'caw'
idly thumbing love leaflets (*U*.69: Bloom reading in jakes)
turning leaves left
casually lavatory thesis
L lama: bog
nr Where Are You Going, My Pretty Maid?: 'My face is my fortune, sir, she said'
fortnights
Du visch: fish *Du* disch: dining table
G ich dien: I Serve (motto of Prince of Wales)
(remember) stone's throw
letting down of trousers
Da liggende gobelined: lying tapestried Gobelin tapestries H . . . EC
limned there
eunuchs Constantinople *G* Kunst: art
Enoch: city built by Cain (Gen 4:17)
General Hugh Gough's statue in Phoenix Park assassinated possibly
U.457 (emended): 'general Gough in the park' as asserted *G* bloss: naked
ambush themselves underneath Howth Hawthorn Glen = Furry Glen, Phoenix Park *F* feuilles
with eye
truly rurally *L* vir: man vegetable
Finnegan week
henceforwards shell shock shall surrender

s I Lift up My Finger & I Say Tweet Tweet (dove)
skylight
involuntary catching snapshots
voluptuary
memoranda of distant relations facsimile
L murmurandum: (something) to be murmured familiar faces
raven/dove
ravishing
shadow lovely line special precisely
space/time
concrete
Cruden's Biblical Concordance
(name 'Earwicker' was gift, 031.28)

sectarian D motto: Obedientia civium urbis felicitas (Citizens' Obedience Is City's Happiness)
Burgage: old name of Blessington, Co. Wicklow burgage: a freehold property *s* Home Sweet Home
happygolucky *L* motu proprio: 'of my own accord': document issued by pope, without cardinals' advice
hope-goal-lucre God's truth
pleased plagued gladdened
Pelagius: heretic; believed in free will *G* Glut: fire, ardour
my hindmost parts
arse
battery *L* columbus: dove *L* corvinus: raven
Gr -philos: -lover *Gr* -phobos: -fearer
Columbus & Magellan, travellers
F se ramasser: to collect oneself
Magellanic clouds: 2 spots formed by nebulae & starclusters, visible in Southern hemisphere

Prophecies of Merlin, by Geoffrey of Monmouth Exod 3:14: 'I AM THAT I AM'

altogether
do-gooder
wife
husband (cultivate) the vine
harbour master Harbour Conservancy Board
Tristan was master of harping
Messiah *I* meiseamhnacht: judgement Finnegan
Yiddish misha mishinnah: an ugly fate, violent death
Persse O'Reilly with all aboard *Per* padar: father *Per* madar: mother
Per biradar: brother *Gr* hals = *L* sal = salt
Per dukhtar: daughter *Alice in Wonderland:* The Mock Turtle & the Gryphon
Gen 6:2: 'the sons of God saw the daughters of men'
with the 2 Lulus
Per maktab: school *s* British Grenadiers: 'with a tow row tow'
s Finnegan's Wake At the annual festival in Basel 2 figures (also names of Basel riverferries), *der wilde Mann* & *Vogel Gryff*, arrive on a float (3rd ferry is 'Leu'–*SwG* 'lion')
superstition that to touch a hunchback's hump brings luck

waxed & waned Bailey light on Howth
Jonah as bringer of ill-luck
Da vokse op: grow up
woke up
St Jerome described Pelagius as 'pultibus praegravatus' ('weighed down with pottage') basketchair
F bas ('Low-Church')
nigh on Haroun-al-Raschid: caliph of Bagdad in *Arabian Nights*
nine & thirty (39 articles of Church of Eng.)
orthodox wholly pleased
ducks & drakes
document number one: the Treaty (term used by De Valera's followers) bears & bulls: speculators on, respectively, falls & rises in Stock Exchange prices
I a chara: friend (voc.) *L* cara: precious

I a grádh: love (voc., endearment)
L genua: knees
tomboy

I slamach: loose handful
Dial slammock: slut
(lucky, .24) *F Sl* drogue: whore in attendance *L* frons: forehead
addenda *F* fesses
frithstool: seat in a church affording privilege of sanctuary hurt
diet (cf. 359.01)

head first wherever VI.B.14.131: 'bullpen (jail)' Caelestius, disciple of Pelagius, was accused of following heretical beliefs: 1) Adam would have died even had he not sinned; 2) his sin only injured himself; 3) newborn infants are in same state as Adam before his fall; (another point, not in all lists); 4) mankind does not wholly die by Adam's fall, nor rise by Christ's resurrection; 5) both Law & Gospel can bring men to kingdom of Heaven; 6) there were sinless men even before Christ Tara: ancient capital of Ir.

law attired *R* taratora: prattler *I* oir: gold honour iron sulphide (ore)

base metal *G* besser territory children mumbo-jumbo

Bessemer process for making wrought iron Chiltern Hundred (conferred on member of Parliament wishing to resign his seat)

Fintan MacBochra: only Irishman to survive the Flood

so he was (Points 5) & 6) above are in reverse order here)

prose quasi verse wasn't

prussiates: cyanides *Sl* arsyversy: head over heels

(before Christ) wasn't

Tom, Dick or Harry Coke, diamond & graphite in pencils are all forms of carbon

G nagelneu: brand new *G* Kohle: coal colouring matter

NaCl: chemical sign for salt chlorine (bleaching)

Du stof: dust tit for tat

G Stoff: material

Old Testament Tyndale's Pentateuch in Coverdale's Bible (early Eng. versions)

Penelope flowers *F Sl* lorette: whore

Dunlop (tyres)

Arthur of the Round Table

Camelot (Arthur's headquarters) Lyonesse, Cornwall: Tristan's home in Malory

tipple: drink in excess

Layamon: *Brut* Jacob & Esau All Saints old salts

layman's brute strength sault: jump

All Souls want gypsies

Aunt Sally: woman's effigy at which balls thrown in game

s Swing Low, Sweet Chariot *s* Knocked 'em in the Old Kent Road

lock him up

radio ham (amateur) just been listening to

ahem!

5 act

John Whiston: C18 London publisher & bookseller

Carlyle (*French Revolution*) describes the coach in which Louis XVI escaped from Paris on the night of 20/6/1791 as having 'six insides' (i.e. 6 inside passengers)

Du hoofd: head *Ice* thing: assembly, parliament

High King of Ireland

pig in a poke Ireland All Souls ghost story by earwigs

I pingin i póca: penny in a pocket Tory/Whig

continued in *Pearson's Weekly* make

breakfast Lucan *s* 'Alouette, gentille Alouette'

F hirondelle

F rondin: breast tantivy: at full gallop

It rondinelle: little swallows

Radio-Diffusion owl: 'to-whit, to-whoo!'

twofold nightingales

B.B.C. live outside broadcast of Surrey nightingales in 1924 naughty girls

Alice Delysia: stage beauty of 1930s Rossini Haydn

'to-whit, to-whoo' (owl) hiding

Valhalla Waterloo Mont St Jean: name Eng. army gave to Waterloo from village

G Wald: forest which Napoleon thought the key to Wellington's position

Jenny Lind: singer, 'the Swedish nightingale' *F* feuille Swift met Stella at Moor Park in Surrey

Alice (Lewis Carroll)

Swift swift (bird) sunset oboe *It* oibò: now then, fie!

F les Parques: the fates Dunsink Time (in D)

hither & thither dots & dashes (Morse code)
zither (mus. instr.)
Florence Nightingale (Crimean War)
'Swedish Nightingale': Jenny Lind, singer
It usignolo: nightingale son of a bitch
owl: 'to-whit, to-whoo!' musical pitch Prime & Tierce: Canonical hours
L primus, secundus, tertius: 1st, 2nd, 3rd Tereus ravished Philomela, who became a nightingale
'Jim Crow': Rice, Am. blackface comedian, performed in D
Du hoe: how woe betide them! theorbo: sort of large lute dulcimer
filthy *U.*256: 'Full throb' dirty
soft pedal (piano) vocalise
VI.C.8.10: 'piano strings respond to different vowels when loud pedal is pressed'
amen Pergolesi: composer Meyerbeer Bellini

Mercadante Beethoven Wagnerians
more by token *s* Whack Fol the Diddle
Bach: *The Well-tempered Clavier* *It* Peana: pæan Gluck
thumped pianos
'jug-jug': sound of nightingale *G* Glück: good luck Bach *It* duol: grief
G gluckgluck: sound of drinking (fox barks, hounds bay)
(035.30)

Du klinkers: vowels John Field: Ir. composer; Mozart (Queen of Night in *The Magic Flute*)
Glinka (composer) developed nocturne
Carmen Sylva: pen name of Queen *s* Questa o quella (from *Rigoletto*)
Elizabeth of Rumania, musician & writer
Tennyson: *The May Queen:* 'Call me early, mother dear'
pyramid of Pepi II, inscription: 'grant that his pyramid . . . may flourish . . . If the name of Nut flourisheth . . . the name of this Pepi . . . shall flourish' Nut: Egyptian sky-goddess
Horus
I toras: weariness Sekhet hetep: Egyptian Elysian Fields

Ragnar Lodbrok: Viking chief
Du naar: nasty
Du vuil: dirt, dirty *Da* far: father

short shirt trooping the colour: Eng. military ceremonial

ventriloquism
truculence
replying

Per bulbul: nightingale Babylon

mesmerism: hypnotism I hope not Pliny describes druid ceremony of gathering mistletoe:
remember a priest cuts it with a golden sickle on the 6th day of
Dean Kinane: *St Patrick* 226: St Aengus's 2nd class of the moon what's
Ir. saints 'are called 'very holy' & are compared to the moon' *F* grappes Gripes . . . Mookse
shit! VI.B.14.29: 'Tiberius fells their forests' (druids) *I* guidhe: prayer,
F gui: mistletoe beseeching O.K.
psalms *Arab* salam: peace
F ô gué, ô gué: jingle in old popular songs
HCE there Moore: *s* I Saw from the Beach [Miss Molly]
hoodie: hooded crow
1, 2, 3 & away! has to

Moore: *s* What the Bee Is to the Flow'ret [The Yellow Horse] Clematis *F* ciel
L celare: to hide seal our ardour
G Erde: earth

earwig Dean Kinane: *St Patrick* 26: 'A person born in Great Britain could scarcely call Ireland the extremity of the world'
dingo: Aust. wild dog *nr* Ding-dong Bell Dingley Dell: country village in *Pickwick Papers*
F élancé: slim
Frazer: *The Golden Bough:* 'The Perils of the Soul': method of abducting human souls in Malay Peninsula: 'sit down on an ant-hill facing the moon, burn incense, & recite the following incantation'
full dress (style of *Egyptian Book of the Dead*)

ant/grasshopper Mr Punch

Harlequin . . . Columbine   combinations
pantomime
Once one is nought, twice two is nil, thrice three makes nine, four's four
ph fair's fair
(legend that King Arthur is sleeping & will return in hour of England's need)   Sir Arthur Guinness   Sen Patrick: foster father of St Patrick
nr This is the way the ladies ride: 'apace, apace'

Guinness's

tongue-twisters

VI.B.14.226: 'Pa let me go too (aeiou)
Letters of Ir. alphabet are names of trees: quicken (L); aspen (E); ash (N); yew (I); willow (S); broom (O); oak (D)
tail about

Manzoni: *I Promessi Sposi*   love all (tennis score, = 0:0)
It spose: brides   *R* promysi: providence
Moore: *s* Nay, Tell Me Not, Dear, That the Goblet Drowns [Dennis, Don't Be Threatening]

I inghean: girl, daughter   *AngI ph* his nose is out of joint: he has been supplanted

everybody's

grasshopper . . . ant   o, bless me!   obelisk
L ovum: egg   aren't they awful   *F Sl* obélisque: penis
Armorica (Tristan)   *nr* 'Ding-dong Bell, Pussy's in the well. Who put her in? . . . Who pulled her out?'   *s* Pretty Kitty Kelly
F amour

Sw kisse: pussy   nice old

nightingale   girl
Da ung: young
full of life

It ombrellone: beach umbrella   parasol   blackthorn stick (shillelagh)

invincible ignorance (theology): that shared by a whole race or class
Shillelagh, village, Co. Wicklow   Invincibles (Phoenix Pk Murders)   *L* immutans: unchanging
Du onze: our   *Du* grootvader: grandfather   *Du* onaangenaam: disagreeable
Du vatter: seizer   *Du* Lodewijk: Lewis   *Du* genaamd: named
Arch twy: 2   Isa Bowman: friend of Lewis Carroll, played Alice in adaptation of *Alice in Wonderland*   *Du* met: with
land   *We* gorsedd: seat, mount; bards' convocation
cursed
F limon   *Du* lurken: to suck
OF godons: English (derogatory)
badly wounded   Buckley   ✠ Boyne, 1690 (Orangemen)
wanted   *Arabian Nights:* 'Tale of the Two Sisters who Envied their Cadette': 'they led the liefest of lives until at last there came to them the Destroyer of delights & the Sunderer of societies . . . & they became as though they never had been'
foliage
Nashe: *Anatomie of Absurditie:* 'The wooers of Penelope will by their Porters, prohibite the poore . . . terming them marrers of mirth'   Jack the Ripper
Ecclus 44:9: '& are become as though they had not been'

unto

many   Hilarion: personification of Science in Flaubert's *St Antoine*

L gestare: to bear   gestures
Gesta Romanorum: medieval collection of stories

Romanov: Russian royal family
L verum: truth   *Arch* swink: to toil   unravel

duty

sorry   *F* gueux: beggar   blue-eyed

○ Dublin cartel: written challenge really
L clam: secretly Clancarthy: Ir. family (McCarthy, 381.02)
roasted barley used in making Guinness condemnation
I Béarla: Eng. language
temptation

'Old Nol' & 'Ironsides': nicknames of Cromwell Cain & Abel
nonconformist cannibal
someone tried HC . . . E
Salmon trout
Finn MacCool roll call

tarpon turbot grampus porpoise

s 'Here Comes the Bride, boys, forty inches wide' (tune: Wedding March) Clancarthy
bridegroom
son of a bitch
British soldier
whereas master to missus

son of a whore

tenth LAP

henpecked kenspeckled: easily recognised
sucker soucar: Indian banker or moneylender
It generose: generous greedyguts

abrasive yous habeas corpus HCE
L umbra: shadow
pr Finders keepers

bowl sold to hold *s* The Wind That Shakes the Barley
barley wine: strong ale
s Peg O' My Heart

deemster: judge

Moore: *s* Like the Bright Lamp (Erin! Oh Erin!) [Thamama Halla]

B.S. Rowntree: *Poverty*. He frequently uses the word 'respectable'

Poverty 156: 'Dirty flock bedding in living-room placed on a box & two chairs' *Poverty* 155: 'Rain coming through ceiling'
Sisters of Charity, religious order

vacuum cleaners back gate

respectable *Poverty* 148: 'Occasionally it is used by the husband when he has writing to do in connection with friendly or other societies, or by the children when practising music. . . . A sofa, albeit of horsehair or American cloth. . . . Upstairs there are three bedrooms, two of them provided with fireplaces'
Poverty 358: 'Sheffield Equitable Druids'
Poverty 136: 'The life of a labourer is marked by five alternating periods of want & comparative plenty'
(Viconian cycle)

G Haar: hair

pay? O, no! paying
piano
Karl Czerny's piano exercises
turning out
respectable *Sl* greenhouse: latrine

respectable

VI.B.14.87: 'kept (lived)'

HCE
nr Ride a Cock Horse
hatch a cock's egg   Cora Pearl: Parisian courtesan whose father wrote   chorus girls
music for *Kathleen Mavourneen*
Prince's St, D (Aeolus)

damn   *s* 'The Wren, the Wren, The king of all birds'
hymn
Newnes, Pearson & Harmsworth: founders of 'popular-style' Eng. journalism
newsboy with armful of papers
ducks & drakes   business
doves & ravens
detective   *s* Old Man River

disguises   shelters   horse chestnut   HCE   excessive (heat)
hoarse chest-notes
s 'But Old Man River, He just keeps rolling along'

Macaulay: *Marriage of Tirzah & Ahirad:* 'How long, O Lord, how long?'

bairn baptised

s Certainly, Lord: 'Has you been redeemed? Certainly, Lord'
renamed
s Phil the Fluter's Ball: 'Ye've got to pay the piper when he toothers on the flute'
paperboy
King Mark of Cornwall   Phil the Fluter

Ir. practice of spitting in hands before shaking them to conclude deal
G spritzen: spray   *It* per bacco!: by Jove (lit. Bacchus)   *F* bis
(083.23–30) spit in his fist   *Da* sprit: alcohol   *L* saltus: a jump   saw to their business
tickled   palm   *L* palam: publicly, openly   Solomon
N tukle: caress
French leave: *I* beannacht leat: 'a blessing with you' (farewell)
departure without notice
'Exsultet': 'O felix culpa!'   indeed

C.M. Doughty: *Travels in Arabia Deserta* (309.09)
ph Dear Dirty Dublin

wanderlust

of   *nr* Humpty Dumpty

hurtled   sod of turf

unheard of trespass   *L* minxi: I have urinated

B.S. Rowntree: *Poverty* 37: 'Sells "hot peas" in the streets at night'

theatricals   impecunious   curious
actresses   precarious
Poverty 34: 'slops being emptied'

arrears   *Poverty* 148: 'midden privies'   appertinent
private apartment
saving the presence   Board of Works, D

inculpable   personal property
incapable   prisoners'
G abfallen: to desert

Flaubert: *Madame Bovary* (adultery)   *G* hinter
hindering
Anglosaxon   *I* Béarla: Eng. language
bare lie
misunderstood   *U*.550 (emended): 'The NANNYGOAT (bleats)
Megeggaggegg!'

God's truth ribald bear witness
mind of God
marines
follower's *L* perambulatrix: female wanderer
20 to 22 thousand mailcoach preparing
lettermail pen . . . post
voluntarily
parcels department with large parcels past
larch (evergreen tree)
branch offices *s* The Green above the Red *G* Baum: tree
offerings
s 'John Brown's body lies a-mouldering in the grave, His soul is marching on'
Du bode: letter carrier *G* Schule: school
would kirtles
bixexual Kipling: Recessional: 'Lest we forget'
bissextile: leap-year
Maggy how do you do Maggy (111.16) attention
r Amazon (February) buxom
amazing
nr Sing a Song of Sixpence: floral Mark 4:9: 'He that hath ears to hear'
'Wasn't that a dainty dish to set before a king?' early C6 Ir. saints had tonsure from ear to ear skull
Gall: founder of phrenology every time he opens his mouth he puts his foot in it
I gall: foreigner
perpetrated
St Patrick: *Confessio* 25: *G* Hochzeit: marriage starvation *M Gr* avrektos: unbroken
'the inner man' hogshead sheet
piece lentils apologist
avoirdupois (pound) Apocalypse
recruiter of conscripts Gen 9:25: 'Cursed be Canaan: a servant of servants shall he be'
ass
ph peace, perfect peace *G* abwarten: wait
Per ab: water
L/R *r* Nile rates & taxes registrar
L res intectis: open statement of affairs
Eblana: name of D used by Ptolemy
ant . . . grasshopper
Sl aunt: whore graverobbers
F par exemple pure & simply *ph* six of one & half a dozen of the other
L perenne: constantly *L* semper: always
Mookse & Gripes *ph* devil take the hindmost
Sp muchas gracias: many thanks
nightmare mare's nest 'Please to remember the 5th of November, Gunpowder, treason & plot' (Guy Fawkes day chant)
G schulden: to owe HCE
Ibsen: *Til min Ven Revolutions-Taleren:* 'I sørger for vandflom til verdensmarken. Jeg lægger med lyst torpédo under Arken' ('You deluge the world to its topmost mark; With pleasure I will torpedo the Ark') *Sl* merken: cunt
G Flaum: fluff *G* merkens: they notice
L turps: shameful *Da* ark: sheet *Per* bas ast: it is enough
(wife) run Sarah . . . Abraham
silly
every home *s* On the Strict Q. T.
man in the street
first liar: the devil banjoist
host Lyra: lyre (constellation)
Manu: Adam in Indian myth
L munda manu: with a clean hand
vacuum cleaner *s* My Old Dutch drives *G* Dreck: dirt drake . . . duck
L victuum: of nourishments *Sl* chuck: term of endearment
showing off Boston, Mass. Lot's wife
henpecked husband
Da hun: she

Father Michael (111.15) wayfarer Marriage Ceremony: 'all my wordly goods'
almighty wafer (Body of Christ)
Book of Common Prayer: Catechism: 'renounce the devil' lovely parcel of cakes (011.23–4)
120.10: 'funferal' *L* sacra religio: holy religion
L sacrilegium: sacrilege
pr Diamonds cut diamonds Molière: *Le bourgeois gentilhomme* born gentleman (111.13)
Gr daimôn: spirit
Hamlet I.4.17: 'to the manner born' Lady Day: feast of the Annunciation philosopher
menhir
Ibsen: *Peer Gynt* Buckley shoots the Russian General
L baculus: stick, staff Bacchus
certain time preaching
Serpentine although
Queen Victoria: 'We are not amused'
very worst
libretto liberator Sebastopol *L* piscis: fish
G lieber *G* Retter: saviour episcopal
Virginia Water (nr Windsor) action bargain basement

Gladstone acquiesced howe: hill, tumulus Howe: site of Thingmote (Viking assembly in D) underwear
D Sl totty: girl (7 adjectives) *Sl* malkin: slut

cold *G* Bauch: belly C . . . EH *Heb* ereṣ: earth
heave coal ears
Du altijd: always *G* Warmer: homosexual Mookse & the Gripes

Hole in the Wall: pub nr Phoenix Park *Per* amir: governor *Per* vilayat: province
ME anent: concerning
prostitution siege of Kars, Crimea *Per* taraf: limit (sb)
Per kashkav: food
Double Dutch uncouth & coldest *Per* bad: wind
Per baran: rain *L* compos mentis: sane *L* novus: new

Mookse & the Gripes
(tyrant dislikes Marxists)
G dank *G* schenk: give
ph do & be damned to you! *G* Schenke: tavern
G hin: thither hither & thither

hand in hand (357.16–17; 358.04–05) ravishing shadows shedder: female salmon after spawning lovely lines
Joseph Jesus
yous
Dubliners called Swift 'Mr Dane' (Dean)

would you not?

Parnell: speech in Cork, 1885: 'No man has a right to fix the boundary of the march of a nation'
put a stop pud: nursery word for child's hand
apprentices Stella . . . Vanessa (Swift) *G* wundervoll
G Nixe: water nymph
W.G. Wills: *A Royal Divorce* deals with . . . Marie Louise . . . Josephine (Napoleon) statues of Marly Horses in Champs Elysées
alderman W.W. Kelly: manager of Evergreen Touring Co., which put on *A Royal Divorce*

Curly Wee: comic strip about a pig, in *Irish Independent* Ossian
Sl salthorse: salt beef dear thirsty

Per aftab: sun
Taylor & Co., mineral waters, 35 Lr Gardiner St, D
Per khavyat: tailor *Per* sard: cold *Per* mah: moon; month tight embracing
child *Sl* sard: fuck Armagh
saith calories false *I* folc: flood
It colori: colours

G Popo: posterior Parnell: 'When you sell get my price' must first guess
F cocottes Swift: 'Ppt' can see
wicketkeeper appeal against light (cricket) *L* nex: murder

L vividus: animated pantomime
evidence suppline: filled up

Sl bottleholder:
second (in a fight)
for aught I know befall
Hearts of Steel: an Ir. secret society

regimental muskets Mass
mascots (bed)
F boule (game) *L* sodalis: companion bended knees
Sackville St, D socialists
rockets regattas Dryden: *Alexander's Feast:* 'None but the brave deserves the
squash rackets fair'

by God *Gr* parthenos: virgin
Per biguidd: to speak
own *G* Mischmasch: hotchpotch *Misch-Masch:* household magazine written by Lewis Carroll
ph tit for tat *G* Matsch: mash, mud (tennis matches)
deepsea borne proudly my dreams
unclothed billowing in my prime
brine
to say

L in re: in the matter Milchu: owner of Patrick in his youth incriminating incorporated
G Milch: milk *G* melken: to milk *Sl* cream: semen

Butt & Taff sod of turf
Isaac Bickerstaff: name used by Swift in parody of Partridge's astrological predictions
Balaclava grapeshot John Bull defalcations
G Krawall: riot Greeks (Greece occupied by Turks from C15) defaecations
pr England's difficulty is Ireland's opportunity
I Tír na Simearóig: Land of the Shamrock
pr What is sauce for the goose is sauce for the gander

charismatic asthma supposedly improper proctor: tithe farmer seducing
Cant ruffin: devil ruffian *T* sippah; *Per* sipah: soldier
It trovatella: foundling *ph* Dear Dirty Dublin

Luke 12:27: 'lilies of the field' *G* Feld Brutus
soothsayer felt
Cassius *L* humandus: requiring burial
eggs
blimey & tarnation Wellington: 'Up, guards, & at them' Kurds
G abkürzen: to shorten
crown prosecutors

Julius Caesar III.2.93: 'Ambition should be made of sterner stuff'
ph the ash on me stump (of cigar) *Sl* blow the gaff: give away a secret
the Ides of March makes a good day to be shot at Falstaff fullstop
fall stiff

s Down Went McGinty to the bottom of the sea wall

dressed in his old suit of clothes

AngI whist!: silence bashaw: pasha, high-ranking Turkish officer
The Weald of Sussex: central region bey: Turkish governor

none *Arab* nun, sad, mim: letters N, S & M
G nun: now

mum (silent) Lokman: Muslim prophet (& title of Sura 31 of Koran)

grocery business

The Grand Remonstrance, 1641: document produced by Parliament giving
account of royal mismanagement & recommending radical reforms

HEC Cincinnatus (030.13)

Sl chin: to converse

The Hague, Holland

G Punkt: full stop

Tut-ankh-amen

It tutti: all

Kallikak: family of U.S. hereditary degenerates

Dún Laoghaire Lyons Corner House for tea

(old spelling: Dun Leary) (lion, Mark's beast) *Du* thee: tea

sixpence *L* lympha: clear water

L avunculus: maternal uncle

evangelists

'The three sorrows of storytelling': 3 well-known Ir. folk stories

Matthew Mark Luke John

Synoptic Gospels: the first 3

John 1:1: 'In the beginning was the Word'

Jukes: family of U.S. hereditary degenerates

HF 19: 'The duke done it'

Deucalion & Pyrrha: equivalent of Noah & his wife, in Ovid Pyrrha

Napoleon ferry

to ship oars: to lift them into boat

aside

I fionn-linn: clear pool dove

I fionn: fair *I* dubh: dark

fair *G* fahre vor: drive on, pass

King Lear III.4.187: 'Fie, foh, & fum' *G* vorn: ahead

delusion *s* The Foggy Dew

Deluge

Johnnie Walker whiskey slogan: 'Still going strong' *G* empor: upward emporia masters

aristocrats *Gr* thalassokratôr: master of the sea 'invisible empire' of Ku Klux Klan

(4 winds)

4 dimensions

mansions

(Viconian cycle) cumulonimbus: thundercloud (marriage) bride

lining (*pr* Every cloud has a silver lining) 'coo' (dove) 'caw' (raven) *I* bréid: kerchief

solid

at home attain a rest *It* atáim: I am

atom a-tombed (burial)

incompatibles

symbols of the Evangelists: angel (Matthew), lion (Mark), calf (Luke), eagle (John)

Kincora: home of Brian Boru behests

Earwicker

R vada: water Behemoth (Job 40:15): prob. the hippopotamus

deepest deeps ever & anon

anonymously

keep back!

against

interrupt foster fathers
underrate ghostly father: father confessor

Sl pad: rob (324.17) *G* Donnerwetter! (expletive)

Buckley shoot the Russian General *G* Wand: wall (Wailing Wall, Jerusalem)
F chute giant
walking marketplace

arrack (rice drink)

nr This Little Pig Went to Market (refers to child's fingers) pedestrians
Sl pinky: little finger *It* porco: pig pederasts
F cul corporation life
L Mona bella: beautiful i) Isle of Man; ii) Anglesey
L perperus: faulty invoking
It culle buone: by fair means
L sic: thus *L* suc: somewhat

G Hummer: lobster
tying themselves
L cave: beware

L quis rebus: by what matters? (12 adverbs)

exits waken up in brothels

fall asleep *G* Putz (frau): char(woman) *G* allerdings: indeed
boots
sardines anything on their conscience

G zum Schluss: finally *Sl* nark: informer

rhythm & rhyme scheme of *Omar Khayyam* stanza, e.g. 'Again to tavern haunts do we repair, & bid 'Adieu' to the five hours of prayer; Where'er we see a long-necked flask of wine, Our necks we elongate that wine to share' *G* Weisheit: wisdom

Koran
K.C.: King's counsel
s 'Casey Jones! Got another papa! Casey Jones! On that Salt Lake Line! Casey Jones! Got another papa! & you've got another papa on that Salt Lake Line'

G Fall: (law) case *s* Willy the Weeper (about an opium smoker)

atlas: satin

bluestocking peek-a-boo

louisine: sort of shimmering largegrained *peau de soie*

(Moscow, Athens, Rome, Dublin) *It* -acci: common pejorative suffix
Matt Gregory, Mark Lyons, Luke Tarpey & Johnny MacDougal
there enduring

(II.1) (II.2) (II.3) (II.4)

G Dial net?: isn't that so? night
Ned: pet name for donkey

Butt & Taff ways & means

G Hinterhand: back of the hand (etwas in der Hinterhand haben: to have something up one's sleeve) explain explication

'on the house': a free drink

his jest has guessed

F geste: gesture, movement

sublation: i) (logic) denial; ii) Hegel's *aufheben,* having opposite meanings of destroy & preserve

ratification

ph by the by (6 names and addresses)

St Bruno: founder of Carthusians Fox Goodman (035.30)

St Bruno pipe tobacco *F* faix: load, burden

chambers Carolan: last of the ancient Ir. bards, blind at 18 gate

People's Park, Dún Laoghaire (478.26) pier Ghazi Power: Ir. journalist (521.22)

F Dieu-donné: God-given; (*Coll*) of uncertain parentage

archdeacon

road

J.F.X.P. (Coppinger, 211.20)

fert: Ir. monument to dead Woeful Dane Bottom: valley in Gloucestershire, possibly site of a Danish defeat

F.E.R.T.: motto of the House of Savoy

Sl tout: informer **S**

told *Sl* Sandy: a Scotsman *Sl* rook: to cheat, defraud

lay *nr* The House That Jack Built

lived

L videlicet: that is to say

L fidelis: faithful

(opening of I.2) Roderick O'Connor: last Ir. high king

Rory O'Connor seized Four Courts, King's Inns Quay, D, during Civil War, 1922

height loofah in form of glove

pr Manners maketh man

you son of a bitch some of us was

point

It tutti: all *It* tempo: time decuman: large, principal

Document no. 2: De Valera's alternative to the Treaty Pandora

(compare 358.36–359.20) secretary bird: African bird, eats snakes

Poulaphuca (chasm on Liffey)

L paula bucca: little mouth

autosuggestions from Shem the Penman

sagas *G* Schelm: rogue, swindler

Pelman Institute: memory training centre 'Jim the Penman': James Townsend Savard, forger

Poolbeg lighthouse, D

F poule *F* bec

majesty post auditress

postulated addressee

Diarmaid & Grania 'Halt! Who goes there?' (sentry)

Father Michael letter capital T 'Capital' Tea

cup of tea

funeral part & parcel

ephemeral

General Post Office, D likewise

who goes there? Michael latter

whither *Dial* mickle: much

letter capital L C . . . H . . . E

L cubitalis: pertaining to the elbow

F comprends because postman

hell because

Amalia Popper inspired *Giacomo Joyce*

Moore: *s* I Once Had a True Love [Through Grief & through Danger] *or* [The Irish Peasant to His Mistress]

nice present divorced

Mother Carey's chickens: stormy petrels *F* carte blanche scattered his letters

Cabra Park, D *G* ungeboren: unborn
born gentleman

Jerry *F* trouver Kevin Howe: site of Thingmote
ph finders keepers howe: hill, tumulus
ph Dear Dirty Dublin cynically

ladylike postscript

remain to be seen fullstop alethiology: that part of logic dealing with truth

sit down

P.B.I.: 'poor bloody infantry' onomatomancy: divination from names

Butt Taff

I duileasc: edible seaweed

milk flowed over Dún Laoghaire (Dun Leary)
dribbling dundreary whiskers

devil a drop

odds on horse Bluebeard The Bleeding Horse: D pub
Blue Boar Alley, old D

Saracen's Head (inn sign) Republican
surprises us *F* tous Invincibles had a last drink at the Royal Oak, Parkgate St, before Phoenix Park murders, 1882

which

polar bear Mullingar Inn, Chapelizod
parlour bar
AngI Lochlann: Scandinavian *King Lear* III.4.187: 'Fie, foh, & fum' farfamed
landlubber
Chapelizod

G Polizeistunde: legal closing hour
(bouncer)
fear of the Lord sons of bitches *G* Bauch: belly *Sl* half seas over: drunk
AngI soulth: formless luminous apparition
Da tilfælde det var nødvendigt: in case it were necessary *Du* een hele tijd: quite a while
not vindicated
& one time he was rinsing their *Da* nedunder: down under
G schmutzig: dirty flasks (glasses)
'Papishers' (Catholics) hell on 'em *Da* fire minutter endnu: 4 minutes to go shut up shop
Maynooth College: training centre for priests
bounce no more clandestine chicken livers
Clondalkin, village, Co. D
aboard Chapelizod stow away Litany of Saints
Catholic steal away

L Pater, Filius & Spiritus Sanctus: Father, Son & Holy Spirit   Amen

vituperation   vipers in his bosom
F petard: fart
Zwingli: Zurich reformer   Sunken Road ('Hohle Gasse'), where William Tell waited for tyrant Gessler
10 o'clock   *G* Glocken: bells   had rinsed bottles up

heard from far
Hord: hero of an Icelandic saga   'coo' (dove)
D street song ridiculing the castrato Tenducci: 'Tenducci was a piper's son, & he was in love when he was young, & all the tunes that he could play Was "Water parted from the say" '
'caw' (raven)

(046.25)   *It* ostia: Host
Ostia: seaport of Rome

remembered   (045.29–30)

Moore: *s* 'Tis the Last Rose of Summer [The Groves of Blarney]
capturing
knocked at the door

certain sure   *N* sture: mope

(.06)   *G* bedauert: regrets

damned

(044.19)

(046.20)   obese   Boniface: generic as proper name of innkeepers
recalcitrant

L pro bono publico: for the public good   C . . . E . . . H
L clamator: bawler   extension (of closing time)
Hosty   Le Fanu: *The House by the Churchyard*   *Da* tid: time
hostelry   (church chiming)   HC . . . E   ears
'Time, gentlemen, please' (closing time in pub)   *G* alle Minuten: any minute
Maynooth College: training centre for priests

Ibsen: *Borte!*: 'farvellets rester tog nattevinden' ('Good-bye–& the rest The night-wind swallowed')
hear not?   *G* Wellen: waves

(.06)   Neck of Sutton joins Howth & mainland
Dunsink Observatory, D   tree/stone

along   *r* Awin-Dhoo, Isle of Man ('Black River')   Rochell Lane: old name of Back Lane, D
r Silverburn, Isle of Man
Mullingar Inn, Chapelizod   Marshelsea Prison, D
Liberties, D, near Back Lane
Mullingar road, D, was a turnpike until 1853   underwear
'Poor Men of Lyons': followers of Peter Waldo, C12   Dick Whittington
Duke of Wellington   HCE
Huguenots

Erin G herkommen: arrive F belles elbows
L hirco: I howl harken to the Bow bells (which told Whittington to turn again)
Mauser rifles used in 1916 Easter Rising in D
'Turn again, Whittington, Lord-Mayor of London' (pantomime)
Kersse the tailor G Toller: mad one plus the daughter dotter of i's
of course G Eidotter: egg yolk
King Mark of Cornwall (021.18) F aime: love
Sl moke: G Wanst: belly
donkey (023.05–08) puts the shutter up

Jonathan (J thought his name was Peter) Sawyer founded Dublin, Georgia, U.S.
F sans Buckley Russian General
1690, Battle of the Boyne, Ir. Jacobite defeat Benjamin Lee Guinness, brewer
Du liefst: dearest
Benjamin Franklin (lightning) granted piece of
Persse O'Reilly
Her supporter: figure on side of shield Jonathan Sawyer, Amos Love, Jeremy Yopp & Hardy Smith: early settlers of Dublin, Georgia

I seanad: senate
Cafe Béranger, Paris (frequented by Hugo, Saint-Beuve, Gautier &c.)
Pierre Jean de Béranger: senators Cicero: *De Senectute* ('On Old Age')
revolutionary songwriter, said to have philosophy of a café concert
gangway ship
gateway Chapelizod
Warburton, Whitelaw & Walsh, I caill: loss
A History of the City of Dublin, 1818
ph safe home Old Ir. name of D means 'brow of a hazelwood'
W.W. Kelly's Evergreen Touring Company performed *A Royal Divorce*
Dinas-Dulin: Welsh name of D S, W, E, N, S, E, W, N Southwester
(compass points)
'Turn again, Whittington' (pantomime)
s 'Westering home' Danesbury, village, Herts
The Flood: rained 40 days & 40 nights
twoly, threely, fourly
CEH Humpty Dumpty
'Forty Bonnets': nickname of Mrs Tommy Healy of Galway
ALP G alle Leute: everyone It passeggieri: passengers Rock Road, D

ahoy!

G Landsmann: fellow countryman inundation mirific: doing wonders
George Alexander Stevens: 'Cease, rude Boreas, blust'ring railer! List, ye landsmen, all to me'
A . . . L . . . P ludification: deception paludine: pertaining to a marsh
L lutus: mud
(371.06) broke

G Klee: clover

Hurray! Three Rock Mountain, D two mile carry on s Garryowen: 'From
It montone: ram s The Mountain Dew Garryowen in glory'
We glowr: collier s Barnaby Finnegan father

luncheon party bugaboo s The Shan Van Vocht

G Wacht: guard ph he died roaring like Doran's bull s The Whistlin' Thief

045.27: 'Rhyme the rann'

four elders were absolutely at their wits' end moiling

I bóthar: road NORTH James H. North, D auctioneer
Battersby Bros: D auctioneers (386.24–26)

Powerscourt House, SOUTH of D (386.18)

Sp nombre: name

EAST

celluloid donkey   dickey: false shirt-front
sailing dinghy

I bóthar mór: highway   WEST
Cliffs of Moher, Co. Clare
Humpty Dumpty

s 'The gangplank's raised & anchor's up, We're leaving sweet Tipperary' (371.06)

ogre
bugger

HCE   *L* Hircus Civis Eblanensis: Goat Citizen of D (215.27)
Horkos: god of oaths
ashamed of himself   shape in his coat
hump   sheep/goat
F rassembler   barefaced
resembling   W.C. Macready: Shakespearean actor
the 3rd   *Richard III* V.4.7: 'A horse, a horse, my kingdom for a horse'
Bruni's history of Florence   Bruno ('Lanno' anagram of 'Nolan')   *L* lana: wool
It orse: she-bears   a Norse   *s* 'Brian O'Linn had no breeches to wear, So he bought him a sheepskin to make him a pair; The skinny side out, & woolly side in, "They are cool & convanient" said Brian O'Linn' (quoted by Boucicault in *The Colleen Bawn*)
insult for

calling   licence

old Dublin taking his leisure

'god on pension' (024.16–17)   divinity defined   *I* páirc: field

mythological   umbrellas
methylated spirit   *L* imber: rain
J.P. Ronayne: M.P. for Cork. According to J, he & Joseph Biggar together invented Parliamentary obstruction   *G* rein: pure
U.446: 'The answer is a lemon' (a derisive reply)   billposters
arder: ploughing   orderlies   beadles
Earwicker   earwigs

I Brugh Ríogh (ancient capital of Munster) abú!: Bruree to victory!   Guinness Brewery, James's Gate, D
brewery   Power's Distillery, John's Lane, D
became

thighs   Solness, in Ibsen's *The Master Builder*, has stopped climbing the towers he builds, because of giddiness. When he tries again, he falls & dies   Disraeli
Gladstone   right as the mail
It pillola: pill
Hudibras's beard is described in detail in Butler's poem   Ragnar Lodbrok: Viking chief   conceals
Du peerd: horse   *G* Loden: coarse woollen cloth
various   Tiernan O'Rourke's wife left him for Dermot MacMurrough, who sought help from the Anglo-Normans against O'Rourke & Roderick O'Connor. This led to Anglo-Norman invasion of Ireland   done
G Musiker: musician
cheques   don't

wather parted (371.06)   bullet   Ballad of Persse O'Reilly

dickens mother Anna Livia

puts into our

manner of man   *pr* What's bred in the bone comes out in the flesh

nr What Are Little Girls Made Of, Made Of
Per mard: man (human male)
C.L. Dodgson ('Lewis Carroll')

Alice in Wonderland *Boston Transcript* postscript
(automatic writing: Yeats' *A Vision*)
Titbits (*U*.67) man
tittivation morn
cards Matt 5:38: 'An eye for an eye, & a tooth for a tooth'
a treat for a throat
Wars of the Roses: York–white; red–Lancaster

anonymous left-handed palinode: poem &c. with retraction of an earlier statement
inspired suspicious
spiderwebbed sib: kinship, concord
Sl notes of admiration: exclamation marks (question marks)

demisemiquavers inverted commas P/Q split *Sl* quoites:
It gomma: rubber quotes buttocks
quite pointless face to face Swift: 'Ppt'
Du punt: point, full stop
aglow J.C. Mardrus translated Koran & *Arabian Nights*
dialect feed Roman Catholicism *Da* fugle: birds gleeman: minstrel
F culotte
inside out (373.16)
outsize
sum

Da lov: law *It* ardor: heat Boy Bishop (on 6 December in Middle ages in Eng. cathedral choirs) *s* The Bay of Biscay
law & order *Da* biskop: bishop
reading pastoral letter epistemology
L lector: reader theology
ph Dear Dirty Dublin *s* The Bay of Biscay
G Dorf: village
s The Death of Nelson: 'For England, home & beauty' Butt Taff

breach of contract byelaw

hide seek *L* hic: here Finn MacCool

Heb namar: tiger; leopard
I namá: alone
no more HCE

presumption Foreign Office
Sl on the shove: on the move
Scotland Yard

s The Peeler & the Goat bearing information

first

Finsbury Park, London backwards

better recent Oscar Wilde is writing
Battersea Park, London Regent's Park, London

Yellow Book of Lecan: Ir. MS Eastcheap, London *Gr* basileus: king
Chapelizod
King's Avenue, Ballybough, D (486.15)
N koldbrann: gangrene
Gen 4:15: 'the Lord set a mark upon Cain' sign of the cross
Sl mo: moment carefully
HCE *C* chung: a crowd *nr* Humpty Dumpty *Tom Sawyer*
number one *C Pi* topside: superior
BLM belong: at, in, on, into, also possessive sign &c. 'noun': name of a person, place or thing

sack of sand saga Sackerson
Da sand: true Saxon

& filling infinity

nr 'Georgie Porgie, pudding & pie'

G Anker: anchor *Du* noord: north
tombstones commemorating Glues, Gravys, Ankers, Northeasts & Earwickers at Sidlesham (030.06–7)
Am. Kallikak & Juke families: hereditary degenerates
nr The House That Jack Built
L juror cruce: I swear by the cross Jesus Christ *nr* Humpty Dumpty

Dunphy's Corner, D

'The Matter of Britain' (Arthurian cycle)

Arthur another wait & see
r Brittas, tributary of Liffey
Sidlesham is in the Hundred of Manhood, W. Sussex womanhoods
parishes
F cent *F* mille *Gr* myrias: 10,000

(O 12 jurymen) correctional court: a lower court, esp. for juveniles
G Dial gell: isn't it? Mount Sackville Convent, Chapelizod
Sl halfmoon: cunt
Gr haimakyklos: blood cycle; menses *Gi* dye: mother
goodness
leap year hearing (in court) H . . . CE
left in camera (process in judge's chambers)
Sir (packed jury) bench

'so help you God & kiss the book' (legal oath) *s* 'Lots of fun at Finnegan's Wake'
G kitzeln: to tickle
It goffo: clumsy
Sl blowing the gaff: giving away the secret
twin *L* nisi prius: unless before (writ of summons to jurors) thought

Da vokse op: grow up *G* Wecker: alarm clock ears
whack Earwicker
H . . . C . . . E Court of Exchequer, D

come

spindles (legs)

Don Giovanni Donal Buckley: last governor-general of Ireland
Dalymount Park: football stadium, D
Tara: ancient capital of Ireland Russian General

Da skærer: cutter
scissors (tailor's daughter)
embarrassment
embezzlement
'Hairy Jaysus': J's nickname for his college acquaintance Francis Skeffington merriment
anvil cloud (cumulonimbus) Barrow-in-Furness, Westmoreland
circus clothes cirrus clouds
cumulus cloud Grannuaile: a name of Grania O'Malley (021.05)
Finn MacCool with Grania of old

G so nimm: do take it nimbus cloud
Nimb took Ossian to the Land of the Ever Young
the Furry Glen, Phoenix Park *I* brí: hillside

dear Wicklow which he loved Parnell: 'When you sell, get my price'
Du lof: praise
tailor coat & trousers caulk: to seal a ship's seams
Sl corking: fine; large
ship at sea womens' wear Wilde edited *Woman's World*, 1887–9

At the first performance of Synge's *The Playboy of the Western World* an uproar was caused by the line 'drifts of Mayo girls standing in their shifts' *Skr* māyā: illusion *AngI* moya!: interj. of doubt

Grania's genealogy: Inghean Cormaic Mhic Airt Mhic Cuinn Céadcathach (daughter of Cormac the son of Art the son of Conn the Hundred Fighter)
(hundred fights) bit

Hillman Minx (small car)

Midgaard: Earth in Norse myth
*372: Midcuart: Cormac MacArt's house, from which Diarmaid & Grania eloped
heresies Walloon Flemish scapular: two squares of cloth, worn on priest's chest & back
nr A Was an Archer: 'H was a hunter' H . . . C . . . E
St Hubert: patron of the chase
F chemin de la croix: Way of the Cross *F* rosaire: rosary

⚔ Clontarf, 1014 ⚔ Waterloo, 1815 Brian Boru

Norse *409–11: Diarmaid's father killed his stepson by squeezing the child
beat (⚔ Clontarf: Brian Boru defeats Vikings) between his knees
Herr Innkeeper *It* vecchio cucco: old dodderer
daughters
D hotels: Dolphin, Gresham, Royal Hibernian *Da* grusom undergang: cruel perdition
wedding-morn *G* dringen: to throng
G streng: stern *G* strengen: to exert
Hymen, god of weddings
holly & mistletoe sod of turf (reverse spelling) jigsaw
L dos: dowry dose of fruit
SwG Sauss: apple juice heavier
*368: Finn performs feat of running carrying 12 balls of lead *G* vollends: entirely
H . . . CE *L* corpus entis: body of a thing serves you right
*362: 'scurvy came upon him . . . whence he used to be called Demne the Bald'
damn you & as English as they make them *Du* oom: uncle *G* Nichte: niece
*359: Demne: Finn's name before eating salmon of wisdom aunt, uncle
*392: 'Diarmaid bound me not to loose any *G* Neffen: nephew
warrior whom he should bind' *375: Grania first saw Diarmaid when he was playing hurley

itch *373: Grania on later seeing Diarmaid: 'Who is that freckled,
*372: Eitche: wife of Cormac MacArt sweet-worded man . . . [with] the two red ruddy cheeks?'

Boucicault: *Arrah-na-Pogue* *AngI* pogue: kiss

*376: Diarmaid, eloping with Grania, leaps out of Cormac MacArt's
house, & also (*382) out of his enclosure in Clan Ricard
couldn't Foote & Sparkes: D actors
cuddled
hance: haunch The Hole in the Wall, pub nr Phoenix Park was *s* Yankee Doodle
known as 'Nancy Hand's', after its hostess *362: 'scurvy came upon him & . . . he
*376: 'a bed of soft rushes & of the tops of the birch' became scald-headed'
*394–6: quicken tree of Dubros is protected by giant who can be killed only by 3 strokes of his iron club
Tom, Dick & Harry

*361: Finn's nurses were his uncle, a druidess named Bodball & 'the Grey One of Luachar'
*394–6: Finn asks for the head of Diarmaid or for a fistful of berries from the quicken tree of Dubros (of
beriberi: vitamin deficiency disease Masses for the dead rejuvenating powers)
*398: Grania wants a portion of the berries
Bran: Finn's dog *ph* never say die
Sherlock Holmes meets Moriarty, his enemy, on precipice tightrope walker
*385–7: Diarmaid performs feats of walking on the edge of his sword, Moralltach, & of balancing on a rolling barrel
s 'Roll out the barrel' Strongbow: chief Anglo-Norman invader of Ireland
Sl longbowman: liar Sitric: name of several Viking kings of D
Blarney Castle *381: Diarmaid: 'O ye of the lie, & of the tracking, & of the one brogue'
*377: 'It is not told how they fared until they arrived at . . . Clan Ricard'
s 'The Wren, the Wren, The king of all birds'
*364: Cruithne (Creena): girl to whom Finn was betrothed as a young man
s Nora Creina *AngI* whist!: silence!
I crú na chríonna: the old man's gore
Mary Virgin forbid! if
*376: 'It is not told how they fared until . . . Diarmaid . . . settled a bed of soft rushes . . . under Grainne'
G Friede: peace fried sole Easter Greeting
*384: Diarmaid left 7 uncooked salmon as a token to Finn that he had not sinned with Grania

*T.P. Cross & C.H. Slover: *Ancient Irish Tales* (1936)

L agnus: lamb 'Sanctus, Sanctus, Sanctus' (prayer) 'The overseer of the house of the overseer of the
*379: Angus: fosterfather of Diarmaid seal, Nu, triumphant, saith:' (frequent introduction
(7 orifices of head, 356.05–06) dromedary dormitory in the *Egyptian Book of the Dead*)
*379: Diarmaid built enclosure with 7 doors while eloping with Grania
HEC ECH

Magrath (060.26) helot H . . . C . . . E *F* champignon: mushroom
hero chest of champion
Gaul *nr* 'The king was in his countinghouse, counting out
*358: 'Cumall fell by Goll . . . (the One-eyed)' his money' *Sl* greenhouse: urinal
R.J. Gatling invented a machine gun *s* Lannigan's Ball

Shelbourne Hotel, D shellshock
Shelbourne Rugby Club, D *s* The Shan Van Vocht
gibbous: hunchbacked (hanging)
gibbet

posthumous (reincarnation)
*361: Finn was born after his father's death
Shiel Martin: one of the summits on Howth

begin three times three

*402: nine of Finn's men, all named Garb, were killed *L* multum in parvo: much in little
by Diarmaid in the quicken tree by his throwing them down in his own appearance so that the others attacked them
impervious Wellesley (Wellington)
Old Wesley; Wanderers: Ir. Rugby football clubs
wagtail (bird) *Portrait* V: 'Pawn to king's fourth'
*400–1: Diarmaid, hiding in the quicken tree from Finn & Oisin playing chess below, throws berries at men
Mendelssohn's Wedding March on the board, prompting Oisin to move & win
honeymoon harmonium
Dubliners: 'Ivy Day in the Committee Room' Eve . . . Adam Vanessa vanities
*357: Almu (a fortress) Hill of Allen: Finn's headquarters finesse *F* fiancailles: betrothal
with *365: Finneces: poet for whom Finn cooked the salmon of wisdom
ph as right as two trivets
ph now or never P/Q split
N knute: knot (i.e. hanging)
s Eileen Alannah

diamond wedding

L gallus: cock C . . . E . . . H hooker: position in rugby

free kick Dublin Dove . . . Raven 417: Diarmaid dies at Rath Finn
massacre by British troops of Irish leaving football game in Croke Park, D, 1920
(Four Horsemen of the Apocalypse)
AngI hike!: stop! (call to horse)

godson *s* Break the News to Mother
AngI gossoon: young lad tomorrow
Ibsen: *The Master Builder* fallen asleep

s Sonny Boy flashlamp (404.13) *I* post pingne: penny post
I Seón Buidhe: 'Yellow John', i.e. Englishman
subconscious (185.35–6) signature *Du* segne:
Da solskin: sunshine sink
stroke of a pen pun *s* One More Drink for the Four of Us
Naut strake: unit of depth
four chorus
F encore
God amen Matthew . . . Mark . . . Luke . . . John
G Mohn: poppy
ph loop the loop

asscart *N* kart: map hip, hip, hurray!
N aas: hill
Allsop's ale four goals to nil

date with a swimmingpool

*T.P. Cross & C.H. Slover: *Ancient Irish Tales* (1936)

ph dead as a doornail LAP once
Anna Dunlap: actress in 1st Italian burletta performed in D, 1761
Bacchus (feasting) imbibe
L bucca: mouthful *It* per Bacco! (exclamation)
L lac: milk one flesh, one blood HCE
lack of godliness
Here comes everybody (032.18–19) traitor

monarch of Ireland
R khorosho: O.K.
ever since he heard Earwicker

written phosphorescence *Sl* fleshmarket: brothel
(lightning flash)
Persse O'Reilly of the Royal Irish artillery Attila (lit. 'little father')
Rollo (Rolf) Ganger: 1st duke of Normandy
G Traum: dream
lightning . . . conductor electrical tramconductor
Greenlander
green islander
making substitutes superstitions false ingots trademark
melting statuettes
King Mark of Cornwall Roderick O'Connor: last high king of Ireland *L* rex *Da* ord: word
Easterling: Viking (used of invaders of Ireland) Sitric: name of several Viking kings of D
Art MacMurrough Kavanagh: C14 king of Leinster *L* adverso ordine: in reversed order *F* coucou: cuckoo
N makt: powr *Da* København: Copenhagen conversion: kick after try in rugby
N morken: decayed cause *U*.335: 'Methusalem' bull & cow
L motus metusolo: moved by fear only
nr Hickory Dickory Dock business as usual
base
alive Michael/Lucifer the Plague, 1665: 'bring out your dead'
(being burned at stake)
tell us

football teams: Partick Thistle, St Mirren, Crystal Palace, Walsall *G* Putsch: revolutionary outbreak
St Michan's Church, D *I* agus: &
Office of the Dead: response to 7th lesson in 3rd nocturn: (plague transmitted by rats)
'Timor Mortis conturbat me' ('the fear of death disquiets me')
let us in get out peaceful possession
Du laat zien: show me *G* geh: go (possession of the ball)
we didn't understand why you said that about 32 11, sir

(13 & a loaf = Last Supper) let us alone language
(13 = baker's dozen)
profound F. Mauthner: *Kritik der* edelweiss: alpine plant idle words
Sprache (1901), 161: 'unsere Worte blosse Gütter Sind' *G* eitel Wort: vain word
learning Ibsen hurry up, grandfather

Sl gurk: belch freebooters *Da* os: us Butt
G Freischütz: marksman
G spuck: spit Taff HCE
speaks
Grimm's Law regarding sound shifts of *I* 'tuigeaan tú Gaedhealg?: do you understand Irish?
mute consonants from pre-Germanic to Gaelic League
historical Teutonic tongues void sentence
John 1:1: 'In the beginning was the Word'
G unbewiesen: unproved
G unbewusst: unconscious
& vice versa *Da* de taler danskernes sprog, men vi: you speak the Danes' language, but we ourselves

speak abstract history court *G* sprich!: speak!

utter nonsense Jespersen: *Language* XXI mentions the 'pooh-pooh' &
L nocentia: guilt 'bow-wow' theories of the origin of speech
N noe brœd: some bread immaterial

enveloped

s Off to Philadelphia in the Morning *G* Mahnung: warning
Gr delphos: brother

Castleknock, W. of Phoenix Park *I* muc: pig
Ticknock: village, Co. D Nick/Mick
Lady Dufferin: *s* Katey's Letter: '& he knows it—oh, he knows it—Without one word from me' (Katey doesn't put her love's name on envelope)
sender to whom

ph take the cake *Bugle & Bitch:* nickname for *Hound & Horn* magazine
pair of drawers
Lordmayor's procession trees
horse & mare
by the same token

what about hesitency *Du* dat: that celebrated
Jespersen: *Language* XXI mentions the 'ding-dong' theory of the origin of speech
(032.02–04) Sechseläuten: Zurich spring festival soldier's pay
Congested Districts Board in Ireland, late C19
loose (Rugby): part of game in which ball is not in possession of any player (063.05)
gun *s* Follow Me up to Carlow *L* vae victis: woe to the vanquished
O'Connell (said to have had numerous illegitimate children)
Hadrian's Wall

s Polly Wolly Doodle
Valhalla

holes
N hores: whores
nice little home of his nice little thoughts 2 eyes, 2 ears, 2 nostrils & mouth (7 holes)
I phúca: hobgoblin boys & girls skirls

stinks *G* Rhein *Du* bok: he-goat bad delusions
rainbow reindeer delirium
Elysian Fields Queen Mab (sleep) Falstaff
fullstop
(7) abdicate gets my goat

death Mt Popocatepetl: volcano some fine day or other
sandblind
It sordo: deaf faith *G* wollen: to want pity our daughter

hen of yourn *Sl* glim: candle
40 candlepower
Du glimlach: smile *G* Rubin: ruby lenses

nr What Are Little Girls Made Of?: 'puppydogs' tails'

wheaten loaf

Gorteen, village, Co. Longford

graciously

majesty

etceteras *L* saturas: stew *s* It's Your Last Trip, Titanic, Fare You Well
L ceterus: the other
referee pass the time

Black Watch, Highland regiment Birgad: female messenger sent by Finn to make terms with his enemies
washerwomen *s* Tea for Two
Armitage, a bookseller, was the last 'king of Dalkey' (087.25) Tammany Hall, N.Y.C.: symbol of corrupt democratic politics
s 'Lots of Fun at Finnegan's Wake'
Tem: creator in *Egyptian Book of the Dead*

Kehoe, Donnelly & Pakenham: D ham curers Dumas: *The Three Musketeers*

I.S. Varian: D brush factory **K**
Kate Strong (079.27)
S

benefit
Heroine of Patrick Kennedy's story *The Twelve Wild Geese* is called Snow-White-and-Rose-Red
ALP
Boniface: generic as proper name of innkeepers
L aqua sancta: holy water
King Mark

Mullingar Inn, Chapelizod

my lords & members of
House of Commons

Thanksgiving Day (U.S. holiday)
I Finnuisce: clear water (anglic. Phoenix)
s Glenfinishk
F en la vallée

first Holy Communion

HCE
*U.*480: 'egg and potato factors'

polemarch: officer in ancient Greece

58 & 57 (Roderick O'Connor was about 60 when he submitted to Henry II)

Last Supper of Jesus & disciples
L umbra: shadow

Conn of the Hundred Battles: Ir. high king
HCE

L equile: a stable

ME whilom: once upon a time
Teheran: capital of Iran
Tara: ancient capital of Ireland

We arth: bear
Art MacMurrough Kavanagh: C14 king of Leinster

Murtagh of the leather cloaks: Ir. high king, 941
leggings
attributed to Henri IV of Fr.: 'I want there to be no peasant in my realm so poor that he will not have a chicken in his pot every Sunday'

palliasse

Marriage Ceremony: 'for better, for worse'

s The Bowld Sojer Boy

J.C. Mangan: *The Woman of Three Cows*
Sterne: *Tristram Shandy* VII.38: 'tis meat, drink, washing & lodging to 'em'

somersaults
sultry summer
s Pastheen Fionn: 'For oh! I would go through snow & sleet, If you would but come with me, brown girl sweet'
s The Widow Nolan's Goat
Nolan/Browne
neats: cattle

'Grand Old Man': Gladstone
hand me down

lack

s McCarthy's Mare

Dermot MacCarthy deserted from Roderick O'Connor's side during the invasion. Justin McCarthy acquired many of Parnell's followers after Parnell's defeat

Goldsmith: *The Deserted Village:* 'Sweet Auburn! loveliest village of the plain'

Lansdowne Rd, D Hibernia vintage

Parthalonians, 2nd group of Ir. colonists, were followed by the Firbolgs, who were themselves defeated by the Tuatha Dé Danann (or Danaan)

AngI mouldy: drunk

AngI googeen: dim, light-headed person

s The Rambler from Clare

Clane, village, Co. Kildare

faith

Dial spilth: waste

L faex: dregs

s A Right Down Regular Royal Queen toper: heavy drinker Smollett: *Roderick Random*

Round Table (King Arthur)

Lanty Leary: character in Samuel Lover

s The Green Linnet (ref. to Napoleon) John of Gaunt (Ghent; born there)

linen collarbone

Macclesfield, town, Cheshire

Presbyterian

Congreve: *The Way of the World*

Scott: *Heart of Midlothian*

Sl blue ruin: bad gin

allocution: address by general to soldiers, hence by pope to clergy

It bel canto

Bell: *Fundamentals of Elocution*

Thomas Hood: *The Dream of Eugene Aram*

humming

s The Ould Plaid Shawl *G* stärken: strengthen

Moore: *s* O Blarney Castle, My Darling [The Blackbird]

s The Lark in the Clear Air

Co. Clare

s I've a Terrible Lot to Do Today

ail

AngI wisha: well, indeed *s* What Irish Boys Can Do

s Smiggy Maglorral

Sl gutrot: bad liquor

Knights of Malta: the Knights Hospitallers, a medieval religious order

relinquished

replenished

mcfirkin: 9 gallons ('firkin' applied jocularly to a person) *Sl* slygrog: illicit, illegal *ph* turn & turn about

It brindisi: toast testified cherubic countenance
brandishing *Macbeth* V.8.12: 'I bear a charmed life'
rubicund Guinness's stout

John Jameson & Sons, Ir. whiskey

O'Connell Ale from Phoenix Brewery, D

than

fullback
Jesuit's tea: S. Am. tea substitute

gill = noggin= ¼ pint

s The Rising of the Moon

Kevin's (110.32) bacon & eggs chapel windows (see 603.35)
(sun) Chapelizod
story historical

eight o'clock Mass newsletter sealed, signed & delivered

blessings almighty
Sl mouldy: drunk
over opposite

Dial forenenst: opposite staircase (556.35–557.04: K with candle)

L pater familias: father of a family millions
forefather

boxing the compass (circled the table)
boat *L* compos mentis
coat & trousers heave ho *s* Larry's on the Force

fo'castle Feagh MacHugh O'Byrne: his attack on the Eng. in 1580 is celebrated in 'Follow Me up to Carlow' *AngI* faugh a ballagh: clear the way

s 'The flea on the hair of the tail of the dog of the nurse of the child of the wife of the wild man from Borneo has just come to town'
s Finnegan's Wake Earwicker

Nancy Hand's: local name of The Hole in the Wall, pub nr Phoenix Park

N natten land: land of night *Da* farvel: farewell *Da* Faerøeren: Faeroe Islands
Da lænder: loins Cape Farvel, Greenland
barque

s Follow Me up to Carlow
starlight

Arch quark: to croak   Sir Dynaden, in Malory's *Tristram*, composes a song
G Muster; paragon   against Mark, which is sung before him

According to a legend the wren became king   skylark
of the birds by flying on the eagle's back   *Dial* un: him
Sl buzzard: fool

Palmerston Park, D

ph cock of the walk

Tristan

t   : to copulate (said of male bird)   redd: to put in order

Da overhoved: chief, head   glee: song, music
overhead   *Da* Hoved: name of Howth in C9

capercailzie: wood grouse
nr Who Killed Cock Robin?: 'All the birds of the air'   ribald
Du smaken: to taste   Tristan & Isolde
G Kuss: kiss
Moore: *s* The Wine-cup Is Circling
white-caps: waves in windy weather
Moore: *s* As Slow Our Ship   *s* The West's Awake
asleep
Gen 1:2: 'the Spirit of God moved upon the face of the waters'   *F* eau
Dublin
Da kæmper: giants   (032.29)
'double u, double u' = w, w; W.W. Kelly, manager of Evergreen Touring Company, who performed *A Royal Divorce*
Du dubbel: double   *Du* donker: dark   donkey   tourney: tournament
Du dorp: village   double Dutch   *r* Tornio, Finland (*Sw* Torneälven)   waterfalls
Fi vuoksi: flood, high tide   oxen   coming in   *Fi* joki: river
r Vuoksen, Finland   *L* vox: voice   *r* Kemi, Finland

(quarter buck per person)
solan-goose: gannet
Solon: Athenian legislator (094.27)
migratory birds

Vico discusses auspices in Roman history
Rugby

Soccer
Associational (football)
Ass
nr Who Killed Cock Robin?: 'All the birds of the air were a-sighing & a-sobbing'

Moore: *s* The Wine-cup Is Circling [Michael Hoy]
Sea of Moyle between Ireland & Scotland
Annals of the Four Masters
The Four Waves of Ireland: 4 points on Ir. coast

I bás na beathadh: death of life

Merrion Square, D (Oscar Wilde's home address)

s One More Drink for the Four of Us: 'Glorious, glorious!
One keg of beer for the four of us!
Glory be to God there are no more of us,
For the four of us will drink it all alone'

Interim of Augsburg: partial halt in the Thirty Years' War, 1555
(Fish is ancient symbol of Christ)
s Auld Lang Syne

palm: symbol of martyrdom
Bunyan: *Pilgrim's Progress*
straining
L pulchrum: beauty
L procul: afar off
Du luisteren: to listen
Bédier, in *Tristan & Iseut,* mentions 4 old felons, who spied on Tristan & Iseut for Mark

bunnyhug: c20 U.S. dance
Boucicault: *The Colleen Bawn*

Sl dinkum: true, genuine
Oscar Wilde (.31)
Tinkerbell: fairy in Barrie's *Peter Pan*
Charles Stewart Parnell ('the Chief')
L cubare: to lie down
cabin
L cubile: bed
only
beau ideal
blue-eyed

L sinister: left
L dexter: right
right & left
rough
Rugby & Associational (footballs)
L vicem versam: turned around
L etiam: & also
off-side (football)
sixfooter
handsome
Sl futter: to fuck
L balbus: stammering

F tout-à-fait charmante
tricked
madonna blue
Isola: sister of Oscar Wilde; died at age of 9
It isola: island

s 'Tea for Two, & two for tea, me for you, & you for me'

Angl pogue: kiss

Boucicault's *Arrah-na-Pogue* was revived annually in D
1st question of Catechism: 'Who made the world?'
remembered
the Vulgar era: The Christian era

Dolphin's Barn, D
Dion Boucicault: *The Colleen Bawn*

In Boucicault's *Arrah-na-Pogue* Arrah's foster brother escaped from prison with help of a message she passed to him in a kiss
underworld

Tut-ankh-amen Sh(a)un (Sean the Post: postman in *Arrah-na-Pogue*)
Tooting Common, London
Shem (penman)
In *Egyptian Book of the Dead,* Thoth holds the reed pen
1st question of Catechism: 'Who made the world?' O'Clery: surname of 3 of the Four Masters
Gerald Griffin: *The Collegians* (source for story of
Da Norsk: Norwegian *The Colleen Bawn*) *Sl* on the nod: on credit
Du neer: down Netherlands Whiteboys: C18 Ir. insurrectionists, dressed in white shirts
land of Nod Oakboys: Ir. insurrectionists of 1763
Peep of Day Boys: Ir. Protestant group, 1784–95 making hay while the sun was shining
s Tom, Tom, the Piper's Son Peeping Tom (spied on Lady Godiva)
Jean de Florian: fabulist

conic sections (maths) vulgar fractions
It vellicar: to tickle
Ultonian: of Ulster
Queen's College, Belfast
L toties quoties: as often as occasion demands tributes
(the Ass) *G* Blut: blood
Brian Boru, the battler of Clontarf *F* livre: pound (money) loaves
(known as 'Brian of the Tributes'; defeated Danes at ⚔ Clontarf, 1014)
crown: 5 shillings mad dean (Swift) eating his victuals
turnover: type of bread loaf
vittles *U.S. Sl* snakepit: madhouse
Ragnar Lodbrok, Viking, cast into snakepit, saved by thickness of his pants
Lord have mercy
It mercia: haberdasher

moods & senses
tenses
mandible: jaw

to sing *ph* six of one to half a dozen of the other

love illicit
Lucan Chapelizod
Gray's *Elegy:* 'Full many a gem of purest ray serene . . . flower is born to bloom unseen'

s 'By the light Of the silvery moon, We loved to spoon, To my honey I'll croon love's tune, Honeymoon'

situation

s One More Drink for the Four of Us: 'Glory be to God there are no more of us'

AngI pogue: kiss mariner
foreigner
Mrs Hemans: 'The warrior bowed his crested head & tamed his heart of fire' *G* Tochter: daughter
Du hoed: hat Tilly the Toiler: Am. comic strip
Da dag: day (daily newspaper)
Roland, Charlemagne's paladin = Ariosto's *Orlando Furioso*
fourmaster (ship) Byron: *Childe Harold:* 'Roll on, thou deep & dark blue ocean, roll'
Master of the Rolls: a judge at Court of Appeal; Keeper of the Records, at the Public Record Office
Macpherson, *Temora* VII, mentions Ossian's 'darkbrown years'

Rudy Bloom

cubbyhole: small, confined room or closet

The Three Jolly Topers: D pub

The Old Man of the Sea

iambic pentameters

pantometer: instrument for measuring angles & distances, & taking deviations

decasyllabics

duck trousers

F salopard: scoundrel

G Wald: wood

Da falde: fall

nr Humpty Dumpty

s Auld Land Syne: 'We'll tak a cup of kindness yet'

lemon squash

straining

(4 hiccups)

bespectacled

respectable

Marcus

Du schoof: sheaf

Da hof: court

L quiescens in pace: resting in peace

Marquis of Powerscourt erected Powerscourt House in S. William St, D

It barge: charcoal embers

L braga: knickers

dormant

F mont

Clery's: department store, O'Connell St

Document No. 1: the Treaty (name used by De Valera's followers)

Dame St, D, runs towards Trinity College

statue of Daniel O'Connell, O'Connell St

ph pros & cons

Dana: mother-goddess of Tuatha Dé Danann

Booterstown: district of D

Battersby Bros: D auctioneers, Westmoreland St

promiscuous caterers

pumiceous craters

creatures

O'Connell was 'The Emancipator'

flowerpots

College Green, the site of the Norwegian Thingmote in D, was called Hoggen Green in C10

James H. North J.P., auctioneer & estate agent, 110 Grafton St, D

century: 100 runs in cricket

Tailtean games in honour of Tailte, queen of the Firbolg

D Horse Show

Anglo-Norman (invasion of Ir.)

active & passive

impulsive

redshanks: original Celtic occupants of Ir.

Sp barranco: ravine; fig. great difficulty

It Cappuccina: Capuchin nun

F jules: chamber pot

cowpunchers

Coppinger

F Sl jules: German

Cotopaxi: volcano (in W.J. Turner's 'Romance')

hours

Peep O'Day Boys called 'houghers' because they hamstrung enemies (hough: back of knee)

(don't step on cracks in pavement)

inasmuch as the weather

horse's withers

D City Corporation

Mt Popocatepetl: volcano (in W.J. Turner's 'Romance')

L jugiter: perpetually

L erumpo: I break out

erupting around

J yama: mountain

Fujiyama, volcano

C Yamen: mandarin's office; hence, any public service department

Curragh of Kildare (racecourse) confession
Priest-hunters claimed bounty on priests under the Penal Laws in C17–18 Ir.
Du noord: north *Du* Amerikaans: American *L* Afer: Africa
'Zuid Afrikaans' is spelled with an 'S' in S. African Dutch
Tierra del Fuego, S. America (7 items of clothing)
It del fuoco: some fire
cut of his jib: his personal appearance
jib: triangular stay-sail
sheepskin *Gr* parapelagios: along the sea (Armorica)
sashes worn by Orangemen
Pelagian heresy pilage: fur J. P. *It* elevato: elevated
gallowglasses: heavily armed Ir. soldiers
Dubliners addressed Swift 'Mr Dane' (Dean)

Sweyn Forkbeard: son of Harald Bluetooth: Danish king

Strathclyde, Aylesbury, Northumberland & Anglesey all ravaged by Vikings
Ivar the Boneless, Viking Liffey St, Ailesbury Rd, Northumberland Rd & Anglesea Rd, D
Ar joghovourt: people sweepstake
Swift's yahoos
Danes
auspices *Ar* Hayasdan: Armenia
vulcanology: study of volcanoes *L* exaestuans: boiling up existence
Du wolk: cloud
L plutor: rainmaker andesite: volcanic rock, Andes Pantelleria: Mediterranean volcanic island
exploiter 'plutonic action' of volcanoes pantellerite: kind of volcanic rock
exploder *L* monasterium: monastery
hysteria

J.C. Mangan: *The Time of the Barmecides*: 'To the old, old time, long, long ago'

Moore: *s* Though Dark Are Our Sorrows [The Prince's Day]
Momonia: Munster
s Fair Margaret & Sweet William
wedded
Black Prince: Longfellow: *The Wreck of the Hesperus:* 'the reef of Norman's
Prince Edward 1330–76, Duke of Cornwall woe'
R.D'A. Williams: *The Barmaid Sighs*
J.C. Mangan: *The Time of the Barmecides* (Barmecides were C8 Persian noble family)

Sir Roger Casement tried to arrange German weapons deal for Ir. rising in 1916, but was arrested on landing

Battersby (386.24)

Henry I's only son William was drowned in the sinking of the White Ship in 1120. It hit a reef because everyone on board was drunk
(Exod 14:28)

Martin Cunningham in *U.* based on Matthew Kane, official in D Castle,
Mark of Cornwall drowned off Dún Laoghaire in 1904

r Suir

someone
Saman: 1st native Persian dynasty
azure
Arthurian
nr Humpty Dumpty widow

writing her memoirs greatest tribute
murmurs Grace's *L* triput: solemn religious dance
monthly *My Man Godfrey* (film)
Da mand: man
Round Table (America)
runt: hag, dwarf

pr As the old cock crows, the young one learns exeunt through *I* doras: door
Sl gink: fellow Hamlet kills Polonius by sword thrust through the arras
Mark of Cornwall, ye king guy, kicked into yard enter at a window
G Kram: rubbish Kierkegaard *Da* jord: earth *Da* nat: night nightshirt
(backwards): nephew, tactful lover . . . Tristan Misunderstood evidence in Parnell court case gave the
impression that he had used a fire escape to leave Mrs O'Shea's room when surprised
Yseut (backwards) Liebestod from Wagner's *Tristan* begins: niece
'Mild und leise wie er lächelt' Isolde, as Mark's wife, was Tristan's aunt
fast behind on continent
within embrace *G* behend: nimble incontinent
F pervenche *Da* elsker: lover worth Tristan thrusting
mulct: fine for offence Selskar Gunn: son of Michael Gunn (025.22) tryst *F* fin
so much per wench
newscasters playbill W.G. Wills' *A Royal Divorce*
was about Josephine & Marie Louise & Napoleon
Sl nippy: penis R. Ord & W. Gayer-Mackay: *Paddy-the-Next-Best-Thing* (play, 1920)
save us knows *G* fing: pret. of fagen, to catch

Annals of the Four Masters record Ir. invasion by a fleet of
Flemings in 1169 (actually the Norman landing at Baginbun)
scattering of the Spanish Armada by a storm off W. Ireland

1132

Cunningham

lacustrine (St Kevin established monastic settlement at Glendalough)
Anabaptists: sect which arose in Germany, 1521 (believed in adult baptism only)
Laurence O'Toole, patron of D, contemporary Powerscourt (386.18) Dana (386.22)
of Thomas à Becket *It* donna: lady
parents Napoleon white horse: emblem of House of Hanover,
also associated with William III (equestrian
hun: pejorative for German Clontarf Wellington's horse Copenhagen statue, Dame St)

G Flut: flood, flood-tide
fleet
sea ⚔ of Helgoland, 1914 freebooter
hidalgo: one of lower Spanish nobility
disembarking

madam Bonaparte 'No Popery!' (slogan)
boche: pejorative for German
F et le voilà: & here he is
VI.C.15.164: 'alevilla: moth'
Narcissus *Angl* pogue: kiss

Du bladeren: leaves *Du* boom: tree Dion Boucicault: *Arrah-na-Pogue*
Sl gallows-bird: person who deserves hanging
G Silvester: New Year's Eve Queen's Colleges: Belfast, Galway & Cork
L silvestris: wooded *Du* neer: down
Bride St, D sentryman

Sylvia Pankhurst: suffragette leader
Ar p'ark': glory
nr Old Mother Hubbard anarchy exequy: funeral rite doxology: hymn ascribing
Hibbert lectureship *Ar* nakhakah: chairman glory to God
Gr doxa: opinion *Gr* arkos: guide, leader

Saxo Grammaticus: Danish historian
Grimm brothers
Latimer: English Church reformer, burned at stake *ME* latimer: an interpreter

vicereine Hugh de Lacy: governor of D for Henry II Rajah
Lord-Lieutenant Buckley shoots the Russian General
ON Ragnarøkr: destruction of the Norse gods
L Regnum: Chichester (390.18)
College Green, D
Gerald Griffin: *The Collegians*
Trinity College, D Ireland, 'Isle of Saints & Sages'

Plymouth Brethren: a religious body which arose in Plymouth ca. 1830; founder was educated at Trinity College, D
Sp zangano: drone

obedient servant 'O pia e pura bella': religious wars of Vico's heroic age
Sp abeja: bee Roman Law of the 12 Tables *Sp* pioja: louse *Sp* pulga: flea
It bolla: blister

I Éire go bráth: Ireland until Judgement Day (i.e. forever) Ulster, Munster, Leinster & Connacht

Matter of Britain (Arthurian cycle) *AngI* kill: church
L super: over, concerning
Kilkenny, on *r* Nore

Rollo (Rolf) Ganger: 1st Duke of Normandy (263.15)
gynecology
Queen's Colleges of Belfast, Galway & Cork, & University College, D, all have medical schools
Elizabeth Anderson: one of first woman physicians
Gr andros: man's
anniversary *s* Auld Lang Syne: 'Should auld acquaintance be forgot'
Unitarians as opposed to Trinitarians
I Banba: Ireland (poetic)
F Sl bambam: lame person
A.D. 1169: Strongbow lands in Ir. (see also 388.10)

Fitzwilliam Square, D

Fatima: daughter of Mohammed (388.32)
divinely

pseudotelephony

trunk line (telephone)

Virgil's *Aeneid* opens 'arma virumque cano' ('I sing of arms & a man') *L* Romano: by a Roman
Moore: *s* 'O Weep for the Hour When to Eveleen's bower'

H . . . CE Eddas (Icelandic & Old Norse sagas)

gaga *F* gnan-gnan: slow, weak & stupid
Ar gagaz: stammer
Sir Galahad (the Grail) *Arthour & Merlin* (anonymous C13 poem) has a true Guinevere whom Arthur distinguishes from her illegitimate half sister, the false Guinevere. Also in earlier Welsh legends & in Tennyson's *Idylls of the King*
triad of Tristans Troad: area around Troy
1132

Byron: *Childe Harold:* 'Roll on, thou deep & dark blue ocean, roll' Ossian

eyeballs Cornelius Nepos: Roman historian & letter writer *L* numquam: never
eyebrows *L* nepos: grandson *L* anumque: & the old woman
L umque: & -um (suffix) Napoleon
L umquam: ever *WWI Sl* napoo: finished, dead

bosun bride baited breath
Brython: a Briton of Wales, Cornwall or Ancient Cumbria
Mother of God! *Ar* aghdod: dirty
Ar mahatsou: mortal *I* ag: at, with, by
$2 \times 2 = 4$ (the ass) *G* Toten: the dead
totem total

feudal manor keep, tower & drawbridge

Saunders Newsletter: D journal 1780–1802
sake

All Danes in England massacred by order of Ethelred the Unready, St Brice's Day, (2 Dec) 1002

Buckley shot the Russian General

ballast master Goatstown, district of D
ballet master Booterstown, district of D
General *AngI* Lochlann: Scandinavian
r Lagan, Ireland
Earwicker Persse O'Reilly *Da* liggende: lying (lighthouse closed)
(wick of lighthouse lamp) piece
Saturday early closing

s Kelly with the Leather Belly Celts
Gr kronios:
old man baldric: pendant belt supporting bugle or sword

AngI bohereen: lane Artichoke Road, old D 'the Mad Mullah': Mohammed bin Abdullah, Somali
We moel: hill rebel, early C20
Alexandre Dumas: *The Man in the Iron Mask* Oran, city, Algeria, has famous mosque *s* Old Folks at Home
Patrick assigned situations for several Gallic priests at Oran, Co. Roscommon
confarreation: most solemn form of ancient Roman marriage
Peregrine O'Duignan: co-author of *Annals of the Four Masters*
Coppinger's Register: chartulary vilest
of St Thomas's Abbey, D cabbage

North, South, East & West Dr Wangel: old man married to younger
woman in Ibsen's *The Lady from the Sea*

The Four Waves of Ireland: 4 points on Ir. coast *s* The Lambeth Walk battledore & shuttlecock
lumbago Lambeg drums in Ulster Protestant marches
F Dial conche: creek, cove

cross In 1700 the lands of Ir. Jacobites publicly auctioned at Chichester House, College
Green (subsequently replaced by Parliament building)

bygone days

s Auld Lang Syne: '& never brought to mind'

Jupiter Pluvius
Sh nup: micturate
privy temporary *Ar* terpay: impersonal verbal form (a which
grammatical category)
foretold Pilgrims with cockleshells in their hats visited the shrine of St James the Greater
Ar or: that
West Indes (Cromwell Ballymacarret, district of Belfast (501.04)
deported many Irish there)
T.P. Cross & C.H. Slover: *Ancient Irish*
Tales (1936), 359: 'So that hence was said this'

We pr I know milk though I am not used to it *It* latte: milk

Dalkey Document No. 2: De Valera's proposed alternative to the Ir. Treaty
Dollymount, district of D
r Ivel

The Holy Maid of Kent: Elizabeth Barton, who incited Catholics against Reformation & was hanged
at Tyburn Connacht Ahriman: Zoroastrian principle of evil
The Coombe, street, D humble petition offices lemon squash
position advice
U.654: '*nisi* was made absolute' (Parnell divorce case)

Goldfish is in the carp family Poland
Cairpre: name of various Ir. kings Cross & Slover 357: 'When Cathar Mor . . . was in the kingship of Tara'
Du voorzitter: chairman full-bottomed wig

(ermine worn by chairman) Armenia *L* regina: queen
In Tasso's *Gerusalemme Liberata,* Erminia disguises herself to enter enemy camp & rescue her beloved
Y.W.C.A.: Young Women's Christian Association
1169 A.D.: Strongbow lands in Ir.
Sl familyman: thief *I* ara na: one given to
Dion Boucicault: *Arrah-na-Pogue*
I scuit: excitement
Du schuit: boat

Johannes
Ar Hovhannès: John
Du zweep: whip
indelible
untellable

attraction *ph* put years on him
atrocity ataxy
Joseph Maas, tenor *Ar* tchors: 4 *Ar* hink: 5 hing: asafoetida
Annals of the Four Masters (the ass) behind
Du borstelen: to brush *Du* schoen: shoe
Du schoon: clean
L materfamilias: matriarch
backscratching: flattering servilely
innocence
in a sense
Middle Temple (law), London

Du stout: bad massacres

Marquis of Powerscourt (386.18) Browne/Nolan
ph brown as a berry
no man's land *Gr* chronometron: time measurer

Moore: *s* Through Erin's Isle [Ally Croker] (390.33) Erin's isle *Da* slide: herrings
G Herrin: mistress
ph between wind & water

Neptune: D rowing club Giant's Causeway
(urination) Diamond Sculls, Henley, London (rowing)

hirsute (wig & beard 390.36–391.01)
suit
Browne/Nolan (writing paper) *Romeo & Juliet* *J* to: &
linoleum Roneo copying machines Gillette razor blades

Dionysius Boucicault
Dion Cassius: Roman historian
ph the world & his wife

ph to have a shingle short: to be mentally deficient

praises be Eph 4:26: 'let not the sun go down upon your wrath'
Peace of Wedmore between King Alfred & the Danes restricted latter to N.E. England
lyre psalms of David
ear Thomas Davis: Ir. nationalist poet

Coleridge: *The Ancient Mariner* 34: 'Red as a rose is she' *It* rosse (f. pl.): red
F rosse: rotter
(Russian General)
room
Sl marrowbones: knees

kalecannon (potatoes & cabbage) traditionally eaten on All Hallows' Eve
midnight
beauty

hansom 'Unfriends' is lit. tr. of *Da* uvenner (enemies)

Mrs Browning: *My Last Duchess* (poem)
Doge of Venice annually wedded the sea in ceremony

letter, 23/10/23, to HSW describes this section: 'a picture of an epicene professor of history in an Irish university college seated in the hospice for the dying etc after "eating a bad crab in the red sea"'

AngI Andrew Martins: pranks
(393.05)
Connacht (Johnny MacDougal)

N hunn: female
eating a bad crab in the Red Sea
Du eten: to eat, eating (gerund)
heaven knows
Dead Sea
Ar hiuantanots: hospital

Our Lady's Hospice for the Dying, Harold's Cross, D
Master Misericordiae Hospital, D (built by Sisters of Mercy, who were founded by Catherine Macauley)
trying
nurse-tender: a sick-nurse

ABC
day
Da død: death
born
1st question of Catechism: 'Who made the world?'

live
L emeritus: retired soldier

Abbottabad, Pakistan
Heb achoth: sister
J.F.M. ffrench: *Prehistoric Faith & Worship: Glimpses of Ancient Irish Life*
sorry
F pourboire
G Sorge: worry
Ar or: that

Cornelius Nepos: Roman historian & letter writer

peregrine
the purple: the cardinalate
Da blusse rød: flush crimson
papal blessing

beaver: a hat of beaver's fur
Caucasus
caucus: committee elected to secure political action
I geasa: magical injunctions (taboos)
mistletoe
Cornelius Nepos says that Themistocles' tombstone had inscriptions in several languages (Themistocles was an Athenian statesman, ca. 527–460 B.C.)
R na vyeleki kamyen: on a big stone

Du rust: rest
oxide of iron (rust)
hospices
s The Exile of Erin
Vico discusses auspices in Roman history
Gr kalos: beautiful
Gr theos: God
Gr spinthêr: spark
Gr chrômato-: colour

Daniel O'Connell
Dana: mother-goddess of Tuatha Dé Danann
New Ireland: island near New Guinea
Henry II gave D to the burghers of Bristol
King Alfred burned the cakes
Anne Lynch's D tea

Shackleton & Sons, D flour millers
I duileasc: edible seaweed
God in Heaven
Gordon Highlanders (regiment)
Malory: *Morte d'Arthur*
G Gott und Heiland
F merde
Sl Act of Parliament: small beer

Adrian IV's bull *Laudabiliter*, granting Ireland to Henry II
lemon squash

Shackleton & Sons, flour millers, D   acid + alkali = a salt + water

AngI signs on: therefore   (Last Supper)

AngI Andrew Martin: prank

last   *Da* koning: king

G Muster: paragon   *G* Bart: beard

Sitric Silkenbeard led Danes at ⚔ Clontarf, 1014   Bartholomew Vanhomrigh: father of Swift's Vanessa, & Lord-Mayor of D   oil

Gr sôtêr: saviour   *G* Bürgermeister

shook hands   Hurdle Ford (*I* Áth Cliath: D)

Moore: *s* When First I Met Her, Warm & Young [Patrick, Fly from Me]

Finnan haddies: haddocks cured with smoke of green wood, turf or peat earth

Noah's Ark   Mock Turtle (*Alice*)   *F* potage

oxtail & turtle soup   caustic potash: potassium hydroxide

grasshopper   *F* bouillon: broth   pulled

G Gries Suppe: semolina soup

bucket of water   *Fi* vuota: to leak   New Year's

It boccata: mouthful   *It* vuota: empty   earwig

HCE

(hiccups)   Shem & Shaun

assisting grace: term used by St Augustine, referring to grace which co-operates with man's good tendencies   *s* Auld Lang Syne   *G* Hosenband: garter

husbands

Glastonbury (according to Giraldus Cambrensis it was once the Isle of Avalon; he recounts the discovery there of King Arthur's grave)

till   mother-of-pearl

latter   catechism

saltpetre: potassium nitrate

middle   maiden

midden   modern

Adam & Eve   *L* malum: apple   *L* ovum: egg   (*ph* from the egg to the apples)

alum: potassium aluminium sulphate

tapestry

kookaburra: Australian bird   ringing

s The Bells of Shandon

punched

knock knees   Moore: *Let Erin Remember the Days of Old:* 'On Lough Neagh's bank as the fisherman strays . . . He sees the round towers of other days, In the wave beneath him shining'

Ar vdankavor: dangerous   *We* ys: it is

Ys: legendary city in Brittany engulfed by ocean

Boston Transcript

Du oorkussens: pillows   oxters   puzzled

Sl puddled: insane, very eccentric

mystified   schooner

Du even rusten: to rest for a minute

G Gastspiel: performance by guest ensemble

gospels   counting the sheep (to get to sleep)

days

sitting

eiderdown

Ar or: that slumber

Synoptic Gospels: the first 3

swallowing

dodging the turkeycock

Du jool: fun

Da fyre: heat, fire *Army Sl* bit of brown: homosexuality

spirits of wine: ethyl alcohol

AngI bawneen: white flannel smock worn by peasants

Sen Patrick (lit. 'Old Patrick').
fosterfather of St Patrick

Dunlop (tyres) *Du* loop: walk
Gr panemmenetikos (artif.): disposed to endure all

s The West's Awake *G* Föhn: S. wind in Switzerland
asleep
Finnegan

left-off bag of dirt Dagobert: C7 king of Franks cheeks

Arthropoda: super-phylum including insects anthroposophy: knowledge of man's nature, human wisdom

preallably: previously, beforehand
telling
dephlegmate: guttural *ph* frog in one's throat *C.f. rom* fong: wind
in Alchemy, to free from phlegm (watery material)

s Coolin Das (means 'pretty fair-haired girl')

L palpebra: eyelid *Da* minder: memories

Tristan

Hungr-vaka: saga of bishops in Skalholt up to 1178
cg 'eenie, meenie, minie, mo'
goose that laid a golden egg (subject of pantomime)
Phoenix Park once known as 'Queen's Gardens'
P/Q split *Da* katte: cat *Da* efter: after EHC Earl of Howth
Prankquean *pr* A cat may look at a queen king Hoved: Danish name of Howth in C9
Heber & Heremon: legendary progenitors of Ir. race
Hobson's choice
I sort of my most inmost *L* ego tum: I then
Isolde binocular
subconsciously upon Wilde: *De Profundis*
L super: above
bejapers! *Gr* pankosmikos: belonging to the whole world

I Sinn Féin, Sinn Féin Amháin: Ourselves, Ourselves Alone (slogan) HCE

s Caller Herring arena

solid, liquid & gaseous Pearl White: film star

It pugno: fist

Milky Way abstruse strew a dim (light) higher dimensional
whey: watery part of milk *L* dimissio: sending forth
seeming Trystan, Isolde (anagrams) meeting
meaning

AngI Johnny Magorey: Prester John: mythical Eastern ruler in whose armies were Gog & Magog.
fruit of dog rose
s Dashing Away with a Smoothing Iron annalists
F pied anal
Da ovenfor: above *Da* nedenfor: below

Da duk: plunge, dive Cicero: *Cat.* I.1: 'Quo usque tandem . . .' four tired schoolmasters
Dunlop (tyres) ('How long at length . . .') 4-masted schooners retired *Du* schoon:
beautiful, pure

narcolepsy: uncontrollable attacks Lake Como
of deep sleep

Sp fumador: smoker modern
Gr dory: ship *It* madornale: huge
cataract: opacity of eye lens (here, window)

Hebrew letter HE *L* qua: in the capacity of *G* oben: over
means 'window'
Moore: *s* She Is Far from the Land [Open the Door]
N hunn: female honeymooners
Alice Springs, Australia *s* She Is Far from the Land

F en famille

sort of made

perfectly sweet beautifully
perfidiously dutifully
Catholic Encyclopaedia, 1911, 'Pelagius' 605a: '*assisting* grace being spoken of more frequently than *preventing* grace'
Gr dory: ship bed verses
in Egyptian theology, the soul travels in a boat after death
Egyptian Book of the Dead XXIII: Chapter of Opening the Mouth
It operare: to work Tut-ankh-amen
AngI pogue: kiss

004.18: 'Stuttering Hand'

Cook's evidence (Parnell divorce case) *Du* poot: foot, leg, paw
courage clap the lid on a pot of porridge
& shut Ibsen: *Et dukkehjem* (*A Doll's House*) death (Liebestod in Wagner's *Tristan & Isolde*)
faithless

even unto death (*L* usque ad mortem) queer little cry of Jesus Christ!
F cri
ruby lips

opportunity of a lover's lifetime

U.S. Sl pigskin: football Armorica (Tristan) champion

arrogant thrust missive (tongue; also the message—see 385.03) flash past
Ar aragan: male virile victory

(teeth) *L* eburnea: of ivory
(forwards in football) Hibernia

Ar abris!: bravo!

Wellington: 'Up, guards, & at them' please

one man or woman to

F mot *Ar* amot': shame *F* comment? *Ar* menk': we *Ar* tou: you
Matt 5:38: 'An eye for an eye' *D Sl* mott: girl
whatyoumaycallit *Sl* strap: fuck

princess hand: unit of measure for horses' height
L priscus: ancient
madapollam: kind of cotton cloth

heart of Moore: *s* By That Lake, Whose Gloomy Shore: 'Eyes of most unholy blue'
Coll ph bedroom eyes: eyes of sexually inviting appearance
627.09: 'My great blue bedroom'

psychological
so-called logical

(kiss) orang-utan
Ar hayrig: little father
(26 shillings & 6 pence) shepherd's

plaid trousers 39 Articles of Church of Eng. please stop

Ar haga: anti, against
Gr hagios: holy *Ar* k'risdonéout'iun: Christianity
to such an individual a pinch of hen shit

meanest *AngI ph* such a thing was never heard of since Adam was a boy
Edem: earth mother in a Jewish heretical tradition navy
AngI ph the dear (deer) knows

tale must be told culpable gullible

purpose *Cz* mha: mist

fashionable

frightful

(spark plugs of car became hot enough not to require choke)

Eccles 1:2: 'Vanity of vanities' brief longings

L lapsus linguae: slip of the tongue

Tristan tongue (mouth) Chapelizod
knight of the true cross chapel-of-ease
Odyssey *It* polpa: flesh, pulp
ph to pop the question (proposal of marriage)

too truly terrific Matthew, Mark, Luke, John

mother-of-pearl buttons

⚔ Clontarf, 1014 *Heb* mem: water beautiful modern
remember

overflowing
Du flauw: faint, weak
oneirist: interpreter of dreams Gregory MacDougal
onliest
Matthew, Mark, Luke, John married

Dion Boucicault: *The Colleen Bawn* *I* a stór: my precious

Moore: *s* O Banquet Not in These Shining Bowers [Planxty Irwine]

(hiccups)

housework

voicebox: larynx Matthew, Mark, Luke, John
It mammalucco: simpleton
Signor Foli: pseudonym of A.J. Foley, Ir. bass, 1835–99 *s* Mother Machree (sung by McCormack)
coxswain *U.S.* hot air register: heating grill in wall of room

'Old Man's House': Royal Hospital, Kilmainham (for military pensioners)

half asleep
L ova: eggs matinée coat worn by babies
brown sugar
Shackleton & Sons, D flour millers
Du boterham: sandwich of peas

Du lepel: spoon *s* Auld Lang Syne: 'We'll tak a cup of kindness yet'

monkeybean

Ar khmel: to drink

heeding skeleton love of Jesus (*I* Iosa)
beheading skillet: longhandled pan *Sl* joss: idol
G Mensch

Pope: *Eloise:* 'the world forgetting, by the world forgot' Flemish (388.10) Boucicault
whooping cough

pissabed eaten a bad crab ABC *AngI* Johnny Magorey: fruit of dog rose (not poisonous)
Du eten: to eat
backscratch farthing dip: homemade tallow candle made from rushes tip *I* Cáisc: Easter (from *L pascha,* by P/K split)
P/K: paschal candle magnesium (flashlight)
Ar megnout'iun: commentary
F faire dodo: go to sleep

Vico discusses auspices in Roman history

L codex old style (Gregorian) calendar
Matthew, Mark, Luke, John
Seanchas Mór: Great Register: corpus of early Ir. law Felicia Hemans: poetess, buried in D
sale *F* ensemble caracul: a kind of astrakhan fur Freud: *Totem & Taboo*
L totam in tutu: the (fem.) whole in safekeeping
tutu: ballet skirt *Du* noenmaal: luncheon

obtainable from the author recall *F* rêve incubism
regulate
green spectacles *Ar* or: that
tentacles
Farfassa O'Mulconry: one of Four Masters
rigorist: believer in religious cult of self-denial

Conary O'Clery: one of the 4 Masters   Merrion, district of D
letter 12/10/23 to HSW: 'The apocrypha are represented by Lally & Roe & Buffler &c.'
L podex: posterior   bag of broth

I scológ: male farm servant   in sum   sept: Ir. clan
beeves: oxen (poetic)
severalty: tenure of property in one's own right   Matthew, Mark, Luke, John
HCE

Gawain: nephew of Arthur
'going, going, gone' (auction)

L in medias res: in the middle of the events (beginning of an epic)
L loquor: to speak   *L* in medios locos: into the middle of places

Liebestod ('love-death', in Wagner: *Tristan & Isolde*)

sallow   *F* sans famille (title of book by Hector Malot)

L oremus: let us pray   *s* Home Sweet Home   homily

HCE   *F* événements

tumble   *Du* slaap: sleep; temple
Du meter: godmother   *Du* peter: godfather   *s* Auld Lang Syne: 'auld acquaintance'
Annals of the Four Masters by Michael O'Clery, Farfassa O'Mulconry, Morris O'Mulconry, Peregrine O'Clery, Peregrine O'Duignan & Conary O'Clery
L pro navigantibus et peregrinantibus: for sailors & travellers (a prayer)   *I* fionnachán: dim. of fionn ('fair')
AngI Faugh a ballagh: clear the way!

Moore: *s* To Ladies' Eyes a Round [Faugh a ballagh]   Tristan   *L* dulcis: sweet
Gr dory: ship   'Here's tricks!' (toast)   Ysolde (anagram)
ph roll one's hoop: go ahead, be successful

doubly blessed

Moore: *s* Oh! The days are gone (Love's Young Dream) [The Old Woman]

King Lear   The Seanchas Mór (corpus of early Ir. lore) was introduced by King Laoghaire ('Leary')

fulfilling

love   *s* Auld Lang Syne
Lazarus raised from the dead (John 11:44)
s 'We'll tak a cup of kindness yet for the sake of auld lang syne'
Kohinor diamond   prize (111.06)
C shanghai: on the sea
Shanghai: type of domestic fowl (117.02)
Lambeg drums played in Ulster on 12 July
Brasenose College, Oxford (i.e. brass instrument)
L anno Domini nostri sancti Jesu Christi: in the year of our blessed Lord Jesus Christ

Ulster (N.)   Ulster Bank, College Green Branch (near Trinity College)

Scot. bawbee: halfpenny   GOLD   SUNDAY
letter 12/10/23 to HSW:

Pronoun	Evangelist		Four Masters	Ore	Evangelist Symbols	Liturgical Colours	Day	Province	Accent
A: thou	Matthew	Matt Gregory	Peregrine O'Clery	gold	—	:blueblack	Palm Sunday	Ulster	Belfast
B: she	Mark	Marcus Lyons	Michael O'Clery	silver	lion	:moonblue	Holy Tuesday	Munster	Cork-Kerry
C: you	Luke	Luke Tarpey	Farfassa O'Mulconry	steel	calf/Ir. tarbh	:red	Spy Wed	Leinster	Dublin
D: I	John	Johnny MacDougall	Peregrine O'Duignan	iron	eagle	:black	Good Friday	Connacht	Galway-Mayo

Sybil Point on Dingle peninsula, Co. Kerry, Munster (S.)

(birth of Aphrodite from foam)

AngI curragh: light canvas boat   *s* By the Light of the Silvery Moon

mother-of-pearl   SILVER

(Women in Co. Kerry traditionally wear blue hooded cloaks)

AngI Yerra!: God! (exclamation)   sloomy: spiritless

barnacle geese

Sl cold meat: corpses

s Widow Machree   snug

Balbriggan: town, Co. D, Leinster (E.); made knit fabrics

surtout: overcoat

AngI wisha: well, indeed   WEDNESDAY

nurse-tender: sicknurse

Sl high-stepper: fashionably dressed or mannered person   *AngI* acushla: my pulse (endearment)

COPPER

FRIDAY   IRON

Maud Gonne: loved by Yeats

Cross of Cong: relic in National Museum   (Resurrection)

Roderick O'Connor (380.12) died at Cong Abbey, Co. Mayo, Connacht (W.)

'Mick, Nick & the Maggies' (219.19)

Moses

I bothar mór: highway (373.05)

Matthew, Mark, Luke, John

(ass)

John-a-dreams (*Hamlet* II.2.295): generic for a 'dreamy fellow'

Da tolv: 12 *G* elf *I* ceathair: 4

G horch: listen

We pedwar: 4 *We* pump: 5 *It* tre: 3
53

fogbow: effect similar to rainbow, produced by fog & light Mark of Cornwall

It naso: nose

RED kepi: military cap ORANGE (gorse)
ruddle: to mark with red ochre
It titubante: hesitating Virgil: *Eclogues* I.1: 'Tityre, tu patulae recubans sub tegmine fagi' ('You, Tityrus, as you lie under the cover of the beech') features
It mobile: capricious Rembrandt *Hamlet* IV.5.174: 'There's rosemarry, that's for remembrance . . . and there is pansies, that's for thoughts . . . violets'
Gr anastasis: resurrection *Du* ziehier: 'voici' GREEN
Du zee: sea
Harald Bluetooth: Danish king; grandfather of Canute
YELLOW (broom) *G* blau: BLUE *Macbeth* I.2.1: 'What bloody man is that?'
Jugurtha: king of Numidia *It* becco: i) beak; ii) cuckold INDIGO
Gogarty
G Hornhaut: horny skin
F pensée: thought
wild, wild world veiled VIOLET kiss kids (goat)
G Veilchen: violets *Midsummer Night's Dream* I.2.75: 'I will roar you as gently as any sucking dove'
F voult: vault palate obsidian: a volcanic glass *G* Aal: eel
obscene lips
Agapemones: C19 religious community practising 'love-feasts' (= Eucharist) back!
It nero: black
Gr apage: go away! no-man's land

zero hour of attack

(035.30: Fox Goodman, hence vixen) (ultraviolet)
'Twelve good men & true': jury (i.e. time is 12 midnight)

letter, 24/5/24, to HSW: 'the copying out of Shawn which is a description of a postman travelling backwards in the night through the events already narrated. It is written in the form of a *via crucis* of 14 stations but in reality it is only a barrel rolling down the river Liffey'

alluvial 004.28: 'Soangso'
(end of I.8) lea, sward

Broadstone railway terminus, D
Dion Boucicault: *Arrah-na-Pogue*
flivvers (1920s): cheap motorcars or aeroplanes
fliers livers
G Hummer: lobster
inchoating Sean the Post: postman in Boucicault's *Arrah-na-Pogue*

meseemed something came from the noise
and someone who might remove all murk

Sp moreno: dark-complexioned verisimilitude
Bre moren: fog *Bre* glao: rain
Sean the Post carries a lamp on his belt
*U.*379: 'nine o'clock postman, the glowworm's lamp at his belt gleaming'
lifesize
going will o' the wisp
Sean the Post carries a whip prompt side: side of stage where prompter sited
hand props (theatre): properties carried on to stage by artistes
ph a belted earl Sean the Post wears a frieze coat
It sipario: curtain indigo blue
in theatre *I* Éire go bráth: Ireland until Judgement Day
terrier *OE* mere-swyn: dolphin, porpoise
ferrier: ferryman Ferrier, Pollock & Co., clothiers, D laces
G Schultern: shoulders welded welt: strip of leather between sole & upper
Sl Scotch mist: rain private sparable: small cobbler's nail
Providence Woollen Mills, Mayo

carat *R* krasnopopskii: papal red
burlap: coarse canvas used for bagging
Sl choker: cravat waistcoat
Tamagno: Italian tenor *It* forte *La Bohème*
L tam magnum: so great *It* sette: 7 4 (084.04: 'seven and four')
Damascus (Paul) *Ms* The Star-spangled Banner sapphire
damask
s Yankee Doodle
embroidered peas, rice, eggs = green, white & orange of Ir. flag
broth
R M Royal Mail, Dublin
F or ready money down
gigot sleeve: 'leg of mutton sleeve'
turnips
perfect absolutely Kersse the tailor (II.3)

'the blessings of God & Mary & Patrick & Brigid on you' (translation
Gr Hagios: saint of Ir. greeting)
turtle soup
I céad míle fáilte: a hundred thousand welcomes (Ir. greeting)

with post haste purchased
post-chaise

Du wijsheid: wisdom

daresay
L orsa: words, speech
Midsummer Night's Dream IV.1: 'Man is but an ass as if he go about to expound this dream. Methought I was—there is no man can tell what' tinkers'
F songe messenger
F Messe: Mass *F* mensonge: falsehood

rods & cones make up the eye retina

F bel Beaux' Walk, D (Stephen's Grn, N.)
Beau-Belle Walk, Phoenix Park
Primas/Caddy (014.12)
(i.e. ace)
Sl fired: damned, infernally

Jabberwocky: 'my beamish boy' Beamish MacCoul: hero to
Beamish stout whom note in kiss passed in
to dine with good Duke Humphrey: to go dinnerless *Arrah-na-Pogue*
nuncheon: light refreshment
eat (no oysters in months without an r)
eight months
Erin *Arch* hem: them fourale: ale sold at 4d a quart
farewell
Ms The Rose of Tralee jovial eyeglasses *s* The Heart of the Roll Is Dicey Riley
L/R Tara Jehovah Jove oval *N* øye: eye
I Trágh Ruadh: Red Bank (famous for oysters)

G Mahlzeit: meal *Arch* porterhouse: house where porter served

A fanatic, preoccupied with murder of Becket, attacked St Wheel of Fortune: Tarot card (X)
Laurence O'Toole on the altar steps of Canterbury Cathedral & beat him with a club
CLUBS cheques

Lazenby's pickles gratis
It graspi: grape stalks
Henry II granted D to the citizens of Bristol Balrothery: village, Co. D
U. 255: 'the house said to have been admired by the late queen'
front door sight

knave HEARTS

s Slattery's Mounted Foot
SPADES
Jewish Feast of Tabernacles (fast of Lent)

It pranza: dinners collation: light meal
St Patrick: *Tripartite Life*
'Bless us O Lord & these Thy gifts' (grace) blood orange
bloodthirsty Blood Thursday: in Ireland, Childermas Day
newlaid *Sl* googs: eggs raspberry pudding *Du* met: with
made of
Du of: or *Du* suiker: sugar godforsaken petrified
Du zonder: without
Tennyson: 'Come into the garden, Maud For the black bat, night, has flown' victuals
prejudice

It merenda: snack

Peter Blong, butcher in Portarlington (town, Co. Laois), 1743 (family name derived from Huguenot *Blanc*)
F récépissé: acknowledgement, receipt   Yorkshire pudding
F à la mélange
more please
Bre mar plich: if you please
s The Owl & the Pussy Cat: 'The turkey who lives on the hill'
rooster
goulash   sop up

L unio: pearl (large)   *L* margarita: pearl
'mea culpa, mea culpa, mea maxima culpa' (*Confiteor*)

eleven o'clock   *SwG* Gitzibraten: roast goat flesh
Bre avalou: apples   *G* Kitze: goats
Du boterham: sandwich   'Exsultet': 'O felix culpa!'
Tartars prepared meat by putting under saddle   Phoenix Ale
just to wet his whistle   *AngI* praties: potatoes   sweet potatoes   Irish stew
Bre sistr: cider   *Bre* gwin: wine   *Bre* gwastell: cake   *We* gwystl: hostage, pledge
turtle   *We* gwên: smile   swallowing   *We* swp: mass, heap

around   Boland's Bread Co., D   *G* Brot: bread

supper   *F* avec   videlicet
F souper   *I* a mhic: my son   *L* vitellus: egg yolk
Caruso   *G* Eier   bacon

Bre kig: meat   *Bre* hag: and   DIAMONDS

Bre tomm: warm

Irish Free State   clyster, suppository   *F* petit pois
(thimbleful of neat gin)   supposedly
G einen Fingerhut   *Dial* fingerhat: thimble   *G* Genever: Dutch gin   *L* pax cum spiritu tuo: peace with thy spirit
voll trinken: to drink a small quantity   *G r* Rhein (wine)   *G* rein: pure, (of wine) unadulterated
truly thankful   *Bre* bara: bread   *AngI* dulse: edible seaweed
(thirst)   Tipperary
F avec
Bre aman: butter   *Sl* avec: spirits
soprano Titiens was described in D as having 'a heart as big as herself'

leaves   *G* Nachtigall: nightingale (says 'jug')   St Julian of Berry: patron of hospitality
floury
Jilian of Bury: barmaid in song in *The Knight of the Burning Pestle*   (toby jug)   Mavrodaphne: a Greek wine
Custom House Quay, D   Litany of the Saints: 'Christ hear us, Christ graciously hear us'

Anne Lynch: D tea   *s* Ever of Thee I'm fondly dreaming

Hosanna in the highest!   *s* Auld Lang Syne
Ms For All Eternity

Swift's Hester Vanhomrigh (Vanessa)
G hungrig
F nourriture: food   merely   mainly
Shem, Ham and Japhet   ingestion: eating
Jaffa oranges
guilty   culpable
Gilbey, wine merchants, D
ph business is business   *AngI* beestings: milk from a cow that has just calved
G Biest: beast
off his oats = no appetite

Du goedkoop: cheap   Fr. Revolutionary Calendar: Thermidor (midsummer month); Floreal (midspring month)
August   *Du* oogst: harvest (in Flemish means August)

(no oysters in months without an r) prairie oyster: raw egg served with vinegar, pepper & salt
Prairial: last spring month in Fr. Revolutionary Calendar
gourmet *Sw* smörgås: open sandwich
I Dia's Muire dhuit: God and Mary to you (greeting)

bottle of Ardilaun = bottle of Guinness *G* lecker: appetising *G* Biss: bite *Du* taart: tart, cake
Da smag af an lækkerbisken: taste of a choice morsel
(Boxers and jockeys weigh in before fight/race) flyweight: boxer weighing 8 stone

G (im) grossen und ganzen: by & large
avoirdupois (weight after eating)
schoolgirl complexion

Easter Monday (Easter Rising began on) tramp and march
Sl on the ramp: engaged in swindling

Sl on the mash: constantly courting or ogling women
'Overture and beginners, please' (call-boy when performance begins)

AngI whist!: silence green rag (theatre): stage curtain

red blue death darkness

St Patrick: *Confessio* 23: '& I read the beginning of the letter containing "The Voice of the Irish"'
While reading it he heard 'the voice of those who were near the Wood of Foclut' Palestrina
L puer: boy

Ms Panis Angelicus Matt 16:18: 'tu es Petrus' ('Thou art Peter')

Michael Kelly: D tenor Mario: Italian tenor, sang in D

G frisch *It* uovo: egg *Bre* Breiz: Brittany

Bre Iverzon: Ireland ozone *s* From Inchigela All the Way
Bre Bro-Zaoz: England
Swift met Stella in Moor Park, Surrey morepork: name of an Australian bird, from its song

lovely Marconi Co. had wireless stations at Clifden, Connemara, & at Glace Bay, Nova Scotia

wireless

(aerials)

Bell's Standard Elocutionist shows 14 positions of the hands to be used by orators as they recite. The ones used here convey negation, affirmation, cautioning, supplication, violent repulsion & apathy or prostration
pr Handsome is that handsome does almost *Du* het: it
Du behulpzame hand: helping hand

hello *L* amo, amas &c. do, si, la, so, fa, me, re, do (solfa)
Alice *Aladdin* (pantomime) lack (something to sit on)
Yawn (474.01) dress rehearsal

(carrier pigeons)

HCE *G* overgestern: day before yesterday
plus
Tuesday's champagne *Ms* There is a Flower That Bloometh: 'the memory of the past'
Sl stews: brothels
L hic et nunc: here & now 'Music of the Future': Wagner's term for his own music
hiccups
It maccheroni: macaroni *L* ex alto: from on high
Mickey Rooney

Sl rag: curtain at theatre *G* Brief Brie, Bel Paese: cheeses billboard pass (theatre): free ticket for tradespeople displaying posters
brief (theatre): pass
deadheads: persons admitted free to theatre today mourn hestern: yester-
s Shule Aroon: 'I'll dye my petticoat' tomorrow Hester Vanhomrigh (Vanessa)

westernmost bread Gen 3:19: 'In the sweat of thy face shalt thou eat bread'
feet
L manducator: chewer

down & out to rest
Bre doaniet: sad de Reszke, tenor

Hundred of Manhood, W. Sussex (030.08)
I Iosa: Jesus *It* a iosa: in plenty

literally *Sl* dished: done for

unworthy *Bre* lous: dirty
lost
Mario the tenor was Count of Candia
It principotto: small fat prince McCormack's papal title 'Count'
prominence

(lying in bed) *G* Weh: woe, pain

might have been Marconi Wilde to Douglas in *De Profundis*: 'but I met you either too late or too soon'
more canny
brother

nickname letter, 14/8/27, to HSW: '[Wyndham Lewis] an "ever devoted friend" (so
G Leichnam: corpse his letters are signed)'
see tomorrow in those days of yore *Vo* lofobs: we love Oscar (Wilde)
Da os saa kær: us so dear
nr 'Simple Simon met a pieman' years
Vo sembal: certain
*U.*393 repeats Aubrey's statement that Beaumont and Fletcher 'had but Shem sows
the one doxy between them'
John Sims Reeves was first a baritone, then a tenor
reap *F* rêver: to dream
St Dizier: town in France where Napoleon defeated *s* Turn On, Old Time (sung 'Ti-hi-hi-hi-hi-me')
Blücher, 1814; *transition* was printed in St. Dizier
hourglass Lough Owel, Co. Westmeath behold!
owlglass (*G* Eulenspiegel): jester, buffoon
Ms Mother of Mine *s* McSorley's Twins
brother
alien *J* banzai: a cheer musical
bull's eye
Siamese (twins) fish's swim-bladder

Iveagh Baths, D (Baron Iveagh was brother of Sir Arthur Guinness) at this stage
G baden: bathing
(musical instruments)

Ms The Wearing of the Green: 'I met with Napper Tandy & he took me by the hand, & he said,
"How's poor ould Ireland, & how does she stand?"' neighbour

'Pansy' derived from *F* pensée (thought) *It* madre patria: motherland
Mother Patrick: pioneer in Gaelic Revival patriarch
John's Lane, D (Power's Whiskey)
John Lane, Eng. publisher of *U.*
s Father O'Flynn: 'Sláinte & sláinte & sláinte again' *s* The Coolin calendar months
colander
hero-worshipper *Bre* koant: gentle
helot: slave
L piscis: fish *It* pescivendolo: fishmonger great *Bre* drouk: wicked
'I have sinned (suffered)' Pisces, constellation Your Grace First Duke of Wellington

Gemini, the twins (constellation)

s The Banshee   Col. Shee embarked in the same boat as Wolfe Tone on the Bantry Bay Expedition
s 'Down among the Dead Men let him lie'   *Sl* dustbin: grave
hear, hear!   aye, aye!

Anthony Trollope reformed Eng. & Ir. postal system
ghost of a notion   *ph* not by a long chalk!
Pious Catholics write 'Saint Anthony Guide' on the backs of letters

sympathy   (permit to be a postman)

ph poor as a church mouse

s Ecco ridente in cielo (*Barber of Seville*)   Catholic
AngI cat's lick: halfhearted attempt at cleaning
capacious

cauliflower   *It* come sta oggi, signor moro mio?: how are you today, my black sir?
s A te o cara (Bellini: *I Puritani*)
G Grüss dich Gott (Bavarian greeting)   *L* columbus: dove   callouses

Lord have mercy
(mustard bath)
L corvus: raven   *Bre* pounner: heavy
curvature   *F* corvée: drudgery
daily

Sl rabbited: confounded, damned

G nichts   tinker's damn
G fort: away
Sl glasshouse: army prison
(2 thieves crucified with Christ)   Hellfire Club, D
believe
Belleek, town, Co. Fermanagh
emolument
emollient: softening
L Deo Gratias

In the Eastern Church, saints are called Hagios

Numerous spurious 'prophecies' attributed to St Colmcille (Columba)   (days of week)
The Book of Kells 'is often called the book of Colum Cille'   *AngI* colleen: girl
Breton *pr* Après le mercredi, le jeudi: *G* Tag   *L* solvitur ambulando: it is solved by walking
Voilà la semaine dans l'étable   *It* sabato: Saturday   *L* palumbes: wood pigeon
L ballando: by dancing   *Ido* (artificial language): til la rivido: au revoir
Ido adie: adieu
L salvator: saviour   Samuel Lover: *Handy Andy*
(solvitur ambulando .29)
(might be postman by order)

Luke 23:34: 'Then said Jesus, Father, forgive them; for they know not what they do'
lips
stroke

John Maddison Morton: *Box & Cox* (a farce)   (a bishop is chief over a see)   H . . . C . . . E
prematurely   initially   *L* praemittere: to send in advance
ECH   Eusebius' *Canons* harmonised the gospels

Book of Breathings: a funeral ritual in the *Egyptian Book of the Dead*

(stud book) John McCormack's papal countship was hereditary of course

Swann in Proust's *À la Recherche du temps perdu*

hindquarters *Sl* old fellow: father *It* orologio: clock, watch
L olor: swan
true trope
F trop
saint time

Hitler's Autobahnen blameless *Bre* erc'h: snow *Bre* skorn: ice
Da hykler: hypocrite *Egyptian Book of the Dead* cv: 'The soul without a name was in a terrible plight in the other world'
Bre grizilh: hail Black Forest, Germany
verbally nonplussed *AngI* craythur: whiskey
veritably
Naut London River (Thames) Catholic Truth Society
cachalot (whale) trout
Ireland's Eye: small island off Howth meson: plane dividing body into symmetrical halves
Lambay Island near Ireland's Eye (045.06: 'Hump, helmet & all')
G Spitze: peak
Gr epi oinopa ponton: upon the wine-coloured sea (Homer)

tight fit

earth

Eddington: *The Expanding Universe*
'Miraculous Medal': Catholic cult, well-established in Ir. omnibus

(we hear that in the end it may well turn out to be you)

beloved
Emania: ancient capital of Ulster the mail
G Email: enamel Aemilia: region in Italy S. of *r* Po
Patrick

damper: snack between meals gunpowder (according to S. Lover's *Handy Andy*, (gum on letters) once sold in Ir. postoffices)
benison: benediction lot
F barbe St Barbara: patron of artillery-men

AngI beg: little

I mór: big

s Whisper & I Shall Hear

hear

cowheel: oxfoot stewed to a jelly

L/R
60 Ir. miles = 75 Eng. miles
L/R chapels of ease
the Rosary is divided into 3 chaplets
pederasts
Egyptian Book of the Dead lxxviii: 'figures of the deceased . . . commonly rendered by . . . "answerers" '
Tom & Sid Sawyer, & Huckleberry Finn Thoth truth Thebes
Tom, Dick & Harry Theban recension of *Egyptian Book of the Dead*

brevet: authoritative written statement, esp. papal indulgence; military grant of nominal rank   vocation

Catechism: 'abstain from unnecessary servile work' on Sundays
Orthodox Jews can't travel beyond a specified distance on Sabbath
F douche: shower

pr when thieves fall out, honest men come into their own   Longfellow: *Excelsior* ('Higher'): poem in which youth carries banner with this device up an Alpine pass
Edward Clodd: *The Story of the Alphabet* 64 deciphers an Alaskan pictogram: 'I there go that island, one sleep there; then I go another that island, there 2 sleeps; I catch 1 sealion, then return mine.'
hour's sleep

G Pfeife: pipe   Ptah: Egyptian god   Amenta: Egyptian underworld
Ammon: Egyptian god   Lord's Prayer: 'Thy will be done, On Earth as it is in Heaven'
Gr (artificial) eirênêsia: peace-island-land   *Ms* In Her Simplicity

declare it
ph turn the other cheek
L declaret: may make clear
Du geit: goat   deity   *Gr* Pantokratôr: Almighty   *G* fett: fat   epistles
Gaiety Theatre, D (Christmas pantomimes)
rosary beads
apostles

G mit   *R* mat: mother   bonze: term applied by Europeans to Buddhist clergy of Japan
Bre mat: good   *Bre* bouzar: deaf
included   Czech national anthem: *Kde domov můj* ('Where Is My Home')

Lord's Prayer: 'Give us this day our daily bread'   *Ms* Ave Maria
Da dag: day
L Gloria Patri: Glory be to the Father

In J's account of the 1870 Vatican Council, in 'Grace', John MacHale shouts '*Credo*!', declaring his submission to doctrine of papal infallibility   tongue
falsehood of a thoroughbred   Tara: ancient capital of Ireland

dogmatic

(with Ir. independence postboxes were painted green)   Little Red Riding Hood (fairy tale)
ph paint the town red   *Ms* The Wearing of the Green
s The Wearing of the Green: 'O Paddy dear, & did you hear'

ph laughing up his sleeve

s The Moon Hath Raised Her Lamp Above

U.39: 'Lump of love'

Diogenes searched with lantern for an honest man   Troubadour   indeed   day
diagnosis   *We* anonest: dishonest   *L* non est: is not
Saxon rule   *Bre* ruz: red
Bre Saoz: English
waistcoat   *s* Stride la vampa (*Il Trovatore*), lit. 'the blaze crackles'
(got paint on his coat)
I focal: word   focal: pertaining to the hearth
It foco: fire
redshank: one of the original Celtic inhabitants of Ir.
mules are sterile

other
G Freude: joy   Freud
(i.e. *felix culpa*)   frightful

'New lamps for old' (*Aladdin*, pantomime)

scotography: X-ray radiography

scripture Newfoundland

gravy (030.06–7) *s* You Are My Heart's Delight
Davy: miners' safety lamp *AngI* Moyard: High Plain
daylight Tom Thumb

F miel melodious *It* bel canto in *The Childermass*, Wyndham
malodorous belch Lewis calls J 'Bel Canto'
exquisite Vulg Ps 80:4: 'Buccinate in neomenia tuba, in insigni die solemnitatis vestrae'
Emania: ancient capital of Ulster ('Blow up the trumpet in the new moon, in the time appointed, on your solemn feast day')

s Pastheen Fionn ('fair-haired child')
F pont *Bre* beleg: priest Cattle Market, N. D *Bre* ledan: broad *Bre* striz: narrow
Belleek: town on border with N. Ireland *Bre* merched: daughters
Portobello: district of S. D (will postboxes or green paint vanish—they question future of Ireland)
virtue

invective fairy

ph to take pepper in the nose: to take offence

mordant: incisive; causing pain; substance that fixes a dye
mortal *Sl* physiog: face
furnished verdure
verjuice: sour juice of unripe fruit
Bre teo: big time being *Bre* bihan: small
Heb teom: abyss
Angra Mainyu = Ahriman, Zoroastrian god of evil

poetry

it is considered unlucky for an actor on stage to whistle or to quote *Macbeth*. VI.B.10.34 adds 'no title with golden' answer me back
post parcels
Patch Purcell: Ir. mailcoach owner
postmistress
G ander: other, second
Ir. legend of Glas Gainach, 'a cow that is better than a thousand cows'
Much Ado About Nothing II.1: 'men were deceivers ever' *L* Scotia: Ireland
U.540: 'His sire's milk record was a thousand gallons of whole milk in forty weeks' *I* a stór: my precious albeit

post

minus one private

F sauve qui peut: save himself who can! largely meddlesome
quipu: ancient Peruvian device for recording events as knots on threads
Sp becco: he-goat *It* colpa di becco: cuckold's fault Buonaparte *It* buon: good
I colpa: unit of grazing animals *It* corpo di bacco: by Jove! *F* bon appetit *It* partita: game; leaving
Wilde: *Avowals; Intentions*

please God please mother of God
Sl POD: Post Office Directory
apt

L capri: goat's

Welsh Fusiliers (have goat for mascot)
G Fusel: bad liquor
G Sündenbock: scapegoat publishers

Browne & Nolan *L* nihil obstat: nothing prevents (form of approval by Church censor)

Verdi: *La Forza del Destino*

peg: wooden leg

s The Memory of the Dead
his race

L [N] salutem dicit: [N] speaks a greeting *G* ander: other, second Lord
Swift called his servant Alexander McGee 'Saunders' Lloyds
G Schuft: scoundrel Esther
to
medical doctors M.D. (.25) Aeschylus (Houyhnhnm) as like
musical high school: the more advanced exercises in horsemanship
Easter eggs
Swift's Stella & Vanessa were both named Esther
Swift: *On the Death of Mrs Johnson*: 'only a little too fat . . . this is the night of her funeral . . . her frequent fits of sickness . . . she had true taste . . . both in poetry & prose'
Dean Swift interment *Da* dag: day
L totidem verbis: in so many words

Aristotle: *Poetics*

U.S. & Dial pilgarlic: poor creature (affectionate; used in *Journal to Stella*)

s John Anderson, My Jo poor late Mrs
broth
Du Mevrouw: Mrs
Mary Anderson, actress, close friend of John McCormack
N stakkers: poor, wretched Exod 20:12: 'Honour thy father & thy mother'
breakfast
dears & testament

street for it Stratford associations *L* sauciatio: wounding
Swift: *On the Death of Mrs Johnson*: 'the truest, most virtuous & reliable friend that I, or perhaps any other person, ever was blessed with'
squat on a tuffet (*nr* Little Miss Muffet)
G Sofakissen: sofa cushion *Du* kussens: cushions *G* Küssen: kisses W.G. Wills: *A Royal Divorce*
real presence: physical presence of Christ's body in Eucharist
Mrs Grundy: character mentioned in Thomas Morton's *Speed the Plough* (1798) as typifying respectability
G Mund: mouth Swift: 'Ppt'

quid Earwicker

Michaelmas March

'Dearly beloved Roger'–Swift praying with his clerk Roger M.D. ('my dears'): Swift's abbreviation in letters to Stella
May Oblong: D whore *Du* droogte: drought

absolutely killing Swift: *Cadenus & Vanessa* (anagram for Decanus = Dean)
Vanessa to Swift: 'those killing, killing words of yours' together
God alone knows
go along now
Vanessas Bickerstaff: name used by Swift in parody of Partridge's astrological predictions
L venustas: beauty *Bre* gwir: true *Bre* gaou: false *Bre* trouz: noise
go on
legal oath: 'the truth, the whole truth & nothing but the truth'
uniform (postman's)

L oremus: let us pray Heaven be thanked

Pasta, soprano Rubini and Winckelman, tenors
It rubini: rubies
rococo

L ex-voto: out of a vow copper coinage for Ir. produced in 1724 by Wm Wood: a swindle. Swift wrote tirades against 'Wood's halfpence'

s Die Wacht am Rhein (cost of his uniform)
Sl rhino: money
G ander: other, second

s She Wore a Wreath of Roses the Night That First We Met *G* Leichnam: corpse
It legname: timber
Van Houtens' Dutch cocoa Clondalkin: village W. of D timberman
Howth (3 castles on D coat of arms) *F* timbre: postage stamp
prodigal neighbours nephews description
nabob: person of great wealth; Indian governor
boys *It* bosco: forest tenants
F bois *Du* baskoor: bass choir *F* bassecour: poultry yard
no one

spent
ghost of a notion
ph like hot cakes *G* Gebäck: baker's goods
Esau's mess of pottage
L quoniam: because

possible probably perceive
parable
Monsieur Guinness's
Mother Goose (pantomime)
'Qui tecum vivit et regnat' (The Mass, Offertory: 'Who with thee lives and reigns')
Tekem: Egyptian god Coopers always test barrels by smelling
so be it Soviet *Du* moed: courage
It vi: you so you are *F* chanson: song
Annals of the Theatre Royal, D 197: 'Viardot held forth'

apologue: allegorical story, fable Spinoza
Du spin: spider
Jakob Grimm's fairy tales Jacob & Esau Aesop's fable of the Ant & the Grasshopper
F gestes: doings, exploits
L casus: calamity *F* cousin: gnat
'my dear little brothers in Christ' (*Portrait* III)
G Husten: cough coughing *L* tussem: cough *I* na casachta: of the cough
It tosse: cough
We peswch: cough *PS* kašel: cough *N* ondt: hard, ill (*'angry)
F toux: cough *M Gr* bêx: cough (pron. 'bix') *M Br* bêchos: of a cough
N graeshoppe: grasshopper

jigger: flea *Tunga penetrans* happy Kant account

fiddlesticks (grasshopper sings with scraping hind legs) support

(Esau's twin Jacob supplants him; name 'Jacob' means 'supplanter')

G Floh: flea *Da* lus: louse *L* (artif.) vespatilla: little wasp *s* Upa-Upa *L* pupa: girl
G Biene: bee pupa: stage in insect development
pulicine: pertaining to fleas antennae pygidium: terminal segment of insect
G lang lawn tennis
commit incest their mouthparts: modified appendages
in sex surrounding mouths of insects
hairy (= Esau) jest among
F Sl gambilles: legs
everlasting (pot with jam in bottom used to trap wasps) of course
*'everlistings = laurel bushes' watering
Gr melissa: bee feelers (antennae) flexors, contractors, depressors & extensors: types of muscles
maliciously
namely (Viconian cycle)

**F* puce: flea *F* fourmi: ant *G* Spinner: silkworm
furnish
hosiery Schopenhauer
shopping hour
called *It* caldo: hot *Da* en ting som ingen ting: a thing like no thing
**F* fourmilière: ant hill
familiarly *Da* bedstefar: grandfather

Zeus *Egyptian Book of the Dead* cxli: earwig wicked albedo: whiteness
G Zeit: time 'the Aged One, i.e. Rā' corolla: ring of petals

*letter, 26/3/28, to HSW

Father Time's scythe inside his electrical
elytra: hardened wing cases of beetles
Delia & Peona in Keats' *Endymion* nymph: immature nonmetamorphosing insect
dahlia peony drupe: stone fruit
insect's compound eyes hornet ALP Puss-in-Boots (pantomime)
CE . . . H hornito: mound of volcanic origin
L cacumen: summit, top end transitus: windpipe *Heb* deborah: bee
cocoon *We* cacynen: wasp tickle diva: prima donna (from *L*, goddess)
It bolle di sapone: soap bubbles *Da* fosfor: phosphorus *G* Furz: fart
boll weevil
sulphur *G* Zucker: sugar *F* douze magnesium *Du* mes: knife
(possibly based on composition of human body)
pitchcap *s* 'The flea on the hair of the tail of the dog of the nurse of the child of the wife of the wild man
madcap from Borneo has just come to town'
F taon: gadfly

tambarines *Cantharides*: genus of beetles *Saturnia*: moth genus exile axle
F tabarin: buffoon *It* canto: song (Phoebe: moon of Saturn; retrograde rotation)
R rogach: stag beetle Saint-Saëns: *Danse Macabre* phobia Beck: expounder of Kant
cockroach (*Periplaneta*, genus of cockroaches) back to back *I* beach: bee
Valentin Le Desossé & Jane Avril painted by Toulouse-Lautrec
diseased Ra: Egyptian sun-god
G langsam: slow *Rigoletto:* 'La, ra, la ra, la ra'

G Mutter Butt & Taff boxing match *Myrmica*: genus of ants
deafmute murmur Myrmidons at Troy
Po pszczoła: bee *Satyr*: genus of butterflies caudle: a warm drink
sozzlers singing Burns: *Cottar's Saturday Night*
nr 'Humpty Dumpty sat on a wall' *s* Tim Finnegan's Wake

L silentium *G* uns

omnibus

harpsichord *Who's Who* something about
Art Accord & Hoot Gibson: cowboy actors
nobodies paunch time

berated *L* Deo gratias: thanks to God thunder & lightning
ME barrat: deception
Anopheles, genus of mosquitoes Cronos dethroned by Zeus, his son *Gr* chronos: time
G alle Leute: everyone *s* 'John Brown's body lies a-mouldering in the grave but his soul is marching on'
C sun: descendants, grandchildren *Heb* ereṣ: earth

anything on earth Book of Breathings: a funeral ritual in the *Egyptian Book of the Dead*
bade
Shem or Shaun *R* zemlya: the earth seemingly to kill time
C liang: to excuse
gracious me! Egyptian my soul bagatelle
sacred scarabs sahu: habitation of the soul, in Egyptian theology
Libellula: genus of dragonflies *Po* pschla: flea what a sight for the gods!
libellous *It* zanzara: gnat *F* pou: louse Ptah: Egyptian god *G* Zeit: time
insincerity *Da* sommerfugl: butterfly

Thoth: Egyptian god of wisdom *Sphex:* genus of solitary wasps isinglass: a variety
thoughtfully making silly faces at himself in front of the looking-glass of his window of gelatine
Wyndham Lewis called *G* nichts
L nix: snow anti-tropical (cold)
N loppe: flea

(ant is a 'social insect') Ba: Egyptian heart-soul & god of the 11th hour
Ulster thon: that
Prov 6:6: 'Go to the ant, thou sluggard' *Da* oldenborre: cockchafer as long as there's a tail on a cat
in Egyptian theology ab: heart; khu: soul; khat: body
Nefer-sent: Egyptian city *Heb* yaar: honeycomb ovipositor: insect's egg-laying structure
nevertheless locked repository
lifted hands *Book of the Dead* lxviii: 'he voideth water' Sekhet Hetep: Egyptian Elysian Fields
Da lofte: raise *PS* voda: water avoid
pigshit on

inscription on pyramid of Pepi II: 'As the name of this Pepi . . . shall flourish, & this pyramid of Pepi . . . shall flourish, & this his work shall flourish for ever & ever'

Hapi: Egyptian god *Da* hävn: vengence Haines (*U.*) Hurrish the sweep: last man
F haine: hatred flogged through streets of D
Amen (humming insect)

G Weltall: universe ablebodied
G Raum: space *Du* bult: hump, hill
G beinah so . . . wie: almost as . . . as tall as a shilling in coppers *G* sehr
Heb sol'am: locust Schelling *G* Kopf *Arab* tsartsur: cockroach
German-looking *G* Spass machen: make jokes
s Sir, Sir Solomon *F* charmant *Gr* eikon: image
Psyche: genus of moths *G* Laus: louse *Sl* ikey: smart, artful
Gr psychê: soul (Freud) *L* laus: praise
F mouche *R* muravei: ant

Du Wim: William

life & death
s Liebestod ('love-death', in *Tristan und Isolde* III.3)
afterwards *G* wetten: to bet bumblebees *Da* drikke: drink
wedding *I* beach: bee
Notonecta: genus of aquatic bugs, 'water-boatmen' daddy-longlegs whoring
bilk: deceive derry down (song refrain) *Da* hor: adultery
Sl ladybirds: lewd women *G* ich nehme die Gelegenheit: I avail myself of the opportunity
ichneumons: parasitic wasps *Gr* oikon: house felt just
G siech: infirm sexton beetle *ph* as poor as a church mouse
sick Satan *It* tanto povero quanto: as poor as Kant
*sylph *R* vosh: louse search grub (larva)
himself *Li* širše: wasp
carapace hospice *Du* wist niet: knew not
L corpus: body nits *Cz* brouk: beetle *It* bruco: caterpillar
It fuco: drone (insect) *Sp* saltamontes: grasshopper *R* osi: wasps
spent *N* sult: hunger *R* osa: wasp (whole world also empty)
kopeck: *Musca*: genus of flies
'Moscow gold' supposedly given to European socialists Russian coin
buy a little bit bee-bread: mixture of honey & pollen Io, chased by Zeus as gadfly
Romeo & Juliet II.2.33: 'Romeo, Romeo' *It* Dio mio!: my God! when cow
corbicula: structure on bee's leg *R* o moi bog: O my God
which carries pollen *N* bog: book
Melanchthon: German theologian sluggard (Prov 6:6)
Sw slug: fly
wallpaper *G* Lüster: chandeliers
while (time) *lustre: 5 years [lustral]
Sl flight of steps: staircases *L* mensa: table
thick slice of bread years months
& butter settles *G* Mund: mouth Ephemeridae: mayflies
F siècles: centuries mothballs mandibles: insect's jaws
Li voras: spider gluttonously timepiece

termitary: termites' nest cicada: type of chitinous: containing chitin, ingredient in insect cuticle
*eternity arboreal bug with loud song
chap mites Christmas chrysalis
so might he Chrysomelidae: a family of beetles

It aver grilli in capo: to have a bee in one's bonnet Leibnitz
(lit. have crickets in the head) live nits
*'Tasmania, he stands on his head to be really "antipodal"' seas of the dead

It tre: 3 *It* verme: grub, maggot heaven
Le Havre *F* havre
angels 'To hell with the pope' (slogan)
engines Hull
Da flue: fly Hegel hailstones

myriapods **It* Luglio: July tornado Bora: Adriatic wind **Aurora borealis* Bora Bora: one of the
*'tournedos (we turn our back to the wind)' *Port* borboleta: butterfly Society Islands (Polynesia)
R bloha: flea *Du* tegel: tile tatters *G* rutschen: to slide slates
*'tilehats: tall hats' *'tetties *It* roofs also *dial.* breasts' *F* ruche: beehive
coffeehouses *ON* Ragnarøkr: Destruction of the Norse gods
*'coppe = rooftiles (*It. dial*)' *It* ragno: spider

*letter, 26/3/28, to HSW

Siphonaptera: fleas   *G* Spuk: ghost; noise, uproar   *G* Graus: horror grasshopper
Pulex irritans & Tunga penetrans: fleas
(chirping)

butterfly
ph blind as a bat
bit   *G* Schmetterling: butterfly   entomology   asked   *G* Nisse: nit
Maeterlinck   smattering   etymology
neither leave nor licence
It nessunissimo: not a single one
Vico   then & there   *Gr* phtheir: louse   dizzily
Gr phthinô: to perish
(021.18)

Aquinas
acquaintance
F mouche   Aquinas: *Summa contra Gentiles*
musichall   musical ensemble   *G* umsummen: buzz around
behold
mighty lucky
R motylek: butterfly
G gross   prostrate   *R* prostranstvo: space   *R* dvor: court   throne (W.C.)
Grace   *R* babochka: butterfly   (space)   drone
L papilio: butterfly   pampooties   smoking a special blend of Havana cigars
Babylonian   babouche: Turkish or Oriental slipper   brand
F cigale: cicada   Wilde on fox hunters: 'the unspeakable in full pursuit of the uneatable'
*'unshrinkables = pyjamas'   *It* farfalla: butterfly   *G* verfallen: to disintegrate
*'Swarming of = Ger to be enthusiastic over (i.e. himself)'

philosophy   Plato   *'Nous rational intelligence of monasticism'
full up   plate of monkey nuts   Confucius
Minthe: nymph turned into that plant by Proserpine   Aristotle
*'confession of mind "infusion de menthe"   Ants secrete formic and acetic acids for defence
happy   honeysuckle   *L* libido: desire
*Lido
*'api = Ital. bee'
right   hugging   left   *Arch* buss: kiss

Mozart: *Cosi Fan Tutte*

Gr entoma: insects

possibly   emmet: ant   damn it!   Jesus Christ

*'By Jaysus wept'   *G* Schnee: snow   *F* guêpe: wasp
Sl jade: whore   agape
jealousy   wittol: a conniving cuckold   *G* Eifersucht: jealousy
R pchela: bee   *ph* at his wits' end   *Du* wat heb ik voorzegd: didn't I tell you
G Spinne: spider

G Spass: joke   (queen ant)   lacewing (in order Neuroptera)

*'spizz = Ital. dialect = itch'
Tingsomingenting
formication: sensation of ants crawling on skin   fornication   Allah
It formicolazione: tingling
houri: nymph of the Mohammedan paradise   *G* Ameisen: ants   *Sp* crabron: hornet
amusing   *Sp* mariposa: butterfly
I Cor 13:13: 'faith, hope, charity'

G jucken: to itch
R zhuk: beetle
chemise   *It* cimice: bedbug   *I* dorsán: grasshopper   *I* Dún Seangáin: Ant's Fort
chimney   *Sp* chinche: bedbug
peripatetic   imago: adult insect
veritable image   *L* imago: imitation
N odde: head   *Da* edderkop: spider   *Da* myre: ant   in Egyptian Judgement of Dead, dead person's heart is weighed against feather
*'odderkop = other head' [*G* Kopf]
Ephemeridae: mayflies   *F* journée: day   *F* sans hantisse ne chouchou: without security or sweetheart
superstition that praying mantis guides lost travellers   featherweight (jockeys, boxers)
actual grace (temporary) & sanctifying grace (permanent)
*'despair and presumption are sins against hope'
too much

*letter, 26/3/28, to HSW

force of gravity U.79: 'Lord Iveagh once cashed a sevenfigure cheque. . . .
L gravitates: weights Still the other brother Lord Ardilaun has to change his Art the Lone: son of Conn
shirt four times a day, they say. Skin breeds lice or vermin'
one of Count John McCormack's bestselling records was *s* Carmè, Canto Sorrentino
s 'Yankee Doodle went to London, just to ride a pony' *It* conte: count *F Sl* carme: money
Coll divi: dividend
L dives: rich *L* Ad Majorem Dei Gloriam: For the Greater Glory of God (Jesuit motto)
L Laus Deo Semper: Praise to God Forever L.S.D.: pounds, shillings & pence
ph darken one's threshold Haru = Horus Osiris *L* oremus: let us pray
Ant: mythological fish in *Egyptian Book of the Dead* which pilots the Sun-god's Ant-boat Sekhet Aaru ('Field of Reeds'): part of Sekhet Hetep *Book of the Dead* CXXII: '"Evil is it" is the name of the rudder. . . .
Let me . . . go in peace into the beautiful Amentet . . . and let me adore
Osiris, the Lord of life' spindrift spendthrift
G empfang: receive *G* meine Weisheit: my wisdom Hru: last word in *Book of the Dead,*
meaning 'day, into day, by day'

he laughed & he laughed & he made such a noise
larvae *F* merde nauseating
misplace his faeces
forces *L* fauces: jaws

Da suk: sigh housekeeping

Smetana: *Luisa's Polka*

ph pay the piper Count McCormack

pr If the mountain will not come to Mohammed, Mohammed will go to the mountain *Arab* massyk bil ẖêr:
Arab ṣabâḥ el ẖêr: good morning! Abraham (anagram) good evening!

We morgrugyn: ant *I* primpeallán: beetle
groggy
pr Never look a gift horse in the mouth

Castor . . . Pollux *MGr* Polydefkis: Pollux bollocks

L culex: gnat itchy *L* pulex: flea
F cul: arse
locust love termite embrace
time
L homo vulgaris: ordinary man
ticks: group of mites
It aquilone: N. wind *It* leone: lion wind to go South
Aquilant (= black) and his brother Gryphon (= white) in *Orlando Furioso*
We gwyfyn: moth *We* drewbryf: bug
griffin drawbridge
Occident (Wyndham Lewis: *Time & Western Man*)
G besiegt: conquered
long suffering zephyrs East audience
ease
pr Waste not, want not

Nolan/Bruno *L* volans: flying
L nolens volens: willy-nilly
gadflies Mookse/Gripes

extension (space), elapsing (time)

tactics *G* Taktstock: baton all's well

partipris: a preconceived opinion, prejudice (my look)

work *F* tout

'Visible Universe' of Aristotle & Aquinas *L* haud: not at all
invisible *L* risus: laughter you'd hardly find
G solch: such ox . . . beef . . . meat . . . veal *G* so viel: so much
G mit
your feet are enormous
G sind: are
send some

species

St Martin
It saltmartino: pop. name of some hopping insects (the metre is that of Goldsmith's *Retaliation*)
'In the name of the Father & of the Son & of the Holy Ghost, Amen' (blessing)

exposition

folklore *r* Loire *Da* velklingende: euphonious vocabulary Volapük: artificial language *L* qui: who
I foclóir: vocabulary *Da* tingeling: onomatopoeia like 'ding-dong'
It chi vive sperando muore cantando: he who lives hoping dies singing
L qua: as far as content
s 'O, Father O'Flynn, you've that wonderful way with you'
G Wandervogel: bird of passage (German hikers, 1920s)
(039.16–18) Tintagel, Cornwall: site of King Mark's castle

Blarney Stone (eloquence) *s* Father O'Flynn: 'in all Donegal'

leprechaun

anaglyptic: pertaining to carving in low relief HCE His M(ajesty)
letters patent (fig.): authority to do something
At the time of their friendship, Gogarty could read Greek; J couldn't

L quisquiliae: fragments, twigs lobe of his ear (acoustic) orthodox
Ms Questa o quella (*Rigoletto*): 'this one or that one' astrolabe
Holy soap (McCormack made a count by the pope)
Julius Caesar V.5.73: 'noblest Roman'
writingpen thank St Laurence (O'Toole; patron of D) patent (.19)

F Sem: Shem Oscar Wilde John St Perse: Fr. poet
Oscan language ancient Persian translating
J's early paper on James Clarence Mangan mentions Mangan's use of phrases such as 'from the Ottoman' & 'from the Coptic'
tips of my fingers draught & bottled stout eyes

F hélas horribly
Gr Hellas: Greece Hebrew

theodicy: work or theory justifying God's ways (title of book by Leibnitz)
The Odyssey purloined
just the position
P.G. = please God; Postmaster General

perfectly awful

actionable Cain & Abel

errors *L* et omnibus: and for all

foulest Oscan (.24) spoken in Lucania Charles Lucas: Ir. pamphleteer whose books were burned by order of House of Lords

flummery: nonsense, humbug; also various sweet dishes for dessert

boxes

Moore: *s* O Breathe Not His Name

pseudonym

slept coachman met a cad with a pipe
F cauchmar: nightmare
there were breakwater
Sl madge: woman

three fellows in the suburbs handmade

K S *Du* keuken: kitchen this
Sl phiz: countenance
here's *F* pauvre petite femme big

lavatory tree/stone epitaph

Vo balsebal: 11 *It* bimbi: babies *Da* tiltops: all the way up
Steyne: pillar in D erected by Vikings *Vo* bim: tree
F combien: *G* wie viel?
laughing

F tout le monde rire

savvy: gumption

J's addresses in D: 29 HARDWICKE ST (1893)

I Baile Átha Cliath: Town of the Ford of the Hurdles (D) HCE
Bre la-ouan: gay
opposite 14 FITZGIBBON ST (1893)
It loco: place *U.S. Sl* loco: crazy
Leopold Bloom
Benjamin Lee Guinness, brewer
17 NORTH RICHMOND ST (1895) name illegible left no address
(Thingmote, Viking assembly-mound in D) *L* Noa: Noah
signed no such person 29 WINDSOR AVE., FAIRVIEW (1896–9)
L non sic possum: not thus can I
L ave: hail! *L* vale: farewell! ⚔ Clontarf, 1014
no such number When J met Nora she worked at Finn's Hotel
FAIRVIEW mistake nine hundred & sixty five
(near Clontarf)
shoot on sight Dunlop tyres

L quod vide 8 ROYAL TERRACE, FAIRVIEW (1900) no such street
L qui vixit: who lived
Dean (Swift: ordeal of dining with) PHIBSBOROUGH

please send on Clontarf
factor: merchant Clonturk Park, D
23 CASTLEWOOD AVE., RATHMINES (1884–7)
3 castles on D coat of arms *L* pax vobiscum: peace be with you Justice of the Peace

City Arms Hotel, D 2 MILLBOURNE AVE., DRUMCONDRA wrongly spelled DRUMCONDRA
(Blooms lived there) Milchbuck: quarter of Zurich *G* Traum
Ir. House of Parliament is now Bank of Ireland, College Green

Adam Findlater: grocery magnate & *G* schon geschossen: already shot
politician in Edwardian D; his granduncle 7 ST PETER'S TERRACE, PHIBSBOROUGH (CABRA);
CABRA built Abbey Presbyterian Church (1902–4)

Sir Arthur Guinness

Paterson & Co. (D): match manufacturers   promised land

Lammas: 1 August   Orange Lodge   SUM   mail   HCE
lemons   *Gr* lemma: preliminary proposition
exiles   *L* aedilis: Roman magistrate   closed for repairs
responsible for buildings
60 SHELBOURNE RD (1904)   Isaac Butt: Nationalist leader ousted by Parnell
(008.08)
kindly forward   Sir Abraham Bradley King: Lord Mayor of D

L salve: be well!   already buried   holly & ivy

overweight   understamped

Bre kaer: beautiful   money order   too late (*U.*41–2: 'money order. . . . *Encore deux minutes*')
care of   *U.*467: 'He implored me to soil his letter'   sold
Sl unfortunates: prostitutes   *U.*568: 'Mamma, the beeftea is fizzing over!'
F bouffi: bloated
G Absender: sender
F destinataire: addressee
raised   lowered   vacant mind

bailiffs   hell

pistol
Sl Bristol: visiting-card
s Come Back to Erin

ten times worse   Tristan died at cliff of Penmarks   Sanskrit

'hesit*e*ncy'   cerebral

Shelta: secret language of Ir. tinkers

Aladdin rubs magic lantern to make genie emerge

HCE   hesit*e*ncy   ears
are: note A in Aretino's 1st, 4th & 7th hexachords

Ossian   'the Drapier': Swift

actually   diagnosis
Guinness
compulsory Irish
Berlitz School (J worked for)

God   high G (note)

roster of fags (at public school)

Reuters & Havas: news agencies   Gilligan's maypole: wireless aerial

U.S. pixillated: whimsical, mildly crazy
ph on his last legs

clergymen

mammifer

deprived of his liberty   silenced: of priest, no longer permitted to say Mass

'the Drapier': Swift (left money to
found lunatic asylum in D)
Antipodes cardsharping clever
Antipope *Bre* klanv: sick
G Fleisch: meat *G* Feldpost: army postal service
(doctors) *Bre* yac'h: healthy
wellknown

Four Courts, D *nr* Humpty Dumpty: 'All the king's horses'
King's Bench Court, D
Macbeth III.2.18: 'We have scotch'd the Snake' 'licence . . . for consumption on the premises'
F ver solitaire: (D.T.s) The Scotch House, pub, D (pub)
tapeworm dolichocephalic & brachycephalic: longskulled & shortskulled back
Dalkey Head syphilis *G* brach: broke
degenerate
F jeune
skeleton drinking
Sl skilly: gruel

Sl bedfellow: penis like unto like

dust unto dust *L* crinis: hair criminal
Sl 'put a nick in the post' (said when unusual event occurs)
ph making the leopard change his spots songbook Gen 4:9: 'Am I my brother's keeper?'

AngI 'on his keeping': on the run am I obnoxious pessimist
housekeeping *I* ar: on army
unicorn Mark Twain: *The Prince & the Pauper* bride
apostles
Samuel Roth pirated J in *Two Worlds Monthly* mussulman's

VI.B.6.79: 'cuistha: hunger voluntarily endured by a person
who will not eat his favorite food prepared for him because [of] the person who prepared it'

Mark Twain: *The Prince & the Pauper* *ph* put one's pride in one's pocket
proper place

Mohammedans ascribe Aesop's fables to Lugman, an Ethiopian

ph eat one's hat

John Braham: tenor melodious & welcome
ham *L* melos: honey
L honoris causa: honorary degree

Gr thelêmôn: willing the elementary long ago
alimentary canal
boys St Dominic supposedly introduced bees into Ireland commonplace
Baden-Baden: German spa Court of Common Pleas, Four Courts, D
Sp pueblo: people Nelson's Pillar, D Trafalgar (Nelson's Column in Trafalgar
Square, London)
la mi si do (564.04) *cg* Blind man's buff *L* (artificial) trifulgureus: thrice charged with lightning

'Old Nol': nickname of Cromwell Matt 6:28: 'lilies of the field' *G* Lilien: lilies
Shakespeare perhaps played Old Knowell in Jonson's *Everyman in His Humour*
knickers *F* jambe Shem, Ham and Japhet
It folletta: sprite *Arch* hem: them
G Wucherer: usurer writing

L nisi prius: unless before (writ of summons to jurors)
nosy pryers Nisi Prius Court, D

James Macpherson, author of Ossianic poems

Garcilasso de la Vega: *The Origin of the Incas* *Sl* anonyma: whore

F Sl garce: whore how anonymous animus

Baltic (man) March Hare periwig W.G. Wills: *A Royal Divorce*

Bre Mac'harid: Marguerite Divorce Court, D

L ferax: fruitful *L* ova: eggs *Sp* Aleman: German Swift: *A Tale of a Tub*

tsetse flies *Bre* tud: people

Bre bourcheoisien: bourgeois cry-baby *Sl* crib-biter: persistant gambler

Sl crib: pub

ambidextrous perspiring *L* decanus: dean (Swift) dickens asleep

It poltrone: armchairs

poltroon

index finger Byron: *Childe Harold's Pilgrimage* CHE

Gr idioglôssa: distinct language, private language

Hyssop twigs used for sprinkling in Jewish rites *G* hocken: to squat I gave him that too

Hu ikrek: twins

hiccup

letter *Twelfth Night* II.3.120: 'Dost thou think because thou art virtuous, there shall be no more cakes & ale?'

G mich: to me King's Bench Court, D

Chancery Court, D

Skrivanitch learnt English from J in Trieste

ph cutting off his nose to spite his face *AngI* begorra!

prose hose

biography

painting

I beo: life

punting: kicking

stop, thief!

L in medias res: into the midst of a subject

Da digter: poet dictator grand tsar

G schick: elegant

Court of Exchequer, D

F jupes (*Portrait* IV) M.D. ('my dears'): Swift's abbreviation in letters to Stella

L cygnus: swan

L ante mortem: before death *Da* syg: sick

post

Nora Barnacle barnacle goose

bow

Sl barnacled: wearing spectacles

ph say boo to a goose

Elm/Stone

pr Marry in haste and repent at leisure

Swift: *A Tale of a Tub*

The Coombe, street & hospital, D Pope: *The Rape of the Lock* Lock Hospital, D

padlock

cough The Age of Reason: time of Pope, C18

age of the use of reason: for Catholics, the age at which

predeceased a child is capable of committing sin

false

medieval *L* vegetabilis anima: vivifying principle

veritable

warned off the racecourse of matrimony

Habeas Corpus HCE

by the same token Buckley shot the Russian General

(Dr Johnson kicking stone to refute Berkeley's immaterialism)

Negus Negesti: (King of Kings), title of Abyssinian Emperor *Da* negertop: Negro head *L* negator: one who denies

L negus: you deny *L* negasti: you have denied *Sl* toby: buttocks

L negarentur: they might be denied Thingmote: Viking parliament in D

mitching HC . . . E erysipelas: St Anthony's fire

Society of Jesus (S.J.) Franciscan Brothers

Bre Bro-C'hall: France *L* frater: brother

G Bruder *R* brat: brother *F* temps failed
Budapest Bratislava: capital of Slovakia

Irish Times Medieval pun made Dominicans *Domini canes*, dogs of God
Skye terrier *U.*591: 'To make the blind see I throw dust in their eyes' Holy Father
*U.*306: 'by the holy farmer'
Farm St, London, Jesuit House avowtried *L* evitandus: to be avoided
avoided
Tristan

School of Medicine, Cecilia St, D Galen: C2 physician, hence, joc., a physician inkpot
⚔Sevastopol & ⚔Inkerman, 1854 incubus
incest utmost
L encaustum: ink
pr Once bitten, twice shy conscientious objectors, 1914–18 Siberia for aristocrats
Proust Christ crucified during reign of Tiberius Tiberias: town on Sea of Galilee
Chekhov: *Chayka* (*The Seagull*) single *It* gattabuia: prison
CheKa: Russian secret police *It* gabbiano: seagull
Moore: *s* Come O'er the Sea, Maiden with Me lover liver Trinity College, D
heathen *L* liber: book
ph your goose is cooked faithfully
AngI ph your bread is baked: you'll die soon damn geese are crammed to make liver paté
F yaourth: yoghurt excommunicated (172.10)
111.17: 'four crosskisses'

rude

Sl crawthumper: ostentatiously devotional Roman Catholic
crossbun act of contrition
James I abolished the old Ir. Brehon dickens *ph* open your mouth & put your foot in it
Laws & published the Act of Oblivion foot and mouth disease
pig latest Ull: Norse patron god of skiing & archery
Hoder: blind god, killed Balder *N* tordenveir: thunderstorm
Midgaard: Earth in Norse myth Urd: a Norse Fate Fenrir: son of Loki bogeyman
Grimnir: Odin Gungnir: Odin's spear Mjollnir: Thor's hammer Oddrun: sister of Atli
Surt: ruler of Norse fire world *ON* Ragnarøkr: destruction of the Norse gods

Sauvé: *Proverbes & dictons de la Basse-Bretagne*, no. 148: 'Paix! Paix! La queue de la vache Est avec vous' ('Peace! Peace! The cow's tail is with you') vulgar (his penultimate speech) velar: a back consonant
Matt 7:6: 'pearls before swine' John Jameson D whiskey

Tristan *G* Zucker: sugar Liebestod in *Tristan & Isolde* begins 'Mild und leise . . .'

Four Waves of Ireland: 4 points on Ir. coast Tibb's Eve: never (there is no St Tibb)

s The West's Awake

incendiary bomb damned

G Silbe: syllable whole
holy words
loquacity three-star whiskey interior monologue monotone
Gr monophthongus: sounded as a single vowel
I tá: it is so! storytelling

(*It* bruno: brown) J: *The Day of the Rabblement* begins 'No man, said the Nolan' (i.e. Bruno)
systematic schismatic thematic robbery writing

letter (I was stealing his pen as he was climbing my ladder)
ph picking a bone

stole the tail of me shirt
saw tore tale off me sure
chemise

literate

I abú: to victory!

so buttermilk
sons of Crimthann suckled by Lugaid Cichech, who gave Laegaire milk (Laegaire's race were
G Muttermilch thrifty) & Aed blood (Aed's race were fierce)
Du melk: milk
Bre fall: bad
foul
peace

words liable convinced
bloody wars

G allergrösste: largest of all soliloquize
enthusiasm
Siamese (twins) openair

(left hand) amanuenses
PS obraz: picture *I* Éire go bráth: Ireland until pencil innuendoes
Bre brâz: big Judgement Day *G* Pinsel: painter's brush menu
Cicero (oration) *L* cicer (pron. 'kiker'): chickpea
Maries *L* trifolium: shamrock libretto St Patrick: *Tripartite Life* orthodox Rev 20:12: 'the book of life'
miracles *It* librotto: small & bad Arthur *L* dux: leader
book

Bolshevik Shem Siamese
so *G* heiss: be called
Guy Fawkes inaudible
Gr ou: not *AngI* feck: steal
print outrage tragedy postcards *Gr* a: not Academy of Letters (Irish; J refused Yeats' invitation to join it)
ink scald: ancient Scandinavian poet *Comedy of Errors*
Tom, Dick & Harry mind's eye

will mayhap

Ormuzd: Zoroastrian principle of good *Du* potlood: pencil *Da* paa tryk: in print
almost pot luck
(signature)

Mark Twain Patrick's Puck in *Midsummer Night's Dream*
Gr ôps: eye
I bruthmhar: ardent, studious amateur neophyte
G Papst: pope
L specimen speciosum: handsome model (111)

D Sl fly: cunning *D Sl* hairy: cunning
Ahriman: Zoroastrian principle of evil
infrared ultraviolet Gen 27:11: 'Esau my brother is a hairy man'
L infra dignitatem: *L* ultra virulentiam: beyond a stink
beneath [one's] dignity ECH *I* piop: pipe

hell

Ahriman: Zoroastrian principle of evil anima

s Little Annie Rooney duly
Ms Mother of Mine
Sl threelegged stool: gallows

usurped
used up
Bre krenf: strong

motherhood *Sl* jerry: mournful
(cow)
Ms Mother Machree: 'I love the dear silver that shines in your hair'

Bre sempl: weak simpleton
Bre gwan: weak

Harley: hero of Mackenzie's *Man of Feeling*; dies when he is accepted in marriage
heavy
Wyndham Lewis: *The Caliph's Design, Architects! Where's Your Vortex?* *Da* sig selv: himself
calf
It allarme: alarm
dashed *F* larme: tear
earning his bread by the sweat of his brow
Moore: *s* Erin, the Tear and the Smile in Thine Eyes [Eileen Aroon]
Du oog: eye *It* sòllo: loose
N øye: eye
G alle balle (dial): all gone *C* fu: happy
'Exsultet': 'O felix culpa!' *C* li: sin, crime
depths of earth although his jaw was too sleepy for talk

anything further

tight (Sean the Post has shackles in part of *Arrah-na-Pogue*)

notion weeds Parsifal Jupiter's

G Vergangenheit: past

sidereal year: time needed for 1 apparent complete cycle of sun standpoint
Sirius
Charles's Wain: Ursa Major (name refers to Charlemagne)
L lacteus: Milky Way *AngI* betune: between *ph* music of the spheres
Fitzball; Wallace: *Maritana*: *s* 'Alas, those chimes *Maritana*: *s* Turn On, Old Time
so sweetly stealing, . . . To the mansions of the blest'
(astrological houses) *Da* drømskvindel: dreamy spiral necklace
spindle *G* Windel: diaper
losing
L lusus: a playing
Sl flash of lightning: glass of gin

Lucifer in Meredith's sonnet 'careened' sins
Luke 10:18: 'I beheld Satan as lightning fall from heaven'

Gr astêr: star

postlude: piece or movement played at end of oratorio &c.

F ensemble

ph Hayfoot! Strawfoot! ('Left!
Right!, in marching)

lapis lazuli Killester: district of D
linkman: torchbearer; (theatre) *s* 'By Killarney's lakes and fells'
L lapis: stone commissionaire tea-leaves

crier
AngI more power to his elbow (encouragement)
s The Keel Row
ph as the crow flies Sitric Mac Aulaf (Silkenbeard) gave the ground for Christ Church Cathedral, D

s Open the Door Softly (sung by Sean in *Arrah-na-Pogue*; Arrah pretends to mistake voice for pig or cow)
Moore: *s* Down in the Valley [Open the Door Softly]
I uile: all *G* spurlos: without a trace
F voilà!

disappeared Vanessa *It* popò: shit *L* per omnia saecula saeculorum: for ever & ever
vanished
Amen *L* circularis circulatio: a round revolution

Da pas paa!: take care!
'going, going, gone' (auctioneer)
It stella: star

I píbroch: bagpipe music *Du* donker: dark

G Luft
Puccini: *Tosca* III: 'E lucevan le stelle e olezzava la terra, stridea l'uscio dell'orto e un passo sfiorava la rena. Entrava ella, fragrante, mi cadea tra le braccia. Oh! dolci baci o languide carezze, mentr'io fremente le belle forme disciogliea dai veli!' ('And the stars shone & the earth was perfumed, the gate to the garden creaked & a footstep rustled the sand on the path. Fragrant, she entered, and fell into my arms. Oh! sweet kisses, languid caresses, as I trembling unloosed her veils and disclosed her beauty') (sung by McCormack)

s 'The cat came back 'cause he couldn't stay away'

Moore: *s* How Dear to Me the Hours when Daylight Dies [The Twisting of the Rope] *I, Bre* dall: blind

dull & yellow *G* es ist zu bedauern: it is regrettable
to bed *s* Thou'rt Passing Hence, My Brother (music by Sir Arthur Sullivan)
G mein Bruder

Moore: *s* In the Morning of Life [The Little Harvest Rose] cod's roe cat's cradle
God's (i.e. sea)
G und
purpose
(i.e. sea)
Da Tyskland: Germany *Arch* oliphant: elephant come *Da* til: to outs
F ouest: west

America tall stories (skyscrapers)
G toll: wild
G so oft

It mano: hand myriads *L* milia: thousands

(Land of the Ever Young in Ir. myth) *I* Sean Magh: Old Plain (Moyelta, where Parthalonian colonisers died of plague & were buried) holy boy

Hittites solace of the weak
L salus: safety, health

(II.1) (II.2) (II.3)

books (II.4)

Du bemind: beloved
AngI musha: if it be (expletive)
nr 'A dillar, a dollar, a ten o'clock scholar'

AngI wisha: well, indeed

*U.*156: 'Milly tucked up in beddyhouse'

palmwine: African illicit spirits   milksop   *Sa* suasusu: milk

Samoa
amnesia
Luke   Mark   John
It giorni: days   Jorn, tenor
ph day in day out   forebear   Matthew
(4 provinces of Ireland)
dickens

Ms Ireland, my Sireland
Marie Louise
saying goodnight   *Ms* Eily Mavourneen, I See Thee before Me   *F* mère l'Oye: Mother Goose

s Thady, You Gander   Uganda   Mosse built Rotunda Hospital, D
G Jugend: youth
pr A rolling stone gathers no moss   *Ms* The Foggy Dew
earth, water, fire, air
(barrel)

Sl bunghole: arse   *s* The Wind That Shakes the Barley   blow
barley wine: strong ale

Notre Dame
Ms Macushla (means 'my pulse')   *F* votre
blancmange

Golden Syrup   Dún Laoghaire was named Kingstown after George IV

'Old Grog': Admiral Vernon

John Joyce: name of J's father & also of a pleasure steamer sailing from Dún Laoghaire   Waterloo   *U*.67: 'On the *Erin's King* that day round the Kish'
(Parnell's death)
skiff   Moyle: sea separating Ireland & Scotland
moiling sea
eschatology   (mailsack)

I cnoc: hill (anglicised 'knock')

L timor: fear

tramtickets   (feet)

RhSl daisy roots: boots   buttercups

cothurnus: thick-soled boot worn anciently by tragic actors; buskin
terminus

shirt

L.F. Sauvé: *Proverbes & dictons de la Basse-Bretagne*, no. 376: 'On a lui fait ses chaussures avant ses bas (se dit d'un homme éconduit)' ('His boots were made before his socks'—said of refused applicant) *G* Hosen
Lazar's Hill, D

(Shaun is rolling along river in barrel)

planimetry: measurement of plane surfaces

heavens

better

St Januarius: patron of Naples, whose blood liquifies

hallux: big toe

F poste restante: post to be collected

I Gárda Síochána: policeman
(síochána = of the peace)
constable S
exserviceman

Bre koz: old

inebriated

hedge schools: private, & at first openair schools in Ir., replaced after 1850 by National Schools

Bre Berched: Brigid

(leap year: February has 29 days)

(a.m.)

It sponda: riverbank
Du sponde: bed

rarest
Yellowstone National Park, U.S.

s 'The Wren, the Wren, The king of all birds, St Stephen's his day, Was caught in the furze'

(2 x 29 feet)

F voulez-vous jouer à la (postman's knock) *Bre* yaouank: young
It allo stesso posto: in the same place *It* misto: mixture
typists *Gr* daktylos: finger dactylogram: fingerprint *Sl* nocturne: whore
F dactylographe: typist
Du log: heavy (sleeping like a log)

Bre vil: ugly

F abasourdir: to dumbfound

Da dette er det bedste, min tykke smukke flaske: this is the best, my fat beautiful bottle
treasure trove belongs to the Crown

(crown of thorns)

beehive

swarm *G* sie *N* bie: bee
busy as she could be

pell-mell jeune premier: juvenile lead in play

trifle

cloud-berry: Eng. wild plant used for making tarts

vowels in Irish divided into broad (*leathan*) & slender (*caol*). Vowels flanking a consonant will always agree, slender with slender & broad with broad ('*caol le caol agus leathan le leathan*')

candied peel *Ms* Panis Angelicus angelica

(stuffing)

Sl jellybags: scrotum
Byron's Don Juan was 16
Sistine Chapel

F froler: brush against

ph killed by kindness

AngI ph how are you at all?

Saints Agatha, Juliana & Eulalia, virgin martyrs. Saint Bernadette, visionary of Lourdes

L columba: dove Toberbunny: village, Co. Dublin ('milk well')

legends

Scots bittock; little bit

spirit

(Christ)

s Old Folks at Home: 'All up & down the whole creation' Samson kills lion (Judg 14:6) Jonah

Inigo Jones and Sir Christopher Wren, architects

s The Wren ('the king of all birds') Infusoria: microscopic animals

s I Know My Love by His Way of Walking

splashing

blushing *Sl* tarnelly: confoundedly (from 'eternally')

Benedict X, antipope (432.04)

L benedictus: blessed

ph the world & his wife

Ms Goodbye, Sweetheart, Goodbye

Bre brao: beautiful

General Deliveries (Post Office)

St Scolastica prayed successfully for a thunderstorm to detain her brother, St Benedict

s The Bells of Shandon: 'With deep affection'

matter to the discharge

Great Harry: a ship in Henry VIII's navy, burnt in 1553

Presentation Order of nuns anon

G nun: now

Dioscuri: the twins Castor & Pollux reiteratedly literally illiterately

G Geschwister: siblings

arithmetic

mainstay Ir. philosopher John Scotus Erigena

original

Sl toss off: masturbate Phoebus Apollo, sungod

Castor . . . Pollux   Parrish's Food (iron)

John Mincius: family name of Benedict X (431.18)
parts of Mass: *It* incomincio: I begin
INTROIT   exordium: introductory part of discourse   Gaiety (Theatre, D)   *L* quid pro quo: something in return
apropos
Swift: *Directions to Menservants*   *s* On the Strict Q.T.
T.T.: teetotal
parish priest   *L* orationes Dominicae: Sunday Prayers
Oratorians: R.C. congregation founded by Sir Philip Neri
D.D.: doctor of divinity   by the by   yerked: lashed
C.C.: Catholic clergyman
offhand   *ph* alike as two peas in a pod
offrande: offering
concupiscent   nuncupative: oral, not written
It non capisco: I don't understand
conferring   *F* tête-à-tête   *L* virgo intacta   virago: manlike woman
confarreation: most solemn form of ancient Roman marriage: bride and groom eat 'mystic bread'
parish priest

I capall: horse   guilders
couple
C . . . E . . . H   consummation with an emission (sexual)   nanny (goats)
F consommation (drink), with an infusion (of tea &c.)
L Di Manes, Lares et Penates: the Ancestral Ghosts, Hearth-Gods and Larder-Gods
It pignatti: cooking-pots   eternal
Sl buckling: marrying

you   OFFERTORY

his & my advice   *ph* please the pigs   parson
Arch an: if
L verba: words

titular bishop: one deriving his title from an ancient see lost to the Roman Pontificate   bishop in partibus: titular bishop whose see is in possession of infidels
indelible   *s* Come All Ye . . .
Sl dell: whore   *It Sl* bella belina: cunt   sit down & listen
MISERERE

practical purposes   *F* soeur: sister   friar
pr practice what you preach
by   a gentleman with a duster: pseudonym of Harold Begbie, C19–20 Eng. journalist & author   Parliament
parlourmaid
speech   apse (on church)
stitch
Da fugtig: damp   *F* feu: fire
G Feuchtigkeit: moisture

St Theresa of Lisieux   *F* liseuse: reader   thing to be done
righteousness
(colours of rainbow)   mandarin oranges   *It* Pasqua: Easter   Vendidads: parts of the Avesta
The Rubrics: C18 building in Trinity College, D, red   *Sp* verde: green   *Sp* verdad: truth
AngI is in it: that exists   livid (blue)   indigo   violet
L indecoris: shameful   intercourse   violence   *F* voyou: hooligan
lethargy   LITURGY   *G* bekannt: famous, known   *F* fête
Gr lithourgia: stonework   Annie Besant: theosophist   feet to be washed
Whitsuntide (7 Sundays after Easter)

server: acolyte (Mass)   Mookse
most
Gripes   economy (theol): judicious presentation of doctrine   XYZ   as I said   Hobson's choice
grace   VI.B.10.32: 'economy of movement—priest on altar'   common: part of Mass which can be used for any feast of a specific type
chouse: swindle   saints in the calendar

L ultra mare: beyond the sea
infrared to ultraviolet
St Ignatius Loyola, born in Pampeluna; feast day 31 July — Proper: that part of Mass which varies with the calendar (opposite of 'common')
St Francis Xavier; feast day 3 December — Litany of Saints: 'Te rogamus, audi, nos' ('we beg Thee, hear us')
L undetricesima: 29th
Isabel — that was — swears
L vicesima nona: 29th — *L* adoremus — *L* oremus — do-re-mi
madonna — Prevost: *Manon Lescaut* — *L* vicisti: thou has conquered
diocese — St Laurence O'Toole (Abbot of Glendalough at age 25, patron of D)
affiance: trust; plighting of troth
Glendalough (in Moore's *s* By That Lake, Whose Gloomy Shore)
Scott: *Lady of the Lake* — *L* manducare: to chew
L feria: holiday — *L* in cena Dominis: to the Lord's supper (Maundy Thursday ceremony)
Sp farrear: celebrate — St Francis Xavier died in China
sisters — sovereign — *L* jocosus: droll

⚔Inkerman (Crimean War) — (Shem the Penman)
acrostic: JIM
s 'Tis the Last Rose of Summer — Myles-na-Coppaleen in Boucicault's *The Colleen Bawn*, stage Irishman — of miles
precepts of the Church: i) hear Mass on Sunday; ii) fast & abstain; iii) confess sins; iv) receive blessed Eucharist worthily; v) contribute to support of pastors; vi) not to solemnise marriage at forbidden times — eat — Moor Park: where Swift met Stella
Benedict: *The Lily of Killarney* (adaptation of *The Colleen Bawn*) — *Sl* lady's game: i) prostitution, ii)copulation
Killiney, Co. D — *Sl* ladies: cards, gambling
Ms When Irish Eyes Are Smiling: 'steal your heart away' — (card game)
Sl stake: penis

DBC (Dublin Bread Company)
Ir. letter-names: dair = D; beith = B; coll = C — *RhSl* Derby Kell: belly
smoker: concert where smoking permitted

Arabian

s White Wings, They Never Grow Weary — *nr* Taffy Was a Welshman
L minxi: I have urinated
by the by — *We* bun: maid — Jacobs' Biscuits, D — biting — HEC

back

laugh — last — commit adultery

buttercups

scissors
saucers
L usufacio: have intercourse with
yous make
(serpent)
(maidenhead) — *ph* thin end of the wedge
sacral vertebrae near base of spine
Boucicault: *The Colleen Bawn* — manslaughter
(Eve) — (apple)
wilful murder — 'Exsultet': 'O felix culpa!' — *s Dies Irae*
copper — cup & dice — *pr* Spit on the iron while it's hot
r Erne — trousers — sweat on your brow (Gen 3:19: 'sweat of thy face')
dig in the earth — urn
silver — gold
Sl key: penis
Parnell: 'When you sell, get my price'
truss: to gird, tie up
dress — circumspect — *pr* Look before you leap
trust — *L* circumspicio: I look around
ph St Swithin is christening the apples — whistle
St Medard: patron of rain — Medlar fruit is eaten only when decayed
L de spinetis: from the thorn bushes
MGr despoinides: ladies (pron. 'despineedes')

I Cor 13:13: 'faith, hope, charity'
ph firm faith
pr Charity begins at home
Da frem: further
Hamlet III.1.57–8: 'Whether 'tis nobler in the mind To suffer the slings & arrows of outrageous fortune'
bows
s Give Back Those Stolen Kisses   *F* restaurer: to restore, refresh

Portrait III: 'restore those illgotten goods'   'yellow peril': supposed danger of Oriental invasion of Europe & U.S.
It iella: bad luck
girls   *It* darà Dora: Dora will give

(pantomime horse)   Bessy Sudlow: wife of Michael Gunn, manager of Gaiety Theatre, D (employed many local girls as seamstresses &c.)
breeches-part: role in which actress dresses as man

Michael Gunn   *Sl* big gun: person of note   leg before wicket (cricket)   *Sl* lag: urinate
The Big Gun: tavern and townland in Fairview, D
nr 'Humpty Dumpty sat on a wall, Humpty Dumpty had a great fall'   *L* femora: thighs

Sl candle: penis   HCE   Hayes, Conyngham & Robinson: D chemists
candlelight
Da forglem mig ej: forget me not   *Da* forstand: reason
Sl glim: candle
Da tilgive: forgive
ph the biter bit
Charlotte Quay, D   Britain Court, D

Magdalene   Crawshaw: *Saint Mary Magdalene, or the weeper*

altar   in the straw: in childbed

L pecunia: money   *King John* IV.2.11–16: 'to paint the lily . . . Is wasteful & ridiculous excess'
ph point a moral
hell   henna: red hairdye   Rev. Francis Finn, S.J.: *The Best Foot Forward*   foolhardy
Gehenna: the underworld   'Oedipus' means 'swollen-footed'   foulard: a silk material
Du scherts: joke   feminine reserve   *L* risus: laugh

s Limerick's Pride
Limerick produces high-quality tambour lace

s Linger Longer, Loo   Santa Claus
lingerie   scented clothes
Thackeray: *Vanity Fair*

diabolical   (whalebone corsets)

Thackeray: *Vanity Fair*
AngI thacka: little girl
Dickens   *Gr* Jonas: Jonah (in whale; name means 'dove')   *U.S.* car barn: place where trams kept   Dolphin's Barn: district of D
tickets please!
Dickens: *Our Mutual Friend*   Dickens: *David Copperfield* (includes Uriah Heep)   composing penitential psalms
F filles
attention span   advertisement   Uriah's wife (involved with biblical David)

Dickens: *The Old Curiosity Shop*
L cupio: I desire
O.W. Holmes: *The Autocrat of the Breakfast-Table*

metamorphosed
Martin Murphy: owner of *Irish Independent*; became antiparnellite
Da kort: short   long

grave sin is committed
*U.*5: 'Algy' (Swinburne)   *L* pulcher   *Sl* performer: whoremonger
artist   autistic
alias
L olea: olive

dilettantes Sp ciudad: town, city Buenos Aires (*Eveline*)
L puella: girl
closing of London playhouses *Merchant of Venice*
during plague birching

AngI tony: fashionable, stylish

model undies

anaesthetic valuable

Hogarth, Botticelli, Tintoretto, Veronese, Correggio

It vergognoso: shameful *It* coraggio: courage, (fig.) effrontery

Masaccio: painter baker's dozen *Gr* dôdekaêmeron: of 12 days
It mazza: cane bilk: deceive Boccaccio's *Decameron*
Lord Byron: *The Waltz* instance
verses (*U.*743: 'he made me the present of lord Byrons poems')
philosophy of Bishop Berkeley *Arch* buss: kiss recklessness fickleness kiddies
Lancelot Bulkeley: C17 bishop of D fecklessness
Art Nouveau *F* nouveautés: icecold globetrotter
nowadays novelties (whitehaired) Globe Playhouse
(waist) Nimrod, the mighty hunter
Sl ramrod: penis *Sl* meat: cunt

Sl hunter: penis *G* Jäger: hunter
eager *ph* the body beautiful
G süsse Mädels: sweet girls Strauss: *The Blue Danube* Danu: Ir. goddess
s Londonderry Air: 'Danny Boy'

Book of Common Prayer: Baptism: 'Grant that the old Adam in this child may be so buried that the new man may be raised up in him. . . . Crucify the old man. . . . Put on Christ'
Nosy Parker
front
Sl nutty: amorous
(rugby football: oval, touch, goal, convert try) *OF* parevis: paradise *N* parvis: in pairs (couples)
evil *F Sl* ovale: cunt parvis: church portico
'The rest is all but leather or Prunella' (Pope) avert your eye wax (Odysseus & the Sirens)
Du opletten!: pay attention! *Sl* leather: cunt *Sl* wick: penis
tempter's beau
boy

(Eve, serpent, fig leaves) 'the strawberry leaves': a dukedom (ducal coronet bears 8 strawberry leaves)
Balfe: *The Bondman* Matt 16:19: '& whatever thou shalt bind on earth shall be bound in heaven'
Du hemel: heaven early hours
hemmel: cowshed *pr* The early bird catches the worm

nr Little Bo Peep fast
F Sl poupée: whore

said
sat on the po
chine: projecting China & Japan *F* jupon: *pr* Go to bed with the lamb & rise with the
rim of cask petticoat lark
wake

G Milchmann *s* The Shan Van Vocht
Sl milkman: penis *Da* mand: man Sullivan
Tim Healy Hail Mary
fingering
societies anonymous
Onanism

unwashed

penchant faggot
puncheon

locusts

loitering with intent

L interstipitalis: between branches

curfew
F couvre *F* feu

ph thin end of the wedge hoyden: ill-bred girl
watch

One tricking

Rossini: *La Gazza Ladra* (*The Thieving Magpie*)
It ragazza: girl *It* ladra: thief
Adam's apples

gee whiz!

G kosen: caress
kissing cousins

hygienically prescribed

two asking
Sl twim: cunt Tommy Atkins
I Béarla: English *Da* snakke: chatter *Da* svare: answer *G* Magd
N snakke: speak snaking forwards *Sl* nurse: whore
Kipling: *Love O'Women* (story)

do: C (sol- fa) sister/brotherly St Jerome: Letter CXXVII: 'Seek in brothels those cisterns of vice'

rest

foretold

fellow especially sluggish

lessons

Sl forty-rod: cheap overproof whiskey
20-odd cherry brandies
The Cat & Cage, pub, D *Sl* coney: simpleton
coney: rabbit
Lotts, street, D

J: *Gas from a Burner:* 'And the foreigner learns the gift of the gab From the drunken draggletail Dublin drab'

Saturday Billy Sunday: Am. evangelist

s The Young May Moon

Navan: Co. seat of Meath Hellfire Club, D go-by
I neamh: heaven Kells, Co. Meath

s 'You may go, darling Nelly, to the wake in Kildare . . . But keep your legs together coming home from the wake'

Byron: 'Maid of Athens, ere we part, Give, oh give me back my heart'

Ms 'Wid my bundle on my shoulder, Faith! there's no man could be boulder, I'm laving dear ould Ireland widout warning, For I lately took the notion For to cross the briny ocean, & I shtart for Philadelphia in the mornin' '

morning ladylike tricks
burning
Gr gymnos: naked

Sl jigger: bicycle bumping races (Oxford & Cambridge rowing)
kick start (cycling)
right lasciviously
point to point: of racing, from one point directly to another acclivity
Rutland Square, D, slopes uphill towards N. side of city
inciting
centre Dr Bereton invented freewheeling
J.B. Dunlop invented pneumatic tyre
G.B.D. tobacco pipes

ptosis: prolapse of any viscera

Magazine Wall (116.18) *F* vin (damages liver)

Duodenum is so-called from its length, that of 12 fingers' breadths

threadworm: intestinal parasite
lector: ecclesiastic who reads lesson ostiary: doorkeeper, esp. of a church
F sportive: sportswoman
Sl greengrocer: cunt Land of Punt: coast of Somaliland, whence ancient Egyptians imported perfumes & resins P/K
ha'penny *AngI* rawny: sickly person
Gi rawnie: lady, wife

ph I never open my mouth but I put my foot in it
natural motion (without laxatives)

F causeries: discussions
Mrs Beeton's Cookery Book
Elizabethans

stupifying
L stuprum: debauchery, disgrace
Po mazurek: masurka, Masovian dance Sackerson
R sukin syn: son of a bitch
son of a bitch *G* kommen *G* alt Pannonia: part of Roman Empire including S.W. Hungary and Austria
stuttering male & female tickles
L femur: thigh
Sl spanks the ivory: plays piano
makes
Da mistro: distrust

inadequately

closeted

Es malbongusta: in bad taste, coarse

(alcohol)

It forte: strong
40

modesty: a slight covering for a low-cut neck

F deux *Arch* twy: 2 (i.e. breasts)

Sl billydoo: loveletter (from *F* billet doux) *Gr* idiotes: peculiarity

G glatt: smooth

got to do

sitting tabernacle turning pictures to the wall

I tobar: well; spring

Gladstone's

Black Watch: 42nd Highland Rgt *Sl* ranger: penis

I go bráth: until Judgement Day

ph out of the frying pan into the fire horrible

communists

Peter Paragraph: name under which Samuel Foote satirised a D bookseller Mr Puff in Sheridan's *The Critic*

SS Peter & Paul keepsake

L pulex: flea *ph* at sixes & sevens

(eggs) below par

Pa

Ma 22,000th 22,000

unladylike Marriage Service: 'to have & to hold'

Lecky (Ir. historian): *History of European Morals*

L qua: in the capacity of intervener: one who interposes in a legal action to which he/she was not originally a partner

VI.A.641: 'intervener (fem corresp)'

Viceregal

vice squad

subpoenas *U.S.* flummoxed: utterly at a loss

penis

company-keeping: revelling; wooing *F* demi-monde

Dublin by Lamplight laundry (employed reformed prostitutes) God

versed *Arch* collions: testicles, rascals

Boucicault: *The Colleen Bawn* (based on Griffin's *The Collegians*)

Sl colleen bawn: erection

Sl nightbird: whore *I* dubh: dark

s Battle of Otterbourne: 'He chose the Gordons & the Graems, With them the Lindsays, light & gay'

Gay Gordons: Scottish dance

fucking tickling
G ficken: to fuck

Ivor Novello: *The Dancing Years*

F cocotte: whore

It sedro: I will sit down
Sedro: prayer in Maronite liturgy
Lucifer White Friars: Carmelites

moonshine whiskey fancyfree

troubadour Thomas Moore: *Irish Melodies*

ph turned his head Swift: *Journal to Stella*
Swift: *A Tale of a Tub* (*It* stella: star)
Prime minister, Gladstone

James Fenimore Cooper: U.S. novelist (cooper makes barrels)

Litany of BVM: 'Seat of wisdom, Cause of our joy'
*U.*569: 'Remember Pasiphae for whose lust my grandoldgrossfather made the first confessionbox' *F* tante
Amen
It amene: pleasant *Gr* mênê: moon
planxty: Ir. harp tune
s All around My Hat I Wear a Tricoloured Ribbon
breath *I* glor go leor: great noise it's long

Henry Cockton: *Valentine Vox:* novel about a ventriloquist Val Vousden: D music hall entertainer
F vaux: valleys (i.e. low notes)
joy must pass away dewdrops

in voice (tenor)

don't know who Falconer: *The O'Donoghue's Warning*; Boucicault: *Daddy O'Dowd* (both played at Theatre Royal, D)
The O'Donoghue: chieftain living under Lake of Killarney

lechery

Browning: *Mr Sludge the Medium*
sledgehammer *G* Hummer: lobster
dickens

operatic
erotic
love
Sl roger: to fuck

brotherly

Issy

Sl chipper: lively massboy
Sl mash: sweetheart
L nostrum: ours
nostrum: quack remedy
believe is

physical high jinks
hygienics *Bookies' Sl*: mugpunter: uninformed backer of horses
Moore: *s* I'd Mourn the Hopes That Leave Me [The Rose Tree] library at Alexandria burned
ph all & sundry
bonfire suffocate Father Finn: *Tom Playfair* Savonarola: bookburner who was himself burned
suffragette *It* zolfanello: match peruse
instead *Weekly Standard*: newspaper Father Finn: *Ethelred Preston*
stand (male organ) *It* veri: true Ethelred the Unready: Eng. king

Rev. R. Archdekin: *Essay on Miracles* (1st book printed in both Ir. & Eng.)
the four last things: death, judgement, hell & heaven (the retreat in *Portrait*)
archdeacon's
I an: the
A Treatise on Dracula
s John Peel: 'view to a death in the morning'
Dickens
L miracula: miracles
priest-hunters claimed bounty on priests under Penal Laws in C17–18 Ir.
Castlebar: town, Co. Mayo
D Castle
William Archer, critic, encouraged J in early days
good Roman Catholic
William Archer, librarian, prepared dictionary catalogue in National Library, D
National Library
Gr labrônios: large cup
It nazional: national
'to the hell with the pope' (slogan)
It denti: teeth
Dante Alighieri's *Divine Comedy* places several popes in hell
Father Finn, S.J.: *Mostly Boys*
Index Expurgatorius
ph a laugh on every page
L risus: laugh
excusing
L arrisus: favoured
bastard: an abbreviated title on page preceding title page

lenten
Cardinal Cullen: archbishop of D
Percy Wyndham Lewis
pottage of lentils for which Jacob sold birthright (Gen 25:34)
Father Finn, S.J.: *Percy Wynn*
peace & plenty
Curé d'Ars: patron of parish priests
warts
peas (lentils)

Du linzen: lentils (.09)
F petit pois
F bois
L licet ut Libanus: it is permitted that Lebanon
Gr libanos: incense (Maronite rite)
consumption on the premises (pub licence)
Father Finn: *His Luckiest Year*
Gill: D publisher & bookseller

decimally
God the Holy Ghost

Immanuel Kant
Lope Felix de Vega: playwright
Du looper: runner
It figa: cunt
nr Mary Had a Little Lamb
Charles & Mary Lamb: *The Adventures of Ulysses*
L nates maximae: biggest buttocks
Alice Liddell: model for *Alice in Wonderland*
L vates: poet
mint sauce (with roast lamb)
spice
sentimental
arse
give a cock's egg: send on a fool's errand
flagellation
heart
F Sl flageolet: penis
St Francis
Father Finn: *Mostly Boys*

sacerdotes

betterment of your thoughts
Moore: *s* Forget Not the Field, Where They Perished
(light a candle)

palmoil: (jocular) money given as bribe
G Hemd: shirt
pr A friend in need is a friend indeed

Ash Wednesday service: 'Remember, man that thou art dust, & unto dust shalt thou return' (from Gen 3:19, said by the celebrant as he puts ashes on heads of laity)
Sl cog: cheat, copy from others
copy that out 10 times
Du broek: trousers
s The Lass That Loves a Sailor

Vestal Virgins

most lamented
It Sl mozza: cunt
ecumenical
It mozzo: docked, cut short
Sp Sl lesma: cunt
Gr oikoumenê: the inhabited world
Hail Mary
prince Hal (*Henry IV*)
merry hell

honest-to-goodness

nudity *L* femina: woman
harness: feminine foundation garment
nullity suit (law): one declaring a marriage null *ph* family hold back: jocular command
Eccles 9:11: 'The race is not to the swift' *s* Green Grow the Rushes-O to leave enough
food for guests

Satan letter, 20/9/28, to HSW: 'three colours of successive stages of cecity as the Germans divide them, namely: green Starr, that is, green blindness, or glaucoma; grey Starr, that is, cataract; and black Starr, that is dissolution of the retina'
Milky Way
St Michael white & yellow: colours of papal flag
G Popo: posterior forget me not *ph* where there's life there's hope *AngI* whist!: silence!
forsake
lunch with good Duke Humphrey: go dinnerless

dripping: fat
appetite from roast meat

tumble *Sl* scouse: stew *L* ad libidinem: at caprice in these latitudes
dumpling *L* ad libitum: as one wishes

Yeats: *Countess Cathleen* (sold soul to aid starving) Theatre Royal, D, in C19, boasted a 'Contessa',
It cantilene: cradlesong *Ms* Cantilene supposedly supporting her husband's gambling debts
Mephistopheles superannuated husbands
soprano gospels
(dripping & suet make her fat)

Wilde on fox hunters: 'the unspeakable in full pursuit of the uneatable'
pure suet
G taucht: dipped white pudding: kind of sausage

Lady Dufferin: *Ms Lament of the Irish Emigrant* : 'I'm sitting on the stile, Mary . . . & the red was in your lips, Mary, & the lovelight in your eye' *Ms* Rose Marie

Sl rollingpin: penis
Moore: *s* Rich & Rare Were the Gems She Wore

Buddhist prayer 'Om Manī Padme Hum' ('Oh Jewel in the flower of the Lotus')
Sl jewel: cunt
pretty few *s* A Ballynure Ballad: 'This cordial that ye talk about there's very few o'them gets it'

suddenly shouted

the devil praying Balaam's ass warned him of Yahweh's wrath
console: key-desk of organ John Braham: Eng. tenor
L vox humana (organ stop) organ keyboards: swell organ & great organ

strung he-man

kinetics bowl

the cur's
gobbed bedtime divulge

surname & address

AngI slieve: mountain

goddamned *s* The Peeler & the Goat: 'They met a goat upon the road & took him for
sex appeal upside down being a-strolling, O'

Shakespeare
pig's cheek
(breasts)

pr Marry in haste & repent at leisure

ministries of Foreign Affairs *G* Fremdling: stranger
I Dubh-ghall: Black-foreigner, i.e. Dane
Ibsen: *An Enemy of the People*
tinker's twopenny damn
Tammany: central organisation of Democratic Party in N.Y.C.; in England associated with political & municipal corruption *I* muc: pig owl: 'tu-whit, tu-whoo!' tongster: member of a tong, Chinese secret society
In legend of the 3 sons of Tuireann the sons had to give 3 shouts on a hill as part of their penance
ph I don't care 2 hoots
namesake Nonesuch: palace of Henry VIII Nolan
Constantine, Roman emperor
Enoch: eldest son of Cain
enough
Tewkesbury: scene of Lancastrian defeat in Wars of Roses, 1471
'Dear Uncle Remus': letters to a children's column in *Weekly Freeman* *Du* baas: master *I* bás: death *L* Eboracum: York (Wars of Roses)
Fi Lissabon: Lisbon *It* Ulisse: Ulysses Lancaster (Wars of Roses) Wolverhampton, town, Staffordshire
Knickerbocker: a New Yorker Lisbon supposedly founded by Ulysses
Bristol soke: district under a particular jurisdiction
brisling: a Norwegian sprat
Matt 16:18: 'Tu es Petrus' Nevsky Prospect: main street of St Petersburg
Peterborough, town, Northamptonshire, in district called the Soke of Peterborough

St Brendan visited the Land of Promise of the Saints in Atlantic *AngI* Hy Brasil: legendary island in Atlantic

assured

of

incest *Du* markt: market
marked man
L quare?: why?

ignoramus
L ignoratis: you misunderstand
dumbshow short way

Jer 8:22: 'Is there no balm in Gilead'

Ms I'll Sing Thee Songs of Araby Ward in Chancery: a minor for whom Court of Chancery has appointed a guardian, or who is subject to that court (maidenhead)
F Sl sanctuaire: cunt (measuring for wedding ring)

It dito: finger *It* ohibò!: now then!, oh! *Ms* Pretty Molly Brannigan: 'Oh, if I had a blunderbuss, I'd go & fight a duel, man'
G sicher: sure

King Laeg aire (Leary), high king of Ir. at coming of St Patrick, was interred facing the men of Leinster, whose enemy he was
'Lineaments of gratified desire' (Blake, quoted in *U.* 199 in connection with Mulligan)
Sean the Post in *Arrah-na-Pogue* sings 'Open the dure softly, Somebody wants ye, dear'

Ms I Hear You Calling Me *G* Blitz muezzin: Moslem public crier
blessing
darkest pillarbox: mailbox scribble

Grand Opera

CheKa: Russian Extraordinary Commission (secret police), founded in 1917. Reorganized & renamed OGPU in 1922
The Coombe, in the Liberties, D
St Patrick's Close, D (in the Liberties, by cathedral; associated with Swift in *U.* 39)
Clos St Patrice: Fr. wine approved of by J *G* Lausbub: rascal

ears

Robert of Retina translated the Koran into Latin brace up
retina of eye *I* amadán: fool *Sl* brass up: pay up

brothelkeeper *U.*308: 'The baby policeman, Constable MacFadden'
Gen 4:9: 'Am I my brother's keeper?'
DORA: Defence of the Realm Act, 1914
Diehards: Anti-Treaty forces of I.R.B. in 1920s

fall upon

floodgates

pogrom

Mountjoy Prison, D
Hep: sacred bull of Memphis
Clontarf means 'bull meadow'
Clonmel, town, Co. Tipperary; means 'meadow of honey' Cromwellian
versus the jewboy
Sl joyboy: homosexual
G strafe: punish 12 good men & true = jury gleeman: minstrel
Maud I. Crofts: *Women Under English Law* 59: 'illegitimate person is . . . for certain purposes, *filius nullius*'
L filius nullius per fas et nefas: the son of no one through right & wrong

whitest feather in my cap *ph* a penny for your thoughts *F* pansement: medical dressing
federal theology: doctrine of covenants between God & man
G Feder: feather
F pensée
Sp pensamiento: pansy; mind, thought
Hamlet IV.5.174: 'pansies, that's for thoughts'
Dr Robert Knox bought corpses stolen by Burke & Hare
I cnoc: hill (*AngI*, knock)
AngI drumlin: little hill

s Charley Is My Darling

Surgeon Gustavus Hume: C18 D property speculator
s Home, Sweet Home

Rolf Ganger (Rollo): 1st Duke of Normandy (theoretically ancestor of Anglo-Norman invaders of Ir.) floorwalker
Arnott's dept. store, D

pithecoid: apelike (possibly a portrait of John Joyce)

Toc H = Talbot House, London *Sl* claret: blood *Sl* in the studbook: of ancient lineage
Sl XYZ: the Y.M.C.A.
stretch (false teeth)

old Finglas May Day revels included grinning through horse-collars for tobacco
Colmans' mustard
(pepper-&-salt suit)
Father Mathew Br., D (Whitworth Br.) named after the Ir. temperance advocate

*U.*81: 'some temperance beverage Wheatley's Dublin Hop Bitters'
Ross's: several D restaurants
people Olaf the Stout: C11 king of Norway purchase *Sl* movables: small objects of value
hebdomadary: one taking weekly turn in performance of R.C. church offices
let
boot
Guinness's

(Rolf Ganger)

film called Finn MacCool mother-of-pearl
Metropole Cinema, D
Henry Arthur Jones: *Michael & His Lost Angels* Los Angeles *F* quelque chose de merveilleuse
St Michan's Church, D: corpses preserved in crypt by dehydration
F morve: snot

L omnibus: for everything

train
claudicant: stammering, limping

Harald Harefoot: C11 Saxon king
be off
Ragnar Lodbrok: Viking chief

tip-&-run: a form of cricket
touch & go

Marie Stopes: advocate of birth control
Sl flute: penis
s Phil the Fluter's Ball: 'With the toot of the flute& the twiddle of the fiddle, O! . . . Up, down, hands aroun' Crossin' to the wall'

let
Da misforstaaelse: misunderstanding
(blame for pregnancy)

cradle
Joseph Biggar: hunchbacked supporter of Parnell
beggar
bugger
coffin
Da vokse: to grow
recommend

bothering
ascertain who struck first

'Who struck Buckley?'(101.15): phrase used in C19 to annoy Irishmen

Sl straphanger: standing passenger in bus, holding strap

G Kuhhandel: shady deal
Sl cowhanded: awkward

Pigeonhouse Fort, D, at mouth of Liffey
Ms 'Plaisir d'amour ne dure qu'un moment'
pledge: (fig.) child

bad manners
tit for tat
auditor
G Minne: love
D Sl micky dazzler: a would-be dandy
corsairs
horsehairs

Barbary (corsairs)
liberally
burberry: type of cloth & clothing
Lupita: sister of St Patrick who became whore & was killed by him
Rosemary Lane, D
Paternoster Row, London

Road

anybody else

Rolf Ganger: 1st Duke of Normandy (theoretically ancestor of Anglo-Norman invaders of Ir.)

Isolde

with friends
droll
G heimsuchen: afflict, punish
Du dol: crazy
Luperca: she-wolf that suckled Romulus & Remus
The Palatinate, Co. Limerick

strict confidence It nerbo: whip Gr bios: life
Sp Nombre di Dios: Name of God
guard *ph* beat about the bush
s I've Been Working on the Railroad
(the parish priest in *Stephen Hero* who collected girls' hats)
lampshades

G Aschenbrödel: Cinderella

I sceilp: slap so help me God kiss the book rod

sadism please *Sl* bishop: penis, condom
satisfaction
plenary indulgence

illicit

John Tobin (1770–1804): *The Honeymoon* II.1: 'the man that lays his hand upon a woman Save in the way of kindness' (*U.* 354)
remember bottom *L* Amor regit Heva: Love rules Eve
motto (backwards)
Mick/Nick next

rhododendrons
Gr rhoda: roses
L calor: heat *L* rubor: redness *L* dolor: pain Caesar: 'I came, I saw, I conquered'

damn stupid puff!
Love's Labour's Lost III.1.169: 'Dan Cupid'
Oedipus
L Gradibus . . . -ibus: 'By degrees to . . .' (old textbook title)
pair of arms

I return

ph from the sublime to the ridiculous

ph times out of number

s Bells of Shandon: 'With deep affection & recollection' Thomas Campbell: 'Far away on the billow'

Ms All through the Night

Dial moider: *G* doppel
worry, brother
Homer Mrs H. Wood: Fred Wetherly: songwriter
Home rule *East Lynne*
s 'I'm sitting on the stile, Mary, Where we sat side by side'
o'er Liffey bank

(my heart)

028.15: 'Airwinger's bride' unceasingly

sons of Abraham Abraham rules the Mohammedan 7th heaven
ampersands
I warrant you, your I.O.U. belittle me
want you & I
Du Ik: I *Sl* purseproud: you 'pansy' derived from *F* pensée
lecherous
Hymen

arch godkin: little god
Sl bodkin: penis weddingnights
satisfaction honour Armorica (Tristan) *F* amour
Sl fight in armour: use condom
belly
F déshabillé
s You Are My Heart's Delight *s* 'It's still I live in hopes to see, The Holy Ground once more'

Da mig: me answer yours so eager for me *G* mich
my wandering hands up in
cheeks plumcake

It zuccheri: sugars so on

belfry

s The Rantin' Dog, the Daddy o't

Moore: *Ms* The Meeting of the Waters

I are you *F* stade: stadium *G* taufen: baptise Fox & Geese, district of D
Ir. Rugby Union
wild geese: Ir. Jacobites who went to continent after defeat in 1591 *ph* 6 of one & half a dozen of the other
Sl green geese: whores

L/R *s* Come Back to Erin
Ealing: suburb of London
present

pursuant

pr Ignorance is bliss *I* capall: horse
G Koppel: paddock
r Suir & *r* Nore are both in S. Ireland King's & Queen's Counties: Offaly & Leix

s Johnny, I Hardly Knew Ye
gamey: spirited
Marlowe: 'Come live with me and be my love' *F Sl* rat: whore
alley cats

Abelites: chaste C4 Christians who adopted children

euphonia: pleasing effect of sounds free from harshness
Murphy, Hernon & Dwyer: D city commissioners 1924–30
Manchester Martyrs: 3 Fenians executed 1867 for short
helping Fenian chiefs to escape

shirtsleeves

ph shoulder to shoulder

'Work in Progress' (J's name for FW during composition)
Tennyson: *Come into the Garden, Maud*: 'I am here at the gate alone'
great unknown county

'I, even I': Pharaoh's inscription unite preparatory
St Ignatius Loyola purgatory

apostles utensil: chamberpot Pascal was converted by his sister Jacqueline jakes
meliorism: doctrine affirming that human effort may improve the world

Hamlet II.2.473–4: 'Break all the spokes & fellies from her wheel, & bowl the round nave down the hill of heaven'
Swift: 'Burn everything English, excepting their coals'
black bile: imaginary fluid supposed anciently to be cause of melancholy

Armorica (Tristan) ore
American
cursorily

Henriette Renan helped her brother write his *Vie de Jésus* mortality
Henrietta St, D natality
juries Sir John Harington: *Metamorphosis of Ajax* (describes water closet)
haar: a cold sea fog Harrington St, D
backwards Dean Kinane: *St Patrick*, 'Approbations': 'I have since tried to run cursorily through the whole of it'
s The Jolly Young Waterman (temperance song)
Waterman pens
F à la coque: of eggs, softboiled (031.18)
Elcock (.15)
dry as dust 4 D streets were named after Henry More, Earl of Drogheda
Drogheda
Talbot St, D look Michael Manning (031.19) done
Luke Elcock (329.26): mayor of Drogheda, 1916
birds of prey
Prince
Castleknock Rd, D
Moore: *s* Though the Last Glimpse of Erin
Ballsbridge Horse Show Dunphy's Corner, D

U.379: 'Mirus bazaar in search of funds for Mercer's hospital'
Marist Fathers, D White Friars: Carmelites
Capuchin trousers (*Portrait* IV)

Sighs
Ballybough Bridge, Fairview, N.E. D (crossed by Stephen in *Portrait* V)
G Platz
John Citizen James (Joyce)
contrast Pierce Egan: *Real Life in Dublin by a Real Paddy* (also wrote *Life in London*)
Liffey dustbin
Egan O Rahilly: Ir. poet
Asia

According to legend, Milesian invasion of Ireland took place because on a certain day Ireland was visible from Spain coast
Da oversæt: translate Matt 16:18: 'thou art Peter & upon this rock'
L perdix: partridge Perdix: nephew & rival of Daedalus, killed by him
partridge *L* oramus: we pray *L* oremus: let us pray *Gr* autotaxis: self-arrangement
William Pett Ridge: author
Town of the Ford of the Hurdles: D *ph* hail fellow well met
Ford cars
boneshaker: old bicycle
(umbrella) Drumcondra, district of D
gondola
Midland Great Western Railway of Ireland
elastic
Aston Quay, D with

1132 Kane & Co, portmanteau & trunkmakers, 11 Aston Quay
Ambrose Keogh, draper, 12 Aston Quay
heels

Dean Kinane: *St Patrick*, preface: 'I shall be greatly mistaken, indeed, if this . . . '

just astonished
Aston
darn well

traffic jam Crosse & Blackwell's jam
St John of the Cross
pr See Naples & then die
Capel St, D
Yeats: *Countess Cathleen* Katherine Strong: C17 D scavenger & tax collector, very inefficient & much disliked Magrath
deface so much loved *L* Troia: Troy *It* tròia: sow; harlot
I muc: pig
L carmen: song mendicants
Bizet: *Carmen*
F laver: to wash

horse races: Grand National, Gold Cup, Derby topsy-turvy
hospital (pregnant women)

meals (D pron. 'males')

speech *L* asper: rough, bitter Avignon (popes lived there 1309–77)
disparage
uproot opium Appian Way, D (J born in Brighton Square; lived later in Bray, 'the Irish Brighton')
Du klaproos: poppy Appian Way: 1st Roman Road paved
bull-baiting Bailey light on Howth Lorcan (Laurence) O'Toole: patron saint of D
s Bill Bailey, Won't You Please Come Home? *Da* by: city
pr It's an ill wind that blows nobody good

pr The labourer is worthy of his hire
cg Ring-a-ring o'roses: 'One for me, & one for you, & one for little Moses'
I Cor 13:3: '& have not charity, it profiteth me nothing'
Du loos: cunning jobless
hardship

Isengrim: wolf in Reynard cycle girls
Jakob Grimm's fairy tales
VI.B.33.106: 'father of curls = wolf'
Oxford Sl sport your oak: shut front door to show visitors not wanted Alice Liddell: friend of Lewis Carroll, model for *Alice in Wonderland*

aloud bloody

badly *F* temps move

discalced: barefoot *F* bourse (Aeolus)
Discalced Carmelites' Church, D
G Baden: bathing Iveagh Baths, D
G Bad-: -Spa Danu: Ir. Goddess
certainly God
Saturn
tax bloody

high fa (Sol-fa) *L* dorsum: back
highfalutin
F ouvre: to open Boosey & Hawkes: Eng. music publishers

It incuriosite: made curious
L incuriosus: negligent
L fulmen: thunderbolt firmament wonderment
fulmar: sea bird bewilderment
uncertain Swift's Stella & Vanessa *'He swallows down an impediment in his throat, looking
Saturn towards a bird that is not there, a projection of the "bird"
Lord Orrery (*Remarks on the Life & Writings of* allusion in "*swift*"'
Dr Jonathan Swift) Eccles 1:2: 'vanity of vanities; all is vanity' *purse
describes vanity as Vanessa's besetting sin *pr* 'Time enough' lost the ducks

Sl blue funk:
extreme fear

L tristis: sad, sorrowful *'O all you who pass by'
Tristan
Deirdre & Conchubar (parallel with Isolde & Mark &c.)
coney: rabbit Wilfred: rabbit in a comic strip 'Pip, Squeak & Wilfred'
spoonfeed

Sl nippy: a Lyons' tea shop girl *L* vera: true 'One True Catholic & Apostolic Church'
It ipostila: hypostyle Tristan of Lyonesse *It* tutti: all (i.e. 'catholic')
Bulwer Lytton: *Lady of Lyons* Lyons' Corner Houses astronomy gastronomics
*'Jaun would like to find a girl with a job of her own to support him. . . . A teashop assistant would do'

brownies: junior girl guides

Jonas Hanway: first man to carry an umbrella in London. Stones were thrown at him. He
wrote against tea drinking gamp: umbrella (from Dickens' Mrs Gamp)
lapidate: to stone Jacob's pipe (607.08) *L* intercisus: cut up *L* purifex: cleaner thurifer
Matt 16:18: 'thou art Peter & upon this rock' shawm: medieval wind instrument crucifix

Sir Boyle Roche, M.P., once said: 'Mr Speaker, it is impossible I could have been in two places at once, unless I were a bird' *We ph* in the bird's lodging: spending night under a hedge
L cubitum: elbow
Sl pheasant: whore *s* 'I dreamt that I dwelt in marble halls With vassals & serfs at my side'

chough: red-legged crow

s Moddereen Rue (means 'little red dog', i.e. fox) Couard: the hare in Reynard cycle
covert: undergrowth & woods sheltering game

St Patrick: *Confessio* 23: 'I saw in the bosom of the night'

(fireflies) *G* Brilliant: diamond
*glowworms
(traffic lights) *'He will catch misty dew on the tip of his tongue'
owl old clock bad cess to it!

owl: 'tu-whit, tu-whoo!'
(2 a.m.)

Drum-salach: land in Armagh given to St Patrick * *F* fleurette

St Grouse's day: beginning of grouse season
11th EB notes that during incubation hoopoe almost never leaves nest Tereus turned into a hoopoe
horizons *'Sheet lightning is to fork lightning as the sheep to the wolf'
arisings *s* On the Road to Mandalay: 'lookin' lazy at the sea'
(thunder) snipe drumming with wings

Erin Ariel in *The Tempest* *'He hears the night mail-trains going along the river *banks*' (*F* rives)
Aeolian harps aerial (wireless)
Swift: 'Ppt' whip-poor-will Moor Park, where Swift met Stella
peewit: lapwing morepork: name of an Aust. bird, cracking jokes
peaceful *Gr* (artificial) philopotamus: from its call
river lover (caddisfly genus) nightingale goes 'jug'
F grenouilles: frogs Belleek: a kind of china made at Belleek, Co. Fermanagh
(town also noted for fishing)
nephoscope: instrument for taking velocity & altitude of
clouds
rugby (hence gibbous moon) Temple Observatory, Rugby School *s* The West's Awake amongst
rockaby *L* cumulus: a heap cumulus clouds
L claustrum: cloister fairy godmother
scrum (rugby) *Mother Goose* (pantomime)

*Stuart Gilbert: *Prolegomena to Work in Progress* (J collaborated)

(sunrise)
ph goose that laid the golden egg *'There is a hole in his trousers on the side towards the river'
poached egg

otter beaver
other breviary
dace (fish) grannom: a fishing fly
Grania . . . Finn
guppies Minnehaha (in *Hiawatha*), 'laughing water' Proust: *Swann's Way*
minnows
J.G. Swift MacNeill: Ir. politician & writer gillaroo: large variety of trout with reddish tinge

Du karper: carp *Aeneid* I.118: 'Rari nantes in gurgite vasto' ('Here & there are seen swimmers astern
carp, perch, tench rods & perches (measure) Swift . . . Sterne in the vast abyss')

Arab naranj: orange lasher: weir-pool lonesome
pear logan-stone: a poised heavy stone at the river's
GBD tobacco pipes sol-fa scale *It* solfanelli: matches edge
*the notes on the 'lines' GBD are between the 'spaces' FACE (tortoiseshell case)
Latakia: a Syrian tobacco nostrils jessamines
It nuvoli: full of clouds
*'The word "delight" is thus stressed in the duet "The Moon hath raised her lamp above"' ('my heart's
September delight')
L humilis: low, near the earth *'Dapping: a method of fishing'
homely
starlight
r Griffeen, Lucan (eels used to be caught by men with lamps & spears)
Royal College of Surgeons, D
sturgeon (a royal fish)
by & by *s* O Twine Me a Bower *F* L'alouette
Moore: *s* O! Weep for the Hour [Eveleen's Bower]
nightingales go 'jug jug' *G* jucken: to itch gamut: the 'great scale' attributed to
s Adelaide (Beethoven tenor aria) *Sl* nightingales: whores Guido d'Arezzo
*'I'd teach my nine-and-twenty blackbirds how to sing' Dorian chthonic: dwelling underground
Wilde: *The Picture of Dorian Gray* mode (music) tonic solfa *Gr* sophia: wisdom
nr Sing a Song of Sixpence music hall variations
**Numerosus* (musical)
*'This is a translation of the "tonic solfa" names of the notes in the scale (as an Italian ear might hear them . . . *I double give*: the high *do* (C)' odes
spinney: small wood echoed along
**F* éclore
*'This is the major chord (do-mi-sol-do: CEGC)'
treble
manage pianoforte
Tamagno: tenor *It* piange: laments
s A Bicycle Built for Two Mario: tenor

Mary & Jesus! John McCormack: tenor
It bemolle: flat; *It* diesis: sharp (music)
latter part of my trousers

phonetics tuning fork *It* naturale: natural (inc. musical)
Sl fork: penis
lower register of voice discord Athlone: birthplace of McCormack
L misericordia: mercy *s* I'm alone (from *The Lily of Killarney*)
The Lily of Killarney (opera based on Boucicault's *The Colleen Bawn*, which is based on Griffin's *The Collegians*)
McCormack's wife was named Lily
pr What's sauce for the goose is sauce for the gander

hemlock (poison) laburnum is poisonous deadly nightshade
G heimlich: secretly loganberries deathcap: poisonous toadstool
bryony (poisonous berries) *Belladonna* (deadly nightshade)

'telling a Greenwood': lying (after chief secretary at D Castle)
business

**sensitive* (note preceding the tonic)

La Touche's bank once largest in Ir.
F touche: piano key
***Gilbert: *Prolegomena* (continued)**

s Dolly Varden; abdominal pattern *AngI* poteen: illicit whiskey
also Calif. species of trout brass farthing subdominant (fa)
bet Chauncy Olcott: actor, played Sean the Post & wrote 'Mother Machree'

s 'Madamina' from *Don Giovanni*
outstrips
G Gott strafe England: God punish England (slogan) Gogarty
cat on a tail (031.2–3)
pr One man's meat is another man's poison *ph* sowing my wild oats
F poisson (Parable of the Plums in *U.*)
horn of plenty VI.B.34.72: 'erbole (wild plum)' (in list of wines)
hydromel: honey & water liquor
bragget: honey & ale fermented together, drunk on Bragget Sunday in mid-Lent Mozart: *The Magic Flute* closing time
Sl flute: penis
top-hole: (fig) the highest point attainable factor: merchant
Bectives: Ir. rugby club

Salmon of Wisdom Solam O Droma: coauthor of *Book of Ballymote* *ph* Ye gods & little fishes (*U*.89)
Solomon Anadromous fish ascend rivers to spawn *It* pesci: fishes
pr money makes money loaves & the fishes (John 6:5–13)
matrimony *AngI ph* ignorant as a kish of brogues
(N, S, E & W)
regiments: Ulster Rifles, Cork Militia, Dublin Fusiliers, Connacht Rangers
F ensemble *r* Shannon

Leixlip *r* Blackwater

G mein Schatz: my treasure, darling fuck

Pope: *Essay on Criticism* 525: 'to err is human, to forgive divine' I.S. Varian: D brush factory
Sl peter: penis Peter denies Christ (Luke 22:57–62)
*'This passage goes to the lilt of an Irish song. Jaun is swinging the girl higher & higher in his arms'
F balayer: to sweep
*affidavit *Rut* divy: virgins *F* cache-cache: hide & seek
Cz divy: wonders catch-as-catch-can
s Roll Me Over, in the Clover snow white

L sponsa: bride 99 (metronome mark)

Peter & Paul

Mumm champagne
damn all

but fill up *It* frullare: to whisk Chartreuses
F brut: extra dry (of champagne)
s 'Take a pair of sparkling eyes, If you can, Happy man'

hide & seek Heidsieck, brand of champagne
s Pretty Molly Brannigan: 'There's not a bit of all me hide the sun'll ever tan again'
K.C.: King's Counsel
Christian name

die *Sl* shoot a bishop: coit
Sl let fly: ejaculate
7th heaven
(never be severed)

luxury simply speechless with admiration *Sp* admiración: wonder, admiration

luxuriously apartments separate
L uxor: wife sybarite: a sensualist (from Sybaris, noted for luxury)

U.S. run my shoestring: make easy money

Vo famik: famous
however famished
L Juppiter Pluvius (rain dispenser) *'Jaun thinks how cold it is out in the night under the stars (assideration)'
consideration *L* sidereus: starry

***Gilbert: *Prolegomena* (continued)**

G Luftzug: draught warbling hydraulics atmosphere
lovesick
*'His cold is getting worse & thus he snuffles "morning"; Dean & his Chapter (Swift)
the Danish prefix for *departure* is *bort-*' *AngI ph* that breeze would perish the Danes
ph a chapter of accidents atramental: inky, black
detrimental
claptrap

ph cat out of the bag
Sl cackle: reveal secrets by indiscrete talk
Du leest: last *'so 'tis fiction'
satisfaction
*I-thou: either *'A sneeze is coming—*Schue*!—Germanically antithetical to "*my hat*", & he foreshortens his mendacious "I am in earnest"'
Ibis (= Thoth in *Egyptian Book of the Dead* LXXXV) *ph* talk through one's hat *G* ernst

Denis Florence MacCarthy: Ir. poet

tripos: final honours examination Thoth
the author
Thoth Chapelizod
Howth *L* focus: fireplace

'His Master's Voice' record trademark: dog listening to gramophone on ground
Thoth

Going Forth (*Egyptian Book of the Dead*)
Ms Mother Machree: '& the brow that's all furrowed'
AngI ph tune the old cow died of (bad slow music) *L* nostra
Moore: *s* O Ye Dead [Plough Tune] (.20)

profane Anna Liffey
Livius's Annals
effervescent beatific
Dean Kinane: *St Patrick*, 'Approbations' 5–6: 'our, as you so often call him, Beloved Apostle'
Pharaoh R. Ord & W. Gayer-Mackay: *Paddy-the-Next-Best-Thing* (play, 1920)
Moore: *s* O Ye Dead far off
Rameses, pharaoh best Vico Road, Dalkey
ramshackle

Peter . . . Paul
It ricorso: reflux (Viconian cycle)

beautiful task
(he is in barrel)
breath blessed be the holy name
praised

F nenni: nay!

Arch pardee: assuredly (lit. 'by God')

newly wed

anamnesis: reminiscence *Sp* abuelos: grandparents
aboulia: loss of will-power
Joshua stopped the sun
Jesu
Norwegian finish

***Gilbert: *Prolegomena* (continued)**

yore

pinafore *s* Finnegan's Wake: 'Miss Biddy Moriarty began to cry' pillow-fighting
It primavera: Spring
Biddy Moriarty: a famous D scold

s Come Back to Erin *G* Hering: herring *s* Impudent Barney O'Hea
clambake: noisy social entertainment
Sl lemoncholic: melancholic
Sl lemon: an unattractive woman
swapping

hose arse

It arricchiransi: they will become rich *Sl* have the painters in: menstruate

worse

breakfasts into Last Suppers Ceylon tea
F soupir *F* salon thé: tearoom
W.G. Wills: *Bolivar* (a play) *Gulliver's Travels* *Du* een blauwe Maandag: a very short time
groaning chair: one on which woman congratulated after successful childbirth *ph* once in a blue moon
ossicles: bones of the middle ear jaundice
John the Baptist Ole Clo: London old clothes seller described by Mayhew (*U*.424) Shep: name for devoted old sheepdog
dyspepsia Clongowes Wood College (*Portrait* I)
Ms Goodbye, Summer
G Sommer

Mistral: Provençal wind (also the poet) *G* Kinder: children vice versa
blue nose
(singer's) benefit telltale
L bene fit: it is made well J: *Tales Told of Shem & Shaun*
tongue Mary Magdalene *Heb* maggal: tickle
L tunc: then (122.23) maggots *Sl* magdalen: whore
'Once upon a time & a very good time it was' (opening *Portrait*)

AngI blatherumskite: blather, yarns *F* chaise

Sean the Post hemisphere

day glass

trimmings inside your head

L Sursum corda: lift up your hearts Heloise (& Abelard)
L omnes: all
plighted

headache

(graveyard)

(married)

HC . . . E Phoenix Elysian Fields
John Field, Irish composer, developed nocturne
Johannesburg

deck: cover *G* Diamant: diamond
Revelation (by St John)

Da Fastetiden: Lent
Du Vastentijd: Lent

upper (of shoe) Byron: 'Fare thee well! and if for ever, Still for ever fare thee well'
s O Sole Mio
G Welt: world welt (of shoe)
ring is

thrust *Ms* Goodbye, Sweetheart, Goodbye: 'For time doth thrust me from thine arms'
G Trost: consolation
(laugh)

love *I* An Posht: the Mail

Sean the Post luck

Westminster
postmaster *G* bloss: naked stentorian
I blas: taste, flavour
lie doggo: hide

deep field (cricket):
fieldsman far from wicket Johnny
rolling his hoop
prototypes midsummer madness
Du samen: together
I splaid: spark *I* spleodar: glee, joy

AngI Johnny Magorey: fruit of dog rose, haw *Gr* hagios: holy
L hic, haec, hoc; hujus, hujus, hujus; huic, huic, huic: this (m., f. & n. nominative, then genitive, then dative, as repeated in schools)
G.P.O.

hymn 'O salutaris hostia' sung at benediction of Blessed Sacrament

Gen 27:11: 'Esau . . . is a hairy man'

parlours
perilous Swift
3 alchemical elements: MERCURY

gimlet-eyes Sterne

G was ist los?: what's going on?

F il souffle: he sighs *F* il souffert: he suffers SALT
suffered *F* soufre: SULPHUR

Moore: *s* Shall the Harp Then Be Silent? beseech *s* Polly Wolly Doodle: 'Fare thee well, fare thee well'
It sorelle: sisters

versus Both Greater & Lesser Doxologies begin 'Gloria'
suburbs *L* Suburra: red-light district of Imperial Rome
Circe

Henry Woodfall: *Darby & Joan*

The Scotch House, D pub *L* 'Sanctus, Sanctus, Sanctus': 'Holy, Holy, Holy' (prayer)

'Exsultet': 'O felix culpa!' Phoenix Park stand at ease Easter

I seanad: senate *G* Pöbel: rabble Tuat: Egyptian otherworld
L Senatus populusque Romanus (Imperial Roman motto)
Sekhet hetep: Egyptian Elysian Fields

Le Fanu: *The House by the Churchyard* hurling cups Apocalypse
courtyard coupling (kissing)
Punch & Judy

Byron's poem at 454.01–2 ('if for ever') idol
begins with motto from Burns
Matt 9:17: 'new wine into old bottles' former sinner
Sl shinner: member of Sinn Féin (Ir. nationalists)
latter-day saints (Mormons) Madame Tussaud's waxworks exhibition
Saturday (suit) Toussaint L'Ouverture: a liberator of Haiti
Dail: Ir. Legislative Assembly Chamber of Horrors (at Madame Tussaud's)
Horus
Saffron cakes in *Egyptian Book of the Dead* represent 'Heaven & Earth', the god 'Shu', or 'the Eye of Horus'
sovran: Milton's spelling of 'sovereign' *AngI* bonham: sucking pig *L* bonum: good
rain *Du* Ier: Irishman *Gr* eirênê: peace
It ieri: yesterday Oliver (Cromwell)
reflection *s* Old Folks at Home
refectory
I Go mbeannuighe Dia dhuit: May God bless you *I* Go mbeannuighe Dia's Muire's Pádraig dhuit: May God &
I Go mbeannuighe Dia's Muire dhuit: May God & Mary bless you Mary & Patrick bless you

(Don) Giovanni

L post Martem: after Mars
postmortem
Macbeth V.1.19: 'Tomorrow and tomorrow and tomorrow' CHE
(quoted by Father Dolan in *Portrait* I) *L* cras: tomorrow *L* heri: yesterday
L hodie: today Paternoster
one fine day fine how-do-you-do (death)
Per sohl: peace *s* The Minstrel Boy: 'And his wild harp slung behind him'

scythe (Father Time)

Adam & Eve *Gloria Patri*: 'World without end, Amen'
God's
AngI moy: plain *s* Here We Sit Like Birds in the Wilderness
Cain mummies in crypt of St Michan's, D
Sl doorstep: thick slice of bread & butter (sentry)

Prospect Cemetery, D Abel
you're able
G neu: new
Sauvé: *Proverbes & dictons de la Basse-Bretagne*, no. 148: 'Paix!
Exod 3:14: 'I AM THAT I AM' Paix! La queue de la vache Est avec vous' (Peace! Peace! The
Heb hyam: life Hyam, B., tailor, Dame St, D tail of the cow is with you'
Humpty Dumpty *It* misero me!: poor me!
L miserrime: most wretchedly
heredity *s* Here We Are Again Gaiety Theatre, D
ph here today, gone tomorrow
afterlife Globe Theatre accidentally burned by discharge of ordnance for king, 1613
(play) W.G. Wills: *A Royal Divorce*
L mea culpa (Confiteor) Christmas pantomime (Gaiety Theatre)
It mio colpo: my shot pandemonium
(Judgement Day) Harlequin S.P.Q.R.: Senatus populusque Romanus (Imperial Roman motto)

Mark Twain time's final joke allspice
King Mark *Hamlet* II.2.257: 'I could be bounded in a nutshell & count myself king of infinite space' 'Thou shalt not . . .' (10 Commandments)

supporting HCE
paten dish

'Patum Peperium, the Gentlemen's Relish': a mixture of anchovies, butter & spices Oonagh made Cuchullain eat a cake with a griddle in it, & he lost some of his teeth great deal

pr The proof of the pudding is in the eating
natives: Eng. oysters
D Sl cup of scald: cup of hot tea *Sp* mozo: waiter
Sp santo: holy Holy Moses!

AngI ph tea so strong you could trot a mouse on it
enjoyed
It ingoiato: swallowed

bully beef
Alleluia
Cork Dial boiled protestants: boiled pigs' trotters
touch too salty
psaltery

godown: in Far East, warehouse
curry favour
Sl godown: gulp; guzzling competition
compliments

omega . . . alpha
colcannon: cabbage, potatoes, & butter cooked together (030.12–13)
L Cincinnatus: curly (hence curly cabbage)
It ci vuol poco: little is needed
Catholic
Annals of Theatre Royal, D, mention difficulty of pronouncing Italian *c*: 'their *cheese*'
Gr Good Friday Mass: 'Hagios o Theos, Hagios ischyros, Hagios athanatos', ('Holy God, Holy strong one, Holy immortal one')
(haggis made from sheep)
L quid: which
Anglican Grace: 'For what we have received . . .'
O Lord
L recipimus: we recover
F jour maigre: day Catholics abstain from meat (i.e. Friday)
too meagre
s Soldier, Soldier, Won't You Marry Me?: 'she brought him a coat of the very, very best & the soldier put it on'
F vair: fur
vairy: variegated
turncoat
ph serve a turn

'Remove these baubles!' (Cromwell ordering removal of mace on dissolution of Rump Parliament)
broadcloth
Samuel Smiles: *Huguenots in England & Ireland* 313 on Portarlington Huguenots: 'their vegetables were unmatched in Ireland'
F legumes
set my teeth on edge
F aigre-doux: bittersweet
G Blumenkohl: cauliflower

'Ite, missa est' (end of Mass)
flitch: side of hog salted & cured

vitamins

tune
chewing
hormones
harmonies
jinglejangle
steak
peas
bacon
rices

onions
duckling
cabbage
boiled protestants
Gr oinos: wine
stuffed
stuffing
Falstaff

Killadoon, Co. Sligo
Letternoosh, Co. Galway
Letterpeak, Co. Galway
II Cor 3:6: 'the letter killeth'
Lettermuck, Co. Derry
Letterananima, Co. Donegal
Castletown House, residence of William Connolly, speaker of Ir. Parliament, said to be largest private house in Ireland
understand

Judas Thaddeus: apochryphal brother of Jesus
debtor
esquire
Am. Juke & Kallikak families: hereditary degenerates

turkeys
Marshalsea Prison, D (debtors' prison)

panes
Castletown House, Co. Kildare, built for William Connolly (457.01), said to have a window for every day of the year
s Widow Machree
stamp

William Connolly: speaker of Ir. Parliament; erected D Hellfire Club in C18
plenty
2 Collopy brothers played for Ireland in a Rugby International seen by J
Collop Monday: day before Pancake Tuesday

Passion Fathers:
discalced missionary order

s The Anchor's Weighed   Hong Kong

grain   the grim reaper (Death)
grame: anger, harm

L in saecula saeculorum: for ever & ever
(*F* aux siècles des siècles)
Father Finn: *Claude Lightfoot*   devil
Claude Duval: highwayman
Dick Turpin (in *s* Turpin Hero he cuts off cape of a lawyer whose gold is stitched in the back of it)   anus
disturbing   own
Eng. sheep tally: 'yan, tyan, tethera, methera, pimp'

I dílis: dearest
G Hure: whore

refund of excise

black & blue

Sunday . . . Monday . . . Tuesday . . . Wednesday

Ms 'Drink to me only with thine eyes & I will pledge with mine'

s Tea for Two   to it   *F* toute
(003.09–10)   off
cigarettes

licks creation

I mise: me   (003.09–10)

I dearbhráthair: brother   dearest

I dubh: black   *I* Dart-shúile: heifer-eyes
(Macpherson's Darthula)
tactfully grabbed   spondee: metrical foot   *G* flüstern: whisper
whisper sweet nothings

nonsense
nun's songs
permitting
I plámás: soft talking, flattery
(she'd thought he'd never be able to stop her speaking)

L tacitum tempus: secret time   angel   engineer
(146.19–20)
throat   last

notepaper

(111.11)   *s* The Heart Bowed Down: 'mem'ry is the only friend That grief can call its own'
G Witwe: widow
widow's mite

widow
between
Rudolf Valentino
love
Linen Hall, D
heavenly benedicted papal bull Father Michael

forty days & forty nights (Christ in Wilderness, Matt 4:2; The Flood, Gen 7:17)

Achille Ratti became Pope Pius XI
It ratti: quick

fiancé
indulge my fancy
end (011.28)
evening

Galway

s Goodbye, Sweetheart, Goodbye: 'The levret bounds o'er earth's soft flooring'

Leslie Stuart: *Florodora* (operetta) 6th Station of the Cross: Veronica wipes Christ's face
speedwell, genus *Veronica*

⊢ (her sister)

Gen 1:2: '& the Spirit of God moved upon the face of the waters'
Mercy (Justice in .17) *F* merci

William Maginn: Ir. poet, died of drink do

debts

Gr pneuma: spirit, breath *F* pneu: same as *petit bleu* (.24)
U.41: '-*C'est le pigeon, Joseph*' (Leo Taxil)
(she gets it back if he dies abroad) *It* curiose (fem. pl.): curious

O.W. Holmes: *The Autocrat of the Breakfast-Table*
eitherways
A.C.W. Harmsworth, Viscount Northcliffe: Ir. newspaper magnate & founder of 'tabloid' journalism
F petit bleu: express letter transmitted by pneumatic tube in Paris

gorgeous

thingumajig
Da silkepapir: tissue paper

answer

(hair)

(414.25)

F chevelure
F bouche

U.348: 'her rosebud mouth was a genuine Cupid's bow, Greekly perfect' *G* Praxis: practice
Gr praxis: business
publicly
omega . . . alpha
oh's ah's

nr Ring-a-ring o'Roses
Rosary (divided into chaplets)
F sauve-qui-peut!: every man for himself! (lit. 'save who can') (003.09–10)
quipu: ancient Peruvian device for recording events as knots on threads
looking-glass (*Alice*)

s My Old Dutch sleepwalking

moustaches (280.23: 'Sally' painted moustaches on 'Christine' while she was asleep)

confess hessians: boots with tassels

*U.*350: 'at last she found what she wanted at Clery's summer sales'
clearance jumble sale

F sosie: double, counterpart

(166.07)

OE athel: prince

Erne St Lower, D

Exiles II: 'I longed to be betrayed . . .'

G betreuen: care for

sure

F Sl petit bonhomme: penis

Swift: 'Ppt'

unlatched garden

Wellington: 'Up, guards, & at them' my adorers obey all my orders
Sl jack: penis Atem (Tem): creator in *Egyptian Book of the Dead*
loudspeaker

Sl candle: penis
ph there's nothing can hold a candle to it

Masterthief: a category of folk tales

passionflower uncle tale

lipsticks (kisses) In Boucicault's *Arrah-na-Pogue* Arrah's foster brother escaped from prison with help of a message she passed to him in a kiss

(rugby) *pr* Love thy neighbour as thyself

patron scent

goodness gracious first murderer = Cain

Da hviske: whisper

*U.*23: '-The Ship, Buck Mulligan cried. Half twelve' *The Ship of Fools*
Ship Hotel & Tavern, Lr Abbey St, D
Mountjoy Square, D
Mountjoy Prison, D

adjust *AngI* caroline: a tall hat

talks to himself louder & louder Co. Louth
F Sem: Shem
*U.*771: 'hes always imitating everybody' Morton Prince: *The Dissociation of A Personality* (280.22) *s* Bid Me to Live
'Love' is '0' in tennis

never

s The Dargle Run Dry

G Ulme: elm
utmost
It amara: bitter
steel our hearts of stone
Gr stêlê: block of stone as stone

G Jungfrau: virgin *F* mensonge
Jung & Freud
telegraph isinglass: a form of gelatin
F morte *Cant* mort: wench
Morton Prince Cedars of Lebanon
F amour cypresses *Gr* libanos: incense (Maronites; see 470)
sycamores (in N. of England confused with plane trees) Babylonians (trees in 470.15–20)
Da ask: ash

in Bédier's account, Hertzian Waves: a class of ether waves *G* Herz: heart
Tristan sent messages carved on twigs to Isolde by dropping them into a stream which ran through her chamber
St Margaret of Hungary received stigmata

L flavus: yellowish *r* Bosphorus

flesh of my flesh *nr* Twinkle, Twinkle, Little Star

L sartor: tailor Leixlip ('salmon leap') on Liffey anon. C19 poem quoted in
L lex: law W. St John Joyce, *Neighbourhood of D*,
At age 4, salmon return to birthplace to spawn 'Howth': 'Or Leixlip smiling on the stream below'
enhanced four-in hand: month's mind: mass for a person celebrated 1 month after his death
(Dean Swift) vehicle with 4 horses driven by 1 person

Thingvellir: seat of ancient Icelandic Parliament D.B.C. (Dublin Bread Co.) *G* süsser: sweeter
Valhalla

Balfe: *The Bohemian Girl*: *Ms* Then You'll Remember Me

J born on Candlemas

(St Joseph) *F* ennui nephew (Tristan legally Isolde's)
annoyed

Emerson: *Civilization:* 'hitch your wagon to a star' *Sl* on the water wagon: teetotal

(Stella) *F* beurre *F* fesses Vanessa (Swift)
Du Barry: brand of cosmetics bury my face (two-faced) Pond's Vanishing Cream
spelling VI.A.901: 'clothes extend personality'
G um zu: in order to

limits buy (mourning if he dies)

Elvery's Elephant House, D (sold raincoats)

Hope Bros: London department store
I Cor 13:13: 'faith, hope, charity'
Honeybee copulates in flight (drone dies immediately after)

(cf. II.1) *D Annals*, 18/8/1897: Duke & Duchess of York visit D & tour Ireland
Duse: Italian actress

Phoenix

(menstruation)

Browne & Nolan/Bruno of Nola

O U T after doing little business steal home

G heimlich: secretly (boots) park
G Heim: home

general

wedding

ladylike
lilac
place

G Fenster: window *s* My Grief on the Sea: 'His breast to my bosom, His mouth to my mouth'
G Eisenbahn: railway train
iron bed

F soie *F* soi-disant Chinese (a foreign male)

mail (308.16)

Ms Then You'll Remember Me: 'When other Lips . . . ' next

eyes *It* toccato: touched
cock-a-doodle-doo cockatoo
talk childish *Ms* The Lost Chord: 'Seated one day at the organ'

going to say prayer going to bed

kiss lassie *It* lui: him *It* tu: you
Scots tassie: a small cup
F j'aime

amen sororal: sisterly

(hookah)

(hand) chalice
cherished

Eucharist use F sacré père F autel: altar
F maître d'hôtel
ladies & gentlemen postmaster brandishing
Annals of the Theatre Royal, D mention the 'brindisi from "Lucrezia Borgia"' *It* brindisi: toast
ph wine, women & song

I Éire go: Ireland until *nr* 'Friday's child is loving & giving'
L mingere: to urinate
(216.04–5) *It* staffetta: courier mulled wine
stiff drink nullified mollified
dreams of harmony Cowper: 'cup that cheers' (tea) *nr* Jack & Jill
Sl cream: semen
I deoch an dorais: parting drink *Port* estrelat: star
F Sl L'estré: cunt
Jonathan (Swift) (falling) *s* The Stirrup Cup
Inisfail (*U.*293, based on Mangan) *s* Love's Young Dream
Sl fizz: champagne *F* douce
Miss Douce (*Sirens*) J. Douce: champagne maker
Piper Heidsieck champagne *Ms* The Snowy-breasted Pearl *G* Brust: breast
s Take a Pair of Sparkling Eyes
Sl pearlies: teeth *ph* nip in the bud nibbling
ph pearls of wisdom wisdom teeth

AngI snaggletooth: gap-toothed salad bowl

goodbye gullible
lullaby
interior monologue 'David' in Hebrew means 'darling' (.30 also)
Gr monophônos: one-toned
II Sam 6:14: 'David danced before the Lord' squamous: scaly
G Kerl: man, guy squeamish

Ms Dear Old Pal of Mine
Fraction (Mass): action of breaking Eucharist Dublin
F Sl doubler: to copulate
Sl tippling: boozing unique

penumbra beyond

doubt *Ms* Il mio tesoro (from *Don Giovanni*)

Leopardstown, D, originally Leperstown, has racecourse

milestones
millstones
Il Trovatore: 'IL CONTE DI LUNA': 'Il Trovator! Io fremo!' ('the troubadour' [his rival] – 'I rage')
tremble *pr* Speak of the devil & he appears
*U.*404: 'a wolf in the stomach' *It* eccolo: here he is
pr A growing youth has a wolf in his belly
athlete

G Österreich: Austria Gaelic League

SwG Schwitz: Switzerland

canton cat o' nine tails
pr cat has 9 lives
mufti: plain clothes worn by one who has right to wear uniform *s* The Mountains of Mourne
s Home to Our Mountains (from *Il Trovatore*)
continent

L quinque: 5 *L* saeculum: century Revolution
(on bicycle)
A.D. 432: St Patrick arrives in Ireland *F* patte: paw

(right hand, cf. 463.02) birdlime

Purge (080.07)

anaglyptograph: machine making relief representations of medals & coins
L sinister: left (left hand)

3 ostrich feathers on badge of Prince of Wales as Heir Apparent
HCE
white feather denotes cowardice
Scott: *The Lay of the Last Minstrel* I.xi: 'He learn'd the art that none may name In Padua far beyond the sea'
L figura porca: sow-shape

lictor: Roman officer executing sentence of judgement
L Rector Magnificus: noble rector
It magnaffica: fig-eater
alter ego
Oxonian
ames-ace: double 1 in dice (bad luck)
L Ausonius: Italian
AngI within an aim's ace: very near
whips
noble a Roman (*Julius Caesar* V.5.73)
(Roman nose)
Jean-Jacques Rousseau
sooner eye his

whip, lashes below
Anna Liffey

G After: anus
impediment

Alfred Jarry: eccentric Fr. dramatist

catanadromous: ascending rivers to spawn
prisoner
cantankerous Cantab.
F poisson
(J wearing dark glasses)
Stanislaus Joyce

fond
God

Shakespeare, *Troilus* III.3.175: 'One touch of nature makes the whole world kin'
nannygoat
Dial twitchbell: earwig
ph through thick & thin
12 Tables of the Law
doorbells
Cain's descendants Jubal & Tubal

heresy
Hennessy brandy
'nasturtium' supposedly derived from *ph* meaning 'nose-torturing'
sinner
brain
thinker
quincunx
Gr diaspora: dispersal (Jews dispersed after Captivity)
desperation
turncoat
Cormac MacArt: Grania's father
camouflage
s Enniscorthy: 'Dimetrius O'Flanigan McCarthy'

R Rossiya: Russia
I Alba: Scotland
L alba: white
E. Hogan: *Distinguished Irishmen* (1896)

half a crown

pebble glasses: thick spectacles for myopia
Jonathan (Swift)

pr 'If "ifs" & "ands" were pots & pans . . .'
F oeufs

James Clarence Mangan died of cholera morbus
eyot: small island
Faroes

St Columba's monastic foundation on Iona
Rockabill Lighthouse off Co. D
'Columba' (Columcille) & 'Jonas' both mean 'dove'

Jonah & the Whale
s Rocked in the Cradle of the Deep
G famos: splendid
It famose (fem. pl.): famous
ph hold a candle to someone

G Postille: book of family sermons
I bréan: putrid
'Prince of triflers' (Swift)
Jonathan
cemented (059.24)
Philip the Good, Duke of Burgundy
good fellows

I abhainn: river

F monsieur

It obbligato: obliged
chums

Sl cog: to cheat by copying
copy

Vicar Rhys Pritchard: *Canwyll y Cymry* ('Candle of Welshman') *F* flamme
mermaid's barmaid's flame
I abú: to victory *G* Servus (greeting)
AngI Hy Brasil: legendary island in Atlantic Diamond sculls (rowing) at Henley

L nuntius: messenger
Pontius Pilate
G Donnerwetter! *G* kaibe, cheibe (Swiss expletive)
Khyber Pass *G* Schinken: ham
It el scapa scansa pagar: he runs away without pay(ing)
Sancho Panza
(J's eye patch)

buttonhole Lemuel Gulliver (*Gulliver's Travels*) *F* sourd: deaf
butting (goat) Shem grandsire
crusader *AngI* caubeen: old hat

Ku Klux Klan
(the girls)
It simpatico: nice
St Patrick
absentminded

hard of hearing EHC

Butter Exchange Band, D fife & drum
G Pfeife: pipe
bowlful *F* moule: mussel *s* Marseillaise *G* Junker: young
F bouillabaisse: boiled fish dish, eaten with its soup aristocrat
Sl doodle: penis *G* wanken: stagger hearing
s 'Yankee Doodle went to London, riding on a pony'
(removed it in .14) right extremity
L dextra: right hand
Claddagh: fishing settlement, Galway City. Claddagh rings display clasped hands
L frater: brother *Ms* The Wearing of the Green: 'I met with Napper Tandy & he took me by the hand'

& *It* mappamondo: geographical globe

(France) (Spain) Austria & Hungary
cock & bull story (*Tristram Shandy*) *G* Auster: oyster
G hungrig: hungry Bulls & bears: speculators on rises & falls, respectively, on Stock Exchange
(Germany) Italy looks like boot kicking ball (Sicily)
Byron: 'The Isles of Greece' (from *Don Juan*) Turkey-in-Europe

G Freischütz: freeshooter; (William Tell: Switzerland): costard: large apple (W.Tell shoots apple)
G feil: mercenary *G* Pfeil & Bogen: arrow & bow
Peter the Great (Russia)

Turgesius: Viking invader of Ireland *s* Mona, My Own Love
(Scandinavia) Jesus (the Moon) better
manner

Breastlaw: Common Law, Isle of Man (mistakenly called Mona)

landscape Lambay Island off Co. D
(postcard he sent his brother)
kidneys *G* du erfreust mich: you make me glad Basil French in Henry James' *Julia Bride*
Michael Davitt: C19 Ir. nationalist devil David

us *Sl* aunt: whore
(Isolde legally Tristan's aunt)

Henry James: *Julia Bride*

delta *Sl* dell: whore recognise
triangle
nr 'Little Jack Horner, Sat in the corner, Eating a Xmas pie' *ph* box his corner: stand up for himself
F Sl jacquot: penis *Sl* box; corner: cunt
brides penis *L* servorum: of servants
penal servitude
drawers *Sl* spinster: whore
sinister
G scheu: shy (pron. 'shoy') *G* Weih: kite (bird) why?
L vir: man
G Weib: woman shamrock womb room
letter, 8/8/28, to HSW: '"Weih? – Up the Shameraugh!" Weihrauch is German for incense'
both of us *r* Bosphorus
AngI smallclothes: knee breeches
enjoy yourselves thoroughly *G* bis: until *G* Biss: bite
L thuris: incense

eyes
frankincense
semiology: branch of pathology concerned with symptoms
Gr idos: incense Ido: an artificial language holly & ivy
I does be asking
(mistletoe–*The Golden Bough*) love tripartite

Charles Reade: *The Lyons Mail*, given at Theatre Royal, D, 1877

Dion Boucicault: *The Corsican Brothers*
Hungry Hill, Co. Cork; *I* name means 'Angry Hill'
Roundhead Byron's relationship with his sister

Shinner: Sinn Féin member *L* tertium quid: a third something

Sl wrinkles: cunning tricks
snakecharmer snail charm: divination of lover's name by initial formed by slug's track

Conte di Luna: brother & rival of hero of *Il Trovatore*

congregation

Da læber: lips
liberally
bilabial: formed by 2 lips

Midas touch
mistletoe
pr The early bird catches the worm woman

hem Little Tich: Eng. music hall comedian
tie
Eccles 9:11: 'The race is not to the swift, nor the battle to the strong'
AngI rossy: impudent girl
unkind (blood brothers)
I Sinn Féin: Ourselves Alone (slogan) kith & kin
I inis: island Ophelia Popish Plot 1678 York & Lancaster (Wars of Roses)
Co. Offaly
Finn . . . Mac . . . Cool (backwards)
I muc: pig Mookse
no matter creature *s* 'Mid pleasures & palaces There's no place like home'
preacher
(152.15) Proust: *Swann's Way*
OE swan's way: sea
time Lady of the Lake gave Arthur Excalibur (in Malory)

Babau: Languedoc bogy to terrify children *Gr* to pan: the all
It babbo: daddy
s Follow Me Up to Carlow

fuck
C fu-chu: to aid
(211.15)

love potion (drunk by Tristan & Isolde) R. Ord & W. Gayer-Mackay: *Paddy-the-Next-Best-Thing* (play, 1920)
L leo (lion, king of beasts)

top full
hopeful
poetry declaring

Manufactured in Europe
Misch-Masch: magazine written by Lewis Carroll when young
Jack the Ripper

Hero & Leander

stave (music)
Jubal Cain: ancestor of those who use harps & organs starveling
jew's harp Wyndham Lewis compared J's style with that of Jingle in *Pickwick Papers*
It rota: wheel *s* Rhoda & Her Pagoda *It* con dio in capo ed il diavolo in coda: with God at the head & the devil at the tail
Cz divá děvucha: mad girl *SC* dobar dan: good day

R.L. Stevenson: *Memories & Portraits* IV: 'I played the sedulous ape' Synge
R pogoda: weather Rota: supreme court of R.C. Church *F* singe: ape
grant *G* verboten: forbidden

I deas: nice *I* deoch an dorais: parting drink
F langue d'oil: dialect of Northern France
s The Death of Nelson coloratura: florid ornaments in vocal music sing
It (Triestine) coraio, fra: courage (i.e. cheer up), brother
(play second fiddle) *s* My Love & Cottage near Rochelle

Fra Diavolo: Italian brigand (also title of opera about him, by Auber)
It diavolo: the deuce!
mashed

Gilbert & Sullivan: *Trial by Jury* *G* wie geht es Ihnen heute, mein dunkler Herr?: how are you today, my dark sir?
G Holmgang: duel to the death
postmaster *F* acheve!: finish!

L taurus periculosus: dangerous bull
L morbus pedeiculosus: lousy disease
L miserere mei in miserabilibus: pity me in my wretchednesses awful *Da* lav: low
It uva: grapes
(translates) *Sl* mob: whore

H.G. Wells: *The Misery of Boots* (pamphlet, 1907) *ph* do you see any green in my eye?: do you take me for a fool?
Moore: *Ms* The Meeting of the Waters: 'valley so sweet' (*r* Avoca, Co. Wicklow) *G* stöhnen: groan
Ireland's Eye: small island nr Howth sings out of tune
kernel (stone)

bite *L* de miserabilibus: concerning the pitiable

leaking may
Lakes of Killarney known as 'Heaven's Reflection' reflex action
'Thy will be done' (Lord's Prayer)

I arís: again interpreter embrace

Arch buss: to kiss flood kissing *G* bissen: to bite

(doomsday) Tristan worried
word
octave
Octavius: hero of *Don Giovanni*
rattlesnake

AngI twig: understand L/R
G Scham: shame shamrock
national emblem *I* arís: again

G scheu: shy (pron. 'shoy') *I* athair: father *G* Onkel: uncle

(used to speak foreign tongue briskly before Tower of Babel fell, & language was confounded) uncle's
AngI bothered: deaf
stone deaf
Sitric Silkenbeard led Danes at ⚔Clontarf, 1014
old fellow Stoneybatter: street, D
Mutt & Jeff
cough up mutton chops
Babel
Balbus: Roman who tried to build a wall in Gaul (name means 'stammering')
lobscouse: salt beef & biscuits (eaten at sea)
cg blind man's buff *Sl* work the oracle: raise money

It diario: diary (185.14–26)
diarrhoea

Riviera

Berlitz schools in Trieste & Pola employed J Holy Ghost
I Beurla: English
reputation Charlie Chaplin Holy Ghost
jactitation: false claim to be married to another cutting chapel (444.32–3)
F gauche learns quickly forgets quickly *F* Allemagne
G alle: all
Da huske: remember Earwicker
Da mand: man
oracles *F* parle Persse O'Reilly Ulster, Munster, Leinster & Connaught
L auricula: outer ear
It quadra: square *L* centum: 100 Trinity College, Cambridge (also D)
Quadrangle, Christ Church College, Oxford (057.24) 432 A.D.: St Patrick arrives in Ir.
It canta: he sings *Sl* chipper: lively oxen moo met tiptop
Cantab, Oxon = Cambridge, Oxford
Priscius Lucius Tarquineus: 5th legendary king of Rome Ireland's Eye: island near Howth
pretty no man better
mimographer: writer of mimes Numa Pompilius: 2nd legendary king of Rome
mimeograph p.p.: pro parte (to the Ancus Martius: 4th legendary king of Rome, a bridge builder encomiums
best of one's ability); pianissimo; past participle (.25) *AngI* Andrew Martin: prank
Roman Roads Paul Aler: *Gradus ad Parnassum* ('Steps to Parnassus'): a textbook of Latin prosody (1680)
Rhea Silva: mother of Romulus & Remus Tarquineus Superbus: 7th legendary king of Rome
Romulus ormolu: gilded metal ware
Servius Tullius & Tullus Hostilius: 6th & 3rd legendary kings of
Rome, respectively

(467.36) *L* recitanda: things worth reading aloud
(stammer) ff: fortissimo
Coll varsity: university
Fukien: province, China piano? forte? *I* bráthair: brother in religion
Gr Sebastos: Augustus *It* Cesare: Caesar
Antony & Cleopatra I.5.86: 'My salad days'
'Au commencement était le Geste'—Udine: *L'art & le geste*, quoted by Marcel Jousse
John 1:1: 'In the beginning was the Word' justly
Word made Flesh (John 1:14)
The 'organ' of *Penelope* in J's table is 'flesh'

F verge: penis *G* taufen: baptise tautological
F verbe: word
singular (might have been) Matt 16:18: thou . . . art . . . Peter
Flournoy (1900) calls the medium Helen Smith 'onomatopoioi' Paul
(3 alternative objects for sentence) onomatopoeic holly & ivy
on a matter poetic
Kennedy: *Latin Primer*: 'Many nouns in *is* we find to the Masculine assigned: amnis, axis, caulis, collis . . . &c'
L amnis: river *L* axis: axle *L* collis: hill *L* sodalis: comrade

snoods nicknames furbelows: flounces on petticoats
moods *F* nœuds: knots
farthingale: arrangement of hoops to support petticoat

pr Seeing is believing *Gr* daktylizô: to finger
point blank
English mnemonic from a Latin schoolbook: 'For *nemo* let me never say *neminis* or *nemine*'

s Ecco ridente in cielo (final scene from *The Barber of Seville*)
It sipario: curtain in theatre
thunder & lightning (naked) microcosm
Nick & Mick
light
ph 'Positively last appearance on any stage' alarm clocks
witchcraft
(they put his watch ahead to stop him)
earphone seamless
mistletoe itching mizzle: run off, disappear suddenly
mitch: play truant
starve Moore: *s* One Bumper at Parting *ph* the more the merrier Moore's Melodies
Moore: *s* Farewell, but Whenever You Welcome the Hour
L tempus fugit: time flees *I* fiacal: tooth, teeth 'Grand Old Man': Gladstone
fiacre: hackney coach *It* fiaccole: torches
monarch *G* Hode: testicle *Arch* tway: 2
man of ark (releasing birds) hoodie: hooded crow
newlaid friar mew: place Carthage-bound
mule let free where hawks kept corsage
beargrease sour puss Androcles removed thorn from
lion's paw & was subsequently not eaten by lion
Daniel in the lion's den
Daniel O'Connell
I a stór: my precious
the Azores, Atlantic islands
I a cháirde: friends (vocative) sister
Sl chorine: chorus girl *F Sl* hourière: whore George Borrow, *Lavengro*: 'There's the wind on the heath,
s The Peeler & the Goat: 'Bansha peelers' *G* Haar: hair Dion Boucicault: *The Octoroon* heaving brother'
houri: nymph of the Mohammedan paradise *Triestine* orco: ogre

A parody of 'The Girl I Left behind Me' includes: 'But when moonlight flits between her tits, Jesus Christ, Almighty!'
F minuit *I* muin: desire
L lux in tenebris: light in darkness

'Adam' means 'man' or 'earth, loam' (earth, fire, air, water)

s The West's Awake 7 hills of Rome

I Banba: Ireland (poetic)

staffette: mounted courier
It staffe: stirrups
(467.01–3)

(Buck Whaley's bet to play handball against the Wailing Wall in Jerusalem) (Mohammed's night journey to Jerusalem on winged horse)
Jehu: name for furious coachman
(hoofbeats) course is courser (horse) *Ms* I'll travel the wide world over
Henry van Dyke: 'It's America for me' (a poem)
Vinland: part of N. America discovered by Norse c. A.D. 1000
Jean-Jacques *G* nett: nice
be-japers!

holy
G Mutter *r* Sereth *r* Maritza
r Olt *r* Altamaha
I Fionn-Gall: Fair Foreigner, i.e. Norwegian

(Aphrodite)

Hazel Ridge: trans. of Drom-Choll-Coil, old name of D all aboard, fuck you
L Ierne: Ireland *L* vale: farewell
Venetian ceremony of Doge wedding Adriatic Sea (013.26)

Macbeth V.8.40–1: 'Lay on, Macduff, & damn'd be him who first cries hold' *G* alt
(macadamised road) *G* danken: thank
I linn dubh: black pool *Angl* lood: ashamed *s* Sweet Innisfallen, fare thee well
It solo: alone *It* solone: mock aug. of solo *I* Rineanna: *r* Shannon

Da søskende: brothers & sisters
L nunc: now *G* nimmer: never Wyndham Lewis: *The Enemy* (1926–7) Benedict composed *The Lily of Killarney*
G süsse Kinder: sweet children how goes the enemy?: what is the time?
The Mass: Last Blessing: 'Benedicat vos omnipotens Deus' ('Almighty God bless you') West

F roman: novel

Kerry boys *s* 'Just before the battle, mother, I am thinking most of you'
cows brother
Da fik: got one two *G* Drei
fuck you!
ph watch my smoke!: see me go quickly!

Shaun the Post wireless fearless postlude: concluding piece at end of oratorio &c.
seven heavens twentyeight & one *L* ludius: actor

Du bijstand: assistance

(430.24) kid gloves

L biga: 2-horse chariot *L* rhaeda: travelling carriage (4-wheeled)
L triga: 3-horse chariot
char-à-banc sitting there

Sp asno: donkey *Sp* no es nada: it's nothing Hermes Psychopompos prods dead along with staff

letter, 8/8/28, to HSW: 'The Maronite [R.C.] liturgy, the language of which is Syrian is at the back of it. On Good Friday the body of Jesus is unscrewed from the cross, placed in a sheet & carried to the sepulchre while girls dressed in white throw flowers at it & a great deal of incense is used. The Maronite ritual is used in Mount Lebanon. Λb departs like Osiris the body of the young god being pelted & incensed. He is seen already as a Yesterday. . . . The choir of girls splits in two = those who pronounce Oahsis & those who pronounce Oeyesis (cf Our Father who/which art etc). The Latin is "Quasi cedrus exaltata sum in Lebanon etc" see A.P.O.T.A.A.A.Y.M. Belvedere College chapter. There are in all 29 words in the threnody 6 × 4 = 24 & the final 5 = 29'

pr February fill dyke, Be it black or be it white

Midnight Sun Peep of Day Boys: Ir. Protestant group, 1784–95 solace in darkness

'heliotrope' orig. meant sunflower & similar plants *I* píopa: pipe *L* sol: sun *I* solas: light *I* dorcha: dark

polylogy: loquacity

polylogue: broadcaster

F Aujourd'hui *G* Weh: woe Osiris Syrian *G* Gestern: yesterday

desirously

Du loflied: hymn tomorrow's

Maronites

It esaltare: to exalt Le Fanu

Vulg Ecclus 24:17–19: 'Quasi cedrus exaltata sum in Libano et quasi cypressus in monte Sion. Quasi palma exaltata sum in Cades et quasi plantatio rosae in Jericho. Quasi oliva speciosa in campis et quasi plantanus exaltata sum juxta aquam in plateis' ('I was like a cedar exalted in Libanus & like a cypress on Mount Zion. I was as a palm-tree exalted in Cades & like the transplanting of a rose in Jericho. Like a splendid olive in the fields & like a plane-tree beside the water in the open spaces I was exalted') (part of lesson read at Assumption of BVM, 15 Aug)

Swift: 'Ppt'

Sl hop off: depart

G Weiner: one who cries; Viennese

(Shaun the Post)

It agnello: lamb

It agnolo: angel

Dean Kinane, *St Patrick*, preface: 'irrepressible piety'

G Tippmamsell:(joc.) lady typist topsy turvy

It manzelle: young cows

John Jameson Ir. whiskey *Sp* hastaluego: so long

bars

s Hands across the Sea

letter, 8/8/28, to HSW: 'This leapyear chorus is repeated lower down in imitation of the Maronite & Latin 'pax'. The girls do nothing really but turn one to another, exclaiming one another's name joyfully'

arms pact widdershins: in contrary direction *G* Friede: peace

G Auf Wiedersehen *Sw* frid: peace

OF pais: peace *Gr* eirênê: peace *Ma* berdamai: make peace *I* sos: peace
Port paz: peace
Hu béke: peace *Ar* khaghaghout'iun: peace *Volof (Senegal)* dama: peace

Li taika: peace
I socair: at peace
R mir: peace *Rut* myr: peace
N. Bre peoc'h: peace *C* ho-p'ing: peace
S. Bre peuc'h: peace
Heb šalom: peace *Ben* sainta: peace *Hin* salāmtī: peace (public tranquillity)

G wider-: mutual
self-righteous
G wieder-: again

Stella & Vanessa (Swift)

Star & Garter (pub name)

(032.34) 'to the off' (cricket)

Naut easting: easterly direction
blessing his stars
Esther (name of both Stella & Vanessa) Southern Cross (constellation) J wore a Borsalino hat
sisters

reward for finder

(green edge) Wyndham Lewis: *Blast*
trover (Law): act of finding & obtaining possession of any personal property Jean-Jacques Rousseau megalomaniac
Mecca
Kincora, where Brian Boru lived Dean Kinane: *St Patrick* 201: 'With an easy rush he planted the cross'
Gr stadion: a measure of distance (606.75 ft)

herm: 4-cornered pillar surmounted by head or bust, usually of Hermes
harm
aqueduct

F mère *Da* far: father *G* fahren: to travel Russian
ph so near and yet so far
garron: small Ir. or Scottish horse

Shanks' mare: one's own legs *G* Windhund: greyhound
Wyndham Lewis

I buachaill: boy

jambo: 'rose-apple' & related species
F jambes
sheriff's

packetship

s Though Lost to Sight, to Memory Dear *L* statumen: support of a floor

(530.22) Brynjolf Bjarme: pen name used by Ibsen *F* la garde auxiliaire
Bjørnstjerne Bjørnson: Ibsen's rival (name means 'son of bear')
Angelical Salutation: 'Hail Mary, full of grace' St Ursula (& her 11,000 virgins)
G heilige Ursula: St Ursula *L* ursus: bear
goodbye

Da Hvor meget har vi knibet tilbage? At ændre kurs og da farvel: How much have we held back? To change course & so goodbye
Bagnal Harvey: United Irishman

Dial whethen: why then *AngI* good people: fairies H . . . E . . . C

Guinness Export Stout

s The Meeting of the Waters: 'Sweet vale of Avoca'

(baby in cot)

barrel-shaped pulpit *AngI* bawn: white
bonny
AngI whiteheaded boy: a favourite

mind your P's & Q's: remember to say 'Please' & 'Thank you' *I* Dún Bláirne: Blarney Castle
Celtic P/Q split Lisdoonvarna, village, Co. Clare
Ms 'The Groves of Blarney They look so charming . . . By the sweet rock close'

It Dial ciesa: church theorbo: a kind of large lute
Caesarea

Ambassador
I a Sheáinín: Johnny (vocative)

s Doran's Ass: 'says he, what use my walking quicker, Sure I know she'll meet me on the way'

s A Long Farewell (J's trial song at Feis Ceoil, 1904): 'A long farewell I send to thee Fair Maigue of corn & fruit & tree . . . my grief, my ruin!'

C. Pi joss = *Heb* El = God, Jehovah, Jove Krishnamurti: Indian sage of early C20
Giovanni Krishna Christ
(his lamp)

(he grows younger through book III)

s While Shepherds Watched their Flocks by Night: 'tidings of great joy' late letter box *pr* It's never too late to mend mansuetude: gentleness
St Mansuetus: C1 Ir. missionary to Lorraine
victorious

ph true as a die sleepwalker

Gi petul-engro: horseshoe-maker, smith, tinker; the name of a gypsy tribe
Gr lampadephoros: 'torch-bearer' *Gi* Romany chal: Gypsy lad
Lake Lucerne (placename derived from *L* lux)

Lake Lucerne = Lake of Four Cantons

patron saint
pattern: in Ireland, a patron saint's day

individuals

L decennia: decades
December

G Silvester: New Year's (St Sylvester's feast day is 31 December)
Whimsical Walker: clown *L* murmuranda: things worth muttering

s When Johnny Comes Marching Home

a vacuum

s Let Erin Remember the Days of Old: 'When Malachy wore the'
Carthaginians sacrificed children to Moloch
DeValera

postmark December straight from
Henry Woodfall: Darby & Joan Ember Days
24 June: feast day of John the Baptist
George R. Sims: *The Dandy Fifth*
dread

8 furlongs = 1 mile

phoenix (Arabian bird) Erebus, son of Chaos, begot Aether, Night & Day on his
Phoenix Park sister
mother Bennu: phoenix (*Egyptian Book of the Dead*) *F* va te faire foutre!
Bre va paotr: my son
Phoenix Park

s Stride la vampa (from *Il Trovatore*), lit. 'the blaze crackles'

'Work in Progress': J's name for FW during composition
s The West's Awake

John 12:35: 'Walk whilst you have the light, that the darkness overtake you not'
John 9:4: 'I must work the works of him that sent me, while it is day: the night cometh, when no man can work'
beast fall fast asleep

[When possible in 477–501 & 519–28, the identity of the members of ✕ speaking are indicated at the beginnings of their speeches. *MW*: Matthew Gregory (Ulster); *MK*: Mark Lyons (Munster); *LU*: Luke Tarpey (Leinster); *JO*: Johnny MacDougal (Connacht). Also *Y*: Yawn]

mid(dle) *ba* or 'heart-soul' in *Egyptian Book of the Dead* landscape

G Brieftasche: wallet

(lit. letter bag) harmless

cause . . . effect paralogism: false reasoning of which reasoner is unconscious

polylogy: much speaking, loquacity

Lucan fillet: headband

L lucens: shining

bedazzled (death)

(pub closing time)

out *G* ebenso: alike

litchi (fruit) *Sl* chow-chow: food

Du zoetheid: sweetness

supposed

pointblank (sticking pin in hypnotic subject (buttocks)

to test depth of trance)

Moore: *The Loves of the Angels* (the wail, .01)

Charge of the Light Brigade

VI.B.10.102: 'buzzer (fire alarm)'

s Keep the Home Fires Burning

(The Magi)

(card suits) points

Dial crowner: coroner

Hill of Uisneach, nr *r* Brosna, junction of the 4 provinces, was regarded as the centre of Ireland,

site of convention each Bealtaine (their feet)

'senator' der. from *L* senex, old man *Scots* skreigh of day: daybreak

faint

ph making a mountain out of a molehill

dews just fear *Gr* phobos: fear

G Furcht: fear *I* eagla: fear *It* paura (child's pronunciation = palula): fear
J ji (shi): death *Assyrian* (C8–5 B.C.) UR.IDIM: 'The Mad Dog' (constellation crossword puzzle
equivalent to Lupus the wolf)
(not counting)

ell: 45 inches

Ireland anciently divided into 'Conn's half' & 'Owen's half', the latter appertaining to Eoghan Mór Mogh-Nuadhat, who divided Munster amongst his 5 sons
Ireland was divided in 5 provinces at one stage; now there are 4

spancel: rope or fetter for hobbling horses &c.

F foule: crowd *s* Daffydowndilly

Narcissus
narcosis: insensibility
potatoes: 'Epicure', 'Aran Chief'

(meteor, nebula, shooting star, comet, asteroid, star chamber)

seedless (skin)

L nebulosus: cloudy (018.28–9)

melanite: a black variety of andradite (garnet)
Phosphor: the planet Venus before sunrise

clomb: climbed Court of Star-chamber in England in C15–16

enquiry quarry

everyman embodiment bodement: presentiment

everyone nation midnight
every woman poems by Browning: 'Any Wife to Any Husband' & 'Meeting at Night, Parting at Morning'
I Eiscir Riada: E.–W. ridge of sandhills ('eskers') Uisneach is nr Mullingar
separating 'Conn's half' & 'Owen's half'
sun's rest *G* klettert: climbs *I* seanadóir: senator

Partition of N. Ireland & Ir. Republic

(St Luke traditionally a doctor)

L caper: goat sheep
paperchase: children's game of 'hare & hounds' using paper scraps as trail
(aniseed used to lay trails for hounds)

Sl legless: drunk

(legs)

AngI ph Paul of Damascus *I* cos dheas, cos clé: right foot, left foot
within the bawl of an ass: too near Verdi: *Ballo in Maschera* (*The Masked Ball*) *G* Kuss: kiss
Es kapr: goat cabbages

s 'Tis the Harp in the Air

Sp diana: reveille

s Dinah, Won't You Blow Your Horn

nr Where Are You Going, My Pretty Maid: 'My face is my fortune, sir, she said'

Per bulbul: nightingale

It proto: foreman

Da bedstefar: godfather

Arch gossip: godfather

Hill of Uisneach (474.20)

I asnach (in placenames): ploughed, ribbed

protended: stretched forth

Mesmer believed that a subtle fluid permitted mutual influence between heavenly & living bodies

(hand of hypnotist [mesmerist])

Sl bucko: swashbuckler

leeside

making obeisance

Prospect Cemetery, D (Glasnevin)

wideawake: soft felt hat with wide brim

firm

prisoner

G Fallen: traps

Insifail: Ireland (poetic)

L quattuor: 4

U.S. Coll stenog: stenographer

solon: sage (from the Greek legislator) (384.01)

sophomore (now U.S.): 2nd-year student

Gr psychomôros: soul-fool

hearts, diamonds, spades & clubs

Patrick

(the donkey)

odd trick: in whist or bridge, one taken after making one's book

AngI forenenst: opposite

(opium)

dear reader

believe

be deaf

Oscar Wilde (trial resulted from Marquis of Queensbury's accusation that he was 'posing' as a sodomite)

satrap: subordinate ruler

Lord Lucan (Crimean War)

L lumen: light

Angel is emblem of St Matthew

Lion is emblem of St Mark

Calf is emblem of St Luke

s The Girl I Left Behind Me

I na h-asailín: of the little asses

ensorcelled: bewitched

encircled

Matthew, Mark, Luke, John

It mammalucco: simpleton

L cubiculum: bedchamber

geography

F chercher

Dial curchy-curchy: to curtsey

Gr pneuma: breath

tetrahedral: 4-sided

Annals of the Four Masters

MW VI.B.10.29: 'He is giving (dying)'

MK *I* a Dhia ara: O God well! (interj.)

Du dat: that

LU *AngI* wisha: well, indeed (interj.) *I* a leanbh: my child

JO Ned of the Hill: Eamonn an Chnuic, C17 outlaw

MW

MK

LU (either he's boosed or he's practicing role of a corpse)

JO *AngI* whist!: silence

(4 people: 8 feet)

Gr chrôma: colour seiner: fisherman using seine net

(childhood) (Viconian cycle)

(marriage) *Sl* chirpy: lively

auspices

(death, i.e. Our Lady's Hospice for the Dying, Harold's Cross, D)

(rebirth)

gentle listener

attentive

quadrilateral

L quadrilibris: weighing 4 pounds

retractable Nansen: Arctic explorer

(FRANKINCENSE in thurible) mystagogue: teacher of mystical doctrine

terrible

puisne (legally applied to a junior judge) (cross on donkey's back)

L cauda: tail

L ex libris: from the books of The Sleeping Beauty (fairy tale)

(rose to take bait)

Max Planck (quantum theory)

plankton

GOLD

Gr chrôma: colour Spanish gold (from wrecked Armada off W. coast of Ir.)

Gr triphthongos: 3-vowel sound

MYRRH

Sl meld: merge Mellifont Lane, D (became Lower Sackville St)

melting (taking bait) Mellifont Abbey, Co. Meath

why?

Yawn?

Y

Moore: *s* How Sweet the Answer Echo Makes

MK *It* ecco: behold

MW (Ulster pron. of 'you')

Y (110.27)

MK

Y thousands Swift: 'Ppt'

MK

Y

MK home

dubious matter
Gr deuteros: second
G Hanner: Johann G Esel: donkey
Rev 13:18: 'the number of the beast . . . is Six hundred threescore & six' L asellus: donkey
ragworts Malherbe: Fr. critic, thought rhymes should be alternately male & female
G Wort: word magi's
one word . . . another reason
G Wald: forest G Wand: wall
you have vale of tears
Sp ya: already, now Sp hace: you have
volumes vellums taught a lot Tallaght, S.W. of D, supposed site of mass burial of Parthalonian colonists, killed by plague
L vallum: rampart Aengus the Culdee: *Martyrology of Tallaght*
Rhaetian Road: chief ancient road across Swiss Alps Tarquentine
L rhaeda: travelling carriage
Aurelian Gate, Rome Sunken Road ('Hohle Gasse') where William Tell waited for tyrant Gessler
L Eleusinia Via: Sacred Way at Eleusis (mysteries) grassgrown
Giant's Causeway, Northern Ir. L via crucis Great Trek (1836–40): Boer migration from Cape Colony
gangplank Copenhagen L unde derivatur: whence [it] is derived

It casamatta: casement, vault L [quo] magis enarratur [eo] minus hoc intellego: the more completely it is explained the less I understand this
F monsieur

Y F comment? c'est mal prononçable It tartagliano: they stutter Sp Francés: Fr. language
(.12) (St Patrick originally from France)
F vous n'avez pas d'eau dans votre bouche provinciale, monsieur: you have no water in your provincial mouth, sir F Boche: German F Provençale 'moosoo' Provence pron. of 'monsieur'
F je m'incline, mais moi, j'ai trouvé la clef dans les champs: I acquiesce, but me, I've found the key in the fields
AngI moy: plain G Klee: clover F avoir la clef des champes: be free to go anywhere
F et çà n'a pas de valure, comment: & that has no value, how
F velours: velvet
MW who's that F dans
F tête: head
F jambes

clever truce trifling (Swift) who are you? (Ulster pron.)
clover & shamrock are trefoils (Patrick & Trinity)
Y Jonathan Swift, Tristan, Patrick F Dieu-donné: God-given; (*Coll*) of uncertain parentage

dactylo (typewriter, cf. .03)

AngI are you in your: are you a . . .

Y God in 3 persons
Tripartite Life of St Patrick
so cold sold
G hold: handsome
MW ultramontane: beyond the mountains; favouring pope's supremacy hound
doraphobia: dread of touching skin or fur of animal Sp primavera: spring

Y Patrick heard 'the voice of those who were near the Wood of Foclut'; caused his return to Ireland Miss Sp mis padres: my ancestors
JO wait grey-lag: common European wild goose (so-called because migrates late)
AngI whist!: silence

I Tir na nÓg: Land of the Young *s* My Little Grey Home in the West

s Follow Me up to Carlow

Poldoody: oyster-producing pool, Co. Clare

Conway, town, Wales

zone of the Zephyrs Sephiroth: 10 emanations of Ain-Soph in Kabbalistic lore

dragoman: interpreter, in Arabic, Persian & Turkish-speaking countries
015.34: 'dragon man' the ass with unpronounceable tail

Y *Du* dood: death, dead Wood of Foclut (Co. Mayo) (478.34)
indeed & I do
Parnell: 'Do not throw me to the wolves'
twelve O

LU *Sp* turca fiera: fierce Turkish woman

I blas: accent in speech
MK
C lin: trees
blather
dunlin & turnstone: wading birds common on Bull Island

advocate

L Auster: the South Wind
G Auster: oyster
Blue Lagoon: projected marina, Dollymount, D

U.142: *'a moment since by my learned friend'*

(The Four Masters derive 'Tallaght' from *I* for 'plague-grave', hence link with Parthalonian burial place)
Vikings commonly interred dead bodies in boats
It battello: boat
'The Boat of Millions of Years' in Egyptian myth transported sun-god & souls of blessed overnight

jackstaff: staff on which the Jack is hoisted

Pourquoi Pas, Antarctic exploration vessel, 1908–10, used by Charcot, Fr. explorer
s Know'st Thou the Land (translation of Goethe's 'Kennst du das Land')
barquentine: small barque
F pourquoi pas: why not
G weisst du was?: you know what? *Annals of the Four Masters*
Webster: *The White Devil:* 'My soul like a ship in a black storm Driven I know not whither'
Webster's Dictionary
boat howe (= boat barrow)

Egyptian Book of the Dead CXXX: 'thou shalt paint a Sektet boat upon the right side and an Ātet boat upon the left'
Hennu: Osiris. In *Egyptian Book of the Dead* the 'Hennu boat' was placed upon its sledge & drawn around the sanctuary at dawn, probably in imitation of sun's course *G* Ablaut aloud
G besuchen: visit ruins
Y (079.25) (018.06–07)
(sickbed, funeral, grave, dungheap)
Long Worm: a Viking ship belonging to Olaf Tryggvason
long urn: type of passage-grave all men
L nauta: sailor S.O.S. *G* warum nicht: why not

s Connais-tu le pays? *Da* Norsker: Norwegian Pirate boats of D Danes had raven flags
Raven Banner, A.D. 878: Ubba defeated by men of Devon
Da Gud, jordens skaber: God, creator of the Earth
(I believe in God) *Da* Guds barnet: God's child
(Holy Ghost) *s* Johnny Come Down from Hilo: 'wake that girl with the blue dress on'
The Three Jolly Pigeons: inn in *The Deserted Village*
temptress Jack London: *The Sea Wolf* *I* faolchú: 'wild hound', wolf
Tantris: name used by Tristan on arrival in Ireland
Patrick left Ireland on a ship carrying Ir. wolfhounds
MK
horse's
permitting
Green Hills: area near Tallaght, Co. D Henry Ireton: Cromwell's 2nd-in-command in Ir.
bona fide heel tappers midden
F midi: noon
levantine: Eastern (of rising sun) ponent: Western (of setting sun) *s* 'In Amsterdam there lived a maid, Mark well what I do say'
oxeyed: epithet of Hera, wife of Zeus
Y *Da* korset: cross perfidious
welsher: one who decamps without paying
Patrick refers to primitive adoption ceremony of sucking male paps: refused to submit to it EHC
L ecce: behold *Gr* hagios: holy
Chrism: consecrated oil used in baptism
JO Jeyes' Fluid: disinfectant
HCE uncle naval manure
hootch: illicit liquor *G* Enkel: grandson
MW *s* Bill Bailey, Won't You Please Come Home? Bailey light on Howth (Ulster pron. of 'who')
Hep: Apis, sacred bull of Memphis Old Bailey court, London
bubs (215.27)
Y HCE *L* avunculus: uncle *s* It's Your Last Trip, Titanic, Fare You Well
G Held: hero
Emania: ancient capital of N. Ireland
LU
AngI acushla: my pulse (endearment) *G Reinecke Fuchs: Reynard the Fox* (poem by Goethe)
wryneck: person with crooked neck
MK best circles Grimbert: badger in the Reynard cycle
circus
G Panzerkreuzer: armoured cruiser
HCE
Cuwart: hare in the Reynard cycle *F* couard: coward
Lyceum: gymnasium where Aristotle taught, named for Apollo Lyceus ('wolf-like')
(Romulus & Remus, also various Ir. saints, suckled by wolves)
cub scouts in Britain: 'DYB': do your best *Da* dyb: deep
It volpe: fox *G* Dieb!: thief!
Y *Heb* dobh: bear boots Curtois: hound in Reynard cycle
cub scouts in Britain: 'DOB DOB DOB': we'll do our best
Heb zeebh: wolf *SC* vuk: wolf
saints & gospels *Du* janken: howl
F goupil: fox
Fingal Harriers: an Ir. hunt hold Animal gangs: D hoodlums in 1930s drawn from men who tended cattle on cross-channel boats
L lupus: wolf
lupus: formerly, cutaneous T.B. caught by people milking infected cows
Wolfgang von Goethe: *Reinecke Fuchs*

Y H
C
E ricorso (Vico) changeling: child left by fairies in place of real child

N eld: (old) age
ithyphallic: composed in the metre of the Bacchic hymns (the trochaic dimeter brachycatalectic)
MW cataleptic: rigid & insensible myth Mass of Immaculate Conception, 8 Dec: 'Tota pulchra es' ('Thou art all
catalectic: of verse, wanting a syllable in last foot totem-pole *L* totum fulcrum est: all is a bed-post loveliness')
s Dies Irae Eire In 1098 William II obtained from Oxmantown the wood for
you had the roof of Westminster Hall 'where no English spider webbeth or breedeth to this day'
L Anno Mundi: year of the world boats Before Christ (B.C.)
(used by old annalists) Ship St, D (name derived from 'Sheep St')
Y Onan

fulfilled

G Sintflut: the Flood *It* fia: be it done
Blake: 'Ah! Sun-flower' (poem) *G* befürchten: to fear that . . .
MK tristich: group of 3 lines of verse
Tristan
Sp fui: I was

coming down abstract
common noun
Ossian was son of Finn *I* claidheamh (pron. clív): sword
Arch yclept: called
vulcanised Dublin town

lava London Underground
Morningside Heights, N.Y.C. subway station
L ad horam: on time Romulus & Remus

to, for or by, with or from: meanings of *L* termination -abus
G ob: whether pope's address: 'Urbi et Orbi' ('To the City & the World')
L ob: for *G* brauchbar: useful Abraham & Sarah *Sp* sierra: mountain
Edmund Brauchbar: a friend of J Apabhraṁsa: a stage in development of Sanskrit sir
God the Father locative case
Lord's Prayer: 'Our Father, Which art in Heaven . . .' *Hin* bap: father
Y *Ali Baba* (pantomime) *It* babbo: daddy
Bre, We tad: father *G* heilig: holy *It* babau: bogey
homeplace HCE *G* Ei: egg Smethwick: suburb of Birmingham Rhondda: town in Wales
St Augustine: *De Civitate Dei* 7 cities have been considered Homer's Temple of Artemis at Kalydôn
birthplace: Smyrna, Rhodes, Kolophon, Salamis, Chios, Argos, Athenae
Salem, Massachusetts
Skt ātman: nature, essence

suffice Edmund Brauchbar: friend of J

Hin bapka: of a father 11th E.B. 'Indo-Aryan languages': 'The past & future participles are passive in their origin . . . for an intransitive verb we have, either "I am gone", or "it is gone by me" '
F Mesdames, Monsieurs! it used to be said in D that Daniel O'Connell *Sp* ahora: now, at present
had fathered so many bastards that one could not throw a stone over a wall without
stepsons *Da* barnebarn: grandchild hitting one

Ir. name of D means 'Town of the Hurdle Ford' Classics: 5 chief Eng. horse races
Sp octubre: October
bounce *Sp* muchas veces: many times *L* dorsus: back
It vecio: old
handicap race: one in which umpire
decides what weights horses must carry
flat race: one without hedges or ditches *Da* tiptipoldefader: great-great-great grandfather

Midas Brodar assassinated Brian Boru father
da: father (used e.g. in Synge's *The Playboy of the Western World*)
s 'The flea on the tail of the dog of the nurse of the child of the wife of the wild man from Borneo has just come to town' father . . . father . . . father *G* Pfänder: bailiff *G* Pfund: pound *G* Fürst: prince
Ranelagh, district of D *L* Pater et Filius Exod 3:14: 'I AM THAT I AM'
Sp fué: he was
Tom Tower on Christ Church, Oxford *Oxford Sl.*: Jagger: Jesus College; Pemmer: Pembroke College; The House: Christ Church College, Oxford

HEC Aedes Christi: Christ Church College, Oxford, where Lewis Carroll (C.L. Dodgson) lived
Mary Baker Eddy founded Christian Science ('Coo'–pigeon–Holy Ghost)
St Edmund's Hall, Oxford Edwin C. Christy Minstrels
L et Spiritus Sancti
L aures: ears *L* aura: breeze *L* aureus: golden *Da* navn: name
pr Silence is golden
Midas has long ears *F* oreilles Persse O'Reilly
(his secret betrayed by breeze) *F* or: gold
eyelashes mudebroth!: ejaculation of St Patrick's big Persse O'Reilly

D Sl chiselur: child

G Haltestelle: bus stop Lucan (coughing)
JO *G* Stille: silence

Galway is on Atlantic coast *Gr* onagros: wild ass Tuam, Co. Galway: name means 'burial mound'
Atlantic City, New Jersey
coffin Co. Cavan *Gr* (artificial) stavrotidês: descendant of a cross
chewing & coughing
Co. Mayo Yokohama fowls
mah jong: old Chinese game played with tiles used like cards
O'Mulconry: one of the Four Masters; also an archbishop of Tuam west coast
VI.B.6.46: 'plucher (cough)' *I* plúchadh: choking, smothering
Glewlwyd of the mighty grasp: Arthur's gateman in *The Mabinogion*

Don Quixote

eagle is emblem of St John
eagle on Galway coat of arms
MW *G* huschen: slip away home Original Sin *We* hin: weather Garden of Eden
home hen
Mrs Hayden: medium *G* Schüler: pupil (automatic writing for Yeats' *A Vision*)
chirography: handwriting (110.22–111.10) as others say
Evan Vaughan: first D postmaster, 1638–46; Post House was in High Street
Guinea fowl
F poule Document No. 1: The Treaty (term used by De Valera's followers)
Pinte: hen in Reynard cycle
Wilde on fox hunters: 'the unspeakable in full pursuit of the uneatable'
dumbfounded
Y *ph* 'Ireland, Land of Saints & Sages'
N sint: angry

ph cry stinking fish

s Cock of the North Matthew Arnold
Armagh in Ulster

MK *Scottish Dial* leal: loyal Ir. Free State

Father Prout wrote 'The Bells of Shandon' (Kevin, who found the document; is he the man who wrote it?)
post(men)
Sp poeta: poet reading

scatology: study of excrement *Book of Kells*
eschatology: study of the Last Four Things (death, judgement, heaven & hell)

pr what can't be cured must be endured *G* greifen: seize
pr What the eye can't see the heart can't grieve for
(they can decode by comparing voice & writing—483.03–4)

cause & effect L alter: other
affect: mental disposition It ricorso: recurring (Vico)
Shem the Penman
ph to twist the lion's tail
Shaun the Post Gen 27:22: 'The voice is Jacob's voice, but the hands are the hands of Esau'
gesture G Schaum: foam, froth

Yeats: *Reveries over Childhood* s The Bells of Shandon

Gen 31:49: 'the Lord watch between me & thee'

Turkey divided into Turkey-in-Europe & Turkey-in-Asia F dinde: turkey
dip (baptise) Indians
Bronze
good
bonze: Japanese Buddhist priest
resurrectionism: grave-robbing

J wore a Borsalino hat (288.18) saint
It borsaiolini: (dim.) pickpockets
hesitency

(are you a postman?) Spell me that without a K (089.18)
It andate: go (pl.) & that

F sans delay

Y F fier: proud Firapeel: leopard in the Reynard cycle J character for 'writing' is interpreted as a
G vier: 4 It fiera: fierce F appel: appeal hand holding a brush
wounder Blarney Castle (Munster, i.e. Mark)
(St Patrick holding crozier)
Mark Antony J mi: I
It marcantonio: tall strong man
do 'Initium' (opening of Mark's gospel in Vulg)
Jacob & Esau struggled in the womb (Gen 25:22)
(Esau means 'hairy'; Jacob 'one who takes by the heel', cf. Gen 25:25–6) alphabet
ALP Rebecca: wife of Isaac It becca (v): pecks
I an: the a Mick . . . a Nick Isaac's sons 'In principio' (opening of John's gospel in Vulg)
unwashables G wachsen: to grow J aniki: elder brother I'm
L puer: boy Patrick: *Confessio* 27: 'I told my most intimate friend what I had one day done in my
Du leperd: cunning boyhood . . . I know not, God knows, whether I was then fifteen years of age' Prime
G lieber G Kalb: calf L ens innocens: innocent thing (canonical hour)
Luke's emblem is calf, Mark's is lion 3 × lustrum (5 years) = 15 years G Realschule: non-classical 2ary
British custom of presenting newborn children with matches, eggs, salt and bread to ensure virtuous life school
Matt. 5:13: 'if the salt hath lost his savour'
G so: as G wie: as
(did I alter my innocent brother towards fatness?)
G hochfahren: to flare up Gen 4:9: 'I know not: Am I my brother's keeper?'
Du ben ik: am I G Kinder
AngI acushla: my pulse (endearment) (I am sure of however this under heaven:
Cashel (in Munster) regarding the first mover [God], He knows
F mes enfants (He by whom I came to be I) that I—not my
F mais enfin brother—was altered first when I entered
religious order)

F plage
air, earth, water (fire in .25)
G Eltern: parents postulant: one who petitions for something, e.g. admission into a religious order
Watford: London suburb
Tierce (canonical hour) childhood

my seniors F sosie: double,
counterpart

converted pilgrim

(tonsure) Lauds (canonical hour) patristic: pertaining to Church fathers

L mea minima culpa: through my least fault a C character for 'I' consists of cocoon sign plus mouth sign
J ikko: oneself
scatology: study of excrement

(5 senses: smell, mouth, finger (touch), audio (ear), eye)
small
(4 people = 8 feet) *J* character for 'speech' interpreted as signs for mouth, four & five
mansuetude: gentleness; meekness St Audoen's (or Audeon's) Church, High St, D
audient: hearer of gospels
G Träne Tropfen: raindrops
teardrops *It* troppo: too much
Iseult (if I crouched down . . . to confess . . . what I did not do . . . why did
J me: eye you . . . blather you would back me for the post)
F essayer adding
so to say
& adding *L* hi allocuti sunt: these have spoken to Sext (canonical hour)
Vulg Ps 21:7: 'locuti sunt labiis' ('they shoot out the lip'—in derision)
delighted
L delatus: accused
G erse Irredentist (Stanislaus Joyce was one), from *It* irredento, 'unredeemed' (big noise)
Tristan, Mark's nephew bachelor
G Laut: sound (writing such letters) (post, 483.13) assuming

476.32: 'mamalujo' (& then you questioned my signature (483.01–6) when you remembered my twin brother & you imply I'm a makebelieve Irish—Patrick the foreign missionary)
catechumen: young Christian convert before baptism
L Quoniam: since, because (first word of Luke's gospel in Vulg)
celebrate
birthday

makebelieve & a *G* nunmehr: henceforth hyper- chuck
Nones (canonical hour) *Du* meer: more Hibernian 'meer Irish': term used by medieval Dubliners to refer to native population
damned cheek *Gr* autokinêton: self-moving thing
(Japan v. China) Chinatown
Luke 1:1: 'Forasmuch as many have taken in hand to set forth'
J to: and
F complet: full
Vespers (canonical hour) Compline (canonical hour)
cardinals a prince (man), a prowler (lion), a prancer (bull), a proud (eagle)—emblems of the evangelists
Improperia ('Reproaches'): Good Friday service: Hittites *Arch* hectates: witches
'I led thee out of Egypt, drowning Pharaoh in the Red Sea: & thou didst deliver me to the chief priests' &c.
Blind Harry: C15 Scottish poet old Dublin
ME mote: mound (i.e. Thingmote)
S.P.Q.R.:Imperial Roman motto

legatine: pertaining to a legate the 4 Christian bishops in Ireland before Patrick: Ailbe, Ciaran, Declan, Ibar
ABCD
Gr episkopeô: to inspect dedition: surrender
L episcopus: bishop Vulg Ps 21:12: 'Circumdederunt me vituli multi' ('Many bulls have compassed me')
ph lap of luxury Lazarus *L* lapsus linguae: slip of the tongue
F loup: wolf *It* lazaroni: the mob *G* lang *C* lang: wolf
J washi: I (abbr. of 'watashi') *J* watashi: I (abbr. of 'watakushi') *J* buku: I (generally used) *J* wachi: I (*Dial.*, used by men) *J* oira: I (form of 'ore') *J* ore: I (used to inferiors) *J* watay: I (familiar, used by women) *J* sessha: I (official, obsolete) *J* jibun: I (obsolete)
J watakushi: I (used with superiors) *C* tsien sing: humble name honorific forms of speech in *J*
ph eat humble cake ruridecanal: pertaining to a rural dean or deanery

Peregrine O'Duignan (398.15) I wish to remain 'Liber generationis' (opening of Matthew's gospel in Vulg) *I* leabhar: book
pilgrims *It* romanesco: modern Roman
Theophrastus: a pupil of Aristotle

Gr pneuma: spirit

ochlocracy: mob rule P/K P/K P/K P/K
It presto: quick *L* columbus: dove *Corvus corone:* hoodie or carrion crow
Terence Kelly: D pawnbroker *L* palumbus: woodpigeon
C ho: I
L ex quovis: from whatever you like I marked

facsimile *It* pappagallo: parrot *L* gallus: cock Pompeius Magnus
St Gallus & St Magnus both connected with Abbey of St Gall
F anglais ascribed to Pythagoras: 'Ex quovis ligno non fit Mercurius' ('You cannot make a Mercury out of just any piece of wood') squawfish: Sacramento pike *Heb* nun (name of letter): fish

I sagart: priest   *L* nihil obstat: nothing prevents   L/R   P/K   L/R   Patrick
G Selbstlaut: vowel   (form of approval by Church censor)
L tripennifer crista: 3-feather-bearing crest (3 ostrich feathers on
It cresta: crest   badge of Prince of Wales)
caudal: of the   *G* Ich dien: I serve (motto   Method Gaspey-Otto-Sauer for study of modern
tail   mottos   of Prince of Wales)   languages, c. 1900 (edited by Motti)
It ecco stesso: behold the same (self)

mine, praise God   *Heb* yod (name of letter): hand
personal pronoun   you'd
Boissy d'Anglas: Fr.   *R* moi bog: my God   Doomsday Book   *Sp* hasta la vista: au revoir
statesman, exiled   *AngI* moy: plain   *R* bozhe bozhe: O God, God   'my God's doom':
Sp alemán: German   Sucat: name St Patrick's parents gave him   expression of St Patrick

LU   *AngI* musha: well, indeed   we were
R misha: bear (animal)
look at   Lucat-Mael: druid defeated by St Patrick
ph 'lick whiskey off a sore leg'
Gr ichthys: fish   God be praised
Ich dien (.03)   have you a tosser (sixpence)
vowels & consonants   confidantes   Tom, Dick & Harry
F voyou: street Arab; corner boy
Wars of Roses: Lancaster (red); York (white)   *F* d'anglais
Blanche of Lancaster: mother of Henry IV
land/sea   *G* sprechen Sie Deutsch?   I say (imitating Eng. accent)
Joyce   *R* bozhe bozhe: O God, God

s 'Come back, Paddy Riley, to Ballyjamesduff, Come home, Paddy Riley, to me' (Ballyjamesduff, town, Co. Cavan)

L tripennifer crista: 3-feather-bearing crest

Dorothy Stuart: *The Boy through the Ages*   *F* vingtetunième
one & only
'Spera in Deo' (Liturgy): Hope in God   spare
L spira in me Domino: breathe into me by the Lord
what price   Polly Peachum in Gay's *The Beggar's Opera*

Sp excusado: privileged, exempt   'The War of Jenkins' Ear': Eng.-Spanish war of 1739, partly provoked by
Sp escusado: privy   Spanish commander cutting off Jenkins' ear
I teanga: language   holly   telephone
VI.B.17.38: 'ivyleaf under tongue = deafness'
best

C shanghai: on the sea   swabber: term of contempt, 1609   2, 3, 1
Sl twicer: cheat   trefoil (shamrock)
heard him   (in outer ear)
otherly
hear him (in labyrinth of inner ear)   rise   *G* Nachtmahl: supper
differently
s Johnny, I Hardly Knew Ye: 'With drums & guns, & guns & drums, The enemy nearly slew ye'
inner ear'd hardly hear
'Chin-chin': Anglo-Chinese phrase of salutation deriving from 'ts'ing ts'ing'

Y   angry   *It* mò: now   yellowman's lingo   St Luke was physician
F anglais   more
'l' for 'r' in Chinese pidgin   ludification: deception   number one
mistletoe   rudiments   *L* ludimentum: toy
C Pi topside: superior

C Pi Joss: God   Adam   Maam Cross (085.23)

G lahm: lame   jack-in-the-box
AngI begorrah!   (his brother)

Bohemian

HCE   Confucius   too much!

Nippon: Japan
China/Japan

granddad's   lambda (Greek letter)   lamb's tail
Charles & Mary Lamb: *Tales from Shakespeare*
P/K   L/R   A.D. 432: Patrick lands in Ireland
L quadrigae: yoke of 4 horses
Patrick was called Cothraige for a time, by P/K split; this was later misinterpreted as meaning 'belonging to 4' & it was held that in his slavery 4 masters had owned him
Tristan
[questioner in 486–91 probably *MK* but hard to demonstrate]
L tandem: at length
AngI ph
James Millington: *English as She Is Spoke:* edited version of a *Port*/Eng. phrasebook by a man who knew almost no English   to the tune the old cow died of (bad slow music)
Sl owl: whore   frow: woman
Tristan called himself Tantris on arrival in Ireland
Patrick   vowelglide: running-together of 2 vowels
killjoy   dragoman: interpreter, in Arabic, Persian & Turkish-speaking countries
understudy   VI.B.23.103: 'plunger (tongue)'   *Sl* paddle: tongue
L studium: inclination, desire; study
God is just   Tennyson: *Morte d'Arthur* 71: 'The old order changeth, yielding place to new, & God fulfils himself in many ways'
Matt 19:30: 'the last shall be first'
(the saying that every 3rd man born is Chinese)

Japan/China   (reflection–hypnotist's technique)
mandrake extract dilates pupil
Mencius: Chinese philosopher; held that man is naturally good   (dragoman)   psychology
Felix Marcus Minucius: *Octavius*   *Arch* drake: dragon   sinology: study of Chinese things
G Armer: poor one   *Du* slang: snake   Lord of Tattu: Osiris
It tutto: all
Ezek 9:6 in Vulg mentions God putting Tau on foreheads of those in Jerusalem who were not to be killed; also mark on Cain (Gen 4:15)   *C* character for 'stone' consists of a T & a square
Knights Templars (unjustly charged with sorcery)

(Tristan–his Fr. influence)   pastrycook

Sl cathedral: high hat   *F* Tiens

PIA   *F* piou-piou: common soldier   distress assails
Tristan & Isolde
G Horizont: horizon   Serpent with ram's head ornament on ancient Celtic monuments   *It* serpe: serpent
Egyptian Book of the Dead I (introduction): 'priest . . . holds . . . the instrument UR HEKA in the form of a ram-headed serpent'

Isis   isinglass: a variety of gelatin from swim bladders of sturgeons   Isolde of the White Hands (Tristan's wife in Brittany)
F O la la!

PURA   *G Arch* sey: be   Swift, Stella, Vanessa

F essayer   *G* (ge)trennt: separated
ph here today, gone tomorrow
Sterne   Patrick was called 'Adzehead' because of tonsure

Patrick's hymn 'Breastplate' (*Cry of the Deer*)

BELLA ('O pia e pura bella': religious wars of Vico's heroic age)
a bollocks
AngI shee: fairy

delysia   picturesqueness   images   *Port* irma: sister   *Imago*: psychoanalytical journal founded 1912
Irma, patient in Freud's *The Interpretation of Dreams*
Gr oneiros: dream
L iter: journey
L qua: in the capacity of

hyperborean

L per accidens: by accident
barring accidents
succession

Gen 27:22: 'The voice is Jacob's voice'
object!

trying God be thanked

In James Hogg's *Confessions of a Justified Sinner,* Wringhim kills his brother & enemy George, in Edinburgh
Gr adelphos: brother 163.05–06: '*Haensli . . . Koebi*' hansom cabby
substitute apart (.04)
It aperto: open

L nex: murder nextdoor neighbour's

Esau sold his birthright for a mess of pottage so to say
qua you (486.36)
birthright (.13)

eric: a blood fine for murdering an Irishman
ridiculous
pottage (.13) Beauty & the Beast (fairy tale)
Bewley's Oriental Tearooms, D
G Gott

S. Lover: *s* I'm not meself at all by myself

John 1:1: 'In the beginning was the Word'
s Finnegan's Wake: 'He'd a drop of the craythur every morn'
OE wyrd: time, change, becoming, *pr* Hood maketh not frere
destiny, fate
Gen 27:22: 'The voice is Jacob's voice, but the hands are the hands of Esau' (R.C.—486.02)
Romanov: Russian Tsar family
Temples of Venus & Rome (AMOR/ROMA) were built sympathy Patrick
as mirror-images Sir Amory Tristram, 1st Earl of Howth

'God save the mark!': expression of impatient scorn

Shem Ham

Da gengang: return Ibsen: *Gengangere* (*Ghosts*)
Rom 12:19: 'Vengence is mine, I will repay'
Charles Leland discovered Shelta, Ir. tinkers' secret language *I* capall: horse
r Lee (Cork)
Chapelizod

L simpliciter arduus: frankly difficult
L magister artes: master of arts
nr 'Friday's child is loving & giving' (a variant
has 'Thursday's child's inclined to thieving')

taken odious

the first liar = the Devil

whether

(tree/stone)
(concerned with 1 thing or said by 2 voices) *L* simplicissime: most simply
Bruno of Nola discussed identity of opposites *F* limon: mud *T* leymon: lemon
layman *Da* bogholder: bookkeeper
orangery (477.36) Oranje Nassau: Dutch Royal family, William III's ancestors
Browne & Nolan, booksellers, Nassau St, D (orig.)
Avicenna: Arabian philosopher *AngI* e'er yesterday: day before yesterday
It a vicenda: each other; in turn
Ibn Sen = Avicenna Ibn Rushd = Averroes (.15)
Ibsen

sees seizes
senses
all in Nola *L* ipso: self *L* id est: that is
ph all in all

L per omnia saecula saeculorum: for ever & ever *G* Löwe: lion
L pro omnibus: for everyone *Bantu* singa: lion

Finn MacCool In Reynard cycle, Bruin = bear, Noble = lion
Felis leo: lion
Averroes: Arabian philosopher itself *L* nolens volens: willing or unwilling
G aber: but Ibsen *L* volans: flying
to stand mute of all malice (law): to refuse to plead
Mutt (Jeff in .29)
Czarnowski: *Le culte des héros* XC: 'croient faire ou justify testify soul
croient souffrir au pluriel et au collectif, les mêmes verbes, mis au singulier, ont pour sujet les héros'
brother brother die

S.O.S. dreamed
'oyez, oyez!' (town crier)
Australia my dearly beloved (.04)
most
alibi *L* nego: I deny

scapegoat expelled

Halloween HEC
(Hallow Eve)
Gr kenographos: empty writing verse All Souls'

Hy-Brasil: legendary island W. of Ireland *Arch* Middle Earth: Earth as between Heaven & Hell
St Brendan supposedly discovered America Co. Clare
(phone number) *G* nein S.S. (steamship) neuropathy: nervous illness *G* Punkt
0009 Europe paths
(172.24–5) plus
please
how to pay
Sl splosh: cash please
L albus: white *Sp* sobrino: nephew

Switzerland

lunch
It coglioni: testicles colonial
It coglione: stupid
It pancia: belly Hail Mary
ph hail fellow well met
Capel St, D Society of United Irishmen: revolutionary movement founded 1791
cabler
endings of foreign surnames: -kov, -ich, -mini, -rati, -opoulos

Albigenses (Fr. heretics)

Emily Monroe Dickinson, Moore: *s* The Harp That Once through Tara's Halls [Gramachree]
sister of Parnell: *A Patriot's Mistake*

Milton: Sonnet XIX: 'They also serve who only stand & wait' *G* Fuchs: fox
fucks
badgers lairs V.C.: Victoria Cross
lodgers B.B.C.: British Broadcasting Corporation
Gripes ant hopper Mookse *M Gr* muxa: mucus, snot
have mercy on his soul hole
last

L oremus pro fratribus: let us pray for [our] brothers

gallows Commemoration of All the Faithful Departed: All Souls' Day

Tass: Russian news agency
air (radio)
someplace antipodes

fondest saved
hush-money: money paid to hush up a crime
light on the subject

L obiit: died Nola, Jerry (⊏) New South Wales

Ham, son of Noah

Castor & Pollux roving eye

excepting claret negus: wine & hot water & lemon & spice teetotum: game of chance in which 4-sided disk is spun
Amharic negus: king total
Shem Shaun
ashamed

beholden namesake

Armorican (Tristan) Dublin television
Amharic: a Semitic language

apricot lumps (sweet) moonshine

Baudelaire: 'Mon semblable,–Mon frère!' (*Fleurs du mal*)

L otium: ease

sanguine brother faith, hope & charity Michael Davitt spent 8 months in Australia in 1895
David (& Jonathan)
United Irishman dearly beloved (488.04)
Sydney & Albany, Australian cities

nursery rhyme
newsreel
old

I bastún: blockhead why was *L* vae victis: woe to the vanquished
Boston (Mass.) (vector of disease)
St Augustine: *Confessions* X.43: 'Pro nobis victor et victima; et ideo victor, quia victima'
('He was for us both a victor & a victim—a victor because a victim')
make way for his vehicle *F* cul *G* Weh: woe
Eugene Sheehy records that J was reading a book in Phibsborough Road when a nursery maid drove a perambulator into his back, so that he fell into it. J turned to her & said 'Are you going far, Miss?'
small of back aloud 2 acolytes (Sheehy & his brother
kick in his arse ever since witnessed incident)

Madonna & Child (the nurse & J) *Scottish* chiel: man, fellow
Thomas MacDonagh: Ir. rebel of 1916 rising
J's early essay, 'The Day of the Rabblement' calls Bruno 'The Nolan'
Nominalism: view that universal or abstract concepts do not correspond to any reality
presumably (his first name is 'Gottgab') *G* Gott gab: God gave (cf. 478.26)
L pro numina: in place of a god Baggot St, D
'Noun' can represent thing, person or place

Eureka Patrick

Yahoos & Houyhnhnms (*Gulliver's Travels*)
homonym
G gab *G* gut memory

personal pronoun *ph* an old head on young shoulders

(305.L1) Emily Monroe Dickinson, sister of Parnell: faithfully
A Patriot's Mistake expatriate
G Doppelgänger: double (sb.)
Dublin
his nibs *G* erst Wort: 1st word
G Antwort: answer

treble stout (drink) Lower Baggot St, D

surprised 4 shillings & sixpence

(dinner) (lookout)

Noah's Ark *F* Nöel: Xmas Foster Place, D
(arch of rainbow)

right . . . left *cg* Jenny is alive again
Jenny Diver: character in Gay's *The Beggar's Opera*
Tat! (postman's knock) letter Bruno Tat-tat! letter
L rediviva: that lives again
Nola *s* 'Here We Go Gathering Nuts in May, On a cold & frosty morning' red letter day
Rat-tat-tat!
I tuar ceatha: rainbow *I* Teamhar (pron. t'our): Tara, ancient capital of Ireland
countryman Cathay: a name for China
writing

sure

'Ireland is the old sow that eats her farrow' (*Portrait* V)
s Peg O'My Heart
F poule

so

L bos: bull

G sag: say *U*.472: 'BLOOM: No, no. Pig's feet. I was at a funeral'

there are two ways of solving *G* Silben: syllables
siblings
come to the same thing

MK (490.08) Christian Socialists: C19 reforming movement
St Crispin, martyr *PS* sokol: falcon *PS* sup: vulture its
Da kamp: fight Irvingites: religious body excommunicated from Church of Scotland in 1833
Sl clapperclaw: thrash soundly orthodox
middle-age spread (putting on weight)

top Acts 9:11: 'the street that is called Straight'
Du straat: street
Patrick St, Cork, is U-shaped

Lismore, town, Co. Waterford (E. of Co. Cork)
Brandon Head, Co. Kerry (W. of Co. Cork)
bend *G* Mittel-: middle Tristan
Sl bint: girl, whore
secrets

L turtur: turtledove *Da* rabrab: duck his
Tartars or Arabs *Du* raaf: raven (*G* Rabe)
marshmallow
Mallow, town, Co. Cork
045.01: 'Have you heard of one Humpty Dumpty' 047.29: 'That's able to raise a Cain'
Abel
383.01: '–Three quarks for Muster Mark!' *Heb* marak: soup

dropped his drawers Mansion House, D

borrow watercress shirtcloths off the

Archbishop of York in yarak: of a hawk, in condition to hunt

Brobdingnag (*Gulliver's Travels*) *G* Bummel: stroll, promenade
Coll bummel: river
Lilliput (*Gulliver's Travels*)

s Sally of the Alley

WW I Allies (England, France &c.) WW I Central Powers (Austro-Hungary, Germany, &c.)

Persse O'Reilly the P/Q split

Tara: ancient capital of Ireland

Green Thursday: Maundy Thursday turd (Earwicker defecating in Phoenix Park)

Scaliger: C15 Italian scholar *nr* 'Do you know the Muffin Man, The Muffin Man, the Muffin Man, Do
bloody *L* scaliger: ladder-carrier (cf. Finnegan) you know the Muffin Man, That lives in Drury Lane?'
King Lear III.4.187: 'Fie, foh, & fum'

Drury Lane *G* viel felicitations deaf Earwicker

girls

Horrocks Ltd, Eng. textile firm Proboer West Briton: Ir. person
affecting Eng. manner

working *G* Donnerstag: Thursday (lit. 'thunder-day')
Da by = *R* grad = city, town
recreation
VI.A.571: 'lord Ashbourne [noted for wearing kilts] put on his trousers when Ireland wouldn't recruit'
s The Bold Boys of Erin

G weiss: know Sandemanians: sect expelled from Church of Scotland in 1730

St Denis: patron of France up through

G womit: with which voice Bass's ale
(491.18)

alpha . . . beta . . . gamma . . . (.09) gamut: the musical scale

Sp lunes: Monday *It* martedi: Tuesday *G* Mittwoch: Wednesday *L* Mehercule!: By Hercules!
lunacy died *Sp* miércoles: Wednesday
F jeudi: Thursday Parasceve: day of preparation for Jewish Sabbath, esp. Good Friday
deceased menaced by a pair of skivvies *Da* lørdag: Saturday
OCS nedelya: Sunday *G* faul: lazy, rotten *OCS* voskresenie: Resurrection
false crescendo *R* voskresen'e: Sunday died
MW *I* Dia Domhnaigh: Sunday *L* dies Domini: Sunday *It* delitto: crime
I Dia's donas: God & evil
L diva: goddess Celtic twilight *G* Russisch: Russian
dainty delta
R vólŭs: hair *R* Krasnoe more: Red Sea

Egyptian Book of the Dead CLIX: 'The Chapter of the
Uatch amulet [made of] mother-of-emerald' (green feldspar)
L ora pro nobis: pray for us
Arrah-na-Pogue
▲ *L* capilla: hairs

delay *L* saxum: stone

Sechseläuten: Zurich spring festival
G Leute: people Black Hole of Calcutta (in which 146 Europeans were kept for 1 night in 1756; only 23 were alive next morning)

Du mijnheer: gentleman (he was in bed because drunk) Hindustani
menhir understand
pilsener: type of beer John Zephaniah Holwell: leader of those imprisoned in the Black Hole of Calcutta
poison
the P/Q split apothecary's

sedan

Surrajah Dowlah was responsible for the Black Hole
Veterinary Surgeon
Dr Achmet Borumborad: pseudonym of Patrick Joyce, C18 D quack. His attraction lay in his hair
Sp afamado: famous *G* Herr Doktor

Seringapatam, Allapalli: Indian towns
G Wasserguss: downpour, sink

pilch: an outer garment of skin or wool

calendar pole, perch (measure) infallible slipper

G Vorfahre: ancestor

Thomas Henry Kavanaugh: leader in Indian Mutiny

Governor-general *G* drei *G* Dreifaltigkeit: trinity
(she brought him the bottle while he was having his picture painted)
G Pinsler: dauber Orpen: painter, died 1931
oil paintings
marry
too many
secular *Per* bad-hazmi: indigestion
bad as my
involvement *G* Priester: priest

St George's Channel between Ireland & Wales Thomas Moore's melodies
aroint: drive away with execration

letters patent: documents from sovereign conferring privilege, title &c.
belt H.R.H.: His Royal Highness

(drink) shirttails
G Brief: letter
(picture) *Per* farangistan: Europe Sunday papers
foreign Afghanistan
aperạtif *Arab* vallad: 'son of' or 'a child' Persse O'Reilly
ballad Bishop Percy's ballad 'Chevy Chase' concerns Earl Percy
ph batted an eyelid

Paradise Lost *F* tout ensemble
A . . . PL *F* Nil: Nile
easychair *Hin* mahārānī: wife of a maharajah

looked Christmas Day

'Sunlight' soap Rawhead-&-bloody bones: a nursery bugbear

rejoice
rajah
perpendicular *Sl* poker: penis
L propendulus: hanging down in front

Hin Vikramaditya: royal patron of arts ('sun of power')
meditationists
Gujarti: an I ran
Indian language Erin
M.D. ('my dears') Swift's abbreviation in letters to Stella
Livia lithia water
Da bort: away

G wem: whom

Eccles 1:2: 'vanity of vanities, all is vanity' *G* Finte: feint; fib
L amnis: river
L nihil: nothing Eccles 1:9: 'there is no new thing under the sun' *G* wie wahr: how true
Ant. & Cl. IV.15.67–8: '& there is nothing left remarkable Beneath the visiting moon'
Ota, wife of Thorgil (Turgesius) the Viking invader, uttered prophecies from the high altar of Clonmacnois Cathedral
Woolsack: seat of Lord Chancellor in House of Lords
G heute: today *G* Leute: people sit up *Scots* sark: a shirt
Sl hoity-toity: supercilious *Sl* girlery: brothel gallery of peeresses
pomposities *G* vierte: 4th frangipanned: perfumed with frangipane
bombasine: a twilled dress material *F* fierté: pride
G Massstab: ruler, measure Otus & Ephialtes: sons of Poseidon; threatened Olympus
Outis: lit. 'no-man'; name used by Ulysses to deceive Cyclops
L simplex mendaciis: simple in [his] lies throat
Horace: *Odes* I.5.5: 'simplex munditiis' (simple in its elegance')
ask away

yes & no *F* vite *F* vide: empty
L vide!: see!
Moore: *s* 'Let Erin remember the days of old, Ere her faithless sons betrayed her'

Isis arise Osiris *Egyptian Book of the Dead* XXII: 'May my mouth be given unto me'
beray: defile Iris: personification of rainbow
(021.18) *F* pont: bridge

vignettes in *Egyptian Book of the Dead*; for XCV 'the vignette is a goose'
rainbow
'The overseer of the house of the overseer of the seal, Nu, triumphant, saith:' (frequent introduction in *Egyptian Book of the Dead*)
Newman
L numen: divine will
Ani: Egyptian scribe, subject of *Papyrus of Ani*
Anne Lynch's D tea ALP

Egyptian Book of the Dead XXX.B: 'My heart, my mother! [twice] My heart whereby I came into being'
Egyptian Book of the Dead: Chapters of Coming Forth by Day
Moore: *s* They Know Not My Heart [Coolin Das] 'Ecclesiastes' means 'Preacher'
glamoury: magic, enchantment

astronomical majesty

(rainbow) *s* Home Sweet Home
Isa Bowman: *The Story of Lewis Carroll* 47: 'a "skew" arch (going slantwise through the wall)'
flabbergasted firmament Matt. 19:24: 'It is easier for a camel to go through the eye of a needle' *U.S.* get the needle: be successfully done down
iridescence indecency (minerals with rainbow colours)
jewels in foundations of Holy City (Rev 21:19–20): i) jasper, ii) sapphire, vii) chrysolyte, viii) beryl
ruby (red), beryl (can be yellow), chrysolite (green), jade (green), sapphire (blue), jasper (can be brown or green), lapis lazuli (dark blue)
It arcobaleno: rainbow *L* orcus: lower world, death HCE Mt Etna, Sicily (volcano) Mt Athos, Macedonia
It orca: sow Bellona: Roman war-goddess extinguish
vulcanology: science of volcanoes love of Moses

interrupting Hekla: volcano in Iceland
HEC heckler
Ophiuchus: the Serpent constellation Vulpecula (constellation)
S *L* muliercula: weak little woman △
rings of Saturn Sata: Egyptian serpent god Pisces (constellation) *L* nova: new
m *It* pesciolini: little fishes nova: new star
Adonis *L* prisca: old Parthenope: siren who drowned herself
⊣⊢
ΛΓ⊏ Earth, Mars & Mercury *L* surgens: rising
towers of Rabelais' Abbey of Thélème: Arctic (N.), Calaer, Anatole (E.), Mesembrine (S.), Hesperia (W.) & Criere
Arcturus: brightest star in Bootes *L* Hesperus: Venus; the West
Anatole, Dusis, Arcis & Mesimbria: mythical stars spelling 'ADAM' *Gr* mesêmbria: noon; the South
Gr Anatolios: the East X North, East, South & West
(astrological houses)
Apep: Egyptian snake-god H . . . C . . . E *ph* chase me Charlie!
Uachet: Egyptian snake-goddess
flounces Ural Mts

Stromboli, volcano *G* Wurst: sausage

Emerald Table of Hermes Trismegistos 2: 'what is above is like that which is below'

bullrushes obsidian: volcanic glass ophidian: snake
bull & lion are evangelical symbols obese end
G Empfang: radio reception *F* Enfants de Marie: Children of Mary, Catholic girls' organisation Belshazzar (writing on wall) *Du* schotschrift: lampoon *G* Kurzschrift: stenography
(disguised as sweets to tempt little girls)
D motto: Obedientia civium urbis felicitas (Citizens' Obedience Is City's Happiness)
Sl sitinems: trousers
L gigas: giant Gyges: Lydian king of proverbial wealth
(244.23)

(038.09ff.) *US Sl* lollapaloosa: 'the cat's pyjamas'
ph bees in her bonnet
Da slanger: serpents *Heb* Hawah: Eve *s* '"Three cheers for old Ireland" says Master McGrath'
Robert E. Service: *Shooting of Dan Magrew* (poem)
△ Daniel McGrath, grocer, 4–5 Charlotte St, D
L emanens: spreading
white dwarf: type of star surrounded sarabande: a slow dance

G kitzel: tickle my elbow
Dial kittle: tickle

entering confessional: 'Bless me father for I have sinned' misdemean: misbehave

Fishamble St, D *F* canailles: rabbles
Grand & Royal Canals, D
dynamite

Da Askepot: Cinderella *r* Nile *RhSl* cash-&-carried: married
Viceregal Lodge ('Healiopolis' 024.18)
r Amazon husband
G Hund: dog
Du baggerman: dredger R.S.V.P.: *F* répondez, s'il vous plaît
beggars

Sullivans Reuters News Agency anonymous
Black Hand: Sicilian Mafia
scurrilous ballads Percy French: Ir. songwriter Magrath (494.26)
(044–047) Parsee: language of Persia under Sassanian kings
chiefly Power's Ir. Whiskey *ph* between the devil & the deep sea (480.28–30)
diver bibber
ph 'not fit to carry guts to a bear' tippler
sylph: slender, graceful woman (fig.)
APL
(170.05)

Solomon

G Henker: hangman Mosaic Dispensation: Moses' religious system
pocket handkerchief
G (ge)froren: frozen *It* patata: potato Church Militant
VI.A.641: 'Mosaic dispensation (hanging)'
Lynch: mayor of Galway; hanged his own son
G Mitarbeiter: colleagues (lit. 'withworkers')
Annals of the Theatre Royal, D 56: 'Revival of "The Warden of Galway" . . . Walter Lynch, T.C. King'

Sl stretch: hang L.B.W.: leg before wicket (cricket)
Lynch Brother, Withworkers
hemp rope (hanging) Captain Moonlight: an unknown leader in the Land League; committed acts of terrorism against those refusing to join it
paliasse *G* schleppen: drag

Holy Paul burying

love Persse O'Reilly

calls Grania
quink: a barnacle goose Goldsmith: *The Deserted Village:* 'Sweet Auburn'
MacCool
call
Finnegan giant

living

40 winks: short sleep

penny in the slot machine *G* Maschine: machine
penis
AngI kish: wicker basket *F* Château La Rose
brack: Ir. speckled cake
Annals of the Theatre Royal, D 61, refer to theatre's activities as 'the "Legitimate"' *G* Bett: bed
Elizabeth & Maria Gunning: Ir. sisters who married C18 Eng. aristocrats, subjects of popular enthusiasm in D *It* Marietta: dim. of Mary *F* noblesse oblige
sexcentenary J.F.M. ffrench: *Prehistoric Faith & Worship: Glimpses of Ancient Irish Life*
six & a tanner: six shillings & sixpence
Motto of the Garter: Honi soit qui mal y pense (Shame Be [to Him] Who Evil Thinks of This)

inches

statutes 082.12–13: 'six victolios fifteen'

R.S.V.P.

I ainm: name
L amnis: river
G Frau F.R.U.I.: Fellow of the Royal Univ. of Ireland ALP *L* artis litterarumque patrona: patroness of arts & letters
M.R.I.A.: Member of the Royal Irish Academy

Theatre Royal, D, had Sullivan, *maître de danse*, who called himself 'Silvain'

ALP pleasures

la-di-da: stuck-up *Uncle Foozle:* play mentioned in *Annals of the Theatre Royal, D* 56
JO Lady Don performed at Theatre Royal, D
Aunt Jack: play mentioned in *Souvenir of the 25th Anniversary of the Gaiety Theatre* 34

deaf & dumb hell & heaven
hill/river
enscribed

L conspuere: to spit upon throwaways
(free pamphlets)
nr 'Humpty Dumpty sat on a wall'

archimandrite: superior of a monastery Manx
Dane's Island off Co. Waterford
Man Lake of 4 cantons = Lake Lucerne
Island of Women is mentioned in *Voyage of Maeldúin*
HEC *L* conciliabulum: place of assembly
ecumenical *Da* nogen: some
Da ingen: none *Du* meid: maid *G* hold: handsome *Da* jord: earth
I inghean: daughter; virgin not any maid on all of the whole surface of the earth
Earwicker

bungalow *L* auxilium meum solo a Domino: my help cometh only from the Lord

rhyme or reason faeces

Earwicker Persse O'Reilly flabbergasted

Macpherson: *Fingal* *nr* 'This little piggy went to market, This little piggy stayed home &c.'
Fingall: ancient name of part of Co. D N. of Howth fingers (played with child's toes)
spilt pee

Peeping Tom spied on Lady Godiva *G* da: there
F tout le temps (.13 Amsad)

L pater patruum cum filiabus familiarum: the father of the uncles with the daughters of the families

I éirghe: rising watersheds
arising
subject dramaturgic
thaumaturgic traumatic

Eoin MacNeill: *Celtic Ireland* 55: 'Lugaid Cichech . . . reared the two sons of Crimthann, Aed & Laegaire, on his breasts. It was new milk he gave from his breast to Laegaire, & blood he gave to Aed. Each of them took after his nurture, the race of Aed being marked by fierceness in arms, the race of Laegaire by thrift'

Motto of City of Paris: Fluctuat nec mergitur (It Is Wave-tossed but Not Overwhelmed) merchant *Da* fadder: godfather

I Abha na Life: River Liffey

(since you can identify yourself both with ᗰ & Δ, let's get back to ᗰ) tears
G Bier: beer onetime *G* ziemlich: rather

(306.03) (Noah sent out birds to see if flood had abated)
Christopher Columbus *L* columba: dove
(Noah's dove returns with olive leaf in beak) unmentionables: underwear
(bespoke tailor)
carrion crow P.C.s: police constables
Henri Le Caron betrayed Am. Fenian plans to invade Canada
G Sieger: victor busybodies

Rota: supreme court of R.C. Church
ME maun: must *Scots* ca'canny: moderation; policy of 'go slow' at work

L Quis est qui non novit Quinnigan: Who is there who did not know Quinnigan?
L qui, quae, quod: who, which *L* quot: how many

s 'Lots of fun at Finnegan's Wake' *Arch* stump: to brag, boast
'examine' derived from hypothetical *L* exagmen, from exigere (to weigh)
Our Exagmination Round His Factification for Incamination of Work in Progress: collection of essays on FW published during its composition fortification
It incamminare: to put on the right road

I a Dhia are: O God now (interj.)

s Ad regias agni dapes ('To the Royal Feast of the Lamb')–hymn used on Low Sunday
imband: form into a band *I* fag a bealach: clear the way
panhibernians fat & lean *G* Jäger: hunter
The Scalp: ridge S. of D

headhunters musicals
Howth
Matt 16:18: 'tu es Petrus' legates & prelates
Rev 1:16: 'two-edged sword'
1132 *L* undecim: 11 *L* centum: 100

L extra omnes: outside of all *L* cunctus: the whole

Rathgar: district of D Roundtown = Terenure, district of D (continents)
Rathangan: town, Co. Kildare Rush: village, Co. D
Appian Way, D

North & South Walls of Liffey, D Mespil Road, D
valleys wallabies of New South Wales no such Vico Road, Dalkey
Sorrento Road, Dalkey
Rock Road, Blackrock
epidemic *Sp* sala de espera: antichamber, waitingroom *Du* keel: throat kraal: in S. Africa, a village or cattle enclosure
L oppidum: town
lodestone (like iron attracted to magnetic mountain)

gonner but afraid Merrion & Dundrum: districts of D

Lucan Ashtown: district of D Battersby & Co.: D auctioneers
Battersea Park, London
Crumlin, Phibsborough, Cabra, Finglas, Ballymun, & Raheny: districts of D
Kremlin boyars Philipsburgh Avenue, Fairview, D
maniacs ⚔ Clontarf, 1014: Brian Boru defeats Danes
G Bettler: beggar

manifest: list of ship's cargo, exhibited at custom house

F vive le roi! *F* roué: profligate, wanton

L usque ad inferos: even unto the dead
I uisce: water *L* usque ad ebrios: even unto the drunk
Epistle of Paul to the Hebrews business premises Delhi

F Sl bazar: shanty Magazine Fort, Phoenix Park

HCE 2 × 566 = 1132 (014.06)

'Grand Old Man': Gladstone *I* mór: great Persse O'Reilly
Parsee: Zoroastrian Indian of Persian descent
Brian Boru called 'Brian of the Tributes' Rimsky Korsakov Peter the Great
pop of cork
durbar: public audience held by native prince or British governor in India Indian empire

Paisley, town, Scotland, formerly known for Paisley shawls mufti: Mohammedan priest (Grand Mufti of Turkey)
muslin Muslim = Moslem
F reine Gordon Highlanders 'Jam Sahib': K.S. Ranjisinhji, cricketer
raisins Jordan almond: a fine variety of almond
It principessa: princess petticoat Queen of Night (*Magic Flute*)

Claddagh rings display 2 hands clasping a heart Salome salami (sausage)
salaam: oriental salutation
Ham, son of Noah Hassan Khan: Persian ambassador, visited D in 1819 maharajahs
German silver: nickel silver rashers of bacon
German Kaiser himself (called British Expeditionary Force in WW I 'contemptible') pro/con tintinabulating
selfish J.B. Dunlop invented pneumatic tyres

Irish Times: newspaper stewards
Stuart & Tudor dynasties
sweepstakes The Autumn Double (horse races): the Cesarewich & the St Leger

L Leodegarius: Leger (saint) sidesaddle
daddy-longlegs
The Oaks (horse race) *Gr* hysteroprôtos: back to front

left handicapped

truly national *s* Horsey, Keep Your Tail Up
trull: strumpet
G Halle: hall throneroom Olaf's
Aleph–B
(Dutch) House of Orange

bitters Brehons: ancient Ir. lawgivers
M.P.: member of parliament
Angl flahoolagh: 'princely', generous Agapemones: C19 religious community
F.P.: Flamen Perpetuus: permanent priest practising 'love-feasts' Antiparnellites
P.P.: Parish Priest Ir. officers of arms: Ulster King of arms, 2 heralds (Cork & D), 1 poursuivant (Athlone)

I Áth Cliath: Hurdle Ford
G Klee: clover
Catherine the Great of Russia *I* féin amhain: self alone *L* geminus: twin Saxons
Gemmy: son of Rossini's *Guillaume Tell*
Iveagh & Ardilaun: sons of Benjamin Lee Guinness (brewing) grand duchy *R* doch: daughter
G Efeu: ivy ephod: Jewish priestly garment Diamond sculls (rowing) at Henley
Adam & Eve *R* lyubov: love *U.*200: 'Murthering Irish' *I* amuigh's amach: altogether, 'out & out', completely
Du boom: chat Punjabi: Indian language doggerel
boon Dogra: Indian language
Tamil: Indian language Gujarti: Indian language
Gogarty
D Sl ball of malt: glass of whiskey *I* móna: of a peat bog Persse
Da øl: beer
O'Reilly *s* Panis Angelicus (Communion wafer) Kennedy: D baker
Cz paní: lady *Sh* pani: water
s At Trinity Church I met My Doom: 'I was an M-U-G'
'lady' der. from *OE* hlæfdige ('dough kneader')
socialism & communism *Egyptian Book of the Dead* cxvii describes protection of deceased's body in Otherworld, by identifying each of its members with that of a god (in text called 'deification of members')
noble savage (Rousseau) poor old
Sl nobble: appropriate dishonestly
Gr basileus: king arteriosclerosis Roderick O'Connor, Rex: last High King of Ireland
I óganach: bachelor
The Round Table (Arthur)

Vernon: Ir. family possessing a sword supposed to have belonged to Brian Boru
tilly: the 13th in a baker's dozen, an additional measure *G* Ringkampf: wrestling match
(candles round corpse at wake)
Da forgifte: to poison

sins

Lord Mayor's hogo: high or putrescent flavour

Communion of Saints 'Italian Warehouses': shops selling Italian groceries in D *It* erica: heather
s Cummilium
ECH *T* hayir: good, prosperity spectrum of his prism
hair
L candidatus: clothed in white daytime black pudding: kind of sausage
(white light split by prism) *Da* tid: time
(celestial hierarchy): Cherubim Seraphim Powers Principalities

Virtues Thrones Dominations Angels Archangels

bottom *L* expositus: set forth
buttoned
s God Save the King: 'Send him victorious, Happy & Glorious' HCE

resurrection of his body PS Bog: God
L eructo: I belch
'life everlasting' (creed)

o happy-go-lucky gaff: stick with an iron hook used for landing salmon F mort
Hin bap: father ph every man for himself & God for us all Cant mort: wench
calisthenics: gymnastic trepas: a sacred dance nine & twenty Gi mulo: dead
exercises for girls L nenia: dirge
(man underground, i.e. buried) Du dood: death I bás: death
dance of death
G böse: evil Sp muerte: death F mort Arab mamât: death Ar mah: death Po śmierć: death
G Mord: murder Arab maut: death Bre maro: death
R smert: death Valhalla Hu halál: death Fi tuoni: Figure of Death
Fi tunteeton: dead G Schmerz: pain We hollol: dead
Gr thanatos: death Cz umarti: death Annamese chết: to die F Merde! early C20 T eulüm: death
you martyr Cambodian damnos: death Per merg: death
Laotian kwamdtai: death Sa maliu: death S.O.S. J sei-shi: life & death J shi: death

Arab mamât: death Introit of Mass for dead: 'Requiem aeternam dona eis, Domine: et lux
Heb hamoves: death L mors: death perpetua luceat eis' ('Grant them eternal rest, O Lord, & may perpetual
dolmen on grave light shine upon them')
sic
s 'Lots of fun at Finnegan's Wake' keen (mourning sound at wakes)

'The king is dead. Long live the king' (Lady Dufferin)

s God Save the King G Muster: pattern, paragon, master

Oedipus Rex
God save you kindly (Irishism) adipose: fat
F saoul: drunk

s Finnegan's Wake: 'Souls to the devil! Did you think I'm dead?' Sl fuddled: drunk
AngI dhoul: devil
MW ph tissue of lies layers liars

Per bazar: market talk-shop (i.e. mouth) Da tolk: interpreter Hindi: 2 Indian dialects
11th E.B.: 'Hindostani': 'it became the bazaar language'
I muc: pig Sorley Boy MacDonnell: opponent of Elizabeth I
(ph pig in a poke)
G alt: old 'Old Nol': nickname of Cromwell
Y Shakespeare perhaps played Old Knowell in Jonson's *Everyman in His Humour*
(.22) homespuns

spinningtop
ph sleep like a top
mound I ollav: sage
pressed olives

'zounds' short for 'God's wounds'

MK (Roland's horn, cf. 073.36–074.05)
(ollaves .26)
Dingle: town, Co. Kerry

Y Matt 26:38 (Vulg): 'tristis est anima mea usque ad mortem' bleeding heart
('my soul is sad even unto death')
lowly head open s Slattery's Mounted Foot I uisce: water
aubain: nonnaturalised foreigner in France wounded
L lignum in: a piece of wood in

LU Rathgar: district of D Donnybrook Fair (noted for public fights)
wrath of God G Donner: thunder at end of *Rheingold*, Donner creates storm
(static on radio) babble resulting in rainbow bridge (Brücke) to Valhalla
Tower of Babel
who is he? AngI wisha: well, indeed (interj.)

MW *Sl* lug: ear to the ground

snare drum: one with strings across it

Clan na nGael: Am. Fenian organisation

thimble & bodkin army: parliamentary army in Eng. civil war

I Dubh-gall: 'Black foreigner', i.e. Dane running

I fionn: fair

F zinzin: onomatopoeia evoking noise

Crom abú: Fitzgerald war cry

York/Lancashire (Wars of the Roses) redshanks: name given to original Celtic inhabitants of Ir.

St Patrick's hymn *Cry of the Deer* slot: footprint of deer (hunting)

The White Hind: R.C. Church, in Dryden's 'Hind & Panther'

Hound & Horn, Eng. hunting journal *L* sanctus: holy

newspapers: *Irish Times, Irish Independent, Freeman's Journal, Daily Express*

St Patrick's *Cry of the Deer*: 'Christ with me, Christ before me, Christ behind me, Christ in me, Christ below me, Christ above me,' &c. chairman

Arch chare: return of a time

Da slog: struck *Da* slagte: slaughter *s* 'Kick the Pope'

I sluagh: host, army

L aude: hear *G* Vater unser: Our Father

Isolde *G* Erster: first one *Da* sidste: last

Esther: name of both Stella & Vanessa (Swift) sister

Isolde

Swift: 'Ppt'

G fort!: away! Bayreuth (Wagnerian opera house)

G bereit, marsch! (*Mil* commands)

Parnell: 'When you sell, get my price'

John 19:26: 'behold thy son'

F forain: wandering; open-air

Da tittit: peekaboo!

Ballymacarret: district of Belfast

time
title
(014.06, 334.31)
[questioner in 501–19 probably *MK* but hard to demonstrate]
act drop (theatre): curtain   juice (theatre): electricity   foots (theatre): footlights
stand by! (theatre): warning that curtain about to rise while scenery is changed   blinders (theatre): bright lights shone on audience
F Ségur cinquante huit (phone no.)

F Gobelins quarante quinze (phone no.)

F parfait   just a jiffy

Challenger Deep, deepest part of Mariana Trench, Pacific Ocean

Swiss

swear
Da svar: answer
Sybil Head, Co. Kerry   (tuning in)   (506.27)   baby spot (theatre): powerful narrow-beam lamp

luke: next midsummer   St Luke's little summer: traditionally warm spell in October

flickers (theatre): slotted disc rotated in front of stage light   dimmer: device for controlling stage lighting
newspapers: *Irish Times, Irish Independent, Freeman's Journal, Daily Express*

somewhere in the Pacific

(Midsummer fire festivals were once universally observed in Europe)

let's continue

bonafides   Bluebeard: wife-killer in story by Perrault

F nuit blanche: sleepless night
The White Knight in *Alice*

s The Lily of the Valley

1st midwinter Ir. campaign: The Hosting of the Frost, 941

marry her mirror   Andes Mts
indiarubber ball

Balkan Mts

Lewis Carroll

went far enough
I fearthanach: rainy
s The Holly & the Ivy

Tree of Jesse (David's father) traces Christ's descent
I clocha sneachta: 'snowstones': hailstones *s* The Holly & the Ivy
I seacht a chlog: 7 o'clock
Himalayas layers
Cz zima: winter

G nass: wet *G* Ost: east
R vesna: spring *R* osen: autumn
s Es ist ein Ros entsprungen (C15 carol)
just

Swift: 'Ppt' Pipette! Isolde. Brinabride, my price! *Da* ny: new
(shivering)
s 'Adeste fideles, laeti triumphantes' ('O come all ye faithful, joyful & triumphant')
It lieto: glad *R* leto: summer Lewis Carroll: *Jabberwocky:* 'galumphing'
Still calling, number please pacific: peaceful

Fi muna: egg *s* Stille Nacht, heilige Nacht *G* nackt: naked
L luna
D Annals, 1339: 'Two moons were seen near Dublin before daybreak, the one bright in the west, the other faint in the east'
I gealach: moon Katty Gollagher: hill near Bray (090.10)
G Gelächter: laughter
L quando: when *L* quondam: once *L* gaudete: rejoice

latterly
L laetare: rejoice
Da latterlig: ridiculous, laughable

ice *L* calidus: hot
G heiss: hot
mostly (Viking boat burial) *It* bruma: haze, depth of winter

(air, earth, fire, water) waterspouts
hailstones *G* stöhnen: groan *PS* voda: water

Angelical Salutation: 'Hail Mary, full of grace! . . . Holy Mary, Mother of God'

please

cold July *Sl* parkiest: chilliest

Eccles 1:2: 'vanity of vanities, all is vanity'
Gr Eumenides: the Furies
s 'The flea on the hair of the tail of the dog of the nurse of the child of the wife of the wild man from Borneo has just come to town'
Maida Vale, London
L fumus: smoke *Skt* maidan: plain (name of great park in Calcutta)
F cache-cache: hide & seek *F* cauchemar: nightmare
. . . has just come to town
A Midsummer Night's Dream midwinter

delirium tremens *L* stramen: straw, litter
Deluge
sere: dry

shire horse: heavy powerful draught horse
G funkel: spark *G* mehr: more
G Rundfunk: wireless
whitecaps: waves in windy weather
Finn MacCool (white hat)
F fuyant Finglas, district of D (N.)
Foxrock, district of D (S.)
landscape panorama paronomasia: word play, pun EHC
(painted backdrop of stage set)

effect . . . cause Giant's Causeway, N. Ireland Dundrum, district of D
effects in theatre: rain drum (grapeshot rattling on parchment), wind machine (canvas rubbing on slats), snow box (clipped paper shaken from box), thunder (shaking suspended sheet of metal)
Roebuck, district of D

stellar
I réaltach: starry
starry auditorium
L oleum: olive oil
L oleo: I smell

everlasting ashtree (the Yggdrasil in Norse myth)

kitchen midden: mound of mesolithic or neolithic kitchen refuse

OE ealdormann: magistrate, chief *G* Junker: young aristocrat

wellknown kikkinmidden

townlands in Fingal area, Co. D: Littlepace, Snugborough, Westereave, Astagob, Slutsend, Stockens, Winnings, Folly, Merryfalls, Skidoo, Skephubble, Goddamendy
The Yellow House: pub, Rathfarnham

Sl skidoo: make off

God Almighty, you're a devil of a talker *Du* tolk: interpreter
Delville: Patrick Delany's house on *r* Tolka, often visited by Swift
the 4 last things: death, judgement, hell & heaven

I Cor 13:13: 'faith, hope, charity'

Stow-on-the-Wold, & Woeful Dane Bottom both in Gloucestershire. The latter is a valley, possibly site of a Danish defeat
OE stow: place
indeed

(green, black & grey stages of blindness; see 441.04) *I* gan ghréin: sunless
I gréinbeach: zodiac gangrene
The Black Sun Press published J's *Tales Told of Shem & Shaun,* 1929
(Ir. tricolour)

Tom, Dick & Harry unfailing

Peter the Great
L petrus: stone
sayeth wooden warning (signpost) *G* Warnung: warning
Wodin = Odin = Ygg
Trespassers will be prosecuted (posted notice)

everlasting ashtree (.07)
G Esche: ashtree
s 'She lived beside the Anner at the foot of Slievenamon . . . A snowdrift 'neath the beechen bough, Her neck & nutbrown hair'
*U.*350: 'ash, oak or elm'
In Norse myth ash was first man, elm first woman
G Beerchen: little berry

rain-laden Wales W.J. Browne: *Botany for Schools,* published by Browne &
Oscar Wilde Nolan
L thesaurus plantarum: a treasury of plants
Frederick Nolan, vicar of Prittlewell: *A Harmonical Grammar of the Principal Ancient & Modern Languages*

F lecture leaf *I* crann: tree
Ir. children used to take a wren fastened in a mass of holly & ivy from door to door collecting money on St Stephen's Day. They chanted: 'The Wren, the Wren, The king of all birds' &c.
squire of dames: one who devotes himself to service of ladies
Matt 5:15: 'Nor do men light a candle & put it under a bushel' Plantagenet: Eng. royal house; name supposedly der. from *L* planta genista, broom

AngI forenenst: opposite

Sumerian
summer
Cimmerians: race fabled to live in perpetual shadows (*Odyssey* XI.14)

downstairs
Luke 2:29: 'Nunc dimittis' (Now thou dost dismiss [thy servant])
L tunc: then Tunc page of *Book of Kells*

Salve (.16)

a little Darwin: *Origin of Species*
r Liffey
F ouragan: hurricane
numbers

L arbor: tree bird's-eye view George Moore: *Ave, Salve, Vale* (*Hail & Farewell*)
L avis: bird Catullus: *Ave atque Vale*
purple *Vatican Sl* purpurandus: one fit to be purpled, i.e. made a cardinal
conclave of cardinals
Italiote: Greek settler in Italy *It* in petto: in (one's) breast

Jack & the Beanstalk (pantomime) Jupiter Tonans: Zeus as thunderer *It* O dite: O say
It Tommaseo: Thomas
I corcair: purple (P/K) *It* udi, udite!: hear! (sing. & pl.)
purpurandus (.17)
cardinals are addressed 'Your Eminence'
fraternities
Tudor *It* odore: odour
L delictum: offence
Idaho *s* Babes in the Wood

(Phoenix) flamingoes Ir. myth of mad King Sweeny who nested in treetops with birds
Bird Flannigan: D wag who appeared at a party dressed as the Holy Ghost & laid an egg *Da* fugle: birds top mast
Urania: muse of astronomy hop to *F* ciel, terre bump to *F* pomme de terre
orange apples (Newton) Emania of the apples: residence of Manannán MacLir
Tyburn, London, place of public executions quicken tree: mountain ash

culprits Erasmus Smith set up grammar schools in C17 Ir.
borstal

Origin of Species Charles Darwin (monkeys with blue arses)
s Charley Is My Darling
Darwin: *The Descent of Man*
gibbons
Guelphs & Ghibellines (Dante) *F* prie-Dieu *Gr* anatolios: East; sunrise
gibbering
(cursing) catastrophes Royal Hospital, Kilmainham, for old soldiers

Wellington Monument, Phoenix Park, once popularly called the 'overgrown milestone'
(knock down)
F pommes Anna: a Fr. dish natural selection

hoyden: ill-bred girl *nr* Who Killed Cock Robin?

mistletoe (*Golden Bough*)
Yggdrasil: the world tree in Norse myth

tom tit (bird) hawks

s The Holly & the Ivy St Jerome learning Hebrew in the Desert (roots in Semitic languages usually have 3 letters)
G mit
Norse world tree Yggdrasil had 3 roots

twenty-two thousand (412.26–7)
atmosphere
twenty-two thousand

(Eve & the Serpent) *Da* Snakke du norsk?: Do you speak Norwegian? *G* wimmern: to whimper
serpent at base of Yggdrasil
G Seele: soul *G* Leib: body fascinating satin

inquisitive

gemination: doubling *Da* onde: evil

L in saeculum saeculi: forever *L* Evoe!: a cry of the Bacchantes

eximious: distinguished *L* excelsior: higher
extraordinary *I* dair: oak

Mark 8:24: 'I see men as trees, walking' *Paradise Lost* I.620: 'Tears such as angels weep' (*U.*184)

nobody ever saw anything to equal it *s* 'Rock of Ages, Cleft for me'
L aviarius: of birds eagle on topmost branch of Yggdrasil

oak

003.09: 'mishe mishe' much of a muchness

tree of liberty Steyne: pillar in D erected by Vikings
G Stein: stone

meaning
L nemus: grove
G Tod: death Matt 16:18: 'thou art Peter'
003.10: 'tauftauf' 'till death do us part' (marriage ceremony)
Da mellemmand: middleman finite *L* mens: mind
Gr melas: black *Manesse Codex:* a collection of Minnelieder *G* mit: with

R dereva: trees
derivative
R. Ord & W. Gayer-Mackay: *Paddy-the-Next-Best-Thing* (play, 1920)
Max Planck (quantum theory)

G Apfelbaum: apple tree (e.g. Newton's)

Moore: *s* The Meeting of the Waters
Luke 23:28: 'Daughters of Jerusalem, weep not for me'

Lucifer
wittol: a conniving cuckold *G* Frau *G* Rausch: drunkenness *Sl* dibble: penis
Book of Common Prayer: Litany: 'the World, the Flesh & the Devil'
brimstone phosphorus
stinks
beam end Nick

G Knechtschaft: servitude

Royal Society for the Prevention of Cruelty to Animals

Gen 2:20: 'Adam gave names . . . to every beast of the field' Tom, Dick & Harry

(Serpent) middle

Sl better half: wife *F* con: cunt

G Bitte: request, prayer

G Muster: pattern, paragon, master
master of the house
called (Serpent) deepest dye

Gen 3:14: 'God said unto the serpent . . . upon thy belly shalt thou go, & dust shalt thou eat all the days of thy life' ashamed
G flachen: flatten, level down
balance of his life

'Exsultet': 'O felix culpa!'
Father Finlay supposedly egged on D students protesting at first performances of Yeats' *Countess Cathleen*
'Exsultet': 'O certe necessarium Adae peccatum' ('Needful indeed was Adam's sin')
Wellington: 'Up, guards, & at them' begot 'em Adam
G hehr: sublime *s* Were You There When They Crucified My Lord?: 'Were you there when they laid him in the tomb . . . Sometimes it causes me to tremble, tremble, tremble'
G eher: sooner *G* Herr
The Coombe, D street
Sl lag: to apprehend (a convict)
C Coll wo: I (1st pers. pron.) *G* grauen: seize with horror

G Fürst: prince *G* Forst: forest

'Prince of triflers' (Swift)
three fellows *G* Holzfäller: wood-cutter
G Esche: ash tree sobriquet: nickname fairest

phalluses *Afrikaans* bomslanger: tree snake
Hin bap: father
It capo: head, cape
(Howth)

s 'There is a boarding house, Far, far away'
lodging house

onion soup
weep

nearer the mark King Mark Lansdowne Road, D
G mehr: more
Pippin apples Ezek 18:2: 'The fathers have eaten sour grapes & the childrens' teeth are set on edge'

Moore: *s* O! Haste & Leave This Sacred Isle [The Brown Thorn]
Cadmus sowed dragon's teeth—armed men sprang up
(spotlight shows exhibits to Yawn)

Finnegan

L inter nubila nimbus: among clouds a splendour

habitat
appetite
advice

ALP Anne Lynch D tea

Pekoe: a superior black tea *AngI* does messages: goes shopping for someone else messuage: dwelling house plus adjacent land & buildings
Dr Johnson struck his foot against a stone to refute Berkeley's proof of the nonexistence of matter

Kimmage: a district of D croft: small farm

ph not all there: mentally deficient

The Green Man: common name of pub

s Brian O'Linn; his breeches had 'The skinny side out & the woolly side in'
apparitions rapparees: Ir. plunderers
outside (elastic-sided boots)

Oxford Sl greats: B.A. course (Hum. lit.)
Cambridge Sl Little Go: classical preliminary exam
Great & Little Belts separating parts of Denmark; Kattegat is channel N.E. of Denmark
2 Sam 6:14: 'David danced before the Lord',
accoutrement i.e. before the tabernacle
I tobar: well
Lugh of the Long Arm: god of the Tuatha Dé Danann

Sl bramble: lawyer

trousers forget-me-nots

Basques invented beret

F drôleries
adultery
Lord *AngI* wait till I tell you!: mark my words!

hardest *Da* ursprog: original language a hundred & one
our brogue
dumbshow

search me

Sl horneys: police *cg* Horneys & Robbers

Lower O'Connell St, D

illuding: mocking

'wash & brush up': notice in Eng. men's conveniences

L pater: father dearly lamented

L qua: in the capacity of (rainbow)
Ark of the Covenant

Booterstown: district of D silliest

fucker EHC *AngI* crannock: piece of wood, chest, box
Sl forker: dockyard thief

The Arch, pub, Henry St, D

nonaryan

above the sea level scatterling: vagabond

buttons

brewer's grains: refuse malt used for feeding livestock

s Then You'll Remember Me

(12 days of Christmas)

Twelfth Night (the P/Q split) Quantum Theory

(= Epiphany) *L* pax: peace in early Christian Church, Epiphany partly commemorated wedding at Cana

s The Holly & the Ivy *L* evoe!: a cry of the Bacchantes

HCE *L* culus: fundament Epiphany: 6 January (means 'showing forth'). In *Stephen Hero*,

curious J uses term to mean 'a sudden spiritual manifestation'

L hodie: today *MGr* esôbrakôn tôn: their underpants

HCE *L* casus: fall *Du* kont: arse

nature Nessus' shirt killed Hercules nether garments

pr necessity knows no law

211.11: 'a pair of Blarney braggs for Wally Meagher' (cf. also 061.13–27)

ph another good fellow gone wrong

cg blind man's buff *G* Blaff!: bang! *Da* skib: ship sneaked into the harbour

pee (leak); pea (lentil)

laden

G leidend: suffering

(the P/Q split, continued down to .28)

(mirrors: mirror images) conversely *U*.734: 'posterior female hemispheres'

semidemihemiquavers: 1/64 notes in music

ministering *L* subligatus: tied on below

G Minne: love

091.06: 'Cliopatrick' *s* Cherry Ripe *L* mutatis mutandis: the necessary

Croagh Patrick: mountain, Co. Mayo *F* chérie: dear changes being made

between

unmentionables:

It mutande: drawers *nr* Little Bo Peep underwear

Sl aunt: whore *nr* 'She sells seashells by the seashore'

Elizabeth & Maria Gunning: Ir. sisters who married C18 Eng. aristocrats, subjects of popular enthusiasm in D

021.15: 'prankquean'

(032.03) Sechseläuten: Zurich spring festival

sex appeal

boy & girl

AngI colleens: girls *AngI* to take leg-bail: to run away

white & black piano keys *It* arpista: harpist *G* Klavierspielen: piano playing

G nicht?: isn't it?

Black Arts

Bach & Liszt *F* études: studies

listed *F* étourdi: scatterbrained

s Where Did You Get That Hat?

watching brief (law): instructions to counsel to attend hearing on behalf of one not a party to case, in case latter's interests affected

(506.28) time how goes the enemy: what is the time?

Tomsk: town, Siberia; Tomsk regiment in Crimean War

Russian

damn

G Schaum: foam

R rossiya moya rodnaya mat: Russia, my native mother

old stager: veteran *pr* What is sauce for the goose is sauce for the gander

South

North gentile Diodorus Siculus reported that in Egypt anyone

giant killing a cat was executed (*History* I.83.8–9)

L galli: cocks

L Galli: Gauls

'Sunflower State': Kansas

drooping hat (.07)

'heliotrope' orig. used for all flowers that turn towards sun, e.g. sunflower

Liburnus: Roman god of lustful enjoyment New Amsterdam became N.Y.C.

Putamayo, Brazil Liburnia, region of N. Illyria (now Yugoslavia)

s Erin, the Tear & the Smile in Thine Eyes

Moore: *s* The Time I've Lost in Wooing: 'The light that lies In woman's eyes, Has been my heart's undoing' *Da* lyd efter lyd: sound after sound

mind's eyes

G Ohrwurm: earwig out of

close both *L* claudere: to close, shut *F* garce: slut

cloudburst

'A man may laugh through the whole of a farce, A man may laugh through the whole of a play, But a man can't laugh through the hole of his arse, 'Cause he just isn't built that way' (Irish, Anon.)

L noli me tangere: touch me not

(John 20:17)

s The Three Ravens: 'Down a down'

poetry (defecation of the Russian General, cf. 344.12–30)

pottery *F* puer: to stink

seen

(215.22-3)

the same to you
anew
mastodon

mammoth   *Da* tropper: troops

trousers   *L* stultiam: folly

in vain   *L* ineptias: absurdities
L in vino veritas
strapping: copulating
AngI ph top of the morning!
turkey drive: whist drive, &c. with turkey as prize

perhaps   for him
G hohe: lofty, exalted   *G* hehr: majestic
Da fra: from   I defy the Lord Mayor
define
& the Lady Mayoress   & the Prince of Wales   Oscar Wilde

G Schottland: Scotland   scenography: presentation of a building &c. in perspective
ballet   *s* The Night of the Ragman's Ball   *R* melay: pleasant, aimiable   L/R
Tailors' Hall, The Liberties, D   mellay: var. of mêlée, fight
ph eat, drink & be merry   *L* gallus: cock

I gall: foreigner   call   nether world
J.H. Todd (ed.): *The War of the Gaedhil with the Gaill*   *The Leather World,* trades journal
in fact   *ph* lock, stock & barrel
Theatre Royal, D, had a 'Stock Company'
thomistic: in manner of St   St Laurence O'Toole: patron of D
Thomas Aquinas or his followers   *I* laircim: I smite, strike
St Thomas à Becket   The Black & Tans: Eng. recruits in 1920-1   'brandy' orig. 'brandewine' from
Butt & Taff (338-55)   serving in Royal Irish Constabulary   *Du* brandewijn
bankrobbers   *F* trou normand: pause in the middle of a long meal; the Calvados one drinks during it

bank clerks   Nast, Kolb & Schumacher: bank in Rome where J worked in 1906

The Bottle Riot, 1822: riot in Theatre Royal, D, in demonstration against leniency to Catholics of Lord-Lieutenant Richard Wellesley. Missiles, including a whiskey bottle, were thrown

G Ehren: honours
Fyn: Danish island
L insula: island   wedding
G Insel: island   *Cant* wap: copulate
radio   Roderick O'Connor: last Ir. high king   broadcast
rainbow covenant between God & Noah (Gen 9:9-17)   *It* eccolo: here he is   hollowing
Eccles 11:1: 'Cast thy bread upon the waters'   *s* Come Back to Erin
Butler: *Erewhon*
Scandinavia   unusual suits of clothes (324.29-30)

Arthur (Wellesley; Richard's brother–Wellington)   (008.21)
white horse: emblem of William III
ladies & gentlemen

Du Kerstfeesttijd: Xmas time   Moore: *s* They Came from a Land beyond the Sea [Song of Innisfail]
crucified
Matt 26:38: 'usque ad mortem' (even unto death)   Pusey led Oxford Movement (R.C. revival)
whiskey & water
Li kapinės: graveyard
L invitus: unwilling   captains
(ship's husband)   elect   Meilhac & Halévy: *Frou Frou* (opera)
G Frau   *F* froufrou: rustle of clothes

widdershins: contrariwise

(494.24) Norwegian Captain best man
Northern Whig: Belfast newspaper batsman

that seems Oscar Slater wrongly convicted of murder with hammer & imprisoned 19 years

search
Li sergas: sick
hardly (midnight)

s Master McGrath

G Kuckuck: cuckoo

(035.30–33)

Beefeater blue & buff: Whig colours; also colours of Duke of Beaufort (& his hunt) Henry Flood: Ir. politician

just like *Li* brolis: brother *Li* sesuo: sister tickling cackles (laughter)

lump in her throat
troth
L cygnus: swan *G* lächel: smile J.M. Barrie: *The Twelve Pound Look*
Du lach: laugh
Royal Irish Roman Catholic whoopingcough *It* cacchi (pl.): euph. for penis
L cachinno: I laugh aloud
s Finnegan's Wake: 'Shillelagh law was all the rage'

epexegesis: addition of words in further explanation

Li perkunas: thunderclap beyond *Li* pinigas: money
peculiar point Yawn
piece of cheese
s I Am Resting in the Arms of Jesus (025.12)

Sackerson (booser) *Li* avis: sheep *Li* oska: goat

Li blogas: bad (laugh)
bloody
186.32: 'Where ladies have they that a dog meansort herring?'
swart: dark
s Finnegan's Wake: ''Twas woman to woman & man to man'

hurley-burley

'tween-decks: space between decks of a ship

regret

G Schublade: drawer; *F* tiroir: drawer (both in furniture sense)
shopladies'
to humour her husband's hobby Massa: town, Tuscany
tantalizer secretaire: piece of furniture with drawers, for papers &c.
bunch of keys *G* Klee: clover *G* Schalter: ticket window *Li* sidabras: silver
shoulder *Li* žiedas: ring
L anulus: ring *AngI* findrinny: silver-bronze *It* croce: affliction curlingtongs
(ring finger) cowslips Croce (expounded Vico)
nr 'the dog that worried the cat that killed the rat that gnawed the rope that tied the sack that held the malt that lay in the house that Jack built'
Sl sap: snake *Cant* mort: woman, wench

jugular
Jacke Jugeler: anon. C16 interlude
Jack the Ripper

Lord God! *s* Old Folks at Home: 'All up & down the whole creation'
followers of Goll killed Finn
seric: silken drysalter: dealer in gums, dyes &c.;
serious *obs* in salted meat & pickles
Izod: Isolde

ph in the pink: in good form almanac

G Brust: breast *Gr* megalo-: great Magellan: 1st man to sail around world
Great Bear (constellation) *U.*327: 'the winebark on the winedark waterway'
Magellanic Clouds: 2 star clusters

Christopher Columbus *Li* žodis: word satisfaction
Kish lightship off D *Sp* caramba!: by Jove! *Sl* pink: hit
Caesar: 'I came, I saw, I conquered'
Li kišu: to stick *Li* varna: crow
glassful Matt 7:3: 'beholdest thou the mote that is in thy brother's eye, but belle
G glanzvoll: glittering considerest not the beam that is in thine own eye'
ALP Annabella, village, Co. Cork
Verdi: *Ballo in Maschera* (*The Masked Ball*)
ten ton (035.31) Santa Sabina, church, Rome A . . . L . . . P
G toller: mad, wild

II Timothy 4:1: 'the quick & the dead' softer *G* Saft: sap mightier the man
deed deaf safer tap staff (blind) main: open sea
pr the more the merrier constricted street Vasco da Gama: navigator
Eccles 9:11: 'The race is not to the swift'
L circumconversio: a revolving ALP (before the stone age) Mt Paganella, Italy huguenot HCE
Lithuanian pagans (converted by Prussians)
Cromwell energuman: one possessed *L* caecus: blind cacodaemon: evil spirit *L* absque: without
juggernaut of a devil *L* deditio: surrender ALP
L litteris: letters Patagonian H . . . C . . . E *Sp* herrero: blacksmith Cabot discovered Newfoundland
Herrera y Tordesillas: *General History of the West Indes* *F* cabotine: strolling player, barnstormer
It putta: wench
explorer exposure
tiptop Persse O'Reilly
Li taip: yes, so
L nautae: sailors

Coleridge: *The Ancient Mariner* 141–2: 'Instead of a cross the Albatross about my neck was hung'
Li kava: coffee *Li* arbata: tea *Li* malkos: firewood
s 'Lots of fun at Finnegan's Wake' *Li* anglys: coal

Persse O'Reilly

Li namas: house *I* súil: eye sorrowful
soulful
s Do Ye Ken John Peel: '& his horn & his hounds in the morning'

L primus auriforasti me: you first earpierced me

Euclid: 5th common notion: 'The whole is greater than the part' Shackleton: explorer

ever thought of being ordained (291.F4)
Artane: district of D (Christian Brothers' school)
s Father O'Flynn: 'Och! Father O'Flynn, you've the wonderful way wid you'
'Town of the Ford of the Hurdles' (D) *s* Johnny, I Hardly Knew Ye

query

Tut-ankh-amen Newcomen Bridge, D

Li tiltas: bridge solar year solemnly shadow of a doubt
Heb salem: perfection *L* num fit: it's not going to happen?
Canicular year: ancient Egyptian year, based on Virgil: *Eclogues* IV.5: 'saeculorum nascitur ordo' ('the
rotation of Sirius order of ages is reborn')

Gr selene: moon St Augustine: 'Securus iudicat orbis terrarum' ('the verdict of
seriously serenely the world is secure')–phrase influenced Newman (cf. *Apologia*)
L securius indicat umbris tellurem: more securely he points out the earth to (or by) the shadows

doubt

L Annus Domini: year Corrig Avenue, Dún Laoghaire
of the Lord *L* Amnis Dominae: River of the Lady marquis Cork
eleven hundred & thirty two

s Crazy-headed John (Russian folk ballad) *G* Weh: woe, pain
Karl Jorn: tenor *Li* bulve: potato
fruitful as his organ *L* ex ungue leonis: we know a lion by its claws (reconstruction of whole
G Orkan: hurricane from part) *L* leno: pimp
Dolphin's Barn: district of D as others say
James (Joyce) performed strange dances when drunk
Tophet: place of burning dead bodies, S.E. of Jerusalem; hell

Nijinsky: Russian dancer *Gr* choreios: pertaining to a choral dance
G Knie: knee episcopally
(some folk- calendar *s* Ta Ra Ra Boom De Ay
dances represent rotation of sun) tarantella: a dance
s 'You should see me dance the polka, You polecat waltz
should see me cover the ground, you should see my petticoats swinging as my partner whirls me round'
G Schrei: cry, shout
Piedigrotta: church in Italy built miraculously in 1 night

Christopher Columbus (birthplace prob. Genoa) (whirling dervishes)
rumba Czardas: a dance
(215.23) se mi ricordo: if I remember pantaglione: pantaloon in the commedia del arte
leaf (shaking)
boiling

Papageno & Papagena in *The Magic Flute* King Priam of Troy
L priscus: old *L* genua: knees
EHC Edwin Hamilton: writer of libretti for *Oedipus Rex* Roxy Theatre, N.Y.C.
Gaiety Theatre, D, famous for Xmas pantomimes Oropus: ancient Greek city with theatre
tripudium: sacred dance tripudiate: dance for joy area
Heraklitos: 'panta rhei' ('all things flow')
years Moore: *s* They May Rail at This Life [Noch bonin shin doe] Noah

L bonum: good

nr 'What are little girls made of, made of? . . . sugar & spice & all things nice' mad

Tristan threne: dirge

Moore: *s* Take Back the Virgin Page [Dermott]

Grania

L pace: by leave of

amnesty metamorphosed
amnesia met & more fussed
U.717: 'flotsam, jetsam, lagan and derelict' (lagan: goods or wreckage lying on seabed; derelict: that which is abandoned)
Listowel, town, Co. Kerry

Die Meistersinger composers supposed to avoid consecutive fifths
lancers: kind of quadrille (the ass)
G weiss: white *Twelve Tables of the Law* O

pedestalled
It podestà: head of medieval free city

(the ass)

(N. S. E. & W.) Desmond: S. Munster Connacht magical medical
Thomond: N. Munster Ormond: E. Munster musical

Coll hum: deceit, hoax marriage feasts

s The Rocky Road to Dublin
s '& the sticks they all went whacking, & the skulls, faith,
they were cracking, When McCarthy took the flure at Enniscorthy'
G Flug: flight
(a brick)

G Stecker: plug his Phoenix Tavern, Werburgh St, kept by James Hoey
chopsticks
certainly suddenly Hellfire Clubs: clubs of reckless young men in early C18 (D had one)
G Schotten: Scotsmen
G was ist das? (term used in France for peephole) *F* vasistas: fanlight over door
s There's Hair Like Wire Coming out of the Empire
HEC Hephaestus: Greek god of fire, thrown down from heaven *Gr* kata: downwards
anvil (Christ descends into hell '3 days' to redeem unbaptised)
Vulcan: Roman god of fire
vacuum

L Noe et: Noah & *L* nonne: isn't it
Ecclesiastes, book of Bible
Fi niin: yes 'A'

Arch an: if

Aquinas name & address
acquaintance
Finn's Hotel (where Nora worked when she met J)

G Schüler: pupil (Viconian cycle)
Sl shuler: beggar, scrounger (birth) (marriage)
(death) *L* et caetera et caeterorum: & the others & the others
L in saecula saeculorum: for ever & ever

L ora pro nobis: pray for us *G* Donnerstag: Thursday *s* A Little Bit of Heaven
Cz hora: mountain *L* hora: hour *L* nubis: tempest
L dei metuus: fearer of god
(marriage announcement) *L* amnis: river
Lower Sackville St, D Westmoreland St, D
(now O'Connell St)
Hospice for the Dying, D Donnybrook: S. D district reverend
Bonnybrook: townland nr Coolock, Co. D
ABC Carlisle Bridge, D (now O'Connell Bridge) bridesmaids

Mass suddenly shot 'the '45': Scotland's Jacobite defeat (1745)
G Schotte: Scotsman fortified
funeral notice: 'No flowers by request'

mayhap ALP
(newspaper advertisements)

Du mof: 'jerry', German swastikas
most of it sweepstakes

(511.10) (512.04) (512.06) (511.19)

G.A.A.: Gaelic Athletic Association Guy Fawkes 'The lady with the lamp': Florence
Da gaa: go (514.13) (511.09) Nightingale (511.12)

Great Scot! him & her

he & she earliest oldest
Eire

ever *Confiteor:* 'mea culpa'

(511.08–9)

L clam: secretly *G* Kram: junk *L* coram: openly spick & span *Sl* cram: lie, falsehood periwinkle whelk

not a word

damn the thing

G. Sigerson ('Erionach'): *Bards of the Gael & Gall* A tale told of Shem or Shaun Nick
J.H. Todd (ed.): *The War of the Gaedhil with the Gaill* *G* nicht: isn't it?
Macbeth V.5.30–2: 'a tale told by an idiot, Full of sound & fury, Signifying nothing' Mick
F sang
motto of the House of Savoy: Fortitudo eius Rhodum tenuit (His Strength Has Held Rhodes)
L Rhodanum: Rhone (*r*)

emphasize euphemize isochronism: property of occupying equal lengths of time
euphonize: render euphonious anachronism
W.G. 'Single Speech' Hamilton: Ir. M.P.; disembowelled (.05–06 have no vowels)
made brilliant maiden speech; said never to have spoken again
Heb laylah: night

ultraviolet
L ultra vires: beyond the powers
F procés verbale: minutes of proceedings &c.

blepharospasm: spasm of eyelid muscle (winking)

Capel Court, London (Stock Exchange)
Capel St, D

Co. Kerry carrier pigeon
Gr kyrie: O lord homing pigeon
massacred Holy Name societies (R.C.)
Mass, Credo
afore last night
after
before

minstrel
s Kafoozalem: '& with a verse of Al Koran, Have managed to bamboozle 'em'
Christy Minstrels doubly known

forget *s* All around My Hat I Wear a Tri-coloured Ribbon
Battersby & Co.: D auctioneers

Matt 5:38: 'an eye for an eye'
'Mister Bones': name for sideman in minstrel show
impediments (of speech) tricks *F* trique: cudgel
F perroquet: parrot

Hawarden: Gladstone's country place *nr* 'Pat-a-cake, pat-a-cake, baker man'

cheerful Prov 6:6: 'Go to the ant, thou sluggard'

Portrait I: 'Once upon a time and a very good time it was'
ant . . . grasshopper

Mr Chairman — *AngI* gag: conceited young fellow
Du meester: master
Bachelor's Walk, D — *Po* wesz: louse — West

MacSuibhne na dTuath Toraighe is sometimes called MacSweeney of the Battleaxes, by mistake of *Tuath* for *Tuagha* ('axes') — 'Henry of the Battleaxes': 12th Earl of Kildare
U.321: 'smashall sweeney's moustaches' — rattlesnake's
Tattersall vest (made of Tattersall)
ragamuffins — whistling

s The Wearing of the Green

Ru plyuskva: bedbug — busby — usual free & easy — Abbé Loisy excommunicated
G Läuse: fleas — *F* loisir: leisure — lousy
good morrow to everybody — boll weevils (pest of cotton)
Po mrowka: ant
Naas, town, Co. Kildare
nice
G Nägel: nails — fix — *L* miles: soldier

forth — comb — (apparently 'grizzly bear' as rhyming sl. for 'hair')
G sofort: immediately — The Coombe, street, D
s There's Hair Like Wire Coming out of the Empire

Major Sirr: British officer who practiced half-hanging in Ireland

1132

Browning automatic pistol — *G* wann: when — once one's one
Major Swann: colleague of Major Sirr
authority — forecasting — Hasculf: last Danish ruler of D — *Da* fanden: the devil
Thor
Miles de Cogan: C12 governor of D — John Donne

Da for sent: too late — waffling

Cains — *G* Patsch: slap, pop, smash

Patch Purcell's Ir. mailcoaches — protagonist — antagonist
factotum — Plantagenet
Book of the Dead

matter of fact

AngI amplush: a fix, difficulty — Talbot St, D
nonplussed
pawnshop — preparing
Sl pumpship: to urinate
L compos mentis
Memphis, Egypt
knew

sarsen: sandstone boulder on Wiltshire chalk downs — *s* The Wearing of the Green: 'I met with Napper Tandy'
s The Rising of the Moon (same melody): 'Shawn O'Farrell'
Moore & Burgess: rivals of Christy's Minstrels
Annu: Heliopolis

usual course of things
L annus cursuus: course of the year

L caelicola: inhabitant of heaven — photo finish
Photoplay: U.S. movie magazine

deaf

mute Adam

dumb
G dumm: stupid
Angelus *Arch* deal: part (082.03)
swede (root vegetable)
America *L* medicus: physician
Medici family, patrons of the magical arts
sure Huguenots were enemies of the Medicis
Juggernaut
just bowdlerize

beholder musket bowling green
black market
Moore: *s* Sublime Was the Warning [The Black Joke]

King Arthur's nephew Modred killed him murdered

Spike Island, Cork Harbour

Mutt & Jeff: Am. comic-strip
characters

together

Black Pig's Dyke: ancient Ir. wall of defence, border of Ulster

eyes (could not speak because biting opponent's head)

John Maddison Morton: *Box & Cox* (play Shaun the Post
about John Box & James Cox)
Shem the Penman
'Jim the Penman': James Townsend Savard, forger
hue & cry W.H. Leverhulme (Sunlight Soap)

Sl bester: swindler sunlight

as best as worst

40 Fort Carlisle & Fort Camden, Cork Harbour pianoforte
It forte: loud *ph* last straw breaking camel's back
G panschen: to mix up

G Bist du meiner Meinung?: Do you agree with me?
Greenwich Mean Time
six o'clock *Sl* pip emma: p.m. Greenwich

G quer: diagonal *L* quercus: oak

heavens

('Half twelve' in Eng. means 12.30, somersault *F* tard
in German 11.30) *Sp* tardes: afternoon
1132 *Sp* reloj: watch

how d'you do?

L ros: dew *ph* nine days' wonder

amity Empties, please *F* merci beaucoup
G Amt: office Armistice signed at 11th hour of 11th day of 11th month of 1918
Martinmas: 11 November

triduum: 3 days, esp. of religious observance *s* The Night before Larry Was Stretched
11 Nov is 3 days before St Lawrence O'Toole's feast day (14 Nov) deathwatch beetle
Gr chronos: time 4 Watches of the Night larboard: port (side) dog watches on ship (4–8 p.m.)
Wyndham Lewis was told that J always carried 4 watches & rarely spoke except to ask the time (1921)

*U.*154: 'After one. Timeball on the ballastoffice is down, Dunsink time' (25 min behind Greenwich time—until 1917)
observatory of Rugby School
warfare love of Moses Mars (war) ambivalent

Virtues & Principalities are orders of angels

Upper O'Connell St, D, was Drogheda St in C18 *Sl* devil's dust: gunpowder

Milesians: last legendary colonists of Ireland

so help me *I* an giolla goillín: the devil
Macgillycuddy's Reeks, Co. Kerry
The Blarney stone is set under battlements from which one leans to kiss it
Long Stone (Steyne): pillar erected by Danes in D kismet: fate, destiny ('Stone of Destiny': Lia Fáil)
St Lorcan (Laurence) O'Toole: patron saint of D

egad! meat eaters

versus vegetarians

HCE hands

revolved

G Ersatz: substitute watering-can
G Elsass-Lothringen: Alsace-Lorraine
It bere: to drink

rebelling

Tolstoy: *Voina i mir* (*War & Peace*) twins Picts & Scots
L merum: wine beer & wine
caricatures *F* roman celebrate
Caractacus: British chieftain, resisted Romans romance
expulsion of the Danes (⚔ Clontarf, 1014) *It* scusa!: I beg your pardon
Gr Danos: Danes *Gr* Danaos: Greeks
Upright Man: The Wooden Man, erected in Essex St, D
Sl upright man: leader of criminal band *Rum* limba: language
Buckley's tuxedo Vercingetorix: Gallic chieftain who revolted against Caesar
It Lingua Romana in bocca Tuscana ('a Roman tongue in a Tuscan mouth'): definition of good Italian
L in fine: in the end

R muzhik: peasant future barbarians of the past
G Zukunftsmusik: music of the future (Wagner's term for his compositions)

Dan Donnelly: C19 Ir. prizefighter
R da: yes
John 1:14: Tolstoy: *Voina i mir* (*War & Peace*) *L* in vino veritas *L* ab chao lex: legislation from chaos
'the Word was made flesh' meed: reward *L* viritim: separately
G nicht wahr?: right?
G Wehr: weapon
'pura e pia bella': religious wars of Vico's heroic age amen
John 1:14: '& dwelt among us'
Balbus: Roman who tried to build wall in Gaul

hellish
howl
Father Pinamonti: *Hell Opened to Christians, to Caution Them from Entering into It* (a source for the hell sermon in *Portrait*) Christmas

CH . . . E   *G* klingen: to sound   *Du* engels: English
G Engel: angel
sinned   all   I Peter 5:8: 'be vigilant; because your adversary the devil . . . walketh about'
AngI pattern: a patron saint's day   *G* Putsch: revolutionary outbreak   pro & con
pantomime
G Minne: love   week
L communis et propria: public & private
s The Night before Larry Was Stretched   Butler family, earls of Ormonde
called
U.306: 'artillery of heaven'
It forte: strong, loud   *Thousand & One Nights*
ph cock & bull story   King Lludd founded London

right   large as   *Sp* largo: long   teetotum: 4-sided disk spun in game
ΛE⊏
(P/Q split)   *Sp* pequeño: small

very funny

funfair   fere: able to go
there it is
MW   brass latten: brass beaten very thin
It lattina: tin, can
wing a part (theatre): learn it in wings before making entrance   rally (theatre): increased tempo, e.g. at climax
pong (theatre): to substitute words for those in the part, if forgotten
ramp (theatre): plank leading to stage
rant (theatre): to act noisily
'Athens of the North': Belfast

Moore: *s* Believe Me, If All Those Endearing Young Charms

ph best foot foremost   (502.11–13)
ph open your mouth & put your foot in it
tor: pile of rocks; abrupt or conical hill

Cork Examiner: newspaper   make water   rain
(Mark Lyons represents Cork & Munster)   (501.36–502.01)
plenty   time
teeming
Y   Grand Jury   Roman Catholic
Calvinist
I Cor 13:13: 'faith, hope, charity'

(Luke Tarpey)

40 days indulgence

(Mark Lyons)   Antarctic   cup & saucer

recusant: one, especially a R.C., who refuses to attend Church of Eng. services
Moore: *s* 'At the mid hour of night, when stars are weeping, I fly'
Dean Kinane: *St Patrick* 201: 'making at the same time two hundred genuflections'

Phoenix Park

Turko the Terrible: 1st Xmas pantomime at Gaiety Theatre, D

begorra! Michael O'Clery: 1 of the Four Masters

(Matt Gregory)
(Johnny MacDougal)
AngI within the bawl of an ass: too near *Coll* stair-rods: heavy rain

cat's paw washing his ear (supposedly a sign of impending rain) Earwicker the convenience

patronised strangers

Sl soup & fish: dinner jacket

J wore a Borsalino hat *G* Tümpel: puddle

lightning

035.11: 'cad with a pipe'

God's truth confessional (038.18–25)

AngI cup-tosser: tea-leaf reader

promised to post Peter's pence: contribution to R.C. church
shieling: hovel pelf: money, riches tocher: dowry
Paradise *G* Alb: elf *G* Tochter: daughter
Paraguay *Sp* paraguas: umbrella alb: priest's white vestment
Father Theobald Mathew: Ir. temperance advocate Mass St Swithin (rain promised)

Thursday Browne . . .

. . . Nolan *F* soldat

nonbelievers disbelievers Notre Dame Ninon de Lenclos: courtesan
F écluse: milldam Church of St Mary del Dam, D
brother

ph rain cats & dogs *Du* foei!: for shame!
'dog-in-the-blanket' (*Portrait* I): roly-poly pudding
F anglais *G* du hast recht: you are right kelt: primitive weapon
MW angry as always
will, can & ought to (051.12) Burns: *For A'That & A'That:* 'That man to man the world o'er Shall brothers be for a' that'
Leinster, Munster & Connacht let yous all
Y *s* 'You take the high road & I'll take the low road & I'll be in Scotland before you, But me & my true love will never meet again On the bonny bonny banks of Loch Lomond' *Da* bil: auto, car
Scots gang: go Trollope

Robert Burns

MW *G* Quatsch: nonsense Loch Lomond

L fiat: let there be

Y really & truly

Ballyhooley, town, Co. Cork oleaginous
ballyhoo: blarney *Gr* hagios: holy
Red Hand of Ulster *The Annals of Ulster*: C15 collection of Ir. annals
lubricated
MW good (Ulster pron.)

L labrosus: with large lips *Sl* (*Canadian*) cabbage: paper money peppermint comfits *Sl* spangle: sovereign (money)

Y *I* rúta práta: potato root airy

L potator: drinker 2 Ir. viceroys were Earls of Essex
Sl to do something for potatoes: to do it for very little
Golden Bridge, Inchicore Road, D
Sl to swallow a hair: get drunk
Sp nada: nothing looking-glass
Lucan
(i.e. nothing—they wear kilts) 3 crowns on flag of Munster

F drapeau: flag

damn bloody

MW the name Sean can be anglicised 'John' motto of Belfast: Pro tanto quid retribuamus (For So Much What Shall We Repay?) Picts & Scots
pigtail
Sl staggerjuice: strong liquor

Sl stripped: (of spirits), neat
Raven & Sugarloaf, grocers, Essex St, D, ca. 1740 VI.B.23.39: 'larges (bottles)' Power's Distillery at intersection of John's Lane & Thomas St, D
Guinness's Brewery, James's Gate, D

Y *Arab* Bismillah: 'In the name of Allah'
Bushmill's whiskey made in Ulster

dove & raven released from the Ark Noah *ph* wet your whistle weasand: throat
MW
wits' end

Y Vartry water (supply to D from Roundwood reservoir) beat we retreat
Chapelizod

MW

Frank 'Ghazi' Power: Ir. journalist & hoaxer Christy Minstrel
Tristan

freck: desirous
Angl freckened: frightened

Y

(Frank Power's phoney bullet wound, a boil, convinced Parnell)

MW

Y

MW Leinster, Connacht, Munster

Y

Du hulst: holly
Ulster
MW (provinces)

Y *F* mais non, par exemple!: but no, indeed Emania: ancient capital of Ulster
It raffa: mob rapparee: Ir. plunderer
fenians
2 Ir. saints named Finnian

I mo rún: my precious Moore: *s* Farewell, but Whenever You Welcome the Hour [Moll Roone]
Queen's Quay Road, Belfast Queen's Road, Dún Laoghaire, near mailboat terminal
selling sailing
goodbye!

MW if I choose

Y

Red Hand of Ulster

certainly wheels within wheels: a complexity of influences (Ezek 1:16)

melano-: (prefix) black
dactylo-: (prefix) finger
(082.04)

seriously Sauvé: *Proverbes & dictons de la Basse-Bretagne,* no. 191: 'Les buissons ont des yeux' ('Bushes have eyes')

Sheba
Bulls & Bears: speculators on rises & falls, respectively, on Stock Exchange
orange v. green *s* The Peeler & the Goat

greengrocers

an ass

have

*U.*512: 'VIRAG . . . Did you hear my brain go snap?'
Souvenir of the 25th Anniversary of the Gaiety Theatre, 1896, 6: 'Thanks to Xrays, the time will come no doubt When he will snappograph you wrong side out'

3rd degree: police intimidation (of witnesses, &c.)

brain

pray HCE
Bray, town, Co. Wicklow cathexis (Freud): concentration of psychic energy on same person &c.
steatopygia: abnormal protuberance of buttocks

psychoanalysed

nurse's sympathy
(J refused to be psychoanalysed by Jung)
quadroon: person with ¾ Caucasian & ¼ Negro blood psychoanalyse
F brun
VI.C.5.30: 'ass = fog ✕'

(061.06) reporter

apropos
G Popo: posterior

pr Haste makes waste

begun

defendant
deponent: one who gives written testimony under oath

St Ives, Cornwall

King Lear III.2.60: 'More sinned against than sinning'

E. Fenollosa: *The Chinese Written Character as a Medium for Poetry:* 'A true noun, an isolated thing, does not exist in nature'

AngI -bally: -town

mufti: in plain clothes

own two

ph a long pull & a strong pull & a pull all together

HCE (announcement of horse sale) own

(horse's height measured in hands)

sire (horse racing)
F sieur

John Jameson & Son D whiskey

Samson & Delilah

horse-bay: stall for horse to stand: (of stallions), be available as a stud

D Bay

9 till 10
noon till dawn

G nun bis dann: now till then

invites inspection
L vice versa

Horace: *Satires* I.1.106: 'est modus in rebus' ('a middle course in all things')

logic: types of propositions by quantity: UNIVERSAL, PARTICULAR, SINGULAR

asseveration: action of confirming generally
ladies & gentlemen

(answers question of Ш being more sinned against, .09)

(039.18) intimate

(tree)
popular

plebiscites

wastepaper basket

Bosquet said of Charge of Light Brigade 'C'est magnifique mais ce n'est pas la guerre'
F bosquet: thicket, shrubbery

12 Dodecanese Islands
r Dodder, D

H . . . CE
host

Middlesex: Anglo-Saxon kingdom

moral turpitude

(12 diseases)

measles
mizzle: drizzle

gleet: morbid discharge from urethra

caries: decay of bones or teeth

sprue: tropical disease with digestive disturbance

mumps

gripe: intestinal pain

jigsaw

not to

barman (040.24)
Du buurman: neighbour

Tower of Babel

fact
fiction
obscene
epicene

NORTH

divisional police force

nouns: masculine, common, neuter or feminine

Essex (Anglo-Saxon kingdom) *F* filles: girls
EAST
(D Metropolitan Police)

Board of Public Works, D, responsible for parks

G Naturpark: natural parkland agents
F agence: bureau, agency

Coppinger's Register of St Thomas's Abbey (the fender)
(Thomas Court, D) (055.18)
'pon my Sam! (expletive)

logic: types of propositions by quality: AFFIRMATIVE, NEGATIVE, LIMITATIVE
(035.17)

bisexualism a proved

lectionary: book with lessons to be read at divine services

resident

L quis ut Deus: who like God Sussex (Downs); Sussex was an Anglo-Saxon kingdom
(attributed to St Michael) SOUTH
logic: types of propositions by relation: CATEGORICAL,

indenture: deed between 2 parties; edges are similarly indented

HYPOTHETICAL,

Da ey: island (Windward Islands, Polynesia; also W. Indies)
DISJUNCTIVE
cuneiform: wedge-shaped
supernatant liquid: in chemistry, that covering the substance under consideration (lit. 'swimming above')
The Naze, headland, Essex
marauding him
ante-meridian (a.m.)
s The Rakes of Mallow: 'Beauing, belleing, dancing, drinking, Breaking windows, cursing, sinking, Ever raking, never thinking'
Zodiac: ram, bull, twins, crab, lion, virgin, scales, scorpion, archer, goat, water-carrier, fishes

It dossi: backs tails

logic: types of propositions by modality: PROBLEMATICAL
somewhat
herrings
Du glad: slippery, cunning Wessex WEST
(Anglo-Saxon kingdom)

sprats
smolt: salmon after parr stage logic: types of propositions by modality: ASSERTORIC
I gealach: brightness; moon
assertative, so help me God (A) alpha be the extent of the superficies
G zwölf: 12 *L* olfactus: smell tench (fish)
fish suppers (L) lambda (293: diagram – *Vesica piscis*) (P) pi
L scaliger: ladder-carrier *It* pesci: fishes
average velocity pectoral fins of fish

logic: types of propositions by modality: APODICTIC *ph* as sure as eggs are eggs

F entre nous

A . . . LP regular

doodah: state of agitation

F rigolo: comical

HCE Ku Klux Klan *G* Watsche: slap delicately

Da mørkning: nightfall toilet
G Brack: refuse twilight
L testificor: testify John Rutty: C18 D doctor who extolled virtues of mineral waters

subjugation of congenital lust (schools of herring)

MW Cromwell: 'Go to Hell or Connacht' (from a Parliamentary Act of 1654) Aryan copulation
many Irish deported by Cromwell to Barbados *Gr* kopros: dung
Pelagius: heretic, perhaps Irish Montgomery St, D (in Nighttown)
Henry Montgomery founded Remonstrant Synod of Ulster
obsessed *Gr* (artificial) makroglôssia: state of having big tongue

microcephalic: small-headed

Leixlip ('salmon leap') on Liffey

Esox lucius: pike *Salmo ferox:* great lake trout (in deep lakes) taking

ready-made

Gr lalia: talkative Lola Montez: Ir. mistress of Ludwig I of Bavaria

L gubernator: steersman

Persse O'Reilly salmon fry 'Merry Monarch': Henry VIII
ova: unfertilized eggs
monachal: monastic a merry-go-round 7 churches at Glendalough
I monach: guileful
Daniel O'Connell Conal: son of Niall of the 9 Hostages
dams *I* óg: young canals
readymade
Magna Carta signed at Runnymede
Du dondervisch: thunder fish Magna Carta ('great carp') *Du* is het niet zoo?: is that not so?
Vishnu (cf. .27)
Arch lax: salmon *Du* hooggeboren heer (Dutch form of address)

G Pluderhose: wide trousers

Arch freck: desirous, lusty
G frech: shameless
r Humber

HCE
MW
Blavatsky: *The Secret Doctrine* II.307: 'Vaivasvata Manu is the Indian Noah connected with the *Matsya* (or the fish) Avatar of Vishnu'; *Ibid.* 313: 'Vishnu is shown in the allegory as guiding, under the form of a *fish*, the ark of Vaivasvata Manu'
fishnet
Vishnu: 2nd god of Vedic triad; reincarnated on earth as half-man, half-fish for some time during & after flood
bullhead: a fish
Malin, Co. Donegal: most northerly point in Ireland
New Ireland, Melanesia

lungfish Finn MacCool
L cumulus: heap

Vaivasvata Manu
man-of-war
St Patrick landed at mouth of Vartry, anciently *r* Dea Romulus
r Dee homunculus
rope *It* bompresso: bowsprit

pull

Scottish burnie: little brook
Scottish byrnie: a coat of mail

Rev 12:14: 'her place, where she is nourished for a time, & times, & half a time, from the face of the serpent'
G Polster: pillow

in 1895 Hogg & Robertson acquired 40 acres at Rush, Co. D, for cultivation of tulips & other flowers: became known as 'Holland in Ireland'

s Tommy, Lad!

(216.04–05)

Pope Gregory I, seeing Eng. captives at Rome, called them 'not Angles but angels'

L tertium quid: a third part

ginger: (fig.) spirit, courage
Da slot: castle
D coat of arms has 3 flaming castles
jinnies (008.31)

reverend
John Walker: founder of a C19 Ir. sect
Apocalypse
Rev 1:9: 'I, John . . . was in the isle that is called Patmos'
utmost

JO naif: naïve *I* Cruachán: ancient royal seat of Connacht
I Naomh: Saint *U.*772: 'worse and worse says Warden Daly'
wander Moore: *s* Gone Where Glory Waits Thee [Maid of the Valley]

trefoil The Furry Glen, Phoenix Park

We glan: riverbank strapping barmaids *It* stilla: drop *Vanessa*, genus of moths
Stella Underwood: heroine of Charlotte M. Yong's *The Pillars of the House* (1873)
underwear Swift's Stella & Vanessa

Gi rawnie: lady, wife *G* Putzfrau: charwoman
superfluous
L fluvius: river
hair
Maud Gonne loved by Yeats

Clovis: king of Salian Franks broadcast
clubs
Carrick-on-Shannon, town, Co. Leitrim nr border with Co. Roscommon
Song of Sol 2:1: 'rose of Sharon'
Pond's cold cream
Coldstream Guards (regiment)
Vesta Tilley: male impersonator of 1890s *G* Bach: brook

(spelled backwards mirror image)

(207.02–03) *L* salices: willows widow's weeds
Alice *G* Weide: willow
G Wehl: bay (water)
veils
(see 527.04) Lough Sheelin, S. of Cavan
Da sælsom: odd *Da* brudlille: little bride narcissism

pr Necessity is the mother of invention Lewis Carroll: *Through the Looking-Glass*
Alices
parlourmaids in later life pools, lakes

the same   Chapelizod   *We* ys: it is   *L* tellus: earth   *Sl* tickey: threepence
It cappella: chapel   Ys: Armorican town swallowed by floods in C5 for sins of townsfolk
ph a penny for your thoughts

⊣   my dearest   horrid   finweed: rest-harrow, a herb
F même
Moore: *s* Come, Rest in This Bosom [Lough Sheeling]

wicked

dear old grandpa
grand passion
pasha: bashaw, high-ranking Turkish officer   (065.12–13)

Rosary is divided into 3 sections (chaplets): SORROWFUL MYSTERIES
(menstruation)
*U.*352: 'little wifey'

Eulogia: Eucharist (from *Gr* eulogia: blessing)

It assoluta: absolute   Boileau & Boyd: D chemists   (nuns as hospital nurses)
absolution
(to relieve her sunburn of a rich egg colour)

cross

very, very, very tiny   *F* froncer: wrinkle, pucker   how d'you do?   shake
F nue: naked

knickers

Isolde Blanchemains, Tristan's wife in Brittany
Isolde la Belle was fairhaired according to Bédier
JOYFUL MYSTERIES   Litany of the BVM: 'Mirror of justice . . . Tower of ivory, House of gold, Ark of the covenant!'
convent
(wedding rings)
F même: *L* idem: same

Tristan returns disguised to Cornwall to meet Isolde   Bartholomew
Bartolo: old man in *The Barber of Seville*
s O Sole Mio   D.V.: Deo volente (God willing)
L columba: dove
It netta: clean   *It* linda: clean

seen something   *G* Marille: apricot   *G* lieben: to love   *F* eau
thank you   (waves)   *Gr* libanus: incense
accents   sombre   each other
amber
rainbow   la belle Isabeau: child prophet of Camisards   *F* reine   learned yester e'en
Isa Bowman: friend of Lewis Carroll who played title role in *Alice in Wonderland* adaptation
moustached lips

suspicious

words all wrong   *L* futuo: I copulate with

child

GLORIOUS MYSTERIES

novena several Loreto convents in D
novice

Clotho: one of the Fates covey: incubate, hatch

banshee Alitta: Babylonian mother-goddess
banish
meantime place as arranged orange blossom (for wedding)
G bloss: naked
L audiens: hearing *I* rosán: shrubbery *G* Diamant: diamond breakfast
St Audoen's Church, D Roman Catholic chapel *G* Blick: glance
my own house BL Add. MS 47486A.54: '○ catclub'
G Minne: love
Mendelssohn (*Wedding March*) *Du* beminnen: to love
G Sinn: sense *Du* bemind: beloved
Gr Kyriê eleêsôn, Christê eleêsôn, *F* kyrielle: form of poetry; litany; rigmarole
Kyriê eleêsôn: Lord have mercy, Christ have mercy, Lord have mercy (prayer)
L Sanctus, Sanctus, Sanctus: Amen my dearest vanished
holy, holy, holy (prayer) *F* même Anguish: father of Isolde
sister

Esther (names of Stella & Vanessa) *G* Magd: maid Matthew, Mark, Luke & John
true you know who Sudermann: *Magda* Mary & Martha
r Tolka, D fay: fairy; doomed

MK Eusapia Palladino: medium *F* elle tait tout: she is silent about all *F* clou
F fais-le: do it!
F hystérique *G* Ding an sich: thing in itself, distinct from perceived thing (Kant)
ph tit for tat prose-poem proem: preface *It* suora: nun, sister

delicious *Through the Looking-Glass*
Alice
s 'Jumbo said to Alice: "I love you"' (032.03) bell
Alice in Wonderland
Sechseläuten: Zurich spring festival think of a number, double it . . . *Sp* presentacion: show, exhibition
Presentation of the Virgin Mary as a child (in Apocryphal Gospels)
Annunciation (to the Virgin Mary by Gabriel) nuptials
apparition of the Virgin at Knock, Co. Mayo, 1879 (Immaculate Conception)
Matt 7:7 & Luke 11:9: 'Knock & it shall be opened unto you' appear Sun-Yat-sen: Chinese revolutionary
G Erscheinung: phenomenon (Kant); apparition *Da* hilde: ensnare
Vaucluse, where Petrarch lived *F* voiler: veil
Cyril & Methodius: principal saints of Eastern Church St Olga 'the Slav'
lyric melodious Anglo-Irish
(527.12: 'Eulogia') Euphemia: Pascal's sister *L* ambidualis: round about 2
Gr euphêmia: use of auspicious language; praise
George Sand: *Consuela* (032.03) *Sp* consuelo: comfort
Angelus: 'et concepit de Spiritu Sancto': '& she conceived of the Holy Ghost'
Gr hoi tettara logioi: the 4 narrators

MW (mimics *MK*'s accent)

Munster 2 R.N.: original call sign of D Broadcasting Co., 1926 ('Come back 2RN')
U.328: 'Cows in Connacht have long horns'

share 1542: general submission of Ir. Lords to Eng. Crown

border between N. Ireland & Ir. Republic
Cobh, Co. Cork (Munster)
Moore: *s* The Minstrel Boy [The Moreen]: 'The Minstrel Boy to the wars is gone' *I* a stoírín: my little treasure
more in store
Munster & Connacht *Sl* moke: donkey

Document no. 1: The Treaty (term used by de Valera's supporters)
G nimmer: never Matt 19:30: 'the last shall be first'
(prisoner—Yawn—railed in by chairs)

answer my questions

100 women & children burned alive at Scullabogue after ⚔ New Ross, 1798

brose: type of porridge commissioners Ida Wombwell (060.22)

Sl raspberry: sound of dislike or contempt sixteen *Du* steen: stone

Maud I. Crofts: *Women under English Law* 13–14: Parnell
'compellable to serve as jurors . . . jury . . . can be empanelled'
(6 counties in Northern Ireland)
Crofts 10: 'the Court of quarter sessions . . . the Sex Disqualification (Removal) Act of 1919'

Committee Room Fifteen (where the vote was taken which ousted Parnell from leadership) pair
Sl general: maid-of-all-work
'nose money' extracted by Vikings: they cut people's noses off if not paid

Martha & Mary Dan Leno monologue: 'The Draper's Assistant'
sisters
J.H. North & Co.: D auctioneers

go up

anteroom 3 tailors of Tooley St sent a petition to Commons beginning: 'We, the people of
Antrim interim England'
Bjørnson: Ibsen's rival, MacMahon: Fr. marshal in Crimea
'son of bear'; also, name MacMahon means 'son of bear'
Isaac Butt was ousted from leadership of Home Rule Party by Parnell
butt & hogsheads *G* Hochzeit: wedding
lawful possession *Sl* bellywash: thin liquor, rinsings

The Coombe, D street
paper-seller
Luke White: D bookseller; became great property owner Isle of Man
lock (of hair) *F* faux: false whoreson
□ Zeppelins were made at Friedrichshafen, Germany

bargain
bullgine: nautical locomotive
arse L/R Glasthule, Dún Laoghaire
Jonah (cab terminus)
ombre: card game for 3 players *Du* ziel: soul *G* Ziel: goal
Sl doughboy: U.S. soldier Cave Hill nr Belfast *Sp* nombre: name
CHE Hernon, Murphy & Dwyer: D city commissioners, 1924–30
Hearts of Steel: Ulster rebels in 1770s V.D. = Vicarus Dei (vicar of God); venereal disease
glengarry: kind of cap, worn by R.I.C. auxillaries, 1920–1
Glenageary, part of Dún Laoghaire
Royal Ulster Constabulary ulster: kind of overcoat made in Belfast

leave off

Du rook: smoke robbing the poor *G* Pfaffe: priest (derogatory) Peterson pipes *L* pater
Sl rook: cheat, defraud Paterson & Co. (D): manufacturers of matches
Father, Son & Holy Ghost actual

ph up to the hilt
(017.11)

nr Bye, Baby Bunting *I* torc: twisted neck decoration
Tom, Dick & Harry
Parthalón, legendary Ir. coloniser, Hengler's Circus was on E. side of Rutland Square, D
has sometimes been anglicised 'Bartholomew' nr Great Denmark St

enjoyable

Sl natural: a simpleton; also a child

falling sickness: epilepsy (hunchbacks) Samuel Roth pirated J in *Two Worlds Monthly*

Sl blind to the world: drunk

s Daffydowndilly

deaf-&-dumb

certiorari: writ issued by a superior court upon party's complaint of injustice in inferior court

(Sunday papers)

F sourd-muet: deaf & dumb lottery St Patrick's Purgatory, Lough Derg

letter distributor (postman) St Patrick's Cathedral, D

Roman Catholic chair go out

Balbriggan, town, Co. D, made hosiery in C18 *s* The Jar of Porter

cruse: drinking vessel

mind the house

s My Lagan Love (*r* Lagan, Belfast)

lady loves

panoply the Phoenix burned at Heliopolis

Dubliners called Viceregal Lodge 'Healiopolis' when Healy was Gov.-General

D Metropolitan Police

F gendarme auxilière

aeronautic sapper: military engineer

artillery

Norse-Erse *Du* woordenboek: dictionary truncheon

G ruf: call Van der Decken: captain in *The Flying Dutchman* *F* mignon: darling

G Deckel: cover, lid *L* magnus: great one

Sackerson: a bear kept near the Globe Theatre in Shakespeare's time

Ibsen: *'Til min Ven Revolutions-Taleren'*: 'I sørger for vandflom til verdensmarken. Jeg lægger med lyst torpédo under Arken' ('You deluge the world to its topmost mark; With pleasure I will torpedo the Ark')

Gr orchis: testicle 'Cyclops' narrator: 'Gob!'

s 'Wid my bundle on my shoulder, Faith! there's no man could be boulder, . . . & I shtart for Philadelphia in the morning'

F tulle: net without

It frulla: (it) whisks

holy preadamite: one who lived before Adam; believer in existence of men before Adam

2-handled sword supposedly used by Sir Amory Tristram is in Howth Castle

(used umbrella to lift girl's skirt)

Walpurgis Night

Ibsen: *Bygmester Solness* (*The Master Builder*)

Kitty the Beads, itinerant, lived nr Ticknock, Co. D Hecuba: queen of Troy

succubus *L* succuba: strumpet

improbable Copenhagen *Sw* röst: voice raised

Hagar: concubine of Abraham *G* rost: roast

Osiris sometimes known as 'the god at the top of the staircase'

K Pater Noster Armenia occupied by Turks from 1405; nationalism in C19–20 met by systematic massacres & starvation

G tückisch: spiteful amenities

'Our Father, Which art in Heaven' down to 'Give us this day our daily bread' (Lord's Prayer)
gibbous: humpbacked *Da* dag: day
Confiteor Pope's indulgence sanctioned
F confiseur: confectioner intelligence *L* panem: bread
Council of Trent, 1545–63 revised missal, breviary &c. P/K P/K *L* cave canem: beware of the dog
Da salmebog: hymn book *Da* omtrent: approximately
G Nummer: number *Da* halvtreds: 50

Michael Gunn managed Gaiety Theatre, D massaged deltoid muscles of shoulders
gone he was the best *Da* bedst: best *Da* sausepander: saucepan
suspender *G* Kisschen: little pillow Iron Duke: Wellington

rolling pin *G* Gänsefett: goose fat
when first discovered, the dodo was called 'vetgans' ('fat goose')

kettledrum (coffeebeans)

Mocha (coffee) ought scourged scratched Abraham's back *Sl* abram: a malingerer
barmbrack: Ir. speckled cake
love Obadiah: servant in *Tristram Shandy* patriarch's nose
L Noa: Noah
flour bucket if the stranger seen you giving squeezes
flower bouquet
queen of my heart *F* reine alone
skillet: stewing-pan reignest
La Goulue: 1890s Moulin Rouge star painted by Toulouse-Lautrec
(tongue & lips glued shut)
Toulouse-Lautrec picture *F* atelier Katti Lanner: ballet mistress
(placenames: Wexford, Toulouse)
*U.*229: 'poster of Marie Kendall, charming soubrette' *F* à la broche: on the spit (cooking)

bedpan *F* matelote: fish stew gigot sleeve: 'leg-of-mutton' sleeve

Toulouse-Lautrec shins chemise
Toulon, Fr. city Shem, Ham & Japhet
F jupon gas meter
(whisks up clothes dancing can-can) gauze by the metre
caught believe ballet *F* balayer: to sweep

It frullini: whisks

F La sauterelle: the grasshopper
Cinderella, Puss-in-Boots (pantomimes)
hobnob ladylike *nr* Highty Tighty

L quamquam: although can-can

P/K P/K horehound: herb used for cough remedy *G* Pförtner: porter, turnkey
s 'Dance to your partner . . . Lots of fun at Finnegan's Wake'

Sl faddle: foolery, trifle

4 elements: sylph: air-spirit; salamander fabled to live in fire, trolls lived under earth, tritons under water
top: (golf) hit ball above centre
(override K's speech & reach the tap—source—m)
Confiteor: 'in thought, word & deed'
dead

Finn MacCool *L* primipatriarches: first patriarch
Coole Park: home of Lady Gregory
Transylvania Tartarus
F terre
Jacob (Shem) Johann (Shaun)
yoke on
Marcel Jousse studied language of gesture Governor-General
date *F* par jesters justice Kovno: Lithuanian city

ECH erenagh: Ir. steward of church lands Sir Edward Carson: Ulster loyalist & opponent of
L custos: guard, keeper *Gr* megas: big Wilde
Gr eirênarchos: police magistrate ('peace ruler')
garrison Persian slippers *F* cherchez la femme
Da synder: sinner sender's Fum: George IV, for whom Kingstown was named
G unterschreiben: to sign *King Lear* III.4.187: 'Fie, foh, & fum' HCE

G Amt: office I'm Adam ECH *It* città: city *s* Here We Are Again
m Amsterdam Eternal City: Rome
Da gammel: old

Sitric Silkenbeard led Danes at ⚔ Clontarf, 1014
Several Sitrics & Olafs were kings of Viking D
Ausculph Mac Torcall, king of D in whose time D became subject to England *L* Pontifex Maximus: high priest, pope
point of fact Mass, I must *It* massimo: greatest
G Altenglisch: Old English

Anglo-Saxon Allen: Lord-Mayor of D *G* soll & will: should & will *L* augustanus: imperial
G Lachs: salmon
L ergastulum: slaves' prison Rathfarnham & Drumcondra: districts of D ('rath' means 'fort'; 'drum' means 'ridge')
L ergastulus: convict
Clondalkin: village W. of D ('clon' means 'meadow') Monkstown: district of Dún Laoghaire township
Clonliffe (Rd, D)

fact *ph* by my life!
fiction

(cricket, cf. 583.24–584.25)

ouija board very life
It vera: true
crim. con.: criminal conversation (i.e. adultery) malfeasance: misconduct, esp. official
G Krim-Krieg: Crimean War
F Sl fri-fri: brief ladies' undergarment, 'G-string'

moustache *F* cousines

Kisilev Park, Bucharest Stottsparken, Oslo Giglottes-Hill (now St Michael's Hill), D
G Lustgarten: pleasure garden giglot: giddy girl
F dot: dowry feed most greedily

nice
annoying
Babylon *Sl* the trade:
Bāb el Mā'la: gate of upper quarter of Mecca prostitution

have her arrested disguise

'Tombs': N.Y.C. prison D.M.P.: D Metropolitan Police
Sl lag: convict lagmen: judges in D Thingmote thinking of such a thing
(.14–15)

G Popo: posterior little wife
It popò: shit
Sl globes: breasts
L Flos mundi: Flower of the world (name applied to Maurice de Portu, archbishop of Tuam, died 1519)
harm's Skinner's Alley, D
Haram: area in Jerusalem Alley: Lord-Mayor of D
(beauty competition) Tennyson: *A Dream of Fair Women* *F Sl* passe: cunt
Manneken-Pis: statue in Brussels of a child urinating

M.R. Werner: *Brigham Young* (1925), 285: During their endowment ceremonies, Mormons received an Endowment garment 'which was always to be worn next to the skin. It . . . was fastened with strings at various places' sport

eyelets

G sowohl: so much her after (follower)
Da saavel her som herefter: now as well as hereafter

Heaven's incomparably

Chinatown Peking (Chinese lisp)
(Chinese women with bound feet)
Da prøvestykke: assay piece (test of skill for apprentice shoemaker)

Lambay Island, N. of Howth Dalkey
Lambeth Palace, residence of Archbishop of Canterbury
John Dowland, supposedly born in Dalkey, wrote lute music, some
celebrating his sadness lutestring: a silk fabric
tabinet: Ir. fabric: Ps 7:9: 'For the righteous God trieth the heart & reins'
watered silk & wool
'laying on of hands' *U.*562: 'His criminal thumbprint on the haddock' (haddock is supposed to bear
five Oslo St Peter's fingerprints) also
Luke 22:12: '& he shall shew you a large upper room furnished' (Last Supper)

Frankfort *G* eins, zwei, drei, vier: 1, 2, 3, 4

ME chantry: singing of Mass (in C16 D guilds organised chantry by 4 priests) Castrucci: C18
(bed) conductor; visited D, where he died in 1752. He was followed by de Mellos,
Wapping Old Stairs, E. London who established opera on Fishamble St
Cant wap: copulate oldsters sycamore
Rowntree: *Poverty* 339: 'Singing from note in *G* Haus: house Ibsen: *Et dukkehjem* (*A Doll's House*)
either notation' (board school curriculum) cage-work timber houses built in C16 D
Gretna Green Cabinteely, village, Co. D
Goose Green Avenue, Drumcondra, D
Howard Payne: *s* Home Sweet Home: marquis Moody & Sankey: U.S. revivalists & hymn writers
heartpains 'There's no place like home' Mark Sankey: Lord-Mayor of D said
O'Clery of the Four Masters Gregorian chant Johannes Sebastian Bach
It Gregorio: Gregory ✕ Matt Gregory . . . John (ass)
there's no such place

Norway *Du* kerk: church The Little Church around the Corner, N.Y.C.
nowhere 'Findlater's Church': Abbey Presbyterian Church, Parnell Square, D
Ku Klux Klan Katechism: booklet with K.K.K. doctrine & hymns
Arch the Belief: the Apostles' Creed

G Jugend: youth Hejaz: province, Saudi Arabia hedge-school: open-air school (formerly in Ireland)

parochially *Per* baji: sister
caliphate: office of spiritual leader of Islam
St Michael *G* Engel: angel

Isthmus of Sutton joining Howth to mainland telephone
Satan Sutton: Lord-Mayor of D
clairvoyance

G reicher: richer superstition raptures
reacher-out
ears Holmenkollen: hill near Oslo
homeland calling
(ordinary shares) four shillings & ninepence halfpenny

Stockholm unsteady (market) Liverpool large hogs
one pound, four shillings & twopence
annoying good, better, best
Big-butter-lane in old D

call goodnight, everybody & a merry Christmas
R noch: night
appreciate New Year customs thank you *Da* tak: thank you
your custom (trade) Kyoto: capital of Japan until 1868
Du tiktak: tick tock

duplicator

s Tramp, Tramp, Tramp, the Boys Are Marching

CHE BBC

G ernst: earnest *Da* morsom: amusing entertainment God's truth!
An old man with a young girl is said to have a colt's tooth
answer *Da* tand: tooth John Luttrel, sheriff of D, 1567–8
give handsel: give pledge literally teaspoonful
Horatio Bottomley: blackmailer & politician
F Sl baba: buttocks
Keemun & Lapsang Souchong: Chinese teas contango: Stock Exchange term for money paid to postpone completion of bargain *L* tango: I touch
39 Articles (Church of Eng.) of clothing Phoenix Park
Sl duds: clothes Pnyx: hill in Athens
prove mercy . . . justice (187.24; 193.31)
The Provost: military prison, D Gramercy Park, N.Y.C.
Everyman Mormon a D deed of 1434: 'said masters shall keep said
woman houses stiff & staunch for ever'
Arab Misr.: Cairo N., S., E. & W.

caveat: warning

Tib & Tom: buildings on Hoggen Green, old D

James Blow: 1st Belfast printer
Bottomley Keyser's Lane in medieval D, vulgarly named Kiss-arse Lane blue-eyed angel wearing
Lane-Joynt: Lord-Mayor of D Waring St, Belfast
libel suit Knockbreckan Reservoir, Belfast water supply Belfast bullrings *ph* run rings round
Falls Road, Belfast (R.C. area) rude accent canvasser *Saunders' News Letter:* D newspaper
Red Hand of Ulster
Nightletter (308.16) *F* noce: marriage *Post Office Directory* (D) business
Sp noche: night *F* lettres Belgrade
'There was a young man from Belgravia, Who believed not in God nor in Saviour, He walked down the Strand with his balls in his hand, & was had up for indecent behaviour'
Thomas Pavier: literary forger Nonesuch: palace of Henry VIII

beauty spots (220.07)

Archer: Lord-Mayor of D (photography, hobby of Lewis Carroll)
Werner: *Brigham Young* 286: Mormon celestial world largely inhabited by spirits 'searching for tabernacles'
G Haben Sie so eines erlebt?: Have you experienced one like that? *Du* beleven: to experience
ph must be seen to be believed *ph* sight for sore eyes *It* caca: shit
North Strand Road, D *Da* domstol: court of justice snake eyes: double 1 in dice
Thom's Dublin Directory (*Post Office Directory*)
F étrangler un perroquet: drink absinthe
suffocated *It* soffiare: to blow Sofia, Bulgaria
'halfwife' (532.15) Dublin
double 'n's
G Dial Tepp: idiot cautioned
Keshan: Lord-Mayor of D
Lorcan Sherlock: Lord-Mayor of D all are Bältespännere ('Belt-Bucklers'): group of statuary, Gothenburg
Sherlock Holmes
hair cut H. Travers Smith: *Psychic Messages from Oscar Wilde* 40: 'Shame upon Joyce, shame on his work, shame on his lying soul'
Atkinson: Lord-Mayor of D *Du Sl* lul: penis
s Çà ira: 'les aristocrates à la lanterne'
Sir William Skeffington, Lord Deputy of D, 1530: 'outcast mastives, littered in currish blood' ECH *Da* til: to
Hanging Tower was on D city walls by Back Lane
G stecken: stick *Arch* avoutry: adultery
(stake in heart: vampires, suicides) Staunton: Lord-Mayor of D
L instanter: urgently ladybird *s* The Night before Larry Was Stretched [i.e. hanged]

dandelion white face *Sl* phiz: countenance
Sl Jack a dandy: insignificant little fellow *r* Wad Fez, Morocco
Bartholomew Vanhomrigh: father of Swift's Vanessa, Man of Sorrows
Lord-Mayor of D Hungary son
G ursprünglich: original Thomas à Kempis: *The Imitation of Christ* imitate my cry us
Marcel Jousse studied language of gesture *L* immitis: harsh initiate

sexcentenary Hell Valhalla The Wooden Man: effigy on Essex St, D
centaur Porte de Hal, Brussels Odin = Wotan
Da hest: horse *Du* op: on *F* maman
Hesten: statue in Copenhagen
L majusculus: somewhat larger *L* magnus: great City Quay, D
majuscule: capital letter majesty leastways
Tara: ancient capital of Ireland *D Annals*, 962: 'the most noble city of D' priceless
L nova terra: new earth horsebacked *G* Ross: steed Ross: Lord-Mayor of D
Ferdinand *G* Pferd: horse alabaster *s* The Midnight Son: 'You needn't go trotting to Norway,
Yeddo: old name of Tokyo You'll find him in every doorway'
fanlight (white horse in fanlight indicates Orange sympathisers)

album greetings premises HCE

congratulations, excellency Eccles: Lord-Mayor of D
Eccles St
nr See Saw, Margery Daw *Sw* att angripa: to attack those
whoso Jack the Ripper *F* Jacquerie: rioting peasants (esp. C14)
Du makkers: friends adversaria: a commonplace book
Du ginder: over there I Pet 5:8: 'your adversary the devil'
speaking *Du* duivel: devil Land's End, Cornwall London
Spuyten Duyvel: area in N.Y.C. *Da* ulv: wolf Skärgaard: islands off Stockholm
Skeppsbro: main quay, Stockholm old city *Du* meisjes: girls *Du* zulke: such silken
Gore: Lord-Mayor of D *G* Meise: titmouse *Du* taart: tart (cake)
Ibsen: *Til min Ven Revolutions-Taleren:* 'De siger, jeg er bleven "konservativ"' ('You say I'm becoming "conservative"')
G Rathaus: city hall
N Bygmester: Masterbuilder *Gr* hystera: womb
business
Ibsen *Da* noksagt: enough said Peter & Paul
obscenest nonsense Nansen: Norwegian explorer
I siogán: ant Peter Paul McSwiney: Lord-Mayor of D
shogun: de facto ruler of Japan before 1869 *I* muc: pig
draff: refuse Enoch: first city, built by Cain (Gen 4:17)
We pr draff is sufficient for pigs
C yü: fish *Da* hed: hot Whitehead, town, Co. Antrim
White Hat (MacCool)

misspelt
Mespil Road, D
Fish is ancient symbol of Christ

H. Travers Smith: *Psychic Messages from Oscar Wilde:* Eustachian tube: passage from larynx to ear
'Oscar is speaking again . . . Pity Oscar Wilde . . . dear lady' Robert Eustace: sheriff of D, 1608–9
White family, owners of Corr Castle, Howth, before reign of James I
memories goodbye

world through

O.W. (Oscar Wilde): *De Profundis* snubbing 39 (articles)

memory failing
(white)
Ps 58:4: 'the deaf adder' *ph* deaf as an adder

Matt 7:20: 'By their fruits ye shall know them' Gen 3:12: 'she gave me of the tree, & I did eat'

friends *L* celeberrimus: most honoured blossoms
F friandise: delicacy, titbit
H.C.E. Childers: M.P. for Pontefract in late C19 womb *Du* boom: tree HCE
Erskine Childers: Republican involved in Howth gunrunning; executed by Free Staters

Sebastian Melmoth: name used by Wilde after trial
The rich went to Fr. Riviera in January Rio de Janeiro
Sl not all there: crazy *G* Fernsprecher: telephone messages departed
messuage: dwelling house plus adjacent land & buildings deported
appointment

HC . . . E *F* butte: hill

Gr psychê: life, soul Real Presence (of Christ in Eucharist)

'miracle wheat' sold by International Bible Students' Association (became Jehovah's Witnesses)
P.P. Quemby inspired Mrs Eddy, founder of Christian Science
Frank Buchman: *Soul Surgery*, handbook of Buchmanist cult
indigestion

babble of tongues (God created different languages after fall of the Tower of Babel)
Cromwell: 'Take away these baubles' 'Exsultet': 'O felix culpa!'
It culo aperto: open arse steeples wool, hides &c. called 'staples' in medieval D, a 'Staple town' bong! Auld Reekie: Edinburgh
ringing the mind: commemoration for deceased member of a D craft guild
bonze: Japanese Buddhist priest
F arrondissements
AngI bally-: -town Kremlin Crumlin: district of D
Gr eleutheria: freedom *Gr* eleaô: to have pity Sechseläuten: Zurich Spring festival
a D bye-law of 1533: 'within the stremmis & libertys graunted to the sayde cyttye'
rue Moncrieffe & Hone: Lord-Mayors of D *G* gestern: yesterday Nobel Prize
truly *AngI* ochone: alas Algernon Moncrieff in Wilde's *Imp. of Being Earnest*
today bronchitic Akershus: country around Oslo, also castle there Oscar Wilde
The Bronx, N.Y.C.
F haute top hat (known in France as 'huit reflets') *G* Stock: stick
White: Lord-Mayor of D Taff (Butt in .04) Hoyte: Lord-Mayor of D 'take off that white hat' (322.01 &c.)
G Eisen: iron *Sl* prop: leg (Order of the Garter)
Stock im Eisen: ancient tree stump in Vienna The Royal Leg: C18 D shop for hosiery
Sp puerto: port *R* dăm: smoke hymnbook *Sp* boccada: mouthful
Sp puros magnos: large cigars *G* dampfig: steamy, smoky *G* Bock: goat
Vereker: Lord-Mayor of D *F* cigare
very carefully
cigar divan: cigar shop *AngI* redden: to light vesta: short match
Vesta: goddess of married chastity
L nepos: grandson *Gr* nephos: cloud nephews *G* Nebel: mist *Da* mest: most *Du* mest: dung
Sl Gladstone: cheap red wine

Mozart: *Zauberflöte* (*The Magic Flute*) Oscarshall: palace in Oslo D Guildhall in C13 in Winetavern St
G sauber: clean (said of wine) Oscar Wilde Buen Retiro: park in Madrid
Boyce: Eng. composer & chorister *G* flau: feeble, flat
Boyce: Lord-Mayor of D boy's voice flattish flute
(grey hair) pepper & salt cloth
It salsedine: saltiness
sent to prison (Wilde)

Du ik miet et well: I know it well depressed depraved
Whitwell: Lord-Mayor of D Wilde: *De Profundis*
Du moed: courage

G Ich kann es nicht Connacht
Kane: Lord-Mayor of D
yeomen

lax: salmon second division: one of the 3 grades of imprisonment
Leixlip *L* lex: law
ph business is business broadcloth: fine black cloth
Haliday: *Scandinavian Kingdom of Dublin* 159: 'Scandinavian Things or Tings' [parliaments]
king of all kings Court of Skivini governed London in A.D. 1191
Allthing: Icelandic national assembly
Merchant's Quay, D Antient Concert Rooms, D Zerubbabel: prince of Judah in Ezra; rebuilt temple after Captivity
Barrington: Lord-Mayor of D
Sir Jonah Barrington: Ir. lawyer & historian X
Dr John Whalley: D astrologer
Jonah & the Whale
jurat: one who has taken an oath
L oremus: let us pray Harald Haarfagre: 1st king of Norway, also called Harald Fairhair
Lord's Prayer: 'Our Father, Which art in Heaven, Hallowed be thy name, Thy kingdom come, Thy will be done'
Harrods: London department store *Da* navn: name *G* Meine Kinder: my children
G Wohl: health *pr* There is nothing like leather Luther O'Shea (Parnell divorce case)
Du leuteren: to drivel *Du* leut: fun *AngI* shee: fairy nasty

pr People in glass houses shouldn't throw stones   *pr* The Englishman's house is his castle
Gladstone   Pigott forged letters implicating Parnell in Phoenix Park murders

EHC Elephant & Castle: area in London
Elvery's Elephant House: D raincoat shop   honest to goodness
VI.B.24.296: 'Taafe's brother Laving attempted   *It* rinunci: you renounce
about this time to take the life of a priest . . .   J.B. Rinuccini, Apostolic Nuncio, visited Ireland 1645–9
discountenanced by all persuasions'   (Mr Kernan in 'Grace' to renounce the devil with a candle in his hand)
Book of Common Prayer: Catechism: 'renounce . . . the pomps & vanities'
thoughtful   *N* døpe: baptise   misprints   virtue
Virchow Hospital, Berlin
Fifth Avenue, N.Y.C.   *r* Ovoca (Avoca)   *L* umbra: shade   Christianity
Ovocna Ulice: street in Prague   *D Annals,* 1535: George Browne, archbishop   Christiania: Oslo
Hu anya: mother   of D, embraces the Reformation   Celt (Eng. mispronunciation)

Mormons baptise their dead by proxy   *It* antenati: ancestors   *Da* stolt: proud

Robin Redbreast
Rabbi   *Arch* leech: doctor
Dr Rutty: D physician   *Du* lijfarts: personal physician   *G* Ehren: honours
Erin to victory
Conrad: *Under Western Eyes*   (English)   *G* ausbreiten: expand   Brighton
Aust sundowner: tramp who arrives at station about sundown, to obtain food & night's lodging
Land's End, Cornwall   England (inverted)   *Sl* stump up: pay up
Du eng: meadow, field
glucose   Peebles: town, Scotland
people
eric: blood fine for murder of an Irishman

enclosed please find my pockethandkerchief
cheque

L in toto: in all   stout . . . fermented
Stoyte: Lord-Mayor of D
L confoederatus: united by a league   *L* bellum: war
(I deny having conspired with Mr Billups to buy a female negro slave or to sell my fourth part in her)
waders: Wellington boots   townsfolk   Nugent: Lord-Mayor of D
Rainsford: Lord-Mayor of D
J. Webb: *The Guilds of Dublin,* 9: 'Osbertus de Kilmainham pulleter': member of Guild of Merchants of D, 1226
Before 1782, D tradesmen paid tax called quarterage, whence they were called quarter brothers
L locum tenens: substitute
Grub Street: literary hack work; term applied by Swift to much of his work
U.S. grubstake: money advanced   *Arch* clepe: to name   constituent
to gold-prospectors   *Du* goedkoop: cheap   *ME* coup: to buy   usucapion: acquisition of ownership by long use

Blanchette = Paris (Rabelais)   Tcherna Djamia: Black Mosque in Sofia, Bulgaria
In C19 *r* Niger believed to have no outlet   Brewster: Lord-Mayor of D   jamjar
N Blaaland: Africa, in the Sagas
Brigstow: old name for Bristol (H.Q. of Eng. slave trade)
Deuteronomy
deuterogamy: marriage after death of first spouse
(Apocrypha)

G verbannt: banished   harrowing
Verbannte: G title of *Exiles*
feelings   pound   *D Annals,* 1300: 'Base coin, called Pollards & Crocards, cried down by
Du punt: point   proclamation'
F frick: cash   *Da* uden: without   (sulphur in matches)
T. Crofton Croker: 'Three Pebbles on the Beach' (folk tale)   Fricka: goddess of marriage vows
matchbox (safety matches)
Da bokse: box

King Cophetua made a beggarmaid his queen
P.T. Barnum's Bearded Lady was vouched for by affadavit: 'in spite of her beard, she is a woman'
were a frolic

Mons Meg: big cannon on parapet of Edinburgh Castle   each   *s* Finnegan's Wake   week
William Fanagan: funeral establishment, Aungier St, D   *G* wecken: wake   Bray, town, Co. Wicklow
Clonsilla, village N.W. of D   *s* Donnybrook Fair
Brooks: Lord-Mayor of D   lacking make in
HCE Edward Cocker: *Arithmetick*   Purdon: Lord-Mayor of D   pre-emption
James Hodder: *Arithmetick, The Penman's Recreation*   unpardonable presumption

Juno was worshipped under title Moneta in Rome & Alba, & her temple used as a mint
Empson: Lord-Mayor of D *L* moneta: money
Maria-Theresa, archduchess of Austria

William Ledwidge (later Ludwig): Ir. baritone dreadfully uninterested
truthfully
talking shop *Da* i hvad mig angaar: in what concerns me
(trying to disguise colour) counters J wanted Nora to drink
cocoa to put on weight (1909)

Miss Travers sued Sir William Wilde, Oscar Wilde's
father, for seduction
fancy nonentities octroy: of governments, to grant, concede
H. Travers Smith (535.26) tried Troy
Isolde borrow some *Du* melk: milk *Du* kaart: card, ticket
resell (the slave, 537.23–5) Melkarth: god of Tyre myself
Bristol (537.25) 100% (*F* cent)
Brixton: London suburb
auction bridge (game) horrible Hannibal (Flaubert's *Salammbô*, set in Carthage, was criticised for its
cruelty when published) *OF* honni: shame *It* crudelta: cruelty
tantamount *G* nackt: naked Borgia popes *Gr* orgia: secret rites *G* wert: worth
Gr skatos: dung
medieval ruins of ancient Carthage Improperia: Reproaches (of Christ from the Cross, Good Friday
G Ruhm: fame Rome *F* enceinte Service) improper
Gr chrysos: gold The Philosopher's Stone is white pebble
Robinson Crusoe Croesus: last Lydian king, world's richest man pimple
penis *Sl* clap: gonorrhea P/K *G* Kanzel: pulpit pox *F* cassé
L panis: bread *Sl* pencil: penis
postern: backdoor *Sl* tester: sixpence *F* cul prick
testicle *Sl* tickey: threepence culprit
F des écus: *Scottish* howff: 'place of resort' so help me God
plenty of money (écu, a coin) Cunzie House: mint in old Edinburgh
Cash: Lord-Mayor of D

G meine Herren!: Gentlemen! absurdity I mean
L surditas: deafness
too too (his one-line advertisement to sell the slave or milk cart)

F saumon: salmon
(second line of advertisement)
A. Peter's *Dublin Fragments* mentions old 'The Cherry-Pickers': Prince Albert's Hussars
D street cry, 'Boyne salmon alive' two Tew: Lord-Mayor of D
F catherinette: woman still unmarried at 25
gathering nets
Fishamble St, D *F* aube: dawn *L* Hesperus: the evening star
I mún: urine
Covent Garden, London wretched
coven (of witches)
youngsters *ph* not know a person from Adam *Du* zuster: sister
A'dam: abbr. for Amsterdam Zuider Zee, Holland
climbing *G* aus: out
Freiung: open space in Vienna
ph out of the frying pan into the fire *F* foyer *F* rassembler resembled
G Freiung: wooing *G* Pfanne: frying pan
G mein anomaly *s* The Man That Broke the Bank at Monte Carlo *It* Conte: Count
Shanks: Lord-Mayor of D
Co. Carlow *Arch* cullions: Deucalion: equivalent of Noah in Ovid *G* annehmend: assuming
testicles *G* ich habe gehört: I have heard
innocent seen *G* mit: those infants
with *F* sosie: double, counterpart
Evening Times (i.e. newspaper) *G* Revolverblatt: scandal sheet
chimes *G* schmutzig: dirty *Da* blotte: to bare thou hast
Mrs Hardcastle in Goldsmith's *She Stoops to Conquer* Schottenhof: Benedictine Abbey in Vienna
upon *Da* kongens: the king's *G* Schutzmann: policeman
Da ikke sandt?: not so? *Da* igen: again goddamn cheek
Gr ekêa: I was burning Gotham: village proverbial for folly of inhabitants; nickname
for N.Y.C.
shabby Howth Head
under white hat (MacCool) *D Annals,* 1029: Aulaffe Sitric 'ransomed on payment of 200 beeves . . . '

G Freiheit: freedom Pelagius: heretic, perhaps Irish

R chistay: pure An 1810 Bible gave for Mark 4:9 ('He that hath ears to hear'), 'He that hath ears to ear'
Roderick O'Connor: last high king of Ireland
Breeches Bible: the Geneva Bible of 1560 Manhattan
Jews take oath with hat on
The Long Stone: pillar in D marking place where the Danes landed Erechtheion: a temple on the Acropolis
erection menhir: tall upright monumental stone
Du een mynheer: a gentleman an Earwicker

Wordsworth

Dante, Goethe & Shakespeare *G* Aktien-Gesellschaft: joint stock company
Napoleon called the English 'nation of shopkeepers'
admires
Moyers: Lord-Mayor of D
card-palmer
palmer: pilgrim

Shinto: native Japanese religious system
4 Horsemen of Apocalypse: Death (*G* Tod), Fire, Plague, War (*G* Krieg) perplexed
G Krim-Krieg: Crimean War dead best Prudential Assurance Co. credentials
prudential: prudent maxim
coalmines
goldmines
G Spanien: Spain *Da* ogsaa: also
Siegfried, forging song: 'Hoho! Hoho!'

sundry Santry, district of D
Sunday closing (of shops)
ph Dear Dirty Dublin *I* Áth Cliath: Hurdle Ford (D)
The Battle of Brunanburgh (Tennyson's translation): '. . . the Norsemen . . . over The jarring breaker, the deep-sea billow. Shaping their way towards Dyflen again, Shamed in their souls'
G irr: confused, wrong
a landing
D Annals, 1801: 'Imperial standard hoisted on Dublin Castle'
advanced Vance: Lord-Mayor of D
G platzt: bursts *G* meine Residenz: my residence *Arch* bourd: jest
G Residenz-Platz: capital square board & lodging
Charter of Henry II granted D to the citizens of Bristol Staréměsto: Old Town, Prague
burgage: tenure whereby lands were held by yearly rent Bridge of Evora, Howth
bag & baggage Tholsel, D (old exchange building) main man in the street average female
Menai Strait *G* Fimmel: sledgehammer; craze
soccage: tenure of lands by determinate services other than knight service
Dunlop car tyre works at Fort Dunlop, nr Birmingham
D once centre for poplin weaving
11th E.B.: 'Washington': 'For many years such characterizations as . . . "City of Magnificent Distances" & "A Mudhole almost Equal to the Great Serbonian Bog" were common'
The Pale: Eng.-occupied part of medieval Ireland
Wallabout Bay, N.Y.C. talus: sloping side of an earthwork The Palisades, New Jersey
counterscarp: slope of the ditch supporting a covered way
Marshelsea Prison, D abattoir *F* blessé: wounded
G Sieg: victory Abbot: Lord-Mayor of D Warren: Lord-Mayor of D
⚔ Clontarf, 1014

L Annus mirabilis: Year of wonders *G* Marken: districts Wenceslaus I, king, first built walls of Prague
Da overdreven: exaggerated sword of
Prussian Albert I ('the Bear'): Margrave of Brandenburg, founded Berlin
G Stock: staff
Du patroonschap: patronage Kensington, London
Du schaap: sheep King's Inns Ward, D
Their Royal Highnesses Pope Urban Charlie Chaplin Charlemagne
Champagne Charlie, nickname of Charles Hardwick, friend of Edward VII
loved hated tenure
Henry the Eighth Terenure: district of D

Da skat og skuld: taxes, treasure & debt, guilt Floki of the Ravens: Norwegian who was guided to Iceland by ravens
In 1528 D visited by a pestilential sickness, the English sweat *G* Englisch: English epidemics
L oppidum: town

D Annals, 897: 'Ireland visited by a plague of strange worms, completely
having two teeth, which devoured everything green in the land; supposed to have been locusts'
Land League: Ir. nationalist body in late C19
League of Nations
Anglican Prayerbook: introductory rubric to 'Holy Communion': 'An open & notorious evil liver . . . truly repented
& amended his former naughty life'

Holinshed: *Chronicles* VI (Ireland), 21: 'DUBLIN . . . The seat of this citie is of all sides pleasant, comfortable, & wholesome. If you would trauerse hils, they are not far off. If champion ground, it lieth of all parts. If you be delited with fresh water, the famous river called the Liffie, named of Ptolome Lybnium, runneth fast by. If you will take the view of the sea, it is at hand' (R. Stanihurst's account)

Percy French: *s* 'There's only one house in Drumcollogher'

F visitez!: visit! *F* la Belle

G Besuchen Sie zuerst: first visit . . .

It Vedi Napoli e poi muori: See Naples & then die Mooney's: several D pubs

proclamation
L clam: secretly, hidden
Swift: 'Ppt' *L* ubi: where *s* Pop! Goes the Weasel
L ibi: there popinjay
Tyburn, place of public executions, now Marble Arch, London

Tempest V.1.88: 'Where the bee sucks, there suck I'
MacMahon (Crimea), asked to leave Malakoff fortification, replied 'J'y suis, j'y reste' ('Here I am, Here I stay')
L esto: thou shalt be *L* estote: you (pl.) shall be *L* sunto: they shall be whole
11th E.B.: 'Rio de Janeiro': Skyline forms 'a huge reclining figure called "the sleeping giant" '
L in altitudine: on high fortification
L caput: head 11th E.B., 'Dublin': Strongbow died of 'a mortification in one of his feet'
G ist disorder
Matt 20:16 &c.: 'last shall be first'
D Annals, 1548, record that the title of Bailiff of D changed to that of Sheriff
Hans Bailie: Lord-Mayor of D *Aladdin* (pantomime): 'New lamps for old!'
Radu Negro: founder of Bucharest back in town Unter den Linden (Berlin main street)
red & black Black & Tans: Eng. recruits in Royal Ir. Constabulary, 1920–1
Sl horney: policeman *G* mit *G* Magd: maid

Ibsen: *Peer Gynt, Caesar & Galilean, The Lady from the Sea*
Gallagher: Lord-Mayor of D fresh lettuce letters
Ibsen: *Hedda Gabler, Ghosts* (*Gengangere*), *When We Dead Awaken* (*Når vi døde vågner*) Wagner
chaingangers
Ibsen: *Pillars of Society, Rosmersholm* D motto: Obedientia civium urbis felicitas (Citizens' Obedience Is City's Happiness)
F bourse: exchange
'Exsultet': 'O felix culpa!' by the ton political economy
Jack Sheppard & Jonathan Wild: Eng. criminals, rivals, hanged unsure

Fielding: *Jonathan Wild the Great* *G* bin so frei: permit me
New Jonathan's became the Stock Exchange
G Danke bestens: many thanks *G* Attentat: assassination attempt *G* blau: blue
Hottentots *G* mindern: lessen
G aus der Mode gegangen: have gone out of fashion 'Hair-Trigger Nick: C18 D duellist
Blue-Blaze-Devil-Bob: an old Galway fighting man
buggery rare as lovers' meetings gloves & mittens
R glovar: leader
Sl better half: wife

Aesculapius: Roman god of medicine The Mall, London my lady discover herself
G Mittagsmahlzeit: midday meal *G* Mahlzeit!: good appetite!
King Ludd: founder of London *F* mignonette Gen 1:31: 'Et erant valde bona' ('&, behold, it was very good)'
m'lord hide & seek *F* minuit *F* midinette: work-girl *G* Wald: forest
Buenos Aires *G* Luft: air Firbolgs: early legendary Ir. colonisers landlubbers
(air, fire, earth, water) lift (our glasses) God bless us 'Bögg' set on fire at Sechseläuten, Zurich festival
pr Keep your powder dry *G* segnen: bless
Sl skivvy: maidservant

7 Hills in Edinburgh: Braid Hills, Blackford Hill, Calton Hill, Liberton Hill, Craiglockhart Hills, Corstophine Hill, Arthur's Seat
Du punt: point
G (ge)habt: had
7 seas
D Annals, 1746: circumference of D found to be 7¼ miles
Prospect Hill, Galway; Peking
Blackrock

R chert: devil
St Nicholas Within, D church
chart
D.A. Chart: *The Story Of Dublin*
St Michan's Church, D
whereabouts

Eiffel Tower
Woolworth Building, N.Y.C.
(004.35–6)
tor: pile of rocks; abrupt or conical hill
Tempest IV.1.174: 'cloud-capp'd towers'
finance
fine ounce: unit of troy measure (gold)
cupolas
The Campanile, Trinity College, D
F impôts: taxes
scruple: small measure
outrageously
imports
by the grace of God
Henry II granted to his burgesses of D in 1174 'freedom from toll, passage, portage, lestage, pavage, murage, quayage, carriage & all custom'
means
overlord
It prender: to take
Brian Boru sometimes known as 'Brian of the Tributes'

nearly out of my mind
Master of the Mint was *percussor monetae*

percussion cap
Morley: *Life of Gladstone*

gambling den
ready money
F Mont-de-Piété: pawnshop

I.O.U.'s
F Pays-Bas: Netherlands
foreigners
Huguenots settled in Ireland in C17 via Holland
F louer
huge knots
met
Matthew
G Papst: pope
St Bartholomew's Day Massacre of Huguenots by papists
G matt: defeated
first to last
face to face
milreis: old Portuguese coin
Mark
Luke
look!
Daniel in lion's den
Belfast envied
G Anfall: attack, seizure
Budapest
Calcutta
attaboy!
Place Atabeth, Cairo
Brian Boru defeated Danes at ⚔ Clontarf, 1014

AngI Lochlann: Scandinavian
r Tolka, D
It fuga: flight
Firbolgs: legendary Ir. colonisers
I fág an bealach: clear the way!
F jusqu'au bout
Ireland
Matt 5:38: 'An eye for an eye, & a tooth for a tooth'
AngI usquebaugh: whiskey
Moore: *s* To Ladies' Eyes a Round [Faugh a Ballagh]
damage
Brian Boru's daughter's remark of approval at ⚔ Clontarf 'is said to have cost the lady one of her front teeth' to her husband, King Sitric
ridotto: entertainment, public assembly (in C18 D)
redoubt: stronghold into which garrison may retire
F roi
G wegschicken: send away
Duke of Wellington
G Walhalla
F plein
Victor Hugo: *L'expiation:* 'Waterloo, Waterloo, Waterloo, morne plaine'
martial law
G Warschau: Warsaw
thole: endure
Marszalkowska: main street, Warsaw
Du schouw: inspection
L plumbum: lead (for bullets)
ping-pong
Cz Praha: Prague
Ernest Renan: *Prière sur L'Acropole* (prose poem)
Acropolis
L corpus: body
Niederdorf: Zurich's old city
Fairview, district of D
breakfast
Thorp: Lord-Mayor of D
'sloblands of Fairview' (*Portrait* V)
Rathgar & Rathmines: districts of D
R sloboda: suburb
I gárdai: police
G badend: bathing
Mendicity Institution, D
innoculated
Baden-Baden, spa
L unoculus: 1-eyed
L ad libitum (ad lib.)
D Annals, 1807: 'Prince of Wales Parkgate packet, & Rochdale transport, with 300 passengers, wrecked at Dunleary; all souls on board lost'
Salisbury Plain, site of army exercises
s 'Wi' a Hundred Pipers & A' & A' '
The Sleeping Beauty (pantomime)
nightingales (nightdresses)
G Murmeln: murmur
Beauty & the Beast (pantomime)
ph turned a deaf ear
muses
L bellua: wild beast
L dulcis: sweet

Tenducci, tenor, made reputation singing 'Water Parted from the Sea'
G Flut: flood
West Indies
St George's-in-the-East, London, scene of anti-Catholic demonstration, 1860: orange-peel thrown during service
Ps 31:20: 'strife of tongues'
orang-utans
Rangoon
G Ofen: oven
G Ofen: Buda
thoroughfare
Mecklenburg St, D (in Nighttown)
making
Sackville St, D
Eskü-Ter: square in Pest
Belváros: Pest's inner city
sight forbid
potato tubers tuberculosis
It belva: wild beast
Da forbedre: improve

G reizen: charm   spitefully   spadefulls   *D Annals,* 1565: 'John Hawkins . . . introduced potatoes into
raised   *Sl* spuds, murphies: potatoes   Ireland'
beriberi: disease caused by vitamin deficiency (potato diet)   *It* pletora: plethora   Irish stew   *F* chou: cabbage
Liberty Lads: D weavers' apprentices (Protestant)   currycombs   The Coombe, D (in the Liberties)
Catacombs, Rome   Curragh of Kildare: racecourse   True Blues: Whigs
Jerusalem   Wellington   Wailing Wall, Jerusalem   Richmond Hill, Rathmines
hooray!   salaam: oriental salutation   Richmond Basin, S. D reservoir
Ranelagh: district of D   Roundwood reservoir, Co. Wicklow, supplies D with water

chairs & tables   spouts   longitudes
crowning of pretender Lambert Simnel in D, 1487, by men 'rearing mighty shoutes & cryes'
Elm pipes used in 1763 to convey water from Grand Canal to Richmond Basin   fondness   *G* Auto: car   outer (those outside central zone)   ozone
trams in Rangoon from Pazundaung to Alôn & Kemmendine   come & dine

It fontane: fountains   *ph* appeal from Philip Drunk to Philip Sober
spontaneously
Cowper: *The Task:* 'the cups That cheer but not inebriate' (i.e. tea), der. from Berkeley
Sir Philip Crampton Monument had drinking fountains with chained cups
confusion   sour grapes
drinking water   (tea is an infusion)
vineyard   *L* obtemperate!: attend!   *Sl* in one's cups: drunk
vinegar   temperance (no alcohol)
coffee cups   Ware: Ir. historian   Beware would you make a mock of me
Mecca   Mocha coffee
Bloom buys coffee in Cabman's shelter   dot the i's   cross the t's
Ka'aba: sacred edifice at Mecca   Shelta: secret language of Ir. tinkers   curse the teas

James St, D   January   syndic: civil magistrate
Janus: Roman god of the doorway   Christmas Steps, Bristol
Sick & Indigent Roomkeepers' Society, D   intendente: municipal
It podestà: head of medieval free city   mayor of Buenos Aires
Demosthenes   Ibsen: *En folkefiende* (*An Enemy of the People*)
Foster Place, D, site of political rallies   friendship   & my pupils
ph his bark is worse than his bite   suffragettes
Burke   John Bright: Eng. politician, opposed home rule
conscientious objectors
Parthenope: old name of Naples
s Mother Machree   Antiparnellites   *G* Schwalbe: swallow (bird)
Gr Parthenôpeia: 'maidenly aspect'   *G* Schwall: flood, flood of words
D sacked in 836: swallows carrying lighted sponges sent over town to burn it   *F* bonbon
s Hokey Pokey   *F* sauve-qui-peut!: every man for himself!
Elizabeth Fletcher: C17 Quaker missionary in D, imprisoned   interrogated
Fleming: Lord-Mayor of D
hesitency   *F* réplique

F Mesdames   *F* leur   *F* monsieur   who in hell said?

firefly   buggers'
At ⚔ Bunker Hill (Am. Rev.) Gen. Israel Putnam supposedly said 'Don't fire until you see the whites of their eyes'
Brigham Young: Mormon leader, founded Salt Lake City
temple of Solomon   *Heb* beth El: house of God
Dr Bethel Solomon: president of Rotunda Maternity Hospital, D   turnkey: jailer
Solyman's Coffee House, D (1691)   *F* accoucher: be confined   *Rape of Lucretia*
Sultan of Turkey   overripe   *L* Lutetia: Paris   *Rape of the Lock*   Lock Hospital, D (for venereal diseases)
Sl turnkey: jailer   insistently
L pax vobiscum: peace be with you   Jacob . . . Esau (mess of pottage for which Esau sold birthright, Gen 25:34)
box of biscuits   Jacobites   cottage cake   exhausted
Delhi   Jacob's Biscuits, D   free & easy

smalls: underclothes   instalments   *ph* tit for tat

It farina: flour   Scipio Slataper: Italian writer & patriot, born in Trieste

Chadni Chauk: street in Delhi   gingerbread   wrapped   *ph* sackcloth & ashes
G Brett: board
Beggar's Bush, D   omnibuses   Billy-in-the-Bowl: legless beggar in old D, strangled passers-by
ambushes
James Collins: *Life in Old Dublin* 78: 'in the humanity of their hearts';   highwaymen
90: ' "curds & whey women" who stood . . . at the corners of the streets to refresh the ball-wearied, or tavern penitents'

Dublin Metropolitan Police
politeness
I Cor 13:13: 'but the greatest of these is charity' devalued base money
De Valera
inner man
square leg: cricket position Botany Bay: quadrangle in Trinity College, D
Dillon Cosgrave (*North Dublin, City & Environs*) *Huckleberry Finn*
claims there are 24 places called 'Dublin' in the U.S. heckling the umpire
receiving anonymous letters
*309 (magistrates) 'Their action in refusing further demands for new licences has been usually supported by widely-signed petitions from the local inhabitants' poetry
symbol *F* causeries: discussions

J sang in the Feis Ceoil (Festival of Music) in Antient Concert Rooms, D, in 1904
G Coll feschest: smartest choirboys
son of a bitch I built I plastered pilaster
birch *G* Palast: palace
F couche *Da* bygget: built Vanderbilt
Thomas à Becket wonder built
midnight encompassed
Hutchinson: Lord-Mayor of D
U. 164: 'Kerwan's mushroom houses' 'Rest & be Thankful': viewpoint, Edinburgh

Luke 12:27: 'Consider the lilies of the field' Balkis: Queen of Sheba
Matt 6:29: 'even Solomon in all his glory was not arrayed like one of these'

fief: an estate in land Oxmantown: part of N. D (named from 'Ostman' – 'Eastman' – Viking) = Villa Ostmannorum
L recte: correctly Thor Stein: centre of worship in Viking D, nr Hoggen Green (site of Parliament house, now College Green)
I Sráid Thomáis: Thomas St, D
Form of riding the franchises in White Book of Christ Church, D, gives 'southward as far as William English his house' Henry de Loundres: Viceroy & Archbishop of D
L saltus: pastureland Ordnance according to which 'Neither "O" nor "Mac" shall strutte ne swagger thro' the streets of Galway'
Baronies of N. Salt & S. Salt, Co. Kildare, from *Saltus Salmonis* (= Leixlip) *Da* bonder: yeoman *F* faubourg
Henry Woodfall: *s* Derby & Joan Drury Jones: Lord-Mayor of D
D'Arcy: Lord-Mayor of D James: Lord-Mayor of D
Blue Coat School, D (King's Hospital) fealty
Brigham Young's account of Noah admitting people to Ark: 'all who have received tickets are aboard' *64 'Fair home' *21 'overcrowded' *17 'tidy' *17 'very little furniture'
(word 'respectable' frequent in Rowntree)

*281 'dead sick of bread & butter'

*255 'A man was confined in a respiration calorimeter for a number of days, & on certain of them he engaged in the severe mental work of reading a German treatise on physics'
*35 'house shares one closet & one water-tap with eight other houses'

*17 'gets parish relief' *17 'young son wants situation, just out of prison'
Montgomery, Lord-Mayor of D
New Departure: make of bicycle brake Montgomery St, D
Secretary Hopgood of American Association for the Advancement of Atheism was described as 'hell-bent to rid the land of the Big-Man-up-in-the-Sky stuff'
'I will not serve, answered Stephen' (*Portrait* V)
*37 'will not work'
*152 'a two-roomed house (usually called "an oop-an'-a-doon")' *L* quasi: as if
*151 'under existing bye-laws, however, a back entrance to every house is insisted upon'
*55–56 'Old garments . . . bought from the ragman . . . older rags & a few bones are given in exchange . . . she once bought a pair of old curtains from the ragman for 3d'

Roe: Lord-Mayor of D
*49 '"house lost in dirt" . . . closets . . . blocked with refuse' Roe's Distillery, James St, D
fire at Marrowbone Lane Distillery, D, ca. 1860: whiskey ran down gutters in Cork St
*50 'slovenly wife' *319 'one adult entered with a jug' (to fetch beer)
ph to get on like a house on fire

*33 'chucked his work over a row'

*B.S. Rowntree: *Poverty: A Study of Town Life* (3rd ed., 1902)

Marquess of Zetland: Ir. Lord-Lieutenant, 1889–92

*46 'The position of these workmen is one of peculiar hopelessness'

*51 'night soil has to be removed through the house'

*19 'not quite steady'   churchwarden: long-stemmed pipe

*3 'before many a house was a clog, or stump of wood, on which its owner often sat & gossipped'

*16 'Widow, chars'   HCE

*66 'tools often in pawn for drink'

Sl unfortunates: whores

*36 'Floor of kitchen full of holes, & dangerous for old men'

*59 'The water-tap is quite 100 yards away'

*289 'bottled gooseberries'

*33 'man "has not had his boots on" for twelve months'

*155 'The accumulation of dust between the banisters & the wall was measured; it was of an average depth of 9 inches, measuring 16 inches in one place'

*33 'wife cleans schools'

*37 'Out of work'   *35 'Regular loafer'   *36 'tumour, which should be operated upon would she consent'

Ottawa, Canada

D Annals, 1490: 'The first importation of claret into D'

*35 'sitting up at night with sick people'

*153 'back-to-back houses in which through ventilation is impossible'   *36 'Harmless imbecile'

*36 'supposed to be weak-minded'

*36 'Neighbours say sons lie in bed most of the day, & go out with sisters at night'

*64 'Resting after a life's hard work'   *22 'Labourer, Plant'

Poverty IV discusses calorie requirements

Rowntree: *Poverty* (uses researches of Dr Dunlop on calorie requirements of Scottish prisoners)

Sunlight soap (Lever Bros)

*268 'The V's live in a four-roomed house, for which they pay 4s, 4½d per week rent'

*Rowntree: *Poverty* (continued)

*268 'Mr. V. became security for a sum of money for a friend of his who afterwards absconded'
*33 'shares . . . one closet with fourteen other tenements'
*17 'probably used as a house of ill-fame' *17 'House cleaner than some'

'Tea pension' explained in Rowntree as a scheme whereby a regular purchaser of a brand of tea is entitled to a pension of 5s. per week on being left a widow

*23 'Query–How they live?' *53 'The last three tenants have been "carried out" (*i.e.* died)'
*77–8 'The husband commonly finds his chief interests among his "mates" & seldom rises even to the idea of mental companionship with his wife'
*156 'large holes admitting numbers of mice'
CHE

amblyopia: defective sensitivity of retina
Goodman's Fields, area in Whitechapel, London

horrible admission
amission: loss

horrors HCE

chartulary: collection of charters tallage: tax levied upon feudal dependants by their superiors

Charter of Henry II granting D to the citizens of Bristol, 1172: 'Wherfore I will & firmly command that they do inhabit it, & hold it for me & of my heirs, well & in peace, freely & quietly, fully & amply & honourably, with all the liberties & free customs which the men of Bristol have at Bristol, & through my whole land'
Great Seal: seal on documents in sovereign's name

Bristol

(witnesses)

G Buch: book
G Büchse: box *King Lear* III.4.187: 'Fie, foh, & fum' Henricus Rex
D Annals, 1217: 'Fee-farm of the city of Dublin granted to the citizens'
furlongs *It* libramento: balancing miles *F* mille
Livramento Hill, Rio de Janeiro
It mancipio: slave Mme de Pompadour *Sl* pumpship: urinate
mancipile: steward
F lieu d'aisances: public convenience drummer: commercial traveller
F lit morganatic marriage: one between man of exalted rank & woman of lower rank, where neither wife nor children share dignities *It* serale: of evening lodged blackmailers
G Morgen: morning *N* litt: a little *F* louche: squint
Parsifal
F siège: seat, chair Virgil: *Aeneid* 6.853: 'Parcere subjectis et debellare superbus' (To spare the defeated & subdue the proud')
Luke 1:52: 'He hath put down the mighty from their seats; *Arch* debell: vanquish draggletail
petticoats *Arch* doomster: judge Pie Poudre (*F* pied poudreux, 'dustyfoot'): court held at fair for quick treatment of hawkers &c.

Guy . . . Fawkes
Guy's Hospital, London
Lynch, mayor of Galway, hanged his own son for murdering a Spaniard, Gomez lawgiver *I* lamh: hand
loy: turf-spade, attempted murder weapon 'eye for an eye' (Matt 5:38) Mag-Mon: Tír na nOg
F loi: law in Synge's *Playboy* magnanimous Mosse built Rotunda Hospital
revolutionized Lucan erections highways & byways waysides W.C.s
volcano . . . eruption *G* Graben: trench; name of main street in Vienna

Sheridan Circle, Washington D.C. Black Pitts: street, D

Pierre L'Enfant planned Washington, D.C. Hearts of Oak Friendly Society rest in peace

*Rowntree: *Poverty* (continued)

Rechabite & Total Abstinence Loan & Investment Society, D *pr* Waste not, want not
D Annals, 1733: 'The custom of burying in wooden shrouds introduced'
Moore: *s* 'Silent, O Moyle!' City Morgue, D *It* lento (music): slow Sullivan: Lord-Mayor of D
D Annals, 1686: 'city charter renewed by James II, under a quo warranto' his grace, my sovereign solivagant: wandering alone
Viking kind regards

nickname *G* flüster: whisper *ph* second to none
ph play second fiddle
L nomen gentilicum: middle name (of free-born Roman) *G* frisch: lively, fresh

F étoile devoid *Her* sable: black
F devoiler: to unveil *Her* fesse-wise: in manner of fesse (⅓ of the field, enclosed by 2 horizontal lines)
Her argent: silver coleopter: beetle *F* fesse
drawers pendant
Her sinister: left *Her* proper: represented in natural colouring
Her blazoned: described so that accurate drawing can be made *Her* terce: division of field in 3
F lancier *Her* saltire: division of field in form of St Andrew's Cross
embusked: placed in ambush *Her* sinople: green *L* heri: yesterday HCE
letters patent: (fig.) authority to do something *L* cras: tomorrow
L hodie: today
Alsergrund: district of Vienna
first

Freud, in *Totem & Taboo,* discusses group marriage of Aborigines HC . . . E Essenes: ancient Jew socialists
holocryptic: of ciphers, wholly hidden cryptogam: non-flowering plant
Ouzel Galley: D society called after ship of same name, believed lost, which reappeared suddenly in 1700
Da tilsammen: altogether

surtout: overcoat wrapped up in each other petticoats

trebled in 3 or doubled in 2 *Sl* abram: naked
trine: triad
Sir Walter Scott: *Rob Roy* Les Rois Fainéants: last of the Merovingian kings 'Fejeean Mermaid', dead specimen with ape's head, exhibited by P.T. Barnum
fenians
L virtus: valour, virtue

Freeman's Journal, newspaper

Mother Church inner

befitteth *L* reclamo: I contradict loudly, cry out against (idle it were to inquire my identity: I am all these things simultaneously)
Song of Sol 2:17: 'Until the day break, & the shadows flee away'

please

(telephone operators) number 1

Catechism in *Book of Common Prayer*: 2
'*Question* What is your name?'
Answer N. or M.
Question Who gave you this name?' 3

4

telephone *L* vox: voice *G* taubstumm: deaf & dumb
G Taube: dove *G* Stimm: voice
Fulvia: 1st wife of Mark Antony
L fulvia: blonde, yellow
G Wien: Vienna
winding
F louve: she-wolf

Ireland *Julius Caesar* III.2.75: 'lend me your ears' (Ulster) *r* Blackwater (Munster)
'Dublin' means 'Black Pool' (Leinster)

Wilhelm Meinhold: *The Amber Witch*
L fluvia: river highwaymen
Stanihurst (in Holinshed) describes E. suburbs of D as 'preyed on by their prolling mountain neighbours'

Cant Moabites: police; Roman Catholics Foxrock, district of D
Moabit: prison in Berlin
Pall Mall, London
where in hell
G sind: are

heartily
my good wife CEH
goods wharf Harty: Lord-Mayor of D
iddle woman (1444): gentle woman
L fulvia fluvia: blonde river *F* née
whereon
instead
Du waarom: why
N tilstede: with others
Du loos: false
found
U.195: 'Perdita, that which was lost' (Shakespeare's Perdita based on Fawnia in Greene's *Pandosto*)
Undine: Greek water sprite lord laws
undies drawers

richest

masked yashmak Maidan i Mashk: military parade ground,
(eyes, mouth, ears & nose covered) Tehran
L flumen: river

Leixlip *r* Liffey describes a 'loop'
Loopline Bridge (last on Liffey)
portreeve: chief officer of town; Kevin's Port, D D, Town of the Ford of the Hurdles
erron. of port
Gardiner's Mall became Sackville Riverside Drive, N.Y.C. Embankment, London
St, then O'Connell St, D *Du* rivier: river
Ringsend: district of D, flotten: flooded *It* flotta: fleet
had ferry *G* flott: fast, buoyant *s* What Ho! She Bumps: 'She began to bump a bit'
In surveying D franchises it was the custom at low-water mark at strand
Ringsend to 'cast the dart', i.e. throw a spear as far as possible into the sea, to delimit as city boundary
L talis . . . qualis: such . . . as
tall as Cuchulain Quaill: Lord-Mayor of D (fearless)
Gr triodontos: 3-pronged
Ajax upraised P/K
G aufgereizt: excited
G Stock: stick ferrule *Gr* polyphloisbos: loud-resounding (applied to sea by
Homer)
Triton: sea-god, son of Poseidon
G rückwarts: backwards
(Canute bids sea retire) *Arch* hem: them
(land reclaimed at Ringsend) *Da* os: us *Du* rook: smoke
stammerer damn fine horsemanship
Stamer: Lord-Mayor of D *G* Dom: cathedral
Donabate: village, Co. D maiden race: one open to horses that have never won prizes berserk (orig. a
Maidan: great park in Calcutta, contains racecourse *Scottish* sark: chemise wild Norse warrior)
Anglican marriage ceremony: 'With my body I thee worship'

Da min bryllup: my wedding Hades Wagner's Rainbow-Bridge is created by Donner,
G Weib: wife *G* hallen: to resound crying: 'Heda! Hedo!'
r Bosphorus tinpan *ph* arse over tip
(10 road bridges over Liffey in D in J's time) *G* Arsch: arse
tup: copulate Echobank Cemetery, Edinburgh Strongbow: leader of Anglo-Norman
(like a ram) invaders of Ireland
'Thalatta! Thalatta!': cry of the 10,000 on reaching the sea maelstrom
Galata: bridge in Istanbul *G* streng: stern, rigorous Gulf Stream
Galatians supposedly Celtic *G* Ringstrasse: circular road Ierne: name for Ireland used by some Latin
(N. & S. Circular Roads, D) writers
all & sundry *Da* idag: today

Da igaar: yesterday *Da* for evigheden: for eternity Ir. P/Q split
Da imorgen: tomorrow Guinness barge lowering funnel to pass under Liffey bridges
to strike one's flag: *G* Dampf: steam
lower it, in submission &c. Stamboul (Istanbul)

Livland: Baltic province hooks G Lettland: Latvia Da skaal!: cheers!
G Hoch! SC zhivio: your health! N viv: wife F vive!
'Empress of Asia' (ship) 'Columbia': 1st U.S. ship to circumnavigate globe paranymph (Gr. antiq.): bridesmaid
'Singing Sands' on Eigg (Hebrides) her brides' Hebrides goosegrease
G uns *F* canaille: rabble *F* canzone: ballad, song *G* Blume: flower
F ailles: wings plumes
put chain & padlock (chastity belt) buttoned Bolton St, D
Bolton: Lord-Mayor of D
Durdin: Lord-Mayor of D ALP Appian Way, D
Darley: Lord-Mayor of D *L* pluvia: rain
G Herr *G* umstellen: alter trained *F Sl* casemate: cunt
I her lover am still *r* Amstel
F grippe *It* fiume: river *G* Brett: board punish
Sp furioso: violent fuming *F* chambrette: little room
G Hochzeit: wedding HCE Mt Everest
Gen 2:24: 'a man . . . shall cleave unto his wife'
ALP *s* Annie Laurie Lorelei *R* pisoved: ant *G* wenn: if
Petrarch's beloved, Laura pissabed
prowess heavenliness
haven (harbour)
bachelor anchorites *ph* ride at anchor *G* frei *G* Pforte: gate, door
G Anker: anchor free ports *s* At Trinity Church I Met My Doom: 'I was an M-U-G'
pr Never buy a pig in a poke
Trinity College, D, faces Dame St
G versuche ich meine List: I try my cunning

Kattegat, strait, Denmark dachshunds *F* crotte: turd

Constantinople fortified
cutaway (kind of coat)
G umgürtle: girdle
F vermicelli à la vinaigrette gyres: conical helices of determined events in Yeats' *A Vision*

Liberty's: London department store
in 'riding the franchises' (or 'fringes') W. fringe of area is in The Liberties
G Lilien: lilies
G Jünger: disciple
L passim: throughout

cocquette Agnès: Parisian milliner
F cocotte: whore
pennyworths
G Pfennig (coin)
Waterhouse & Co.: D jewellers
Rose: Lord-Mayor of D
Redfern: C19 Parisian fashion house transparencies

Pile: Lord-Mayor of D Pim's: D drapers
peltry: furs piled: hairy
Slyne's; Sparrows: D ladies' tailors *F* lumineuse 'Grace': '*Lux upon Lux*'
Credo: 'lumen de lumine' Luxor: town on site of Thebes
hooks *It* primavera: spring Pyrrha: wife of Deucalion *F* or *F* reine *F* beau
(4 seasons) *F* mère *Gr* pyrinos: fiery rainbow *F* sourire
F d'Hiver (a shire wide) *Sl* trilby: a woman's foot

torture of the Spanish boot (legscrew) bede: prayer

wampum: beads worn by N. Am. Indians today mercury under glass of mirror tomorrow
shard: broken fragment (here, of glazed pottery)
Du thee: tea Copenhagen

G Schwänchen: little swan Royal Marine School, D
(By legend, swans sing only when about to die)
F moules marinières Moore: *s* Silent, O Moyle sea songs swan-upping: marking swans with nick on beak as sign of royal ownership
Children of Lir spent 300 years as swans on Moyle (sea between Ireland & Scotland)
King's County: Co. Offaly eldritch *L* olor: swan
court Aldrich: Lord-Mayor of D alas unheeding

order of Dannebrog: Danish distinction G soll leben!: hail! *Mother Goose,* pantomime
G König: king grave *F* lever (i.e. sunrise) bear's
cresset: vessel holding burning oil; torch Leonard's & Dunphy's corners, on S.& N. Circ. Roads
11th E.B.: 'Paris': till close of C16 only lamps those in front of madonnas at street corners
Arch lanthorn: lantern *It* quinta casa: 5th house Tallon: Lord-Mayor of D J.M. Synge
Chart: *The Story of Dublin* 92: every 5th house in Quin: Lord-Mayor of D tallow candles
D had to put out a candle or lantern mutton-fat candles Lightburne: Lord-Mayer of D dip:
knickerbockers bookends Booker: Lord-Mayor of D Hutton: Lord-Mayor of D cheap candle
Blackhall: Lord-Mayor of D tope: drink copiously (flagpole)
Black Hole of Calcutta

Haliday: *Scandinavian Kingdom of Dublin* 54n: 'Ulf, a black pagan' (i.e. Dane)
Blackheath: H.Q. of Kentish rebels in 1381 & 1450
Chart: *The Story of Dublin* 6: 'from 875 to 915, the historians record "rest from the Danes" ' *L* pacis: of peace
Annals of the Four Masters 1171: 'Diarmaid . . . by whom a trembling sod was made of all Ireland'
Chart: *The Story of Dublin* 7: 'The stream of warriors which the North had so long poured from her "frozen loins" showed signs of exhaustion' septuor: septet

Ku Klux Klan days of the week: dark, deadly, *Da* tolv: 12 *Da* maane: moon
dismal, doleful, desolate, dreadful, desperate; months of the year: bloody, gloomy, hideous, fearful, furious,
alarming, terrible, horrible, mournful, sorrowful, frightful, appalling
s (hymn) Peace, perfect peace

dwindling *L* luna Ketil Flatneb: a Viking king of Hebrides
Larry Kettle, Tom's brother, chief engineer for Poulaphouca hydroelectric scheme in 1920s
supper hour *L* columba mea, formosa mea: my dove, my beautiful one
F frimas: hoarfrost Les Halles, Paris
W. 23rd St, N.Y.C. Elgin Marbles, part of Parthenon, in British Museum
West wind Wyndham Lewis: *Tarr* *s* I Dreamt That I Dwelt in Marble Halls
back to back vaulted empire
(blocks blacked out by power cuts) volts & ampères
electrodes: anode (+ve), cathode (–ve) Topazolites occur in Mourne Mts

Arklow, town, Co. Wicklow; lighthouse there fitted out by E. & W. Siemens
Wykingloe: Viking name of Wicklow town polder: *Sw* sjömen: seaman Wexford
Henry II landed in Ireland at the Crook reclaimed land Hy Kinsella: tribal land, Co. Wexford
over against Hook Tower, Waterford Bay: supposed origin of phrase 'by hook or by crook'
haven't you seen
Avenue C, N.Y.C.
munificence fourths drift nets
municipality draught beer
Fi enempi: more Portobello, district of D, also
empties (bottles) town 3 miles from Edinburgh
submarine C.R. Maturin: Ir. novelist; wrote *Melmoth the Wanderer,* from which Wilde derived his
Sl Jack: *F* matelot assumed name Sebastian Melmoth. Maturin's Melmoth sells soul to devil & dies in St Petersburg
Peter, Jack & Martin: Catholic, Anglican & Lutheran Churches in Swift's *Tale of a Tub*
sink *G* Sankt: saint St Petersburg *F* barque
Caesar Sawyer founded Dublin, Georgia
Old World
Hy Brasil: legendary island W. of Ireland wealth

pleasure *pr* (orig. *F*) The English amuse themselves sadly
Isa 2:4: 'They shall beat their swords into plowshares'
It alta (f.): open (of the sea) *I* máthair: mother
It mare (m.): sea D, Georgia, is on Oconee, tributary of *r* Altamaha
O'Connell: Lord-Mayor of D creature cricket on the hearth
AngI crith: hump
It calle: narrow street in Venice

1331: a school of turlehide whales stranded *L* potatum: *D Annals,* 1802: 'Peace of Amiens proclaimed
at D; mentioned in *D Annals* & in *U*.45 drink in D' Amiens St, D
ph peace & plenty biblus: papyrus Bedell's Bible D Craft Guilds organised C16 Xmas pageants
bibulous beadles Stanihurst (in Holinshed): 'great triumphs & pageants'
Adam Loftus: Lord-Chancellor of Ireland Lough Conn, Co. Mayo Cain & Abel
Adam Duff O'Toole, burned for heresy, D, 1327 Ireland anciently divided into Conn's half &
Turgesius (Thorgil), the Viking, was drowned in Lough Owel Mogh's (Owen's) half
Guinness barges on Liffey Sir Arthur Guinness & James Stirling ousted by Liberals in 1880
G Kartoffel: potato general election, when J's father was secretary of United Liberal Club, D
C16 D Xmas pageants had glovers portraying Adam & H . . . C . . . E
Eve, basketmakers Cain & Abel, & skinners providing ninepence nine pins (bowling game)
'the body of the camell'. Pageant of St George's Day had an emperor

C16 D Xmas pageants featured the 6 & the 9 Worthies. halfpennies on corpse's eyes *F* bis
The '9 Worthies' included Joshua (biblical) & Godfrey of Bouillon, being chronologically the first & last
L processus prophetarum: 'procession of prophets' (in mystery plays)
be sure to book

bum & belly

s Johnny, I Hardly Knew Ye fit him

86 Stephen's Green, D, original University College building *L* collegium: partnership
College Green, D, by Trinity College
Padraic Colum, poet & friend of J

ME carline: old woman *I* Bearla: Eng. language
Berlin Leinster
G Knoblauch: garlic

marrow bone
Marylebone (London suburb & railway station)
G Kraut: cabbage, herb Piccadilly dill (herb)
AngI dislisk: edible seaweed
Peter: *Dublin Fragments* 2: 'subtleties' (prophets, ships &c., in jelly for Xmas dinners)

St Pancras: patron of children; London borough & railway station *Du* Paas: Easter *Du* Pinkster: Whitsun
pancreas: digestive organ (sweetbread) *Sw* Pingst: Whitsuntide
pease pudding Brady: Lord-Mayor of D Nuttal: Lord Mayor of D *Da* stor: great
U.675: 'an empty pot of Plumtree's potted meat'
G Dampfküche: steam kitchen coffee jalap shallot: onion *Allium ascalonicum* (name now obs.)
Dampkjökken: public kitchen for poor, Oslo
Kava root used to make intoxicating drink
Ascalon, port, Palestine

Da skinsyg: jealous *Da* syg: sick

Borwick's Baking Powder *It* uliva: olive Cuticura skin ointments
Björvik: main part of Oslo harbour *L* pulver: powder
Sl scrubber: female pubic hair

currycomb Song of Sol 1:5: 'I am black but comely'
Sl tuzzi-muzzi: cunt
s Mopsa dust her seat spores of clubmoss *Lycopodium* were used in surgery as absorbant
mop

Sl soiled dove: whore

Escurial Palace: chief palace of Spanish kings, near Madrid Finglas: N. district of D
bow windows bay windows
L librarium: bookcase
Tailtean Games: annual games established in honour of Queen Tailte
G Abendbrot: supper withers: part of horse's back between shoulder blades *ph* to wring someone's withers: to cause someone distress
Dean Swift: *The Drapier's Letters*
wheatear: small bird
nap: a cardgame VI.B.11.45: 'old games/ . . . Ranter-go-Round/Spinado/Bray'
Lord-Mayors Lady-Mayoresses kow-tow: Chinese custom of touching ground with forehead: mark of respect
Kyoto: old capital of Japan
smiling famous likenesses late: dead
framed
oilpainted by hand Tamerlane
Thomas Cusack: first Mayor of D
Larry O'Neill: Lord-Mayor of D, insisted on retaining title while D Corporation suspended 1924–30
Michael Cusack: original of 'the Citizen' in *Cyclops* Hugh O'Niell outlawed in 1613
Dick Whittington: Lord-Mayor of London Pieter Stuyvesant: governor of New Amsterdam
currants raisins figs *It* datteri: dates *F* prune: plum
Reyson: Lord-Mayor of D Prunikos: sister of Jesus
in whom
F quetsche: damson
Amos 5:6: 'Seek ye the Lord, & ye shall live; lest he break out like fire in the house of Joseph, & devour it, & there be none to quench it in Beth-el'
double time
Hu alj: bottom Alhambra: palace of the Moorish Kings at Granada; music hall name (Paris & London) dancing the *Blue Danube* Dunsink Observatory, D
F jambes Vauxhall Gardens, London
Humpty Dumpty

Telegraph line between Dunsink & Ballast Office made Winter Palace, St Petersburg
time ball drop at 1 pm GMT Windsor *G* Palast: palace
It vampa: blaze, flash *G* lübden: vow *G* loben: praise *Da* Gud: God sheep & the goats
G elend: miserable; (etymologically) exiled *G* sehr gut: very well (Matt 25:31–46)
F chauffer: to warm footsies jewels of Wigan: coal

skald; ancient Scandinavian poet memories Snorri Sturlason: *Heimskringla* (saga)
Atti Mermer: palace in Constantinople murmurers (i.e. lips)
G Thronsaal: throne room *G* lecken: lick dormer window
Peacock: throne in Delhi
camise: shirt worn by Arabs *s* A-roving: 'In Amsterdam there dwelt a maid, Mark well what I do say'
chemises *F* rideau: curtain Rue Rideau, Ottawa Diana duenna
G merken: notice *Du* let wel!: mark you! Church of Pantocrator (*Gr*, 'Almighty'), Constantinople
sights *Little Red Riding Hood* (pantomime)
G ritt: rode
pantomimes: *Cinderella, Hansel & Gretel, Babes in the Wood*

Champ de Mars, Paris piddled
use *F* d'amour
G verträumt: lost in reverie

Du volmaakt: perfect *Sl* frails: women
prevene: act in anticipation
tradesmen Horace: *Odes* IV.7.16: 'pulvis et umbra sumus' ('we are dust & shadow')
ph lights o'love *L* pelves ad homines sumus: we are basins to men
(without her shift) father

Du prater: talker *It* ciao! CE . . . H
Prater: great park in Vienna *G* Kamerad: comrade

(12 '-ation' words)

L (artificial) latificatio: broadening

2nd Adam: Christ coming
I Cor 15:22: 'For as in Adam all die, even so in Christ shall all be made alive'
Grand & Royal Canals, D
Canal Grande, Venice
'Rus in Urbe': inscription on Aldborough House, D, is from
Virginia Water (nr Windsor) Martial, ep. XII.57 (lit. 'country in city')
G Minne: love *Da* min elskede: my loved one
astrolabe observatory
G Erd-: earth

U.131: '*It is meet to be here. Let us construct a watercloset*'

coven of witches
convenience
G fest: firmly (building)
It gotta: gout
National University of Ireland *G* göttlich: divine sizar: scholarship student at Trinity College, D
sophister: 3rd or 4th year student at Trinity against lifesize
Swift's Stella stele: upright stone
Inscription on the Rosetta Stone is in *It* stella: star Little Egypt: dancer at a Chicago World Fair
Hieroglyphic, Greek & Demotic Democritus (3 castles on D coat of arms)
Reader: Lord-Mayor of D *Gr* hieros: holy, divine
bimetallism: unrestricted 2-metal currency Seven Dials: place in Holborn Chart: D historian
Hibernská Ulice: Prague Street with former Ir. Franciscan College
Matt 19:24: 'It is easier for a camel to go through the eye of a needle'
Love Lane, D, also London, not far from the Bank of England, Threadneedle St
Newgate, Prison, D Vico coincide
Da gade: street *L* vicus Veneris: Venus's street
'Thalatta! Thalatta!': cry of the 10,000 on seeing the sea Hindus must wash in Ganges at Ghats of Benares some time in life
G kolossal: colossal Sublime Porte: Ottoman Court *Gr* hoi polloi: the many
Matt 20:16: 'many be called but few chosen' *G* Vater: father

Old Sarum constituency (1 house on a hill) before 1832 Reform Bill stations

D railways serving 4 provinces: Great Northern; Great Southern & Western; D, Wicklow & Wexford; Midland Great Western

Procathedral, Marlborough St, D (R.C.)
ph pros & cons Christ Church Cathedral, D (Church of Ireland)
Roger de Hoveden says Henry II built outside D 'a royal palace constructed with wonderful skill of peeled wands'
Stavekirke: wooden church in Oslo nicely *r* Chattahoochie
Norse *G* fest: solid Freemasonry
Sl Shinner: member
Ark of the Covenant of Sinn Féin *It* rifugio: refuge
Covenanter: Scottish presbyterian Litany of BVM: 'Refuge of sinners'
Hagia Sofia (Holy Wisdom): mosque in Istanbul
apses
ABCDs
steadfast radio hams (amateurs)
Ham & Shem (sons of Noah)
Barkey: Lord-Mayor of D (no dogs)
F Sl truande: whore *Sl* trull: whore (silence in cathedral)
go, go trolls compel
Nibelung gnomes
D architects &c.: Richard Cassels (Leinster House), Mary Redmond (Fr Mathew's statue), James Gandon (Custom House & Four Courts), Sir Thomas Deane (Nat. Library & Museum), Oliver Shepperd (statue in GPO), Edward Smyth (sculptures on Custom House), Parke Neville (Vartry Waterworks), Thomas Heaton (Findlater's Church), B.B. Stoney (Essex Bridge), John Henry Foley (O'Connell's & Grattan's statues), Sir Thomas Farrell (Wm Smith O'Brien's statue), John Van Nost (statues at D Castle), Hamo Thorneycroft (Plunkett's statue), John Hogan (statue of O'Connell in City Hall)
spirits goblins Gobelins: district of Paris
L tectum: roof tilery: place where Tuileries, Paris R.L. Hine: *The History of Hitchin* I.277: ' "the peace
protect tiles are made *L* gentes: race of the four great ways" in which . . . Hitchin shared'
Four Waves of Ireland: 4 points on Ir. coast boost William Booth founded Salvation Army
(.02) otiose: idle, sterile, useless (hellish roads to heaven; heavenly roads to hell)
Swedenborg: *Arcana Coelestia* Valhalla
(reached by rainbow bridge)
s 'As I was going to St Ives, I met a man with seven wives, & every wife had seven' &c. saving clauses
amaze wynd: narrow cross lane close: passage to house
(215.15–18)
(effects of gusts)

Niblo's Garden: N.Y.C. music hall 'Balbus was building a wall' (*Portrait* I)

G Eltern: parents Susanna, in book of Apocrypha, propositioned by 2 Elders
N elte: knead altering
G ewig: ever, eternal
Da smukke: beautiful

Chaucer: *Miller's Tale* 1.82: 'She was a prymerole, Goldsmith: *Deserted Village:* 'Sweet Auburn'
a pigges-nye' (i.e. flower) Coolock: N.E. D suburb Quaill: Lord-Mayor of D
St Patrick's Cathedral, D, restored by Benjamin Lee Guinness
Sexton: Lord-Mayor of D
Petit Palais, Paris Bell: Lord-Mayor of D Moscow
I cloisint: hearing *It* duomo: cathedral muezzin Caliph: 'Commander of the Faithful'
(chiming 6) *It* mezzatinta: half-tint *It* comminare: threaten
oracle Angel of the Lord (Matt 1:20)
G Orgel: organ *L* laudo: I praise
Telford & Telford made organ in St Patrick's laver: large vessel for ritual washing
Thomas Telford: bridge builder
Hellfire Club, D rose windows Oriel: N.E. Ir. principality
oriel windows
OCS gospodi pomilui ny, khriste pomilui ny: Kyrie eleison, Christe eleison Bab Azoun, street, Algiers
rolled *It* sasso: stone sackbut: kind of trumpet, obsolete *F* baba: astounded organs
Tara: ancient Ir. capital *G* sass: sat *G* hernach: afterwards Forty Bonnets: nickname of Mrs Tommy
Ali Baba & the Forty Thieves (pantomime) *I* Sasanach: Englishman Healy, Galway
Ota, wife of Thorgil (Turgesius), the Viking invader, uttered prophecies from the high altar of Clonmacnois
Cathedral May the Lord have mercy on us chilly bum *Sl* I love my Chilibombom
G Hoch!: Hail!

all hail! Snaefell: mt, Isle of Man *s* Showers of Blessings
snowfall
chalice *Da* eller: or foreskin Fagrskinna: compendium of lives of Norse kings

Moore: *s* Take Back the Virgin Page HCE
F verge: rod Page: Lord-Mayor of D
Ana: earth-goddess of Tuatha Dé Danann alpha, beta, gamma, delta
yew ALP
alphabet *G* Birke: birch tree *G* Tanne: pine *I* mí-rath: misfortune rattan: palm used for switch
Ir. alphabet has 18 letters & runs from A (ailm: elm), B (beith: birch) to T (teithne: furze), U (ur: heath)
Dundrum: district of D
OF oyez!: hear!
Camomile St & Primrose St, London (near each other)
Coney Island, N.Y.C. Mulberry Bend Park, N.Y.C.

blade bled or budded Gore: Lord-Mayor of D
ago
Bloody Acre, Glasnevin Cemetery, D bloody well pissed over *It* selva: wood
Passover (blood on doorposts, Exod 12:22–3) salvage
Letchworth, the first Garden City guerdon: reward
(Seven Wonders of the World)
Cheops' Pyramid, Mausoleum at Halicarnassus, Lighthouse at Alexandria, Colossus of Rhodes (7 wonders)
F mousseline: muslin *Gr* pharos: lighthouse fires
pensile: hanging *L* turris: tower *Arch* buss: kiss Semiramis: princess of Assyria
terraces *G* Busse: repentance pledges
(D statues Hanging Gardens of Babylon, Statue of Zeus, Temple of Artemis (7 wonders)
from Parnell Square to College Green) Templeogue ('church of virgin'): district of D
PARNELL FATHER THEOBALD MATHEW: Ir. temperance advocate NELSON rearadmiral *G* eilig
Pardon of Maynooth: massacre of Irish in 1535 *It* Fra Teobaldo: brother Theobald *G* heilig
SIR JOHN GRAY: head of D waterworks *F* porte l'eau *L* Guglielmus: William (WILLIAM SMITH *L* caulis:
U. 93: 'the hugecloaked Liberator's form' (O'CONNELL) O'BRIEN of 1848 'Cabbage Patch rebellion') cabbage
MOORE's statue over pub. convenience (*F* édicule) glorietas: open spaces with statues, Mexico City
highly ridiculous Pass if you can: *L* gloria in excelsis workdays
road intersection N. of Finglas *L* annus: year *It* calendario: calendar
holidays *Sp* compleaños: birthday
Gregorian Calendar: modification of Julian Calendar made in 1582 by Gregory XIII
Romany *Romeo & Juliet*
Lisbon

HCE Chesterfield planted elms in Phoenix Park
hops grown in Kent
s The Rakes of Mallow The Bowery, N.Y.C. Greenwich Village, N.Y.C.
rigs of barley Barlow: Lord-Mayor of D washed
Sp pampo: plain *Port* animo: life *Port* necessidade: necessity ponds *L* pons: bridge
Paço das Necessidades: royal palace, Lisbon *Port* ingles: English *Sp* iglesia: church
Aqueducto das *Port* agua: water Hawthorn Glen = Furry Glen, Phoenix Park Valhalla
Aguas Livres: aqueduct, Lisbon Hawthornden House, Edinburgh
deer chase Howe: site of the Viking parliament (Thingmote) in D
Finmark, S. Norway How: Lord-Mayor of D howe: hill, tumulus
Magazine Fort, Phoenix Park

'The Queen's Garden at the Phoenix': old name for Phoenix Park

ALP wigwam speak-easy (in Prohibition in U.S.) Granville: Lord-Lieutenant of Ireland

I lionn dubh: porter, stout *G* froh: merry

U.S. Sl pussyfoot: prohibitionist

F trottoir Eblana: Ptolemy's name for D Stoneybatter, street, D

F nord, sud N. & S. Circular Roads, D Eastmoreland Pl. & Westmoreland St, D
L circulum: circle Westland Row, D
boulevard *Da* syd: South Sydney Parade, D (shouting D.U.T.C.
suddenly timekeeper)
Opslo: old spelling of Oslo Storthing: Norwegian parliament mantra
up slow starting tram
s The Memory of the Dead: D United Tramways Co. conductor
'true men, like you, men' Swift's Yahoos
all fares *Da* velkommen: welcome *Da* vogn: carriage
G Fahrt: journey hanging (passengers holding straps)
Hosea HCE Clydesdale: Arabin: Lord-Mayor of D *G* Römerreich: Roman Empire
L claudus: lame breed of heavy draught horse 'The Arab's Farewell to His Steed' (*Araby*)
rickshaws Hispanic: pertaining to Spain street Arabs Madrid
Shaw: Lord-Mayor of D

Bucharest post chaise shay: chaise Thurn und Taxis: a German family (ran postal service)
bucking
tilburies & noddies: types of carriage gig: light 2-wheeled buggy

sedan chairs prick up Roger de Coverley: Eng. country dance; character in Addison's essays
Přikopy: main street, Prague prick: ride quickly
la-di-da

hinny: offspring of stallion & she-ass
jennet: a small Spanish horse
Shetland (ponies) Orkneys (ponies)
R zholtay: yellow
I rinnce: dance pleasure

G lalageô: to babble

Matthew, Mark, Luke, John *Cz* hana: shame
I lua: a kick

What was that? What was what? tumult
Du waas: fog too much

expatiate: speak or write copiously

Da nat: night *s* The Good Old Days Gone By

G Kinder: children

pr Quartan agues kill old men & cure young

sagamore: Red Indian tribal chief

Balearic Islands: Majorca, Minorca, Iviza, Formentera are the 4 largest

fermentarian: term of reproach applied by Latin to Greek Christians, as using fermented bread

s The Ballyhooly Blue Ribbon Army *G* nicht: not *L* nox: night

Ballyhoura Mts, Co. Cork *G* Nacht: night *Gr* tetra-: four-

cg Pussy Four-corners palaeologers coper: horse dealer

palliasse: mattress foursome

Sl cuddy: ass

Dion Boucicault From lands of Viking kings of D, Henry II formed his 4 royal manors of Esker, Newcastle, Saggard & Crumlin (018.06–7) *F* donc

nr 'See-saw, sacradown, Which is the way to London town?'

Kevin Barry died for Ireland, aged 18, in 1920

commander-in-chief

Irish mile = 2240 yards

Vico discusses auspices in Roman history

dribble orange custard cabbage (Ir. tricolour)

onager: wild ass

R brat: brother

Cardinal Cullen: archbishop of D *G* bald: soon

'The Night Refuge': Night Asylum for Houseless Poor, Bow St, D

foreign

Sl lemoncholy: melancholy

L rhus barbarorum: rhubarb

(rhythm of Byrd's 'Woods So Wild'–cf. .16) ⊣

s The Holly & the Ivy

Presentation Order of nuns

Michaelmas
mistletoe

HCE *s* She Wore a Wreath of Roses the Night That First We Met

F veuve
Isa Bowman, friend of Lewis Carroll, played title role in *Alice in Wonderland* adaptation
Isolde la Belle lissom *nr* Little Boy Blue
buxom
(orange blossom for wedding)

s O Song of Songs: 'Do you recall the night that first we met'
s Sally in our Alley: 'She is the darling of my heart' apricot

chamber
Da seng: bed
(stuck) William Byrd: *s* 'Shall I go walk the woods so wild, Wand'ring, wand'ring here & there, As I was once full sore beguiled, Alas! for love! I die with woe'

daffodils daphne: kind of laurel, bay
s (anon.) I sing of a maiden that is makeless: 'He came al so stille'

(Viconian cycle)

Howth *G* Nacht: night S *G* wacht: guards *The Lay of Havelok* (C14)
Rembrandt's painting 'Nachtwacht' tumbril: cart emptying by tipping back
sees queer scenes Sackerson *G* Punkt: point
L sequester: umpire, mediator punctual
G Kursbuch: train schedule *G* gross: big *G* Strasse: street *N* hende: to happen

G Pöbel: rabble *Da* for at: in order to
pub
ph wet his whistle *F* escroquerie: fraud

leavings Walpurgis Night *Da* og: & gneiss: a metamorphic rock
I agus: & *Da* kikkert: binoculars *Da* knapper: buttons *G* Handschuhe: gloves
Da briller: eyeglasses *Da* baand: ribbons
Da strømper: stockings *Da* sminke: rouge, makeup *Da* eddikeflasker: vinegar bottles

K *F* chambre à coucher

I mo mhíle stór: my thousand treasures (endearment) pillowslip
basking Basque language
thought a knock came at the downstairs door at that hour
Persse O'Reilly the air down she went *G* Schritt: step *G* Schrat: imp

Schweppes mineral waters Shaun the Post with a telegram
L mingere: to urinate tilly: an extra measure, 13th to the dozen

HCE *Bas* Eskuara: Basque The Four Horsemen of the Apocalypse
esquire
North, South, East & West

glory be to the saints in heaven *Heb* hevel: nothingness staircase
AngI galore: in plenty
rose the candle glory down

bless herself knocking

milkjugs Longfellow: *The Wreck of the Hesperus* *Da* kong: king
Hapsburgs
Samuel Lover: 'King O'Toole & St Kevin' in *Legends & Stories*. King O'Toole's goose was made young by St Kevin
ghost

seen sliding
skiving
everyones' in turn

G Hals: neck *G* Klo: privy clock key (had tocher: dowry
Lord Iveagh: Edward Cecil Guinness, philanthropist gone down to wind) *G* Tochter: daughter
AngI whist!: silence
Litany of BVM: 'Tower of David', 'Tower of Ivory'
ph silence in court

o Fox & Geese: district of D
cg Fox & Geese
Du overboord: overboard d'you remember *F* jure: juror
jury members

referendum
L reverendum: inspiring awe
fornication 'Exsultet': 'O felix culpa' *L* albo-: white crural: of the leg
copulation

L amo, amas, amat, amamus, amatis, amant (present tense of v. to love)

It deretano: posterior

tweeds suedes

festination: haste

L comploro: I bewail

obsecration: earnest entreaty

Jas. Sammon, grocer, 167 King St N., D
Sammon's Horse Repository, 35 King St N., D

Gilbey's gin (D)   whey: the watery part of milk

eructation: belching

nepman: follower of New Economic Policy in U.S.S.R. in 1920s

please

Adam Findlater: grocery magnate & politician in Edwardian D

(573.06)   extenuation

(383.01)

Jeroboam sought to take Solomon's place, but failed   jeroboam: wine bottle holding 4/5 gallon

Sl park-pest: man who accosts girls in park

jarkman: carrier or fabricator of false papers

L nolens volens: willing or unwilling   *L* volans: flying   East wind

The Nolan (Bruno), burned at the stake   yeast, hops, malt, barley (brewing)

have mercy on his soul   Clonmel prison, Co. Tipperary; name means 'Meadow of Honey'

(death sentence)   mead is made from honey

Sir Edward Clarke defended Wilde

F reverie

Leixlip   leap year (29 day February) ○

(year old salmon)   *Sl* darters: daughters

nr 'What are little girls made of, made of?'

albatross   Albert & Victoria Nyanza: the 2 western reservoirs of the Nile

m

Δ   *L* victa: defeated   (penis)   (gown)

fell: animal skin

s Moddereen Rue (means 'little red dog'; last word is reiterated)

Holy Ghost   *AngI ph* by the holy poker!

I duine: person

(offstage)

see   daresay

HC(E)   Garden of Eden   *I* fíonghort: vineyard

Teach Miodhchuarta, the Banqueting Hall at Tara—name means 'house of the circulation of mead'

chamber scene (theatre): old name for 'room' scene

box scene (theatre): one made of flats, as opposed to a backcloth & wings

Robert Adam fireplace

argentine: material giving glass effect in stage windows

party-wall: one jointly owned by persons on either side

vamp (theatre): spring door cut in a flat

G Klubsessel: easy chair

Strawberry Beds, Chapelizod

Millikin wrote The Groves of Blarney (*s*)
milkingstool

tabret: timbrel, small stool

seven acre

seapen: squid's internal shell

taces: in plate armour, overlapping pieces forming a skirt

nacre: mother-of-pearl

eiderdown

limes: stage lights

F éventail: fan

(condom)

dumb-show: in medieval theatre, mimed preamble summarising action of a play

leads (theatre): 2 main players

discovered check (chess): check given by a piece, the action of which has been unmasked by the moving of another piece
CEH (564.04)

parallel lipped
parallelepiped

omoplate: shoulder blade

L pondus: weight

Arab ghazi: fighting

Gr metron: measure

Armenian bole (theatre): powder used for sunburn effect

bar wig
earwig

CHE

Da trekant: triangle

featherweight

Welsh rabbit = Welsh rarebit

F fossette: dimple

F teint: complexion

U.530: 'Nubian slave'

Free Kirk: Free Church of Scotland, as opposed to Episcopalian

tableau

F tablier: board (chess)

callboy (theatre): a boy who calls the acts

footage: (cinema) instruction to cameraman to proceed

Pocahontas: mother of Eng. race horses

Finnuala: daughter of Lir (the name means 'white shoulders'), changed into a swan until coming of Christianity to Ireland

gallowglass: heavily-armed Ir. soldier

(goat's leap)

bed

gambit (chess opening)

Name Mesopotamia applied allusively to any tract between rivers

r Potomac

64 squares of chessboard

nightlight

Sl progging: foraging

Shelley: *Prometheus Unbound* female
It fiamma: flame *It* fiammetta: lover, mistress
diva: prima donna *It* diva: goddess
huff: to capture opponent's pieces in draughts/checkers
to circus a scene (theatre): to turn it round

flies: space above stage where scenery hung until needed
flats: flat pieces of scenery in theatre
Da spille: play rooks & bishops (chess) bridge (theatre): part of stage that can be raised
spill (theatre): the 'throw' of light from a lamp or lowered automatically
Ps & Qs

humbug on its dead (theatre): of newly hung cloth, level, with bottom just touching stage
II Tim 4:1: 'the quick & the dead'

quicklime (burial) chess–pawn, castle, stalemate
checkers
to be sure

notwithstanding backgammon upstairs

Da til: to top double corner on chess/checker board whist (game)
snakes & ladders (game)
scenic artist (theatre): *I* realta: star realtor: dealer in real estate
scene painter real tar
Du ingang: entrance *L* limen: threshold *PS* Bog: God
F limon: mud
Earwicker *G* Lingling: onomatopoeic description Magazine Wall
be awake of bell ringing or water falling (doorbell) *F* magasin: shop
effort stop
Ephor: one of Spartan magistrates who controlled kings, hence, an overseer
ominous hain't it?
F homme
Da nogen er begravet: someone is buried *Du* beneden: below
noggin engraved *I* Binn Éadair: Howth
Aladdin's lamp

Bluebeard: *Beauty & the Beast* (pantomime) Anglican Grace: 'For what we are about to receive may the
wife-killer in Perrault's story *Da* bedst: best Lord make us truly thankful'
G vertan: wasted, destroyed

(photographs) newspapers

N forlike: reconcile, accommodate *G* auf diese Weise: in this way
Da alvorlig: serious *Da* talt: counted, told
Bartholomew Vanhomrigh: father of Swift's Vanessa VI.B.44.97: peruke: natural head of hair;
Parthalón, Ir. coloniser, sometimes anglicised Bartholomew 'hayamat (hairy)' periwig
heavy man: actor cast as Mackerel: Bloom's nickname at school (*U.*162)
villain in melodrama
poppyhead Chapelizod *F* chevelure

L pater & mater

paper masterkey
Sl key: penis
wedlock *AngI* bally-: town- (river)
Sl lock: cunt

It porto: port

It da: from Brozzo: village, Italy Cain
It corpo di Bacco!: by Jove!
really

Du toegeven: admit *G* Tonart: musical key A to Z

Da snakke: talk, chatter

as soon as I'm able *Sp* hablo: I speak
Abel

Sp derecho: right *Da* skeer: spoons still higher *Da* til hφjre, til venstre: right, left
Sp izquierdo: left (left hand holds fork, right knife)
G Kante: edge

world *Babes in the Wood* (pantomime) to be sure

coeducation bottom
We coed: wood tomboy
ought to know *ph* once upon a time

nowadays *G* Ach so? Boucicault: *The Corsican Brothers*

guess beehive
bless

Elizabeth *Da* sov: sleep

pure & simple Cunina, Statulina & Edulia: Roman goddesses connected with up-
F par exemple bringing of children
petname

L passim: throughout *It* novelletta: little short story

Gilbert & Sullivan: *H.M.S. Pinafore*: 'I'm called little Buttercup, sweet little Buttercup, Although I could never tell why'

(Isolde's love philtre)

think *F* coup de grâce grace cup: cup used
in drinking final health after grace at end of a meal
Gen 19:36: 'Thus were both the daughters of Lot with child by their father'

G Bruder: brother (Isolde theoretically Tristan's aunt)

G Freundin: girl friend

Golden Legend: C13 collection of saints' lives, by
Jacobus de Voragine
laurels, lilies *L* arrosas: nibbled at *F* arroser: to
It lilla: lilac sprinkle, bedew
New Year's Day pasque flower: type of purple anemone (7 colours)
Hamlet IV.5.174: 'There's rosemarry . . . ' indigo
Sweet William: pink flower amaranth: imaginary never-fading flower marigold
Lord's Prayer: '& lead us not into temptation'
Charis: one of the Graces
L carissima: dearest
It bambola: doll dressed as grown-up woman conjure
bambina
Boccaccio's *Decameron* enamour little bit
It boccuccia: little mouth *Da* lillebitte: tiny
virginals (Elizabethan keyboard instrument)

Gripes . . . Mookse hair (pubic)
(tried with her hand) to grasp the moth (in flight)
Mother of God! John 1:14: 'the word was made flesh'
Vanessa, genus of moths
The Dormition: falling asleep of the Virgin Mary; (fig.) sleep of the righteous

(impregnation)

F s'il vous plaît

pussy cat's

It bimbi: children
husband Presentation of BVM (in Apocryphal New Testament)
of course Wellington: 'Up, guards, & at them'

40 winks
bimbashi: a middle East military officer

F chambrette: little room

Tiddles (cat)

playfellow

G es min (*Dial.* for *ist mein*)   I play with my Tiddles

Da gifte: marry   misnomer

baritone

(7 adjectives)   buttercups

L dulce: sweetly

L delicatissima: most alluring

Du allerliefst(e): dearest

Da ønske: wish, desire

tiptoe   to her christening

Gr chrisma: annointing

Book of James (*Protevangelium*) in the Apocryphal New Testament states that BVM walked 7 steps at age of 6 months, that she danced when brought to the temple at the age of 3, that when enlisted to help spin a veil for the temple she was to spin the purple & scarlet, & that during Herod's massacre, Elizabeth, mother of John the Baptist, was concealed within the mountain of God, which clave asunder to take her in

believe   marigolds

Heb blee: without   St Brigid, 'Mary of the Gael'

saucepan   matchbox   *nr* Little Polly Flinders

G platsch: splash

aimlessly   broken sleep   cradle days

amnesia

is   *F* bis

doze

F chair

'Les Deux Magots', Blvd St Germain, Paris   each

The *Táin Bó Cúailgne*, Ir. epic, deals with war of Connacht on Ulster to capture 1 of an antagonistic pair of bulls. They had been conceived by 2 cows in those 2 provinces, which had swallowed 2 antagonistic pigkeepers in the shape of 2 maggots

U.113: 'The Sacred Heart that is: showing it. Heart on his sleeve' (statues in Glasnevin of this type extend *right* arm)

fairhaired boy   *Du* bode: postman

AngI white-headed boy: a favorite

Chart: *Story of D* 46: 'The wonder-working Bacall-Iosa, the sacred staff of Jesus, in Christ Church, was burned at the Reformation'   *I* buachaill: boy   blessed

mouth is semiopen   J.C. Mangan: *My Bugle & How I Blow It*

yodelling   pedalling

bicycle   Moore: *s* Whene'er I See Those Smiling Eyes [Father Quinn]   Finnegan

bugle

smile   have a world to win

'weird' der. from *OE* wyrd (fate, destiny)

Da han blir: he will be   night

dean's (D pron.)   *F* Angleterre

America   cushy

Armorica (Tristan)

(Swift)   vain insolence   nonsense   profane

nonchalance

'The Almighty Dollar' (expression first used by Washington Irving)

audible   adorable   eunuch   unique

venial sins

weaned on codliver oil liver in cod mostly to *left* side of body
twin
shipshape incisors

stick-in-the-mud
snake in our midst
graven image (Exod 20:4)
teasing
Swift: 'Ppt' pipette: instrument for transferring liquids
posthumous

fountainpen ink spilt from an inkhorn

James Joyce *R* sobrat: fellow, brother jehu: furious driver

P/K
L caper: GOAT Gen 25:26: 'his hand took hold on Esau's heel; & his name was called Jacob'
SHEEP right

'Exsultet': 'O felix culpa!'

Ireland lost The Pale: Eng.-occupied part of medieval Ir.

dedication of Blake's *The Ghost of Abel*: 'To LORD BYRON in the Wilderness' *Da* tosset: mad
G Lorbeeren: laurels brew
Moore: *s* When through Life Unblest We Rove [The Banks of Banna]
Blake: one of tribes of Galway
vulgar 'Bugger' derived from Bulgarus, a Bulgarian heretic accused of perversions vowels
Da blæk: ink

hyacinth
G Tintenfass: inkpot have sent
anonymous Mark decided to marry Isolde after seeing 1 of her hairs, which a swallow dropped
brightest
Donatus: *Ars Grammatica*
Donatus: 1st bishop of D
The Cat & Cage Tavern, D sweat of his brow (Adam)

Gipsy Devereux & Lilias Walsingham: lovers in Le Fanu's *The House by the Churchyard*

hell

preterite: past tense

R blizko: close, intimate

breadcrumbs Jacob & Esau
scrum in rugby football
custard

s Donnybrook Fair

High Court thrilled tale told
Swift born in Hoey's Court
Romeo & Juliet holy sweet
Pro fournigo: ant *Pro* cigalo: cicada La Fontaine: *La cigale & la fourmi*
G barmherzig: charitable
barmbrack: Ir. speckled cake
breakfast

Rosencrantz & Guildenstern (*Hamlet*) *G* Blech: tin Black & Tans: Eng. recruits in Royal Ir. Constabulary, 1920–1
It soldi: money
wheels in a snuffbox *Da* som: sold *Da* als: parted

ph neither fish nor flesh nor good red herring

Serbian Velika noc: Easter *G* nicht: not forgives
Da tak: thanks vellicate: to tickle, irritate *Du* vergeefs: in vain
II Tim 4:1: 'the quick & the dead'
the present till tomorrow

Gemini (twins)

feme covert (law): woman under cover or protection of her husband

In fixed-do system of solmization, C = do, E = mi, B (called H in German terminology) = si; therefore, 'mi-si-do' = EHC

Tim Healy, Ir. Gov.-General HC . . . E chryselephantine (gold & ivory) statue of Zeus at Olympia

Croesus: richest man in the world, last Lydian king

zoo in Phoenix Park

weather

full back (football position)

F beau Phoenix Park

Greek & Roman

Chesterfield Road bisects Phoenix Park: Viceregal Lodge & Chief Secretary's Lodge are on either side of it

Viceregal Lodge

EHC

Chief Secretary

sacristan

G man: one (indef. pronoun) *Du* bewonderen: admire bosk: bush, thicket

alfresco: in the open air

Warburton, Whitelaw & Walsh: *A History of the City of D* II.1311: [country round Phoenix Park is] 'highly embellished with country seats'

100 heirs 10,000 (people)

L super: over

F tu as raison *G* Wort: word worts: medicinal plants Jews . . . Gentiles

stalwarts

Paynim: pagan; Mohammedan true *I* ollav: sage

papooses papisher: R.C. (derisive) *F* triste olive tree

L membrum virile: penis Liffeyside *G* Tannenbaum: pinetree

firtree

ton of bloom *Du* rood: red

Arch rood: cross

L silva: weed

Mascagni: *Cavalleria Rusticana* Moore: *s* In Yonder Valley There Dwelt Alone [The Mountain Sprite]

Baroness Orczy: *The Scarlet Pimpernel* (flower)

Cities of the Plain (Sodom, Gomorrah &c.) pimple Parnell

rules 1882, Phoenix Park murders wont

I fionghal: fratricide tree/stone

eavesdropping

Swift, dean of St Patrick's Cathedral

advenement: superaddition

naked eyes

Du hoor eens!: listen!

L fundus: foundation, field *Du* bodem: bottom

G Gardinen: curtains

cicatrices

Sl sit-astrides: horse riders

pedestrians
pederasts
Valhalla G Götterdämmerung
Du hol: hole; hollow (adj.)
It duolo: grief Valkyries *Gr* kyrios: lord, master *F Sl* bander; to have erection
gives one curious thoughts
Pentapolis: district on Dead Sea
The Hollow in Phoenix Park was used by D Metropolitan Police band
Wednesdays (called after Woden) Wolfe Tone: founder of United Irishmen
Ulverton Road, Dalkey *Da* ulve: wolves
wherefore dost thou *G* Volk: people *R* volk: wolf overtones
Du dorst: pret. of *durven,* to dare

s A-roving: 'In Amsterdam there lived a maid, Mark well what I do say'

F trembloter: to tremble
wretch jelly *Du* niet: you don't? *Du* genever (drink)
G Staubbeutel: anther *R* niet: no
Guinness a bottle of stout *G* Staub: dust
G Geniesser: sensualist *Du* gij: you *G* Beutel: bag *Du* te veel: too much
Vortigern (Guorthigirn): king of Britain when Hengest & Horsa arrived Our lord have mercy!
Mercia: Anglo-Saxon kingdom in N. England (much later than Vortigern) Gortighern: the Adamic
G Gehirnhaut: meninges *Du* stemming: mood, atmosphere *R* bojazn: fear language before the
confusion of tongues

s Finnegan's Wake
Lewis Carroll: *Jabberwocky*
keep *R* pochemu: why
Kevin (Jerry in .10) Putamayo

light up *U.*3: 'Slow music' thunder in the air
Du Let op!: attention!
dreaming *I* Pádraig: Patrick

I phantar: clumsy thing, thick-set person *I* a mhicín: my little son
*U.*4: 'He was raving all night about a black panther' phantasms
I capall: horse *R* moi malen'kii malchik: my little boy
It cavallo: horse melancholy
R gorod: town godown: in Far East, warehouse
L/R far away tomorrow
s The Rocky Road to Dublin Lublin: town, Poland thoroughbred grocery business
thoroughbass: a bass continuo
F honte: shame

Es Li ne dormis?: He hasn't slept?

Es S! Malbone dormas.: S! Sleeps badly.

Es Kion li krias nokte?: What is he crying in the night?

Es Parolas infanete.: Speaks childishly.

it's only

imagination

Elvery's Elephant House, D sailing
N elv: river elver: young eel eel

There was a sulphur spa at Lucan
Chapelizod

s The Heavens Are Telling the Glories Picts Saxons
L saxum: stone

Snugborough: townland, Castleknock, D

ph face to face   *F* hostie: Eucharist   *pr* All roads lead to Rome
horses
fried onions

L unio: onion   Berkeley valued tar water as a cure-all

I Bi i dho husht: be quiet!

half mourning

Seneschals of Esker, Newcastle, Saggard & Crumlin were appointed by Eng. sovereign   ✕   (the ass)
salaam   *F* selle: saddle   pencils
Balaam's ass warned him of Yahweh's wrath   penises

beefeater   *It* bouffe: comic   S   *Da* tændstikker: matches   swastika
Skt kātyā: widow   K   *I* dún: fort   Dundalk, town, Co. Louth   Drogheda, town, Co. Louth   drawers
Katya: Russian nickname for Catherine   done (finished)
O   duodecimally

Arum: genus of plants with phallic appearance (Cuckoo-Pint &c.)

Magna Carta signed at Runnymede   farms

L magnum chartarium: great archive

harm   *s* The Bridal of Malahide: 'The joybells are ringing In gay Malahide' (about a bride whose husband was killed on day of wedding)   O

s She Was Poor but She Was Honest: 'stands & wrings her ringless hands'   △
murderer   God in *F* ciel

Tower Royal: palace in Cannon St, London   Develin Tower in Tower of London
Princes murdered in Tower of London (*Richard III*)   *F* dauphin   Λ   ⊏
AngI duff: black   gerent: manager, ruler   Lord Dufferin, Ir. viceroy
m

Sl weapon: penis
G Wappen: insignia

⊣
father

full mourning

Es Vidu, porkego! Ili vin rigardas. Returnu, porkego! Maldelikate!: See, big pig! They are looking at you. Turn back, big pig! How coarse!
heaven (theatre): alcove at back of stage
God of Heaven   Moore: O, the Sight Entrancing [Planxty Sudley]
vision (theatre): effect where character seen through gauze
hummel: antlerless stag   *G* Hummel: bumblebee   Osiris (his phallus)
EH . . . C   *G* Himmel!: heavens!

Du donker: dark   *Du* roovers: robbers

God grant it!   *G* finster: dark
how does it finish?
Finisterre, Spain   *G* anschauen: look at
sinister

Sl pole; tube: penis   *Sl* pointer: penis
Egyptian Book of the Dead, lxxiv: 'the god who is the lord of the ladder' (joining heaven & earth) = Osiris   longitude   verst: Russian land measure   first
Du verst: farthest
father   mist   agreed!
Hathor: Egyptian goddess

Dún Laoghaire obelisk commemorating   Blackrock   eight miles no furlongs
George IV's visit, erected by Abraham Bradley King   *F Sl* obelisque: penis   knots
General Post Office, O'Connell St   thousands of paces   Wellington Memorial, Phoenix Park
Tennyson: *The Charge of the Light Brigade*: 'Half a league onwards'   Sarah Bridge, D

metres
Sl pointer: penis   *Arch* yard: penis
G mit einem solch: with such an

R o moi bog: o my God
Egyptian Book of the Dead lxix: 'solemn ceremony of setting up the . . . backbone
(condom)   of Osiris'
Fox hunters' red coats are called 'pink'
lover's meeting   *Oxford Sl* Greats: final B.A. exam

great gross: 12 gross   *F* tête-à-tête
tet: upright tree trunk containing body of Osiris

G König: king
Elizabeth & Maria Gunning: Ir. sisters who married   *I* céad míle fáilte: 100,000 welcomes
Eng. aristocrats, subjects of popular enthusiasm in C18 D
Humpty Dumpty   *Du* bemerk je: do you notice?   Hanover, Royal house

visit of George IV to D, 1821: the Queen was dying and remained in Eng. Contrary winds caused the Royal Party
to turn back to Holyhead on 1st attempt to cross Ir. Sea
nickname   Mock Turtle (*Alice in Wonderland*)

s No, No, Nanette   late   18th dynasty
It nanetta: (f.) little dwarf   lateen: triangular sail
Da mellem: between
way   Michaelmas: 29 September
nr Humpty Dumpty: 'All the king's horses & all the king's men'

Knights Templars   Harald Gray Cloak ruled W. Norway   Olaf
G Knecht: servant, groom
Da dog! dog! (eq. of *G* doch! doch!): o yes!
locks   loft: flock of pigeons
tumbler: *Du* broodkast: cupboard   'Work in Progress': J's name for FW during composition
part of lock   *Du* brood: bread   broadcast   *F* accosté: alongside
Da uge: week

jubilarian: priest or   Brigadier-General Nolan: head of U.S. Intelligence, 1917–18
nun who has been so for 50 years   Browne & Nolan
(031.18–20)

Luke Elcock: mayor of Drogheda, 1916   income taxes
Cambridge Sl Little Go: 1st exam for B.A.
G Faxen: buffoonery   Beaufort: an Eng. hunt
foxes   blue & buff: Whig colours   *Arch* beaufort: material used for flags
F noblesse oblige   *F* hommes
G Pöbel: rabble   *I* pobel: people
L Mehercule!: By Hercules!   Rip Van Winkle slept under Catskill Mts
Eccles St, D   *Da* kattekillinger overalt: pussy cats all over the place

guillotine windows: (jocular) sash windows

Zozimus: D bard & beggar   *We* crwth: bowed lyre   Southwester (wind & hat)

Arch gantlets: gauntlets   *L* Pontifex Maximus: high priest; pope

entrapped   detained   bicycles
trams & trains
tricycles   penny farthings: old bicycles with 1 large & 1 small wheel (& solid tyres)
R troika: 3 horses harnessed abreast   *G* Fahrt: journey
North Pole   Hibernian   pelota: Basque game
L castrum: fort   Siberian
behold   York & Lancaster (Wars of Roses)   gambolling   Ghibellines & Guelphs: warring factions in C13 Italy
bowl, yorker (cricket)   yerk: lash, jerk   *L* ne . . . ne: neither . . . nor   gambling on golflinks

Howth Mausers (rifles) used in 1916 Easter Rising
mouser (cat)
what the dickens!
(rainbow colours) fulvid: yellow *L* viridis: green
L ruber: red orange *F* vide: empty
L caerulus: blue
credulous
Adam
damson (purple)
slowcoach Blessed Virgin Mary (BVM) animation A . . . L . . . P liveliness
sloe (dark violet-blue) everybody loveliness
patience

please remain Victoria: 4-wheeled carriage landowner Londoner
landau: 4-wheeled carriage
dickey: seat at back
of carriage for servants
Brutus & Cassius
British v. Goths
G Sonne: sun atonement autonomy
ph place in the sun Mark Antony sigh
Aqua Claudia: Roman aqueduct dewdrop
L dulcis: sweet *It* duolo: grief
Mookse Gripes
G süss von ihr: sweet of her
Sp muchas gracias
siblings *F* sauterelle: grasshopper
G Ameise: ant mouse
Moore: *s* It Is Not the Tear at This Moment Shed [The Sixpence]
G ist
nr Cock Robin: 'Who'll toll the bell? . . . I, said the bull, Because I can pull'
poll: remove horns

pleasure
stop press *Du* mijnheer: sir mayor
Insuppressible: Antiparnellite newspaper
G Bürgermeister *Ulster* thon: that Thon, once worshipped in England, may be Thor
s Billy Boy: '& my Nancy tickled the fancy'
nanny & billy goats
Sl best bib & tucker: best clothes
Wellington boots
F botte
baboosh: heelless oriental slipper
babushka: triangular headscarf
clouded canes (variegated with dark
patches) were fashionable in C18–19
D city corporation
Sl fixed bayonets: among *G* Menge: crowd *Sp* pueblo: people
brand of rum
Pinchgut Lane, Hog Hill, Dark Lane, Gibbet's Mead, Beaux Walk, Bumbailiff's Lane, all in medieval D

Lad Lane, D Abraham Bradley King, Lord-Mayor of D, presented keys of city to George IV, kissing his hand, on his arrival in city centre, & was knighted on the spot
Broadstone railway terminus, D
G mit kiss

humble duty gracious majesty
Humpty Dumpty
hear! hear! Earwicker illness

HEC Le Fanu: *The House by the Churchyard*
N lik: corpse
F cherchant
Cabbage Garden: D Capuchin cemetery near St Patrick's
foison: abundance Copenhagen
cabbaging (030.12)
AngI caubeen: old hat *G* Hauben: hoods
topic
Da sol: sun
Solomon
nightmare

miniated: illuminated
alpha, beta, gamma, delta, epsilon, zeta, eta, theta, iota, kappa,
Alfie Byrne: Lord-Mayor of D in 1930s
lambda, nu

illnatured papyrus Pepin the Short: Frankish king
OF roy: king Pepi: Egyptian king (415.36)
Rex Ingram: Am. actor, played God in *Green Pastures*, 1936
L rex: king
F canule: nozzle

breeches poking *Da* tungespids: tip of tongue
G spitz: sharp
Crimea *G* Balkon: balcony *s* Here's a Health unto His Majesty modesty: slight covering
Arch crimosin: Balkans *F* balcon: prominent female bust for lowcut neck
crimson furbelow: flounce odds bods

carillon: set of hung bells *G* Glückspiel: game of luck
glockenspiels peals
D churches: Presbyterian on N.E. corner of Rutland Sq. St Mark's, beside loopline bridge
(Findlater's; NORTH) (SOUTH)
St Laurence O'Toole's was, in 1904, 2 doors from an engineering works in Seville Pl. (EAST)
St Nicholas of Myra, Francis St (WEST)
St Francis Xavier's, Upper Gardiner St St George's, Hardwicke Pl.
have anon St Joseph's, Berkeley St
martyr All Saints, Phibsborough Rd St Paul's, N. King St
St Columba's, Iona Rd, Glasnevin *G* Aposteln: apostles
on the other hand St Jude's, Inchicore Rd (nr gates of Royal Hospital)
(i.e. S. Side of D) Brown Friars', Church St *PS* weslen: oar
St Andrew's, Westland Row Stella Maris, Sandymount
Molyneux Church, Bride St
St Bride's & St Audoen's are nr St Werburgh's HCE
Wardrobe Tower, D Castle charming
Anna Livia Plurabelle

June July

Tranquilla Convent, Rathmines (Carmelite) unclosed
St Agatha's, N. William St
St Thomas's on Marlborough St, which also contains the Catholic Pro-Cathedral
Christ Church Cathedral St Patrick's Cathedral
L beata: blessed

G doch! doch!: o yes! primarily
pontifex . . . primate
Canterbury & York (archdioceses) L/R *L* precare: to pray vespers
Canberra & New York
swastika

hieroglyph for Egyptian *khaibit*, shadow, is in
form of a parasol or umbrella (*Book of the Dead* cxlvii)
Anglican grace at meals: 'Benedictus benedicat' ('May the blessed one bless') *G* Mahlzeit: Good appetite!

Randle Holme: *The Academy of Armory & Blazonry* III.3.78: 'Terms for Carving . . . *Unlace* that Coney . . . *Chine* that Salmon . . . *Culpon* that Trout . . . *Tranch* that Sturgeon . . . *Barb* that Lobster . . . *Sauce* that Capon . . . *Frust* that Chicken . . . *Display* that Crane . . . *Unjoynt* that Bittern . . . *Allay* that Pheasant . . . *Thigh* that Pigeon'
Finn MacCool
nr 'Old King Cole was a merry old soul . . . & he sent for his fiddlers three'
F saoul: drunk
hip, hip, hurray! *s* 'For he's a jolly good fellow . . . Which nobody can deny'
ph hail fellow well met
(.21–3)

CHE Hilton Edwards: C20 D Mumm Champagne tell me no
actor/manager
Thalia: muse of comedy Melpomenê: muse of tragedy

EHC cash Gate Theatre, D Henry Mossop & Spranger Barry: rival & contrasting actor/
gatecrashers managers in C18 D
Two Gentlemen of Verona *It* veruno: anyone, no-one

Bruno of Nola; Browne & Nolan finale John Dryden: *All for Love*

Rowe: *The Fair Penitent* Rhoda Broughton: *Red As a Rose Is She* (novel)
(performed in D) brought on (to stage)
scenes Synge: *The Playboy of the Western World*
G gatten: fuck by-play: acting carried on aside, during
Dion Boucicault culture Tyrone Power: Am. actor by my faith! main action
F bouche W.&F. Fay: actors of early Abbey Theatre
J. Home: *Douglas*: 'My name is Norval; on the Grampian hills My father feeds his flocks; a frugal swain'

abnormal

It bravissimo! music

L dolenda: things to be lamented
ph Dear Dirty Dublin *I* dailce: moroseness
John Dowland (Doulandus), composer, perhaps born in Dalkey
Moore: *s* My Gentle Harp Once More I Waken [The Dirge] *Da* tumleplads: playground
F adieu *N* pike: girl turnpikes *Sw* tummelplats: battlefield
F forain: wandering, open air *G* doll: wild *G* Manöver: manoeuver
rain dances D is 'Town of the Ford of the Hurdles' Vesuvius
hieroglyphics Grace O'Malley: Ir. pirate (amnesty: 023.12–14)
pyrotechnics gracious majesty
F assombrir: darken
assembled
s There'll Be a Hot Time in the Old Town Tonight *G* es steht im Buch: it is written in the book

Egyptian Book of the Dead xliii: 'The Book
of that which is in the Underworld'
courier brassard: armlet giving sign of special appointment
(Shaun the Post) currier: man armed with ancient gun

We ys: is *G* morgen: tomorrow were *G* war: was
Morgana le Fay: King Arthur's sister, sorceress
I toth-ball: cunt

St Peter *G* Tonbild: tone poem

G Es gibt . . . zu denken: that makes one think
esquire
Du integendeel: on the contrary
ECH Herculaneum buried with Pompeii by Vesuvius (.05) Lot

G sag ihm: tell him literature

apron
Abraham (.29)
L pater familias

Hurdle Ford (D)

s John Reilly the Active (.28) *I* mic: of a son

I mac: son make

beg your pardon

(to urinal)

Moore: *s* O! Think Not My Spirits Are Always as Light [John Reilly the Active]
G verdenken: blame
Middle Egyptian khaibit: shadow Sarah: wife of Abraham
cubit: about 20 inches *Sl* number one: urination Sarah Place, D
Isis

route *1001 Nights*

Ford of the Hurdles (D)
Decline & Fall of the Roman Empire, ch. XXIXn: [Saint]
hardly 'Sylvania . . . At the age of threescore she could boast that
the steps of the Annointed she had never washed . . . any part of her whole body,
crocodile (Christ) except the tips of her fingers, to receive the communion' *L* retrorsum: backwards
brimstone
F garde à feu Eater of the Dead (in *Egyptian Book of the Dead*)
It guarda: look (throw salt over shoulder for luck)
pillar of salt (Lot's wife, Gen 19:26) salt cellar do so
Sui: crocodile fiend in *Egyptian Book of the Dead* XXXI, steals words of power

G sag mir: tell me
deafmute
Tefnut: Egyptian goddess   Lewis Carroll: *Jabberwocky:* 'brillig'
sekhem: Egyptian name for power or vital force of man   Phoenix Park derived from *I* Páirc an Fionnuisce ('Clear-water Field'), referring to a spring there
deaf   blind

In Bédier's account, Tristan sent messages carved on twigs to Isolde by dropping them into a stream springing at the base of a pine tree
G Buchstabe: letter (of alphabet)
drugget: orig. material for wearing, half wool
loves
Tristan on arrival in Ir. called himself Tantris   *G* lesen: read   schoolmistress
ken   Tantrist: of class of Hindu religious works
Ir. letters: A (ailm: elm); B (beith: birch); C (coll: hazel); D (dair: oak); T (teithne: furze); S (sail: willow)
*U.*726: 'Brigid's elm in Kildare'   TAMTRIS   ilex: holm oak

maidenhair fern

St Mary's Chapel of Ease, D   *Sl* chapel of ease: water closet
Chapelizod
Parnell: 'When you sell get my price'   Moore: *s* Yes, Sad One of Zion [I Would Rather Than Ireland]   Izod
Tell   soldier   drooping
Isolde
monkshood: plant from which aconite extracted (*U.*684)   *F* triste   *Arch* ivytod: ivy bush   *G* Tod: death
Moore: *s* When Cold in Earth Lies the Friend Thou Hast Loved [Limerick's Lamentation]
Isolde Blanchemains
underclothes   *Arch* kirtle: skirt

mistletoe   Swift: 'Ppt'

trust   (must also enter urinal)   Little Ease: a dungeon in the Tower of London
thrust
s I Would Rather Than Ireland (.12)   business

s O Mister Porter, Whatever Shall I Do?

lifesize

s Limerick's Lamentation (.15)
Lac Leman, Switzerland (*Gr* limnos: lake)

Saar: wife of Finn   Sarah Place, D   (021.02–3)
Sarah: wife of Abraham
HCE

ALP   & she   privy
banshee

Anglican marriage ceremony: (not) 'like brute beasts that have no understanding . . . they 2 shall be one flesh . . . to have & to hold'

sleeps

Quick   girl

John Keble: *The Christian Year:* 'Hues of the rich unfolding morn. . . . New every morning is the Love, Our wakening & uprising prove . . . God will provide for sacrifice'

friends   *ph* fighting tooth & nail

G Tod: death

underfoot

G hinter: behind *N* ungdommer: youths

Ibsen: *The Master Builder* I: 'I tell you the younger generation will one day come & thunder at my door'

HEARTS *G* pochen: beat, knock doorknockers

G Jungfer: maiden *G* Backfisch: teenage girl DIAMONDS

span

SPADES

four-in-hand: vehicle with 4 horses driven by 1 person CLUBS

Wolfe Tone: founder of United Irishmen

11th E.B.: 'Eskimo': 'On leaving a place they sometimes say 'inûvdluaritse', *i.e.* live well' (215.31–216.05)

Eskimo

tell me stone

Da elsk: love

alter ego

M.M. Matharan: *Casus de matrimonio* (gives examples of church pronouncements on matrimonial cases in form resembling that used here)

HCE

ex-sergeant major

F droit d'oreiller: pillow-right

L eugenius: wellborn ('Kevin' means 'of comely birth')

Gr philadelphoi: those who love their brothers

tirewoman: lady's maid

It fortezza: strength, courage

L Mauritius: Maurice

Magrath (584.05) CEH

Sir James Ware: *The Antiquities & History of Ireland*

It giglio: lily (white is blend of spectrum colours)

Cad's name is Gill (036.35, 244.23)

John D'Alton: *The History of the County of Dublin* Poppaea: Nero's wife *It* gialla: yellow

It aranciata: orange juice

Low L ex equo: out of fairness poppy red (rainbow colours) *Gr* chlôris: greenness

blue sea (marine) indigo Iodine vapour is violet
It Marinuzza: dim. of Marina
C. Haliday: *The Scandinavian Kingdom of Dublin*

Michael Cerularius established Greek church
L vulgo: commonly

Lucius Cornelius Sulla: Roman dictator
Sully (495.01, 618.08)

Matthew Gregory *L* vitellus: calf (beast of Luke) Johnny MacDougal
L leo: lion (beast of Mark)

Gilbert & Sullivan

J.T. Gilbert: *History of Dublin*
Stuart Gilbert: commentator on J

39 articles of Anglican Church *L* turpiter: shamefully, basely

L ex cathedra: from the chair, with authority
L ex cathedris: from the chairs

Giraldus Cambrensis: wrote on Ireland in C12
General Cambronne: famous for using word *merde*
Gr gerontes: old men; senators

subdolous: crafty, cunning

comminate: threaten

L Guglielmus: William
ordinary: a judge of ecclesiastical & other causes

pious fraud: one practised for sake of religion

affricate: combination of stop & following homorganic fricative *L* affricare: to rub against
Luke Wadding: *Annales Minorum* (annals of Franciscan order)
nullity (law): total absence of legal effect or existence

L vitellus: calf

L turpissima: most foul *L* Canicula: The Dog Star

abnegand: one who renounces or abjures
hegemony: predominance; orig. of 1 state in a confederacy in Ancient Greece

lax: salmon *I* bradán: salmon 'In the goods of' (law) indicates the name of a lawsuit brought in connection with the proving of a will

ladies & gentlemen
lay reader: layman authorised to read public service of (Anglican) church
(Umbrella is a contraceptive symbol)

*U.*622: 'Jesus, Mr Doyle' (Christ = Anointed = oiled = Doyle)
I dáil: assembly D'Oyly Carte Opera Company
Finn MacCool

G Fuchs: fox
Brer Fox & Brer Rabbit in Joel Chandler Harris's *Uncle Remus* stories
deceased *L* tango: tetigi: I touch, cheat; I have touched, cheated
disseize: wrongfully dispossess

HCE

L jucundus: pleasant *L* pecuniosus: rich
L fecundus: fruitful
Coppinger (055.18)

Wilhelm Harold's Cross: district of D
William

lodgement of the species (law): act of depositing money

particularise (law): allege special matter in defence

trustee

fun

dud 1132

39 Articles of Anglican Church

L pango; pepigi: I fasten, promise, drive in; I have fastened, I have promised, driven in

I Saorstát Éireann: Ir. Free State
a dozen of stout: crate of Guinness bottles
jointly & severally (law): both as members of a group & as individuals

garnishee attachment (law): act giving notice to a person for purpose of attaching money or property for which he or she is liable to another

mandamus: writ, letter or mandate issued by sovereign, demanding certain acts

Arch whilom: former Brer Fox Guy Fawkes
depletion (accounting): impairment of capital

moratorium: legal authorisation to a debtor to postpone payment

martyrs

In law, appearance is entered by the defendant delivering to the proper officer a memorandum stating the name of his solicitor, or that he will defend in person

motion (law): application to obtain ruling in favour of applicant

service of a motion (law): act of bringing to notice, or executing, any writ or process

interlocatory injunction: an intermediate injunction made during the progress of an action

obsolete

I an Dáil (pron. 'doyle') Éireann: the Ir. Legislative Assembly

FB: *James Joyce & the Making of Ulysses* XIV: 'I painted a picture . . . in front of a row of cottages–Coppinger's, perhaps'

ph odd man out

jeremiad

crossed cheques

L in re: in the matter

brisk
brusque

boiling
bullion

discount

Brer Fox

(pregnancy)

without issue (finance): the first delivery of a negotiable instrument, complete in form, to a person who takes it as a holder

rubber (condom)
Sl rubber: a swindling trick

(bank account)

paid

at sight (law): as soon as seen

to assign in blank (Stock Exchange): to execute an assignment of stock, leaving the name of the assignee to be entered by a succeeding owner

F crème de citron: lemon cream
OF vair: varicoloured

F émail: enamel
F paoncoque: peacock

L tango, tetigi

City & Suburban: an Eng. horse race

wrote

L in camera: privately

alias

dear

Kersse the Tailor's daughter (327.04)
Jerry/Kevin

PS dar: gift

Mick, Nick & Maggy
Tom, Dick & Harry

Green St Courthouse, D
Little Green, D: site of Newgate Prison

settlement (law): act or process by which transactions for the account are settled

Act of Settlement, 1652, legalised Cromwellian confiscations in Ireland

perforce: forcibly

pardoner: person licenced to sell papal pardons
partnership

Da fond: fund

L pango, pepigi

*U.*738: 'he never did a thing like that before as ask to get his breakfast in bed'

Brer Fox & Warren

to estreat a cognisance (law): mode by which a recognizance is ordered forfeited after default

G Popo: posterior

Jeremy Taylor: C17 Eng. theologian, bishop of Down & Connor

course

lower correctional (law): court punishing delinquents by detention in a house of correction

G treu: loyal
treason

pending the decision

packed jury

L judices (Roman Law): judges, jurymen
Judas

thumbs (down to convict)

L occupante extremum scabie: an itching having seized the end

fact

Calf of Man, on the Isle of Man   *F* eau de vie: brandy   Lusk, village, Co. D
odalisque: concubine in harem   *I* duileasc: edible seaweed
L mancipium (Roman Law): legal purchase, right of ownership

(Henry VIII)   Anne Boleyn   *It* una bellina: a pretty tale   *L* pepigi: I have fastened, promised, driven in
Kilbride, village, Co. Wicklow   Ballina, town, Co. Mayo
Sl rhino: money

Lewis Carroll: *Lobster Quadrille* (in *Alice*): 'Will you, won't you, will you, won't you, will you join the dance?'   how do you do

G verwachen: stay awake

Manneken-Pis: statue in Brussels of a child urinating

F mon beau

G Baumeister: master builder   Giant's Causeway, Co. Antrim
Ibsen: *The Master Builder*
hopping-off point

Sw strax: at once   corpsestrewn   *G* Ziel: goal

pr Many a little makes a mickle (sometimes 'many a mickle makes a muckle', although both mean 'much')
ph As different as chalk from cheese

ways   *I* muc: pig

myriadminded (159.07)   curiosities   world
tease
mountains to Mohammed   Stevenson: '& the hunter home from the hill'   Matt 7:6: 'pearls before swine'
ph making a mountain out of a molehill
Hurdle Ford (D)
Hungerford: 3 Eng. villages & towns
first parents   *Sl* bow: penis

F cauchemar   Ibsen: *Bygmester Solness* (*The Master Builder*)   Phoenix Park
Finnegan

sometime   *Dial* gang: walk, go
bottom rung

alter egos

Mark 5:9: 'My name is Legion'
It ligio: faithful, obedient

magdalen: a repentant prostitute
Neolithic   Magdalenian culture in Upper Paleolithic
duty-free goods on voyage   Jenny Jones: character in *Tom Jones*

Dioscorides' *Greek Herbal* IV.76: mandragora (mandrake)—distinguishes Norion (male mandrake),
dragon man (015.34) *I* mór: great wee Morion (a similar plant) & Thridacias (female mandrake)
basilisk: legendary dragon with lethal breath & glance *Annals of Tigernach* (Ir. MS)
maid *Gr* basilikos: kingly *I* tigerna: lord
pr A man is as old as his arteries vervain: herb once supposed aphrodisiac
white arsenic: arsenious oxide bismuth (in same group of elements as arsenic)
bismite: bismuth oxide
mortal sin peccadillo: trifling sin dowser: water diviner
Piccadilly, London
F douce white feather (cowardice)

lambs' wool *AngI* great gas: great fun
Landsmaal: 'New Norse', based on rural dialects
Solomon & Sheba
grand slam: in whist, taking every trick
coney: rabbit cash-&-carry shop
Sl cod; coney: simpleton *RhSl* cash-&-carried: married
corsair: pirate imbiber
G Biber: beaver
Margaret Kennedy: *The Constant Nymph* Boniface: generic as proper name of innkeepers *G* Hose: trousers
L lympha: clear water St Bonaventura The Naze: headland, Essex
'The Big Smoke': London

G rösten: to roast *G* Fährmann: ferryman Wagner
N vogn: wagon
Sl trull: whore 111 *G* elf: 11 Tullamore, town, Co. Offaly Maryborough, town, Co. Leix
Leix & Offaly (Queen's & King's Counties) Bunyan: *Grace Abounding* Regius Professor
L abunda: copious
F vedette: film star *s* Peg o' My Heart
vedette: mounted sentry
caw (raven) . . . coo (dove) rockdove: rock-pigeon *G* Tag: day Frygga: Odin's wife
C16 D markets on Wednesday & Friday
baron & feme (law): husband & wife discover (Viconian cycle)

W.G. Wills (wrote *A Royal Divorce*) Eno's Fruit Salts (hangover)
I Neamh: heaven Bushmill's whiskey
Goerz: town, Italy Hearts of Oak Friendly Society, & Scottish Widows: Life Assurance Societies
Haarlem, town, Holland
Khyber Pass HEC ALP
Via Mala, Switzerland
Kipling: *s* The Road to Mandalay
G Landweg: country road
ph highways & byeways *N* pen: pretty

Jean Ingelow: *High Tide on the Coast of Lincolnshire:* '. . . mellow, mellow . . . Quit your cowslips, cowslips yellow'
pinguid: fat *Sl* whacked to the wide: utterly exhausted *G* oder: or
Arthur's Seat: hill in Edinburgh on which, in Hogg's *Confessions of a Justified Sinner,* Wringhim tries to kill his brother
Da til sengentid: till bedtime
Henry Woodfall: *s* Derby & Joan *I* codlaim: I sleep Unter den Linden: Berlin Street
G Linnen: linen rue de Toulouse Cheapside & Covent Garden, London
ca'canny: 'go-slow' at work

Strangford Lough, Co. Down: scene of C17 plantations (Ulster) Protestant

Cork (Munster) Liberties, D (Leinster)
Carcer (Mamertine): Roman prison dryfooting
Co. Sligo (Connacht) *I* slighe: way, road

Snorri Sturluson: Norse historian
Du oom: uncle (pope with mitre)
G um Gottes Willen: for God's sake
East Great Brunswick St, D
chrism: holy oil
Caspian Sea

Pharaoh Levite Tom, Dick & Harry Finnan haddy: haddock cured with smoke of
G Pfarrer: pastor fin—gill—lung (evolution of green wood, turf or peat Finn MacCool
herring respiratory surfaces) teacosy

surplice *F* plisser: pleat peascod: pea pod
codpiece
Parnell's death resulted from his not changing wet socks

blankets coffin Finn MacCool Mithra: Persian god of light
finnoc: a white trout *It* finocchio: homosexual
s 'Are you the O'Reilly that keeps this hotel?, . . . Begorra, O'Reilly, you're looking right well'
Ibsen: *John Gabriel Borkman* North South Man of Sorrows (Sorgmann)
HCE Hekla: volcano, Iceland Mt Etna, volcano

G Fuchs: fox *G* schauen: look devil's Doge: ruler of Venice
Du schouw: fireplace, chimney
decent

r Voulzie *r* Valsch

Ys & Zs up
r Ybbs *r* Zab *ph* dibs & dabs *r* Vop
ph for the love of Mike loop

r Wells *r* Sow *G* Donau: Danube

G Donnerwetter! husband
r Ardèche
r Alabama *Du* bek: mouth *It* ninna nanna: lullaby
r Troutbeck like
Septuagesima calendar puzzle *G* Habe die Ehre, gnädige Frau!: I have the honour, gracious lady
F cul bustle (conventional salutation)
Sunlight Soap wenches Wagner: *Das Rheingold*
r Rhine Rheingold beer (American)
tried lapping the swills

Islandbridge: district of D (lit. *F* pont de l'isle) Bournemouth

buried Heytesbury St, D Hatch St, D loaned
borrowed *ph* bury the hatchet
feet Love Lane, D (Old Love Lane became Sackville Avenue) halfpennyworth

dripping: browned
fat from *r* Brent
roast meat The Angel, Islington, London

Amen Corner, London, nr North, South, East & West servant
St Paul's Norwood, Southwark & Euston (London)
gambeson: C14 military tunic

woman of the house *Du* terug: back

inch by vesting: dressing
ell: 45 inches
devilment Kierkegaard: *Enten-Eller* (*Either/Or*) Mt Athos, Greece *r* Dayman
r Devol *Da* anden: other *G* aller: of all *Da* er: are Mt Err, Switzerland
r Aller *F* avec cette ECH
Luxembourg is on *r* Alzette
G königlich: royal King's & Queen's Counties (Offaly & Leix)
Stepney, London

Dr Barnardo's Homes, for stray & waif children, had house at Stepney Causeway, London
wife of his bosom
Little Dunmow, Essex, had custom of presenting flitch of bacon to couples who could prove 1st year of marriage spent in harmony
L scala: stairs
marriage on the rocks
satraps
tormentors (theatre): first wings inside proscenium arch

A . . . LP *F* la purée: the mash escaping Diamond is crystalline carbon

HCE (water) electricity

ALP

F boutique *Da* grinden: the garden gate *L* cave canem: beware of the dog
boot: profit eke: to add to

'Take away these baubles' (Cromwell ordering removal of mace on dissolution of Rump Parliament)
Sl brass: money

Prov 6:6: 'Go to the ant, thou sluggard'

Mookse & the Gripes soles (of boots)

Da raaber: crier
nuisance Post no Bills (notice)
pr Respect the uniform, not the man ravens
robes *G* König: king plethron: ancient Greek linear measure, c. 101 ft
plethora pleasure doves
queen her court *pr* Waste not, want not *pr* Spare the rod & spoil the child
coyne & livery: billeting practiced under Brehon laws by Ir. chiefs
pr Tell the truth & shame the devil Tom the Devil: Eng. sergeant in 1798 Ir. rising

Matt 19:19, 22:39; Mark 12:31; Gal 5:14: 'Love thy neighbour as thyself'

Sauvé: *Proverbes & dictons de la Basse-Bretagne*, no. 310: 'Ne vends rien à un ami & n'achète pas d'un homme riche' ('Sell nothing to a friend & do not buy from a rich man')
ph follow my leader
Parnell: 'When you sell, get my price' tell not *G* Freund: friend
L dives: rich Freud HCE
ALP

pr Practise what you preach
Exod 20:3: 'Thou shalt have no other gods before me'
Gomorrah

Sodom Lot (escaped before Cities of Plain destroyed) *pr* All's well that ends well

lord

buckle: unite in marriage

Heb har: mountain

Hardanger fjord, Norway

Cripplegate, London

Piccadilly Line of London Underground runs under length of Long Acre
Seven Sisters Rd, London
Wormwood Scrubs, London (prison) turncoats

foals'
ph to feather one's nest

waylaid Arnott's department store, D (bridged) waterfalls vaudeville
pr It is a foul bird that fouls its own nest *R* voda: water
G Zollgebühr: import duty Job 19:20: 'I am escaped with the skin of my teeth'
burdened
Congested Districts Board in W. of Ireland, late C19
St Peter's Church, Wood Wharf, London, united with St Benet's, Paul's Wharf
old Jonathan Sawyer founded **Dublin, Georgia** *Du* verf: paint *Du* werf: wharf
(J thought his name was Peter) *G* werfen: throw
Paul used Rachel & Leah: wives & nieces of Jacob
de Paolis, tenor
haggard: wild female hawk when caught in adult plumage *ph* looked daggers at 88
winners rock oil: crude oil police force

collapsed *Sl* phiz: face Tobias: son of Apocryphal figure Tobit
Zachary: John the Baptist's father

pole *Du* diergaarde: zoo

ghost Mullafarry, townland, Co. Mayo, ⚔, 1798 *L* fero, tuli, latum: principal parts of v. 'to bear'
It qual: as immortality
G immer: ever
Beelzebub

G durch: through slumber
dark somewhere
Book of the Dead is closed

seen *F* tour d'adieu *L* pervinca: periwinkle

Selskar Gunn: son of Michael Gunn (025.22) Chapelizod

U.553: 'THE YEWS: . . . Deciduously!'
insidiously
s Old Michael Finnegan (117.06–7)

Dollymount: district of D

Niall of the Nine Hostages: Ir. High King
ph a host in himself
HCE ALP
Hydropathic Spa, Lucan *L* lympha: clear water
sleeping *nr* The House That Jack Built
Alaeddin in *Arabian Nights* controls 2 spirits, 'The Slave of the Ring' & 'The Slave of the Lamp', summoned by rubbing those objects

businessman (035.01–044.21) cad Phoenix Park

Persse O'Reilly

O'Connell Bridge, D Burke & Hare robbed graves in Edinburgh; **they were Irish**
Sl doss: bed
Butt Bridge, D Henry Grattan: Ir. statesman *We* crwth: bowed lyre
Grattan Bridge, D
Henry Flood: associate of Grattan
jigger: one who dances jig *I* rann: verse rain
Malin Head: extreme N. point of Ir. (Ulster) Carnsore Point: extreme S.E. of Ireland (Leinster)
Cape Clear: extreme S. point of Ireland (Munster) Slyne Head, Co. Galway (Connacht)
I na Gaillimhe: of Galway

Arch lewd: lay, secular

perilous

vehmic: pertaining to the Vehmgericht. Westphalian secret tribunal, C12–16

Bectives: Ir. rugby club

Du uitlander: foreigner

invective

invader

s Slattery's Mounted Foot

(573.07)

HCE

Heinz canned foods

s Swanee River

Scots her ainsel': herself

AngI betune: between

(383.01–3)

Mark of Cornwall

banshee

queer old bit

fart

wended

Oliver Wendell Holmes (home in .12): author of *The Professor at the Breakfast-Table* (124.09–10) & *The Autocrat of the Breakfast-Table* (434.31)

Finn MacCool

most

Zingari Cricket Club, London

neck & neck

expostulating

cold comfort

collations

L sursum corda: lift up your hearts

G Funke: spark

Big Dipper constellation (Great Bear)

Sl blue funk: extreme fear

unregenerated

'brogue' fr. *I* barróg, speech defect

kenneth

Du donderslag: thunderclap

understanding

Virgil: *Aeneid* I.604: 'mens sibi conscia recti' ('mind informed with the right')

G Unterscheidung: distinction

embracing

L omnis: all

ph dropping his H's

Maida Vale, London

hiding hole

(sighs of ✕, II.4)

Low L ilium: groin, flank

Matthew, Mark

Luke & John

F carrefour: crossroads (4)

Aulus Plautius: Roman general invading Britain for Claudius, A.D. 43; also a donkey owned by Phyllis Moss, friend of J in 1920s

habeas corpus

one & two

(3)

s Green Grow the Rushes-O: 'Three, three, the rivals'

(2)

Appius Claudius built first veritable Roman road, the Via Appia, in 312 B.C.

L trivialis: pertaining to crossroads

monolith

(1)

Gr monomythos: single word

G gibt es da nicht auch: is there not there too?

hebdomadary: member of R.C. chapter &c., taking weekly turn in performance of sacred offices

Revue Hebdomadaire, Paris (weekly)

s Swanee River: 'All up & down the whole creation'

4 Aristotelian causes: efficient, final, material & formal

asphalt

Da far: father

F grippe

Greeks & Romans

Arch eld: old

L alter: other

G Alter: old man

paint

G einander: another, each other

Gr anandros: unmanly

F même

F encore

G immerhin: in spite of everything

nr 'This is the way we wash our clothes . . . So early in the morning'

therefore *AngI ph* tare & ages! propose
preposterous
HCE

chancery

Cant fambles: hands
Sl fambly: family
Devil's Punchbowl: chasm nr Killarney
ph between the devil & the deep sea
Anglesey, Wales *I* cluas: ear
closed
desperado Hebrew alphabet runs from Aleph to Tav
Esperanto
Amlave or Aulaffe: Danish invader of D

Shem, Ham & Japhet

(Ir. tricolor) attached
wagtail: small bird with protruding tail
(scrotum) *Da* ennver: every, any
F enver: wrong side

EHC *L* semper: always
L identidem: repeatedly
piecemeal vegetables

overtakes (*F* sur: over; prendre: take)

Aust larrikin: hooligan
James Larkin: C20 Ir. labour leader
Gr megaron: bedchamber eternity
world
s 'There was a raughty tinker Who in London town did dwell & when he had no work 'Dyflin' on C11 D coins
to do His meat ax he did sell. With me solderin' iron & taraway Hammer legs & saw . . . Came up a gay old lady &c.'
Da borg: castle (D Castle)

I iar-: West; remote

Maidenhead, town, Berkshire HCE
Mizen Head to Youghal = entire S. coast of Cork
MacMahon (Crimea), asked to leave Malakoff fortification, replied 'J'y suis, j'y reste'

I dearg: red Lough Derg: site of St Patrick's Purgatory

sark: nightshirt

In fixed-do system of solmization, C = do, E = mi, B (called H in German terminology) = si;
therefore 'si-do-mi' = HCE
respect
red spot on planet Jupiter
Ulster thon: that Dalkey *Da* Kongeby: Kingstown Blackrock
Da og: & wagonline
(protestants) Dalkey, Kingstown & Blackrock Tram Line passes Booterstown Luther Holy Romans
P.W. Joyce: *English as we Speak it in Ireland* V: railway to hell: 'porters ran round shouting out, "Catholics change
here for Purgatory; Protestants keep your places!" ' metropolis
ALP
Dún Laoghaire Larry Twentyman: character in Trollope's *The American Senator*
(= Dun Leary = Kingstown) Kingstown

breeches
Jupiter: planet, also Temple of Jupiter, on the Arx (*L*, castle), Capitoline Hill, Rome
Dardanelles (straits) tartanelle: small sailing vessel
L dentes: teeth
(Jupiter as bull carries off Europa) reaching
smeech: smoke
heels mobcap: indoor cap worn by women in C18
gait
things
Jove
Brobdingnag & Lilliput (*Gulliver's Travels*)
It puttana: whore
bar *Da* datter: daughter
Sl bore: fuck *L* io, io: ho, ho! Io: beloved of Zeus; satellite of Jupiter
Da twilling: twin Ganymede: cupbearer to Zeus; satellite of Jupiter
nr This is the way the ladies ride: 'A gallop a trot, a gallop a trot'
F père et mère paramour
paramere: half of a bilaterally symmetrical animal
Proserpine
Phosphor: the planet Venus before sunrise
Mrs O'Shea's biography of Parnell, II.109. says he often used the codeword 'Satellite' when telegraphing her
set alight Satellites of Jupiter cast shadows on surface
far & wide Urania: muse of astronomy
Uranus, panet
tightening Rhea: satellite of Saturn
Titan: satellite of Saturn *Gr* rhe: (root) run
snapdragon Japan *Gr* rhoda: roses
Japetus: satellite of Saturn
Saturday best *s* Phoebe Dearest
Saturn Phoebe: satellite of Saturn (the furthest from it)
G Irland: Ireland
G irre: confused, crazy
Malahide: town, Co. D *s* Who'll Buy My Rosebuds
hide *Da* liv: life
s Little Black Rose *L* nivea: snowy Paps of Ana: mts, Co. Kerry
fall of the flag: start of horse race ephemeris: astronomical almanac
(from Genesis to Judgement Day)
Sl peelers: policemen
Co. Dublin
Sl stick: penis
Da kikke: peep *ph* stick-in-the-mud
block: in cricket, position where bat rests slog (cricket): hit hard L.B.W. (leg before wicket): mode of dismissal
Sl block: fuck *F Sl* doubler: fuck
cricket positions: mid off, mid on C. Stewart Cain edited *Cricketers*
King Willow: cricket bat
cap-à-pie: from head to foot; refers to arming
tyrant's hand Tarrant, Brand: cricketers
hot & wet six
Ottowey: cricketer
Askew, Trumble, Ranjitsinnji: cricketers *Sl* wick: penis
trembly fucking
Spofforth: cricketer sick to think
lamp while Jessup: cricketer *I* simné: chimney
a wide (in cricket) just up *Sl* chimney: cunt
I dubh: black cover point (position) *Sl* wicket: cunt
Duff: cricketer *Sl* cover: fuck
drove stumps (cricket) Tyldesley, Tunnicliffe: cricketers
tiddly winks
slips (position) yorker (cricket): Studd: cricketer
Sl slops: baggy trousers ball which pitches about batting crease

Stoddart, Trott, Trumper, Lord Harris: cricketers
stuttered
Blackham, Abel: cricketers innings (cricket)
pitch (cricket) *Sl* lock: cunt
concert pitch: one slightly higher than normal, used in concert six o'clock in the morning
Pidgin English bails (cricket)
L lingua: tongue balls
U.497: 'You hig, you hog, you dirty dog!' ironmonger (615.30)
Huckey, Iremonger: cricketers
Sl peg: fuck; cricket stump *s* Knocked 'em in the Old Kent Road
prick
toss (cricket) tombola *s* 'Here a sheer hulk lies poor Tom Bowling'
flog the bowling (cricket): hit hard & often dare
Buller: cricketer love lob (cricket): bowl underarm
break his duck (cricket): score his first run
Parr: cricketer Easter M.C.C. (Marylebone Cricket Club) googlie (cricket): offbreak bowled with
pairing *Du* oogst: harvest *s* My Love Is Like a Red Red Rose: 'till all the seas gang dry' legbreak action
the Ashes contested for at Test Match (cricket) 3 for 2 (cricket): 2 wickets for 3 runs declare (cricket):
s 'Tea for Two, & two for tea, Me for you & you for me close innings
W.G. Grace: cricketer
Gracie Fields, singer
Pooley, Gubby Allen: cricketers bye (cricket): run scored caught in the slips (cricket): mode of
AngI hooley pooley: hubbub without batsman hitting ball dismissal
Dunlop tyres (condom)
Dunlop: cricketer
Merriman (cricketer)
'Grand Old Man' (Gladstone) *Sl* merryman: penis
Mynn, Lillywhite, Hobbs: cricketers
square leg (cricket position)
Wisden founded *Cricketer's Almanac* The 'Nursery end' of Lord's Cricket Ground
wisdom *F* bosse (7 items of clothing)
Cricketers divided into 'gentlemen' (amateurs) & 'players' (professionals)

'flannelled fool' (Kipling, referring to cricketers) Hambledon: Hampshire village noted for cricket team in C18
tread: copulate (said of male bird) maiden over (cricket): one in which no runs scored
The Oval, cricket ground, London *F Sl* ovale: cunt pads (cricket)
over & over over (cricket) crease (cricket): white line on pitch
well held! (cricket): said when difficult ball caught keek: peep
(111.05) dawn's chanticleer: proper name applied to a cock
G kikiriki: cock-a-doodle-doo
wont to do

Sl bird: penis no ball (cricket): ball unfairly delivered
L gallus: cock how's that? (cricket): Noble: cricketer carries his bat (cricket):
932 not out (cricket) appeal for dismissal keeps batting through
innings without dismissal
AngI ph top of the morning *Da* morgan: morning

F cocorico: cock-a-doodle-doo

Almighty & everlasting Lord Armageddon gerent: ruling Bow Bells, London
armiger: one entitled to bear heraldic arms
F belle, beau

Telamon: father of Ajax tabernacle Co. Tipperary
F tel . . . tel: such . . . such; as . . . so *F* amie
marriageable daughters *G* Tochter: daughter
thanks to
L contractatio: theft tug-o'war *Du* personeel: staff of servants
ECH
I.O.U.

L gratias: thanks

repast
pictorial

recreations

(203.12–13) Neptune: planet; rowing club, Ringsend Tritonville Rd, D
Freeman's Journal Triton: satellite of Neptune
ECH
It eccolo: here he (it) is

Sl glim: candle

services
(the mattress)
F Sl le mettre: fuck
damosel–maid of honour (wedding) trainbearer (wedding)

G dankeschön: thank you very much

Ringsend: district of D Dean Kinane: *St Patrick* 203:
'prevenient inspiration'
(condom) *Da* tusind tak: a thousand thanks

Malthus (birth control) *G* Donnerwetter!
F paratonnerre: lightning conductor
It prego: you're welcome

G bitteschön: you're welcome *F* merci beaucoup

godfathers & grandmothers

Sl piledriver: penis

devices laden
(contraceptives) Leyden Jar stores static electricity
condole

G eingeboren: inborn *L* verbum sap.: a word is enough to the wise (verbum sapienti sat est)
I indé: yesterday

anastomosis: connection of 2 vessels, esp. blood vessels, placenta *AngI* usquebaugh: whiskey
by a cross branch
belladonna *L* totus: all *L* vir: man
Sl donah: girl-friend *Sp* esquema: plan
Act of Union (of Ireland & England), 1801

OF oyez!: hear!

F Sl chambre: cunt adjourned abjuration: official repudiation on oath of a principle

Donnelly's Orchard, Clonliffe, D Fairbrother's Fields, the Liberties, D

s 'Polly, put the kettle on, Polly, put the kettle on, Polly, put the kettle on, We'll all have tea'
Sl kettle: cunt *Sl* wick: penis

antediluvian
Anna Livia

disturbing

Kierkegaard: *Either/Or* ('The Rotation Method'): 'Those who bore themselves are the elect, the aristocracy; & it is a curious fact that those who do not bore themselves usually bore others, while those who bore themselves entertain others'
Val Vousden: *s* 'Let Each Man Learn to Know Himself'

corn-cob (used as pipe)

L coram: before   Tristram Shandy, in Sterne's novel, lost his foreskin while urinating from a window

(condom)

(maid will find it while making bed)   *G* Omama: grandmother (children's language)

(045.01)

Hambledon: Hampshire village noted for cricket team in C18   gentleman   met   Burning Bush (Moses)

pap & mom   Magdalen

G Ding: thing   two   *Sl* laundress: whore

Sl maggie: whore   bonny   *AngI* bawn: white   Madge Ellis: D actress

Magdelene   bitch's bastard   Dublin

mulct: fine imposed for offence

milkman

Hamlet   *Othello*

brothel

G irgendwas: anything

curfew   *F* couver: hatch

Da for at samle op: to gather together

G sammeln: gather

1724–copper coinage for Ireland produced by Wm Wood; a swindle. Swift wrote tirades against 'Wood's halfpence'

Du rivier: river   *F* argent: money

Da halvtredsindstyve: 50 or thereabouts   +5

G Gang: way

+2   in   *G* Römer: Roman   50 + 5 + 2 = LVII

F caboche: head   mistle thrush   *Du* oud: old

missiles (excrement)

parasang: Persian measure, between 3 & 3½ miles   coinage   *s* (Swiss) 'Min Vatter ischt en Appenzeller, Er frisst de Chäs mit samt em Teller' ('My father is from the canton of Appenzell, He eats up the cheese & the plate as well')

(yodelling)   *G* sicher sein: be secure

G Polizei: police   *G* Senn: cowherd

L tanquam: as; as if   Crumlin: district of D   *Du* hoon: scorn

Du honger: hunger

Arch mak sicca.. make sure   *Da* sikker af intet gudsfordømt: certain of no goddamned

G Erscheinungen: apparitions

uncle's window

(stopped walking)   *ph* to pass in peace

Da vand: water

what

(196.01–3)   Anna Livia   tea

marmalade

Quaker Oats (213.14) 4 a.m.
F aurore: dawn
s Lobet Gott, den Herrn At end of *The Master Builder* Hilda mistakes wind in trees for Solness singing
In Goethe's *The Erlking* a father tells his child not to listen to the Erlking luring him to death, & that it is only the wind in the trees

Auxies: Auxiliaries, British officers serving in Ir. from 1920

Captain Kidd, pirate

Mountjoy Prison, D Mountjoy Brewery, D

Woodbine cigarettes Cadbury's chocolate jocular

Gr theos: God *F* drôleries Theatre Royal, Hawkins St, noted for pantomimes snug: secluded area in pub
It punto: point, passage in story or play

Cambridge Arms, pub, D widower

Moore & Burgess, minstrels, had catchline 'Take off that white hat!'
Ir. tonsure an issue at Synod of Whitby, A.D. 659

Moore: *s* Before the Battle: 'Tomorrow, Comrades, we' [The Cruiskeen Lawn] *F* cuir
'Cruiskeen Lawn' means 'little full jug'
s The picture with its face turned to the wall
pitcher . . . well

towards

butcher whole bleeding church-ale: periodic church festival
Blücher: Prussian marshal at Waterloo

Sl palships: friendships trousers

Fred Atkins: blackmailer, claimed at Wilde's 2nd trial to have been entertained & propositioned by Wilde, but then perjured himself
Sebastian Melmoth: name used by Wilde after imprisonment dip the colours: naval salute
Melmoth: town, Natal

F vis-à-vis
sitting Isthmus of Sutton joins Howth to mainland

cigarettes

Phoenix Park supervised by Rangers Moore: *s* The Meeting of the Waters

dandelions *s* Elsie from Chelsea *s* Two Little Girls in Blue

bloomers Wilde was convicted of indecent practices with Charles Parker twitch: couch-grass
Sl park-pest: man who accosts girls in park
charlock: field mustard fucking
Lord's Prayer: 'As we forgive those who trespass against us'
G versammelt: gathered together

P/K L/R
Catholic
with

grandpapa Aubrey Beardsley (homosexual)

accomplished burgomaster

sainted mouth

G Weihnacht: Xmas

Four Masters Jibbo Nolan: hero of O'Flaherty's *The Informer*
Nolan (Browne at 588.13)

Sl feeler: hand

Boucicault
Beggar's Bush, D: area with barracks
s At Trinity Church I Met My Doom: 'I was an M-U-G'
Garryowen
s We May Roam through This World [Garryowen]

Lord Ardilaun of Guinness's
G Waffenstillstand: armistice

Swift: 'Ppt'

F retroussé: of skirts, tucked up

away
thrush
G Frosch: frog
forgetmenots
musical
bare

thighs
s 'The cat came back . . . thought he was a gonner'
'corkiness' of sherry

D Sl joy: ale from Mountjoy Brewery
Sp fino: dry; *Sp* oloroso: sweet (inscriptions on sherry bottles)

am I right?
Brown Friars
F frère

Sp doloroso: sorrowful
fine
oloroso, fino (.12)
Seapoint, district of Dún Laoghaire

each
anathema
anthem's
Du hoofd: head
welkin
Da varsel: warning
s The Holly & the Ivy
welcome
wassail
Holy Mary
Du hoer: whore
Black & Tans: Eng. recruits serving in Royal Ir. Constabulary, 1920–1
ten a penny
Tommy Atkins
Fred Atkins, blackmailer (587.20)
s Were You There When They Crucified My Lord?

G Wolken: clouds
through
L fulmen: lightning; thunderbolt
Vulcan
Sl number two: defaecation

Sl pall: stop
Heb mispeh ('Mizpah'): watchtower

humility
Sl number one: urination
mistletoe
listen to

F Nöel: Xmas

Book of Common Prayer: Burial of the Dead: 'Ashes to ashes, dust to dust'
L dulce: sweetly
G Esche: ash tree
Moore: *s* O! Arranmore, Loved Arranmore [Killdroughalt Fair]
Boucicault: *Arrah-na-Pogue*

Edmund Burke

William Smith O'Brien: 1848 insurrectionist
Daniel O'Connell
Archibald Hamilton Rowan: United Irishman
Gr megalodendron: big tree
Windy Arbour, district of D near Dundrum
I mór: big
humbled
s Were You There &c. (.19): 'tremble, tremble, tremble'
doomsday's
G Urwald: jungle
Illustrated Sunday Herald, London paper
nr 'Two little dickybirds, Sitting on a wall, One named Peter, One named Paul' &c.
mistletoe
'The Liberator': Daniel O'Connell
three

s The Maypole: 'Come lasses & lads, take leave of your dads'

Chiltern Hundreds, Stewardship of: conferred on member of Parliament wishing to resign his seat

pr Look after the pence & the pounds will look after themselves

Congreve: *The Way of the World*

forced

the pope's address: 'Urbi et Orbi' ('To the City & the World')

trouble
treble stout
billiards

L meum, tuum: mine, yours

Co. Mayo
'Mayo & Tuam' = the archdiocese of Tuam

Tuam: town, Co. Galway

3 golden balls: pawnbroker's sign
Golden Ball (Kilternan): village, Co. D

cg Three Golden Balls

F bourse

HCE

imperialist

him

finners: a genus of whales

s The Peeler & the Goat
pound

(finger on the scales)

Dr Jekyll

Mr Hyde

Du overmorgen: day after tomorrow

pr Early to bed & early to rise makes a man healthy & wealthy & wise
H . . . C . . . E
General O'Duffy led Ir. fascist ('Blueshirt') movement in 1930s

s The Band Played On

s After the Ball

insurance policy cover: SICKNESS

earthly paradise

Finland

accidentally
Occident (West)

F jeune

FIRE

Wilde

personified

sleeveless

nights

inundated

probably

FLOOD

writing

fives-court: prepared court for 'fives', a ball game

Four Courts, D

standing
pr birds of a feather flock together
hurricane
(the four winds)

STORM

reflection

pr People who live in glass houses shouldn't throw stones

cook was keeping
cook (falsify) accounts
embezzled

burglars
nr Little Boy Blue

BURGLARY

Hussites: followers of John Huss, C15 Bohemian religious reformer

hussies

ENCROACHMENT

ultimately
ultimatum

EXPLOSION

ph last straw that breaks the camel's back
s The Barley Straw

deaf & dumb *U.S.* dry goods store: draper's shop *G* Sintflut: the Flood

'Heptarchy' refers especially to the 7 kingdoms founded by Angles & Saxons bleary-eyed & liverish

moribund bankrupt

pr Honesty is the best policy

G Polizist: policeman Phoenix Assurance Co., 10 Trinity St, D Lloyds of London (insurance)

forbidden fruit Joseph Meade: Lord-Mayor of D

rainbow a covenant between God & Noah (Gen 9:13–17)

Ark of the Covenant Covenanter: Scottish presbyterian

ultraviolet to infrared

ph tissue of lies try-on

triune

Arc de Triomphe rainbow

ph to shoot one's bolt

timepiece young *R* plemyannitsy: nieces prepaid

premiums (insurance)

R promysi: providence

policies

to welsh: fail to keep promise chock-full *I* beach: bee Lord's Prayer: 'on earth as it is in heaven'

you backside *I* beac: mushroom

L integer integerrimus: perfect most perfect foremost foreman

It integerrimo: strictly honest *L* formaster: dandy

Da folkemøde: popular assembly farewell accumulated

George Moore: *Hail & Farewell* cumulus cloud

Nuadha: king of Tuatha Dé Danann *Heb* Nephilim: giants (Gen 6:4; Num 13:33)

conclave nabob: person of great wealth *ON* Niflheim: Home of Mist

appearance (282.04) (realm of ice-giants)

G jetzt: now *G* hin: away jeepers! Ptah: Egyptian god

Du boos: bad, angry *G* fürwahr: indeed Swedish *Da* mand: man

jawbone

bedad!

HCE Eastman: Viking

Christmastide & Easter

jolly

In fixed-do system of solmization, C = do; E = mi; B (called H in German terminology) = si; therefore 'do-mi-si' = CEH Begum: queen, in Islamic countries

Gen 1:27: 'male & female created He them' Michael Gunn: manager of Gaiety Theatre, D

breathes (4 statements from ✕) *Arch* hem: them

broods Oldbawn: village on *r* Dodder

(disk of sun appears) *Da* drømt: dreamed Dundrum, district of D

Inchicore: district of D

G Tag: day

(theatre: tiers of seats & rounds of applause)

L 'Sanctus, Sanctus, Sanctus': 'Holy, Holy, Holy' (prayer) *Skt* saṁdhi: peace
Isis Unveiled I.32: 'a sandhi (or the time when day & night border on each other, morning & evening twilight)'
J told Mercanton 'Sandhyas' was *Skt* for 'the twilight of dawn' today dawn resurrection
'calling all cars' (police in films) towns ray (of light)
Earwicker *G* wohl: well Dublyn (anagram) Persse O'Reilly
whole bloody world
Moore: *s* What Life Like That of the Bard Can Be [Planxty O'Reilly]

HCE Oceania: general name for Pacific islands
Ossian
Tass, Havas, Reuter: news agencies bread & butter
Hear hear!
lifting alderman gotten up
Da løfte: lift gentleman's gentleman: valet
litany *G* Sonne: sun *I* Sinn Féin, Sinn Féin Amháin: Ouselves, Ourselves
(on other mornings) *F* bon amour *G* feine: fine Alone! (slogan) *F* somme: nap, snooze
G Föhn: S. wind avaunt!: 'Good Morning, have you used Pears' soap?' (advert) Persse O'Reilly
in Switzerland begone! *Da* guld: gold *Da* modning: ripening *F* aube orb
Three years ago I used your soap since when I have used no other (tramp depicted in a *Punch* cartoon)

whole bleeding blasted commonwealth of nations Finn MacCool
B.B.C. culmination Culmin: person mentioned in Macpherson's *Temora*
letter 'Thalatta! Thalatta!' (cry of the 10,000 on sighting the sea) *L* timorem: fear
St Augustine: 'Securus iudicat orbis terrarum' ('the verdict of the world is *L* albus: white
secure')—phrase influenced Newman (cf. *Apologia*) 'Move up, Mick [Michael Collins], make way for
Macpherson: *Temora* *I* clogán: little bell or clock wake up Dick [Richard Mulcahy, his successor]': D graffito
Da baal: bonfire after Collins' death, 1922
ballad (of Finnegan's Wake) humiliation
Jurchen: a tribe of Tartars humus

G P.T. Publikum: audience, clientele *AngI* praty: potato
future publication patrician
'Guinness is good for you' (advert)
Genghis Khan *Weekly Irish Times* 19/7/36: Finnegan
HCE HCE family crest: 'Out of a cloud a hand erect,
holding a book expanded proper'
s I Sowed the Seeds of Love cold old souls
overseer
St Domnat of Gheel (Ir.): Tefnut: Egyptian goddess
tutelar saint of lunatics dormitory deaf-mute
Noah Shaun Nu: Egyptian sky-god Shem *I* codul: sleep
I nuadhacht: news
coffeepot the sunup Pu: solar deity in Vedas otherworld underworld
AngI coddle: type of stew nu: now *G* seht: sees 'The overseer of the house of the overseer of the
in *MGr*, 'd' written 'nt'; *Gr* photo-: light- seal, Nu, triumphant, saith:' (frequent introduction
'b' written 'mp' *Heb* toph: good in *Egyptian Book of the Dead*)

Skt vah: to flow, carry *Skt* Suvarn sur: 'God of good shape', i.e. golden
sovereign sir scatterbrain *Da* brand: fire renewer
agnition: recognition *Skt* dah: to burn, scorch *Gr* arcturos: guardian
Agni: Hindu god of fire Arthur is coming John 1:1 (Vulg): 'In Principio erat Verbum'
ignites transitive verb killed *ph* kith & kin
kelt: prehistoric instrument used as chisel or axe
I tir: land Tintagel, Cornwall (site of Mark's castle & birthplace of Arthur; a 'rotten borough' before 1832)
Dubliners adjure thee *F* jour *Hin* Svadesia: self-government *L* salve: hail!
Skt durbala: of little strength *G* morgen: tomorrow *Skt* mārga: way, path
Lord's Prayer: 'kingdom come' Newman: *Lead Kindly Light* *Sw* hoppas: hope

Sw hämta: fetch Geryon: monster killed by Hercules *L* iter, itineris: journey
F journée: day *Skt* kal: supreme spirit regarded as destroyer VI.C.15.177: 'kal = gill'
seminary cemetery heliotrope When Tim Healy became Ir. Free State's Gov.-General, Dubliners called
L semita: path *L* somnium: a dream Viceregal Lodge 'Healiopolis'; the Phoenix burned HCE
3 castles on D coat of arms & resurrected at Heliopolis towel
fetched filched *Sw* tvål: soap
someone else warmed water *Da* smudsig: dirty
Sw varmet vatten: warm water
Margaret Mary Smith, Brown & Robinson *Sw* brunt: brown Sunlight Soap
Sw mörkret: the dark
on *pr* Charity begins at home
Woeful Dane Bottom: valley in Gloucestershire, possibly site of a Danish defeat
Du zie maar (lit. 'see but'): just have a look
W.H. Leverhulme (Sunlight Soap)
Trespassers will be prosecuted *L* qui stabat: who was *G* mein
Sw respass: travel ticket accoutred: dressed standing
G Pein: pain yore Annu: Heliopolis *Sw* ännu: yet, still
L quantum: as much as *Sw* ånyo: again
G mengen: mix hip, hip, hurray! *G* Flasche: bottle

G rasch: quickly *G* Pasch: dice heart
come to pass *L* pascha: Easter
tenderest Hill of Allen: Finn's H.Q., Co. Kildare
N tander: delicate *G* Ahle: awl
afterwards Lugh Lámh-fhada: god of sun & genius
L atria: the whole house
I bráth: judgement, doom
Earwicker *G* wacker: brave
I teine: fire *Da* spids: point, tip in
tiny
I áth: ford (midsummer sunrise at Stonehenge)

Heliopolis, Egypt (lit. 'sun town') peneplain: tract of land almost a plain
hell's bells! (oath)
bight: bay HCE Horned cairns have 2 stone 'horns' when seen in plan; some in Ireland
Fangelava Bay, New Ireland, Melanesia *Gr* ergon: work standing stones *N* stanse: stop, check
G froh: merry Isthmian Games celebrated in 1st & 3rd years of each Olympiad, in honour of Poseidon
s 'John Brown's body lies a-mouldering in the grave' post no bills
VI.B.14.112: 'the gossips (menhirs)' *G* grob: coarse
L cur: why? great dane (dog) trespass

if he's not byelaws *I* Beinn Éadair: Howth *Sw* humoristisk: humorous
ECH *Sw* eder: your (polite use)
ph put the cart before the horse *L* nox: night *I* duan: poem
their dawn chorus
L gallus: cock *Sw* han: he *r* Susquehanna duck: out for no runs (cricket)
G Hahn: cock *Sw* hon: she who, the hen
cricket (ringing) chambermaid porter
(crowing)
waiter
Wilde on fox hunters: 'the unspeakable in full pursuit of the uneatable'
(daylight) (night) (*Sw* words sometimes begin with letters 'kv')

F Allemagne sailor (606.35) turkey trot: U.S. ballroom dance introduced ca. 1912 Pierrot
aliment *Sw* säljare: seller Seapoint, district of Dún Laoghaire
Punch & Judy George Simon Tappertit: anarchical apprentice in Dickens'
Noel = Yule = Xmas = *Da* jul *G* Punsch: Punch *Barnaby Rudge*
Kersse, the tailor (II.3) HCE Stonehenge *I* ceol: music, singing
curses *Sw* kurs: course (of instruction) *N* henge: hang

Exmouth, town, Ostman: Viking for us (193.29; 195.05) bane: kill, harm
Devonshire *Sw* östby: east-village (Oxmantown, part of N. D) *Sw* var och en: 'each & one', i.e.
Hu domb: hill everybody

Howth *G* nach und nach: by & by *I* sasanach: English
Hafiz: Persian poet *AngI* knock: hill
G lang landscape *G* straucheln: stumble, trip stretches his limbs on Gazelle Channel, New
Cape Strauch, New Ireland Lamusong, town, New Ireland Ireland
399.03: 'Brinabride' *Sw* dotter: daughter

Eve Adam a dance with her father Lambel, Mt, New Ireland
damsel
presently hear *Gr* geôglyphê: earth-carving
geography
goodbye & wishing to see you soon 40 winks
G Bett: bed *Da* liv: life
majesty *s* 'It's a Long Way to Tipperary'

New Ireland CORK (Co.) steamed fish *Sw* strömming: herring
VI.B.14.112: 'Tipperary (I's premier Co)' *Sw* korv: sausage *Sw* konfekt: sweetmeats
Sw buljong: clear soup *Du* smeerworst: sausage spread *It* patate: potatoes *Sw* stekt: roasted
(bouillon) *Sw* smörsås: sauce made with butter steak stuck pig
Ir. Counties: MAYO LIMERICK WATERFORD WEXFORD LOUTH

KILDARE LEITRIM KERRY CARLOW LEIX

OFFALY DONEGAL CLARE GALWAY LONGFORD
tunny (fish) Claregalway, town, Co. Galway
MONAGHAN FERMANAGH CAVAN ANTRIM

ARMAGH WICKLOW ROSCOMMON SLIGO

MEATH WESTMEATH KILKENNY
Sw kvällsmat: supper
cromlech: prehistoric structure–large flat stone supported by 3 or more upright ones

Sir Richard Burton withdrew his theory ALP absolutely right
of the Nile's source & accompanied Speke part of the way wrong
L perporto: I transport boring you perhaps? Namantanai: town on New Ireland

Skt namana: bending, bowing *G* also
Kavieng: chief town on New Ireland
Skt āpad: calamity *Da* opad: at the top of Wellington's Monument, Iron Duke
L apud: with, at, by, near about Muniment Room, City Hall, D
HCE Horse Shows (D) charioteers heterogeneous

over & under
Sw över och under: up & down
modern
midden
It topaia: rats' nest, (fig.) hovel Mankai: town, New Ireland
Topaia: district of New Ireland
lava *It* marame: residues, rubbish melma: effluent from volcanoes
New Ireland natives *SC* marama: hard *It* amara: bitter
divided into 2 classes: Maramara *s* 'It's a long long way to Tipperary, But my heart's–right there'
& Pikalaba

cock-a-doodle-doo *Skt* svap: to sleep
Sl conk: nose *Sl* dook: large nose
sleep shutter from his shop

shop HCE Pekinese full stop

Australian friarbird ('four o'clock bird') Sydney (Aust.)
repeats 'four o'clock' *Da* syd: South
then known *Skt* aya: going

sleight of hand

*U.*446: 'The answer is a lemon' (a derisive reply) *G* Milch: milk
Gr theatron: theatre Roman theatre at Orange
Goat Fair of Killorglin kermesse: fair, carnival Dagda: father of Aengus, Ir. love-god
(087.26) *Skt* dogdhrī: giving milk *nr* 'Humpty Dumpty sat on a wall'
Hundred of Manhood, Sussex (030.08)
Du donder: thunder founder
renascent Finn incarnate *Da* fortælle: tell
ascendent
stone (037.24) HCE matins: morning prayers
as a matter of fact Erskine Childers helped run guns to Howth for Easter Rising
thumb in his mouth Viking *It* risurgere: rise again, revive crest *L* victis poenis hesternis: yesterday's
(Finn & the Salmon) Fum: George IV *N* fram: forth, out punishments having been overcome
foster father *I* solas: light J.H. Voss: 'wine, women & song'
first father
Da sogn: parish *I* Banba: Ireland (poetic) 39 Articles (of Church of Eng.)
It sogno: dream *Da* til: to
L consecrandus: (one) to be made sacred
*459: St Patrick 'was chanting the Lord's order of the canon'
angel (303.F1) Paternoster Unknown Warrior

Tumbarumba, town, N.S.W., Australia

Lancelot Czar of all the Russias *It* razzia: raid Dún Laoghaire
Da slot: castle *Da* forbi: past *433: 'Loegaire of the Swift Blows the son of Dub'
Woodhenge, not far from Stonehenge *U.*327: 'Spanish ale in Galway' *Da* øl: beer for
Mangan: *My Dark Rosaleen:* 'Spanish ale' *G* Öl: oil
I aingealach: numbness *I* sasanach: English(man) gnome sylph salamander merman
Anglo- (English) *458: Finn's 'Angalach or drinking horn'
fert: Ir. monument to dead Gunnar: character in Njal's Saga
bruiser F.E.R.T.: motto of House of Savoy C18 Ir. Gunning sisters married Eng. aristocrats
Edward & Robert Bruce went to Ireland in 1315 'going, going, gone' (auction) HCE

kilderkin: cask holding 16–18 gallons

Pamphilius died while asking the time
F pamphile: jack of clubs in game of pamphile
HC . . . E
L nivis: of snow
*432 *The Death of* know
Finn: 'from the thick of his thighs'
green, white & blue maypole

Inis Elga: old name of Ireland CEH *427 *The Death of Finn*: '& then he spoke the lay'
*422: a hag warning Diarmaid & Grania of the approach of Finn, during their hiding on Howth: 'there
is not a smooth plain in all Elga . . . not a The Gyres in Yeats' *A Vision*
bell is heard, no crane talks' *Gr* gigantogyroi: giant circles
Gr parasama: emblems 'Atman: the spiritual self recognised as God' (*Isis Unveiled,* index)
King Lear III.4.187: 'Fie, foh, & fum' *Skt* atma eva: becoming even the self Adam & Eve
paladin

(031.15) *L* soleo tempora: accustomed to the times

stutters (Parnell, Carroll &c.)

L inspectorum: of observers sergeant HCE holocaust cist: sepulchral
dahlias eaten by earwigs police inspector searching Holy Ghost chamber
(constellation) *Skt* Jambudvīpa: central continent round Mt Meru
L fabula: story Giambattista Vico *Skt* Vipra: wise,
versicle: short sentence said or sung antiphonally in divine service inspired; a Brahman

Søren Kierkegaard: *Either/Or*

ph pot calling the kettle black milkwhite
G Pfanne: frying pan
Swift (595.35) was kidnapped within a year of his birth & kept for 3 years

Skt antar: within, between, amongst
altar of Jesus *Skt* yaśas: beautiful appearance, splendour, renown
(Judg 6:37–8: dew on fleece; dry on all ground)

G gut! *F* goutte *AngI* Lochlann: Scandinavian of anyone
Fingal: area N. of D *F* goûte!: taste!

*T. P. Cross & C. H. Slover: *Ancient Irish Tales* (1936)

so, la (Sol-fa) Lugh Lámh-fhada ('Long-Arm'): god of sun & genius
I lá: day *ph* the long arm of coincidence
say Hadding: mythical Danish king, visited the other world

Skt svapnaj: asleep *Skt* svap: to sleep
strangest
G rund: round hundred best pages of *1001 Nights*
Da bedst: best pagans
The Eddas *The Book of the Dead* Tom, Dick & Harry
odds & ends sagas written at Oddi, Iceland
entireties

dreams tale told

grace of God

John 1:1: 'In the beginning was the Word' sides (turn over in bed)

West East
yesterday (past) *G* ist (present)
falling asleep & waking up, so on, so forth South
F sourd
Moscow ginpalace djinns: order of Moslem spirits; 360 images of djinns in Great
kiosk *G* Palast: palace (hell) Mosque at Mecca
*U.*86: 'mosque of the baths' (muezzin's call) *It* sponda: riverbank other side
Fred Barrett's Bazaar next to Turkish Baths, Stephen's Green, D Valhalla
bathos bizarre Alcoran (The Koran) (heaven) *It* buona notte: goodnight
alcove
pure poetry once upon a time bed & breakfast

parricide *F* se coucher thole: to endure, undergo
It combattere ad armi pari: to fight on equal terms holes
wornout chaffer: to trade or barter HCE

pr Every dog has his day witness
Skt shava sam-jīvana: corpse being restored to life
John-a-dreams (*Hamlet* II.2.295): generic for a 'dreamy fellow' Leixlip Loopline railway bridge, D
Sw under dagens lopp: during the course of the day true
systole diastole

does search me

upsy-daisy!
how sad to say
look! (shaft of light) *It* lancinante: stabbing (of pain), penetrating God's truth!
Old Ice lok: lock
Skt vayuna: moving, agitated that
Vayu: Vedic god of wind *F* voyons!: let's look!
G Reisefieber: nervousness before a journey
It una corrente d'aria: a draught Bach cantata 'The Sleeper Wakes'
coranto: dance in triple time
N geip: wry mouth, grimace
Skt Māyā: illusion *Old Ice* vindr: wind
window
Old Ice vildr: agreeable; good choice *G* Wirbel: whirl
G Welt: world

degrees Celsius (centigrade) jackdaw (still does not sing)
L excelsius: higher *Skt* jaladevatā: a water-goddess, naiad
they mackerel cloud: cirrocumulus (heralds depression) temperature
anemone: windflower
normal human
morn
alfresco: in the open air vervain: plant once thought aphrodisiac
fresco: fresh air
eaten
Eden
so what? snacked *Da* snakket med: talked with
say what snake (garden of Eden) (Salmon of Wisdom) tell which

Substantives represent persons, places, objects & things

Gr dromos: race dream *Sp* todos: all
Dromios: twins in *Comedy of Errors* drama of today
out & about *G* verschwunden: disappeared had
held
tip of the tongue *Da* tang: tongs solitary syllable sense

Matt 5:38: 'An eye for an eye, & a tooth for a tooth' cumulonimbus: thundercloud
noctambulation: sleepwalking
F Nil Victoria & Albert Nyanza: the 2 Western reservoirs of the Nile *F* néant: nothingness
I ní h-annsa: not hard (formula for answering riddles)
all but unending

Macpherson, footnote to *Croma:* 'the waves dark-tumble . . . various is the night'

I indé: yesterday *I* indiu: today *It* Dio: my God!
I diu: day
G gestern: yesterday hi! *G* heute morgen: this morning

yesterday *It* destati: awakened well done!
L dormite: sleep ye! destiny
Skt divas: day *Skt* padma: lotus
Isis Unveiled I.92–3: 'the mystic water-lily (lotus) . . . signifies the emanation of the objective from the concealed . . . (and) is worked into the earliest dogma of the baptismal sacrament' brother & sister of orisons
'Let us pray' *Sw* til härnäst: until next time *Skt* adya: today, now *It* addio: goodbye
Sw tack: thanks *Skt* tamas: darkness European

India

supernatural
('above the night')
It dire pane al pane e vino al vino: to call a spade a spade (transubstantiation of bread & wine)

Tamil: S. Indian language *ph* French without tears

other other yesterday

Swift: *A Tale of a Tub* picture turned to the wall atoms
ph the pitcher went too often to the well (said when it breaks)
well 'Matthew, Mark, Luke & John, Bless the bed that I lie on' (trad. prayer)

comparative
It campare: to live
G Kraft durch Freude: Strength through Joy (Nazi slogan)

Skt adya: today, now Matt 5:38: 'An eye for an eye, & a tooth for a tooth'
Skt anta: end

Tim Finnegan
time
Skt Loka: the universe or any division of it orbit
Chapelizod Lucan Erin 'Urbi et Orbi': the pope's address 'To the City [Rome] & the World'
ears
heard The Speaking Clock, telephone service: 'On the third stroke it will be . . . hours, . . . minutes & . . . seconds' chime
Matt 11:15: 'he who hath ears to hear, let him hear'

hour *Arch* sennight: week *Da* maaned: month year
L diurnus: of the day
Mahamanvantara: Hindu great year

L -ibus: dative & ablative plural *Sw* äktaman: husband
BLM wee-wee: French (oui, oui) *Sw* hustru: wife
neighbours

Exod 20:17: 'Thou shalt not covet thy neighbour's . . . manservant &c.'

L cognatii: kinsmen *U.*214: 'orts and offals'
ins & outs *G* Ort: place
Exod 20:17: 'Thou shalt not covet thy neighbour's house . . . nor his ox, nor his ass, nor anything that is thy neighbour's'
Timothy (Finnegan) what o'clock
time of day where?
Skt vartman: path, road, course (do you not see?) *G* Pfad: path
Lord's Prayer: 'Our Father, Which art in Heaven, Hallowed be Thy name'
founded found Vata: Vayu spirit of wind in Vedic myth horrid *I* bóthar: road
G Pfund: pound avatars *G* Vater: father erred *G* Himmel: Heaven Himalaya Mts *I* ruadh: red
cow steer
I gabhar: goat tiger lion elephant thirst
Under the name Athar, Ishtar became a male god in Saudi Arabia at time of abandonment of matriarchy
at their vittles Finnegan family arms: 'argent a lion rampant sable between
padding on foot (4 hoofs) 3 trefoils slipped gules'
Skt pada: a step
tongues may talk *r* Tolka, D *Sw* tolka: to interpret, translate
(tongues silenced 598.04)

(Viconian cycle) Solomon salmon
L fulmen: thunderbolt
divine providence (Vico)

hesitency

economic

come on George Moore
Sl gammon: humbug, chatter
Morpheus (sleep) let's not be unguardsmanlike
morphemes
touch stomach *Sw* ångare: *G* Anker: anchor *L* aequus: level, equal
F tache *pr* An army marches on its stomach steamer aquatints: type of graphics
seaworthy *Sw* lots: pilot persons
Sw sevärd: worth seeing, lit. 'see-worthy'
s There Is a Tavern in the Town

Sl topical tip: tip to back horse, based on Browne & Nolan
fortuitous coincidence Bruno of Nola

CHE cumulus, cirrus & nimbus clouds
nubilous: cloudy
Blake: *Milton,* preface: 'Arrows of desire' poplar trees

picnic
panicstricken
(hydrologic cycle)

done

Old Man of the Sea *s* Old Man River: 'don't say nothing'
mounted shoulders of Sinbad in *Arabian Nights*, and would not get off
jest

simply & solely

Drury Lane Theatre, London time/space
dreary Drury Lane, D

St Polycarp: bishop of Smyrna Anna Livia *G* Saft: juice
(pool with many carp) *Skt* sara: liquid, fluid
marge: margin Pisces & Sagittarius: signs of the zodiac
Gr astrion: little star
live George Moore: *Hail & Farewell* ('Ave', 'Vale') Minnehaha (Hiawatha's sweetheart;
F laver *L* alvus: womb *It* alveo: riverbed Catullus: *Ave* name means 'laughing water')
Hiawatha *r* Poddle, D pissabed *atque Vale*
her water

apparitions

Finn & Ann *I* Baile Átha Cliath: Town of the Ford of the Hurdles (D)
Da kongdømme: kingdom
accursed corsair Dublin Moyle: sea between Ir. & Scotland
L alieni: foreigners
Albert & Victoria Nyanza: the 2 Western reservoirs of the Nile vignette
I ní h-annsa: not hard; formula for answering riddles Neanderthal
F née in sea (Aphrodite) Tom, Dick & Harry

Cataracts of Nile Cothraige: early name for St Patrick
G Schluss: ending *ph* God speed the plough!
Moore: *s* 'Tis Believed That This Harp' [Gage Fane]
happened
beauty spot (220.07, 291.F7)

ECH Colonel House: President Wilson's advisor
praeter-: beyond, more than
Michael Dwyer: C19 Ir. rebel

blunderbuss *Sl* pike: penis

long afterwards elmtree *Du* alom: everywhere grow
almond tree
Søren (Kierkegaard)

Ascension MacCool *Sw* vit: white *L* alba: white
essential sentence of law *It* vitalba: old man's beard; clematis
bloomers *Sw* tvätterska: washerwoman hobgoblins
Dublin
L saxum: stone like our ancestors thought so dearly of
Saxons . . . Angles . . . Jutes *Sw* saxen: the scissors
over Anglesey, Wales free of duties *Sw* dyrt: expensive
dirt cheap
sleeps *G* immer: always
immemorial

(shivering)

White Horse of Wansted celebrated Alfred's victory over Danes ought to have at least

butcher's apron (213.16) HCE *Angl* Lochlann: Scandinavian
L homo: man *L* circa: in the neighbourhood *L* -ensis: pertaining to
Lambay Island, off D coast George Borrow: *Romany Rye* *G* Pfiff: whistle
I Liam: William *r* Wye
swim shamrock

whiskey steal *Angl* pogue: kiss
I Páidín: dim. of Pádraig (Patrick)
Dolly Varden in Dickens' *Barnaby Rudge* Boucicault: *Arrah-na-Pogue* Proper: that part of Mass
which varies with calendar
G feist: corpulent ferial days: ones that are not feast-days he
feast Cardinal Cullen: archbishop of D
celebrate peregrine pilgrim
celibate Uí Maine: tribal lands along the Shannon
Land's End, Cornwall Moore: *s* By That Lake Whose Gloomy Shore [The Brown Irish Girl] (about St Kevin
palm of Glendalough) glaum: snatch

business empower yogi
Empire bogpriest
decked leaves offrande: offering
okey doke fondest love
AngI owen: river *Skt* Tasyām kuru salilakriyam: In her (river?) perform water-rite
G Pfaffe: priest (derogatory)
look, our late lamented
Lac Leman: Lake Geneva Isis a king of Atlantis supposedly buried under Lough Neagh
Ys: legendary city in Brittany engulfed by ocean at last
'Urbi et Orbi': the pope's address 'To the City [Rome] & the World' *G* Wasser: water Lake Erie, U.S.
sleep from slumber
Giraldus Cambrensis says that in clear weather fishermen see buildings (round towers) under Lough Neagh

G wo: where *We* hwy: they, them *s* Dermot Asthore
I dair: oak (.02) dear Astaroth, Ashtoreth: names of Astarte, Babylonian fertility goddess

Hell's angels Macpherson (*The Songs of Selma*) glosses 'mac alla' as meaning 'son of a cliff'
G Engel: angel *G* langsam: slow
samphire: maritime plant; leaves used for pickles *s* Tea for Two
Samphire Island, Tralee Bay *Skt* tat-tuam-asi: 'that thou art': aphorism identifying Brahma with the individual
F sosie: counterpart, double
I Clann na nGaedheal: 'Children of the Irish': U.S. society supporting Fenians

15 + 14 = 9 + 20 = 8 + 21 = 28 + 1 = 29
novena *F* vingt
(628.15)

L sicut campanulae petalliferentes: just like petal-bearing little bells
family Campanulae includes Canterbury bells corolla of flower
Botany Bay: quadrangle at Trinity College, D
Botany Bay, prison colony, N.S.W., Australia dream of those
girls

Moore: *s* Sing, Sing, Music Was Given [The Old Langolee] little

G Klagelied: lamentation
I Clann na nGaedheal (.13)
D churches: St Agatha's, William St N. St Peter's, Phibsborough
St Francis Xavier's, Gardiner St St Andrew's, Westland Row
Discalced Carmelites, Clarendon St (Clarinda Pk, Dún Laoghaire) Our Lady of Dolours, Dolphin's Barn
Immaculate Heart of Mary Church, City Quay St Joseph's, Portland Row
St Paul's, Arran Quay Adam & Eve's (St Francis of Assisi) Out Lady of Refuge, Rathmines
St Kevin's Chapel, Cath. University Ch., St Stephen's Green
Church of the 3 Patrons, Rathgar
Corpus Christi, Drumcondra *It* vestiti: clothes St Paul's College, Mt Argus
St Michan's (known for its vaults) St Mary of the Angels, Church St Milltown Park Chapel, Clonskeagh
Church of the Visitation, Fairview
Star of the Sea, Sandymount St Patrick's, Ringsend St Mary's, Haddington Rd
It bella vista: good view
Our Lady of Dolours, Glasnevin White Friars (Carmelite Priory, Aungier St) Abbey of St Thomas à Becket, Thomas St
G Umlaut St Laurence O'Toole's, Seville Pl.
It trema: it trembles Swift: 'Ppt'
pray for us

St Laurence O'Toole buried at Eu, Normandy
F midinettes: work-girls so what
maiden *I* óg: young
G meiden: avoid St Kevin supposed to have slept in hollow of tree in Glendalough
Isa 60:1: 'Arise, shine' Cathleen, rejected by St Kevin
St Kevin's bed (hollow in rock), Glendalough St Kevin's Kitchen: church, Glendalough
I mo bhrón: my sorrow *L* ex terra: from land
L interirrigo: I conduct water along
archipelagos Dr John Whalley, Australian astrologer, fled from D to England
wallaby (Australian) Toland, deist, fled from D to England
forsook our shores (A is next after Z)
New Zealand
Bismarck Archipelago, Melanesia, includes New Ireland

second

Leeward Islands, Polynesia

Grania on seeing Diarmaid: 'Who is that freckled, sweet-worded man?'

Windward Islands, Polynesia

in particular summarize

Coemghen: Old Ir. spelling of Kevin do-gooder
Macpherson: *War of Caros*, 360: 'What does Caros' morality
The Pursuit of Diarmaid & Grainne 'As for Finn, I will tell his tidings clearly'
I Móralltach: 'Very wild': name of Diarmaid's sword
Grania first saw Diarmaid at a 'goaling match' *pr* A rolling stone gathers no moss Diarmaid performed feat rolling a tun up & down a hill
must: mould
Skt rāga: attachment Macpherson: *Cathlin of Clutha* 336: 'be thine the secret hill'

r Jarama Macpherson: *Comala* 26: 'let one virgin mourn thee'
Skt amar: deathless *Skt* aj-: birthless *L* adeste!: come! *s* John O'Dwyer of the Glen
Macpherson: *Conlath & Cuthona* 370: 'Cuthona sits at a distance & weeps'
Macpherson: *The War of Caros:* 'stream of Balva' (M. notes this means 'a silent stream') Macpherson: *Colna-dona:* 'Crona of the streams'
F terroir: soil
Dwyer Gray: owner of *Freeman's Journal* (214.33) about to bray afeared Macpherson: *Comala*: 'in his terrors' Potter's Field: frequent name for pauper cemetery
I Béarla: Eng. language
four corners rigs of barley
Irish Independent, newspaper (067.25) tomorrow morning

letter-man's *I* gortán: miser inquest
It questure: police headquarters
makes the following *Durban Gazette:* S. African periodical
Dublin Gazette, newspaper forthcoming
correspondent anywhere *G* Dienstag: Tuesday *F* bosse: hump
L collis: hill doomsday
Upper & Lower Baggot St, D Earwicke (anagram) ever
Da bygge: build *It* strade: streets
funeral games *Saturday Evening Post*, newspaper ECH

VI.B.41.123: 'ass = caricature of a horse' (111.27) camera obscura *G* Kamerad: comrade
It coricatore: loader ass Oscar Wilde
Dutch Schultz: U.S. gangster pipe dream
G Schuld: guilt

(Sullivani 573.07)
silence
body conic section (geometry) Pathé news
Buddha Macpherson glosses 'Car-avon' as a 'winding river' caravan
I scuit: excitement, fuss *Gr* skotia: darkness Macpherson: *Cathloda* II.10: 'misty Loda: the house of the spirits of men!'
Macpherson glosses 'scuite' as 'wandering nation' city London
Macpherson glosses Concathlin, a star, as 'mild beam of the wave'
Macpherson: *Cathloda* II: 'Thou art with the years that are gone'
polar bear *Sw* stjärnar: stars Macpherson: *Cathlin of Clutha* 335n: 'Ton-thena, fire of the wave . . . star . . . directed the course of Larthon to Ireland'
Pole Star

always to himself *F* foule

hopping home *Sw* nyckel: key
knuckle

Grimstad, where Ibsen worked as druggist's assistant
Old Parr: Eng. centenarian accused of incontinence frieze coat fed up *L* nox: night
s Oats, Peas, Beans & Barley Grow once upon a time
G . . . P . . . O Moore: *s* The Time I've Lost in Wooing [Pease upon a Trencher]

women smile grease of bacon & eggs
beckoning

eclipse moonshine

gasmask letter man improvement right

ph right as the mail *G* schön: good *Du* schoon: clean *Sl* shoon: lout, fool
ph fit as a fiddle *Du* schoen: shoe *Gi* shoon: listen Shaun the Post
G putzen: to clean *L* te, tibi

nr A Was an Archer (e.g. 'T was a tinker & mended a pot') butters *Arch* baxter: baker
bakes
heavenly Lord's Prayer: 'Our Father . . . Give us this day our daily bread,
& deliver us from evil' *Sw* bulta: knock
Macpherson: footnote to *Croma:* 'receive me, my friends, from night'
relieve *Sl* doss: sleep eiderdowns
*U.*327: 'the winebark Thomas of Ercildoune was taken under Eildon Hill by a female elf (Scott:
on the winedark waterway' *Minstrelsy of the Scottish Border*)
Du dat is het dus: that's how it is *Sw* sångare: singer eiderdown
G dass: that *G* singen: singing
try

postmaster general say *I* sé: him *I* sí: her
Parnell: 'get my price' *s* 'Tea for Two & two for tea'
Parnell's brothers & sisters called him 'butt-head'

makeshift *G* nackt: naked *G* älter: older took keepsake
s 'Tea for Two & two for tea' altarboy *L* alter: other
beautiful weather for the Ides of March
walker
I a mhic: my boy (rumour) *s* Sonny Boy

guilty ladies of the jury *It* letti: beds persuaded
lettuce Gideon . . . dew . . . (.22 fleece)–Judg 6:39–40 *F* Suède: Sweden
F entre nous *Sl* dago: Spaniard
(7 girls)
U.S. College Sl well-stacked filler-outer *U.S. College Sl* fever frau: lively lady
U.S. College Sl plush: posh plus
U.S. College Sl dope = clonk = stupid person *U.S. College Sl* pig: girl
U.S. Sl pigskin: football *U.S. College Sl* muffle: fumble
P/K P/K *U.S. College Sl* pipe: easy course Anguish: father of Isolde
U.S. College Sl Anguish: Eng. course
G fliessen: flow fall D.A. Chart: *The Story of Dublin* Charles S. Parnell
Petrie lived at 21 Great Charles St, Topographical Office of Ir. Ordnance Survey
declination
inclination
G Fuss: foot fay: fairy
Parnell died as result of wet feet face
U.S. College Sl hang a goober: kiss *Sw* lag: law
Sw var . . . än: where . . . then lagmen: judges in D Thingmote
Macpherson's *Carthon* uses tradition that deer can see ghosts

Dublin

Great Heavens! Hesitency with heliotropes (both flowers supposed metamorphosed persons)
events *U.*374: 'What is it? Heliotrope? No. Hyacinth? Hm'
Sw fullvuxen frökener: full-grown young ladies libel action
Sw dubbel: double hobbledehoys double decoys
part of the Catholic Church someone must atone
F porte: door *L* summum: whole Aquinas: *Summa theologica*
'blankety blank' (euphemistic) hound *Sl* peeler: policeman
sound
son of a gun *G* Hund: dog Fox Goodman (035.30)
N sunt: sound

Coemghen: Old Ir. spelling of Kevin Wyndham Lewis edited *Tyro* (1921–2)
Macpherson: *War of Caros* 360: 'What does Caros?' *r* Tora in Macpherson's *Carric-Thura*
novena iconostasis: screen bearing blue & green vitriols: sulphates of copper & iron
icons in Eastern Church *F* vitrail (see letter to FB, quoted 613.15)
faint *Gr* Phôsphoron: 'torch-bearing', epithet of Artemis
U.S. Sl peachy: good

during Diarmaid's pursuit he was asked after by foreigners who failed to recognise him. 'I have seen him that saw him today' said Diarmaid
gentlemen Kevin/Jerry *L* roga: ask
Jeremiah
son of a bitch *PS* bog: god
pice: Indian coin Finnegan family said to descend from Heremon *Sl* puckaroo: to seize
Heremon & Heber: legendary Bregia: tribal land, Co. Meath, orig. Heber's; taken by Heremon;
progenitors of Ir. race Teffia: tribal land, Co. Westmeath, W. of Bregia
Her inverted: turned inward Finnegans originated in Bregia & may have spread to Teffia
left ancient crest of Finnegan family: a vine branch leaved fructed proper P/K CHE public houses are not
early risers' Mass HCE John Eliot Cairns: Ir. political economist
Higgins & Egan families figure in lineage of Finnegans
T.R. Malthus (population control) Moore: *s* How Sweet the Answer Echo Makes [The Wren]
Da hus: house *Da* lukket: shut within
Sw besökare: visitor
soakers (boozers)
silicates silica, lime & soda fused in manufacture of glass
(first) libation *F* limon lemon sodas
Matt 1:20: 'angel of the Lord' 'Hail Mary, full of grace!' (morning prayers)
lorries
It (apoc.) mattin: morning Lord's Prayer: 'Thy Kingdom come'
matins: morning prayers
Great Siberian Railway *I* réal: star happens *N* avvente: await
sideral: sent from the stars
Sw hästkraft: horsepower *Sl* buzzer: motorcar buses

violet *Sw* fartyget: the vessel, ship
L Via Lactea: Milky Way fare ticket
Milky Way (our galaxy)
collection potato
small train *G* Eltern: parents cream
Sw smultron: wild strawberry *Sw* eldaren: the stoker (whistle)
Strawberry Beds, Chapelizod
Ursa Major also called The Waggon
shamrock *F* or
It aspetta!: wait!
L tacete: be silent! HCE John Aubrey: *Brief Lives*
L hagiographice canat Ecclesia: the church sings hagiographically *F* aube: dawn

(470.15–20: 'Oasis . . . Oisis') primate
'Oyez' (town crier)
protonotary: member of college of 12 prelates who register papal acts, keep records, &c.
Exod 3:14 'I AM THAT I AM' free nitrogen (atmospheric) Irish Free State
Popeye: 'I yam what I yam' gale
about
eyot: small island Ireland's Eye: small island off Howth *1001 Nights* *G* Insel: island
Gr mega: big Melanesia Thousand Islands, *r* St Lawrence, Canada
G Ostern: Easter Eastern
Western Approaches: Atlantic searoutes to British & Ir. ports

FEAR OF THE LORD (gift of Holy Spirit; cf. 605)

Tom . . . Dick . . . Harry Springheeled Dick: character in boys' comics

Anglican Grace: 'For what we have received may the Lord make us truly thankful'

Lupita proved her chastity by carrying live coals without getting burned

(003.09–10) *R* dusha: soul
F douche (*G* taufen: baptise)
ECCLESIASTICAL HIERARCHY | CELESTIAL HIERARCHY | LITURGICAL COLOURS | CANONICAL HOURS | GIFTS OF HOLY SPIRIT | SACRAMENTS
(7 words in paragraph based on 'create')

papal encyclical

ANGELS WHITE

PRIEST monkish vows: voluntary poverty privilege *R* pravilo: rule
(Kevin named 7 times in increasing states of sanctity)
L altare cum balneo: altar together with bath
(bath named 7 times)
MATINS MATRIMONY

ROSE alb: priest's tunic
GOLD cloth of gold: cloth partly woven with gold threads
ARCHANGELS GREEN (*F* vert)
St Kevin lived 7 years as hermit at Glendalough, Co. Wicklow
Meeting of the Waters, Co. Wicklow *I* ise: she (emphatic)
I eisin: he (emphatic)
(2 lakes at Glendalough) PIETY

lauding *Gr* Trishagion: Holy Trinity LAUDS
L triunus: three-one
DEACON diaconal: pertaining to a deacon HOLY ORDERS
Ancient Order of Hibernians
epicentrum: point above centre
PRINCIPALITIES
Yeats: *The Lake Isle of Innisfree* (poem)
POWERS PRIME KNOWLEDGE

I uisce fian: wild water

I uisce fionn: clear water

SUBDEACON *L* propter: beside

EXTREME UNCTION

RED TIERCE PENANCE

ACOLYTE Yeats: *Innisfree:* 'a hive for the honeybee' FORTITUDE (1 of Cardinal Virtues, .25)
Ancient Ir. beehive hut enclosures (mentioned in Yeats' *Innisfree*)
VIRTUES *L* arenaria: sandpit

COUNSEL

monkish vows: entire obedience

Gregorian & Ambrosian chant SEXT

EUCHARIST

L una cumque: one, however
(DOMINATIONS; in line omitted from published text)
LECTOR

CONFIRMATION

EXORCIST

ECCLESIASTICAL HIERARCHY | CELESTIAL HIERARCHY | LITURGICAL COLOURS | CANONICAL HOURS | GIFTS OF HOLY SPIRIT | SACRAMENTS

monkish vows: perpetual chastity UNDERSTANDING

THRONES NONES (ninthly)
L translatus: carried across
VIOLET VESPERS
vail: lower, descend
Gr hydrophilos: water lover BLACK (sable) cappa magna: nonliturgical cope worn by popes, cardinals & bishops
CHERUBIM COMPLINE WISDOM
Angelical Salutation: 'Seat of wisdom'
L doctor insularis: insular doctor

DOORKEEPER (Ostiary)

extempore: unpremeditated

SERAPHIM

BAPTISM

Bishop Rock Lighthouse, Scilly Isles server boy (Mass) *L* nota bene
bishops . . . rook's right (chess) *It* nuota bene: it, he, swims well
(notice to shipping, on rock)
rear Ben of Howth (3 distinct peaks visible)
Sw åskan: the thunder *Sw* blixten: the lightning damn & blast
asking your blessing *Sw* dimman: the fog *Sw* blåsten: the wind
write home Hume (philosopher) E . . . C . . . H previous

hen coop Henry II gave D to citizens of Bristol: subsequent
Hellfire Club, on hill over D migration to D
30 11 2
trolls elves cobolds (earth spirits) cobbled
artificially

franklin: freeholder
Benjamin Franklin (lightning)
household word

pr Familiarity breeds contempt

'Exsultet': 'O felix culpa!' explorer
L ferax: fruitful *I* cúpla: pair
ablation: taking away, surgical removal
oblations ablutions parts

Sw ark papper: a sheet of paper undecidedly Tristan died at Cliff of Penmarks, Brittany
antecedently
Sw prov: sample *G* Kuvert: envelope *G* gefaltet: folded (124: paper wounds made by professor)
covertly stylus, ink *Gr* stigmatophoron: thing bearing tattoo marks
(Holy Trinity) flower pollinated through stigma, connected to carpel by style

Sw tofflor: slippers *G* Teufel: devil
021.15: 'prankquean' *Da* tøfler: one who shuffles, trudges
It panni: clothes the P/Q split talents
talons
G wandl-: transform, cast a spell *G* Rute: wand, rod
wanderer *Sw* sjuk: ill, sick route
G Unterrock: petticoat *Sw* kläder: clothes Claddagh: fishing community in Galway; women once all
Sw utter: otter *Sw* rock: coat *F* appeler: invite wore red flannel skirts
played that polka as well as I *Sw* flickor: girls
poker *Sw* pojkar: boys
fore floor *nr* Humpty Dumpty
L flores: flowers

U.S. ph a sailor on horseback

G gehen: go *G* wie geht's?: how are you? Parnell: 'When you sell, get my price'
saw him going we gets a surprise (003.09–10)

F en masse *ph* tell that to the marines *It* marino: of the sea
Marino, district of D
Eccles 1:2: 'vanity of vanities' lustre: 5-year period

Maximilian debility fact Moore & Burgess, minstrels, had catchline: 'Take off that white hat'
emollient: softening , Laudabiliter (papal bull granting Ireland to Henry II)
L (artif.) ludibilitas: playfulness *Da* sønner: sons

MacCool *Mil. Sl* scrimshanker: shirker
Thor spent night sleeping in the glove of a giant, Skrimm, thinking it was a sleeping hall
L socer: father-in-law
sacerdotal
horologer: clockmaker going west
Gen 35:1: '& God said unto Jacob, Arise, go up to Beth-el, & dwell there'
Heb beth-el: house of God *R* smolkat: to fall silent Jacob . . . Esau Jacob's pipe: pipe
Jacob of Edessa (Mesopotamia) sulking *G* behing: covered with porcelain head representing one of the
founded Jacobite sect Lent lending ladling chafing dish: vessel to hold burning fuel patriarchs
Gen 25:34: mess of pottage of lentils *It* Postumia: Postojina, Yugoslav caves
symbolising the Apostles = Credo EHC
'cymbal' der. from *Gr* for 'cup' *Cymbeline* (includes Posthumus)
Haeckel: *The Riddle of the Universe* *Sl* nam: man *We* nam: sin, fault
Arch nam: I am not *I* an am: the time *I* anam: soul, life

Moore: *s* Fill the Bumper Fair [Bob & Joan] *G* Fleischer: butcher
Sw boning: dwelling (place)
signal Chapelizod
G segnen: bless Champs Elysées, Paris
around teach

s 'Lots of fun at Finnegan's Wake'

Rom 13:11: 'It is high time' *I* tig: house title (*Finnegans Wake*) *Sl* dick: penis

Sw dag: day *G* genug: enough old Nick *Sw* gnid mig bra: rub me well beg your pardon
Sw gnugga: to rub *Sw* Ni: you *Sw* gnid: rub *Sw* mig: my good my bag: steal
body ourselves

Svea: region in central Sweden incongruity coupling
contiguity inferiority complex
he upon her marriage must subliminate apology for my English
mirage *L* sublumbo: under the loin epilogue
G Engel: angel I'm still so sorry While I'm still so tired *Da* om til ti: about till 10
excuse *Da* sove: to sleep what is the time

I deo-gréine: spark of the sun *G* schlimm: evil summer, winter, spring, fall
Sw daggryning: dawn *Sw* skymningen: the dusk *G* Wind
Da regn: rain reign of darkness, slowly receding
G durchnässt: drenched reassessing
livening below stairs Amenta: Egyptian underworld
stars
hit or miss Hill of Howth hotel
The Hollow, Phoenix Park
Da solskin: sunshine *G* Frist: time limit attended admiral captain
W.S. Gilbert: First *Da* friste: to tempt actor 'attempts' part
The Bab Ballads: 'Lieutenant-Colonel Flare'
Da løfte: raise *F* corne: horn
Temple Bar, D & London *F* pont Boer *G* Bürgermeister
Dublin Bar (across Liffey)
Isolde *G* Eis: ice pleased nonplussed
It isole: islands
Tempest IV.1.174: 'cloud-capp'd towers' sunbonnet unaccompanied
39 Articles of Church of Eng. canopied pony
big white horse. Tip (008–010)
equine sequined torse: torso
Blanchardstown: newspapers please copy goodness gracious!
village N.W. of D *I* capall: horse W.G. Grace, cricketer
have mercy upon us 'Grand Old Man': Gladstone
L mensa: table *L* mens: mind, judgement
balls

mannerism F vague

meteorologist Brehon Law: ancient Ir. legal system sorcerers
(hostility of C19 scientific bodies to spiritualists) British Association for the Advancement of Science

essence
L esse: to be
dissolving *Dial* forenenst: over against Swift, 'the Drapier'

Dan Leno monologue: 'The Draper's Assistant'
pair of drawers

We arth: a bear coz: cousin
Arthur
Nice conject *s* The Ballyhooly Blue Ribbon Army
uncle/niece

sphygmomanometer: instrument for measuring blood pressure
George Sigerson: C19 D professor of biology
Prussians

G nichts mehr: not more Aventine: 1 of the 7 hills of Rome; (fig.), a secure position
nightmare, haven't I (had one)

Anna Livia

Du baas: boss, master *I* bás: death
B.A.A.S.: British Association for the Advancement of Science
Da sten: stone the matter
Skt stena: thief
placed into the hands of our solicitors salacity *F* messieurs

Son & Son *N* alm: elm Aline, wife of Ibsen's Master Builder
so-&-so *It* alina: little wing
ph gladdens the cockles of the heart morning
Thomas Mann: *The Magic Mountain*
chop suey *C* kao lao: apply for leave to resign on account of old age
cow Foochow, Chinese tea port
Becker Bros (D), sold tea future Jonathan Sawyer sawest? *R* nyet: no
brose: type of porridge founded Dublin, Georgia
I think I seem to remember some such

threelegged probably it resembles *Da* kvinde: woman
pubic symbols
perhaps triangle (293) *G* Hahn: cock
plus a sort of a
whatyoumaycallher

Du thee: tea *AngI* signs are on: therefore more by token

tealeaves wreck
Stanley Houghton: *Hindle Wakes*
The White Ship sank because everyone on board was drunk; Henry I's only son was drowned
Ibsen: *Borte!:* 'før natten den sorte' ('with the dark coming on') Hurdle Ford (D)
'over & out' (intercom) Firth of Forth, Scotland
Wakes week: holiday period in N. of England
innumerable Asias *King Lear* III.4.187: 'Fie, foh, & fum' Tem: creator in *Egyptian Book of the Dead*
embers ashes
Finnegan
Phoenix

wide awake

I a Dhia: o God

agreeable L sine: without (gearless clutchless car)
pr No time like the present sinecure (from L sine cura, without care)
absolent = erron. for absolute & obsolete Petty: survey of Ireland
s 'There's no place like home' I bhán: white s Polly Vaughan F petit
populace L magnus gentry whitehaired missionary blokes
I mór: great VI.B.41.132: 'lloyd (grey)' mercenary
(St Patrick) I buidhe: yellow (i.e. Chinese druid of 611.05) We gwyn: white
Gen. Blücher (Waterloo)
I dubh: black Wilde on fox hunters: 'The unspeakable in full pursuit of the uneatable'
dove-eyed
Mata: 7-headed tortoise; offspring of Eve & the Serpent

Matthew, Mark, Luke & John

ah yes A, double S = ASS

grogram: a coarse fabric G laut: loud
I gruagán gré: grey-hairdye hue
Minister of Transport Rosina: girl in *The Barber of Seville*
G Rosine: raisin
Amaryllis belladonna: belladonna lily, pink flower I sail: willow
named from a country girl in Theocritus & Virgil
seven

It attraverso: across F mille (Castletown House said to have 1 window It ricorso: recurring (Vico)
multitudinous for every day of the year) testudineous rococo crossing
stained glass in plain English Wynn's Hotel, D

branches places in Proust's *A la Recherche du temps perdu:* Balbec, Elbeuf, Sissonne, Jersey,
Heudicourt, Braquetuit, Orgeville, Forcheville

G Wille: will, desire Valhalla

opening shortly Da sanger: singer
Thingmote: Viking parliament in D
oriel window (see letter to FB, quoted at 613.15) ECH (215.15–17)
Oriel: ancient Ir. principality hue & cry

EHC

L horam: hour

him

L muta!: change!
L quod est nunc fumus iste volvens ex Domino: R domoi: home
what now is that smoke rolling out of the Lord? (smoke from St Patrick's paschal fire, lit in defiance of
L iuva!: help! Royal orders)
Old Head of Kinsale, promontory, Co. Cork AngI ph the top of the morning to you
Edda Thor
ought to thoroughly

letter, 20/8/39, to FB: '= Deus est Dominus noster plus the day is Lord over sleep. i.e. when it days'
L Deus est Dominus noster et commandat ille tenebras: God is our Lord & He commands the darkness

L Dominus noster: Our Lord Arch an: if perceive amongst
diminished Gr astêr: star aster (flower)
walk Du wolk: cloud procession
'Work in Progress': J's name for FW during composition
Per khub: good chrysanthemum anthem
Christian (St Patrick)
bonze: Japanese Buddhist priest Per ghar: cave AngInd wallah: fellow
pom-pom (machine gun) AngInd gharry: horsed vehicle
manoeuvring Cabra: district of D Patrick lit paschal fire at Slane, challenging druids at Tara
battlefield
It pongo da panza: I put from belly Arch an: if

Berkeley (denied existence of matter) disgusted oesophagus
theosophy (mystic leanings of druids & followers of George Russell)
horse race (.34–6)

Harald Fair Hair: 1st king of Norway who the dickens
L -ibus (dative & ablative plural) *Da* ild: fire Huns
resurrects *L* -orum (genitive plural)
rearises *L* rex: king
believe firmly *G* fing: caught
motto of House of Savoy: Fortitudo eius Rhodum tenuit (His Strength Has Held Rhodes)
Oliver all over 'em
L ullo verum: for anyone, certainly *L* fulgor: lightning Rhedones: Celtic people near Rennes
relentlessly tip of his staff D motto: Obedientia civium urbis felicitas (Citizens' Obedience Is City's Happiness)
ph a Roland for an Oliver *L* ubi: where *L* deinde: next
L suavium: kiss *It* Fenicio: Phoenician Felix & Regula (.10): patron saints of Zurich
earwig's *It* fenice: phoenix
High King Laoghaire (Leary)—after defying his orders St Patrick defeated his druids
regular *L* ruga: wrinkle
Rugular: king of Huns
every time half a crown (Leary's crown)
ph bet your bottom dollar
G geholfen: helped H . . . C . . . E
Buckley shot the Russian General (II.3)

Irish twilight valid paradisiacal *F* parier: to bet
truly *G* Wehleid: self-pity *G* vielleicht: perhaps

L ut vivat volumen sic pereat paradisus: that the book may live let paradise be lost

even

10 to 1 outsider in horse race, also St Patrick (foreigner)

Sucat: name given St Patrick by his parents
quaffs (031.11–12)
Berkeley valued tar water as a cure-all *G* wett-: bet
F sec *G* warte: wait
L sic 'Pia e pura bella!': religious wars of Vico's heroic age

J.H. Voss: 'wine, women & song' *Da* og seng: & bed
G (ge)winne!: win!

descends
day sends

hotwaterbottle
Da ord: word

warmingpan, ironmonger

Moor Park, where Swift met Stella *Paradise Lost*
Arch moot: meeting, assembly Peredos (= *Gr* 'seat of the Gods'): race horse
Grand National television
Caesar: 'veni, vedi, vici' (' I came, I saw, I conquered')
(039.02–11) drawers
J.W. Widger: most famous of Waterford racing-associated family, amateur rider

Jack the Ripper

Patrick & Berkeley

'& here are the details' is a Radio Athlone expression

L tunc: then (122.23) *It* vampa: flame, blaze *C Pi* topside: superior
BLM bymby (used to indicate future tense) *CPi* joss: God twopenny *Sl* bob: shilling
Berkeley L/R Ir. *C Pi* chin chin joss: religious worship

Gr heptachrômatikos: 7-coloured: *L* septicoloratus (rainbow colours)
(King's Ollave [master poet] in ancient Ireland wore 7 colours)
(to) Patrick

(Patrick's throat hums with chant sung also by his monks, who fast with him)
alb: priest's white tunic (monotone)

Grey Friars: Franciscans *G* fast: nearly
Saint P/K L/R *L* quoniam: since now
Catholic
Japanese Nōh plays influenced Yeats *L* scilicet: certainly, it is evident,
no man is free namely
It illusione: illusion

prism splits light *L* velamina: coverings, veils *Gr* panepiphanês: all-visible
(Berkeley's *Theory of Vision*) 'epiphany': J's term (*U.*40 &c.)
spectrum *Gr* zôon: animal *Gr* anthos: flower *Gr* lithos: stone
L spectaculum: stage play Berkeley used phrase 'furniture of earth' to refer to totality of material objects

('Colour' of an object is that part of the spectrum which it reflects & does not absorb)
iridal: pertaining to rainbow
(.13) *Gr* eu: good *Gr* pan: all *Gr* epi: upon

L absorbere: to swallow; engross number one paradised
paradoxed
Seven Degrees of Wisdom: 12-year programme incumbent upon ollaves in ancient Ireland
L dux: leader *L* entis: of a being *Gr* ontôn: of beings *Sl* savvy: know
Kant: 'Ding an sich' (thing in itself) *L* id est: that is
Da hvad: what

L in coloribus: in colours *L* gloria

one tint opposite Roman Catholic
L intus: within ruminant Patrick
stereotypical (didn't understand) *L* utpiam: anyway
stare optical

(.04–5) (said to Patrick)

verbigerating: repeating same word *L* verbi gratia: for instance *It* lento: slow *It* celeri: quick
or phrase in meaningless fashion (Patrick's chant goes from quiet to loud) stridulent
r Hwang-Ho (China) changed course *L* (artif.) comprehenduriens: longing to grasp
in 1852, seizing bed of *r* Tsing singsong
clarity *Arch* actinism: philosophy of radiant heat & light

L calor: heat *G* durchsichtig: transparent

G über Laoghaire (Leary): Ir. High King in time of (red) (hair)
Patrick
(All objects appear green to Ir. archdruid) wood sorrel (sometimes knickerbocker
mistaken for shamrock) *L* niger: black
F blanc ECH 6-coloured (7 colours of spectrum minus green)
2 Ir. viceroys were earls of Essex *G* Holm: hill homegrown green
saffron kilts traditional Ir. costume spinach
(orange)

L mutis: you are mumbling comprehend
mutism: dumbness
(yellow) *I* torc: twisted neck ornament *SwG* Kabis: cabbage; tits
curly cabbage
(green) rainproof (coat) (belonging to) *G* über
L pace tua: with your permission
G ober-: upper; supreme the dead spit of: just like

(blue eyes) *I* Árd Rí: High King
open bull's eyes Tsar

soul of a bitch's bastard 'indigo' means 'the Indian
bishop pastor substance'
forefinger HCE

G kikiriki: cock-a-doodle-doo (violet) *L* contusiones: bruisings
J kiri: fog
L sublimissime: most loftily

Colour variables are hue, intensity & saturation

L sicut: as for example *Sl* chow-chow: food
like you see cut (leaves)
medicinal *Senna* leaves of HCE Sucat: name St Patrick's parents gave him Succoth
some *Cassia* species *I* baile: town Here Comes Everybody *G* Kot: filth (613.09)
G Punkt: point; reflects *G* wacklig: tottering
full stop refraction of light

poor chiaroscuro (orig. meant black & white pictorial style) *Da* dynger: scrap heaps
J shiroi: white *J* kuroi: black
L a posteriori: empirical apostrophied paralogism: false reasoning of which reasoner is unconscious

paralysed *J* iro: colour rainbow (pot of gold at end)
Iris (rainbow *Du* boon: bean
for the time being goddess) complementarily
It completamente: completely
blankminded electrolysis
blinkered neutrality
verity *G* Sager: sayer *G* erobern: conquer
L viridis: green *ph* 'Ireland, Isle of Saints & Sages' *L* ruber: red
It t'appropinqui: come near! wife & myself knows *Gr* gnôsis: knowledge
nosegays
handkerchief shamrock (supposedly used by Patrick to demonstrate Trinity)
chamois: wash-leather
A.D. 432: Patrick lands in Ireland

It arcobaleno: rainbow (Gen 9:13–16)

simple: healing plant wide wide world

blessing: 'In the name of the Father and of the Son and of the Holy Ghost, Amen'

G Götter: gods begotten
begetter begorrah! *PS* bog: god
begat!

shutting shutter love of Jesus (Laoghaire's druid performed
Aust sweat on: wait anxiously *G* Schatten: shadow, lamb miracle of botting out sun)
Aust stonker: defeat, outwit shade stuck his thumb & four fingers up
(352.28–9)
Da Højhed: Highness arse (exposed when Patrick kneels)
(as a title) *I* Ard: High The Ards: baronies, Co. Down

s God Save Ireland [Tramp, Tramp, Tramp]: '"God save Ireland," said the heroes; "God save Ireland," said they all; "Whether on the scaffold high, or the battlefield we die" ' helots *Gr* hêlios: sun

(Patrick caused reappearance of sun blotted out by Laoghaire's druid; onlookers glorified Patrick's God) (sun in sky)

L a die: from the day

L per jucundum Dominum nostrum Jesum Christum Filium Tuum: through our dear Lord Jesus Christ Thy Son to whom?

tar water (Berkeley)

Tara, ancient capital of Ireland

saints & sages Lewis Carroll: 'The Walrus & the Carpenter' in *Through the Looking-Glass:* 'cabbages & kings'

Moore: *s* 'Tis Gone, & Forever, the Light We Saw Breaking [Savourneen Deelish]

F pour today

transfiguration *G* feist: corpulent Feast of Tabernacles (i.e. tents): Succoth

I feis: festival *Gr* skênopêgia: setting up of tents

shamrock *G* Erscheinung: appearance, phenomenon

shining

Du ons: us yolk *Du* melk: milk *G* farbig: coloured

egos you & me far bigger

394.32: 'pancosmic' ham & eggs God's truth!

Da Guds: God's

dictated to FB: 'In Part IV there is in fact a triptych–though the central window is scarcely illuminated. Namely the supposed windows of the village church gradually lit up by the dawn, the windows, i.e., representing on one side the meeting of St Patrick (Japanese) & the (Chinese) Archdruid Bulkely (this by the way is all about colour) & the legend of the progressive isolation of St Kevin, the third being St Lawrence O'Toole, patron saint of Dublin; buried in Eu in Normandy' His heart is preserved in Chapel of St Laud, Christ Church Cathedral, D (017.31)

L fuit fiat: as it was, let it be

(botany) spathe: sheathing leaf glume: husk of grain perianth: floral envelope

calyptra: hood of spore case in mosses involucre: whorl of bracts

amentum: catkin fungi, algae filical: pertaining to ferns plantain

Amenti: Egyptian underworld *Musci:* mosses *Gramineae:* grasses

thingumajigs *L* luxurio: I am rank

(612.29)

joyride *Gr* thea: goddess

U.179: 'a ravenous terrier choked up a sick knuckly cud on the cobble stones & lapped it with new zest' ere breakfast boomerang

bark

Da pænt: nice; pretty Moore: *s* Wreathe the Bowl [Nora Kista]

ph neat as paint

rancour a million

Gr amulion: cake

HCE chalice *pr* Don't buy a pig in a poke

ALP *Da* lykke: luck

It folgore: thunderbolt (Viconian cycle) optimistically

frightful

ominous lovely marriages

Da lovlig: legal, lawful

morning & evening undertaken bury the hatchet

I múirnín: sweetheart Moore & Aveling: 1st translators of *Das Kapital* orchard

breeches

sailor *s* Home Sweet Home tailor

tailor (sews seams) port helm harbour master

ph got up to kill: very welldressed as bid

a shit

I a rún: my secret (endearment)

Skt aruna: the dawn

definitively *Gr* gynê: woman Linnaean classification of flowering plants: genus *Jasminum* belongs to order *Monogynia* (having 1 pistil), part of the class *Diandria* (having 2 stamens)

in Linnaean account of flowers, the corolla has 3 parts, the *tubus*, *limbus* & *nectarium*

Ant

Grasshopper Da ædel: nobleman Mookse & Gripes Gracchi: Roman politicians
grazing heifer Da bonde: peasant Mopsus: soothsayer of Argonauts; also Apollo's son
heredities incessantly Annona: Roman çorn-goddess
Herodotus, Greek historian
wash house F orme: elm F pierre Dundrum: district of D
(clothes washed in I.8)
bleaches beautifully nicely
F blanche
(215.14–23)

different G Rolle: roll; role; me thee kick in the pants
dapper mangle Sl choker: cravat

been G Morgenland: the Orient Mourne Mts, Co. Down
Arch bane: death G Laune: mood
G fordern: demand A . . . L . . . P

Sl kaffir: low fellow 'Collars & Cuffs': nickname of Duke of Clarence Sl cull: fool (sb.)
ph survival of the fittest (best-fitting) 'blue-bag' (washing) I íorna: hank
blood, iron
starch (074.17–9) iron (for pressing)

clothes Manor Mill Steam Laundry, Dundrum, D L nox: night
Angl clipeclash: gossip next day
I Sinn Féin, Sinn Féin Amhain: Ourselves, Ourselves Alone (slogan) Moore & Burgess minstrels' catchline: 'Take off that white hat!'
pick of the basket give: elasticity

wear Parnell: 'When you sell, get my price' F guetter: to watch

Parnell, speech in Cork, 1885: 'No man has a right to fix the boundary of the march of a nation'
marge: margin
s A Nation Once Again

G gestern: yesterday

HCE ALP

(uncensored reading) APL plain of the Liffey

ECH river delta ph dear dirty Dublin
Eblana: Ptolemy's name for D PS deva: girl
Deva: old name of Chester (r Deva = r Dee)

wholemeal Vico's cycles 4-dimensional
cyclometer: instrument attached to wheel, measuring revolutions dominational
gazebo: turret or lantern on housetop

Sheridan: *School for Scandal* John-a-dreams (*Hamlet* II.2.295): generic for 'a dreamy fellow'
Matthew, Mark, Luke & John
autokinesy: spontaneous motion
donkey

Father, Son &
Work in Progress: J's name for FW during its composition
Holy Ghost HC . . . E (Viconian cycle) E . . . H . . . C

catch-as-catch-can (hepatic) portal vein takes products of digestion from gut to liver
dialysis: separation of colloids & crystalloids through membrane
dialectical

HCE

ALP

Gr topos: place

ascendence (281.04–13) Pliny & Columella

It giacinto: hyacinth *F* marguerite: daisy
F pervenche: periwinkle
F les Gaules Illyria Numantia *G* Mutter

anastomosis: connection of 2 vessels, esp. blood vessels, by a cross branch *L* praeter: previously
Gr (artif.) paraidiôtikos: almost privately
atomic structure
Adam
HCE haphazard

HCE

Gr menos: strength, spirit

puts pen to paper (drawings on Easter eggs)

of course! cause & effect

ph Dear . . . Dirty Dublin

(120.17–18)

delighted right
last lifetime
Magrath (060.26) *G* Uhr: clock *G* Wecker: alarm clock
muckrakes (448.10) Earwicker

salmon (of knowledge, eaten by Finn)

2-handled weapon (2-handled sword supposedly used by Sir Amory Tristram is in Howth Castle)
Merrion & Ailesbury Roads intersect just N. of Williamstown, D
William III & Queen Mary
s 'Merrily we roll along'
(tram on Merrion Road)
Job 30:15: 'my welfare passeth away as a cloud'

beside us *Goldilocks & the Three Bears* (pantomime)
heaven on earth
pantomime

Jack & the Beanstalk (pantomime) *Paradise Lost*
Gr palai: long ago

s On the Banks of the Wabash

cause

In pantomime &c. *The Sleeping Beauty,* the heroine falls asleep after pricking her finger on a spinning wheel spindle
s I Will Give You the Keys to Heaven snakes
AngI caffler: contemptible, cheeky little fellow said

Daniel McGrath, grocer & publican, 4–5 Charlotte St, D (in J's time)

Magazine Wall
margarine
G strengstens verboten: strictly forbidden
9th Commandment: 'Thou shalt not covet thy neighbour's wife'
8th Commandment: 'Thou shalt not bear false witness'
10th Commandment: 'Thou shalt not covet thy neighbour's goods'
keening: wailing for the dead (in Ireland)

Lord forgive him his trespasses

Milord Persse O'Reilly *Huckleberry Finn*
I fann: weak
HCE Coolock: district of D an out-&-out
hardiest
I inis: island Earwicker first mate on ship
Irishman *Da* evig: eternal
doubters HSW came from Oldham, Lancashire *G* Widmung: dedication
F douter: to doubt fancy women
twist: cord tobacco

HF 32: 'by jings' *L* corpus
corpse

slatters: waste, spillings Peter the Painter: anarchist, involved in Siege of Sidney St
'Peter the Packer': Lord Peter O'Brien, C19 judge, 'packed' juries *G* drei
seventy-fifths *Da* Gud ved: God knows! *F* délit: crime, offence
tailor 'the ninth part of a man' (316.11)
annual coronation of King Parnell: 'When you sell, get my price' peri: one of a race of Persian
of Dalkey: burlesque ceremony Sultans of Turkey surprise superhuman beings, fairies
Co. Monaghan sugar of lead: lead acetate caustic potash: potassium hydroxide
It monachina: little nun *Gr* chlôra: pale green
valency: of an element, the combinative power of its ion, i.e. the
number of electrons changed in its formation
ECH CHE

W.G. Wills: *A Royal Divorce*

snakes prostituting not withstanding

posted notice: 'Commit no Nuisance'

CH . . . E ('Which came first, the chicken or the egg?')
Original Sin erogenous *Da* hun: she
salesman *AngI* cloon: piece of fertile land
Cloon: townland nr Glencree, Co. Wicklow
Joe Cuffe (fired Bloom for giving lip) statistics
Sl guff: impudence sage used in sausage manufacture
hiccups sausages spit fat when fried
teacups
polony: Polish sausage
metropolitan (dwellers)
draw Workman's Compensation Act, 1897 magnates
Du wolk: cloud
parasites
space

king's evil: scrofula, formerly supposed stared
curable by regent's touch
gate stand of trees
I brad: thieving God Mananaan MacLir: Ir. sea-god

bulletproof unpierceable Persse O'Reilly holly, ivy & mistletoe
Thomas Percy: ballad collector (Norse god Balder killed by thrown mistletoe)
(Ir. bards rhymed their enemies to death) Beggar's Bush, D, near Lansdowne Road rugby stadium, home
of Ir. Rugby Union
St Laurence O'Toole: patron saint of D

God in Heaven, Livia, my cheque is a complete blank
evil
thumb fingers *G* Hose: pants

his arse (352.28–9) 111 plus
hussars
1001 Nights conclude

that trouble to take

Fintona, town, Co. Tyrone ourselves (Sinn Féin)
It fintona: deceitful
dearest of husbands, who will be true until life's end

ph pocket full of brass (wealth)

(hence confusion of MacCool & Magrath)

bellow (snakecharmer)

Finn MacCool Finn MacCool
McGrath (snake crawls)
(Phoenix) Park Murders, 1882 Vercingetorix: Gallic chieftain who revolted against Caesar St Thomas à Becket
St Laurence O'Toole: patron saint of D

characters *F* culs (sleep) cannonballs punch
Caractacus: British chieftain, resisted Roman invasion Conan Doyle
daylight out of him

s Music, Maestro, Please band *Du* brand: fire *G* fing: caught
grand Ibsen: *Brand* sing
Finnegan good luck!

make wake Fairy Godmother (in *Cinderella,* pantomime)
G gut murderer
AngI gillie: servant, lad Gaping Ghyl: vertical shaft in Yorkshire
(get dressed) *AngI* man in the gap: a sturdy defender
fool funeral take place
Finn
six Tuesday *G* willkommen: welcome Allsop's Ale
today *Sw* -en: the Bluebeard: wife-killer in story by Perrault
pen . . . post Mansion House: Lord-Mayor's residence, D Horse Guards
Boston Transcript *F* femelles predominant
Morning Post: London newspaper Adam
28 to 12 = 11.32

(111.09–17) lovely parcel of cakes born gentleman poor Father Michael

foon .20

eight hours sharp

ECH

Skt māyā: illusion May Day your Majesty's
L Meus Deus Bridges: 'The duteous day now closeth'
anonymously anent: concerning
erroneously
Da fand: devil alleged Moore: *s* I Wish I Was by That Dim Lake [I Wish I Was on Yonder Hill]
liege *AngI* whist!: silence! *Sl* tyke: dog
other Jacob (heel, Gen 25:26) *s* The Sweetest Song in All the World

native copper: unrefined copper

Married Womens' Property Act, 1883 points
impropriety
Goldsmith: *The Deserted Village:* 'Sweet Auburn!' straight
Swiss Autumn

'Exsultet': 'O felix culpa!'

virgins Viscount Harmsworth: Ir. newspaper magnate *Hansel & Gretel* (pantomime)
Virgil's *Aeneid* opens 'I sing of arms & the man' girls handsel: first specimen of something, auspicious

milkman Michaelmas
cad with the pipe (205.11) Lilith: Adam's first wife (Kabbalah)

snake

just a prince for tonight (pantomime & fairy tale motif)
(belly of pork, lightly cured) back & streaky bacon ninepence

thugs Bully's Acre: oldest D cemetery, Kilmainham Boot Lane, old D

AngI waxy: cobbler St Patrick's Hospital, D, founded by Swift
Ir. Hospital Sweepstakes
letterbox

A.D. 432: St Patrick lands in Ireland 8 & 20 to 5 = 4.32

court of quarter sessions bevy BVM

L Maria Reparatrix: Mary the Restoress St Patrick's Purgatory: tunnel on island in Lough Derg, supposed real entrance to Purgatory
s Lily Is a Lady

s 'Lilliburlero, bullen a law' *s* What Ho! She Bumps: 'She began to bump a bit'

s Love Walked In solicitor's

Sl buss: kiss

Waterloo Road, D *s* The Cubanola Glide
Wonderland

bows arse Hill of Allen: Finn's H.Q., Co. Kildare
F beaux Alice
opening nighters
Apennines

Thanksgiving Day

Dial forenenst: over against

(.08)

bookmaker
(.11)
hereafter larceny
U.586 (emended): 'superintendent Laracy'
constantly

pots & pans *It* pance: bellies
Peter's pence: contribution to R.C. church
Norwegian
expelled Christianity
St Crispin & St Crispinian: patron saints of shoemakers
Swift: *Polite Conversation*

100% business & pleasure

shag tobacco
Sl humpty-dumpty: ale boiled with brandy
L uro: I burn original sin
Gr gynê: woman
Alex Findlater: founder of Findlater & Co., grocers, built Abbey Presbyterian Church, D. Adam Findlater: subsequent manager of same firm, politician in Edwardian D; involved in revision of Griffith's Valuation (a rent reduced to the government rating valuation of the farm) *L* varus: contrary
Christmas parcel *G* Parzelle: parcel (land)
crossword puzzle
damn cheek Rathgar: district of D
alphabet
amphibious bed
D Sl bothered: deaf possibly filth *nr* Humpty Dumpty
certified insane
profitably deaf
Picts & Scots Samuel Roth pirated J in *Two Worlds Monthly*
Hill of Howth Earwicker
namesake
ECH
confessional
Alma Mater (school) *It* pollo: spring of water
Anna Livia Plurabelle *It* polla: fowl, chicken
Rolf (Rollo) Ganger: 1st Duke of Normandy (theoretically ancestor of Anglo-Norman invaders of Ir.) fed up
G fett: fat
nursery rhymes *ph* rags to riches (Cinderella) *Sl* ritzy: stylishly well off
Ritz: common hotel name
Document No. 2: De Valera's proposed alternative to the Treaty decuman: large wave (supposedly every 10th)
lisp Liffey speaking
AngI soft day: light drizzle
I foltach: long-haired *It* capelli folti: thick hair
Gen 7:17: 'the flood was forty days upon the earth'
listen
Babes in the Wood (pantomime)
Robinson Crusoe (pantomime) golden wedding
house
Howth
meseems
cap-à-pie: head to foot Tierce, Sext, Nones (canonical hours)
Finn . . . Mac . . . Cool *nr* 'Old King Cole was a merry old soul & a merry old soul was he, He sent for his pipe & he sent for his bowl & he sent for his fiddlers three'
arise novena
Nirvana
U.580: 'I was once the beautiful May Goulding' exaggerator
Arch soger: soldier
F charmante
Whitley Stokes: Celtic authority Co. Offaly (tidal bore)
sleep *Da* tak: thank you
s Johnny, I Hardly Knew Ye
YHWH: Tetragrammaton
Es (synthetic) helpunto min, helpas vin: one who would help me helps you nightshirt (Parnell)
stock: a tight-fitting neckcloth
(from laundry)
overall nevertheless

umbrella

green belt (city planning)

latest Dublin (backwards) *We* budd: profit, gain
lotus (598.14)
Buckley shot the Russian General 57 shillings & 3 pence
birthday suit Song of Sol 2:1: 'I am the rose of Sharon, & the lily of the valleys'
cash (for his hump) *ph* Perfidious Albion *s* Eileen Aroon
Sl purseproud: lecherous (rich England & poor Ireland)
L/R Éireann deadly sins: pride, covetousness, envy
Irene, heroine of Ibsen's *When We Dead Awaken*
Van der Decken: the *Flying Dutchman* *Sinbad the Sailor* (pantomime)
Du wonderdokter: quack *G* decken: copulate *G* Balt: native of one of Baltic States
Magellan, explorer Patrick Sarsfield, Earl of Lucan, 'wild goose'

Iron Duke: Wellington somebody else
G Iren: Irishmen ass (bray)

When Diarmaid & Grania agreed to make peace with Finn they settled at a place called Rath Grainne fast asleep

'High Heels & Low Heels': Lilliputian political parties in Swift's *Gulliver's Travels*
he'll
Jacob (heel, Gen 25:26)

I Cor 15:51–2: 'We shall not all sleep, but we shall all be changed, In a moment, in the twinkling of an eye, at the last trump' twins *Da* som: like Tom Tim Shem/Shaun
same anew *Du* doffer: pigeon brothers as different as North from South *Du* zoen (pron. 'soon'): kiss,
G sehen: see *N* bredder: riverbanks *Du* nors: surly peace, reconciliation
Christ

crones

font II Tim 4:1: 'the quick & the dead'
quicken tree
(stone)

laundry
Arthur Symons lived at Lauderdale Mansions, Maida Vale, London

whistle

Persse O'Reilly *Angl* jackeen: countryman's derisive term for Dubliner
Patrick Pearse: 1916 Easter insurrectionist: oration at grave of O'Donovan Rossa, 1915
wanting

Judy (Punch .23)
Holy Jesus

E . . . C . . . H

motherwit foundlings

ph as merry as a grig ('grig' perhaps in sense 'hen')
Greek
Latin lighten
G Leiden: suffering
Isis (also name of upper Thames) *Cz* hospoda: pub hopscotch
S hotchpotch
K *s* 'Tea for Two, & two for tea'

Copenhagen parts
Cobh, Co. Cork, pron. 'Cove'
switchback

The Sleeping Beauty (pantomime) *ph* let bygones by bygones finished
pr business is business
Sterne: *A Sentimental Journey*
F journée St Michael
Lucifer *Book of the Dead*

finger

Aladdin's lamp (in *Aladdin*, pantomime)
Our Lady's 'lady with the lamp': Florence Nightingale
gusts of air rucksack, looks like
hump
Danny Mann: hunchback in Boucicault's *The Colleen Bawn*
Arcturus: star in Bootes
Arthur Guinness *It* ismo: isthmus
S.A.G. ('St Anthony guide'), written on letters by pious Catholics
surely *Fi* ilma: air, weather

s The Ould Plaid Shawl: 'Not far from old Kinvara'
Finvarra: village, Co. Clare
shoulders breakfast
roly-poly: steamed
jam-pudding 'Black Pool' (meaning of word 'Dublin')
polony: Polish sausage black pudding: type of sausage
I Is tú féin: It is yourself *G* Rostbrot: toast Oxmantown: part of N. D
Du brood: bread *L* me alterum: another me
woodpile poppinjays
Coppingers (575.06 &c.)
clotted cream

list!

Nol: nickname of Cromwell Mark of Cornwall

North Wall, D *Da* -sen: son of (Isaac's sons, Isaac Butt: Parnell's predecessor
Jacob & Esau) Butt Bridge, D
Loopline railway bridge, D *We* fy: my *We* arth: bear
(alongside Butt Br.) Mark fie! art thou Arthur
L pater: father *I* a mhic: my son for my tiny (hand) notes: fa, mi, ti, do, la
Sl padder: highwayman Nancy Hand's: name of The Hole in the Wall, pub nr Phoenix Park
language of flowers Jorgen Jorgensen studied Aborigines' vocabulary
It languo: I languish

little more *Arch* glave: sword
glove *PS* glava: head
King Hugon: Fr. hobgoblin foreskin smooth as an infant's
huge one *Da* falsk: false, forged

likeness

Finnegan's hod
head

florimel (Spenser): virginity
Florizel: prince of Bohemia in *The Winter's Tale*
(child on a white horse on Tarot Card XIX, The Sun)

Butler: *The Way of All Flesh* leave
F laver
Rum timpul: time temple early E . . . C . . . H
I teampal: church
Le Fanu: *The House by the Churchyard* 035.30: 'Fox Goodman'
Luke 2:14: 'Glory to God in the highest, & on earth peace, good will toward men'
Sterne: *Tristram Shandy* end of Wagner's *Ring:* Wotan's ravens fly off
Noah loosed a dove & raven from Ark

coo (dove) caw (raven) Finn MacCool

raven Peter & Paul
driven snae (Scots, = snow) poll (election)
solicitous bride elect *G* Weib: woman

(618.04) seduce McGrath

cockadoodling cheeping (chicks)

I na nGall: of the foreigners putting

F pot de chambre to shame When Tim Healy became governor-general of the Ir. Free State, Dubliners called the Viceregal Lodge 'Uncle Tim's Cabin'
Viceregal (after H.B. Stowe, *Uncle Tom's Cabin*) *AngI* caubeen: old hat
fuddy-duddy

Goody Two-Shoes (children's story, perhaps by Goldsmith) knot = nautical mile per hour
It penisole: peninsulae
Puss in Boots (pantomime)

Ma buah: fruit
I buadh: victory
ALP HCE

forty days & forty nights (the Flood, Gen 7:17)

Huckleberry (Finn)
hurrying
hips & haws: fruit of dog rose

hammock

go Dutch: to pay for oneself D.U.T.C.: Dublin United Tramways Company (ran tram to Howth summit)
L nos: we Duncriffan: promontory on Howth

ph time hangs on one's hands

Sullivans (006.15, 573.07) *Ali Baba & the Forty Thieves* (pantomime)
Sp lobo: wolf
Teague: nickname for Ir. peasant *s* The Masked Ball
bail
G Wald: forest Naul: village, Co. D
Ward Union Staghounds, Ashbourne, Co. Meath (nr Naul) draws
whip (assists Master of Hounds)

tally-ho! Ballyhaunis: town, Co. Mayo
Tallaght
Little Red Riding Hood (pantomime) *s* Here's a Heath unto His Majesty

roebuck even ECH hoist

I deoch an dorais: parting drink cap-à-pie: head to foot

(194.06–7)

Earwicker

EHC hue-&-cry
enlarged: set free
Townlands in barony of Duleek Upper, nr Naul, Co. D: Heathtown, Harbourstown, Fourknocks, Flemingstown, Bodingtown Snowton Castle across *r* Delvin from Naul
Ford of Finn on *r* Delvin nr Naul

Botanic Gardens (adjoins Glasnevin Cemetery, D)

lost in her reflection (mirror) ECH Earwicker come home
conditioned reflex (Pavlov's dogs) *F* cocorico: cock-a-doodle-doo
handsome coach

E . . . HC *nr* 'Little Jack Horner, Sat in the corner' *G* Mutter
Mother Goose (pantomime)

(316.11–12)

moiety

promontory (Howth)
prominent tory

New Year's Day
Door of Howth Castle traditionally left open since Grace O'Malley kidnapped the heir in revenge for being refused admission
HCE
invited Easter hot cockles
Moore & Burgess, minstrels, had catchline 'Take off that white hat!' ECH

how d'you do, his majesty?
Howth isthmus (Sutton)
House of Lords Grace O'Malley curtsey
gracious
pr If the mountain will not come to Mohammed, Mohammed will go to the mountain
kow-tow: Chinese custom of touching ground with forehead as mark of respect

(021.18) bring to light

knight in armour Armorica (Brittany), *Hu* elsö̋: first dub
home of Sir Amory Tristram, 1st Earl of Howth
chief magistrate Bartholomew Vanhomrigh: Lord-Mayor of D & father of Swift's
Magyar (Hungarian) Vanessa; was given collar of SS. by William III G vom
G hungrig: hungry HCE epaulettes *King Lear* III.4.187: 'Fie, foh, & fum'
Du hongerig: hungry Lord-Mayor's chain
Royal Highness

ph castles in the air *Rh Sl* currant bread: cinematograph *pr* Enough is enough
Howth Castle head (many craft in current of river)
Ruff: *Guide to the Turf*

followed folly *G* klatschen: applaud
'Exsultet': 'O felix culpa!' *R* clyatcha: jaded nag
Dollymount: region on coast Struldbrugs: decrepit men incapable of dying,
between central D & Howth in Swift's *Gulliver's Travels*
Houyhnhnms (*Gulliver's Travels*) *s* The Rocky Road to Dublin
Du donder: thunder
I Beinn Éadair: Howth Head me & you calm
qualms of conscience
scan the horizon Drumleck: point on S. side of Howth Head
rising sun
Sir Amory Tristram, 1st Earl of Howth, supposedly defeated Danes at Bridge of Evora morning

Glen of the Downs: valley, Co. Wicklow *I* Sinn Féin, Sinn Féin Amháin:
dunes luna (anagram) Ourselves, Ourselves Alone (slogan)
salvation

the man of my dreams
by means main drains
strips Nut: Egyptian sky-goddess picked
Nuts of knowledge eaten by Salmon which Finn catches
HCE
by

Anne Hathaway hesitency
Heb letters: 'aleph' means 'ox'; 'vau' means 'hook'
ph signed, sealed & delivered

Boston Transcript from Boston, Mass.
based on transcript *G* Traum: dream

Daniel 7:9: 'the Ancient of days' (God) 014.12: Caddy, & (623.32) Primas (letter in bottle)
tea caddy
On His Majesty's Service *F* mugissement: roaring, bellowing (often used of sea)
Book of Common Prayer: Burial at Sea: 'when the sea shall give up her dead' *WWI Sl* blob: glass of beer

Roderick O'Connor: last High King of Ireland (family has 2 branches, 'the red' & 'the brown') *G* Donner: thunder *Sl* dunner: importunate creditor
Christmas

bungalow
loan from bank

Tower of Babel round tower *nr* Little Bo Peep *It* sterro: excavation
Swift: 'Ppt' *Du* ster: star
Jack & the Beanstalk (pantomime)

The Master Builder, in Ibsen's *Bygmester Solness,* has stopped climbing the towers he builds, for fear of giddiness, but at the play's end tries again (& falls to his death) *Da* til: to The Summit, Howth
ground-plot: plot of land on which building stands

nr Humpty Dumpty *Dial* hise: hoist

Sarah . . . Abraham rambling damn
AngI sorra: not
patriarch *s* At Trinity Church I Met My Doom: 'I was an M-U-G'
marge: margin home
donkey's years ago

taught Tefnut: Egyptian goddess
tough
St Fintan's Church (ruins), Howth
I Sinn Féin: We Ourselves (slogan)
*U.*308: 'baby policeman'
Bailey Lighthouse, Howth
lady-killer reform

Sheilmartin: a peak on Howth
St Martin
loveliest

darling wonderful old boy

object to my perfume eau de Cologne Collooney, village, Co. Sligo
paraffin Killarney maraschino (liqueur)
pine smell Swift's Esthers (Stella & Vanessa)

everyone's nostrils Swift: *Cadenus & Vanessa*
nasturtiums Nose of Howth: N.E. tip of Howth *L* medeus condignus: by the most worthy god!
Swift: *A Tale of a Tub* 'Grand Old Man': Gladstone M.D. ('my dears'): Swift's abbreviation in letters to Stella
town
s 'Tis the Harp in the Air [Cummilium] Finn MacCool (MacCumhail)

Da meget: very (Norwegian Captain's suit)

(tailor's daughter had to stand on pile to answer phone)

finger went into me ear
(Certain old theologians held that Mary was impregnated through her ear)
Bray, town, Co. Wicklow *Da* bragt op: brought up
dragged up
in Borstal (reformatory)
Bristol
fireplace petticoats taking the pledge: swearing to give up drink
pentecost
howsomever

crusts

F Marianne chérie = Fr. Republic

cousin-german (205.09) earwig

Gladstone bag perhaps Pharaoh
Clarkson: London wigmaker
Egypt
I Aos-sidhe: fairy folk
dangerous

I céad míle fáilte: 100,000 welcomes *F* bienvenu: welcome
Bellevue: place in Zurich where *r* Limmat meets lake
Cromwell 'Quis Separabit?': motto of Order of St Patrick ('Who Shall Separate?')
L quid superabit: what shall surpass? Eccles 1:2: 'vanity of vanities'
Sl murphies: potatoes Mrs Spendlove: D prostitute; mourned Edward VII

CHE undertaking

pump torrent

J wore a Borsalino hat
snug: secluded area in pub saloon bar
Daniel O'Connell
Conal: son of High King Niall of the Nine Hostages
Finglas: district of D 'Work in Progress' : J's name for FW during composition
tomorrow

stone/tree *G* Rasse: race, breed
rustling write your sermon
suck (Finn burnt his thumb while cooking Salmon of Knowledge & in sucking it to relieve pain he acquired wisdom. In some accounts, he subsequently sucked thumb when great decisions were required)
⚔ Clontarf, 1014: Brian Boru defeats Danes Earwicker
sniff Clane, village, Co. Kildare
Butt & Taff

Brian Boru *U.* 164: 'Kerwan's mushroom houses'

acres, rods & perches *G* Dom: cathedral
parishes patches
Rut dim: house *Rut* dym: smoke Capitol play: Olympic games; races were held in the stadion

MacCool
Colossus
ALP lentil
little
caraway seed *It* cara: dear
I cara: friend
all the wide world neighbourhoods nebulae for Newton
Lotts, street, D *F* boulotte: i) work, toil; ii) food
Eblana: Ptolemy's name for D looming
L magna *L* lumen: light
Li dumblinas: muddy, dirty *It* città: city *G* Sitte: custom slept
Dublin dumbness *Skt* sama: same Attis (backwards)
Cockney ph it fair takes your breath away *D Annals,* 1452: 'The Liffey was entirely dry at Dublin for the space of two minutes'

suffering beloved *U.* 286: 'To wipe away a tear for martyrs'
Dryden: *Alexander's Feast:* 'None but the brave deserves the fair'
ph gave their own
were Michael Gunn, manager of Gaiety Theatre, D

Liffey *We* nâd: cry, howl
nod

Dick Whittington (pantomime): 'Turn again Whittington, Lord-Mayor of London'
Dublin

r Annamoe Bow Bells told Whittington to turn again Strongbow: Anglo-Norman invader of Ireland
AngI Annaghmore: Great Fen (625.35)
timer girls weak Adam & Eve
wee
whoops North-West Norway *D Annals*, 1839: 'Dublin visited by an awful storm on the night
r Nore nowhere of the sixth January' (Epiphany)
Apocalypse

AngI pogue: kiss bow & arrow *AngI* Lochlann: Scandinavian
Boucicault: *Arrah-na-Pogue* Lord God
'Thalatta! Thalatta!' ('Sea! Sea!'): cry of *r* Liffey tidal to Islandbridge
Xenophon's 10,000 on sighting the sea
G mit

ten tailor's daughter
tiny tot
father
dad
Kerse, tailor, Sackville St, D (became O'Connell St)

supper

'prince of triflers' (Swift) atlas: satin

goose: tailor's smoothing iron Singer: make of sewing machine
duets

L/R

Finn MacCool heliotrope
(see letter to HSW quoted on p. 219)
Wicklow hills (where Liffey rises) 'To be continued' (printed at end of installment)

bluebells grow Selskar Gunn: son of Michael Gunn
bugles bubbles *Da* elskere: lovers

U. 273: 'Too late. She longed to go. That's why. Woman. As easy stop the sea. Yes: all is lost'

AngI forenenst: opposite barkentine Black & Tans: Eng. recruits serving in Royal Ir.
Constabulary, 1920–1
Finn MacCool mouse

J told Mercanton he would use H. Zimmer's
phrase 'a great shadow' for Finn
Persse O'Reilly *D Annals* say the Liffey was frozen in
1338 & 1739
thaw
thee
principal boy (pantomime) Viking

invasion of Ireland Thorir: Viking invader of Ireland
terror

s I Will Give You the Keys to Heaven

Marriage Ceremony: 'till death us do part'
delta

did Dub . . . lin ('Black Pool') *Da* farvel: goodbye
I inn: we, us Black Linn: highest point on Howth
alas glasses appear daylight
AngI whist: silence
AngI acushla: my pulse (endearment)

'Imla' (II Chron 18:7–8) means 'fullness'
ph let the devil take the hindmost
Skt māyā: illusion
Himalaya Mts
(202.27)

somersault
sauntering
F sauterelle: grasshopper
Cinderella (pantomime)
Saltarello: a dance (267.07–08)

reign

Boccaccio says Dante was asked to undertake an embassy to the pope, & replied 'If I go, who remains? If I remain, who goes?' Yeats quoted this to J in asking him to join the Academy of Irish Letters. J declined
100 + 10 + 1 = 111
1001 Nights

Cinderella's carriage turned back into a pumpkin at midnight

nr Humpty Dumpty: 'All the king's horses & all the king's men'

Anna Livia Plurabelle
r Amazon
anew
L pulchra: beautiful
Amazons had 1 breast cauterized to shoot & fight better
worth

r Nile

r Hoang Ho

L aura: breeze
heard
L voles: you may fly

(627.25–6)

eyes miles & miles moaning monotoning
Moyle: sea between Ireland & Scotland Mananaan MacLir: Ir. sea-god
seasick

treble (Neptune's trident)
terrible (N. & S. Walls of Liffey)
I Muir Meann: Limpid Sea: the Ir. Sea *L* ave et vale: hail & farewell
moments Anna Livia *F* l'aval: downstream direction
(last leaf of this book) *r* Liffey

We tad: father

Noah released birds from ark to find land Matt 1:20: 'angel of the Lord' (Annunciation) think
Archangel, Russia (named for St Michael)
lie *nr* Humpty Dumpty worship
Luke 7:38: Mary Magdalen washes Christ's feet wake up (resurrection)
Da tid: time hair

AngI whist!: silence! *Da* far: father

Finnegans Wake but softly remember me
Sl buss: kiss *Heb* mem: water
thousand years (156.19; 627.15) *s* I Will Give You the Keys to Heaven
thou sendest thee